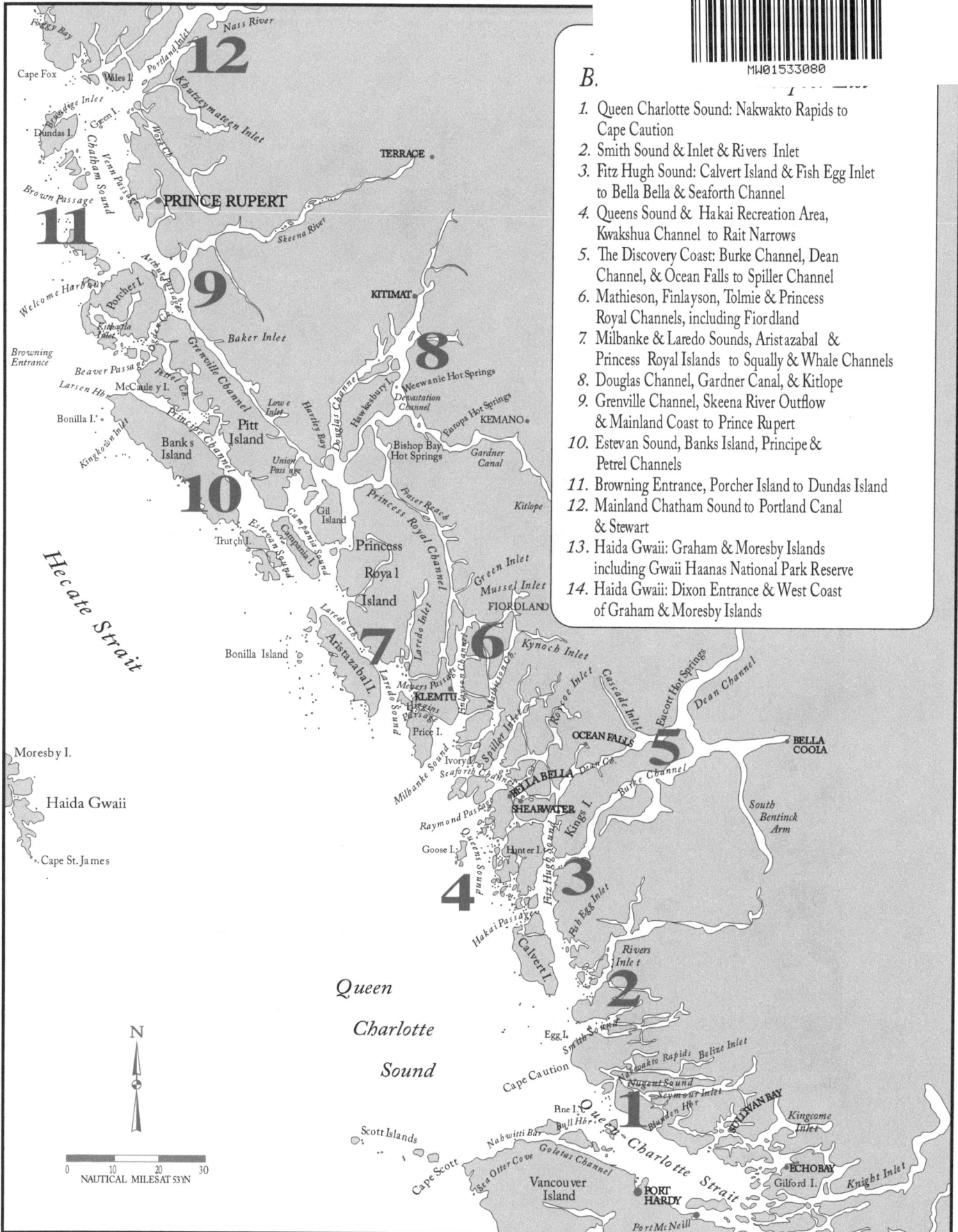

MW01533080

54°N

53°N

52°N

51°N

12

11

9

8

10

7

6

5

4

3

2

1

Nass River

Foggy Bay

Cape Fox

Wales I.

Portland Inlet

Khutzeymateen Inlet

TERRACE

Dundas I.

Green I.

North

Chatham Sound

Venn Pass

Brown Passage

PRINCE RUPERT

KITIMAT

Skeena River

Welcome Harbour

Porcher I.

Arthur Passage

Kitkatla Inlet

Browning Entrance

Beaver Passage

Baker Inlet

Grenville Channel

Weewanie Hot Springs

McCauley I.

Larsen Hbr.

Petrel Ch.

Lowe Inlet

Hartley Bay

Hawkesbury I.

Devastation Channel

Europa Hot Springs

KEMANO

Bonilla I.

Pitt Island

Kingkown Inlet

Principe Channel

Banks Island

Union Passage

Bishop Bay Hot Springs

Gardner Canal

Kitlope

10

Estevan Sound

Campania Sound

Campania I.

Gil Island

Fraser Reach

Trutch I.

Princess Royal Channel

Princess Royal Island

Green Inlet

Mussel Inlet

FIORDLAND

Hecate Strait

Laredo Cr.

Laredo Inlet

Bonilla Island

Aristazabal I.

Laredo Sound

Meyers Passage

Kynoch Inlet

Cascade Inlet

Eucott Hot Springs

Dean Channel

Finlayson Channel

Mathieson Ch.

Roscoe Inlet

KLEMTU

Higgins Passage

Price I.

Ivory I.

Spiller Inlet

Seaforth Channel

OCEAN FALLS

Dean Ch.

BELLA COOLA

Moresby I.

Haida Gwaii

Milbanke Sound

BELLA BELLA

SHEARWATER

Kings I.

Burke Channel

South Bentinck Arm

Cape St. James

Raymond Passage

Goose I.

Queens Sound

Hunter I.

Fitz Hugh Sound

3

Fish Egg Inlet

4

Hakai Passage

Calvert I.

Rivers Inlet

Queen

Charlotte

Sound

2

Egg I.

Smith Sound

N

Scott Islands

Nahwitti Bar

Pine I.

Bull Hbr.

Cape Caution

Nakwakto Rapids

Belize Inlet

Nugent Sound

Seymour Inlet

Blunden Hbr.

SULLIVAN BAY

Kingcome Inlet

Cape Scott

Sea Otter Cove

Goletas Channel

Vancouver Island

Queen Charlotte Strait

PORT HARDY

ECHO BAY

Gilford I.

Knight Inlet

Port McNeill

0 10 20 30
NAUTICAL MILES AT 53°N

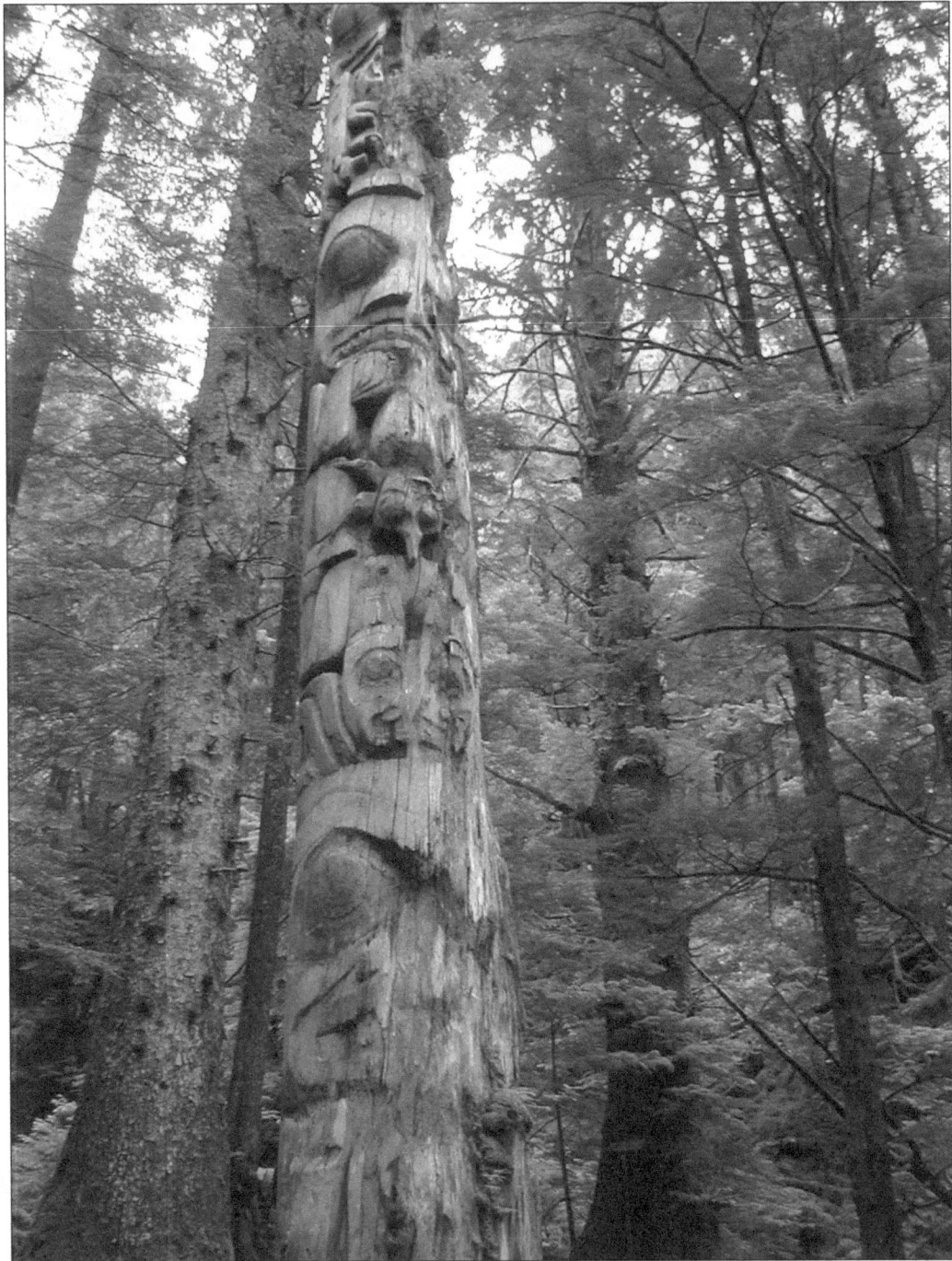

Unique Mosquito Totem in Buck Channel, West Coast, Haida Gwaii

EXPLORING
THE

NORTH COAST

OF

BRITISH COLUMBIA

Blunden Harbour to Dixon Entrance
Including Haida Gwaii

FOURTH EDITION

BY DON DOUGLASS & RÉANNE HEMINGWAY-DOUGLASS

FOREWORD TO THE FOURTH EDITION BY LORENA LANDON
PREFACE BY NEIL CAREY
GUEST ESSAY BY RODERICK FRAZIER NASH

Fine Edge
Nautical & Recreational Publishing

Contact the Canadian Hydrographic Service to obtain information on local dealers and available charts and publications or to order charts and publications directly:

Chart Sales and Distribution Office, Canadian Hydrographic Service
Department of Fisheries and Oceans, Institute of Ocean Sciences, Patricia Bay
9860 West Saanich Road, Sidney B.C., V8L 4B2 Telephone (250) 363-6358: FAX (250) 363-6841

Important Legal Disclaimer

This book is designed to provide experienced skippers with planning information on the coast of British Columbia. Every effort has been made, within limited resources, to make this book complete and accurate. There may well be mistakes, both typographical and in content. Therefore this book should be used only as a general guide, not as the ultimate source of information on the areas covered. Much of what is presented in this book is local knowledge based upon personal observation and is subject to human error. The authors, editors, publisher, and local authorities assume no liability for errors or omissions, or for any loss or damages incurred from using this information.

Credits:
Book design: Melanie Haage Design
Edited by Leonard Landon, Lorena Landon, Lisa Wright, Rae Kozloff, and Arlene Cook
Diagrams & maps: Sue Athmann; Melanie Haage
Front Cover Photo: Lorena Landon
Back Cover Photos: the authors, Chris Cheadle, Elsie Hulsizer, and Iain McAllister
with permission of Pacific Wild
All photos by the authors unless otherwise credited
Sidebar authors include Réanne Hemingway Douglass, Don Douglass, Arlene Cook,
Kathleen Kaska, and Lisa Wright, among others.

Library of Congress Cataloging-in-Publication Data

Douglass, Don.
  Exploring the north coast of British Columbia : Blunden Harbour to Dixon Entrance,
including the Queen Charlotte Islands / by Don Douglass & Réanne Hemingway-Douglass ;
2nd Ed. Foreword by George Eaton ; 3rd Ed. Foreword by Marianne Scott ; 3rd Guest Essay by Roderick Frazier Nash.
    p. cm.
  Includes bibliographical references and index.
  ISBN (first edition): 0-938665-80-4   (second edition): 978-0-996979-92-4   (third edition): 978-1-934199-25-1
  1. Pilot guides—British Columbia.   I. Hemingway-Douglass, Réanne.   II. Title.
VK945.D684   2001
623.89'29711—dc21   00-050412

Fourth Edition ISBN 978-1-734131-29-1

Copyright © 2024 Don Douglass & Réanne Hemingway-Douglass
All rights strictly reserved under the International and Pan-American Copyright Conventions.
The anchor diagrams, local knowledge, and GPS waypoints are all original data and no part of this book, including diagrams, may be reproduced or transmitted in any form or by any means, electronic or mechanical, including photocopying, recording, or by any information storage and retrieval system except as may be expressly permitted by the 1976 Copyright Act or in writing from the publisher.

Address requests for permission to FineEdge.com LLC,
P.O. Box 726, Anacortes, WA 98221
FineEdge.com
Printed in the United States of America

Contents

Appendices and References

Foreword to the Fourth Edition

by Lorena Landon

The popular Exploring Series guidebooks, written by the late Don Douglass and the late Reanne Hemingway-Douglass, are used by serious boaters looking for numerous anchoring options between major destinations. These valued resources are published by Fine Edge Nautical Publishing. This 4th Edition of Exploring the North Coast of British Columbia has been updated by the editors of the Waggoner Cruising Guide, Lorena and Leonard Landon. Information on marinas, marine parks, and select destinations have been revised where applicable, while maintaining the original research, writing style and character of the series. Information about wildlife viewing areas is now included, along with the latest changes at destinations such as Butedale, Pruth Bay, Klemtu, Cow Bay Marina, and Haida Gwaii. The text narrative regarding charts has been updated to reflect recent changes in NOAA and CHS charting. Anchorages have been updated as known and where needed. Maps have been positioned in the page layout near/next to the related text for easy reference. Most personal sidebar stories and photos by the Douglasses have been retained to maintain the character of the guidebook, with new photos added where sites have changed significantly.

The Douglass' Exploring Series of nautical guidebooks remain a valuable resource for boaters who love discovering Northwest remote destinations and quiet anchorages. It should be noted that not all anchorages were visited for this 4th edition. We would like to thank Waggoner volunteer field correspondents who submitted contributions to this 4th edition of Exploring the North Coast of British Columbia.

Editors: 4th Edition; Leonard and Lorena Landon, Managing Editors of the Waggoner Cruising Guide, published by Fine Edge.

Maps: 4th Edition; Melanie Haage and Leonard Landon

Layout: 4th Edition; Leonard Landon

Preface

by Neil G. Carey

Over a half-century ago my wife, Betty, and I were hooked by the unparalleled magnificence of the North Coast of British Columbia. I first saw this coast as a young sailor standing watch on a U.S. Navy tanker plying the coast between Seattle and Alaska during the winter of 1947-48. Speckled with countless verdant islands, confusing channels and inlets, these unique waterways—all with little evidence of human activity—intrigued me. As a young woman, Betty was also bewitched by this country when she rowed an Indian dugout canoe—alone—from Anacortes, Washington to Ketchikan in 63 days.

That lure eventually pulled our family from an ocean-front home in Southern California to settle in a solitary cabin on the rugged west coast of the beguiling Queen Charlotte Islands. We have made these enchanting and challenging islands our home for the past 35 years.

Over the years we have been privileged to observe and study the varied beauty of the Charlottes, traveling by water, by air or by land. I have a special place in my heart for Puffin Cove, our cabin home overlooking the unfettered North Pacific on the isolated and wild west coast of Moresby Island. Based there, we cruised the Charlottes in all months, enjoyed the great forests, and walked through all of the hauntingly memorable Haida villages—a few with totems still standing. We have watched grey whales feeding and blowing, humpback whales leaping, bald eagles soaring on thermal drafts, salmon fighting their way upstream to spawn, large black bear flipping rocks over in search of crabs, and the dwarfed Columbian blacktail deer feeding on kelp at low tide. And, of course, we have endured fierce, destructive storms. You, too, may enjoy all of this, and more.

The new Third Edition of *Exploring the North Coast of British Columbia,* which is a veritable storehouse of local knowledge, includes 2,000 entries on B.C.'s remote north coast and the Queen Charlotte Islands—information not found elsewhere. For the first time ever, the Douglasses documented dozens of major inlets and anchorages along the west coasts of Graham and Moresby islands, and they have included many detailed diagrams and photographs based on their research. This cruise-tested book, which gives you accurate local knowledge, is a necessary supplement to enhance other information, including that found in official Canadian publications.

With over 175,000 miles of worldwide cruising, Don and Réanne Douglass are well qualified to know what a sailor needs and how to supply it in a readily useable form—they are sailors' sailors and have shown they have what it takes to survive in high latitudes. If you are in doubt, read Réanne's book *Cape Horn: One Man's Dream, One Woman's Nightmare.* In helping bring you this book I have enjoyed working with Don and Réanne to share as much as possible of our experiences along the coasts of Graham and Moresby islands that we love so dearly.

Local knowledge is vital to anyone setting forth on the Inside Passage. To obtain local knowledge about these wild and wonderful waterways, the Douglasses—over a period of thirty years in their research vessels, *Baidarka* or by kayak—have personally investigated the coast, performed thousands of test-anchorings recorded GPS data, photographed and documented their information. In essence, they have hazarded their vessels for this local knowledge so that you may cruise in safety and comfort through these wondrous and ever-changing North Coast waters. I would not veer off the ferry-boat route to Alaska without the Douglass's guidebooks and route maps.

Neil Carey is the author of A Guide to the Queen Charlotte Islands *and* Puffin Cove. *Neil Carey lives on Moresby Island.*

Photo courtesy Pacific Voyager/Sea Cabana

Betty Lowman Carey in her dugout canoe Bijaboji during her 1937 solo voyage from Anacortes, Washington to Alaska. Bijaboji is on permanent display at the Anacortes Museum. Betty's book Bijaboji *is a wonderful account of a fearless young woman's journey the summer after she graduated from college.*

   Coincidentally, Don Douglass's uncle Phil "Chip" Douglass is also shown in this picture. He and three buddies spent the summer of 1937 canoeing from Seattle to Skagway. Their journey is described in Ken Wise's book, Cruise of the Blue Flujin.

Introduction

The North Coast of British Columbia is an enchanted cruising ground considered by many experienced mariners to be the best in the world. The Guest Essay following this section speaks eloquently about the unique environment of the North Coast that touches any boater fortunate enough to visit its pristine waterways. We agree that it is a *Great Place* that must be saved so future generations can admire its magnificent scenery and, as boaters, we must all help do our part to conserve this wilderness. To paraphrase the backpacker's ethic: Proceed slowly, take only photographs and leave only a small wake.

Our goal in this guidebook is to help you explore and enjoy these remote waters by sharing our "local knowledge." While the beautiful, convoluted coastline of the North Coast is, for the most part, a user-friendly boating environment, it is wilderness nonetheless, and requires careful and vigilant navigation. Boaters must respect its wild and unpredictable nature and be prepared to handle whatever comes. On the North Coast, response time for assistance in an emergency can be hours or even days, rather than the minutes found in less remote cruising areas. Preparation, self-sufficiency, and constant vigilance are required to make a visit to the North Coast incident-free as well as carefree. (Please see the Appendix for weather information and cruising tips.)

In providing up-to-date pilothouse information, we have tried to anticipate both general and navigational concerns that might arise as you plan and execute your cruise. While our information does not replace official charts and *Sailing Directions,* and is not to be used for navigation, it reports useful local knowledge discovered in personal visits to the more than 2,000 sites described in this book.

We believe that, in thousands of miles of coastline from the Mexican Border to Lituya Bay in the Gulf of Alaska, there are a number of alternative places where you can find shelter if the fog rolls in, the chop picks up, or currents or tides are unfavorable. This is particularly true along the Inside Passage to Alaska, where you are seldom more than an hour from an anchor site that offers temporary shelter. In this book we have tried to document all coves and anchor sites found along B.C.'s North Coast to help minimize undue hardship on your boat and crew.

Our *Baidarka* research vessels—used in documenting nearly 5,000 places along the West Coast in over nineteen years—have been 32- and 40-foot diesel trawlers and a 21-foot kayak. We have always preferred to keep "one foot on the beach" to get the feel of a cove, view the wildlife, and enjoy the sights, sounds, and scents of the land; however some of you may find our routes or anchor sites uncomfortably tight for the size of your vessel or crew's skill level. If you're a newcomer, or have a boat over 40 feet, you may want to reconnoiter a small cove or channel by dinghy before entering. In any case, don't hesitate to turn around and use a safe alternative whenever you or your crew become anxious. You, as skipper, must exercise judgment and determine what is appropriate for your circumstances.

Our detailed diagrams are a reflection of the particular route and anchor site we used. We always enter a small cove or anchorage at a very slow speed with one or more alert crew on the bow watching for submerged rocks or other hazards. We circle around our expected swinging radius, but there's always a possibility that we could miss a potential hazard. At times, we do not remain over an entire tide cycle and, because of that, we could miss additional data. Our local knowledge reflects personal observations as well as follow-up discussions with mariners we trust. In certain areas, the North Coast of B.C. is rather poorly charted and there are few large-scale charts of the smaller coves and channels used in recreational cruising. Indeed, some of the best places for exploring have not been charted at all! The Haida Gwaii archipelago (formerly the Queen Charlotte Islands), where many miles of the west coast have no soundings within a mile or more of the shore, are an extreme example of this. Furthermore, there is no data on more than a dozen inlets and harbors.

We consider the North Coast of British Columbia to have some of the best cruising waters in the world. But when you venture forth, take nothing for granted, beware of potential hazards at all times, and be prepared for the challenges and rewards that await you!

Using This Book
Each chapter in this book covers a separate cruising area (usually proceeding from south to north). An **area map** is included at the beginning of each chapter to serve as a quick reference to location of channels, passages, and coves found within the text. **Place names** are shown in bold type. We have tried

in all cases to use established or local names for the documented coves and bays; however, where we could find no reference to a name on either Canadian charts or in Canadian Hydrographic Survey (C.H.S.) sources *(Sailing Directions)*, we assigned a new name that seemed appropriate. **GPS coordinates** for **Position, Entrance** and **Anchor** sites are adjusted to NAD83.

The **main body of the text** describes the local knowledge we have discovered through personal observation or in conjunction with sources we believe to be reliable and knowledgeable. The last entry under each place-name gives specific **Anchor** information for the Anchor Site Waypoint identified at the heading and/or on the detailed diagram for that site. If you find conditions different from those described, double-check your position on the chart and make your own judgment about suitability.

Anchoring Information

The last paragraph lists depth(s) at zero tide, followed by specific bottom material (sand, mud, clay, rocks, gravel, kelp), and our estimate of the relative anchor holding power. Whenever depth, bottom type and holding power are specified, we have personally anchored there and this information is from our log. In places where we have not personally anchored, or where our records are incomplete, we have stated the bottom or its holding power as *unrecorded*.

Anchor Diagrams

We have included detailed diagrams for some of the more popular coves—many of which have not previously been covered by charts or other publications. These diagrams show the approximate routes we took, the typical depths we found, and the places we anchored. Please note that these diagrams are non-representational and not to scale; they do not include all known or unknown hazards and should always be used with caution and self-verification.

Please note: A detailed diagram does not imply that a site is suitable for your particular boat or circumstances. Whenever you are faced with critical judgments involving navigation or anchoring, you should be the sole judge of what is appropriate and assume full responsibility for using this book.

Definitions Used for Holding Power

- **Excellent—very good holding:** Anchor digs in deeper as you pull on it—the preferred bottom in a blow, but a rare find— usually thick sticky mud or clay.

- **Good holding:** Generally sufficient for over-

Sample Layout Selection

Place name (Body of water or island)

Jones Cove (Smith Sound) — Distance from known place
2.7 mi E of Egg Island
Entrance: 51°15.09'N, 127°45.86'W
Anchor: 51°14.93'N, 127°45.75'W

All GPS coordinates adjusted to NAD83

Jones Cove, 2.5 miles due east of Egg Island, offers good protection for small craft with somewhat limited swinging room. Ropes on a piling near the entrance can be used in conjunction with a second anchor or to tie up. Inside the piling there is room for two or three small boats to anchor. In the past this cove was used as a logboom storage area, but small craft and fishing boats now use it frequently. Millbrook Cove, on the north side of Smith Sound, has more swinging room and is more popular with larger pleasure craft.

Our own recorded local knowledge based on personal experience

Jones Cove is easy to enter but avoid the rocks off the north point or those extending from Turner Islands. The pass inside Turner Islands has a fairway depth of about 20 fathoms and inside Chest Island about 6 fathoms. Avoid the rocks off Chest Island.

Anchor in 2 to 3 fathoms over soft mud with good holding.

Describes depth(s), bottom material and holding power

night anchorage in fair weather—anchor digs in but may drag or pull out on strong pull. Common in mud/sand combinations or hard sand.

- **Fair holding:** Adequate for temporary anchorage in fair weather, but boat should not be left unattended. Bottom of light sand, gravel with some rocks, grass or kelp or a thin layer of mud over a hard bottom. Anchor watch desirable.

- **Poor holding:** Can be used for a temporary stop in fair weather only. Bottom is typically rocky with a lot of grass or kelp, or a very thin layer of mud and sand—insufficient to bury anchor properly. Anchor watch recommended at all times.

- **Steep-to:** Depth of water may decrease from 10 fathoms to ½ fathom in as little as one boat length! (Approach at dead-slow recommended.) Use shore tie to minimize swinging and to keep anchor pulling uphill.

Anchoring in the Pacific Northwest

Cruising in the Pacific Northwest is all about anchoring. Once beyond marinas and fishing resorts, you must have confidence in your own anchoring skills. Nothing assures a restful night in a secluded cove better than a well-set oversized anchor. A conventional cruising anchor (not a lightweight folding version), a boat length of chain, and a good stretchable nylon rode are indispensable equipment. Supplement these essentials with a smaller lunch hook to use for temporary stops or to restrict swinging room. Commonly seen in close quarters and deep, steep-to anchorages, an additional stern-tie to shore can often be the only method that will reliably secure a boat. Many Northwestern boaters keep a stern-tie line on a mounted reel for easy deployment and recovery. In shared anchorages, minimize intrusion on your neighbors by observing and matching the mooring techniques and swinging radii of other boats.

The new Baidarka *explores the North Coast*

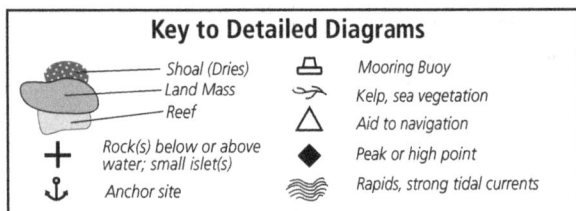

Learn from the local knowledge and experience of your fellow mariners. Be aware of the potential for downslope winds or williwaws. Choose your spot carefully, set your anchor well, and enjoy the challenges and rewards of cruising in this remote and isolated wonderland.

Mooring buoys

Public mooring buoys may be found in many of British Columbia's Provincial Parks, as well as in non-park waters. Park mooring buoys are supposed to be inspected annually, but many other buoys are not, and their security is undetermined. Buoys may be removed seasonally or permanently. The prudent mariner will always conduct a thorough test of the suitability of any mooring before depending on it.

Navigational Charts

In the past, Canadian and US government navigational charts were available in three formats: Paper, digital Raster, and digital Electronic charts. Paper charts have not been available from Canadian or US government sources for many years. Until about 2020, digital images of paper charts were available from both Canadian and US government sources.

In 2020, both Canadian and US government agencies responsible for nautical chart information started a program to sunset their support for and updating of all Raster charting products. Both Canadian and US agencies are currently engaged in a process of enhancing their digital Electronic Navigational Charts (ENCs) and they have been canceling digital Raster charts as the enhanced ENCs become available for the equivalent geographic area.

The hydrographic agencies of both countries maintain and distribute two types of digital charts, raster and vector, for electronic navigation applications.

- Charts are still available on paper. Paper charts are printed versions of the ENC charts and look considerably different than their first generation cousins. Booklets are available from third party venders with images of out-of-date historical paper charts. Use these booklet charts with a large degree of caution as they all have old information. While the rocks may not move, existing rocks are newly discovered and new navigational information is added or changed (such as new restricted areas and Aids To Navigation - ATONs).

- Raster charts are electronic images of paper charts created by scanning and digitizing paper charts. When you zoom into a raster chart, everything on the image will get larger, but no further information is available unless there is a larger scale chart that covers the same geograph-

Canadian Chart Tidal Water Symbols

feet or meters

Ocean level

(4)

_ feet or meters

HIGH WATER

CHART DATUM "0"

fathoms or meters

Depth	Island	Awash	Drying height
7₃	4•	·I·	(4) ✳4)

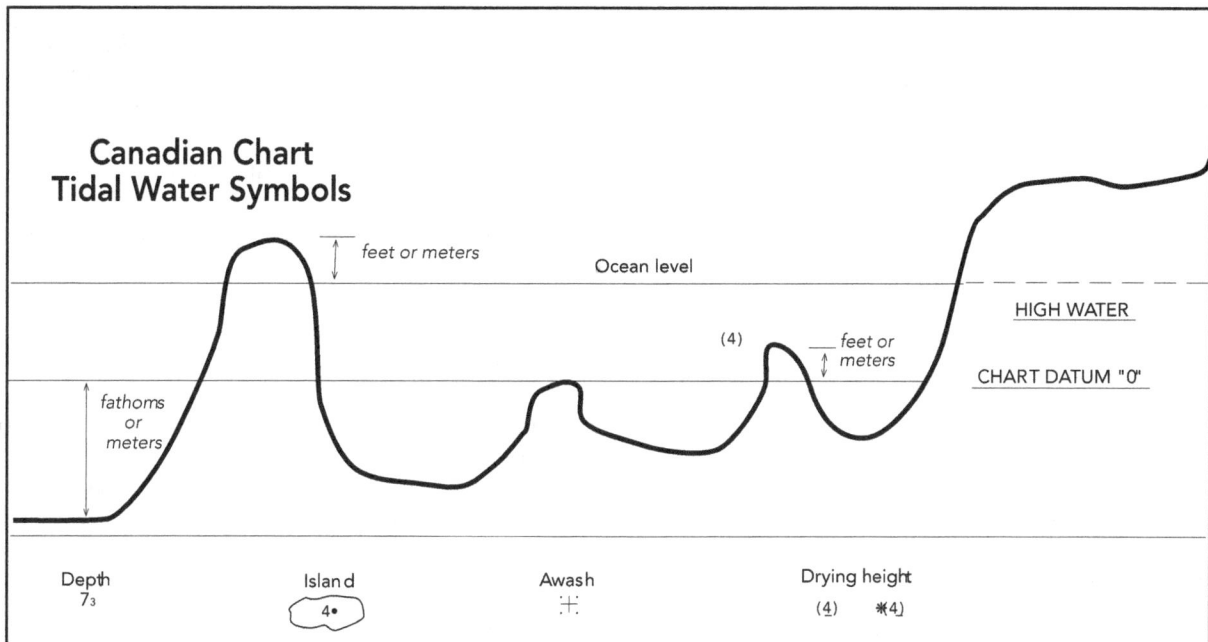

ic area and your computer-based navigation system has the capability to electronically stitch charts together. The digitized image is usually geo-referenced, and displays a vessel's position on the chart image of your computer-based navigation system that is connected to GPS.

• Electronic Navigational Charts (ENCs) are vector charts. Vector charts are not scans of paper charts. Rather, they are built from points, lines, and polygons representing various kinds of navigational information stored in a database and retrieved for display. ENCs carry suppplemental geo-spatial information not available in paper or raster charts that can be displayed by clicking on a particular feature. The user can customize the image to display only desired information. ENCs can be combined with GPS, radar, ship course, speed, and draft in an Electronic Chart Display and Information System (ECDIS). This is a powerful system that instantly and accurately informs mariners of their ship's position.

• Legacy ENCs and Reschemed ENCs. Legacy ENCs were created in the 1990's from paper charts. As such, Legacy ENCs are in a wide range of scales and dimensions. Legacy ENCs are the electronic Vector charts that we have been using for decades. Reschemed ENCs are the latest digital Vector charts that are of a uniform size and set of scales. Reschemed charts are built on a more comprehensive data definition that will allow each chart to have more information.

Canadian Charts

The Canadian Hydrographic Service maintains Canadian charts. Be sure and register electronic charts with C.H.S. to ensure you receive updates, and consider subscribing to the email Notices to Mariners service. **As a result of C.H.S. initiative to phase out all Raster charts, enhance Legacy ENC charts and transition to Reschemed ENC, the majority of Pacific Canadian charts have been or will be updated and re-issued with new chart numbers. Older guidebooks will refer to outdated chart numbers.** Visit the C.H.S. website to learn how to obtain current charts and updates. *https://www.charts.gc.ca/charts-cartes/index-eng.html*

Canadian Metric Charts

As noted above, C.H.S. is in the process of canceling all Raster charts, enhancing Legacy ENCs, and moving to Reschemed ENC charts. Prior to this recent ENC charts initiative, C.H.S. embarked on an earlier process of making Raster charts metric. These metric charts are now out-of-date. However, if you are using any of these charts, take note that measurements are metric. Pay close attention to every chart used, since some may be fathoms and the older horizontal datum of NAD27. The metric charts have "Metric" printed in red in the lower right-hand corner. These metric charts will also be in digital Raster format.

Changes on metric charts involve more than just a substitution of depth numbers—the *symbols* for depth and height have changed as well. For instance, [1₃] on old Canadian and American charts means a depth of 1 fathom and 3 feet, for a total depth of 9 feet (1.5 fathoms). An islet shown as (45) means a height of 45 feet. On the metric charts, the symbol |1₃] means 1.3 meters or about 4 feet. The elevation of an island or islet is usually shown as a number followed by a dot [57•]; the elevation at the top of trees is a number with a line over it [$\overline{57}$]; a number preceded by a dot indicates spot elevation, such as the elevation of a peak [•57].

Since many of these differences can be confusing, be sure to purchase and study *Canadian Chart 1* (Symbols, Abbreviations and Terms) to familiarize yourself with current Canadian symbols.

U.S. Charts

Thomas Jefferson founded the Coast Survey in 1807. Now part of the National Oceanographic and Atmospheric Administration (NOAA), the Office of Coast Survey is the nation's chartmaker, with over a thousand charts covering 95,000 miles of shoreline and 3.4 million square nautical miles of waters within the U.S. Exclusive Economic Zone. Below is an overview of the types of nautical charts that NOAA produces. For more information, see NOAA's website, which contains links to the various chart products: *https://www.charts.noaa.gov/InteractiveCatalog/nrnc.shtml*

- NOAA has authorized certified agents to sell NOAA's paper nautical charts that are printed when the customer orders them—or "print on demand." The information on the charts is maintained by NOAA. Charts with updated information will be printed from ENCs.

- NOAA Raster Navigational Charts (NOAA RNC®) are digital images of NOAA's entire suite of paper charts, updated continually with critical corrections. NOAA RNC® are geo-referenced, digital images of NOAA navigational charts. NOAA RNC® are available for free download in BSB format. Note: All Raster chart products will be canceled by January 1, 2025. *https://www.charts.noaa.gov/InteractiveCatalog/nrnc.shtml*

- Legacy ENCs are NOAA's Vector electronic charting product created in the 1990's from paper charts. These layered vector charts can be used in Electronic Chart Display and Information Systems (ECDIS). The ENC charts and weekly updates are available for free download for incorporation into ECDIS. These Legacy ENCs are in a number of different shapes, sizes, and scales that corresponded to the origin Raster charts. *https://www.charts.noaa.gov/InteractiveCatalog/nrnc.shtml*

- Reschemed ENCs are NOAA's newest Vector elec-

tronic charting product that is replacing Legacy ENCs. Reschemed ENCs are built in one of a uniform set of sizes, consistent rectangular shape and in one of six scales. Reschemed ENCs data content data architecture is enhanced with the ability to carry more information on each chart. NOAA is in the process of replacing Legacy ENCs with Reschemed ENCs with up-to-date informationand more content. *https://www.charts.noaa.gov/InteractiveCatalog/nrnc.shtml*

- BookletCharts™ are free, print-at-home products to help recreational boaters locate themselves on the water. BookletCharts, in letter-sized format, contain all of the information on full-scale nautical charts. Booklet Charts are not up-to-date and do not meet US Coast Guard carriage requirements. *https://www.charts.noaa.gov/InteractiveCatalog/nrnc.shtml*

- NOAA's Historical Maps and Charts Collection contains over 35,000 images, including some of the nation's earliest nautical charts. *https://www.charts.noaa.gov/InteractiveCatalog/nrnc.shtml*

- *United States Coast Pilot*® comprises ten volumes of supplemental information important to navigation. PDFs are updated regularly and are free for download. *https://www.charts.noaa.gov/InteractiveCatalog/nrnc.shtml*

Measurements Used in this Book

Spelling and use of place names follow—as closely as possible—local tradition and the lead of the Canadian *Sailing Directions*.

The authors have chosen use of fathoms, nautical miles, yards, feet, degrees in Fahrenheit. We urge all navigators to double-check each chart, echo sounder readings, and GPS initial settings for consistent use of measurement units.

Unless otherwise noted, depths listed in the text or shown on diagrams are always given in fathoms, regardless of the measurement units on cited charts; depths are reduced to approximate zero tide. You should add the amount of tide listed in the corrected tide tables when you use these numbers. In Canada, zero tide data is given as the lowest expected tide for the year; therefore tide tables almost always appear as a positive number rather than the frequent minus tides of the United States. The depths shown on diagrams or mentioned in the text are typical of what we observed and do not represent exact minimums for any given area.

Bearings and courses, when given, are generally magnetic and identified as such. Courses are taken off the chart compass rose; they are approximate and are to be "made good." No allowances have been made for deviation, possible current, or drift. When compass cardinal points are used (example NW or SE), these refer to true bearings and should be taken as approximate only.

Distances are expressed in nautical miles, and speed is expressed in knots unless otherwise stated. Scales on the diagrams are expressed in yards, meters, and miles as noted and are approximate only. Time is given in four-digit 24-hour clock numbers, and all courses are given in three digits.

Unnamed islands and islets are referred to in the text by the height of the island enclosed in parentheses [e.g., island (45)].

The Bibliography contains references on general cruising. If you are unsure of your cruising skills or the suitability of your vessel, we recommend that you consult local experts—cruising instructors, the Coast Guard, yacht clubs, experienced North Coast mariners, commercial fishermen—and that you consult and read many of the texts listed in the Bibliography.

In discussing local knowledge concerning routes, coves or anchoring, we make the assumption that you, as skipper, have the proper largest-scale chart available for the area you plan to visit, as well as the latest edition of Canadian Tide and Current Tables and that you are skilled in using these tools. By knowing your own abilities and interests and matching them to the unlimited cruising opportunities for exploring the North Coast, you can enjoy the trip of a lifetime.

Waypoints and GPS

GPS is an excellent tool for navigating the North Coast. Nav-Aids are uncommon and many passages and islets can be confusing. GPS will help locate the proper entrances, detect cross-track errors, provide speed over the ground, and hence determine tidal currents.

Latitude and longitude for waypoints in this book—given to the nearest one-hundredth of a minute of latitude—are taken from the largest scale charts available at the time of writing and are referenced to NAD83 which, for practical purposes, are identical to the GPS default horizontal datum of WSG84. These Lat/Longs—which are to be treated as approximate only—should be verified by each user. Many charts are not accurate to one-hundredth of a minute. We have approximated this last digit—which is about a boat's length—to provide as complete a picture as possible. With the removal of Selective Availability (SA), *Baidarka* has found both differential GPS and WASS GPS to be stable to within a boat's length, and accurate to a very high degree. Note: In Haida Gwaii

we have discovered major errors in both paper and electronic charts that require extreme caution. Use care in plotting GPS position on NAD27 charts, as the difference in position is from 300 to as much as 600 feet.

Errata and Updates

When a new edition is published, it supersedes the older edition, which is no longer valid. Your comments, corrections or suggestions are welcomed. Please send them to info@waggonerguide.com

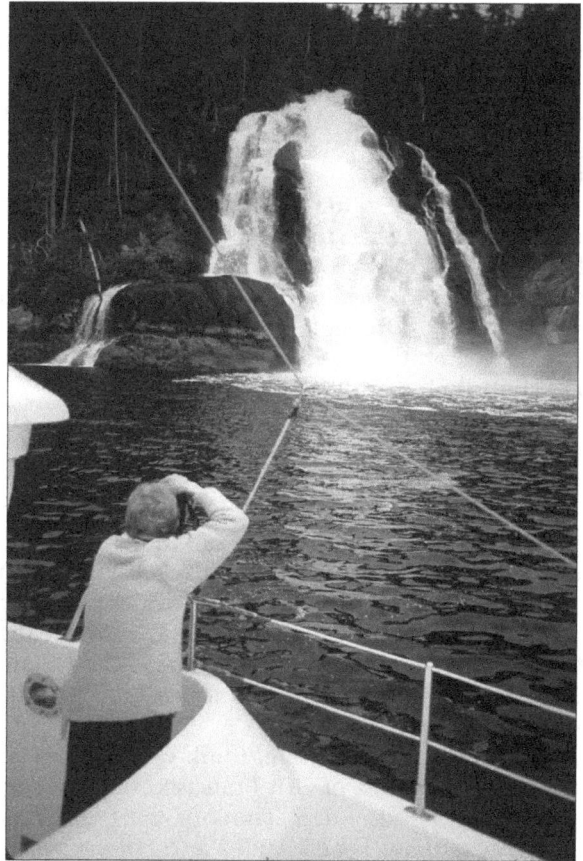

Visiting Kynoch Falls in Fiordland

GUEST ESSAY

The Last Great Place
by Roderick Frazier Nash

From a mariner's point of view, the most significant landmarks are called "capes."
Horn, Good Hope, Cod, Hatteras . . . the list is well known. Cape Caution marks the most
significant passage on the British Columbia coast; rounding it is a nautical coming of age.
Weekend warriors and two-week charterers don't make it this far. Serious cruisers who do, enter
a fraternity of mutual respect where they experience the space, the solitude, and the
silence of one of the world's wildest coastlines. Cape Caution is a gateway
to the last great place – British Columbia's North Coast.

Time was, and not so long ago, that one of the largest conifer forests on the planet stretched in an unbroken green carpet from the Gulf of Alaska all the way south to the central California coast. Salmon and steelhead runs occurred in rivers as far as Southern California. Grizzly bears and wolves roamed the entire North American coastline.

People lived here too, but their lifestyle centered on complementing, rather than conquering nature. These First People saw nature as a community to which they belonged, rather than a commodity to possess. Their numbers, however, were small, and their impact on the environment could be sustained in perpetuity—over thousands of years.

Change came to the west coast with the arrival of Europeans. Capitalism, Christianity and industrial civilization quickly ripped the fabric of the primeval ecosystem. Dams blocked rivers and ended salmon runs; old-growth forests disappeared; highways and railroads paralleled the coast; and subdivisions and airports replaced nutrient-rich saltwater wetlands. From Los Angeles to Vancouver, we are now dealing with fragments of ecosystems. In the United States, the vast coastal temperate rain forest has dwindled to a few tiny preserves.

For historical perspective, think of the biological richness and beauty of San Francisco Bay or Puget Sound just 150 years ago. Think of the food chains involving salmon, bears, eagles and native peoples along rivers like the Sacramento and the Columbia. It is twilight for those miracles now. Wild salmon seem headed on the same course as the buffalo. Management efforts have been too little, too late and piecemeal.

But on its central and northern coast, British Columbia has an opportunity to protect what California,

Oregon and Washington squandered. The intricate, wild coastline north of Cape Caution is a remnant, a reminder and, hopefully, an inspiration. Thousands of miles of island and mainland coastline have changed little since the glaciers rolled back 15,000 years ago. The massive old-growth Sitka spruce, western red cedar and eastern hemlock crowd the water's edge as they did for Vancouver's crew in the 1790s. The largest virgin timber stands in North America are here. Although the last grizzly (the fabled "golden bear") disappeared from California in 1922, the big carnivores thrive on the north coast, as do whales, salmon, and eagles. First Nations People are still here too, some of them trying to cling to the shreds of their traditional and splendid cultural heritage.

The north coast is a land hanging in the balance between wilderness and civilization. While there is vast wilderness, there is also intense pressure for environmental transformation. British Columbian policy is still largely driven by the old frontier land-use priorities. Moving up from the south coast and Vancouver Island, giant lumber companies have laid bare huge tracts of land, sometimes entire watersheds, from the mountain ridges right down to salt water. Of course, not just the trees disappear. Entire ecosystems unravel; biodiversity takes a heavy beating.

The full scale of this war against the Earth may not be apparent to the casual observer. The cutting is often cleverly done and not visible from the decks of cruise ships on the Inside Passage. But get in a smaller boat and look behind the "tourist fringe" of waterline trees, back into the bays, and you see a war between wilderness and civilization. Here are the simple numbers: British Columbia has 25% of all the coastal temperate rain forest in the world; 39% of that has been logged. There is intense pressure to extract the rest of the prime old growth. Others feel it is time to establish a balance between human needs and the natural ways.

Of course, the lumber companies say the forest will recover, and demonstration reforestation projects support the idea of tree farming. But farms are not wilderness, either ecologically or spiritually.

For its part the British Columbia government proudly claims that it is committed to placing 12% of the province in protected status by the year 2000. However, most of the established and proposed parks are or will be swamps, scrub forest and snow peaks. The critical low elevation temperate rain forest is notable for its absence in the province's plans. There is a shortage of large habitats so critical to free-ranging creatures like bears, wolves and salmon. Also lacking are the corridors or bridges from one protected sanctuary to another which conservation biologists believe are vital to the health of wildlife populations.

In particular, friends of wildness in British Columbia covet a chain of environmental reserves extending from Tweedsmuir Provincial Park in the interior, through the Kitlope and Fjordland protected areas, and on to the proposed Spirit Bear Park. It is this last site that is the most exciting. While Kitlope and Fjordland touch a small portion of the mainland coast, Spirit Bear is *entirely* marine oriented. Included in the 265,000 hectare proposal are Campania, Princess Royal, and Swindle islands, as well as a substantial reach of the mainland coast centered on Green and Khutze inlets with their extensive saltwater marshes. The final link in the chain is Gwaii Haanas National Park Reserve on South Moresby Island, Queen Charlotte group. Taken together, this is a preservation vision that does justice to the scale and variety of this immense land.

Spirit Bear, the common name for the *Ursus kermodei*, was the focus of an exploratory cruise we made in the summer of 1996 when we circumnavigated the fabulous Princess Royal Island. The island is huge (over 100 miles long) and, except for its north end fronting Whale Channel where clearcutters have been at work, it is pristine.

The star of the wildlife show in this region, and

The North Coast and particularly the islands of Haida Gwaii, are the future cruising frontier. Pacific Voyager *and* Sea Cabana *explore Skedans.*

namesake of the proposed park, is the Kermode bear (spirit bear). Its coat ranges from a dazzling white to a rich caramel, but it is not an albino. Rather, biologists think this white phase of the black bear results from occasional manifestations of a recessive gene that has persisted since the ice age when it had an evolutionary advantage. Although there are only an estimated 100 spirit bears alive, patient study by Charles Russel and Jeff and Sue Turner has brought international attention to the animal. Russel's book *Spirit Bear: Encounters with the White Bear of the Western Rain Forest* (1994), and the Turners' outstanding documentary film, will enrich any cruise in the Princess Royal area.

Although few in number, the spirit bear has come to symbolize the fragile wilderness of the northern coast and its uncertain future. The white bear lives only on the islands and the mainland north of Bella Bella. If this area continues to be logged, the bear will go, along with the giant trees. Also at stake in the Spirit Bear proposal is the economic and cultural vitality of the Kitasoo First People, centered in the village of Klemtu on Swindle Island. Along with the Heiltsuk of Bella Bella and the Haida of the Queen Charlotte Islands, the identity of the Kitasoo is tied closely to the wildness of their coastal environment. True, some natives welcome the logging that is moving north from Roderick Island and

Griffin Passage, but increasing numbers are aware that logging jobs are ephemeral. Sustainability lies in a productive ecosystem and ecotourism. Moreover, if the Kermodei country and the spectacular Spiller Channel-Ellerslie Lake region is clearcut, deep-rooted spiritual values will be jeopardized.

The big picture shows that a corridor of protection—from the interior plateaus, over the coastal ranges and down to the ocean islands—could be a splendid monument to the human capacity for restraint, and a gesture of planetary modesty.

In April 2001 the British Columbia government approved in principal the idea of expanded protection for the Spirit Bear and its wilderness ecosystem. The area of permanent protection rose to 1.5 million acres while logging on another two million acres was deferred. While certainly a step

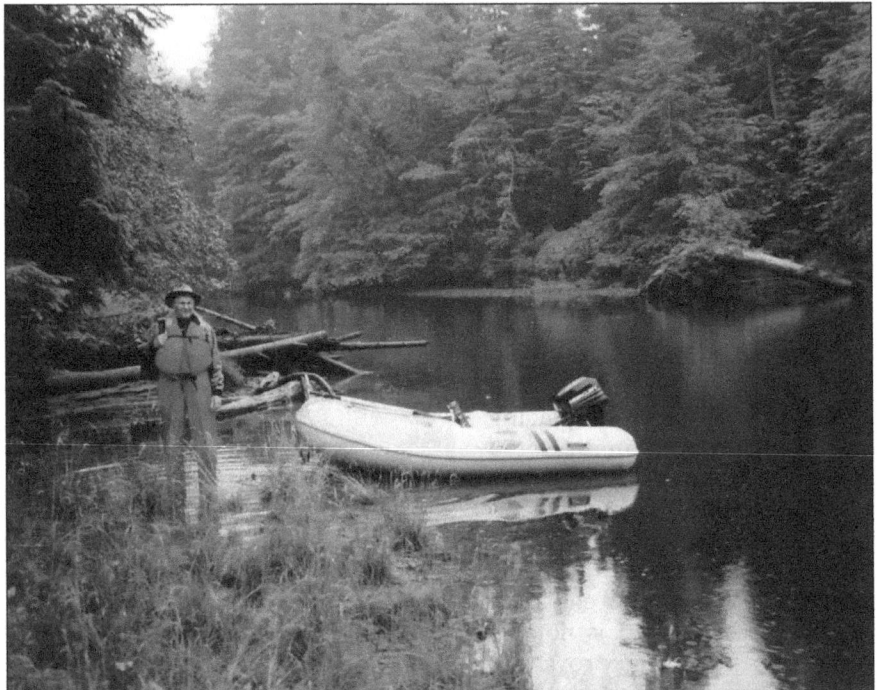

Baidarka *crew member Francis Caldwell exploring the rainforest on Graham Island's West Coast. We are grateful to have had his help and friendship on numerous voyages.*

in the right direction, the land protection is only a proposal, not a law. Friends of the bears and old growth/ estuarine environment must not relax their pressure on British Columbia. They must continue to call attention to the fact that time is running out on the opportunity for permanent, large-scale wildland preservation on the northern coast.

Wilderness holds the answers to questions we have not yet learned how to ask. If we destroy the last of the planet's great wild places, we cut ourselves off from the evolutionary path that ours and all species have followed. On the large scale of time, technological civilization is a perilous new experiment. In the sea of monumental changes in which we will live during the next millenium, wilderness, like that of the northern British Columbia coast, is both an ecological and psychological anchor.

Environmental historian Roderick Frazier Nash is a frequent visitor to the waterways of northern British Columbia on his boat Forevergreen. *Nash's works include the well known,* Wilderness and the American Mind.

(For more information about environmental organizations, please see the Appendix.)

Editor's note: Since Professor Nash's essay was written in

2001, the government of British Columbia has expanded its parks and protected-area system. In 2016, after more than a decade of complex negotiations between First Nations, industry, conservation organizations, and the provincial government, an agreement was reached that permanently protects 85% of the coastal temperate Great Bear Rainforest from industrial logging. More than 15% per cent of the entire province has been dedicated to protected status. Along with the adjacent Tweedsmuir Provincial Park, the Fiordlands Conservancy, and some additional preserves, more than 9,000 square miles of generally contiguous wild lands have been protected from mining and timbering. In addition, the Tatshenshini-Alsek park, along with adjacent parks in Alaska and the Yukon Territory form the world's largest international World Heritage Site. Studies show that conservation lands are providing a significant boost to rural employment as well as economic benefit to the provincial GDP.

Beware of Paralytic Shellfish Poisoning

The shellfish of the Pacific Northwest, including bivalves like clams, mussels, oysters, scallops, as well as some whelks and snails, are filter feeders. They pump sea water through their digestive systems, filtering out and consuming algae and other food particles. This process can make shellfish dangerous to humans and other creatures that eat shellfish, because certain species of algae produce poisonous biotoxins. These single-celled dinoflagellates are generally present in sea water at low concentrations year-round. However, during algal "blooms," the concentration of toxin-producing algae in the water increases, and large amounts of biotoxin accumulate in shellfish tissues. It can take several days to months, or even longer, for shellfish to flush the toxins from their systems. Although there are anecdotal accounts of lower-risk months, the exact combination of factors that contribute to algal blooms is not yet known.

Paralytic Shellfish Poisoning (PSP) results from consumption of these biotoxins. The biotoxins block normal neuron function and can lead to death from paralysis of the breathing muscles. Some biotoxins are 1,000 times more potent than cyanide, and the toxin levels contained in a single shellfish can be fatal to humans. In 1793, PSP poisoned members of Captain George Vancouver's survey crews after the men gathered and consumed mussels. One man died. This incident is memorialized at Poison Cove, in Mussel Inlet. PSP deaths have also been documented in wildlife populations such as sea otters and humpback whales.

In humans, symptoms of PSP include tingling or numbness that starts around the lips and mouth and spreads to the face and neck. Prickly sensations occur in the fingertips and toes, accompanied with headache and dizziness. Muscle weakness, nausea, and vomiting can also occur. Severe poisoning can produce tingling or burning in the arms and legs, incoherent speech, lack of coordination and breathing difficulties.

Do not underestimate the seriousness of PSP. There is no antidote. If you suspect that someone has PSP, seek immediate medical attention. Induce vomiting to expel shellfish from the stomach. Treat for shock and transport the victim as quickly as possible to a medical facility. Life support services may be necessary to sustain the victim's life. Once treated, the reduction of symptoms usually occurs within nine hours, with complete recovery in 24 hours.

To reduce your risk of PSP, you should not eat self-harvested shellfish, but purchase it from a reputable seafood retailer or shellfish farm that is required to sell only tested products. Neither cooking nor freezing eliminates the biotoxin from shellfish. Since crabs feed on shellfish, the guts/butter of crabs has been found to contain the biotoxin, although it is not known to accumulate in crab meat. Therefore, consumers of non-commercially harvested crab should clean the meat thoroughly, discard the guts/butter before boiling, and avoid drinking the broth in which the crab was boiled.

If you consider harvesting shellfish, you should, at a minimum, take into account the recent history of PSP in the area, the species harvested and their ability to concentrate and retain biotoxins, and the method of cleaning and preparing the shellfish. You should also be aware that the color of the seawater is not a reliable indicator of toxic shellfish. Just because red tide is not present does not mean absence of danger. Listen regularly for local PSP alerts on the weather channel. Shellfish closure notices are updated on the Fishing Information Lines at 604-666-2828 / 1-800-431-3474; and notices are available online. You should consult the map of Biotoxin Management Areas and be aware of closure notices.

—LW

Map of Biotoxin Management Areas:
http://www.pac.dfo-mpo.gc.ca/fm-gp/contamination/biotox/index-eng.htm

Biotoxin and Sanitary Contamination Closure notices:
http://www-ops2.pac.dfo-mpo.gc.ca/fns-sap/index-eng.cfm?pg=view_notice&lang=en&ID=recreational&ispsp=1

State of Alaska Epidemiology Section PSP Fact Sheet:
https://dec.alaska.gov/eh/fss/shellfish/paralytic-shellfish-poisoning/

Washington State Department of Health: http://https://doh.wa.gov/community-and-environment/shellfish/recreational-shellfish

BC Centre for Disease Control
http://www.bccdc.ca/health-info/diseases-conditions/paralytic-shellfish-poisoning

Queen Charlotte Sound:
Nakwakto Rapids to Cape Caution
(large numbers refer to chapters)

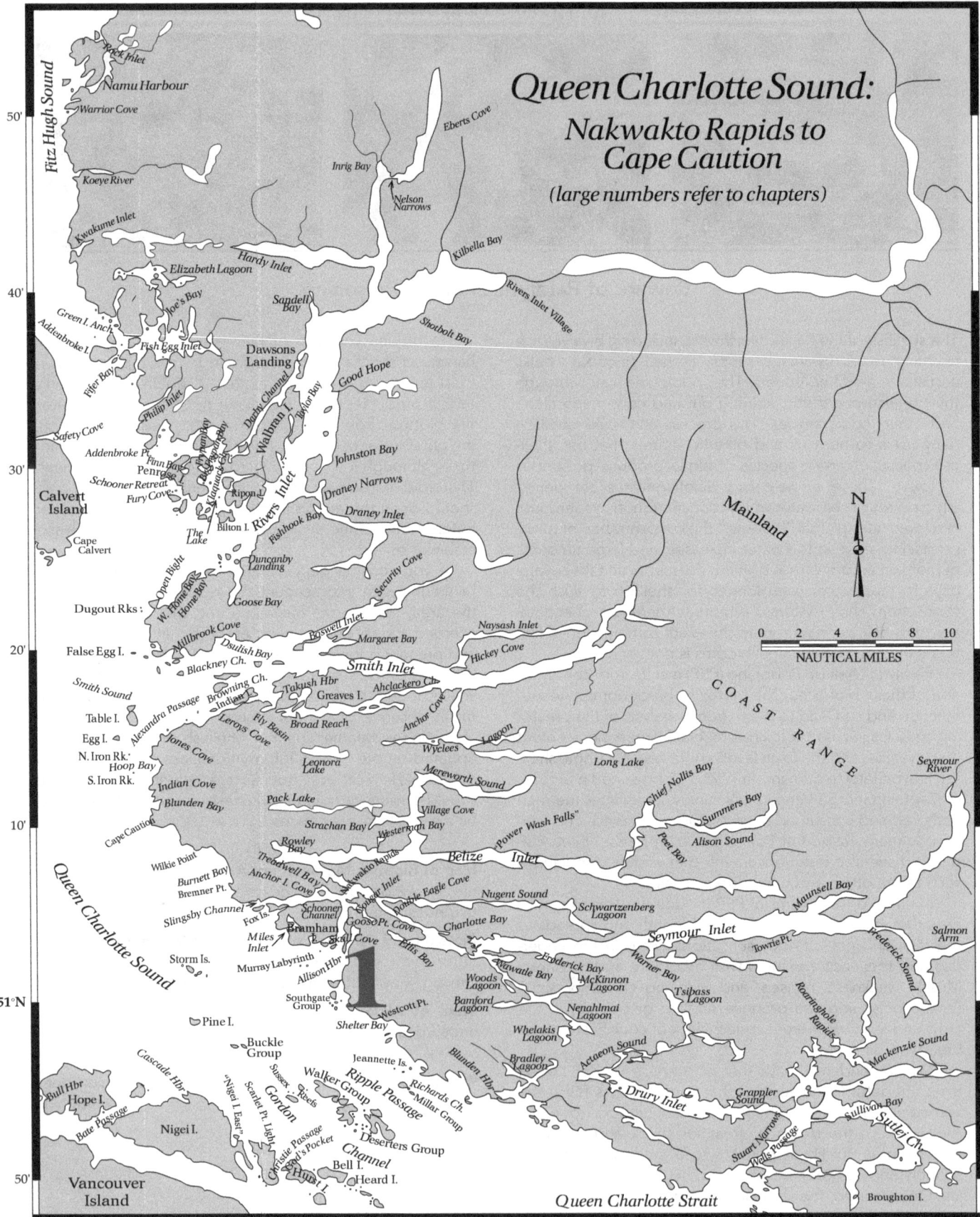

Fitz Hugh Sound

Rock Inlet
Namu Harbour
Warrior Cove
Koeye River
Kwakume Inlet
Elizabeth Lagoon
Hardy Inlet
Joe's Bay
Sandell Bay
Green I. Anch.
Addenbroke I.
Fish Egg Inlet
Fisher Bay
Philip Inlet
Safety Cove
Addenbroke Pt.
Penrose
Finn Bay
Schooner Retreat
Fury Cove
Klaquaek Channel
Calvert Island
The Lake
Bilton I.
Ripon I.
Cape Calvert
Open Bight
W. Home Bay
Home Bay
Dugout Rks.
Millbrook Cove
Dsulish Bay
False Egg I.
Blackney Ch.
Smith Sound
Alexandra Passage
Browning Ch.
Indian I.
Table I.
Egg I.
N. Iron Rk.
Hoop Bay
S. Iron Rk.
Jones Cove
Leroys Cove
Indian Cove
Blunden Bay
Cape Caution

Dawsons Landing
Walbran I.
Dachu Channel
Taylor Bay
Good Hope
Johnston Bay
Draney Narrows
Draney Inlet
Fishhook Bay
Duncanby Landing
Goose Bay
Boswell Inlet
Margaret Bay
Smith Inlet
Takush Hbr
Greaves I.
Ahclackero Ch.
Fly Basin
Broad Reach
Anchor Cove
Leonora Lake
Pack Lake
Wyclees
Lagoon
Mereworth Sound
Village Cove
Strachan Bay
Westernan Bay
Rowley Bay
Treadwell Bay
Anchor I. Cove
Nakwakto Rapids
Wilkie Point
Burnett Bay
Bremner Pt.
Slingsby Channel
Fox Is.
Schooner Channel
Bramham I.
Miles Inlet
Skull Cove
Goose Pt. Cove
Kapper Inlet
Double Eagle Cove
Storm Is.
Murray Labyrinth
Allison Hbr
Southgate Group
Shelter Bay
Nestcott Pt.
Pine I.
Buckle Group
Jeannette Is.
Richards Ch.
Millar Group
Blunden Hbr
Cascade Hbr
Bull Hbr
Hope I.
"Nigei I. East"
Gordon
Sussex Reefs
Scarlet Pt. Light
Walker Group
Ripple Passage
Nigei I.
Christie Passage
"God's Pocket"
Deserters Group
Bate Passage
Goletas Channel
Bell I.
Heard I.
Hunt I.
Vancouver Island

Eberts Cove
Inrig Bay
Nelson Narrows
Kilbella Bay
Rivers Inlet Village
Shotbolt Bay
Rivers Inlet
Naysash Inlet
Hickey Cove
Security Cove
Long Lake
Chief Nollis Bay
Summers Bay
Alison Sound
Peet Bay
"Power Wash Falls"
Belize Inlet
Nugent Sound
Schwartzenberg Lagoon
Maunsell Bay
Charlotte Bay
Seymour Inlet
Frederick Bay
Warner Bay
Towrie Pt.
Ellis Bay
Ahwatle Bay
McKinnon Lagoon
Woods Lagoon
Bamford Lagoon
Nenahlmai Lagoon
Tsibass Lagoon
Whelakis Lagoon
Bradley Lagoon
Actaeon Sound
Drury Inlet
Grappler Sound
Roaringhole Rapids
Mackenzie Sound
Stuart Narrows
Wells Passage
Sullivan Bay
Sutlej Ch.
Frederick Sound
Salmon Arm
Seymour River

Mainland

N

COAST RANGE

Queen Charlotte Sound

Queen Charlotte Strait

Broughton I.

1

50'
40'
30'
20'
10'
51°N
50'

0 2 4 6 8 10
NAUTICAL MILES

©2024 Don and Réanne Douglass • Diagram not for navigation

1

Queen Charlotte Sound:
Nakwakto Rapids to Cape Caution

Some of the most fascinating and least known waters of British Columbia lie between Wells Passage and Cape Caution. The area has often been ignored by northbound cruising boats that want to cross Queen Charlotte Sound as quickly as possible, but little by little, adventurous boaters are beginning to discover the beautiful fiords that lie in Seymour and Belize inlets. Here, behind swift-flowing Nakwakto Rapids, in Smith Sound, in Rivers and Fish Egg inlets, you find fantastic fishing grounds, and remote, quiet lagoons. Some boaters have also discovered that in addition to being destinations in themselves, these inlets offer sheltered steppingstones to Fitz Hugh Sound that break up the "dreaded crossing."

For years, the standard northbound route along the Inside Passage followed the eastern shore of

Low tide in Blunden Harbour

Vancouver Island to its very tip; Port Hardy was the traditional last stop for provisioning and fueling, with God's Pocket or Bull Harbour the jumping-off sites for an early morning crossing of Queen Charlotte Sound. For powerboats, this was the shortest distance to the lee of Calvert Island in Fitz Hugh Sound; for sailboats it was just a close-hauled reach. Because so many boats took the standard route, the area between Wells Passage and Cape Caution remained one of the last on the coast to be explored and charted.

These days, however, many cruising boats leave Port McNeill and head for Blunden Harbour; or they use the Broughton Archipelago for shelter as far as Wells Passage, then Blunden Harbour, Miles Inlet, and Penrose Island Marine Park as steppingstones to Cape Caution and Fitz Hugh Sound. Be aware that strong ebb currents flowing out of Slingsby Channel create some of the biggest swells along this part of the coast.

With electronic charts, you can safely expand your cruising itineraries to include the seldom-visited waters east and north of Egg Island along the mainland shore of British Columbia and well beyond the northern tip of Vancouver Island.

Blunden Harbour (Queen Charlotte Strait)
12 mi NW of Wells Passage, 25 mi SE of Cape Caution
Entrance: 50°53.90'N, 127°16.12'W
Anchor: (Byrnes Island bears 060°T @ 0.11 Nm); 50°54.41'N, 127°17.74'W

Blunden Harbour, a wonderful, well-sheltered anchorage, is a favorite of cruising boats that head north following the mainland coast. Although the bay is quite shallow on its north side, there is adequate swinging room for various-sized boats and you can easily have good scope ratio. If the weather forecast calls for gales in either Queen Charlotte Strait or Sound, Blunden Harbour is a protected, landlocked basin. Upon entering, follow a mid-channel route avoiding charted rocks and shoals. Boaters who remain here for a day or two may be

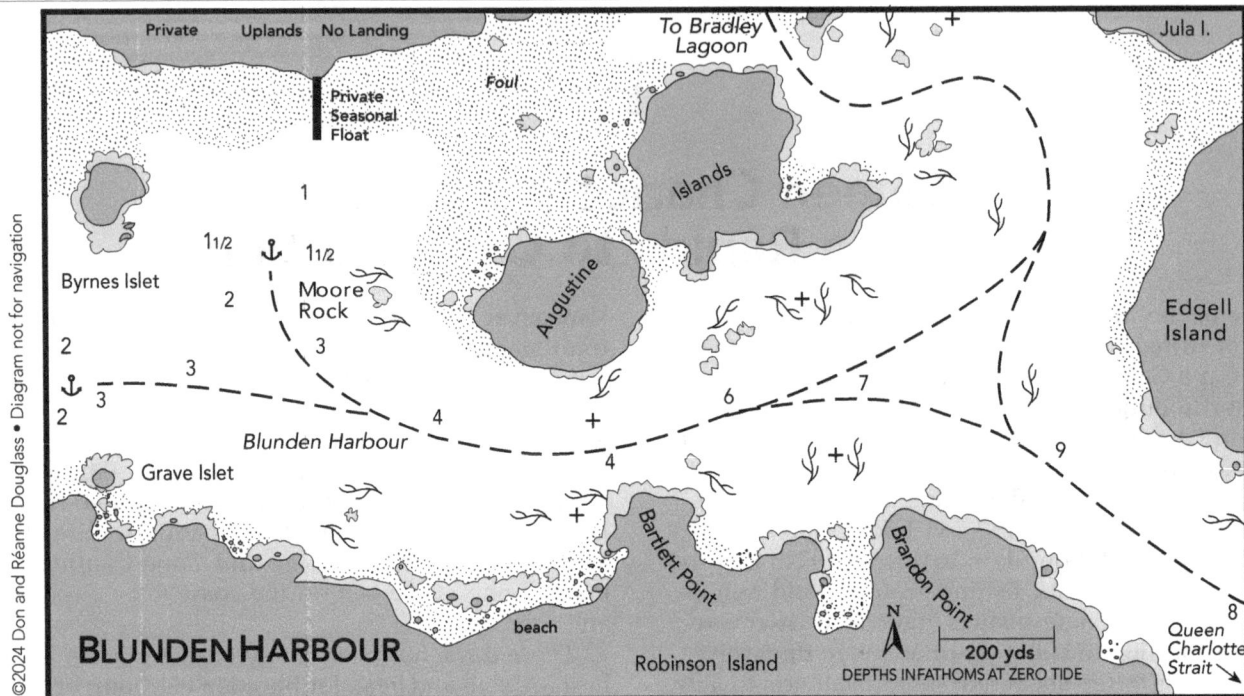

interested in exploring Bradley Lagoon by dinghy or kayak as noted below.

A thriving native culture once existed in this rain forest. Currently, nearly all of the north shore and its uplands are Indian Reserve lands that are private, no trespassing. A seasonal private float along the north shore provides access for the caretakers and onshore buildings. This is the traditional territory & homeland of the Nakwaxdaxw People. It is regularly monitored by guardians. No camping or digging."

Anchor in 1½ fathoms, mud bottom with very good holding.

Bradley Lagoon (Blunden Harbour)
1.5 mi NE of Blunden Harbour
Entrance: 50°55.01'N, 127°15.72'W
Anchor: (far E end): 50°56.51'N, 127°13.77'W

Bradley Lagoon is a large, quiet and beautiful, inland "lake" that extends northerly to less than a mile from Whelakis Lagoon, at the bitter south end of Seymour Inlet. We have entered by dinghy only and immensely enjoyed a pristine wilderness, populated by seals and various species of birds that seldom see visitors. There is no sign of civilization inside the lagoon until the bitter end where you can see evidence of past logging on the ridge at the far south reaches of Seymour Inlet.

Access to Bradley Lagoon is blocked by a strong tidal rapids that allows access for just a short duration at slack water. According to our experiences, high-water slack occurs about 2 hours after high water in

Blunden Harbour; and low-water slack occurs about 2 hours before high water outside. This is due to the fact that the lagoon tidewater level changes half or less than that outside the rapids. These slack-water times occur later during spring tides and earlier during neap tides. The narrows are about 40 feet wide and, during spring tides, the ebb current resembles a continuous waterfall. The ebb current may run for 8 to 9 hours or more with a large amount of foam covering the approach for several hundred yards.

Getting a good fix on depth in the rapids fairway, even near slack, is difficult due to underwater turbulence. The bottom has a number of small- to medium-sized boulders below the surface of the water, with about 3 to 4 feet depth at low-water slack and perhaps 6 feet depth in the fairway at high-water slack. The actual amount depends upon rain runoff levels, as well as the lunar cycle.

One difficulty here is that the muskeg water inside the lagoon is nearly opaque, limiting underwater visibility to just a few inches. As you proceed into the second narrows the surface water becomes fresher and turns to the color of root beer. Although we once witnessed another couple take their 40-foot vessel into the lagoon, we definitely do not recommend it. However, we do recommend reconnoitering the lagoon by dinghy or kayak from a base camp in Blunden Harbour.

Inside the rapids a large basin, 2.5 miles long trends northwest to southeast. This first basin, which has a long, mid-channel rock awash near high water at its northwest end, has an average depth of about

50 feet. We call this mid-channel rock Seal Rock since it is a favorite "hangout" for seals. Sheltered anchorage can be found anywhere in the north end of the basin, avoiding Seal Rock. If southeast winds are expected, we would anchor in the southeast corner.

On the east side of the first basin, a narrow channel leads northeast 3 miles from the rapids to a second much smaller basin. This channel, which passes through a series of narrows 20 to 50 yards wide before entering the second basin, has a fairway depth of 2 to 3 fathoms. The second smaller basin (also trending northwest to southeast) is extremely calm with little water movement. The north end of this small shallow basin has a number of isolated granite erratics that are not visible in the muskeg water until you are upon them. This basin, which ends in small streams at its north and east sides, is less than a mile from Whelakis Lagoon reached from behind Nakwakto Rapids. You will find animal tracks here along the soft sandy-mud beaches.

Waiting for slack water, Bradley Lagoon

Bradley Lagoon is just one of more than a dozen large, poorly or uncharted lagoons in northern B.C. that are seldom, if ever, visited. If this kind of adventure appeals to you, you might want to explore other lagoons such as Whelakis Lagoon in Seymour Inlet, Drury Lagoon to the South, the much larger and complex Elizabeth Lagoon behind Fish Egg Inlet, Campbell Inlet and Lagoon off Hunter Channel, and beautiful Ellerslie Lagoon off Spiller Channel.

Jeannette Islands

(Queen Charlotte Sound)
6 mi NW of Blunden Harbour
Entrance (SW): 50°55.38'N, 127°25.09'W
Anchor: 50°55.70'N, 127°24.28'W

Jeannette Islands are well placed for a temporary stop but not recommended for overnight anchorage due to chop from prevailing northwest winds. Avoid the large drying rock off the cove point, and favor the north wall for a less rocky bottom. We have found Jeannette Islands to be calm and comfortable in moderate southerly winds.

Anchor in 3 fathoms over a mixed bottom with fair holding.

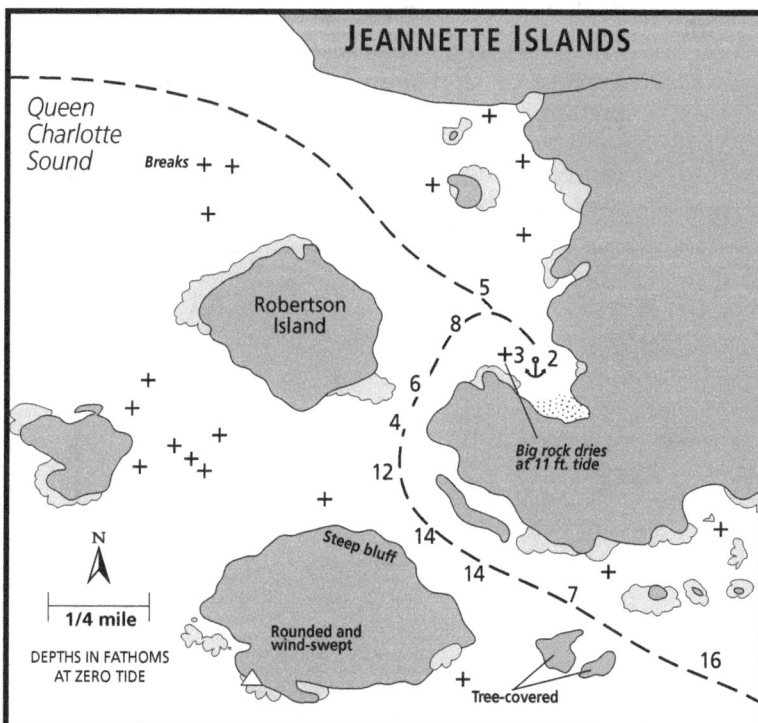

JEANNETTE ISLANDS

Queen Charlotte Sound

Breaks

Robertson Island

5
8
+3 ⚓ 2
6
4
12
Big rock dries at 11 ft. tide

N
14
Steep bluff
14
7
16

1/4 mile
DEPTHS IN FATHOMS AT ZERO TIDE

Rounded and wind-swept

Tree-covered

©2024 Don and Réanne Douglass • Diagram not for navigation

Shelter Bay North

(Queen Charlotte Sound)
8 mi NW of Blunden Harbour
Outer Entrance: 50°58.18'N, 127°28.13'W
Entrance (N branch): 50°58.23'N, 127°26.76'W
Anchor: 50°58.10'N, 127°25.49'W

The north branch of Shelter Bay offers good protection in almost all weather and excellent shelter from southerly storm winds. Northwest swell is greatly diminished by the nearly landlocked entrance. The lack of driftwood indicates that the bay is not greatly affected by storms, and the lower branches of the trees, cut evenly along the high tide line, suggest a lack of chop or swell. Shelter Bay's north branch is strategically located halfway between Blunden Harbour and Miles Inlet, the two main anchorages for cruising boats along this part of the coast.

You can find good anchoring a quarter-mile from the head of the bay, on a line from the rock on the south shore to the tree-covered island on the north shore. We found the bay easy to enter; the fairway to the north branch is a flat 10 fathoms with no sign of rocks except along shore. Although we recommend this as an overnight anchorage, its biggest drawback is that, deep in the bay, you can't see or guess the conditions outside.

Anchor in 4 fathoms over soft mud and clay with good holding.

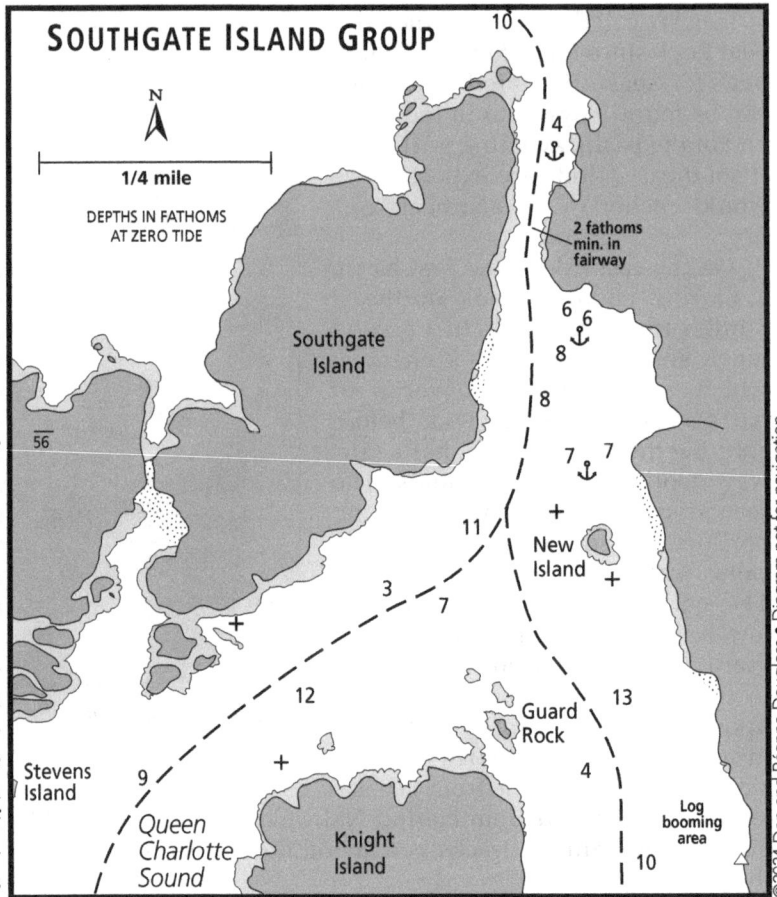

SOUTHGATE ISLAND GROUP

N

1/4 mile

DEPTHS IN FATHOMS AT ZERO TIDE

Southgate Island

2 fathoms min. in fairway

New Island

Guard Rock

Stevens Island

Queen Charlotte Sound

Knight Island

Log booming area

©2024 Don and Réanne Douglass • Diagram not for navigation

Entrance: 50°58.27'N, 127°27.21'W
Anchor (small boats): 50°58.53'N, 127°27.33'W

The small, scenic cove east of Westcott Point makes a great lunch stop or an overnighter for small boats in prevailing northwest conditions. We enjoy its lovely sand beach and lack of swell or chop. From here, you can easily determine outside conditions by hiking over the spit for a view.

Westcott Point, East Cove

(Seymour Inlet)
On the N side of Shelter Bay

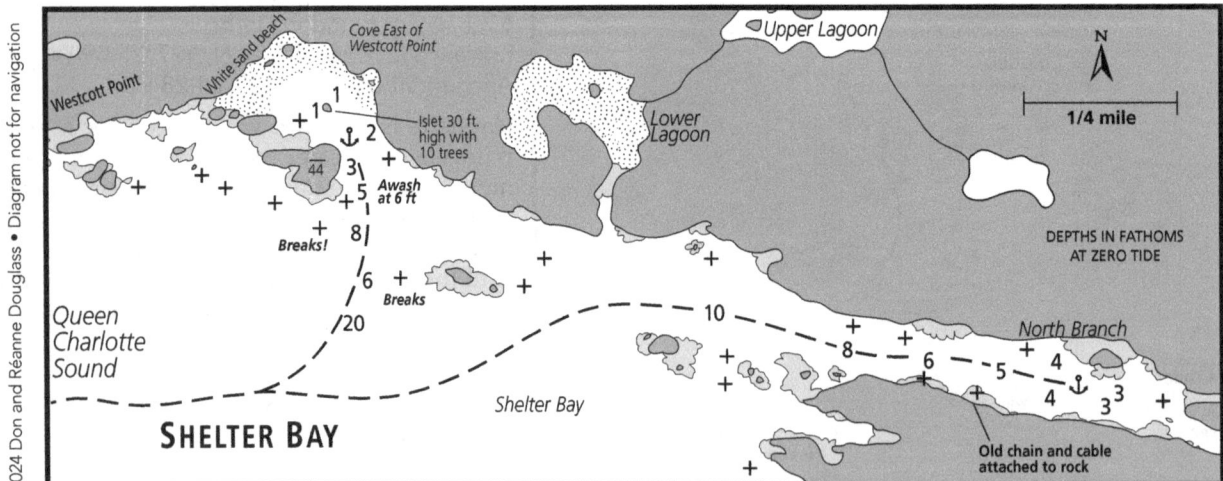

Cove East of Westcott Point

Westcott Point

White sand beach

Islet 30 ft. high with 10 trees

Awash at 6 ft

Breaks!

Breaks

Queen Charlotte Sound

Upper Lagoon

Lower Lagoon

N

1/4 mile

DEPTHS IN FATHOMS AT ZERO TIDE

North Branch

Shelter Bay

SHELTER BAY

Old chain and cable attached to rock

©2024 Don and Réanne Douglass • Diagram not for navigation

The entrance to Westcott Point, East Cove lies between two rocks across which swells occasionally break. The easternmost rock, which dries on a 6-foot tide, is particularly dangerous. Anchor on a line between the small 30-foot high islet with ten trees on it and island (44) to the south. Swinging room is limited.

Anchor in 2 fathoms over sand with good holding.

Southgate Island Group
(Queen Charlotte Sound)
11 mi NW of Blunden Harbour
Entrance (SW): 51°00.08'N, 127°32.30'W
Anchor: 51°00.68'N, 127°31.41'W

Exploring the bitter end of Bradley Lagoon

The passage between Southgate Island and Knight Island offers a "flat-water" shortcut of sorts for boats heading to Allison Harbour. It can also be used in fair weather as a lunch stop or an overnighter. Sheltered anchorage for small boats using a stern tie to shore can be found on either side of the narrows; the north end is suitable for small boats only.

Anchor (larger boats) in 7 fathoms over a mud bottom with good holding.

Allison Harbour, East Cove
(Queen Charlotte Sound)
13 mi NW of Blunden Harbour
Entrance (mid-channel City Point to Ray Island):
51°02.15'N, 127°31.24'W
Anchor (head of bay): 51°03.43'N, 127°30.44'W
Anchor (East Cove): 51°02.98'N, 127°30.53'W

Allison Harbour, a long north-south inlet extending nearly two miles, provides good shelter in most weather. The entrances to Allison Harbour and Schooner Channel are encumbered with offshore rocks and reefs and, in foul weather or limited visibility, entering can be risky.

Halfway into the harbor there's a dangerous rock, awash on a 6-foot tide, which can easily be avoided by staying to the west. In stable weather, anchor at the head of the bay favoring the west side. In unsettled weather, small boats can anchor in one of the two small coves. Set your anchor well—it's sometimes hard to get a good hold on the clay bottom.

Anchor (head of the bay) in 3 to 4 fathoms over clay and mud with good holding.
Anchor (east cove) in 3 to 4 fathoms over soft mud with poor-to-fair holding.

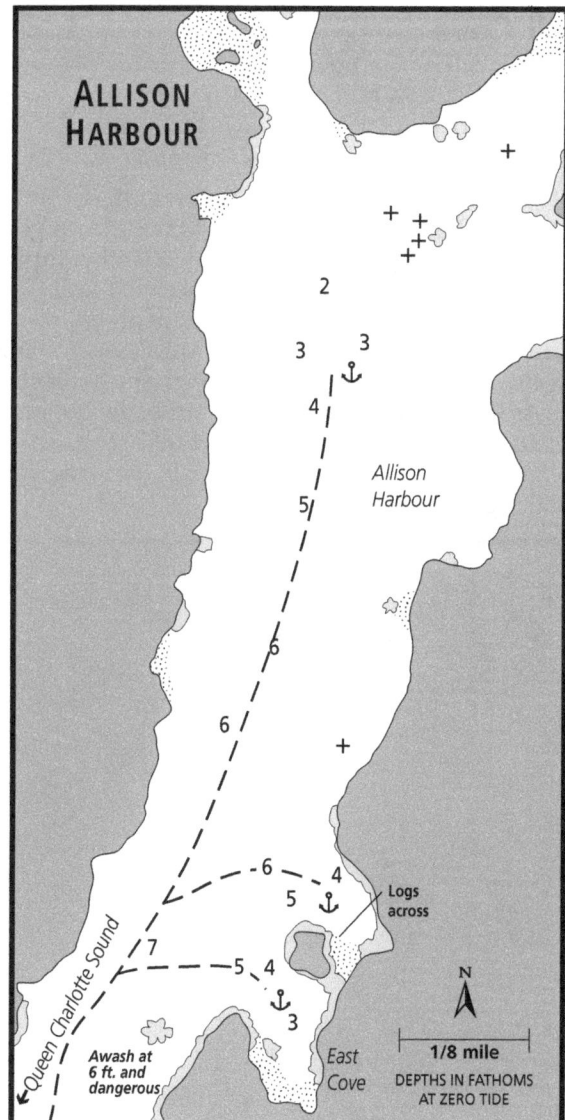

Murray Labyrinth

(Queen Charlotte Sound)
1 mi W of Allison Harbour
Entrance: 51°02.60'N, 127°32.39'W
Anchor: 51°02.81'N, 127°31.91'W

Murray Labyrinth is truly a well-sheltered maze of islands, islets and rocks, in a pristine setting. There's a protected spot in the center of Murray Labyrinth where small boats can anchor and explore by dinghy or kayak, but proceed dead slow, posting alert lookouts on the bow. The bottom is more irregular than indicated on the chart and not all hazards are noted.

Anchor in 1.5 fathoms over soft bottom with good holding.

Skull Cove (Schooner Channel)

2 mi W of Allison Harbour
Entrance: 51°02.94'N, 127°33.28'W
Anchor (N cove): 51°03.21'N, 127°33.72'W
Anchor (S cove): 53°03.01'N, 127°33.66'W

Skull Cove, just west of Murray Labyrinth, is another favorite, well-sheltered anchorage that makes a good base camp for exploring the nearby island complex. Small boats can anchor in many places in Skull Cove since the water is quite shallow. Midden Hill, on the east side of the bay, composed of a large heap of shells, indicates that this was once an important harvesting area. As in the case of Murray Labyrinth, the bottom is somewhat irregular and not all hazards are shown on the chart. Particularly avoid the rock in the center, just west of Ten Tree Islet.

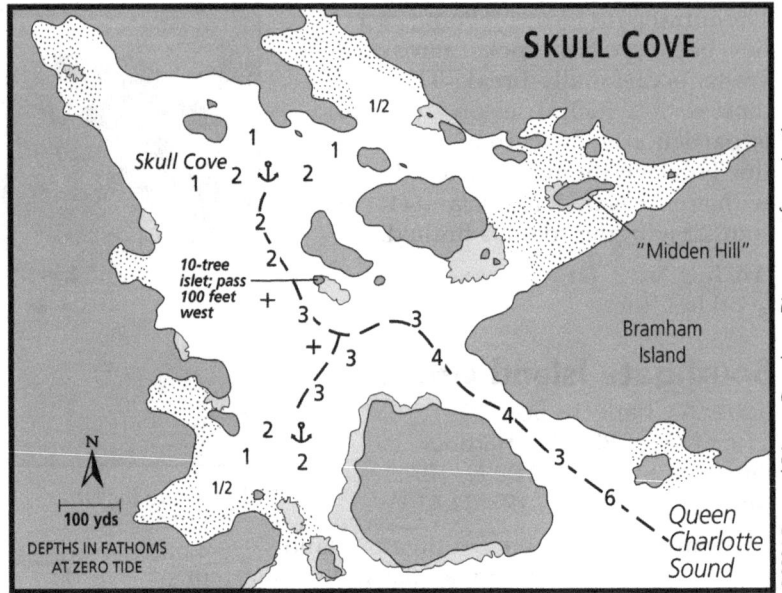

Anchor in 1 to 2 fathoms over mud and sand with good holding.

Schooner Channel

(Queen Charlotte Sound)
The S entrance to Nakwakto Rapids, 0.5 mi W of Allison Harbour
Entrance (S): 51°02.27'N, 127°31.46'W
Entrance (N): 51°05.12'N, 127°30.72'W

Schooner Channel is a narrow 3-mile-long channel between Bramham Island and Allison Harbour. To navigate it safely requires constant vigilance. Although we have transited Schooner Channel and

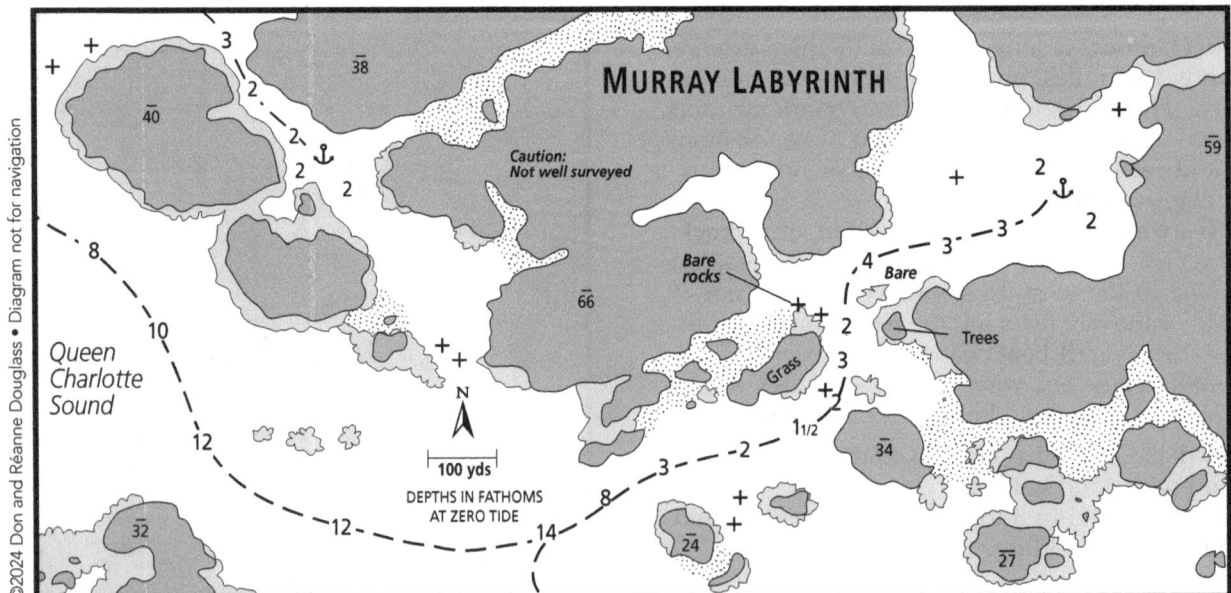

Nakwakto Rapids in fog under radar and GPS, we do not recommend it. The current—which can run five knots on a flood and six on an ebb—can easily set you on the rocks or on shore. When tugs use Schooner Channel to tow log booms out of Seymour Inlet to the storage area at Southgate Island, they have limited maneuverability when the current is flowing, so stay clear!

Tiny Goose Point Cove on the east shore, 0.8 mile south of the point, can be used as an anchorage. Avoid two uncharted rocks a quarter-mile south of Goose Point close to the west shore.

Goose Point Cove (Schooner Channel)

At the NE end of Schooner Channel
Entrance: 51°04.92'N, 127°30.70'W
Anchor: 51°04.93'N, 127°30.58'W

Goose Point Cove, well protected from all weather, is removed from the heavy currents that flow outside. If you plan to visit Nakwakto Rapids or Seymour Inlet it's a good place to stay overnight to catch slack water. Two small boats can anchor in mid-channel south of the islet just west of the drying shoal to the east. You can also leave your boat here if you want to explore Nakwakto Rapids by high-speed inflatable.

Anchor in 1 to 2 fathoms over mud with good holding; since swinging room is limited consider using a second anchor if there are other boats in the cove.

Tying to a log dog

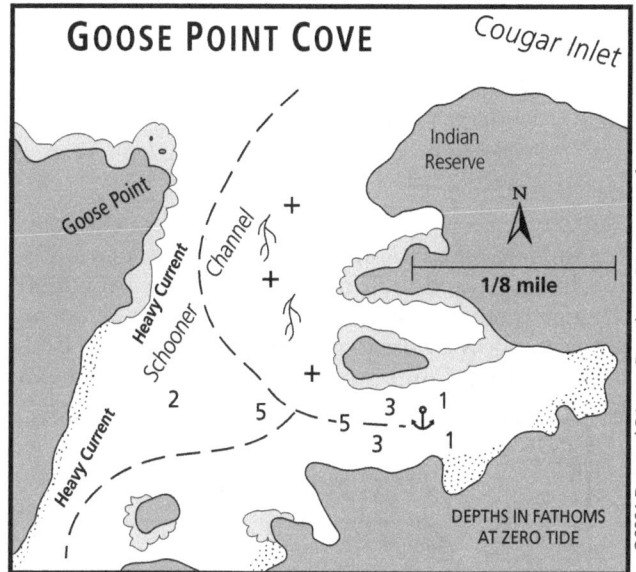

GOOSE POINT COVE   Cougar Inlet

Goose Point

Indian Reserve

N

Schooner Channel

Heavy Current

Heavy Current

1/8 mile

2   5   -5   3   1
                                  3   1

DEPTHS IN FATHOMS
AT ZERO TIDE

©2024 Don and Réanne Douglass • Diagram not for navigation

British Columbia Provincial Parks

Visitors to British Columbia are fortunate that the provincial government has displayed both foresight and commitment in establishing well over 600 provincial parks. Fundamental to implementing BC Park's mission is integrating reconciliation with Indigenous Peoples.

The government has promised to set aside 13 percent of the total area of Vancouver Island for parks; their goal for the entire province is that 12 percent of all the land will be designated as provincial parks or ecological reserves. Over 148 parks have been added since 1991, and they range from the Tatshenshini wilderness area of 2.4 million acres to a 5-acre parcel near Nanaimo for the protection of an important breeding colony of pelagic cormorants. On Quadra Island, 7,400 acres in the Main Lakes area has been set aside as a park.

Seventy of the Provincial Parks are Marine Parks. Although the exact definition of a marine park is not clear, many—but not all—are accessible only by boat. About 10 percent of these have wharves or floats, 70 percent provide all-weather anchorage. Many are highly developed, with camping and picnic sites, toilets and drinking water. Others provide only some facilities, while still others remain completely undeveloped at this time. Most of the parks are free; a moderate moorage fee is charged at a few of them.

Travel to Marine Parks by cruising boat and visit prehistoric middens, Indigenous settlements, shipwrecks, pristine beaches, thick forests, clear blue lakes and rugged mountains. You can canoe, kayak, swim, SCUBA dive, hike, fish, and watch birds and other wildlife—thanks to the government and the people of British Columbia.

Cougar Inlet

(Schooner Channel)

½ mi S of Nakwakto Rapids

Entrance: 51°05.19'N, 127°30.56'W

Anchor (outside narrows): 51°05.04'N, 127°30.17'W

Anchor (head of inlet): 51°04.17'N, 127°28.61'W

The entrance to Cougar Inlet is the closest anchor site to Nakwakto Rapids. Over the years, many vessels have painted their names on the vertical wall of the north shore just east of Barrow Point. Mooring here can allow a boat to remain out of the main body of the current. Compared to the waters of Nakwakto Rapids that surge past its entrance, it is relatively calm inside the inlet.

Small boats can anchor in shallower water close to the narrows. Larger vessels can anchor in 10 fathoms and use a stern tie to the steep-to vertical wall. Shallow-draft vessels can also find excellent protection out of the current, deep inside the inlet.

Minimum depth in the fairway of Cougar Narrows is about 3 feet at zero tide, with current about 3 knots; width is about 45 feet. The current changes to flood about the time of high water at Alert Bay, and 2 hours before slack at Nakwakto Rapids. To avoid uncharted rocks we advise reconnoitering prior to

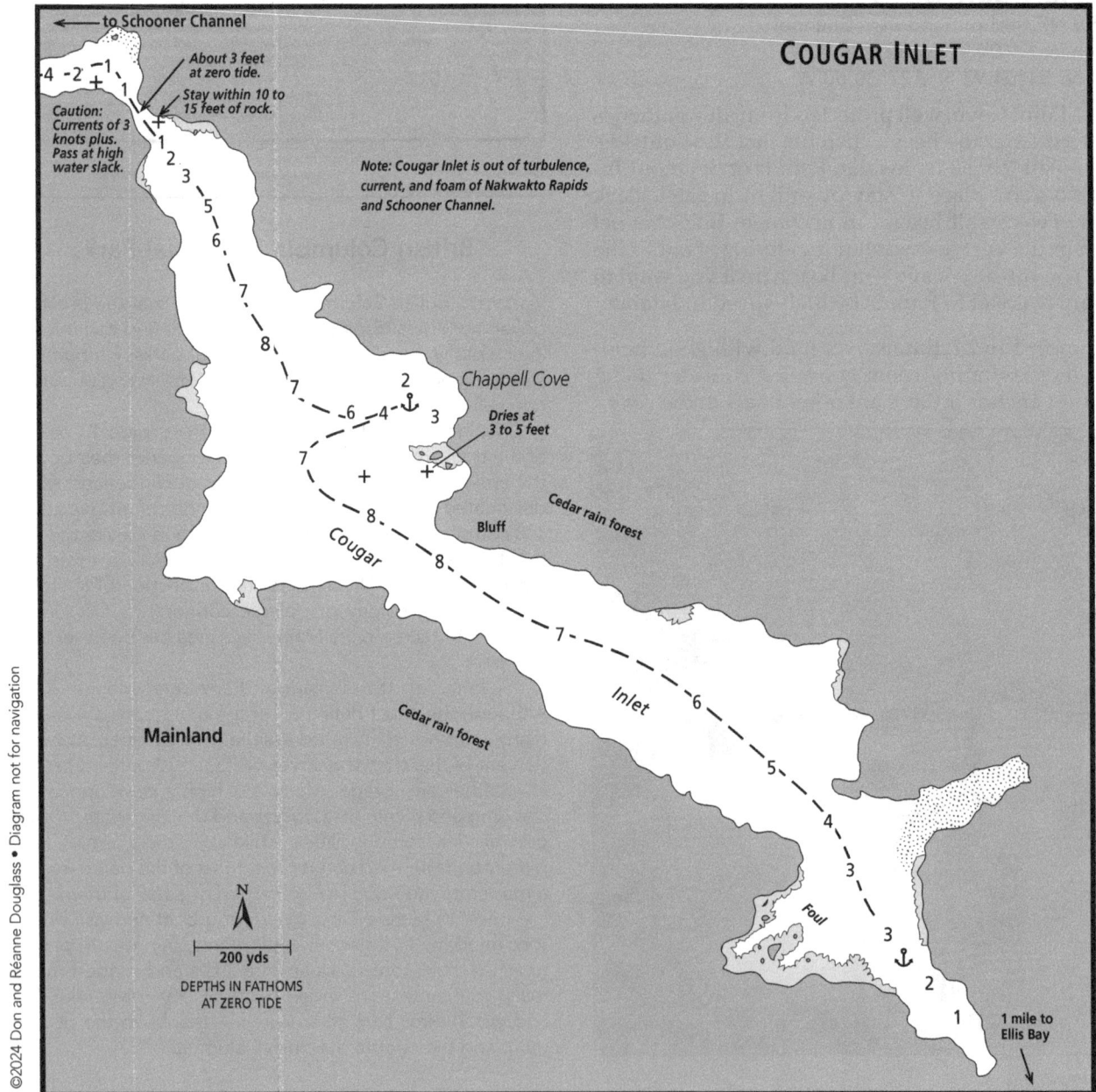

COUGAR INLET

to Schooner Channel

About 3 feet at zero tide.

Stay within 10 to 15 feet of rock.

Caution: Currents of 3 knots plus. Pass at high water slack.

Note: Cougar Inlet is out of turbulence, current, and foam of Nakwakto Rapids and Schooner Channel.

Chappell Cove

Dries at 3 to 5 feet

Cedar rain forest

Bluff

Cougar

Inlet

Cedar rain forest

Mainland

Foul

N

200 yds

DEPTHS IN FATHOMS AT ZERO TIDE

1 mile to Ellis Bay

©2024 Don and Reanne Douglass • Diagram not for navigation

transiting the narrows of Cougar Inlet. At the west entrance, favor the south shore, staying within about 15 feet of one of the rocks to avoid kelp on the north shore. In the center of the narrows, favor the south shore to avoid a dangerous rock on the north shore.

Anchor (outside narrows) in 4 fathoms over sand with fair holding.

Anchor (head of inlet) in 6 fathoms over mud and sand; good holding.

Chappell Cove
(Cougar Inlet)
1 mi SE of Cougar Inlet entrance
Entrance: 51°05.19'N, 127°30.56'W
Anchor (N of spit): 51°04.68'N, 127°29.36'W

Chappell Cove is the anchor site 0.4 mile on the northeast shore inside Cougar Inlet, just above a spit that extends from shore. We named this cove in honor of early sailing explorer, John Chappell, who in his wonderful book, *Cruising Beyond Desolation Sound,* speculated that this inlet might be an interesting place to explore. If his sailboat had had a shallower draft, he, too, might have been able to enjoy the wild nature of Cougar Inlet. Surrounded by old-growth rain forest where time stands still, the quiet is overpowering.

Anchor (north of spit) in 4 fathoms, soft mud and sand with good holding.

Nakwakto Rapids (Seymour Inlet)
4 mi NE of Miles Inlet
Entrance (S): 51°05.61'N, 127°30.58'W
Entrance (N): 51°05.96'N, 127°30.18'W

Nakwakto Rapids—one of the world's fastest rapids where the flood can attain 14 knots and the ebb 16 knots—should set your adrenaline pumping.

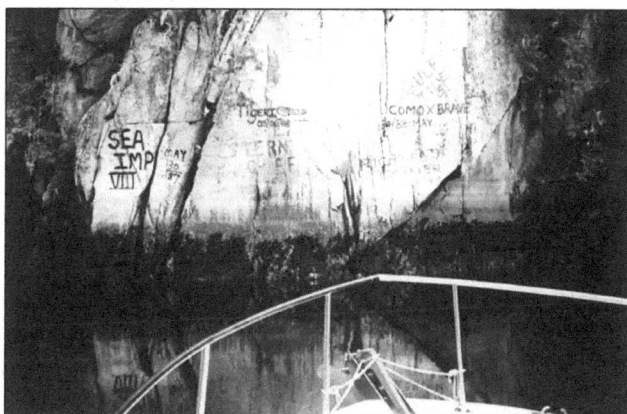

Cougar Inlet, boat names on outer wall

Caution: Nakwakto Rapids has extremely hazardous eddies and turbulence when the current exceeds more than a few knots. During neap tides and near slack water, Nakwakto is not difficult to transit at either high or low water. And when you are east of the rapids, a magical world opens up.

On spring tides, foam obscures much of the rapids and transit should be timed close to slack water. Although passage can be taken on either side of Tremble Island, we have generally approached the rapids from the south and find the wider, slightly shallower route east of the island perfectly acceptable.

One strategy to enjoy the incredible sight of the rapids in full ebb is to take a dependable high-speed inflatable from Treadwell Bay or Goose Point Cove and land on a rock shelf on the northwest corner of island (49), 0.18 mile due west of Turret Island. Tie your dinghy well and follow the primitive trail southeast across the top of the island to a 10-foot-square viewing-platform, 100 feet above the seething rapids! As you approach the haul-out rock, be careful not to get sucked into the tight 4-foot-wide slot at the north end of the island where water, rushing through, creates falls of 3 feet or more in either direction!

Seymour Inlet
Trends NW and E of Nakwakto Rapids
Entrance (N of Nakwakto Rapids): 51°05.96'N, 127°30.18'W

Seymour Inlet, a major fiord of the British Columbia coast, leads 12 miles southeast from the junction of Belize Inlet (northwest of Nakwakto Rapids) to Harriet Point. Seymour Inlet then turns east for 21 miles to Eclipse Narrows, then northeast for another 13 miles to its head at the outlet of Seymour River—a total of 46 miles to the mainland mountain range.

Eclipse Narrows marks the beginning of Frederick Sound, a deep, scenic fiord that cuts 7 miles to the southeast. For several miles Seymour Inlet has depths in excess of 2,000 feet, particularly impressive because the inlet is a mile wide or less.

The tidal range in Seymour Inlet is seldom more than 4 feet, or less than a third of that found west of Nakwatko Rapids. The waters, though generally calm, are subject to occasional up- or downslope williwaws, especially in winter. The water is a muskeg brown with limited underwater visibility, particularly in the nearly stagnant lagoons. Tidal currents are generally weak except at a few narrows. Logging activity comes and goes in the inlet and you may find active logging, clear-cut areas, and old sites with remaining logging debris.

We describe Seymour Inlet from the northwest to the east before venturing into the other inlets.

Access the Cruising Wonderland Beyond Nakwakto Rapids

The world's fastest tidal rapids are found 28 miles north of Port Hardy, where four major watersheds drain an area of roughly 1,000 square miles through Nakwakto Narrows, a passage less than 400 meters wide where the currents can attain a velocity of up to 16 knots on a spring ebb tide. This is a totally landlocked area, where two major fjords—Seymour and Belize inlets—cut deep into the mainland coast range. Since all the water behind Nakwakto Narrows flows in and out via Schooner or Slingsby Channel, tidal streams are strong on all tides, regularly reaching 5 to 9 knots. So much water empties out of the area that the tidal range inside Seymour and Belize inlets never has a chance to fluctuate more than four feet before the outside tide—more than 14 feet in range—comes roaring back in.

These waters were among the last areas to be explored along the British Columbia coast. The area provided a refuge for indigenous people who moved further into the backcountry as Europeans arrived. Both inlets were named in honor of Frederick Seymour who was appointed governor of B.C in 1865. The unlikely name, Belize, comes from the fact that Seymour had previously served as lieutenant governor of British Honduras where he was based in the capital city (the name of the now-independent country). He died of acute alcoholism about four years after his appointment, but no one thought it appropriate to rename the inlets.

Schooner Channel—the more direct route if you're approaching from the south—leads directly north between Bramham Island and the mainland. This is the channel used by small tugs towing log booms out of Seymour Inlet. Although it is much narrower and more intricate than Slingsby Channel, the current is not as strong here. If you use Schooner, navigate with vigilance and post an alert lookout on your bow.

Slingsby Channel, northwest of the Fox Islands and Bramham Island, leads directly east from Queen Charlotte Sound into Nakwakto Narrows; it is much wider and deeper than Schooner Channel. Although the Sailing Directions favor Slingsby, beware of large threatening waves at its entrance during west winds and spring ebb tides.

When heading northward upcoast, we usually enter through Schooner and exit through Slingsby, using favorable currents on both passages.

To approach Nakwakto from the south, leave early in the morning to beat the prevailing northwesterlies that build in mid-morning and produce an uncomfortable ride when they meet contrary currents. Spending the night in a nearby anchorage along the mainland shore gives you a better chance of avoiding these conditions. Blunden Harbour, 14 miles southeast of Schooner Channel, and Allison Harbour, off the south entrance to Schooner are the most "bomb-proof" anchorages. Shelter Bay North,

the cove east of Wescott Point and the Southgate Group (Southgate and Knight islands) are also acceptable. Despite their daunting names, Murray Labyrinth (just around the corner to the northwest of Allison Harbour) and Skull Cove (west of Murray) can provide good shelter for small craft. Enter in daylight and post a bow lookout.

Miles Inlet, between Bramham and McEwan points, south of Slingsby, is the safest, most secure anchorage along this stretch of the coast. Its entrance is narrow and if a following sea is running, you may get a little excited when you see waves breaking over the rocks. But the seas calm immediately once you enter the T-shaped sanctuary. To enter Slingsby Channel from Miles Inlet, we prefer the small channel leading between Bramham and Fox Islands. Although this channel is narrow, with shoals and some current, it is totally protected from seas and winds. Whatever current you encounter will certainly be weaker than at the entrance to Slingsby.

The preferred anchor sites closest to Nakwakto—ideal for awaiting slack water—are Cougar Inlet, just southeast of the rapids, and Treadwell Bay to the northwest. Treadwell Bay is straightforward with good protection and little current. If you want an easy start to cross Nakwakto, anchor in the outer entrance to Cougar Inlet using a stern tie to the steep wall on the north side. Boat names painted on this wall attest to previous visitors.

A landlocked anchorage south of Cougar Narrows provides very good protection and a place to leave your boat if you wish to explore by a high-speed dinghy. The entrance, which is tricky, requires advance planning because of its narrow width (45 feet) and shallow depth (3 feet at zero tide). Enter only during high-water slack. During neap tides, deep-draft boats should not attempt to enter. Inside Cougar Inlet, depths range from two to eight fathoms, and the calm water and cedar-lined shores give you a taste of the lagoons that lie inside Seymour Inlet. In addition, Goose Point Cove, just south of Nakwakto, and the area west of Anchor Island on its north side, are out of the main current and offer sheltered sites for one or two boats.   —RHD

Tremble Island, Nakwakto Rapids at slack water

Lassiter Bay (Seymour Inlet)
5 mi NW of Nakwakto Rapids
Entrance: 51°08.13'N, 127°35.33'W

Lassiter Bay, immediately north of Rowley Bay, collects a lot of logs, stumps, and trees that drift ashore from Belize and Seymour inlets during southeast storm winds. Bleached silver logs are piled deep, one on top of another, around the head of Lassiter Bay. We did not find suitable anchorage here.

Rowley Bay (Seymour Inlet)
4 mi NW of Nakwakto Rapids
Entrance: 51°07.71'N, 127°35.22'W
Anchor: 51°07.66'N, 127°36.66'W

Rowley Bay, at the northwest corner of Seymour Inlet, offers protection from all but easterly winds. The head of the bay widens slightly and has a 2- to 4-fathom bottom. The shore at the head contains a number of drift logs, and isolated rocks lie under water along both the north and south shores.

There is room for one small boat, or two to three boats using stern ties. Larger boats can anchor farther east in deeper water with more swinging room.

Anchor in 2 to 4 fathoms over a mixed bottom of sand and mud; fair-to-good holding.

Harvell Islet Cove (Nakwakto Rapids)
Immediately E of Nakwakto Rapids
Entrance: 51°06.14'N, 127°29.33'W
Anchor (N of Harvell Islet and the reefs): 51°06.19'N, 127°29.08'W

Anchorage can be taken to the northeast of Nakwakto Rapids in the small cove 0.3 mile north of Harvell Islet. This is a good place to wait for slack water and watch the rapids. Swinging room is limited. Larger vessels can anchor east of Harvell Islet.

Anchor (north of Harvell Islet and the reefs) in 2 fathoms over sand and mud with good holding.

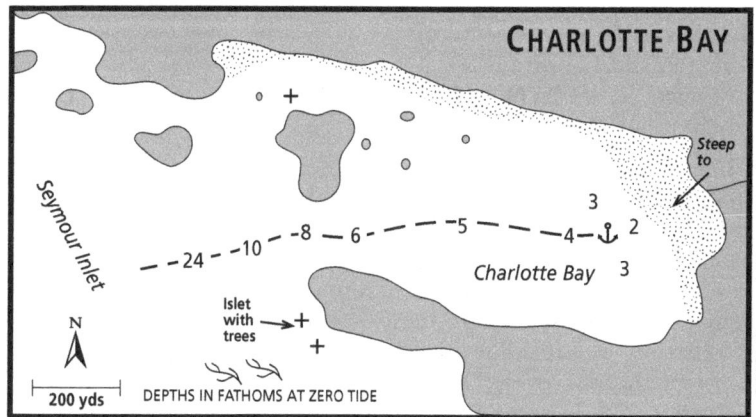

CHARLOTTE BAY

©2024 Don and Réanne Douglass
Diagram not for navigation

Double Eagle Cove
(Seymour Inlet)
1.5 miles W of Charlotte Bay
Anchor: 51°03.91'N, 127°25.26'W

Double Eagle Cove, on the west shore of Seymour Inlet, is a convenient lunch stop protected by several islets. Eagles often use this area as a vantage-point to watch for prey up and down the inlet.

Anchor in about 1½ fathoms over gravel and some kelp; fair holding; limited swinging room.

Charlotte Bay
(Seymour Inlet)
5 mi SE of Nakwakto Rapids
Entrance: 51°03.59'N, 127°23.14'W
Anchor: 51°03.58'N, 127°22.54'W

Charlotte Bay, protected from most of the easterly winds, has many drift logs on shore indicating that strong westerlies blow here. However, this is one of the better anchorages in the area.

Anchor in 4 to 6 fathoms over sand and gravel with fair holding.

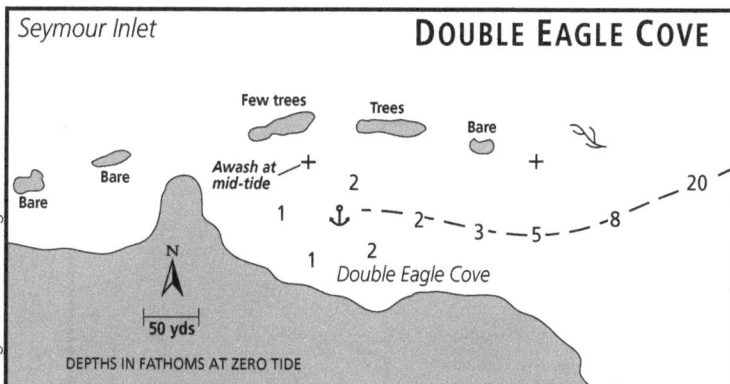

DOUBLE EAGLE COVE

©2024 Don and Réanne Douglass
Diagram not for navigation

Bow watch in Seymour Inlet

Ellis Bay (Seymour Inlet)
1 mi SW of Charlotte Bay
Entrance: 51°03.04'N, 127°23.69'W
Anchor: 51°02.96'N, 127°25.19'W

Ellis Bay is a good introduction to the fascinating lagoons that lie along the south shore of Seymour Inlet. Extra caution or prior reconnoitering by dinghy is advised in these shallow, rocky waters. The narrows are very shallow and currents can be a problem. Shallow-draft, small boats can find very good protection in Ellis Bay along the south shore, just west of the narrows. The upper end of Ellis Bay is less than a mile away from the bitter end of Cougar Inlet.

Anchor in 2 fathoms over soft mud with isolated rocks; fair-to-good holding.

Wawatle Bay (Seymour Inlet)
4 mi SE of Charlotte Bay
Entrance: 51°02.14'N, 127°19.10'W
Anchor: 51°02.05'N, 127°16.85'W

Wawatle Bay, which offers good shelter in southerly or downslope weather, makes a good base from which larger boats can explore, by dinghy or kayak, the wonderful lagoons to the southeast.

Halfway into the bay a shoal area extends into mid-channel. At this point, boats should favor the south shore, perhaps 200 feet off. The water in Wawatle Bay is brackish (muskeg brown), limiting visibility to 2 to 3 feet. Anchor directly off the outlet of the creek, south of the treed islet and a rock that extends about 60 feet to the west of shore.

Anchor in 5 fathoms over mud with good holding.

Safe Cove (Seymour Inlet)
7 mi NE of Warner Bay
Entrance: 51°05.01'N, 126°55.03'W

Safe Cove, little more than a bight in the north side of Seymour Inlet, can be used as an anchorage in fair weather tucked in near shore. Jesus Pocket, just to the east, offers better protection from wind and chop for small boats.

Jesus Pocket (Seymour Inlet)
8 mi NW of Warner Bay
Entrance: 51°04.93'N, 126°53.80'W
Anchor: 51°05.00'N, 126°53.88'W

Undoubtedly named by someone thankful for finding good shelter in an otherwise deep and steep fiord, Jesus Pocket reminds us of the size and shape of Cathedral Point Cove in Burke Channel. The pocket can handle just one or two boats with swinging room limited.

Anchor in about 4 fathoms over a sandy bottom with fair holding.

Towry Point, West Cove
(Seymour Inlet)
7.1 mi E of Warner Bay
Position: 51°03.75'N, 126°54.37'W

A small boat can find shelter from east winds squeezed in close to shore, 0.35 mile west of Towry Point.

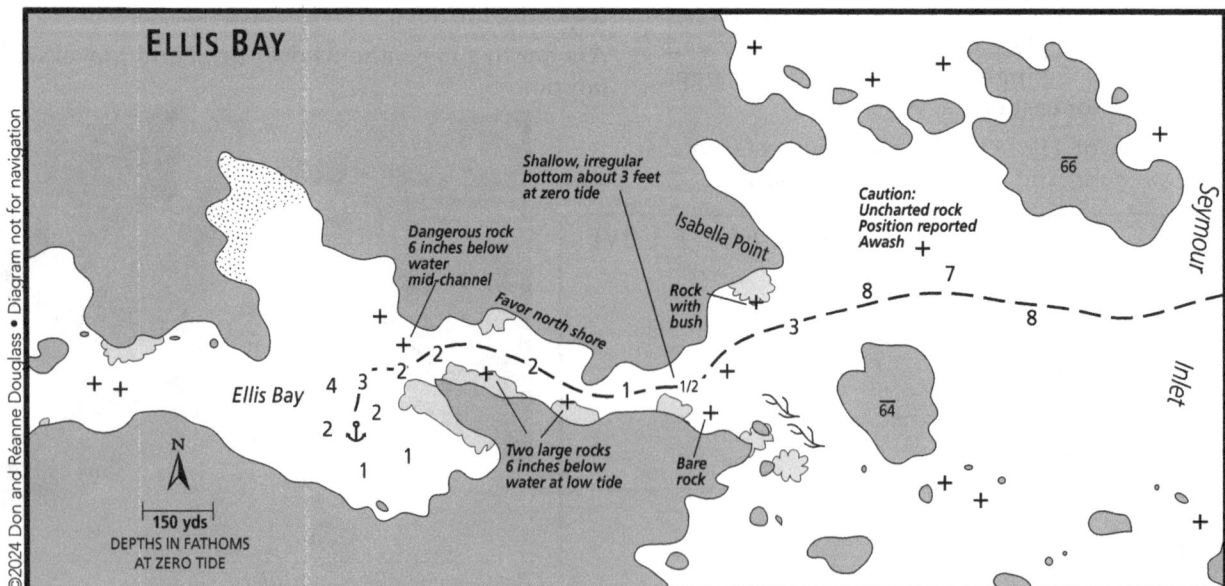

ELLIS BAY

Shallow, irregular bottom about 3 feet at zero tide

Dangerous rock 6 inches below water mid-channel

Favor north shore

Isabella Point

Rock with bush

Caution: Uncharted rock Position reported Awash

66

Seymour Inlet

Ellis Bay

Two large rocks 6 inches below water at low tide

Bare rock

64

N

150 yds
DEPTHS IN FATHOMS AT ZERO TIDE

©2024 Don and Réanne Douglass • Diagram not for navigation

Planning tomorrow's route

Towry Point, East Cove (Seymour Inlet)

7.6 mi E of Warner Bay
Entrance: 51°03.7'N, 126°53.57'W
Anchor: 51°03.72'N, 126°53.72'W

Towry Point East Cove—a more sizeable cove than the west cove—provides good protection in most westerly weather, but it is open to down-slope winds.

Anchor in 5 to 10 fathoms over mud with good holding.

Maunsell Bay (Seymour Inlet)

10 mi NE of Warner Bay
Entrance: 51°04.97'N, 126°51.82'W
Anchor: 51°05.85'N, 126°47.62'W

The tiny inlet on the east end of Maunsell Bay offers welcome shelter for small boats, although it has limited swinging room. However, the plus side is that any wind entering this well-hidden spot can flow only lengthwise in the inlet while you're tethered nicely into it.

Anchor in 12 fathoms over mud and gravel with good holding.

Eclipse Narrows (Seymour Inlet)

12 mi E of Warner Bay
Entrance: 51°04.09'N, 126°45.51'W

Eclipse Narrows, a stunning hole-in-the-wall on the east shore of Seymour Inlet, lies at the point where the inlet turns abruptly northeast to its head at Seymour River. Behind Eclipse Narrows there are two more fiords—Frederick Sound and Salmon Arm. The narrows are formed by the terminal moraine of this system.

Frederick Sound (Seymour Inlet)

E and S of Eclipse Narrows
Entrance: 51°04.09'N, 126°45.51'W
Anchor (basin at SW head of sound): 50°59.30'N, 126°44.58'W

Although Frederick Sound has seen the effects of loggers' saws, views of the high coastal peaks from this area are magnificent. The narrow end of Frederick Bay is only 1.5 air miles from Nepah Lagoon, north of Sullivan Bay, but this area is a long way from civilization!

The western curve of Frederick Sound forms its own landlocked basin that shoals gradually to the head, offering very good protection in any weather.

Anchor (basin at southwest head of sound) in 10 fathoms over mud with good holding.

Seymour River (Seymour Inlet)

Head of Seymour Inlet
Position: 51°11.67'N, 126°39.40'W

The bottom is steep-to and there is little shelter from downslope winds except what can be found behind the shallow point. If you travel two miles up-river you can view a 50-foot waterfall.

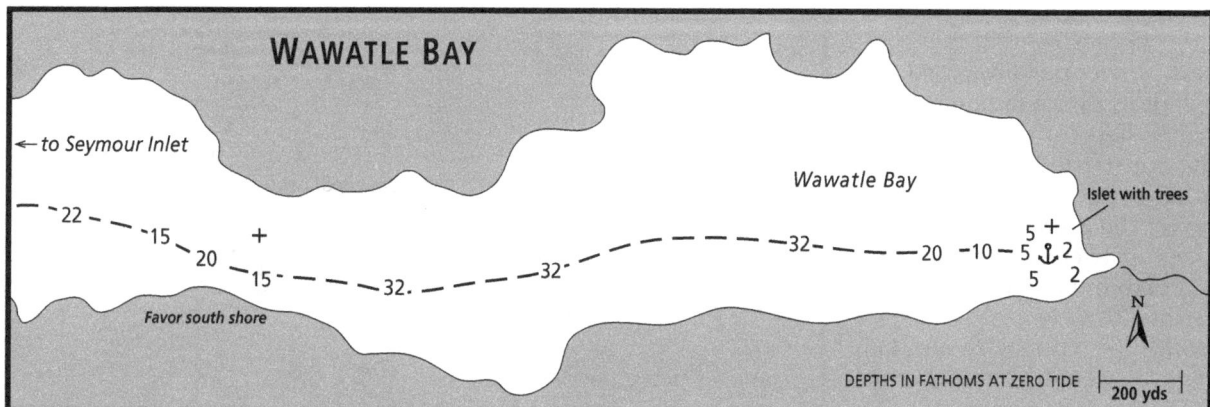

WAWATLE BAY

← to Seymour Inlet

Wawatle Bay

Islet with trees

22   15   20   15   32   32   32   20   10   5   2   5   2   5   2

Favor south shore

DEPTHS IN FATHOMS AT ZERO TIDE   200 yds

N

©2024 Don and Réanne Douglass • Diagram not for navigation

Nugent Sound & Nugent Sound Cove (Seymour Inlet & Nugent Sound Cove)

1.5 mi E of Nakwakto Rapids; 3 mi E of Holmes Point
Anchor (NW of island 69): 51°05.55'N, 127°23.33'W
Entrance: 51°05.51'N, 127°28.07'W

Nugent Sound, more of an inlet than a sound, is the first major indentation east of Nakwakto Rapids. Narrow and picturesque, it offers two coves for exploration.

Nugent Sound Cove, east of Holmes Point and northwest of island (69), is a comfortable anchorage. When northwest winds blow on the outside, this cove is perfectly calm and offers good protection from most winds. This cove and Westerman Bay in Belize Inlet offer the best choice of anchor sites near Nakwakto Rapids. The water within the cove is muskeg brown and tastes of a mixture of saltwater and fresh water. Summer water temperatures hover in the mid- to high 50s (F). An old steam boiler and a 4-foot steel gear can be seen on the north shore.

Anchor in 3 to 4 fathoms over sand and small wood debris with good holding.

Explorers Inlet (Seymour Inlet)

2.5 mi SE of the S entrance point of Wawatle Bay
Entrance: 51°02.04'N, 127°19.12'W

"Explorers Inlet" is what we call the narrow, unnamed inlet 8 miles southeast of Nakwakto Rapids. It is a great place for serious exploring. While *Sailing Directions* warns that the inlet is not suitable for navigation, we think it should be considered by cruising boaters who like a good challenge. This area is primitive, and can feel "spooky" when you're deep inside without reference to the outside world.

An extensive log dump and log booming operation occupies the south shore just before the entrance to Woods Lagoon. Beyond this point, Explorers Inlet narrows and becomes shallow (3 to 4 fathoms). Boats can anchor here in mid-channel or near the constricted south narrows (in 4 fathoms, sticky mud) in order to reconnoiter the route ahead.

In the constricted south narrows of Unnamed Inlet, favor the north shore to avoid rocks awash that extend from the south shore and kelp that clogs the center of the channel.

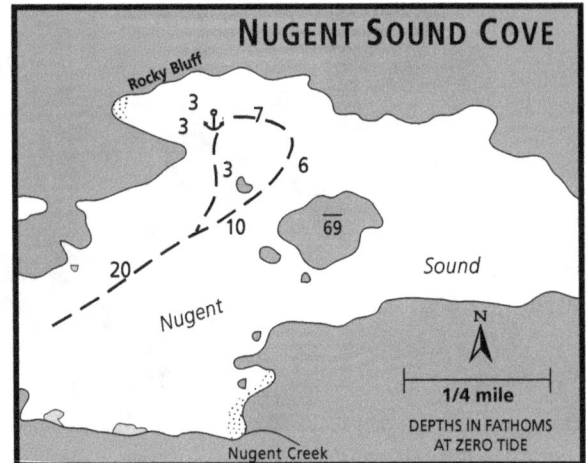

NUGENT SOUND COVE

Rocky Bluff

3
3
7
3
6
10
69
20
Nugent   Sound

N

1/4 mile
DEPTHS IN FATHOMS AT ZERO TIDE

Nugent Creek

©2024 Don and Réanne Douglass • Diagram not for navigation

About 30 feet from the trees on the north shore we found a route 5 feet deep near low water.

Don't be surprised if the tides here and farther south are confusing and seem to reverse at will. Strange tidal dynamics appear to be at work in both this narrows and in Whelakis Lagoon, suggesting a kind of resonance or oscillation. Please share your observations with us.

Once you pass through the constricted narrows, you arrive at what we call "Four Lagoon Intersection." Bamford, McKinnon, and Nenahlmai lagoons all offer good anchorage near their head. Whelakis Lagoon, an offshoot of Nenahlmai Lagoon, is a wild place unto itself.

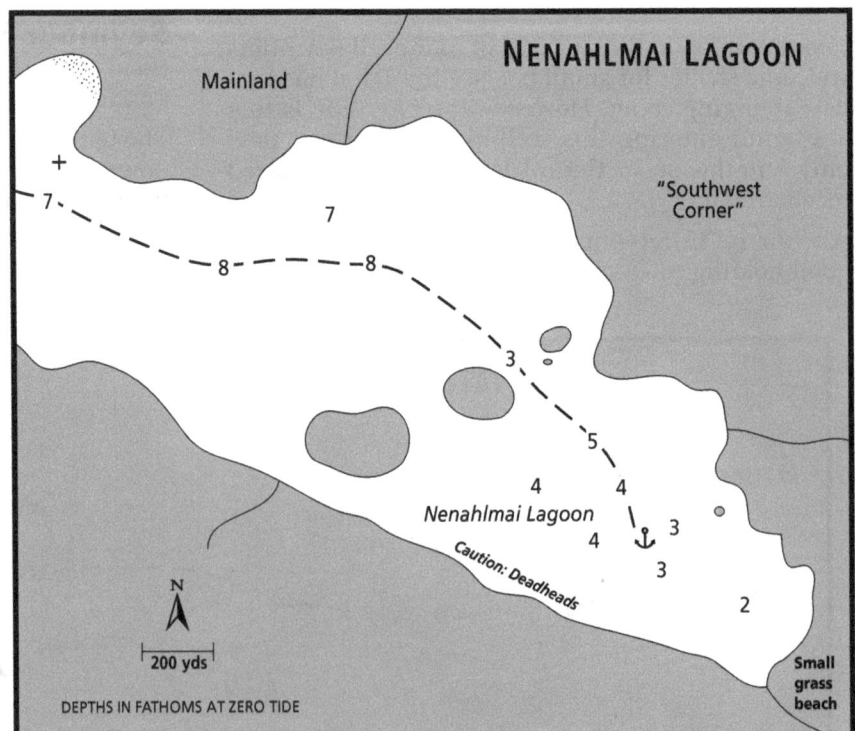

NENAHLMAI LAGOON

Mainland

"Southwest Corner"

+
7
7
8 — 8
3
5
4   4
Nenahlmai Lagoon
Caution: Deadheads   4   3
4
3
2

N

200 yds

DEPTHS IN FATHOMS AT ZERO TIDE

Small grass beach

©2024 Don and Réanne Douglass • Diagram not for navigation

Bamford Lagoon (Seymour Inlet)

2.5 mi SE of Wawatle Bay
Entrance: 50°59.89'N, 127°15.19'W
Anchor: 50°59.42'N, 127°18.19'W

The entrance to Bamford Lagoon has several obstacles: an uncharted 10-foot shoal, about 150 feet off the northeast point, and islets and rocks on its south side. You can avoid these islets and rocks by favoring island (40) which marks the south side of the first cove on the north shore.

The head of Bamford Lagoon offers good anchorage with the added attraction of a creek that can be explored by dinghy for several hundred yards. Partway up this creek are the wooden remains of an old dam, and on the south shore you can find the ribs of an old shipwreck.

Anchor in about 7 fathoms over sand and gravel with fair-to-good holding.

McKinnon Lagoon (Seymour Inlet)

3 mi SE of Wawatle Bay
Entrance: 50°59.84'N, 127°14.09'W
Anchor: 51°01.25'N, 127°12.08'W

McKinnon Lagoon has a large inner basin beyond its narrows. Although deep, this remote basin offers some anchor sites using stern ties, with little chance of crowding.

Nenahlmai Lagoon (Seymour Inlet)

3.5 mi SE of Wawatle Bay
Entrance: 50°59.56'N, 127°14.14'W
Anchor: 50°58.04'N, 127°10.57'W

Nenahlmai Lagoon is fairly deep up to the basin at its southeast head. By keeping the two biggest islands to starboard, you can enter a well-sheltered basin with excellent protection from all weather over a nearly flat 4- to 6-fathom bottom.

Anchor in 4 fathoms over soft mud and sand with good to very good holding.

Whelakis Lagoon (Seymour Inlet)

5 mi SE of Wawatle Bay
Entrance: 50°58.32'N, 127°11.75'W
Anchor: 50°57.95'N, 127°12.30'W

Whelakis Lagoon is an end in itself: cedar and muskeg rain forest where strange patterns of pollen weave their way across the lagoon and around the point, as if they were lateral moraines on a frozen glacier. The water is so still we felt almost guilty disturbing it.

We recommend reconnoitering the narrows (or the lagoon itself!) by dinghy before you enter it. We did this on our first transit and were able to assure ourselves that, at high water, we had 10 feet of water in the shallowest spot on the east side of the narrows near the living horizontal tree.

You cannot see the entrance to Whelakis Lagoon from either the north or south when passing it in Nenahlmai Lagoon. Use GPS to keep you headed in the right direction. As you approach the narrows, avoid two uncharted rocks just below the surface at high water, off the west point. Favor the south shore in the narrows to avoid a live tree that extends about 30 feet into mid-channel. We found minimum depth in the fairway at high water to be about 10 feet on either side of the horizontal tree, with current weak at this time.

You can find good shelter in the first cove on the south side of the narrows or farther in at the head of the lagoon.

Anchor in 1 to 2 fathoms over sticky mud with very good holding.

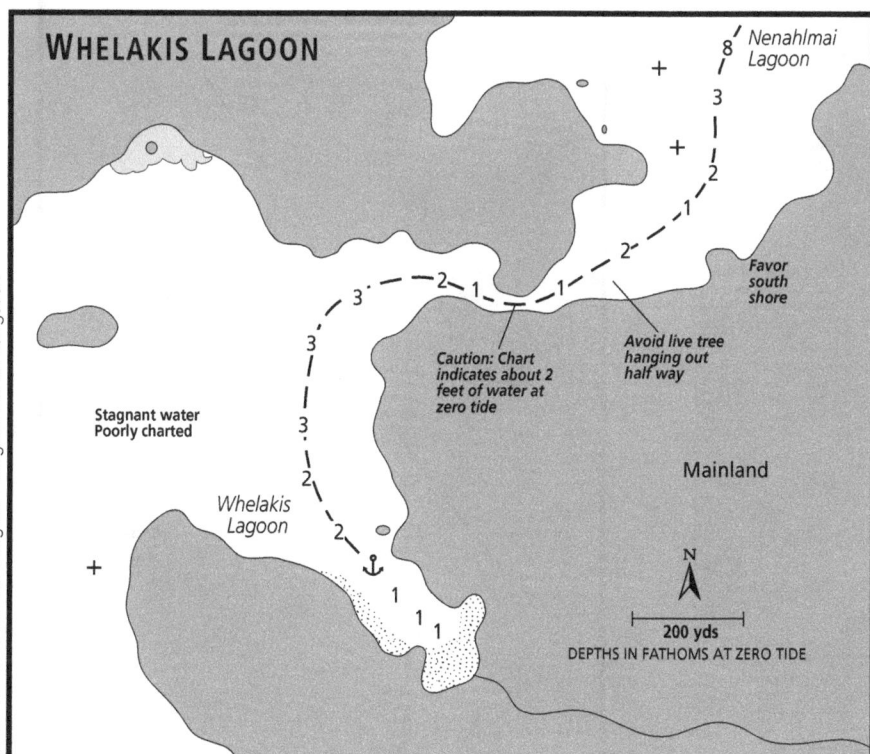

WHELAKIS LAGOON

©2024 Don and Réanne Douglass • Diagram not for navigation

Nenahlmai Lagoon

Whelakis Lagoon

Stagnant water
Poorly charted

Caution: Chart indicates about 2 feet of water at zero tide

Avoid live tree hanging out half way

Favor south shore

Mainland

N

200 yds
DEPTHS IN FATHOMS AT ZERO TIDE

Belize Inlet

3 mi N of Nakwakto Rapids
Entrance: 51°07.74'N, 127°33.39'W

Belize Inlet—a beautiful fiord that extends 25 miles due east from its junction with Seymour Inlet—gradually becomes narrower and more precipitous, showing little evidence of man's travels.

As you enter the inlet, give Mignon Point a wide berth since several submerged rocks lie off its west and north sides. About a mile northeast of Mignon Point, there is a sheer black granite cliff on the north side of Belize Inlet that we call "Echo Rock;" try your echoing powers as you glide closely by. This remarkable overhanging rock which focuses the sound directly back to you is covered with bright white stains. Seals congregate on a 2-meter rock islet a half-mile east of Echo Rock, making themselves comfortable in its wide grooves. The seals here and in Seymour Inlet seem less concerned about passing boats than in other areas—perhaps they haven't been shot at for their consumption of fish!

Overhanging "echo" rock, entrance to Belize Inlet

Westerman Bay (Belize Inlet)

3.5 mi NE of Nakwakto Rapids
Entrance: 51°08.22'N, 127°28.13'W
Anchor: 51°09.11'N, 127°27.30'W

Westerman Bay offers very good protection from up- and downslope winds. It has easy access and convenient depths.

Anchor in 4 fathoms over sand and mud with good holding.

Mereworth Sound (Belize Inlet)

4.5 mi NE of Nakwakto Rapids
Entrance: 51°08.10'N, 127°24.97'W

Mereworth Sound has good anchorage in Strachan Bay or Village Cove.

Strachan Bay, Southwest Cove

(Belize Inlet)
1 mi NW of Westerman Bay
Entrance: 51°09.98'N, 127°25.45'W
Anchor: 51°09.52'N, 127°28.49'W

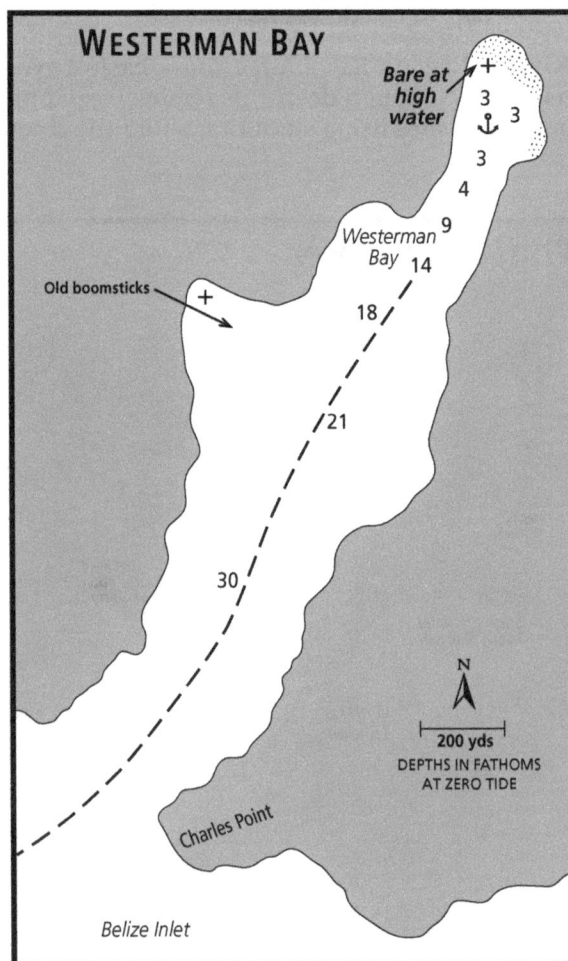

WESTERMAN BAY

Bare at high water

3
3
3
4
9
14
18
21
30

Westerman Bay

Old boomsticks

Charles Point

Belize Inlet

N

200 yds
DEPTHS IN FATHOMS AT ZERO TIDE

©2024 Don and Réanne Douglass • Diagram not for navigation

Strachan Cove is landlocked and almost perfectly sheltered from all weather. During outside southeast gales some wind sneaks across the isthmus from Belize Inlet. However, the fetch is minimal and the effect is small.

The entrance to Strachan Cove is about two hundred feet wide with a fairway depth of 4 fathoms at mid-tide. There is swinging room for several boats over a large flat bottom.

Note: Charlie Chilson, who had lived here since he was a youngster, passed away since our last edition. We were privileged to have been able to visit him at his float camp several times before he passed away in 2005.

A trail at the western leading to Pack Lake is now quite rough and covered with windfalls.

Anchor in 5 fathoms over sticky brown mud with very good holding.

Village Cove (Mereworth Sound)
2.5 mi NE of Westerman Bay
Entrance: 51°10.26'N, 127°24.85'W
Anchor: 51°10.47'N, 127°24.72'W

Village Cove, a small cove on the east side of the entrance to Mereworth Sound, has two islets lying along its west side. There is a grassy beach on its east side where a substantial creek flows out. Anchorage can be found west of the small grassy beach, north of the innermost island. Heavy Spanish moss droops from the trees above the beach from where an old logging road heads east up the creek. We found large cedar trees among the stumps; one is perhaps 10 feet in diameter and worth the short hike uphill from the creek outlet.

Anchor in 8 to 12 fathoms over a mud bottom; fair-to-good holding.

Power Wash Waterfall (Belize Inlet)
4 mi E of the entrance to Mereworth Sound
Position: 51°08.27'N, 127°18.55'W

"Power Wash" is our name for the spectacular waterfall that originates from Trevor Lake on the north shore of Belize Inlet. This powerhouse of water that falls directly into the saltwater could swamp your boat if you were forced in against it by a strong wind or current.

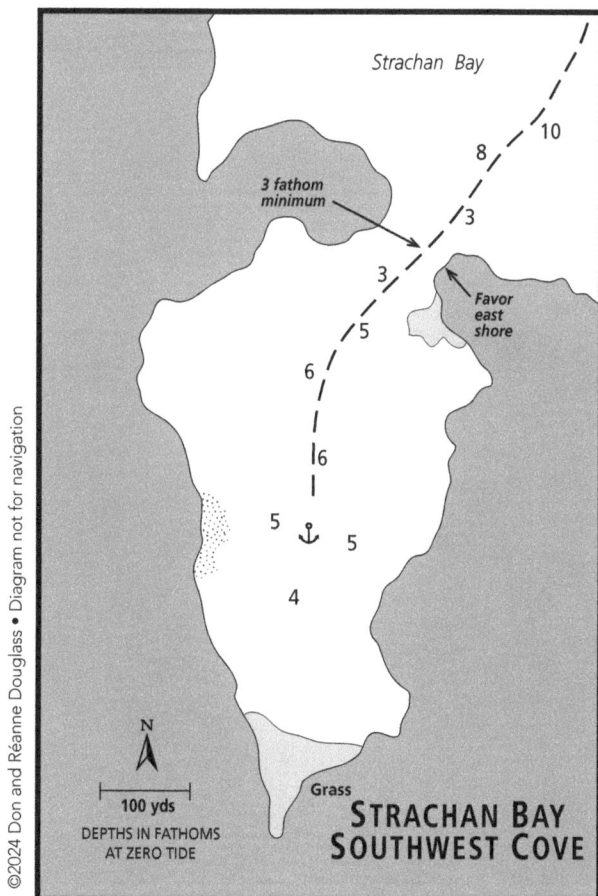

Fending off in Belize Inlet

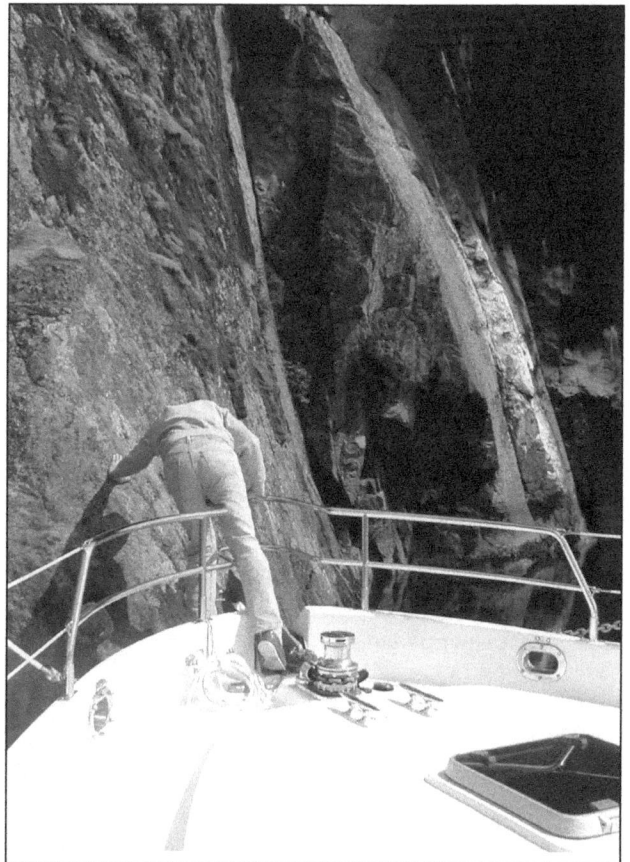

Strachan Bay

10
8
3 fathom minimum
3
3
Favor east shore
5
6
6
5 ⚓ 5
4

N

100 yds
DEPTHS IN FATHOMS
AT ZERO TIDE

Grass
STRACHAN BAY SOUTHWEST COVE

©2024 Don and Réanne Douglass • Diagram not for navigation

Half-Dome Waterfall (Belize Inlet)
4.6 mi E of Power Wash Waterfall
Position: 51°07.91'N, 127°11.39'W

"Half-Dome Waterfall" is our name for another lovely waterfall that spills out of the U-shaped valley on the north shore of Belize, east of Power Wash Waterfall. This valley has some spectacular scenery, including an almost-perfect, half-dome-shaped vertical granite monolith at least 1,000 feet high. Note the green "toupée" of evergreens growing along the very edge of the drop-off.

Alison Sound (Belize Inlet)
11 mi E of Mereworth Sound
Entrance: 51°07.41'N, 127°08.39'W

Alison Sound is considered the most scenic of the inlets behind Nakwakto Rapids. Misnamed sound in the traditional sense, it is more similar in shape to two freshwater lakes connected by a narrow bar that, in turn, connects to Belize Inlet via a "river gorge." The shores are steep with granite slabs and overhanging cliffs where evergreens attempt to grow on nearly all the vertical surfaces. As you proceed up the inlet, you have views of snow-covered peaks and ridges to the north and east. This lovely sound seems so remote from civilization and the Pacific Ocean, that you can hardly believe it's just miles away from Queen Charlotte Sound. Until recently, the narrows has kept out the effects of both weather and man. But Alison Sound is losing some of its pristine quality as small clear-cuts have begun to appear.

A 3-fathom rock shoal, part of a submerged terminal moraine, crosses the entrance to Alison Sound.

"Half-dome," north shore Belize Inlet

Pictographs

High on a vertical face in Belize Inlet near Alison Sound, a series of pictographs executed in ochre paint depict what appears to be an early encounter between indigenous people and European explorers. (See photo.) The paintings seem to represent a square-rigged sailboat, perhaps anchored offshore; a long boat with numerous oars and a couple of sailors or militia men wearing wide-brimmed hats and carrying rifles; a third small vessel appears to be a native canoe; off to the side, orcas leap across the rock face. The paintings are well preserved, due probably to their location below an overhanging cliff where they have escaped rain damage. Belize Inlet was surveyed for the first time in 1865. In 1869, a government party in a warship was dispatched to this area to put down a skirmish between Natives and Whites. These pictographs may possibly date from that era or from an earlier encounter with White Man in Queen Charlotte Sound—perhaps even as early as Vancouver's time.

—RHD

Overhanging garden, Belize Inlet

Obstruction Islet (Alison Sound)

1.3 mi NE of Belize Inlet
Position: 51°08.56'N, 127°06.88'W

Obstruction Islet lies in the middle of Alison Narrows. The fairway of the entrance to Alison Sound is about 100 yards wide and 5 fathoms deep. Favor the west shore as you pass the islet. Currents can reach 5 to 6 knots alongside Obstruction Islet, but the flow is generally laminar with minimal turbulence.

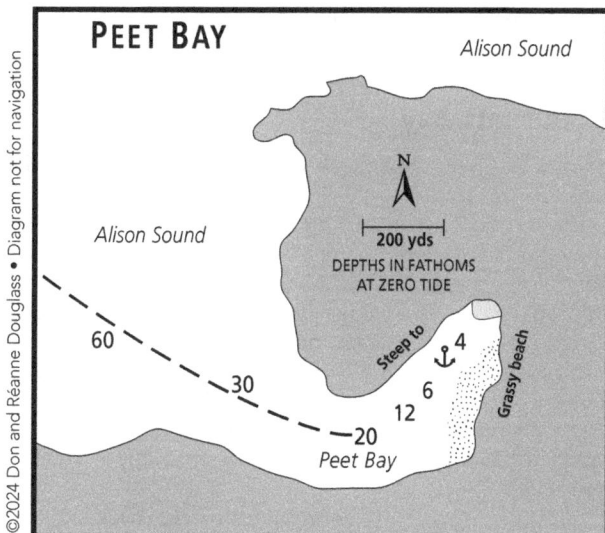

No Name Bay (Alison Sound)

0.8 mi north of Obstruction Inlet
Entrance: 51°09.39'N, 127°06.64'W

No Name Bay—at the north end of the narrows. It is well sheltered and offers good protection from all winds. Because the small bay is steep-to, you must look carefully to find an anchor site off the tiny grass beach at the outlet of the creek.

Chief Nollis Bay (Alison Sound)

2 mi N of Obstruction Islet
Entrance: 51°10.51'N, 127°05.85'W
Anchor: 51°11.08'N, 127°05.46'W

Chief Nollis Bay is the largest body of open water in Alison Sound. It has a long, grassy beach with many stumps and trees stranded along its shore. A sizeable creek that drains a large area enters the bay on the west end of the beach. Although boats can find anchorage near the head of Chief Nollis Bay, there is little protection from the south.

Anchor in 10 to 15 fathoms over mud.

Peet Bay (Alison Sound)

1.5 mi SE of Chief Nollis Bay
Entrance: 51°09.87'N, 127°04.60'W
Anchor: 51°09.83'N, 127°04.29'W

Peet Bay, a small, attractive anchorage, offers very good protection deep in its north corner where it is completely landlocked with no evidence of chop. As you head in to the anchor site, you'll notice a beautiful waterfall along the south shore. Anchorage for one vessel can be found north of the grassy beach but swinging room is limited, so larger vessels should consider using a shore-tie.

Anchor in 4 to 5 fathoms over soft brown mud and sand with fair-to-good holding.

Log bridge at Village Cove Creek

Summers Bay (Alison Sound)
2 mi E of Peet Bay
Entrance: 51°10.15'N, 127°01.96'W
Anchor: 51°10.20'N, 127°01.52'W

Summers Bay is a picturesque anchorage with very good protection from downslope winds. High, snowy peaks tower above the bay; a white bluff rises above the cove's north side and a black bluff lies to its south.

Anchor off the grassy flat in about 12 fathoms over mud with fair-to-good holding.

Waump Creek (Alison Sound)
4 mi NE of Summers Bay
Position: 51°11.13'N, 126°55.50'W

Slingsby Channel (Queen Charlotte Sound)
W entrance to Nakwakto Rapids
Entrance (W): 51°05.04'N, 127°39.16'W
Entrance (E): 51°05.50'N, 127°31.10'W

Slingsby Channel, the northern channel for entering or exiting Seymour Inlet, faces directly into Queen Charlotte Strait and is notorious for rough seas when a strong spring ebb tide opposes westerly wind and swells. Seas that can heap up to dangerous proportions extend a mile or more west of Fox Islands. The same effects can be noted between McEwan Rock, on the south, and Bremner Islet, on the north. The most confused seas lie west of Vigilance Point.

Turbulence and breaking chop in Outer Narrows, between Fox Islands and Vigilance Point, can be both frightening and dangerous to small craft; currents at this point can run 5 knots or more on a spring ebb; 3 to 4 knots on spring floods. The flow is largely laminar with moderate turbulence. All chop and swells disappear a half-mile or so east of Vigilance Point.

The best way to avoid uncomfortable conditions in normal weather is to leave at dawn and round Cape Caution before the westerlies pick up. Under unfavorable conditions it is best to turn around and wait for better conditions, or consider following the route on the south side of Fox Islands and work your way into Miles Inlet. Vigilance Cove provides a modicum of temporary shelter because it is out of the current, and you might duck in here to help turn around if necessary. If you have a boat and crew that can keep going in heavy weather, it's best to quarter the seas to avoid violent rolling.

Named for a now-obscure baron, we feel that Slingsby Channel would be more aptly named Slingshot!

Fox Islands Channel (Slingsby Channel)
1 mi NW of Miles Inlet
Entrance (W): 51°04.55'N, 127°36.70'W
Entrance (E): 51°05.06'N, 127°35.45'W

Note: If you wish to proceed west down Slingsby Channel from Nakwakto Rapids and enter Miles Inlet, consider using the narrow channel between Fox Islands and Bramham Island, west of Outer Narrows. In marginal weather, this route avoids some of the spectacular current and swells that occur at Outer Narrows.

Contrary to the chart, we found a minimum depth of 5 fathoms (not 5 meters) in the fairway at the east end of the passage, and 8 fathoms at the west end, with a smooth ride on an ebb current. But use caution for a safe passage!

Vigilance Cove (Slingsby Channel)
2.5 mi NW of Miles Inlet
Entrance: 51°05.33'N, 127°38.37'W
Anchor (temporary): 51°05.43'N, 127°38.13'W

B.C.'s Coast by Kayak: Burnett Bay

Heading north from Allison Harbor, I rounded Bremner Point and paddled into the south end of Burnett Bay, timing a surf-landing onto its sandy beach.

I camped on shore just north of the point from where I watched an osprey trying to fish in the surf. The bird battled the waves, getting rolled over time and time again and, at last, surfacing with a fish his talons. Just as he was flapping his wings for take off, another wave hit him and he disappeared into the surf.

He emerged finally and took off—without his fish. Later, I scrambled out through salal to Bremner Point and spotted him nesting with his mate in the nearby trees. The following morning I walked up Evader Creek at dawn, sighting

bear tracks. River otters played in a pond at an elbow of the creek.

Burnett Bay has a moody beauty: dreamy on a misty windy evening; gloomy on a rainy morning; bright and cheerful on a sunny day. And its scrawny trees—wind-sculpted, ground-hugging, aerodynamic forms—lend a mysterious air to its various moods.

I packed up and left Burnett Bay to round Cape Caution. For several miles I followed a pod of gray whales, spouting and diving, and I marvelled in their proximity, happy in the knowledge that only from a kayak would I have such a view!

—John McCormack, kayak explorer

Vigilance Cove can serve as an emergency anchorage or temporary stop or turnaround when strong currents in Slingsby Channel meet the swell and chop in Queen Charlotte Strait. When conditions off Vigilance Point are threatening, you may get marginal and temporary relief in Vigilance Cove because it is out of the ebb current, and swells and chop diminish the further in you go. However, the only good shelter in the immediate area is Miles Inlet, 2 miles to the southeast.

The north shore of Vigilance Cove is steep-to and the bottom flat. Favor the north shore. A low swell enters the cove making it somewhat uncomfortable for anything but a short stay. Beware of an uncharted rock surrounded by kelp, awash on an 8-foot tide, just east of the knob on the south shore.

Anchor (marginal and temporary) in the middle of the cove in 6 fathoms over an unrecorded bottom.

Anchor Islands Cove (Slingsby Channel)

2 mi W of Nakwakto Rapids
Entrance: 51°05.79'N, 127°33.30'W
Anchor: 51°05.96'N, 127°33.12'W

Anchor Islands Cove, immediately west of Treadwell Bay at the northwest extremity of Anchor Islands, is suitable for a number of small vessels and offers very good shelter from all weather. Since the cove is effectively blocked from any major wind, and currents attain a half-knot at most, there is little exchange of water and the cove is full of small flotsam. Moss-cov-

Photo courtesy CHS, Pacific Region

Cape Caution

ered cedars bend low over the water, giving the cove a primeval aspect.

Anchor just west of a line between the drying spit—which nearly connects the main island with the island to its west—and the small creek on the north shore.

Anchor in 4 fathoms over sand and mud with good holding; limited swinging room.

Treadwell Bay (Slingsby Channel)

1.5 mi W of Nakwakto Rapids
Entrance: 51°05.80'N, 127°32.03'W
Anchor: 51°06.17'N, 127°32.66'W

Treadwell Bay is a good place to spend the night in order to be near Nakwakto Rapids. The far northwest corner of the bay is out of the current (2.5 knots ebb off Stream Point). Favor the right shore upon entering to avoid two rocks in the main channel that dry at mid-tide. Anchor deep in the cove for good shelter from all winds. You may experience some chop on strong southeast or outflow winds.

Anchor in 5 to 6 fathoms over mud with fair-to-good holding.

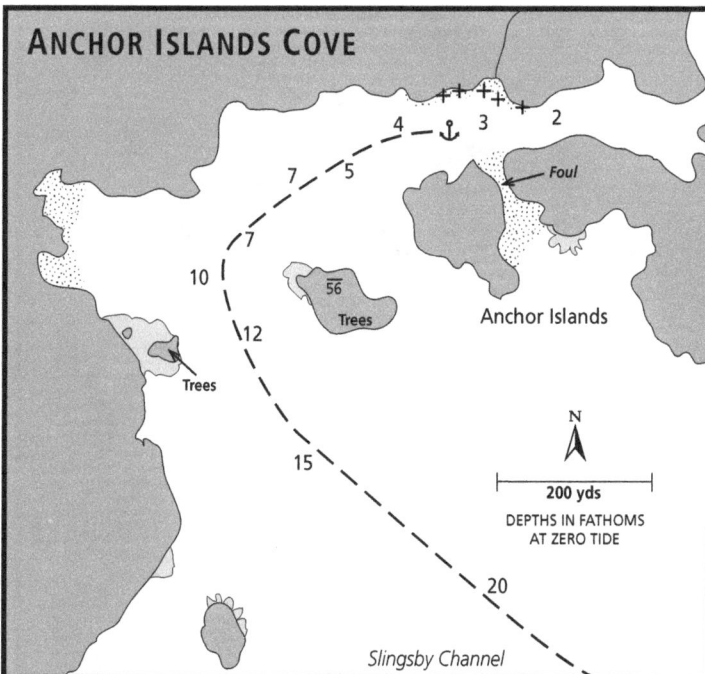

ANCHOR ISLANDS COVE

4 ⚓ 3   2
7 5
Foul
7
10   56
Trees   Anchor Islands
12
Trees
15
N
200 yds
DEPTHS IN FATHOMS
AT ZERO TIDE
20
Slingsby Channel

©2024 Don and Réanne Douglass • Diagram not for navigation

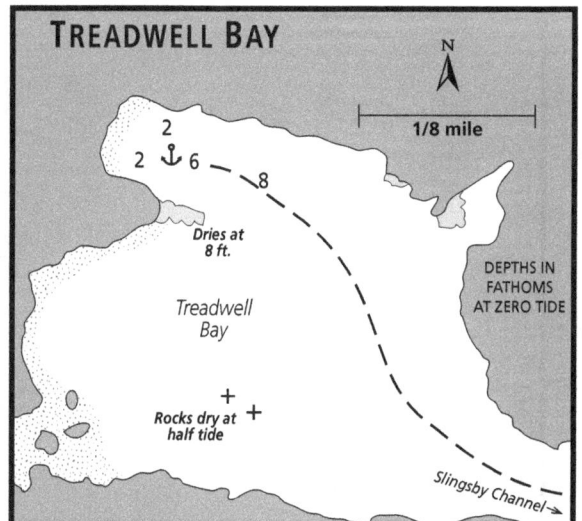

TREADWELL BAY

N
2
2 ⚓ 6
8
1/8 mile
Dries at
8 ft.
DEPTHS IN
FATHOMS
AT ZERO TIDE
*Treadwell
Bay*
+
Rocks dry at   +
half tide
Slingsby Channel

©2024 Don and Réanne Douglass • Diagram not for navigation

Miles Inlet (Queen Charlotte Sound)

3 mi W of Allison Harbour
Entrance: 51°03.61'N, 127°36.26'W
Anchor (N arm): 51°04.05'N, 127°34.93'W
Anchor (S arm): 51°03.90'N, 127°34.70'W

Miles Inlet is one of the best small-craft anchorages along this section of coast. Its proximity to Cape Caution makes feasible an early morning transit to Fitz Hugh Sound during calm weather. Although the narrow entrance to Miles Inlet may cause anxiety when a following sea is running and waves break over the entrance rocks, foam and swell quickly die off toward the head of the inlet. On a northbound passage, from a quarter-mile south of McEwan Rock, the course is approximately 043°M. Use the light on McEwan Rock as your entrance mark, and avoid the detached rocks on either side of the entrance to the inlet.

On a clear day, the inlet lines up perfectly with a high, snow-covered peak to the northeast (north of Nugent Sound). McEwan Rock Light (51°.06N, 127°.63W) or GPS can help you identify the opening and the straight channel that leads northeast. Beautiful, old-growth cedars line the 75-foot wide channel—a forest noteworthy for silver snags that point toward the sky. A few hundred yards into the northern arm of the T-intersection, Miles Inlet dries.

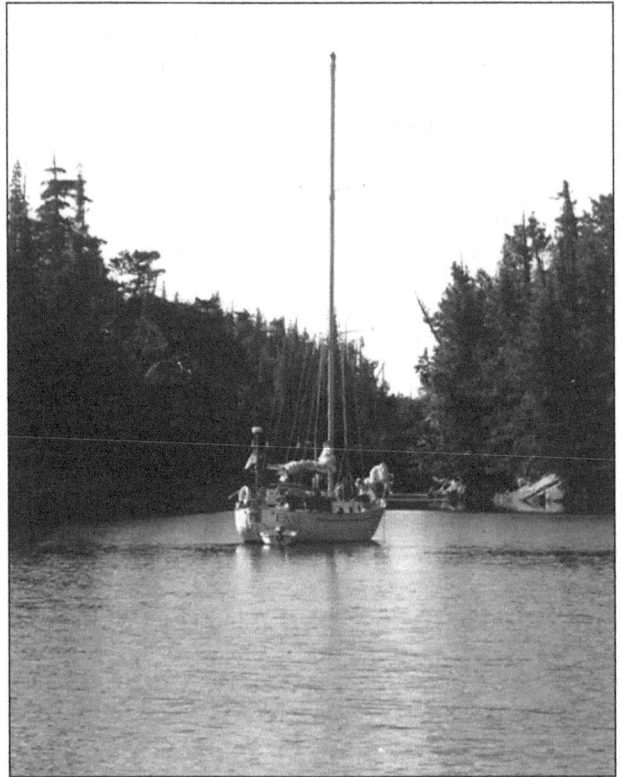

Elyxir *anchored in Miles Inlet at start of worldwide voyage*

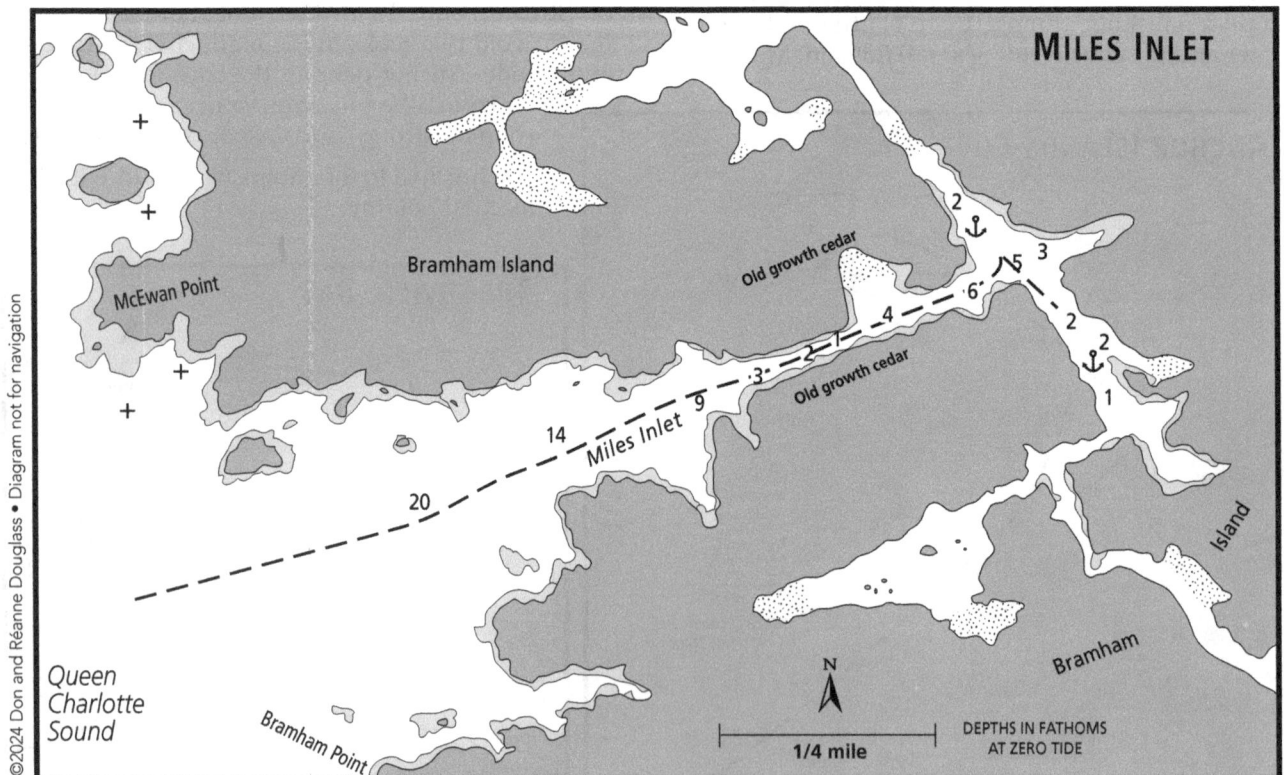

The head of the south arm divides into several shallow passages that can be explored by dinghy. The inlet, which is well protected from swell and chop, is a quiet sanctuary, undisturbed by man. Several boats can anchor at the head of the inlet, using short rodes. In May and June, when cruising and fishing boats head north, the inlet may get a little crowded. In this case a stern tie is useful.

Anchor in either arm in 2 to 3 fathoms over mud with good holding; limited swinging room.

Burnett Bay (Queen Charlotte Sound)
5 mi NW of Miles Inlet
Position: 51°07.22′N, 127°41.61′W

Burnett Bay, open to Queen Charlotte Sound, looks—most of the time—like a surfing beach. With the exception of expert kayakers, cruising vessels are advised to keep well offshore.

Réanne autographing her book

Miles Inlet Rapids

Wilkie Point Cove (Queen Charlotte Strait)

2.75 miles SE of Cape Caution
Entrance (S): 51°08.24'N, 127°43.61'W
Entrance (N): 51°08.36'N, 127°43.83'W
Anchor: 51°08.42'N, 127°43.51'W

"Wilkie Point Cove" is our name for the small, rather well-protected cove between Burnett Bay and Silvester Bay. Its strategic location near Cape Caution makes it useful as an emergency shelter during east winds or as a lunch stop where you can get relief from the perpetual westerly swells and southeast chop. A sizeable ledge of rocks, backed by large patches of bull kelp, extends from the north shore. The ledge, the kelp, and a treed islet to the immediate south cut prevailing westerly swells to almost nothing. The beautiful sandy beach allows landing a dinghy in fair weather, in contrast to the wider, more exposed beaches to the north and south.

We have used the north entrance when a 2-meter swell was running outside. However, the entrance is quite narrow and the whitewater can be intimidating. Favor the island side. Using the north entrance, you must work your way through kelp where the fairway carries minimum depths of 3 to 4 fathoms. We found enough shelter under these conditions to land a dinghy on the beach (no more than a foot or two of breakers).

The south entrance is free of kelp, and easier to enter with a depth of 4 to 5 fathoms in the fairway.

Anchorage can be found east of the unnamed island, anywhere off the beach, just inside a secondary line of kelp in about 1 to 2 fathoms at zero tide. By anchoring next to the rock in the south corner, the bluffs may give some protection from southeast chop.

Anchor in 2 fathoms over sand with some kelp; fair-to-good holding.

Spirit of the Coast Canoe Voyage

During the summer of 2014, a group of voyageurs from around the world undertook a journey along the entire length of the British Columbia coast. They paddled 1,200 km from Fort Langley to Prince Rupert in a 25-foot long canoe called *Chief of the River*, seeking the spirit of the British Columbia coast and connecting with the First Nations Peoples who have inhabited and cared for it since time immemorial. The Spirit of the Coast journey was designed as a consciousness-raising exercise, meant to draw attention to the cultural importance of the coast to British Columbians, both native and non-native, and to the world at large, as well as emphasizing its beauty and fragility. Chris Cooper of Spirit Dancer Canoe Journeys was the primary organizer of the trip, and twenty-six different paddlers from five nations participated in various segments of the 76 day long journey. Supported by a 22-foot long support and safety sailboat carrying their extra gear and supplies, the crew camped on shore most nights, experiencing the rugged coastal landscape up close. Along the way, they saw both unspoiled wilderness and massive environmental degradation due to poor management of resource exploitation. The paddlers visited fourteen First Nations communities along the way where they were welcomed into community centers to testify about their observations and share their goals of education, awareness, environmental stewardship, and culture. LW

Photo credit Donald Jonasson

WILKIE POINT COVE

Alders

Alders

Sandy beach

Alders

2

2   2

2   1

2   2

3

6 — 4   3

3

⚓

N

200 yds
DEPTHS IN FATHOMS
AT ZERO TIDE

4

5

Queen Charlotte Sound

©2024 Don and Réanne Douglass • Diagram not for navigation

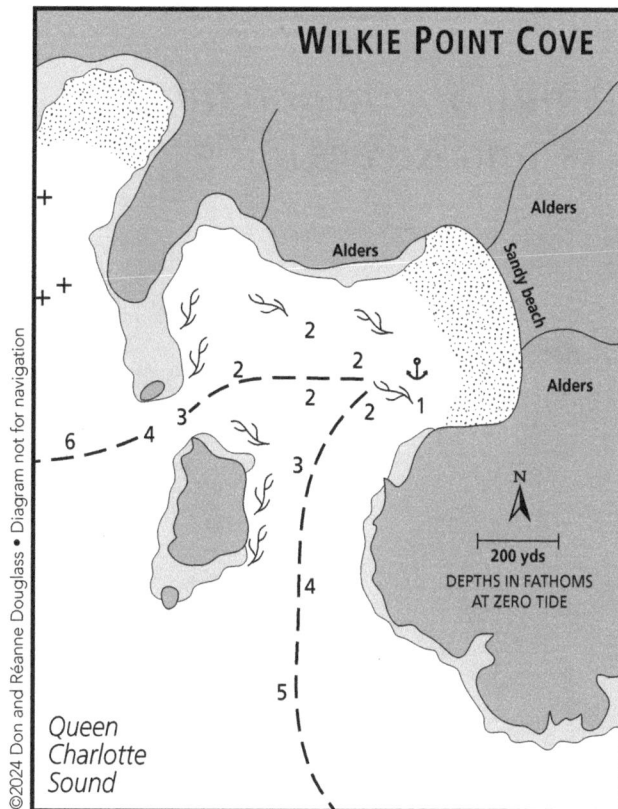

Silvester Bay (Queen Charlotte Sound)
1 mi E of Cape Caution
Position: 51°09.29'N, 127°45.39'W

Silvester Bay, along with Blunden Bay and Indian Cove, 3 miles north, have lovely beaches and campsites for skilled kayakers. The surf tends to keep small boats well to windward.

Cape Caution

16 mi S of Calvert Island; 10.5 mi NW of Miles Inlet
Position (10-fm patch 1.2 mi SW of light): 51°09.26'N, 127°48.94'W

During strong southwest winds and/or conditions of high westerly swell, swells reflecting off Cape Caution cause confused sea conditions for at least 1 mile to seaward. This condition is accentuated by shallow water directly off the cape.

Barbecued Salmon, Native Style

In this traditional method of barbecuing, the salmon is propped over smoldering coals in a cedar frame, giving it a delicious smoky flavor.

For each 4–6 lb. salmon, you need:

- straight-grained cedar stake 4'–5' long by $1\frac{1}{2}$" square
- 8 to 12 cedar sticks 16"–18" long and $\frac{1}{2}$" square
- short length of wire (14 gauge copper works well)
- condiments of your choice

Pre-soak the cedar for several hours before using it to minimize the risk of its igniting during the cooking process.

Slit the fresh salmon down the back, rather than the belly. Clean the fish and remove the backbone, keeping the belly skin intact so that both halves are still joined. If the fish has already been cleaned in the usual manner by slitting its belly, you can still cook it Native style, although the thickest part of the fish will be partially shielded from the heat by the central stake, rather than being positioned toward the edges where it gets more direct heat.

Wrap a piece of wire around the stake, a quarter of the way from the bottom. Then split the stake from the top down to the wire. The wire will keep the stake from splitting all the way. Rub the salmon with a mixture of brown sugar, Dijon mustard and lemon juice, or cook as is. Lay the salm-on between the two halves of the split stake. Then slide the smaller cedar sticks between the salmon and the stake on both sides. For a large salmon, you may need additional sticks woven parallel to the split stake. Once you have all the cross-pieces in place, pinch the top of the split stake together and secure with a loop of wire.

To cook the salmon, incline the fish toward the wood fire coals, either by propping the bottom of the stake against a support such as a rock, or by pushing it into the ground. Watch your fire carefully to keep it hot but smoldering. Turn the fish occasionally. Don't worry if the cedar stake becomes blackened by the heat, but make sure it does not ignite. A 4–6 lb. salmon takes about 40 minutes to cook.

Courtesy of Noreen Rudd, M.D. and David Hoar, Ph.D.,
Cooks Afloat! Harbour Publishing

Photo courtesy of Noreen Rudd & David Hoar

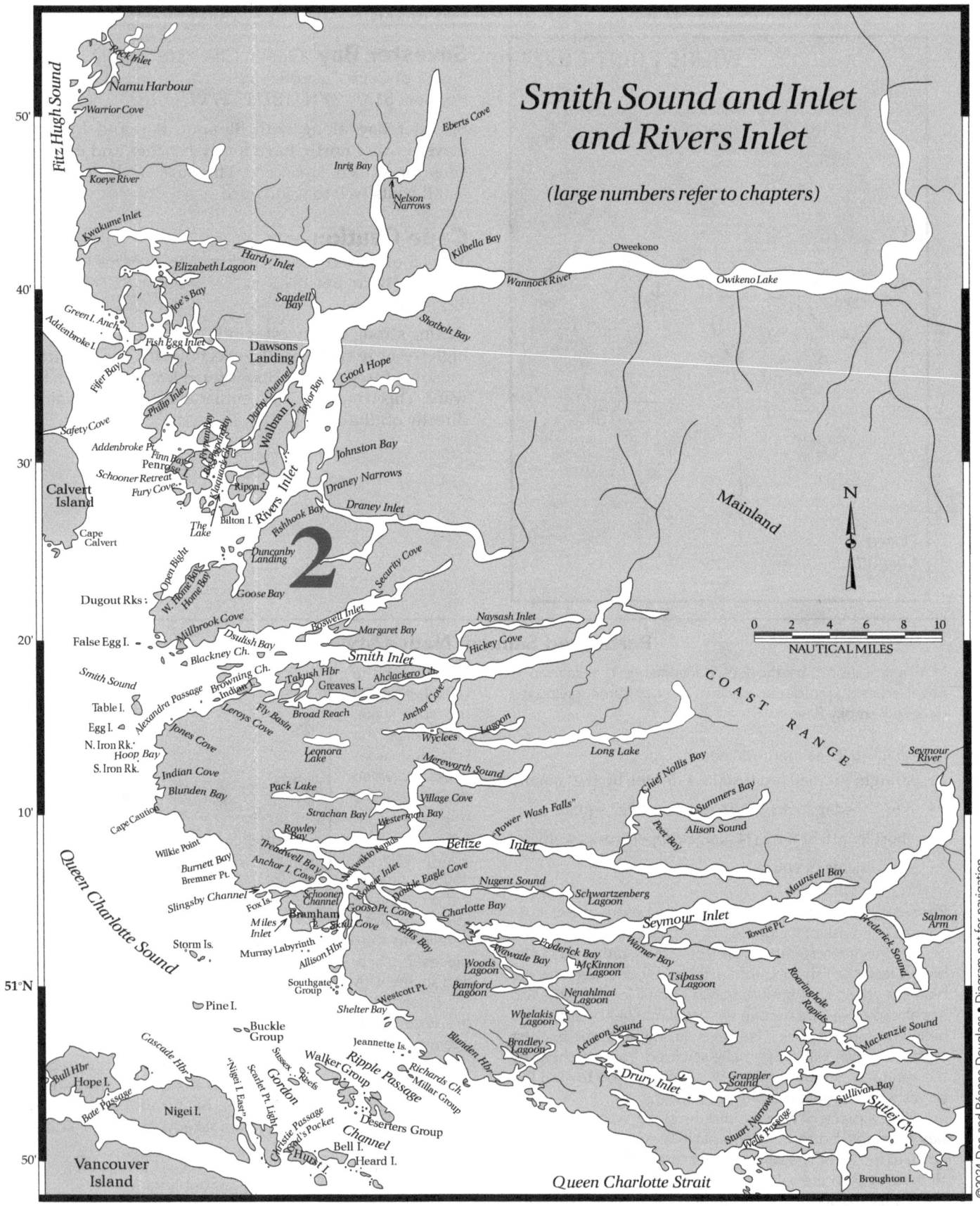

Smith Sound and Inlet and Rivers Inlet

(large numbers refer to chapters)

2

Fitz Hugh Sound

Rock Inlet
Namu Harbour
Warrior Cove
Koeye River
Kwakume Inlet
Elizabeth Lagoon
Joe's Bay
Hardy Inlet
Sandell Bay
Green I. Anch.
Addenbroke I.
Fish Egg Inlet
Dawsons Landing
Fifer Bay
Philip Inlet
Safety Cove
Addenbroke Pt.
Finn Bay
Penrose
Schooner Retreat
Fury Cove
Darby Channel
Taylor Bay
Walbran I.
Calvert Island
Cape Calvert
The Lake
Bilton I.
Ripon I.
Rivers Inlet
Fishhook Bay
Draney Narrows
Draney Inlet
Open Bight
W. Home Bay
Home Bay
Goose Bay
Duncanby Landing
Security Cove
Dugout Rks.
Millbrook Cove
Dsulish Bay
Boswell Inlet
Margaret Bay
Naysash Inlet
Hickey Cove
False Egg I.
Blackney Ch.
Smith Inlet
Smith Sound
Browning Ch.
Indian I.
Takush Hbr
Greaves I.
Ahclackero Ch.
Table I.
Alexandra Passage
Fly Basin
Broad Reach
Anchor Cove
Egg I.
Leroys Cove
Wyclees
Lagoon
N. Iron Rk.
Hoop Bay
S. Iron Rk.
Jones Cove
Leonora Lake
Mereworth Sound
Long Lake
Indian Cove
Pack Lake
Village Cove
Blunden Bay
Strachan Bay
Westernam Bay
Cape Caution
Rowley Bay
Belize Inlet
"Power Wash Falls"
Chief Nollis Bay
Summers Bay
Peet Bay
Alison Sound
Wilkie Point
Treadwell Bay
Burnett Bay
Bremner Pt.
Anchor I. Cove
Nakwakto Rapids
Maunsell Bay
Slingsby Channel
Schooner Channel
Seymour Sinlet
Double Eagle Cove
Nugent Sound
Schwartzenberg Lagoon
Seymour Inlet
Fox Is.
Bramham
Goose Pt. Cove
Skull Cove
Charlotte Bay
Warner Bay
Towrie Pt.
Salmon Arm
Miles Inlet
Storm Is.
Ellis Bay
Frederick Bay
McKinnon Lagoon
Tsibass Lagoon
Frederick Sound
Murray Labyrinth
Allison Hbr
Nawatle Bay
Woods Lagoon
Bamford Lagoon
Nenahlmai Lagoon
Roaringhole Rapids
Southgate Group
Westcott Pt.
Whelakis Lagoon
Artaeon Sound
Mackenzie Sound
Pine I.
Shelter Bay
Bradley Lagoon
Grappler Sound
Sullivan Bay
Buckle Group
Jeannette Is.
Blunden Hbr
Drury Inlet
Sutlej Ch.
Cascade Hbr
Sussex Reefs
Walker Group
Gordon
Ripple Passage
Richards Ch.
Millar Group
Bull Hbr
Hope I.
"Nigei I. East"
Scarlet Pt. Light
Stuart Narrows
Wells Passage
Bate Passage
Nigei I.
Christie Passage
Seagul's Pocket
Channel
Deserters Group
Bell I.
Heard I.
Hunt I.
Vancouver Island
Queen Charlotte Strait
Broughton I.
Queen Charlotte Sound

Eberts Cove
Inrig Bay
Nelson Narrows
Kilbella Bay
Oweekono
Wannock River
Owikeno Lake
Shotbolt Bay
Good Hope
Johnston Bay
Mainland
COAST RANGE
Seymour River

N

0 2 4 6 8 10
NAUTICAL MILES

50'
40'
30'
20'
10'
51°N
50'

©2024 Don and Réanne Douglass • Diagram not for navigation

2

Smith Sound, Smith Inlet, and Rivers Inlet

North of Cape Caution, there are a number of good, sheltered anchor sites, beginning with Jones Cove, just 5.2 miles northeast of the cape. Smith Inlet, east of Egg Island, offers several sheltered anchorages along both its north and south shores, facing Queen Charlotte Sound. Farther east, interesting and rarely-visited sites can be found: Takush Harbour and Village Island which had some of the longest continuously inhabited native sites in the area; the bay with its beautiful sandy beach marked only by bear and cougar tracks; Boswell Inlet and the inlets and lagoon to the east offer excellent sportfishing. Because Smith Inlet trends east and west, you can generally cruise here when southeast weather makes it impractical to head south or north along the outer coast.

Rivers Inlet, especially popular with sportfishing enthusiasts, is busier than Smith Sound. During high season, sportfishing boats from numerous fishing resorts zip around the lower reaches of the inlet from dawn to dusk, sometimes making Channel 16 sound like CB radios on a major freeway. Kayakers and cruising boats find pleasure in the lovely archipelago centered around the marine park at Penrose Island and Klaquaek Channel, as well as farther east. The upper reaches of Rivers Inlet penetrate forty miles into the mainland where a number of rivers culminate—and grizzlies abound. (Note: The inlet was named, not for the many rivers that flow into it, but by Vancouver in the late 1700s, after George Pitt, Baron Rivers.)

Dawsons Landing, on Darby Channel, caters to sportfishing and cruising boaters with moorage, fuel, general store provisions, beer, and wine. Boats that carry limited fuel supplies can fill up and easily continue their northward journey to the next fuel supply in Bella Bella and Shearwater.

On a northbound trip, when conditions in Queen Charlotte Sound and Fitz Hugh Sound grow nasty, Rivers Inlet and Darby Channel are a welcome alternative to Fitz Hugh Sound (or the reverse on a southbound trip).

Blunden Bay (Queen Charlotte Sound)
1.1 mi NE of Cape Caution Light
Entrance: 51°10.77'N, 127°47.03'W

Blunden Bay, immediately north of Cape Caution, is a half-moon-shaped indentation in the mainland. Exposed to western breakers, it is shallow and surf breaks heavily on its beautiful sandy beaches. Its north and south points must have given protection to early canoeists as well as present-day sea-kayakers. This and the next three coves are useful for kayakers or small craft only in calm weather. Although the beach looks inviting, cruising boats generally give the coast from Cape Caution to Alexandra Passage a wide berth due to the heaping and breaking swells along the rocks and reefs extending from the shore. Indian Cove, immediately north, offers more protection for kayakers.

Indian Cove (Queen Charlotte Sound)
1.5 mi N of Cape Caution Light
Entrance: 51°11.24'N, 127°47.20'W
Neck Ness Position: 51°11.85'N, 127°47.97'W; 2.1 mi N of Cape Caution Light

CHS's inflatable measuring speed of the rapids

Photo courtesy Michael Woodward, CHS, Pacific Region

Hoop Bay (Queen Charlotte Sound)
3.3 mi N of Cape Caution Light
Hoop Bay Position: 51°13.11'N, 127°46.88'W

Hoop Bay, east of South Iron Rock, can provide temporary, rolly anchorage in moderate weather. The bay behind the outlying rocks and reefs can be calm and enticing as a good camp site for kayakers, but it is best explored by high-speed inflatable from a mothership safely anchored in Jones Cove. Avoid nasty rocks NW of the islet and shoals northeast of the islet.

Protection Cove
(Queen Charlotte Sound)
4.3 mi N of Cape Caution Light
Entrance: 51°14.18'N, 127°47.06'W

Protection Cove is too small and shallow to offer much protection from heavy westerly swells to anything but kayaks. We once entered here under difficult conditions and got "spooked" by the solid white foam filling the cove, and strong surges from the crashing reefs close on our starboard hand. The cove clearly offers little protection except when small seas are running. Jones Cove, a mile north, offers much better protection and significantly more room to maneuver.

Alexandra Passage (Smith Sound)
Between Egg Island and Jones Cove
Entrance (SW): 51°14.03'N, 127°49.95'W
Entrance (NW): 51°15.81'N, 127°46.21'W

Boats crossing Queen Charlotte Sound bound directly for Fitz Hugh Sound pass roughly a mile west of Egg Island as do the ferries and cruise ships. Those wishing to enter Smith Sound can use Alexandra Passage by carefully passing between Egg Rocks and North Iron Rock, or closer to shore between South Iron Rock and Hoop Reef.

The seas around both North and South Iron rocks generally break or heap up so you can spot them easily. If you take the inside route, monitor your position carefully. In rare calm weather, when the rocks aren't easily spotted, watch your chart plotter carefully to double-check your progress.

During southeast gales, Alexandra Passage and Browning Channel are somewhat protected by the lee of the mainland coast, and have less chop than Queen Charlotte Sound or the more exposed parts of Blackney Channel and Smith Inlet. Because the same lee effect takes place in Open Bight in Rivers Inlet, small southbound cruising boats sometimes take advantage of these conditions to move down to Millbrook Cove or Jones Cove, shortening their transit of Queen Charlotte Sound and Cape Caution.

South and North Iron Rocks
(Queen Charlotte Sound)
South Iron Rock Position: 51°13.24'N, 127°49.13'W;
1.6 mi NE of Neck Ness
North Iron Rock Center Position: 51°13.93'N, 127°49.10'W; 2.2 mi NE of Neck Ness

The shoals around South Iron Rock break at low water; North Iron Rock bares on a six-foot tide.

Egg Island (Queen Charlotte Sound)
5.3 mi N of Cape Caution
Light: 51°14.90'N, 127°50.02'W
Anchor: 51°14.95'N, 127°49.88'W

Egg Island Light Station's timely weather reports are critical to the success and comfort of cruising boats that cross Queen Charlotte Sound. Although many of the original light stations were de-staffed some years ago, Egg Island, and many others, remain in operation. With 24 years service on the island, Stan and Judy Westhaver were the longest-serving lightkeepers since its inception in the late 1800s. Over a period of ten years we were privileged to have yearly visits with the Westhavers and to hear some of the stories of the island's history.

If you wish to visit the Light Station, when weather and sea conditions allow it, call ahead on Channel 82A to inquire if it is a suitable time. If so, respect the government property.

The cove east of Egg Island is extremely small and subject to heavy 2- to 3-foot surge caused by the

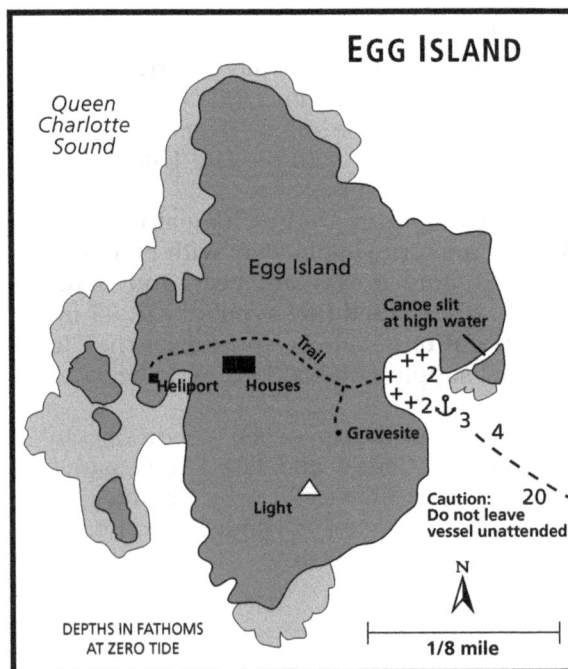

EGG ISLAND

Queen Charlotte Sound

Egg Island

Canoe slit at high water

Trail

Heliport   Houses

Gravesite

Light

Caution:
Do not leave
vessel unattended

DEPTHS IN FATHOMS
AT ZERO TIDE

1/8 mile

©2024 Don and Réanne Douglass • Diagram not for navigation

many ships passing a mile or so to the west. A small 4-fathom shelf, 75 feet wide, ringed with above- and below-water rocks, can be used as temporary anchorage in calm weather. For success, use a stern line to shore here. Your boat should lie on a line from the canoe slit of the islet to the southern point, with about 160 feet of line to shore. The unpredictable surge and lack of swinging room make this shelf rather dangerous.

It is better to anchor off the shelf farther east in about 8 to 12 fathoms (rocky bottom, poor holding). Leave an experienced crew member aboard as anchor watch, or drift or circle farther outside while your party is ashore. If you survive the challenge of landing on the rocky beach in surge, the 118 steps to the top of the island will be easy! The shore party should carry a hand-held VHF for communicating with the boat.

An alternative and safer plan is to anchor in Jones Cove and shoot across in a fast inflatable.

Anchor (tiny east cove) in 4 to 6 fathoms over a mixed rocky bottom; fair holding if your anchor is well set. Larger boats can anchor farther out in 8 to 12 fathoms.

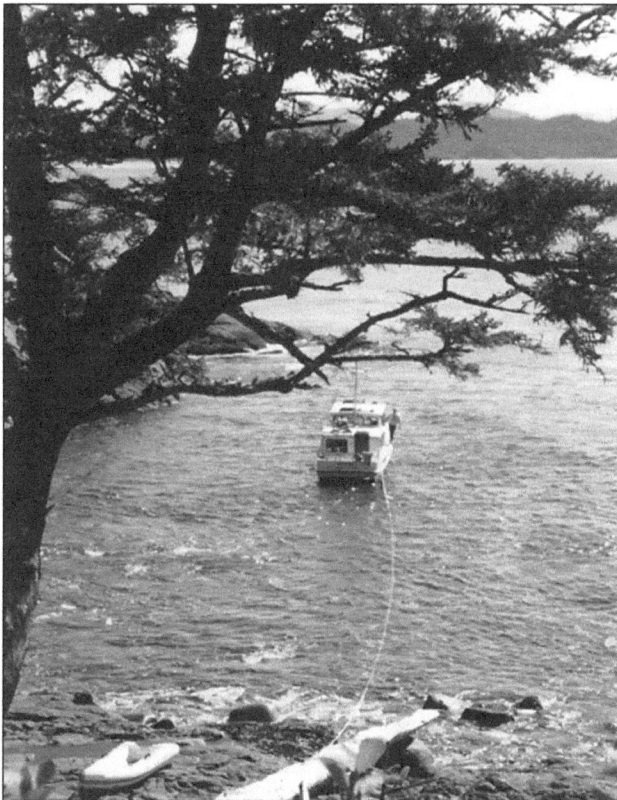

Egg Island, temporary anchorage in fair weather only

Table Island Anchorage
(Queen Charlotte Sound)
1.5 mi NE off Egg Island
Anchor: 51°16.39'N, 127°48.48'W

In northwestern weather, the east and northeastern side of thickly-wooded Table Island can provide anchorage. Small boats can anchor in about 2 fathoms between Table Island and small Ann Island. Larger boats should anchor along the east side of Table Island in 3 to 4 fathoms. We do not recommend these anchorages in easterlies.

Jones Cove (Smith Sound)
2.7 mi E of Egg Island
Entrance: 51°15.09'N, 127°45.86'W
Anchor: 51°14.93'N, 127°45.75'W

Jones Cove, 2.5 miles due east of Egg Island, offers good protection for small craft with somewhat limited swinging room. Ropes on a piling near the entrance can be used in conjunction with a second anchor or to tie up. Inside the piling, there is room for two or three small boats to anchor. In the past, this cove was used as a log boom storage area, but small craft and fishing boats now use it regularly. Millbrook Cove, on the north side of Smith Sound, has more swinging room than Jones, and is a better choice for larger pleasure craft.

Jones Cove is easy to enter but avoid the rocks off the north point or those extending from Turner Islands. The pass inside Turner Islands has a fairway depth of about 20 fathoms and inside Chest Island about 6 fathoms. Avoid the rocks off Chest Island.

Anchor in 2 to 3 fathoms over a soft mud bottom with good holding.

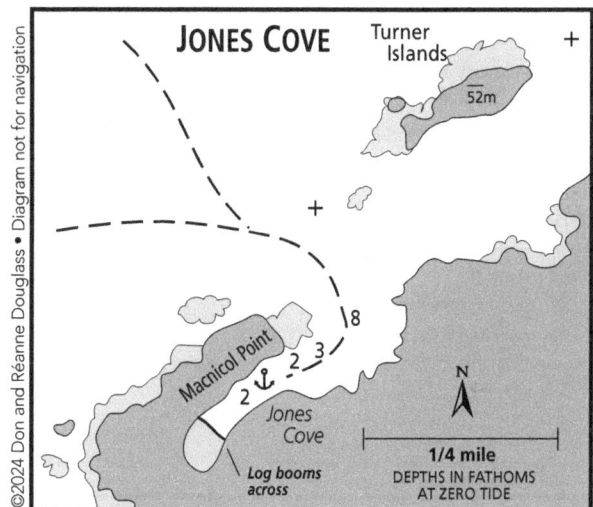

Egg Island Lighthouse Tribulations

I would sooner die than live without you.

In the past, the life of a lighthouse keeper and his family was one of peril and loneliness. Months often passed without contact from the outside world. Illnesses went untreated. The isolation caused emotional depression. Bad weather often stalled supplies from reaching the island as scheduled. Wives grew despondent; children succumbed to illnesses; keepers became desperate.

Widower William Brown, the first Egg Island lighthouse keeper, arrived along with his young son and an assistant after the lighthouse was built in 1898. A fierce storm smashed the windows and flooded the basement that first summer on the island. The assistant quit soon after, abandoning Brown to man the lighthouse alone. In November 1899, he became too sick for his duties, leaving the lighthouse unattended for twenty-seven days. His distress flag went unnoticed until Christmas Day, when the *Quadra* sailed by. Brown and his son were rescued, never to return.

The story behind the grave within the picket fence at Egg Island.

Robert Scarlett brought his family to the island in 1900. When delivery of supplies failed to arrive due to bad weather in November 1904, the Scarlett family faced starvation. When supplies finally arrived, the Scarletts discovered everything had spoiled. They boarded the supply boat and left the island for good.

It is uncertain who took over immediately after Scarlett. In 1919, William Hartin resigned, claiming his wife had "gone crazy." In came Arnold Moran, who was confident he could handle life on a lonely island since he'd been raised at an isolated station. He lasted from 1923 to 1930. His resignation letter stated, "I found that the cruel isolation of Egg Island affected my wife's health. It is no light thing, Sir, for a woman to be cut off entirely from all social and religious contacts; to be immured in what is virtually a prison during the term of her husband's service. Should she be blamed for trying to induce me to seek a position where conditions of life are more human?"

The two men hired as temporary replacements for Moran mysteriously disappeared. It is believed they drowned while braving the turbulent waters in an attempt to take their boat out to fish.

During a monstrous storm in November 1948, lighthouse keeper Robert Laurence Wilkins, his wife Ada Marie, and nine-year-old son, Dennis, escaped minutes before the structure washed away. The family, dressed only in their pajamas, found shelter in a chicken coop. After six days without food and water, Wilkins spotted a fishing boat, the *Sunny Boy*. The family jumped into their rowboat to meet the vessel and was taken to nearby Bella Bella. During their escape, Wilkins broke both arms, permanently damaging his elbows. Mrs. Wilkins had a nervous breakdown from which she never fully recovered. Once more, Egg Island Lighthouse was without a keeper.

Lawrence Dupuis replaced Robert Wilkins. Dupuis brought along his girlfriend, Peggy, and her fourteen-year-old son, Stanley. The story goes that Peggy was estranged from her husband and looking for a romantic adventure on Egg Island. The bad weather and isolation sent Peggy into a depression and caused Dupuis to fear she would leave him. When a storm damaged the lighthouse, they were forced to evacuate the island for Port Hardy, where Peggy's husband lived. Dupuis threatened suicide if Peggy refused to return to the lighthouse after it was repaired. She acquiesced. The following spring Peggy needed surgery and she and Stanley left for Vancouver. Eight weeks later, a letter arrived from Peggy's husband, addressed to his son, Stanley. Dupuis opened the letter and misread its meaning. He assumed Peggy had reunited with her husband. Despondent, Dupuis shot himself. The following day Peggy found a captain to take Stanley and her back to the island. When Dupuis failed to greet their return, the captain went ashore and found a stack of letters Dupuis had written during Peggy's absence. Peggy rushed to the lighthouse but was unable to locate her lover. Instead she found a letter that read, "I would sooner die than live without you." Stanley found Dupuis' body on the rocky shore. He was buried on the island.

Advanced technology affords today's lighthouse keepers timelier rescues. Surviving the weather and isolation is still an ongoing battle.

—KK

The Westhavers were the longest-serving Egg Island Light-keepers

Narwhal *anchored off Egg Island on a rare, calm day*

Millbrook Cove (Smith Sound)

6 mi NE of Egg Island
Entrance: 51°19.12'N, 127°43.93'W
Anchor: 51°19.66'N, 127°44.20'W

Millbrook Cove offers excellent protection, with room for a number of good-sized vessels. Entering requires careful navigation in shallow water, but the calm, well-protected waters inside are worth the effort. We have taken refuge here more than once, and while the wind may howl, the shallow water, good holding, and swinging room should make you happy. On a southbound crossing to Cape Scott you can pick up weather briefings from Egg Island to determine conditions.

Enter Millbrook Cove by using buoy "E6" to line you up for a direct course toward island (30). Post a sharp bow lookout to avoid rocks and reefs. Just before island (30), turn right and circle around islet (34) to the north side, anchoring where convenient.

We have entered Millbrook Cove on the west side of island (30) and have exited by staying to the far east side, although both of these routes are subject to irregular bottoms and shallow depths. Note that the back bay appears shallower than depths indicated on the chart.

Anchor in 3 to 4 fathoms over a soft mud bottom with fair-to-good holding.

Dsulish Bay (Smith Sound)

2.5 mi NE of Millbrook Cove
Entrance: 51°20.01'N, 127°40.48'W
Anchor: 51°20.33'N, 127°40.57'W

Dsulish Bay, northeast of Millbrook, is known for its beautiful, wide sandy beach. We have seen dozens of puffins here, as well as tracks of cougar and deer on the beach. You can enjoy browsing among the driftwood on shore or taking long walks.

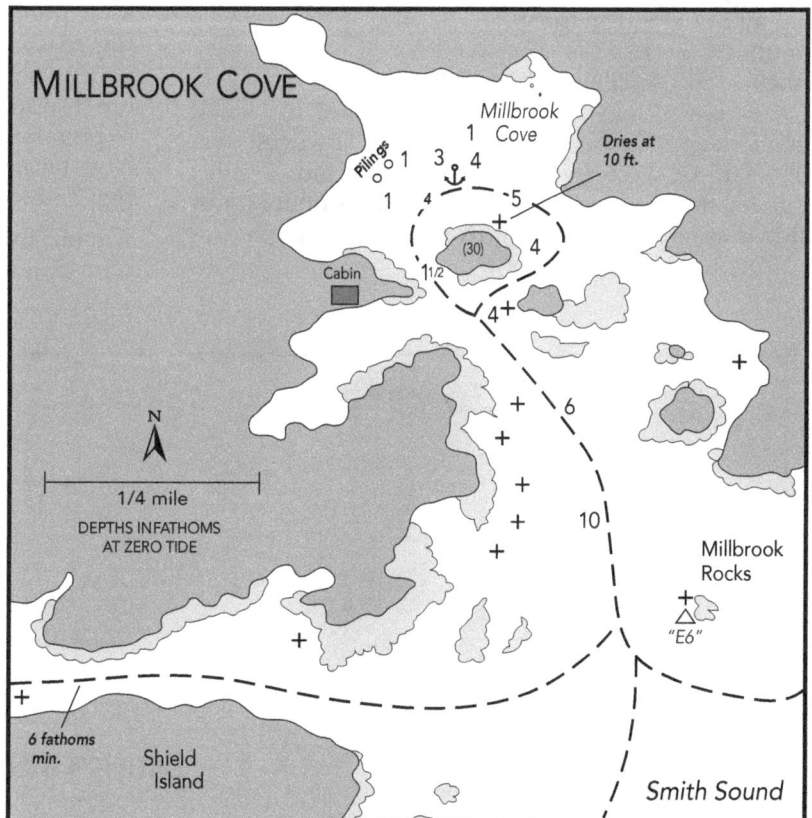

MILLBROOK COVE

Millbrook Cove

Pilings

Dries at 10 ft.

Cabin

(30)

Millbrook Rocks

"E6"

N

1/4 mile

DEPTHS IN FATHOMS AT ZERO TIDE

6 fathoms min.

Shield Island

Smith Sound

©2024 Don and Réanne Douglass • Diagram not for navigation

Although Dsulish Island provides protection from prevailing winds on its northeast side, it is open to the southeast. We recommend this site in stable weather only.

Anchor a short distance anywhere off the beach if you are stopping for lunch or beach-combing. (If you remain overnight, consider staying behind Dsulish Island, or in East Cove.)

Anchor in 2 to 3 fathoms over a sandy bottom with good holding.

Dsulish Bay, East Cove (Smith Sound)
0.5 mi E of Dsulish Island
Anchor: 51°20.38′N, 127°40.02′W
Entrance: 51°20.25′N, 127°39.89′W

Sandy Beach in Dsulish Bay

More protection from northwest winds can be found behind the small peninsula at the east side of Dsulish Bay. Avoid the rock that breaks on an 8-foot tide off the peninsula and another rock just north when entering. Anchor off the small creek at the head of the bay. Driftwood along shore indicates that this bay is exposed to southerly winds.

Anchor in 1 to 2 fathoms over a sandy bottom with some grass; holding is fair to good.

Leroy Bay (Smith Sound)
0.5 mi SW of Indian Island
Entrance: 51°16.43′N, 127°40.40′W
Anchor: 51°16.35′N, 127°40.08′W

Leroy Bay offers fairly good protection for small boats deep in the bay. The outer bay, however, gets its share of westerly chop. Cathcart Island, 2 miles due north of Leroy Bay, has a small nook on its south side that makes a good temporary anchorage in prevailing west winds.

Indian Island (Browning Channel)
7.5 mi NE of Egg Island
Entrance: via Takush Harbour
Anchor: 51°17.09′N, 127°38.42′W

Indian Island is an Indian Reserve. Middens attest to its long history of habitation, and the integrity of the island should be respected. The cove on the east side of Indian Island, which can be entered via Ship Passage, offers good protection but with limited swinging room. The bottom is very soft and may make getting a good hold difficult. We recommend it as a lunch stop only. Fly Basin, 1.5 miles to the southeast, is preferable as an overnighter. Enter Indian Island cove by favoring the north point and avoiding the reef and rocks off the south point.

Anchor in 2 fathoms over a soft and difficult bottom with poor-to-fair holding.

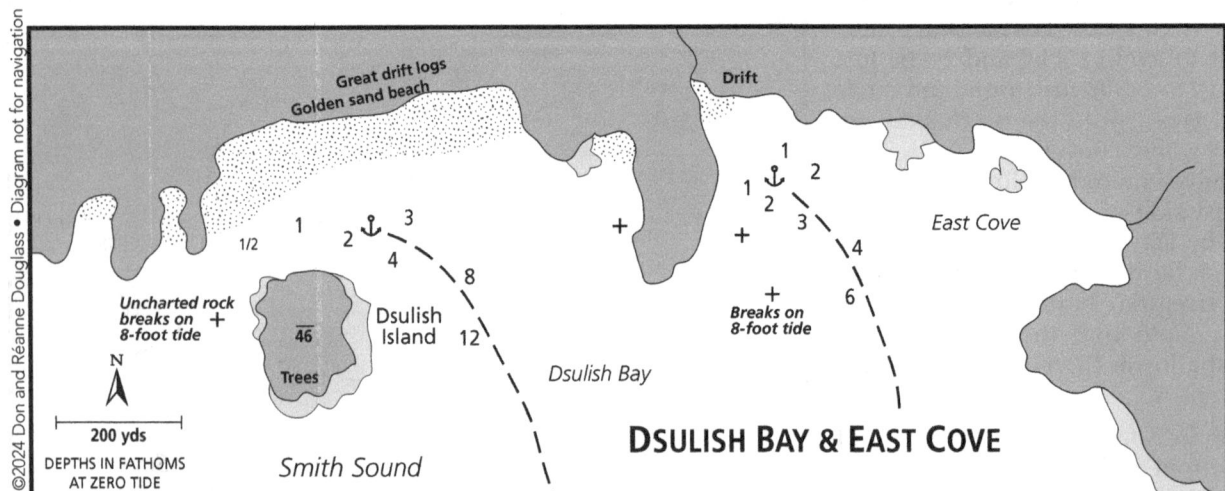
DSULISH BAY & EAST COVE

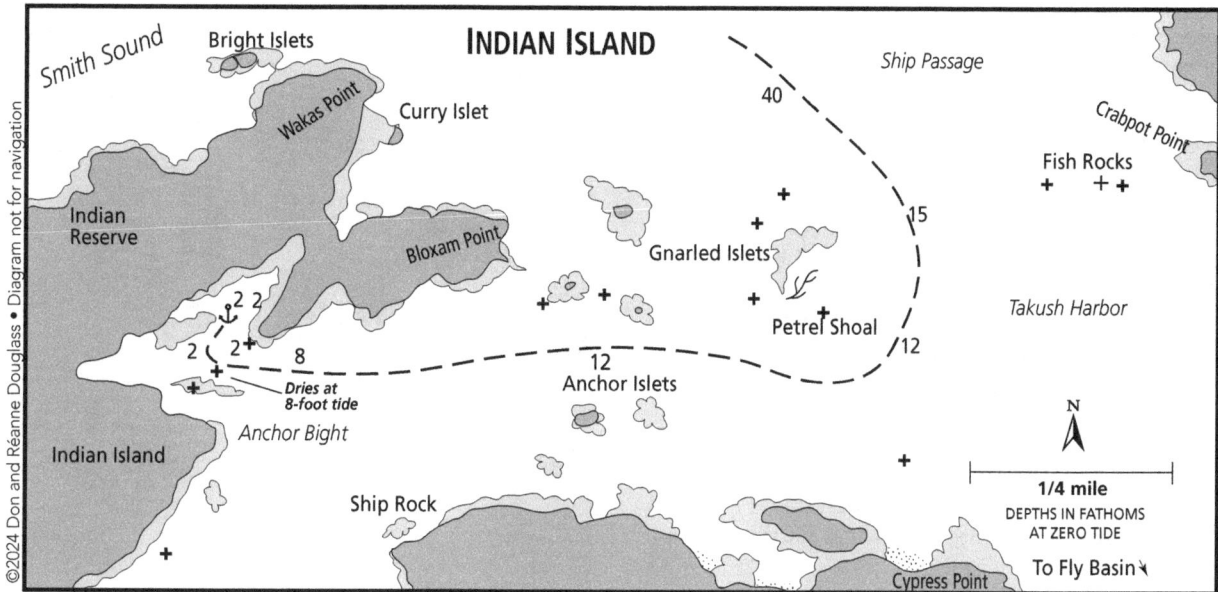

©2024 Don and Réanne Douglass • Diagram not for navigation

Smith Sound • Bright Islets • **INDIAN ISLAND** • Ship Passage • 40 • Crabpot Point • Wakas Point • Curry Islet • Fish Rocks • Indian Reserve • Bloxam Point • Gnarled Islets • 15 • Takush Harbor • Petrel Shoal • 12 • 2 2 2 • 2 2 • 8 • 12 • Anchor Islets • *Dries at 8-foot tide* • *Anchor Bight* • Indian Island • Ship Rock • Cypress Point • To Fly Basin • N • 1/4 mile • DEPTHS IN FATHOMS AT ZERO TIDE

B.C.'s Coast by Kayak—Indian Cove to Hoop Bay

Indian Cove is a haven for kayakers. I paddled through its narrow mouth and set up camp on its sandy beach just in time to enjoy a lovely sunset.

The next morning, I got off to a late start. The wind had been forecast to be 15-20 knots from the northwest, but it was blowing harder—probably a steady 25 knots. As I left the mouth of Indian Cove, I encountered a southwest swell, 6-8 feet high, with wind waves from the northwest and waves that reflected off Neck Ness, a point a half-mile to the north with an extensive shoal. Every fifth or sixth wave broke 18 to 24 inches from the top. The intersection of the three wave patterns formed ugly pyramids, steep on all sides. Within 15 minutes of leaving the Indian Cove, I decided to return, but I couldn't see its narrow entrance for the bouncy water, so I turned around again and headed back toward Neck Ness, taking water in the chest and mouth. I braced into the face of one particularly ugly wave but couldn't recover in time for its steep back face, and my kayak flipped.

I quickly remounted the boat using a technique called a "cowboy," but water had swamped the cockpit and I needed to bale. My bilge pump was mounted on the back deck. I had to get back in the water to fetch it, then climb back into the cockpit, fasten my spray skirt and begin alternately paddling, bracing and pumping, in stormy conditions.

Water poured into the cockpit over the gap in my sprayskirt where I'd inserted the bilge pump. But I discovered that the boat was more stable with the cockpit full of water rather than half-full and sloshing. I could feel the cold water splashing over my thighs inside my wetsuit but, for the most part, I was warm. I decided to paddle on and look for a safe place to land.

I rounded Neck Ness and looked for a sheltered beach. I saw nothing promising, and kept paddling, searching the chart and shore for a refuge. It was still rough and the boat was low in the water—the cockpit coaming and the bow were nearly awash. Hoop Reef lay ahead and, as I approached it, I could see sheltered water to its lee. Studying the chart I noticed a sand beach in Hoop Bay; I could enter the middle of Hoop Reef without broaching and be sheltered from the seas.

I approached the reef and dashed through the middle between waves, narrowly avoiding a couple of shallow rocks on either side. In the excitement I realized that I had been clenching my sunglasses in my teeth and I finally relaxed.

I approached the beach in Hoop Bay, got out of the kayak, and stood in the shallows pumping out the cockpit. A red and yellow Canadian Coast Guard propjet passed by overhead—probably called out by the lighthouse keepers at nearby Egg Island to help me. A grayish, immature puffin was sitting on the rocks inside Hoop Reef, and I happily watched him from the calmer waters.

I set up camp on the beach above the high-tide line and rested, watching the lovely sunset, grateful for my survival.

—John McCormack, kayak explorer

Takush Harbour (Smith Inlet)
8.5 mi E of Egg Island
Entrance: 51°17.29'N, 127°37.03'W

Takush Harbour, a large indentation on the south side of Browning Channel, offers a choice of anchor sites for good protection from southeast storms; Fly Basin and Bull Cove are convenient anchor sites on its south corner. Ship Passage is the deep-water route between Gnarled Islets and Petrel Shoal on the west and Fish Rocks on the east.

There are many detached rocks and reefs in Takush Harbour and its bottom is uneven; careful piloting is required, especially in poor visibility. When entering the harbor, watch for Fish Rocks that extend a quarter-mile due west of Crab Pot Point and are awash on a five-foot tide. Largely untouched by modern development, the harbor is a quiet, scenic anchorage. Perhaps the most interesting feature in Takush Harbour is Indian Island.

Anchor Bight (Smith Sound)
Close S of Indian Island
Entrance: 51°17.29'N, 127°37.43'W
Anchor: 51°16.76'N, 127°38.69'W

Anchor Bight is located in the western section of Takush Harbour between Ship Rock and Indian Island. Protection can be found in shallow water close to the spit connecting the two. The recommended anchorage for smaller boats in a southeast gale or storm force winds would be Fly Basin. Large fishing boats frequently use the entrance west of the connecting spit to anchor at night.

Anchor in 4 to 7 fathoms over mud and sand bottom with good holding.

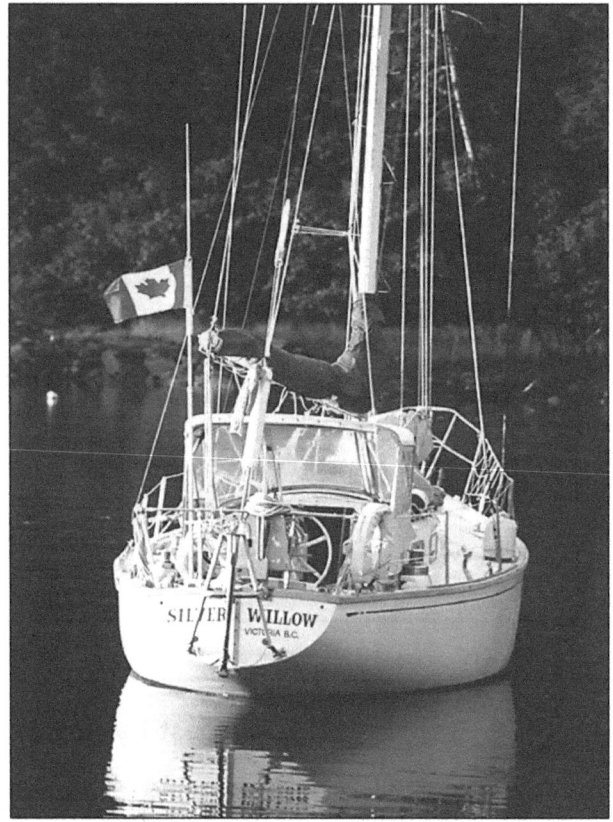

Anchored in a quiet cove

Fly Basin (Smith Inlet)
S side of Takush Harbour
Entrance: 51°16.68'N, 127°36.60'W
Anchor: 51°16.31'N, 127°36.07'W

Fly Basin is a wonderful landlocked shelter that has a large, flat, shallow bottom with lots of swinging room but a rocky entrance. This tranquil place is disturbed only by the sounds of birds and inquisitive seals. Surrounded by old-growth cedar, you feel as though you're in a landlocked swimming pool. Underwater visibility in the basin is good to about 15 feet.

Entering Fly Basin, favor the west shore as you cross the 2-fathom bar to avoid a rock complex off the east entrance point. Then favor the east shore until you enter the 5-fathom basin proper. We prefer the eastern section of the cove.

Anchor in 4 fathoms over sticky gray mud with worms; very good holding.

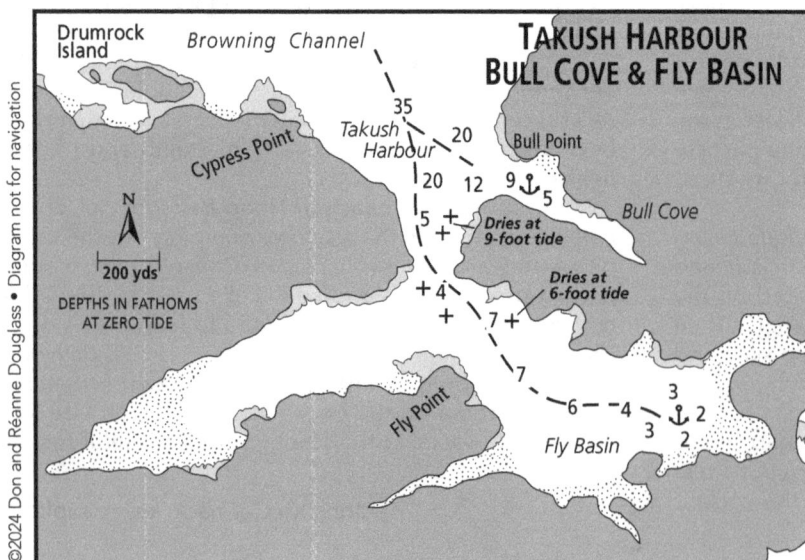

Broad Bay

(Takush Harbour)
E corner of Takush Harbour
Anchor: 51°17.28'N, 127°35.77'W

Broad Bay, 0.5 mile due east of Crabpot Point, offers good shelter from all winds and is almost land-locked. Its south side is the western high-water dinghy entrance to tortuous 10-mile-long Ahclakerho Channel that leads along Greaves Island's south side.

Anchor in the head of the bay in 7 to 9 fathoms, hard bottom, fair holding.

BS Cove

(Smith Inlet)
2 mi NE of Takush Harbour
Entrance: 51°18.30'N, 127°34.38'W
Anchor: 51°18.24'N, 127°34.51'W

BS Cove is the local name for the cove 0.7 mile east of Birkby Point on the north shore of Greaves Island. This cove has excellent views of snowy peaks of the high country behind Boswell Inlet. The head of the bay is mostly a drying flat with a large beach that provides easy landing access. The islets across the north end keep out the westerly chop.

Although the cove is a good anchorage in prevailing westerlies or fair weather, it is a poor choice in easterlies. (In Smith Inlet and the north side of Smith Sound, southeast gales usually occur as easterlies.) "Gill Net Cove," east of BS Cove, offers better protection under east winds.

Anchor in 2 to 3 fathoms over a mud bottom with good holding.

Gill Net Cove

(Smith Inlet)
3 mi SW of Margaret Bay
Entrance: 51°18.25'N, 127°34.06'W
Anchor: 51°18.09'N, 127°34.14'W

"Gill Net Cove," our name for the cove that nearly cuts Greaves Island in half at its western end, derived from the fact that there was once a small float anchored here, used by fishermen to unload and work on their gill nets.

Upon entering, favor the west shore to avoid a detached rock on the east entrance. Larger vessels prefer to anchor in McBride Bay.

Anchor in 2 to 4 fathoms over a mud bottom with good holding.

McBride Bay (Smith Inlet)

2 mi S of Margaret Bay
Entrance: 51°18.60'N, 127°32.51'W

McBride Bay, a large, well-sheltered bay at the north end of Greaves Island is deep with an irregular bottom. There is plenty of swinging room for boats with lots of anchor rode. Locals report that anchorage can be taken in 12 to 20 fathoms over an irregular bottom with fair-to-good holding; larger vessels anchor mid-bay, avoiding the rocky patch south of Middle Patch.

Margaret Bay (Smith Inlet)

5 mi NE of Takush Harbour
Entrance: 51°19.88'N, 127°31.44'W
Anchor: 51°19.96'N, 127°29.66'W

Margaret Bay lies at the west end of a peninsula that separates Smith Inlet from Boswell Inlet. Small boats can find good protection in all but very strong westerlies at the far east end of the bay.

When entering the bay, favor the north shore near Mills Point to avoid Camosun Rock which extends beyond mid-channel from the south shore. Prevailing westerly chop dies at the head of the bay. When entering the inner basin, avoid the dangerous rock awash at 11 feet by favoring the south side of the channel. Use a stern tie to the islet just west of the cannery ruins for more security.

Anchor in 1 to 3 fathoms over a sand and mud bottom with good holding.

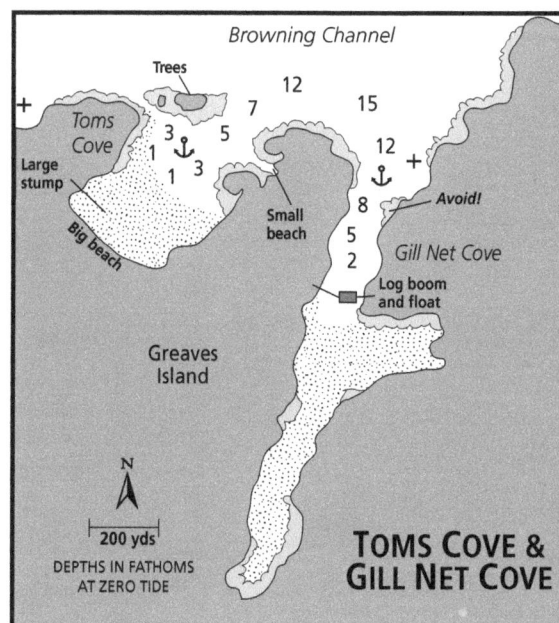

TOMS COVE & GILL NET COVE

Ethel Cove (Smith Inlet)
0.5 miles NW of Margaret Bay
Entrance: 51°20.05'N, 127°31.62'W
Anchor: 51°20.25'N, 127°31.31'W

Ethel Cove, immediately north of Margaret Bay, offers good protection in all but strong southwest weather. Anchor off a small, sandy beach. Larger boats will like the additional swinging room found here, in contrast to that of Margaret Bay.

Anchor in 3 to 6 fathoms over sand and mud with fair-to-good holding.

Smith Inlet (Smith Sound)
E of Browning Channel
Entrance: 51°18.93'N, 127°32.92'W

Smith Inlet begins at McBride Bay on Greaves Island and continues 20 miles east, deep into the coast mountains where Nekite River flows into the salt water. Proceeding eastward along the inlet, a series of channels and lagoons offer interesting exploration: Naysash Inlet on the north side of Smith, Ahclakerho Channel and Wyclees Lagoon to the south and farther up-inlet Burnt Island Harbour and Walkum Bay.

Ahclakerho Channel (Smith Inlet)
6.3 mi E of McBride Bay
Entrance (E): 51°17.46'N, 127°23.20'W
Entrance (W): 51°17.08'N, 127°35.85'W

The western entrance rapids to Ahclakerho Channel at the east end of Takush Harbour are navigable by dinghies at adequate high-water slack. Times of slack water are unpredictable. Boulders that extend across the channel completely block access at moderate tidal heights and cause cascades of water until the channel dries. Local knowledge is recommended before you attempt to enter the western entrance, but if you decide you want to give it a try, do so on an ebb tide when the current is flowing slowly west. That way, if you bump a rock, you will be swept back out to the west, instead of being sucked further into the rapids.

Fishing vessels and boats up to medium size enter the eastern end of the channel at Quascilla Bay at medium to low tide when the rocks are visible; more care must be taken at high water. The only good anchor site within the channel lies at the western end of Broad Reach. Within the channel, it is beautifully calm and protected; however the anchor site is exposed to southeast and outflow winds.

Quascilla Bay (Smith Inlet)
6.5 mi E of McBride Bay
Entrance: 51°17.65'N, 127°22.18'W

Quascilla Bay, the eastern entrance to Ahclakerho Channel, has Anchor Cove in its southwest corner.

Naysash Inlet (Smith Inlet)
N of Cape Anne
Entrance: 51°18.35'N, 127°22.16'W

Naysash Inlet is a long, narrow inlet with convenient depths for anchoring only east of the spit at Naysash Creek. This large spit extends well into the inlet at

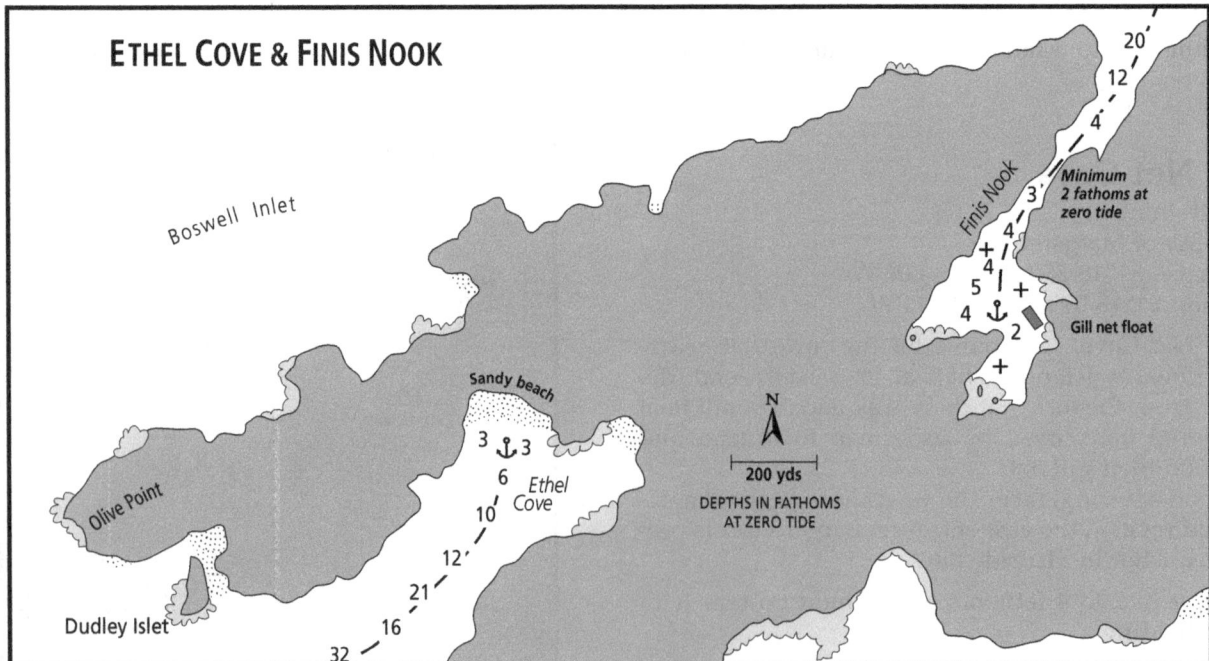

ETHEL COVE & FINIS NOOK

Boswell Inlet

Olive Point

Dudley Islet

Sandy beach

3 ⚓ 3
6
10
12
21
16
32

Ethel Cove

N

200 yds
DEPTHS IN FATHOMS
AT ZERO TIDE

Finis Nook

20
12
4

3
4
4
5
4
2

Minimum 2 fathoms at zero tide

Gill net float

©2024 Don and Réanne Douglass • Diagram not for navigation

the outlet of the creek almost closing off access to the east; favor the south shore at this point. Anchorage can be found above the spit in moderate to deep water. The bitter end of the inlet opens into a large basin about 20 fathoms deep. On the north shore of this terminal basin, an impressive landslide—formed by a stream of rubble that jumped a cliff and flowed down into the inlet—is visible. The waters of Naysash Inlet, which have very little exchange with outside waters, serve as a breeding ground for plankton and algae that discolor the water. There is no VHF radio reception or satellite communication within most of the inlet. Even GPS may be affected due to masking of satellites by the high mountains. Nonetheless, Naysash Inlet is an interesting place to visit.

Hickey Cove (Naysash Bay)
1 mi E of Adelaide Point
Entrance: 51°18.46'N, 127°20.75'W

Hickey Cove, 1 mile inside Naysash Inlet, can offer good protection for small boats only from downslope or east winds close to the drying flat at the head of the cove. Swinging room is limited.

Naysash Bay (Naysash Inlet)
0.5 mi N of Hickey Cove
Entrance: 51°18.97'N, 127°20.61'W

Naysash Bay is a broad bight, too deep for convenient anchorage.

Wyclees Lagoon (Smith Inlet)
1 mi E of Quascilla Bay
Entrance: 51°17.42'N, 127°20.85'W

Wyclees Lagoon is an extraordinary example of the distance and remoteness of the Pacific Ocean stretching into the mainland coast, flooding steep-walled canyons. Access to the lagoon is possible only at high-water slack. On spring tides the entrance bar can be hazardous, with an overfall of up to 6-foot for a distance of 50 yards. Within the lagoon, the tidal level varies just 1 to 2 feet regardless of the level of the ocean tide. You can enter rather easily when the water in Smith Inlet is near the level inside the lagoon. At other times there can be very strong currents in the narrows.

The Docee River, which drains Long Lake, is considered one of the most important sockeye salmon rivers between the Fraser and the Skeena. Department of Fisheries maintains a seasonal counting fence near the outlet to the river. Small and medium-size fishing vessels sometimes enter lagoon during fishing season, anchoring in reasonable depths at the head of either arm of the lagoon.

Anchorage is reported to be in the "Seine Hole"—so named because it's deep enough for a seine boat to anchor—0.3 mile inside the entrance and north of the rapids where charted depth is 7.4 meters on the west side of the shallow reef. Boats that anchor here swing with the turn of the tide. The reported current in Seine Hole may run to 2 knots or more at spring tides. The drying rocks to the east and north of the Hole are extremely hazardous.

Smith Inlet, east of Wyclees Lagoon, terminates at the Nekite River and in steep-sided, landlocked fiords too deep for anchoring. Burnt Island Harbour, Walkam Bay and Nelos Landing are the arms of this remote, scenic area.

Finis Nook (Boswell Inlet)
0.5 mi N of Margaret Bay
Entrance: 51°20.85'N, 127°30.07'W
Anchor: 51°20.48'N, 127°30.39'W

Finis Nook is an "out-of-this-world" place, hidden from view and protected from outside weather. Anchorage can be taken in the center of the bay. Small boats can anchor closer to the southeast corner, avoiding old structures.

The narrow entrance, with its overhanging trees, offers no particular problem. Mid-channel fairway depth is about 2 fathoms minimum. The narrows has an irregular bottom; avoid the rock 10 feet from shore at the south side of the entrance.

Anchor in 2 to 4 fathoms over soft mud with good holding.

Security Bay (Boswell Inlet)
2 mi NE of Finis Nook
Entrance: 51°22.02'N, 127°28.30'W

The depths are too great for most pleasure craft.

Boswell Cove (Boswell Inlet)
0.7 mi NE of Security Bay
Anchor: 51°22.52'N, 127°26.46'W
Entrance (Boswell Inlet): 51°22.65'N, 127°25.90'W

"Boswell Cove" is what we call the unnamed cove on the north shore, 1.5 miles east of Security Bay. Wonderfully quiet and secluded, it offers very good protection from all weather. Tuck into the landlocked north corner and enjoy the scenic old-growth forest. This is one of our favorites.

Slightly favor the south shore when entering. Minimum depth in the fairway is 3 fathoms.

Anchor in 2 to 3 fathoms over soft mud, sand and some grass; good-to-very good holding.

PASSAGES FROM SMITH SOUND TO RIVERS INLET

Boats using Millbrook Cove or continuing north from Smith Sound can exit via Radar Passage or Irving Passage to rejoin the ferryboat route to Fitz Hugh Sound.

Edward and Wood rocks, 1.5 miles northeast of Table Island, can be hazards upon leaving or entering Smith Sound. Earlier editions of charts show Edward Rock with an inaccurate drying height of 2.1 meters, the same as Wood Rock. Be sure to verify that your chart has the correct information.

Boats wishing a challenge or those wanting to stay close to shore to avoid chop may find that the passage north of Shield Island, around Ada Rock, inside False Egg Island and Dugout Rocks, is more comfortable. Ada Rock is generally marked by kelp or breaking waves. While this route may be shorter, it can cause high anxiety unless you are certain of your position at all times. Use GPS to identify proper turning points.

We have passed inside Spur Rocks during a southeast blow, but because there are many breaking rocks off Kelp Head, this route requires precise navigation and a stomach for white water when swells are running.

Eliza Bay and Lucy Bay (Smith Sound)
2 mi W of Millbrooke Cove
Entrance (Eliza Bay): 51°19.30′N, 127°44.67′W
Entrance (Lucy Bay): 51°19.57′N, 127°47.07′W

Both Eliza and Lucy Bays are exposed to southwest swell, which is felt at almost all times, and they offer little or no protection for cruising boats. Millbrook Cove, 2 miles east, is greatly preferred.

Rivers Inlet (Fitz Hugh Sound)
E of Cape Calvert
Entrance: 51°25.00′N, 127°46.82′W

Rivers Inlet, on the east side of the entrance to Fitz Hugh Sound, is entered between Cranstown Point and Addenbroke Point, 8.7 miles north. The two entrance channels to Rivers Inlet are separated by a group of islands. The main entrance channel lies south of this group; Darby Channel, which is narrow, lies north of it.

Once you have passed the choppy entrance of Rivers Inlet, wonderful opportunities for exploration open up. Although the lower reaches of the inlet abound with fishing lodges where small sportfishing boats zip around at high speed, you can find peaceful anchorages and lovely coves and bays. The area around Penrose and Walbran islands is particularly appealing to pleasure craft and kayakers.

Often ignored by cruising boats heading to Alaska, Rivers Inlet can be used as an alternative to crossing the bouncy lower part of Fitz Hugh Sound either on a northbound or southbound voyage by using Darby Channel and Penrose and Walbran Islands.

Open Bight (Rivers Inlet)
1.3 mi E of Dugout Rocks
Entrance: 51°22.45′N, 127°46.05′W
Anchor: 51°22.16′N, 127°46.42′W

Open Bight, in the lee of Cranstown Point, has a lovely, wide, white sand beach where you can take temporary shelter in all but northerly and northeast winds and chop. Outflow winds generate a bad chop against the beach here, setting you against a lee shore, but during a southerly, there is just a hint of swell here and the waters are nearly flat. Although there are several kelp patches in the bight they present little trouble in finding a clear anchor site.

A 40-yard-long primitive trail heads south across the spit to a rugged, exposed beach facing southwest; the contrast is remarkable. This beach has white sand and the driftwood is worn and scattered. We call the trail "Cougar Trail" because of the tracks we've noticed. Make lots of noise when you hike or climb around here.

Anchor in 1 to 2 fathoms near shore over a sandy bottom with good holding.

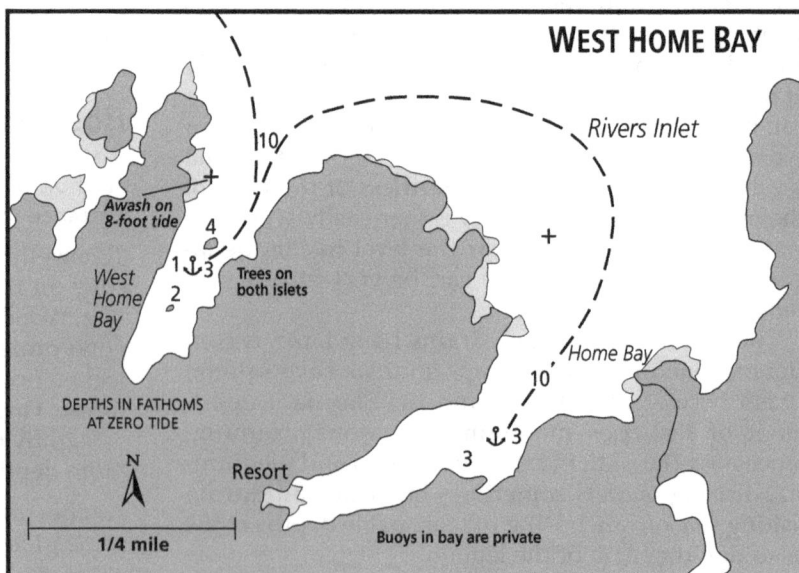

WEST HOME BAY

Awash on 8-foot tide

West Home Bay

Trees on both islets

Rivers Inlet

Home Bay

DEPTHS IN FATHOMS AT ZERO TIDE

N

Resort

1/4 mile

Buoys in bay are private

©2024 Don and Reanne Douglass • Diagram not for navigation

West Home Bay (Rivers Inlet)
2.8 mi NE of Open Bight
Entrance: 51°24.04'N, 127°43.11'W
Anchor: 51°23.85'N, 127°43.27'W

West Home Bay provides a quiet retreat and good shelter for one small vessel from all but down-inlet winds. Enter using the east side of the bay and anchor between the two treed islets. Swinging room is limited.

Anchor in 2 fathoms over a soft mud bottom with fair-to-good holding.

Duncanby Cove (Rivers Inlet)
0.9 mi W of Duncanby Lodge
Entrance (S): 51°24.25'N, 127°40.21'W
Anchor: 51°24.39'N, 127°40.13'W

Duncanby Cove is our name for the snug anchor site situated inside the small island due west of Duncanby Lodge.

The south entrance to the cove is clear. However, if you use the north entrance, favor the east shore to avoid a dangerous rock awash on a 4.8-foot tide off the small north islet.

Anchor near the center of the bay in about 10 fathoms over a mixed bottom; fair-to-good holding; a stern tie to shore is useful for anchoring farther north.

Duncanby Lodge (Rivers Inlet)
6.2 mi NE of Dugout Rocks
Floats: 51°24.35'N, 127°38.75'W

Duncanby Lodge is an all-inclusive fishing resort with no services or facilities for boaters. For complete information see the Website: www.duncanby.com; or phone 1-877-846-6548; 604-628-9822.

Open Bight, looking out toward Queen Charlotte Sound

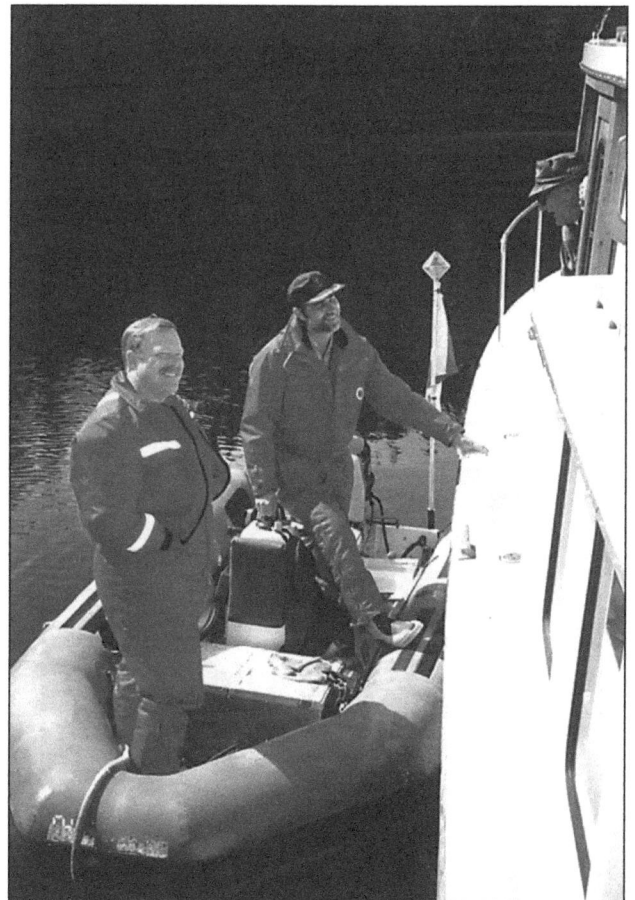

OPEN BIGHT

20

Rivers Inlet

Cranstown Point

10

N

3
2
1   2
1

3

1/4 mile

DEPTHS IN FATHOMS
AT ZERO TIDE

White sand beaches

Trail: 40 yards long

Drift logs

©2024 Don and Réanne Douglass • Diagram not for navigation

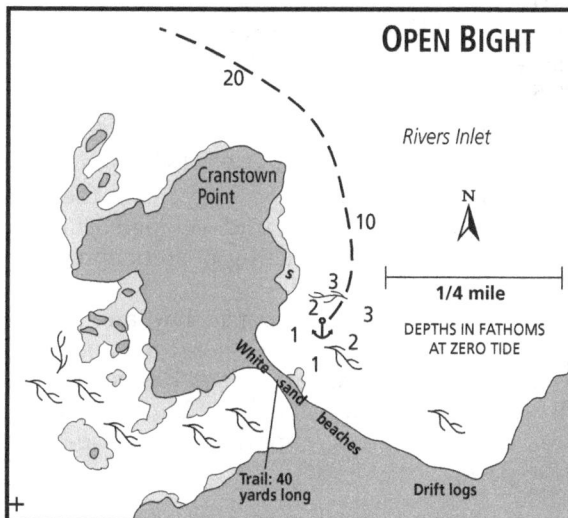

A friendly visit by Fisheries & Oceans

Goose Bay (Rivers Inlet)
2 mi SE of Duncanby Lodge
Entrance: 51°24.23'N, 127°39.50'W
Anchor: 51°22.48'N, 127°40.05'W

We feel that small boats can find the best storm shelter in the vicinity anchored deep in Goose Bay, on either the north or southeast side of island (53). The water at this particular spot is shallow, the fetch minimal, and holding ground good. You can make your boat additionally secure if you use a stern tie to the south side of island (53), with your main anchor set well out in the mud flat.

The water in Goose Bay is muskeg color with visibility limited to 1 to 2 feet. The area is a major bird area where you can hear songbirds in the trees along shore or view eagles, blue herons, and gulls poking about the greenish mud flats. At low water, a pervasive musty odor fills the air.

Although Goose Bay is fully protected from westerly summer winds, furious gusts can occur in a southeast storm. Because there is little fetch and good holding in southerly weather, in foul weather, this is a good choice, along with Klaquaek Channel.

The old cannery was restored by a group of BC firemen. The restored cannery is now a fishing resort

Goose Bay, looking north

with no facilities for transient boaters. The dock and uplands are posted with No Treaspassing signs.

Anchor in 3-4 fathoms north of island (53) or in 1½ fathoms south of island (53) over soft brown mud with very good holding.

Penrose, Walbran and Ripon Islands
(Rivers Inlet)
10 mi SE of Addenbroke Lighthouse
Position (Rouse Reef): 51°29.37'N, 127°46.10'W

Penrose, Walbran and Ripon islands form a unique archipelago of small coves and narrow channels best enjoyed by kayak or dinghy.

Just south of Bilton Island, south of Ripon Island, you may be able to observe a "herring ball" feeding frenzy—hundreds of screaming rhinoceros auklets, gulls, and bald eagles churning the water in search of their main meal.

Penrose Island Marine Park
(Penrose Island)
9.3 mi SE of Addenbroke Lighthouse
Entrance (Schooner Retreat): 51°28.67'N, 127°45.43'W
Anchor (Fury Cove): 51°29.26'N, 127°45.57'W

Penrose Island was established as a British Columbia Marine Park in 1992, encompassing all but the north coast. Penrose Island and its undeveloped 5000 acres are quite popular with cruising boaters and kayakers.

In this area, Fury Cove, Frypan Bay, and Big Frypan Bay are favorite anchor sites for good storm anchorages. Fury Cove sometimes has restrictions, advisories, and closures, check the BC Parks website for the latest at: https://bparks.ca/penrose-island-marine-park/.

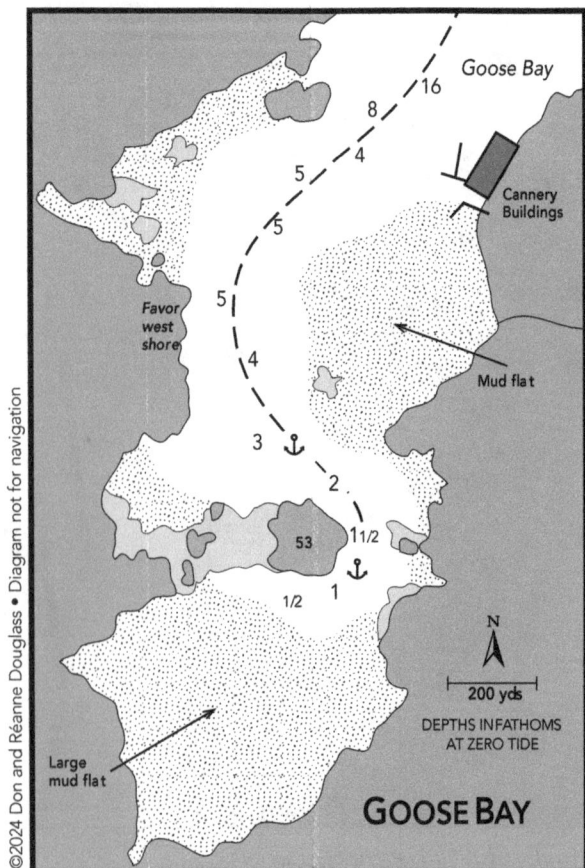

GOOSE BAY

Fury Cove (Penrose Island Marine Park)

8.5 mi SE of Addenbroke Lighthouse
Entrance: 51°28.67'N, 127°45.43'W
Anchor (Fury Cove): 51°29.26'N, 127°45.57'W

Fury Cove, the landlocked cove on the far west end of Penrose Island, is a popular anchorage for north- or southbound boaters and often has a number of boats at anchor. Nearby Frypan and Big Frypan bays are less crowded options. Its strategic location can provide relief from outside weather. From the west end of the anchorage, you can view conditions outside on Fitz Hugh Sound. Fury Cove is within the Penrose Island Marine Park and makes a good base from which to explore the entire park by kayak or skiff.

Entering Schooner Retreat and Fury Cove for the first time can be a hair-raising experience that should be avoided in stormy weather. It's difficult to identify all the islands and openings but, with experience, it becomes easier. The fairway is deep and we have not yet seen waves break across the entrance (unlike Breaker Pass, the next pass north, which can be used safely only in calm weather). However, if there is a big southwest swell running outside with wind blowing, white water and foam do blow across the outer entrance to Schooner Retreat, making it more difficult and dangerous to enter. You should not attempt to enter in poor visibility.

Cleve Island, with Fury Point on its south end, lies

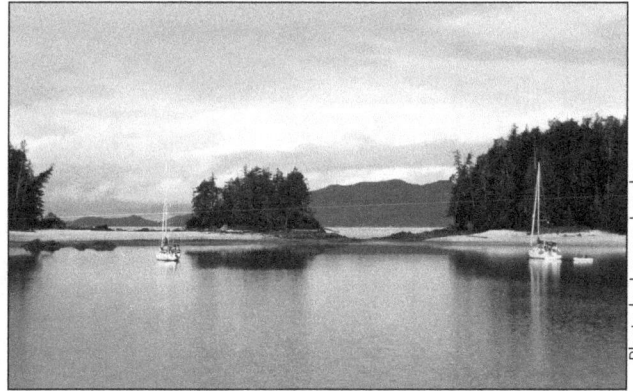

Fury Cove anchorage looking west to Fitz Hugh Sound.

southwest of Fury Island. Vertical walls on its northwest side look as if they have been cleft from Fury Island. Stay east of Cleve, noting the white paint on the islet north of Folly Islet that marks the entrance.

In poor visibility avoid Rouse Reef, which is awash on about a 14-foot tide. The waves heaping and breaking on this reef show up on radar at high tide. Rouse Island is covered with trees. Rouse Point lies on its southern tip. When you are correctly lined up to enter Exposed Anchorage—the outer chamber for Fury Cove—your heading should be about 015° magnetic. On this heading you are directly in line with Dyer Islets at the north center end of Exposed Anchorage. When you are about 250 yards in front of Dyer Islets, execute a sharp left turn. The swell diminishes at once as you pass through the narrow opening to calm Fury Cove.

Anchor in 3 to 5 fathoms over sand and mud with good holding, avoiding the rock close to the beach.

Frigate Bay

(Penrose Island Marine Park)
NE side of Joachim Island
Entrance (Safe Entrance): 51°27.93'N, 127°44.62'W
Anchor: 51°28.41'N, 127°43.73'W

Frigate Bay provides good protection for small craft deep in its north corner. Enter by way of Safe Entrance and avoid the mid-channel Fire Islets and rocks on the north side. We prefer the view from Fury Cove but this is a nearby alternative when Fury is crowded. Anchor tucked into the north end for maximum shelter.

Anchor in 7 to 10 fathoms over sand and mud with good holding.

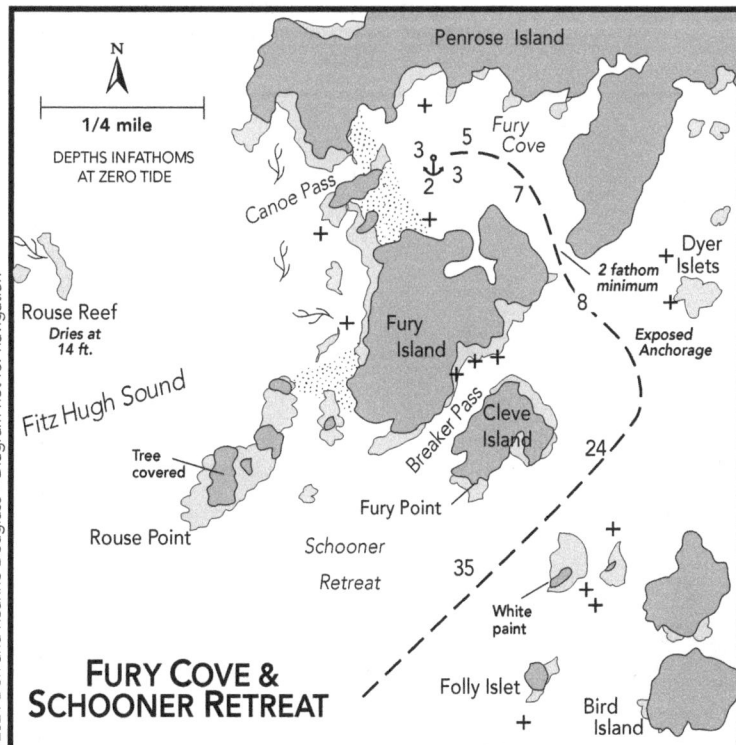

Map labels:
N
1/4 mile
DEPTHS IN FATHOMS AT ZERO TIDE
Penrose Island
Fury Cove
Canoe Pass
3 5
2 3
7
Dyer Islets
2 fathom minimum
8
Exposed Anchorage
Fury Island
Breaker Pass
Cleve Island
24
Rouse Reef Dries at 14 ft.
Fitz Hugh Sound
Tree covered
Rouse Point
Fury Point
Schooner Retreat
35
White paint
Folly Islet
Bird Island
FURY COVE & SCHOONER RETREAT
©2024 Don and Réanne Douglass • Diagram not for navigation

Big Frypan Bay has plenty of room for many boats

Secure Anchorage

(Penrose Island Marine Park)
NE side of Ironside Island
Entrance (SE): 51°28.33'N, 127°44.33'W
Entrance (W): 51°28.53'N, 127°45.36'W
Anchor: 51°28.45'N, 127°44.41'W

Secure Anchorage offers very good shelter, especially for larger vessels and those wishing more swinging room. The bottom is deeper and it is difficult to tell what the weather is doing due to its landlocked position.

We prefer to enter via the north side of Folly Islet, following the deeper Edmond Passage from Schooner Retreat on the north side of Ironside Island. Your chart plotter will help in locating the many rocks and shoals you must avoid in navigating this beautiful convoluted area. An alert bow watch is a must when exploring this wonderful coast.

Rocky Bay (Penrose Island Marine Park)
E of Exposed Anchorage
Position: 51°28.82'N, 127°44.45'W

Rocky Bay is a sheltered cove, best explored by dinghy or kayak.

Klaquaek Channel (Penrose Island)
10 mi SE of Addenbroke Light
Entrance (SW): 51°27.20'N, 127°44.01'W
Entrance (NE): 51°30.57'N, 127°40.85'W

Klaquaek Channel separates Penrose Island from Walbran and Ripon islands. Both the north and south entrances to the channel are encumbered with small islands. Klaquaek Channel waters are surrounded by islands and are so well protected that it looks like a big lake. There are a number of secure anchorages on either side of the channel, namely Frypan, Big Frypan, Magee Channel, Five Windows Cove and Sunshine Bay. The entire area is a fantastic exploring ground for kayaks or dinghies.

The north entrance, known as "Slaughter Alley" or "Slaughter Illahie" was the site—in the mid-1800s—

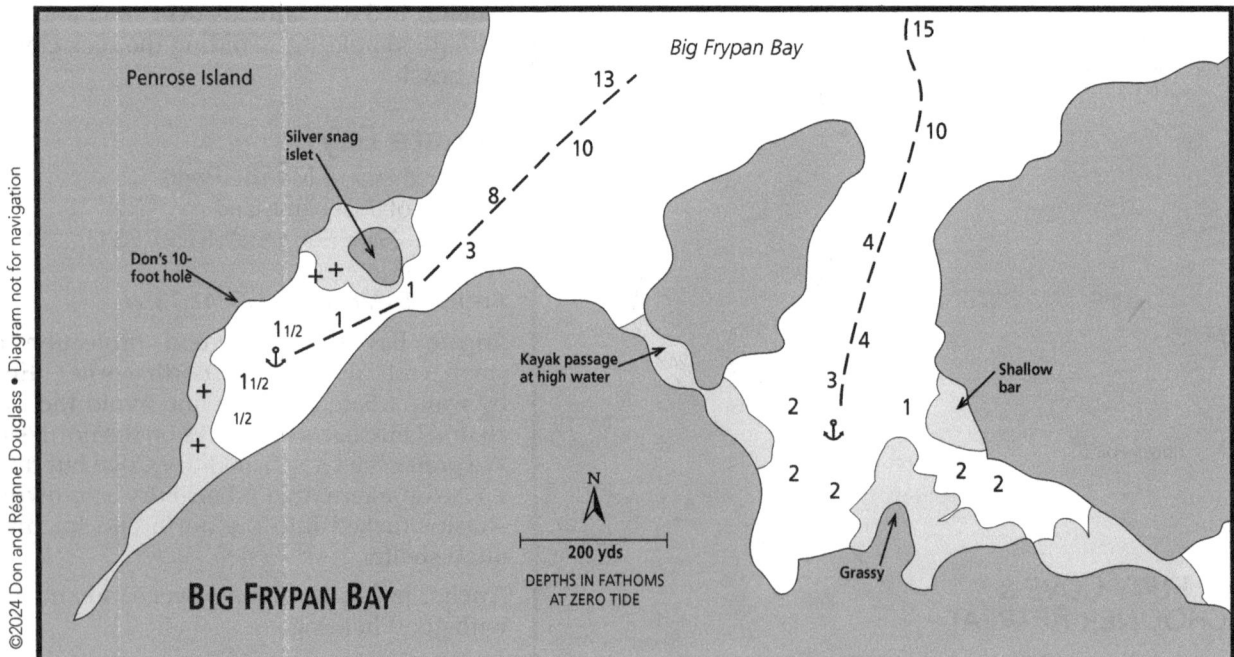

of a massacre of the local Oweekeno by the Heiltsuk of Bella Bella.

Approaching the north entrance to Klaquaek Channel from Darby Channel, the northeastern entrance is generally preferred; but avoid submerged rocks on either side of the fairway at the entrance.

Approaching from Fitz Hugh Sound, in good visibility, we suggest taking the northwestern entrance which requires an exaggerated S-turn to avoid two charted, mid-channel rocks. Southbound, favor the east shore of island (96) and stay within about 60 feet from shore until abeam the north rock, awash on a 13-foot tide. Then cross over smartly to the west shore (Penrose Island) to pass the south rock that bares 2 feet above high water. This south rock has a tuft of grass on its summit and a long underwater shoal that extends from its north side. Minimum depths in the fairway are 3 to 4 fathoms.

Frypan Bay (Penrose Island Marine Park)
NW corner of Klaquaek Channel
Entrance: 51°29.70'N, 127°42.18'W
Anchor: 51°29.98'N, 127°42.70'W

Frypan Bay, on the northeast corner of Penrose Island, offers good protection in all weather. Only occasional gusts with little chop are found here when gales blow up Fitz Hugh Sound. Anchorage can be taken over a generally flat 9-fathom bottom with good swinging room for a number of boats. Large boats can anchor in the middle of the bay, while smaller boats may want to use the cove just inside the entrance. The south shore offers good protection but the bottom is rocky. Avoid several small rocks along the shore.

Anchor in 3-4 fathoms over brown mud, twigs and rocks; good holding if you set your anchor well.

Big Frypan Bay
(Penrose Island Marine Park)
2 mi E of Fury Cove
Entrance: 51°29.17'N, 127°42.26'W
Anchor: (larger boats): 51°29.22'N, 127°42.83'W
Anchor (small boats): 51°28.88'N, 127°42.83'W

Big Frypan Bay offers excellent protection from southerly weather along its south shore. Large boats or those wanting more swinging room can anchor in the center of the bay in about 15 fathoms, while small boats have a choice of anchor sites closer to shore. The narrow entrance to Big Frypan carries a minimum depth of 6½ fathoms in its fairway.

Pleasant anchorage can be found off the entrance to the lagoon between a small grassy peninsula and a high-water kayak route south of the island to the

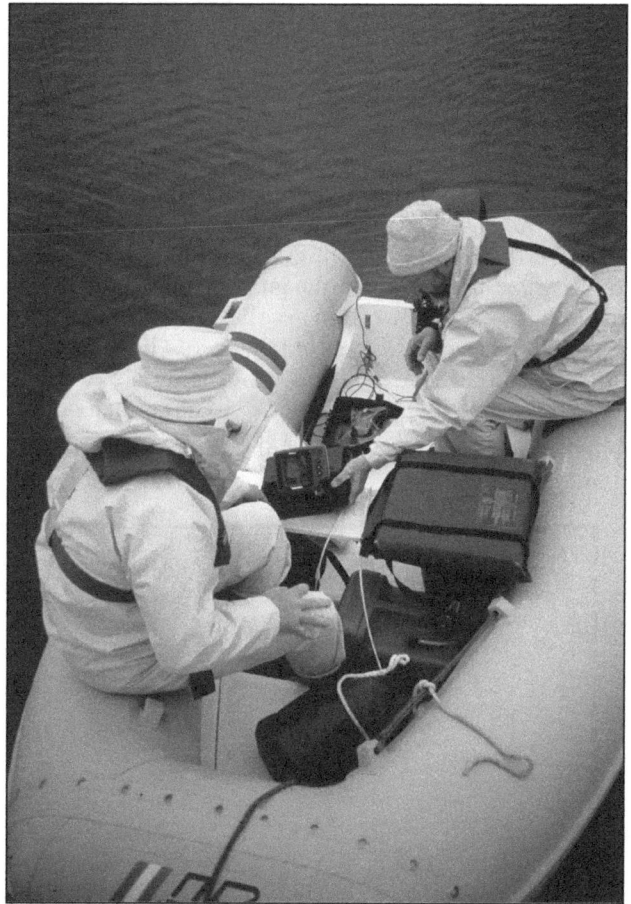

Baidarka's *crew goes exploring*

west. Small boats may anchor in the lagoon entrance east of the grassy peninsula and the 1-fathom entrance bar.

A more secluded anchorage for one or two small boats can be found in the very southwest corner of Big Frypan Bay behind what we call "Silver Snag Islet." A narrow passage on the east side of Silver Snag Islet carries about 4 feet at zero tide. To the southwest of the islet is a small, flat-bottom area with a depth of 10 feet at zero tide which we named "Don's 10-Foot Hole."

The sun seldom reaches this nook; tree branches overhang the water and there is no beach. But it's a good place to sit out a storm. Avoid the foul area west of the islet and two large rocks on the southwest side of the nook. If more than one boat uses this nook, consider using a stern tie.

Anchor (small boats) in 4 fathoms over sand and mud with good holding.
Anchor (larger boats) in 12 to 15 fathoms, sand and mud with good holding.

Sunshine Bay (Ripon Island)

2 mi W of Big Frypan Bay
Entrance: 51°28.52'N, 127°40.72'W
Anchor: 51°28.64'N, 127°40.02'W

Sunshine Bay has a narrow entrance with an irregular bottom and a minimum depth of about 2 fathoms. Inside the bay there is room for several boats over a flat 5-fathom bottom. A number of floathomes occupy the northeast and southeast shores and the bay is quite busy. While it offers excellent protection, it no longer offers a wilderness experience. Those seeking such an experience can find it in the next bay north which we call "Five Window Cove." (See diagram.)

Anchor in 5 fathoms in the center of the bay over soft sand with grass; fair holding.

Five Windows Cove (Ripon Island)

0.3 mi N of Sunshine Bay
Entrance: 51°28.72'N, 127°40.69'W
Anchor: 51°29.06'N, 127°39.94'W

"Five Windows Cove," immediately north of Sunshine Bay, is formed by the intersection of five islands, hence our name. The "windows" represent the extremely narrow passages between the islands. Five Windows Cove offers a quiet and pristine experience and is a good getaway for smaller boats.

The southwest passage indicated on the diagram is the only viable small-boat passage since the others can be used only at high water by kayaks. The water in Five Windows Cove is calm with overhanging cedar, hemlock and alder branches along the shore.

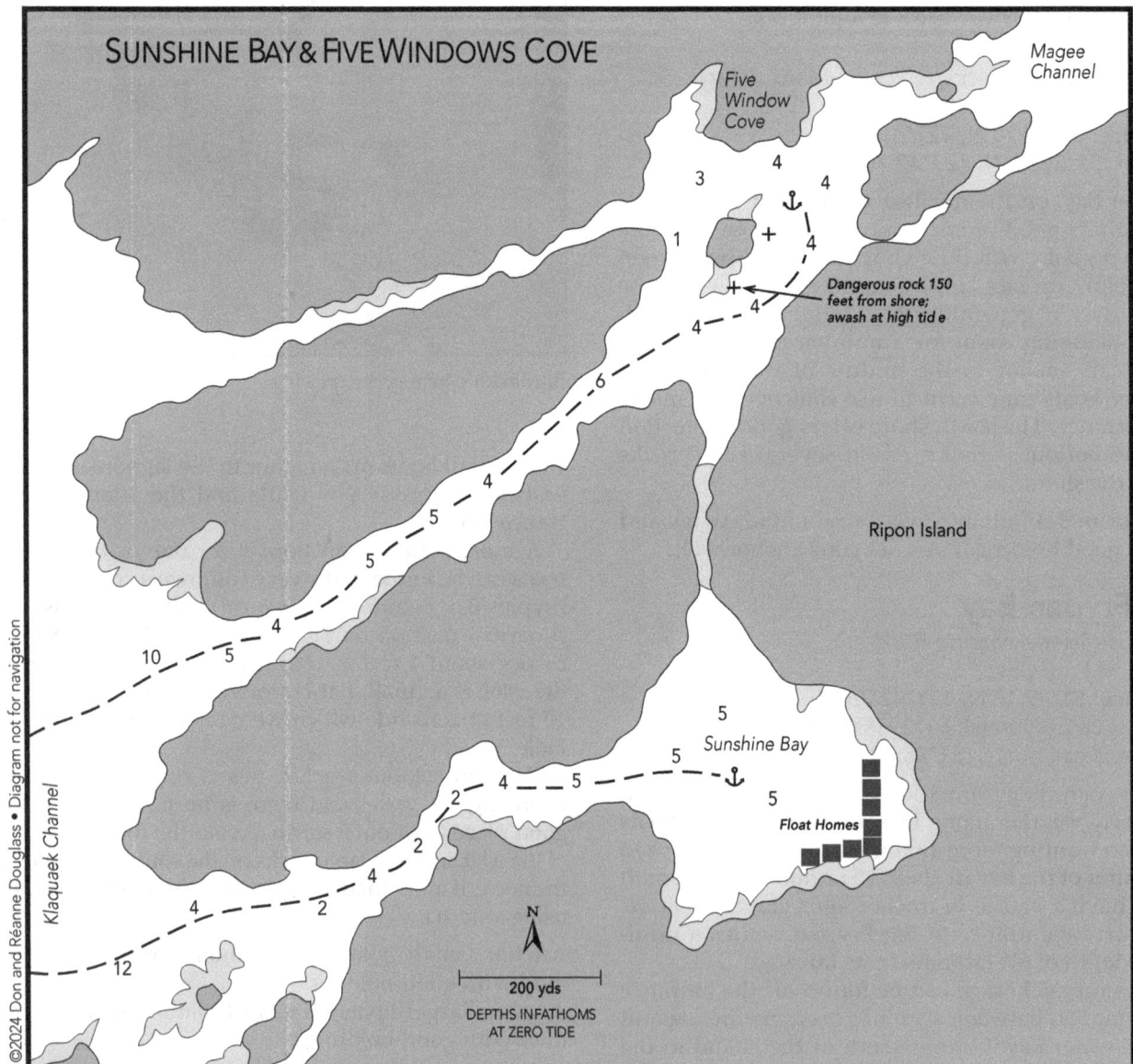

SUNSHINE BAY & FIVE WINDOWS COVE

Five Window Cove

Magee Channel

Dangerous rock 150 feet from shore; awash at high tide

Ripon Island

Sunshine Bay

Float Homes

Klaquaek Channel

©2024 Don and Réanne Douglass • Diagram not for navigation

N

200 yds

DEPTHS IN FATHOMS AT ZERO TIDE

The best anchorage is on the east side of the center islet, avoiding its two rocks, especially the rock 150 feet from the south shore.

Anchor in 4 fathoms over a mostly sandy bottom with some grass; fair-to-good holding.

Magee Channel (between Ripon and Walbran islands)
N shore of Ripon Island
West entrance: 51°29.49'N, 127°40.97'W
Anchor (large vessel): 51°29.32'N, 127°39.32'W
Anchor (small vessel): 51°29.35'N, 127°38.65'W

The western end of Magee Channel is easily navi-

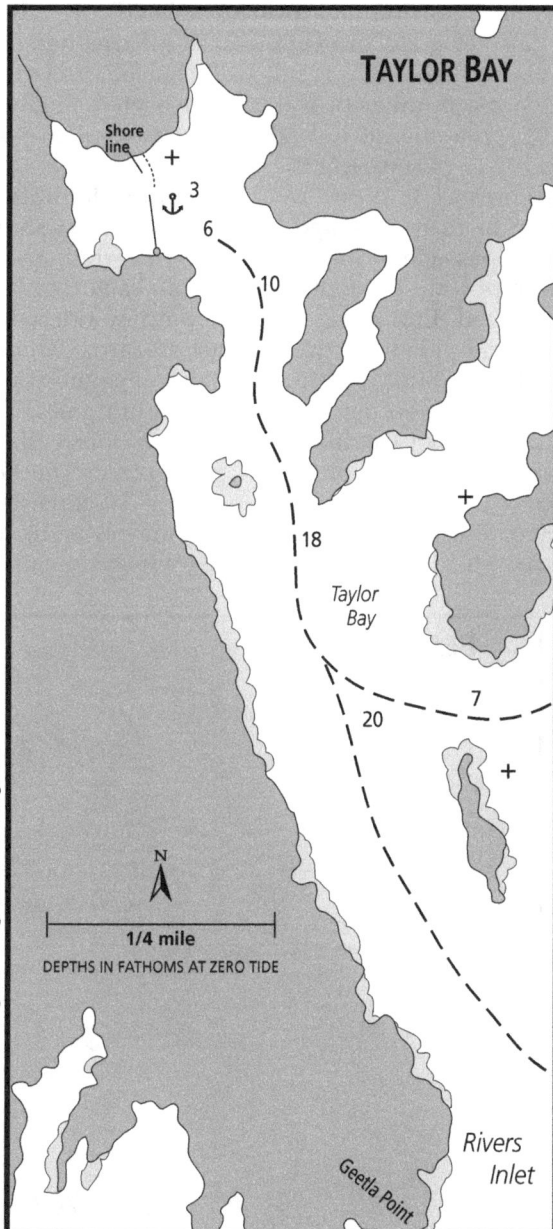

gable and well protected. The eastern end, which has foul ground, is suitable only for dinghies. Small boats can find yet another wilderness experience in the center portion of Magee Channel east of the second narrows and east of the mid-channel islet. Spruce, cedar and hemlock branches hang low over the saltwater at high tide.

The islet just east of the second narrows has a canoe pass on its south side that is blocked by limbs. Small boats can pass north of the islet in a passage about 50 feet wide between the tree branches. Favor the north shore. Anchor between the islet and the rock at the east end of the basin which bares 1 foot above high water. Larger boats can anchor just west of the second narrows on either side of the channel in 12 fathoms.

Anchor (small boats) in about 6 fathoms over a soft bottom; good holding.

Anchor (larger boats) in 10 to 12 fathoms over a mixed bottom; fair holding.

Wilson Bay (Ripon Island)
0.7 mi N of Canniff Point
Entrance: 51°27.54'N, 127°39.00'W

Wilson Bay has a small basin in its northwest corner that can be entered by small craft at high water.

Geetla Inlet (Walbran Island)
E end of Magee Channel
Entrance: 51°28.92, 127°37.36'W

Geetla Inlet, connected to Magee Channel at high water, is an interesting place to explore by kayak.

Taylor Bay (Walbran Island)
N of Geetla Point
Entrance: 51°29.76'N, 127°35.65'W
Anchor: 51°30.66'N, 127°36.29'W

Taylor Bay, on the east side of Walbran Island, is typical of the myriad small inlets, channels, and lagoons found in Rivers Inlet. From the east side of Walbran Island to the west side of Penrose Island, you can explore narrow, shallow channels by kayak or dinghy but, if you do, don't be surprised by an outboard that occasionally whizzes by.

Good protection with limited swinging room is afforded for small craft at the far northwest end of Taylor Bay. Larger boats can find good protection and more swinging room in deeper water northwest of the island.

Anchor as far west as appropriate in 2 to 7 fathoms over mud with good holding.

Hemasila Inlet (Walbran Island)
1.2 mi NE of Taylor Bay
Entrance: 51°31.24'N, 127°35.18'W

Hemasila Inlet is exposed to southerly winds. Its high bluffs and deep water make it accessible and scenic. Avoid mid-channel rocks if entering the basin at the north end.

Darby Channel (Rivers Inlet)
NW shore of Walbran Island
Entrance (W): 51°30.54'N, 127°46.48'W
Entrance (E): 51°34.60'N, 127°34.80'W

Darby Channel, also known as Schooner Pass, is the northern route connecting Fitz Hugh Sound to Dawsons Landing and the upper part of Rivers Inlet. The north side of the channel has rocky cliffs; the south side is lined with trees that hang low, trim and horizontal over the water, indicating protection from all weather. The smooth water of the channel mirrors the trees.

You can hug the north side of the channel inside Stevens Rocks or follow a mid-channel course. The southernmost Stevens Rocks are bare; islet (16) is treed. The narrows west of Pendleton Island offers little problem to cruising boats. See large scale chart to help avoid Stevens Rocks.

Pierce Bay (Darby Channel)
1.5 mi NE of Addenbroke Point
Entrance: 51°31.17'N, 127°45.57'W
Anchor (West Cove): 51°31.95'N, 127°46.04'W
Anchor (East Cove): 51°32.23'N, 127°45.03'W

Pierce Bay, the first bay on the north shore east of Addenbroke Point, has a number of small islands in its western portion that form an isolated cove where you can get good protection from all weather. The bottom of Pierce Bay is not well charted, and since there are a number of isolated uncharted shoals in the bay you should not attempt to enter it in poor visibility or foul weather.

The entrance to West Cove has an irregular bottom and an intricate passage that hugs the west shore. This passage is not for the faint-hearted, and it is important to identify and avoid each rock and kelp bed. Entry may be easiest at low tide when you can identify the various hazards. Underwater visibility is poor due to the opaque water. Seagulls often use this cove to sit out gales, and during quiet weather you can hear loons calling, so you know it must be a good place. The bottom—extremely soft black mud—is the consistency of jello so be sure to set your anchor well, and use a stern tie to shore if strong winds prevail.

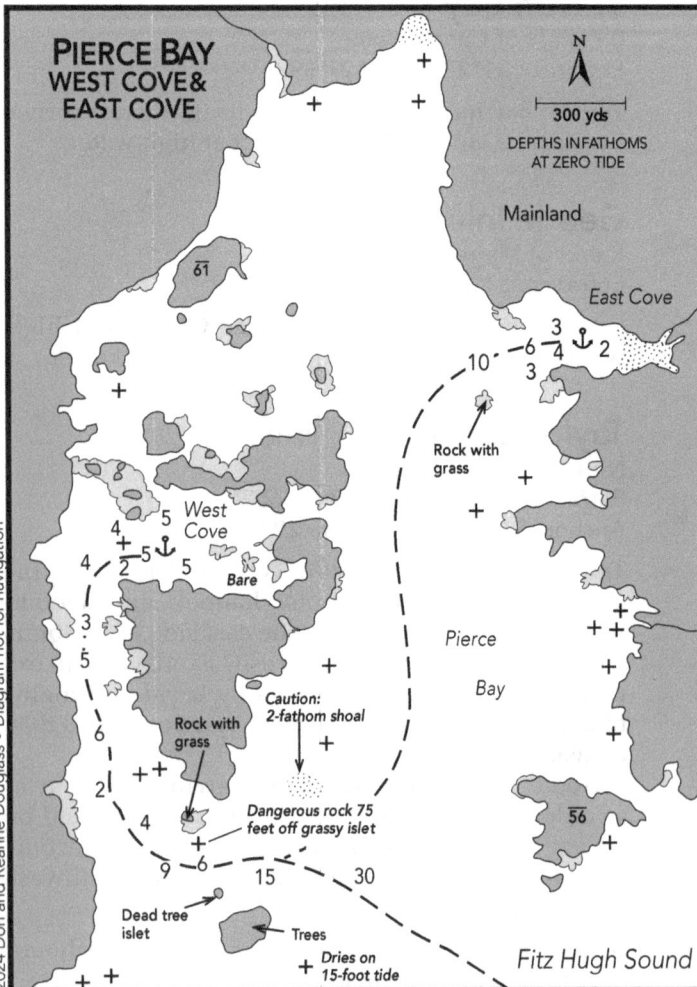

PIERCE BAY WEST COVE & EAST COVE

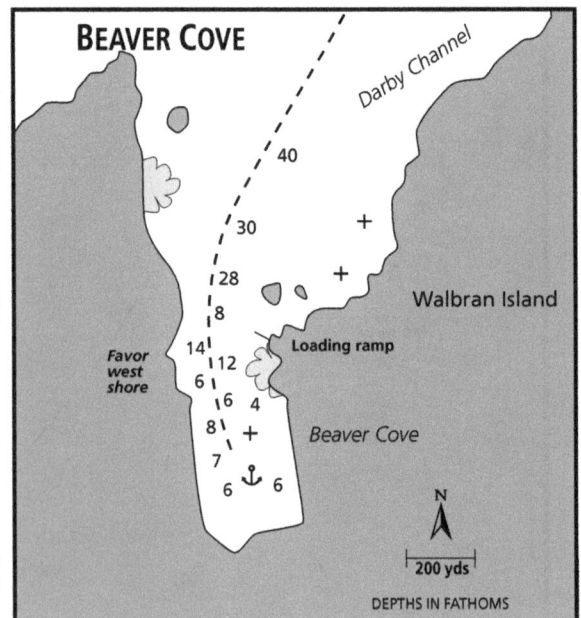

BEAVER COVE

East Cove offers good protection in most weather, if you anchor just short of the drying flat, deep in the cove. Old-growth trees line the shore, and a stream from Elsie Lake comes in at the head of the cove. Avoid the rock SW of the entrance.

Anchor (West Cove) in about 4 fathoms over soft black mud; poor holding unless you set your anchor well.

Anchor (East Cove) in about 4 fathoms over sand and gravel bottom with fair holding.

Finn Bay (Penrose Island)
8 mi SE of Addenbroke Light
Entrance: 51°30.43'N, 127°43.35'W
Finn Bay Resort Float: 51°30.23'N, 127°43.85'W

Finn Bay, the first possible moorage at the west end of Darby Channel, is a convenient place to wait for favorable conditions to cross Queen Charlotte Sound on a southbound voyage.

Beaver Cove (Darby Channel)
1.5 mi S of Duncanby Landing
Entrance: 51°33.44'N, 127°35.89'W
Anchor: 51°33.06'N, 127°35.95'W

Beaver Cove provides very good protection in all weather. A buffer of trees hides the devastation from older clearcutting when you are tucked into the head of the cove.

The old cannery (indicated on the chart) is long gone, but an old loading ramp, once used by logging concerns, lies along the eastern shore; an anchored log is off this ramp. The logs removed from the shore were loaded directly onto barges and locals claim no slash built up along the bottom of the cove. Although the bottom off the ramp is uneven, the head of the bay has a fairly large and flat anchoring area. The water is an almost olive drab color with reduced visibility.

The west shore has remained uncut and its evergreens, which touch the water at high tide, perfume the air, making this a lovely anchor site overall.

Anchor in about 8 fathoms over a mixed bottom with fair to good holding.

Dawsons Landing (Darby Channel)
10.5 mi E of Addenbroke Light
Float: 51°34.52'N, 127°35.52'W

Dawsons Landing (Dawsons Landing General Store), owned by Nola and Rob Bachen, is a popular year-round resort and supply center that caters to pleasure, sport fishing and commercial vessels. Facilities include diesel and gasoline, post office, WiFi, water, showers, laundry and a store that stocks everything from soup to liquor to outboard motor parts. Its inventory is the best north of Port Hardy and south of Bella Bella and Shearwater. Moorage can be obtained, with reservations recommended. There is a heli-pad for scheduled flights by Pacific Coastal Airlines. Dawsons monitors VHF Channel 06, or call 604-629-9897. Website: dawsonslanding.ca; email: dawsonslanding@gmail.com

Dawsons Landing

Bickle Passage Cove (Darby Channel)
0.6 mi E of Dawsons Landing
Entrance: 51°34.44'N, 127°34.54'W

Bickle Passage Cove offers protection from southerly weather. Although it is a little deep it makes a good short-term anchor site close to Dawsons Landing.

Draney Narrows (Draney Inlet)
5 mi SE of Dawsons Landing
Position (shoal rock): 51°28.41'N, 127°33.78'W

Draney Inlet, which penetrates the mainland coastal mountains for 14 miles, is seldom visited by cruising boats. The water in Draney Narrows is turbulent but not particularly dangerous for well-powered boats. At low current, or near slack water, the passage is quite easy. By approaching the narrows from the north during ebb flow, it is possible to stay out of the tidal stream and observe conditions before entering. The fairway carries 6 fathoms or more but pay attention to the turbulence over the small 2-fathom shoal. Remember that turbulence occurs some distance *down-current* from the rock. Due to the curves in the channel, it is not always easy to judge the conditions in the narrows from the west when the tide is flooding.

Fishhook Bay (Draney Inlet)
1.2 mi SE of Draney Narrows
Entrance 51°27.42, 127°32.46'W
Anchor: 51°27.70'N, 127°33.07'W

Fishhook Bay offers landlocked shelter at its far west end.

Anchor in 3 fathoms over a mixed bottom.

Allard Bay (Draney Inlet)
9 mi inside Draney Inlet
Entrance: 51°26.47'N, 127°19.14'W

Allard Bay, a narrow cut in the high peaks, offers good protection from westerly winds. Although it may offer protection from other winds we have no knowledge of what happens in southeast storms. It may get downslope winds from Allard Lake. There is a 6 fathom mud hole across the shallow bar.

Johnston Bay (Rivers Inlet)
4.5 mi. SE of Dawsons Landing
Entrance: 51°30.40'N, 127°31.98'W
Anchor: 51°29.56'N, 127°32.68'W

Johnston Bay offers excellent anchorage in most weather. Enter west of the reef in the middle of the

Side tie guest moorage at Dawsons Landing is immediately in front of the general store and guest cabins

Photo by Lorena Landon

Constant maintenance!

Heading north past False Egg Island

entrance, favoring the west shore as you approach the inner basin.

Anchor in 5 to 6 fathoms over a mud bottom with good holding.

Good Hope (Rivers Inlet)
2.7 mi E of Dawsons Landing
Position: 51°34.29'N, 127°31.02'W

Good Hope offers good protection from outflow winds in Rivers Inlet. Water is rather deep over a mud bottom.

Sandell Bay (Rivers Inlet)
5 mi N of Dawsons Landing
Entrance: 51°38.39'N, 127°32.46'W

Sandell Bay, exposed to southerly inflow winds, is a fair-weather anchorage only.

Kilbella Bay (Rivers Inlet)
12 mi NE of Dawsons Landing
Entrance: 51°41.62'N, 127°20.80'W

Kilbella Bay provides useful anchorage in settled weather; but during southeasterlies or conditions of outflow winds, avoid it. In the past, the bay had a log dump and booming facility on its east shore. Sport-

fishing is restricted in this area; be sure to consult the *Tidal Waters Sport Fishing Guide*. The Kilbella and Chuckwalla rivers flow into Kilbella Bay through a large U-shaped valley where grizzly bear can frequently be sighted feeding along shore.

Oweekeno (Wannock River)
14 mi NE of Dawsons Landing
Entrance: 51°41.05'N, 127°15.71'W

There are no facilities for pleasure craft at Oweekeno. This small First Nations village sits on the north bank of the Wannock River just inside the entrance to Owikeno Lake. For the latest information about facilities, check the website: http://www.ccrd-bc.ca or try the Band Administration office at 250.949.8625.

Hardy Inlet (Rivers Inlet)
8.5 mi NE of Dawsons Landing
Entrance: 51°41.39'N, 127°27.50'W

The area from Hardy Inlet north is grizzly bear country and, in the fall, you can generally find them scavenging for shellfish along the mud flats or fattening themselves on salmon along the streams. There are no useful anchorages in Hardy Inlet.

Moses Inlet (Rivers Inlet)
N of Hardy Inlet
Entrance: 51°41.57'N, 127°26.95'W

Moses Inlet—a steep-sided fiord with high bluffs along its shores—cuts deep into the coast range and is too deep for convenient pleasure-craft anchorage.

Milbanke Sound
Seaforth Channel
Mouat Cove
Chatfield I.
Johnson Channel
Dean Channel
Rattenbury Pt.
Jenny Inlet
Dutton I.
Rait Narrows
Lockhart Bay
Lagoon Cove
Bart Bay
St. John Harbour
The Nook
Gale Passage
Kynumpt Hbr
Cavin Cove
Gosse Bay
Cathedral Point Cove
Bardswell Group
Raymond Passage
BELLA BELLA
McLoughlin Bay
SHEARWATER
Kakushdish Harbour
Hampden Bay
King Island
Port John
Farewell Pt.
Thompson Bay
Hochstader Cove
Denny I.
Evans Inlet
Kwatna Inlet
Campbell I.
Sugar Lake
Stryker I. Nook
Joassa Channel
Lama Passage
Canal Bight
Long Point Cove
Lagoon Bay
Burke Channel
McMullin Group
Tribal Group
Wide Awake Cove
Bob Bay
Ada Cove
Nancy Cove
COBVILLE LAGOON M.P.
Admiral Group
Jane Cove
Fisher Channel
Restoration Bay
Dodwell North & South Coves
52°N
Hunter Channel
Baas Peur Passage
Kisameet Bay
Haakswold Point
Goose I.
Hunter Island
McNaughton Gp.
De Cosmos Lagoon
Windsor Cove
N
Cultus Sound
Spitfire Lagoon
Spitfire Channel
Ripbud Bay
Kildidt Inlet
Kiltik Cove
Fougner Bay
Goose I. Anchorage
Kayak Cove
Bremner Bay
Domestic Tranquility
Harlequin Basin
Duck Island
Brydon Channel
Crab Cove
Rock Inlet
Namu Harbour
50'
Gosling Island
Huricane Anch.
Spider Anch.
Sea Otter Inlet
Warrior Cove
0 2 4 6 8 10
NAUTICAL MILES
Queens Sound
Nalau Passage
3
Koeye River
Lewall Inlet
Stirling I.
Namu Inlet
Fitz Hugh Sound
Kwakume Inlet
Turnbull Inlet
Hakai Passage
Kwakume Pt.
Elizabeth's Lagoon
Adams Harbour
Goldstream Hbr.
Illahie Inlet
The Rapids
Joe's Bay
Waterfall Inlet
Crooked Passage
Hecate I.
Green I. Anch.
Remotesville Cove
Oyster Bay
West Beach
Kwakshua Channel
Patrol Passage
Addenbroke I.
Fish Egg Inlet
Fishtrap Bay
Pruth Bay
Fifer Bay
Convoy Passage
Gildersleeve Bay
Manarapy Inlee
Dawsons Landing
Calvert Island
Philip Inlet
Darby Channel
Walbran I.
Taylor Bay
Addenbroke Pt.
Safety Cove
Fanny Bay
Fougan Bay
Cypher Bay
Ripon I.
Penrose I.
Kwakwack Cove
Rivers Inlet
Schooner Retreat
Fury Cove
Duncanby Lodge
Cape Calvert
Open Bight
Grief Bay
W. Home Bay
Home Bay
Goose Bay
Pears Rocks

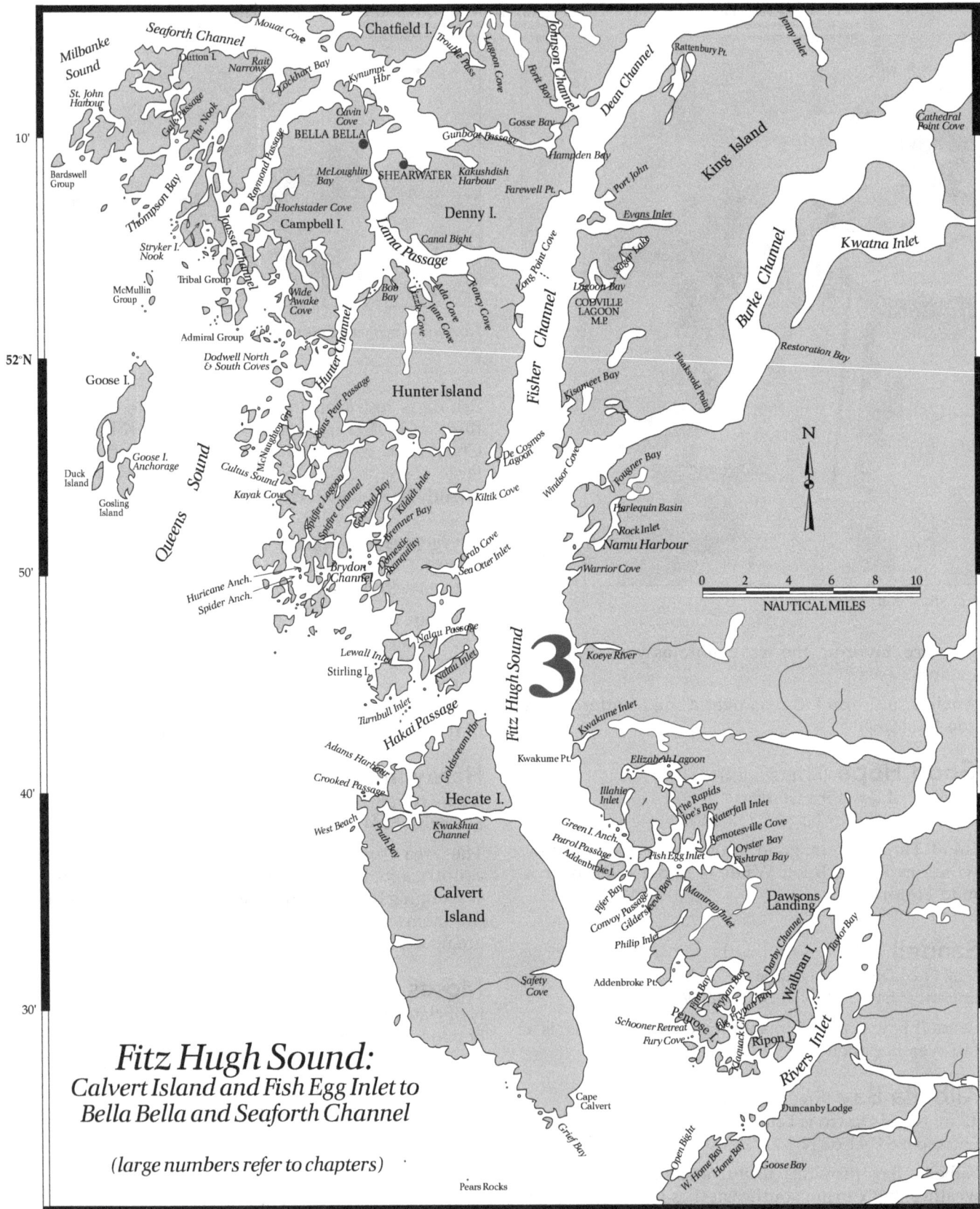

Fitz Hugh Sound:
Calvert Island and Fish Egg Inlet to
Bella Bella and Seaforth Channel

(large numbers refer to chapters)

3

Fitz Hugh Sound: Calvert Island and Fish Egg Inlet to Bella Bella and Seaforth Channel

Fitz Hugh Sound, on the east side of Calvert Island, marks the continuation of the Inland Passage smooth-water route. A number of good anchorages along Fitz Hugh Sound and Fitz Hugh Channel allow you to cruise at a leisurely pace after you cross Queen Charlotte Sound. For years Safety Cove, on the east side of Calvert Island, was the most popular anchorage. However, favorable anchor sites are located in Fury Cove, Green Island Anchorage at the entrance to Fish Egg Inlet, or Goldstream Harbour at the north end of Calvert Island—all quieter and more scenic than Safety Cove. Farther north, Codville Lagoon Marine Provincial Park, in Fisher Channel, is a favorite site.

Fitz Hugh Sound, Lama Passage, and Seaforth Channel have ferry, cruising ship and commercial traffic at all hours of the day and night, so you need to be alert at all times.

Fitz Hugh Sound
(Calvert Island)
Extends N of Cape Calvert to Burke Channel
Entrance (S): 51°23.66'N, 127°51.5'W
Entrance (N): 51°55.33'N, 127°56.49'W

The westerly swells quickly die off as you proceed north of Cape Calvert in Fitz Hugh Sound. However, a nasty chop can be found southeast of Cape Calvert on westerly or southwest winds when large ebb currents flow out of Rivers Inlet. Tidal streams in Fitz Hugh Sound and the channels north and east flow south at up to 2 knots. North/south winds enhance or retard this current, and during times of heavy runoff, the north-bound flood all but disappears. When the current and wind are in opposition, a nasty chop can develop and a quick duck into one of the nearby coves is highly recommended.

Cape Calvert Light (Clark Point)
1 mi NE of Cape Calvert
Clark Pt. lt.: 51°25.78'N, 127°53.21'W

Cape Calvert, at the southern end of steep, high Calvert Island, marks the beginning of Fitz Hugh Sound and the smooth-water route to Prince Rupert. There is a weather repeater atop Calvert Island. As you head north, Safety Cove offers the first shelter along Calvert Island, however, we prefer Penrose Island Marine Park (Chapter 2) or Pruth Bay (Chapter 4).

Grief Bay (Calvert Island)
1.1 mi SW of Clark Pt. lt.
Entrance: 51°24.93'N, 127°54.42'W
Anchor: 51°25.30'N, 127°54.71'W

Grief Bay, at the southern tip of Calvert Island, offers an interesting temporary anchorage in the lee of Sor-

Grief Bay, Calvert Island

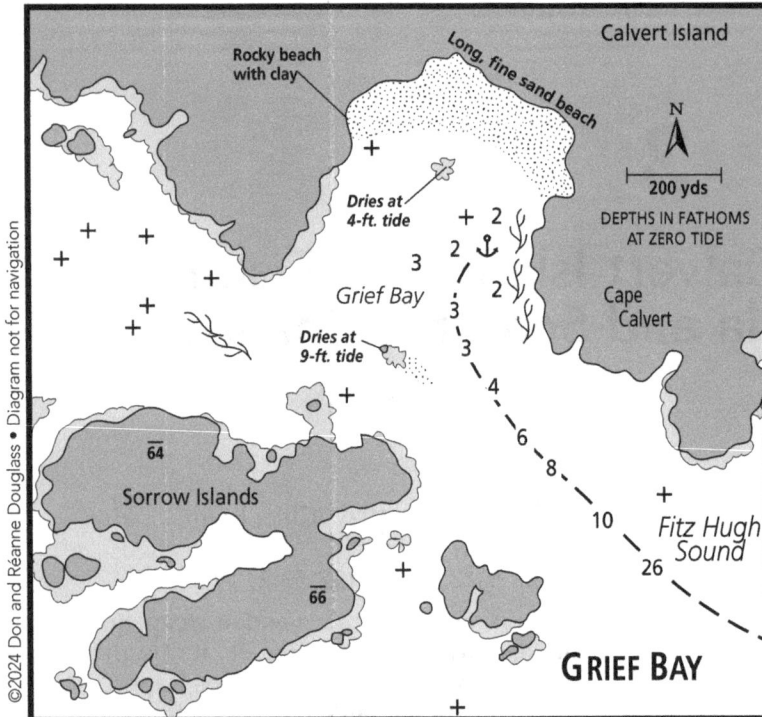

Rocky beach with clay

Long, fine sand beach

Calvert Island

Dries at 4-ft. tide

N

200 yds

DEPTHS IN FATHOMS AT ZERO TIDE

Grief Bay

Cape Calvert

Dries at 9-ft. tide

64

Sorrow Islands

66

Fitz Hugh Sound

GRIEF BAY

©2024 Don and Réanne Douglass • Diagram not for navigation

Canoe Cove (Calvert Island)

2.2 mi N of Clark Pt. lt.
Entrance: 51°28.01'N, 127°52.59'W

Canoe Cove is just that—a good place to haul out a canoe or a kayak, but too small for cruising boats, other than as a lunch stop.

Safety Cove (Calvert Island)

6 mi N of Clark Pt. lt.
Entrance: 51°31.75'N, 127°54.56'W
Anchor: 51°31.71'N, 127°55.87'W

Although Safety Cove is easy to enter and provides good protection in most weather, it isn't our favorite anchorage. It is too deep for convenient anchorage and, because large vessels tend to choose this site, smaller boats are subjected to the noise of generators and the glare of deck lights. Add to this the fact that the cove is subject to swells from Queen Charlotte Sound and may be uncomfortable at night. We prefer to anchor in the smaller, more scenic coves on the east side of Fitz Hugh Sound, such as Penrose Island (Chapter 2), or in sites farther north, such as Pruth Bay (Chapter 4) and Goldstream Harbour.

Anchor in 10 fathoms at the steep-to head of the cove over mud with fair holding.

Addenbroke Point Cove

(Fitz Hugh Sound)
5.5 mi SE of Addenbroke Isl. light
Entrance: 51°31.60'N, 127°47.01'W
Anchor: 51°31.59'N, 127°46.70'W

Addenbroke Point Cove, our name for the small bowl-shaped basin 0.6 mile north of Addenbroke Point, offers good protection from up- and down-channel wind and chop. The bowl has no beach and is steep-to right up to the rocky shore where old-growth forest surrounds the cove. Entering the cove is easy but avoid the large bare rock and two additional small rocks awash on a 12 to 13-foot tide off the south entrance point.

Anchor in 2 fathoms over a hard mud bottom with fair-to-good holding.

Philip Inlet (Fitz Hugh Sound)

2.2 mi N of Addenbroke Pt.
Entrance: 51°33.28'N, 127°47.27'W
Anchor: 51°34.17'N, 127°45.32'W

Philip Inlet, 5 miles northeast of Safety Cove, is a narrow inlet cutting into the mainland coast that has

row Islands, but this is not a good place to be caught in a southeast storm, hence its name. Grief Bay can also offer protection from outflow winds although the surge of northeast seas can make things uncomfortable. While history suggests that the coast along the west shore of Calvert Island is foul and treacherous, we find Grief Bay a wonderful place to spend an afternoon. A large, sandy beach with a varied collection of driftwood, flotsam and jetsam surrounds the bay. Because of the large kelp beds between Sorrow Island and Calvert Island, westerly swells don't penetrate.

Anchor in 2 to 3 fathoms over a sand bottom with fair holding.

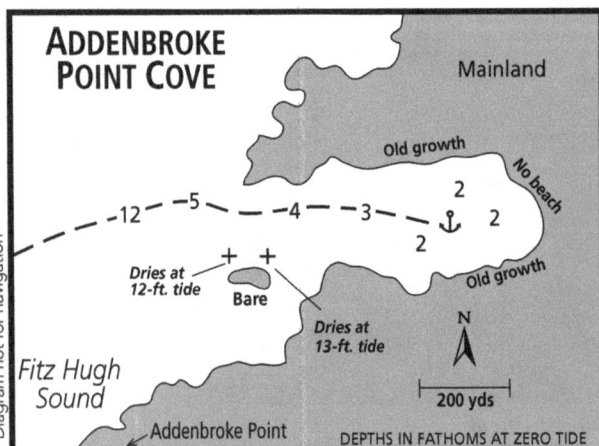

ADDENBROKE POINT COVE

Mainland

Old growth

No beach

Dries at 12-ft. tide

Bare

Dries at 13-ft. tide

Old growth

N

Fitz Hugh Sound

Addenbroke Point

200 yds

DEPTHS IN FATHOMS AT ZERO TIDE

©2024 Don and Réanne Douglass • Diagram not for navigation

an entrance largely hidden from Fitz Hugh Sound. Inside the inlet you have total protection from all weather, and it's calm and quiet even when chop outside is heavy. The shores of the entire inlet are lined with overhanging trees.

The entrance to Philip Inlet is straightforward, but the bottom is irregular as you approach the narrows. West of the narrows, favor the south shore to avoid a rock and a shoal that extends to mid-channel from the north shore. The narrow fairway north of the islet has a minimum depth of 3 fathoms. Or you can anchor anywhere in the inner basin or at the north end as indicated in the diagram.

Anchor in 3 to 6 fathoms over a mixed hard bottom; fair holding with a well-set anchor.

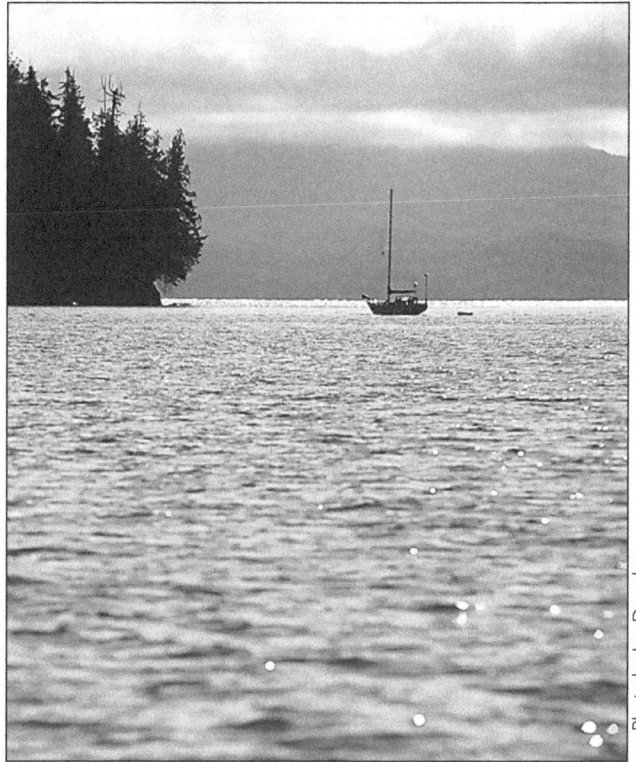

Photo by Ian Douglas

Entrance to Philip Inlet

Anchored in popular Safety Cove

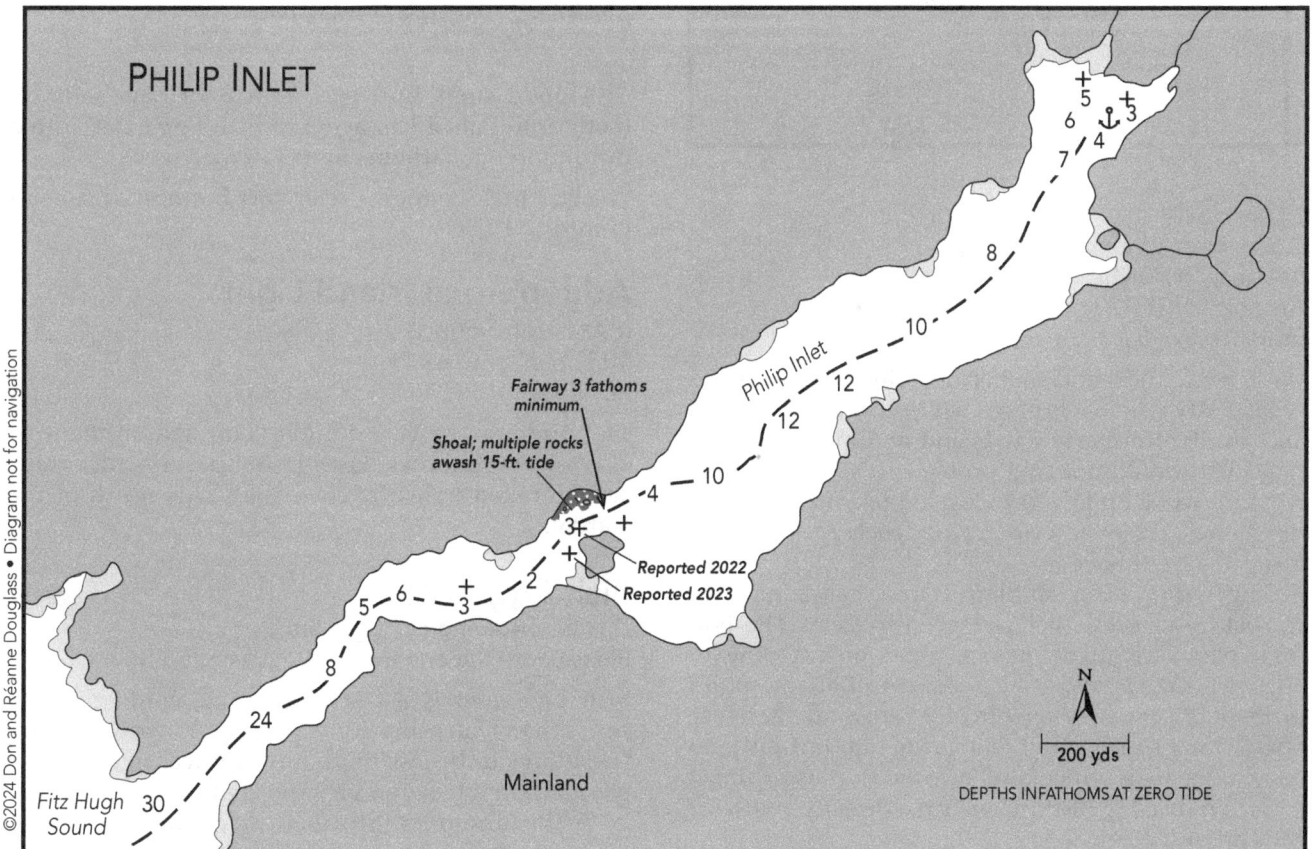

PHILIP INLET

Philip Inlet

Fairway 3 fathoms minimum

Shoal; multiple rocks awash 15-ft. tide

Reported 2022

Reported 2023

Mainland

Fitz Hugh Sound

N

200 yds

DEPTHS IN FATHOMS AT ZERO TIDE

©2024 Don and Réanne Douglass • Diagram not for navigation

FIFER BAY

No Trees Islet

Fitz Hugh Sound

12

20

8

+ + +
Danger:
Dries at
4-ft. tide

15

+

20

Dries at
7-ft. tide
150 ft. from
shore

10

+ 4

Islet with
6 trees

+

*Fifer
Bay*

Blair
Island

15

+ +

4

3

⚓

2 2

1

DEPTHS IN FATHOMS
AT ZERO TIDE

N

1/4 mile

©2024 Don and Réanne Douglass • Diagram not for navigation

Moored to a boomstick in Philip Inlet

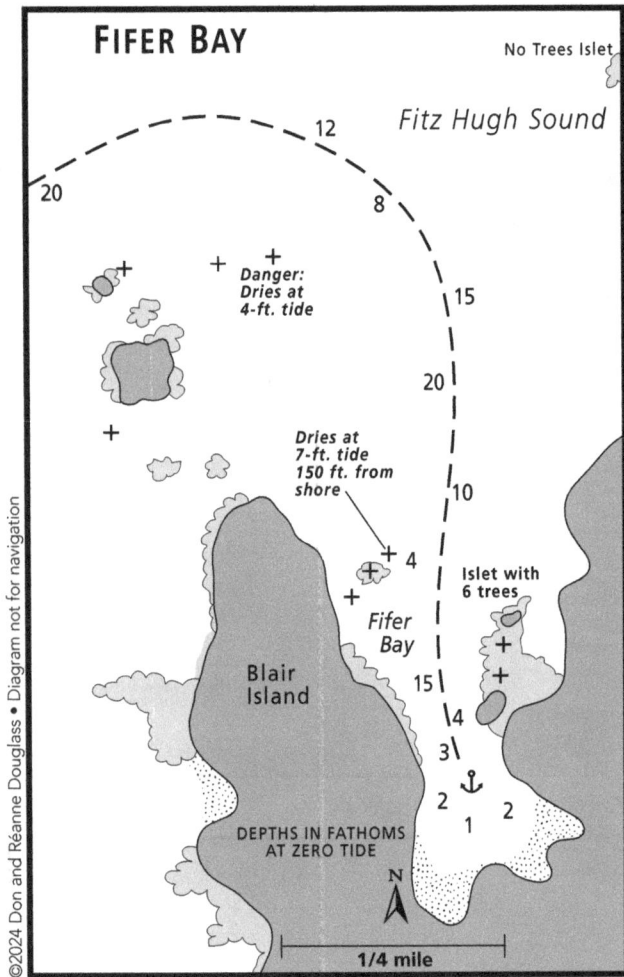

Fifer Bay (Fitz Hugh Sound)
1.6 mi E of Addenbroke Isl. light
Entrance: 51°35.82'N, 127°49.87'W
Anchor: 51°35.42'N, 127°49.50'W
Entrance (N): 51°36.30'N, 127°49.50'W

We have found good shelter deep in the south head of Fifer Bay where it is protected from all south winds and swells. Northerly winds and outflows from Fish Egg Inlet should not be a problem. It's so quiet here we once woke up to what sounded like machine-gun fire, only to discover it was a woodpecker hammering away at a tree above us.

The western tip of Blair Island has a number of rocks and islets that you need to clear. The bottom, which is quite uneven, gives no warning of approaching shoals. Set a course well off the point of Blair Island, steering directly for small "No Tree Islet." Turn south about 100 yards out, but only after you have identified and avoided the easternmost rock that dries at 4 feet. Then, turn directly south for the end of the bay.

A good small-boat exit from Fifer Bay leads directly into Patrol Passage and Fish Egg Inlet with a minimum of 6 fathoms in its fairway.

Anchor in 1½ fathoms over soft bottom with good holding.

Addenbroke Island Light
(Fitz Hugh Sound)
10.5 mi N of Clark Pt. lt.
Position: 51°36.21'N, 127°51.83'W

The Addenbroke Island Light is located on the west side of Addenbroke Island. Temporary anchorage can be taken in a tiny cove 300 yards north of the station.

Fish Egg Inlet
Due E of Addenbroke Light Sta.
Please note the entrance waypoints listed below.

Fish Egg Inlet is a fascinating and wild area that holds many surprises for exploring. We found many soundings to be less than those shown on charts, so use caution when you visit the area.

Within the inlet, Elizabeth Lagoon is a particu-

Addenbroke Island Light Station

larly interesting site to explore but it should not be entered without prior reconnoitering and with substantial preparation. It is easy to get caught in or above the rapids without the ability to return to your boat safely.

Convoy, Patrol, Fairmile, Souvenir, and Sweeper Island Passages
(Fish Egg Inlet)
Entrance (S): (Convoy Pass): 51°34.77'N, 127°48.87'W
Entrance (W): (Patrol Pass): 51°36.92'N, 127°51.19'W
Entrance (N): (Fairmile Pass): 51°37.95'N, 127°50.50'W
Entrance (W): (Souvenir Passage): 51°37.31'N, 127°48.73'W

Gildersleeve Bay, West Cove
(Fish Egg Inlet)
3.5 mi E of Addenbroke Isl. lt.
Entrance: 51°36.57'N, 127°46.20'W
Anchor (W): 51°36.06'N, 127°46.52'W

Gildersleeve Bay is the first bay inside Fish Egg Inlet on the south shore. It is too deep for convenient anchorage except in tiny "West Cove" where you can anchor in 2 fathoms when the cove isn't filled with log-booms, as it sometimes has been in the past.

The lagoon at the south end of Gildersleeve Bay, which we call "Every Nook and Cranny," has a very tight entrance suitable only for very small boats or dinghies at high water. Small boats with draft less than 4 feet can enter the lagoon at high water. On a 3-foot tide only a dinghy can make it through, and at zero tide just a kayak. One or two boats can find room to anchor inside the lagoon in 1 to 2 fathoms.

Anchor (West Cove) in 2 fathoms over sand with fair holding.

Mantrap Inlet (Fish Egg Inlet)
0.6 mi SE of Gildersleeve Bay
Entrance: 51°36.19'N, 127°45.16'W
Anchor (N): 51°35.82'N, 127°44.80'W
Anchor (S): 51°35.27'N, 127°45.42'W

Mantrap Inlet, located one mile southeast of Gildersleeve Bay, is an isolated and primitive inlet suitable only for small craft. Because of uncharted rocks in the narrows, you can, in fact, be trapped inside the inlet at low water. The fairway is less than 20 feet wide and should be reconnoitered first by dinghy to determine suitabil-

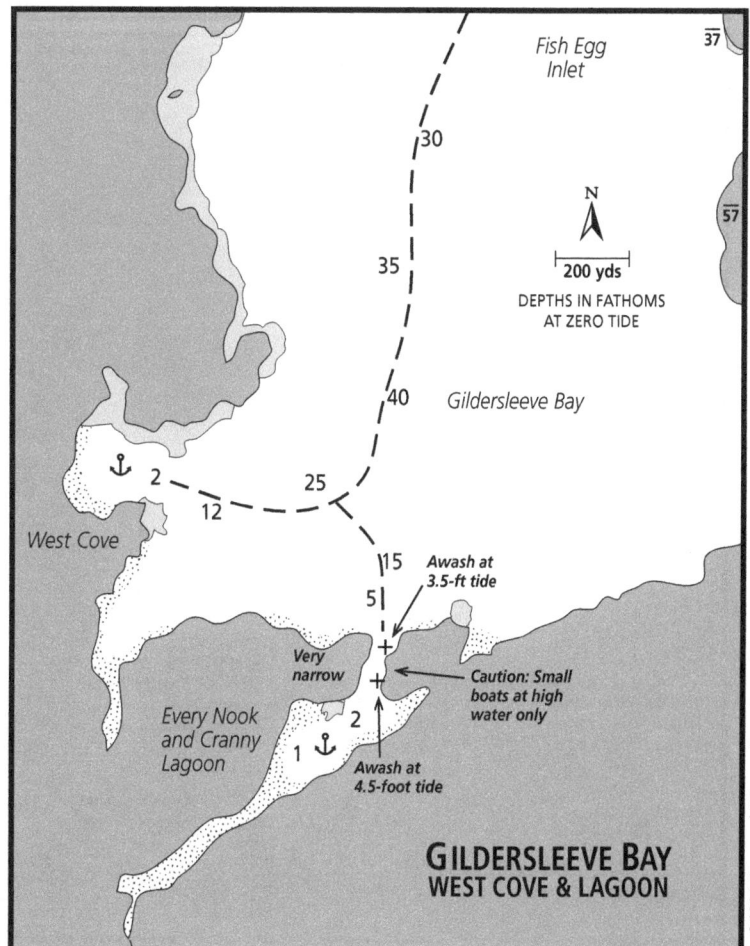

GILDERSLEEVE BAY
WEST COVE & LAGOON

©2024 Don and Réanne Douglass • Diagram not for navigation

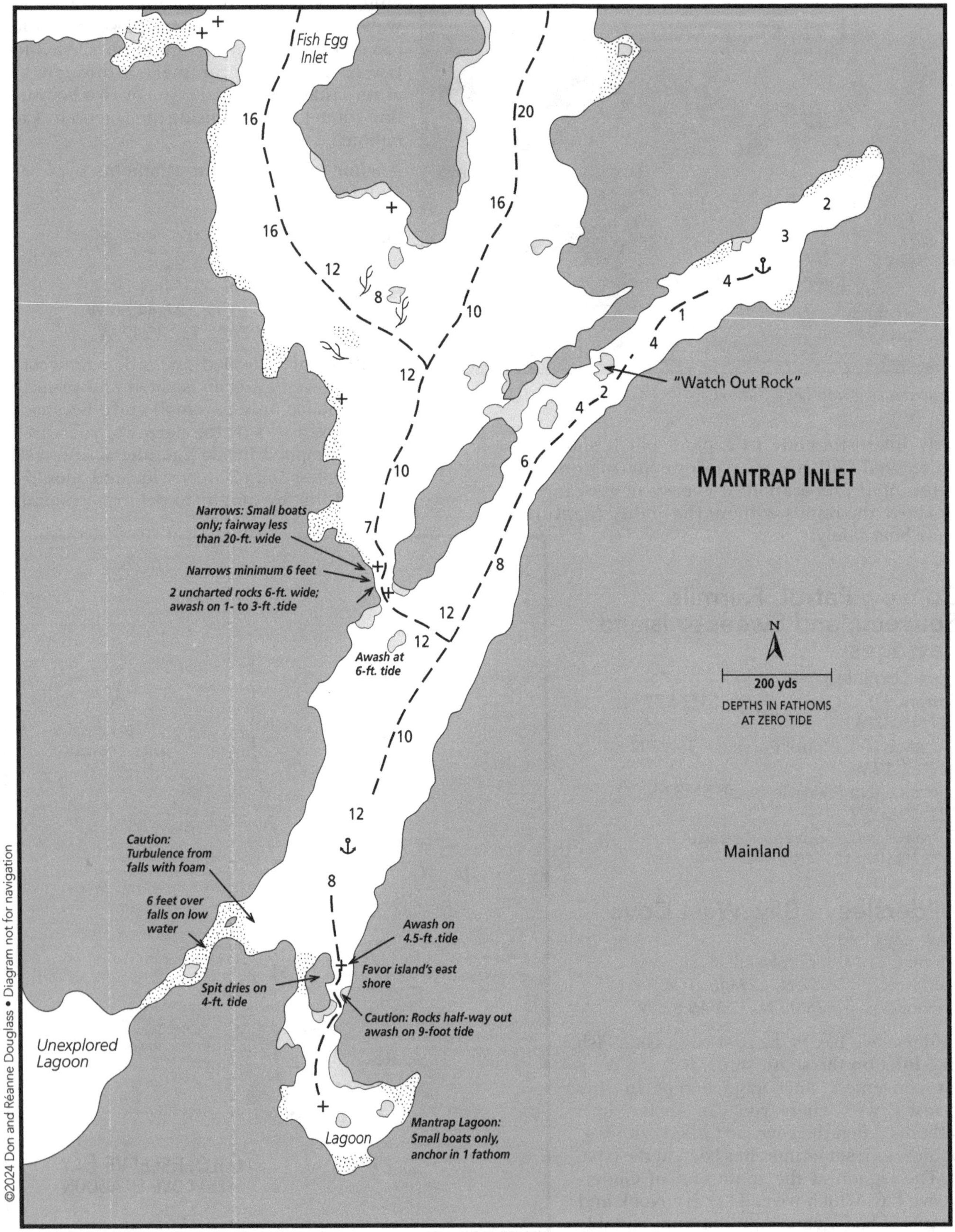

Fish Egg
Inlet

16

20

16

2

3

16

16

4

12

1

8

4

10

2   "Watch Out Rock"

12

4

MANTRAP INLET

2

6

10

8

Narrows: Small boats
only; fairway less
than 20-ft. wide

N

Narrows minimum 6 feet

8

7

200 yds

2 uncharted rocks 6-ft. wide;
awash on 1- to 3-ft .tide

12

DEPTHS IN FATHOMS
AT ZERO TIDE

Awash at
6-ft. tide

12

10

12

Caution:
Turbulence from
falls with foam

Mainland

6 feet over
falls on low
water

8

Awash on
4.5-ft .tide

Favor island's east
shore

Spit dries on
4-ft. tide

Caution: Rocks half-way out
awash on 9-foot tide

*Unexplored
Lagoon*

Mantrap Lagoon:
Small boats only,
anchor in 1 fathom

Lagoon

©2024 Don and Réanne Douglass • Diagram not for navigation

ity for entering. There is a 3-knot current on ebb tide.

Anchorage can be taken almost anywhere in the inlet, with the far north end the most secluded. You can carefully enter the lagoon at the south end of the inlet realizing that not all hazards are charted. We have not explored the large body of water to the southwest and were unable to determine whether it is a freshwater lake or a saltwater lagoon. We did, however, hike to the 6-foot overfalls to have a look; it appears to be a lagoon that can be entered at high water. Along the edge of the overfalls we saw a colorful display of small starfish—orange, blue, grey, red and purple—as well as sea anemones in all colors, green, white, beige, brown and orange. This inlet would be an excellent place for a boardwalk nature trail.

Anchor (north) in about 3 fathoms over soft mud; fair-to-good holding; a shore tie is helpful.
Anchor (south) in about 9 fathoms over soft mud; fair-to-good holding.

McClusky Bay (Fish Egg Inlet)
3.5 mi NE of Addenbroke Isl. lt.
Entrance: 51°37.59'N, 127°47.32'W
Anchor: 51°38.65'N, 127°47.40'W

McClusky Bay is exposed to the south and, except for temporary anchorage in the northeast corner, there is little protection available unless you anchor in the lagoon at the north end of the bay. This interesting double lagoon offers very good protection to small boats which can carefully enter its narrow, rock-strewn entrance.

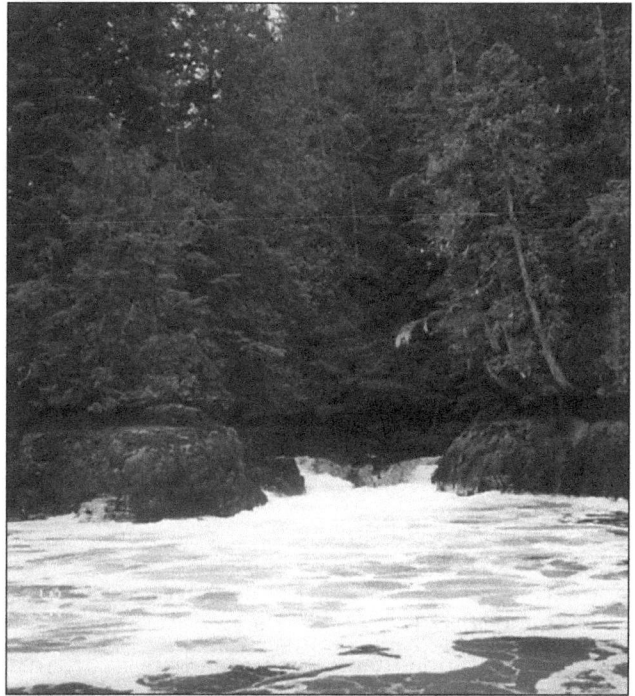
Mantrap Inlet, entrance to unexplored lagoon

The fairway to the lagoon, which is lined on both sides by reefs, has about 1 fathom at zero tide. The currents run at about 2 knots. The mid-channel rock at the north end of the entrance, awash on a 12-foot tide at Bella Bella, can be passed by favoring the west side of the channel, keeping the rock close to starboard. In the first lagoon, there is enough room for several boats in 1 to 3 fathoms. Some shallow-draft small boats could anchor in parts of the second lagoon since depths are greater than shown on charts.

If you enter the second lagoon, favor the west side of the fairway to avoid rocks on the north side. We recommend that you reconnoiter both lagoons by dinghy before entering to properly identify the fairway, its hazards, and the amount of current.

Anchor in 2 fathoms (inside the first lagoon) over sand and shell with good holding.

Middle Cove (Fish Egg Inlet)
1 mi NE of Gildersleeve Bay
Entrance: 51°37.31'N, 127°45.82'W
Anchor: 51°37.27'N, 127°45.70'W

Middle Cove is our name for the small cove located almost in the middle of Fish Egg Inlet. The cove, formed by three islands, although open to the northwest, offers good shelter for one boat in stable weather.

Anchor in 3 fathoms over soft brown mud with broken shells; fair-to-good holding.

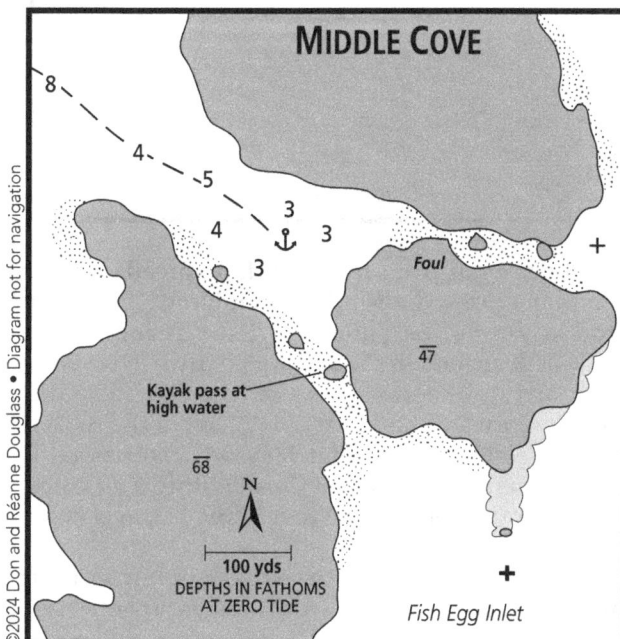

MIDDLE COVE

8
4
-5
3
3
4
⚓ 3
3
Foul
+
47
Kayak pass at high water
68
N
100 yds
DEPTHS IN FATHOMS
AT ZERO TIDE
Fish Egg Inlet

©2024 Don and Réanne Douglass • Diagram not for navigation

Joe's Bay, entrance to Elizabeth Lagoon

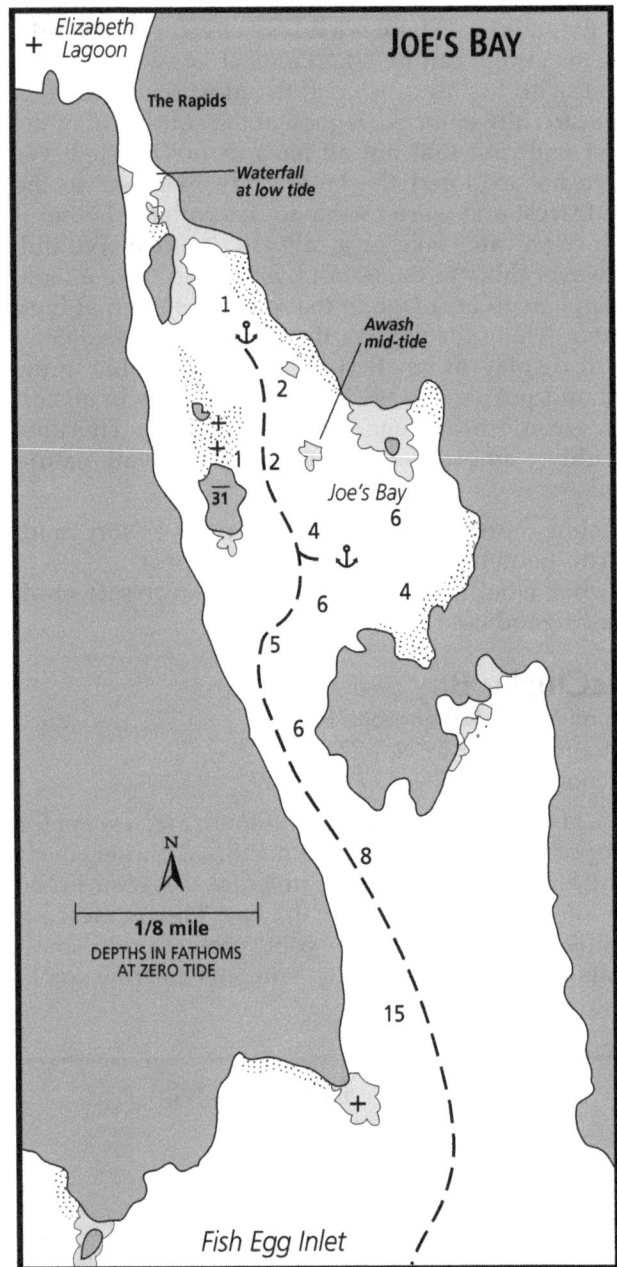

Joe's Bay (Fish Egg Inlet)
4.8 mi NE of Addenbroke Isl. light
Entrance (SW): 51°37.91'N, 127°46.06'W
Anchor: 51°38.97'N, 127°45.57'W

Joe's Bay is decidedly off the beaten path in an area of wild territory. You and your crew need to be alert at all times, because the hazards may not all be visible or even shown on the chart.

Entering Joe's Bay is straightforward. Small boats may find anchorage in shallow water between the islands and shoals, as shown on the diagram; this more northerly anchor site has several below-water rocks, so you should approach it slowly and carefully. During spring tides the waterfall at the entrance to Elizabeth Lagoon generates a tremendous amount of foam, creating current. At such times it's a good idea to anchor farther south, away from the narrows. Larger boats can anchor in deeper water, as noted on the diagram, where there is more swinging room.

Anchor (north end) in 2 to 3 fathoms over mud; fair-to-good holding.

Elizabeth Lagoon (Fish Egg Inlet)
Inside head of Joe's Bay
Entrance: 51°39.23'N, 127°45.85'W

Elizabeth Lagoon is a fascinating "lake", pristine and wild, but it should not be entered without prior reconnoitering and substantial preparation. It is easy to get caught in or above the rapids without the ability to return to your boat safely. Within the lagoon, there are at least 30 miles of shoreline. We found no cut logs, no shell middens, no clearings inside. It was a thrill to visit an area that appears to be untouched.

The challenge to entering Elizabeth Lagoon is negotiating the rapids, which look like a major waterfall most of the time except at high water slack. At low tide, foam from the waterfall spreads out over the water for a half-mile, resembling "bergy-bits" from a glacier. Be patient—it took us four tries to make it over the rapids, and we nearly destroyed our outboard in 2 feet of water on the "lip." The dark, discolored water makes trying to avoid the rocks all the more challenging. But once we had passed beyond the entrance bar and shoal, within a mile north the water deepened and we felt free to travel at high speed.

In the bay to the northeast of Sulphur Arm, the mud is so soft that boots are an absolute necessity for getting around. Water level in the lagoon appears to move up and down just a few inches with each tidal change.

Sulphur Arm (Elizabeth Lagoon)
1.5 mi NE of Elizabeth Rapids
Entrance: 51°40.68'N, 127°46.21'W

Sulphur Arm is pristine wilderness that appears to be frozen in time; however, it is an interesting study in biological diversity. Its entrance is narrow with about 4 to 12 feet in the fairway. The bottom along the shore is so soft it hardly supports a person's weight. Although it acts like quicksand, it is just *very* soft mud. You will find no evidence of human presence here; please help keep it that way.

Narrows Cove (Fish Egg Inlet)
1.4 mi E of Gildersleeve Bay
Entrance: 51°36.39'N, 127°44.17'W
Anchor: 51°36.24'N, 127°44.02'W

The Narrows is the route to the eastern part of Fish Egg Inlet and Oyster Bay. The island at the east side of The Narrows can be passed on either side, avoiding an uncharted rock off the southeast corner of the island, awash on a 6-foot tide. Good shelter from all weather can be found in the island complex directly south of The Narrows which we call "Narrows Cove." Choose the depth and proximity to shore you desire. The bottom is irregular with a number of rocks, so scout out your swinging room and make sure your anchor is well set.

Anchor in about 8 fathoms over a mixed bottom with fair-to-good holding.

Gee Whiz Nook (Narrows Cove)
0.2 mi S of The Narrows
Anchor: 51°36.38'N, 127°43.83'W

"Gee Whiz Nook" is our name for the eastern end of Narrows Cove. Small boats can find very good shelter here with limited swinging room. A shore tie will make your boat steady as a rock. Enter slowly with an alert lookout on the bow,

remembering that not all hazards are charted, and enjoy the pristine surroundings in this quiet, secure anchorage.

Anchor in about 2 fathoms over soft mud with good holding.

Waterfall Inlet (Fish Egg Inlet)
2 mi NE of Gildersleeve Bay
Entrance (S): 51°37.09'N, 127°43.57'W
Entrance (SW): 51°37.62'N, 127°43.77'W

Landlocked Waterfall Inlet, north of The Narrows, is a beautiful site surrounded by old-growth forest. The muskeg water has restricted turnover and is almost without a ripple. There is little evidence of wind or chop in the inlet so anchorage can be found at any appropriate depth.

Enter from the south in a fairway of about 1 fathom, favoring the west shore to avoid a mid-channel rock awash on a 9-foot tide. Or, enter from the southwest where the fairway carries a minimum of about

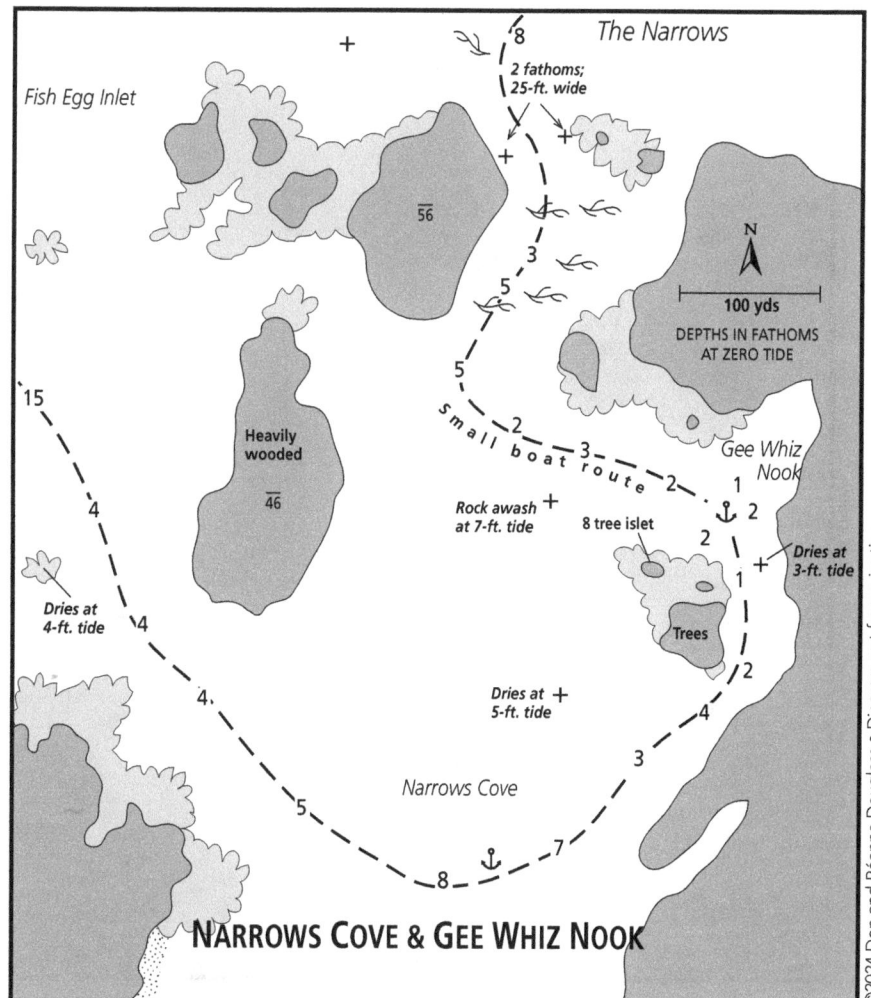

NARROWS COVE & GEE WHIZ NOOK

OYSTER BAY,
FISH TRAP BAY &
BITTER END COVE

Waterfall

Oyster
Bay

2

2   2

3   3

2   One fathom
     minimum   22
                   (Island 22)

2

3   3

4   +
         3   +
     35   ⚓
              4

4

7   6
6   Dries at
     6   12-ft. tide

Fish Trap   3   3
Bay   6
          8   7   7   "Stone
                             Face
          7   Point"
     10

14

     10

     10

     6

          12

          18

               18

                    8

                         10   High dark granite bluffs

Fish Egg
Inlet
                              12
← to entrance
                              7
30   25   3
          30
                              ⚓ 3
          30   25
                    10   8   5   7   Bitter End Cove
Old cedar cut to water +   +   5   6 5 4 3 ⚓ 3
                                                         2

N
↑

⊢—— 200 yds ——⊣

DEPTHS IN FATHOMS AT ZERO TIDE

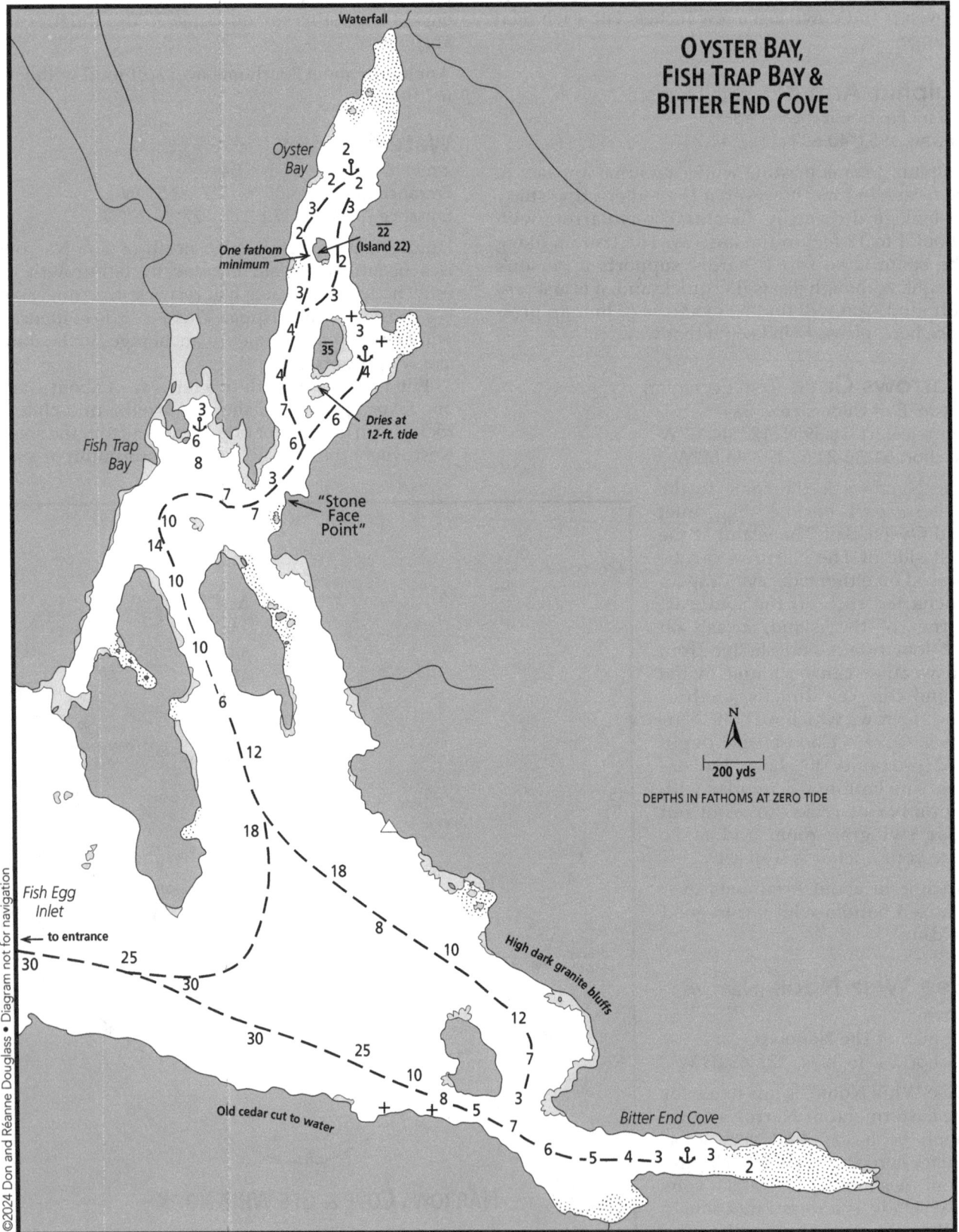

©2024 Don and Réanne Douglass • Diagram not for navigation

2 fathoms and about a 2-knot current. Although the inlet is fairly deep, a shore tie can be used almost anywhere. We prefer the northwest corner of the inlet or the small cove in the southeast corner that we call Remotesville Cove.

Remotesville Cove (Waterfall Inlet)
1.1 mi NE of The Narrows
Entrance: 51°37.73'N, 127°43.26'W

"Remotesville Cove" and Oyster Bay to the east are about as remote and intimate as you can find. The area, which is surrounded by the mainland coastal mountains, is filled with innumerable lakes and thick rain forests and dinghy exploring is at its best. It is quiet here to the extreme, and there is little water turnover.

We like to anchor in the east nook off the drying flat at the head of the creek; a shore tie is useful. Entry from either the north or south side of island (27) is possible; however, proceed slowly and maintain a sharp lookout. This entire area is inadequately charted.

Anchor in 3 fathoms over soft mud with broken shells; fair-to-good holding.

Oyster Bay (Fish Egg Inlet)
1.8 mi NE of The Narrows
Entrance: 51°37.28'N, 127°41.58'W
Anchor (N): 51°37.86'N, 127°41.34'W
Anchor (E): 51°37.55'N, 127°41.29'W

Oyster Bay is well-sheltered and shallow and you can anchor almost anywhere. We prefer the cove east of island (35) or north of island (22) at the head of the bay where there is a view of the waterfall that tumbles from the lake above. Note that island (22) has about a 1-fathom shoal on its west side; its east

Réanne finds another smooth-water route.

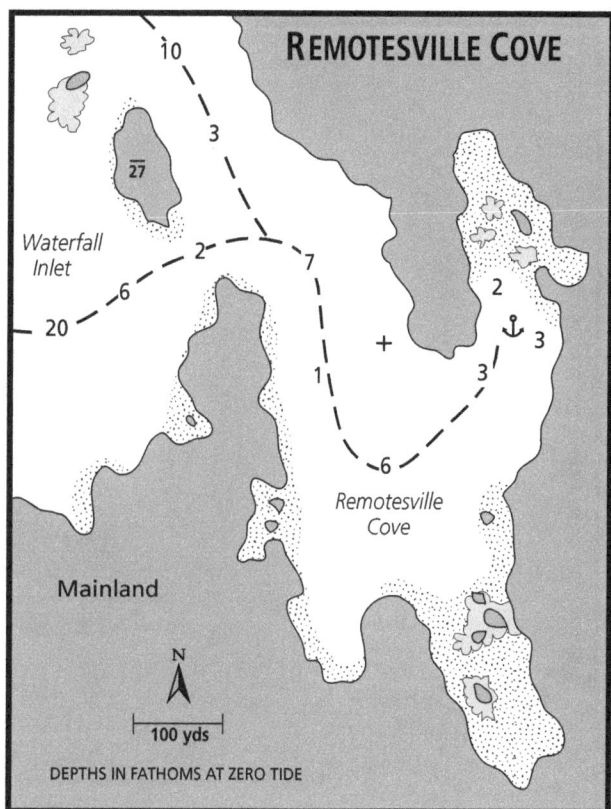

side is deeper.

The water in the bay is calm without signs that chop ever invades this quiet place. Note the lifelike "Face" reflection of the rock surface in still water at the entrance along the east shore.

Anchor (N) in 2 fathoms over a soft mud bottom with good holding.
Anchor (E) in 4 fathoms over a soft mud bottom with good holding.

Bitter End Cove (Fish Egg Inlet)
2.1 mi E of The Narrows
Entrance: 51°36.23'N, 127°40.84'W
Anchor: 51°36.18'N, 127°40.40'W

Bitter End Cove is our name for the eastern end of Fish Egg Inlet. This quiet, well-sheltered anchorage has granite bluffs to its north, a long drying flat to its east, and a large stream that tumbles down from Doris Lake to its south. It makes a good base camp from which to explore the surrounding nooks and crannies by dinghy. We wouldn't be surprised to find williwaws blowing off Doris Lake or the high ridges to the east and south when a low pressure system passes through the area.

Anchor off the flat in 3 fathoms over mud with shells; good holding.

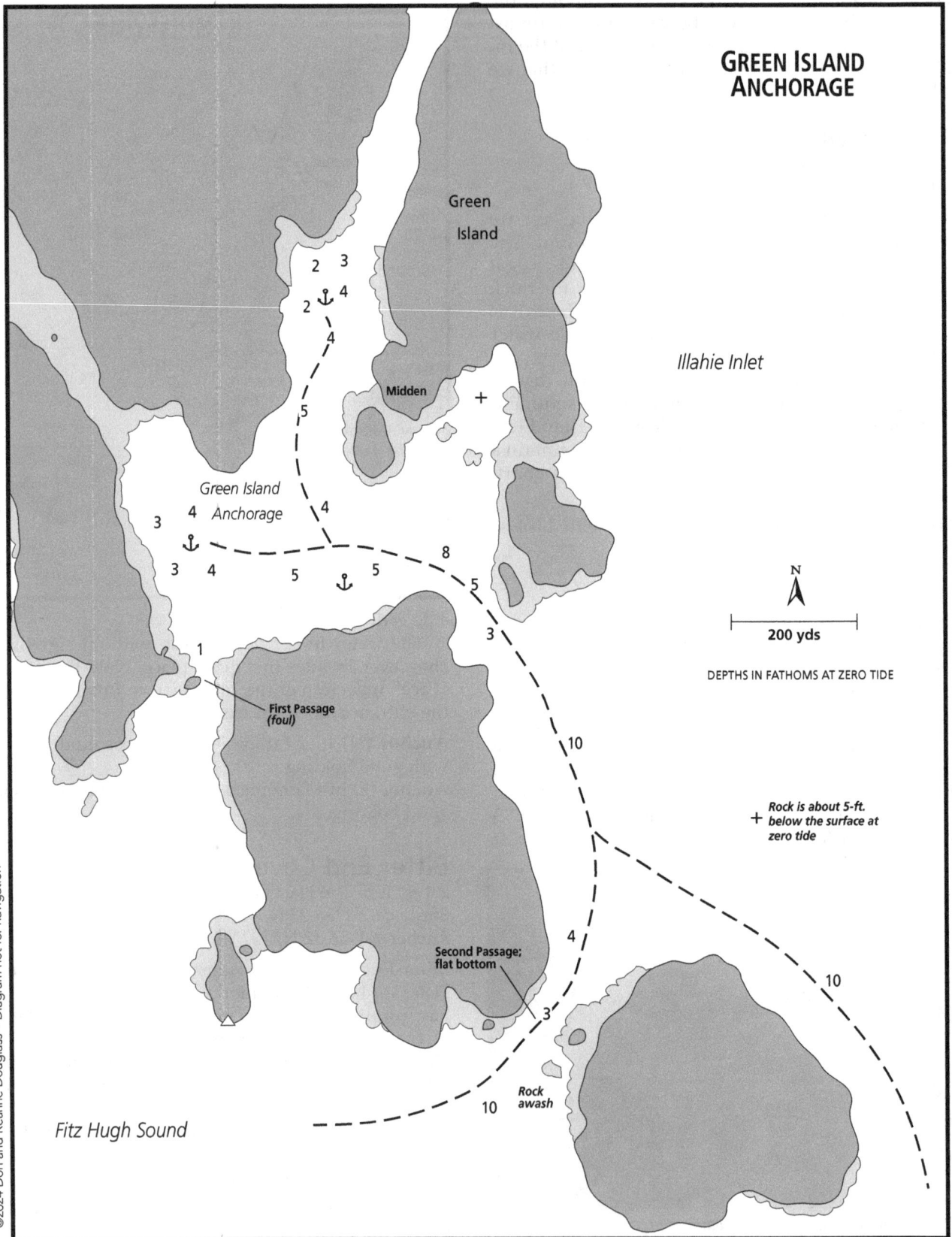

**GREEN ISLAND
ANCHORAGE**

Green
Island

Illahie Inlet

2 3
2 ⚓ 4
2
4

5

Midden

+

*Green Island
Anchorage*

3   4   4
⚓
3   4   5   ⚓   5   8

5

3

1

**First Passage
*(foul)***

N

200 yds

DEPTHS IN FATHOMS AT ZERO TIDE

10

+ *Rock is about 5-ft.
below the surface at
zero tide*

**Second Passage;
flat bottom**

4

3

10

*Rock
awash*

Fitz Hugh Sound

10

©2024 Don and Réanne Douglass • Diagram not for navigation

Illahie Inlet
(Fish Egg Inlet)
3 mi NE of Addenbroke Isl. lt.
Entrance (S): 51°37.80'N, 127°49.46'W

Good anchorage can be found in the landlocked basin at the head of Illahie Inlet. However, Green Island Anchorage is closer to Fitz Hugh Sound.

Green Island Anchorage
(Illahie Inlet)
2.5 mi NE of Addenbroke Isl. lt.
Entrance: 51°38.42'N, 127°50.00'W
Anchor (W): 51°38.54'N, 127°50.37'W
Anchor (N): 51°38.69'N, 127°50.21'W

Green Island Anchorage is quite well protected from weather and conveniently close to Fitz Hugh Sound. The first passage to the west is a canoe pass filled with foul rocks; the second passage has a flat bottom of about 3 fathoms (the chart says 3 meters); the south passage is clear and can be entered using radar. Avoid the rock with 5 feet over it at zero tide.

The south anchor site is roomier and deeper than the north site; however the north side is slightly more protected and shallower. The small island covered with brambles on the east side of the anchorage is a midden.

Anchor (west) in 4 fathoms over sand, mud, shells, and grass with good holding.
Anchor (north) in 2-4 fathoms over sand, mud, shells, and grass with good holding.

Goldstream Harbour
(Hecate Island)
12.3 mi N of Safety Cove
Entrance: 51°43.72'N, 127°59.73'W
Anchor: 51°43.57'N, 128°00.28'W

Well protected from all seas, Goldstream Harbour has rugged, beautiful surroundings. You can make this a good base-anchorage for exploring Queens Sound to the northwest or Koeye River to the east. At the very northeast end of Hecate Island there is a small convoluted island appropriately called Hat Island. Hat and Hecate islands create a cozy anchorage for small craft. Be careful upon entering. We have found the bottom to be irregular, indicating that it is poorly surveyed with uncharted rocks. Small boats can anchor farther north than

indicated in the diagram, giving wonderful views of a sunset. However, swinging room is limited; check for rocks. Pruth Bay has more swinging room and can handle more boats.

Anchor in 8 fathoms over sand and mud with some rocks; good holding.

Kwakume Point Cove
(Fitz Hugh Sound)
(E of Kwakume Pt.) 12.3 mi N of Safety Cove
Entrance: 51°41.52'N, 127°53.02'W
Anchor: 51°41.61'N, 127°52.93'W

Kwakume Point, 4.6 miles southeast of Goldstream Harbour, has a flashing light (3) on its western extremity. Behind the point to the east, is a cove we call Kwakume Point Cove that offers good temporary protection from downslope northerly winds, but drift logs on shore indicate there is no shelter from southerly winds. Kwakume Inlet, a mile north, offers better shelter.

In fair weather, the northeast corner, close to the drying lagoon, makes a good lunch stop in 7 fathoms. Two treed islets, 0.7 mile south of Kwakume Point, are connected to shore by a white sandy beach. This is also an excellent kayak haul-out point. The cove behind the islets is too shallow for anything but a small-boat lunch stop near high water.

Anchor in 1 to 4 fathoms, over a bottom of mud and clamshells.

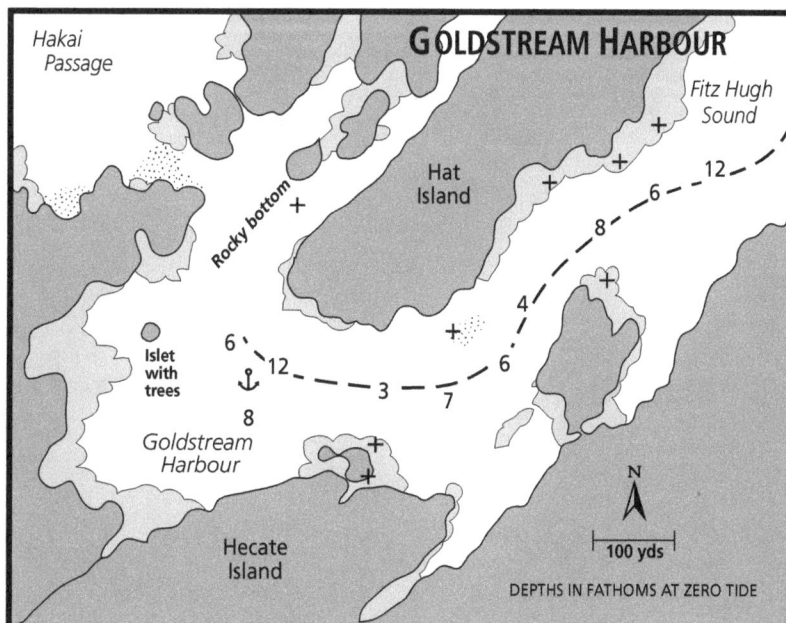

GOLDSTREAM HARBOUR

Hakai Passage — Fitz Hugh Sound — Hat Island — Rocky bottom — Islet with trees — Goldstream Harbour — Hecate Island — 100 yds — DEPTHS IN FATHOMS AT ZERO TIDE — ©2024 Don and Réanne Douglass • Diagram not for navigation

Kwakume Inlet

(Fitz Hugh Sound)
0.8 mi N of Kwakume Light
Entrance: 51°42.41'N, 127°53.33'W
Anchor (S): 51°42.21'N, 127°52.74'W
Anchor (inner cove): 51°42.76'N, 127°51.68'W

Kwakume Inlet is pretty and well protected. Entry requires avoiding a mid-channel, below-water rock that is difficult to locate since it can be seen only at low water. You can pass on either its north or south side. Favoring the north shore may be easier.

Once past the entrance rock, pass midway between the 4-treed islet and the larger island with many trees immediately north. The fairway has a minimum depth of about 3 fathoms; slightly favor the north side of mid-channel. (The anchor site on the north, just inside the entrance, is quite shallow, and while the view of the channel is good, at low water you may find your keel kissing the mud bottom.) Do not pass south of the islet with four trees—the passage is foul. What we show on the diagram as a dangerous rock awash on the north shore (on about a 7-foot tide), sits on a reef that extends southward about 300 feet from shore. Large boats will find good anchorage almost anywhere inside. Small boats wanting bombproof shelter may prefer the inner basin.

Longhouse in the bay at the mouth of the Koeye River

Photo by Lorena Landon

The inner basin has a narrow, shallow entrance that can be tricky. Avoid the mid-channel rock pile by favoring the north shore and proceed at dead-slow with an alert bow watch. Inside, it is well protected from all weather and it has ample swinging room for good scope. If a major storm were approaching, we wouldn't hesitate to anchor against the south shore as indicated on the diagram, or inside the inner cove.

Anchor (south) near shore in 2 to 3 fathoms over a mud bottom with good holding.

Anchor (inner cove) in 3 to 4 fathoms over a mud bottom with good holding.

©2024 Don and Réanne Douglass • Diagram not for navigation

KWAKUME INLET

Whidbey Point

Fitz Hugh Sound

N

1/4 mile

DEPTHS IN FATHOMS
AT ZERO TIDE

Note:
Very narrow
and shallow

See detail
below

Inner Cove

2   2
4
3
3

4 ft.
min.

10

Below
water

5

3

5

4 trees

Foul

3

1   1

3

Dangerous
rock awash

6

0

3

5

Awash at
5.5-ft. tide

5

6

3   3

1

Awash

Depths in feet

12'

6'

4'

6'

40-ft. wide —
favor north
side

12'

20'

Photo by Lorena Landon

Buildings on Koeye Point

Koeye River

(Fitz Hugh Sound)
4.9 mi N of Kwakume Point
Entrance: 51°46.48'N, 127°52.89'W

Koeye River (pronounced Kwy) is a wonderful place for viewing animal and bird life. However, it is a marginal anchorage. We've anchored here twice overnight, and each time spent a rolly, uncomfortable night. It's far better to use Koeye River as a temporary anchorage and take a kayak or inflatable upstream. It may be possible to take a small craft just beyond the old mill site at high water, but we don't recommend it.

There are several rocks awash off the shoal at the river's outlet. Consider tucking just inside the south point, dropping the hook for a while, and having a look around. (See Sidebar.) The old fishing lodge on Koeye Point burned down in 2011 but was rebuilt and opened in 2014. The new structure was designed and built by the Heiltsuk people, the timber harvested from their lands and milled with their own mill.

Anchor in 1 to 2 fathoms over a sand bottom with fair-to-good holding.

Celebration at the Koeye River

The Koeye River, a traditional home of the Heiltsuk and Owikeeno peoples, is a lovely, pristine place where grizzlies wander its moss-draped old-growth forest, sedge marsh, and tidal seashores. Five species of salmon that run the Koeye still feed both Natives and bears.

The Raincoast Conservation Society, together with Ecotrust Canada, and the Land Conservancy of B.C., purchased a 74-hectare parcel and lodge at the mouth of the Koeye which, in turn, were given to their original owner, the people of the Heiltsuk and Owikeeno First Nations. On Saturday, August 11, 2001, more than 300 people gathered at the Koeye to celebrate the transfer of ownership; they had traveled more than 30 miles by boat from the nearest settlements of Waglisla (Bella Bella) and Rivers Inlet—there is no ferry service to the Koeye.

The previous afternoon and evening saw the arrival of sailboats, aluminum ocean-going fishboats and little skiffs. Many Natives were already there since the Heiltsuk maintain a summer camp on the beach where they teach the children their traditions. Other native people had come to visit the camp too—a group of Ainu kids from the island of Hokkaido in Japan, and a group of Agua Caliente Native Americans from Palm Springs, California.

That night we travelers came ashore and were welcomed to the camp by the First Nations peoples who sang, told stories and danced. Saturday morning the celebration began with traditional cedar bark weavers giving lessons in their craft; there was drumming, singing and a traditional bear dance. After a picnic, the First Nations elders, Hereditary Chiefs, and Tribal Council members dressed in full regalia and separated into two groups. One group remained on shore. The second group boarded a pair of replica Native canoes that had been lashed together to form a catamaran. They paddled downstream then returned to shore where the others greeted them with more singing, drumming, and speeches.

The First Nations leaders then led a processional along the shore and up the hill to the Lodge. More speeches followed, and a braided cedar bark "ribbon" was cut, opening the lodge, and signaling the start of a feast. We ate, talked and enjoyed the views from the hillside lodge site. The next morning, we awoke early and motored back to Waglisla in the fog. It was wonderful to witness the Koeye land and lodge being returned to its traditional owners. The lodge will be used as a research center in the summer and a healing center in the winter. In addition the Koeye has also been protected from further logging.

I first paddled into the Koeye in the summer of 2000 on the second of three trips along the Inside Passage, during which I paddled from Bellingham, Washington to Hartley Bay, B.C.—about 100 nautical miles south of the Alaska Border. I have come to admire the First Nations people of Canada's West Coast for their art, their rich culture, and for their tenacious survival. These people are moving toward a renaissance culturally, artistically, politically and, in fact, numerically. I look forward to returning to the Koeye again, enjoying its rare, old-growth forest, and visiting with some of these resourceful Native peoples.

—John McCormack, kayak explorer

Sea Otter Inlet, South Arm

(Fitz Hugh Sound)
1.2 mi N of Hergest Pt.
Entrance: 51°50.10'N, 128°01.66'W
Anchor: 51°49.51'N, 128°01.66'W

Unfortunately sea otters are nowhere to be seen in Sea Otter Inlet, but the south arm offers very good protection from all weather. You can anchor north of the high-water canoe pass to Target Bay. The "window" to the east allows you to determine conditions in Fitz Hugh Sound. Swinging room is somewhat limited.

Anchor (South Arm) in 5 to 6 fathoms over mud with good holding.

Crab Cove (Sea Otter Inlet)

0.5 mi N of South Arm
Entrance: 51°50.45'N, 128°01.51'W
Anchor: 51°50.87'N, 128°01.37'W

Crab Cove, opposite Sea Otter South Arm, is partially exposed to south winds as driftwood at the head of the cove suggests. It is a good anchorage for small boats in prevailing northwest winds. Anchor mid-channel on the north side of the 2-fathom bar where it drops down to 3 to 4 fathoms.

Anchor in 3 to 4 fathoms over sand and mud with good holding.

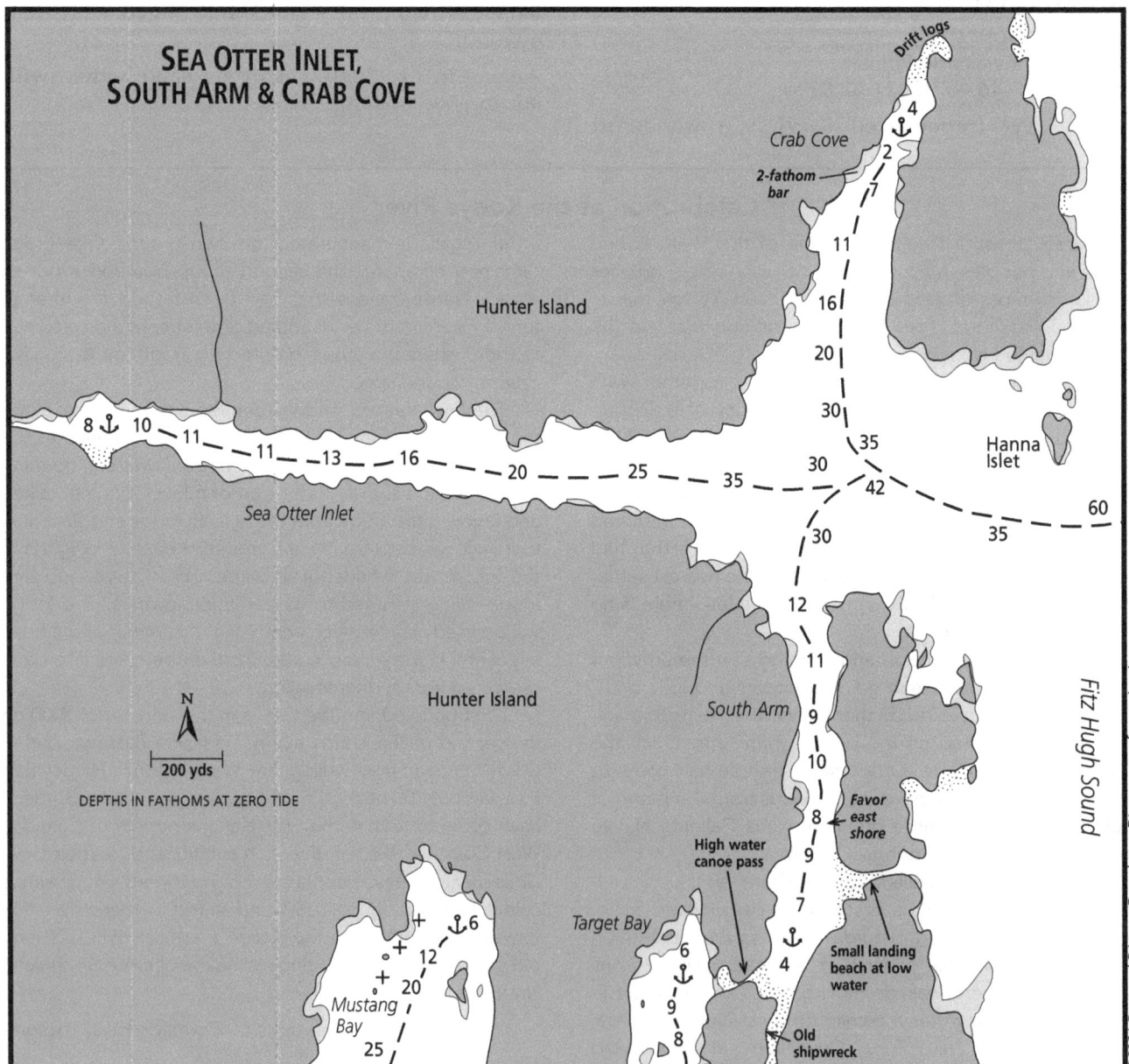

SEA OTTER INLET, SOUTH ARM & CRAB COVE

©2024 Don and Reanne Douglass • Diagram not for navigation

Warrior Cove (Fitz Hugh Sound)
1.5 mi S of Namu
Entrance: 51°49.90'N, 127°53.43'W
Anchor: 51°50.44'N, 127°52.59'W

Warrior Cove offers some surprisingly good protection from channel winds and seas in its inner basin. Entry is straightforward and can be made by radar if necessary. The fairway appears to have a flat bottom with no sign of rocks except at its outer entrance.

Chop from Fitz Hugh Sound completely dies off once you pass island (270). Under stable conditions, anchor mid-channel at the head of the bay where there are minimal drift logs on shore. Small boats can tuck into the little bight at the west wall and become almost landlocked.

Anchor, as indicated, in 2 to 3 fathoms over mud and sand with some kelp; good holding if you set your anchor well.

Kiwash Cove (Fitz Hugh Sound)
0.7 mi N of Warrior Cove
Entrance: 51°50.68'N, 127°53.24'W
Anchor (SE): 51°50.75'N, 127°52.25'W

Kiwash Cove makes a good lunch stop in fair weather between the islands that form the northwest corner of the cove. Unfortunately, this scenic spot has a gravel and kelp bottom with poor holding. You can find moderate protection from southeast winds in the southeastern end of the cove, off a steep-to, drying gravel flat at the outlet of a little creek; it's easy to detect the shallows by the light-colored water. This is not a good spot to anchor in westerlies.

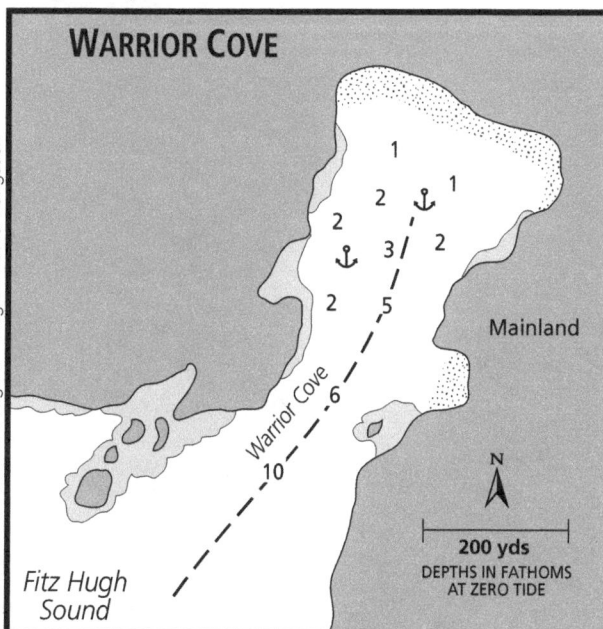

Namu Harbour and village building ruins
Photo by Leonard Landon

Anchor (southeast corner) in 4 fathoms over a mixed bottom with poor-to-fair holding.

Morehouse Passage (Fitz Hugh Sound)
0.8 mi W of Namu
Morehouse Pass (S entr): 51°51.30'N, 127°53.50'W

Morehouse Passage is the route to Namu that passes south of Kiwash Island. From outside Kiwash Cove, you can head directly toward the old Namu fuel dock by passing between Lapwing Island and the mainland, then passing north of Calm Island to avoid the charted shoal. Least depth in the fairway is 4 fathoms.

Namu Harbour (Fitz Hugh Sound)
9.4 mi NE of Goldstream Harbour
Entrance (SW): 51°51.34'N, 127°53.44'W
Entrance (NW): 51°52.20'N, 127°53.41'W

Namu Harbour, the site of an old, formerly successful cannery has had a "rocky" history in recent years. Two revitalization projects in the 1990s failed. The compound has deteriorated and is off-limits or closed due to hazards.

Namu was once a thriving community with attractive houses and gardens that have all fallen into ruin. Hopeful past attempts to revive Namu have been unsuccessful.

Whirlwind Bay (Namu Harbour)
In front of Namu
Entrance: 51°51.81'N, 127°52.10'W

Whirlwind Bay, aptly named for the waterspouts often seen here in southeast storms, is a poor place to anchor in such conditions. Rock Inlet to the northeast offers better shelter.

WARRIOR COVE

1
2 ⚓ 1
2 ⚓
3 / 2
2   5
2
Mainland

Warrior Cove
.6
10

N

200 yds
DEPTHS IN FATHOMS
AT ZERO TIDE

Fitz Hugh
Sound

©2024 Don and Réanne Douglass • Diagram not for navigation

Rock Inlet (Namu Harbour)
0.8 mi NE of Namu
Entrance: 51°51.92'N, 127°51.85'W
Anchor: 51°52.36'N, 127°51.27'W

Rock Inlet offers almost complete protection from weather and is close to good fishing grounds. Make a careful entry to identify and avoid the many islets and rocks. You can anchor almost anywhere in the inner basin, but we like the notch on the north shore as shown in the diagram. For larger boats, the south side has more swinging room in 4 to 7 fathoms.

Anchor in 2 fathoms over mud and gravel with fair-to-good holding.

Harlequin Basin (Namu Harbour)
1.5 mi N of Namu
Entrance: 51°52.60'N, 127° 52.30'W

Anchor: 51°53.23'N, 127°51.73'W

Harlequin Basin is protected from most weather, much of it is too deep for small-craft anchorage. In addition, old logs and branches that float around the basin collect at the north end present a nuisance for anchoring. The fairway in the entrance narrows has a least depth of 9 fathoms in its center. The bottom rises rapidly from 16 to 4 fathoms, and the small 4-fathom bench near shore has poor holding with a rock and gravel bottom.

Anchor in 4 to 16 fathoms over gravel and rock with poor holding.

Kiltik Cove (Hunter Island)
3.5 mi N of Sea Otter Inlet
Entrance: 51°53.82'N, 128°00.21'W
Anchor (S): 51°53.75'N, 128°00.70'W

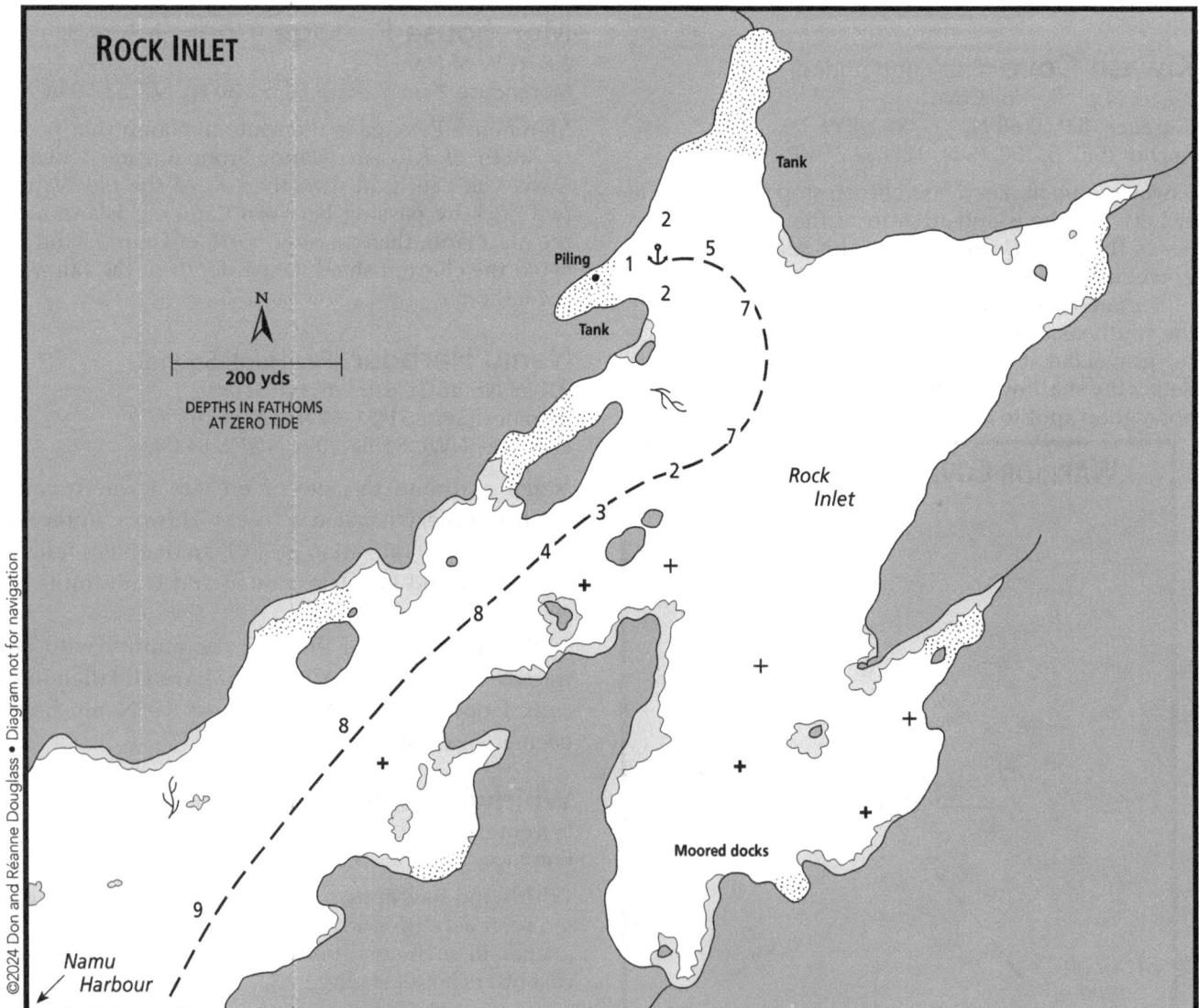

ROCK INLET

N

200 yds

DEPTHS IN FATHOMS
AT ZERO TIDE

Tank

Piling

Tank

Rock Inlet

Moored docks

Namu Harbour

©2024 Don and Réanne Douglass • Diagram not for navigation

The southern arm of Kiltik Cove is well protected from all weather. You can find good shelter in the south cove by anchoring west of the large rock that bares at high water; the cove dries just south of this rock. Kiltik is a snug anchorage when a south wind kicks up a chop on an ebb tide.

Anchor (south cove) in 5 fathoms over a soft bottom with fair-to-good holding; limited swinging room.

De Cosmos Lagoon (Fisher Channel)
2.8 mi N of Kiltik Cove
Entrance: 51°56.29'N, 127°57.91'W

Landlocked De Cosmos Lagoon, part of the Hakai Lúxvbálís Conservancy Area is a wildlife refuge where tree limbs nearly meet in the center of its narrows. The tiny entrance is choked with kelp and tidal currents are strong. In fair weather only, you can anchor outside the entrance to the lagoon in about 6 fathoms (no protection). Entry by pleasure craft is not advised.

Fisher Channel
Entrance (S): 51°52.87'N, 127°55.07'W
Entrance (N): 52°15.47'N, 127°45.45'W

The south end of Fisher Channel marks the entrance to Burke Channel and the route to Bella Coola. (See Chapter 5.) Fog Rocks, which lie almost mid-channel near the south end of Fisher Channel, can be passed on either side. Along the channel Kisameet Bay and Codville Lagoon Marine Park are favorite cruising anchor sites.

Kisameet Bay (Fisher Channel)
1.2 mi E of Fog Rocks
Entrance: 51°57.72'N, 127°53.51'W
Anchor: 51°58.13'N, 127°53.10'W

Kisameet Bay, which offers very good shelter on the northwest side of the easternmost Kisameet Island, is a lovely, quiet setting. The stream that enters the east side of the bay will lull you to sleep.

Enter southeast of Kipling Island or immediately south of the largest Kisameet Island. The bay is poorly charted, so use caution to avoid the rocks and kelp patches.

Anchor in 6 fathoms over mud with good holding.

Long Point Cove (Fisher Channel)
4.8 mi NW of Fog Rocks
Entrance: 52°03.21'N, 127°57.06'W
Anchor: 52°02.83'N, 127°57.13'W

Long Point Cove, on the northwest corner of Hunter Island, is an excellent anchorage for small craft that want to escape southerly chop coming up Fisher Channel. The cove, which is easy to miss, is located one mile south of the Pointer Island light where you turn west into Lama Passage.

Long Point Cove affords good protection from southerly storms or chop but, because the head of the cove has been used from time to time to store float houses or commercial operations, it's not the most scenic anchorage. It is, however, a good place to hide on a southbound passage if you're hit in the face coming out of Lama Passage into Fisher Channel.

Namu Slips Away

Eleven thousand years ago, maritime hunters launched their boats and fished for sockeye salmon in the waters along British Columbia's Central Coast. Archeologists who discovered microblades (small blades made of chipped stones like chert and quartz) and shell middens near the village of Namu, have theorized that a thriving population once existed there. In more modern times, Namu became a flourishing community when a cannery opened in 1893. BC Packers purchased the business in 1928 and built a salmon and herring processing plant, warehouses, bunkhouses for workers and their families, an icehouse, wharves, hydro power plant, and fuel stations. With declining salmon population, the cannery was closed in 1970 and citizens began to leave the area in search of other employment. Today, no one lives in Namu and the crumbling town has become an environmental concern. Many of the buildings contain asbestos insulation; rusting fuel tanks sit on a rotting wharf;

machinery and cannery supplies sit in decaying warehouse buildings. Nature is slowly taking Namu back.

Nearby communities are pleading for the current owner of the site and the Canadian government to clean up the mess. The present owner purchased the site in the early 2000s with the intention of restoring the historic buildings and boardwalk and turning the place into a resort, but his plans failed. The Heilsuk First Nations considered buying and reestablishing the village, but the clean-up alone was estimated at $400,000 to $600,000, Canadian. Along with the Heilsuk First Nations, Pacific Wild, Environmental Law Center, and the Hakai Institute lobbied for funds to save what's left of Namu.

In the meantime, what remains of the village is slipping away.

—KK

Entry to the cove is easy, but watch out for a small, mid-channel rock 300 yards north-northwest of Long Point that dries on a 3-foot tide. There is another rock near the head of the cove dries on a 2-foot tide. Walbran Rock, 0.6 mile northeast of Long Point and marked with a buoy, can be passed on either side.

Anchor in 6 to 8 fathoms, well into the cove; unrecorded bottom.

Codville Lagoon Marine Provincial Park (Lagoon Bay)
3.3 mi E of Lama Passage
Entrance: 52°03.28'N, 127°51.76'W
Anchor (E basin): 52°03.64'N, 127°50.30'W
Anchor (N basin): 52°04.41'N, 127°50.30'W

Codville Lagoon Marine Park is a natural harbor and a good place to head whenever a major blow develops while you're in Fisher Channel. If you're not paying attention to the chart, you could easily pass its entrance at Lagoon Bay without realizing that such a great anchorage lies nearby. Codville Lagoon is a large, saltwater "lake," surrounded entirely by old-growth cedar and lots of silver snags. Wildlife viewing, especially birding, is a pastime here at the lagoon. Watch out for bears.

A difficult trail with many tree roots leads from the lagoon to 3-mile long Sagar Lake. While you may have a rough time getting to the lake, it's beautiful and well worth the hike. Be sure to wear rubber boots. In warm weather a dip in the lake is pleasant.

Entry to Codville Lagoon lies through a narrow passage that has a minimum depth of about 5-fathoms. Avoid a rock underwater at zero tide on the north side of the narrows by favoring the south shore. From the south, Codville Hill is a leading landmark, noticeable as a series of lumpy, bald rock knobs. Most of the lagoon is too deep for convenient anchoring, but the east basin has a shoal where you can find good anchorage and almost complete shelter. The north basin also has favorable anchoring depths but is open to south winds. Deep in the east basin there is no driftwood or shoreline stress, indicating lack of heavy weather. It is peaceful, pristine and quiet; so quiet, in fact, that it's difficult to tell when southeast gales are blowing in Fisher Channel.

This is a heritage site for the Heiltsuk People. Do not disturb this site or remove any artifacts. Sleeping on board your boat is preferred rather than camping ashore.

Anchor (east basin) in 4 to 6 fathoms over a mud bottom with fair-to-good holding. Larger boats requiring more swinging room may want to anchor in depths of 8 to 10 fathoms.

Anchor (north basin) in 8 to 10 fathoms over a mud bottom with fair holding. Open to south winds with considerable fetch.

Evans Inlet (Fisher Channel)
3 mi N of Codville Lagoon
Entrance: 52°06.06'N, 127°52.80'W

Evans Inlet—rather a long way off Fisher Channel (4.5 miles)—is seldom used by cruising boats. Although its depths are too great for small boats, larger boats can find plenty of swinging room. Well-sheltered anchorage is reported behind Boot Island near the head of the bay on its south side in 15 to 20 fathoms. The bottom is rocky with fair holding.

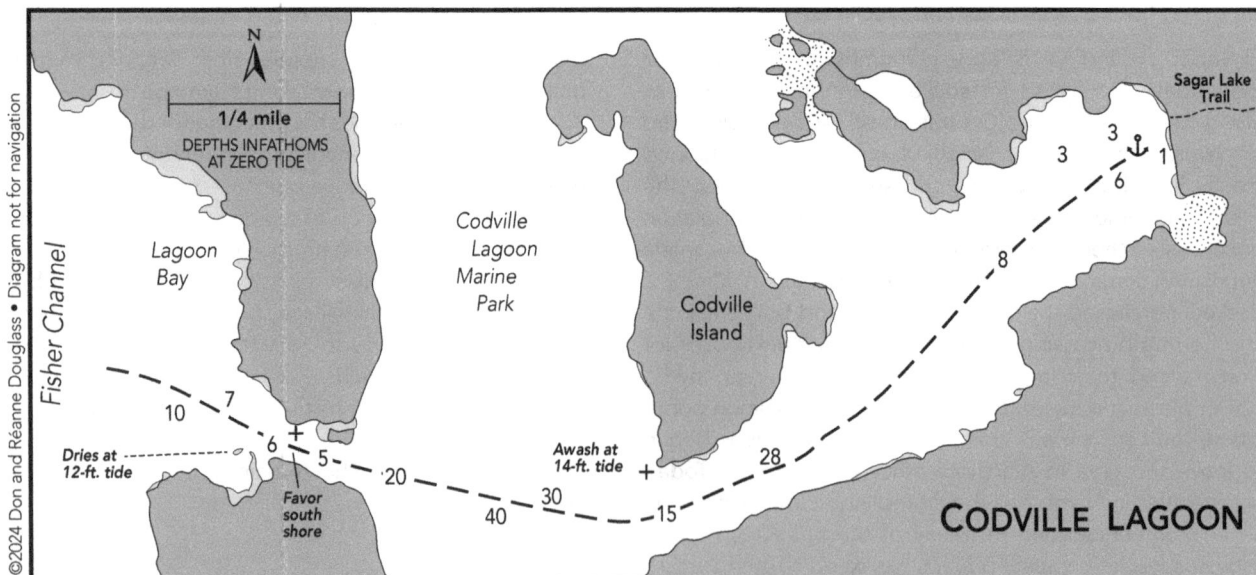

©2024 Don and Réanne Douglass • Diagram not for navigation

N

1/4 mile
DEPTHS IN FATHOMS
AT ZERO TIDE

Fisher Channel

Lagoon Bay

Codville Lagoon Marine Park

Codville Island

Sagar Lake Trail

Dries at 12-ft. tide

Favor south shore

Awash at 14-ft. tide

CODVILLE LAGOON

Port John (Fisher Channel)
5 mi NE of Lama Passage
Entrance: 52°07.15'N, 127°51.28'W
Anchor: 52°07.31'N, 127°50.50'W

Port John can offer shelter in fair weather tucked close to shore between Hook Nose Creek and the south shore, but it is exposed to southwest chop and you may find it rolly. This site does avoid the reef mentioned in *Sailing Directions;* however, the water is deep and the shore steep-to. Small boats can use the piling in the southeast corner for a stern tie (the pilings are in just a few feet of water at zero tide) and set a main hook to the west.

Anchor in 4 to 10 fathoms over sand and mud with fair-to-good holding.

Lama Passage (Hunter Island)
5.8 mi N of Fog Rocks
Entrance (E): 52°04.19'N, 127°56.76'W Entrance (N, Dryad Point): 52°11.00'N, 128°06.46'W

Lama Passage, largely free of chop, has several good anchorages along the north shore of Hunter Island. Since nearly all north- or southbound traffic uses this narrow passage, be on the lookout for vessels of all sizes, including cruise ships. Gunboat Passage, 8 miles north and far less travelled, is a scenic small-boat passage that comes out just east of Shearwater. (Gunboat Passage, see Chapter 5.) Cell service in the area is spotty with signal coming from Shearwater and Bella Bella.

Fancy Cove (Lama Passage)
2.5 W of Pointer Isl.
Entrance: 52°03.95'N, 128°01.27'W
Anchor: 52°03.65'N, 128°00.73'W

Fancy Cove is a fine, scenic cove where small craft can find good protection from southerly weather, and where most westerly chop passes by. The cove behind the islet offers solitude and a small landing beach.

Anchor in 2 fathoms over sand and shell with good holding.

Cooper Inlet (Lama Passage)
6.5 mi SE of Bella Bella
Entrance: 52°03.97'N, 128°04.54'W

Cooper Inlet has an irregular bottom and is poorly charted. The scale on current chart is still too small to provide for adequate navigation. The cove offers good shelter, but when you enter, approach slowly and use an alert bow watch.

Sagar Lake Trail

The 1.2 km trail to 3-mile-long Sagar Lake begins at the sign as shown in the Codville Lagoon diagram. The trail has sections of boardwalk, but much of the trail is wet and muddy, requiring boots. Elevation rise is plus or minus 300 vertical feet. At the lake, there's a wide, sandy beach about 200 yards long with a gently sloping sand bottom—a big treat and ideal for swimming. The beach can be infested with sand flies at certain times. Fishing did not appear promising off the beach, but a small inflatable kayak could access the upper lake, narrows, and second lake (really the same lake) which almost touches Evans Inlet to the north.

   You need an hour and a half for the full round trip with time for a dip at the lake. The sand on this superb beach looks like brown sugar and is rare in this part of the Northwest, where the trees usually meet the water.   —Rod Nash

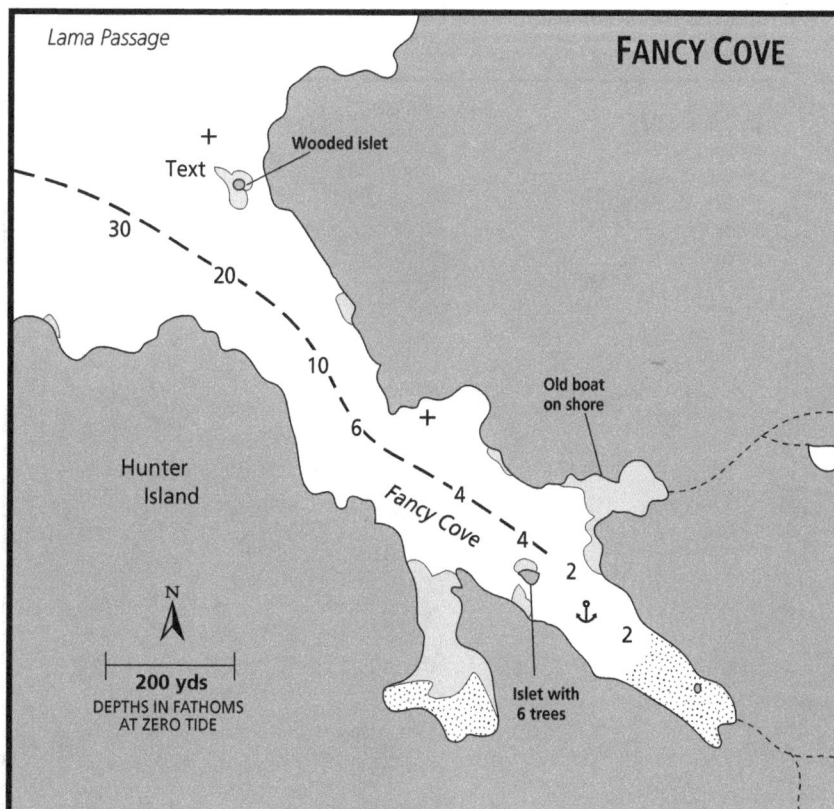

FANCY COVE

Lama Passage

Wooded islet

Text

30

20

10

6

Hunter Island

4

4

Fancy Cove

2

Old boat on shore

2

Islet with 6 trees

0

N

200 yds
DEPTHS IN FATHOMS AT ZERO TIDE

©2024 Don and Réanne Douglass • Diagram not for navigation

Ada Cove (Lama Passage)
0.3 mi S of Harbourmaster Light
Entrance: 52°03.74'N, 128°03.71'W
Anchor: 52°03.50'N, 128°03.19'W

Ada Cove is a good calm anchorage in southerly weather. Like Cooper Inlet, it is poorly charted so use caution. The small anchor-hole just inside the narrows is adequate for several boats. The head of the cove shoals rapidly and dries at about 10 feet.

Entry should be made as indicated on the diagram, avoiding the rock off Strom Point and the foul ground between the cove and Harbourmaster Point. Harbourmaster Point is marked with a white light.

Anchor in 4 to 5 fathoms over soft sand and shells with fair-to-good holding.

Jane Cove
(Cooper Inlet)
0.8 mi SW of Harbourmaster Light
Entrance: 52°03.60'N, 128°04.05'W

Jane Cove is the third of five coves located along the north side of Hunter Island. Like Ada and Fancy Coves, it too offers good shelter from southerly weather, but it is poorly charted. Entry requires avoiding several shoals and rocks. Favor the south shore and anchor near the head of the cove in about 8 fathoms over an unrecorded bottom.

Fannie Cove (Cooper Inlet)
1.1 mi SE of Harbourmaster Light
Entrance: 52°03.58'N, 128°04.72'W

Fannie Cove, although well sheltered in all weather, is poorly charted. While Fannie and Lizzie are recommended in some books for small craft, we *do not recommend* either one as a cruising anchorage, especially Lizzie Cove. Furthermore, the bottom in both Fannie Cove and Lizzie Cove is rocky and uneven. We were unable to get a satisfactory set on our anchor despite several determined tries.

Lizzie Cove (Cooper Inlet)
1.5 mi SE of Harbourmaster Light
Entrance: 52°03.78'N, 128°05.07'W

Lizzie Cove is well sheltered but poorly charted with an uneven, rocky bottom. While the cove looks good on paper, it is very difficult to determine the position of the dangerous entrance rocks in order to avoid them.

Canal Bight (Lama Passage)
2 mi NW of Harbourmaster Light
Entrance: 52°05.28'N, 128°05.19'W
Anchor: 52°05.46'N, 128°05.27'W

Canal Bight is exposed to south winds and has limited swinging room, but it's a delightful place to take a lunch stop in stable weather and explore the nearby lagoon-like mud flats. Avoid the large rock deep in the cove, as well as rocks on the south side. In fair weather you may find, as we have, that a 2-fathom spot on the northwest corner makes a nice rest stop.

Anchor in two to four fathoms over sand with fair holding.

McLoughlin Bay (Lama Passage)
1.4 mi S of Bella Bella
Entrance: 52°08.32'N, 128°08.38'W

McLoughlin Bay—the Bella Bella stop for the seasonal Discovery Coast and Inside Passage ferries—is growing busier. Although local fishermen have traditionally anchored north of the fish plant in 14 fathoms, the site is exposed to southeast winds and swells from channel traffic. Avoid the pipeline in the bay that extends underwater northeast from the shore.

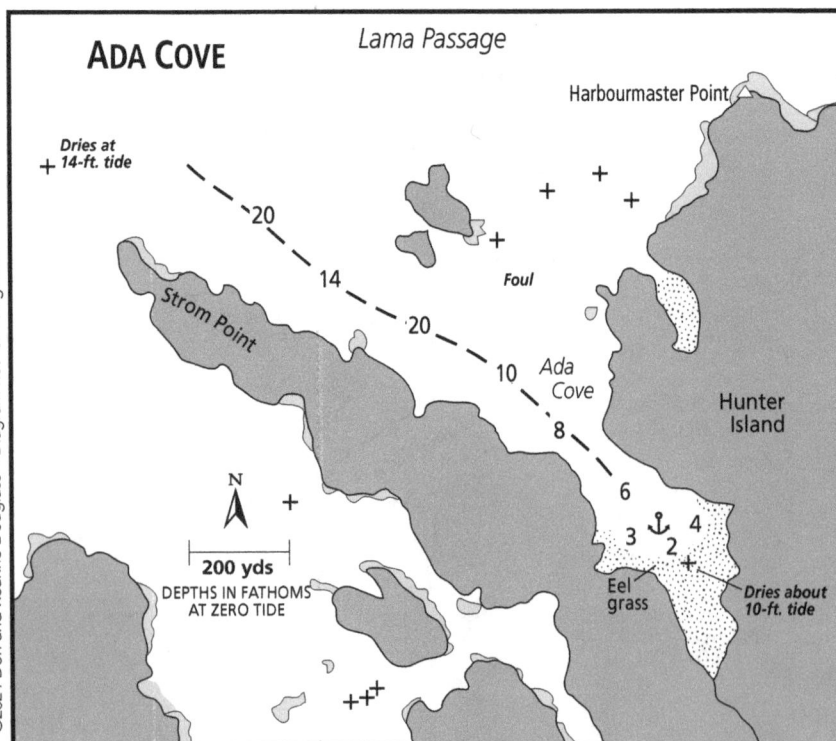

ADA COVE

Lama Passage

Harbourmaster Point

Dries at + 14-ft. tide

20

14

Foul

Strom Point

20

10 Ada Cove

8

Hunter Island

N

6

200 yds
DEPTHS IN FATHOMS AT ZERO TIDE

3 ⚓ 4
2

Eel grass

Dries about 10-ft. tide

©2024 Don and Réanne Douglass • Diagram not for navigation

Bella Bella (Waglisla) (Lama Passage)
Float: 52°09.77'N, 128°08.51'W

Bella Bella, known also by its native name Waglisla, has grown considerably. Now that the Discovery Coast Connector Ferry makes frequent stops at Bella Bella (McLoughlin Bay) and Shearwater, the town will continue to serve as the main supply and communication center for the north-central coast of British Columbia. A water treatment system provides good, filtered fresh water.

In season, the public docks are quite busy and tend to be crowded. The Band Store, liquor store, and post office all were destroyed by a fire in the summer of 2013, but the store has reopened across the street from the old location. It usually has a good selection of groceries, bakery bread, and general merchandise.

The community has a small hospital as well as a RCMP detachment and airport with convenient flight schedules in the summer. There is also a Canadian Coast Guard lifeboat station here. A shuttle taxi runs between town and the airport which is located about two miles away. There is excellent cell phone coverage. For a laundromat, serious marine repair work, good float space, and a less frantic pace, visit Shearwater, 2 miles to the southeast.

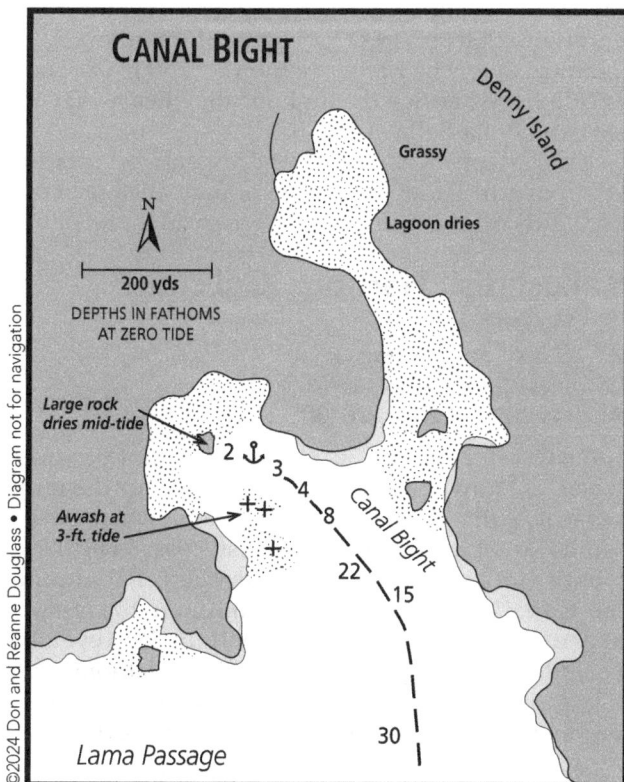

CANAL BIGHT

Denny Island

Grassy

Lagoon dries

N

200 yds
DEPTHS IN FATHOMS
AT ZERO TIDE

Large rock
dries mid-tide

Awash at
3-ft. tide

2 ⚓ 3 4 8

22

15

30

Canal Bight

Lama Passage

©2024 Don and Reanne Douglass • Diagram not for navigation

Rebuilding Bella Bella

The small Heiltsuk First Nation community of Bella Bella is in the heart of the Great Bear Rainforest on the east side of Campbell Island, BC. The Heiltsuk people are descendents of the nomadic tribes who once roamed the 6,000-square miles of British Columbia's Central Coast. In the 1800's, the Heilsuk began to settle, relying on fishing for their livelihood. Today, they claim 4,000 acres of Campbell Island's shoreline. Bella Bella is the only established town. In the 1970's, the village council sought government assistance to repair the old houses and build new ones and a cultural center. They also strove to revive and preserve their ancient culture by teaching their children the native language, dances, and customs. The elders even created the first Heilsuk dictionary.

When the government cut back funding, the Heilsuk decided to create their own non-profit entity to operate, and solicit ongoing support for youth and cultural programs. In 1999, Larry Jorgenson, the project founder, spearheaded its formation, named the Qqs Projects Society. Pronounced "kucks," the Heilsuk word means "eyes." The organization assumed responsibility for the two-year-old Koeye Camp, designed to teach young people about their culture and to understand and respect their environment. In 2001, the Koeye Lodge was added and five years later, the Koeye Bighouse. Soon the Qqs's office in Bella Bella near the government wharf became the focal point of the community. The Koeye Café opened inside the office and locals began to gather to discuss future programs. The Thistalalh Memorial Library was established here in 2007.

On July 12, 2013, disaster struck. A fire roared through the town, destroying the Qqs's office and café, Bella Bella's post office, the library, and the town's only grocery store. Donations poured in from surrounding communities to help Bella Bella rebuild. Bob Adams, a resident of Whistler, organized a book drive to help replace the 3,500 books that were destroyed. The residents of Kitimat donated one hundred and twenty-five boxes of books. The Government House, Rotary Club, and locals businesses donated a trailer that was outfitted with computers and shelving made from local Heilsuk cedar. The new library holds nearly 4,000 books.

Bella Bella is accessible only by air and water. Pacific Coastal Airlines offers daily flights from Vancouver to Bella Bella with a stop at Port Hardy. BC Ferries provides passenger and vehicle service from Prince Rupert and Port Hardy. Both companies serve Bella Bella year round.

—RHD

Martins Cove (Lama Passage)
0.6 mi N of Bella Bella
Entrance: 52°10.37'N, 128°08.46'W

Martins Cove, where the Bella Bella fishing fleet moors, has little room and does not hold much interest for private cruising boats.

Cavin Cove (Lama Passage)
0.8 mi N of Bella Bella
Entrance: 52°10.62'N, 128°08.19'W

Cavin Cove, a storage area for floats, boomsticks and other equipment, is sometimes used as an anchorage for small boats wishing to remain close to Bella Bella.

Shearwater Resort & Marina on Kliksoatli Harbour

Whisky Cove (Shearwater)
1.5 mi E of Bella Bella
Entrance: 52°09.48'N, 128°06.02'W

Whisky Cove has a number of private homes, floats and buoys. Boats may find anchorage in the middle of the cove taking care to avoid the private floats and buoys.

Kliktsoatli Harbour (Shearwater)
2.5 mi SE of Bella Bella
Entrance (NW): 52°09.17'N, 128°05.51'W
Anchor: 52°08.74'N, 128°04.66'W

Kliktsoatli Harbour provides good protection from southerly weather. Pleasure craft can anchor in the southeast corner, just inside the 10-fathom curve, avoiding private floats, and the ferry docking area. Additional small-boat protection from northerly winds can be found behind Klik Island in 5 fathoms at the east end of the harbour or in the lee of Shearwater Island.

Most boats go through Clayton Passage between Shearwater and Shearwater Island - Slow No Wake south of Shearwater Island. With the advent of ferry stops, there is now a range and a red buoy one mile east of Shearwater Island in Wheelock Pass.

Anchor in 6 to 8 fathoms, mud bottom, good holding.

Shearwater (Kliktsoatli Harbour)
2.2 mi SE of Bella Bella
Position: 52°08.82'N, 128°05.29'W

Shearwater, located on the west side of Kliktsoatli Harbour, is the only serious repair and haul-out operation between Campbell River and Prince Rupert. (Please note that haul-out capabilities for sailboats at Shearwater Marine may be limited by a vessel's depth or keel configuration.)

The resort has 1,700 feet of moorage on a concrete float with 15, 30 and 50-amp power. The fuel dock and the moorage docks have potable water. There are showers, laundry, ice, and propane on shore. There is a grocery store, liquor store, ATM, and recycling is available. The pub was recently expanded, and a gift shop opened next door to the marine supply store; the Post Office is located inside the store. A water taxi makes regular runs (10 minutes) between Shearwater and Bella Bella or you can use a dinghy in calm weather. The resort suggests that if you wish moorage during summer, you phone ahead for reservations 250-957-2666. Shearwater monitors VHF Channel 66A. The fuel dock monitors VHF 08. There is cellphone service throughout the Shearwater Resort and Bella Bella area.

The Discovery Coast Connector ferry docks just south of Atli Point. Two large orange anchor buoys, 150 yards off the terminal, are reserved for ferry use.

Kakushdish Harbour, Gullchuck
(Denny Island)
2.5 mi E of Shearwater
Entrance: 52°09.46'N, 128°02.75'W
Anchor: 52°09.02'N, 128°00.91'W

Kakushdish Harbour, located 3 miles east of Shearwater, is known locally as "Gullchuck" for the numbers of gulls that seek shelter here when strong winds are blowing on the west coast. The landlocked harbor offers good protection. Its entrance bar is shallow (about 7 feet minimum in the fairway at zero tide), with an irregular bottom. However, the basin has a nearly-flat bottom of 3 to 5 fathoms over a large area. There is plenty of swinging room for a number of boats. Avoid the mid-basin rock that dries on a 3-foot tide.

The cove in the entrance on the south shore largely dries. Powerlines from Ocean Falls, with 83 feet (25 meters) of overhead clearance, cross the harbor at its entrance bar. The *very soft* mud bottom has a consistency that resembles jello (the locals have a crude name for it!), so you may have difficulty setting anchor.

Anchor in about 3 fathoms over very soft mud with fair-to-good holding, only with a well-set anchor.

Seaforth Channel

(Milbanke Sound)
Turning point: 52°11.11'N, 128°06.2'W

Seaforth Channel is a busy area where almost all north- or southbound boats converge. There are several isolated rocks and reefs in the channel, some of which are marked. Alert navigation is required as you pass through this channel. The waters are generally smooth until your reach Milbanke Sound. Kynumpt Harbour (Strom Bay) is a popular anchor site in this area.

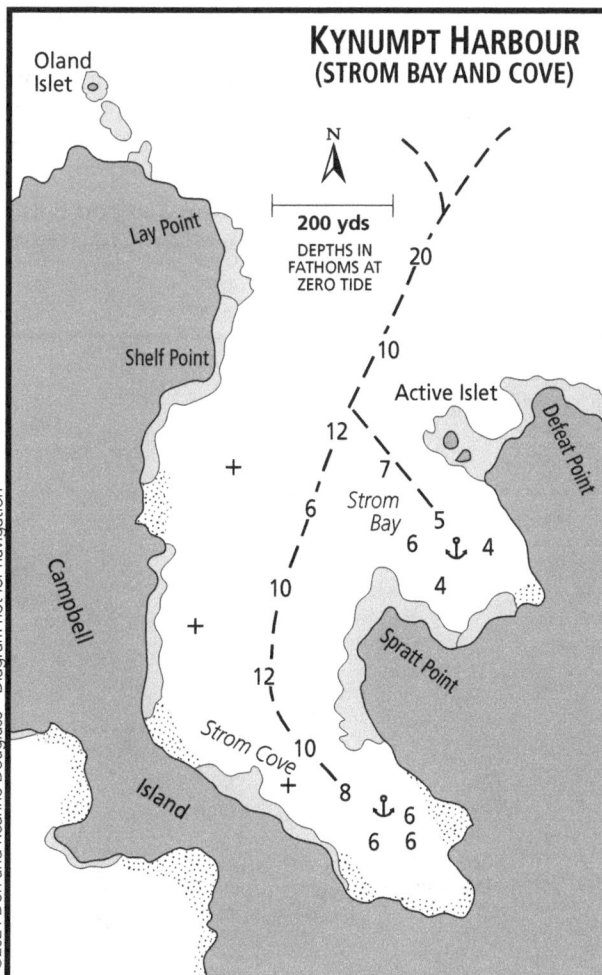

KYNUMPT HARBOUR
(STROM BAY AND COVE)

N

200 yds
DEPTHS IN FATHOMS AT ZERO TIDE

Oland Islet
Lay Point
Shelf Point
Active Islet
Defeat Point
Strom Bay
Spratt Point
Campbell Island
Strom Cove

©2024 Don and Réanne Douglass • Diagram not for navigation

Ormidale Harbour

(Seaforth Channel)
1.8 mi NE of Dryad Point
Entrance: 52°12.37'N, 128°09.07'W

Ormidale Harbour is a harbour for large vessels only. With the exception of the tiny lagoon area at its south end, where small boats might find limited anchorage, we couldn't find any reasonable anchorage along shore.

Kynumpt Harbour

("Strom Bay and Cove")
(Seaforth Channel)
2.5 mi NE of Dryad Point
Entrance: 52°12.62'N, 128°10.05'W
Anchor (Strom Bay): 52°12.38'N, 128°10.16'W
Anchor (Strom Cove): 52°12.16'N, 128°10.00'W

Strom Bay and Strom Cove in Kynumpt Harbour are well-protected anchorages with calm waters in most weather. Just an occasional wake of a cruise ship is felt in here.

Entry is easy, even by radar. Avoid Active Islet and its reef which form a natural breakwater for the outer Strom Bay anchorage. If you are headed deep into Strom Bay, give wide clearance to the rocks on the west shore.

Anchor (Strom Bay) in 5 to 6 fathoms over mud with good holding.

Anchor (Strom Cove) in 6 to 8 fathoms over mud with good holding.

Odin Cove (Seaforth Channel)

0.5 mi W of Kynumpt Harbour
Entrance: 52°12.73'N, 128°10.79'W
Anchor: 52°12.56'N, 128°10.77'W

Odin Cove offers good protection to smaller vessels in southerly weather and fair protection in strong westerlies. The westerly chop in Seaforth Channel tends to flow right by Odin Cove and, although some wind penetrates the cove, it slowly dies off. The charted rock mentioned with 3 feet over it at zero tide presents little concern except on low tides. The bottom gradually shoals, and good anchorage can be found south of the treed islet in the center of the cove. The bottom of sand and shells has large areas of iridescent seaweed that can foul some anchors; verify that yours is well set.

Anchor in 3 fathoms over sand and shell with some seaweed; holding depends on set of anchor.

Bella Bella—returning from trip to Queens Sound

Dundivan Inlet (Seaforth Channel)
3.5 mi NW of Kynumpt Harbour
Entrance (N): 52°13.66'N, 128°15.40'W

Dundivan Inlet is the entrance to Rait Narrows and the route to Queen Sound. (See Chapter 4.) Temporary anchorage can be found in the cove southwest of Penny Point where you can wait for proper tide conditions in Rait Narrows. The first cove east of Kimlock Point is poorly charted, and we felt uncomfortable there.

Lockhart Bay (Dundivan Inlet)
0.9 mi E of Rait Narrows
Entrance 52°12.55'N, 128°15.61'W
Anchor (unnamed cove): 52°12.31'N, 128° 15.97'W

Lockhart Bay has an irregular bottom and was too rocky for our tastes. Temporary anchorage with good shelter from all weather can be found at the head of the unnamed cove southwest of Penny Point where it is nearly landlocked. Swinging room is limited and a stern tie is useful for a stay of any length. (*Note:* Lockhart Bay is also covered in Chapter 4.)

Anchor (unnamed cove) in 2 to 3 fathoms over sand and mud with good holding.

Berry Inlet (Seaforth Channel)
3.3 mi E of Ivory Isl. Light
Entrance: 52°16.01'N, 128°19.73'W
Anchor: 52°16.99'N, 128°17.95'W

The head of Berry Inlet provides good anchorage since moderate wind and chop die off before you reach the far end. However, it offers inadequate protection in a southeast or southwest storm and, if strong winds are expected, you can find better shelter in Mouat Cove.

Anchor in 5 fathoms over a soft mud bottom (somewhat stinky) with good holding.

Mouat Cove (Berry Inlet)
3 mi E of Ivory Isl. Light
Entrance: 52°16.37'N, 128°19.17'W
Anchor: 52°16.52'N, 128°19.54'W

Mouat Cove is a small labyrinth of islets, reefs and rocks worth exploring. The anchor site is not self-evident. Anchoring here is sort of a find-it-yourself game. In any case, Mouat Cove offers good shelter from all weather and it is *quiet*, except for the occasional moan of Ivory Island's foghorn. We once stopped here after a disagreeable all-night run from Cape Saint James, and it was a stable non-rocking paradise that we didn't leave for 24 hours!

Cruise slowly around Mouat Cove and pick your own flat spot. We followed the north shore to near the head of the cove. The bottom in the cove is uneven, with plenty of surprises here and there, especially when you think you've just it figured out. It is essential to proceed at dead-slow with an alert bow watch. You may also enjoy the islets which Iain Lawrence describes in *Far Away Places* ". . . capped by twisted trees that sprout from a shag of bushes and lichen, crowding on the rock like shipwrecked sailors atop a raft."

Birds rule here, with kingfishers setting their typical staccato beat. Ravens chortle, Canada geese honk, loons cry and small deer graze on the grassy margins of the cove.

Anchor in about 4 to 6 fathoms over a mixed bottom with sandy spots; holding depends on finding the flat sand and mud spots!

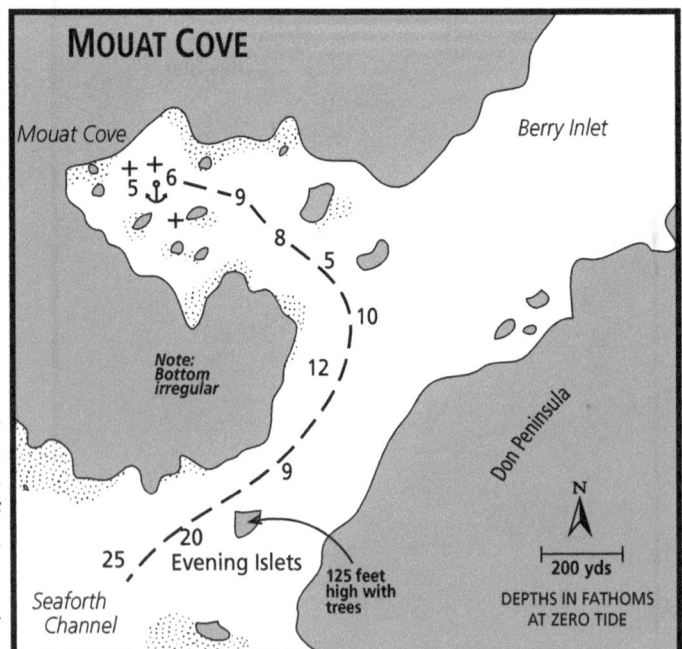

Fisher Point (Seaforth Channel)
2.2 mi E of Ivory Isl. Light
Position: 52°15.82'N, 128°20.87'W

Fisher Point was the home of two totems known locally as the "The Watchmen," located high on the granite face of Fisher Point. Recent reports indicate that the totems have deteriorated and are no longer clearly visible.

Gale Passage (Seaforth Channel)
2.3 mi SE of Ivory Isl. Light
Entrance (N): 52°14.46'N, 128°22.40'W

Gale Passage is very narrow, fraught with hazards and suitable only for experienced kayakers at high-water slack. The passage leads to Queen Sound via Thompson Bay.

Note: St. Johns Harbour, 5 miles west of Gale Passage, and Ivory Island Light station are discussed in Chapter 7. Blair Inlet and Reid Passage are discussed in Chapter 6.

"Watchman" on duty, Fisher Point

Otoliths

Otoliths—the balance organs of fish—which occur as paired bonelike structures at the base of the brain have growth rings that biologists can study to determine the age of a fish. The otoliths are delicate, lacey structures that can be made into jewelry. It takes a little know-how to extract the otoliths from the fish, but once you have learned the technique, you will prize these beautiful little treasures, the prettiest of which come from large snapper, rockfish and true cod.

One morning as we were jigging for bottom fish a friend hooked into a big one. "What do you think it is?" I asked. "Another pair of otoliths," was her prompt reply.

To extract otoliths, use a sturdy knife to cut off the top of the fish's skull just at the top of the eye socket, exposing the brain. Lift the brain and gently free the otoliths from their sockets below, using the tip of the knife. The otoliths lie on edge, with a front-to-back longitudinal axis, on either side of the midline. If they are tight in their sockets, tease them out gently with the tip of the knife or a pair of forceps (pressure may break them).

Courtesy Noreen Rudd and David Hoar, M/V *Pacific High*, authors of *Cooks Afloat!*, Harbour Publishing

Preparing the catch of the day

Milbanke Sound

Seaforth Channel

Mouat Cove

Chatfield I.

Jenny Inlet

Dutton I.

Rait Narrows

Lockhart Bay

Kynumpt Hbr

Trouble Pass

Lagoon Cove

Fort Bay

Johnson Channel

Dean Channel

Rattenbury Pt.

St. John Harbour

Gale Passage

The Nook

Clovin Cove

BELLA BELLA

Gunboat Passage

Gosse Bay

Hampden Bay

Cathedral Point Cove

Bardswell Group

Raymond Passage

McLoughlin Bay

SHEARWATER

Kakushdish Harbour

Farewell Pt.

Port John

King Island

Hochstader Cove

Campbell I.

Denny I.

Evans Inlet

Kwatna Inlet

Thompson Bay

Joassa Channel

Canal Bight

Lama Passage

Stager Lake

Burke Channel

Stryker I. Nook

Tribal Group

Wide Awake Cove

Bob Bay

Alta Cove

Nancy Cove

Long Point Cove

Lagoon Bay

COLVILLE LAGOON M.P.

Restoration Bay

McMullin Group

Admiral Group

Hunter Channel

Jane Cove

Jans Cove

Fisher Channel

52°N

Dodwell North & South Coves

Haaksvold Point

Goose I.

Jans Peur Passage

Hunter Island

De Cosmos Lagoon

Kisameet Bay

Duck Island

Goose I. Anchorage

McNaughton Gro.

Cultus Sound

Kayak Cove

Spitfire Lagoon

Spitfire Channel

Sound Bay

Kildidh Inlet

Bremner Bay

Kiltik Cove

Windsor Cove

Fougner Bay

Harlequin Basin

Rock Inlet

Namu Harbour

N

Gosling Island

Queens Sound

4

Domestic Tranquility

Crab Cove

Sea Otter Inlet

Warrior Cove

Huricane Anch.
Spider Anch.

Brydon Channel

0 2 4 6 8 10
NAUTICAL MILES

Nalau Passage

Lewall Inlet

Stirling I.

Nalau Inlet

Koeye River

Fitz Hugh Sound

Kwakume Inlet

Turnbull Inlet

Hakai Passage

Adams Harbour

Goldstream Hbr.

Kwakume Pt.

Elizabeth Lagoon

Illahie Inlet

The Rapids
Joe's Bay

Waterfall Inlet

Remotesville Cove

Oyster Bay

Crooked Passage

Hecate I.

Green I. Anch.

Patrol Passage

Addenbroke I.

Fish Egg Inlet

Fishtrap Bay

Dawsons Landing

West Beach

Pruth Bay

Kwakshua Channel

Fifer Bay

Convoy Passage

Gilden Sleeve Bay

Mantrap Inlet

Derby Channel

Walbran I.

Taylor Bay

Philip Inlet

Calvert Island

Addenbroke Pt.

Fury Bay

Frypan Bay

Ripon I.

Rivers Inlet

Safety Cove

Schooner Retreat

Penrose I.

Fury Cove

Duncanby Lodge

Cape Calvert

Open Bight

W. Home Bay

Home Bay

Goose Bay

Grief Bay

Pears Rocks

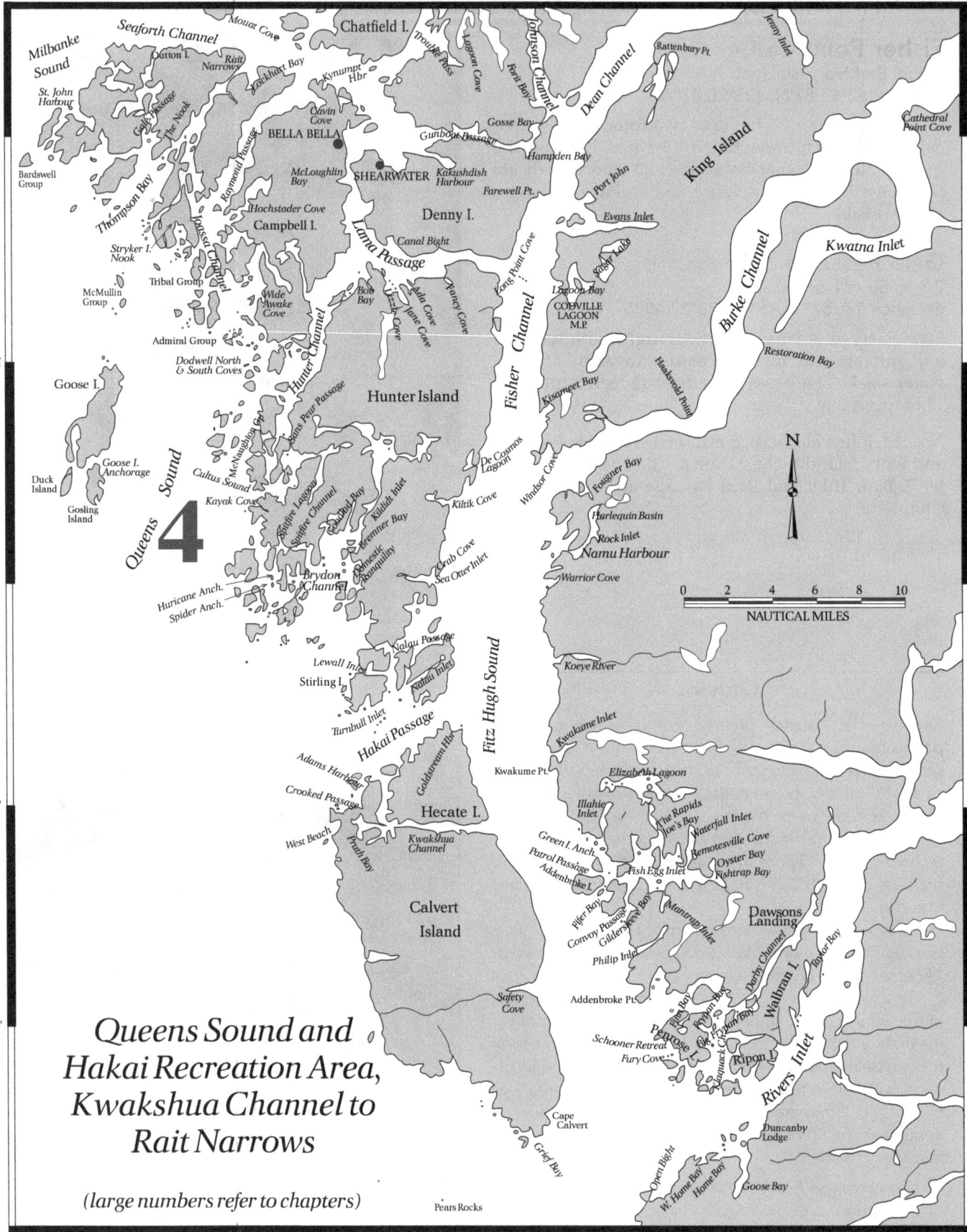

Queens Sound and Hakai Recreation Area, Kwakshua Channel to Rait Narrows

(large numbers refer to chapters)

©2024 Don and Réanne Douglass • Diagram not for navigation

4

Queens Sound and Hakai Lúxvbális Conservancy Area, Kwakshua Channel to Rait Narrows

Queens Sound includes the outer coastal islands between Calvert Island and Seaforth Channel. Seldom described in cruising circles, this unique archipelago offers outstanding recreational opportunities for boaters, canoeists and kayakers. Untold passages, coves, and nooks are waiting to be discovered and enjoyed. This is a kayaker's paradise.

The southern half of Queens Sound, designated as the Hakai Lúxvbális Conservancy Area (formerly the Hakai Recreation Area), encompasses over a quarter-million acres of land and sea. It is the largest provincial marine park on the coast of British Columbia and, with the exception of the Hakai Beach Institute at the head of Pruth Bay, it is undeveloped wilderness cruising at its best. Self-sufficiency is mandatory and some tolerance for swells and surge is needed as these are outside waters.

Dramatic contrasts, from fully exposed shorelines to rolling, forested hills and 1,000-meter summits, create some of the most varied and scenic coastline in the province. Lagoons and reversing tidal rapids, beaches, all-weather anchorages and tombolos (sand spits) make this area an ideal cruising ground for boaters, anglers, kayakers, scuba divers and naturalists. Please be aware that the outer coast is subject to sudden and dramatic changes in weather; fog can roll in quickly and sea conditions can change dramatically within a few hours.

Caution: Charts for Queens Sound, while much better than before, may still be derived from old surveys; they are small-scale and hazards are not well defined. A vigilant bow watch and slow speed are critical when exploring this magnificent area. Nearshore exploration is best done by kayak. The text that follows is a modest attempt at describing what this area has to offer.

Kwakshua Channel

(Fitz Hugh Sound)
4.5 mi NW of Addenbroke Light
Entrance (E, Fitz Hugh): 51°39.05'N, 127°57.52'W
Entrance (NW, Hakai Passage): 51°41.57'N, 128°05.72'W

Kwakshua Channel, on the west side of Fitz Hugh Sound, is the 7-mile-long, east-west channel between Calvert and Hecate Islands. This channel marks the southern end of the Outer Passage for vessels following the west coast route to Prince Rupert. Out of the current and chop found in Fitz Hugh Sound, the west end of the channel gives excellent protection for cruising boats. Pruth Bay at the far west end is also a favorite anchorage for north-bound vessels following the conventional ferry-boat route.

Unnamed Cove

(Calvert Island)
1.5 mi E of Pruth Bay
Entrance: 51°39.08'N, 128°04.67'W
Anchor: 51°38.91'N, 128°04.62'W

Unnamed Cove, a small indentation in Calvert Island immediately east of Keith Anchorage, offers more solitude for small boats than the anchor sites farther west. During southeast storms the cove may be subject to gusts that deflect off the high peak on Calvert Island, but we still consider this a very good anchorage.

Anchor in 4 fathoms over sand and mud with eel grass; good holding.

Pruth Bay, looking east down Kwakshua Channel

Pruth Bay, art found on the south face of a tree at Hakai Beach Institute cluster of buildings

Keith Anchorage (Calvert Island)
1.1 mi E of Pruth Bay
Entrance: 51°39.05'N, 128°05.35'W
Anchor: 51°38.79'N, 128°05.58'W

Keith Anchorage offers good protection in most summer weather, especially in its western portion.

Anchor in 2 to 5 fathoms over sand and mud with fair holding.

Hakai Institute; guest dinghies only at designated dock

Pruth Bay (Calvert Island)
10.5 mi NW of Safety Cove
Entrance: 51°39.26'N, 128°05.87'W
Anchor: 51°39.28'N, 128°07.37'W

Pruth Bay has always been a popular anchorage for cruising boats as well as a base for sportfishing. Shelter in the bay is very good and there is adequate swinging room for a number of boats. If strong easterlies are expected, several small anchorages along the south shore offer more protection from chop.

In 2010, the fishing resort at the head of Pruth Bay was sold to the Tula Foundation and became the Hakai Beach Institute, a private research and conference center. The Institute lies within the Hakai Lúxvbális Conservancy, the largest provincial marine protected area on the BC coast.

Visitors are welcome to tie their dinghy at the designated "dinghy dock", sign in at the visitor bulletin board upland from the wharf, and hike the trails. The 0.75 km trail to the west beach is flat and easy. A trail leads from west beach to north beach, and another more challenging trail leads south to several beaches and a lookout.

Boats must anchor at least 100 meters away from the Institute docks. No fuel or any commercial services are available.

The inner bay on the north shore is interesting to explore by dinghy or kayak at high water; at low water the bay becomes a drying mud flat.

Hakai Passage [Hakai Pass] (Calvert Isl.)
Between Hecate and Nalau Islands
Entrance (NE): 51°44.70'N, 128°00.08'W
Entrance (SW): 51°42.20'N, 128°08.75'W

Hakai Passage is renowned for its salmon fishing, particularly Chinook (Spring), but all five species of salmon migrate through here (Coho, Chum, Pink, Sockeye, and Chinook). Located in the Hakai Lúxvbális Conservancy Area and thus closed to commercial fishing, these resorts offer superb opportunities for sport fishermen. Popular fishing spots are Odlum Point, The Gap, Foster Rocks and Barney Point. Salmon are commonly caught on cut-plug herring. The area also has good fishing for halibut, Ling cod, and rock fish.

The outer portion of Hakai Passage can be extremely dangerous on large ebb tides when strong southwest winds and westerly swells oppose the 4-knot current. Twenty-foot breaking seas mid-channel north of Odlum Point have been reported.

Hakai Passage leads to Choked Passage where wonderful fair-weather cruising and anchoring opportunities exist.

Photo by Lorena Landon

Choked Passage, northwest tip Calvert Island

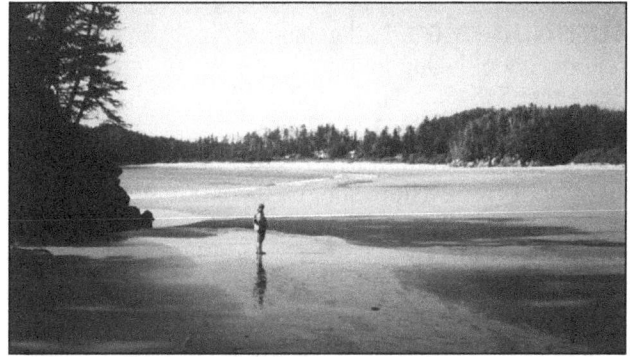

Pruth Bay, west beach at low tide

Choked Passage (Calvert Island)
1 mi N of Pruth Bay
Entrance (N): 51°41.44'N, 128°06.18'W
Entrance (SW): 51°40.16'N, 128°07.90'W

This area is a popular sportfishing area offering great opportunities for exploration by dinghy or kayak—there are beautiful beaches along the Calvert Island shore at the south end of the passage. The best reported anchorage lies in a nook between Starfish and Odlum Islands on the Choked Passage side.

Adams Harbour (Calvert Island)
0.6 mi SW of Rattenbury Island
Entrance: 51°41.28'N, 128°06.24'W
Anchor: 51°41.14'N, 128°06.26'W

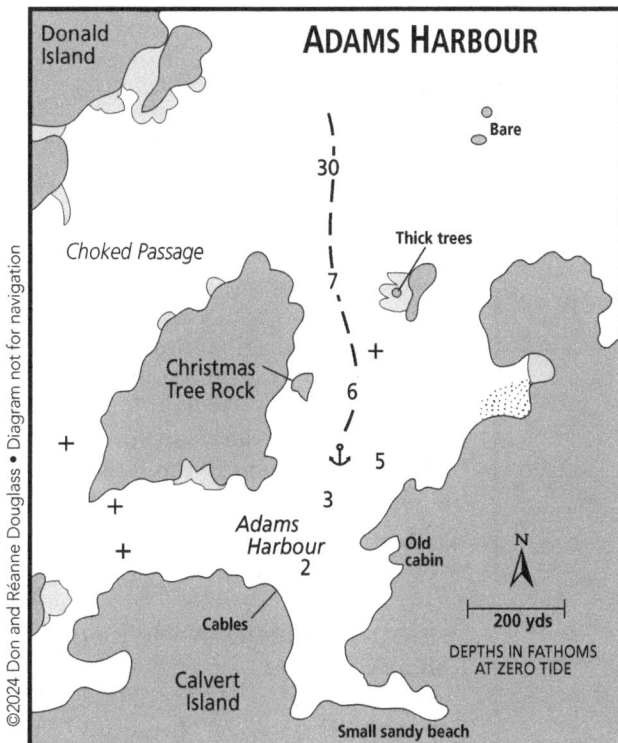

The east shore of Adams Harbour, southeast of Donald Island, offers good protection close to the fishing and recreation area of Choked Passage. There is far less westerly chop here than further west. Fishing resorts sometimes moor in the very southern end of this tiny bay, and at times it may be plugged with fishing boats. Use caution as unmarked steel cables may foul the bottom. Swinging room is limited.

Anchor in 3 to 5 fathoms over sand with fair-to-good holding.

Barney Point Cove
0.5 mi SE of Barney Point
Entrance: 51°42.70'N, 128°03.11'W
Anchor: 51°42.18'N, 128°03.21'W

Barney Point Cove is the name we give to the well-hidden anchorage a half-mile southeast of Barney Point at the northwest end of Hecate Island. Shelter deep in the cove is excellent, but avoid the fish camp sometimes located here during the summer.

Anchor in 4 to 5 fathoms over sand and mud with fair-to-good holding.

Nalau Inlet (Hakai Pass)
3.3 mi NE of Rattenbury Island
Entrance: 51°44.57'N, 128°02.60'W
Anchor: 51°45.10'N, 128°02.07'W

Nalau Inlet is our name for the indentation on the southwest end of Nalau Island. The inlet provides excellent anchorage in all weather. There are two very narrow entrances with poorly charted shoals; we prefer the eastern entrance. Avoid the mid-channel rock upon entering from the west. The east entrance carries about 2 fathoms in the fairway.

Anchor (small boats) in 4 fathoms close to shore; larger boats anchor in the middle of the inlet in 8 fathoms over mud.

Turnbull Inlet (Nalau Island)

0.8 mi NW of Nalau Inlet
Entrance: 51°45.25'N, 128°03.31'W
Anchor: 51°45.81'N, 128°02.39'W

River-like and remote, Turnbull Inlet is lined with a variety of trees where songbirds make their summer home. The inlet and the lagoon at its head almost cut Nalau Island in two. This is a good temporary lunch stop or an overnighter in fair weather. Some southwest gusts may enter but there is very little chop, as the lack of drift logs indicates.

Upon entering Turnbull Inlet, favor the east shore to avoid rocks and kelp off the north shore. At the narrows, favor the north shore to avoid kelp and rocks at the bend in the inlet. Flood currents run from 1 to 2 knots in the narrows. Anchor in the basin and explore the lagoon to the north by dinghy for an adventure that brings to mind *African Queen*.

Anchor in 2 fathoms over mud and decaying vegetation; good holding.

Ward Channel (Nalau Island)

Between Nalau and Underhill islands
Entrance (S): 51°45.56'N, 128°03.57'W
Entrance (N): 51°47.05'N, 128°02.68'W

Ward Channel is the easy way to transit from Hakai Passage to Nalau Passage. The small bight on the east side of the channel should be well suited as an anchor site for small boats. Avoid several rocks along the east shore by favoring the steep-to west shore.

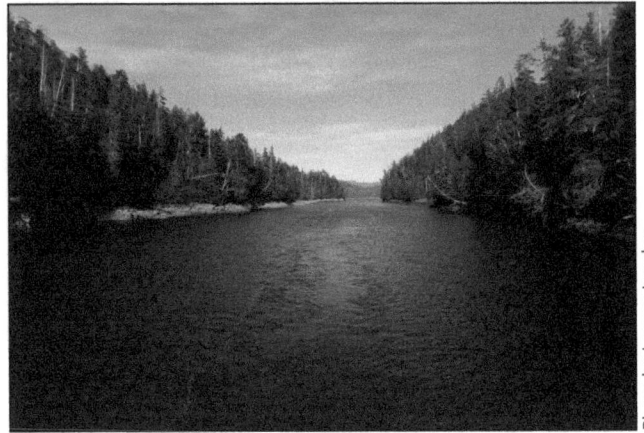
Lewall Inlet, looking east toward the entrance

Photo by Lorena Landon

Edward Channel (Nalau Passage)

Between Underhill and Stirling islands
Entrance (S): 51°44.97'N, 128°04.55'W
Entrance (N): 51°47.01'N, 128°04.47'W

Edward Channel is entered a half-mile northwest of the Planet Group of islands, with the simplest entrance utilizing the channel with the 10-foot depth mentioned above.

The small cove at the northeast end of Edward Channel is well sheltered. However, we found the bottom rocky with poor holding. Lewall Inlet, however, offers very good protection without this problem.

Lewall Inlet (Stirling Island)

1 mi S of Nalau Passage
Entrance: 51°45.97'N, 128°04.84'W
Anchor: 51°46.07'N, 128°06.29'W

Lewall Inlet is extremely well sheltered from all chop, and because its waters are so calm you get wonderful reflections along the rocky shore. Human profiles and aboriginal designs are evident in the rocks on the south shore as you approach the basin with tide level near 4 feet. Excellent anchorage can be found anywhere in the inner basin. Swinging room is somewhat limited.

Anchor in 2 to 3 fathoms over soft mud with very good holding.

Nalau Passage (Nalau Island)

S shore of Hunter Island
Entrance (W): 51°47.11'N, 128°07.34'W
Entrance NE: 51°48.38'N, 128°00.79'W

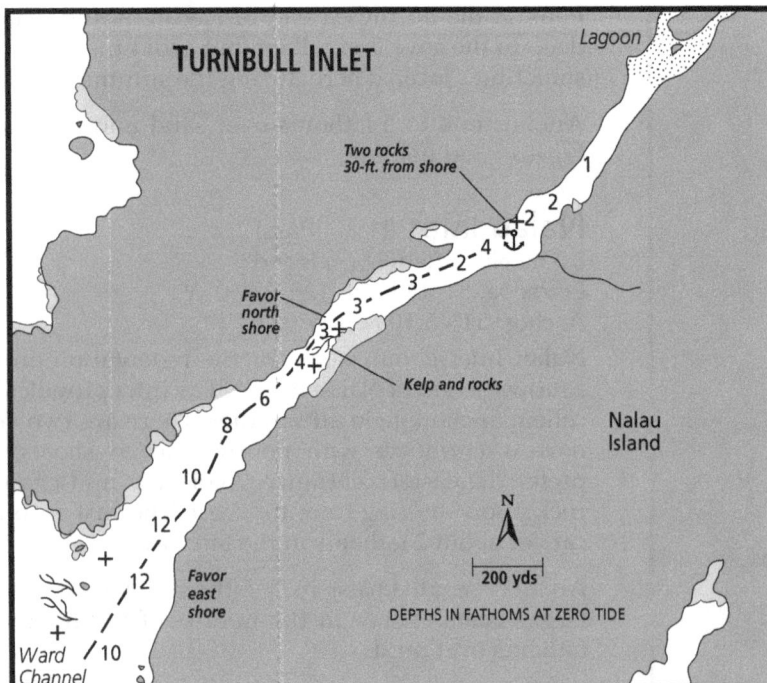

TURNBULL INLET

Lagoon

Two rocks 30-ft. from shore

Favor north shore

Kelp and rocks

Nalau Island

N

200 yds

DEPTHS IN FATHOMS AT ZERO TIDE

Favor east shore

Ward Channel

©2024 Don and Réanne Douglass • Diagram not for navigation

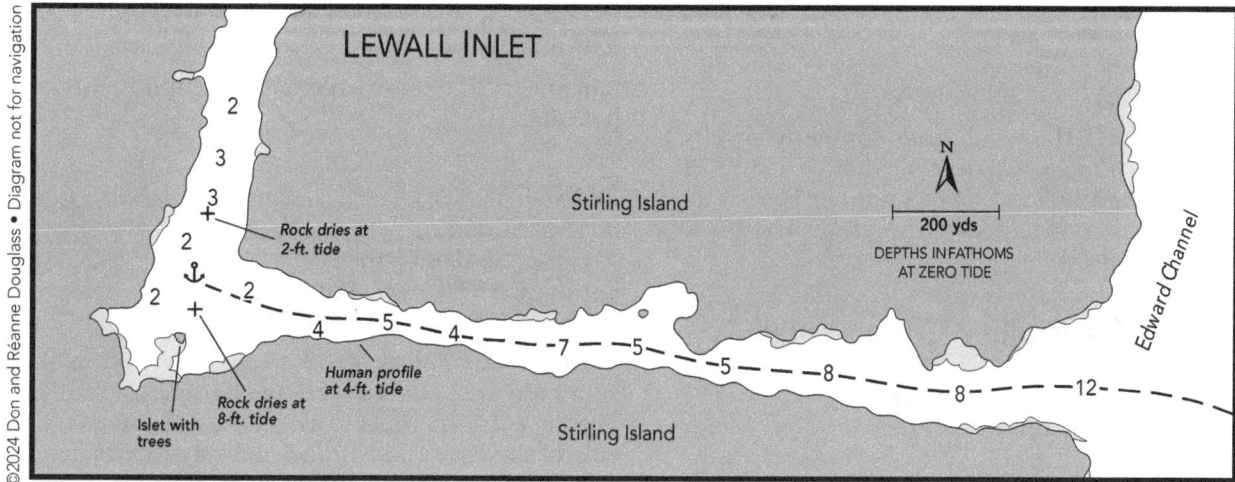

©2024 Don and Réanne Douglass • Diagram not for navigation

LEWALL INLET

Stirling Island

Rock dries at
2-ft. tide

N

200 yds

DEPTHS IN FATHOMS
AT ZERO TIDE

Edward Channel

Human profile
at 4-ft. tide

Rock dries at
8-ft. tide

Islet with
trees

Stirling Island

Nalau Passage offers no difficulty to cruising boats unless it is open-season for gill-netters. In this case, the boats and their nets nearly close off the passage north of Edward Channel. Moderate to strong currents (especially ebb on spring tides) of 3-4 knots are common. The flow is largely laminar with minimal turbulence.

Mustang Bay

(Nalau Passage)
1.5 mi SW of Sea Otter Inlet
Entrance: 51°49.14'N, 128°02.85'W

Mustang Bay offers fair anchorage in stable weather at its head, but it is exposed in southerly winds.

Target Bay

(Nalau Passage)
0.7 mi SE of Sea Otter Cove
Entrance: 51°49.04'N, 128°02.09'W

Target Bay—a small cove filled with reefs—like Mustang, is open to southerly winds. It offers very good protection in northeasterlies. (For protection from southeast gales see Tomahawk Island below.)

Tomahawk Island Anchorage

(Nalau Passage)
0.9 mi SW of Daedalus Pt.
Anchor: 51°47.32'N, 128°01.50'W

Tomahawk Island Anchorage, between Tomahawk Island and the islands to its south, provides very good protection in southeast gales.

Anchor in 5 to 7 fathoms over gravel and rock; fair holding.

Kildidt Sound (Hakai Passage)

12 mi N of Pruth Bay
Entrance: 51°47.71'N, 128°08.66'W

Kildidt Sound is the beginning of the fascinating Queens Sound archipelago. The primary cruising route for small to medium boats leads through Spitfire Channel on the north side of Hurricane Island. Large boats must pass farther west.

Leckie Bay Cove (Kildidt Sound)

1.5 mi N of Nalau Passage
Entrance: 51°47.70'N, 128°07.15'W
Anchor: 51°49.17'N, 128°06.66'W

"Leckie Bay Cove" is our name for the small inlet at the north end of Leckie Bay. It is scenic and intimate with reefs along its eastern shore. Open to south winds and any storm swells from the southwest, it is a marginal anchorage. In fair weather, you can use it as a good lunch stop or temporary anchorage. It's best to enter at low tide so you can see the rocks that lie in the eastern basin and along the channel to the east side.

Anchor in the west basin over soft mud on a 4-fathom shelf or in deeper water over rocks with fair holding.

Rupert Island Passage (Kildidt Sound)

S corner of Watt Bay
Entrance (S): 51°48.85'N, 128°08.21'W
Entrance (N): 51°49.92'N, 128°07.10'W

"Rupert Island Passage" is what we call the interesting, L-shaped passage to Watt and Bremner Bays, where the waters are well protected. A rocky path lies midway through the north leg so favor the east shore slightly. The elbow carries a minimum of 3 fathoms in its fairway.

Watt Bay (Kildidt Sound)
1.5 mi E of Spitfire Channel
Entrance: 51°50.31'N, 128°08.32'W

Watt Bay is well sheltered from southerly swells, with good anchorage available in what we call "Domestic Tranquility Cove" or in Bremner Bay on its north side. This entire area is poorly charted and vigilance is advised.

Domestic Tranquility Cove (Watt Bay)
0.5 mi S of Bremner Bay
Entrance: 51°50.30'N, 128°06.83'W
Anchor: 51°50.40'N, 128°06.79'W

The first time we transited Spitfire Channel we were on the return leg of a trip to Alaska. Don, busily shooting video from atop the pilothouse, told Réanne to head for the extremely narrow western entrance of Spitfire Channel. She thought Don had gone mad with his filming since his directions seemed to lead straight to a rock pile. She worked her way through with flying colors but had a few unkind words to say to the nonchalant captain. An hour later, well anchored in what we now call "Domestic Tranquility Cove," and after we had opened and sampled a bottle of Dubonnet, peace and quiet returned to *Baidarka*.

Domestic Tranquility Cove is the scenic indentation a half-mile north of Rupert Island Passage, at the east end of Watt Bay. You enter the cove by staying east of the bare, grassy rock we call Flower Pot Rock, favoring the east shore to avoid rocks off its north side. As you approach the basin, avoid rocks off the spit on the east shore. The basin itself has a flat bottom of 3 to 4 fathoms and anchorage can be taken anywhere in the east side behind the rocky spit, with somewhat limited room. Larger boats, or those seek-

ing more swinging room, may stay in Bremner Bay a half-mile to the north.

Anchor in 3 fathoms over sand and mud with good holding.

Bremner Bay
(Kildidt Sound)
2 mi E of Spitfire Channel
Entrance: 51°50.90'N, 128°07.19'W,
Anchor: 51°50.83'N, 128°06.84'W

Bremner Bay offers good protection over a large swinging area but it is poorly charted. Carefully favor the entrance islets to avoid the rock on the south side of the bay. The entrance fairway carries about 3 fathoms. For best protection, anchor in the south portion of the bay. This is a well-sheltered place to base an exploration of Kildidt Inlet and the surrounding areas.

Anchor in 9 to 12 fathoms over mud with good holding.

Kildidt Inlet and Lagoon (Hunter Island)
2 mi N of Bremner Bay
Inlet entrance: 51°52.34'N, 128°06.86'W
Lagoon entrance: 51°56.15'N, 128°05.44'W

Kildidt Inlet and Lagoon appear to be a fascinating cruising destination; unfortunately, you must transit dangerous Kildidt Narrows. This is a wonderful place for bird watching and nature viewing; you may even spot a wolf or a black bear along shore.

Kildidt Narrows
(Hunter Island)
1.5 mi N of Bremner Bay
Entrance: 51°52.82'N, 128°06.83'W

Kildidt Narrows is daunting at best. Currents as high as 12 knots on spring tides are reported on charts. Overfalls are said to form on both flood and ebb tides.

Brydon Channel (Hurricane Island)
S shore of Hurricane Island
Entrance (E): 51°50.16'N, 128°10.85'W
Entrance (W): 51°49.81'N, 128°12.39'W

Brydon Channel is navigable by vessels of all sizes. But use caution if you enter; trying to avoid the 8- and 10-foot drying rocks in the channel northwest of 72-meter island makes this a particularly interesting experience at high tides. If you are nervous about using the channel, enter it only when the tide levels are below 8 feet—then it's a relative piece-of-cake. Elec-

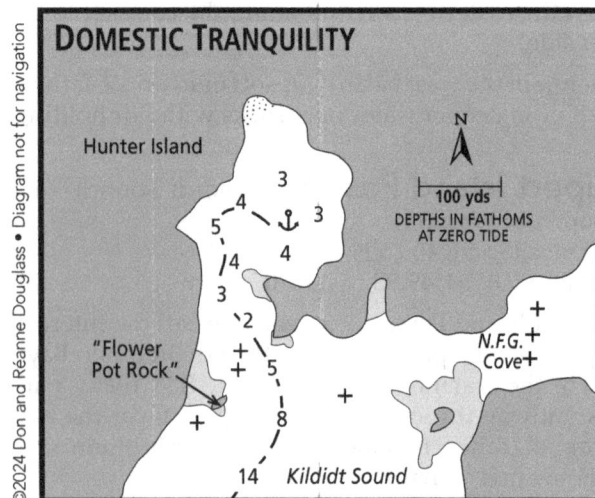

DOMESTIC TRANQUILITY

tronic charts and GPS help take a shallow pass close to 72-meter island.

Brydon Channel is the main protected (east) entrance into Spider Anchorage, and Fulton Passage is the west entrance. The area around Breadner Point on the west side of Spider Island has confused wave patterns, even on a calm day. Stay either well out to sea or transit through Spider Channel. This is dinghy and kayak country, and the routes for shallow-draft small craft are endless. It's also a favorite place for scuba divers.

Kildidt Narrows, south entrance

Brydon Anchorage (Kildidt Sound)
1 mi NE of Spider Anchorage
Entrance: 51°50.28'N, 128°12.26'W
Anchor: 51°50.50'N, 128°12.04'W

Brydon Anchorage is the local name for the nearly-enclosed bay north of Brydon Channel just before it turns south into Spider Anchorage. The anchorage is well protected and has a deep sticky mud bottom—be prepared to wash off your foredeck after hoisting anchor. Avoid a charted rock off the south shore.

Anchor in 10-12 fathoms over deep mud with very good holding.

Kittyhawk Cove (Kildidt Sound)
1 mi W of Mosquito Islets
Anchor: 51°49.80'N, 128°11.25'W

"Kittyhawk Cove" is what we call the well-sheltered cove in the center of the Kittyhawk Group. It is best to enter Kittyhawk Cove from the northwest channel leading to and from Brydon Channel.

Anchor in 8 to 10 fathoms over sand and rocks.

Spider Channel
Between Spitfire and Spider islands
Entrance (S): 51°50.29'N, 128°14.07'W
Entrance (N): 51°51.67'N, 128°14.30'W

Spider Channel is a smooth-water alternative to tiny Spitfire Channel. A narrow, shallow route can be found keeping all but the westerly Round Island (and its south islet) of the Stopper Group to your east side. Minimum in the fairway at zero tide is reported to be 10 to 12 feet.

Spider Anchorage (Kildidt Sound)
SE of Spider Island
Anchor: 51°49.48'N, 128°14.50'W

Of the anchor sites mentioned above, the bay between Edna Islands and Anne Islands is reported to be the best. There is plenty of anchoring room for several boats here. On a nice day, you can carry your

dinghy across the tombolo between the Edna Islands and row out to weather-beaten Typhoon Island.

Anchor in about 10 fathoms over sand with fair holding.

Hurricane Channel (Kildidt Sound)
etween Hurricane & Spitfire Islands
Entrance (S): 51°50.24'N, 128°13.16'W
Entrance (N): 51°51.56'N, 128°12.85'W

An unnamed channel we call "Hurricane Channel" connects Brydon Channel with Spitfire Channel. This channel allows small or mid-sized boats to

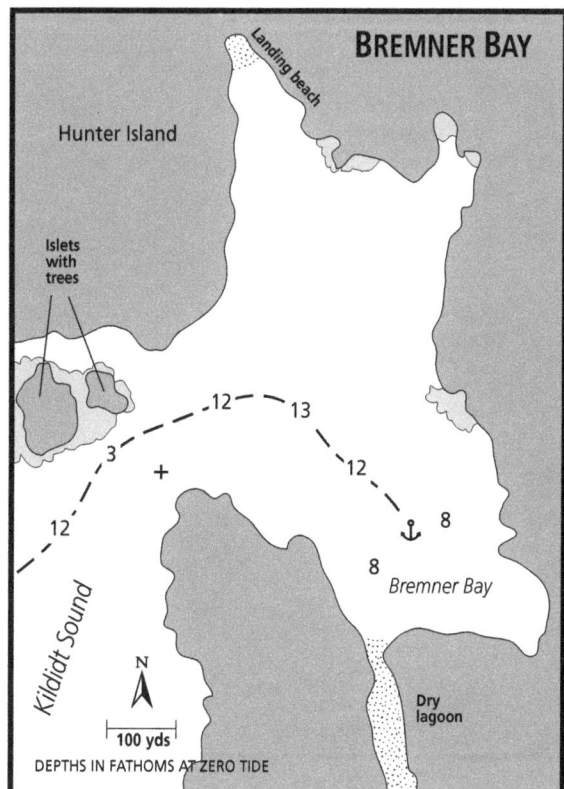

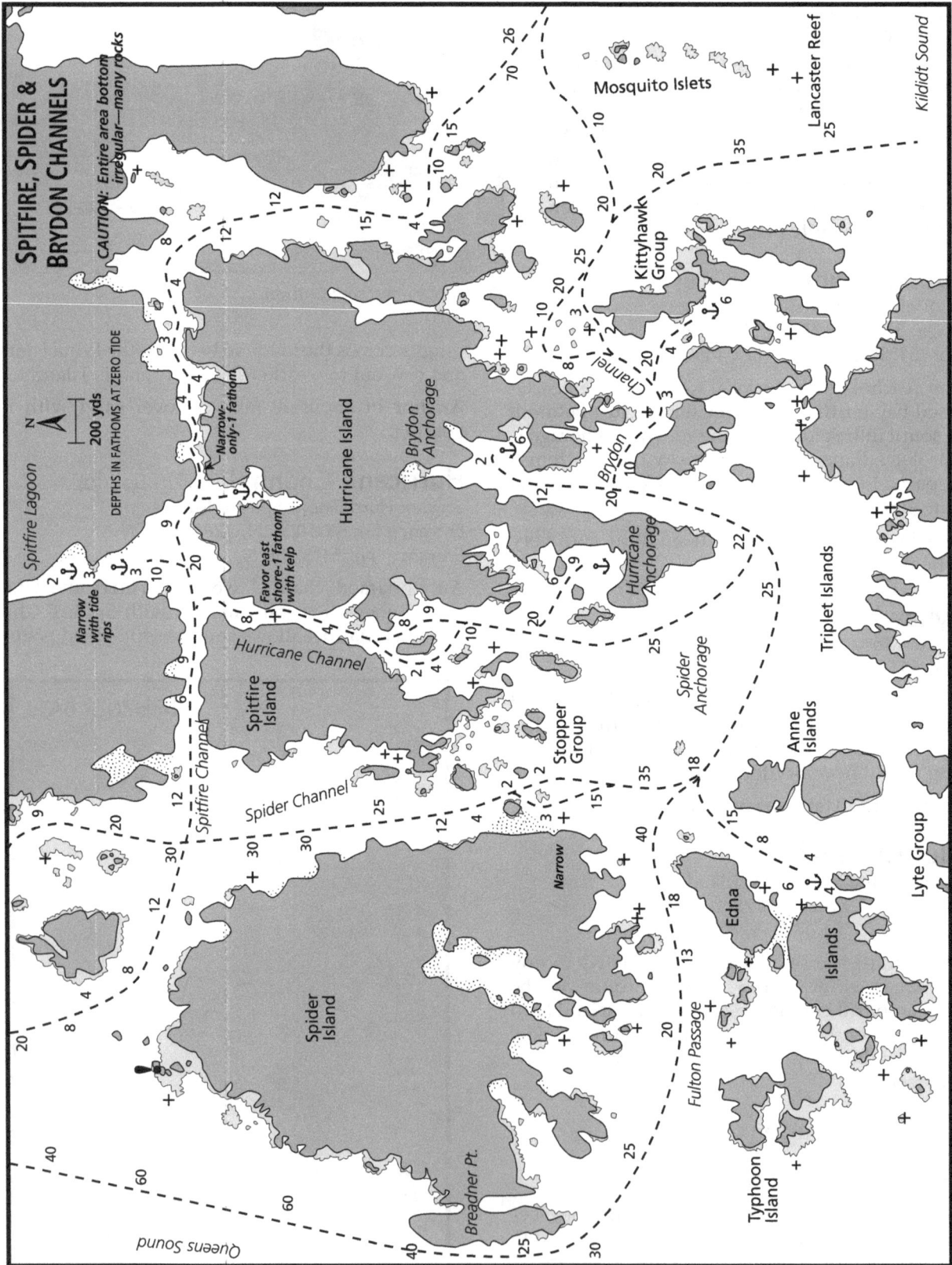

SPITFIRE, SPIDER & BRYDON CHANNELS

CAUTION: Entire area bottom irregular—many rocks

DEPTHS IN FATHOMS AT ZERO TIDE

N

200 yds

Spitfire Lagoon

Narrow—only-1 fathom

Narrow with tide rips

Favor east shore-1 fathom with kelp

Hurricane Island

Brydon Anchorage

Brydon Channel

Mosquito Islets

Lancaster Reef

Kildidt Sound

Kittyhawk Group

Hurricane Channel

Spitfire Island

Hurricane Anchorage

Triplet Islands

Spider Channel

Stopper Group

Spider Anchorage

Anne Islands

Lyte Group

Narrow

Edna

Islands

Fulton Passage

Spider Island

Typhoon Island

Breadner Pt.

Queens Sound

©2024 Don and Réanne Douglass • Diagram not for navigation

cross to Queen Sound without going through Spitfire Narrows. It is outside Spider Island and more protected than Fulton Passage and a little quicker than using Spider Channel due to the constriction in the Stopper Group of islets. Hurricane Channel is restricted by a shoal and mid-channel rock 0.21 mile off its north entrance. This shoal is choked with kelp—especially in late summer—but you can slide through in neutral favoring the east shore to avoid the rock. There is about 7 feet at zero tide. At high water there is less problem with kelp and the current is moderate.

Once past the two center islets, 0.5 mile northwest of Hurricane Anchorage, when headed north, favor the west shore until you reach the shoal, then favor the east shore until past the rock and kelp. We prefer the route east of the center islets because the water is deeper and the route is more direct.

Hurricane Anchorage
(Hurricane Island)
0.8 mi NW of Manley Island
Anchor: 51°50.21'N, 128°12.72'W

Very good shelter from all weather can be found in what we call "Hurricane Anchorage," a cove created by the hook at the very southern tip of Hurricane Island. Named after the famous British fighter plane, this is a bomb-proof anchorage with room for several boats. It is landlocked and the most secure place to anchor for miles around. The easiest entrance lies north of the islets.

Anchor in 8 to 10 fathoms over mud with good holding; good swinging room.

World War II Names

Have you noticed the number of islands on the west side of Kildidt Sound with names of famous World War II aircraft? During the early years of the war when these islands were still unnamed, Canadian and U.S. pilots were based at Shearwater east of Bella Bella. As the pilots began flight patrols over the coast they gave names to each island to help identify coastal checkpoints—Airacobra, Spider, Spitfire, Mosquito, Lancaster, Kittyhawk, Typhoon, etc. all legendary airplanes used in the Battle of Britain.

—RHD

Spitfire Narrows (Hunter Island)
3.1 mi W of Bremner Bay
Entrance (E): 51°50.72'N, 128°10.21'W
Entrance (W): 51°51.65'N, 128°13.88'W

Spitfire Channel is the smooth-water route for small boats from central Kildidt Sound to Spider Channel and around Superstition Point into Cultus Sound—Spitfire Narrows defines a narrow, tiny channel. We have heard that the biggest vessel to make the transit was a 50-footer whose skipper claimed he made it only because the underwater configuration of his hull happened to correspond exactly to the shape of the rocks on either side of the narrows! Any boat over 30 feet should proceed *very* cautiously because there is no maneuvering room. *Caution:* Spitfire Narrows requires high performance!

The key to transiting is to identify visually the rock on the north shore at the east end of the narrow portion and stay close, halfway to the rock ledge on the south shore. The depth of 9 feet occurs only in the center of the V-shaped channel. At low water the narrowest part is perhaps 15 feet wide at the top of the V-channel. At highwater slack the narrows is about 25-feet wide which allows more maneuvering room. Once you are safely past this rock, the rest is a straight shot and not particularly difficult. Reconnoiter first by dinghy and if you don't feel comfortable with this route, consider using Spider Channel or pass west of Spider Island via Brydon Channel and Fulton Passage.

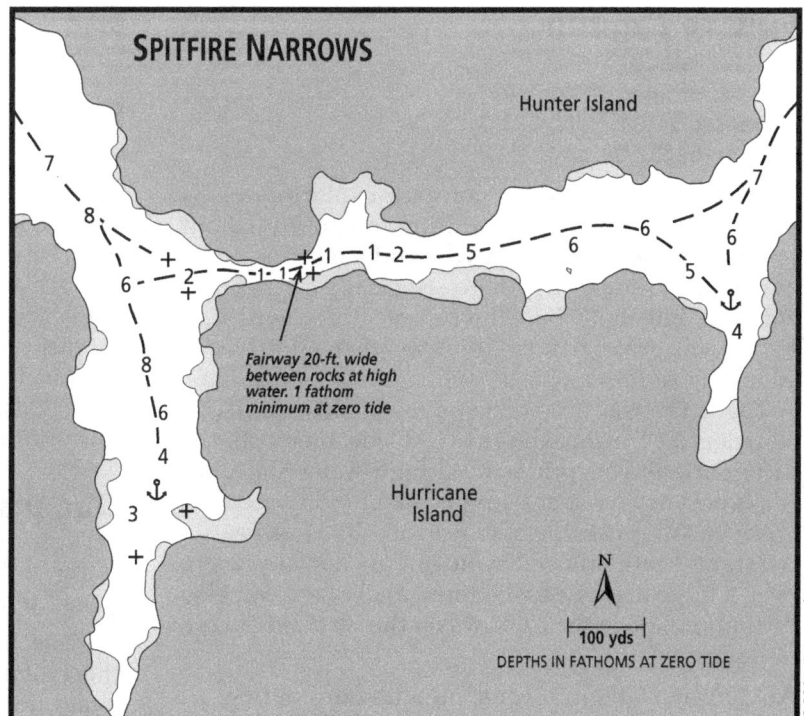

SPITFIRE NARROWS

Hunter Island

Fairway 20-ft. wide between rocks at high water. 1 fathom minimum at zero tide

Hurricane Island

N

100 yds

DEPTHS IN FATHOMS AT ZERO TIDE

©2024 Don and Réanne Douglass • Diagram not for navigation

Spitfire East Cove (Hunter Island)

0.3 mi E of Spitfire Narrows
Anchor: 51°51.60'N, 128°11.58'W

"Spitfire East Cove" is the name we've given the tiny cove east of the narrows on the south shore. This is a good place to anchor and wait for the correct tide conditions in Spitfire Channel. It is a well-sheltered anchorage although swinging room is restricted. If you plan to stay long, a stern tie to shore is advisable. Current in this channel, usually moderate, does not present a problem.

Anchor in 3 fathoms over mud and sand with good holding.

Spitfire West Cove

(Hunter Island)
0.1 mi W of Spitfire Narrows
Anchor: 51°51.49'N, 128°12.30'W

"Spitfire West Cove" is what we call the small cove on the south shore of Spitfire Channel's west side. This is a good place to reconnoiter the narrows or to wait for proper tidal conditions before proceeding.

Anchor in 4 to 6 fathoms over a gravel and rocky bottom; poor-to-fair holding.

Spitfire Lagoon

(Hunter Island)
0.5 NW of Spitfire Narrows
Entrance: 51°51.91'N, 128°12.69'W
Anchor: 51°52.06'N, 128°12.72'W

Spitfire Lagoon is a great place for exploring, viewing wildlife, rowing or paddling, or poking about on shore. Its entrance is narrow and a bit tricky, and current can flow swiftly here, especially on a spring ebb tide, but that's half the fun of it! You will find very good protection from all weather with lots of swinging room.

Favor the islet on your starboard side until you can identify the shoal on the west side, then split the difference as you proceed. At high-water slack entry is easy for most cruising boats of moderate size. Once you're inside the narrows, depths are a nearly-constant 3 fathoms, and you can anchor anywhere over a large area. Less-sheltered anchorage can also be found outside the narrows on the west side in 6-8 fathoms.

Anchor in 3 fathoms over sand with fair holding.

Goose Islands

Swordfish Bay (Hunter Island)

1 mi N of Spitfire Channel
Entrance: 51°52.53'N, 128°14.38'W

Swordfish Bay is a small bay with several tiny arms just made for exploring or hiding out. It offers shelter in stable weather to small boats and kayaks if the surge isn't bothersome. However, since Swordfish Bay is open to prevailing southwest swells, it is not to be trusted. During periods of southeast or southwest gales the seas are reported to break right into the entrance. The bottom of the bay appears to be rocky.

Superstition Point Cove (Hunter Island)

0.5 mi NE of Superstition Point
Entrance: 51°53.63'N, 128°14.92'W

The intricate cove and lagoon just north of Superstition Point is another place that appears to offer good exploring in fair weather. It has a remarkable beach, but because it is open to the west, large swells, chop, or surge can easily enter the cove. The low hills around this cove would make it of doubtful value in heavy weather. We prefer Kayak Cove just inside Cultus Sound, a half-mile northeast. (See below.)

Queens Sound (Goose Island)

Between Hunter and Goose islands
Entrance (S): 51°50.00'N, 128°22.00'W
Entrance (N): 52°01.75'N, 128°26.19'W

Queens Sound is a fascinating place and digital charts have made navigating the area considerably easier. In calm weather, the sound can be benign, and under such conditions kayaks, inflatables, and small boats cross over to the Goose Group. However, the weather can change quickly, becoming a nightmare if a southerly kicks up. Trying to return to protected waters on the east side of the sound under poor conditions is dangerous because of the many off-lying rocks and reefs which, with a southwest swell and wind, create an ugly lee shore. It can be particularly hazardous entering or exiting Cultus Sound when the 3-knot current is running.

Goose Group (Queens Sound)
Forms the W side of Queens Sound
Position: 51°56.00'N, 128°25.00'W

The Goose Islands, the westernmost islands within the Hakai Lúxvbálís Conservancy Area, receive the brunt of the storms that blow through Queens Sound. Windswept trees, polished silver snags, glistening beaches—some piled high with drift logs—show the effects of strong storm winds. The low-lying topography of the Goose Group is perfect for getting around by small boat and the area is particularly popular amongst kayakers. There is no fresh water in these islands; bring your own drinking water.

Watch the weather carefully, and monitor the weather channels for any sign of change in stable conditions. There is no safe storm anchorage for small craft in the Goose Group. Kayakers or people travelling in inflatables can carry their craft up to high, dry turf and make the best of it. The north side of Snipe Island has a lovely sand beach where kayakers can camp. The north tip of Goose Island has a beautiful sandy beach as well.

The only confirmed sea otter colony on the north coast has taken up residence around the Goose Group in recent years. Please do not disturb these wonderful, amusing mammals.

Goose Island Anchorage (Goose Island)
8.5 mi NW of Spitfire Channel
Entrance: 51°56.23'N, 128°25.20'W
Anchor: 51°55.90'N, 128°26.03'W

A visit to Goose Island Anchorage can be a rather lonely, sobering experience when blue skies turn to grey or fog rolls in. Stunted trees and the gentle, but ominous, surge are a constant reminder that you really are exposed to the forces of the Pacific Ocean. It's particularly unnerving when the tide rises and you watch the beach you've just walked on disappear under water.

You can anchor deep in the west or southwest corner of Goose Island Anchorage over a flat shallow

bottom during prevailing northwesterlies when seas are flat calm. Avoid the charted shoals and rocks. However, this is a poor site in any other weather and can be extremely bumpy. Small boats can anchor about 0.2 mile northwest of Gull Island, larger ones north of Gull Island.

Anchor in 3 to 4 fathoms over sand and mud, with occasional gravel and kelp; fair-to-good holding.

Cultus Sound
(Queens Sound)
1 mi NE of Superstition Pt.
Entrance (SW): 51°54.05'N, 128°15.10'W

The turn into Cultus Sound (when you're northbound) brings welcome calm water again and a choice of several fine anchor sites. One of the more popular, which we refer to as "Kayak Cove," is just inside the sound on the south shore.

Kayak Cove (Hunter Island)
1 mi NE of Superstition Pt.
Entrance: 51°54.01'N, 128°14.04'W
Anchor: 51°53.90'N, 128°13.97'W

Kayak Cove is well known to kayakers as a great haul-out place and campsite, and it probably has been used as a kayak and canoe base camp for centuries. The sandy beach—one of the best in these parts—is large, easy to land on, and well protected. Although some swell and surge can be felt here, especially in a strong Norwester, it is a safe place to anchor in any summer weather. The cove can accommodate several boats including a few big ones.

Anchor in 4 to 5 fathoms over sand with fair holding.

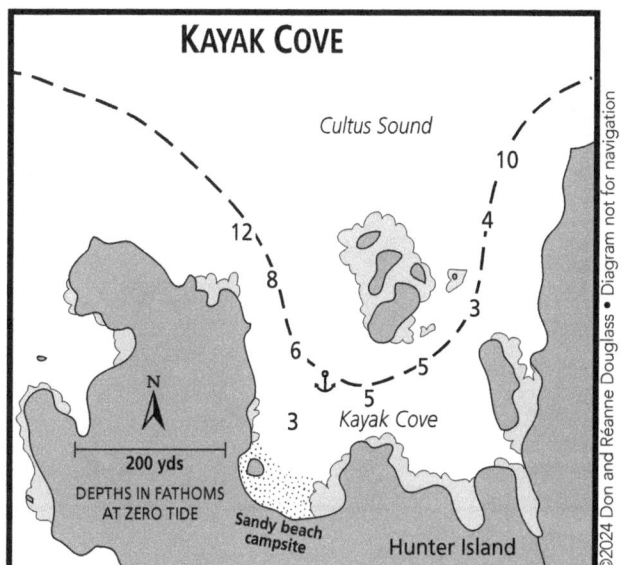

KAYAK COVE

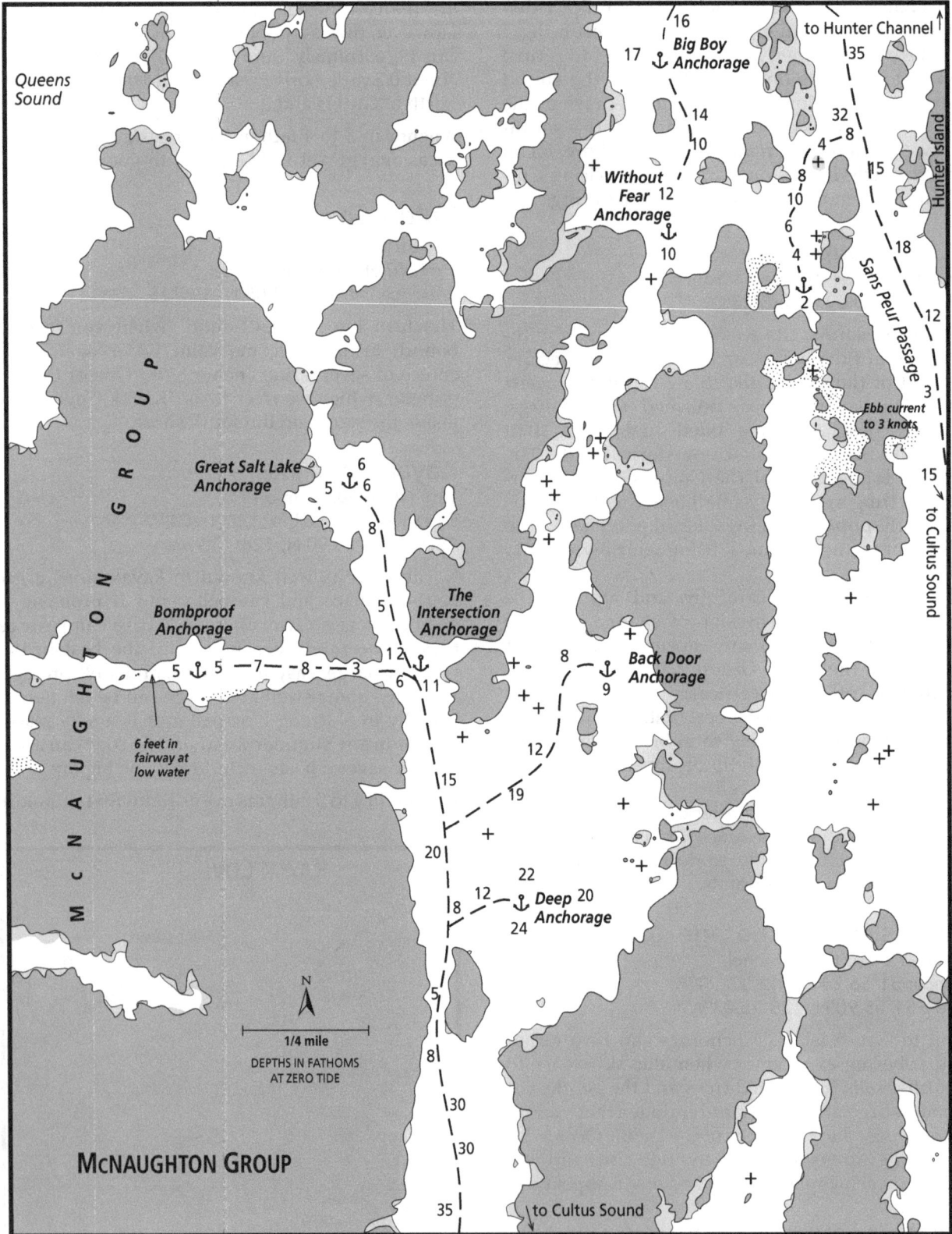

Queens
Sound

16
Big Boy
Anchorage
17

to Hunter Channel
35

14
10

32
4 8

15

8

Without
Fear 12
Anchorage

10
6

4

18

2

12

Sans Peur Passage

3

Ebb current
to 3 knots

M c N A U G H T O N   G R O U P

Great Salt Lake
Anchorage

6

5 6

8

5

15

The
Intersection
Anchorage

Bombproof
Anchorage

5 5 — 7 — 8 — 3
12
6 11

8

Back Door
Anchorage

9

6 feet in
fairway at
low water

12

19

15

20

8 12
22

Deep 20
Anchorage

24

N

5

1/4 mile
DEPTHS IN FATHOMS
AT ZERO TIDE

8

30

30

McNAUGHTON GROUP

35

to Cultus Sound

to Cultus Sound

Hunter Island

©2024 Don and Réanne Douglass • Diagram not for navigation

McNaughton Group Anchor Sites
(Queens Sound)
1.2 mi SW of Sans Peur Passage
Entrance: 51°54.65'N, 128°13.53'W

McNaughton Group Anchorage is a maze of narrow passages in a marine wilderness, many of which are great landlocked anchorages for cruising boats. You can choose a depth and swinging room to suit your purpose. All anchorages have good holding if your anchor is well set.

We rank the anchorages as follows:
1. **Bombproof Anchorage**: Anchor in 5 fathoms, 51°55.95'N, 128°14.38'W
2. **Great Salt Lake Anchorage**: Anchor in 7 fathoms, 51°56.29'N, 128°13.89'W
3. **Intersection Anchorage**: Anchor in 14 fathoms, 51°55.98'N, 128°13.70'W
4. **Back Door Anchorage**: Anchor in 10 fathoms, 51°55.93'N, 128°13.06'W
5. **Deep Anchorage**: Anchor in 24 fathoms, 51°55.52'N, 128°13.27'W
6. **Big Boy Anchorage** (Sans Peur Passage): Anchor: 51°57.18'N, 128°12.89'W; excellent shelter for larger boats over mud in 15-17 fathoms.

Cultus Bay (Hunter Island)
1.6 mi NE of Kayak Cove
Entrance: 51°54.75'N, 128°11.69'W
Anchor: 51°54.45'N, 128°11.66'W

Cultus Bay offers very good protection from southerly weather and is considered a safe place by fishing boats to stay during the summer. This is our name for the small unnamed bay 1.7 mile south of Sans Peur Passage. Avoid a mid-channel rock at its entrance and in the bay by favoring the west shore. A large lagoon to the east with several islets and an entrance that dries at 10 feet looks like an interesting place to explore by kayak. Avoid a large mid-channel rock in the middle of Cultus Sound. We anchor at the southeast corner of island (55) m where no southwest swell is felt. Cultus is a good base camp from which to explore this entire marvelous wilderness.

Anchor in 6 fathoms over mud with good holding.

Kinsman Inlet (Cultus Sound)
0.5 mi SE of Sans Peur Passage
Entrance: 51°55.87'N, 128°11.44'W

Kinsman Inlet is surrounded by low-lying land, and the water within the inlet is a typical muskeg brown with little turnover. It is perhaps best explored by a high-speed inflatable with due caution for its many rocks and shoals. The air is still and heavy with moisture. Kinsman Lagoon with its 10-knot rapids is truly wild!

Sans Peur Passage (Hunter Island)
Connects Cultus Sound & Hunter Channel
Entrance (S): 51°56.18'N, 128°12.04'W
Entrance (N): 51°57.39'N, 128°12.44'W
Anchor: 51°56.74'N, 128°12.52'W

Sans Peur ("without fear") Passage has moderately strong current and turbulence, but it can generally be transited on any stage of the tide. (See McNaughton Group diagram.) There is a small cove immediately west of the passage which is out of the current and can be used by small craft tucked deep in the south end, as indicated in the diagram. The bottom is irregular with marginal holding, so set your anchor well or use a shore tie. This is a nice, quiet landlocked place for one small boat to hide out. Boats much over 30 feet might want to check out the roomier anchorages called Without Fear and Big Boy, in the basin to the west, as indicated on the McNaughton Group diagram.

Anchor in 4 fathoms over sand and gravel with kelp; fair holding.

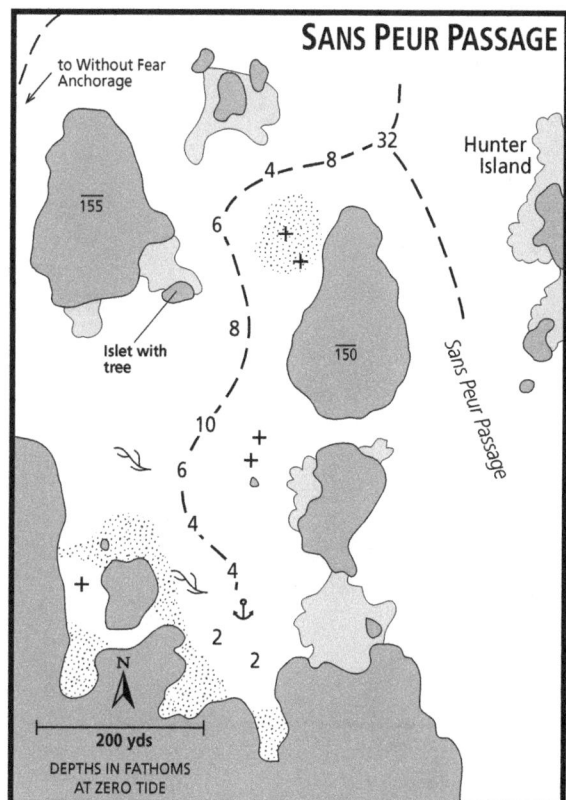

SANS PEUR PASSAGE

to Without Fear Anchorage

Hunter Island

155

Islet with tree

150

Sans Peur Passage

200 yds

DEPTHS IN FATHOMS AT ZERO TIDE

N

©2024 Don and Réanne Douglass • Diagram not for navigation

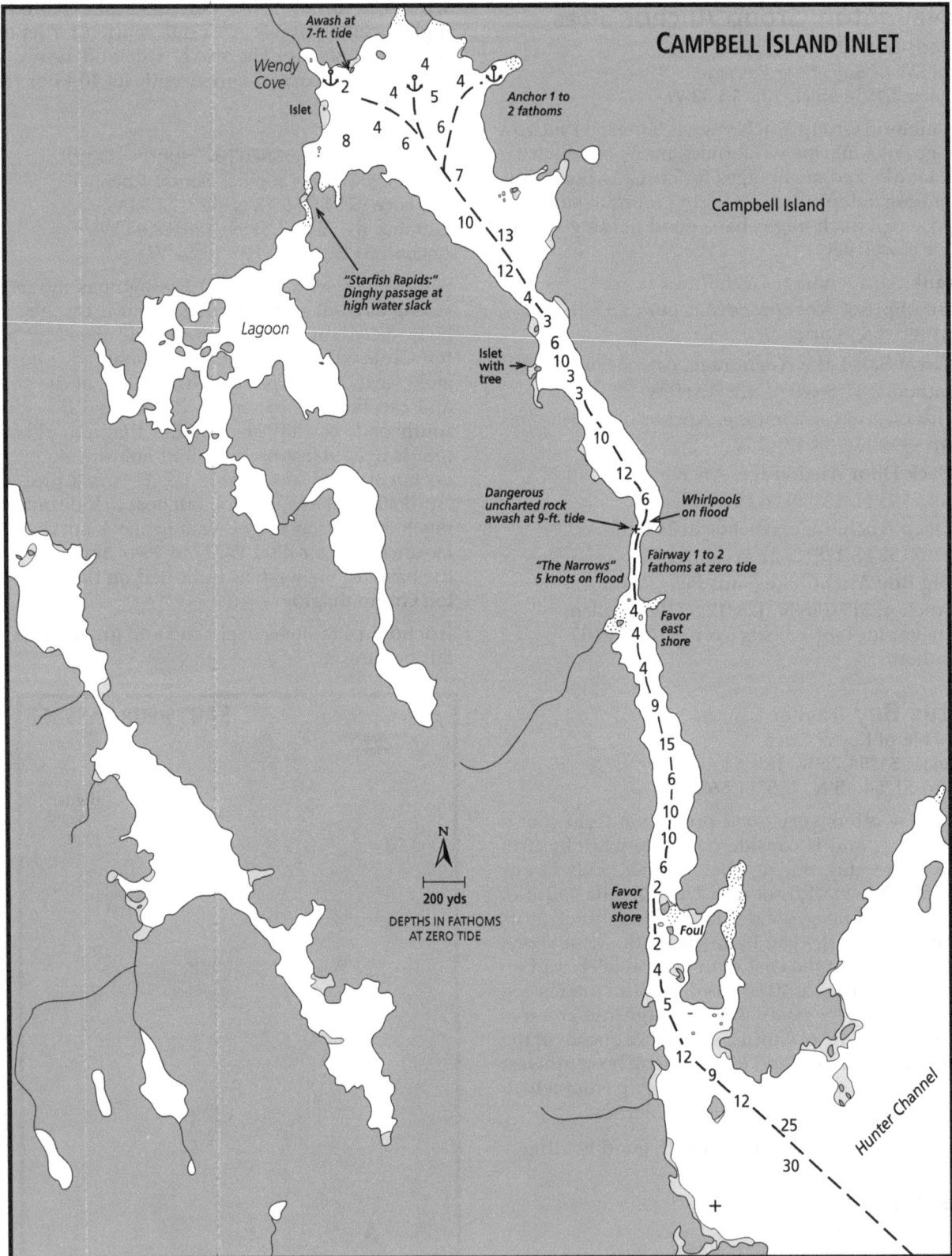

CAMPBELL ISLAND INLET

Awash at
7-ft. tide

Wendy
Cove

2

Islet

8   4

Anchor 1 to
2 fathoms

4   5   4

4

4

6

6

7

Campbell Island

10

13

12

4

3

6

"Starfish Rapids:"
Dinghy passage at
high water slack

Lagoon

Islet
with
tree

10

3

3

10

12

Dangerous
uncharted rock
awash at 9-ft. tide

6

Whirlpools
on flood

"The Narrows"
5 knots on flood

Fairway 1 to 2
fathoms at zero tide

4

4

Favor
east
shore

4

9

15

6

10

10

6

Favor
west
shore

2

2

Foul

4

5

N

12

200 yds

DEPTHS IN FATHOMS
AT ZERO TIDE

9

12

25

Hunter Channel

30

+

©2024 Don and Réanne Douglass • Diagram not for navigation

Hunter Channel (Hunter Island)
Connects Sans Peur Passage with Lama Passage
Entrance (S): 51°59.82'N, 128°11.18'W
Entrance (N): 52°04.83'N, 128°07.48'W

You can proceed north of Latta Island into Hunter Channel and directly to Bella Bella, or turn west and continue along the east side of Prince Group Islands, heading northwest to Raymond Passage via Brown Narrows; or for an intimate, highly sheltered route, pass east of Dodwell Island and island (44) m on its east shore and follow an intricate route west along the north shore of Dodwell Island.

Hunter Channel is the main channel connecting Queens Sound with Lama Passage and Bella Bella. Latta Island is just inside the north border of Hakai Lúxvbálís Conservancy Area, where the boundary turns east. Good protection can be found in Bob Bay and in the unnamed inlet on Campbell Island. At the south end of Hunter Channel there are moderate tide rips with collected flotsam as well as the first hint of the Pacific swell which pervades Queens Sound. These waters, now the Hakai Lúxvbálís Conservancy Area, are a perfect place to explore by kayak or small vessel.

Dodwell South Cove (Hunter Channel)
0.5 mi N of Latta Island
Entrance: 51°59.82'N, 128°13.75'W
Anchor: 51°59.83'N, 128°13.17'W

Scenic but indifferent anchorage can be taken in what we call "Dodwell South Cove." It is tiny, out of the current, and offers moderate protection from southerly weather. The west entrance is the preferred approach. Since this entrance is narrow and fringed with rocks and kelp on its south side, stay close to the southwest point of Dodwell Island and its south shore all the way in. The center of the cove is deep, with a depth of about 14 fathoms. Small boats using shore ties can find temporary anchorage in either the north-northwest nook or in the tiny notch in the island on the south side. Avoid all kelp patches, which mark submerged rocks.

Anchor, as you choose, between 3 and 14 fathoms over sand, mud and rocks; a stern tie to shore is helpful.

Dodwell North Cove (Dodwell Island)
Position: 52°00.49'N, 128°13.53'W

The well-protected cove in the northwest corner of Dodwell Island that we call "Dodwell North Cove" could provide shelter from any southerly weather; however, it's open to the prevailing northwest winds and afternoon chop. We have not used this cove; however, we have used the small cove in the center of the maze of islets 0.6 mile to the northeast and found it very well protected.

Maze Cove (Queens Sound)
0.2 mi NE of Dodwell Island
Entrance: 52°00.77'N, 128°12.95'W
Anchor: 52°00.93'N, 128°12.90'W

The maze of islets north and east of Dodwell Island form a tiny, intricate, smooth-water route from Hunter Channel to Queens Sound to the north. Depths are sometimes less than those indicated on the chart, but small boats can make a safe passage with alert bow lookouts and by approaching at slow speeds. We have anchored in what we call "Maze Cove" in the shallow, flat-bottom area to the northwest of island (61) m on the south side of Campbell Island. This is a calm, peaceful spot.

You can enter on either side of the treed islet but stay south of the rock that dries on about a 16-foot tide. When passing the northern tip of Dodwell Island, favor the south side of the channel to avoid the large underwater rock on the north side.

Anchor in 4 to 6 fathoms over mud with good holding.

Campbell Island Inlet (Hunter Channel)
4 mi N of Latta Island
Entrance: 52°02.95'N, 128°11.08'W
Anchor (Wendy Cove): 52°05.35'N, 128°12.71'W

The west side of Hunter Channel has a major unnamed inlet that leads 3-miles deep into Campbell Island, terminating in a lagoon. This inlet nearly divides the island in two. We refer to this anchorage as "Campbell Island Inlet." It is wild and made for intrepid explorers and recommended for small vessels only due to the narrows.

Seldom visited, the inlet provides excellent protection from all weather deep in its labyrinth and is a rare find for cruising boats that want solitude and wilderness. We found no sign of man here—no stumps, middens, cables, or pollution of any kind. There are signs of deer but no bear, and ravens and eagles abound. The lagoon receives saltwater on spring tides only.

Because the south end of Campbell Island is so low and flat, the inlet is easy to miss. You can enter from either side of the island located in the entrance, avoiding the reefs along the Hunter Channel side. The inlet narrows rapidly, and you should favor the west shore until you've passed the chain of treed islets which, while scenic, have foul water behind them. The bottom is irregular but deep until you reach the narrows, recognizable by the small islet on its west shore, with a big tree and rocks alongside. The narrows have strong currents, and if you don't want to enter, you can anchor south of the islet in 4 fathoms.

The narrows is a picturesque channel with minimum depths of 3 to 6 feet at zero tide. A rock, about 10 feet in length, awash on a 9-foot tide, lies crosswise to the channel on the west side at the north end of the narrows. This rock—dangerous because it extends about a third of the way into the narrow channel—is dark-colored and hard to see. During flood currents, the current glancing off the rock could easily set a boat toward the east shore.

Safe passage through the narrows is possible at or near high-water slack when there is less current and you can go dead-slow. We have traversed the narrows during the middle of a 10-foot tidal range and found 4 knots of flood in the narrows, with a stronger current adjacent to the north-end rock.

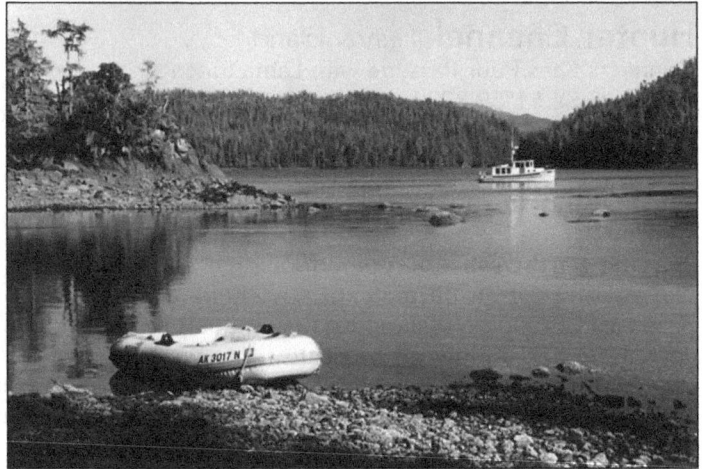

Campbell Island Inlet

North of the narrows, the bottom continues to be irregular, but it is fairly deep until you reach the large basin at the head of the inlet. This basin offers fine anchorage over a large area in 5 to 10 fathoms. (Avoid the charted reefs along shore.)

Small boats may want to use either the northwest

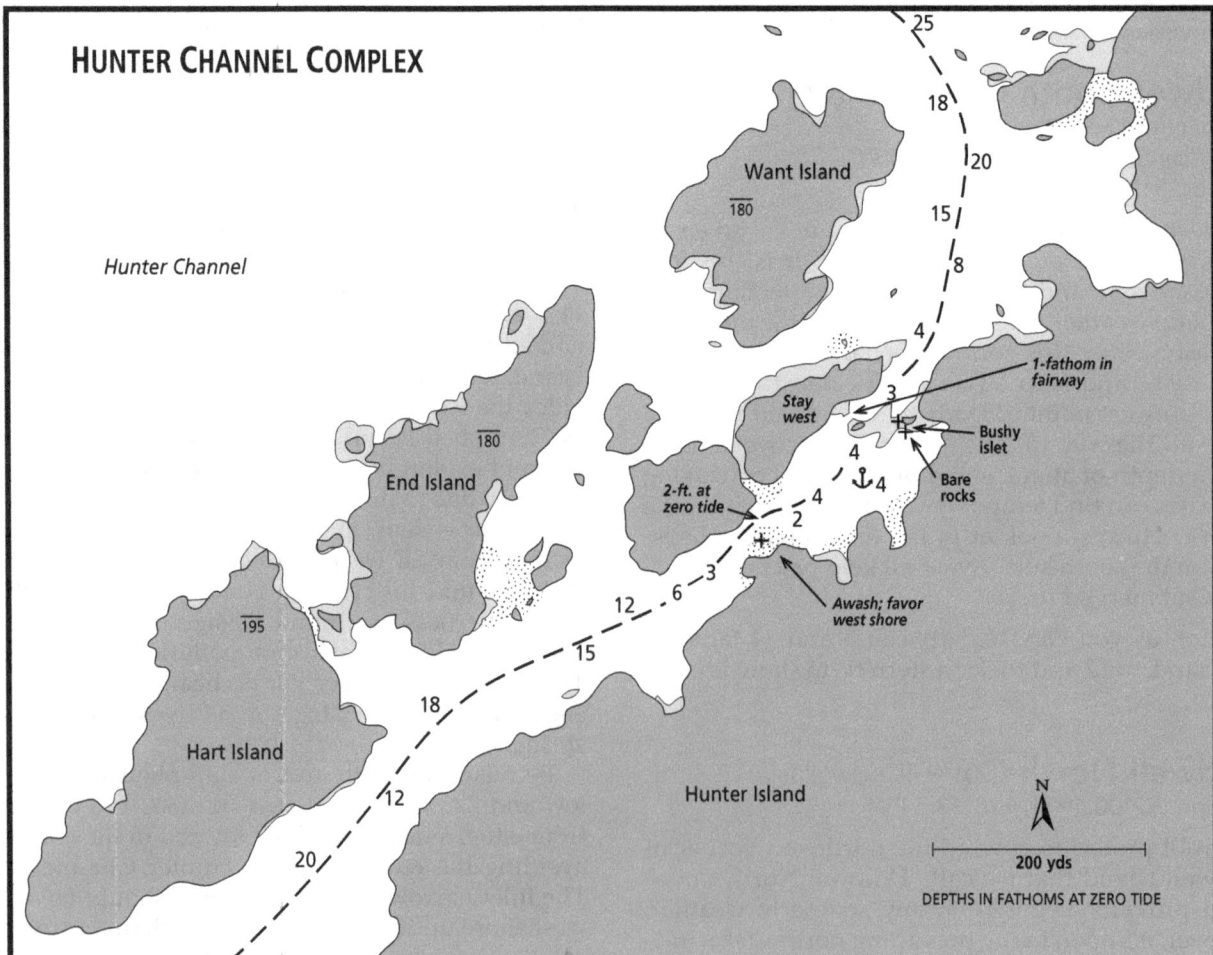

cove we call Wendy Cove (after our intrepid bow watch), or the east cove.

Boats using Wendy Cove should anchor on a line between the tall-treed islet and the east point to avoid a steep-to shelf; at low water, this shelf is a living aquarium, and a great place to study the interaction of Dungeness crabs, fingerlings, flounders, sea anemones, and eel grass.

Anchor (Wendy Cove) in 4 to 5 fathoms over a brownish-black, primordial, stinky mud that's thick with clamshells and debris; very good holding.

Hunter Channel Complex
6.5 mi S of Bella Bella
Entrance (S): 52°02.47'N, 128°09.44'W
Entrance (N): 52°03.60'N, 128°07.90'W
Anchor: 52°03.07'N, 128°08.05'W

At the north end of Hunter Channel, due east of the entrance to Campbell Inlet, lies a complex of islands that create sheltered waters. Southwest winds in Hunter Channel sometimes blow through this complex, but no chop enters. The innermost basin, formed by Hunter Island and two small unnamed islands, can provide good anchorage for two or three small boats in a 4-fathom hole. This is a good area for sportfishing or exploring by dinghy or kayak.

The south entrance can be entered keeping Hart Island to port and favoring the Hunter Island shore until you reach the southernmost unnamed island east of End Island. Hug the east shore of this unnamed island to avoid a mid-channel-rock awash. The fairway is about 2 feet deep at zero tide.

For the north entrance, pass Want Island to starboard and close to the Hunter Island shore. (The basin east of Want Island has an irregular bottom.) Approach the northernmost unnamed island, avoiding rocks that bare on a 2-foot tide off its north end. Enter the narrow channel, favoring the northernmost unnamed island on your starboard. The fairway has a minimum of about one fathom west of the bushy islet and the rocks on its west side. This is a remote hideaway for small boats using careful piloting.

Anchor in 4 fathoms over sand and mud with some rocks; fair-to-good holding.

Bob Bay (Hunter Channel)
1 mi W of Lizzie Cove
Entrance: 52°03.95'N, 128°07.06'W
Anchor (S): 52°03.23'N, 128°06.49'W

Bob Bay is a long narrow bay offering good protection from southerly weather; the prevailing winds die out before reaching the head of the bay. Spindly

Réanne enjoying a sunny day on the west coast

cedars, thick with moss, overhang the rocky shore—scenery typical of the flat land and thick forests found in Queens Sound to the west.

Small boats can find temporary shelter on the north side of the island north of Spire Point in 2 fathoms with limited swinging room. Larger boats and those wanting more protection can proceed to the head of the bay and anchor on or near the shoal off the east shore. Avoid the cluster of rocks near the small peninsula.

Anchor in 2 fathoms (south end) over gravel and small rock with iridescent seaweed; poor-to-good holding depending on set.

Admiral Group
(Queens Sound)
1.5 mi NW of Dodwell Island
Position: 52°01.24'N, 128°15.45'W

Northward from Dodwell Island you can proceed more or less directly toward the upper end of Athabaskan Island headed for Brown Narrows and Raymond Passage. Or turn northeast and work your way toward Redford Point, or follow the smooth-water route which turns north a half-mile northwest of Dodwell Island and proceed along the west Campbell Island shore.

Wide Awake Cove (Campbell Island)
1.2 mi SE of Piddington Island
Entrance: 52°02.96'N, 128°14.67'W
Anchor: 52°02.75'N, 128°14.44'W

"Wide Awake Cove" is our name for the secure anchor site on the Campbell Island shore, 1.2 miles southeast of Piddington Island and 2.2 miles east of the north end of Athabaskan Island.

We found good shelter here from gale-force winds that were blowing down the coast on a clear day, when thermal heating over the mainland was sucking cooler marine air eastward. The cove should be equally as good in southeast or southwest gales.

As indicated on the chart, the entrance to the cove is intricate and dangerous unless you carefully identify and avoid the rocks. Upon entering, first favor the islet with trees located on the east side of the entrance and continue southeast until you sight the large, light-colored, underwater rock that dries at about 9 feet. Turn west into the cove, avoiding the rocky ledge that extends east about 100 feet from the trees, and tuck in behind the point. You may want to use a stern tie to assure a bombproof anchorage in this landlocked cove. Avoid the tiny lagoon at the south end of the cove—it is foul. Loons, eagles, and seals will entertain you as gusts of wind blow by outside.

Anchor in 5 fathoms over sand with small rocks; good holding.

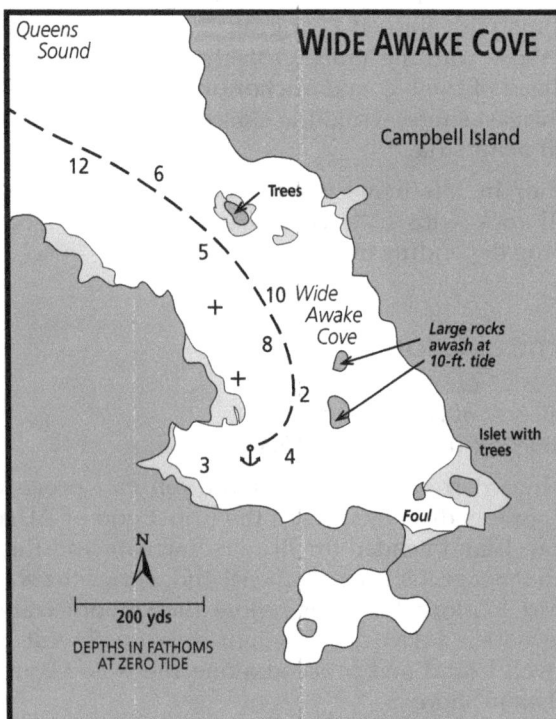

Pictograph Passage (Piddington Island)
Between Campbell & Piddington islands
Entrance (N): 52°04.95'N, 128°14.85'W
The channel east of Piddington Island is encumbered with islands and rocks at its south end.

Continue north from Wide Awake Cove, through the islets and reefs along Campbell Island shore. At the north end of these islands and reefs you can see some rock paintings of faces and hands executed in red ochre—hence our name "Pictograph Passage." These paintings are located above waterline approximately 1 mile south of Redford Point on Campbell Island.

End of the World Inlet (Campbell Island)
2 mi N of Wide Awake Cove
Entrance: 52°04.97'N, 128°14.34'W

From Redford Point, a narrow, 2.5-mile long inlet proceeds southeast, deep into Campbell Island. We call this "End of the World Inlet" due to its remoteness and windswept appearance. Except for four narrows with shallow bars, the inlet is deep. At the first narrows avoid the "unicorn" tree, a silver snag projecting from the east shore at a 45° angle. Cedar trees extend over the water, adding an eerie quality as you penetrate this world of stillness and mystery. The lagoon in Campbell Inlet reaches to within 0.25 mile of End of the World Inlet.

Peter Bay (Piddington Island)
2 mi SE of Raymond Passage
Entrance (NE): 52°06.22'N, 128°17.11'W
Anchor: 52°04.55'N, 128°17.07'W

Peter Bay is reported to offer good protection from southeast winds deep in the south end of the bay. Its northwest entrance is easy to use if you favor the west shore, avoiding a string of rocks and reefs that extend south from island (210). We found a much shallower and more intimate anchor site suitable for small craft in the small channel between two unnamed islands 2 to 4 fathoms.

Anchor in about 12 fathoms over mud with very good holding.

Hochstader Basin (Campbell Island)
1.2 mi SE of Raymond Passage
Entrance: 52°06.38'N, 128°16.94'W

Hochstader Basin, which penetrates deep into Campbell Island, is too deep for convenient anchoring except along its margins; its entrance is confusing and very shallow. For secure anchorage use Hochstader Cove.

Hochstader Cove (Campbell Island)
0.9 mi NE Hochstader entrance
Entrance: 52°06.90'N, 128°15.87'W
Anchor: 52°06.77'N, 128°15.79'W

"Hochstader Cove" is what we call the small, land-locked cove on the east shore of the channel that leads into Hochstader Basin. The cove provides very good shelter from all weather, but it is poorly charted, so use caution.

The route into the outermost entrance follows the east shore of island (200) in a fairway of 9 fathoms minimum. Continue north, favoring the west shore to avoid a rock pile in the center of the channel. To the west of the rock pile, the fairway carries a minimum of 6 fathoms. Before entering the basin narrows, turn east. The entrance to the cove lies 0.4 mile northeast of the rock pile and is 50 to 60 feet wide, with a minimum depth of 2 fathoms in its fairway. Turn south into the cove and anchor over a 2- to 3-fathom bottom, avoiding a large flat rock in the western part of the cove which dries on a 3-foot tide—the rock is covered with purple and ochre sea stars. Three or four boats can anchor here; however, there isn't any good landing beach.

Anchor in 2 to 3 fathoms over brown mud and clamshells; very good holding.

Raymond Passage (Campbell Island)
1.1 mi W of Kynumpt Harbour
Entrance (S): 52°07.16'N, 128°18.46'W
Entrance (N): 52°12.97'N, 128°11.66'W

Raymond Passage (via Codfish Passage) is the easiest and quickest way to get to the Bella Bella area from

Island Roamer *in Cultus Sound*

the north end of Queens Sound. If you're looking for shelter from northwest winds, consider the two tiny coves just north of Kingsley Point; in south winds, the Raymond Passage Cove, east of the north end of Matilda Island.

Raymond Passage Cove (Campbell Island)
0.25 mi E of Matilda Island
Anchor: 52°07.12'N, 128°17.20'W

"Raymond Passage Cove" is the name we give to this tiny cove that provides very good protection for a small boat in southeast weather—the lack of drift logs on its shore indicate its safety. The cove is small with limited swinging room. If strong westerlies pose a problem, consider the tiny Kingsley Point Coves on the west side of Raymond Passage.

Anchor in about 4 fathoms over sand and shells; fair-to-good holding.

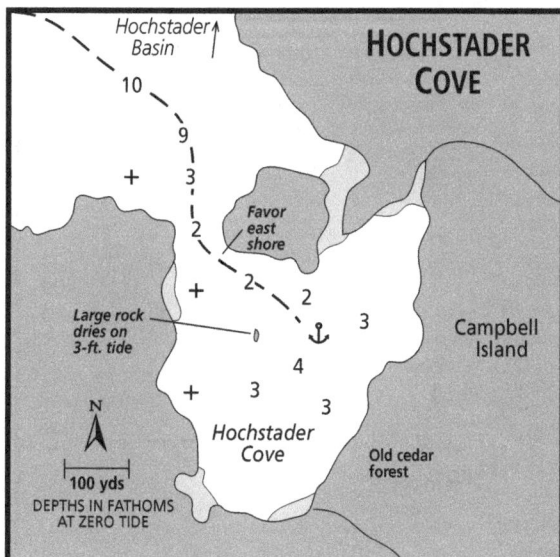

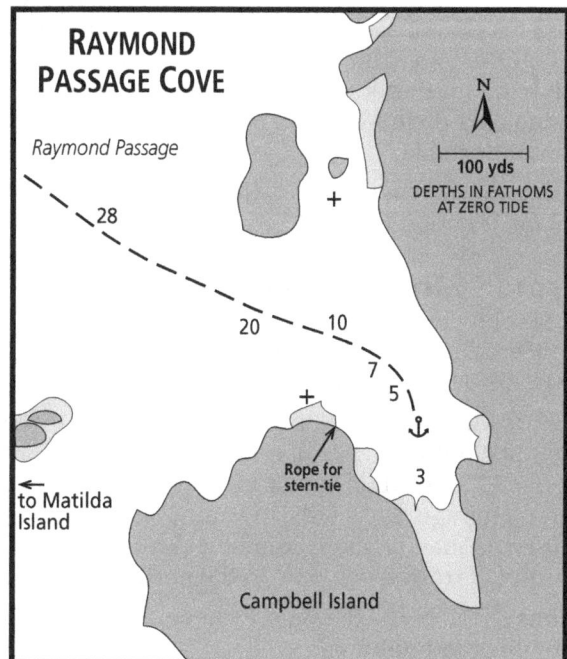

Kingsley Point Coves (Horsfall Island)
0.75 mi NW of Matilda Island
Entrance (S cove): 52°07.55'N, 128°18.63'W
Entrance (N cove): 52°07.65'N, 128°18.55'W

The first tiny cove north of Kingsley Point (south cove) is essentially landlocked, affording very good protection for small boats in most weather. However, entering can be difficult and dangerous, due to several drying rocks. Only small boats should attempt it—and then preferably near low water when you can clearly identify the entrance reefs. Larger boats can easily find protection from northwest winds in Cundall Bay, 1.9 miles north, where the water is deeper and the entrance more straight forward. Entering the south cove, avoid the rock close to the west shore that dries near 12 feet, a zero-tide reef in the southeast corner of the bay, and a reef south of the entrance reef.

The fairway leads through a narrow channel, 35 feet wide, between the large light-colored reef that dries on about a 4- or 5-foot tide, and the rock that projects from the southwest corner of the island at the north side of the entrance. Minimum depth in the fairway is about 10 feet at zero tide.

Anchor (south cove) in 3 fathoms over a bottom of brown mud and shells with small rocks; good holding.

The second cove north of Kingsley Point (north cove) is much easier to enter and affords good protection for small boats when northwest winds are howling. Avoid a rocky complex along the north shore by favoring the south shore until you're well inside the cove. This cove is easy to enter and exit and affords good protection from northwest winds. We have used both of these small coves when gales were blowing outside in Milbanke Sound and found them quite comfortable.

Anchor (north cove) in 3 fathoms over sand and shell; fair-to-good holding.

Norman Morrison Bay (Campbell Island)
1 mi SE of Kynumpt Hbr
Entrance: 52°12.09'N, 128°11.61'W
Anchor: 52°11.47'N, 128°10.63'W

Norman Morrison Bay is located at the north entrance of Raymond Passage just south of Seaforth Channel. The southernmost arm of the bay offers good anchorage, especially in southeast storms, but small boats may be more comfortable at the head of Kynumpt Harbour, one mile to the north.

Anchor in 12 to 15 fathoms over mud, gravel and shell with good holding.

Joassa Channel
(Horsfall Island)
W of Raymond Channel
Entrance (S): 52°07.33'N, 128°18.97'W

Joassa Channel is a scenic, smooth-water route that leads from upper Queens Sound to Seaforth Channel. Rait Narrows, lying at the upper end of Joassa, while not particularly difficult, should not be attempted by larger boats with limited maneuvering or by skippers who lack experience transiting narrows or fast-moving waters.

Boddy Narrows
(Joassa Channel)
5 mi S of Rait Narrows
Entrance (S): 52°07.33'N, 128°18.97'W

Boddy Narrows is the south entrance to Joassa Channel, and the rocks at the turning point, 0.5 mile north of Reba Point are a frequent haul-out place for seals. Southeast winds funneling through Boddy Narrows have sometimes been recorded at over 100 knots, while just a few miles away, reported velocity was 60 knots. Protection can be found in the cove just west of Reba Point.

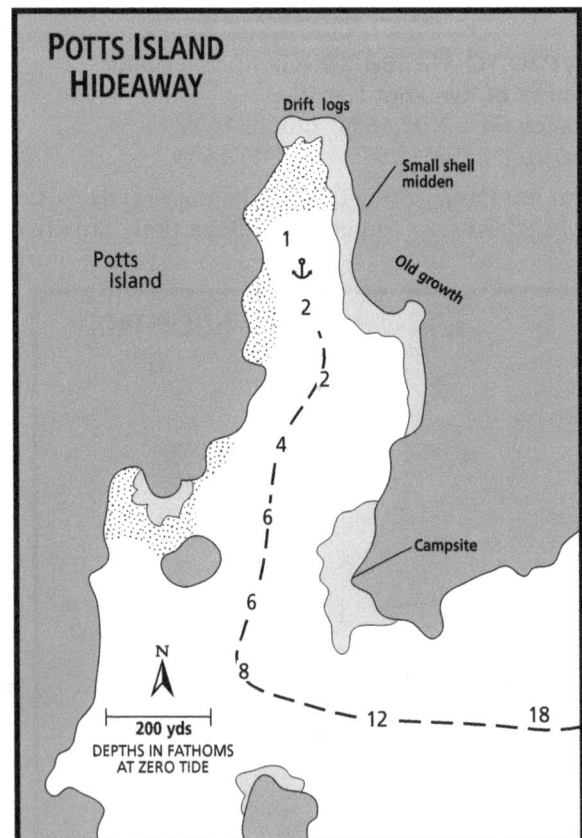

POTTS ISLAND HIDEAWAY

Baidarka *at anchor*

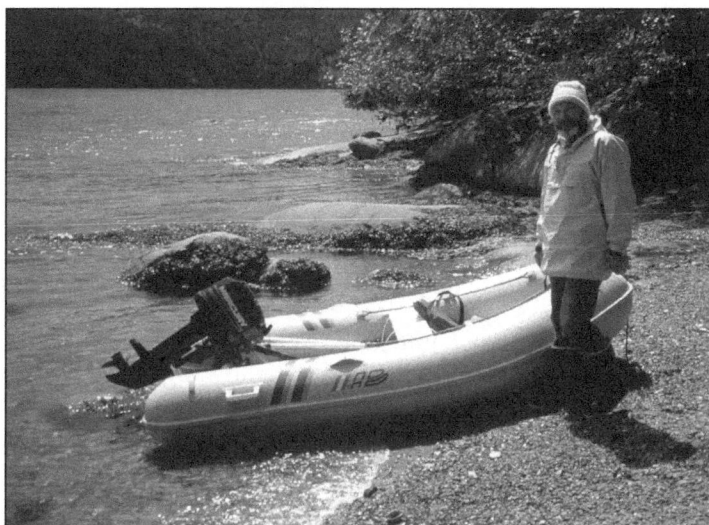

Baidarka's *crewman John Leone searching for petroglyphs*

Potts Island Hideaway (Joassa Channel)

4.3 mi SW of Rait Narrows
Entrance: 52°08.52'N, 128°19.98'W
Anchor: 52°08.61'N, 128°20.52'W

"Potts Island Hideaway" is our name for the cove in Louise Channel North to the west of Boddy Narrows. The cove makes a good lunch stop or an overnight stay in fair weather. It is partially exposed to the south but it would take a good blow to affect the cove from that direction. As you leave Boddy Narrows, you must work your way carefully though a rocky patch in order to enter this cove. Despite its trickiness, the cove is centrally located. It has a small beach and campsite, and can be quite comfortable in prevailing northwesterlies. Swinging room is limited and a shore tie can be useful.

Louise Channel Narrows is blocked to all but skiffs at high water.

Anchor in 2 fathoms over sand and mud with good holding.

Reba Point Cove (Potts Island)

0.1 mi W of Reba Pt.
Entrance: 52°09.17'N, 128°20.43'W
Anchor: 52°09.03'N, 128°20.45'W

Reba Point Cove, immediately west of Reba Point, is a small indentation in Potts Island's east shore reported to offer protection for small boats from southeast winds. Seals haul out on the various reefs and rocks in the vicinity of Reba Point.

Anchor in 12 fathoms over a reportedly good bottom.

The Small Boat People

They travel by day, close to the land. At night they haul their frail little boats up on the beach and light fires of driftwood and bark. For years we knew they were there. We stumbled on their campsites, on those magical circles of stones in the moss. On sandy beaches we found their mysterious markings still not erased by the tide, as though they had fled at our coming.

And then one morning they rounded the point in a steamy calm, emerging from the morning mist. Their boats were long and sleek, open to the sun and the rain, driven by oars in delicate frames.

Kayakers and rowers, the sailors of very small boats, travel in an intimate way, learning each indent and point, every outcropping, rock, and overhung tree. Those marks in the sand are the tracks of their keels. The beaten-down patches of moss were their beds for the night.

They're friendly folk, the small boat people. They'll gladly let you look inside their small boats. They'll spend hours telling of their travels and adventures. If they seem elusive and shy, it's because they're not used to being seen. Two of them in a boat like a peashell told us they used to wave at everyone they saw. But the only people who ever waved back were lost and needed rescuing.

Now we don't pass them at sea without waving. We never meet them on shore without stopping to talk. And we've learned a bit of the lore, a bit of the wisdom of the Small Boat People.

—by Iain Lawrence,
author of *Sea Stories of the Inside Passage*

Rait Narrows, South Cove (Horsfall Isl.)

0.4 mi S of Rait Narrows
Entrance: 52°12.36'N, 128°17.36'W
Anchor (S cove): 52°12.03'N, 128° 16.93'W

Immediately southeast of Rait Narrows there is a deep cove that offers very good protection in all weather. Avoid several rocks on the south shore awash on a 14- to 15-foot tide. This is a good place to wait for proper tidal conditions in the narrows on a northbound passage.

Small boats can tuck into a nook on the north side of this cove and anchor with a stern tie to shore in a calm, quiet setting. The entrance into the nook carries a depth of about 3 feet at zero tide with a little over 6 feet in its center. Eelgrass growing in the channel makes entering appear more difficult than it really is.

Anchor (south cove) in 5 to 7 fathoms over a relatively flat, mixed bottom; fair holding.

Anchor (nook) in 1 fathom over sand, mud, and eel grass; fair holding.

Rait Narrows (Joassa Channel)

1.3 mi S of Dundivan Inlet
Entrance (S): 52°12.46'N, 128°17.35'W
Entrance (N): 52°13.05'N, 128°16.46'W

Rait Narrows is a picturesque passage that can serve as either the finale or the overture for a cruise through beautiful Queens Sound. Moderate currents through

Rait Narrows, north entrance with rock showing

Rait Narrows appear to flow in a direction determined as much by outside wind as by the tide. (We've seen the current reverse one or two hours after high or low water.)

Before you enter the narrows, determine the direction and strength of the current in order to gauge its impact on your maneuverability. You may want to sound a horn or announce your presence on Channel 16 before entering Rait Narrows since there is little passing room. Avoid the submerged rocks on the southwest side of the channel south of the south entrance.

The fairway in the narrows has a minimum depth of about 3 fathoms just south of the small dog-leg near the north end of the narrows where a bushy islet and large rock extend nearly to mid-channel from the west shore. This rock dries at about 14 feet so it is easy to identify. Overhanging trees line much of the narrows, and there is seldom any chop through here.

Lockhart Bay

(Dundivan Inlet)
S end of Inlet
Entrance: 52°12.55'N, 128°15.61'W
Anchor: 52°12.31'N, 128°15.97'W

Lockhart Bay, at the north end of Rait Narrows, offers good shelter for larger boats waiting to enter the narrows. For small boats, temporary anchorage with good shelter from all weather can be found at the head of the cove southwest of Penny Point. Swinging room is limited and a stern tie is useful if you stay any length of time. (Lockhart Bay is also covered in Chapter 3.)

Anchor in 2 to 3 fathoms over sand and mud with good holding.

RAIT NARROWS SOUTH COVE

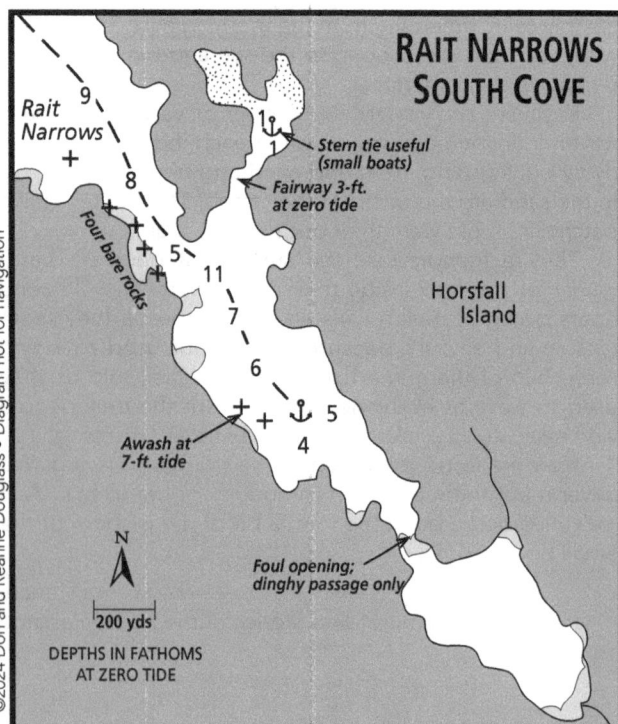

Rait Narrows

Stryker Nook, 1.5 miles north of Alleyne Island, is the small, well-protected cove off the bottom of Stryker Island. (It is located behind the island which, on the chart, looks like water wings.) Although the cove is somewhat difficult to enter, its security and scenic views through the "windows" to the west make it one of our favorites.

From Alleyne Island, turn north along its west shore and continue generally true north for 1.6 miles. Avoid the dangerous isolated rock 300 yards southeast of the water-wing island

Favor the east shore until you reach the top of "water wings" island, then turn southwest toward the islets which form the "windows." Minimum depth in the narrows is about 3 fathoms. Anchor as depth and swinging room allow. Small boats can anchor off the head of the cove and use a stern tie for a happy, bombproof sleep.

Anchor in 2 fathoms over mud and shells with good holding.

Tribal Group (Queens Sound)
2 mi SW of Piddington Island
Entrance (N): 52°03.46'N, 128°18.72'W

The Tribal Group, a good jumping off point for boats wishing to head to Goose Islands, is interesting in its own right. The waters are largely sheltered although strong currents and concentrated patches of logs and driftwood can be encountered. Small Iroquois Cove on the north side of Iroquois Island makes a good anchorage from which to explore the region.

Iroquois Cove (Tribal Group)
0.5 mi W of Athabaskan Island
Entrance: 52°02.71'N, 128°18.94'W
Anchor: 52°02.53'N, 128°19.21'W

Two small, unnamed islands off the north side of Iroquois Island form a well sheltered cove that we call "Iroquois Cove." This cove lies in the basin between the three islands. The east entrance to the cove is choked with kelp and may be foul. The north entrance is clear, but you must avoid the rocks and reefs upon entering. The bottom is irregular, and a shore tie can effectively be used on the west side of the basin. Anchor in the cove just north of the high-water kayak passage to the west.

Anchor in about 8 fathoms over a mixed bottom; fair holding with a well-set anchor.

Stryker Nook (Stryker Island)
1.1 mi E of Codfish Passage
Entrance: 52°05.88'N, 128°20.36'W
Anchor: 52°06.03'N, 128°20.66'W

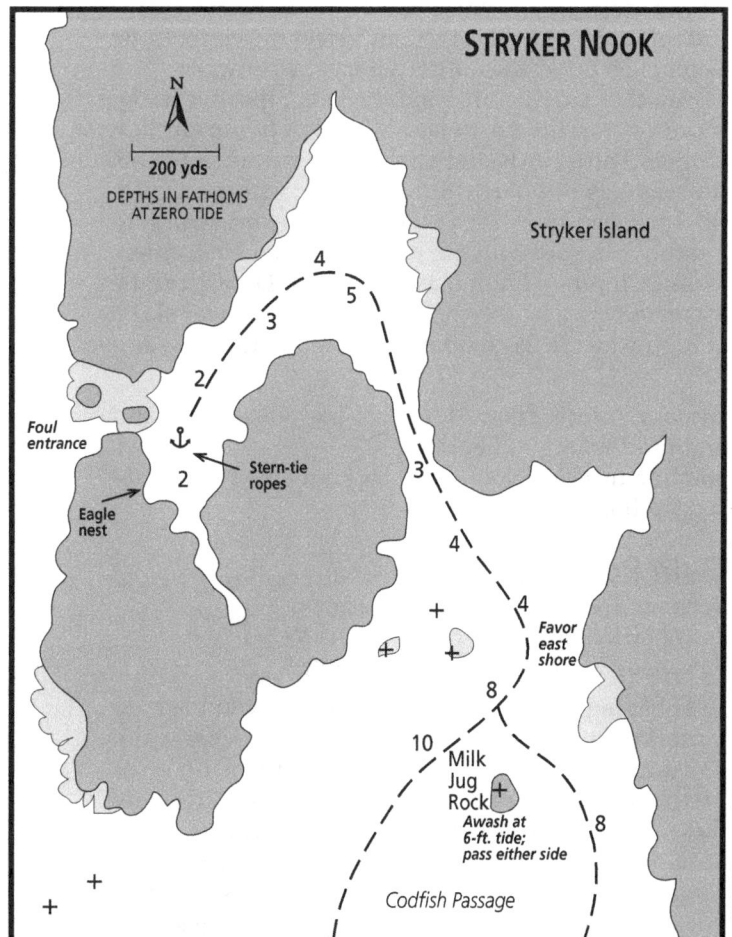

STRYKER NOOK

N

200 yds

DEPTHS IN FATHOMS
AT ZERO TIDE

Stryker Island

4
5
3
2
2
Foul entrance
Stern-tie ropes
2
3
Eagle nest
4
4
Favor east shore
8
10
Milk Jug Rock
Awash at 6-ft. tide; pass either side
8
Codfish Passage

©2024 Don and Réanne Douglass • Diagram not for navigation

Thompson Bay & Little Thompson

(Thompson Bay)
1 mi E of Cree Pt.
Entrance: 52°09.70'N, 128°20.79'W
Anchor (Little Thompson): 52°09.34'N, 128°20.87'W
Anchor ("The Nook"): 52°09.97'N, 128°21.17'W

Thompson Bay and Little Thompson, located at the north end of Thompson Bay, provide sheltered anchorage for large and small craft respectively. Little Thompson is the local name for the area north of the three islands in the northeast corner of Thompson Bay, deep in the labyrinth at the northwest corner of Potts Island. The entrance to both anchor sites starts at the north end of Thompson Bay, avoiding the mid-channel rock east of Cree Point and entering Little Thompson. Large vessels can find anchorage here in mostly very deep water. Small boats will find more suitable anchorage by continuing northeast then turning east, before circling south into the indent in Potts Island. As you turn south, avoid the islets and rocks by favoring the east shore and then avoid the rocks on the east shore as you enter the inner basin. This is suitable only for boats less than 35 feet in length. Little Thompson Cove is secure from most weather.

Another small craft anchor site is reported in the small cove at the north end of Little Thompson that indents Dufferin Island shore. The entrance to this tiny nook is littered with rocks and requires a careful approach near high water. This cove has a 2- to 3-fathom depth. The far north channel that enters Joassa Channel, known as "The Back Door," can be traversed only by dinghies, kayaks and power skiffs at high water; this channel is choked with rocks and kelp.

Anchor (Little Thompson) in 5 fathoms over sand and mud with good holding.
Anchor in (The Nook) in 2 fathoms over an unrecorded bottom.

Gale Passage (Seaforth Channel)

Between Dufferin and Athlone islands
Entrance (N): 52°14.46'N, 128°22.40'W
Entrance (S): 52°09.61'N. 128°22.90'W

Gale Passage should be avoided unless you have experience and equipment for wilderness, whitewater kayaking or high-speed inflatables. If you do enter the passage, plan plenty of time to reconnoiter both the north and south rapids and determine when high-water slack occurs in order to wait for proper conditions before attempting a transit. A steep tidal fall 6 feet high is reported at the rapids during spring tides. This should be considered serious wilderness exploration.

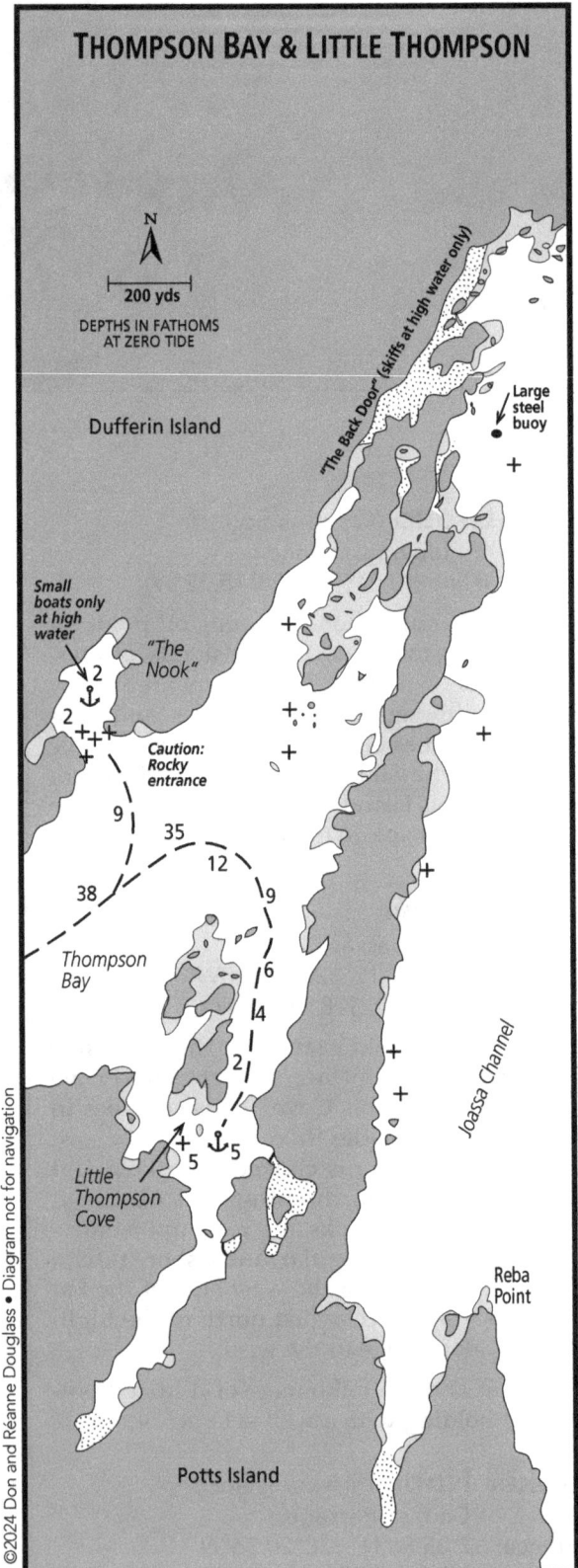

THOMPSON BAY & LITTLE THOMPSON

N

200 yds

DEPTHS IN FATHOMS
AT ZERO TIDE

Dufferin Island

"The Back Door" (skiffs at high water only)

Large steel buoy

Small boats only at high water

"The Nook"

Caution: Rocky entrance

Thompson Bay

Little Thompson Cove

Joassa Channel

Reba Point

Potts Island

©2024 Don and Réanne Douglass • Diagram not for navigation

Gale Passage Landlocked South Cove

1.7 mi NW of Cree Pt.
Position: 52°10.94'N, 128°23.12'W

A well-sheltered, but poorly charted anchor site for intrepid explorers is reported to lie just south of the south rapids in Gale Passage. To reach this cove requires transiting an intricate and narrow passage with mid-channel rocks. Great caution and skill are necessary. This is a site where small craft can observe the rapids and perhaps explore the inner basin, but little is known about it. There may also be a similar anchor site at the north entrance. At this time, we have no local knowledge to offer. Fast water flows (see tidal fall above) among the islets and rocks, making maneuvering dangerous or impossible. A large-scale chart of this area is not currently available.

Note: Saint Johns Harbour, on the west side of Athlone Island, which fronts Milbanke Sound, is discussed in Chapter 7.

Hakai Passage looking north

Ivory Island Light Station on Seaforth Channel overlooking Milbank Sound

The Discovery Coast:
Burke Channel, Dean Channel, and Ocean Falls to Spiller Channel

5

FIORDLAND

53°N
50'
40'
30'
20'
10'
52°N
50'

Kimsquit River
Kimsquit Bay
Dean River
Bolin Bay
Mathieson Narrows
Sheep Passage
Windy Bay
Waterfall
Culpepper Lagoon
Kynoch Inlet
Griffin Passage
Purcell Rock
Skowquiltz Bay
Carlson Inlet
Mathieson Channel
Spiller Inlet
Ellerslie Lagoon
Ellerslie Lake
Nascall Bay
Rescue Bay
Nash Passage
Neck*s* of the Roscoe
Eucott Bay
Brynelson Bay
Arthur T. Cove
Links Lake
Cascade Inlet
Bachelor Bay
Neekas Cove
Roscoe Inlet
Elcho Hbr
SIR ALEXANDER MACKENZIE PARK
Labouchere Channel
Mesachie Nose
Green Bay
Don Peninsula
Emily Bay
Florence Penin.
Briggs Inlet & Lagoon
Yeo I.
Clatse Bay
Beaumont Cove
OCEAN FALLS
North Bentinck Arm
Bullock Channel
Cousins Inlet
Wallace Bay
BELLA COOLA
Whiskey Bay
Neo Cove
Wigham Cove
Return Channel
Troup Narrows
Windy Bay
Spiller Channel
Raven Cove
Tankeeah Channel
Dean Channel
King Island
Croydon Bay
Chatfield I.
Troup Pass
Font Bay
Lagoon Cove
Jenny Inlet
Rattenbury Pt.
Burke Channel
Seaforth Channel
Kynumpt Hbr
Sanctuary
Cunningham I.
Gunboat Lagoon Cove
Cathedral Point Cove
BELLA BELLA
Gunboat Passage
Tallheo Hot Springs
South Bentinck Arm
McLoughlin Bay
SHEARWATER
Denny I.
Evans Inlet
Campbell I.
Canal Bight
Long Point Cove
Larso Bay
Lama Passage
Fancy Cove
CODVILLE LAGOON M.P.
Haakswold Point
Kwatna Inlet
Ada Cove
Jane Cove
Lizzie Cove
Fisher Channel
Kisameet Bay
Restoration Bay
Hunter Island
Windsor Cove
Fougner Bay
Spitfire Channel
Harlequin Basin
Rock Inlet
Namu Hbr

N

0 2 4 6 8 10
NAUTICAL MILES

©2024 Don and Réanne Douglass • Diagram not for navigation

5

Discovery Coast: Burke Channel, Dean Channel, and Ocean Falls to Spiller Channel

From Hakai Lúxvbálís Conservancy Area, with its innumerable rugged islets and remote lagoons, to the fjords and inlets that penetrate deep into the mainland coastal range, the Discovery Coast encompasses some of the best cruising grounds found along the British Columbia coast and perhaps along the entire Inside Passage. Many boaters familiar with the entire Inside Passage consider these quiet, uncrowded waters their favorite cruising grounds. Boaters can easily spend weeks and months exploring the wild and solitary Discovery Coast. There is much to do and see here. One of our favorite trips is a circle route traveling north along Burke Channel, across Labouchere Channel and southward down Dean Channel, north and through Johnson Channel, then choosing from

Every mile a surprise, Burke Channel

among myriad inlets, such as Roscoe Inlet and Spiller Channel.

Upper Burke Channel, north of Cathedral Point, offers spectacular scenery—multi-hued rock cliffs, vertical granite faces, and breathtaking waterfalls. Labouchere Channel continues to amaze us with some of the most stunning topography along the Discovery Coast. Tenaciously nestled in high-granite cliffs, tiny plants and trees sprout from the rock fissures and jut out over the water. Nearby, Sir Alexander MacKenzie Provincial Park is home to a piece of North American history. This park commemorates the site where, in July 1793, fur trader Alexander Mackenzie—along with a small party—was the first to cross the mainland of North America. In the village of Ocean Falls, at the head of beautiful Cousins Inlet in Dean Channel, you can take a historic walking tour of the former mill town. Bella Coola, a logging and fishing town at the end of North Bentinck Arm, features a museum dedicated to the area's Norwegian history.

Travelling up Spiller Channel and pristine Roscoe Inlet, you'll find even more beautiful scenery and anchorages. Waterfalls, tidal lagoons, primitive hiking trails, solitude and quiet are yours to enjoy. Roscoe Inlet has some of the most scenic and striking granite faces and domes along the Inside Passage. Summer waters even warm up enough to allow you to swim off your boat during the long, sunlit days. To the west, at the head of Spiller Channel lies the gem of the region—Ellerslie Falls inside Ellerslie Lagoon. You can approach this roaring cascade—one of the loveliest we've seen on the B.C. coast—by dinghy or kayak. From the falls you can take a primitive trail through the rainforest to lovely Ellerslie Lake.

Boaters planning to travel in this area should exercise caution in using the information on charts as well as the local knowledge presented in this chapter, since not all hazards to navigation are correctly or completely identified. The Discovery Coast, formerly thought of as the undiscovered coast, has been discovered!

The Discovery Coast Connector is BC Ferries' summer service (mid-June to mid-September) between Port Hardy and Mid-Coast ports Bella Bella, Shearwater, Klemtu, Ocean Falls and Bella Coola.

FOUGNER BAY

Burke Channel

Fougner Bay

150

160

20

12

5

7

8

7

9

9

6

5

4

3

3

Dries at
2-ft. tide

1
1

2

4

← Caution: Fast,
turbulent water

2

3

2

1

N

200 yds
DEPTHS IN FATHOMS
AT ZERO TIDE

©2024 Don and Réanne Douglass • Diagram not for navigation

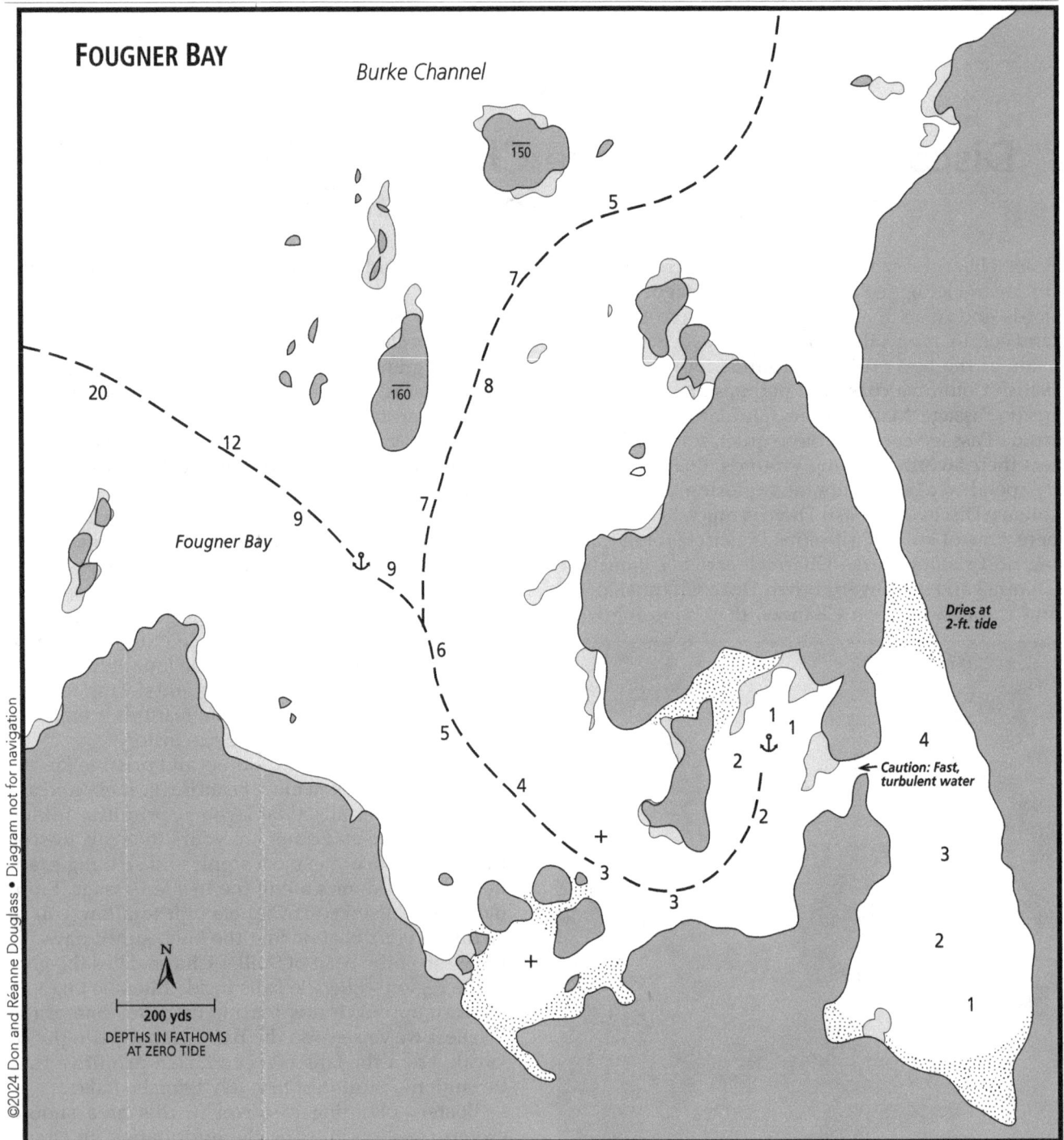

Burke Channel (King Island)

Starts 3 mi N of Namu
Entrance (SW): 51°54.68'N, 127°53.67'W

Burke Channel is a beautiful, glacier-cut inlet between the mainland and King Island. Its outlet at Fitz Hugh Sound has an entrance bar between 20 and 70 fathoms. Once you are north of Haaksvold Point, the water deepens gradually to 300 fathoms. The shores on either side of the channel are steep-to, with depths of 50 to 100 fathoms frequently just 50 yards offshore. Strong westerly winds tend to build up on summer afternoons; during such conditions, it's a good idea to get an early morning start. Squamish outflow winds are gale force winds that occur when high pressure over the interior flows through the channels to a low-pressure area offshore. These winds are most prevalent in winter. However, they can occur in summer, and in such conditions, it's better to wait, seek shelter, and wait until they die down, usually in the afternoon.

You can escape prevailing strong ebb currents in Burke Channel by playing the back eddies and lesser ebb current along the steep shores. Kelkpa Point, 19 miles from Fitz Hugh Sound, marks the beginning of the rougher waters for which Burke Channel is known. The S-shaped curve of the channel creates turbulence and back eddies—appreciated by any river runner—that result in a confused surface full of whitecaps, even though up-inlet-wind may be light. Kwatna Inlet, entered just east of Mapalaklenk Point, offers quick relief from these confused seas. Monitor VHF channels for information on the latest weather conditions at Cathedral Point.

Fougner Bay (Burke Channel)
2.6 mi N of Namu
Entrance: 51°54.61'N, 127°51.65'W
Anchor (outer): 51°54.33'N, 127°51.22'W
Anchor (inner): 51°54.23'N, 127°50.72'W

Fougner Bay, on the south shore of the entrance to Burke Channel, contains an intricate group of islands, islets and rocks and is one of the more well-protected anchorages along this part of the coast. Heads-up navigation and an alert bow lookout are required to enter the bay.

Large boats can anchor in the outer anchorage in 5 to 9 fathoms northeast of a 12-foot drying rock where holding power is good holding in southeasterly winds. The bottom is relatively flat over a large area with good protection from southerly weather, but with moderate exposure to downslope and westerly winds.

A very scenic and secluded anchor site can be found in the south portion of Fougner Bay west of the mainland peninsula, east of the small unnamed island, and south of the large unnamed island. The inner cove is landlocked, with cedar, hemlock, and old silver cedar snags over 6 feet in diameter. Anchor just south of a line from the south end of the tiny tree-filled rock islet in the head of the cove west of a 30-foot white granite wall. The anchor site is out of the current flowing through the passage. We heard loon calls and those of other birds echoing off the trees.

Anchor (outer anchorage) in 9 fathoms over an unrecorded bottom, with fair-to-good holding.

Anchor (inner cove) in 1 to 2 fathoms over brown sand covered with extensive lettuce kelp; poor-to-good holding depending on set of your anchor.

Windsor Cove (Burke Channel)
4.6 mi N of Namu
Entrance: 51°55.80'N, 127°52.94'W

Protection from strong westerlies can be found in Windsor Cove deep in the head of the cove. A temporary anchorage and good lunch stop can be taken north of Sagen Islet between the rocks and the southern tip of King Island.

Haaksvold Point (Burke Channel)
6.3 mi NE of Fougner Cove
Position: 51°57.49'N, 127°42.59'W

On spring tides at Haaksvold Point we have seen a small tidal bore. Although the bore was only a few inches high it reminded us of a 3-foot tidal bore we witnessed 100 miles off the Amazon River outlet several decades ago.

In this case, the tidal bore occurs where the outflow of fresh water creates a standing wave on top of the heavier incoming saltwater. Below the bore, the flood moves northeast at about 1 to 1.5 knots; along the top, the freshwater flows southwest at about 2 knots. If you observe this phenomenon, it's worth stopping to watch. At Haaksvold Point you may find an uncomfortable chop during the summer when afternoon inflow winds pick up.

Calm anchorage, Fitz Hugh Sound

Restoration Bay (Burke Channel)
10.4 mi NE of Fougner Bay
Entrance: 52°01.06′N, 127°39.16′W
Anchor: 52°01.51′N, 127°38.10′W

Restoration Bay was named by George Vancouver who anchored here May 29, 1793, during his explorations of the coast. The date represented the 133rd anniversary of the restoration of Charles II.

Because it is exposed to winds that blow up the inlet, Restoration Bay is a fair-weather stop. Tuck close into the northeast corner where you can find protection from down-slope gales. The shoreline of the bay is steep-to with high granite cliffs that rise about a thousand feet vertically to Sharp Cone—the 2,970-foot peak on the north side of Restoration Bay. Trees grow out of nearly every crack along these ramparts. The east side of the bay is less precipitous and falls more gently to the shore of Kwatna Inlet. During times of heavy rain or runoff, Quatlena River, one mile east of Restoration Bay, comes charging out of a saddle between 2,000- to 3,000-foot peaks and cascades down the face in a series of waterfalls on its way to sea level in Kwatna Inlet.

Anchor southeast of the yellow triangle on a sloping bottom, or close-in to the 1½-fathom shelf, just below the outlet of the creek where holding is reported to be good.

Anchor in 4 to 8 fathoms over an unrecorded bottom.

Kwatna Inlet
10.5 mi NE of Restoration Bay
Entrance: 52°09.89′N, 127°28.62′W

The entrance to Kwatna Inlet is just above Mapalaklenk Point, where Burke Channel follows an S-shaped curve. As you approach Mapalaklenk Point, stay well out from Odegaard Rocks that extend 400 yards northwest of the point. This is high, steep country with little VHF reception.

The inlet curves south, then west and southwest to a large, drying mud flat at the base of Quatlena River. The inlet is 13 miles long, with steep sides that rise to 3,000-foot peaks less than a mile from the saltwater. Until you reach the far southwest end, depths are too great for anchoring.

Kwatna Bay (Kwatna Inlet)
5.5 mi SE of Cathedral Pt.
Entrance: 52°06.77′N, 127°26.14′W

Kwatna Bay is well protected from outside chop, but it is open to downslope winds that blow down the large, drying mudflat at the outlet of the Kwatna River. Avoid the mid-channel Kwatna Rocks when entering. Kwatna Bay is also too deep for convenient anchorage. We prefer tiny Cathedral Point Cove.

Cathedral Point Cove (Burke Channel)
11.6 mi NE of Restoration Bay
Anchor: 52°11.20′N, 127°28.09′W

Cathedral Point is a landmark remarkable for its rosy-orange cliffs that face southwest; "Cathedral Point Cove" is our name for this tiny remarkable topographic feature. The cove is surrounded by granite walls and a stand of old-growth hemlock and spruce. Just west of the point, the bold cliffs give way to a circular bay which provides welcome relief from the channel chop and good protection from both up- and downslope summer weather. The cove has a large, flat 4-fathom bottom with swinging room for two or three small boats. The south end of the cove gives the best protection from up-inlet winds. Notice, however, the large tree roots collected on the south beach, and low windswept trees that bend southward, attesting to terrific Arctic outflow winds in winter. If downslope winds are anticipated during the night, the east center of the cove is a better place to anchor, with a shore-tie advised since swinging room is limited.

Photo courtesy CHS, Pacific Region

Kwatna Bay

Cathedral Point Cove, north end

Winds in the vicinity of the point swirl into the cove periodically and you can expect some rocking. During inflow gales this anchorage may be uncomfortable. However, chop largely blows by and you should have a fine view of the channel, and the pink granite and tree-covered mountain on the western shore. To minimize rocking, consider a stern anchor to keep your bow pointed toward the opening. All in all, Cathedral Point Cove is a welcome respite in an otherwise steep and beautiful fjord cut deep into the coast mountains.

Anchor in 4 fathoms over mud with some rocks; good holding.

The Crack, Upper Burke Channel
0.7 mi NE of Gibraltar Pt.
Position: 52°13.32'N, 127°22.95'W

North of Cathedral Point, the east side of Burke Channel has some of the most spectacular scenery we've encountered.

In the rain, small streams develop and race down rounded slabs of boulder—formations so smooth and rounded that soil cannot develop, and the tiny plants and trees frequently found in crevices along vertical faces have no chance along this two-mile stretch. The rock cliffs are paintings in themselves—some mauve, some ochre or violet-hued; some heavily glaciated with white and grey striations. Then, 0.7 mile east of Gibraltar Point, the first of many beautiful surprises—a waterfall we call "The Crack" drops out of a narrow fissure 70 feet above; sometimes in mid-summer, snow still remains wedged in the fissure,

Avalanche chute, The Sanctuary

just 200 feet from the water.

The scenery is so magnificent we're loathe to attempt describing it. Instead, take pleasure in your own discovery of upper Burke Channel. Stay within 50 to 100 yards from the east shore for the full impact of the peaks and overhanging cliffs.

The Sanctuary (Burke Channel)
1.5 mi NE of Gibraltar Pt.
Entrance: 52°13.41'N, 127°21.53'W

"The Sanctuary" is what we call the small indentation 1.5 miles east of Gibraltar Point on the south shore of Burke Channel. Approximately 300 yards deep by 75 yards wide and carved out of granite and conglomerate cliffs, there is a large avalanche chute where a seasonal stream flows underneath snow-bridges that descend to within 200 feet of the water. The head of the bay at the foot of the chute is choked with chunks of yellow granite that contrast dramatically with grey granite slabs, brilliant green trees and bushes, and patches of pure white snow.

As you approach Kwaspala Point, the water becomes greener, announcing glacier run-off from North Bentinck and South Bentinck arms, and a promise of more grandiose scenery.

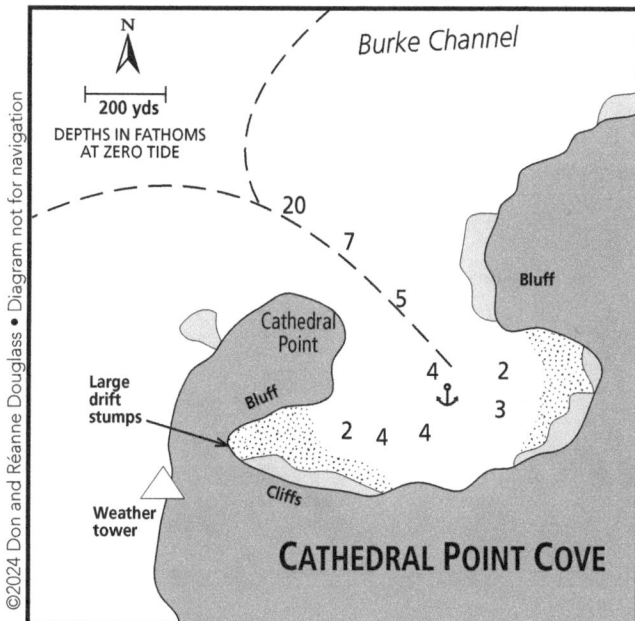

N

200 yds

DEPTHS IN FATHOMS
AT ZERO TIDE

Burke Channel

20

7

5

Bluff

Cathedral
Point

Large
drift
stumps

Bluff

4   2
⚓
2
3

2   4   4

Cliffs

Weather
tower

CATHEDRAL POINT COVE

©2024 Don and Réanne Douglass • Diagram not for navigation

Croyden Bay (Burke Channel)
0.5 mi E of Kwaspala Pt.
Entrance: 52°18.89'N, 127°10.22'W
Anchor: 52°18.63'N, 127°09.68'W

Croyden Bay is a wide, deep bay that offers some relief from outside weather and chop. There are two beaches at the head of the bay. The western beach is steep-to with a rocky bottom, 5 fathoms deep, 60 feet from shore. The eastern beach, at the outlet of a small creek, has small grassy patches. A temporary stop can be found in favorable weather in 4 fathoms, about 100 feet from the beach. The islet off the east point provides fair protection on the east side of the bay from downslope chop.

Anchor in 4 fathoms over mud, gravel and rocks with some grass and wood debris; poor-to-fair holding.

Jacobsen Bay (Burke Channel)
E of Kwaspala Pt.
Entrance: 52°18.95'N, 127°09.51'W

Jacobsen Bay provides less protection than Croyden Bay and is equally steep-to. Depths 60 feet from shore are about 60 feet, indicating a 45-degree slope. A major creek empties into the head of the bay, flowing between two patches of green grass and some driftwood.

Glacier-carved rock, upper Burke Channel

A temporary stop can be found in calm weather with your bow headed into the outflow of the creek.

Anchor in about 12 fathoms over a mixed bottom of gravel and rock; poor holding.

North Bentinck Arm (Burke Channel)
7.3 mi E of Kwaspala Pt.
Entrance: 52°19.40'N, 126°58.71'W

North Bentinck Arm is entered between Tallheo Point and Loiyentsi Point. It is deep throughout with no off-lying dangers, and its shores are moderately steep-to. At the head of the arm a mud and sand flat extends from low, swampy ground which is submerged at HW. The Bella Coola River, a stream of considerable size and velocity, flows through the flat which, from recent surveys, shows indications of extending west. The Necleetsconnay River flows into the NE side of the head of the inlet.

North Bentinck Arm cuts east 8 miles with magnificent peaks and ridges rising over a mile high directly out of the salt water. Bella Coola lies at the head of North Bentinck Arm.

Green Bay (North Bentinck Arm)
7.5 mi E of Kwaspala Pt.
Entrance: 52°20.55'N, 126°58.73'W

Green Bay lies at the bottom of a classic U-shaped, glacier-carved valley which is the outlet of the Nooseseck River. The river outlet is at the far west side of the bay and we could not find the 6-fathom shoal shown on the chart. Instead we found depths of 20 fathoms up to the very edge of the rapidly flowing river. A house is located on the east side of the bay 100 yards from the beach.

Loiyentsi Point offers some protection from west winds blowing up Burke Channel. We would consider this a temporary anchorage only. A small 4- to 6-fathom shelf, 50 yards west of the end of the old

Bella Coola public floats

pier pilings, extends to the front of the pier and can be used for temporary anchorage in fair weather. The saltwater is milky green color from glacier water with poor underwater visibility.

Anchor in 4 to 6 fathoms over rocky bottom with poor holding.

Bella Coola (North Bentinck Arm)
52 mi NE of Namu
Entrance: 52°22.58'N, 126°47.72'W

The harbor for Bella Coola lies outside the delta of the river of the same name. Its entrance is protected by a rock breakwater marked by a quick-flashing red light. The public floats are located east of the ferry dock and wharf and are managed by the Bella Coola Harbour Authority. The harbormaster's office lies at the head of the gangway (closed during the noon lunch hour). The Harbour Authority tries to monitor VHF 06 and 16. Pay phones (land phones) are located just behind the office. The Columbia Fuels fuel dock, on a small float at the foot of the wharf, is open Monday–Friday but is closed during lunch.

The Discovery Coast ferry calls at Bella Coola several times a week from the end of May to the latter part of September. The road to Williams Lake, 283 miles (456 kilometers) east, leads up the beautiful Bella Coola Valley, and passes through Tweedsmuir Park, the largest provincial park in British Columbia. This is big mountain and grizzly country. Hagensborg, 15 kilometers east of Bella Coola, is home to the central coast Ministry of Forestry office.

Ice can be purchased on the Bella Coola Harbour wharf. Groceries, hardware and liquor are available at the co-op in town, about two miles from the harbor. Repair shops, a post office, motels, guides, credit union, hospital, showers and a laundromat are found in town. Both B.C. Parks and Conservation Service have offices in town where you can obtain information on recreational possibilities in the region. Bella Coola Valley Museum, located at the west entrance to town is worth visiting. The Thorsen Creek petroglyph site, one of the largest in B.C and with spiritual significance to the Nuxalk people, is located on private land. Contact Bella Coola Valley Tourism about the possibility of a guided tour, but note that, in an effort to protect the petroglyphs, public access is restricted.

Good-tasting water is available on the landing zone float and along some of the other floats; power is available as well. There is no water at the fuel dock. A tidal grid and launching ramp are also provided.

While the majority of boats in the harbor are fishing vessels, the Harbormaster has seen a dramatic increase in visits from pleasure boats over the last 10 years. A few even winter over. Moorage can be crowded with rafting required; windy conditions are the norm; watch for strong outflow current when docking. (The bay has no ice in the winter, we were told.)

South Bentinck Arm
7 mi E of Kwaspala Pt.
Entrance: 52°18.45'N, 126°59.20'W

South Bentinck Arm is the continuation of Burke Channel. Inflow winds that blow northeast in lower Burke Channel frequently turn and follow South Bentinck Arm to the southeast.

Snow-capped mountains rise to 7,000 feet on both sides of the arm, providing a continuation of the spectacular scenery found in Burke Channel. There are well over a dozen glaciers visible from salt water on a rare clear day. Until mid-summer, the entire arm has snowy peaks that nearly overhang the channel, and you feel you could reach out and grab a handful of snow.

The only reasonable anchorage for small boats in the entire arm is 10 miles within the inlet on the east shore of Larso Bay. It is strange to see the strong west wind blow northeast in Burke Channel, then turn

Hanging glacier, South Bentinck Arm

and be blowing southeast in South Bentinck Arm at the same time. Local weather conditions are quite variable, with different microclimate zones in close proximity.

One of the dangers of traversing Burke Channel and Bentinck Arms in times of spring tide is that the 16-foot tide lifts many logs, branches, and tree stumps off beaches and river flats and fills the channels with debris. You could easily damage your propeller if you take your eyes off-course for a minute. In the channel chop, the drift is hidden from view 90 percent of the time.

South Bentinck Arm is seldom visited by cruising boats and its outstanding scenery and solitude are well worth the effort and risks.

Tallheo Hot Springs (South Bentinck Arm)
6.5 mi SE of arm entrance
Position: 52°12.20'N, 126°56.14'W

Tallheo Hot Springs is one mile south of Bensins Island. Logs and debris tend to collect in the area on either side of Bensins Island, so use caution in traversing this area.

The hot springs, popular with locals, is located just inside the outlet of Hot Springs Creek. There is a cabin on shore at the outlet; however, there is no dock or easy access since the water is relatively deep,

Lunch break at Larso Bay

and there is no protection from inflow or outflow winds. Temporary anchorage in fair weather may be found in about 14 fathoms immediately off the creek over an unrecorded bottom.

Larso Bay (South Bentinck Arm)
9.1 mi SE of arm entrance
Float position: 52°10.79'N, 126°51.66'W

Larso Bay, 15 miles from the head of the arm, gives welcome relief from up-channel wind and chop. Anchoring is possible in 8 fathoms between the float and the shoal at the outlet of the creek.

On shore, wild strawberry, salmonberry, clover, daisies, and salal grow amidst the hemlock, cedar, spruce and alder. High on the ridge are clear-cut scars. On the west shore there is a remarkable waterfall that cascades from the snowfield on a 4,200-foot peak above.

Larso Bay, the best place in the south arm for small boats to anchor, has very good protection from upslope winds that flow from the northwest in this area. Only moderate protection from downslope winds is offered by the point and the logbooms on the southeast side of the bay. Anchorage can be taken between the logging float and the shoal off the small creek at the head of the bay.

The head of South Bentinck Arm ends in two small basins reached by very narrow channels. Mile-high peaks hang overhead. The water is too deep for convenient anchorage.

Anchor in 5 to 10 fathoms at the head of the bay over sand, mud and gravel with fair holding.

Labouchere Channel (King Island)
15 mi W of Bella Coola
Entrance (S): 52°21.01'N, 127°10.95'W
Entrance(N): 52°26.66'N, 127°15.26'W

The calm waters of Labouchere Channel offer welcome relief from Burke Channel chop as soon as you pass Mesachie Nose—a spectacular cliff—on the east side of the south entrance. Southeast and southwest

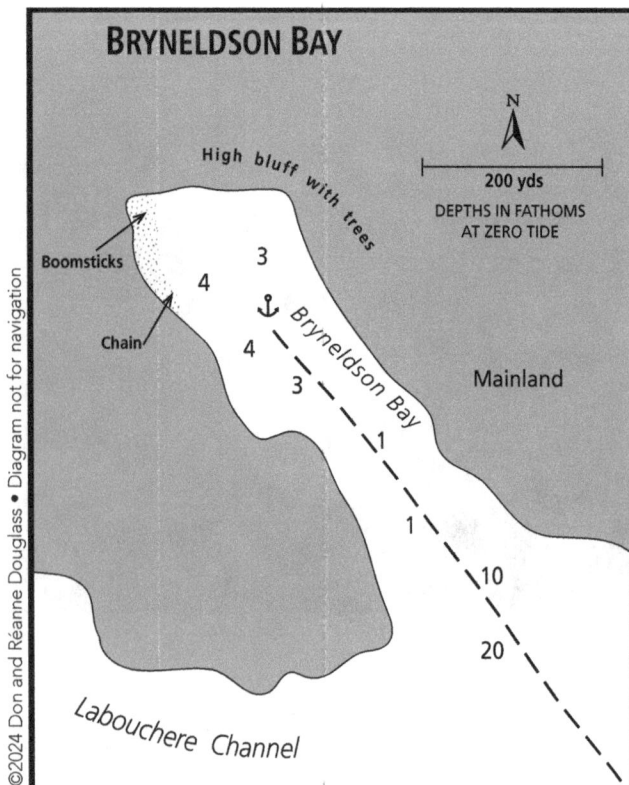

BRYNELDSON BAY

N

200 yds
DEPTHS IN FATHOMS
AT ZERO TIDE

High bluff with trees

Boomsticks

3

4

⚓

Bryneldson Bay

Chain

4

3

Mainland

1

1

10

20

Labouchere Channel

©2024 Don and Réanne Douglass • Diagram not for navigation

Cousins Inlet and Martin Valley

winds blowing up Burke Channel strike the cliff and the waves rebound, causing a confused sea in the immediate vicinity.

Bryneldson Bay (Labouchere Channel)
2 mi E of Dean Channel
Entrance: 52°26.62'N, 127°13.12'W
Anchor: 52°26.80'N, 127°13.31'W

Bryneldson Bay offers very good protection deep in the small cove located one mile southeast of Ram Bluff. There are very few drift logs in the bay and the grassy margins show no signs of chop. This is a tranquil anchorage with lovely trees and striking granite bluffs.

The west shore is sometimes used as a log storage area; you may find boomsticks tied along shore. A sandbar lies approximately one-third of the way into the bay. Minimum depth is about 7 feet across the bar. North of the bar the bay has an almost flat bottom of 3 to 5 fathoms.

Anchor near the head of the bay in 4 fathoms over mud and some wood debris; good-to-very-good holding.

Dean Channel (King Island, north side)
W and N of Bella Coola
Entrance (W): 52°15.44'N, 127°45.66'W

Dean Channel begins east of Rattenbury Point in rugged, scenic cruising grounds. During periods of strong runoff, the ebb currents completely override the flooding currents on the surface, and it is not uncommon to have a ¼- to ¾-knot down-channel current the entire time the tide is rising! The saltwater temperature runs around 50° F, a good 10° colder than Seaforth Channel a few miles west! Upslope winds, which start about 10 a.m. and usually blow fresh all afternoon, can cause a nasty chop on a strong ebb current.

The color of the water in upper Dean Channel is not as light-colored or opaque as the water in the Bentinck Arms, indicating less glacier activity.

The route from Bella Bella to the town of Bella Coola, and the deep channels to the east, follows Dean Channel. Bella Coola, at the head of Burke Channel and North Bentinck Arm, on the river of the same name, is connected to the British Columbia highway system at Williams Lake, 479 kilometers inland.

Cousins Inlet, 1 mile north of Rattenbury Point, is known as a sportfishing area, and Ocean Falls is a cruising destination with modest facilities and a Discovery Coast ferry stop.

Rattenbury Point (Dean Channel)
6.8 mi SW of Ocean Falls
Anchor: 52°14.67'N, 127°45.29'W

We have found temporary shelter on the east side of Rattenbury Point. Since the winds and seas can change dramatically in this area, it's a good place to take a break.

One-half mile east of Rattenbury Point, a small collection of islets makes a lee for small craft during southerly and westerly weather. The inside islet has a pleasant sandy beach that serves as a campsite for fishing and hunting parties. Old-growth hemlock, cedar, and alder that grow on the point show the effects of the strong winter outflow winds. The peaks to the east are high and steep. In this remote area we have seen dolphins, orcas, seals, and numerous species of birds, including puffins.

Avoid the small rock that dries at about 10 feet and anchor on the 2- to 4-fathom shelf just southeast of the islets. You may be able to find some protection from downslope winds on the west side of the islets, but we found foul ground there and would recommend a run into Cousins Inlet, Wallace Bay, or Ocean Falls.

Anchor in 2 fathoms over sand and gravel with fair holding.

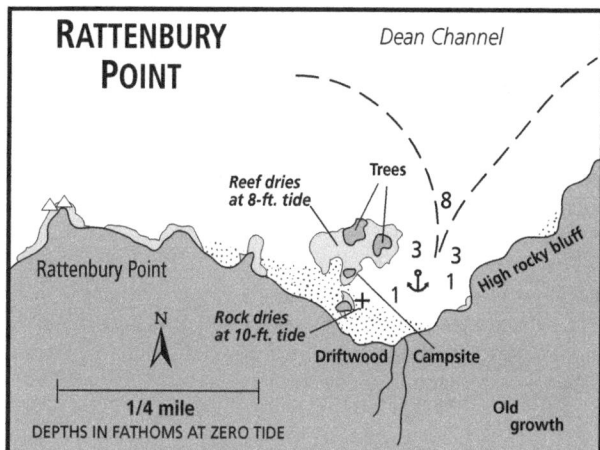

RATTENBURY POINT

Dean Channel

Reef dries at 8-ft. tide
Trees
8
3 / 3
1
Rattenbury Point
High rocky bluff
N
Rock dries at 10-ft. tide
Driftwood / Campsite
1/4 mile
DEPTHS IN FATHOMS AT ZERO TIDE
Old growth

©2024 Don and Reanne Douglass • not for navigation

Cousins Inlet (Dean Channel)
1.5 mi N of Rattenbury Pt.
Entrance Position: 52°16.10'N, 127°46.20'W

Cousins Inlet, at the junction of Fisher and Dean channels, leads north to Ocean Falls where visiting boats can find moorage at good, uncrowded floats. Up- or downslope chop in Dean Channel quickly dies as you pass north of Wallace Bay.

Wallace Bay (Cousins Inlet)
4 mi S of Ocean Falls
Anchor: 52°17.50'N, 127°45.04'W

Wallace Bay is a shallow bight on the east shore of Cousins Inlet just inside the entrance. A number of old cabins on shore formerly served as summer and weekend homesites for the residents of Ocean Falls. The bay affords moderate protection close inshore from southerly winds. You can find a good lunch stop at the head of the bight, south of a large green patch of alder trees. Avoid Guns Rock at the north end of the bight.

Anchor in 12 fathoms; unrecorded bottom.

Cousins Inlet Labor Day "Storm"

Ocean Falls is one of those sleepy places you head for to escape the growing chop and big winds. We had taken a 960mb low for three days on the west coast of Moresby Island 12 days earlier and wanted some peace and quiet to get some work done.

There was no VHF radio reception in Cousins Inlet, and the Calvert Island and Klemtu repeaters were inoperable for several weeks, so we were somewhat surprised when the barometer took a nose dive as a 980mb low turned northeast from Hecate Strait toward Alaska. Before long, the chop came over the floating log breakwater that protects the Ocean Falls floats. Sea smoke developed as williwaws bounced off the high peak to the north, hitting the Ocean Falls floats as 40-plus knots gusts. It was strange to be taking northwest winds when Cousins Inlet and Fisher Channel were white from southeast gales.

The stronger storm from the williwaws hit the face of the dam, creating a great white plume that rose a hundred feet or more and, as the wind opposed the cascading water spray shot up and over the structure like snow banners in a Sierra Nevada snowstorm.

The two floats bobbed and swayed as buckets of water fell. Other than some torn canvas on some of the sportfishing boats, there was no damage. Everyone had doubled their mooring lines and hunkered down, thankful to have a relatively safe place to enjoy the show.

—RHD

Labor Day Storm in Cousins Inlet

Ocean Falls (Cousins Inlet)
14 mi NE of Gunboat Passage
Floats: 52°21.15'N, 127°41.90'W

Ocean Falls welcomes cruising boaters, and the docks have excellent purified water from Link Lake. Weather channel WX1 has a spotty signal.

Ocean Falls has a post office, city hall, and pleasure boat dock with 20- and 30-amp power, good water and reasonable moorage fees. No garbage drop but some recyclable items are accepted. Free seasonal WiFi. In the recent past, several businesses have come and gone that served food and provided services for visitors, including an inn, cafe, pub, gift shop, convenience store, and baked goods. Check with one of the locals to discover what might be open for business.

Old roads around town, and the trail to Link Lake above the falls, offer the best opportunity for exercise for miles around. A controversial multi-million dollar fish farm (for Atlantic salmon) is located beside the old Crown Zellerbach mill and gets its water and power from the dam.

A 4-wheel drive road from Martin Valley leads across to Shack Bay in Roscoe Inlet, passing Twin Lakes (Ikt and Mokst lakes). Past the lakes the road becomes little more than a hiking trail.

Elcho Harbour (Dean Channel)
8 mi E of Ocean Falls
Entrance: 52°22.40'N, 127°29.07'W
Anchor: 52°23.84'N, 127°31.92'W

Elcho Harbour is a scenic fjord which affords good protection from inflow and outflow wind and chop. The head of the harbor is a good place to anchor while visiting Mackenzie Park. The harbor has depths of 10 to 20 fathoms. The valley behind the head is V-shaped with very steep sides.

Anchor in about 12 fathoms over mud with very good holding.

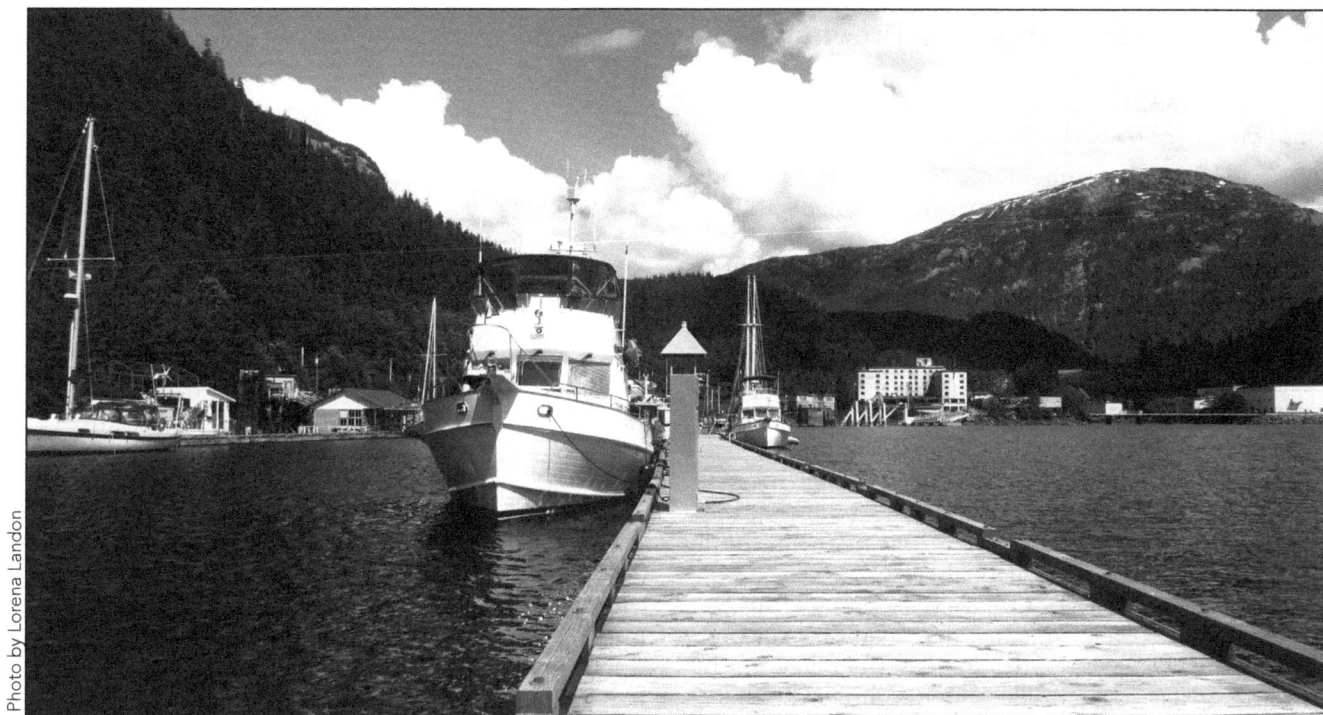

Photo by Lorena Landon

Ocean Falls Small Craft Docks with Ocean Falls town buildings in the distance

Ocean Falls - Ghost Town

Ocean Falls was once a mill town, home to 4,000 people. The pulp and paper mill town that started in 1906 grew quickly. Initially, the mill's location with low labor costs, inexpensive hydro power, and low infrastructure costs made it financially viable. By 1970, however, labor and other costs increased making the mill unprofitable. Crown Zellerback, the then current owner, decided to shut down the mill, effectively shutting down the main industry and labor force of the town. The BC province attempted to save the town by operating the mill for a period of time in the 1970's; but by 1980, the province gave up trying to make a profit.

When the mill closed, homes and buildings were abandoned. Today, the town's few year-round residents keep the remaining town assets active. The hydro electric power generators provide power for Ocean Falls and the nearby towns of Bella Bella and Shearwater.

At its peak, the Ocean Falls 600-bed hotel was the second largest hotel in British Columbia. The proud remains of this hotel can be seen today and is one of the most prominent buildings still standing. During the 1940s, 50s, and 60s, the Swim Team earned world recognition, turning out Pan-American and Olympic champions.

Today, Ocean Falls is a favorite stop for boaters along the Inside Passage, where crabbing is good, power and water are plentiful, and where walking the once busy streets of this modern-day ghost town stirs the imagination and vision of the people whose "home town" has been etched in history.

— Lorena Landon

Ocean Falls - For Sheer Pleasure

Mention Ocean Falls almost anywhere and you hear, "Oh—my uncle worked at the mill" or "I went to grade school there!" Visitors' fascination with the old buildings vies with a compelling urge to own a piece of this fjord-like setting where fishing and seaside adventure abounds!

Americans and Albertans especially have found the locale's affordability alluring. Where else could you buy a seaside home with hardwood flooring, fireplace, and a million-dollar view that fits a budget! Plus, the heavy daily decision of "Should I go deep for halibut, run to the point for salmon OR explore and flyfish up Link Lake" keeps newcomers grinning. But no hurry, these plans can be clinched over breakfast at the Old Bank Inn, where you can purchase freshly baked cinnamon buns.

The buzz is about "change"—crafts and secondhand booths in the old Co-op, eco-tourism and artwork projects, paint cans and brooms to sweep out old corners, private enterprise vs. government hangovers. The place isn't jumping but it's *humming*, and the whisper among the old buildings is "Don't count me out—I'm still here— but *now* just for the *sheer pleasure* of it!"

— Sally Rivenes Isaksen

Sir Alexander Mackenzie Provincial Park (Dean Channel)
13.3 mi NE of Rattenbury Pt.
Position: 52°22.65'N, 127°28.32'W

This small park, commemorating the first recorded walk across the North American continent, is the place where Alexander Mackenzie became convinced that the Bella Coola River did in fact flow into the Pacific Ocean. Interestingly, Mackenzie just missed sighting George Vancouver who was on his first sailing expedition to this area in July 1793.

When you're approaching the park, the obelisk monument makes a good landmark. The shoreline off Mackenzie Rock is steep-to and, in calm weather, you can anchor off the small beach, climb the rocks to the monument, then scramble down to look at the message. However, if you prefer not to anchor and go ashore, the inscription on Mackenzie Rock can easily be seen from your boat. Mackenzie wrote on the rock: "Alex Mackenzie from Canada by land 22 July 1793." The message, originally written in vermilion grease, has been chiseled into the stone.

The anchor site off the beach, while good in calm weather, affords little shelter in any winds. If you anchor here, be prepared to leave at any moment. Better protection can be found nearby at the head of Elcho Harbour.

From the beach, you have a wonderful panorama of snow-clad peaks that rim the nearby fjords. A high waterfall across Elcho Harbour on the west shore breaks the perfect silence, a silence otherwise so profound that you can hear the sound of bird wings and the swoop of hawks between the trees. Notice how the hemlock roots on the west side of the bight cling like large spider webs to the granite walls. This is a nice place to contemplate the heroic feats accomplished by the area's native peoples and early explorers.

Anchor (temporarily) in 2 to 3 fathoms over gravel and rock; fair holding with a well-set anchor; limited swinging room.

McKay Bay (Dean Channel)
0.7 mi NW of Cape McKay
Entrance: 52°24.08'N, 127°26.46'W
Anchor: 52°24.75'N, 127°26.16'W

McKay Bay is out of the current and outflow winds of Dean Channel. Temporary shelter may be obtained in the small nook at the head of the bay, avoiding drift logs that indicate exposure to southerly winds.

Anchor in 10 fathoms over sand and gravel; fair holding.

Mackenzie Rock

Cascade Inlet (Dean Channel)
11.2 mi E of Ocean Falls
Entrance: 52°24.79'N, 127°24.86'W
Anchor: 52°36.34'N, 127°37.34'W

Cascade Inlet has majestic scenery similar to that of upper Dean Channel and South Bentinck Arm. The inlet is only half the width of Dean or Burke channels so the steep slopes, some of which exceed 45-degree angles, appear all the more impressive. Roughly every half-mile of its 13-mile length there is a spectacular cascade or waterfall. Some of the crevasses or canyons are seldom touched by sunlight and reveal patches of snow lasting into late summer when the peaks are bare.

Deep Cascade Inlet can provide welcome escape from the afternoon inflow winds and chop in Dean Channel. The inlet was named by George Vancouver, for obvious reasons, and he considered it one of the loveliest he had seen.

Anchor in 10 fathoms at the head of the inlet on the east shore, soft bottom.

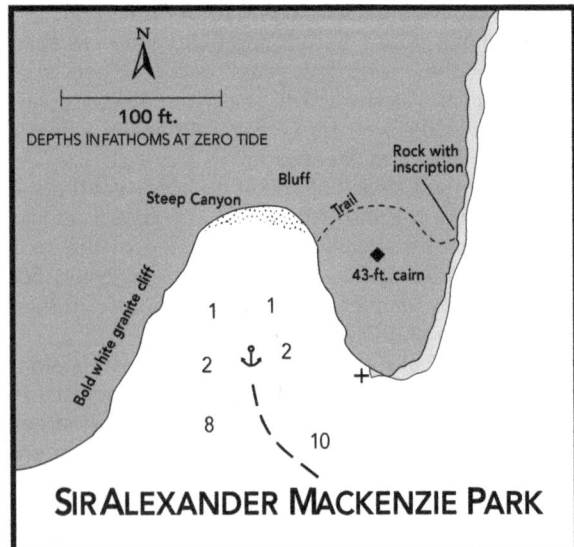

SIR ALEXANDER MACKENZIE PARK

©2024 Don and Réanne Douglass • Diagram not for navigation

Rain doesn't stop a "seasoned" fisherman, Ocean Falls

Ocean Falls Voices from the Past?

Réanne and I woke up to voices at 1 a.m. Instantly I got up and locked our saloon door—perhaps the first time this summer. The voices, which were quite audible, sounded like drunken fishermen who had gotten into a pushing and shoving match at the end of the main float. I climbed up the stairs into the pilothouse and looked around. No one there—the float was empty in both directions.

I went below and reported to Réanne. "How can that be?" she asked. "They're still talking." I went back upstairs and opened the pilothouse door—voices all right, with a limited vocabulary. "Uh, ah, arump, gurah," interspersed by "ha" and "oh," and punctuated with gurgling and thudding sounds.

Voices of the past? No. I finally realized the sounds were coming from a dozen or more harbor seals underneath the float walkway; they had been cavorting and carrying on for about five hours.

The next morning twenty thoroughly exhausted seals lay on the log breakwater, 50 yards west, where they remained all day, not moving a muscle.

—DD

Sir Alexander Mackenzie Provincial Park

I now mixed up some vermillion in melted grease, and inscribed in large characters on the face of the rock on which we slept last night, this brief memorial; "Alexander Mackenzie from Canada, by land, the twenty-second of July, one thousand, seven hundred and ninety three."
—Sir Alexander Mackenzie

Twelve years before Lewis and Clark viewed the Pacific Ocean from these shores of northwestern North America, Sir Alexander Mackenzie spotted these western waters near a village known today as Bella Coola, BC. The Mackenzie Party had begun their trek from Montreal. Upon entering British Columbia, they located and followed the Frazier River, trekked the Interior Plateau over the Rainbow Mountains, and finally traveled down Burnt Bridge Creek, which flows into the Bella Coola River. Mackenzie encountered the Nuxalk People who guided him and his party down the river into Dean Channel. His intention was to reach the ocean's shore, but the coastal Heilsuk people, who had been in a dispute with the Nuxalk, prevented Mackenzie's party from continuing. Nevertheless, Mackenzie proclaimed his mission complete and commemorated the occasion with the above inscription on a rock. Also marking the location is a forty-foot cairn and plaque that was erected by the Historic Sites and Monuments Board of Canada in 1926. The rock on which Mackenzie wrote his inscription is situated on the water's edge in what is now the Sir Alexander Mackenzie Provincial Park. The park is located near Elcho Harbour, sixty-five kilometers northwest of Bella Coola on Dean Channel. Visitors can access the park by air or boat charters from Bella Coola or Bella Bella. The park is a cultural heritage site and is restricted to day-excursions only.

Long before Mackenzie made his wilderness trek to the Pacific Ocean, First Nations people blazed this interior trail network to trade eulachon oil, a grease made from a smelt-like fish (*Thaleichthys pacificus*). Hence, the trail was named "grease trail," but is now officially noted as the Alexander Mackenzie Heritage (Grease) Trail. Hikers can access the 420-kilometer (260 mile) historic wilderness trail in Quesnel, and hike to Bella Coola where charter boats will ferry them to the park. Because of the ruggedness of the trail, hikers should be prepared for a two to three week trip. Visit the park's web site for more information: *http://www.env.gov.bc.ca/bcparks/explore/parkpgs/sir_alex/*.

—KK

Eucott Bay (Dean Channel)

3.5 mi W of Bryneldson Bay
Entrance: 52°26.51'N, 127°19.23'W
Anchor: 52°27.21'N, 127°19.07'W

Eucott Bay is the best-protected anchorage in this immediate area. Green grass rings the high-tide line and spindly trees cling tenaciously to vertical cracks along the steep granite cliffs. On the south shore, a remarkable stream cascades a thousand feet down from snowy peaks, emptying directly into the saltwater. The unnamed 4,665-foot peak to the southwest has a cirque on its eastern side that holds snow patches until late summer. The 2,000-foot vertical grey monolith on the northeast side of the bay rises from a talus and treed slope in a bold face reminiscent of Yosemite's Half Dome, while the rugged volcanic ridge of the 3,780-foot peak to the northwest plays hide-and-seek with scudding clouds. The grassy meadows echo with bird calls while a seal scans the bay waiting for the incoming tide to bring fresh fish. Giant mussels grow at the bottom of the bay in great clusters.

In the crater-like basin, the hot springs emerge from a rock wall below the southwest base of "Half Dome." The hot pool, formed of natural rock augmented with some concrete slabs, is large enough for about six people. Porcelain pipe carries the water to the pools. There is a wading pool below, not far from the high-tide line. The location of the pools is in line with the old pilings at the northeast corner of the bay. Since the bay is quite flat and silted, it may be best to visit the pools at high water and carry your dinghy back to the water, or tie it to one of the pilings, so you can retrieve it after your soak. The water is very hot and you may want to remove the inlet hose to allow the pool to cool off a bit. Enter at high water.

The view from the hot tub and the upper end of the bay looks out onto the beautiful valley and peaks to the northwest. Eucott Bay and Hot Springs should be preserved for public use in its present form—it is too valuable to squander.

The bay is too shallow to anchor off the upper end. The inner bay is reported to be nearly calm when a 40-knot westerly is blowing in the outside channel. The inner bay largely dries at zero tide; however, there is a large flat-bottomed area of 1.5 fathoms (we measured it on a 1.8-foot tide) where you can find very good holding in a mud bottom.

Eucott Hot Springs

Photo courtesy R & J Sanger

Anchor in 1.5 fathoms over brown sand and soft mud; very good holding. There is enough swinging room for a number of boats, even at zero tide.

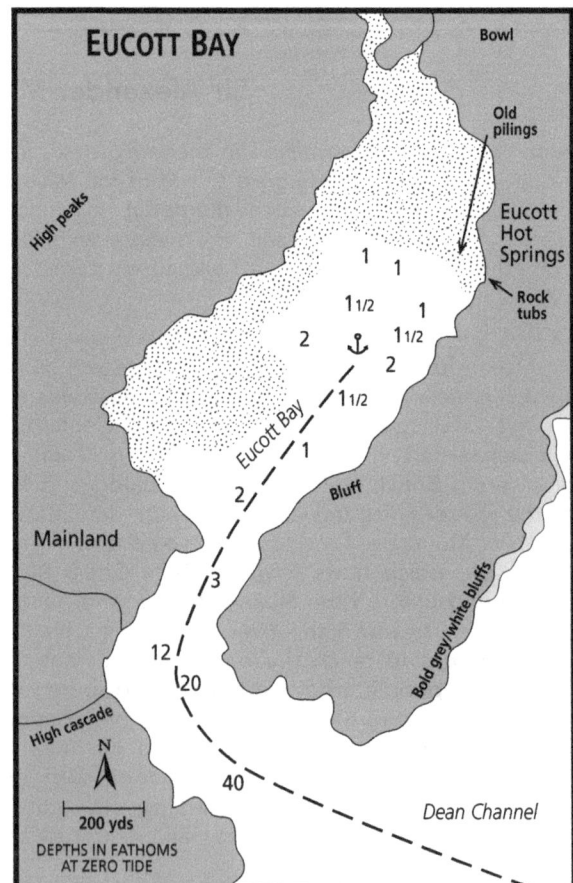

©2024 Don and Réanne Douglass • Diagram not for navigation

Nascall Bay (Dean Channel)
3.6 mi NE of Eucott Bay
Entrance: 52°29.59'N, 127°16.10'W
Anchor: 52°29.68'N, 127°16.55'W
Nascall Bay is 3 miles NNW of Ram Bluff. . .

Nascall Bay, on the west shore of Upper Dean Channel, lies 2.8 miles northwest of Ram Bluff. The outer bay is deep, but the inner bay which is the delta of the Nascall River, is quite shallow. When entering the inner bay, avoid the mid-bay rock on the drying spit by staying close to the north shore. The current here can be quite strong, making maneuvering difficult. Good anchorage can be obtained, out of the current, on the south side of the drying spit in 7 fathoms.

The land around Nascall Bay, an original land grant dating back to 1906, is privately owned and the land is posted with no trespassing signs. Pleasure boaters wishing to anchor are advised to do so on the south side of the bay protected from the river stream by the rock and gravel peninsula. Boats unfamiliar with the area should inquire on-site.

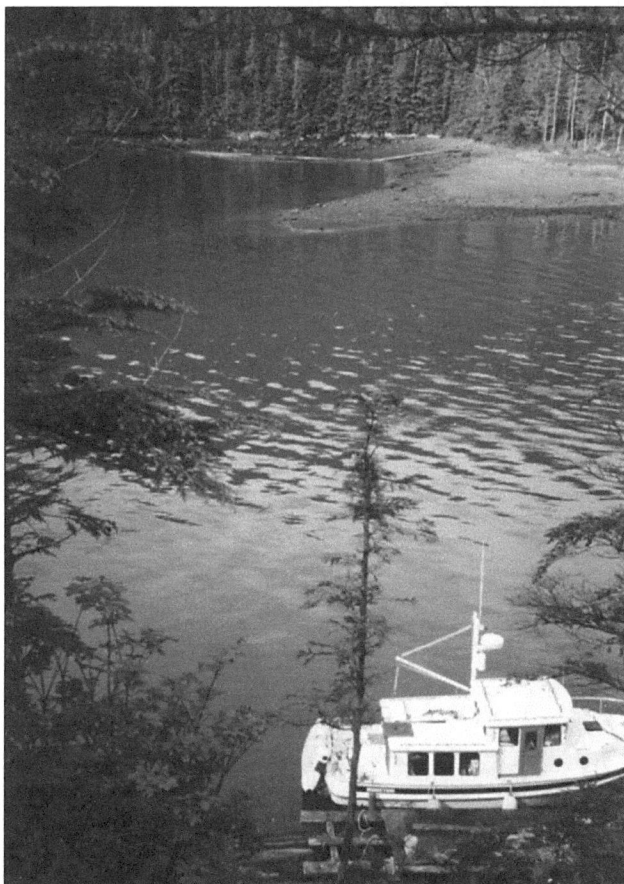

Nascall Bay, anchorage behind spit

Carlson Inlet (Dean Channel)
5 mi N of Nascall Bay
Entrance: 52°33.86'N, 127°13.20'W
Anchor: 52°34.51'N, 127°14.21'W

Carlson Inlet is the most sheltered spot in upper Dean Channel, out of both up- and downslope winds and the current. The head of the inlet stretches back into a series of V-shaped valleys where waterfalls cascade down on both sides. This is a scenic, quiet and serene place. The south entrance point has bright white rock cliffs. North of here, the rocks are darker in color.

Upper Dean Channel has high mountains on either side which, as in South Bentinck Arm, reach to over 7,000 feet. The peaks have perpetual snow patches, and some of the gullies are filled with snow well into the summer. It is so deep and steep-to that we were only able to get one good set out of nearly a dozen tries in 4 to 10 fathoms just off the drying flat. We could not get a bottom sample, but it was consistent with soft sand.

A small 6-fathom shelf is just west of the charted 15-foot rock on the south shore. A small creek comes to the west side of the rock, and there is a very small bench of 6 fathoms, brown sand and mud, that gives fair holding. It would be convenient and easy to use a stern tie to one of the vertical tree snags along shore, since the shore is so steep-to.

Anchor in 4 to 10 fathoms over a soft bottom; holding depends on how well you set your anchor.

Kimsquit Bay (Dean Channel)
18 mi NE of Carlson Inlet
Entrance: 52°49.72'N, 126°59.49'W

Kimsquit Bay lies on the north side of the Dean River outlet immediately north of the old village site of the same name. The water here and near the outlet of the Kimsquit River at the head of Dean Channel is too deep for convenient anchorage. However, this remote and picturesque area is worth a day trip from the more protected anchorages in Carlson Inlet and Nascall Bay.

Gunboat Passage (Denny Island)
8 mi E of Bella Bella
Entrance (E): 52°09.64'N, 127°54.95'W
Entrance (W): 52°10.14'N, 127°58.17'W

While Lama Passage is the route used by all cruise ships and ferries, Gunboat Passage is far more scenic and interesting; it is also protected from the effects of most weather. We do not recommend entering it without consulting charts. The range markers are the key to the western part of the passage, while careful judgment of the position of the notch in the bar just south of Maria Island is the key to the eastern entrance. *Caution:* You can't see the bottom through the muskeg water even crossing on a 6-foot tide.

At Draney Point the power lines from the Ocean Falls power station cross under Gunboat Passage. On the east side of Gunboat Passage, consider anchoring at Forit Bay.

Forit Bay (Gunboat Passage)
0.9 mi N of Gunboat Passage
Entrance: 52°10.41'N, 127°54.45'W
Anchor: 52°10.42'N, 127°54.72'W

Forit Bay is a well-protected anchorage with excellent shelter from southerlies. While it may get some outflow gusts, it receives little chop. It is quiet and secluded and, if not for the power lines on the west shore, the setting would be pristine.

To enter, stay well north of Flirt Island, passing between the large 75-foot-long rock, 200 feet off the north shore, and an underwater rock to the south, visible at low tide. If you stay within about 50 feet of the large rock you should have no problems with a 2-fathom minimum in the fairway. The bottom of the bay is flat and is 3 to 5 fathoms deep.

Anchor west of Flirt Island in 3 to 4 fathoms over a mud-and-pebble bottom with good holding.

Hampden Bay (Gunboat Passage)
0.5 mi S of E Gunboat entr
Entrance: 52°09.46'N, 127°54.77'W
Anchor: 52°09.14'N, 127°54.80'W

Hampden Bay, on the south side of the east entrance to Gunboat Passage, affords excellent protection in southerly weather and good protection in all other weather. It's a good place to anchor while you wait for proper tides and currents in Gunboat Passage. The foreshore is steep-to off the gravel beach, with eel grass lining the one-fathom curve. The head of the beach is grassy and is a good kayak haul-out spot.

When traversing Gunboat Passage, favor a mid-channel course between Denny Point and Maria Island, passing south of the rock that dries on a one-foot tide.

Anchor in 10 fathoms off the head of the easternmost creek that drains into the bay; mud bottom, good holding.

Gosse Bay (Gunboat Passage)
1.5 mi E of W Gunboat entr
Entrance: 52°09.87'N, 127°55.64'W
Anchor: 52°09.92'N, 127°55.79'W

Gosse Bay, off the west shore in the middle of Gunboat Passage, is a safe anchorage. It is out of the current, in 7 fathoms over a fairly large area. Anchor in a well-protected cove about 200 yards northeast of Algerine Island, avoiding the large grass-covered rock east of the island.

Anchor in 7 fathoms, brown mud, shells, and some kelp with fair-to-good holding.

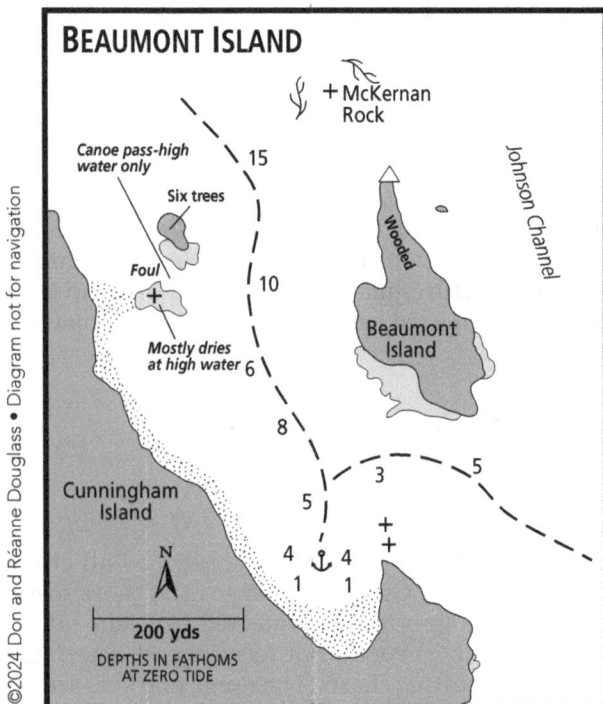

BEAUMONT ISLAND

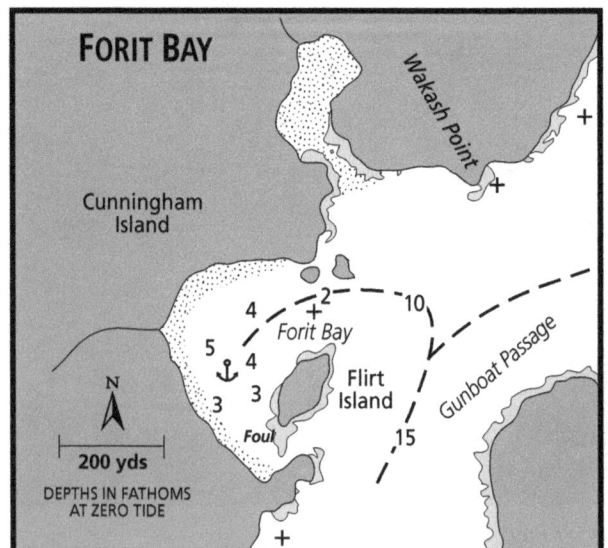

FORIT BAY

Gunboat Lagoon Cove

(Gunboat Passage)
4.5 mi NE of Shearwater
Entrance: 52°10.42'N, 127°58.86'W
Anchor: 52°10.58'N, 127°58.68'W

The best-protected anchorage in Gunboat Passage can be found in what we call Gunboat Lagoon Cove. The cove, located a half-mile northwest of Dunn Point and one mile east of Manson Point on the north shore of Gunboat Passage, offers excellent shelter from all winds and seas. Upon entering the cove from Gunboat Passage, pass east of an islet with two small trees. The fairway has 2 to 3 fathoms minimum midway between the islet and the eastern shore. (We tried the passage on the northwest side of the islet but when we found 1.9 fathoms we decided to back out.)

Avoid two submerged rocks, awash on about a 10-foot tide, that extend 75 yards—and nearly 200 yards on a zero tide—from the west shore at the entrance to the lagoon rapids. The rapids and lagoons can be explored by dinghy at slack water only. The outer lagoon, at cove height, has a very narrow entrance of about 25 feet with rocks on its west side—favor the east shore. The inner lagoon is four-to-five feet higher than cove level.

Anchor in 5 fathoms slightly east of the lagoon entrance over stiff brown mud with very good holding.

Johnson Channel

(E side of Cunningham Island)
Between Fisher & Return channels
Entrance (S): 52°11.08'N, 127°52.49'W
Entrance (N): 52°18.41'N, 127°57.36'W

Johnson Channel connects Fisher Channel to scenic Roscoe Inlet and Bullock Channel for those headed toward Spiller Channel.

Beaumont Island Cove

(Johnson Channel)
8.1 mi N of Gunboat Passage
Entrance (S): 52°17.41'N, 127°56.51'W
Entrance (N): 52°17.71'N, 127°56.91'W
Anchor: 52°17.40'N, 127°56.80'W

On the northwest corner of Johnson Channel, "Beaumont Island Cove" offers good protection from southerly storms. It is well sheltered from all weather except when strong williwaws sweep down the 3,000- to 4,000-foot peaks to the north.

The rocks off the southeast point extend about 100 yards beyond the trees. The spit at the north end provides more shelter than indicated, and you can anchor off its southern side. All-in-all, this cove provides welcome shelter and a comfortable anchorage in an impressive setting.

Anchor (south end) in 4 fathoms over a sandy bottom with good holding.

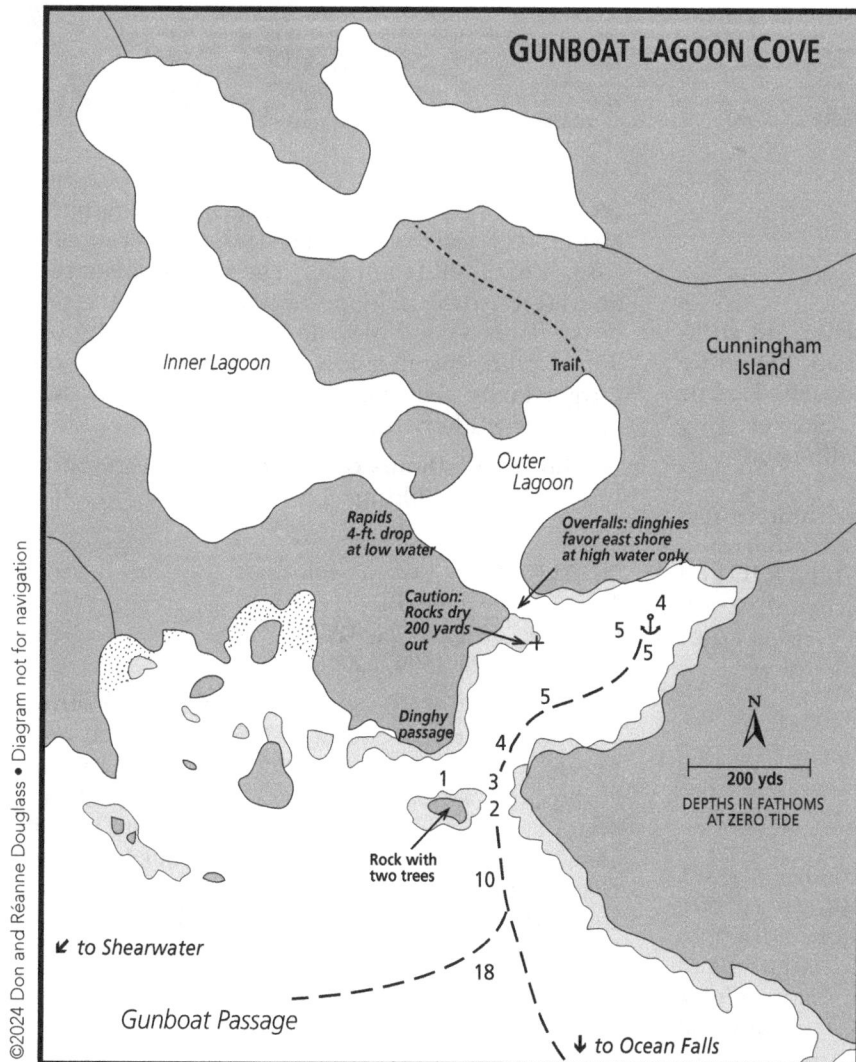

GUNBOAT LAGOON COVE

Inner Lagoon

Trail

Cunningham Island

Outer Lagoon

Rapids 4-ft. drop at low water

Overfalls: dinghies favor east shore at high water only

Caution: Rocks dry 200 yards out

Dinghy passage

Rock with two trees

N

200 yds
DEPTHS IN FATHOMS
AT ZERO TIDE

↙ to Shearwater

Gunboat Passage

↓ to Ocean Falls

©2024 Don and Réanne Douglass • Diagram not for navigation

Courtesy Randi Sanger

Roscoe Inlet

Roscoe Inlet
12 mi NE of Shearwater
Entrance: 52°19.32'N, 127°56.31'W

Roscoe Inlet has some of the most scenic and striking granite faces and domes found along the entire Inside Passage. Since our Second Edition, Roscoe Inlet's magnificent scenery has been discovered by cruising boaters. The entire inlet is pristine and worthy of park status.

Strong summer westerlies rarely have much effect past Clatse Bay and definitely not past the narrows. The head of Roscoe Inlet receives little tidal flow and swimming off your boat is a real joy when the fresh surface-water reaches depths of 3-4 feet with a water temperature of 75°F during long summer days.

Clatse Bay (Roscoe Inlet)
7 mi NE of Troup Narrows
Entrance: 52°21.78'N, 127°51.48'W
Anchor: 52°20.53'N, 127°50.51'W

Clatse Bay, on the south shore of Roscoe Inlet, offers good anchorage in all weather except strong outflow gales. The bay is a small classic fjord with high snowy peaks to the southeast. Loons, seagulls and honkers find the bay and the flat off Clatse Creek desirable. This spit provides a kayak haul-out and campsite with anchorage possible in 1 or 2 fathoms off the grassy point. The most secure anchorage can be found off the drying flat near the east shore not far from a bare white boulder. The mud flat is steep-to and largely dries. The point with trees in the center of the flat is a good place to leave your dinghy while you explore the meadows and creek to the south. Larger boats needing more swinging room should anchor in mid-channel.

Anchor in 3 fathoms over mud and some wood debris with good holding.

Shack Bay (Roscoe Inlet)
1.5 mi N of Clatse Pt.
Entrance: 52°22.94'N, 127°51.65'W
Anchor: 52°23.34'N, 127°51.63'W

Shack Bay offers good protection from northwest winds at the north end of the bay off a small grassy beach. This place has an excellent view of the snow cornices on 4,010-foot Mount Keys four miles to the south and the perpendicular grey granite wall just east of Shack Bay. Avoid the natural rock breakwater that extends about 300 feet from the grassy point on the northwest corner of the bay. Although we liked Shack Bay, some readers have disagreed with our perception.

Anchor in 6 fathoms over mud with good holding.

Time for a swim, head of Roscoe Inlet

Photo by Herb Nickles

Photo by Herb Nickles

Rock wall, east side Florence Peninsula, Roscoe Inlet

Ripley Bay (Roscoe Inlet)
4 mi N of Clatse Bay
Entrance: 52°24.68'N, 127°53.30'W
Anchor: 52°25.39'N, 127°53.34'W

Ripley Bay, 2 miles north of Shack Bay is too deep for convenient anchorage but it can offer temporary anchorage off the steep-to drying flat at the northeast corner of the bay. A rock with less than 6 feet over it, lies about 0.1 mile from the east shore and 0.8 mile NW of the west entrance point of Ripley Bay.

There is a waterfall on the west side of the bay as well as a large creek at the head.

Anchor in about 6 fathoms, over smooth mud with fair holding but, if you choose to anchor here, consider using a stern anchor on the flat to maintain a good bite on the steep-to face.

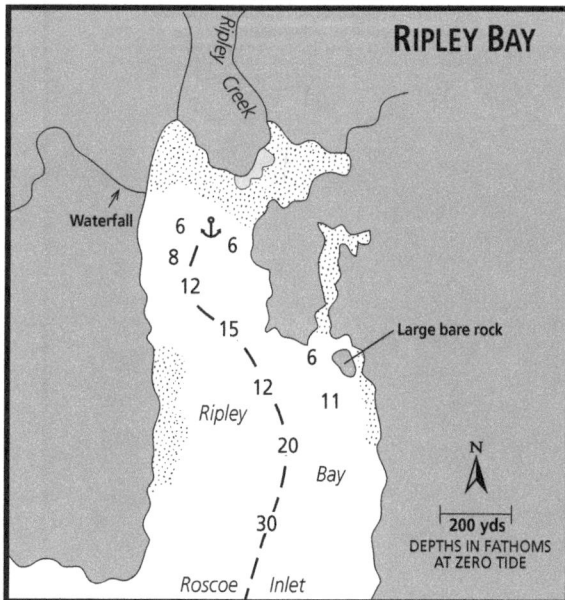

RIPLEY BAY

Ripley Creek

Waterfall

6 ⚓ 6
8
12
15
12
11
6
Large bare rock

Ripley

20

Bay

30

N

Roscoe Inlet

200 yds
DEPTHS IN FATHOMS
AT ZERO TIDE

©2024 Don and Réanne Douglass • Diagram not for navigation

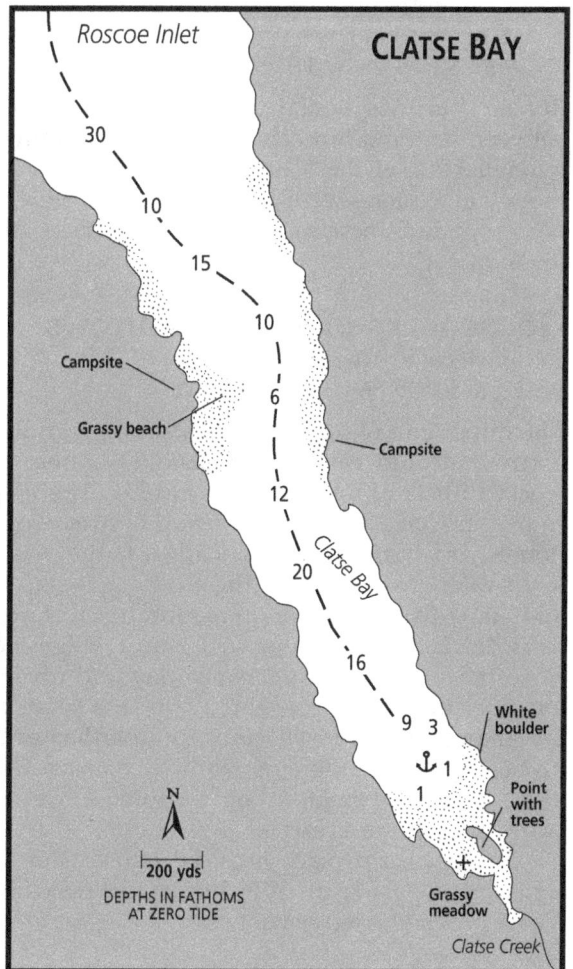

Roscoe Inlet

CLATSE BAY

30
10
15
10

Campsite

6

Grassy beach

Campsite

12

Clatse Bay

20

16

9 3
White
boulder

⚓ 1

1

Point
with
trees

N

200 yds
DEPTHS IN FATHOMS
AT ZERO TIDE

Grassy
meadow

Clatse Creek

©2024 Don and Réanne Douglass • Diagram not for navigation

Boukind Bay

(Roscoe Inlet)
6.8 mi N of Clatse Bay
Entrance: 52°26.99'N, 127°56.23'W
Anchor: 52°27.75'N, 127°56.25'W

Boukind Bay, one mile north of Roscoe Narrows, provides very good anchorage in most weather. The anchor site is on a flat shelf that starts approximately 300 yards off the shore and gently tapers to a small creek outlet. We find Boukind Bay to be the most convenient anchorage in Roscoe Inlet.

There is a primitive animal trail that extends a quarter-mile due north to Briggs Lagoon. This is a scenic and interesting hike through the rain forest, but you should carry a whistle or noisemaker to alert the bears that frequent this trail. Boots are advised due to the muskeg terrain.

Anchor in 5 fathoms over mud and sand with very good holding.

Roscoe Narrows

(Roscoe Inlet)
1 mi S of Boukind Bay
Position: 52°26.85'N, 127°55.71'W

Roscoe Narrows is the quarter-mile-wide channel between Boukind Bluff and Home Point leading east into what we call the "Goosenecks of the Roscoe." Although in winter, several inches of ice in the inlet have been reported, these same waters reach over 70°F in midsummer!

Goosenecks of Roscoe Narrows

3.6 mi NE of Roscoe Narrows
Position: 52°29.86'N, 127°52.41'W

The upper end of Roscoe Inlet, starting with Roscoe Narrows, could easily be mistaken for one of the world's finest alpine freshwater lakes. The serpentine route up Roscoe Inlet flows between granite domes which disappear vertically into the ocean below. Water streams down the cracks and slab faces, and snow patches linger on mountain summits and in gullies into late summer. The granite ridges nearly close the inlet east of Quartcha Bay and divert the currents the way "goosenecks" do in a giant river. Overhanging granite chimneys, amphitheaters, and arches dot the landscape. Nothing manmade is in sight. Without icefields to cool the inlet, summer saltwater temperatures exceed 70°F.

This beautiful place received conservancy designation as part of the 2016 British Columbia North Coast protection agreement.

Quartcha Bay (Roscoe Inlet)

4.5 mi NE of Boukind Bay
Entrance: 52°30.06'N, 127°50.63'W
Anchor: 52°30.62'N, 127°50.21'W

Quartcha Bay is a beautiful cul-de-sac with high granite mountains on each side and two main U-shaped valleys emptying into its head that reminds some visitors of Yosemite Valley. The western valley follows Quartcha Creek, winding in a broad turn to the north. A large grassy flat hides the creek behind a small peninsula. The northeast canyon is a classic glacier-carved shape with a high cascade falling 2,000 feet down from an alpine lake high in a granite bowl above.

If you enjoy alpine mountains, Quartcha Bay is one of the most spectacular anchorages in B.C.'s Inside Passage. Bold dark grey granite walls overhang the bay while evergreens cling to vertical ledges, filling the valleys and spreading their branches over saltwater in a perfectly horizontal line. There are no drift logs or evidence of chop. On a sunny day, serenity rules. The saltwater is 68°F (near the surface!) and swimming is in order. There are some pesky deer flies, but luckily, they can easily be captured or driven off.

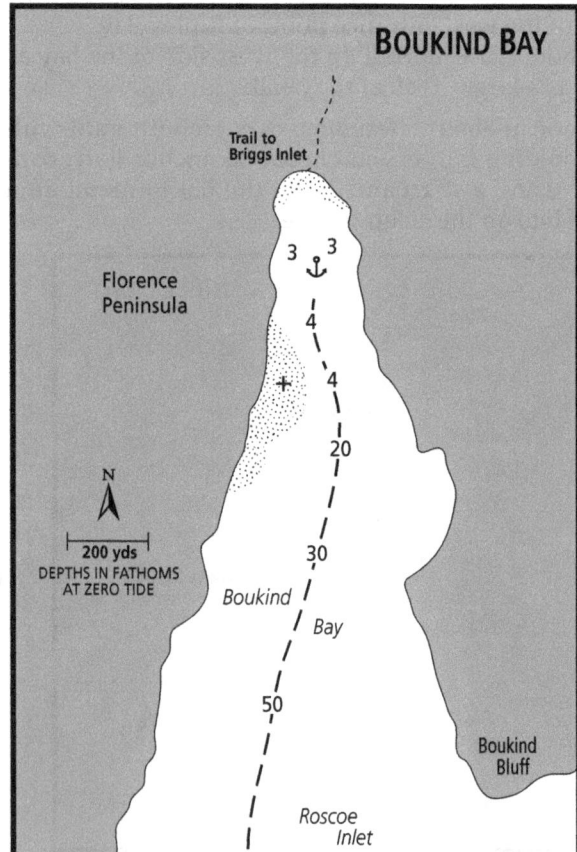

BOUKIND BAY

Trail to Briggs Inlet

Florence Peninsula

3   3

4

4

20

30

Boukind Bay

50

Boukind Bluff

Roscoe Inlet

N

200 yds
DEPTHS IN FATHOMS
AT ZERO TIDE

©2024 Don and Réanne Douglass • Diagram not for navigation

Temporary anchorage can be found along the steep margins of the drying flat along a 2- fathom shelf. Watch the tide level and signs of upslope winds. During heavy downslope winds holding is marginal on the steep-to slopes.

Anchor in 2 to 4 fathoms on the steep-to shore over sand and mud with fair-to-good holding.

Roscoe Creek

(Roscoe Inlet)
4.2 mi SE of Quartcha Bay
Entrance: 52°28.19'N, 127°44.62'W

Roscoe Creek flows from another beautiful 5-mile-long U-shaped valley. The shore is steep-to and extends into the bay on its west margin.

The fairway between treed Latch Island and the grassy delta on the south side of the narrow channel is 12 fathoms. Anchorage can be found 1.4 miles south at the bitter end.

Bitter End of Roscoe Inlet

8 mi E of Boukind Bay
Anchor: 52°27.09'N, 127°43.01'W

At its head, the finale of Roscoe Inlet features a crescendo of snow-covered ridge to the east, large grassy meadow on the valley delta to the southwest, high peaks, and silence. Bears roam the high meadows. With a water temperature as high as 75°F, swimming is refreshing in the saltwater topped with a layer of fresh water. No signs of serious weather reach this far end of the inlet and winds largely die out along the way.

Anchorage can be found at the bitter end of the bay, or temporarily for bear watching, off the steep-to creek delta to the west.

Anchor in 8 to 10 fathoms at the head of the inlet over a bottom of brown sand and mud with occasional rocks and wood debris; generally very good holding.

Troup Narrows

(Troup Passage)
9 mi N of Shearwater
Position: 52°17.08'N, 128°00.10'W

Troup Narrows (Deer Passage) is a calm, well-sheltered destination that makes a good overnight stop or an extended base camp for further exploration. The beautiful bay is landlocked and has a mostly flat, sandy bottom that is 5 fathoms deep with plenty of swinging room. On the west side of the narrows, you may find pictographs suggesting large human and animal shapes. (We transit the north end, keeping close to the east shore of Cunningham Island all the way.) We prefer to anchor on the north side of the narrows in a cove to the east, safe from all southerly storms.

Caution: There are many small underwater rocks and obstructions in this area, so move slowly with good bow lookouts and scout out your projected swinging area. The current is moderate and the narrows are not difficult to transit, but the fairway is narrow and an alert crew is essential. Favor the west shore on the north side, and the east shore on the south, but beware of rocks close off both shores. We have found the water to be clear to about 3 fathoms, so you can see most of the bottom as you transit the center of the passage.

Troup Narrows Cove

(Troup Passage)
0.3 mi E of Troup Narrows
Anchor: 52°16.98'N, 127°59.59'W

We call the first cove east of Troup Narrows on the north side "Troup Narrows Cove" and find it offers excellent protection in all weather. When approaching from the narrows, enter north of the 19-foot island (shown as 17 meters on charts) because the area south of it is foul. Avoid the shoaling flat off the creek on the east side of the bay.

Anchor in 5 fathoms over brown sand, shells, small rocks and kelp. Fair-to-good holding.

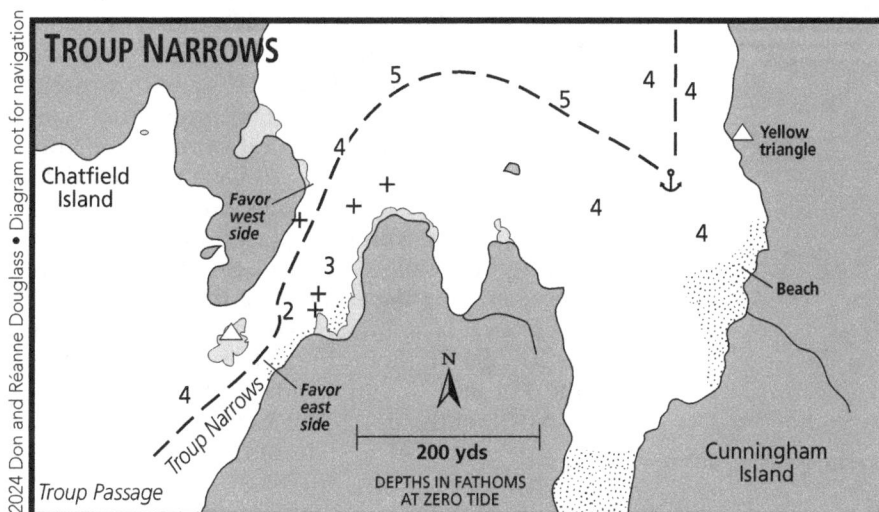

TROUP NARROWS

©2024 Don and Réanne Douglass • Diagram not for navigation

Chatfield Island — Favor west side — Favor east side — Troup Narrows — Troup Passage — Yellow triangle — Beach — Cunningham Island — N — 200 yds — DEPTHS IN FATHOMS AT ZERO TIDE

Discovery Cove (Troup Passage)
6 mi N of Shearwater
Entrance: 52°14.19'N, 128°01.18'W
Anchor: 52°13.76'N, 128°00.42'W

"Discovery Cove" is our name for the unnamed and undocumented cove on the west side of Cunningham Island. This overlooked and seldom-visited cove is centrally located in the middle of the Discovery Coast and provides very good shelter in all weather. High peaks and granite ridges form a landlocked bowl here in this pristine environment. The entrance bar has irregular depths and, in keeping with the spirit of exploration, we recommend you enter slowly with alert lookouts on the bow. Anchorage can be found almost anywhere in the bay. We prefer to anchor in either of the two nooks on the north side of the cove. This is a good, quiet place to explore by dinghy or kayak and it's only 8 miles from bustling New Bella Bella.

Anchor (north nook) in 4 fathoms over sand and mud with good holding.

Briggs Inlet (Return Channel)
2 mi N of Troup Narrows
Entrance: 52°19.15'N, 128°00.85'W
Briggs Inlet is entered east of Coldwell Point, the south end of Coldwell Peninsula.

From its entrance, Briggs Inlet appears to be a deep bay 2.5 miles long. In reality, you can see only the first quarter of the inlet because the first narrows makes a jog to the west, then resumes its northward path. It forms a fjord that ends less than 0.75 mile from the south end of Ellerslie Lake and 300 yards from Roscoe Inlet at Boukind Bay. The inlet has high angular mountains with exposed granite walls. Because of its position, Briggs Inlet is not subject to strong inflow or outflow winds. Drift trees collect on the beach on the west shore at Lat 52°21.04'N. Some protection from northerly winds may be found here.

First Narrows Cove
(Briggs Inlet)
0.2 mi E of First Narrows
Anchor: 52°21.78'N, 128°00.28'W

"First Narrows Cove" is what we call the cove directly east of First Narrows in Briggs Inlet. This is a good place to wait for proper tide conditions, and it is out of the current and any westerly or northerly winds. It is exposed to southerly winds as shown by the thick collection of derelict trees, stumps and driftwood.

Temporary anchorage can be found 100 yards off the beach.

Anchor in 6 fathoms over sand and gravel with fair holding.

Briggs First Narrows (Briggs Inlet)
2.5 mi N of entrance
Position: 52°21.68'N, 128°00.61

Favor the west shore to avoid the rocks off the southern end of the small peninsula. Water flow is laminar on a moderate flood with no apparent motion unless you look along the shore and see how fast the trees are flying by. On a 3-knot flood current, a large area of turbulent water starts just north of the narrows and lasts for the next half-mile or so with upwellings and small whirlpools; nothing dangerous, but enough to require a positive response from the helmsman. *Caution*: We have measured 4.1 knots through the narrows on an 8-foot tidal range that would suggest 5 or so knots on spring tidal range of 16 feet. Small waves were present along the east side of the fairway, with a current of 4 knots. We found a minimum depth of 3.5 fathoms in the fairway, rather than the 5 or more fathoms indicated on the chart.

North of the first narrows the shores become steep, with treeless slabs of dark granite rising high above.

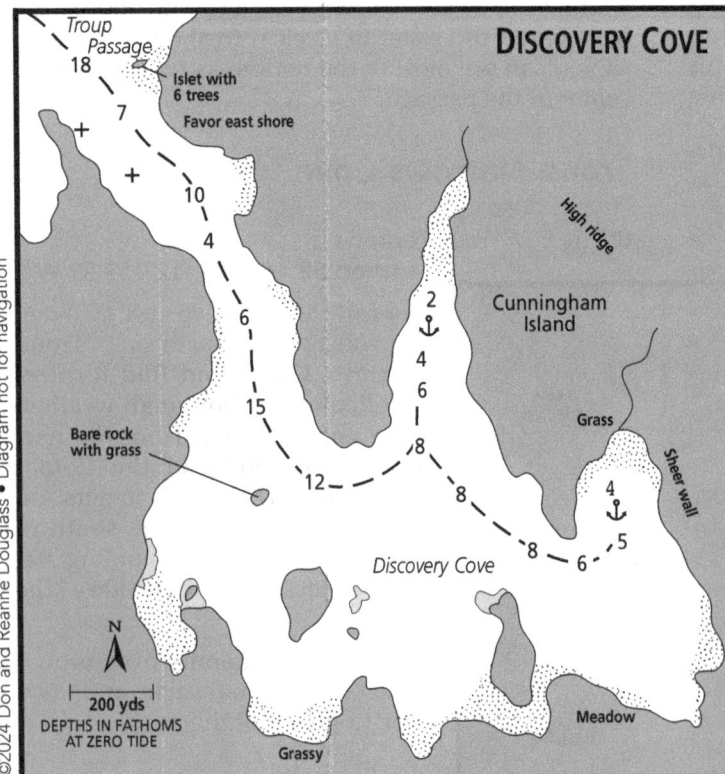

DISCOVERY COVE

Troup Passage
18
Islet with 6 trees
Favor east shore
7
10
4
High ridge
2
Cunningham Island
4
6
6
Grass
15
Bare rock with grass
8
Sheer wall
12
8
4
8
5
Discovery Cove
8
6
Meadow
Grassy

N
200 yds
DEPTHS IN FATHOMS
AT ZERO TIDE

©2024 Don and Réanne Douglass • Diagram not for navigation

Emily Bay

(Briggs Inlet)
1.8 mi N of Narrows
Entrance: 52°23.50'N, 128°00.00'W
Anchor: 52°23.53'N, 128°00.83'W

Emily Bay offers good protection from any weather. It is a scenic anchorage surrounded by high mountains. Ravens, crows, bald eagles and songbirds fill the air with calls and songs while seals cruise in the bay. A sharp-pointed peak lies directly behind the long lake that feeds the creek a short distance inland.

A difficult and overgrown primitive trail leads to Emily Lake, west of Emily Bay. Land your dinghy near the outlet of the creek, do not use the private mooring buoy. A raised boardwalk leads from the beach landing to a cabin. The trail continues on the far side of the cabin to a foot bridge over the creek. From the foot bridge to the lake is a difficult, primitive, muddy trail that follows two black plastic water pipes.

In the bay, avoid the rock off the south entrance that bares on a 2.5-foot tide as well as the two rocks on the north entrance that dry on an 11-foot tide. The fairway between the rocks has a depth of 12 fathoms and lies about 40 percent of the distance from the south shore to the north. We have entered carefully in pea soup fog proceeding slowly and measuring distances from the charted rocks. Emily Bay has an almost flat bottom of 9 fathoms, sand and shell. We found no signs of isolated rocks in our research, other than a one-fathom shoal on the north side of the bay near the entrance. Where the bottom slopes upward at the head of the bay off the creek, small boats can find anchorage. The creek has substantial flow

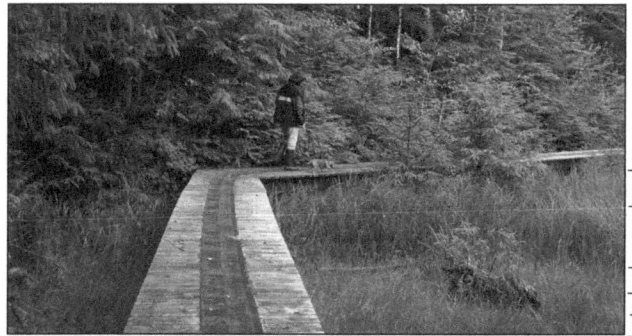
Boardwalk path from Emily Bay beach landing to the cabin

Primitive trail from cabin to lake follows plastic water pipes

and will keep your boat tethered in, even on a flood tide. An occasional back eddy may cause your boat to drift in toward the two rocky patches (with many small sharp barnacles) on either side of the creek exit or the mud flat with eel grass on the south shore. For this reason you may not want to anchor in less than 6 or 7 fathoms.

Anchor in 7 fathoms over sand and shell with good-to-very-good holding.

Anchor in 10 fathoms with good holding.

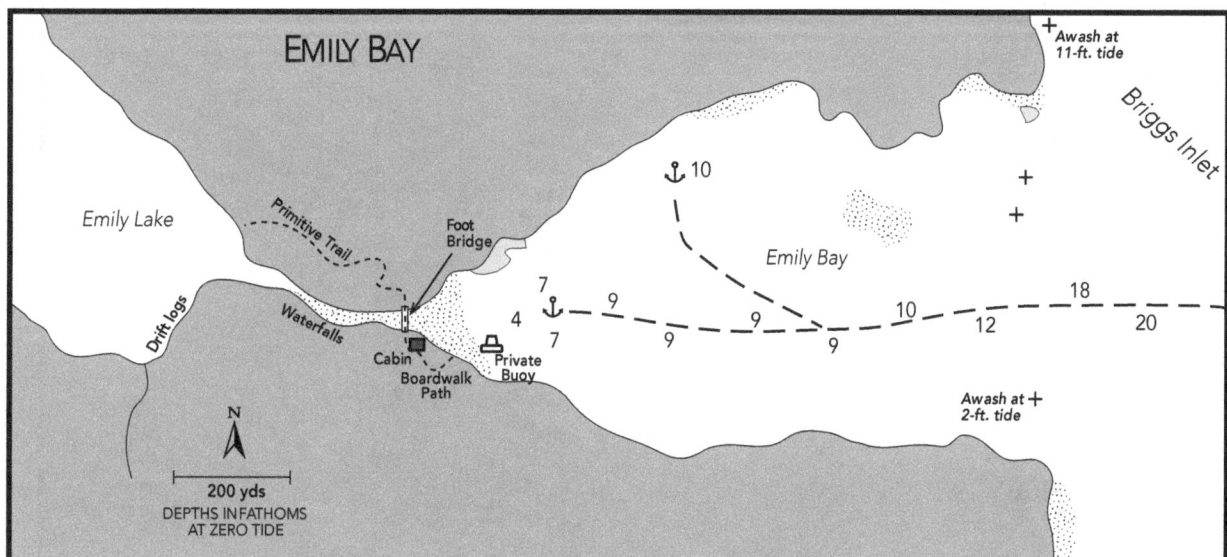
EMILY BAY

Emily Lake

Primitive Trail

Foot Bridge

Awash at 11-ft. tide

Briggs Inlet

Emily Bay

Drift logs

Waterfalls

Cabin

Boardwalk Path

Private Buoy

Awash at 2-ft. tide

N

200 yds
DEPTHS IN FATHOMS
AT ZERO TIDE

©2024 Don and Réanne Douglass • Diagram not for navigation

Briggs Second Narrows

5.5 mi N of Emily Bay
Entrance (W): 52°28.67'N, 127°57.60'W

The "Second Narrows" is what we call the entrance to Briggs Lagoon. The Narrows are tidal rapids of fast-moving water on large tides and care must be taken not to be swept into the rock attached to the north shore at the entrance or the more dangerous rock farther east and almost exactly mid-channel. *Note*: The isolated rock is not a continuation of the rock attached to shore.

Entry should be made at or near high-water slack only. Larger boats may find this site uncomfortable; reconnoiter first if doubtful. Due to the brown, opaque water, visual sighting of the mid-channel rock cannot be counted upon. We have exited Briggs Lagoon at low-water slack with the mid-channel rock showing 2 inches just an hour and 20 minutes after a low tide of 3.9 feet at New Bella Bella. We passed between the isolated rock and the south shore with only 10 feet between our boat and the rock to starboard and 10 feet to the south shore to port. Slack water at low tide lasts for only a few minutes and the current builds quickly. The foam generated on the lee of the rock on the last of the ebb will stop moving and then start moving east indicating slack water. The flood current makes a sweeping turn tending to

set you over the mid-channel rock—so beware! Minimum depth in the fairway at low water was about 8 feet, *not* the 6 meters (19 feet) indicated on the chart. Second Narrows is short and brief and you soon encounter deep water again.

Fisheries boats sometimes anchor overnight west of the narrows and report calm anchorage even when a southeast gale is blowing in the outer channels.

Briggs Lagoon

(Briggs Inlet)
10 mi N of Briggs Entrance
Entrance (Second Narrows): 52°28.71'N, 127°57.49'W

Briggs Lagoon is entered through Second Narrows at the head of Briggs Inlet at the east side. This is a true "hole-in-the-wall" experience. You can see only high granite ridges in all directions until you are directly in front of the narrow opening. The lagoon has poor water exchange creating opaque water and there is no freshwater creek to provide an outflow current. Inside, the water deepens and trees, limbs, rockweed and other flotsam are permanently caught in the lagoon. There are plenty of protected anchor sites here, such as the southeast lagoon cove, the northeast cove, or the central south portion used occasionally by fishing boats.

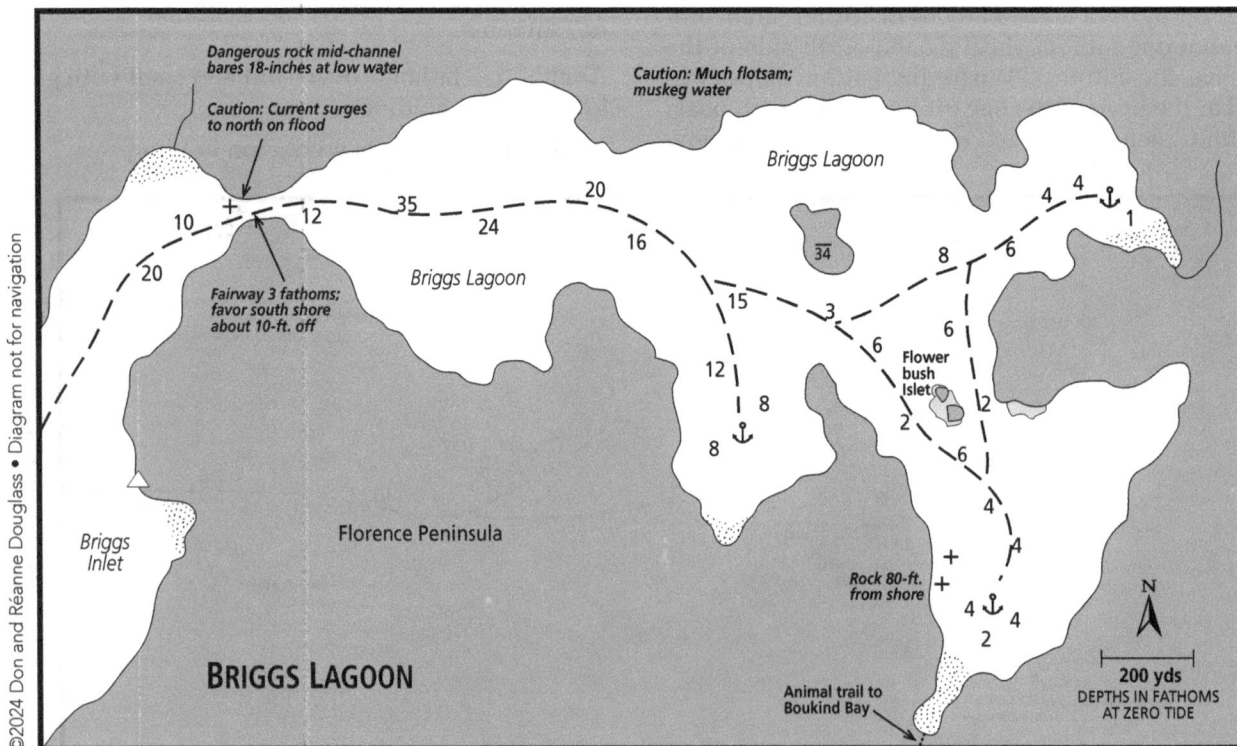

Southeast Lagoon Cove

(Briggs Lagoon)
1 mi E of Second Narrows
Anchor: 52°28.24'N, 127°56.22'W

The southeast corner of Briggs Lagoon, which we call "Southeast Lagoon Cove," offers very good protection off the drying flat. Enter on the south side of island (34) over a shoal of about 2 fathoms. Once past either side of "Flower Rock," the bottom is a flat 4 to 5 fathoms. There is extensive flotsam throughout Briggs Lagoon—trees, branches and small patches of floating rockweed—so careful helmsmanship is required. In this quiet place ravens chortle, crows caw-caw, loons croon their forlorn cry, kingfishers issue staccato alarms, woodpeckers hammer, and songbirds sing, while man-o-war pulse by, and small jellyfish wander in all directions.

Geza and Don input info on the latest anchorage

Boukind Bay lies just 300 yards due south of the bitter end of Southeast Lagoon across a small low spit of rainforest. A bear trail can be followed through the rain forest, but boots are a necessity. Make lots of noise here—we use a police whistle which we keep in our mouth all the time! There is an elevation gain of about 60 feet or so to the saddle. If you find yourself climbing more, you are off-route. Favor the west side of the very small creek on the Briggs Lagoon side and the east side of a small creek on the Roscoe Inlet side. The only annoying thing about this lovely, quiet place is the small black flies that find the boat when the wind stops—they love to bite.

Anchoring can be found almost anywhere in the eastern part of Briggs Lagoon in moderate depths. Larger boats may want to use the cove south southwest of island (34) where anchorage can be found in 8 fathoms off the small gravel beach. The best anchorage is in the far southeast corner near where the short hike to Boukind Bay begins. In Southeast Lagoon Cove, an uncharted rock extends about 80 feet from the west shore and a bare rock extends from the east shore at the head.

Anchor (southeast corner) in 4 fathoms over soft black mud with very good holding.

Choosing to Go Remote

A biology teacher and a college manager speculating on retirement: what to do for the next 30 years? Play bingo at the Seniors' Centre, or . . .?

Joe, the son of a Norwegian fisherman, and a commercial fisherman, himself, from an early age, and I—having grown up at the water's edge on a large lake—felt the need to rehydrate after having lived on the Alberta prairie for 28 years.

I thought Kootenay Lake would be a nice choice. But then a chance real estate advertisement tempted us with "three bedroom ocean waterfront home, $39,000." After a dozen phone calls we flew to Ocean Falls along the Discovery Coast to check out the property—in February, no less!

Awaiting us was sun on newly fallen snow, mirrored in a fjord where halibut and shellfish reside, and an opportunity to live an adventure in a setting that reminded us both of our childhood. And . . . the price was right!

Could we survive without a mall nearby—hmph? Is it forever? As long as we want it to be! Comparing this luscious vacation setting to a traditional residential suburb—bingo versus all this?

If this is a dream, don't wake me up too soon!

—Sally Isaksen
Note: Sally and Joe Isaksen made Ocean Falls their home for a number of years.

SPILLER CHANNEL

N

1/2 mile

to Ingram Bay

Spiller Inlet

Ellerslie Lagoon

Ellerslie Falls

Ellerslie Bay

Tidal Falls

"East Anchorage"

Ellerslie Lake

Cheenis Lake

Cheenis Lake Cove

Nash Passage

Nash Cove

Nash

"Second Narrows"

Briggs Lagoon

Neekas Cove

"Fish Weir Cove"

Trail

S.E. Lagoon Cove

Neekas Inlet

Spiller Channel

"Bullock Channel North Cove"

Briggs Inlet

Boukind Bay

Roscoe Inlet

Don Peninsula

"Island 45 Cove"

Florence Peninsula

"Island 35 Cove"

Coldwell Peninsula

"Five Meter Hole"

Mosquito Bay

Emily Bay

Spiller Lagoon

Spiller Channel

Yeo Island

Bullock Channel

"First Narrows"

"First Narrows Cove"

"Bullock Spit Cove"

Tankeeah River

Return Channel

Johnson Channel

to Seaforth Channel

Yeo Cove

Chatfield Island

Troup Narrows

Cunningham Island

Roscoe Inlet

Wigham Cove

Morehouse Bay

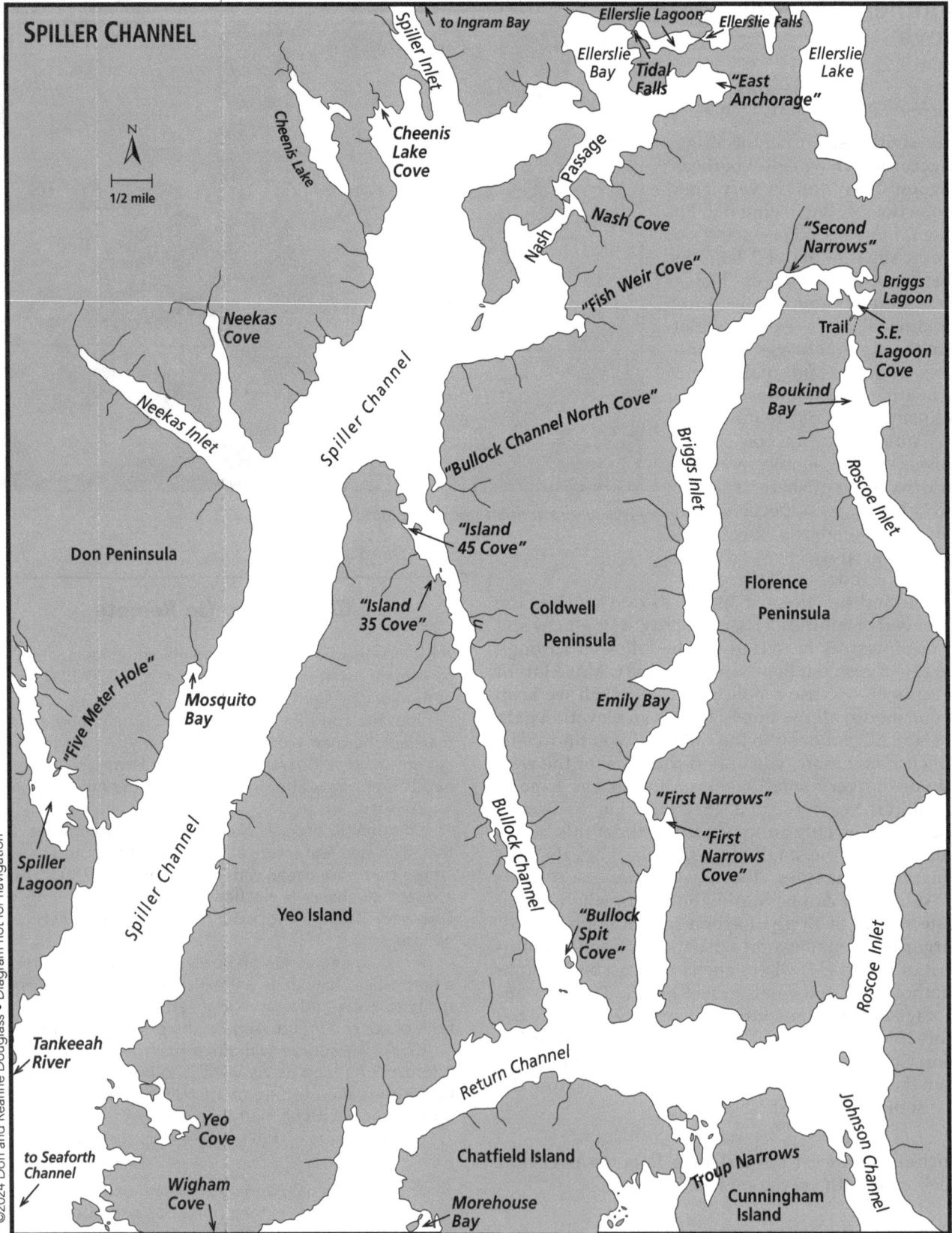

©2024 Don and Reanne Douglass • Diagram not for navigation

Return Channel (Yeo and Chatfield islands)
S side of Yeo Island
Entrance (E): 52°18.20'N, 127°58.20'
Entrance (W): 52°16.90'N, 128°12.60'W

Return Channel connects Roscoe Inlet, Briggs Inlet, Bullock Channel and Spiller Channels. There are several good anchorages along the way (east to west), namely Beaumont Island, Troup Narrows, Morehouse Bay, Wigham Cove and Raven Cove. Return Channel has protected waters and is usually quite calm.

Morehouse Bay (Return Channel)
3 mi E of Wigham Cove
Entrance: 52°16.62'N, 128°06.16'W
Anchor: 52°16.28'N, 128°05.08'W

Morehouse Bay, 4 miles within the west entrance of Return Channel, has good protection from all weather deep at the head of the bay. The southwest cove in Morehouse Bay is easy to enter and provides good shelter in 12 to 15 fathoms. The cove in the southeast portion of the bay has very good land-locked shelter in 7 to 9 fathoms, but you must cross or avoid the two shoal areas shown on charts, that are covered with water at about 4 feet at zero tide.

Anchor in 9 fathoms over mud and sand with very good holding.

Raven Cove (Return Channel)
1.9 mi S of Wigham Cove
Entrance: 52°15.11'N, 128°09.49'W
Anchor: 52°14.90'N, 128°09.08'W

Raven Cove offers good shelter deep in the southeast corner of the bay. The bottom is somewhat irregular and rocky so you need to avoid the rocks in the approach.

Anchor in 6 to 7 fathoms over a mixed bottom with good holding if well set.

Dearth Island Cove (Seaforth Channel)
2.7 mi NW of Kynumpt Hbr
Entrance: 52°14.88'N, 128°12.49'W
Anchor: 52°15.00'N, 127°12.06'W

The south side of Dearth Island has a small cove we call "Dearth Island Cove." While open to the west and not generally considered a viable anchorage, it is, in fact, an intimate scenic cove in calm weather, offering good protection from everything except strong westerlies. The cove is almost landlocked and shows little evidence of exposure to anything except southwest chop. This is one of the few anchor sites

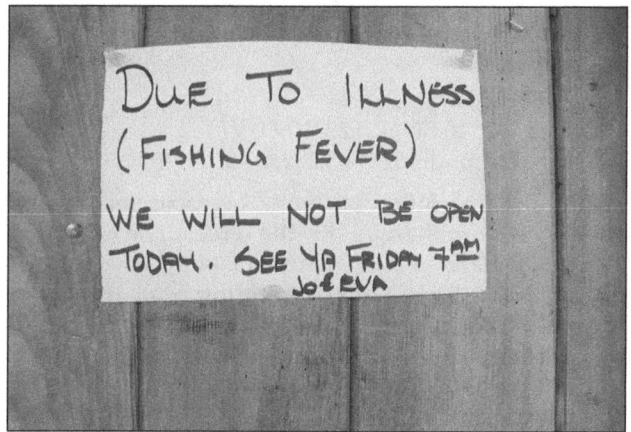

Contagious "disease" in many North Coast villages

along Seaforth Channel where you will not feel the wake of passing cruise ships or large commercial craft.

Anchorage can be found on the north side of island (140) opposite a canoe passage and a small peninsula on the south side of Dearth Island, just north of Beazley Island. Approach from the west only; the area north of Beazley Island is foul.

Anchor in 7 fathoms over mud with good holding.

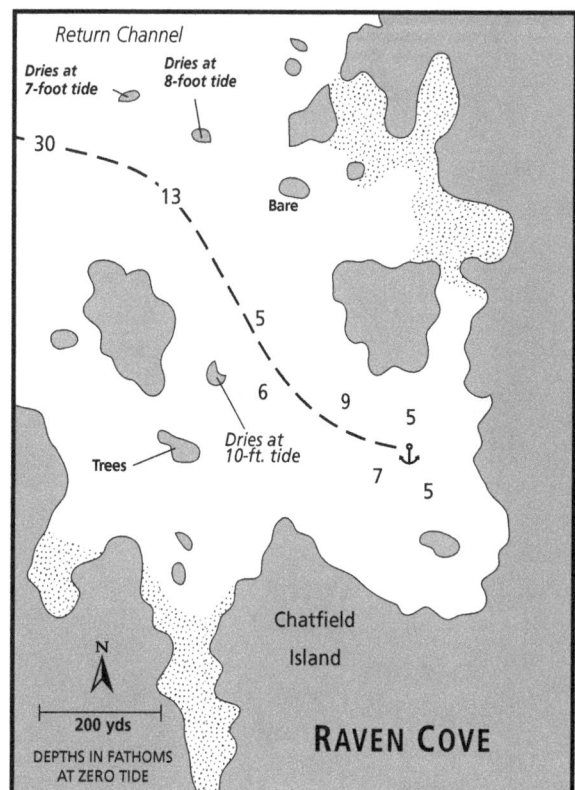

Wigham Cove

(Yeo Island)
1 mi NE of Dearth Island
Entrance: 52°16.50'N, 128°10.60'W
Anchor (east end): 52°16.92'N, 128°09.96'W

Wigham Cove offers perhaps the most secure and easy-access anchorage in the area. The entrance channel is narrow and you must favor the west shore to avoid the large shoal extending well into mid-channel. Commercial and larger boats find anchorage in the north end of the cove while smaller boats find a little more shelter in the east end of the cove. The bottom in Wigham Cove is a flat 10 to 15 fathoms, and there is room for a number of boats. This is a popular place when the west end of Seaforth Channel is fog-bound.

Anchor in 5 fathoms over stinky mud with very good holding.

Bullock Channel

(Yeo Island/Coldwell Peninsula)
5.6 mi NE of Wigham Cove
Entrance (S): 52°19.20'N, 128°02.30'W
Entrance (W): 52°26.40'N, 128°05.50'W

Bullock Channel, on the east side of Yeo Island, is

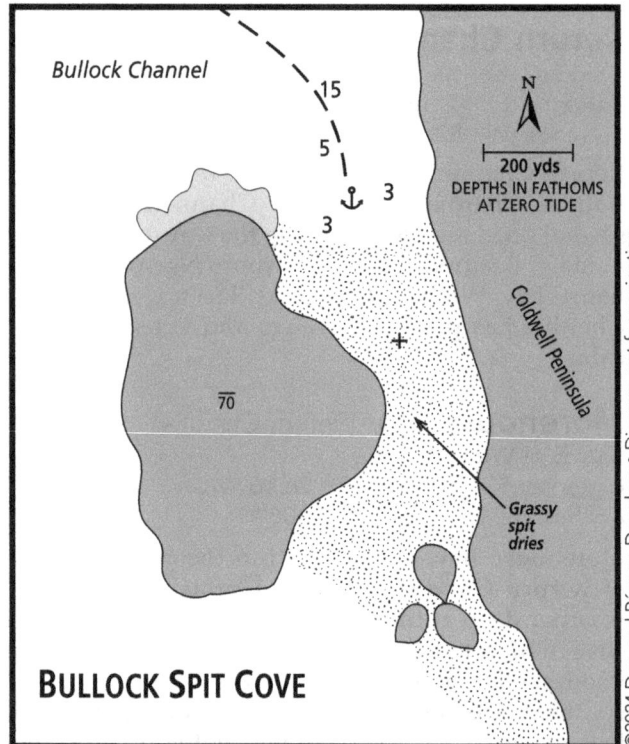

BULLOCK SPIT COVE

©2024 Don and Réanne Douglass • Diagram not for navigation

the quickest way to reach the upper reaches of Spiller Channel from New Bella Bella. The currents are moderate, there is less wind and chop than Spiller Channel, and once north of the entrance islets, a mid-channel course is free of dangers. We have found a north-flowing ebb on occasion, which is a little difficult to understand, so don't be surprised. Along the way, several places make good temporary stops.

Bullock Spit Cove (Bullock Channel)

0.9 mi N of Bullock entr
Anchor: 52°20.00'N, 128°02.27'W

"Bullock Spit Cove" is our name for the small nook on the north side of island (70), on the east side of Bullock Channel, 0.75 mile inside its south entrance. The spit gives good protection from southerly weather.

A grassy spit between the island and the peninsula is navigable only by kayak on 14-foot spring tides.

Anchor in 5 fathoms, over brown sand, small rocks, and mud with good holding.

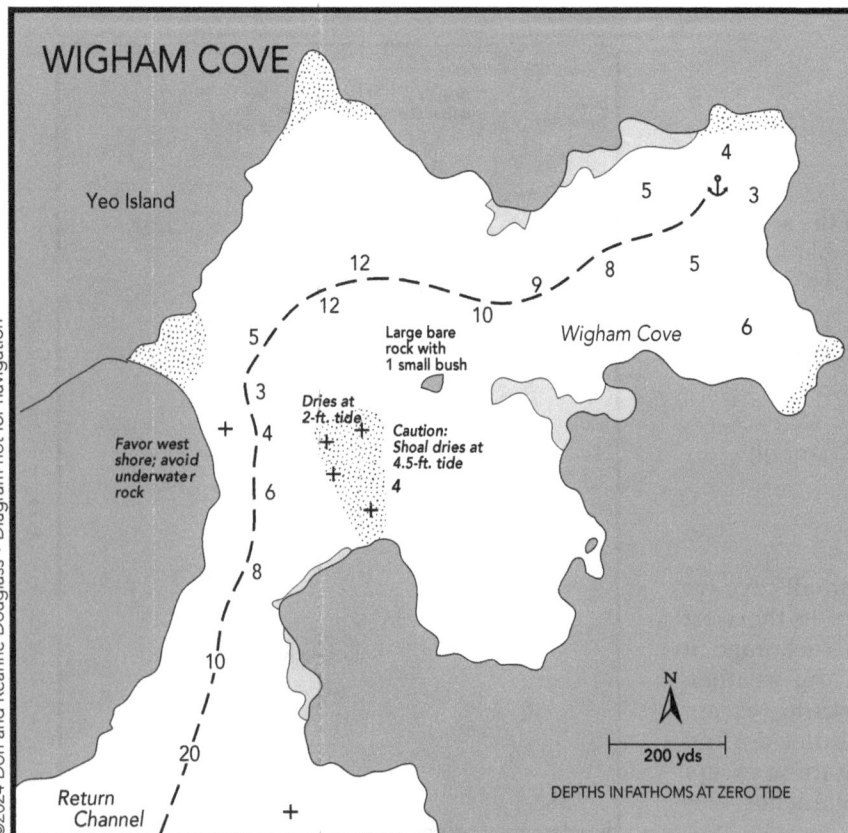

WIGHAM COVE

Mouth of Bay (Bullock Channel)
2.7 mi S of N entrance
Anchor: 52°23.68'N, 128°04.54'W

Two-thirds of the way up Bullock Channel, a small bay on the west shore that can offer anchorage in fair weather makes a good lunch stop. The bay is one-half mile north of a small grass-covered rock that dries at 14 feet close along the west shore. The beach of the bay is fairly steep-to and has eel grass marking the low-tide line. You'll probably see a seal cruising the bay.

Tuck in close to the south point, avoiding a rock about 75 feet northwest of the south point. Underwater visibility is limited to about six feet due to the muskeg water.

Anchor in 4 fathoms over sand and gravel with good holding.

Island (35) Cove (Bullock Channel)
1.4 mi S of north entrance
Anchor: 52°24.94'N, 128°04.99'W

The cove on the west side of island (35) can be used by small boats for protection against southerlies, but it is open to the north. This cove has a nice view and makes a good lunch stop.

Anchor in 3 fathoms on a shelf off the southwest shore over sand with worm casings; fair holding.

Island (45) Cove (Bullock Channel)
0.9 mi S of N entrance
Anchor: 52°25.48'N, 128°05.53'W

Island (45) Cove, located one mile southeast of Gerald Point, provides moderate protection from southerly weather due to its extensive drying reefs and rocks between island (45) and the shore. It is open to outflow winds from the north. The preferred entry is from the north side of island (45).

Anchor in 4 fathoms over sand with eel grass that marks the low-tide line; fair holding.

Bullock Channel North Cove
0.4 mi SE of N entrance
Anchor: 52°26.14'N, 128°04.89'W

Enter west of island (39) by staying north of a line extending west from the south tip of island (39) until you are close aboard the island, then head southeast into the cove, avoiding the rock on the south tip of the island. Larger boats can simply round island (39) on the north side. There is very good protection from southerlies and moderate protection from downslope northerly winds. Anchor anywhere in the cove over a relatively flat 6- to 7-fathom bottom. The south end of the cove dries, so do not anchor south of the line

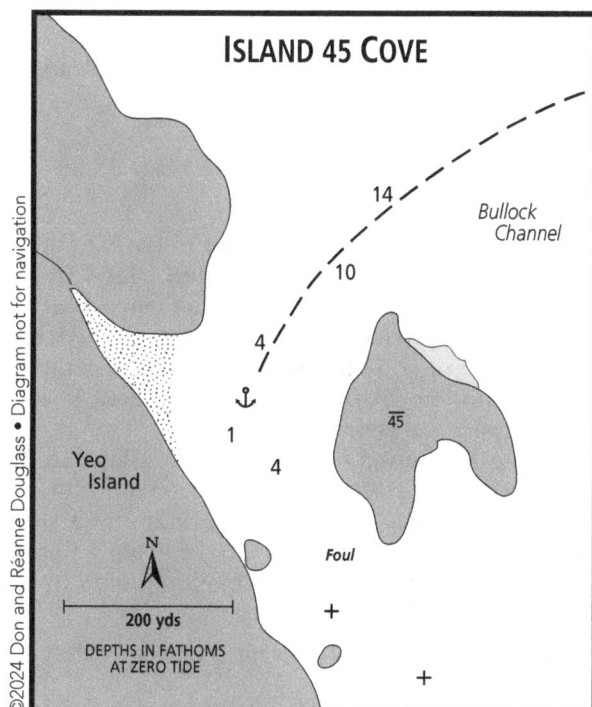

ISLAND 45 COVE

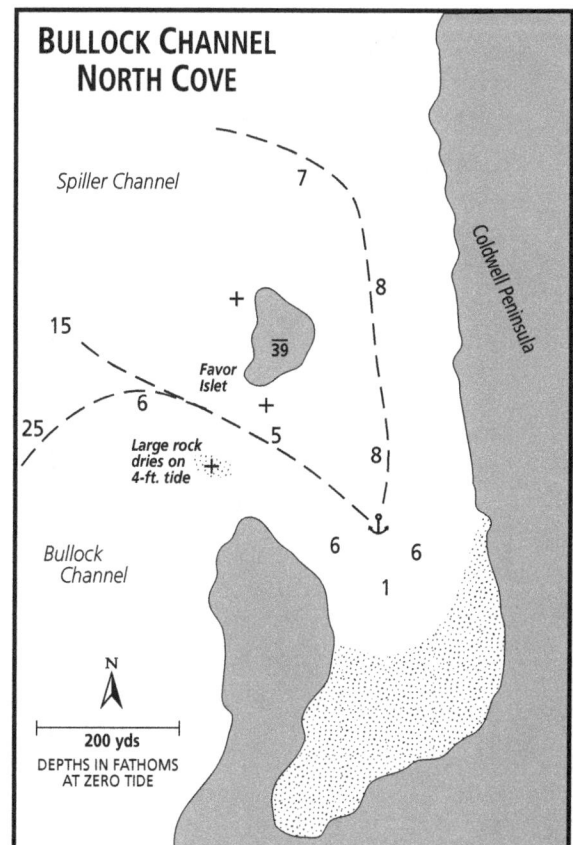

BULLOCK CHANNEL NORTH COVE

between the point of the peninsula and the creek on the east shore.

Caution: The mid-channel entrance rock extends well west of a line between the peninsula and island (39) and can be dangerous in poor visibility.

Anchor in 6 fathoms over sand and shell with good holding.

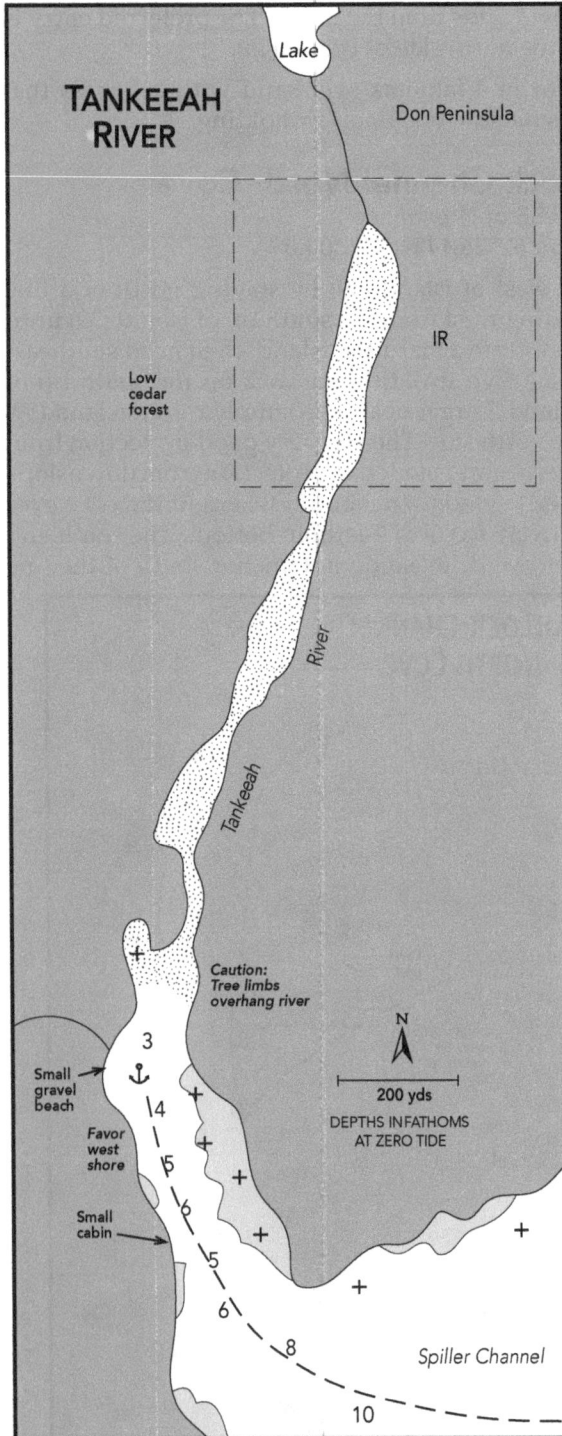

TANKEEAH RIVER

Lake

Don Peninsula

IR

Low cedar forest

River

Tankeeah

Caution: Tree limbs overhang river

N

3

Small gravel beach

4

Favor west shore

5

Small cabin

6

5

6

8

10

200 yds

DEPTHS IN FATHOMS AT ZERO TIDE

Spiller Channel

©2024 Don and Réanne Douglass • Diagram not for navigation

Spiller Channel

6.4 mi E of Ivory Island lt.
Entrance (S): 52°17.00'N, 128°14.20'W

Spiller Channel is wide and very deep with a strong ebb flow that can quickly kick up a chop when moderate south upslope winds prevail. Spiller Channel leads to some fine cruising in the area of Ellerslie Bay and in the Ingram Arm of Spiller Inlet. Yeo Cove is a well-sheltered anchorage that makes a good base camp for exploring the area.

Tankeeah River (Spiller Channel)

2.4 mi SW of Yeo Cove
Anchor: 52°17.74'N, 128°15.70'W

Tankeeah River, known locally as "Tinkey," is 2 miles due west of Grief Island. It is a shallow river flowing out of the low, flat, south end of Don Peninsula 4 miles south of Lake Mountain. Cruising boats can anchor temporarily off a small gravel beach on the west shore a quarter-mile inside the entrance. This anchorage is well out of the chop frequently found in this part of Spiller Channel.

On entering Tankeeah River, avoid the rocks near shore and fallen silver snags that point directly out into the river. You can explore the upper reaches of the river at high water by dinghy, paddling through a narrow channel with cedar branches nearly filling the route. This is not mountainous like the area to the north, but a swampy muskeg environment of thick cedar rain forest with dark brown water. Eagles and seals patrol the river.

Anchor in 3 fathoms over gravel with fair holding.

Yeo Cove (Spiller Channel)

1.9 mi NE of Spiller Entrance
Anchor: 52°17.78'N, 128°10.98'W

Very good protection can be found in the far end of Yeo Cove tucked in behind the small island in the southwest corner. The approach is on the west side of island (72). The fairway is located between the rocks alongside island (72) and the rock and reef complex which extends north from the south shore. A slow, cautious approach is prudent.

The small secluded nook behind the island in the southwest corner of the cove is hidden from the logging activity. Swinging room is limited and a stern tie to the island can be useful. Larger boats will find adequate swinging room in 10 to 12 fathoms in the northeast part of the cove.

Anchor in 2 to 3 fathoms over mud bottom with very good holding.

Spiller Lagoon (Spiller Channel)
3.5 mi NW of Yeo Cove
Entrance: 52°21.68'N, 128°12.10'W

Spiller Lagoon is the local name for a 3-mile deep penetration of Don Peninsula—the waterway on the west shore of Spiller Channel, 3.5 miles due north of Yeo Cove. This was probably a freshwater lake until recent geologic time. It has a difficult and dangerous entrance and we do not recommend it to general cruising boats, especially larger boats. The current is quite strong in the entrance and it's a good idea to reconnoiter first by dinghy before entering. Rocks and reefs fill the narrow and shallow entrance to the inlet, and currents on flood and ebb run 2 to 3 knots, pulling the thick kelp under and interfering with steerage. At high water, many of the key rocks are submerged and are particularly dangerous. At low water, the rocks are generally visible but do not seem to be in their relative position on the chart because of the chart scale and current. Because of these difficulties, there has been no commercial exploitation and the inlet is filled with more than its share of seals, eagles, loons and other fauna. We recommend it only to explorers who are comfortable with the entrance.

Favor the west shore at the entrance until the large drying rock system clogging the mid-channel is passed, then immediately favor the east shore to avoid the rock that protrudes from the south shore. The route requires a significant left turn prior to reaching island (21) and its shallow bar, and staying between two rocks that submerge at about 10 feet on the south side and 13 feet on the north side. The bar has a minimum depth of about 6 feet at zero tide. A strong flood current will quickly carry you into foul ground between the dangerous dry reef that dries at about 13 feet, and the small island directly east. Both of these rocks are part of a larger shoal complex marked with substantial patches of bull kelp, visible when the current is minimum but pulled under and invisible on spring tides. Anchorage can be taken at the deep southern end of the inlet or in either of the two shallow coves at the north end of the inlet. Five Meter Hole, a half-mile north of the shallow bar, is centrally located for convenient anchorage.

Five Meter Hole
(Spiller Lagoon)
1 mi NW of entrance
Entrance: 52°22.35'N, 128°12.83'W
Anchor: 52°22.53'N, 128°12.81'W

There is a shallow gunk hole on the north shore of Spiller Lagoon which provides good protection in stable weather. It is sheltered by a number of rocks and reefs which must be carefully negotiated. Enter from the south avoiding the charted rocks as well as an uncharted rock near the southeast corner of the hole off the peninsula.

Because the inlet/lagoon has been uncharted and lacks commercial interest, it is pristine and has an abundance of fauna. Seals, loons, eagles and ducks find refuge here. Five Meter Hole is a good base camp for exploring the inlet but swinging room is limited for larger vessels. Additional anchor sites can be found in both the north and south end of the inlet.

Anchor in 2 fathoms over mud with good holding.

Mosquito Bay
(Spiller Channel)
2.4 mi N of Spiller Lagoon
Position: 52°23.70'N, 128°10.10'W

Mosquito Bay, 2.5 miles south of Neekas Inlet, offers no protection from southerly weather, but it does make a good lunch stop in prevailing northwest winds if you anchor close to the rocky beach. The shore is steep-to, rising dramatically from a depth of 16 fathoms to one fathom. Avoid the two rocks due south of Mosquito Bay that dry at about 2 feet at zero tide. The bottom has poor holding.

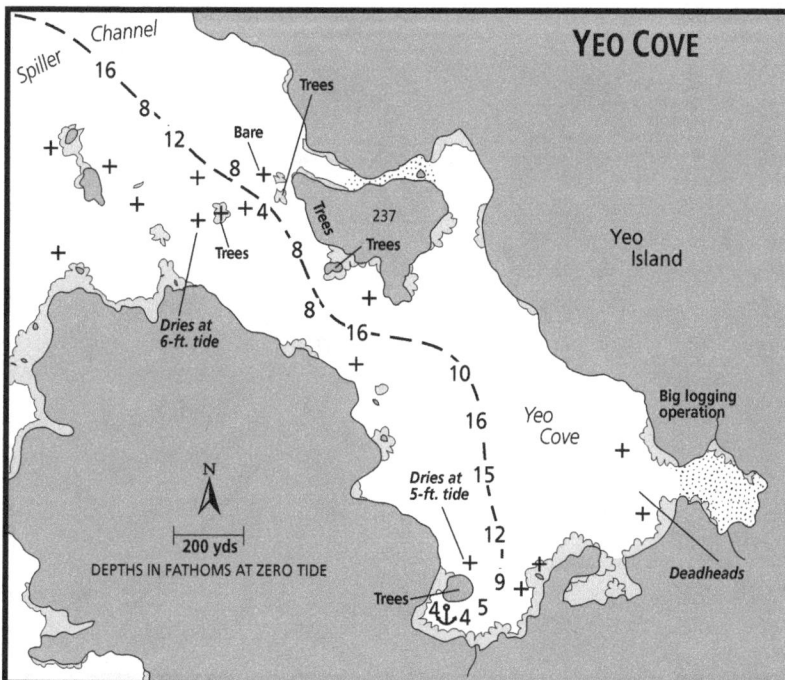

YEO COVE

Spiller Channel
16
8
12
Bare
8
4
Trees
Trees
237
Trees
Yeo Island
8
8
Dries at 6-ft. tide
16
10
Yeo Cove
16
Big logging operation
Dries at 5-ft. tide
15
12
Deadheads
9
Trees
4 4 5

N

200 yds
DEPTHS IN FATHOMS AT ZERO TIDE

©2024 Don and Réanne Douglass • Diagram not for navigation

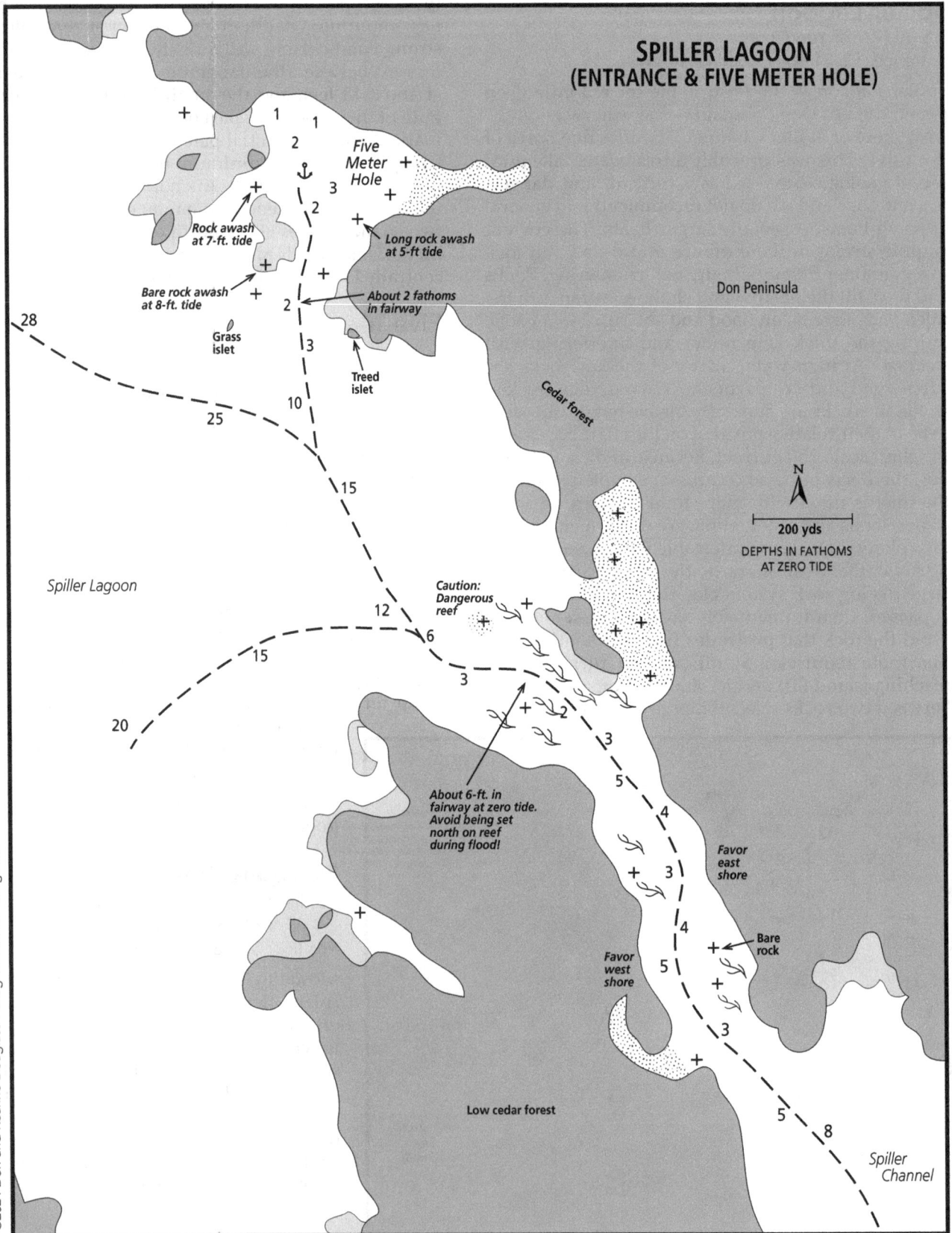

SPILLER LAGOON
(ENTRANCE & FIVE METER HOLE)

1   1
2
Five
Meter
Hole
3
2
Rock awash
at 7-ft. tide
Long rock awash
at 5-ft tide

Don Peninsula

Bare rock awash
at 8-ft. tide
About 2 fathoms
in fairway

2

Grass
islet

3

28

Treed
islet

10

Cedar forest

25

15

N

200 yds

DEPTHS IN FATHOMS
AT ZERO TIDE

Spiller Lagoon

Caution:
Dangerous
reef

12

15

6

20

3

2

3

About 6-ft. in
fairway at zero tide.
Avoid being set
north on reef
during flood!

5

4

Favor
east
shore

3

Favor
west
shore

4

Bare
rock

5

3

Low cedar forest

5

8

Spiller
Channel

©2024 Don and Réanne Douglass • Diagram not for navigation

Neekas Inlet (Spiller Channel)
8.5 mi N of Yeo Cove
Entrance: 52°26.10'N, 128°08.70'W
Anchor: 52°27.72'N, 128°12.30'W

Neekas Inlet is easy to enter and provides fair protection for all but southeast winds. However, we prefer to anchor in nearby Neekas Cove where there is better protection and more scenic surroundings.

Anchor (head of inlet) in 7 fathoms over mud and gravel with unrecorded holding.

Neekas Cove (Neekas Inlet)
N side of Neekas Inlet
Entrance: 52°26.64'N, 128°09.19'W
Anchor: 52°27.99'N, 128°09.57'W

Neekas Cove offers surprisingly good protection, even when Spiller Channel kicks up a nasty up-channel chop. Southerly winds die down as you proceed up the cove and there is little driftwood or indication of exposure common to south-facing coves. Local knowledge, however, relates that this is not a good place to be caught in a southeast storm, but up to about 30 knots southeasterlies this is a fine anchor site.

At the head of the cove is a large drying flat with a few stumps, rocks, and lots of flat grassy areas. This scenic, quiet place is easy to enter. A shoaling area halfway up the cove should be of no concern when you keep a mid-channel route.

Anchor in 4 fathoms over sand and mud with good holding.

Nash Passage (Spiller Channel)
1.5 mi S of Ellerslie Bay
Entrance (S): 52°27.90'N, 128°04.00'W
Entrance (N): 52°30.40'N, 128°01.60'W

There is a small, well-sheltered passage east of the large unnamed island at the head of Spiller Channel which we named "Nash Passage" after Professor Roderick Frazier Nash who, aboard his trawler *Forevergreen,* assisted in our research of this area.

Nash Passage, entered from the south between two rocky projections, appears, at first, to be a dead-end. After 0.6 mile there are a number of large rocks requiring sharp, elbow turns. Turn east and pass the rocks on your port side. When abeam the deep valley to the south ("Nash Narrows Cove"), turn hard left at the "elbow" and proceed up the channel. The east shore is a bold overhanging granite bluff.

Caution: We found an uncharted one-fathom shoal on the north side of the easternmost rock near the east

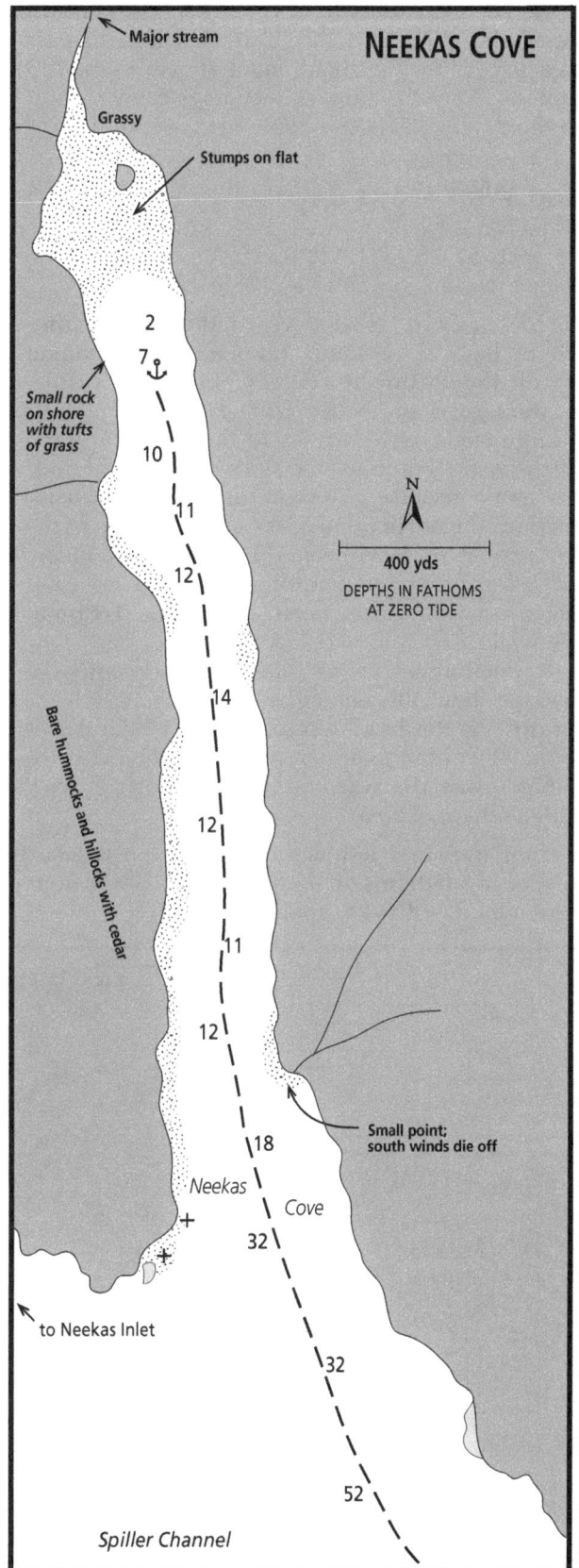

NEEKAS COVE

400 yds
DEPTHS IN FATHOMS
AT ZERO TIDE

©2024 Don and Réanne Douglass • Diagram not for navigation

shore. There are several rocks close ashore beneath the overhanging bluff. Minimum depth in the passage, except for the shoal noted above, is about 3 fathoms. A scenic and safe anchorage can be found off the drying flat at the elbow turning point.

Fish Weir Cove (Spiller Channel)
4.6 mi NE of Neekas Cove
Entrance: 52°28.05'N, 128°02.20'W
Anchor (N side): 52°28.15'N, 128°01.98'W

"Fish Weir Cove," is what we call the small, round-shaped bight at the south end of a large, unnamed bay off the northwest side of Coldwell Peninsula. It offers good protection from almost all winds. A large avalanche scar lies to the east, along the north-facing granite slope. We've given the cove this name because of the prehistoric fish weir located off the north point of the cove. It is one of the best preserved we've seen. Ed and Virginia Lester on *Cadenza* reported that they observed a second intact fish weir on the north side of the stream at low water.

A one-fathom, sandy shoal extends into the cove for about 100 feet midway between two large stumps on the beach. You can see to depths of about 12 feet in the brown water; the temperature—at 67°F—was the warmest we encountered in the Spiller Channel area.

Anchor in 3 to 4 fathoms on a shelf on the north side, or in 8 fathoms on the south side. The bottom is brown mud, with very good holding.

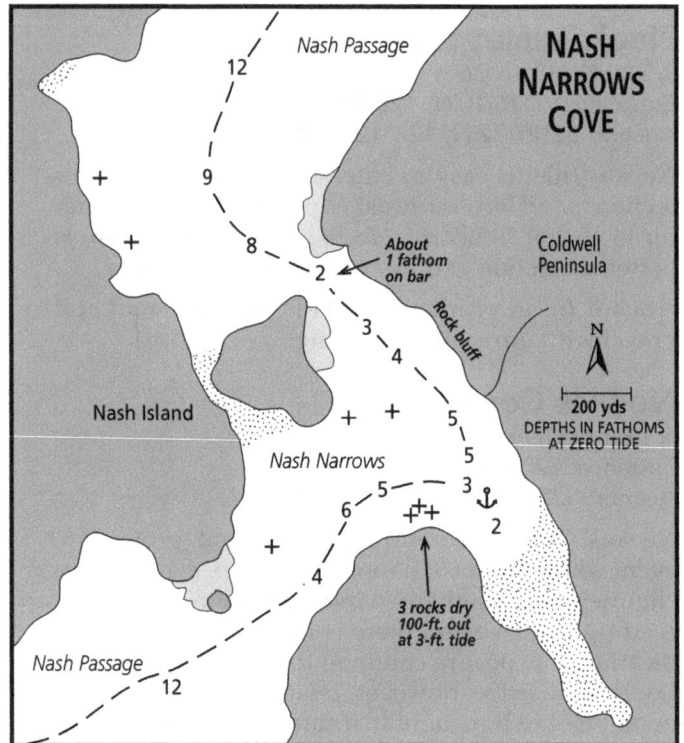

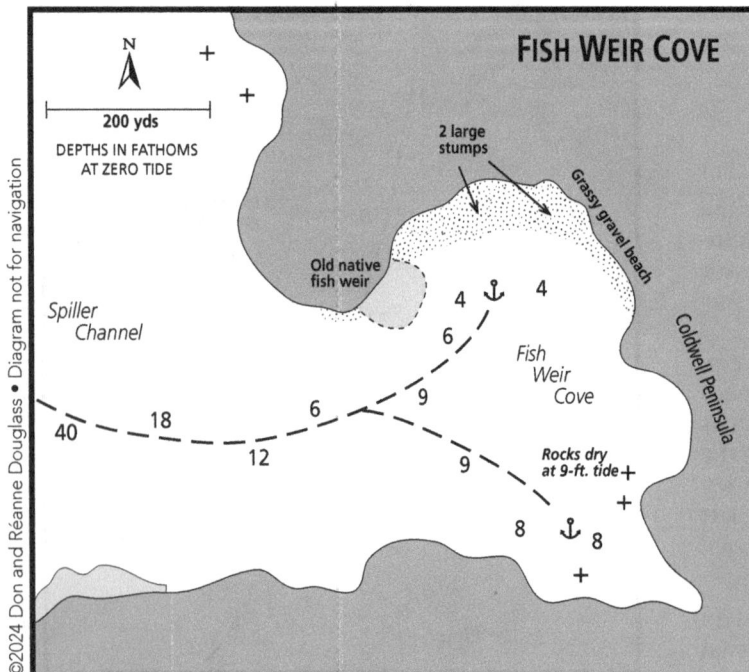

Nash Narrows Cove (Spiller Channel)
0.2 mi SE of Narrows
Anchor: 52°30.45'N, 128°01.96'W

The small cove at the narrows between Coldwell Peninsula and the large unnamed island provides good anchorage for small boats in almost all weather. We find it scenic with a lot of interesting flora and fauna. Water temperature reaches a balmy 67°F in the summertime and masses of small fish live in the eelgrass off the steep-to beach.

Anchor in 2 to 5 fathoms off the creek delta over brown sand with shells; fair-to-good holding.

Ellerslie Bay, East Anchorage
(Spiller Channel)
1 mi S of lagoon entrance
Entrance: 52°30.90'N, 128°00.38'W
Anchor (N shore): 52°31.27'N, 127°59.39'W

"Ellerslie Bay, East Anchorage," known locally as Ellerslie, is a well-protected anchorage and a convenient place to stay while you reconnoiter Ellerslie Lagoon or wait for favorable tidal conditions to enter the lagoon's narrows. You can enter on either side of the small treed islet. However, the channel is deeper close to the south side, and you avoid the rock 150 yards south of the islet.

Anchorage can be taken either along the north shore, if fair weather is expected, or along the south shore, if winds are expected from that quarter. There is ample swinging room for several boats in East Anchorage and this is one of the most popular anchor sites in Spiller Channel.

Anchor (north shore) in 7 fathoms over sand, mud and shell with good-to-very-good holding.

Ellerslie Bay (Spiller Channel)

14 mi NE of Yeo Bay
Entrance (S): 52°31.00'N, 128°01.00'W

Ellerslie Bay is surrounded by high peaks with a wooded dome on the east side, the end of a peninsula forming the south shore of Ellerslie Lagoon. The dome has a 200-foot granite slab wall on its northwest corner, a half-mile south of the entrance to the narrows of Ellerslie Lagoon.

The entrance to Ellerslie Lagoon, via a narrow tidal rapids, is on the east shore of Ellerslie Bay. The bay is generally too deep for anchorage; however, temporary anchorage to reconnoiter the lagoon entrance can be taken directly off the entrance. Avoid the rocks on the south side of the narrows that extend almost 100 yards into Ellerslie Bay.

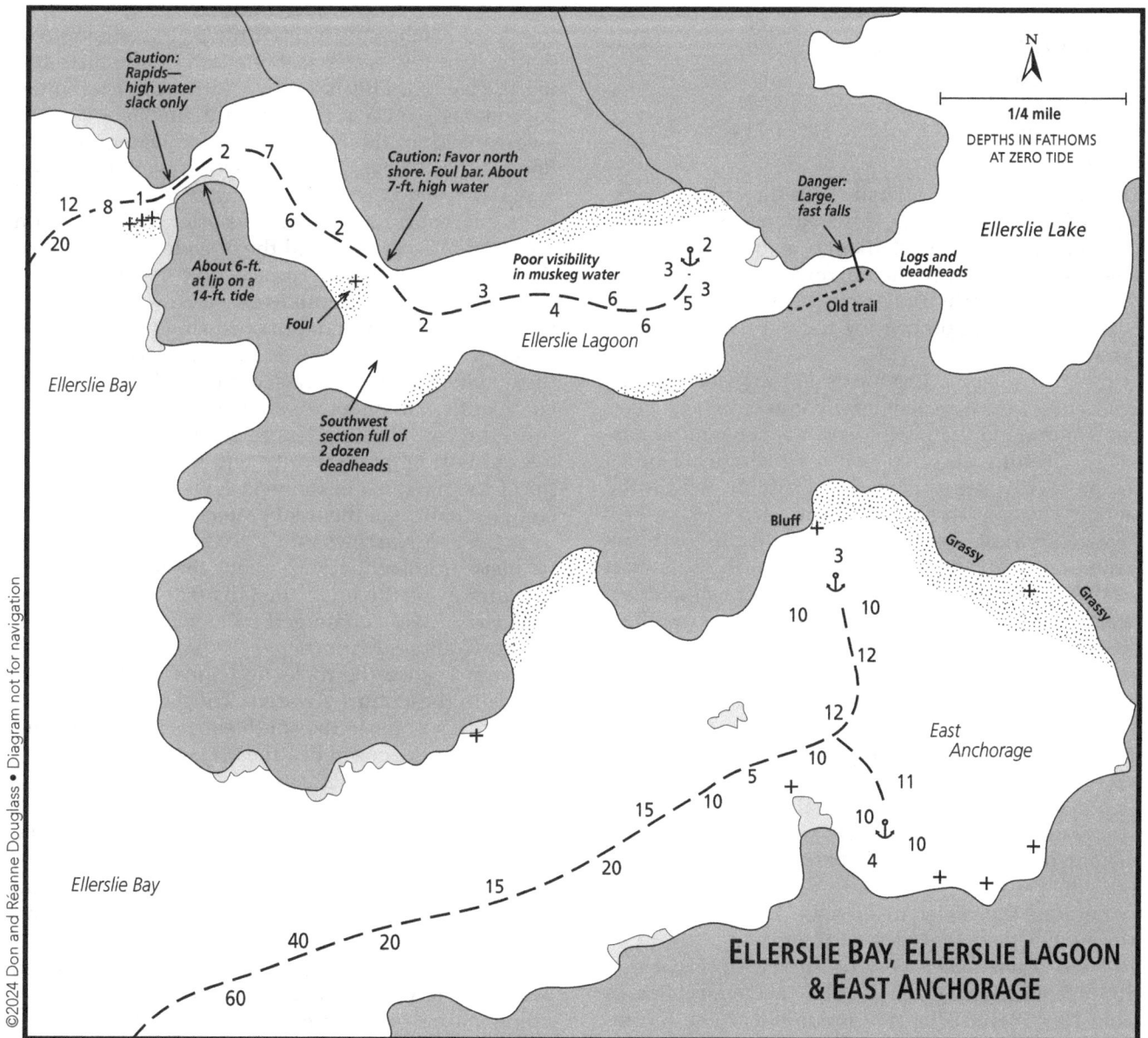

ELLERSLIE BAY, ELLERSLIE LAGOON & EAST ANCHORAGE

©2024 Don and Réanne Douglass • Diagram not for navigation

Ellerslie Lagoon Narrows at low tide

Ellerslie Lagoon—"Seabird Rock" turbulence,
first narrows upper lip, ebb tide

Ellerslie Lagoon (Ellerslie Bay)
14.7 mi NE of Yeo Cove
Entrance: 52°31.78'N, 128°00.96'W
Anchor (northwest of the falls): 52°31.71'N,
127°59.75'W

Ellerslie Lagoon and Ellerslie Falls have all the makings of classic cruising destinations: outstanding scenery and a major challenge of navigating two sets of narrows. Until the narrows have been better charted, and depths and hazards are understood, all boaters should approach the narrows with healthy skepticism.

Caution: Ellerslie Lagoon is not advised for any vessel other than a small, easily maneuverable boat. We recommend that, before *any* boat enters the narrows, carefully reconnoitering by dinghy. Due to the muskeg water, underwater visibility within the lagoon is poor, and the rocks are difficult to see. Boats with limited maneuvering ability, larger boats (around 40 feet or more), those with vulnerable twin screws, or those drawing 4 feet or more should anchor in East Anchorage and visit the lagoon and falls by dinghy.

To enter the lagoon at high-water slack, favor the north shore at the west outer entrance since a dyke of rocks extends about 50 yards from the south shore. Pass through the rapids slightly south of mid-channel, then favor the south shore as you pass into the lagoon to avoid a rock we call Seabird Rock that projects from the north shore. Do not attempt to enter the narrows when there are barnacles visible on the shore rocks.

Because the water in Ellerslie Lagoon is generally higher than that west of the tidal rapids, there are two slack water periods in the narrows that differ from high and low water in Ellerslie Bay or from New Bella Bella tide predictions. The incoming flood reaches the level of the lagoon a couple of hours after low water in Bella Bella and starts filling the lagoon. This is a very short slack. Due to the narrow restriction at the entrance, the lagoon water level is seldom the same as outside water, and the flood current flows into the lagoon well after high water is reached in Ellerslie Bay. There is a second slack current for a few minutes after high water on the outside is reached and the outside level drops to the lagoon level. This is the second time of slack water with maximum depth in the narrows fairway. At this time the fairway depth on spring tides is on the order of 7 feet; it can be as little as 4 feet or less if the outside tide has not raised the inside lagoon level sufficiently. This is precisely why we recommend a careful reconnoitering before entry—we expect that a lot of bottom paint will be left on the rocks at the lip of the narrows in the next few years due to the complex nature of the tidal patterns.

A Second Narrows and a shallow area 0.25 mile lie inside the lagoon with about the same depth in the fairway as the lip of the falls. The fairway passes between two submerged rocks near the point on the north shore. Favor the north shore and approach dead slow since the rocks and shoal water are not visible in these murky waters. The entire area, from just off this point to the south shore, is shallow and fouled with dozens of deadheads.

Past the Second Narrows, the lagoon appears to be clear. Some boats may want to anchor in the outflow of stunning Ellerslie Falls, but at that point the bottom is shallow and rocky. We suggest anchoring north of the current in about 2 fathoms over a mud bottom. Ellerslie Lagoon is well sheltered from wind and chop.

About 200 yards south of the falls, there's a small beach where you can haul-out your dinghy and hike uphill on an old primitive logging trail that leads

Entering Ellerslie Lagoon, high-waer slack tide

to 10-mile-long Ellerslie Lake. Much of the trail is muddy and slippery, so wear boots. If you take children or pets on the trail supervise them closely. It's possible to walk to the water's edge at several places along the falls but a slip or fall could be fatal.

Anchor (northwest of the falls) in 2 to 3 fathoms over soft mud with good holding.

Cove East of Cheenis Lake
(Spiller Channel)
4.5 mi N of Gerald Pt.
Anchor: 52°30.88'N, 128°06.07'W

Temporary anchorage can be found with shelter from northwest winds in the cove east of Cheenis Lake. The pebble beach is strewn with drift logs indicating serious exposure to southeast and up-channel winds. The shore is fairly steep-to but it has a good bottom that should hold you against prevailing northwest winds.

Forevergreen and friends exploring Ellerslie Lagoon

Anchor in 4 fathoms over a mud, gravel, eelgrass and clamshells with fair-to-good holding.

Spiller Inlet

2.1 mi E of Ellerslie Bay
Entrance: 52°30.70'N, 128°04.60'W
Anchor: 52°38.92'N, 128°03.03'W

Spiller Inlet is the continuation of Spiller Channel north of the large unnamed island and heading due north for 10 miles. Nine miles inside the inlet is a large cove to the east at the outlet of Ingram Creek.

As you enter the narrow tip of Spiller Inlet, watch for the overhanging granite slabs high up the east shore. You will see a large granite shelf that appears to be the sculptured face of a weeping woman, Picasso style. The weeping woman is quite striking when observed from mid-channel. The mixed forest on shore appears to be old growth. On the hill above the west side of the bay, a large, white granite slab in the shape of a boomerang about 200 feet long also makes a good landmark.

The very head of Spiller Inlet is steep-to; 100 yards from shore a shelf rises from 10 fathoms to just one! A grassy margin lines the shore, and the bay has very little driftwood, indicating that the anchorage is fairly safe in most weather and offers moderate protec-

tion in southerly weather. Anchorage can be found on the west side of the head of the inlet, south of the orange-colored rocks, in the lee of a small point.

Anchor in 7 fathoms, soft brown mud and large clam shells; holding is very good.

Ingram Bay (Spiller Channel)

7.2 mi N of inlet entr
Entrance: 52°37.80'N, 128°02.20'W
Anchor: 52°37.63'N, 128°01.72'W

"Ingram Bay" is what we call the sheltered anchorage 350 yards north of a spectacular waterfall. The

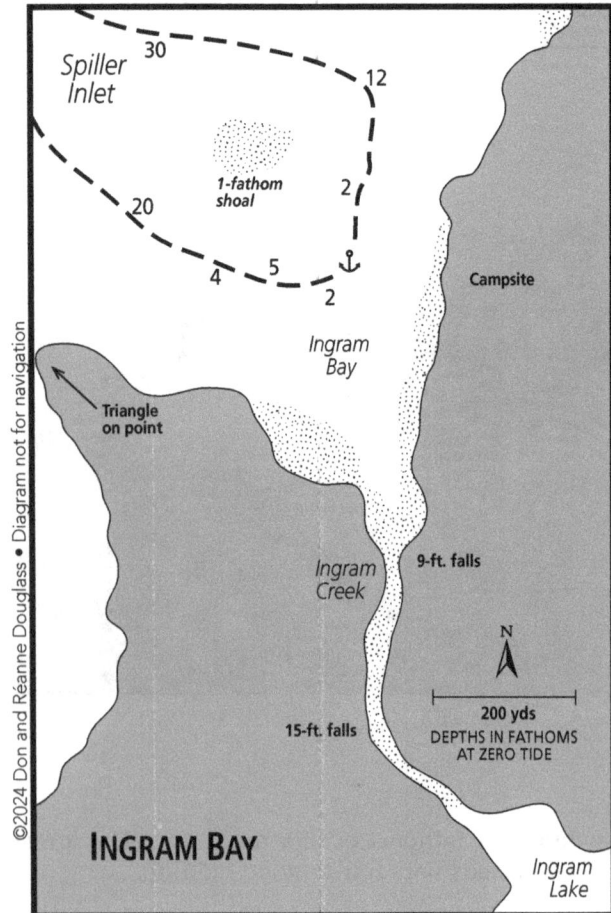

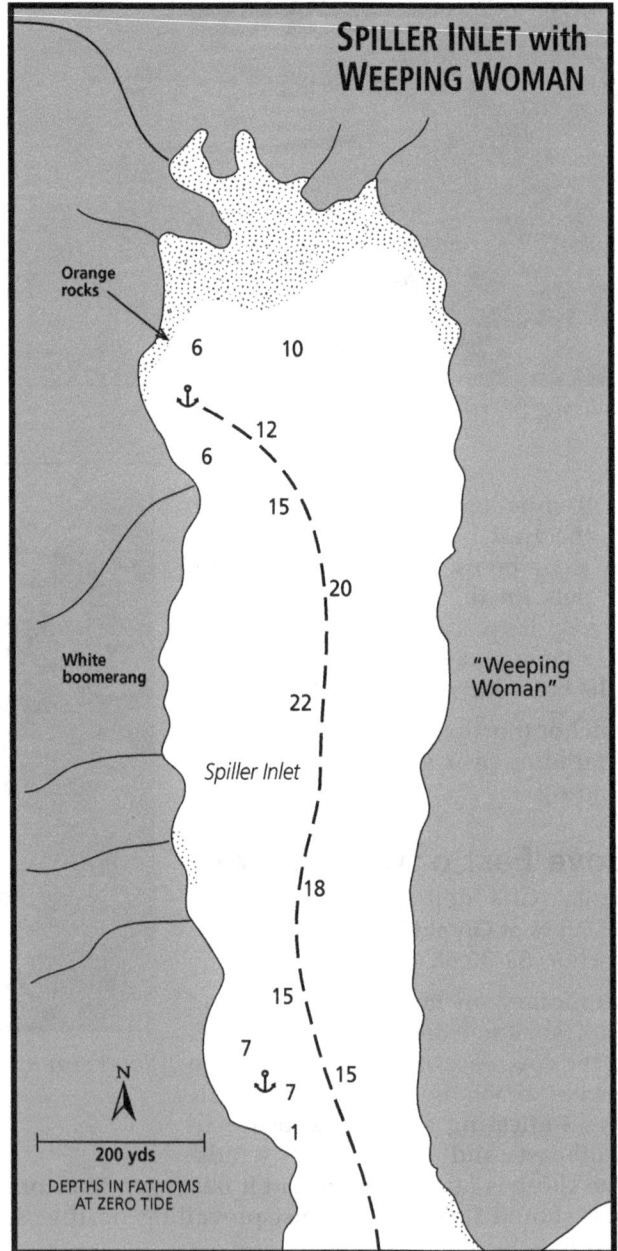

waterfall is a two-stage affair; the upper part falls 15 feet and the lower part 9 feet before plunging directly into Ingram Bay. Ingram Lake, several miles long and immediately behind the falls, is said to be colder than the bay (about 66°F in the summer).

Good protection can be found from prevailing weather. Anchorage close off the small gravel and grass beach offers a good view of the falls with easy access to the beach. Although the chart shows a 3-meter shoal in the center of Ingram Bay, we disagree. Avoid it, regardless. The inner cove, south and east of this 3-meter shoal, is considerably more shallow in general than shown on the chart. *Use caution:* the water is opaque brown and the bottom difficult to discern even in less than 10 feet. The small beach at the outlet of Ingram Creek is used occasionally as a campsite.

Anchor in 2 to 3 fathoms over gravel and sand with fair-to-good holding.

Raison d'Etre *in Gunboat Passage headed for Bella Bella*

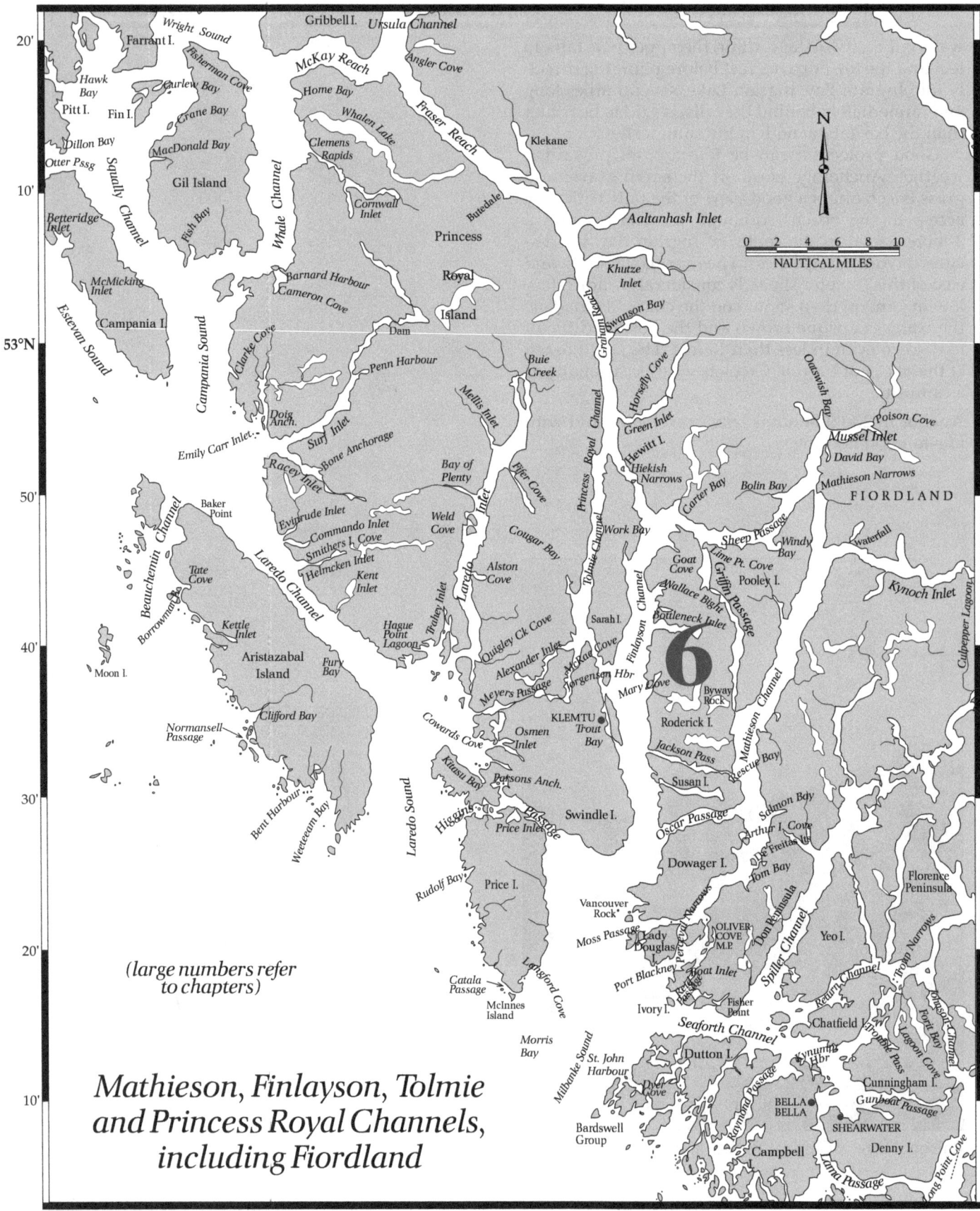

Wright Sound
Farrant I.
Gribbell I.
Uksula Channel
McKay Reach
Angler Cove
Hawk Bay
Fisherman Cove
Curlew Bay
Home Bay
Pitt I.
Fin I.
Crane Bay
Whalen Lake
Fraser Reach
Klekane
Dillon Bay
MacDonald Bay
Clemens Rapids
Aaltanhash Inlet
Otter Pssg
Gil Island
Fish Bay
Whale Channel
Cornwall Inlet
Butedale
Betteridge Inlet
Princess
Khutze Inlet
McMicking Inlet
Barnard Harbour
Cameron Cove
Royal
Swanson Bay
Campania I.
Island
Campania Sound
Clarke Cove
Dam
Horsefly Cove
Oaswish Bay
Estevan Sound
Penn Harbour
Buie Creek
Graham Reach
Green Inlet
Poison Cove
Doig Anch.
Mellis Inlet
Mussel Inlet
David Bay
Emily Carr Inlet
Surf Inlet
Hewitt I.
Mathieson Narrows
Bone Anchorage
Hiekish Narrows
FIORDLAND
Racey Inlet
Bay of Plenty
Fifer Cove
Bolin Bay
Baker Point
Carter Bay
Waterfall
Evinrude Inlet
Weld Cove
Cougar Bay
Sheep Passage
Windy Bay
Commando Inlet
Tate Cove
Smithers Cove
Work Bay
Lime Pt. Cove
Pooley I.
Helmcken Inlet
Alston Cove
Goat Cove
Griffin Passage
Kynoch Inlet
Beauchemin Channel
Kent Inlet
Wallace Bight
Laredo Channel
Kettle Inlet
Hague Point Lagoon
Turkey Inlet
Bottleneck Inlet
Borrowman
Laredo Inlet
6
Aristazabal Island
Fury Bay
Quigley Ck Cove
McKay Cove
Byway Rock
Moon I.
Alexander Inlet
Jorgenson Hbr
Meyers Passage
Mary Cove
Clifford Bay
KLEMTU
Roderick I.
Trout Bay
Normansell Passage
Cowards Cove
Osmen Inlet
Jackson Pass
Bent Harbour
Kitasu Bay
Parsons Anch.
Susan I.
Rescue Bay
Weetceam Bay
Higgins
Oscar Passage
Mathieson Channel
Salmon Bay
Laredo Sound
Price Inlet
Swindle I.
Arthur I. Cove
Florence Peninsula
De Freitas Inlet
Rudolf Bay
Price I.
Dowager I.
Tom Bay
Vancouver Rock
Perceval Narrows
Don Peninsula
Yeo I.
Tsibon Narrows
(large numbers refer to chapters)
Moss Passage
Lady Douglas
OLIVER COVE M.P.
Spiller Channel
Return Channel
Port Blackney
Boat Inlet
Lagoon Cove
Forit Bay
Catala Passage
Longford Cove
Ivory I.
Fisher Point
Chatfield I.
Lafroghe Pass
Jackson Channel
McInnes Island
Seaforth Channel
Cunningham I.
Morris Bay
Milbanke Sound
St. John Harbour
Dutton I.
Kynumpt Hbr
Raymond Passage
Gunboat Passage
Mathieson, Finlayson, Tolmie and Princess Royal Channels, including Fiordland
Dixie Cove
BELLA BELLA
SHEARWATER
Bardswell Group
Campbell
Denny I.
Land Passage
Long Point Cove

N

0 2 4 6 8 10
NAUTICAL MILES

20'
10'
53°N
50'
40'
30'
20'
10'

©2024 Don and Reanne Douglass • Diagram not for navigation

6

Mathieson, Finlayson, Tolmie, and Princess Royal Channels, including Fiordland

Finlayson, Tolmie and Princess Royal channels—the main channels leading north to Grenville Channel along the Inside Passage—have a lot of traffic at all hours. Mathieson Channel, whose smooth waters lead to magnificent Fiordland Recreational Area, draws less traffic. If you're fortunate you may see more Dall porpoises, seals and bird life than people.

A visit to Fiordland—particularly Kynoch Inlet and Culpepper Lagoon—whose beauty is yet undiscovered by cruising boaters that follow the ferry-boat route, is a must if time permits this detour. Outstanding waterfalls and overhanging granite walls are the mark of Fiordland, and in some areas you can take the bow of your boat alongside without concern.

There is even more to explore along this stretch of the coast: Lombard Inlet and Lady Trutch Passage are still uncharted, and the newly charted 13-mile-long Griffin Passage awaits intrepid explorers. Klemtu, the home of the Kitasoo Band, is the only settlement in the area, and its telephone, store, and fuel dock can be a welcome sight. In addition, a number of coves offer outstanding shelter, such as Bottleneck Inlet along the route north to Princess Royal Channel. Venture forth off the well-travelled routes to explore some of these seldom-visited areas and you won't be disappointed!

Reid Passage (Ivory Island)
1.5 mi NE of Ivory Island lt.
Entrance (S): 52°16.04'N, 128°23.35'W
Entrance (N): 52°19.60'N, 128°21.35'W

The smooth waters of Reid Passage allow you to avoid the swells occasionally found near Ivory Island Lighthouse and in Milbanke Sound. While most commercial fishing boats round Ivory Island and cross Milbanke Sound directly, cruising boats usually take the scenic route north through Reid Passage, then up through Mathieson Channel. Numerous reefs at the south entrance to Reid Passage make entering it a bit dicey, and you should first study the large-scale chart before transiting. We have seen waves heap up and break on these reefs and spew sea-foam clear across the entrance. At such times (fortunately they're rare) you risk raising the ire of your crew—if not threatening the survival of your boat—by surfing the entrance. At such times it's better to wait in Kynumpt Harbour (northbound) or in Oliver Cove (southbound).

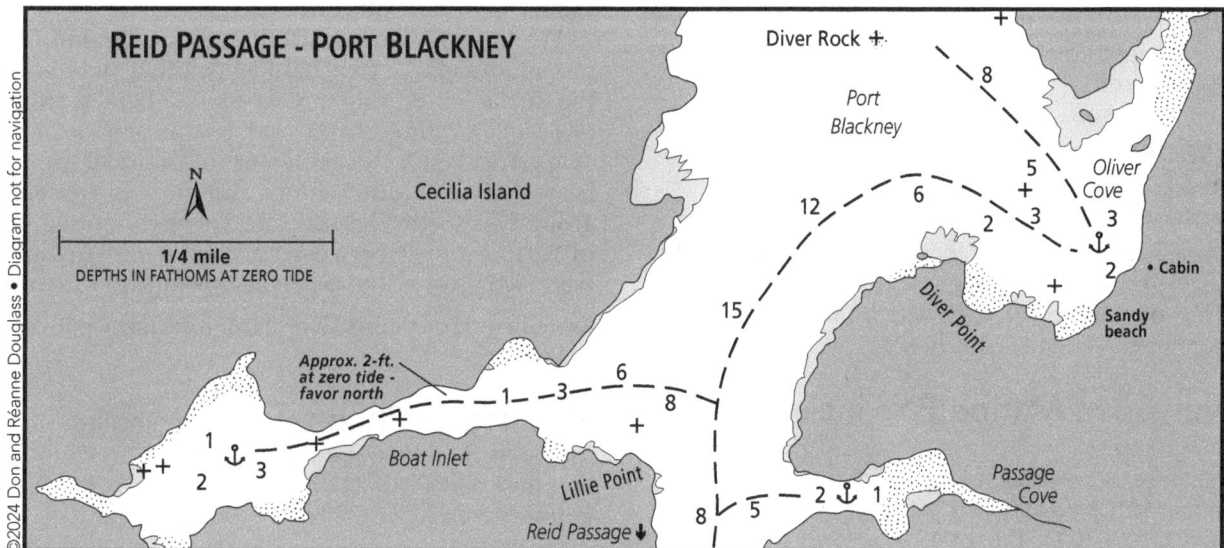

REID PASSAGE - PORT BLACKNEY

©2024 Don and Réanne Douglass • Diagram not for navigation

Hobbit *heading through Reid Passage*

Approaching Reid Passage from Seaforth Channel, continue west until you are due south of red buoy "E50." Turn north, passing the buoy to starboard. In this manner, and in most sea conditions, you can run with the swells on your port quarter making a more comfortable ride. Once you have passed the red buoy, travelling is fine even in 30 knots of wind. On calm days, most of the numerous reefs and rocks in this area are marked by breaking or heaping swells, which do a good job of dissipating the southerly swells. Once you are in Reid Passage, proper, the seas calm and there are no swells north of Carne Rock. When passing Carne Rock, favor the east shore. Both ebb and flood currents seem to flow north through Reid Passage — hydraulic effects that make you scratch your head.

Southbound from Perceval Narrows, be sure to identify Promise Point at the north end of Cecilia Island; it is easy to confuse the rock piles there at the north entrance to Reid Passage.

Charting errors have been noted at the south end of Reid Passage into Mathieson Channel. Visual navigation is required.

Passage Cove (Reid Passage)
0.4 mi NE of Carne Rock
Entrance: 52°18.47'N, 128°21.55'W

Passage Cove, a nice small cove 0.3 mile south of Oliver Cove, nearly dries on low water, but a small boat can find pleasant anchorage here by using a stern tie to shore just inside the entrance.

Oliver Cove Marine Provincial Park
(Reid Passage)
3.2 mi NE of Ivory Island Light
Entrance: 52°18.78'N, 128°21.27'W
Anchor: 52°18.70'N, 128°21.13'W

Oliver Cove, in the east side of Port Blackney, is a B.C.

Provincial Marine Park. It is a popular, well-protected layover for both north- and southbound cruising boats. There is a small, sandy beach backed by woods, where you can spot deer and sometimes find evidence of early habitation; but there are no landing docks or other facilities.

Enter Oliver Cove by passing Carne Rock to your port side. Avoid Diver Rock (marked by kelp) and a small, underwater rock in Oliver Cove itself. Logs and debris find their way into Oliver Cove and seldom escape. While you can anchor over a fairly wide area, some boaters tie a line to the spike-shaped rock on shore.

Some locals prefer to pass Boat Inlet and Oliver Cove and continue north for 2 miles into Lombard Inlet where the mud is said to be "deep and stinky" but holding is good.

Anchor in 3 to 4 fathoms over gravel with fair holding.

Boat Inlet (Reid Passage)
0.5 mi SW of Oliver Cove
Entrance: 52°18.56'N, 128°21.84'W
Anchor: 52°18.51'N, 128°22.33'W

Boat Inlet is one of those quiet places where you feel you're the only people left on the planet. There is never a ripple here, but during a storm you can hear the surf crashing on the outside. The entrance is quite shallow (about 2 feet at zero tide!) and a bit tricky. Favor the north shore the entire route. We once had to remain inside for several hours waiting for the tide to rise so we could exit. The bottom through the passage is visible the entire way and, since the current is slight, you can enter slowly. Inside, there is ample swinging room over a flat bottom.

We have sighted sandhill cranes here and "Penpoint Gunnels," a blue eel-like fish that swims along the surface scooping up its food. There were also *thousands* of fingerlings that left an expanding V-shaped wake on the calm surface. A small group of four or five sandhill cranes summers in the region around Seaforth Channel, and we have spotted them in various coves between Boat Inlet and Ardmillan Bay. Please do not disturb these beautiful rare birds.

Anchor in 2 fathoms over sand and mud with good holding.

Mathieson Channel (Don Peninsula)
Connects Reid Passage to Fiordland
Entrance (S): 52°18.21'N, 128°25.55'W
Entrance (N): 52°50.70'N, 128°08.70'W

Mathieson Channel — a well-protected, smooth-water route all the way to its end in Fiordland — offers a sheltered route east of Milbanke Sound for those headed to Klemtu via Jackson Passage.

Perceval Narrows (Mathieson Channel)
4.1 mi N of Ivory Island Light
Entrance (S): 52°19.83'N, 128°22.69'W
Entrance (N): 52°20.32'N, 128°22.69'W

From Reid Passage to Perceval Narrows, you cross the southern part of Mathieson Channel which is exposed to southwest and southeasterly weather, conditions that will put your boat broadside to the waves and in their trough for a short distance. When southwest swells are running in lower Mathieson Channel, with opposing strong ebb currents in Perceval Narrows, large standing waves that form off Martha Island can be extremely dangerous to small craft. During times like this, it is a good idea for small boats to wait out the weather in Port Blackney.

Cockle Bay (Mathieson Channel)
1 mi NW of Perceval Narrows
Entrance: 52°20.88'N, 128°23.17'W
Anchor: 52°20.77'N, 128°23.32'W

Cockle Bay, on the east side of Lady Douglas Island, offers protection close to its long, sandy beach and makes a good lunch stop. Several boats of various sizes can find anchorage here. This is also an excellent kayak haul-out and camping spot where you can stretch your legs and enjoy the large beach with its collection of logs and stumps that blow south from Fiordland during winter storm winds. Cockle Bay, which is out of the major current of Perceval Narrows, also benefits somewhat from the lee effect of Alec Islet.

Anchor in 4-10 fathoms over sand and shells with fair holding; avoid a rock at the north end which dries on four feet.

Moss Passage, Sloop Narrows
(Mathieson Channel)
3.5 mi NW of Oliver Cove
Entrance (E): 52°21.68'N, 128°22.77'W
Entrance (W): 52°21.29'N, 128°28.57'W

Moss Passage, although not usually found on anyone's route to anywhere, has a charm of its own. Small Sloop Narrows on the south side of Squaw Island is choked with a patch of large bull kelp that weaves an almost hypnotic pattern in the moderately turbulent water. The fairway in Moss Passage is about 50 yards wide and about 6 fathoms deep. It is protected from major winds and chop and, along with Merilia Passage on its northwest corner, can

offer a semi-protected route for those headed north to Higgins Passage. There are several small, sandy kayak haul-out beaches in Moss Passage. We like to anchor in Morris Bay.

Morris Bay (Moss Passage)
1.9 mi W of Sloop Narrows
Entrance: 52°21.12'N, 128°26.90'W
Anchor: 52°20.87'N, 128°26.84'W

Morris Bay, a small scenic bay on the south shore of Moss Passage, 2 miles east of Vancouver Rock, provides secure anchorage in gale-force southeast and southwest weather and fair-to-good protection in strong westerlies. The lack of drift logs on the beach indicates its level of protection. Tuck in at its southern end and, if the weather is heavy, use a stern tie. Avoid the large, dark rock complex awash on 14 feet on the southeast side of the bay. From Morris Bay you can gauge conditions in Milbanke Sound.

Anchor in 3 to 5 fathoms over sand and mud with good holding.

Lady Trutch Passage
(Mathieson Channel)
2 mi NE of Perceval Narrows
Entrance (N): 52°21.97'N, 128°20.74'W
Anchor: 52°21.80'N, 128°20.50'W

We advise extreme caution when entering Lady Trutch Pssage. We have anchored in the north end of the passage on the west side of Nathan Island and found it well sheltered. There is also shelter among the islets on the north side of Nathan Island. Although Lady Trutch Passage may be a less exposed alternative to Perceval Narrows, its south end is choked with large rocks and a number of reefs that make navigation difficult, especially when the current is running. The passage should be attempted only by small boats at slack tide and in good weather.

Anchor in about 6 to 8 fathoms over sand and gravel with fair holding.

Tom Bay
(Mathieson Channel)
5.8 mi NE of Perceval Narrows
Entrance: 52°24.37'N, 128°16.16'W Anchor: 52°23.65'N, 128°15.74'W

Tom Bay, reported to offer good shelter from southeast storms, is subject to down drafts from the high peaks above its shores.

Anchor in 8 to 10 fathoms over an unrecorded bottom.

Arthur Island Cove (Mathieson Channel)
3.6 mi S of Rescue Bay
Entrance (S): 52°26.68'N, 128°16.46'W
Anchor: 52°27.41'N, 128°16.79'W

"Arthur Island Cove," our name for the westernmost of two small coves northwest of Arthur Island, offers protection from strong northwest winds or chop for small boats. Heavy driftwood on the shore of both coves indicates that these are not favorable anchorages in a southerly gale. In such weather, you should head quickly to Rescue Bay.

Entry to Cove Northwest of Arthur Island is over a deep, uneven bottom, indicative of a rocky surface. Be sure to avoid the rocks off Dowager Island. Rescue Bay on Jackson Passage is better in all weather.

Anchor in 4 fathoms over a mixed bottom of sand, rock, grass, and shells; good holding if you set your anchor well; swinging room is limited.

Salmon Bay (Mathieson Channel)
3 mi SE of Rescue Bay
Entrance: 52°28.85'N, 128°13.36'W
Anchor: 52°29.07'N, 128°12.07'W

Salmon Bay is seldom visited because it is off the regular route and because Rescue Bay is so close.

Anchor at the head of the inlet in 10 fathoms over an unrecorded bottom.

Oscar Passage to Klemtu (Susan/Dowager islands)
7.5 mi N of Moss Passage
Entrance (E): 52°28.96'N, 128°16.82'W
Entrance (W): 52°27.41'N, 128°25.10'W

Oscar Passage is an easy way to cross from Mathieson to Finlayson Channel and Klemtu, especially in east winds or in limited visibility. During strong southerly weather, the west entrance of Oscar Passage receives heavy swells. Jackson Passage (3 miles north) generally provides a better and shorter, but narrower route; however, your boat will still lie in the trough of the swells.

Bulley Bay (Oscar Passage)
1.3 mi west of Buckley Head
Entrance: 52°28.26'N, 128°19.25'W

Bulley Bay, although not well charted, is sheltered in most weather. A better anchorage for this area is Rescue Bay.

Rescue Bay (Jackson Narrows)
15.5 mi N of Ivory Island Light
Entrance: 52°31.23'N, 128°17.30'W
Anchor: 52°30.92'N, 128°17.29'W

As its name indicates, Rescue Bay provides the best protection from stormy weather in Mathieson Channel. It can accommodate a number of small and large boats, and you usually find all sorts of vessels here in any weather. Entry requires care to avoid reefs off the islets and shoal areas around the bay, but you can enter at night with radar if necessary.

Since Rescue Bay shoals rapidly, stay in the middle toward the east side. Avoid the isolated rock at the eastern side of the head of the bay that dries on a four-foot tide. The bottom is mostly flat with good swinging room. When leaving Rescue Bay, northbound, you can pass on either side of Miall Island but avoid two submerged reefs on the north side (marked by kelp).

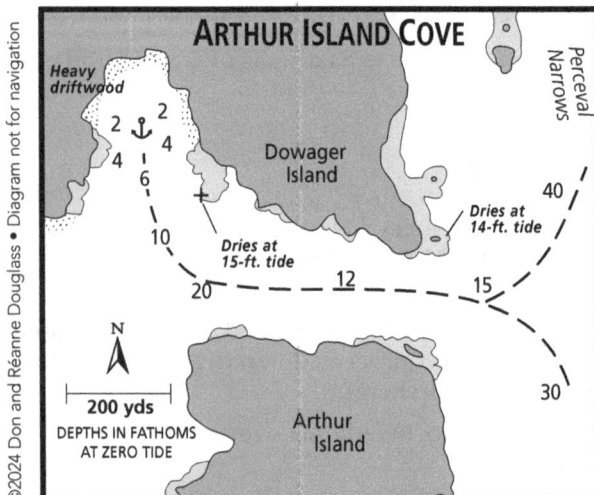

ARTHUR ISLAND COVE

Heavy driftwood
Dowager Island
Perceval Narrows
2   2
4   4
6
10
Dries at 15-ft. tide
Dries at 14-ft. tide
40
12
20   15
30
N
200 yds
DEPTHS IN FATHOMS AT ZERO TIDE
Arthur Island
©2024 Don and Réanne Douglass • Diagram not for navigation

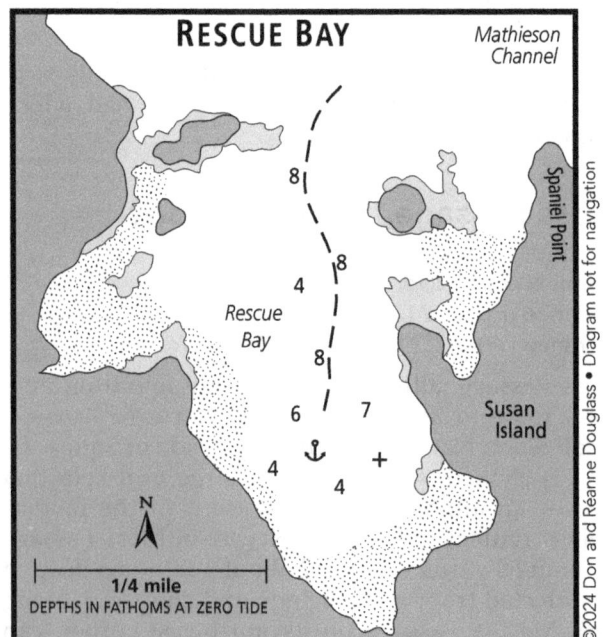

RESCUE BAY

Mathieson Channel
Rescue Bay
Spaniel Point
8
8
4
8
6   7
4
4
Susan Island
N
1/4 mile
DEPTHS IN FATHOMS AT ZERO TIDE
©2024 Don and Réanne Douglass • Diagram not for navigation

Griffin Passage, south entrance at beginning of ebb

Griffin Passage, south entrance rapids

Anchor in 4 fathoms over brown, sticky mud with broken shells and twigs; very good holding.

Jackson Passage (Susan Island)
8.9 mi SW of Klemtu
Entrance (E): 52°31.33'N, 128°17.44'W
Entrance (W): 52°32.75'N, 128°26.56'W

Jackson Passage is a shorter, more scenic route to Klemtu than Oscar Passage but it requires careful navigation of Jackson Narrows. The waters, which are quite calm, provide picturesque reflections of the surrounding scenery. When southeast winds howl as you exit the west end of Jackson Passage, you will encounter beam seas. In this case, you may want to turn north for the comfort of your crew or boat and run with the seas to Jane Passage.

Jackson Narrows (Jackson Passage)
0.5 mi NW of Rescue Bay
Position: 52°31.44'N, 128°18.01'W
Entrance (E narrows): 52°31.33'N, 128°17.70'W
Entrance (W narrows): 52°31.47'N, 128°18.36'W

Jackson Narrows Marine Provincial Park, at the east end of Jackson Passage, offers anchorage, fishing and diving in an attractive little bay suitable for small boats. There is a small beach here, but no facilities. The passage is narrow at the east end with rocks and drying reefs. Navigate only at high slack.

Jackson Narrows requires some tight maneuvering—especially when current is running and a local sportfishing boat from Klemtu happens to come screaming through at 20 knots! We have transited Jackson Narrows on a 3-foot tide and found 1.6 fathoms under our echo sounder. All the rocks are visible at low tide, and the fairway is usually clear of kelp in the summer months. When kelp is present, you can glide through it, following paths that are mostly open. Proceed slowly.

The width of the fairway in the narrows is not as great as has been reported—we would guess no more than 65 feet. The fairway through the narrows favors the south shore avoiding mid-channel reefs and rocks. Minimum depth in the fairway is about 2 fathoms. When westbound, at the narrowest point be sure to execute a turn to the left and favor the south shore in order to safely pass the last reef and rock to your starboard. These hazards, just outside the fairway, are marked by kelp during the summer. Current through the narrows is generally moderate (1-3 knots), and the time of slack water depends on tide levels in Finlayson and Mathieson channels.

When transiting the narrows, watch for opposing traffic. Fast, small commercial fishing boats often roar through at top speed, passing just a few yards away! Larger boats should sound their horn and/or make a sécurité call on Channel 16.

Griffin Passage (South Entrance)
S entrance 4.5 mi N of Rescue Bay
Entrance: 52°35.17'N, 128°17.42'W
South rapids: 52°36.97'N, 128°17.59'W

As you continue north in Mathieson Channel, 4 miles north of Jackson Narrows, you pass the south entrance to Griffin Passage.

Thirteen miles long, Griffin Passage connects Mathieson Channel to Sheep Channel, four miles southeast of the entrance to Hiekish Narrows. Cruising boats have long speculated whether Griffin Passage could be used as a pleasure-craft route.

During our first visit, we were on the very upper lip of the south narrows when Gloria Burke, our sharp-eyed bow lookout, went "ballistic" pointing straight into the water. We were able to stop just inches from hitting a large uncharted rock we now call "Byway Rock" (see sidebar). Since the ebb was quickly becoming a fast-moving river, we backed down to the basin and anchored.

Don made the transit by inflatable the full length to the north narrows and back, reporting the route as very sheltered and quiet with the only signs of civilization a few old hand-logged stumps.

Between the two narrows he found a remote and deep saltwater "lake" where there are a couple of possible anchor sites. This 6-mile-long "lake" varies little in depth from tide to tide and is full of giant starfish and sea urchins; there were signs of deer crossing the channel at the middle narrows. Anchor sites can be found in the basin just south of North Falls and at the narrows 0.9 mile south. These sites look promising and there is little sign of chop or strong weather in the basins.

While we believe technically that a safe transit can be made by small boats at high-water slack, there are three major obstacles: 1) The narrows becomes a roaring tidal rapids (waterfall) at anything less than high water; 2) the rapids at the north end become an extremely narrow and dangerous cataract less than 20 yards wide; and 3) north of the north tidal rapids there is a two-mile-long narrow, shallow channel choked with bull kelp and grass. Until Griffin Passage is completely charted in large scale and its tidal mechanisms well understood, it is an intrepid explorer's dream, but it cannot be recommended as a cruising-boat route.

May Day in Griffin Passage

At the upper end of the south tidal rapids in Griffin Passage, there's a rock we now call "Byway Rock." At 1500 hours on July 16, 1996, while we were in Higgins Passage, we heard a MAYDAY sent by the Byway, a 42-foot fishing boat with two persons aboard. The Byway had hit a rock located at 52°37.13'N, 128°17.53'W and was listing at a 45-degree angle. (This was the same uncharted rock that had alarmed my crew and me the previous summer at the same spot!) The Prince Rupert Coast Guard sent the Kitasu Responder to their rescue.

Later, we talked with Joe Tobacco, skipper of the Byway, in a call from Victoria. He told us that a small, log-salvage tug from Bella Bella, operated by Jim Darwin, did a marvelous job pulling the boat off the rock at high water in the midnight darkness, and towing it to Shearwater where the boat was repaired.

Joe told us that Byway had arrived in the area at low water and, although he had checked out the narrows through his binoculars, he thought the rock was farther away. But it was lurking just 18 inches below the surface (awash on about an 11-foot tide) right in the center of the channel at the edge of the narrows. Joe struck the rock on the last of the flood and with power on. In future attempts, he suggests staying on the west side of Byway Rock. Until there is definite information to confirm these observations, beware! —DD

Griffin Passage south entrance at low tide, "Byway Rock" showing in center

James Bay

(Mathieson Channel)
5 mi SW of Kynoch Inlet
Entrance: 52°41.46'N, 128°12.27'W
Anchor: 52°42.56'N, 128°12.73'W

James Bay is exposed to southerly weather but protected from westerlies or downslope winds. Rescue Cove is the preferred anchorage in the southern portion of this area; Windy Bay is the preferred anchor site to the north.

Anchor in 13 fathoms over mud and sand with good holding.

Kynoch Inlet

(Fiordland)
5 mi S of Mathieson Narrows
Entrance: 52°45.82'N, 128°07.33'W
Waterfall: 52°44.64'N, 128°07.52'W

Kynoch Inlet, part of Fiordland Conservancy, contains wild and magnificent scenery. High snow-covered peaks and ridges with vertical granite ramparts rise 3,500 feet above its shores. Visit here on a rising barometer on a day when the low clouds break up to reveal a startling vertical rock cliff rising to the sky. Kynoch Inlet is a special place to enjoy the wilderness with all its complexities and beauty. A stunningly beautiful waterfall that tumbles from Lessom Creek lies on the north shore of Kynoch. Upon approach the view of the waterfall may call to mind different images—a shaman? a priestess? a gingerbread woman? a graduate in mortarboard? You can get close to this waterfall, but be careful not to swamp your boat!

There are no shallow anchorages within Kynoch Inlet except what can be found along the shore in Culpepper Lagoon.

Wolves and Rainforests

Ian MacAllister and I spent the morning bushwhacking and scrambling up to the very top of a 2,000-foot ridge that rises straight from sea level, and overlooks the stunning expanse of the James Bay Creek watershed on Pooley Island. Ian and I had sailed to Pooley Island to do reconnaissance for the Raincoast Conservation Society.

Pooley Island is one of the jewels in British Columbia's Great Bear Rainforest, the largest network of intact coastal temperate rainforest left on earth. To put the Great Bear Rainforest's global importance in context, coastal temperate rainforests originally covered less than one-half of one percent of the earth's land base. Close to sixty percent of these rainforests are now gone.

Sitting atop the ridge, we gazed out across the gentle beauty that is the James Bay Creek watershed with its winding streams and rivers, old growth spruce, delicate bog forests and wetlands. From this elevation, Ian's trimaran, the Companion, anchored in the inlet, looked like a miniature replica. James Bay Creek has runs of pink, chum, coho and sockeye salmon, and serves as habitat for the spirit bear (the rare white phase of the coastal black bear), and grizzly bears as well. This watershed is also prime wolf country.

On the scramble down, we stopped at an extraordinary alpine lake frequented by mew gulls. Hot and sweaty with clothes and boots full of twigs, leaves, stones and dirt, we decided to take a swim.

Afterwards, as we made our descent from the lake to the boat, we began to notice the tracks. There were deer tracks everywhere, followed by the unmistakable paw prints of Canis Lupus.

We came to a mossy bench along a steep ridge above the river and stopped. Out of the rainforest, almost preternaturally, like figures revealing themselves in a dream, the wolves appeared. A large, beautiful, jet-black adult meandered along the river's sandy spit, eventually plopping down on a bed of lush grass, rolling over on his back and squirming about, satisfying an intense itch. Then two black pups ambled out and played a game of wolf tag as they chased each other's tails. Then another pup and a big tawny-coloured adult emerged. More adults and pups followed in this wolf parade until we counted ten in all. A long time passed while we watched from our perch as the wolves splashed in the river and lolled about in the late afternoon sunshine.

That evening, from the deck of the Companion, we watched a sunset of gold streaks turning to red and then purple, with broken clouds backlit by the dying sun. As the last slivers of daylight faded into darkness, we heard a wolf howl somewhere up the valley.

—Christopher Genovali

Christopher Genovali lives in British Columbia. He is the executive director of the Raincoast Conservation Society. Please see the Appendix for the Society's contact information.

Approaching Kynoch Falls

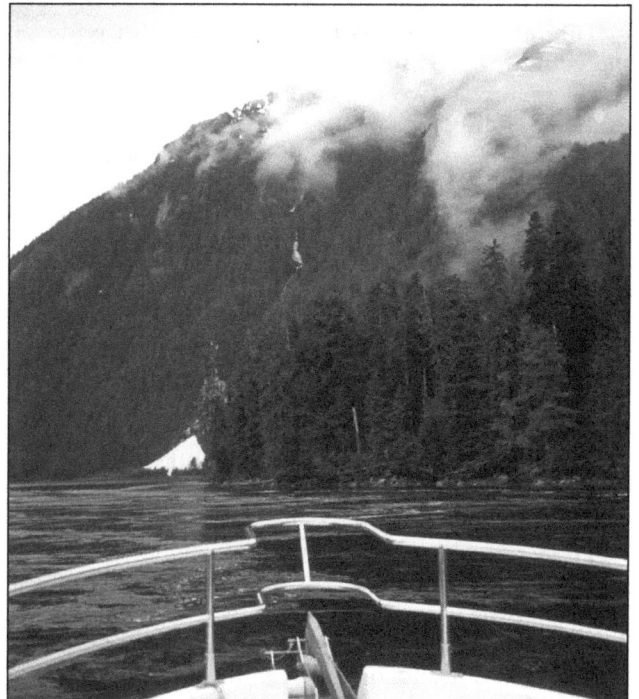

Snowfield at salt water, Kynoch Inlet

Desbrisay Bay, "Big Bay" (Fiordland)
4.4 mi E of Kynoch Point
Entrance: 52°45.48'N, 127°59.57'W

Debrisay Bay is cleft deep into the granite mainland shore forming a grand amphitheater stretching to the sky. A prominent avalanche scar on the east side, at least 1000 feet or more in length, gives the appearance of a snowfield. The head of the bay terminates in grassy mud flats.

Culpepper Lagoon (Fiordland)
8.5 mi E of Kynoch Point
Entrance: 52°45.14'N, 127°52.79'W
Anchor (Kainet Creek): 52°45.27'N, 127°53.32'W
Anchor (lagoon head): 52°43.94'N, 127°49.88'W

Culpepper Lagoon extends 2.25 miles southeast of the head of Kynoch Inlet. Cut deep into the center of the snow-laden Coast Range, it is one of the least visited places along this part of the B.C. coast. Fiordland is one of the most scenic parts of the B.C. coast, and Culpepper Lagoon is arguably the best part of Fiordland.

Culpepper Lagoon, entered by means of a shallow 100-yard-long narrows, is poorly charted and can be intimidating. It has traditionally discouraged more than a few visitors. We found most cruising boats can enter near high-water slack without difficulty. Here is what we learned in several transits and with verification by trusted experts.

The fairway appears to be about 30 feet wide in the center of the approximately 80-foot wide fairly short narrows. Two large tooth-shaped rocks with green tops lie close on the south shore as you approach the narrows. Some submerged rocks that lie close to the east shore contribute to the turbulence in the narrows. There are more rocks along the north shore, some of which extend north 50 yards. At this point, the depths are shallower. Avoid this area by favoring the south shore slightly until you are in the middle of the narrows. We looked for the one-foot depth indicated on the chart just inside the entrance on the south side and couldn't find it. However, we found some moderate whirlpools there on flood currents that raise havoc with the echo sounder.

There are no significant rocks or kelp mid-channel in the 30-foot-wide fairway, and minimum depths appear to be about 10 feet at low water. At neap tides (first and third quarter of moon), current and turbulence are moderate and the time-window for safe transit is fairly wide. On spring tides (new and full moon)

High peaks pierce the clouds, Desbrisay Bay

current and turbulence are strong and dangerous to any size vessel except at high water slack.

On the latter part of the flood, as the water covers the outer bay mud flat, it turns more southward and consequently has an increasing tendency to push boats toward the south shore and into the bluff at the south point.

If you are transiting the lagoon narrows at the head of Kynoch Inlet on the last of the flood, follow the center of the fast-moving water. Once you approach the sharpest point on your starboard hand, make a slight turn to the north (left) to avoid the small but strong whirlpools caused by the point; a shoal area is found in its lee. Once past the tongue of the flood in about 60 feet of water, make a turn to the right (south) to head down the center of the lagoon.

We recommend the following strategy for first-time visitors. Arrive early and anchor in the 14-fathom anchor site off Kainet Creek, off the mud flat (GPS

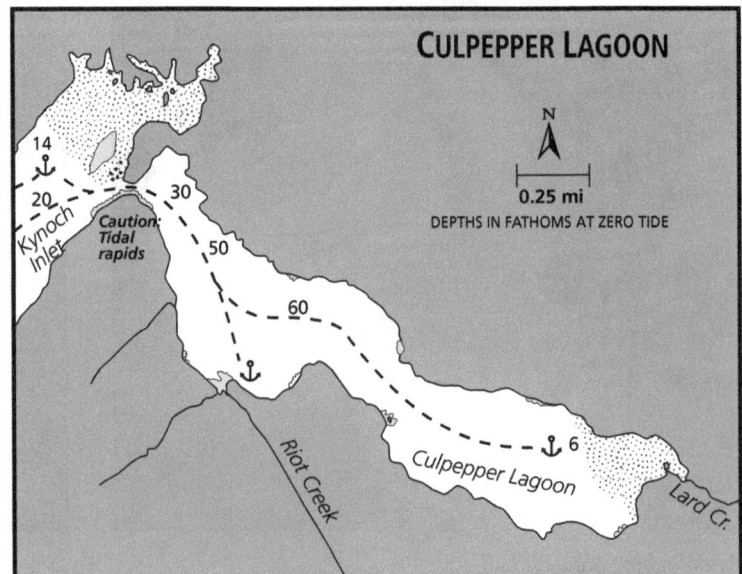

CULPEPPER LAGOON

N

0.25 mi

DEPTHS IN FATHOMS AT ZERO TIDE

14

20

30

Kynoch Inlet

Caution: Tidal rapids

50

60

6

Culpepper Lagoon

Riot Creek

Lard Cr.

©2024 Don and Réanne Douglass • Diagram not for navigation

Culpepper Narrows

Going upstream in Culpepper Lagoon

position above). Reconnoiter the narrows by dinghy and gauge for yourself conditions in the narrows. Proceed when you are satisfied. If the vertical drop across the rapids is over a foot, to minimize maneuvering problems you may want to wait until the lagoon level more closely matches that of Kynoch Inlet

Exiting Culpepper Lagoon on moderate ebb current is fairly easy. We exited on a 6-knot current (a one- to two-foot drop across the length of the narrows) with a fairly laminar flow and little problem. However, when the drop is 3 to 4 vertical feet as on some spring tides, we estimate that current reaches 9 knots or more—very dangerous for most vesssels.

Inside Culpepper Lagoon it is calm, totally landlocked and pleasant. After the excitement of negotiating the entrance narrows, beautiful views unfold in all directions. Now it's time to relax in quiet and solitude.

Look toward the northeast and take in the view of the 2,000-foot-high cascade that flows down the flank of the granite ridge a half-mile away. This is a favorite of bears that like to dig up skunk cabbage roots.

Explore Culpepper Lagoon to your heart's content. The water is deep and free of dangers. The two anchor sites we used lie off the mud flat at the bitter end of the Lagoon (a good base camp for visiting Lard and Levi creeks by dinghy on the upper half of flooding tides) and just off the north side of Riot Creek. The large spruce grove to the right of Lard Creek is particularly attractive. Alder limbs almost bridge the creek and bear bones can be found along the many mossy animal trails on the east shore.

Heathorn Bay (Fiordland)
0.4 mi SE of Mathieson Narrows
Entrance: 52°50.28'N, 128°08.13'W

Crystal-clear Heathorn Bay, at the north end of Mathieson Channel, can provide protection from northerly winds if necessary, but the beach is so steep-to, it's difficult to find anchorage. In calm weather you can literally run your bow to the beach and hold it there, because there is absolutely no wave action, or you can drift around and just enjoy the scenery.

It may be possible to get a line ashore and put a stern anchor into deep water if the situation requires it, but it's easier to pass through Mathieson Narrows and head into Windy Bay for shelter.

Mathieson Narrows
(Fiordland)
35 mi N of Perceval Narrows
Position: 52°50.73'N, 128°08.71'W

Mussel Inlet is north and Sheep Passage turns west. We once saw a flock of at least 500, if not 1,000, puffins in the narrows here, frolicking in the slight turbulence. Not normally sighted along inner waterways, the puffins must have been sitting out a storm.

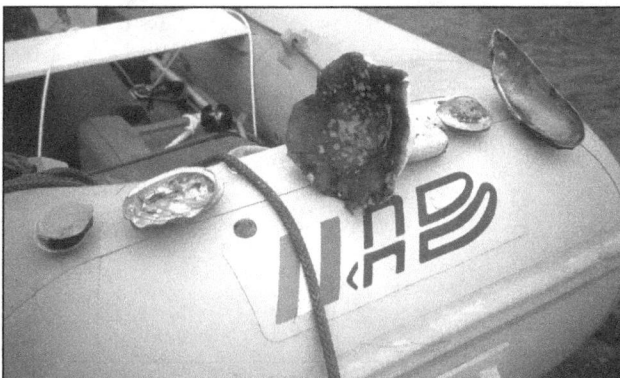

Culpepper's shells, bones and mushrooms

Finlayson Channel

9.5 mi NW of Ivory Island lt.
Entrance (S): 52°24.94'N, 128°28.86'W
Entrance (N): 52°48.35'N, 128°26.09'W

The upper portion of Finlayson Channel is seldom used by pleasure craft that normally make the turn into Tolmie Channel. However, Finlayson offers solitude, natural beauty and a better choice of anchor sites. To visit Fiordland, combine an inbound trip up Mathieson Channel with an outbound via Sheep Passage and Finlayson, or the reverse. Rejoining upper Tolmie Channel through Hiekish Narrows is not difficult.

Red tides are commonly encountered in Finlayson Channel from May to August and, although not all red tides are toxic, it is unwise to eat clams taken from areas not regularly tested (i.e., the entire North Coast).

Nowish Cove (Susan Island)

5.5 mi SE of Klemtu
Entrance (N): 52°31.53'N, 128°26.20'W
Anchor: 52°31.33'N, 128°25.72'W

Nowish Cove offers essentially complete protection from all weather. However, since the drying mud flat off Salmon Creek is steep-to, you have to anchor in the center of the cove in depths of 11 to 12 fathoms, with limited swinging room. Nowish Narrows, a tidal rapids with 6 knots current, is about 50 feet wide. The inlet behind the narrows, which is 4 miles

Klemtu fuel dock and store in the building above the fuel dock

long and surrounded by steep, high peaks, appears to be too deep for convenient anchorage.

Moderate eddies from current in the channel may cause your vessel to swing and risk fouling your anchor.

Anchor in about 12 fathoms over a rocky bottom with fair holding.

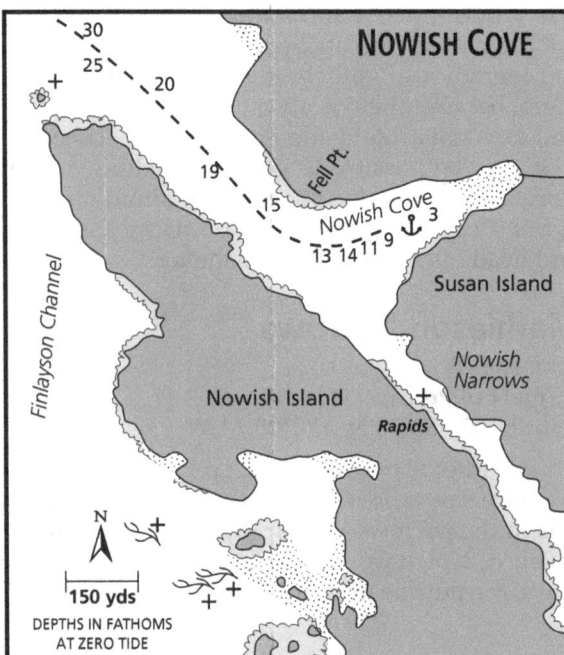

NOWISH COVE

Finlayson Channel

30
25
20
19
15
Fell Pt.
Nowish Cove ⚓ 3
13 14 11 9
Susan Island
Nowish Island
Nowish Narrows
Rapids

N

150 yds
DEPTHS IN FATHOMS
AT ZERO TIDE

©2024 Don and Réanne Douglass • Diagram not for navigation

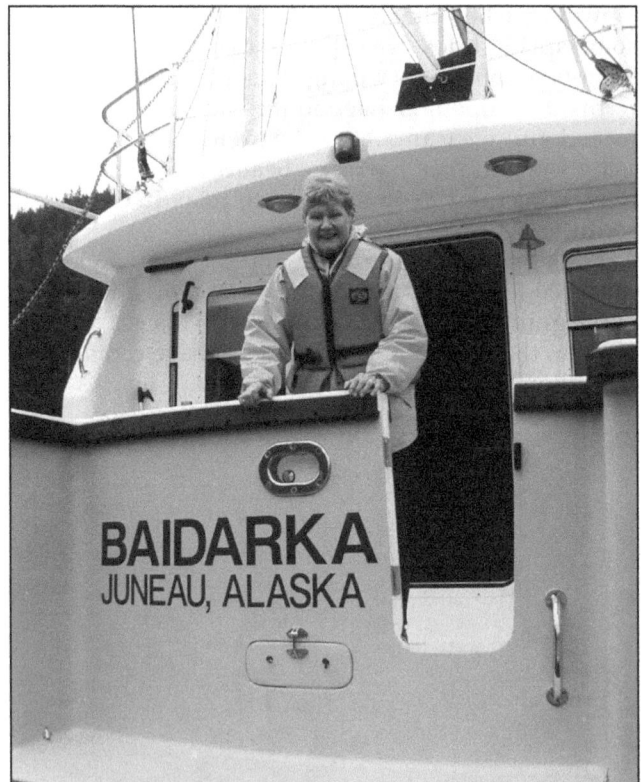

BAIDARKA
JUNEAU, ALASKA

Réanne greets the dinghy crew

Klemtu Passage

17 mi N of Ivory Island Light
Entrance (S): 52°33.06'N, 128°29.60'W
Entrance (N): 52°36.63'N, 128°31.34'W

Klemtu Passage is a well-sheltered channel.

If you see a ferry or cruise ship in narrow Klemtu Passage, be sure to give the vessel as much clearance as possible. Courtesy requires a no-wake speed when you pass Trout Bay or the facilities on the north side.

Klemtu Anchorage (Clothes Bay)

1.2 mi S of Klemtu
Anchor (Clothes Bay): 52°34.34'N, 128°30.92'W

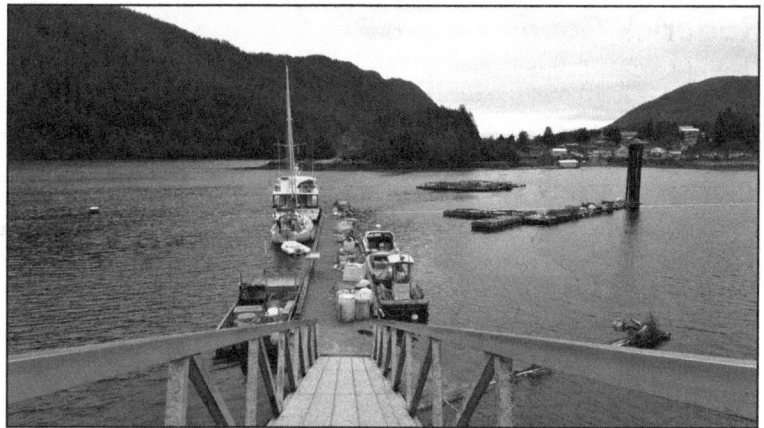

Klemtu public float, village in the distance to the right and Longhouse on far shore strait off the float

Good protection can be found in Clothes Bay northwest of Star Island in 3 to 4 fathoms, over sand with fair-to-good holding. Southwest of Star Island is good protected anchoreage in 5 to 8 fathoms. Both of these locations have cell service from Klemtu.

Klemtu (Swindle Island)

3 mi S of Boat Bluff lt.
Entrance: 52°35.58'N, 128°31.23'W
Fuel dock: 52°35.65'N, 128°31.28'W

Klemtu, a Kitasoo village on the west side of Finlayson Channel, is the only fuel stop between New Bella Bella, 30 miles south, and Hartley Bay, 65 miles to the north. The fuel dock, at the north side of the village, is exposed to the wake of passing boats, so be sure to secure your boat well. Fuel is available, but it's a good idea to call ahead for hours and availability. The store in the warehouse building above the fuel dock has supplies and groceries (depending upon the supply barge delivery), and an ATM. Good water is available via the village's water treatment system.

There is good cell phone coverage in and around Klemtu. There is no power on the 210-foot concrete dock inside the bay. If you have time to spend in the village, we recommend that you visit the Kitasoo Band office in the village and arrange a tour of the Band's Big House. (Reasonable fee charged.)

Anchorage is good in Trout Bay between the fuel dock and the village. Scheduled floatplane service frequents the docks on the west side of Trout Bay. B.C. Ferries serves Klemtu from the ferry dock 1.3 miles north of town.

Mary Cove (Finlayson Channel)

3.1 mi NE of Klemtu
Entrance: 52°36.63'N, 128°26.72'W
Anchor: 52°36.83'N, 128°26.29'W

Mary Cove, on the west shore of Roderick Island, 3.5 miles southeast of Boat Bluff, offers good shelter and is close for a run into Klemtu. Most weather seems to blow by outside, while inside you're snug. However, if a storm were expected, we would head for Bottleneck Inlet, 4 miles north.

Once you've crossed the shallow bar of Mary Cove, you can anchor anywhere near a 9-fathom hole or on the north side off the beach.

Anchor in 7 to 9 fathoms over sand and mud with good holding.

Watson Bay (Finlayson Channel)

4 mi N of Mary Cove
Entrance: 52°41.20'N, 128°26.03'W

Watson Bay is entered between Bancroft Point and Howay Point. Roderick Cove at its head offers moderate protection for small boats.

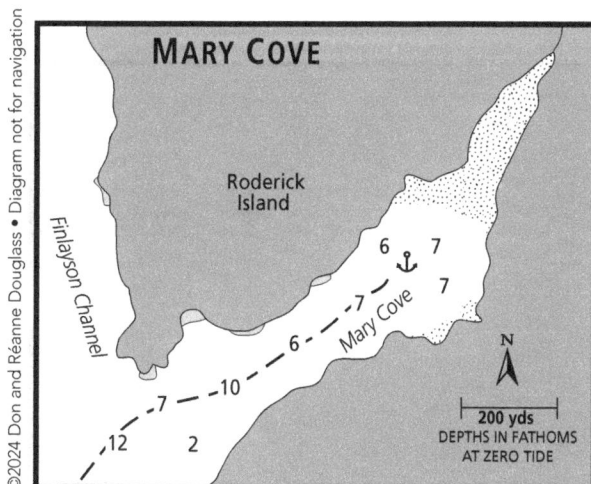

©2024 Don and Reanne Douglass • Diagram not for navigation

MARY COVE

Roderick Island

Finlayson Channel

Mary Cove

6   7
7

6
10
7

12   2

N

200 yds
DEPTHS IN FATHOMS
AT ZERO TIDE

Roderick Cove (Watson Bay)
Head of Watson Bay
Entrance: 52°40.65'N, 128°21.60'W

Although small boats may be able to find good shelter in the south nook of Roderick Cove using a stern tie, Bottleneck Inlet, one mile to the north, offers better protection and more swinging room.

Bottleneck Inlet (Finlayson Channel)
8.1 mi NE of Klemtu
Entrance: 52°42.81'N, 128°25.63'W
Anchor: 52°41.59'N, 128°24.10'W

Bottleneck Inlet, one of the more peaceful anchor sites in this area, is easy to enter and provides excellent storm shelter. The narrow entrance to the inlet is easy to miss because it's well disguised. Use your chart plotter to locate the entrance, or remain close to Roderick Island as you head north. While depth over the entrance bar is only one fathom or so at zero tide, it is not difficult to cross, and you can enter under radar if necessary. The mud flat at the head of the inlet is quite large but because depths shoal slowly, you can find very good anchorage at any depth you please. There is plenty of room for several boats to swing and only radio reception suffers here. A deadhead at the head of the inlet at location 52°42.597'N, 128°24.009'W was noted in earlier editions of this guidebook. It was marked with a flag. There have been no recent reports of the deadhead and we assume it is no longer a factor.

Anchor in 3 to 4 fathoms over black mud with very good holding.

Wallace Bight (Finlayson Channel)
1.3 mi N of Bottle Inlet
Entrance: 52°43.75'N, 128°26.22'W
Anchor (Lagoon S bight): 52°43.64'N, 128°24.04'W

Wallace Bight, although not recommended as an anchorage, has a lagoon inside its east end that offers excellent shelter and solitude. The lagoon draws 4 to 6 feet on a high tide and we found excellent anchor sites on the northwest and south bights. The shoal at the narrows has one foot of water at zero tide so you must be sure the tide level is adequate before you attempt to enter. The current is a laminar flow with moderate turbulence. Other than the shoal in the narrows we know of no other special hazards.

Anchor in 4 fathoms over a mud bottom; good holding.

Work Bay (Finlayson Channel)
4 mi NW of Bottle Inlet
Entrance: 52°45.84'N, 128°28.91'W
Anchor: 52°47.00'N, 128°28.89'W

Work Bay is largely ignored by the cruising public because it appears too exposed to the south. However, it does offer good shelter near its head. In moderate southerly wind little chop enters the almost land-locked northern basin. A beautiful 200-foot cascade tumbles directly into the saltwater from the edge of the lake high above.

Goat Cove (Finlayson Channel)
2.9 mi NE of Work Bay
Entrance: 52°47.15'N, 128°24.79'W
Anchor: 52°46.39'N, 128°23.49'W

Goat Cove is easy to enter and its inner cove very well protected from any serious weather. The narrows carries 4 to 5 fathoms in its fairway and, while depths in the basin are a little deep for convenient anchoring, we have been able to stay off the steep-to flat in the south end off the creek entrance.

Anchor in 4 to 8 fathoms over sloping mud; fair-to-good holding with a well-set anchor.

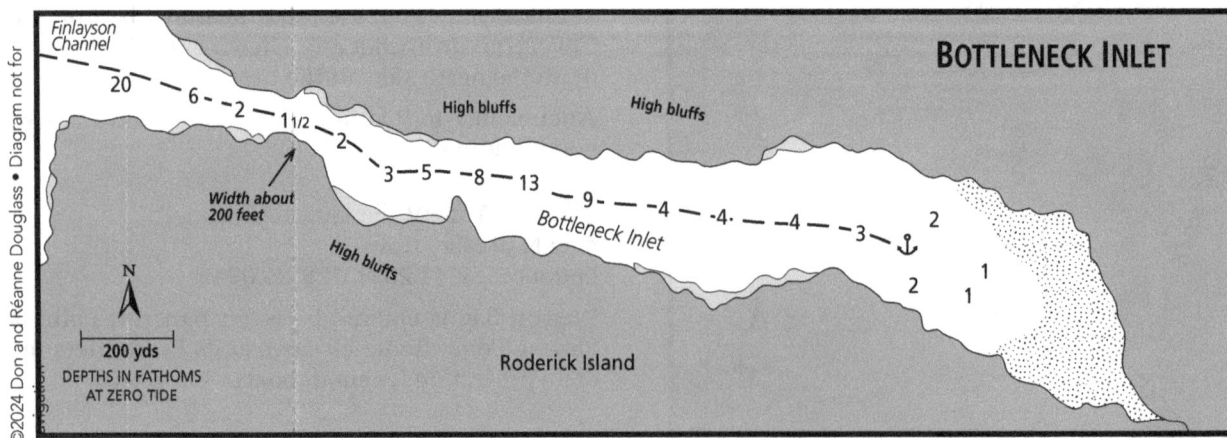

BOTTLENECK INLET

Finlayson Channel

©2024 Don and Réanne Douglass • Diagram not for

Width about 200 feet

High bluffs   High bluffs

High bluffs

Bottleneck Inlet

High bluffs

N

200 yds
DEPTHS IN FATHOMS
AT ZERO TIDE

Roderick Island

Kid Bay (Finlayson Channel)
1 mi NE of Goat Bay
Entrance: 52°48.00'N, 128°23.89'W

Kid Bay is exposed to prevailing westerlies; we prefer the coves to the south.

Sheep Passage (Pooley Island)
14 mi NE of Klemtu
Entrance (W): 52°48.56'N, 128°24.58'W
Entrance (E): 52°51.00'N, 128°09.20'W

Sheep Passage leads east 10 miles to scenic Fiordland and the upper end of Mathieson Channel.

Carter Bay (Sheep Passage)
4.5 mi SE of Heikish Narrows
Entrance: 52°49.30'N, 128°23.86'W
Anchor: 52°49.81'N, 128°23.78'W

The bow section of the wreck of the *S/S
Ohio* lies in the east side of the head of Carter Bay at
52°49.86'N, 128°23.44'W. In 1909, after hitting what
was then an uncharted rock off the southwest corner
of Hiekish Narrows, the captain of the sinking steam-
ship made a critical decision to cross Finlayson Channel and beach the boat in Carter Bay. His quick think-
ing was successful in saving the lives of all but four
crew. The bow section of the steel ship lies in about
5 fathoms. Carter Bay is exposed to southerly winds
and chop but temporary shelter from prevailing westerlies can be found in the northwest corner.

Anchor in 8-10 fathoms over sand with fair holding.

Griffin Passage, north narrows

Griffin Passage (North Entrance)
4.6 mi W of Windy Bay
Entrance: 52°47.05'N, 128°20.93'W

Griffin Passage was home to logging operations over
the years, discouraging pleasure vessels from using
it as an anchor site. However, "Logboom Bay" offers
protection from all weather. Shelter from downslope
winds or strong westerlies can be taken within the
north entrance to Griffin Passage in what we call
"Lime Point Cove."

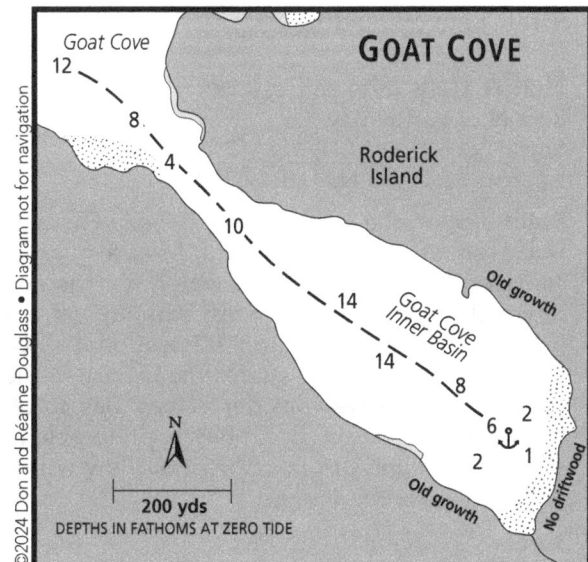

GOAT COVE

Goat Cove
12
8
4
Roderick
Island
10
14
Goat Cove
Inner Basin
Old growth
14
8
2
6
1
2
Old growth
No driftwood
N
200 yds
DEPTHS IN FATHOMS AT ZERO TIDE
©2024 Don and Réanne Douglass • Diagram not for navigation

Guess what's for dinner?

Lime Point Cove (North Griffin Passage)

0.4 mi SE of Lime Pt.
Entrance: 52°46.65'N, 128°20.28'W
Anchor: 52°46.65'N, 128°20.21'W

By tucking inside the very northwest tip of Pooley Island in Sheep Passage, you can find shelter in Lime Point Cove from all but southerly winds. The water in this part of Griffin Passage is quite deep, and you can find convenient anchoring only by staying close to shore, as indicated on the diagram.

The shore is steep-to (4 fathoms, 60 feet from shore) and covered with large sea stars and sea cucumbers; a stern tie to shore is recommended.

Anchor in 4 to 12 fathoms over sand, shell, rock, and kelp; fair holding with a well-set anchor.

North Griffin Narrows Anchorage (Roderick Island)

3.3 mi S of Lime Point
Anchor: 52°43.72'N, 128°19.83'W

Entrance to what we call "North Griffin Narrows Anchorage" is very shallow requiring adequate tide level. Favor the east shore. The north-south trend of this anchorage and its position in a long north-south valley means it can be exposed to outflow winds in the winter, but otherwise it offers excellent shelter.

Anchor in 2 fathoms or more (to avoid disturbing the eelgrass) over mud and sand; good holding.

Windy Bay (Sheep Passage)

4.5 mi SW of Mathieson Narrows
Entrance: 52°47.28'N, 128°13.78'W

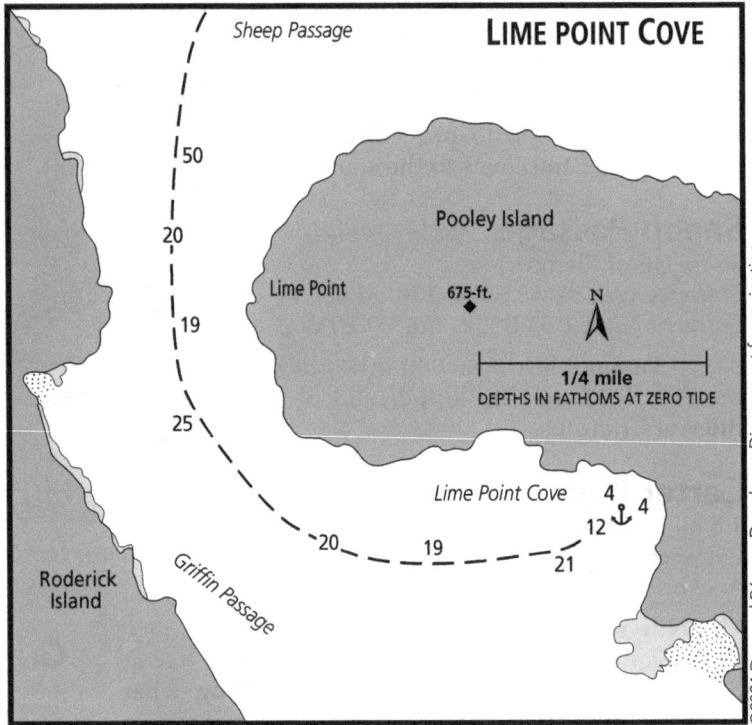

LIME POINT COVE

©2024 Don and Réanne Douglass • Diagram not for navigation

Anchor: 52°47.08'N, 128°12.86'W

Windy Bay, surrounded by high peaks, is the easiest, most accessible place to anchor in this area. Although it is open to some winds that blow off these peaks, it offers good protection in almost all weather. Despite its name, it is our choice as an anchor site when the wind picks up. Tuck in east of the small island. We experienced some downslope winds from the southeast so we would anchor in the southeast corner when winds are expected from that quarter.

Anchor east of the islet in 10 fathoms over sand and gravel; fair-to-good holding.

Bolin Bay (Sheep Passage)

3 mi N of Windy Bay
Entrance: 52°50.24'N, 128°12.15'W
Anchor: 52°50.15'N, 128°12.97'W

Bolin Bay, on the north shore of Sheep Passage, is a lovely, small bay that lies at the base of high, snow-covered peaks where waterfalls cascade down the sheer granite sides. Although it lies just outside the Fiordland Recreational Area boundaries, its setting shares the beauty of the park. Although we consider Windy Bay to offer better protection, Bolin Bay is preferable in strong westerlies or in northeast outflow winds when chop can be severe.

Anchor in about 15 fathoms.

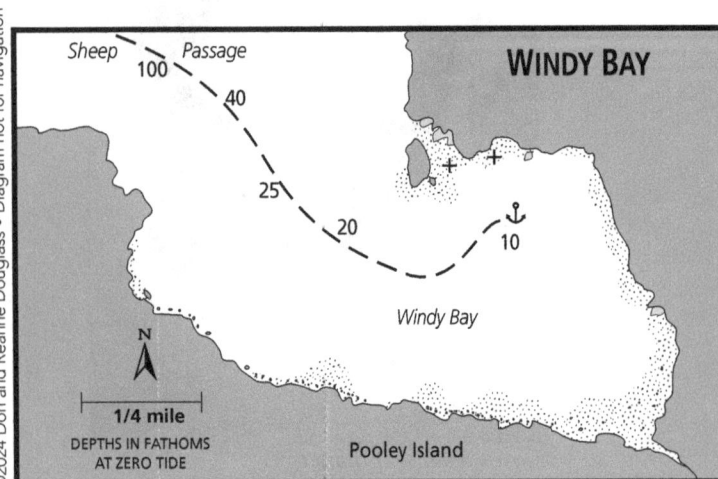

WINDY BAY

©2024 Don and Réanne Douglass • Diagram not for navigation

Magnificent Fiordland Conservancy

Mussel Inlet (Fiordland)
N of Mathieson Narrows
Entrance: 52°51.24'N, 128°09.10'W

The western boundary of Fiordland Conservancy lies along this inlet east of Bolin Bay. Two areas in Mussel Inlet have been set aside for wildlife. The Mussel Estuary and the Poison Cove Estuary are designated wildlife areas set aside with special provisions. From May through August 14, boaters may enter these estuaries for water-based wildlife viewing with a maximum of 16 people at a time. During Peak Season August 15 through October 15th, all access to the estuaries requires a permitted guide (Kitasoo Guardians or BC Park Rangers). During this period boaters are to contact the Kitasoo Guardians on VHF Ch 6 about 1 mile east of Barrie Point at David Bay to declare their intentions of entering the estuary area. Going ashore in the estuary areas is not permitted at any time. The estuaries are closed to all bear and wildlife viewing October 16 through April 31st.

Mussel Inlet is famous for alpine scenery, the shellfish poisoning of Vancouver's crew, and fierce winter outflow winds. Evidence of winter storms can be seen as ice-carved markings along the steep, granite shore.

SESAME SEED-CRUSTED HALIBUT WITH SUN-DRIED CRANBERRY SALSA

3 Tbsp.	dried cranberries
1 C.	cranberry juice or apple juice
1 tsp.	minced shallot
1 tsp.	butter
1 Tbsp.	white wine or water
1 tsp.	chopped chives
salt and pepper to taste	
2 tsp.	cornstarch
4 - 5 oz.	pieces fresh halibut, identical thickness
1 Tbsp.	white sesame seeds, toasted
1 Tbsp.	black sesame seeds, toasted
1/2 tsp.	butter
1/2 tsp.	olive oil

To make salsa, refresh the dried cranberries by bringing them to a boil in the cranberry juice. Set aside for 30 minutes to plump up and cool. In a small pot, sauté the shallot in butter. Reduce heat and add wine, chives, salt and pepper. Continue to cook for 3 minutes. Mix the cornstarch into the cooled cranberries. Add this to the shallot mixture, stirring constantly over low heat until thickened. Set aside and keep warm.

Pat the halibut dry. Mix the toasted white and black sesame seeds together and coat one side of the fish with the seeds. In an ovenproof frying pan, heat butter and olive oil until hot. Fry the seeded side of the halibut for 1 minute, then flip the halibut over, put the pan into a preheated 350°F oven. Bake until the halibut is done to your taste, about 8 minutes per 1" or internal temperature of 140°F. Don't overcook! Serves 4.

Courtesy of Noreen Rudd and David Hoar,
Cooks Afloat! Harbour Publishing
Editor's Note: This is one of Réanne's favorite recipes!

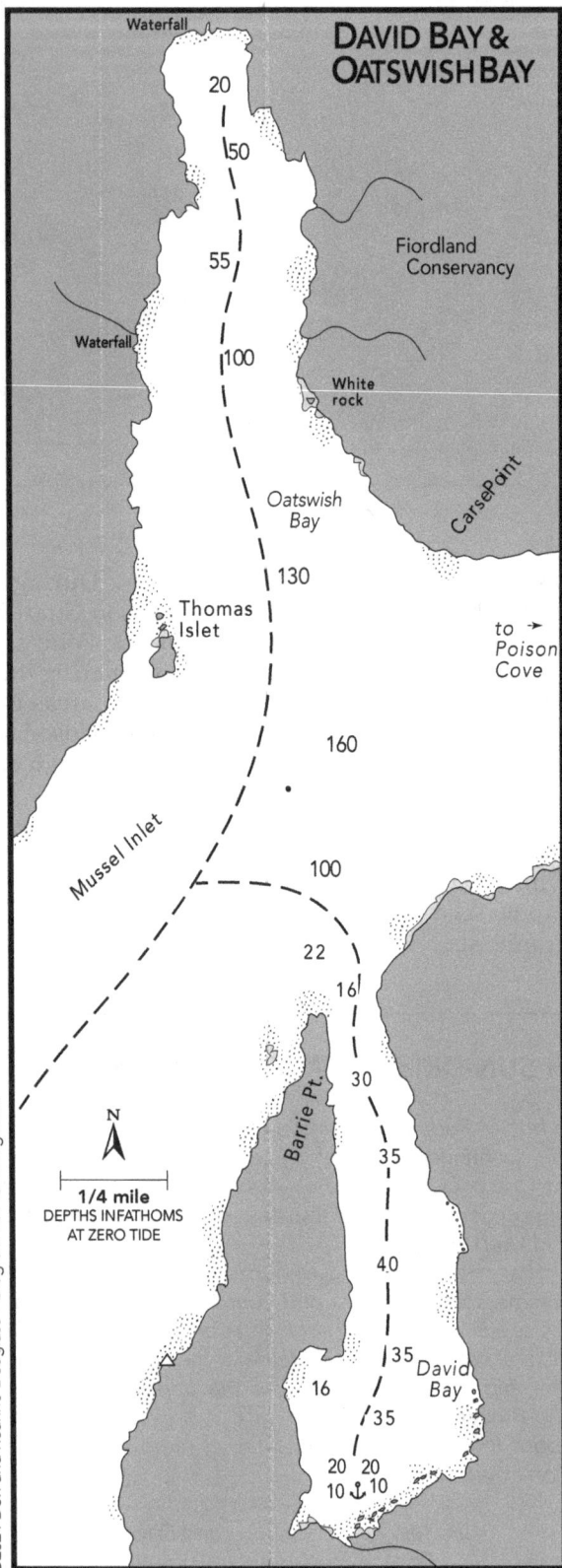

DAVID BAY &
OATSWISH BAY

Waterfall

20

50

55

100

Fiordland
Conservancy

Waterfall

White
rock

Oatswish
Bay

Carse Point

130

Thomas
Islet

to →
Poison
Cove

160

Mussel Inlet

100

22

16

Barrie Pt.

30

35

N

40

1/4 mile
DEPTHS IN FATHOMS
AT ZERO TIDE

35 David
Bay

16   35

20 20
10 ⚓ 10

©2024 Don and Réanne Douglass • Diagram not for navigation

David Bay (Mussel Inlet Fiordland)
3 mi N of Mathieson Narrows
Entrance: 52°53.60'N, 128°07.40'W
Anchor: 52°52.43'N, 128°07.43'W

David Bay, an attractive inlet on the south side of Mussel Inlet, offers good southerly protection. The head of the bay shoals so rapidly that the anchorage is marginal, unless you like to anchor in 100- to 200-foot-deep water. We anchored off the outlet to the creek in 10 fathoms and, with 90 feet of rode out, our vessel swung around and around with our stern, alternately, in 14 feet of water or 100 feet. While this can work in the calm weather it would be unsafe in windy conditions. Fifty feet from shore in the first bight on the west side of David Bay, there's an 8-fathom "hole" where you might be able to tie a stern line to the trees. This would be our first choice in any weather.

The granite rock along the shores of the bay has several parallel white lines that appear to have been incised by winter ice. This is spectacular country and well worth the short detour!

Anchor off the steep-to creek in about 10 fathoms over sand and gravel with fair holding; limited swinging room.

Mussel Bay (Mussel Inlet Fiordland)
3.3 mi NE of David Bay
Position: 52°54.82'N, 128°02.39'W

Mussel Bay Estuary is a protected area for wildlife with special provisions for boaters wishing to visit the area; see the Mussel Inlet section.

Mussel Bay is a flat bight at the bottom of a V-shaped valley cut by the Mussel River. This is wild scenery and, as the treetops on shore indicate here and farther south near Crosson Point, downslope winds blow hard during winter storms.

Poison Cove (Mussel Inlet Fiordland)
3.3 mi E of David Bay
Entrance: 52°54.62'N, 128°02.37'W

Poison Cove Estuary is a protected area for wildlife with special provisions for boaters wishing to visit the area; see the Mussel Inlet section.

Poison Cove, affords more protection than nearby Mussel Bay. The scenery is alpine but the cove is ice-carved and very deep. Poison Cove was named by Captain George Vancouver when several of his crew became ill, and one died, after eating mussels contaminated with red tide (paralytic shellfish poisoning—PSP).

Tolmie Channel (Princess Royal Island)

Leads N of Klemtu
Entrance (S): 52°38.57'N, 128°31.80'W
Entrance (N): 52°53.17'N, 128°31.11'W

Tolmie Channel, the main route for cruise ships and commercial boats, can have heavy traffic day or night. Visibility in the channel is limited during periods of foul weather, particularly fog around Boat Bluff, the south entrance. *Caution:* There can be tiderips and turbulence mid-channel from Parry Patch to Split Head.

Split Head (Tolmie Channel)

2.3 mi NW of Boat Bluff
Position: 52°40.37'N, 128°33.25'W

Heavy traffic, combined with reduced visibility in drizzle or fog, is frequently found here. For a lunch stop, consider either of the two small nooks just west of Separation Point. Anchor close to shore in 4 to 5 fathoms.

Alexander Inlet (Princess Royal Island)

5.3 mi NW of Klemtu
Entrance: 52°40.44'N, 128°34.51'W
Anchor: 52°38.50'N, 128°40.63'W

Infrequently used as a cruising destination, Alexander Inlet is lined on its north shore by high, granite peaks and overhanging cliffs of yellow and grey rock. The inlet is attractive and unspoiled. Cone Mountain to the west at 2,540 feet is an impressive monolith, its walls too steep to hold soil. A quarter-mile north of Bingham Narrows, a bare, solid ridge of rocks extends from the west shore to mid-channel; favor the east shore at this point. As you approach the narrows, favor the west shore, remaining about 75 feet off the rock wall to avoid the western end of an underwater ledge. The ledge extends three-quarters of the way across the channel; a rock that dries on a 4-foot tide marks the west end of this ledge. The ledge is not marked by kelp except near the rock that dries on a 4-foot tide. The

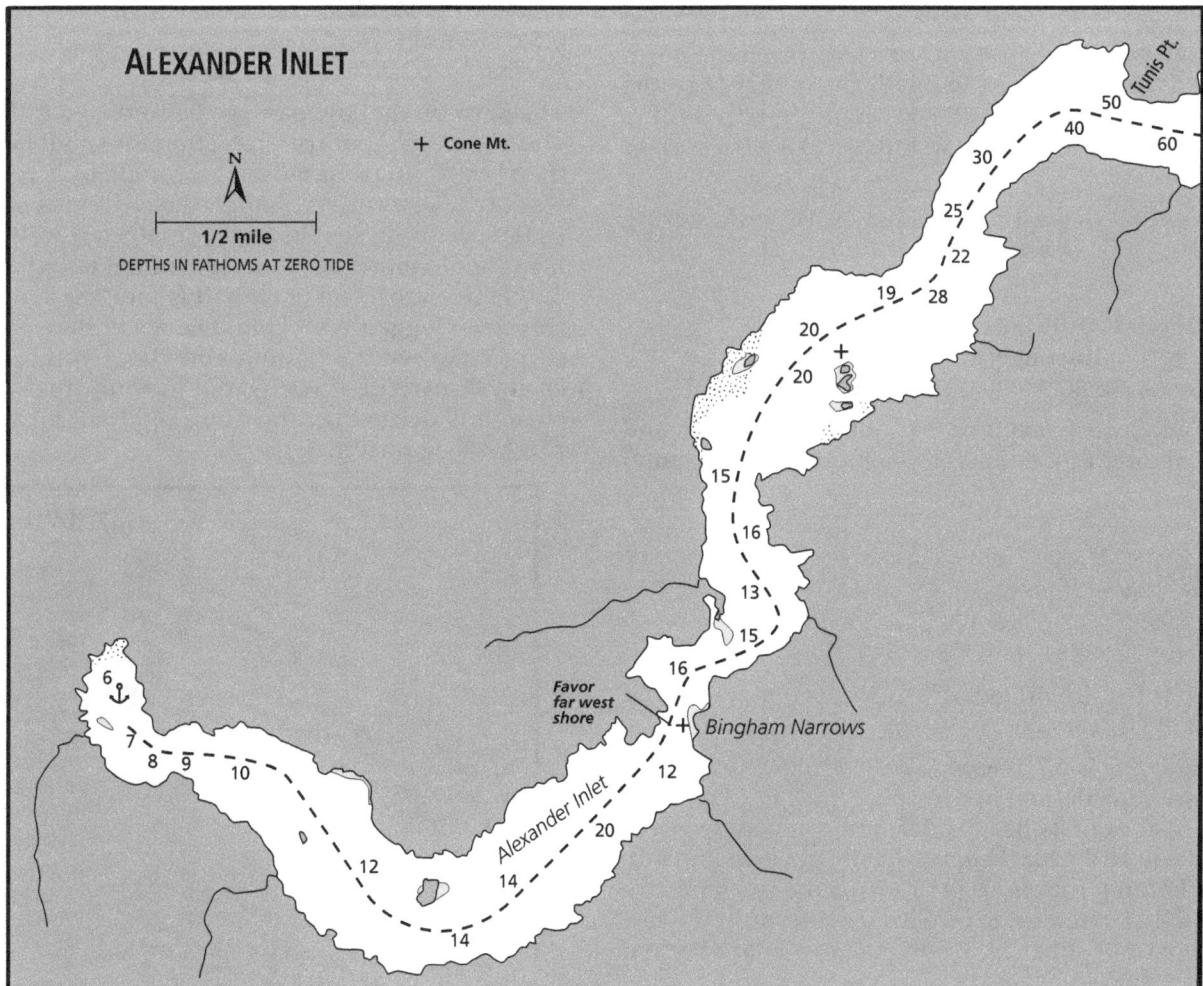

ALEXANDER INLET

N

1/2 mile
DEPTHS IN FATHOMS AT ZERO TIDE

+ Cone Mt.

Favor far west shore

Bingham Narrows

Alexander Inlet

Tunis Pt.

©2024 Don and Réanne Douglass • Diagram not for navigation

Tolmie Channel, looking north

narrows carries about 4 fathoms of water at zero tide with a route about 20 yards parallel to the west wall.

South of Bingham Narrows, Alexander Inlet is quiet and landlocked and an odor of earthy, decaying matter permeates the air. You can anchor anywhere north of the rapids that flows into the head of the inlet from the west. The rapids originate in a lagoon that can be entered only by dinghy on a 12-foot high tide or more. The rapids create a lot of foam and we found the best anchor site to lie on the north side of this foam in 4 to 6 fathoms. Other than the foam, the water is so still you can see hundreds of v-patterns created by little waterbugs along the surface of the water.

Anchor in about 6 fathoms over soft, thick, oozing brown mud with very good holding.

Brown Cove (Alexander Inlet)
3 mi NW of Boat Bluff
Entrance: 52°40.91'N, 128°34.55'W

Brown Cove is exposed to southeast weather and useful only as a temporary stop off its drying mud flat.

Cougar Bay (Tolmie Channel)
5.6 mi NW of Boat Bluff
Entrance: 52°43.65'N, 128°34.72'W
Anchor: 52°44.51'N, 128°34.75'W

Cougar Bay, 2.6 miles north of Nash Point, is entered west of Ditmars Point.

Cougar Bay is often used as an overnight anchorage, but we can't figure out why. We saw a large commercial boat drag its heavy hook and chain all over the east side of the bay before it finally gave up and left. The holding ground is poor—hard rock as far as we can tell. If you want to give it a try, anchor in the east part of Cougar Bay in 10 fathoms over a hard bottom with *poor* holding.

Hiekish Narrows (Finlayson Channel)
Entrance (S): 52°48.68'N, 128°26.54'W
Entrance (N): 52°53.11'N, 128°30.29'W
Hewitt Rock light: 52°52.14'N, 128°29.33'W

Hiekish Narrows is a deep-water passage to Princess Royal Channel; Hewitt Rock, mid-channel, marked by a red/green/red buoy can be passed on either side. Avoid Ohio Rock at the south entrance. Don't cut the corner like the *Ohio* did. (See Carter Bay)

Since there is minimal turbulence, you can transit Hiekish Narrows on all tides if you have sufficient power. In summer of 2000 a new NOAA research vessel ran aground here on its maiden voyage. The helmsman apparently underestimated the power of the current in the narrows and slammed into the east shore scraping the rocks clean of vegetation. This site is visible at 52°51.93'N, 128°28.93'W.

The small channel behind Hewitt Island offers a convenient temporary stop for small boats. Enter from the north side.

Hewitt Island (Hiekish Narrows)
0.5 mi NW of Hewitt Rock
Anchor: 52°52.50'N, 128°30.25'W

The narrow, shallow passage behind Hewitt Island offers good temporary protection for small boats if there's a storm front moving through, or if you just want to take a rest. Although the current is strong, its flow is linear, so if you set your anchor well, your boat should tether very nicely without budging. Enter via the north end of Hewitt Island; the south entrance is clogged with kelp. The water here is clear, so you can see the bottom and check your anchor easily. Be careful; if you go out in your dinghy—the current is deceiving, and you might not be able to row back against it!

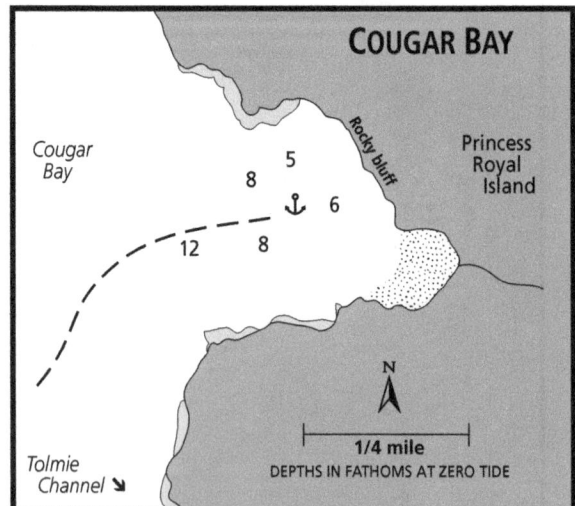

COUGAR BAY

Cougar
Bay

Princess
Royal
Island

Rocky bluff

5
8
⚓ 6
12   8

Tolmie
Channel ↘

N

1/4 mile
DEPTHS IN FATHOMS AT ZERO TIDE

©2024 Don and Reanne Douglass • Diagram not for navigation

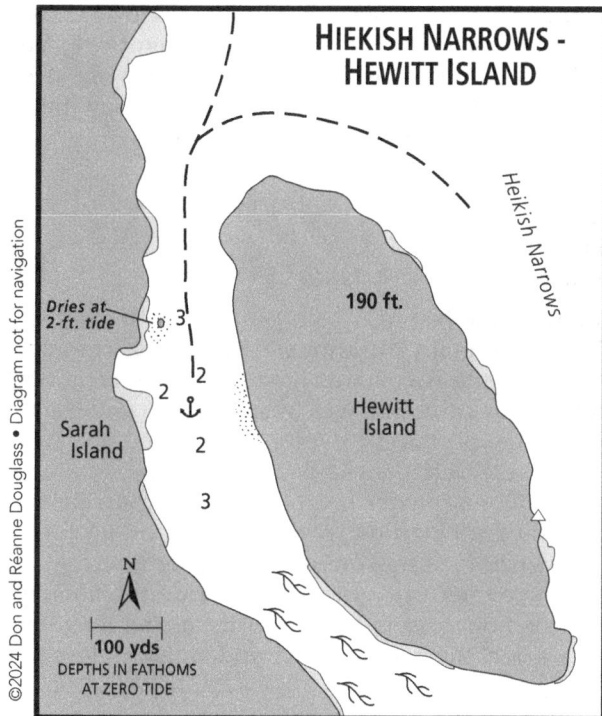

Anchor mid-channel in 2 fathoms over sand and grass; good holding with a well-set anchor.

Princess Royal Channel
1.5 mi NW of Hiekish Narrows
Entrance (S): 52°53.52'N, 128°30.76'W

Green Inlet (Princess Royal Channel)
3.2 mi N of Hiekish Narrows
Entrance: 52°55.45'N, 128°30.06'W

Green Inlet is another Cougar Bay as far as we can tell. Horsefly Cove proved too deep and difficult, so we visited the shoal just south of Baffle Point where we enjoyed the view of the ebb current at the rapids—it was like watching a jet fighter with its after-burner ignited. The rooster tails of the waterfall pulsate for perhaps 100 yards on a good low tide. For the life of us, we couldn't get our trusty CQR to hold on the shoal close south, so we gave up and spent the night poorly secured to a spit that extends from the stream on the south shore across from Horsefly Cove.

Horsefly Cove (Green Inlet)
0.6 mi E of Green Inlet entr
Anchor: 52°55.22'N, 128°29.00'W

Anchor in 13 to 15 fathoms over a hard bottom in the middle of the cove if you have lots of chain; poor holding.

Swanson Bay (Princess Royal Channel)
5.2 mi N of Green Inlet
Entrance: 53°00.59'N, 128°30.94'W
Anchor (S): 53°00.78'N, 128°30.36'W
Anchor (N): 53°01.93'N, 128°30.62'W

You can find moderate protection from channel winds and chop at either of the two indicated sites in Swanson Bay. There is a large shoal off the beach, and caution is advised. The southern anchorage seems to be the better because the creek has created a small area with a sandy bottom. Both sites have limited swinging room.

Anchor (S) in 3 to 4 fathoms over sand and grass with good holding.

Anchor (N) in 6 to 8 fathoms over sand and gravel with fair holding.

Khutze Inlet (Princess Royal Channel)
13.1 mi N of Hiekish Narrows
Entrance: 53°04.84'N, 128°33.13'W
Anchor: 53°05.42'N, 128°31.10'W

Some boaters consider Khutze Inlet (pronounced Kootz) on the east side of Green Spit to be one of the best anchorages in Graham Reach. Be careful not to anchor too deep (over 10 fathoms) or the length of your anchor line will allow you to swing onto the spit. If you have a larger vessel with an anchor winch, it is best to anchor in 10 to 15 fathoms north of the spit in the fairway where it's protected from most winds and swinging room is more ample.

Khutze Conservancy encompasses Khutze Inlet, Khutze River watershed, and 85,00 acres of uplands around the Inlet and river. Khutze Conservancy is jointly managed by the BC Parks and the Kitasoo Xai'xais Band. From July to October 15th, boaters are

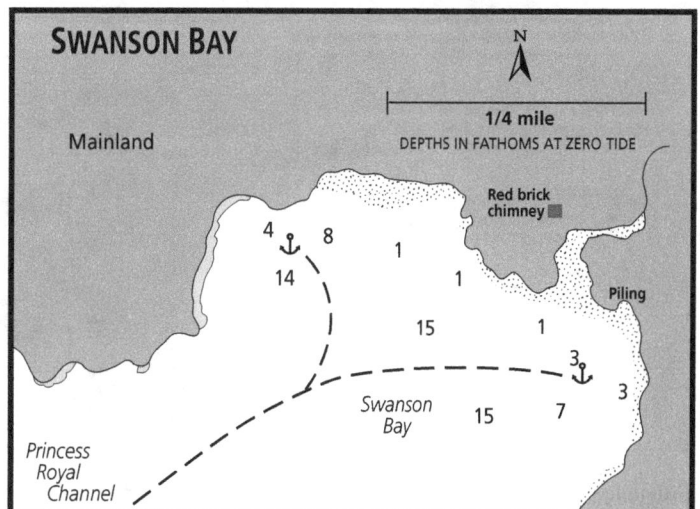

to contact the Kitasoo Guardians on VHF Ch 6 before entering the Khutze water-based wildlife viewing area at the Khutze River esturary at the head of Khutze Inlet.

When permitted by the Khutze Conservancy access limitations, anchorage can also be found just off the river mouth, but the mud flats are steep-to and there is danger that the river's current could cause you to drag anchor.

West of the entrance to Khutze Inlet is the outlet of Canoona River/Lake—a beautiful, wide falls created by a coffer dam.

Anchor (east of spit) in about 6 to 8 fathoms over mud, shell and kelp; fair holding; limited swinging room.

Aaltanhash Inlet (Princess Royal Channel)
2.6 mi N of Khutze Inlet
Entrance: 53°07.42'N, 128°34.44'W

If you want to turn off your engine and just drift a while for respite from chop or traffic in the channel, Aaltanhash Inlet is not a bad place to do so. It is a beautiful U-shaped valley off the beaten track. You might even find a "big one" lurking here in the deep waters, but it's too deep for an overnight stay unless you use a shore tie.

Butedale (Princess Royal Island)
35 mi NW of Klemtu
Entrance: 53°09.71'N, 128°41.59'W

Butedale, like Namu, was a cannery with extensive wharfs, and many buildings. After the cannery shut down, the site was a welcome stop for recreational boaters. The caretaker welcomed boaters and shared some of the past and recent history of the site. After the caretaker left, the site decayed.

The current owner has been cleaning up the site and added a new float with space for about 5 or 6 boats. Visitors must contact the owner and register with the owner prior to using the side-tie moorage. Construction vessels have priority at the float. Uplands are a construction site and remain closed to

Butedale - unusually busy with Waggoner's SE Alaska Flotilla group. Moorage is by permission only in advance from owner

Photo by Mike Beemer

visitors.

Contact Shawn Kennedy at the Inside Passage Marine Corp. for permission to use the float - skennedyau@gmail.com.

The Butedale waterfall is still an inspiring sight when it is at full rush, and big halibut can sometimes be caught just offshore.

Klekane Inlet, Marmot Cove and Scow Bay (Butedale Passage)
Entrance: 53°10.86'N, 128°38.87'W

Scow Bay and Marmot Cove in Klekane Inlet have drying flats with steep-to shores. Neither offers serious anchoring opportunities other than as a lunch stop. Some boats have used the pilings in Marmot Cove for moorage; however, it is not considered trustworthy protection.

Boat Bluff light station, Sarah Island

BBQ SALMON WITHOUT A BBQ

4 - 6 oz.	salmon steaks
2 Tbsp.	melted butter
2 Tbsp.	lemon juice
2 Tbsp.	ketchup
1 Tbsp.	Worcestershire sauce
2 Tbsp.	minced shallot
1 Tbsp.	brown sugar
1/2 tsp.	dry mustard
1/4 tsp.	salt

Place salmon steaks on a greased, foil-lined baking sheet. In a small saucepan, mix together the rest of the ingredients and heat gently. Spoon the marinade carefully onto the top of each salmon steak. (If there is any left over, it can be refrigerated for future use.) Let the salmon marinate at room temperature for 30 minutes. Preheat broiler and place steaks 3" from the broiler element. Cook on one side only, allowing 10 minutes per 1" of thickness. Serves 4.

Courtesy of Noreen Rudd and David Hoar,
Cooks Afloat! Harbour Publishing

Graham Reach, waterfall

20'

10'

53°N

50'

40'

30'

20'

10'

N

0 2 4 6 8 10
NAUTICAL MILES

Wright Sound
Farrant I.
Gribbell I.
Ursula Channel
McKay Reach
Angler Cove
Fisherman Cove
Hawk Bay
Pitt I.
Curlew Bay
Fin I.
Crane Bay
Home Bay
Whalen Lake
Klekane
Dillon Bay
MacDonald Bay
Clemens Rapids
Fraser Reach
Aaltanhash Inlet
Otter Pssg.
Squally Channel
Gil Island
Cornwall Inlet
Betteridge Inlet
Fish Bay
Whale Channel
Princess
Butedale
Khutze Inlet
McMicking Inlet
Barnard Harbour
Royal
Swanson Bay
Campania I.
Cameron Cove
Island
Graham Reach
Horsefly Cove
Estevan Sound
Campania Sound
Clarke Cove
Dam
Ouswish Bay
Penn Harbour
Buie Creek
Green Inlet
Poison Cove
Emily Carr Inlet
Doig Anch.
Mellis Inlet
Princess Royal Channel
Hewitt I.
Mussel Inlet
David Bay
Surf Inlet
Hiekish Narrows
Mathieson Narrows
Racey Inlet
Bone Anchorage
7
Bay of Plenty
Fifer Cove
Carter Bay
Bolin Bay
FIORDLAND
Baker Point
Evinrude Inlet
Weld Cove
Laredo Inlet
Cougar Bay
Tolmie Channel
Work Bay
Sheep Passage
Windy Bay
Waterfall
Commando Inlet
Smithers I. Cove
Alston Cove
Goat Cove
Lime Pt. Cove
Pooley I.
Kynoch Inlet
Tate Cove
Helmcken Inlet
Kent Inlet
Wallace Bight
Griffin Passage
Borrowman
Beauchemin Channel
Laredo Channel
Trahey Inlet
Quigley Ck Cove
Sarah I.
Finlayson Channel
Bottleneck Inlet
Kettle Inlet
Hague Point Lagoon
Alexander Inlet
McRae Cove
Byway Rock
Mathieson Channel
Culpepper Lagoon
Moon I.
Aristazabal Island
Fury Bay
Meyers Passage
Jorgensen Hbr
Mary Cove
Roderick I.
Rescue Bay
Clifford Bay
KLEMTU
Trout Bay
Jackson Pass
Normansell Passage
Cowards Cove
Osmen Inlet
Susan I.
Salmon Bay
Kitasu Bay
Parsons Anch.
Swindle I.
Oscar Passage
Arthur I. Cove
De Freitas I.
Bent Harbour
Higgins Passage
Price Inlet
Dowager I.
Tom Bay
Florence Peninsula
Weeteeam Bay
Laredo Sound
Don Peninsula
Spiller Channel
Yeo I.
Rudolf Bay
Price I.
Vancouver Rock
Moss Passage
Perceval Narrows
OLIVER COVE M.P.
Return Channel
Johnson Channel
Lagoon Cove
Port Blackney
Goat Inlet
Chatfield I.
Fort Bay
Catala Passage
Langford Cove
Lady Douglas
Reid Passage
Fisher Point
Ivory I.
Seaforth Channel
Kynumpt Hbr
Cunningham I.
McInnes Island
Morris Bay
Milbanke Sound
St. John Harbour
Dutton I.
Raymond Passage
Kakushdish Pass
Gunboat Passage
(large numbers refer to chapters)
Dyer Cove
BELLA BELLA
Bardswell Group
Campbell I.
SHEARWATER
Denny I.
Lama Passage
Long Point Cove

Milbanke and Laredo Sounds, Aristazabal and Princess Royal Islands to Squally and Whale Channels

©2024 Don and Réanne Douglass • Diagram not for navigation

7

Milbanke and Laredo Sounds, Aristazabal and Princess Royal Islands to Squally and Whale Channels

Crossing Milbanke and Laredo Sounds gives cruising boats a good introduction to the "wild west" coast. The most direct route northbound—and what we call the Outer Passage—crosses south of Price Island and is exposed to southerly swells and chop. Although Catala Passage can minimize this exposure, smaller boats should use it in fair weather only. Meyers Passage is a smooth-water route.

The west coast of both Aristazabal (pronounced A-*ris*-ta-bal) and Princess Royal islands have the most interesting inlets for pleasure craft. (There are few anchor sites along the east coast of Aristazabal.) Add to these two islands the west coast of Price Island, and boaters can find outstanding opportunities for kayaking, beachcombing, scuba diving or just observing nature within a multitude of small islands, islets, and reefs. Weeteeam Bay and Borrowman Bay at the southwest end of Aristazabal are well-protected base camps from which the marvels of the Outer Coast can be explored. Princess Royal and Gribbel Islands have the largest concentration of Kermode bears (*Ursus kermodei*)—the beautiful cream-colored bear known as the Spirit Bear. This island will provide the keystone to the wilderness corridor connecting Tweedsmuir Park and the Kitlope to the east, with Gwaii Haanas National Park Reserve (South Moresby Island) directly to the west across Hecate Strait.

Higgins Passage and Meyers Passage can both be used to cross from east to west to enter Laredo Sound. Higgins Passage, the more challenging of the two passages for small- and medium-sized vessels, should be attempted only with careful study of the chart. (See cautions later in this chapter.) Meyers Passage is an easier route that can be transited by most boats at mid-tide and above.

The area from Laredo Channel to Principe Channel and Dundas Island, along with Haida Gwaii is a major flyway for wild birds. Infrequently visited by cruising boats, the area sustains the highest concentration of flora and fauna along the Inside Passage.

Note: Charts 3726 and 3737 were drawn prior to the adoption of NAD 27, thus all latitudes and longitudes derived from these charts should be used with caution, and allowance made for an adequate margin of safety.

Milbanke Sound

10 mi SW of Ivory Island lt.
Entrance (S): 52°12.02'N, 128°38.00'W
Entrance (N): 52°25.00'N, 128°29.12'W

Milbanke Sound is exposed to southeast weather or remnant swells from that direction. In fair weather, it's a 10-mile run from Seaforth Channel across to Catala Passage and up into Laredo Sound. Check conditions at McInnes Island Light Station before attempting this route as Milbank Sound and Laredo Sound are open to ocean swell and wind. If you're headed for Higgins Passage, you can cross Milbanke Sound, keeping Vancouver Rock to starboard. For more protection, you can take Reid Passage to Moss Passage or Oscar Passage, then west through Higgins Passage. Heading to Klemtu and Meyers Passage, Milbanke Sound is the most direct route, however the most protected route leads through Mathieson Channel and Jackson Narrows.

If you are southbound from Higgins Passage and a southerly swell or chop develops in Milbanke Sound, you can follow a smooth-water route east that hugs the Swindle Island shore, passing inside Pidwell Reef and around Jorkins Point into Finlayson Channel. From there you can cross Oscar Passage or Moss Passage, heading south in Mathieson Channel and Reid Passage to Seaforth Channel.

Gulls in Milbanke Sound

St. John Harbour (Milbanke Sound)

4.6 mi SW of Ivory Island lt.
Entrance: 52°12.18'N, 128°28.54'W

St. John Harbour, on the west shore of Athlone Island, offers very good protection in all weather. Use caution to identify the entrance since red buoy "E46" is not visible until you are close to Rage Reefs. The prevailing southwest swells that break so vigorously on the reefs die off as soon as you are abeam of "E46." Within St. John Harbour, there are two basins: Louisa Cove to the southwest and Dyer Cove to the southeast. St. John Lagoon lies to the south of Dyer Cove.

Several fishing lodges are located in the area. Be careful to avoid congestion around the lodges.

What's So *Hot* About These Volcanoes?

Underneath mature coniferous forests growing in the Kitimat and Coastal Mountains of Northwest British Columbia sleeps a group of five small basaltic volcanoes unlike any others in Canada. The Milbanke Sound Cones spread across four small islands: Swindle, Price, Lady Douglas, and Lake. Geologists disagree about when and how these basaltic volcanoes were formed. Due to the small amount of erosion, the most accepted theory is that they formed after the last glacial period, about 10,000 years ago. Some scientists group the Milbanke Sound Cones with the nearby, but much older, Anahim Volcanic Belt that formed when the North American Plate moved across "hotspots" (mantle plumes like the ones that formed the Hawaiian Islands). Another possible theory suggests that the Milbanke Sound Cones are the northern extension of the Garibaldi Volcanic Belt formed by northwest subduction (collision between two tectonic plates); or other tectonic processes not yet understood. Compositional analysis does not distinguish between possible origins.

The northernmost and best-preserved cone, Kitasu Hill, on the southwest shore of Swindle Island rises 250 meters (820 feet) and rests on bedrock scoured by glacial movement.

Covering Lake Island on the southwest side of Don Peninsula, Helmet Peak's steep-sided formation makes it the largest, at 335 meters (1,099 feet). Kitasu Hill and Helmet Peak are the only two named cones.

On Finngal Island, the basalt lava flows have resulted in a unique formation called columnar joints, a geological structure formed as rocks cool and contract into intricate polygonal prisms. Seen from the air, these well-preserved geological features appear like beehive honeycombs.

The smallest two cinder cones of the Milbanke Sound Cones are on Price Island and Dufferin Island, with elevations of forty meters (130 feet) and fifty meters (160 feet), respectively. Erosion has greatly scoured both cones, allowing dense forest to cover each. Remnants of lava flows are visible on the island's beaches.

While the Geological Survey of Canada monitors the five volcanoes' magma chambers, the seismographs are located too far away to predict what's brewing beneath the cones.

—KK

Dyer Cove (St. John Harbour)

1 mi S of St. John Harbour entrance
Entrance: 52°11.59'N, 128°28.48'W
Anchor: 52°11.29'N, 128°28.28'W

Dyer Cove can be entered on either side of Raby Islet; the west side is the deeper of the two. Well-sheltered anchorage can be taken anywhere in Dyer Cove.

Anchor in about 12 fathoms over sand and mud with some rocks; fair-to-good holding.

Louisa Cove

(St. John Harbour)
0.6 mi SW of Dyer Cove
Entrance: 52°11.62'N, 128°28.87'W
Anchor: 52°11.02'N, 128°29.49'W

St. John Lagoon entrance

Louisa Cove, less busy than Dyer Cove, holds more attraction for many boaters, although it does receive more wind and chop under northeast conditions. Inside Wurtele Island, there is a small high-water route that skiffs can use to go back and forth from Queens Sound; this route is choked with kelp.

Anchor in about 5 fathoms over sand and gravel with fair-to-good holding.

St. John Lagoon

(St. John Harbour)
0.5 mi SE of Dyer Cove
Entrance: 52°11.01'N, 128°28.02'W
Anchor: 52°10.75'N, 128°27.41'W

"St. John Lagoon" is what we call the two well-protected basins, entered just east of the fishing resorts through a small channel. Both basins are removed from the noise and bustle of sportfishing boats. The entrance narrows carries about 7 feet minimum in its fairway. The shores of the lagoon are lined by small cedars so typical of the west coast, making a dinghy landing difficult. Anchorage can be taken anywhere in the first basin; we prefer the entrance to the nook on the southeast corner. Since swinging room is limited, a stern tie to shore is effective.

The entrance to the second basin to the southeast contains an islet and is choked with kelp. Small boats can pass to the south side of the islet near high water.

Anchor (first basin) in 4 fathoms over sand, mud, and grass with good-to-very-good holding.

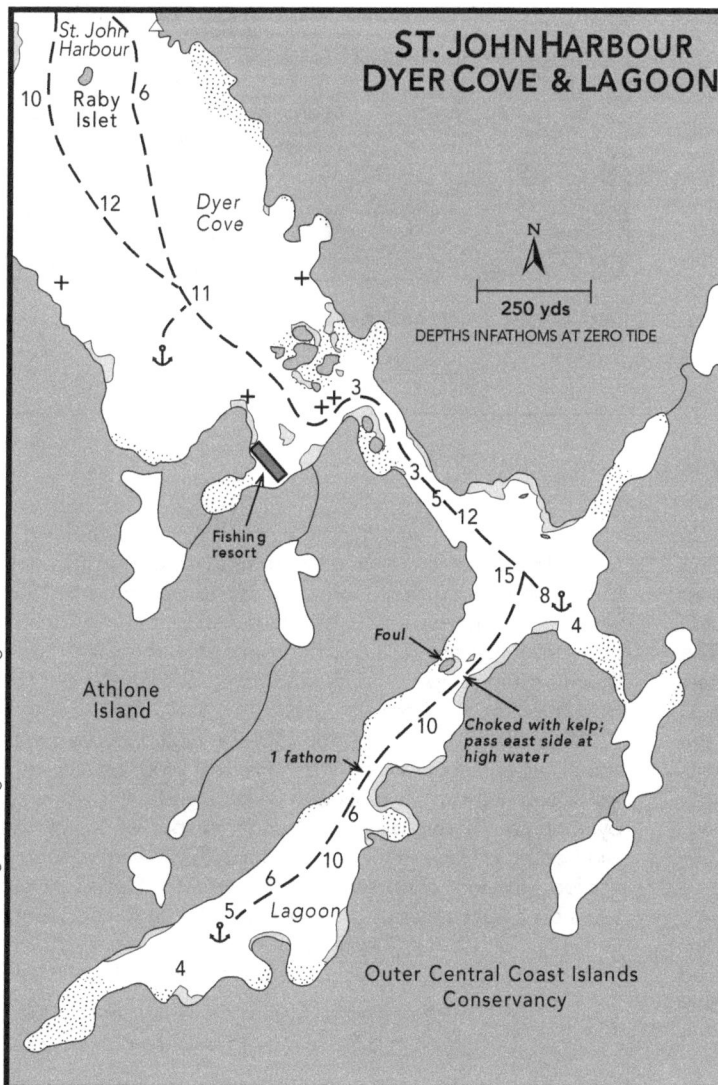

ST. JOHN HARBOUR
DYER COVE & LAGOON

St. John Harbour
Raby Islet
10   6
12
Dyer Cove
11
N
250 yds
DEPTHS IN FATHOMS AT ZERO TIDE
3
3
5
12
Fishing resort
15   8
4
Foul
Choked with kelp; pass east side at high water
Athlone Island
10
1 fathom
6
10
6
5   Lagoon
4
Outer Central Coast Islands Conservancy

©2024 Don and Reanne Douglass • Diagram not for navigation

Ivory Island (Seaforth Channel)
12 mi NW of Bella Bella
Light (position): 52°16.18'N, 128°24.40'W
Anchor: 52°16.67'N, 128°23.77'W

Ivory Island, at the west entrance of Seaforth Channel, is the site of a classic red and white lighthouse, located on Robb Point with a clear view of Milbanke Sound. The station monitors Channel 82A when the lightkeepers are free from their duties. Small boats can anchor in fair weather in a tiny cove on the northeast corner of Ivory Island. On the shore of this cove, a walkway leads 0.6 mile to the lighthouse where you get a spectacular 270°-view across Milbanke Sound.

Anchor in about 3 fathoms over a mixed bottom of sand, gravel and rocks with fair holding. Swinging room is limited and the site is subject to surge or swell. Be careful not to leave your boat out of sight as surge can cause your anchor to drag, so leave a responsible party aboard.

Powell Anchorage (Blair Inlet)
0.25 mi NE of Watch Island
Position: 52°16.98'N, 128°21.15'W

Powell Anchorage, east of Knarled Point, can provide good anchorage for larger boats, but southerly swells occur during unsettled weather. Small boats will find better shelter in Oliver Cove or at the far east end west of Tuno Creek in 8 fathoms.

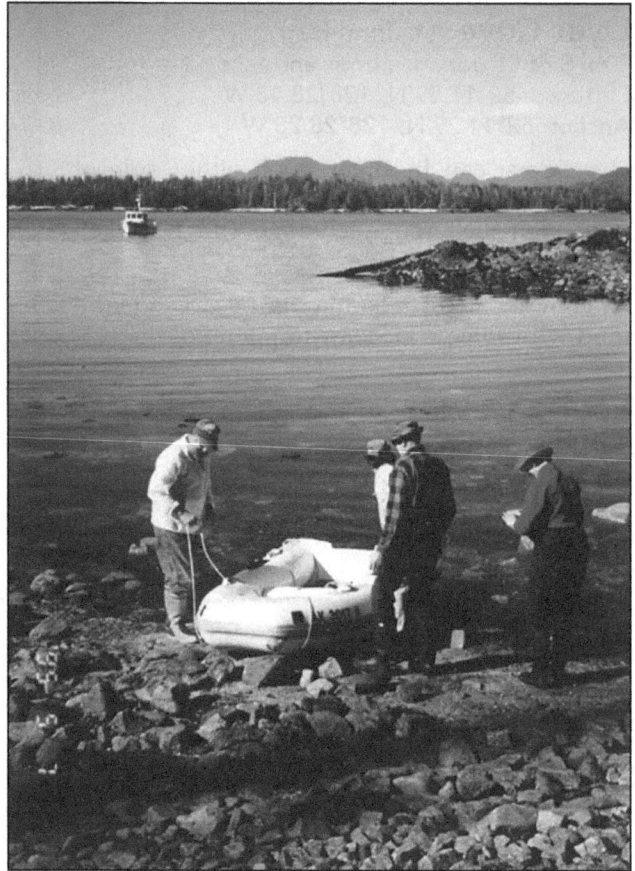

Ivory Island, fair-weather anchorage

High Waves on Ivory Island

Rene and I were alone on station that day in April, and I was on morning shift. At 0340 (PST), we reported winds blowing east at 18 knots, with gusts to 23 knots. By 0600 the wind had turned to southeast, 18-20 knots and, by 0940, we were recording southeast winds at 25 knots, with gusts of 31. The swell started building and I reported a low/moderate sea. At 1010 I had to file a special weather report: southeast 34 knots, gusting to 46 knots. For the following 8 hours, the winds never dropped below 30 knots, with steady gusts in the 40s, and occasional 50-55 knots. Around 1500, the wind was blowing from the south and swell was moderate. By 1800 hours, swells had built to heavy level. About 1830, swells started coming over the sea wall, rising up and over our satellite dish and slamming into the livingroom windows. Spray blew clear over the roof of our house. The back steps were covered in ebbing seawater, and Rene narrowly missed being hit by a wave while doing his 1840 hours observations! We had been on Ivory since June 22, 1992, and we had never seen such a swell.

The "system" was mostly cumulonimbus clouds—the most dangerous of clouds. We'd had hail during the day, but no thunderstorms. Normally I go to bed around 1900 when I'm on morning shift, but Rene and I sat at our kitchen table until just after 2100, when the tide turned. We knew that if nothing happened by high tide, we'd be all right (no wave through the house)!

Weather remained unsettled for the next two days, with southwest and south winds. On the 28th at 0640, we recorded winds southeast at 25 knots with 36-knot gusts, and 46 knots by noon. Swells were back up to moderate, but fortunately the wind eased off later in the day. By the 30th we were reporting rippled, one-foot chop seas with a low swell. During all our years on a light station, I'd never before felt frightened. But I certainly did that day of April 25!

—Sherrill Kitson, Ivory Island

Editor's note: After their retirement in 2002, Sherrill and Rene moved back to Nova Scotia.

McInnes Island Light Station (Milbanke Sound)

11.8 mi W of Ivory Island lt.
Position: 52°15.65'N, 128°43.34'W

McInnes Island, strategically located between Milbanke and Laredo Sounds, is a manned lightstation. It is important to monitor their timely weather reports before attempting to round the south end of Price Island. Since the seas around McInnes Island frequently carry a lot of drift logs and flotsam, especially on spring tides, use caution in this area. Catala Passage, on the north side of McInnes Island, is a smooth-water route between Milbanke and Laredo Sound in fair weather. Be careful to identify each rock and reef in this somewhat confusing area. *Note:* The longitude of McInnes Light varies +/- 300 feet on different electronic charts.

Ivory Island Lightstation, looking toward Reid Passage

Ivory Island Lighthouse—More Tribulations

British Columbia's Inside Passage offers protection for vessels sailing along most of the province's coastline. Concern for the safety of vessels along some exposed areas caused the British Columbia Board of Trade to petition the government to build a lighthouse on Ivory Island, where Milbanke Sound opens to the rough waters of the Pacific. Construction began in February 1894, and the Ivory Island Lighthouse on Surf Point began operation on October 1, 1898. The white wooden structure, topped with a bright red roof, stood thirty feet high and rose sixty-six feet above the waterline. Its illuminating dioptric lens was considered state-of-the-art.

Several storms hit the island soon after the lighthouse was completed, causing Peter Wylie, the first keeper, to question his decision to take the job. During that first month, severe winds and swells destroyed the boathouse. Wylie came dangerously close to losing his life when he waded into the surf to salvage what he could of the battered structure. Claiming the storms were too much, he soon tendered his resignation. Many suspected it was really the isolation that drove his decision.

With a new boat and boathouse, the Ivory Island Lighthouse once again began operations. J.C. Thompson, the new keeper, blamed his resignation, a little more than a year later, on his wife's poor health. "I am sorry but my wife absolutely refuses to leave unless I go with her, and it would be unkind on my part to stay here against her wishes. She dreads her attacks because we are so far away from her Doctor or any medical assistance." Accepting the responsibility of his decision, his letter

ends with, "The fact of it is I should never have brought a sick woman out here."

The next keeper to take over was James Forsythe whose wife and baby contracted an almost fatal case of dysentery from the station's contaminated water supply, resulting in his resignation in November 1904.

F. Reuter, a German, reputed as one of the best boatmen on the Pacific Coast, was recruited to replace Forsythe. A new state-of-the-art fog alarm installed in 1908 offered a sense of safety for Reuter. One year later, an earthquake sent a tidal wave crashing into the fog alarm building, rendering the alarm inoperable. A new protective breakwater was then constructed and all was well. Reuter handled the challenging lifestyle with ease, for almost ten years before he was dismissed despite his stellar service. At the onset of World War I, isolation struck again. Reuter, a German immigrant, had failed to fill out his naturalization papers. The Canadian government dismissed him for being an alien and enemy subject.

Several more lighthouse keepers succeeded Wylie, Thompson, Forsythe, and Reuter, including Charlie Hoy, who arrived in 1942 with his wife, a canary, four cats, and dog Rusty. Gordon Schweers arrived in 1981 just a few months before his fiancée. The day she set foot on the island to marry Schweers was the first time she had laid eyes on him.

Despite the tribulations of life on Ivory Island, the lighthouse remains staffed to this day.

—KK

Catala Passage (McInnes Island)
N of McInnes lt. Sta.
Entrance (W): 52°16.20'N, 128°43.96'W
Entrance (E): 52°15.64'N, 128°41.44'W

Catala Passage gives valuable relief from southwest swells in a crossing from Milbanke to Laredo Sound. During strong southerly weather this area is sometimes covered with sheets of white foam and, at such times, small craft should not attempt a crossing.

The area from Catala Passage to Higgins Passage, on the west side of Price Island, is a maze of islets, rocks and reefs. To explore the region by kayak or inflatable, you can use the anchorage at Rudolf Bay as a base camp in fair weather. Higgins Passage is a viable alternative for small craft wishing to avoid passing south of Price Island.

At the south end of Price Island, ebbing tidal currents interact with southerly seas, creating nasty conditions off McInnes Island. Though large seas may be running in Milbanke and Laredo sounds, the waters of Catala Pass are relatively quiet.

To the north of Catala Pass and along the southwest shore of Price Island, a series of reefs enclose an area of quiet water. We have been present in this area when an uncomfortable swell was running in Laredo Sound and surf was breaking on the reefs, but the inner waters where we were anchored were quite placid. However, since there are numerous isolated rocks, any vessel using Catala Pass should exercise caution and enter only in good visibility.

To the northeast of Day Point, between a triangular-shaped island and the southern point of Price Island, lies Day Point Anchorage. Although swell does penetrate this anchorage somewhat, there is, at best, moderate holding in 8 fathoms; this is reported to be an ideal place to stay if you wish to get the flavor of the wild marine environment. Two rocks bracket the entrance (one which dries at one foot), but since there is usually a swell running, the waves breaking over the top of the rocks help identify them during the lower half of the tide. The passage from the anchorage to the southwest side of Price Island dries at low tide. Take your dinghy and pass into the area protected by the reef—there's enough exploring and beachcombing to keep you busy for several days.

Langford Cove (Milbanke Sound)
6 mi NE of McInnes Island lt.
Entrance: 52° 20.45'N, 128°37.05'W
Anchor (SW nook): 52°20.31'N, 128°37.32'W

Higgins Passage, view of the narrows from west anchor site

Photo courtesy CHS, Pacific Region

Langford Cove can be used as an emergency anchorage if you're caught on the west side of Milbanke Sound. Protection from strong northwest winds can be found in the small northwest bight close to the rocky shore (favor the south side). Anchor in 4 fathoms over an irregular and rocky bottom with poor-to-fair holding. For protection from chop with southeast through west winds, tuck tightly into the small nook on the southwest side. Avoid the bare rocks at the north entrance and a large patch of kelp. At the south entrance, there is a rock awash on a 12-foot tide. Both nooks have many drift logs, so we rate this site as a temporary anchorage only.

Anchor (southwest nook) in 2 fathoms over brown sand, stones, kelp, and eelgrass; fair-to-good holding.

Higgins Passage (Laredo Sound)
13.5 mi N of McInnes Island lt.
Entrance (E): 52°29.37'N, 128°41.85'W
Entrance (SW) (0.4 mile SW of Kipp Islet): 52°28.57'N, 128°47.30'W
Anchor (E side narrows): 52°28.84'N, 128°43.58'W
Anchor (W side narrows): 52°28.64'N, 128°44.24'W;

Higgins Passage is an explorer's dream or a marginal navigator's nightmare. While approaching Higgins from the east is straightforward, entering from Laredo Sound is more of a challenge. The east side of Laredo Sound, between Price and Swindle islands, is a labyrinth of islands, islets and rocks that offers scenic, well-protected cruising waters and excellent sportfishing.

The narrows has a land bridge that dries on a 5-foot tide. *Large boats not advised!* Thick kelp grows in the area of this land bridge. We suggest that you anchor, then reconnoiter the area by dinghy and proceed when the tide is sufficiently high. There is

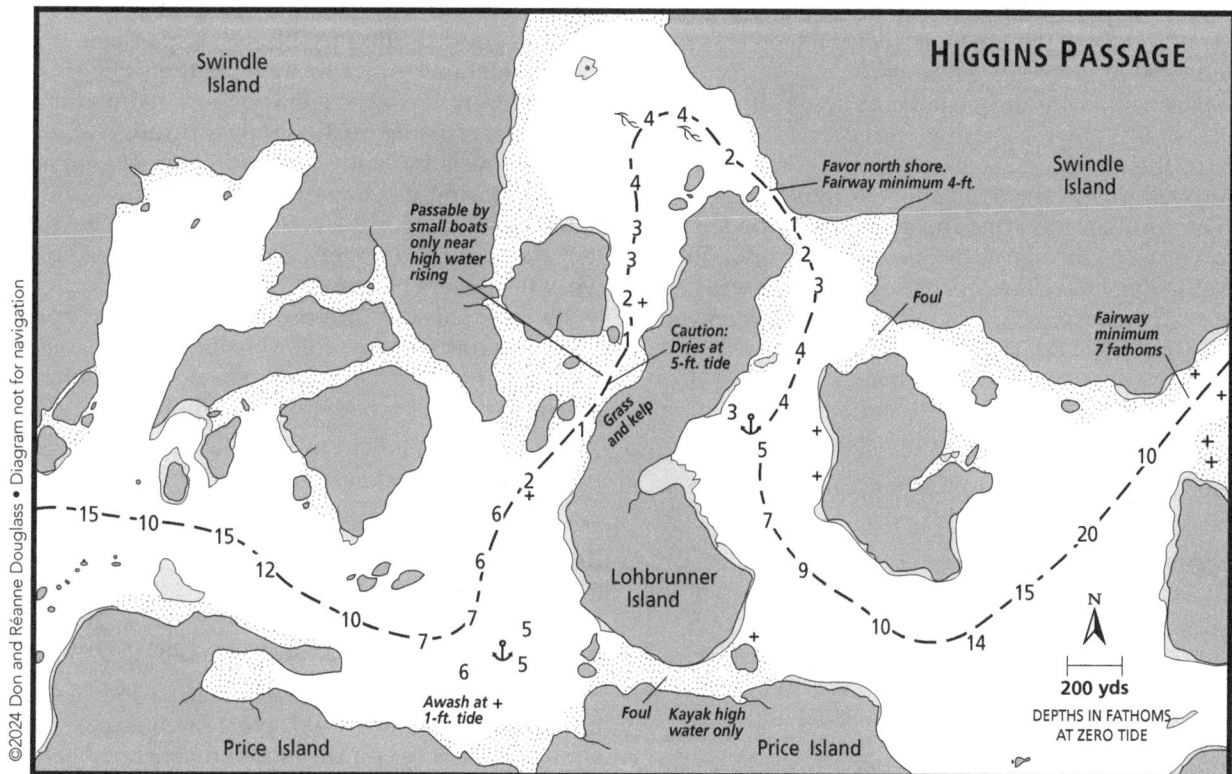

substantial current with little turning room. Good, sheltered anchor sites, where you can wait for the tide to rise, lie on both the east and west sides of the narrows. (Meyers Passage, seven miles to the north, is a much safer transit.)

Swells that break on the outer rocks of Laredo Sound obstruct the view of the intricate western entrance to Higgins Passage. GPS can help locate the turning points to the entrance. Swells quickly die down inside the first islets. The southwestern entrance is a maze of islets and reefs that requires careful plotting of your exact position. The key to entering is to identify Kipp Islet.

The *approximate* route we follow starts at the Higgins Passage entrance point, 0.4 mile southwest of Kipp Islet at 52°28.47'N, 128°47.25'W. From here, it proceeds at 026°M for 0.51 nautical mile, avoiding the rocks close south of Kipp Islet, to a position 0.25 mile east of Kipp Islet. From this point, the course changes to 335°M for 0.30 nautical mile then east to 065°M for a distance of 0.30 nautical mile, then southeast at 169°M, passing close to the peninsula that forms the western side of Grant Anchorage.

A shorter but narrower route starts from 1.0 mile northwest of Kipp Islet, then passes east through an intricate passage, taking many of the small rocks and islets on their north side. The position for entering this route is: 52°29.28'N, 128°48.10'W.

Tidal rapids in Higgins Passage, at the north end of Lohbrunner Island, create a lot of foam. An hour before high water, flood tide flows west here and has a drop of about one foot over its 300-yard length. Since current is substantial, it's difficult to turn around inside the narrows.

Anchor (west side of narrows) in 6 fathoms over sand and gravel with good holding.

Anchor (east side of narrows) in 4 fathoms over mud with good holding.

Grant Anchorage (Higgins Passage)
1.2 mi W of Lohbrunner Island
Anchor: 52°28.87'N, 128°45.89'W

Grant Anchorage is the basin to the northwest of Higgins Passage. Our favorite anchorage is in front of the rapids where you have a good view of the narrows.

Price Inlet (Higgins Passage)
7 mi W of Jorkins Pt.
Entrance: 52°29.01'N, 128°40.39'W

"Price Inlet," on the north corner of Price Island, is a charming area and the only secure anchorage on the west side of Milbanke Sound. Easy to enter, it has reasonable depths and offers good shelter. Unlike Higgins Lagoon to the north, it does not have a kelp-choked tidal rapids at its entrance.

Central depths are about 8 fathoms over a large area. Because of unknown risks there has been little exploitation of this remote area. The shore is covered with mature old-growth forest and lots of moss and muskeg. There are several arms and a couple of wooded islands. The tree limbs grow in a normal horizontal line, indicating that little chop ever develops here. It was late in the day when we pulled into Price Inlet and we were running out of time, so we checked the bottom not far from the entrance on the west shore, where a tiny stream caught our eye. The bottom had good holding and we swung all night on our lunch hook.

Anchor in 5 fathoms over mud with good holding.

Meyers Passage (Princess Royal Island)
2.5 mi W of Klemtu
Entrance (NE) (Tolmie Channel): 52°40.20'N, 128°34.00'W
Entrance (W): 52°35.88'N, 128°45.34'W
Anchor (elbow): 52°36.13'N, 128°35.35'W

Meyers Passage, the preferred smooth-water route from Laredo Sound to Seaforth Channel, is particularly convenient when a southerly wind is blowing in Laredo Sound. Passage between Princess Royal Island and Swindle Island is easy, with the exception of the one-mile, shallow, kelp-filled shoal at Meyers Narrows. The shallowest point, in the vicinity of Buoy "E70," is approximately one fathom at zero tide. Although the kelp beds can cause anxiety, the bottom in the narrows is fairly flat and it's easy to guide between the patches. Visibility through the water is good, adding to the ease of passage.

Considerably easier to traverse than Higgins Passage, Meyers Passage demands less tedious navigation. Most cruising boats can pass through at moderate tide levels by holding a mid-channel course and slowly passing on the north side of buoy "E70" that marks a submerged rock. Small boats can find excellent shelter in the center of Meyers Narrows in what we call "Meyers Narrows Cove" (see below).

Larger boats can find protection in all but northerly weather at the elbow of Meyers Passage, one mile east of buoy "E70," although we find the bottom irregular and rocky with poor holding.

Anchor (elbow) in 8 to 10 fathoms over a hard, rocky bottom with poor holding.

Jorgensen Harbour (Meyers Passage)
2.5 mi SW of Split Head
Entrance: 52°38.47'N, 128°35.14'W
Anchor (shallow bar): 52° 38.63'N, 128°35.01'W

Although Jorgensen Harbour itself is too deep and open for convenient small-craft anchorage, the flat, shallow bar between the island to the northeast and Princess Royal Island makes a great anchor site.

Anchor (shallow bar) in 4 fathoms over sand and mud with good holding.

Meyers Narrows (Meyers Passage)
5 mi SW of Split Head
Entrance (E): 52°36.21'N, 128°35.55'W
Entrance (W): 52°36.55'N, 128°37.91'W

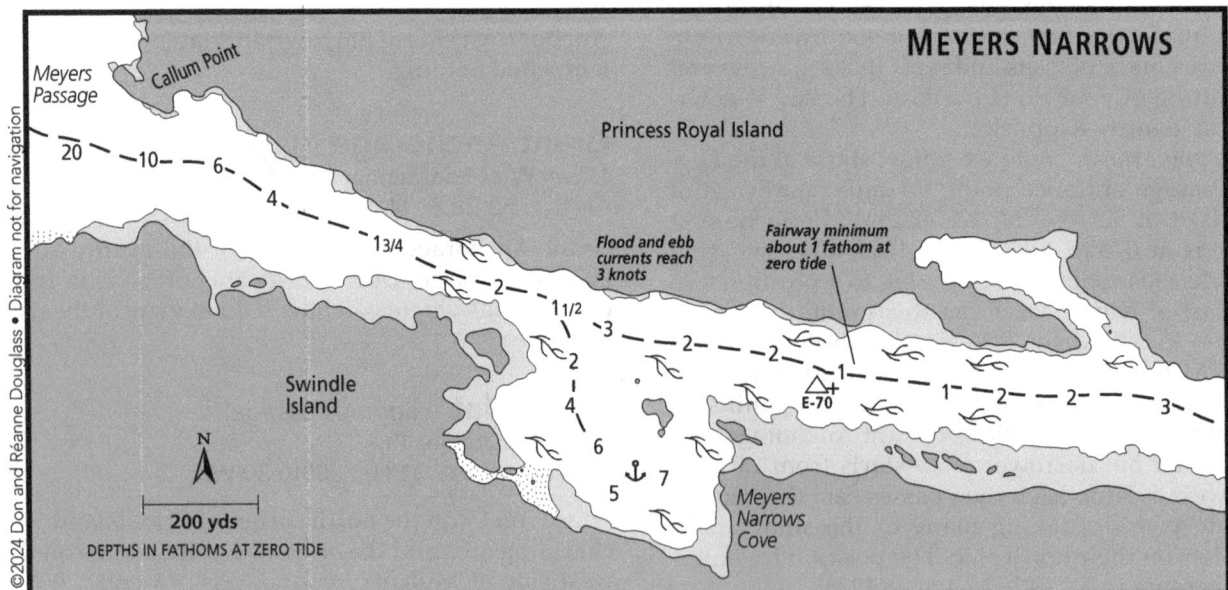

Cruising boats can transit Meyers Narrows at all but the lowest tide levels due to moderate current and a relatively flat bottom. Late in the summer, patches of intimidating-looking bull kelp may be prevalent but, by keeping your speed low, you can easily pass through these patches. We once transited the Narrows on a full moon—no artificial light and perfectly quiet— which was a magical experience.

Passing from west to east in sunny weather you have a view of peaks that rise from 800 feet to over 2,000. Directly east of the narrows, where the channel turns north, two peaks over 2,000 feet on Swindell Island form a saddleback ridge. Meyers Passage appears to dead end below this ridge.

Meyers Narrows Cove

(Meyers Passage)
3.4 mi E of Corney Cove
Anchor (small boat): 52°36.27'N, 128°37.15'W
Anchor (large boat): 52°36.19'N, 128°35.04'W

"Meyers Narrows Cove," our name for the unnamed cove in the center of Meyers Passage, just west of the shallowest spot, provides the best storm anchorage in the vicinity. Small craft can find complete shelter from all weather in the cove on the south shore. The bottom is largely flat with depths of 6 to 7 fathoms, and there is adequate swinging room for several boats. Enter west of islet (18); the east side is foul. The entrance fairway carries 2 fathoms, with kelp patches on either side and, at times, in the center. Eastbound, this cove is a good place to wait for a favorable tide to pass over the shoal just east of buoy "E 70;" the current here is much diminished. Deep draft boats can anchor southeast of Saunders Point, 150 feet northwest of a yellow on-shore triangle in 8 to 10 fathoms.

Anchor in 6 fathoms, over brown mud with good holding.

Corney Cove (Meyers Passage)

3.4 mi W of Meyers Narrows
Entrance: 52°36.53'N, 128°42.76'W
Anchor: 52°36.93'N, 128°42.79'W

Corney Cove, located on the north side of Meyers Passage inside its western entrance, is a well-sheltered and scenic anchorage for one or two boats. Boats with deep draft can wait here for the proper tide level before continuing an eastbound transit. A small creek drains into the head of the cove, and no driftwood on shore indicates good shelter. Avoid a rock near shore off the creek.

Anchor in 8 to 10 to fathoms over gravel with fair holding.

Laredo Sound (Price Island)

15 mi SW of Klemtu
Entrance (S): 52°18.05'N, 128°52.86'W

Laredo Sound is subject to southerly swells that heap up on an ebb tide in a southerly wind. Crossing Laredo Sound can be uncomfortable, but there are coves on either side of the sound where you can await better conditions.

Rudolf Bay (Price Island)

4.2 mi S of Higgins Passage
Entrance: 52°24.43'N, 128°46.15'W
Anchor (head of bay): 52° 24.91'N, 128°45.39'W

Uncharted Rudolf Bay is the only shelter on the west side of Price Island. If you want to explore the west coast of Price Island by kayak and dinghy, this tiny bay offers moderately good protection to small boats and a chance to get out of swell and chop. Pass the mid-channel island on its north side via a very narrow channel and anchor in the inner basin where swinging room is limited. While the rocks and reefs to the south of Rudolf Bay may offer opportunities for exploration, use extreme caution.

Anchor (head of the bay) in 2 to 3 fathoms over sand; fair-to-good holding.

Larkin Point Basin (Swindle Island)

5.4 mi S of Meyers Passage
Entrance: 52°29.86'N, 128°48.89'W
Anchor: 52°30.89'N, 128°48.84'W

"Larkin Point Basin" is a strategically located shelter in the center of Laredo Sound. This highly-protected basin, due east of Larkin Point on the east shore of Laredo Sound, provides good shelter in most summer weather. Larkin Point Basin has an exposed southerly entrance, so use caution when exploring the area. A fairway with depths of about 12 fathoms can be found leading north into the basin, keeping most of the islets to port. Anchor on the northeast side of the islet in the center of the basin.

Anchor in 9 fathoms over a mixed bottom with good holding.

Kitasu Bay (Swindle Island)

3 mi S of Meyers Passage
Entrance: 52°33.59'N, 128°46.73'W

Kitasu Bay, which provides protection from southerly swells, has anchor sites in Cowards Cove, Parsons Anchorage, Osment Inlet or Cann Inlet. This is a major herring spawning area in late March when grey whales are a common sight.

Cowards Cove (Kitasu Bay)

2.2 mi S of Meyers Passage
Entrance: 52°33.55'N, 128°44.60'W
Anchor (head of cove): 52°33.92'N, 128°44.34'W

Cowards Cove, a tiny inlet 0.4 mile east of Jamieson Point on the north side of Kitasu Bay, is well sheltered in most weather, but it is only charted at a small scale, so caution is required. Over the years small fishing boats that use Meyers Passage have found comfortable shelter here when they want to avoid crossing Laredo Sound with large beam seas. The entrance is narrow with about 3 fathoms in the 40-foot wide fairway. Avoid the kelp and a rock on the west shore by favoring the east shore in the narrows.

Anchorage can be found for small vessels east of the tidal rapids of the lagoon on the west shore. Avoid a white rock awash on a 3-foot tide in the east nook. Smaller cruising boats can anchor deep in the head of the cove where it is quiet and scenic. The lagoon can be entered at high water by dinghy only.

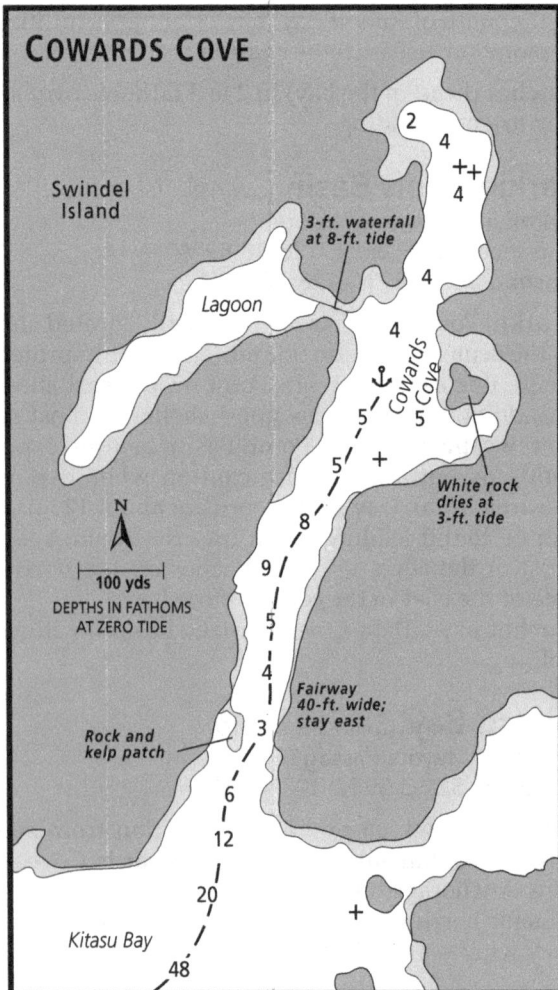

COWARDS COVE

Swindel Island

Lagoon

3-ft. waterfall at 8-ft. tide

Cowards Cove

White rock dries at 3-ft. tide

Fairway 40-ft. wide; stay east

Rock and kelp patch

N

100 yds
DEPTHS IN FATHOMS
AT ZERO TIDE

Kitasu Bay

©2024 Don and Réanne Douglass • Diagram not for navigation

Anchor (head of cove) in 2 fathoms over a rocky bottom; poor-to-fair holding.

Anchor (east of lagoon) in 5 fathoms over soft mud with good holding.

Parsons Anchorage (Kitasu Bay)

5 mi S of Meyers Passage
Entrance: 52° 31.30'N, 128° 44.91'W

Parsons Anchorage, deep in Kitasu Bay, offers very good shelter in heavy southerly weather, but it is open to strong westerlies. This site has good holding with lots of swinging room.

Anchor deep in the cove in 7 to 10 fathoms, over sand and gravel; good holding.

Osment Inlet (Kitasu Bay)

1.5 mi NE of Parsons Anchorage
Entrance: 52°32.21'N, 128°43.30'W

Well-sheltered anchorage is reported in the inner basin of Osment Inlet. The bottom is largely flat with occasional irregularities. Watch for shallow areas with rocks. Scenic and secure in all winds. Fishing boats anchor near the two mid-channel islets in about 6 fathoms; small boats anchor in the north nook farther east in 3 fathoms with a mud bottom.

Cann Inlet (Kitasu Bay)

2.3 mi NE of Parsons Anchorage
Entrance: 52°33.36'N, 128°44.35'W

Entering Cann Inlet from the north is straight forward. Correspondents Michael Boyd and Karen Johnson reported that the passage is wide, deep, and mostly straight. The easternmost basin before the unsurveyed portion has a sounding of 13 fathoms with other areas deeper. Northwest winds can make their way into the basin.

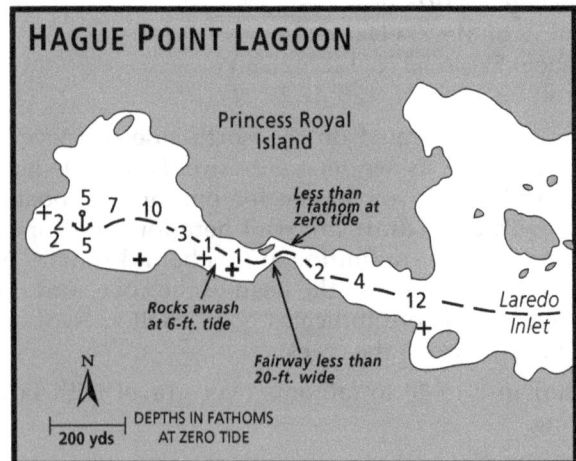

HAGUE POINT LAGOON

Princess Royal Island

Less than 1 fathom at zero tide

Rocks awash at 6-ft. tide

Fairway less than 20-ft. wide

Laredo Inlet

N

200 yds
DEPTHS IN FATHOMS
AT ZERO TIDE

©2024 Don and Réanne Douglass • Diagram not for navigation

Laredo Inlet (Princess Royal Inlet)
3.5 mi NW of Meyers Passage
Entrance: 52°37.55'N, 129°48.74'W

Laredo Inlet, at the south end of Princess Royal Island, is a deep fiord with striking high peaks and ridges and cleft gullies on both sides. Southerly swell diminishes quickly as you enter the inlet. The river outlets and grassy meadows of Princess Royal Island are good places to observe bear. The cream-colored Kermode bear is more common here than anywhere else in the world. Laredo Inlet has several attractive anchor sites, the most popular being Alston Cove and Bay of Plenty.

Hague Point Lagoon (Laredo Inlet)
0.8 mi N of Monk Bay
Entrance: 52°40.00'N, 128°51.09'W
Anchor: 52°40.14'N, 128°51.91'W

"Hague Point Lagoon," the small landlocked basin one mile northwest of Hague Point, offers excellent protection for small boats in all weather.

If Cowards Cove where northbound skippers head to avoid the seas in Laredo Sound, Hague Point Lagoon (aka "Chicken Cove") is the equivalent for southbound "chickens" who've had it with the Sound.

Entering the lagoon, however, does require a measure of courage. It is extremely narrow with less than 20 feet between the rocks on a 9-foot tide, with a depth of less than one fathom at zero tide. An S-turn is required to avoid the initial rock on the south side of the channel, followed by two rocks on the north side. Current in the narrows is moderate, but underwater visibility is good to 25 feet. The lagoon has a large, flat bottom with swinging room for several vessels. Large concentrations of sea nettles are sometimes found in the lagoon.

Anchor in 6 to 9 fathoms over soft mud, sand, kelp and some wood debris; fair-to-very good holding.

Thistle Passage (Hastings Island)
1.25 mi NW of Meyers
Entrance (S): 52°36.20'N, 128°45.90'W
Entrance (N): 52°39.45'N, 128°45.32'W

Thistle Passage can be used as a smooth-water route for entering Laredo Inlet from Meyers Passage when Laredo Sound kicks up. Minimum depth of the fairway at the south end of the narrows is 4½ fathoms. Avoid a rock awash on a 4-foot tide, 30 feet off the east shore. Just north of this rock there is another near the west shore—awash at 12 feet—that extends about 90 feet from the trees. The north end of the narrows carries about 3 fathoms in the fairway, less than the depth indicated on the chart.

Quigley Creek Cove (Laredo Inlet)
3.5 mi N of Meyers Passage
Entrance: 52°39.38'N, 128°45.15'W
Anchor: 52°39.40'N, 128°44.69'W

Quigley Creek has a group of small islets near its outlet that provide good shelter to cruising boats; caution is required. The extensive islets in the vicinity offer better protection than you might guess from studying the chart—the cove is essentially landlocked.

From Thistle Passage, enter what we call "Quigley Creek Cove," passing north of the westernmost islet that lies close to the point on Princess Royal Island. The entrance is irregular, with many isolated underwater rocks. "Elephant Rock" lies off the northeast corner of the westernmost islet and extends approximately a third of the way into the channel. Depths are considerably less than those indicated on the chart. The bottom is irregular until you have passed all the islets.

A large, drying flat lies off the north shore of Quigley Creek, and the bottom is steep-to. Anchor off the flat in the center of the cove where there is swinging room for two or three boats. Local fishing boats frequently use this cove.

Anchor in 8 fathoms, over brown sand with shells; good holding.

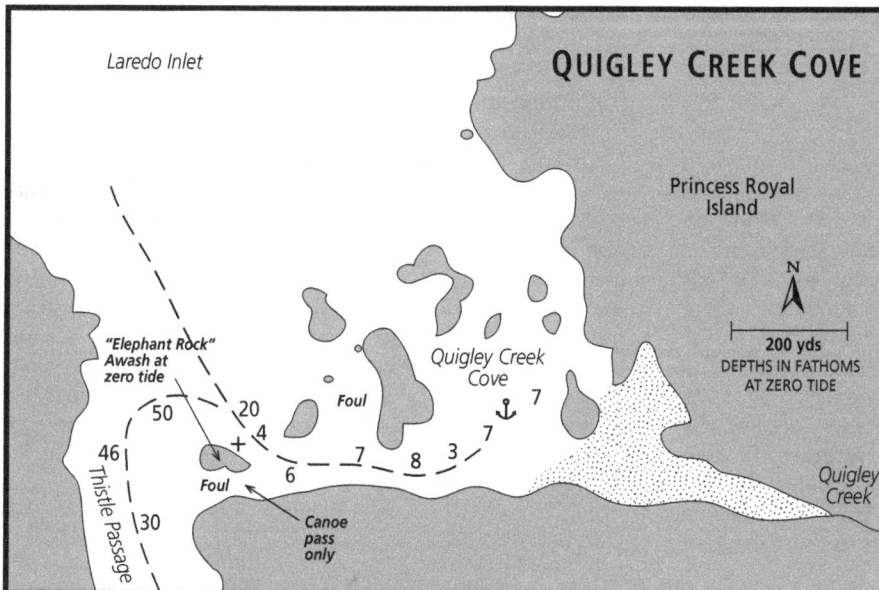

©2024 Don and Réanne Douglass • Diagram not for navigation

Unnamed Cove (Laredo Inlet)

1.8 mi SW of Alston Cove
Entrance: 52°43.72'N, 128°47.02'W
Anchor: 52°43.53'N, 128°47.16'W

An unnamed Cove, located between two treed islets on the west of Laredo Inlet, provides excellent protection from southerly weather with good views north up Laredo Inlet. Although the cove is open to downslope winds, the shore shows little evidence of drift logs.

A large rock, awash at 12 feet, extends about 100 feet from the trees on the east shore of the peninsula. South of this rock, the bottom is a flat 5 fathoms.

Anchor in 6 fathoms over grey mud with very good holding.

Alston Cove (Laredo Inlet)

5.8 mi N of Quigley Creek
Entrance: 52°45.04'N, 128°45.55'W
Anchor: 52°44.84'N, 128°44.68'W

Alston Cove is a beautiful cove, well protected from all weather. High peaks and deep valleys make this site particularly scenic. A rock slide extends from the north shore at the entrance, and a bar of 3.5 fathoms crosses the opening. Near the head of the cove, the bottom is steep-to at the drying mud flat off Blee Creek. There is swinging room for several boats. Kamin Cove, 1.4 miles north, offers shelter for small boats in southerly winds with limited swinging room.

Anchor in about 6 fathoms over sand and mud with good-to-very-good holding.

Weld Cove (Laredo Inlet)

4 mi N of Alston Cove
Entrance: 52°47.47'N, 128°46.23'W
Anchor: 52°48.94'N, 128°46.07'W

Weld Cove, well protected in all weather, can be entered from either the west side of Kohl Island or a passage between Kohl and Pocock Islands. However, passing between the two islands is the easier of the two routes. The fairway between the two islands carries a minimum depth of 3½ fathoms. Be careful to avoid two dangerous charted rocks awash on about a 7-foot tide about 400 yards northwest of Kohl Island. You can pass between the charted rocks and

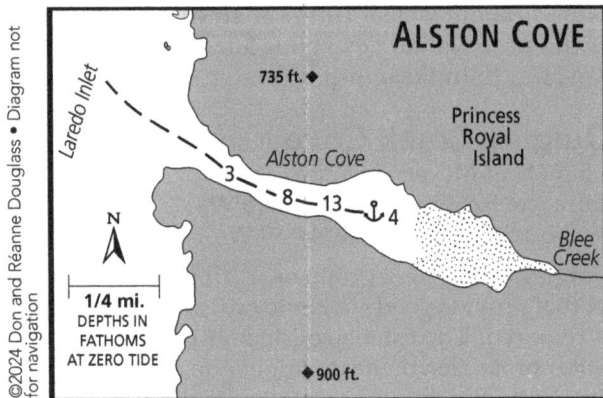

©2024 Don and Réanne Douglass • Diagram not for navigation

ALSTON COVE

Laredo Inlet

735 ft. ◆

Princess Royal Island

Alston Cove

3
8 — 13 — ⚓ 4

Blee Creek

N

1/4 mi.
DEPTHS IN FATHOMS AT ZERO TIDE

◆ 900 ft.

The Spirit Bear—British Columbia's Official Animal

If you're near a stream on Princess Royal or Gribble Islands while the salmon are running, you might come upon a sight few ever see: a ghostly white bear fishing for a meal. The males stand up to six feet tall and can weigh nearly 500 pounds; the females are about half that size.

In April 2006, British Columbia designated the Kermode Bear, also called the "Spirit Bear," as its official animal. First Nations people, who have resided along British Columbia's Northwest Coast for hundreds of years, include stories of this mysterious bear in their oral folklore, although some believe speaking of the Spirit Bear is taboo.

The Kermode Bear is a subspecies of the black bear whose range extends from Southeast Alaska to the northern part of Vancouver Island. Overall, only 1-2% of British Columbia's black bear population display the cream-colored coat of the Spirit Bear. However, the trait is especially concentrated on Princess Royal and Gribbell Islands, where as many as 30% of the bears display the white or cream-colored coat that is the result of a double-recessive gene. While all bears are skilled at catching fish, researchers have demonstrated that the Kermode Bear is thirty percent more proficient than black bears at catching fish during the day, likely because the light color of their fur makes them less visible to fish.

If you fail to spot a Spirit Bear in the wild, you can view one in captivity. The British Columbia Wildlife Park in Kamloops houses the only captive Spirit Bear. An abandoned yearling male was discovered near Terrace Mountain and sent to the park in October 2012 after several unsuccessful attempts to rehabilitate him and return him to the wild. Named Clover, the young bear moved into his new 2.7-acre enclosure in mid-May 2015. A stream connecting two pools runs through his habitat. When he is not sleeping in his den, park visitors can observe Clover from an elevated viewing platform. Visit the park's website for the latest information on Clover: http://www.bczoo.org/

—KK

Pocock Island in 5 fathoms by favoring the Pocock shore. Once inside, you can anchor anywhere in the northern end of Weld Cove, where there's room for a number of boats along an 11-fathom bottom.

Entrance west of Kohl Island is more intricate and carries less water than indicated. Entering from the south, stay close to the Princess Royal shore on your port hand to avoid a rock that dries at 2 feet off Busey Creek; continue to favor this shore until you're about to enter the small cove formed by a short peninsula directly ahead. You will notice a large rock-reef complex that nearly connects to the peninsula from Kohl Island. The slot between this rock complex and the peninsula is only about 25 feet wide and has a mid-channel depth of about 2 fathoms. You must turn due east and pass within about 15 feet of the peninsula to avoid the rock extending from the unnamed island, before turning north again to enter Weld Cove.

Anchor in 10 fathoms over mud with good holding.

Bay of Plenty (Laredo Inlet)
1 mi N of Pocock
Entrance: 52°49.84'N, 128°45.14'W
Anchor: 52°50.44'N, 128°46.21'W

The Bay of Plenty is a favorite among cruising boaters for its good protection and extensive area of shallow water. The bay has been known for its abundance of crab, which seem to have dimished over the years.

As you enter the bay, favor the south shore, taking the first island (120) inside the entrance to your starboard, and the small treed islet in the center of the bay to port by favoring the north shore. The area between the small center islet and the south shore is foul on low water.

You can explore Pyne Creek by dinghy for over a mile—a good place to observe wildlife—or you can sit in your stern and admire the steep bluffs on the north side of the creek. There is adequate swinging room here for several boats.

Anchor in 6 to 8 fathoms over soft brown mud with very good holding.

Fifer Cove (Laredo Inlet)
3 mi NE of Bay of Plenty
Entrance: 52°52.17'N, 128°41.66'W
Anchor: 52°51.61'N, 128°40.96'W

Picturesque Fifer Cove, on the east shore of Laredo Inlet, is surrounded by high peaks, so characteristic

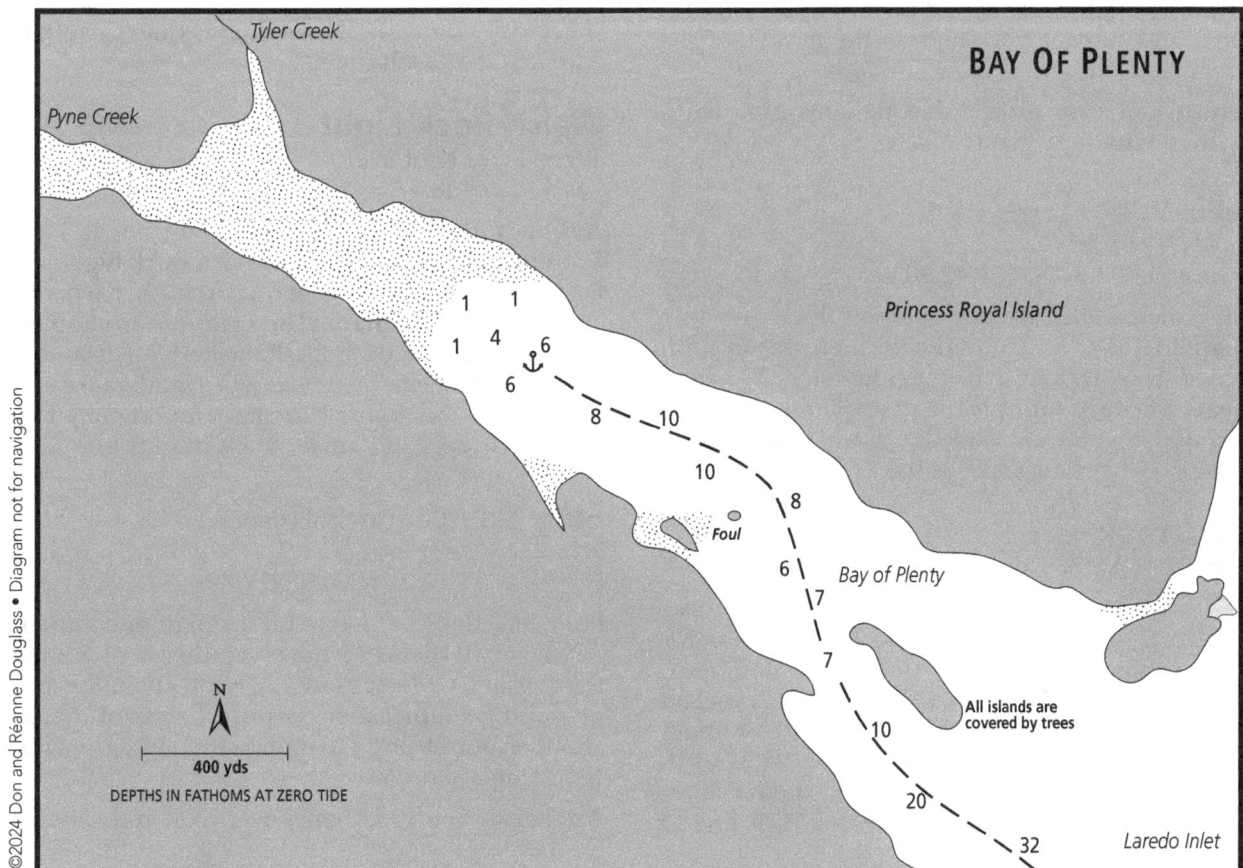

Philip Narrows, looking south

of Laredo Inlet. The inlet between Tuite Point and the entrance islands has a minimum depth of about 4 fathoms. The cove itself is fairly deep and its shores steep-to and well protected with no indication of driftwood or chop. Reported to be breezy in westerly winds, Fifer Cove may not offer adequate shelter in storms.

The creek from Bloomfield Lake has created a large drying flat on the southwest shore. The grassy shore here, and the flat-bottomed creek, are known as good bear habitat.

Small boats can anchor in about 8 fathoms in the southeast corner with limited swinging room; larger boats can anchor anywhere in the middle of the cove.

Anchor (southeast corner) in 8 fathoms over dark-grey mud with very good holding.

Mellis Inlet (Laredo Inlet)
1.7 mi NW of Fifer Cove
Entrance: 52°53.27'N, 128°42.90'W

Mellis Inlet, a 2.2-mile-long inlet on the west shore of Laredo Inlet, has remarkable high peaks with exposed grey granite slabs on either side. The inlet appears too deep for convenient anchorage, and we have no further local knowledge to add. We prefer to anchor in either Fifer Cove or Bay of Plenty.

Buie Creek (Laredo Inlet)
13.6 mi N of Alston Cove
Anchor: 52°58.13'N, 128°40.01'W

Buie Creek, at the head of Laredo Inlet, is an indifferent anchorage, useful only for bear-watching or for exploring the creek in calm weather. The head of the inlet is steep-to, but there is a small 4-fathom shoal at the northwest corner of the inlet, due north of Brew Island, where anchorage can be taken. Summer water temperatures here can reach 70°F, higher than elsewhere in Laredo Inlet.

Westbound, north of Brew Island, there is a dinghy-route of not much more than one fathom. If you use this route, avoid two large rocks off the north side of Brew Island.

The cove at the head of Arnoup Creek has a large shallow bar on its east side. If you wish to anchor here, consider using a stern-tie to a tree on the west shore in 7 fathoms since poor underwater visibility and a dark bottom make anchoring difficult. We recommend this site only as a lunch stop or for investigating the drying flat off the creek.

Anchor (northwest corner) in 4 fathoms over sand and gravel; poor-to-fair holding.

Laredo Channel (Aristazabal Island)
Between Aristazabal & Princess Royal islands
Entrance (SE): 52°37.68'N, 128°54.17'W
Entrance (NW): 52°51.17'N, 129°13.08'W

Laredo Channel is a continuation of the outside smooth-water route. The eastern shores of Aristazabal Island, along the channel, have few significant indentations where you can find shelter. The Princess Royal Island shore does not offer easy anchorage until the vicinity of Surf Inlet. Smithers Island Cove, on the east shore of Laredo Channel, is the most accessible anchor site in this area. *Caution:* The charts may show shallower depths than exist in Laredo Sound and Channel.

Walsh Rock Light (Laredo Channel)
4.5 mi SE of Kent Inlet
Position: 52°38.17'N, 128°57.33'W

Although there are few places to anchor in Laredo Channel, we would not put Walsh Rock high on our list. The south-flowing ebb current is particularly strong in Laredo Channel and we've seen chop build very quickly inside both Ramsbotham Island and Walsh Rock, when there was just a moderate easterly blowing up the channel. We have found more hospitable anchorage in Ramsbotham Islands (see below).

Fury Bay (Aristazabal Island)
2.1 mi S of Kent Inlet
Entrance: 52°40.22'N, 129°00.70'W

Fury Bay, the local name for a small indentation on Aristazabal Island, 2 miles southeast of Ramsbotham Islands, offers moderate protection. It is out of prevailing southeast or northwest chop of the main channel but strong current limits swinging room, requiring a shore tie.

Anchor in 5 to 10 fathoms over rock and sand with fair holding.

Ramsbotham Islands (Laredo Channel)

1.4 mi W of Kent Inlet
Entrance: 52°41.86'N, 129°02.93'W
Anchor: 52°42.02'N, 129°02.94'W

Anchorage can be found on the west side in the crux of the two northernmost Ramsbotham Islands, tucked in between. Although we don't recommend this site in southeast storms, it is quite well protected by kelp from normal up- and down-channel chop.

Anchor (northeast of the rock patch) in 6 to 8 fathoms over rocky sand; fair holding.

Kent Inlet (Laredo Channel)

11.4 mi NW of Meyers Passage
Entrance: 52°42.32'N, 129°00.76'W
Anchor: 52°43.25'N, 128°58.91'W

Kent Inlet is located on the east shore of Laredo Channel, opposite Ramsbotham Island. It is a picturesque inlet where deer often graze along shore. The inlet—which should be entered near slack water—has a narrow, intricate entrance with several drying rocks and two additional narrows that require careful navigation (see Philip Narrows below). Study the chart carefully before entering. Avoid the rock marked by kelp on the south side of the entrance and the dangerous rock mid-channel that dries at 8 feet, 200 yards east of Loap Point; this mid-channel rock should be passed on the east side in about 5 fathoms of water.

The second narrows, 0.3 mile north of Philip Narrows, carries 3.5 fathoms minimum. Favor the west shore, avoiding the islets. Kent Inlet is totally landlocked with calm waters. Very good protection can be found in the inner basin at the eastern head of the inlet; favor the north shore to avoid the mid-channel rocks. This remote and beautiful area is seldom visited and it's well worth the time it takes to transit at slack water.

Anchor (inner basin) in 6 to 10 fathoms over a sandy bottom; fair-to-good holding.

Philip Narrows

(Princess Royal Island)
0.4 mi inside Kent Inlet
Position: 52°42.66'N, 129°00.34'W

Philip Narrows, an extremely narrow passage about 100 yards in length, is probably best transited at low-water slack so you can see the rocks or at least the turbulence surrounding them. The mid-channel fairway is only about 30 feet wide with a minimum depth of about 6 feet at zero tide. (We found 1.5 fath-

Helmcken Inlet, entrance to lagoon

Photo courtesy CHS, Pacific Region

oms on a 2.2-foot tide with slack water 30 minutes after New Bella Bella.) Strong currents through the narrows make navigation hazardous at any time other than *at* or *near* slack water. Although boats up to 100 feet are said to have navigated the entrance, any size boat requires careful attention.

Helmcken Inlet

(Princess Royal Island)
3.7 mi NW of Kent Inlet
Entrance: 52°45.24'N, 129°04.54'W
Anchor: 52°45.88'N, 129°01.82'W

Helmcken Inlet is entered through a narrows on the south side of Smithers Island. Favor the north shore of the narrows for the deepest water. The shallowest part is in the east end of the narrows. Kelp lines both shores of the narrows. Minimum depth on the north side of the narrows is 4 fathoms at zero tide, 30 feet or so off Smithers Island. Current in the narrows appears to be moderate.

The large lagoon at the head of the inlet can be entered by cruising boats at high-water slack. Caution is advised because currents at springs attain 6 to 8 knots through the narrows, but the flow appears to be quite laminar. The lagoon, which is uncharted and may provide some interesting sheltered anchorage, appears to be about five miles long. From the lagoon entrance you can see a large tree-covered island inside.

Temporary anchorage can be found on the 2.5-fathom flat off the entrance to the lagoon. The lagoon is quite large and is seldom visited. Due to the current into the lagoon, you must be sure your anchor is well set.

Anchor in 2½ fathoms over sand and gravel with some grass; fair-to-good holding.

Smithers Island Cove
(Helmcken Inlet)
Entrance to Helmcken Inlet
Entrance: 52°45.44'N, 129°04.54'W
Anchor: 52°45.52'N, 129°04.24'W

Smithers Island Cove, on the outer side of the first narrows to Helmcken Inlet, is fairly easy to enter and is fairly well sheltered. However, the bottom is rocky, and it's difficult to get a good bite with your anchor. In moderate weather, there is not much strain on your anchor, but in a blow we'd look elsewhere, such as Hague Point Lagoon, Meyers Passage or Racey Inlet.

Anchor in 8 to 10 fathoms over a rocky bottom with poor holding, unless you set your anchor well.

Commando Inlet (Princess Royal Island)
2 mi N of Helmcken Inlet
Entrance: 52°47.12'N, 129°06.23'W

Commando Inlet is difficult to enter unless conditions are nearly optimal. One to 2-foot overfalls at the mid-channel islet create a lot of foam and turbulence in the entrance. In addition, there is inadequate turning room in the entrance, and the channel on the north side of the islet is very narrow. This route is for small, easily maneuverable boats only. We went only to the islet and retreated because of less-than-optimal conditions. A slow approach with bow lookouts is required since there is an underwater rock off the west end of the islet; favor the north shore, avoiding overhanging branches. During spring tides there are overfalls on either side of the islet and passage should only be attempted very close to high water slack. Good shelter, protected from all weather is reported in a small basin at the extreme eastern end of Commando Inlet; however, we can't add any additional local knowledge.

Evinrude Inlet (Laredo Channel)
0.25 mi N of Commando Inlet
Entrance: 52°47.42'N, 129°06.18'W
Shore tie-up: 52°48.17'N, 129°04.93'W

Evinrude Inlet provides excellent shelter from northwest and southeast gales since the outside chop rolls by the entrance. Silver snags covering the granite outcroppings of the inlet give it a wild look. On the north shore, near the outlet of the creek, there is a rusty donkey with a V-8 engine, remains of past logging days. The inlet can be entered at all tide levels because there is minimal current. Favor the south shore at the second narrows to avoid a 3-fathom shoal.

A log tied to shore can be used for moorage as there is approximately one fathom or more of water along the steep-to rock. Depths elsewhere are too deep for convenient anchorage, unless you use a stern-tie to shore. The bottom is reported to be sticky mud with very good holding.

Baker Point (Laredo Channel)
4.1 mi W of Evinrude Inlet
Light Position: 52°48.13'N, 129°12.99'W

Baker Point is an open roadstead where you can obtain temporary anchorage in 2 fathoms off the long and lovely stretch of sandy beach, *but only in fair weather*. It is not much more than a lunch stop and a place to stretch your legs. However, in westerly weather, it can be surprisingly comfortable.

Anchor (as convenient) on either side of the light in 3 fathoms over sand; fair holding.

Aristazabal Island, West Coast (Hecate Strait)
W side of Princess Royal Island
Position (Prior Passage): 52°26.49'N, 128°59.96'W
Entrance (N): 52°49.78'N, 129°17.92'W

Aristazabal Island faces Hecate Strait, but it is surprisingly well protected by innumerable islets, reefs and rocks. A favorite destination of fishermen and intrepid kayakers, this coast offers great fishing, wildlife viewing and exploration of the rugged inner tidal zone by kayak or inflatable. The routes described below follow a south to north orientation.

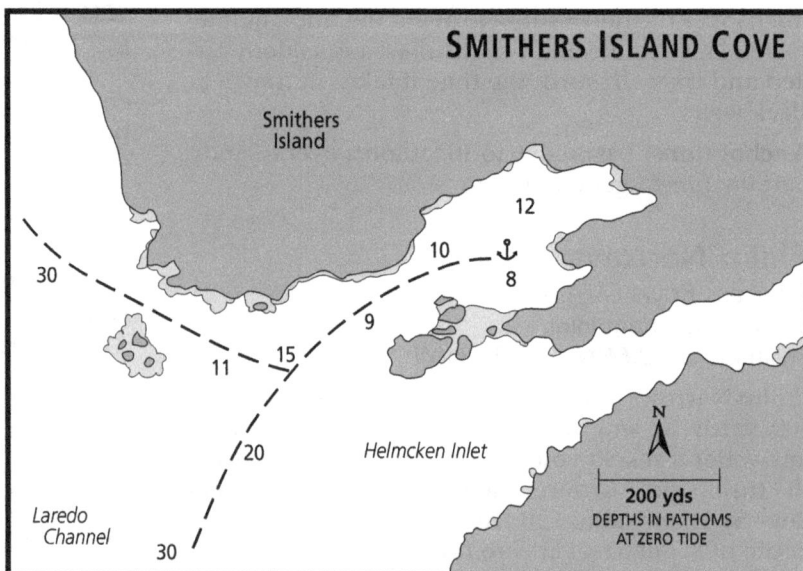

SMITHERS ISLAND COVE

Smithers Island

Helmcken Inlet

Laredo Channel

200 yds
DEPTHS IN FATHOMS
AT ZERO TIDE

©2024 Don and Réanne Douglass • Diagram not for navigation

Prior Passage, in the lee of Munro Island, provides some relief from southerly swell when rounding the south end of Aristazabal Island. Avoid a shoal and foul area marked by kelp on the south side of the channel, east of Munro Island.

Weeteeam Bay (Aristazabal Island)

9.5 mi W of Higgins Passage
Entrance: 52°29.64'N, 129°02.30'W

Weeteeam Bay, on the south tip of Aristazabal Island, offers good shelter behind its many islands and islets. The bay should not be entered without consulting large scale charts. Anchorage can be found in Weeteeam Bay at the entrance to Noble Lagoon and in Bent Harbour. We find the shelter afforded by Bent Harbour and its close access to the outer coast make it a favorite spot in this area.

Bent Harbour (Aristazabal Island)

0.6 mi NW of Thistleton Islands
Entrance: 52°30.70'N, 129°02.71'W
Anchor: 52°30.78'N, 129°03.27'W

Bent Harbour is the small basin between Thistleton Islands and Aristazabal Island at the west side of Weeteeam Bay. While no swell or chop enters the harbor, it is exposed to southeast winds. A shore tie can make this a reasonably secure anchorage; however, large seiners are reported to have parted 1½ inch shore ties during southeast storms—caused perhaps by surge. We really liked the rugged atmosphere here and felt very comfortable.

Small boats can use the smooth-water passage near high water north of the big Thistleton Island; however, underwater rocks and kelp highly restrict the narrows to just a few feet in width, requiring adroit navigation. The simpler way on a northbound

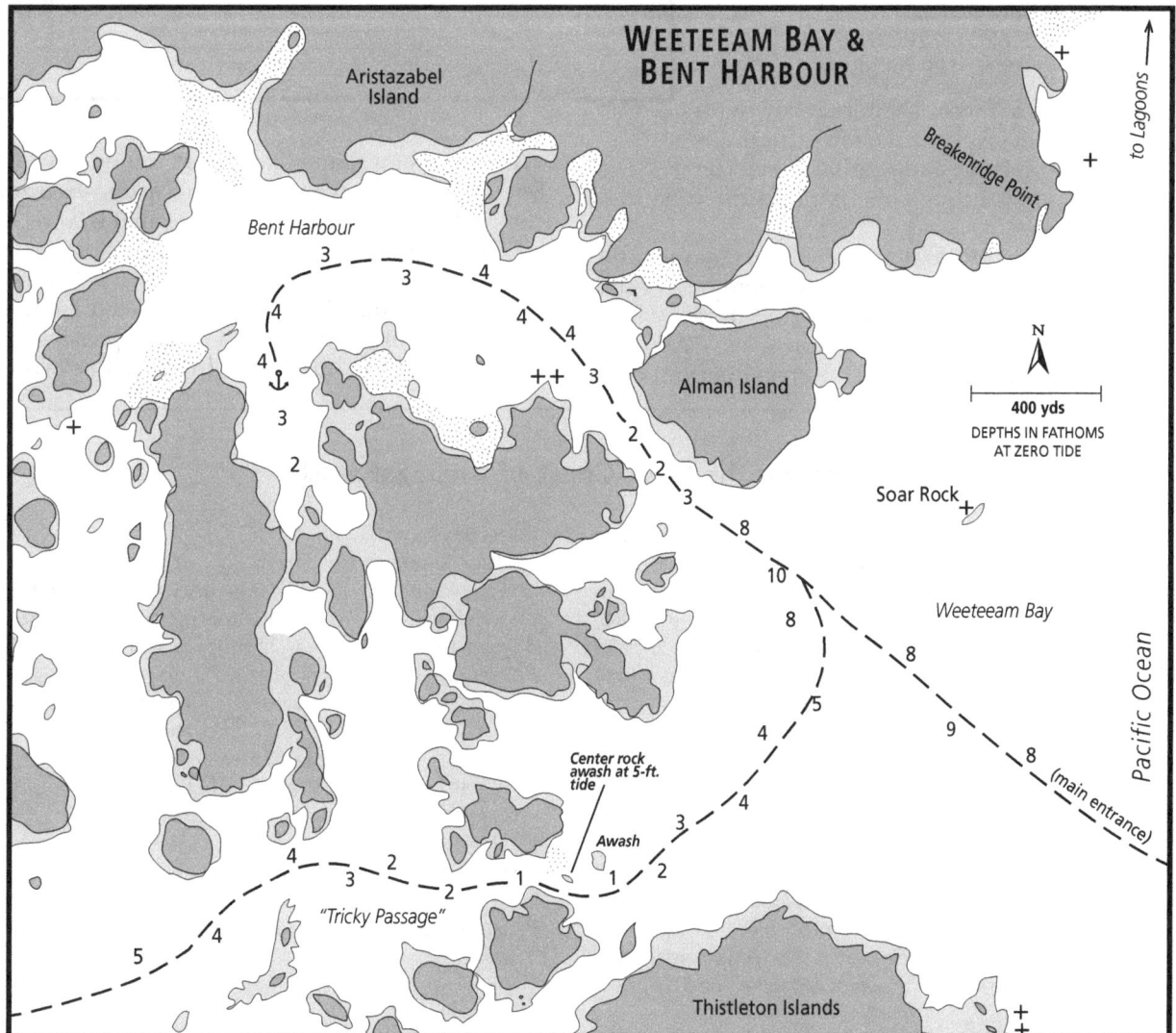

WEETEEAM BAY & BENT HARBOUR

to Lagoons

Aristazabel Island

Bent Harbour

Breakenridge Point

Alman Island

N

400 yds
DEPTHS IN FATHOMS
AT ZERO TIDE

Soar Rock

Weeteeam Bay

Pacific Ocean

(main entrance)

Center rock awash at 5-ft. tide

Awash

"Tricky Passage"

Thistleton Islands

©2024 Don and Reanne Douglass • Diagram not for navigation

route is to use the entrance to Weeteeam Bay.

Anchor in 4 fathoms over mud with good holding.

Archer Islets (Weeteeam Bay)
0.9 mi NE of Bent Harbour
Anchor: 52°31.52'N, 129°02.30'W

The area located outside the entrance to the common basin Noble Lagoon and Kdalmishan Creek northwest of Archer Islets, is a great base from which to explore Noble Lagoon and the outstanding maze of islets located within a few miles.

Anchor in 5 fathoms over mud with good holding.

Clifford Bay (Aristazabal Island)
6.1 mi NW of Bent Harbour
Entrance: 52°35.62'N, 129°09.69'W
Anchor: 52°35.39'N, 129°08.58'W

Clifford Bay—a large, sheltered bay with protection from swells and chop—offers anchorage to both large and small vessels. The wind may howl through the islets to the west and south, however.

The west side of Craft Island, the recommended anchorage, has plenty of swinging room over a flat shallow bottom. Small boats may find more protection southeast of Craft Island; however, we found poor holding over the sand and gravel bottom cov-

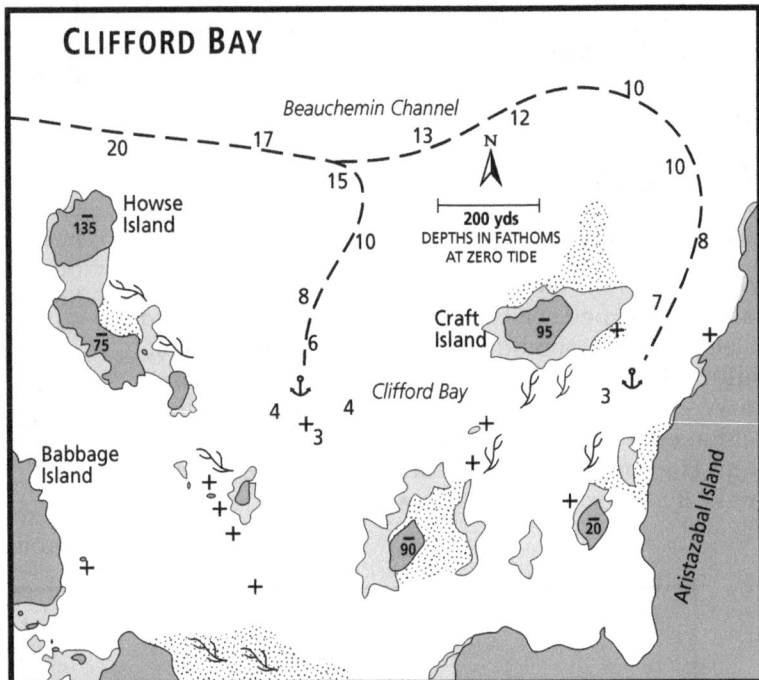

ered with newspaper kelp that fouled our anchor. Small boats may want to look for a kelp-free zone, as the shelter is best close to Aristazabal Island.

The Normansell Islands offer a sheltered route for boats heading to or from Clifford Bay. The passage inside Normansell Islands is protected from southerly swells and you can find several possible anchor sites with good exploring within this network. No-

Exploring the West Coast of Aristazabal Island

After leaving the security of Clark Cove, one morning in early September, Réanne and I encountered brisk southerly weather and dropped our plan to explore the west coast of Aristazabal Island. We decided, instead, to explore the Estevan Group and took secure refuge in Gillen Harbour that night. The next morning was misty and foggy so we crossed Campania Sound under radar and GPS and found our way into Barkley Passage among the biggest flock of loons we have ever seen.

We resumed our original plan and continued south along the west coast of Aristazabal Island, keeping as many islands to windward as possible to avoid southerly chop. We found the smooth-water route on the north side of Thistleton Islands and, after a tricky passage through a maze of islets, we worked our way into Weeteeam Bay. We found the small gaff-headed ketch *Endymion* anchored securely in Bent Harbor—the first boat we had seen in

three days.

Its owners were canoeing in the rain, combing the remote beaches for flotsam and jetsam, as they had been doing for 10 years. We invited Don and Gwen Burton aboard for tea. They said that, when they saw *Baidarka* through one of the "windows" in the maze of islands, they had to fight the urge to paddle out and tell us we were crazy fools and should head out to sea as quickly as possible. They confessed that they had second thoughts as their heads filled with visions of the jetsam they could pick up if we grounded!

The weather eased after tea and Réanne and I sailed through Prior Passage north of Munro Island and crossed bouncy Laredo Sound to the west side of Higgins Passage where we were stormbound for 24 hours.

—DD

tice, however, disfigured tree limbs that indicate the strength of southeast storms!

Anchor (west side of Craft Island) in 5 fathoms over sand and kelp; fair-to-good holding.

Kettle Inlet (Aristazabal Island)
2 mi S of Borrowman Bay
Entrance: 52°42.71'N, 129°17.40'W
Anchor: 52°41.82'N, 129°14.06'W

Kettle Inlet is a long, narrow indentation in the west coast of Aristazabal Island. However, the inlet is exposed to winds from the northwest or southeast.

When entering Kettle Inlet, take a mid-channel course and anchor west of longitude 129°12.50'W in 8 to 10 fathoms. The best anchor site in the inlet is located in the nook on the east shore, just east of the tip of the peninsula that forms the south shore of the inlet. Tuck in behind a small islet on the south shore of this nook; a stern tie to the south shore makes it almost bombproof. Our friend Kevin Monahan once anchored in Kettle Inlet during 60-knot southeasterly winds. Within five minutes, the wind switched to

Endymion in Bent Harbour, Weeteeam Bay

60 knots from the northwest, and although his anchor did drag, there was plenty of dragging room.

Anchor (east shore) in 6 fathoms over sand and mud with good holding.

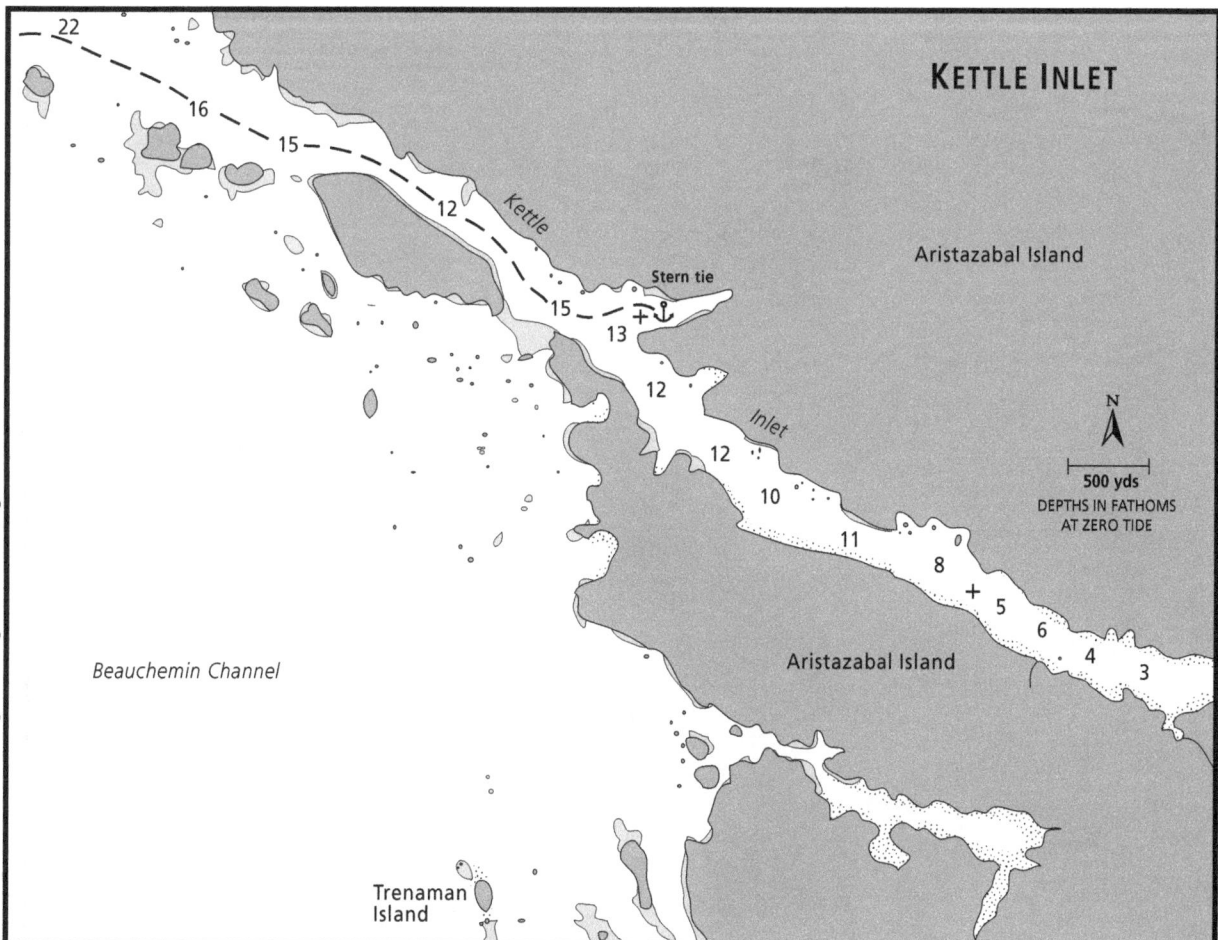

©2024 Don and Réanne Douglass • Diagram not for navigation

KETTLE INLET

22
16
15
12
Kettle
15
Stern tie
13
12
Inlet
12
10
11
8
5
6
4
3

Aristazabal Island

Aristazabal Island

N
500 yds
DEPTHS IN FATHOMS
AT ZERO TIDE

Beauchemin Channel

Trenaman Island

Borrowman Bay, Turtish Harbour

(Aristazabal Island)
11 mi S of Surf Inlet
Entrance: 52°44.48'N, 129°18.39'W

Borrowman Bay offers the best protection for small craft along the entire west coast of Aristazabal Island, particularly in Tate Cove. Upon approaching the bay from the southwest, Trickey Island fades into the shore and is almost invisible. Wall Islets and the reef to Mesher Rock are also difficult to identify clearly; use caution when entering Morison Passage or Meiss Passage. GPS helps to identify the route.

Turtish Harbour provides very good anchorage for larger vessels. Wind shifts can cause vessels to swing, so avoid anchoring near Sere Rock or the 3-fathom patch to its west. Otherwise holding is good in 8 to 10 fathoms over a mud bottom, but small boats can find even better protection in Tate Cove, immediately south.

Tate Cove (Borrowman Bay)

0.25 mi S of Turtish Hbr.
Entrance: 52°44.10'N, 129°16.68'W
Anchor: 52°44.02'N, 129°16.62'W

Tate Cove offers virtually bombproof shelter for small boats. Wilks Island has a tree on its north point shaped like a Chinese parasol (we call this Parasol Point) that provides a landmark. Just beyond this point, you turn southeast into Tate Cove. There is a kayak haul-out beach at the head of the cove. The water here has better than 10-foot visibility, and it's a

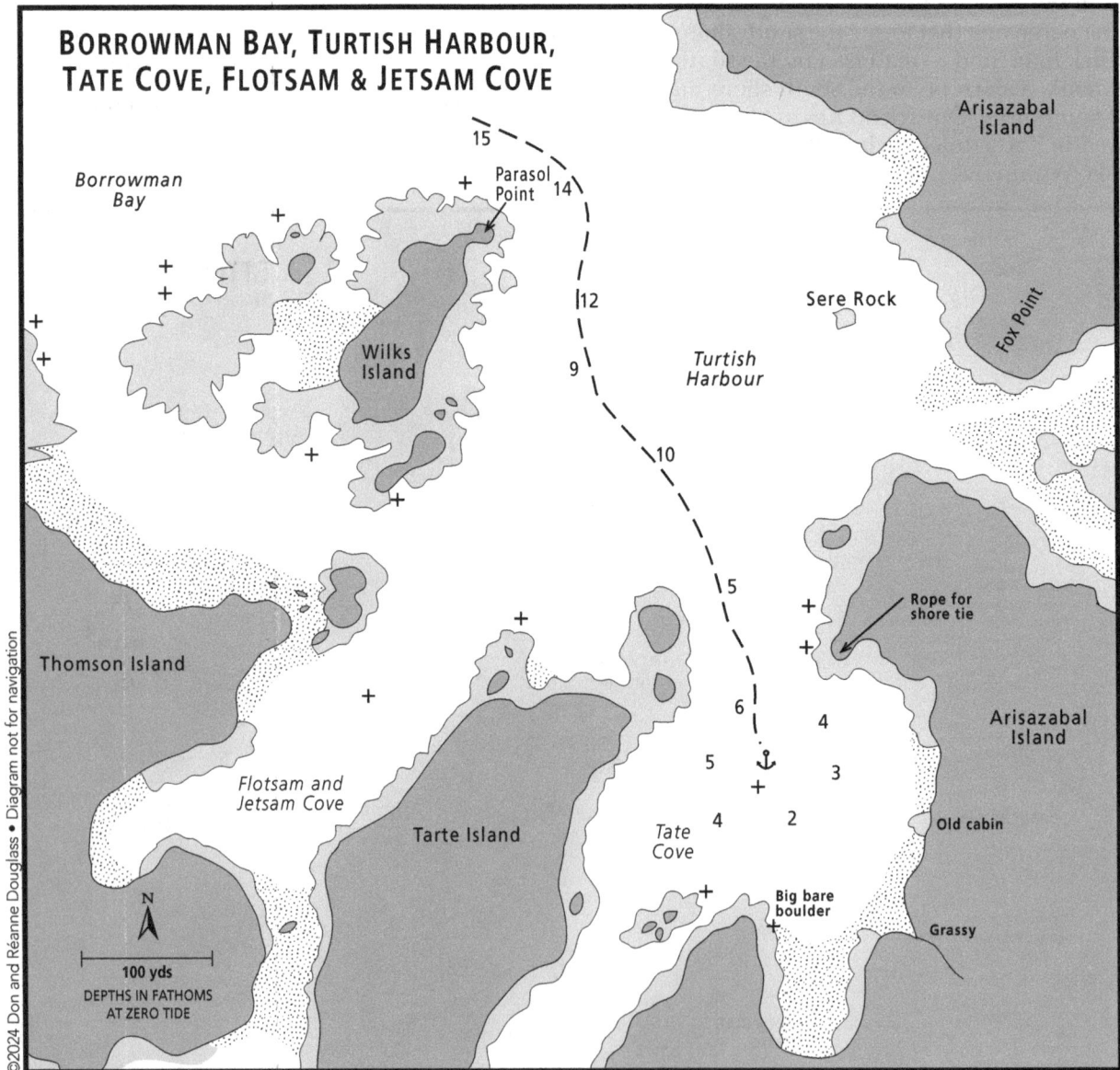

BORROWMAN BAY, TURTISH HARBOUR, TATE COVE, FLOTSAM & JETSAM COVE

Borrowman Bay

Parasol Point

Arisazabal Island

Wilks Island

Sere Rock

Fox Point

Turtish Harbour

Thomson Island

Rope for shore tie

Arisazabal Island

Flotsam and Jetsam Cove

Tarte Island

Tate Cove

Old cabin

Big bare boulder

Grassy

N

100 yds
DEPTHS IN FATHOMS
AT ZERO TIDE

©2024 Don and Réanne Douglass • Diagram not for navigation

good place to observe bald eagles, grebes, and gulls. This spot is so comfortable you won't realize you're next to Hecate Strait!

Anchor in 3 to 5 fathoms over brown mud, with shells and sea lettuce; very good holding.

Surf Inlet
(Princess Royal Island)
6 mi N of Evinrude Inlet
Entrance: 52°53.34'N, 129°08.85'W

You will consider Surf Inlet aptly named if you enter when a strong westerly is blowing in against an ebb tide; however, it is known principally as a scenic, narrow fiord with steep peaks towering above its shores. Favor slack water for entering. Bears are known to inhabit this side of Princess Royal Island and this is a favorite place to look for them. Racey Inlet, entered southeast of Surf Inlet entrance, offers good shelter in its south end.

Surf Inlet extends about 13 miles northeastward from its entrance point off Johnstone Point to its head. Penn Harbour, 8 miles northeast of the entrance to Surf Inlet, provides excellent anchorage.

Penn Harbour (Surf Inlet)
7.4 mi NE of Surf Inlet entrance
Entrance: 52°57.96'N, 128°58.33'W
Anchor: 52°58.40'N, 128°57.25'W

Penn Harbour, 7.5 miles northeast of the entrance to Surf Inlet, provides excellent anchorage and is the safest anchorage in Surf Inlet. Its narrow entrance is clear on all tides, and inside you can find protection in all weather. While gales or storms blow outside in Hecate Strait, flags barely flutter inside Penn Harbour.

The harbor is landlocked. There is a lovely falls at its head which you can explore by dinghy or you can run 4 miles up to the head of Surf Inlet to explore an abandoned hydro-dam.

Anchor in 10 fathoms over mud with good holding.

Racey Inlet (Princess Royal Island)
5.7 mi N of Evinrude Inlet
Entrance: 52°52.99'N, 129°06.66'W

Racey Inlet is strategically positioned to offer shelter when Campania Sound and Laredo Channel start kicking up or when entering Emily Carr Inlet is risky. (Penn Harbour, 7.5 miles up Surf Inlet, offers the best all-weather protection in the immediate area.) Deep in the head of Racey Inlet, Bone Anchorage is nearly landlocked and offers shelter in moderate depths; the bay has a large creek with waterfalls.

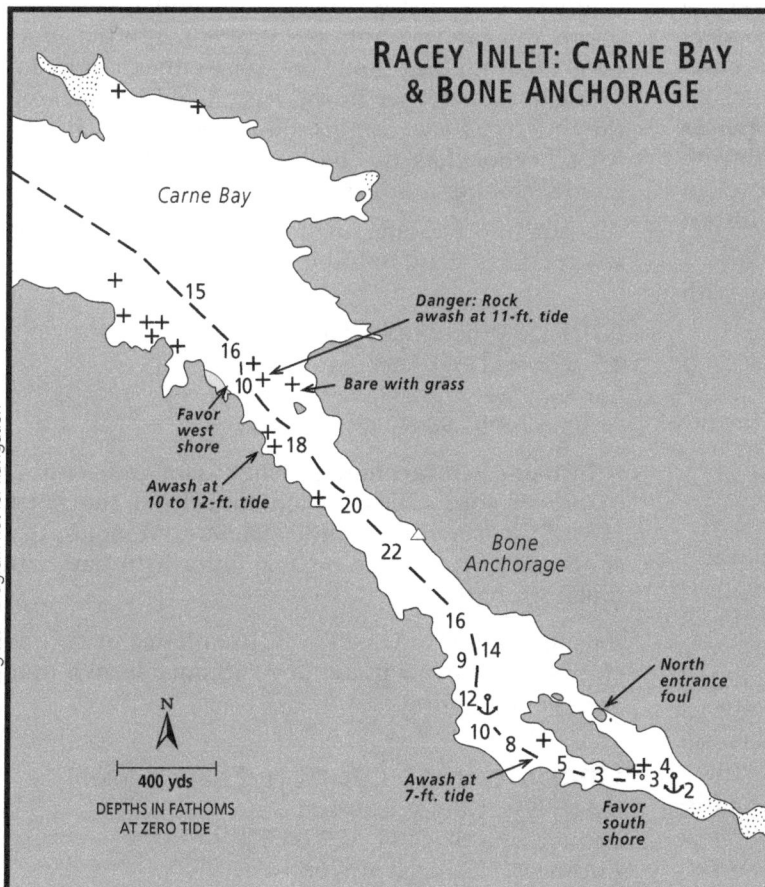

RACEY INLET: CARNE BAY & BONE ANCHORAGE

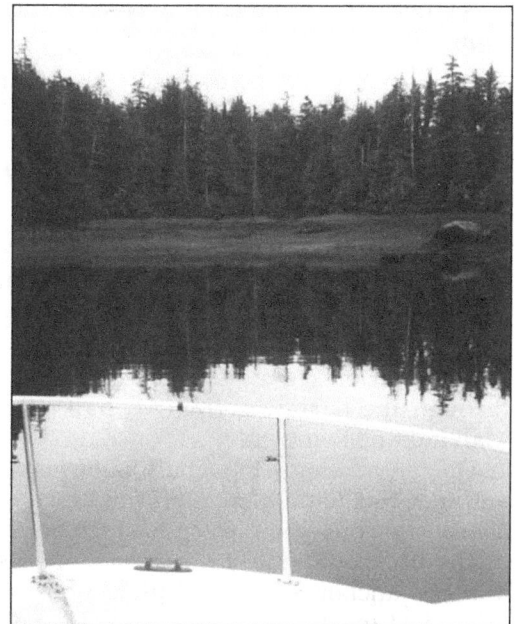

Tate Cove head

Carne Bay (Racey Inlet)

2.9 mi SE of Racey Inlet entrance
Entrance: 52°51.81'N, 129°02.77'W
Anchor: 51°51.88'N, 129°02.25'W

Although Carne Bay reportedly has satisfactory anchorage for larger boats in moderate winds avoid this bay in storm-force southeasterlies, where severe downdrafts make it unsafe.

Anchor in 10 fathoms with mud and very good holding.

Bone Anchorage (Racey Inlet)

1.7 mi SE of Carney Bay
Anchor: 52°50.40'N, 129°00.66'W

Bone Anchorage, at the very head of Racey Inlet, has swinging room for several small boats with good scope ratios. Anchorage can be taken between the bare rock just southeast of Wale Island and the drying flat in front of the creek. This is a quiet, secluded wilderness anchorage that offers very good protection in all weather, but use caution.

As you pass Carne Bay, Racey Inlet necks down; at this point you must avoid Cox Rocks to safely enter Bone Anchorage. Cox Rocks lie mid-channel; perhaps the most dangerous one is the northerly rock, awash on about an 11-foot tide. Once you have passed the bare 5-foot-high rock with grass, the channel appears clear. Favor the south shore but avoid the rocks close along shore.

Kevin Monahan once observed a seiche (water surge or oscillation) near Bone Anchorage during strong south winds that caused the water level in Racey Inlet to rise and fall slowly—18 inches within a 20-minute period.

Anchor in 3 fathoms, over soft brown mud with worms; good holding.

Doig Anchorage, Chapple Inlet

(Princess Royal Island)
1.3 mi N of Mallandaine Point
Entrance: 52°54.42'N, 129°07.92'W
Anchor: 52°55.10'N, 129°07.83'W

Chapple Inlet provides surprisingly smooth water and protection from weather as soon as you pass through the narrow entrance a half-mile north of Mallandaine Point.

Doig Anchorage, the small bight just inside the entrance to Chapple Inlet, off the beach of the east shore, is a convenient place to stage an exploration of the backcountry bear areas or upper Surf Inlet. You can anchor, with good protection from southerlies, just inside Doig Anchorage. The cove west of Chettleburgh Point has more protection and swing-

"Parasol Point," entrance to Tate Cove

ing room.

Anchor in about 9 fathoms over sand and mud with good holding.

Chettleburgh Point Cove (Chapple Inlet)

1.6 mi N of Doig Anchorage
Anchor: 52°56.60'N, 129°08.65'W

Chettleburgh Point Cove offers protection from southerlies for just one boat with limited swinging room. You can tuck into the tiny notch in the south corner behind the point. We advise either a shore tie, or anchoring deeper in the bay. Avoid the rock off the tiny treed islet as you round the point. Chapple Inlet Lagoon has the best overall protection with good swinging room and holding.

Anchor in 6 fathoms, over brown sand, shells and wood debris; good holding.

Kiln Bay (Chapple Inlet)

2.9 mi N of Doig Anchorage
Entrance: 52°57.82'N, 129°08.74'W
Anchor: 52°57.93'N, 129°08.91'W

Kiln Bay offers anchorage where you can weather plenty of southerlies tucked in behind the north side of the island in about 6 fathoms. We doubt that southeast gales on the outside enter Kiln Bay with much strength.

Anchor (center of the bay) in 10 fathoms or tuck in close to the island in about 5 fathoms; brown mud with good holding.

Chapple Inlet Lagoon (Chapple Inlet)

3.3 mi N of Doig Anchorage
Entrance: 52°57.41'N, 129°08.30'W
Anchor: 52°58.43'N, 129°08.18'W

"Chapple Inlet Lagoon," our name for the basin at the head of the inlet, is technically not a lagoon, although its narrow entrance and labyrinth of islands and nooks give it that feeling. Lovely old-growth, no evidence of logging, and granite bluffs along the eastern shore all contribute to making Chapple Inlet Lagoon a wonderful place to anchor.

The head of the bay is a large, drying flat with grassy margins that contain no driftwood, indicating utter stillness. This site—West Coast environment at its best—is the most protected.

It is imperative to use a large scale chart if you wish to enter the lagoon and avoid the obstacles. Entrance is made east of Baile Island, favoring the east shore, in 2 fathoms minimum. There is a narrows east of McKechnie Point which carries a minimum of 4 fathoms in the fairway.

Anchor in 5 fathoms, brown mud with clam shells; very good holding. There is plenty of swinging room for a number of boats over a flat bottom.

Emily Carr Cove (Emily Carr Inlet)
1.6 mi N of Surf Inlet entr.
Entrance (inlet): 52°54.84'N, 129°09.00'W
Entrance (cove): 52°55.36'N, 129°08.93'W
Anchor: 52°55.39'N, 129°09.53'W

Emily Carr Inlet, named for British Columbia's famous artist, is formed by a complex group of islands, islets and rocks. Cruising boats can find both a well-sheltered anchorage and an explorer's challenge here. Use a large scale chart and extra caution in traversing this area, since it is easy to become confused, turning room in the channel is very limited, and is encumbered with rocks.

The lagoon at the head of the inlet offers excellent protection for a small boat from all weather. Its entrance is intricate, with about one fathom in the fairway and mid-lagoon rocks to avoid. The anchor site has limited swinging room.

We prefer to anchor in the northwest corner of Emily Carr Inlet in what we call "Emily Carr Cove." This cove, which also has a narrow, intricate entrance with less than one fathom in its fairway and very limited turning room, is equally well protected. There is more swinging room here than that in the lagoon. Old-growth trees lining its shores make it a nice anchorage. There are two rocks at the west end of the entrance narrows which you must locate and pass between.

Anchor (NW cove) in 4 fathoms over sticky mud with very good holding.

Note: 2022 Sailing Directions has the following warning: "Groundings have occurred by vessels attempting to enter the unnamed cove on the west side of Emily Carr Inlet near the entrance. The passage on the north side of the large island in the entrance to this cove is narrow, shallow and obstructed by drying rocks. The west end of this passage has a large drying rock in the centre. Mariners must favour the south side and go close to a large fallen tree. Local knowledge and prior reconnaissance at low water is recommended before any attempt is made to enter this cove."

Campania Sound
(Campania Island)
SE of Campania Island
Position: 52°58.00'N, 129°15.00'W

Strong ebb current on the order of 3 knots flowing south in Campania Sound can cause nasty chop in south winds or confused seas in westerlies. The southwest swell sometimes felt in Caamaño Sound dies off as you head north toward Ashdown Island. Clarke Cove, on the Princess Royal Island coast of Campania Sound, is an outstanding anchor site.

Around the Next Point

I imagine people travel for hundreds of miles saying to each other, "Let's just see what's around that next point."

Sometimes there's a house in the woods, a lonely homestead left abandoned. Sometimes there's a fish camp or lodge, a bustle of people and noise. But often, at first glance, there's nothing. You pass the point and a cove appears, a sheltered place where every tree and rock is doubled on the water. It spreads before you like a pushed-open door. So you go in and anchor, and you wonder if it's possible that no one has been here before.

We've passed that next point and found a family of wolves so unaccustomed to people that they lounged on the beach like cats on a windowsill. We found ravens who mimicked the strange sounds of the anchor chain, a sea lion that came right to the boat, songbirds that perched like pilots by the tiller. In this sort of place the trees still grow to a monstrous size. The rocks at low tide are covered by incredible things. The water's so clear that you can watch the anchor dig in fathoms and fathoms below.

For thousands of years the forest has grown and died and grown again, untouched and maybe unseen. The cliffs and the beaches have only slightly given way to the sea. For all this time nothing has changed. Night falls, and the light at your masthead adds one more star to the hundreds of others that have filled this place every night through the centuries.

It's not empty at all.

—Iain Lawrence, author of *Far Away Places*

Clarke Cove (Princess Royal Island)

3.9 mi NW of Emily Carr Inlet
Entrance: 52°58.34'N, 129°11.72'W
Anchor: 52°57.90'N, 129°11.03'W

Clarke Cove, along with MacDonald Bay on Gil Island, may be one of the best-kept secrets for cruising boats on the entire coast. Tucked behind the three-islet-and-rock complex just inside the narrows, this landlocked cove offers perfect protection for a small boat from all weather. Its entrance is so small you need GPS to locate it. When you're 100 yards off the shore, you still can't see its opening.

On spring tides, the current in the narrows, which runs 2 to 3 knots, can be turbulent. The fairway narrows to about 25 feet or less with underwater rocks evident on both sides. The fairway carries only about 3 feet of water at zero tide. Larger boats can transit best at high-water slack. Favor the north shore inside of the narrows; there are several square rocks off the south shore. Once inside, pass south of the islets in the middle of the cove.

The cove is surrounded by old-growth forest where tree branches extend horizontally over the water and chop appears never to enter. During gales, the wind inside is probably felt only as gusts along

Entrance to Clarke Cove

the surface, while overhead it howls.

There is plenty of swinging room for three or four small boats. The bottom, initially 12 fathoms, bounces between 10 and 6 near the islets then slopes upward to a nearly flat 7 fathoms well east of the islets. There is no landing beach here other than a small rocky shoal where two small creeks empty into its head. Radio reception inside the cove is nil.

Anchor (head of the cove) in 6 to 7 fathoms over mud with good holding.

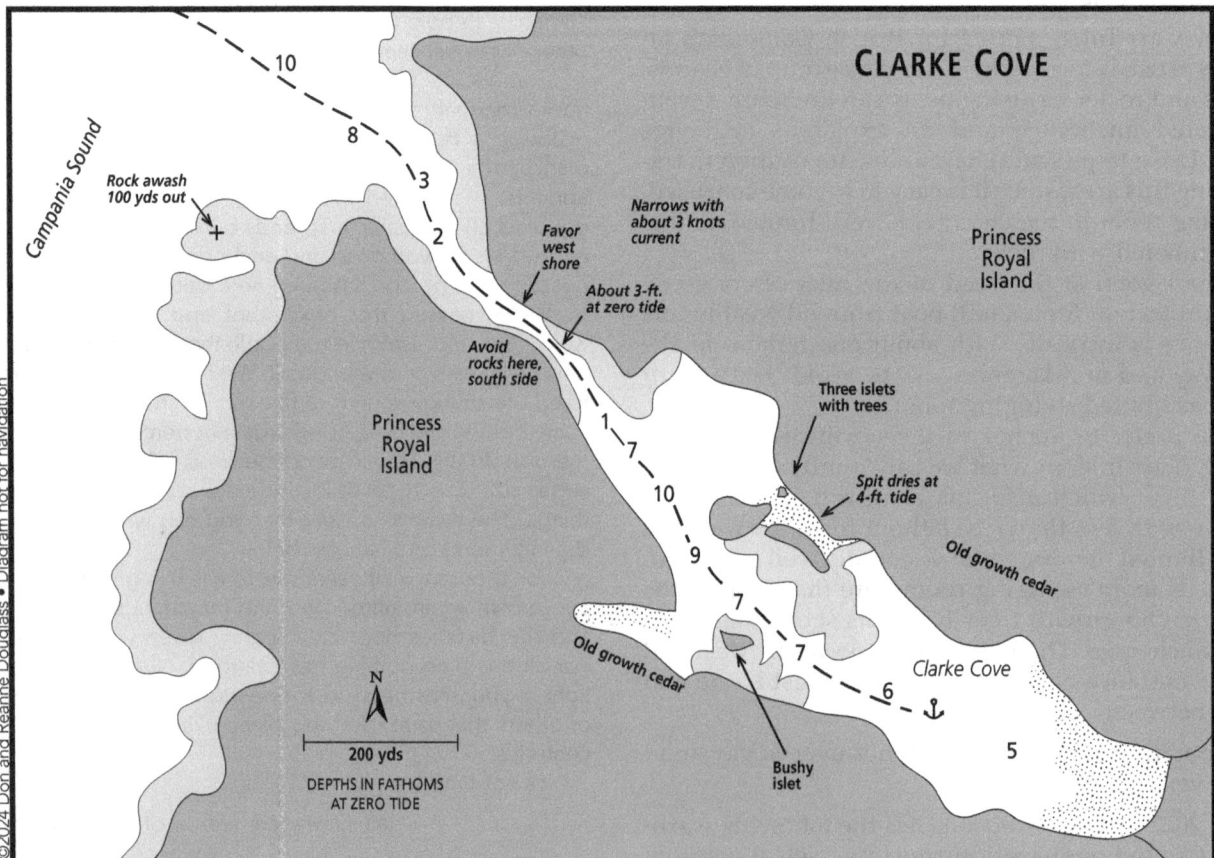

Clarke Cove, looking out from inside

Whale Channel (Wright Sound)
NW Princess Royal Island
Entrance (SW): 53°04.34'N, 129°15.46'W
Entrance (NE): 53°17.10'N, 129°07.90'W

Whale Channel is fairly well protected and has considerably less chop than Squally Channel. Cameron Cove on its south shore provides good protection with easy access.

Barnard Harbour (Whale Channel)
9.5 N of Emily Carr Inlet
Aikman Passage entr: 53°04.77'N, 129°07.54'W
Burnes Passage entr: 53°05.12'N, 129°06.65'W
Anchor: 53°04.16'N, 129°05.83'W

Barnard Harbour, with Cameron Cove, lies on the northwest corner of Princess Royal Island off Whale Channel and provides excellent anchorage for cruising boats. You can enter the harbor on either side of Borde Island.

Although depths in most of Barnard Harbour are too great for convenient small-boat anchoring, you can find good spots on the west side of Cameron Cove (the western lobe of the harbor) near the head of the cove. Be aware, however, of the rapidly shoaling bottom. In southeast storms, large boats are advised to anchor at the extreme east of Barnard Harbour close to shore.

Anchor (extreme east) in about 10 fathoms; bottom not recorded.

Cameron Cove (Barnard Harbour)
0.5 mi W of Barnard Harbour
Anchor: 53°03.85'N, 129°07.03'W

Strong southerly winds are known to blow down Barnard Creek into Barnard Harbour and Cameron Cove. To reduce the fetch and the effects of the gusty wind during southeast storms, anchor just outside of a line between the treed island and Uren Point in 3 to 4 fathoms.

Anchor in 3 to 4 fathoms, over mud, sand, shells and eelgrass; fair-to-good holding. Larger boats can anchor in the middle of the bay in 15 fathoms.

Cornwall Inlet and Drake Inlet (Princess Royal Island)
3.7 mi S of Home Bay
Entrance (Cornwall Inlet): 53°12.83'N, 129°03.33'W
Entrance (Drake Inlet): 53°10.52'N, 128°59.40'W

Cornwall and Drake inlets offer beautiful, well-protected cruising, although Clement Rapids is wicked and its entrance not well charted. The inlets are surrounded by 3,000-foot peaks and high ridges and are quiet, scenic places. This is Princess Royal Island bear country with anchor sites reported to be near the heads of both inlets in about 10 to 15 fathoms.

River Bight and Clement Rapids
8.5 mi N of Barnard Harbour
Anchor (near Salmon Point): 53°12.63'N, 129°03.12'W

Dangerous Clement Rapids has been the site of nasty surprises for small boats that try to enter. On spring tides, the rapids attain an 8-foot overfall with 6-foot standing waves at the bottom. The surprise comes because, approaching on a flood tide, you can see nothing except the laminar flow disappearing into a very narrow tree-lined passage. The waterfall and its heavy foam and turbulence are out of sight until it's too late! Enter Clement Rapids at high-water slack only!

It's possible to anchor temporarily at the small basin immediately southeast of Salmon Point and reconnoiter the rapids ahead of time while you wait for slack water. We have been comfortable here, but we don't recommend leaving your boat unattended. Home Bay offers more security as an anchor site.

Anchor in 4 to 6 fathoms over sand, gravel and mud; fair-to-good holding.

Entrance to Clement Rapids, Cornwall Inlet

Home Bay (Princess Royal Island)
0.9 mi S of Nelly Point
Entrance: 53°16.55'N, 129°05.42'W
Anchor (SW corner): 53°16.30'N, 129°04.85'W

Home Bay can provide some shelter from southwest to southeast winds but it is exposed to outflow winds and northwesterlies. Large driftlogs lining the shore indicate heavy weather in the bay.

Anchor (southwest corner) in about 10 fathoms over sand and some eelgrass; fair-to-good holding.

Fisherman Cove (Gil Island)
2.6 mi S of Coghlan Anchorage
Position: 53°19.50'N, 129°16.80'W

Fisherman Cove, at the north end of Gil Island, lies between Turtle Point and Blackfly Point. Most of the cove dries and anchorage off its entrance is indifferent and not recommended due to the steep drop-off in depths.

Fisherman Cove is open to chop from Wright Sound and offers little protection. It can serve as a lunch stop in fair weather. Large boats can anchor in 15 fathoms off the steep-to beach; small boats can anchor temporarily over the drying mud flat, visible in 12 feet of water. The bottom is composed of small stones, sand, and shells, with some grass; fair holding. Coghlan Anchorage is the preferred anchor site in this area.

MacDonald Bay (Gil Island)
2.3 mi S of Fin Island
Entrance: 53°11.81'N, 129°20.55'W
Anchor (E end): 53°11.87'N, 129°19.73'W

MacDonald Bay, the small bay a half-mile south of Blackrock Point on Gil Island, is a bombproof anchorage once you're inside, but entering requires caution and an adequate tide level. Totally landlocked, the bay provides excellent protection from all weather. Moderate-sized cruising boats can enter on the upper half of the tide. Near slack water the entire world could be blowing away outside the bay and you'd never know it.

You can anchor temporarily in the outer bay in 7-8 fathoms while you're waiting for a favorable tide level to pass through the narrows, but the bottom is rocky so be sure to set your anchor well. We have measured minimum depth in the narrows fairway at 2 feet at zero tide.

The shallowest spots are located just inside the west entrance, and again at the east end of the 500-yard-long narrows. Due to the dark rocks and muskeg water, underwater visibility is limited to about one foot. The bottom along the narrows is composed of basketball-sized rocks; however, we couldn't detect any sign of isolated rocks when the tide level was at 3.5 feet in Bella Bella. Currents through the narrows are relatively moderate with laminar flow.

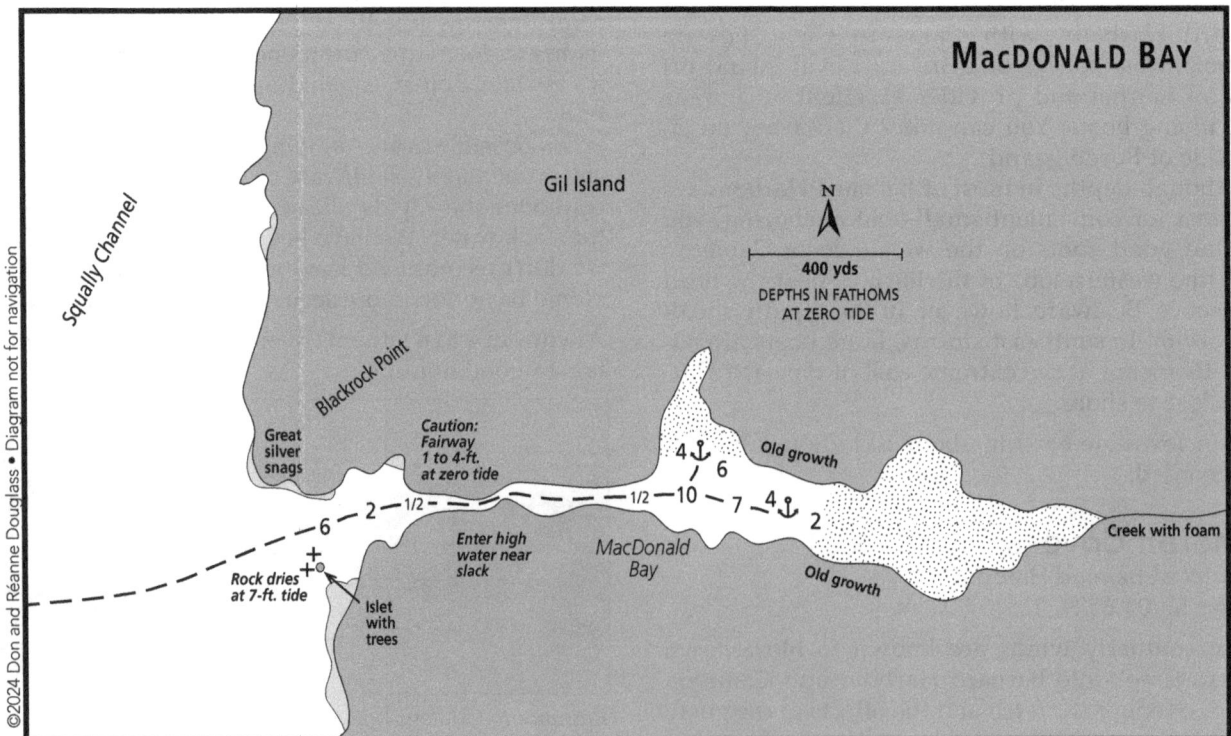

MacDonald Bay entrance

MacDonald Bay, looking out toward entrance

Large boats that want maximum swinging room can anchor in the widest part of the bay in 10 fathoms. Smaller boats can anchor farther east on the 3-fathom flat in front of the drying flat that fills the eastern portion of the bay. Old-growth forest lines the shores, and there is a grassy beach at the head of the bay where you can land a dinghy or kayak. We saw Canada geese and grebes, kingfishers, and seagulls diving for their food, and heard wolves howling in the early morning hours.

Anchor (east end) in 3 fathoms over sticky mud with very good holding.

Dillon Bay
(Otter Channel on Pitt Island)
3.7 mi S of Tuwartz Inlet
Entrance: 53°12.99'N, 129°29.74'W

Dillon Bay, located at the east end of Otter Channel, in the lee of McCreight Point, can provide good temporary protection for a small boat at its head from strong northwest winds and southwest swells. It is open to the southeast, however, and not secure in such conditions. *Caution:* The bay is very small and poorly charted. Small Sharp Bay on the north side of Campania may afford some temporary shelter to small boats.

Crane Bay (Gil Island)
3 mi S of Curlew Bay
Entrance: 53°13.73'N, 129°18.55'W

Crane Bay, three miles north of MacDonald Bay on the south shore of Lewis Passage, offers some protection from northwest and outflow winds and chop. However, fishermen report that winds blow through the pass and that Crane Bay receives swells from inflow and outflow winds, making the anchorage rolly.

We found the bay too deep and steep-to for convenient anchorage. In calm weather, anchorage can be taken between Williams Islet and Gil Island over a large 3-fathom flat. Avoid the dangerous rock that lies about 100 yards south of the rock islet near the south center of the pass which dries on a 10-foot tide.

Primordial Wolf Calls

I stood on the foredeck at 0400, wondering what all the commotion was about, shivering with excitement and cold. Somewhere in the dense brush 50 yards away, on the shore of MacDonald Bay, was an alpha-male wolf howling in the dark late August night. The stars were as clear as I had ever seen them. Orion was rising in the east and Cassiopeia and the Pleiades were overhead. Ursa minor and Polaris defied identification due to the abundant lower magnitude stars that filled the cold, clear northern sky.

As I waited on deck, there came another long burst, a four-pitch howl similar to an air-driven lighthouse foghorn needing maintenance. A quick shiver shot through me from head to toe. This wild animal, only yards from me, was a descendant of those who freely roamed the entire North American continent two centuries ago. I was glad I was in my small boat surrounded by a saltwater moat, not camped on shore in a thin nylon tent.

Long howls of slightly varying pitch and duration echoed through the hills, then there was silence as the wolf listened for a reply. Sometimes he gave a few short yelps; sometimes a series of mournful calls, powerful and long-lasting. Was he lonely and longing for the company of the pack or was he broadcasting his position, alerting them to an upcoming feast? His was a 30-minute performance that I shall long remember—a highlight of sailing the waters of northern British Columbia.

—DD

Curlew Bay (Fin Island)

5 mi S of Coghlan Anchorage
Entrance: 53°17.10′N, 129°18.56′W
Anchor: 53°16.71′N, 129°19.36′W

Curlew Bay provides welcome relief from southerly storms or inflow winds, although it is open to the northeast and susceptible to outflow chop. Large boats can anchor at the entrance to the bay in 10 fathoms with plenty of swinging room. Smaller boats anchor at the west side of the narrows in 3 fathoms with limited swinging room. Two grassy beaches on shore can be used as kayak haul-out campsites or for landing a dinghy.

Anchor (west side) in 3 fathoms over a stony, gravel bottom, with fair-to-good holding depending on the set of your anchor.

Brant Bay (Fin Island)

2.7 mi SW of Curlew Bay
Entrance: 53°15.45′N, 129°22.25′W

Brant Bay, on the southwest side of Fin Island, offers good shelter and easy access from northerly or outflow winds. The very head of the bay has a 5-fathom flat where a small boat may find anchorage with limited swinging room.

The bay, however, is open to the southwest and westerly chop enters it. Hawk Bay, immediately to the north, and Curlew Bay on the northeast corner of the island, provide better anchorages in most conditions.

Anchor in 5 fathoms, over a bottom we classify as poor holding.

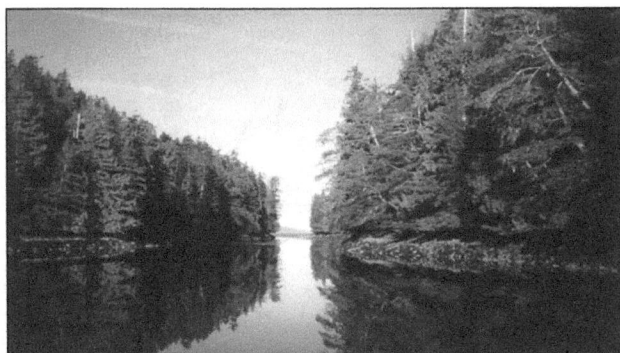

Curlew Bay, looking north

Hawk Bay (Fin Island)

0.75 mi N of Brant Bay
Entrance: 53°16.16′N, 129°22.41′W
Anchor (E): 53°16.24′N, 129°21.24′W

Hawk Bay is a small, picturesque inlet on the west side of Fin Island, 0.7 mile north of Buckle Point. The bay is surrounded by old-growth cedar and silver snags, with some spruce and hemlock. The bay is open to strong westerlies, although moderate westerlies die off before they penetrate the inner basin. The inner basin breaks into two coves: the north cove largely dries, but small boats can find protection from westerlies behind the treed islet, or south of the islets in the eastern cove.

Larger boats, or those wishing more swinging room, can anchor over a flat bottom in the widest part of the bay in 8 fathoms.

Anchor (east) in 4 fathoms over stones, sand, and kelp.

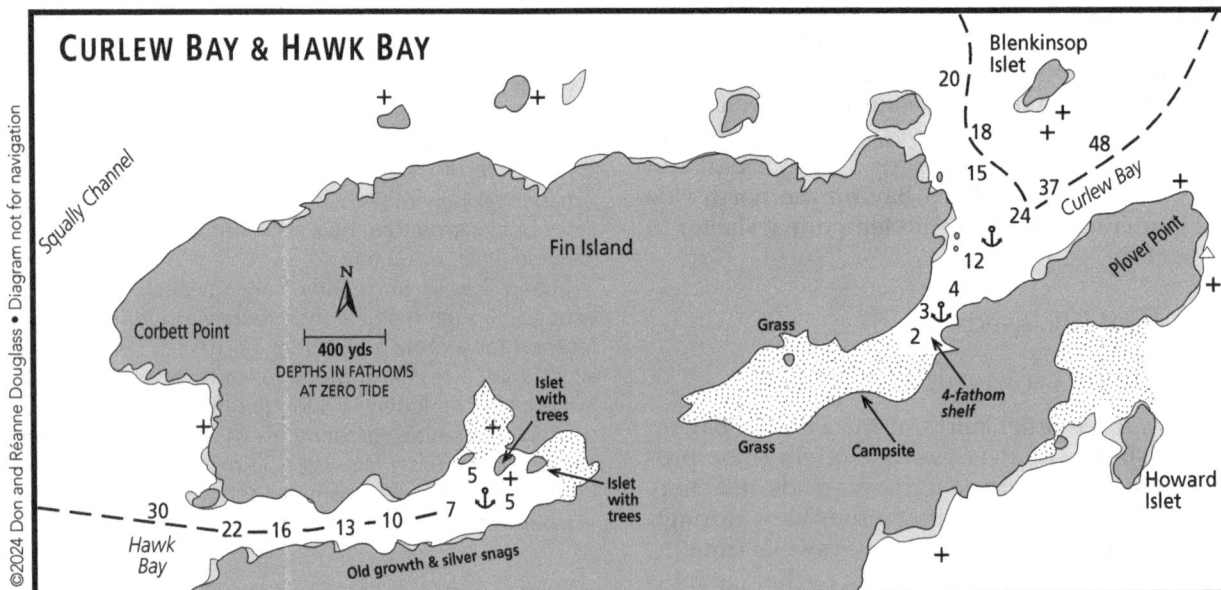

Caption: CURLEW BAY & HAWK BAY map

Tuwartz Inlet (Pitt Island)
4.5 mi W of Fin Island
Entrance: 53°16.75'N, 129°30.07'W

Tuwartz Inlet is an interesting, seldom-visited inlet in the southwest corner of Pitt Island. The best cruising boat anchor sites are located north of Tuwartz Narrows. Anchorage can also be found just north of Wilman Point with good protection in southeast gales.

Tuwartz Narrows (Tuwartz Inlet)
2 mi NW of inlet entrance
Entrance (S): 53°18.36'N, 129°31.42'W

When entering Tuwartz Narrows from the south, favor the west shore to avoid the large mid-channel rock that dries at 15 feet. When you have passed the rock, favor the east shore and keep the three-treed islet at the north end of the entrance on your port hand passing to the east of the islet. Although the channel on the west side of the three islets is wider, the depths there are one fathom or less and it appears to be foul. Current is about 3 knots in the narrows.

Tuwartz Lagoon Cove (Tuwartz Inlet)
NW of narrows
Anchor (3 fathoms): 53°19.31'N, 129°32.83'W
Anchor (7 fathoms): 53°19.26'N, 129°32.41'W

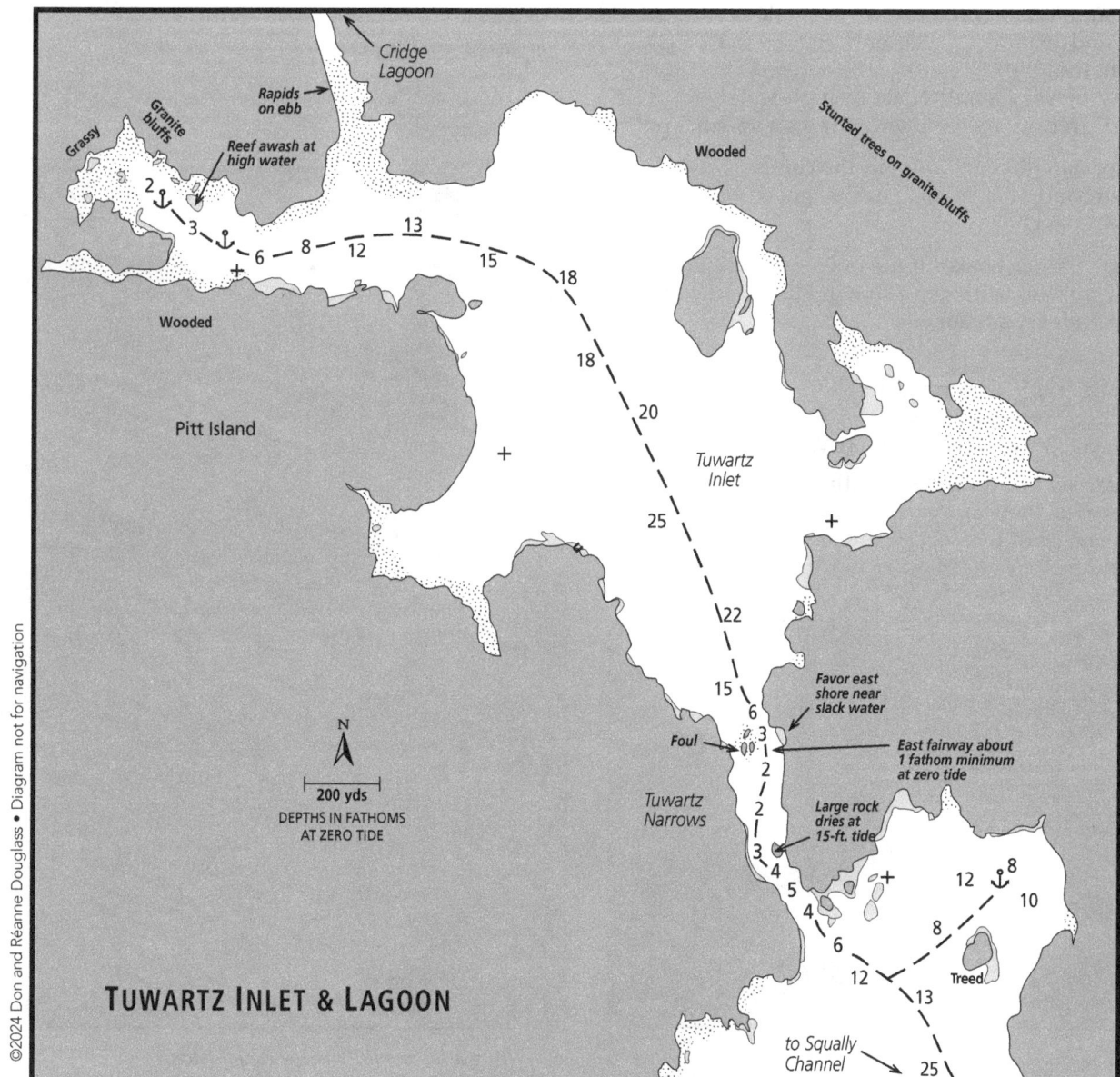

TUWARTZ INLET & LAGOON

"Tuwartz Lagoon Cove" is what we call the well-sheltered cove on the west side of the entrance to Cridge Lagoon. Totally landlocked and calm when gales blow in Squally Channel, the cove has the appearance of an alpine lake near timberline. Bold granite bluffs with stunted trees cover the nearby peaks. At low water, the cove is considerably reduced in size by a number of glaciated rocks covered with golden rockweed. There is no driftwood along the grassy margins of the shore—an added indication of its good protection and remoteness.

Cridge Lagoon is fed by a series of lakes four miles away in the interior of Pitt Island, and the terrain to the north looks like good exploring. The entrance to the lagoon, foul with rocks, can be entered by dinghy or very small boats at high-water slack. Carefully reconnoiter your own anchor spot.

Tuwartz Narrows, looking north

Photo courtesy CHS, Pacific Region

Anchor (small boats only) in the center of the "rock pile" in 3 fathoms, mixed bottom; good holding with a well-set anchor.

Anchor (larger boats) in the outer bay in 7 fathoms, mixed bottom with mud and rocks; good holding with a well-set anchor.

Minnis Bay (Hinton Island)
2.9 mi S of Peters Narrows
Entrance: 53°19.26'N, 129°27.37'W

Minnis Bay is exposed to southerlies that moderate or die off as they approach the head of the bay. Small boats may find temporary shelter at the head of the bay. Mitchell Cove, 2.5 miles north, offers better protection.

Bagan heading north

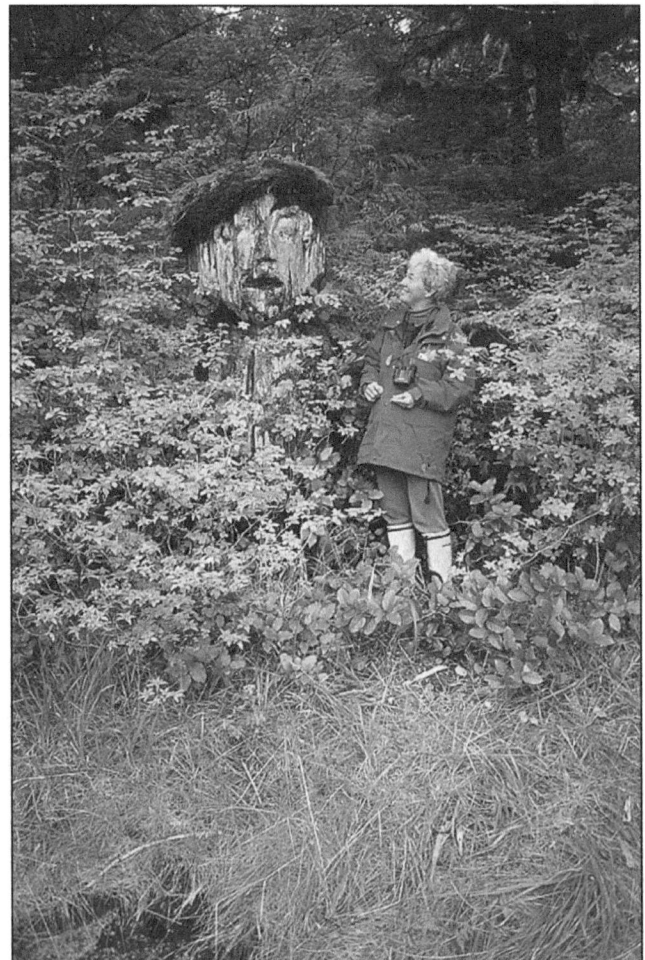
Admiring a totem on Princess Royal Island

Photo by Ron Thiele

Mitchell Cove (Payne Channel)

1 mi SW of Peters Narrows
Entrance: 53°21.76'N, 129°28.22'W
Anchor (two-snag island): 53°21.82'N, 129°28.42'W

Mitchell Cove, at the head of Payne Channel, offers protection from all winds except southerlies, but it is poorly charted. Small boats can find some protection from southerlies by tucking in behind the "two-snag islet" avoiding the rock on the west side of the cove that dries at 6 feet. Larger boats should anchor farther out in 8 fathoms. Those seeking storm shelter would do well to use the cove on the north side of Peters Narrows or the lagoon immediately north which has a large and shallow swinging area with excellent holding. (See Chapter 9, Union Passage area.)

Anchor (two-snag island) in about 6 fathoms over a mixed bottom; fair-to-good holding.

Unbeatable Outer Passage

Commando Inlet, entrance east end

Photo courtesy CHS, Pacific Region

One of the Worst Nights in My Life

I knew a storm was coming, so I tucked *Babine Post* into the southeast corner of Carne Bay in about 15 fathoms. The wind rapidly peaked and kept up for 36 hours. (Bonilla Island reported gusts to 94 knots that night!) Carne Bay was abominable. The gusts in the bay came from northeast to southwest, straight down out of the hills. The boat horsed around so much she swung through more than 240°. She received such violent squalls and heeled so far that galley lockers burst open, spewing everything across the cabin sole. I maintained an anchor watch for 36 hours, regularly refitting the chafing guard and letting out anchor line. During those two days we lost two antennas and a canoe. None of us got much sleep, and we had some bruises, but I can report that the anchor held throughout, and that the bottom is rich dense mud with excellent holding power.

—Kevin Monahan

Normansell Passage, Normansell Islands

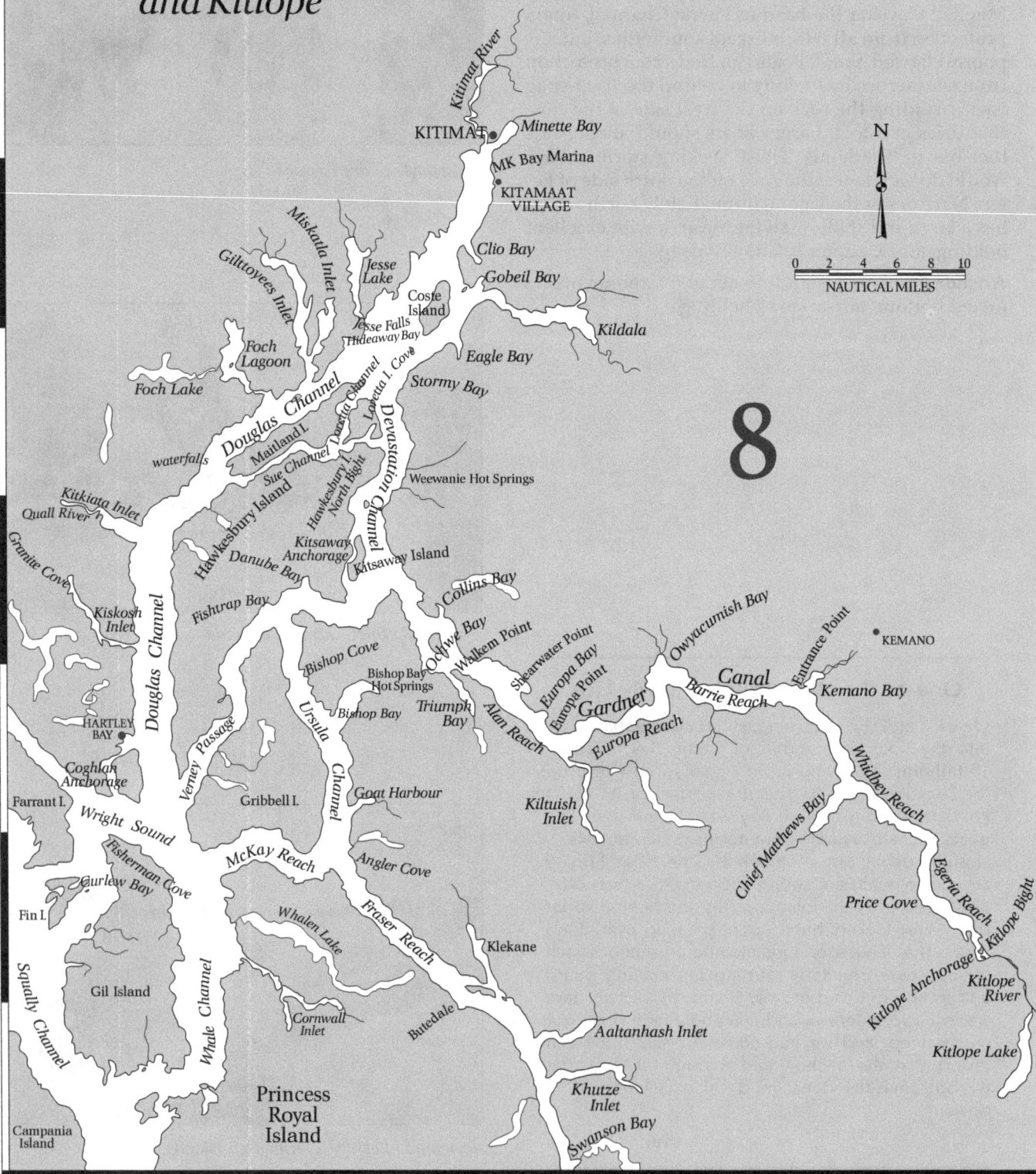

Douglas Channel,
Gardner Canal,
and Kitlope

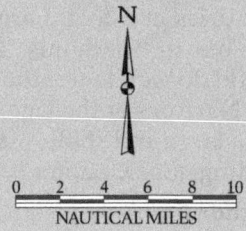

N

0 2 4 6 8 10
NAUTICAL MILES

8

Kitimat River

KITIMAT • Minette Bay

MK Bay Marina

KITAMAAT VILLAGE

Clio Bay

Gobeil Bay

Miskatla Inlet

Jesse Lake

Coste Island

Kildala

Gilttoyees Inlet

Jesse Falls
Hideaway Bay

Eagle Bay

Foch Lagoon

Loretta I. Cove

Stormy Bay

Foch Lake

Douglas Channel

Devastation Channel

waterfalls

Maitland I.

Sue Channel

Loretta Channel

Weewanie Hot Springs

Kitkiata Inlet

Hawkesbury I.
North Bight

Quall River

Hawkesbury Island

Kitsaway Anchorage

Kitsaway Island

Granite Cove

Danube Bay

Collins Bay

Owyacumish Bay

Kiskosh Inlet

Fishtrap Bay

Ocjwe Bay

Walkem Point

Shearwater Point

Europa Bay

Europa Point

Entrance Point

KEMANO

Gardner   Canal

Bishop Cove

Bishop Bay
Hot Springs

Triumph Bay

Alan Reach

Barrie Reach

Kemano Bay

HARTLEY BAY •

Ursula Channel

Bishop Bay

Europa Reach

Europa Reach

Coghlan Anchorage

Verney Passage

Goat Harbour

Kiltuish Inlet

Chief Matthews Bay

Whidbey Reach

Farrant I.

Wright Sound

McKay Reach

Angler Cove

Fisherman Cove

Curlew Bay

Whalen Lake

Fraser Reach

Klekane

Price Cove

Egeria Reach

Fin I.

Squally Channel

Gil Island

Cornwall Inlet

Butedale

Aaltanhash Inlet

Kitlope Anchorage & Kitlope Bight

Kitlope River

Whale Channel

Kitlope Lake

Princess Royal Island

Khutze Inlet

Campania Island

Swanson Bay

10'

54°N

50'

40'

30'

20'

10'

53°N

©2024 Don and Réanne Douglass • Diagram not for navigation

8

Douglas Channel, Gardner Canal, and Kitlope

Some of the most stunning scenery along the north coast of British Columbia lies just miles to the northeast of the Inside Passage. Douglas Channel, which stretches 60 miles from its south end to Kitimat at its head, is one of the longest fiords along the coast; Gardner Canal runs east then southeast to its head at Kitlope—over a hundred miles from the ocean. Wonderful surprises greet visitors of this region: spectacular waterfalls, granite domes and vertical faces, hanging glaciers, turquoise glacial melt, and miniscule plants that peek out of dark granite crevices. The area also hosts three of the best hot springs on the coast—Bishop Bay, Weewanie, and Europa.

Cruising boaters who have shied away from this area as too remote will be happy to find that Hartley Bay, at the south end of Douglas Channel, has fueling facilities. The city of Kitimat (population about 10,000), at the north end of the channel, has a government dock and a full-service pleasure craft

Baidarka enjoys a smooth anchorage—fenders down, awaiting friends

marina, 7 miles south of town at Minette Bay.

At the head of Gardner Channel lies the gem of North American forests—the Kitlope Valley, ancestral home of the Haisla People—considered the world's largest undeveloped coastal temperate rain forest. In 1994, nearly 700,000 acres of this valley, which contains stands of trees over 800 years old, were set aside to protect it against future logging.

McKay Reach (Wright Sound)
11 mi NW of Butedale
Entrance (E): 53°18.30'N, 128°55.76'W
Entrance (W): 53°18.20'N, 129°07.00'W

McKay Reach—the "express route" connecting Princess Royal Channel to Grenville Channel—is out of the major inflow-outflow wind patterns and generally calmer than the south end of Douglas or Ursula channels. Because of this, it frequently collects large patches of driftwood. Keep a sharp lookout when you transit the area.

Ursula Channel (Gribbell Island)
12 mi E of Hartley Bay
Entrance (S): 53°18.90'N, 128°54.77'W

Ursula Channel heads north leaving the ferryboat route into outstanding territory. Popular Bishop Hot Springs lies on the east side of Ursula Channel.

Angler Cove (Ursula Channel)
10 mi S of Bishop Hot Springs
Entrance: 53°18.95'N, 128°53.29'W

Angler Cove, with a small sandy beach on its south side and a favorite campsite for kayakers, offers marginal respite from strong southerly winds that blow northward in Princess Royal Channel. Angler Cove was called Fisherman Cove in Vancouver's time. (Fisherman Cove is actually 15 miles west on the north tip of Gil Island. (See Chapter 9.) Although temporary anchorage can be taken off the sandy beach or the flat to the east, depths are too great for convenience.

Bishop Bay Hot Springs

(Ursula Channel)
20 mi NW of Butedale
Entrance: 53°26.25'N, 128°54.50'W
Anchor (SW of float): 53°28.19'N, 128°50.20'W

Bishop Bay Hot Springs, which sits in a beautiful bowl at the head of Bishop Bay, is a well-known attraction of the Inside Passage. In 2006, the recreation site was established as the Bishop Bay-Monkey Beach Conservancy, an area that encompasses 3374 hectares (8337 acres) of upland and foreshore. The dock is rather short so rafting is encouraged. Boats over 36 feet are asked to anchor offshore after their crew have had their soaks in the hot springs. If you anchor, be careful to avoid a shoal south of the dock.

The original bathhouse was built just above the high tide line by the Kitimat Yacht Club and other private groups. The site now includes the bathhouse, a boardwalk, tent platforms, a pit toilet, and picnic spots.

We hope that Bishop Bay Hot Springs will continue to serve as a pleasant stop along the Inside Passage and that boaters will do their part to keep the area clean and prevent deterioration. Please pack out your refuse as you do everywhere else.

When a major storm front passes, strong westerly winds sometimes penetrate Bishop Bay, rendering the anchorage untenable. On occasion, gale force southwesterlies follow a deep depression.

Anchor southwest of the float in 8 to 15 fathoms over a mixed bottom with fair holding. Avoid the shoal that extends from shore about 100 feet east of the float ramp. Mooring buoy(s) are available south of the dock. There were originally 3 buoys; recent reports indicate only one remains.

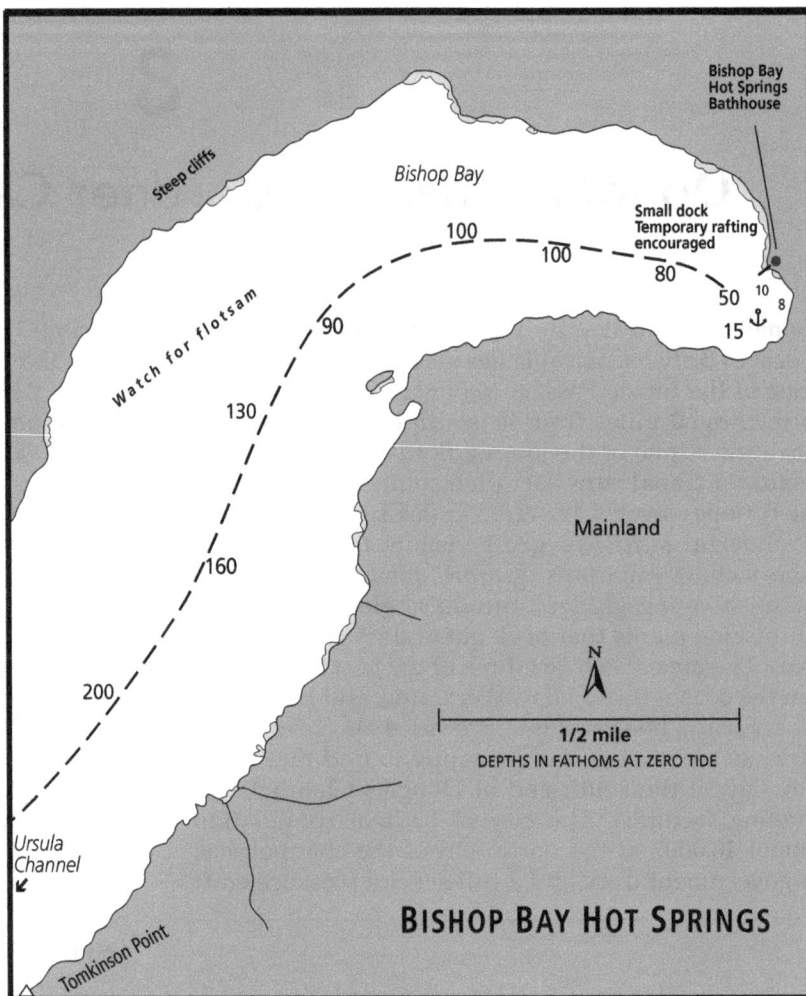

BISHOP BAY HOT SPRINGS

DEPTHS IN FATHOMS AT ZERO TIDE

©2024 Don and Reanne Douglass • Diagram not for navigation

From Vancouver's Voyage of Discovery to the North Pacific Ocean and Round the World, Vol. II, 1798, p. 299

[Editor's note: We have kept the original 18th Century type style used for the double s and st.] . . . *The next morning (june 24th) as they [Whidbey and Johnstone] were preparing to proceed, a ſmoke was diſcovered iſſuing from amongſt the ſtones on the ſhore, that, at low tide, formed a kind of beach. On examination, a run of hot water was found paſſing amongſt the ſtones, which at high tide muſt be at leaſt ſix feet beneath the ſurface of the ſea. They were not able to diſcover its ſource, and having no thermometer, its degree of heat could not be aſcertained. Some of the ſeamen attempted to waſh their hands in it, but found the heat inconvenient. It had the ſaltiſh taſte, and Mr. Whidbey was of opinion, that the rapidity with which it flowed could ſcarecely permit of its receiving its ſavour from the ſea water. Its colour and taſte were thought to reſemble much the waters at Cheltenham.*

—Submitted courtesy of Brian Gisbourne from a copy in the B.C. Archives

Bishop Cove (Ursula Channel)
3.7 mi NW of Bishop Bay
Entrance: 53°29.28'N, 128°58.15'W

Bishop Cove is a bight on the east shore 0.4 mi south of Egerton Point. Fair, temporary anchorage can be found in stable weather close to shore as shown on the diagram. Swinging room is limited. Sport fishing boats can also find temporary shelter from souther-lies in the tiny cove immediately north of Egerton Point.

Verney Passage (Hawkesbury Island)
6.8 mi NW of Bishop Hot Springs
Entrance (SW): 53°22.48'N, 129°09.41'W
Entrance (NE): 53°35.02'N, 128°50.30'W

Verney Passage is a scenic and pleasant way to cross over to Hartley Bay on the way to Grenville Channel. The sill is considered by Kitimat sport fishermen to be the center of a very productive salmon area; there can be significant turbulence here on spring tides.

Fishtrap Bay (Verney Channel)
7.8 mi NW of Bishop Bay
Entrance: 53°32.92'N, 129°01.37'W

Use caution when approaching Fishtrap Bay from the north. Give wide berth to the shoal on the east side of the bay which extends into Verney Channel. The upper end of the shoal is marked by a collection of stumps and trees and by water turbulence at the outer end.

Small sportfishing boats anchor overnight in Fishtrap Bay in fair weather, tucked in behind the stumps, or close to shore in Danube Bay, 3 miles north; or on the southwest side of Kitsaway Island. We prefer Kitsaway Anchorage, seven miles north-east.

Gardner Canal (Devastation Channel)
17 mi N of Princess Royal Channel
Entrance: 53°34.54'N, 128°48.03'W

Gardner Canal is a major fiord of the British Colum-bia coast and, with the exception of clear-cut patches at its west entrance, is perhaps the most pristine and scenic in North America. As soon as you enter Gard-ner Canal, the chop in Devastation Channel dies off and the east-west-lying waterway is calm. Here, the water turns a clear, greenish-blue—glacial melt from the mountains towering above. During spring and summer, a constant overlay of fresh water in the canal creates a continuous ebb that attains 2 knots or more. VHF weather channels die out quickly as you enter Gardner Canal, but it is possible to contact

Bishop Bay Hot Spring soaking tub is covered

Prince Rupert Coast Guard on VHF Channels 16 and 22A throughout most of Alan Reach. East of Europa Point there is no radio reception and anchorages are marginal; mariners should be self-sufficient with fuel and supplies and use caution at all times.

Alan Reach, the first part of Gardner Canal, trends southeastward. High peaks with snow and icefields, seen directly ahead, are the 5,000-foot peaks imme-diately behind the entrance to Kiltuish Inlet. These icefields are remnants of the same glaciers that

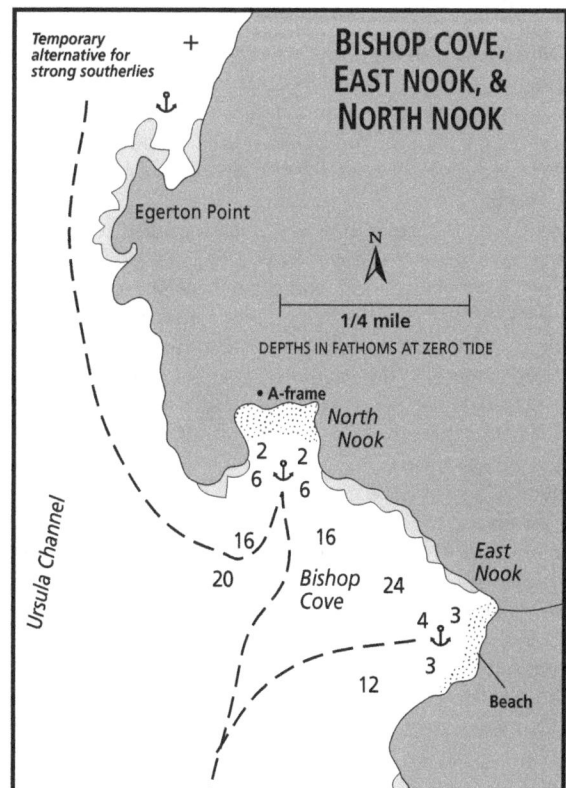

helped carve this great fiord.

At Europa Point, where the canal narrows and some majestic gooseneck turns begin, the saltwater becomes decidedly more milky in color and water temperatures drop to 52°F. Deep grooves in the granite cliffs just east of Europa Point give evidence of the power of the moving glaciers and ice that cut this channel. The walls of the canal become increasingly sheer with vertical slabs that, in places, reach all the way to bare ridges above. Europa Point also marks the end of the severe clearcutting in the western part of the canal.

We call the beautiful area between Europa and Icy Points the "Goosenecks to the Kitlope." Here, there is a continuous ebb of surface current regardless of tide; we have seen it flow as high as 2.5 knots on springs.

Collins Bay

(Gardner Canal)
3 mi E of Staniforth Point
Entrance: 53°32.62'N, 128°43.87'W

Due to its depths, Collins Bay is a marginal anchorage where driftwood lines the beach. We found that the small bight between the creek and the small point on the east side of the bay, where it is slightly less steep-to, could provide temporary anchorage in about 10 fathoms.

The cove off Crab River to the north is sometimes used by locals for temporary anchorage. Although its shores are equally steep-to, fewer drift logs along shore indicate less severe weather.

Gardner Canal: All You Need is a Lot of Anchor Chain and a Bit of Courage.

"Better than Fiordland and Misty Fjords." With that recommendation from a friend who'd visited all three, we had to see Gardner Canal.

As we entered the canal, the water turned turquoise from glacial silt, the hillsides steepened and stately hemlocks and spruce replaced scraggly cedars. Our first anchorage was Europa Bay where we relaxed in the steaming waters of Shearwater Hot Springs while admiring the artful arrangement of stones around the open-sided shelter.

Mists swirled around mountain tops as we pushed farther up Gardner Canal two days later. Sculpted stone walls, u-shaped valleys and imposing rock domes awed us. Near the tops of the 5,000 – 6,000 ft peaks, remnants of the glaciers that once filled these fjords peeked out of the clouds.

In Chief Mathews Bay, we anchored in the southeast corner with a marsh at our bow, deep water at our stern, a sheer rock cliff to port and a fetch of several miles. We put all 275 feet of Osprey's anchor chain out and wished for at least 30 feet more. But our anchor held, even in the offshore breeze. In the morning we woke to the tangy smell of a tide flat just a few feet away. At half-tide-rising tide, we motored the dinghy to the mouth of the Kowesas River where we stopped at Kowesas Lodge, built by the Kitimaat Native village. Inside the unlocked cabin we found varnished floors, tables and chairs, a complete set of kitchen appliances and a full pantry – ready for the next campers.

From the lodge we motored upriver through swirling currents along banks bordered with blue lupine flowers. "I wouldn't want to get into trouble out here," said Steve, as we wound our way through a maze of channels. "It might be a week before somebody came by."

Our next stop was Kitlope Anchorage at the head of the Canal. As we approached, we saw two powerboats anchored off the mouth of the Kitlope River. I looked at the chart plotter, then at the boats. Could they really be anchored in several hundred feet of water? Or had the inlet silted in?

"How much anchor line do you have out?" Steve asked the occupants of one of the boats as we passed. "One hundred fifty feet," was the reply. We eyed the steep angle of the boat's anchor line and noted the 100 feet depth on our sounder. We continued on to the anchorage's southwest corner, putting down 210 feet of chain in 53 feet of water where the chart gave the depth of 50 m (165 feet).

In the morning, low tide revealed a branch of the Kitlope River racing by only 40 feet off our side while fog swirled around the tide flats. We looked down inlet to see the other two boats dragging anchor fast. A radio call confirmed their crews were awake and okay.

Returning down-Canal we stopped at Owyacumish Bay. I paddled my kayak up the Brim River and admired the contrast of stark gray walls, bright green marsh, white clouds and blue sky. When I returned to Osprey, Steve reported we were drifting across what would become shallows at low tide. We up-anchored to try again but everywhere we tried was too deep, except where it was too shallow.

"I'd vote for another soak in the hot springs instead of staying here," I told Steve.

As we left Gardner Canal two days later, we reflected on how few other boats we'd seen. Boaters are missing out on a place of beauty. All you need is a lot of anchor chain and a bit of courage.

—Elsie Hulsizer

Elsie Hulsizer is the author of Glaciers, Bears and Totems: Sailing in Search of the Real Southeast Alaska (Harbour Publishing, 2010) and Voyages to Windward: Sailing Adventures on Vancouver Island's West Coast (Harbour Publishing, 2015).

A relaxing soak! Europa Hot Springs

Baidarka *visits* Poplar II, *Europa Bay*

Europa Bay (Gardner Canal)
11.8 mi SE of Staniforth Point
Entrance: 53°26.74'N, 128°33.59'W

Europa Bay is the local name for the bight between Shearwater and Europa Points. Due to its uneven rocky bottom, anchoring is poor in Europa Bay, but the bay has the hottest springs and most artistically-designed facilities in the area. Rock handiwork at Shearwater, also known as Europa Hot Springs, and the tasteful structure above it, are located on the west side of the bay about 3 feet above the high-water mark. This is by far the most pleasant hot-spring experience on the North Coast.

Anchor in 6 to 12 fathoms over an irregular rocky bottom with poor holding. BC parks added two mooring buoys to the bay in 2010.

Kiltuish Inlet (Gardner Canal)
14.2 mi SE of Staniforth Point
Entrance: 53°24.31'N, 128°31.72'W
Anchor: 53°23.79'N, 128°31.19'W

Kiltuish Inlet is a narrow, shallow inlet that penetrates 6 miles into the south shore at the east end of Alan Reach. High, snow-covered ridges to the south and east create an attractive setting, combined with an ice field that runs southeast from the head of the inlet. The south basin in Kiltuish Inlet is surrounded by snow- and icefields on both sides; a high glacier lies above the Kiltuish River. The current is reported to run at 5 to 6 knots at springs, and the inlet should be entered with care at or near high water, *only after proper reconnoitering.*

In approaching Kiltuish Inlet, be particularly careful to avoid a rock that reportedly dries at 11

A Weather Puzzle

Gardner Canal is a fairly narrow east-west inlet with snow- and ice-capped mountain ranges that generate their own microclimate. Normal summer up- and downslope winds in Douglas Channel tend to peter out before reaching the goosenecks of the canal. Mist and patchy layers of fog, with little or no wind, are the most prevalent summer condition. Bright sunny days are a rare treat.

In general, summer winds are light and variable and only faintly resemble those of the outside in strength and direction. Local boaters tell us that different sections of each arm can have contrary winds, and that winds in Whidbey Reach actually blow from the southeast toward Kemano Bay while, on the outside, they blow from the north. We found that when southeast gales blow in Grenville Channel and Hecate Strait, Gardner Canal experiences little wind. When a low-pressure front moved over Kemano Bay during the night,

and the barometer rose 6 mb, a local 20-knot wind blew up Kemano River for about two hours and the waters became lumpy, before resuming their normally calm conditions.

Trees and branches from the wild Kitlope River, frequent mist and fog patches, and opaque glacial water are perhaps the most pressing hazards in the canal. There is no VHF weather reception in the east end of Gardner Canal, and we have been unsuccessful in raising Prince Rupert Coast Guard on either Channel 16 or 22A—or anyone else! There are no nav-aids or signs of civilization east of Kemano Bay. In Chief Mathews Bay and at the approach to the Kitlope River, there are a number of active avalanche chutes into April or May of each year; the amount of snow and ice they dump into the canal can be as dangerous as icefalls from tidewater glaciers.

—DD

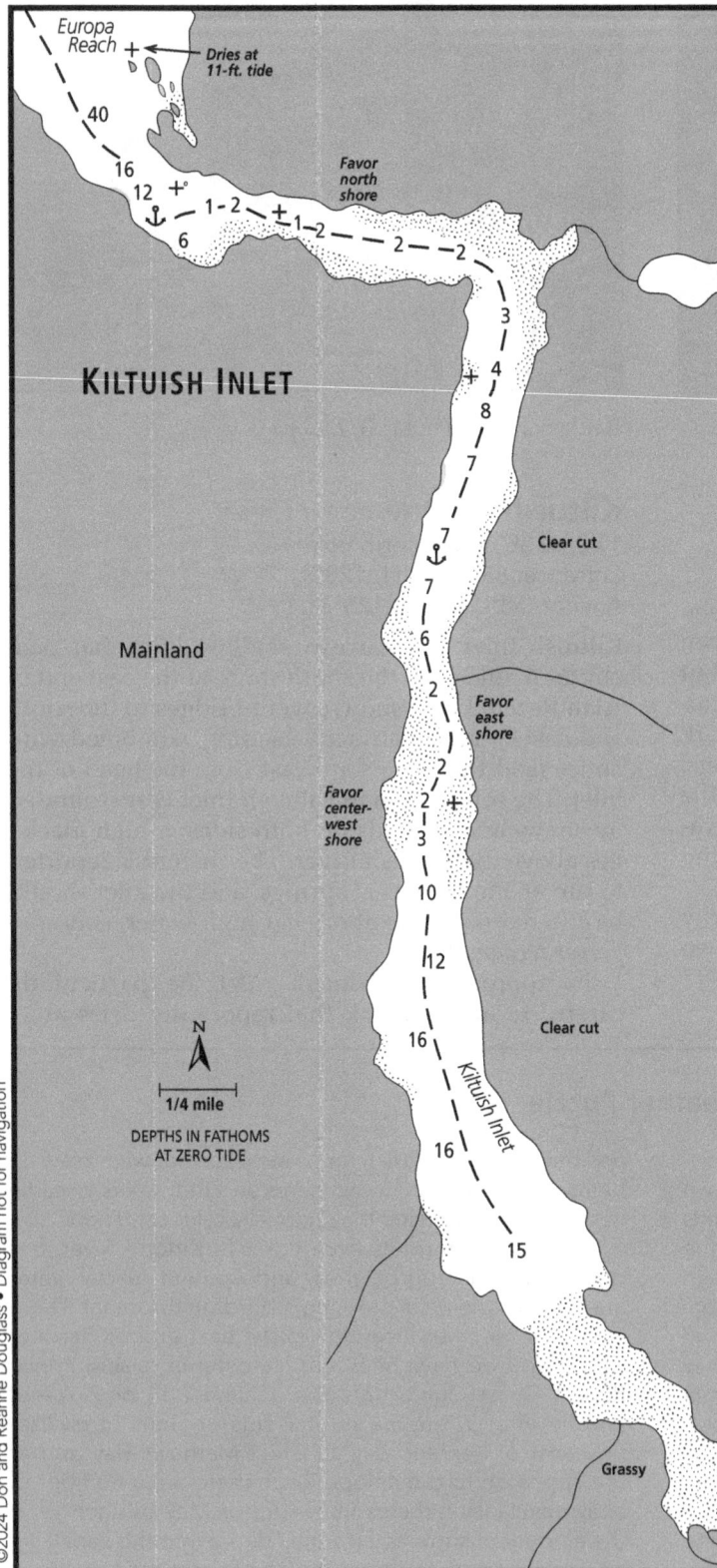

Europa
Reach
Dries at
11-ft. tide
40
16
12
1-2
6
1-2
2
2
Favor
north
shore
3
4
8
7
KILTUISH INLET
7
7
6
Clear cut
2
Mainland
2
Favor
east
shore
Favor
center-
west
shore
2
2
3
10
12
16
Clear cut
N
1/4 mile
16
DEPTHS IN FATHOMS
AT ZERO TIDE
Kiltuish Inlet
15
Grassy

©2024 Don and Réanne Douglass • Diagram not for navigation

Kiltuish Inlet, south of Europa Point

feet about 200 yards northwest of the small islet close north of the north entrance point; this rock is not visible in the glacial water. The submerged rock south of the north entrance point can be detected by the ripple it makes on strong current-flows at lower water.

In entering, keep a mid-channel course through the first narrows, favoring the north and east shore slightly. The irregular bottom at the entrance will give you some anxiety even on high water; we found a minimum depth of about 4 feet at zero tide at the entrance. East of here, the fairway bounces between 2 and 4 fathoms until you reach the deeper sections. The fairway through the second narrows starts from mid-channel, then favors the east side near an obvious white rock slab, avoiding the large shoal that extends from the west shore. South of the slab, begin to favor the west shore to avoid a shoal and rock along the east shore. The milky-green water has limited underwater visibility.

The recommended anchorage near the entrance lies on the south shore just west of the drying treed point. Anchorage can be found close to shore in a small back eddy in 7 to 9 fathoms with about one knot of counter-current. The bottom is steep but holding is good. You may swing round and round with the eddy but you can watch the seals thrashing about as they feed on salmon headed upstream.

Check each site carefully before you anchor in order to properly identify the changing bottom.

Anchor (outside narrows) in 7 to 9 fathoms over silt, mud and sand with good holding.

Owyacumish Bay (Gardner Canal)

16.5 mi E of Staniforth Point
Entrance: 53°29.95'N, 128°22.05'W
Anchor: 53°30.48'N, 128°22.11'W

We feel Owyacumish Bay, known locally as Brim River, is one of the most scenic and enjoyable anchorages imaginable. Located north of Cornwall Point and across from the sharpest of the gooseneck turns, Owyacumish Bay is a delightful place for cruising boats and an excellent haul-out spot for kayakers. The bay which gets little direct chop or high winds is comfortable in fair weather. The Brim River enters the bay from a low valley on the north. On its northeast side, this valley is backed by an impressive high, sheer granite "half-dome." The half-dome is obscured from view in the canal by what we call the abrupt "Wow Ridge" which extends eastward along the banks of the canal. Owyacumish Creek drops into the west side of the bay in a beautiful cascade. In between, there is a grassy shore with little driftwood or storm debris.

In approaching Brim River, avoid the steep-to shoal that extends several hundred yards into the center of the bay and separates the two fresh-water courses. Anchorage can be found on the sloping bottom in front of Owyacumish Bay waterfall in about 5 to 7 fathoms or, as locals suggest, against the east wall in appropriate depths. On neap tides small boats may be able to take advantage of the 3-foot deep, mud-and-shell shelf at the head of the bay on the east side in front of the Brim River.

Anchor (waterfall) in 5 to 7 fathoms over silt and soft mud with fair-to-good holding.

Owyacumish Bay

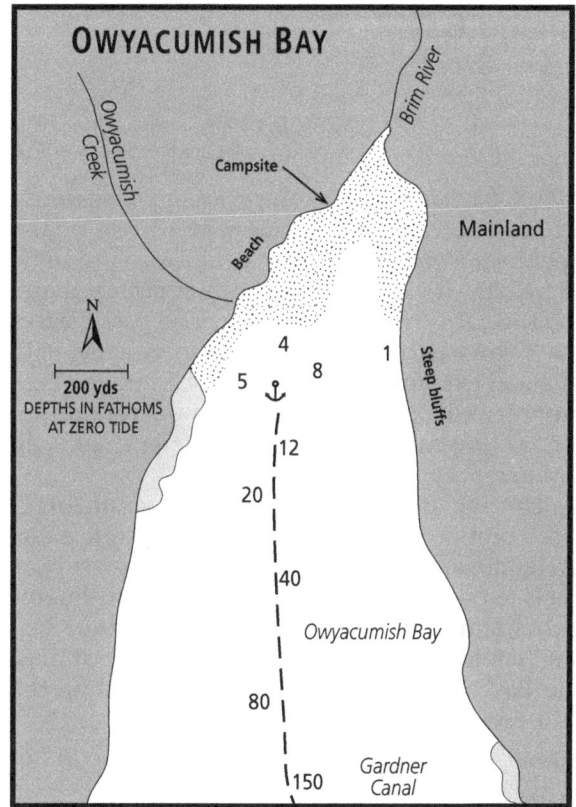

Observations from Owyacumish Bay

We were warned that winds in Gardner Canal are brisk, especially in the afternoon, but during our two-week kayak expedition, it was remarkably calm. Tides rose without a ripple, sometimes catching us unaware.

Owyacumish Bay, where we were camped one night, receives so much fresh input from Brim River that we couldn't taste salt at the surface. Much of Gardner Canal is overlaid with an ebbing fresh-water current several feet deep. This has the perverse effect of allowing fresh-water plant life to grow *below* the high-tide line. Judging the high-water mark at a new campsite was a bit dicey. One night, my friend Tom looked out from his hammock to find himself swinging over the water.

Overland travel was a big difficulty here. We found it almost impossible to travel up creeks, and life-threatening to try to climb above the timber to open alpine areas. Our peak-bagging plans, made in the warmth of our livingrooms studying topo maps, became climbs of Himalayan proportions—45-degree slopes, log jams, lethal berry patches that caused our feet to shoot out from under us just as we tried to contour the cliffs. We managed to climb 2,200 feet one day carrying light packs and had just broken out of the timber when we had to bivouac. It rained that night and the next morning we were socked in by fog, forcing us to descend with worse footing than before.

—David Scharf, Portland, Oregon

Kemano Bay

(Gardner Canal)
25 mi E of Staniforth Point E
Entrance: 53°28.32'N, 128°08.14'W;
Anchor (SE Entrance Bluff): 53°27.90'N, 128°07.28'W

Kemano Bay, behind Entrance Point, is somewhat protected from upslope winds in Gardner Canal by the peninsula on the west. The peninsula is an Indian Reserve. Alcan's powerhouse lies 7 miles up the Kemano River. In an emergency it may be possible to tie at the Alcan wharf, but there are no services available.

A shoal extends 0.2 mile south of Entrance Point. Temporary anchorage can be taken north of Entrance Point, paying careful attention to water depths and river current.

Anchoring depths are reasonable south of Entrance Point peninsula, with protection from Kemano River current and downslope winds; however, the point is exposed to fickle winds of the main channel. A better temporary anchor site is the shallow bight immediately southeast of Entrance Bluff, east of Kemano Bay which receives less wind and chop than the area around the point.

Anchor (southeast Entrance Bluff) in 10 to 20 fathoms over an unrecorded bottom.

Private Alcan docks at Kemano Bay

Chief Mathews Bay (Gardner Canal)

25.5 mi SE of Staniforth Point
Entrance: 53°22.51'N, 128°03.51'W
Anchor: 53°20.17'N, 128°06.18'W

Chief Mathews Bay, in the center of the most beautiful and spectacular part of Gardner Canal, is a center for environmental studies. A beautiful longhouse built by the Haisla people stands at the southwest corner of the river outlet.

Each spring avalanche chutes clear all vegeta-

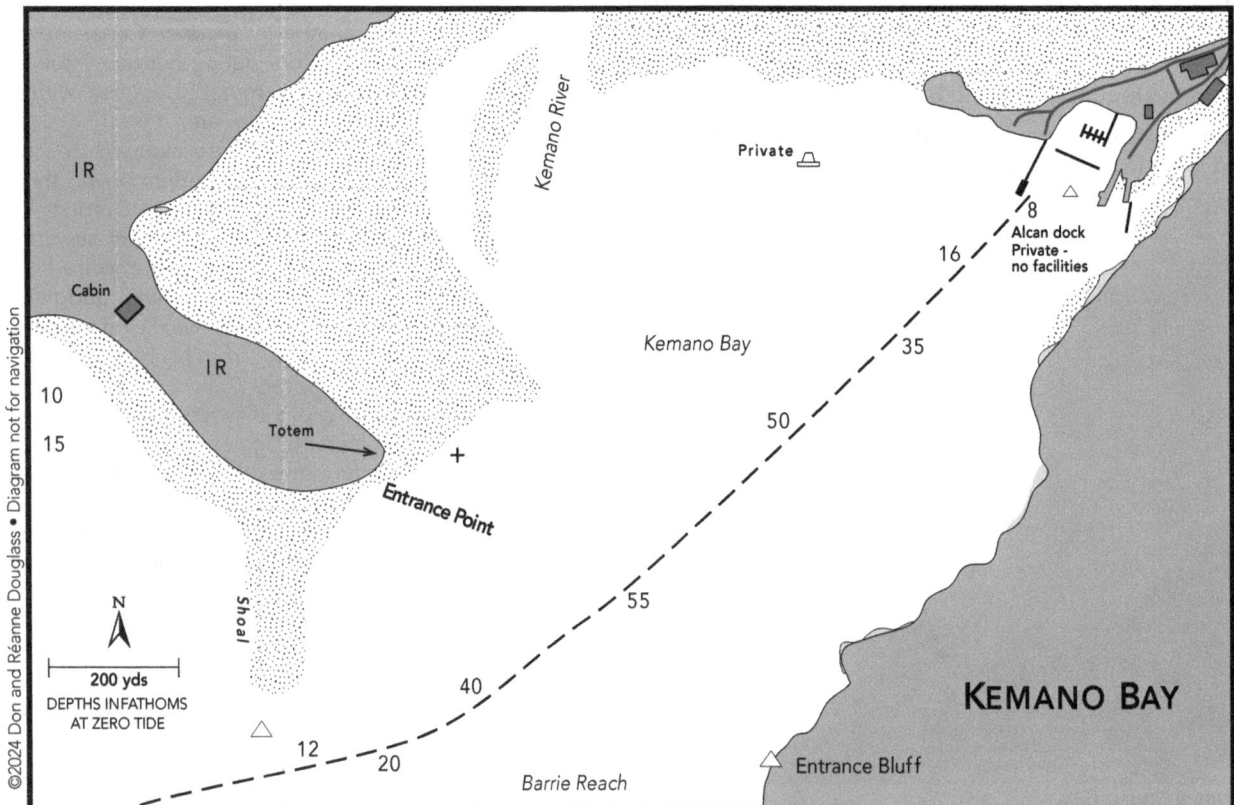

©2024 Don and Réanne Douglass • Diagram not for navigation

IR

Kemano River

Private

Cabin

IR

Totem

Entrance Point

Shoal

N

200 yds
DEPTHS IN FATHOMS
AT ZERO TIDE

12
20

Barrie Reach

10
15

8
Alcan dock
Private -
no facilities

16

35

Kemano Bay

50

55

40

Entrance Bluff

KEMANO BAY

Chief Mathews Bay enshrouded in fog

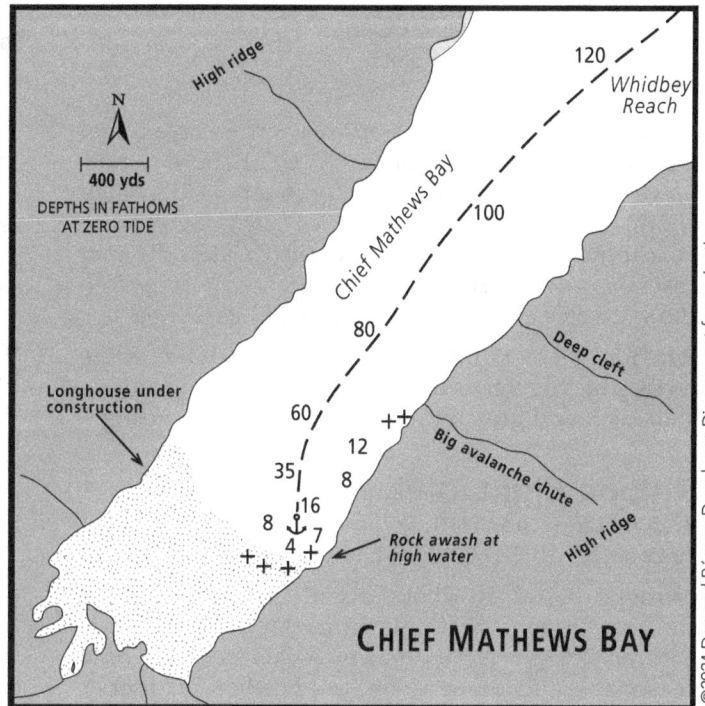

CHIEF MATHEWS BAY

tion from the high ridges down to the saltwater. Hanging glaciers tower over the head and sides of the bay, and the sound of waterfalls lulls you to sleep. This anchor site or Kemano Bay would be the preferred anchor sites for day trips to the Kitlope area. (Less driftwood, current, exposure to wind and chop than the bitter end of Gardner Canal.)

Chief Mathews Bay is less exposed than Gardner Canal itself. You can find fair shelter on the east shore, south of the rock fall, north of the drying flat at its head. Although locals prefer the 12-fathom area just south of the rockfall, we found this place to

be steep-to without any flat surface. We prefer a spot about 0.5 mile south, where you can anchor in about 10 fathoms—a safer distance from shore if you need to let out some scope.

Anchor in 10 fathoms over mud with good holding.

An Engineering Feat: Kemano Generating Station

Talk about an engineering feat—the Kemano Generating Station built by Alcan takes the prize! The Kemano hydro-electric power station was built in the 1950s to provide energy for an aluminum smelter about 50 miles to the northwest, in the town of Kitimat. The smelter's raw material is imported by ship from around the world for processing in Kitimat due to the abundance of relatively low-cost hydroelectric power. The generating project began with construction of the Kenney Dam, which created a 350 square mile reservoir by diverting 75% of the outflow of the Nechako River. At the time of its construction, the Kenney Dam was the largest rock-fill dam in the world. The water exits the reservoir through a ten-mile long tunnel the width of a two-lane highway that was drilled and blasted through the coastal mountains. The tunnel took more than 1,000 workers and twenty months to complete. The water drops 2,600 feet to a generating plant in a cavern that was blasted from solid granite inside the base of Mt. Dubose. The plant produces 896 MW from eight huge generator units. The power is transmitted to the Rio Tinto-Alcan aluminum smelter in Kitimat over 50 miles of transmission lines that cross hazardous terrain, including Kildala Pass (elevation 5,350 feet).

The village of Kemano was built to house the workers and their families from 1952 until 2000. It was a completely self-contained town, with family homes, school, church and recreational facilities for a population of about 280 people. The town was demobilized in 2000 when the the powerhouse was automated and control went to Kitimat. A training exercise involving hundreds of firefighters from across Canada provided valuable experience in fire suppression techniques when the town was destroyed by deliberate fire. There is still a remote work camp and private dock on site, accommodating about 30 shift workers who maintain the power facilities.

Alcan began planning an expansion to the tunnel system in the late 1980s, but the Provincial government withheld permits, delaying the project until a recent restart. Rio Tinto acquired Alcan in 2007. The first phase of a backup tunnel project was completed in 2012. Rio Tinto-Alcan has recently committed nearly US $5 billion to modernize the Kitimat smelter, offering increases in efficiency and production capacity, and reducion of greenhouse gas emissions by more than 50%.

—LW

Price Cove (Gardner Canal)

36 mi SE of Staniforth Point
Position: 53°16.07'N, 127°56.92'W

Although Price Cove is steep-to, we were able to get a good set in about 6 fathoms. With offshore winds, however, holding may be suspect on such a steep shore. A large glacier west of Price Cove is the source of a number of strikingly beautiful waterfalls that cascade down vertical granite faces, dropping into the saltwater along the west shore of Egeria Reach.

Anchor in 6 to 12 fathoms between the outlet of the creek and the vertical crack on the rock face along shore; silt and grey mud with fair-to-good holding.

Kitlope Bight (Gardner Canal)

37.5 mi SE of Staniforth Point
Anchor: 53°15.57'N, 127°54.34'W

"Kitlope Bight" is what we call the tiny bight on the east shore, a half-mile from the drying flats of Kitlope River; it is reported by locals to be the only reasonable anchorage at the very head of Gardner Canal. This bight is said to receive protection from the river's current and from large trees that frequently wash down the river.

We recorded depths between 10 and 20 fathoms, one to three boat-lengths off the steep rocky cliffs. The opaque glacial water gives only one-foot visibility, and we found inconsistencies between the 50kc and 200kc echo sounders. Some of these readings may be due to the incomplete mixture of fresh and saltwater.

Larger boats that have anchored here reportedly set their anchors in 10 to 30 fathoms using a stern-tie to shore. We found two old cables, indicated on the diagram, which may be useful for stern-ties. We had trouble getting a good set in the area between the sheer south wall and the creek to the north. The bottom was silt with occasional bumps indicating rocks or stumps, and our anchor brought up a lot of twigs.

During our first visit to Kitlope Bight, we made a valiant effort to reach the deep hole and possible bombproof anchor site in the lee of a mile-long peninsula extending from the south shore of the Kitlope River. We kept running into dead-end leads on

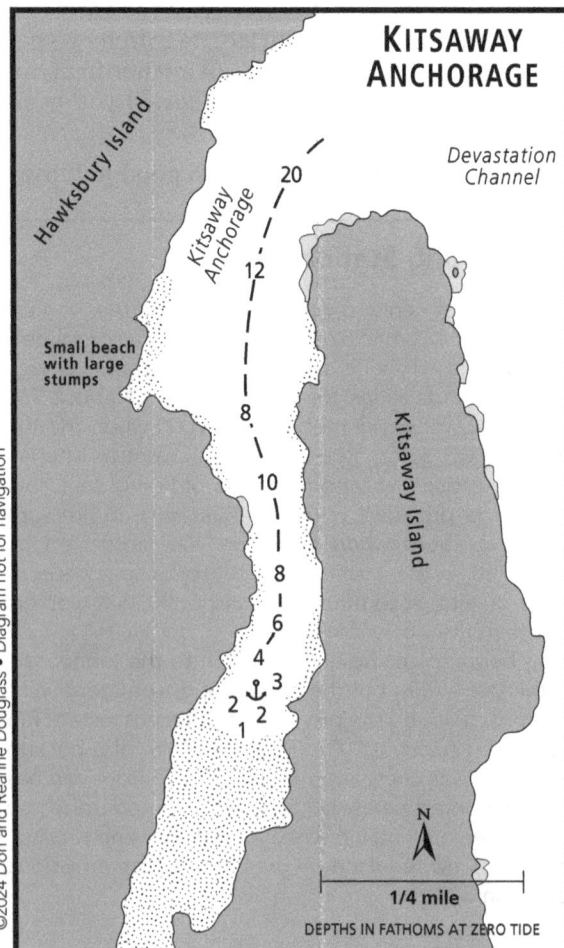

KITSAWAY ANCHORAGE

Hawksbury Island

Kitsaway Anchorage

Devastation Channel

20

12

Small beach with large stumps

8.

10

8

6

4

2 3
1 2

Kitsaway Island

N

1/4 mile

DEPTHS IN FATHOMS AT ZERO TIDE

©2024 Don and Réanne Douglass • Diagram not for navigation

Saving the Kitlope

The Kitlope Heritage Conservancy Protected Area has been found to have *the largest undeveloped coastal temperate watershed in the world*. It was scheduled to be logged, but local community groups and lobbying helped set aside 317,000 hectares of land to be protected from roads and chainsaws.

During this period the local First Nations opposed the logging of this area. Even when offered a share of the profits, they had never accepted the loss of their rights to their ancestral lands. The Haisla were central to the research, planning and lobbying that resulted in saving this priceless treasure, and they are equal partners with the province of British Columbia in its perpetual co-management. —RHD

The Kitlope River meets Gardner Canal

Photo by Ron Thiele

the mud flat and finally gave up. The opaque water and current was too nerve-racking.

Kitlope Valley (Gardner Canal)
38 mi SE of Staniforth Point
Position: 53°14.53'N, 127°54.24'W

Kitlope Valley, (the Kitlope Heritage Conservancy) is considered to be the world's largest undisturbed coastal temperate rain forest. In 1996, 795,700 acres (322,020 ha) were set aside as a reserve to protect this area. The valley which lies inland from the mouth of the Kitlope River is jointly administered by BC Parks and the Haisla. The region falls within the Haisla Nation which welcomes visitors and gives guided tours during the summer months. Their name for the valley (Husduwachsdu) means "source of the milky blue waters" and we can attest to that after viewing the outlet of the river.

Another organization based in the Kitlope is the Haisla Nation Rediscovery Society that sets up camp on the beach at Kitlope Lake. The group welcomes youths and adults of all peoples to participate in their rediscovery camp which highlights Haisla culture. For information, see haisla.ca or phone 250.639.9361.

Kitsaway Anchorage (Devastation Channel)
4 mi NW of Staniforth Point
Entrance: 53°37.72'N, 128°52.25'W
Anchor: 53°36.35'N, 128°52.65'W

Kitsaway Anchorage, which is deep and well sheltered with excellent protection from southerly storms, appears to be subject to just moderate chop on outflow conditions. We prefer to anchor deep in the bay off the drying grassy flat. The water is opaque, so you need to monitor your echo sounder carefully. Notice the size of some of the old stumps on the small beach halfway down the bay.

Anchor in 2 to 3 fathoms deep in the bay over oozy, soft mud with grass and shells; use a soft touch when you set your anchor in this soft bottom.

Weewanie Hot Springs Provincial Park (Devastation Channel)
7.6 mi N of Staniforth Point
Entrance: 53°41.78'N, 128°47.52'W

Weewanie Hot Springs was designated a Provincial Park in 2004, and for the improvements, we must thank Kitimat Aquanauts Scuba Club. There is now a Plexiglas window in the hot springs hut that allows you to keep your eye on your boat as you're soaking. In addition to the cement bathhouse, the park has a pit toilet and a small campsite with a picnic table. There are two tubs side by side, a smaller one for washing yourself, and a larger one for soaking. Protocol calls for opening the valve on the outside of the hut and draining the smaller tub while you're soaking in the larger one. Don't forget to close the valve before you leave so the washing tub fills up again. If you feel the need to take any containers inside, please remember to pack everything out with you, along with any refuse "inadvertently" left by others.

You can land your dinghy on the gravel beach at the head of the cove and take the trail that leads west past a picnic and campsite area to the bathhouse. Or, at high tide, you can take your dinghy to the rocks

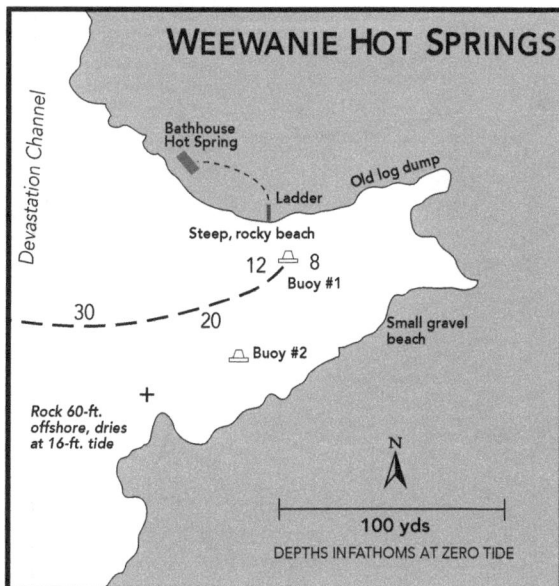

WEEWANIE HOT SPRINGS

Devastation Channel

Bathhouse Hot Spring

Ladder

Old log dump

Steep, rocky beach

12 ⚓ 8
Buoy #1

30   20

⚓ Buoy #2

Small gravel beach

Rock 60-ft. offshore, dries at 16-ft. tide

N

100 yds

DEPTHS IN FATHOMS AT ZERO TIDE

©2024 Don and Réanne Douglass • Diagram not for navigation

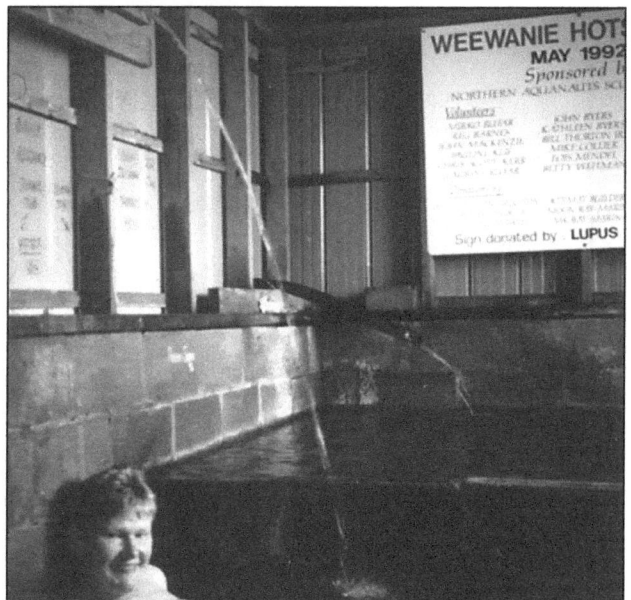

"I could stay here forever . . ."

directly below the bathhouse and tie to a log.

One buoy in the cove offers convenient moorage. Entering the cove is easy; however, watch for a rock that dries at about 14 feet, 60 feet off the south point.

Anchoring is possible between the buoy and the head of the bay in 6 to 12 fathoms, over a rocky bottom with poor holding.

Sue Channel (Hawkesbury Island)
8.9 mi N of Staniforth Point
Entrance (NE): 53°42.92'N, 128°49.95'W
Entrance (SW): 53°40.77'N, 128°04.68'W

Sue Channel, a convenient route for cutting across to Douglas Channel, gives a fast ride down-channel on ebb current, especially with a tailwind. The flip side is that an upslope wind can create a nasty chop. In case of bad weather, you can find anchoring sites in two places. The first, at the head of the bay on the south side of Loretta Island; the second is in Hawkesbury Island North Bight.

Loretta Island Anchorage
(Sue Channel)
9.5 mi N of Staniforth Point
Entrance: 53°43.29'N, 128°51.67'W
Anchor: 53°43.83'N, 128 50.82'W

Very good protection from outflow winds, as well as southeast winds, can be found on the south side of Loretta Island at the head of the bay.

Anchor in 10 to 16 fathoms over mud with good holding.

Hawkesbury Island North Bight
(Sue Channel)
8.8 mi NW of Staniforth Point
Anchor: 53°42.44'N, 128°53.59'W

"Hawkesbury Island North Bight" is our name for the bay located directly south of the west tip of Loretta Island. We've tried out this anchorage in a

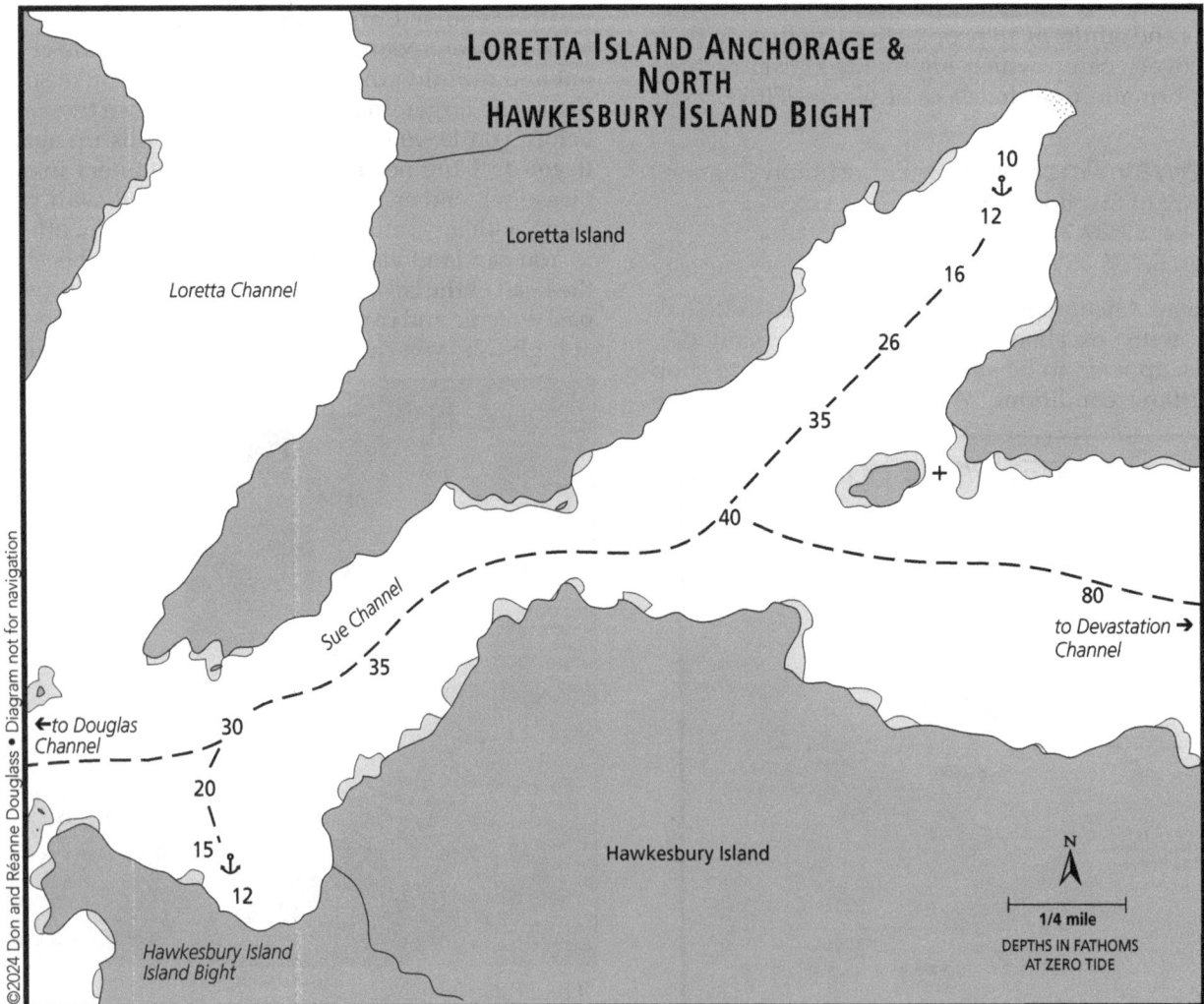

LORETTA ISLAND ANCHORAGE & NORTH HAWKESBURY ISLAND BIGHT

Loretta Island

Loretta Channel

Sue Channel

←to Douglas Channel

to Devastation → Channel

Hawkesbury Island

Hawkesbury Island Island Bight

1/4 mile

DEPTHS IN FATHOMS AT ZERO TIDE

©2024 Don and Réanne Douglass • Diagram not for navigation

southerly blow and found it almost calm. Although the water is deep, we felt little strain on our anchor.

Anchor in 12 to 15 fathoms over a hard bottom with fair holding.

Stormy Bay
(Devastation Channel)
12.3 mi N of Staniforth Point
Entrance: 53°46.40'N, 128°48.25'W

Stormy Bay, the local name for a tiny notch on the north side of Hopkins Point at the entrance to Devastation Channel, offers emergency shelter for *small sportfishing boats* that need to get out of severe upslope chop or wind. This very shallow notch, which is only about 120-feet wide, has a rock pile at its head, with large drift stumps, evidence of strong downslope winds.

We found the bottom to be entirely stony. A couple of sportfishing boats could fit into the middle of the notch over a bottom that nearly dries at zero tide. You may be able to use stern-ties to the small trees on the white rocky shore. A single small cruising boat might find temporary shelter at the entrance in one fathom, but you would need to keep a constant anchor watch and use one or two stern ties to shore.

Anchor in 1 fathom over a stony bottom with poor holding.

Eagle Bay
(Amos Passage)
10.6 mi S of Kitimat
Entrance: 53°48.97'N, 128°42.75'W
Anchor: 53° 48.02'N, 128° 42.36'W

Eagle Bay is one of our favorite anchorages in Kitimat Arm. The bay gives good shelter and is an attractive anchorage with a view of a high snowy ridge. Small boats can anchor near the head of the bay on a flat 3- to 5-fathom shelf. Larger boats can anchor just outside the shelf with plenty of swinging room. Avoid the rocky bottom on the west shore off the creek outlet.

At the entrance to Eagle Bay, the outflow of a large creek on the east shore creates a shallow flat with stones and mud that makes a good kayak haul-out point. However, give it wide berth if you're going to the head of the bay. There's a light gravel beach at the head of the bay with a few drift logs where you can land your dinghy. Avoid the rock awash on a 10-foot tide, approximately 100 feet off Legeak Point.

Anchor in about 5 fathoms over dark mud with very good holding.

Kildala Arm (Douglas Channel)
8 mi S of Kitimat
Entrance: 53° 51.56'N, 128° 40.55'W

Kildala Arm has a striking skyline to the east with several sharp peaks that jut above large permanent snowfields.

Closer in, the steep sides are tree-lined to the top. High-tension power lines for the Alcan smelter in Kitimat cross the head of the arm on their way, and many slopes show the loggers' handiwork. The arm is somewhat protected from heavy weather, but the north shore may be taken up by log-boom storage.

Gobeil Bay
7.5 mi S of Kitimat
Entrance: 53°52.02'N, 128°40.73'W
Anchor: 53°52.59'N, 128°40.35'W

Gobeil Bay, on the north side of Kildala Arm, is known locally as Mud Bay. Although open to the south, it can offer quiet anchorage in fair weather in a 6-fathom hole deep in the bay between the west shore and the drying creek delta. Its shores are steep-to and swinging room is limited, so larger boats would need a stern-tie to shore. The bay is open to wake from passing work boats, but upslope chop is somewhat diminished by the lee formed by Coste Island.

Anchor in 6 fathoms over soft mud with twigs; good holding.

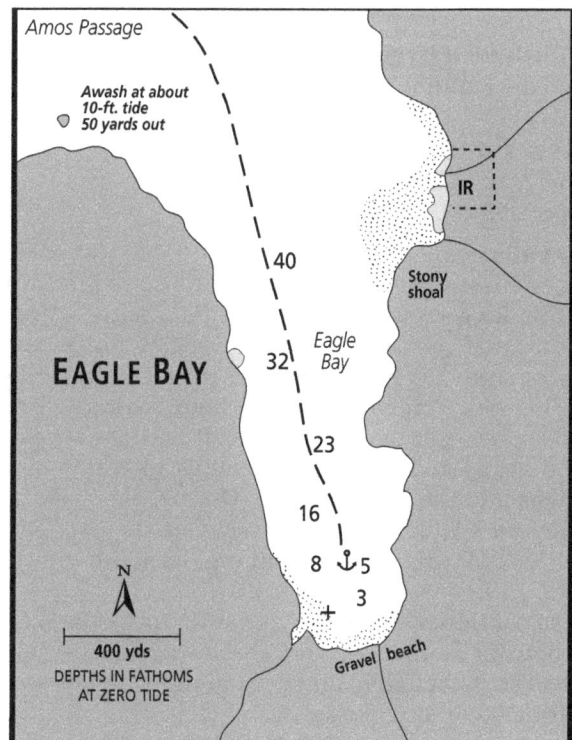

Looking north, Kitimat Arm

Atkins Bay (Kildala Arm)
4.5 mi E of Gobeil Bay
Position: 53°50.85'N, 128°33.63'W

Atkins Bay is steep-to with a beach that drops off at a 45° slope. The only possible anchorage would be with a shore tie along the west shore of the bay. On a clear day, there is a great view to the east of high, snowy peaks. This site does offer some shelter from upslope winds behind the peninsula.

Kitimat Arm
(Douglas Channel)
11.6 mi SE of Kitimat
Entrance: 53°49.01'N, 128°50.00'W

Kitimat Arm is the extension of Douglas Channel that reaches to Kitimat at the outflow of Kitimat River. Watch for a large, mid-channel weather buoy just inside the Kitimat Harbour limit east of Hilton Point.

Jesse Falls (Kitimat Arm)
5.6 mi W of Eagle Bay
Position: 53°50.03'N, 128°51.86'W

Jesse Falls is one of the more remarkable waterfalls on the British Columbia coast. The falls are fed from six-mile-long Jesse Lake, held in by a natural rock dike located just above the high-water mark over which massive volumes of water tumble into Douglas Channel. You can carefully land a dinghy and climb up the slippery granite wall on the east side of the smaller of the two waterfalls to watch as it plunges into the Pacific Ocean. *Use extreme caution if you do climb up to the lake; the rocks are slippery!* Don experienced this when climbing back down the wall.

Use caution, also, when you motor near the falls; the bottom is uneven and shallow, and the falls cause a strong current and a shoal that extends well out into Douglas Channel.

Jesse Falls; Jesse Lake to right, Douglas Channel to left

Kitamaat Village (Kitimat Arm)
0.9 mi S of MK Marina
Position: 53°58.06'N, 128°39.12'W

Kitamaat Village, the primary residence of the Haisla First Nation, is located 11km south of Kitimat, on the east side of Kitimat Arm. Visitors will find a marina, a number of First Nations' artisan shops, and cafes in the village.

The Haisla are actively leading the region in eco- and adventure tourism.

MK Bay Marina
1.4 mi SE of Kitimat Terminal
Entrance: 53°59.04'N, 128°39.27'W

MK Bay Marina, an attractive marina, open all year and located on the east side of Kitimat Arm north of Kitamaat Village, can handle pleasure boats of all sizes. MK Bay has 140 slips with full amenities that include water and 20, 30, & 50 amp power on concrete floats, laundry and shower facilities, ice, and fuel. Monitors VHF channel 68. Used oil disposal, a boat-launching ramp, large parking lot for boaters with trailerable boats, and a convenience store.

The marina is located 11 kilometers from town—a good bicycle ride—but a bit far if you're carrying groceries or supplies. Taxi service is available, but you can sometimes hitch a ride with a local.

Telephone: 250-632-6401; email: contact@mkbay.ca; website: mkbaymarina.ca

Minette Bay (Kitimat Arm)
0.6 mi N of MK Marina
Entrance: 53°59.40'N, 128°39.65'W
Position (float): 54°01.60'N, 128°36.67'W

Minette Bay, accessible only at high water, has a private float used for a few commercial and pleasure craft. An active log dump is just south of the float.

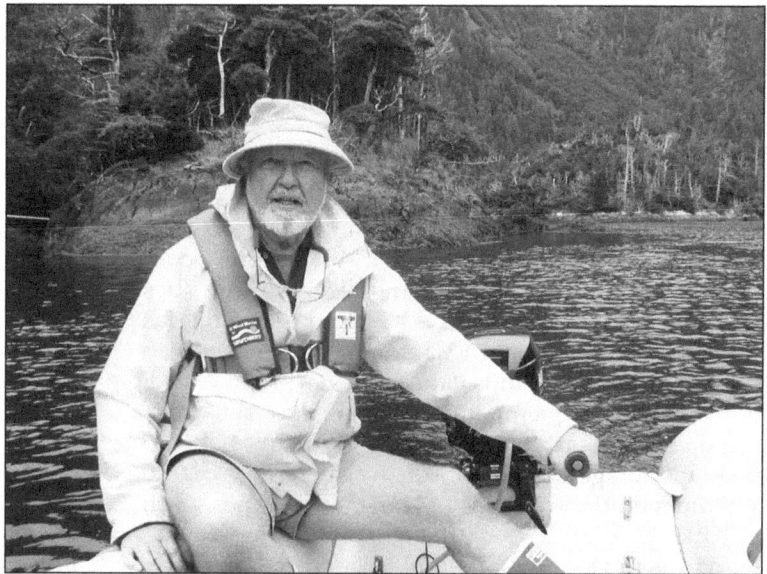

Don exploring the backwaters.

Kitimat Harbour (Kitimat Arm)
44 mi NE of Grenville Channel
Position (Yacht Club): 53°59.96'N, 128°41.58'W

Kitimat, a community of about 10,000, is quite attuned to outdoor activities, and in the last decade it has made a big push to develop tourism for both land- and water-users. Sportfishing—both saltwater and freshwater—is reputed to be some of the best in British Columbia waters. Kayaking, whale watching, camping, and hiking are all popular activities in the area. For more information about the entire area, contact Kitimat Visitor Centre, tel: 250-632-6294 or 1-800-664-6554 (within North America). Their staff is efficient, helpful and friendly!

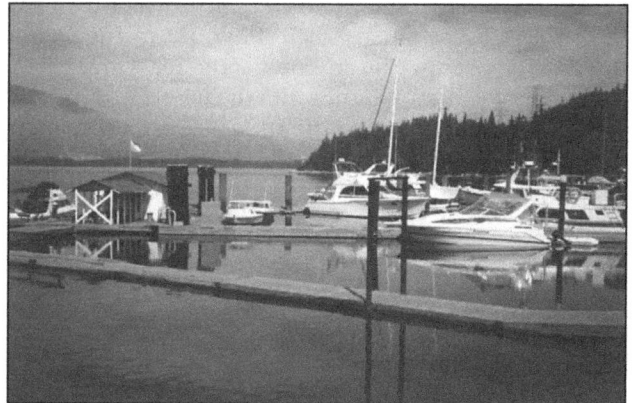

MK Bay Marina, east side Kitimat Arm

Jesse Falls

Jesse Falls, a prominent landmark for boaters in the Douglas Channel, is the spectacular end to the world's shortest river. Jesse Lake turns very briefly into a hungry current before roaring 20 to 30 meters down into the ocean.

A young Kitimat teacher once underestimated the power of Jesse Falls. Tania Chisholme, outfitted in a wet suit, was enjoying a swim in Jesse Lake near the falls when the current overpowered her and swept her over the main falls. She was spotted just once before she finally came to the surface in the channel off the falls and was rescued. She was badly injured but fortunately lived to tell the tale.

I was in my early teens when I had my first canoeing experience at Jesse Lake. Portaging gear up to the lake across the rock face next to the falls was tough work, but it was well worth it because very few people ever make this trip. My brother and I spent a week exploring the lake and gorging on its trout supply. Most of the lake's shoreline is steep and rocky, yet the trees and brush are quite dense right to the water's edge. A substantial river [Jesse Creek] feeds into the far end of the lake, about 8 kilometers from Douglas Channel. The only feasible campsites with sandy beaches are found at this end. About one kilometer up the river, amongst stands of massive old-growth forest, is Jesse's best-kept secret, a most impressive waterfall.

—Norman Wagner, Kitimat Guide

In 2005, Jesse Falls and Lake were designated a Protected Area that encompasses 32 hectares (79 acres).

Douglas Channel

Route to Kitimat
Entrance (S): 53°22.06'N, 129°11.72'W
Entrance (N): 53°48.00'N 128°52.00'W

Douglas Channel deserves serious respect year round. In the summer months, prevailing westerlies funnel up the channel, often reaching gale force and raising seas of 4, 6, or even 8 feet. When inflow conditions are expected (i.e. during clear, sunny skies June through September), it is best to transit Douglas Channel before noon. In winter, and sometimes in summer, outflow winds can reach storm force and, with subfreezing temperatures, can cause severe icing on small craft. It's possible for cruising boats to take advantage of a north-setting current of one to 1.5 knots on the west side of Douglas Channel south of Kitkiata Inlet.

Winds in Douglas Channel blow from two directions—in and out. Low pressure over the British Columbia interior plateau, caused by intense summer-time heating, causes air to rise and winds to roar up Douglas Channel. In Arctic outflow conditions, the cold interior causes air to flow out of the inlets toward the ocean. The channel is the termination of a long valley that extends northeast from Kitimat to Terrace all the way to the interior plateau. Listen for weather conditions at Nanakwa Shoal (one mile east of Jesse Falls). Due to its unique weather patterns, Douglas Channel has its own Marine Weather Forecast Area.

Hideaway Bay (Douglas Channel)

0.8 mi SW of Hilton Point
Entrance: 53°48.56'N, 128°53.71'W
Anchor: 53°48.52'N, 128°53.90'W

Hideaway Bay is the local name for the small notch, 0.9 mile southwest of Hilton Point (not to be confused with the larger, deeper cove west of Hilton Point). The roughest water in Douglas Channel can be found at the intersection of Kitimat Arm and Devastation Channel. Hideaway Bay, and Stormy Bay on the east shore, both offer protection from southerly storms or excessive chop in the channel.

White rocks on both sides of the notch mark the entrance point. The head of the notch dries and has a steep-to flat; do not proceed beyond the white-capped rock on the east shore which is 2 feet above high water. The northern half of the bay has a nearly flat 5- to 7-fathom bottom with swinging room for a couple of boats.

Anchor in 6 fathoms over grey mud with shells, good holding.

Gilttoyees Inlet

(Douglas Channel)
27.4 mi NE of Grenville Channel
Entrance: 53°45.42'N, 128°59.72'W
Anchor (outer anchorage): 53°46.89'N, 128°56.87'W

Gilttoyees Inlet is a beautiful inlet with high peaks and steep granite faces above both shores. Snowfields and perpetual icefields hang on the north side of the 4- to 5,000-foot peaks. Alas, depths in this inlet are too great for convenient anchoring, with little shelter along its sheer walls, although there may be anchorage at the head of the narrow bay halfway up the east shore.

Anchorage can be found in fair weather on a 3-fathom shelf in the entrance, 0.9 mile north of Point Ashton; protected from downslope winds, this spot is open to the southwest. From here you can conveniently explore Gilttoyees or Miskatla inlets.

Anchor (outer anchorage) in 3 fathoms over a stony bottom with grey silt and broken shells; holding is fair-to-good depending on how well your anchor is set.

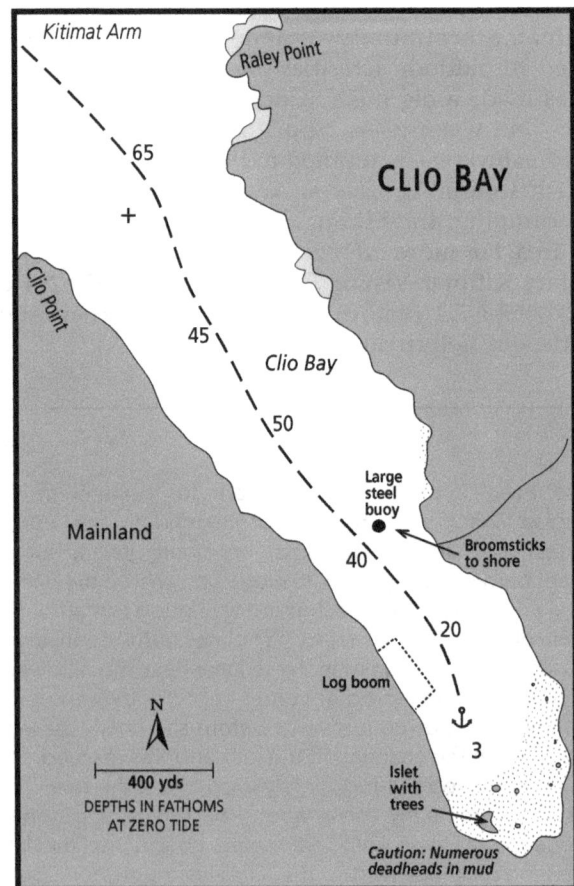

Kitimat Arm
Raley Point
65
+
Clio Point
45
Clio Bay
50
CLIO BAY
Mainland
Large steel buoy
Broomsticks to shore
40
20
Log boom
N
3
Islet with trees
400 yds
DEPTHS IN FATHOMS AT ZERO TIDE
Caution: Numerous deadheads in mud

©2024 Don and Réanne Douglass • Diagram not for navigation

Gilttoyees Inlet

Foch Lagoon, looking out at entrance

Miskatla Inlet (Douglas Channel)

1.7 mi N of Ashton Point
Entrance: 53°47.75'N, 128°57.34'W
Anchor (inlet head): 53°50.97'N, 128°55.25'W

Miskatla Inlet lies immediately east of Gilttoyees Inlet, and they share a common entrance. The western shore of Miskatla Inlet is high and bold; the eastern shore is lower and flat in places. There may be good anchorage at the head of the inlet in 8 fathoms. Fishermen report that the charted anchor site at the mouth of Miskatla Inlet provides a pleasant stay in moderate summer weather when there are upslope evening winds.

Anchor (inlet head) in 8 fathoms; unrecorded bottom.

Anchor (fishermen's site) in 14 fathoms over an unrecorded bottom with good holding.

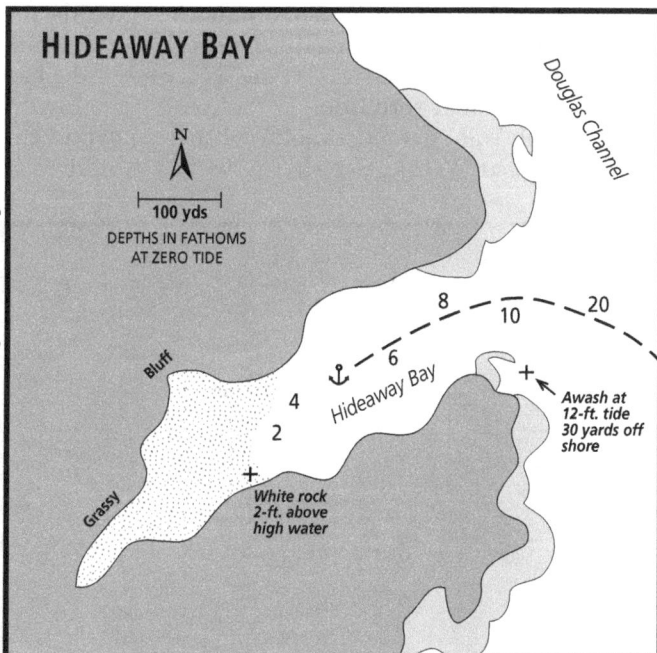

Foch Lagoon, Drumlummon Bay

(Douglas Channel)
25.7 mi NE of Grenville Channel
Entrance: 53°45.84'N, 129°01.49'W

Foch Lagoon, nearly 6 miles long, is one of the largest lagoons on the coast and also one of the best-kept cruising secrets. High granite peaks, with snowfields that melt and cascade into the saltwater, form the backdrop to this lagoon. Islands, islets, cliffs, waterfalls and a major river make Foch Lagoon a destination for cruising boats that want to visit pristine wilderness.

The fairway follows a mid-channel course through the narrows, and rocks lie on either side. The very strong currents make control difficult. Arrive early in Drumlummon Bay, anchor, and reconnoiter for slack water for that day's tidal range. We have not researched good anchor sites here; however, this deep land-locked lagoon may have a number of shore stern-tie possibilities.

Kitkiata Inlet (Douglas Channel)

15.8 mi NE of Grenville Channel
Entrance: 53°37.35'N, 129°14.11'W

The shore of Kitkiata Inlet is steep-to with little chance for anchoring except off the large drying mud flat. Fishermen report that Kitkiata is an exposed anchorage and not a good choice in doubtful weather. A bridge that crosses the outlet to Kitkiata Creek allows access to the log dump on the north side of the bay.

The waterfall is not only conspicuous, it is a majestic sight as it tumbles down, step after step. There is also a perfectly round, U-shaped bowl across the channel from Kihess Creek, and a double waterfall in the next valley north. From Kitkiata Inlet northward, the water in Douglas Channel becomes more opaque from silt and glacier melt.

The Quaal River flows into Kitkiata Inlet's west

Pacer Chant *hauling bauxite to Alcan smelter, Kitimat*

Entrance to Kiskosh Lagoon

end. On an 8-foot tide or better, a small outboard-powered boat can travel 8 kilometers up-river; a canoe can travel almost 12; be careful not to get stranded in the river or drying flats on a falling tide. Favor the south shore at the river outlet. The best time to explore the river is on a rising tide in the morning, and it's worth a visit! The river, which follows a series of oxbows for at least 8 kilometers, is backed by high mountains and bordered by meadows where you may catch sight of a moose.

The inlet is a poor anchorage which has one of the most extensive areas of mud flats on the North Coast. The distance from the river mouth to the edge of the flats is almost 2 miles. On a rising tide, in a canoe or kayak drifting above these intertidal waters in just one or two feet of water, you can watch sole, flounder and crab carry on their daily lives.

Kiskosh Inlet (Douglas Channel)
9.6 mi NE of Grenville Channel
Entrance: 53°30.91'N, 129°14.05'W
Anchor (bar): 53°30.85'N, 129°16.06'W

Strategically located Kiskosh Inlet provides short-term protection from uncomfortable conditions in Douglas Channel. As mentioned above, Douglas Channel has only two wind directions—outflow (downchannel) and inflow (upchannel). These winds, along with the strong currents (mostly ebb), can create a sharp, nasty 6-foot chop that makes headway difficult. When this happened to us, we ducked into Kiskosh Inlet and spent a calm afternoon anchored on the inside of the entrance bar.

The entrance bar has a flat 1½ to 2-fathom, sandy bottom. Dropping your lunch hook on the west side of the inlet, just out of the chop, will give you a secure afternoon. When the wind dies or the current lessens, it is easy to move to good shelter in Coghlan Anchorage.

To enter Kiskosh Inlet and cross the 2-mile-long entrance bar, start from a point in the center of the entrance, and head for the far end of the clearcut on the south shore, 1.5 miles. Continue along the treed south shore until you reach the point, avoiding the drying flat that extends halfway from the north shore. (Current here sometimes runs 2½ knots or more.) Cross to favor the north shore, heading for a green, brushy patch. Favor the north shore in a northwesterly direction until you reach a clear-cut area and deeper water. This maneuver avoids the rock and large shoal area on the south shore. Minimum depth in the fairway at the west end of the bay is one fathom at zero tide.

Kiskosh Inlet extends another 4 miles beyond the shallow bar. While the shores were clearcut near

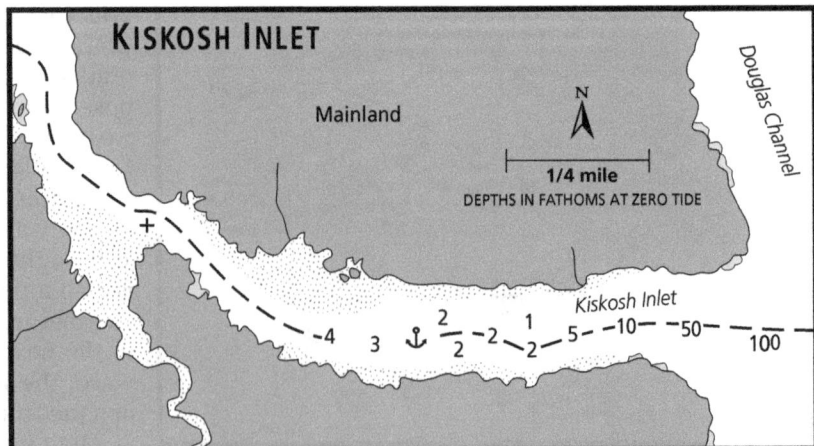

KISKOSH INLET

Mainland

Douglas Channel

N

1/4 mile
DEPTHS IN FATHOMS AT ZERO TIDE

Kiskosh Inlet

—4   3   ⚓ 2/2 —2   1/2   —5— —10— —50—   100

©2024 Don and Réanne Douglass • Diagram not for navigation

the entrance in the past, there are some outstanding high glacial domes and bowls that make a visit worthwhile. If you have time and proper tide, cruise up to Granite Cove near the head of the inlet.

Anchor (on bar) in about 2 fathoms, sandy bottom with good holding.

Granite Cove (Kiskosh Inlet)
5 mi NW of inlet entrance
Anchor: 53°33.85'N, 129°20.79'W

The small, remote cove at the foot of a granite bowl, southwest of the entrance to the lagoon in Kiskosh Inlet, is what we call "Granite Cove." The cove offers shelter from all weather and is a wonderful destination for a wilderness cruising experience. Tucked inside the south point of this cove, you have a magnificent view of the granite mountains towering several thousand feet above. Avoid the uncharted rocks, awash on a 9-foot tide, that extend about 250 feet from the south point.

Kiskosh Lagoon, at the very head of the inlet, becomes a grassy meadow that collects stumps and

Petroglyphs near Douglas Channel

logs at the foot of another granite bowl. The entrance to the lagoon has a sharp S-shaped turn with rocks that extend to mid-channel on both shores. Reconnoiter at low water by inflatable and enter only on slack water when depths are adequate.

Anchor in 7 fathoms over stones, gravel, and mud; holding depends on the set of your anchor.

A Long Journey Home

In 1929, the Haisla Nation's mortuary totem pole, the G'psgolox, was taken from its location at Misk'usa, at the entrance to the Kitlope wilderness near the village of Kitamaat, BC. The tribe's Eagle Chief, G'psgolox, who had lost his family and entire clan in a smallpox epidemic, erected the totem pole in 1872. When he walked into the forest to grieve, a being he referred to as "little man" appeared and told him if he returned to the burial site and took a bite of a crystal, he could wake up his deceased family. The Chief did as he was instructed and his family came down from the treetops with "little man." In gratitude, G'psgolox commissioned two Raven Chiefs to carve a totem pole in the image of "little man."

The traditional fate of a totem pole is to allow the totem to stand in the location where it was erected until it falls, decomposes, and returns to the earth, allowing the memorialized ancestors to rest peacefully. However, the G'psgolox Totem Pole was removed under dubious circumstances in 1929. It was sold to the government of Sweden and displayed in an ethnographic museum for more than sixty years.

In 1991, the tribal council, led by Gerald Amos, chairman of the totem committee, and Louisa Smith, spokesperson and direct descendant of Chief G'psgolox, began repatriation efforts. The tribal leaders visited the Folkens Museum Ethnografiska in Stockholm, and were overcome with emotion upon seeing their artifact "on display" some 4,500 miles from home. Several years of discussion between the tribal council and the Swedish government

ensued. Eventually, the museum's director recommended the totem pole's return based on ethical considerations. However, the Swedish Minister of Culture added a proviso: the totem pole would be returned only if it were to be housed in a protective shelter. This was not in keeping with the tribe's intention to return the artifact to Misk'usa, but after much deliberation, the tribal council reluctantly accepted these terms and commissioned the carving of not one replica, but two. One would be traded for the original and the second would be mounted at Misk'usa.

Haisla Master Carver Henry Robertson, whose grandfather had carved the original pole more than a hundred years earlier, went to work along with his nephews. Shortly thereafter, the Haisla people realized that they would have to cover the entire cost of the project: building the replica pole and the protective structure; transporting a second replica to Sweden; and transporting the original pole back to Kitimaat. Fundraisers, private donations, and financial assistance from Canada's Eco Trust helped offset the $300,000 cost. On August 25, 2000, an unfinished nine-meter replica was loaded onto a brand new Lufthansa aircraft on its maiden voyage to Stockholm. Accompanying the replica were Robertson and his team of carvers. They added the finishing touches in Stockholm, where the official exchange was made in a formal tribal ceremony on October 1. The second replica was raised four days later at Misk'usa, as tribal members and a delegation of Swedish visitors watched. In 2006 the original G'psgolox pole finally returned home. —KK

©2024 Don and Réanne Douglass • Diagram not for navigation

HARTLEY BAY

Kukayu River

Fish Hatchery

Village

N

100 yds

DEPTHS IN FATHOMS AT ZERO TIDE

Village

School

Government Dock

Fuel

2

2

Hartley Bay

10

20

Douglas Channel

30

©2024 Don and Réanne Douglass • Diagram not for navigation

COGHLAN ANCHORAGE

to Hartley Bay↗

15

Mainland

Stewart Narrows

12

10

8

Otter Shoal

White gravel beach

Letitia Point

7

3   5

6

8

4

6

7

Promise Land

Brodie Point

10

12

15

10

Harbour Rock

16

N

1/4 mile

DEPTHS IN FATHOMS AT ZERO TIDE

12

Wright Sound

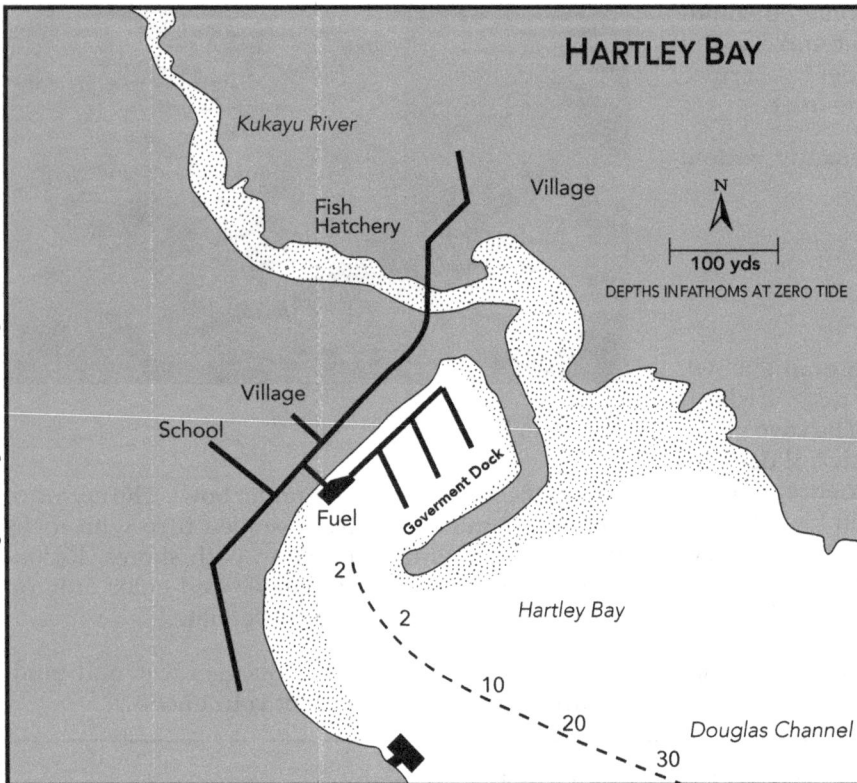

Hartley Bay (Douglas Channel)

4.2 mi NE of Grenville Channel
Entrance: 53°25.35'N, 129°14.94'W

Hartley Bay is a well-maintained First Nations boardwalk settlement with a small but well-protected harbor. It is often crowded when the fishing fleet is in, but you can raft to other boats. Although the dock is open all year, fuel availability may be limited. Be sure to call ahead. This small community has a medical clinic, Tsimshian Cultural Center, and a fish hatchery that may be possible to visit. Cell phone coverage is available. No grocery store or supplies. Telephone for the marina and fuel sales: (251) 841-2500, hvbc@gitgaat.ca.

Coghlan Anchorage (Wright Sound)

2 mi SW of Hartley Bay
Entrance (S): 53°21.98'N, 129°15.93'W
Entrance (N): 53°24.51'N, 129°15.11'W
Harbour Rock Light: 53°23.26'N. 129°16.64'W
Anchor: 53°23.88'N, 129°17.14'W

Coghlan Anchorage, at the south end of Grenville and Douglas channels, covers a large, loosely defined area that can accommodate a number of anchored craft off the white gravel beach on the west side of the channel (Otter Shoal). The bottom is flat at about 5 fathoms with kelp growing along the 2-fathom line. The water is muskeg, and there is little driftwood on shore. Although used principally by fishing boats, we find it convenient on either north- or southbound passages.

If strong southerly winds are expected, you could retreat into Stewart Narrows for more protection against chop.

Entry to Coghlan Anchorage can be made from the north via Stewart Narrows or from the south via Wright Sound. South of Brodie Point, avoid Harbour Rock which is passable on ei-

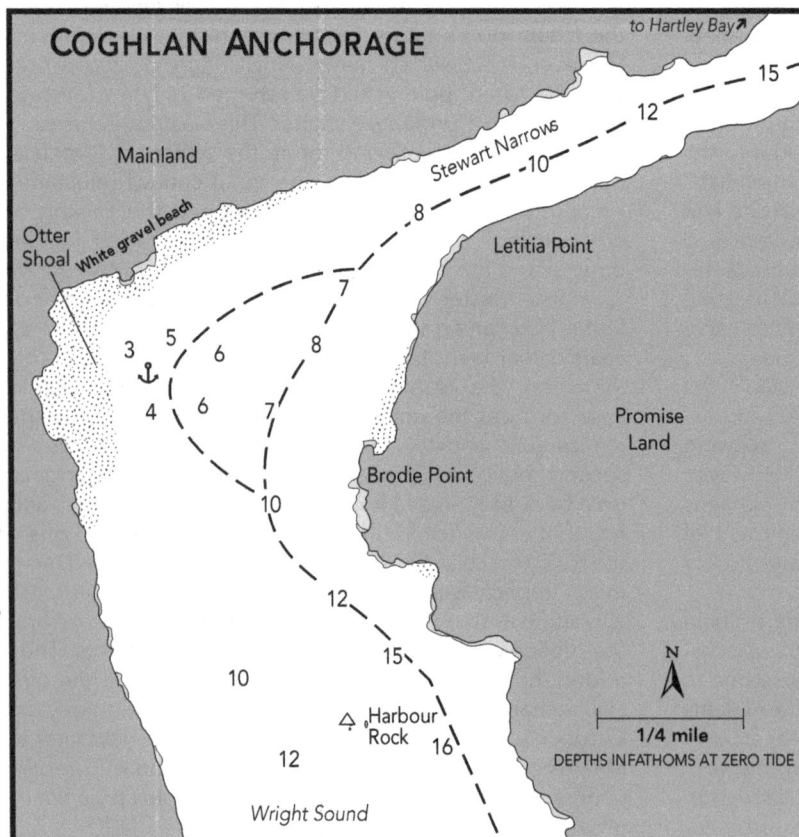

ther side. Access is easy either day or night, and it's as good place to wait for correct tide conditions in Grenville Channel. Currents are moderate.

Anchor (Otter Shoal) in 4 fathoms over sand, gravel, and some kelp with good holding.

Hartley Bay breakwater & public floats

Bella Via *moored in Coghlan Anchorage*

Collecting Oysters

What you need:
- Saltwater sport fishing license
- Information on closures (check with local government agency regarding shellfish testing and closures)
- Information on daily limit and possession limit
- Heavy gloves
- Oyster shucking knife
- Plastic container with lid, if shucking on the beach
- Bucket, if taking oysters in their shells

Your choice of oysters depends on what size you prefer and how you are planning to eat them. Oysters come in all shapes, so if you plan to barbecue them, choose ones where the bottom shell has a deep cup and a flat bottom. This configuration allows the shell to sit flat on the barbecue with the cup up to hold the oyster and sauce without tipping. The size of the cup gives an indication of the size of the oyster. If you are planning to pressure can, freeze or use the oysters in a stew, large flat shells are as good as cupped ones.

Opening Oysters
Shucking
Ensure that the shells are clean and, if necessary, scrub them in sea water. Hold the shell on a firm surface with a heavy gloved hand, deep half down. Position your hand so that if the oyster knife slips, it will not hit your hand. Insert the strong blunt blade between the shells near the hinge (narrow end). With a twisting motion, pop the hinge. Slide the knife forward, keeping the sharpened point tight against the top (flat) shell and sever the muscle that holds the halves together. Open the shell and cut the muscle on

the lower shell to release the oyster. Slide the oyster and liquor into a container.

On the barbecue
Place oysters in a pan containing 1/2" (1 cm) of water. Bake at 400°F for about 20 minutes or until shells open.

Be sure shells are tightly closed before using the oyster. If in doubt, discard.

Remember to discard shells in the intertidal zone, preferably on the beach where they came from so that juvenile oysters (called "spat") can settle and survive.

Storing Oysters
In the shell
Store cup side down, covered with a damp cloth in the refrigerator for up to 10 days. Ensure that the container is not sealed so that the oysters can breathe.

In oyster liquor
Strain liquor through a cloth to remove particles of shell or sand, store oysters and liquor in a tightly covered container in the refrigerator until ready to use (2 to 3 days.)

Freezing
Freezing oysters in their shell is not recommended. Shucked oysters may be frozen after being washing in brine—1 Tbsp. (15 mL) salt for each quart (litre) of water. Drain and pack in freezer containers, covering oysters with the strained liquor. Seal tightly and freeze immediately.

Thawing
Thaw frozen oysters overnight in the refrigerator or in a cold water bath for a few hours unless microwave defrosting is available. Never re-freeze thawed oysters.

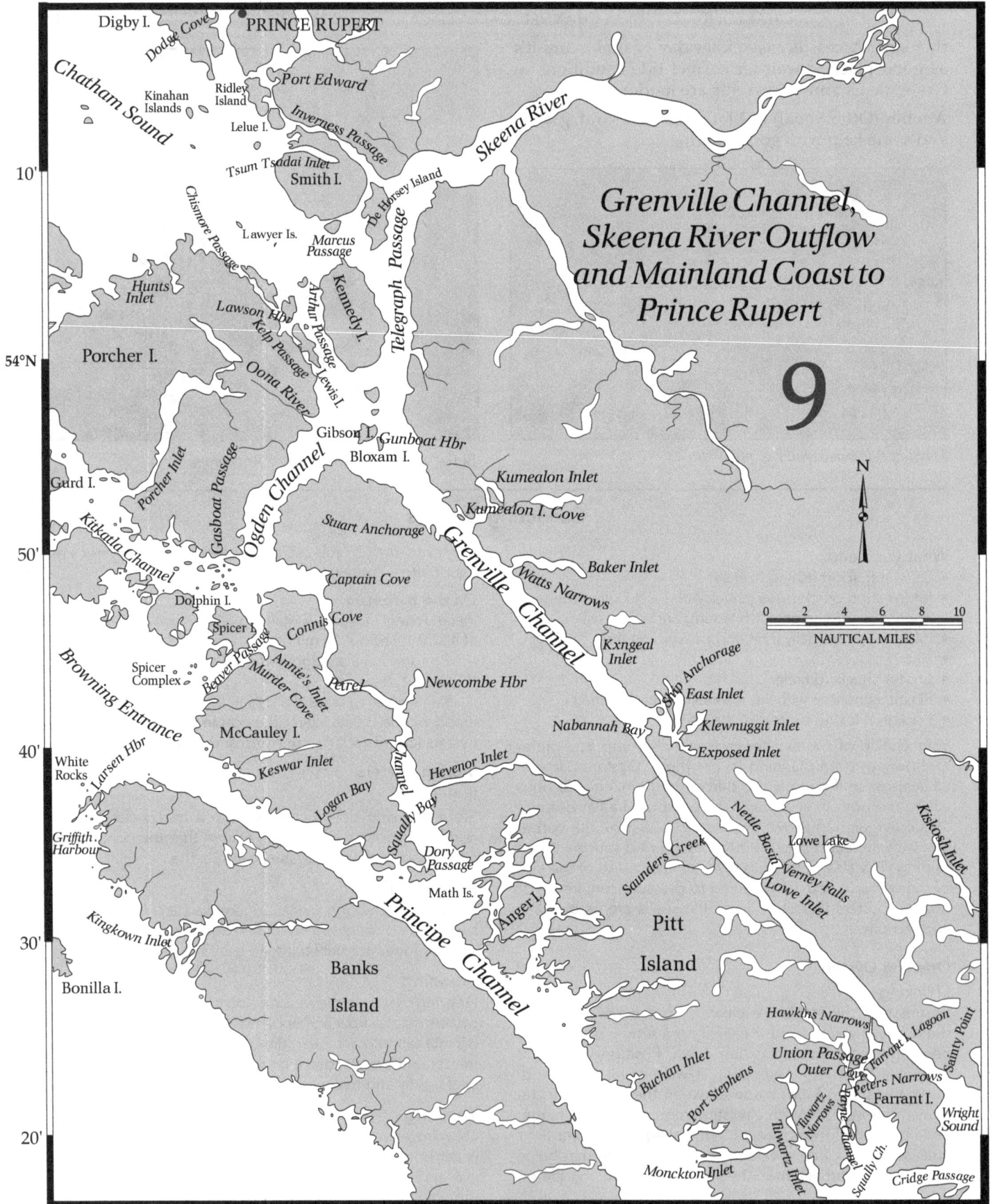

Digby I.
Dodge Cove
PRINCE RUPERT
Chatham Sound
Kinahan Islands
Ridley Island
Port Edward
Lelue I.
Inverness Passage
Tsum Tsadai Inlet
Smith I.
Chismore Passage
Lawyer Is.
Marcus Passage
Hunts Inlet
Lawson Hbr
Arthur Passage
Kennedy I.
De Horsey Island
Skeena River
Telegraph Passage

*Grenville Channel,
Skeena River Outflow
and Mainland Coast to
Prince Rupert*

9

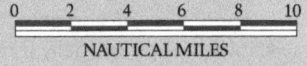

N

10'

54°N

Porcher I.
Oona River
Kelp Passage
Lewis I.
Gibson I.
Gunboat Hbr
Bloxam I.
Kumealon Inlet
Kumealon I. Cove

Gurd I.
Gasboat Passage
Ogden Channel
Stuart Anchorage
Grenville Channel
Baker Inlet
Watts Narrows

Kikatla Channel
Porcher Inlet
Captain Cove
Kxngeal Inlet

50'
Dolphin I.
Connis Cove
Skip Anchorage
East Inlet

Spicer I.
Beaver Passage
Annie's Inlet
Parel
Newcombe Hbr
Klewnuggit Inlet

Spicer Complex
Murder Cove
Nabannah Bay
Exposed Inlet

Browning Entrance
McCauley I.
Channel
Hevenor Inlet
Saunders Creek
Nettle Basin
Lowe Lake

40'
White Rocks
Larsen Hbr
Keswar Inlet
Logan Bay
Squally Bay
Verney Falls
Lowe Inlet
Kiskeosh Inlet

Griffith Harbour
Dory Passage
Math Is.
Anger I.
Pitt Island

Kingkown Inlet
Principe Channel
Hawkins Narrows

30'
Banks Island
Union Passage
Outer Cove
Peters Narrows
Sainty Point

Bonilla I.
Buchan Inlet
Port Stephens
Tuwartz Narrows
Farrant I. Lagoon
Farrant I.

20'
Monckton Inlet
Tuwartz Inlet
Union Channel
Squally Ch.
Wright Sound
Cridge Passage

0 2 4 6 8 10
NAUTICAL MILES

©2024 Don and Réanne Douglass • Diagram not for navigation

9

Grenville Channel, Skeena River Outflow, and Mainland Coast to Prince Rupert

A crowd-pleaser for passengers of ferryboats and cruise ships, 45-mile-long Grenville Channel is about as narrow a channel as these large vessels use on the entire Inside Passage. (The exception is Wrangell Narrows in Alaska, a dredged, man-made wonder.) In early summer, snowmelt from steep, granite peaks above Grenville Channel feeds waterfalls that tumble a thousand feet—one of the most thrilling sights in upper British Columbia—especially after a heavy rainfall.

Like Johnstone Strait, nearly all traffic travelling this route to and from Alaska must fit into a single channel and, after days of solitude, you may suddenly find yourself in a crowd of vessels—particularly in Wright Sound. Stay sharp and glance aft frequently to avoid being startled by the sudden blast of a horn! Northbound, fast, large, commercial and pleasure vessels keep slightly right of center-channel, while low-powered boats normally travel close to the right-hand shore. As you near Prince Rupert, the waters in Chatham Sound—influenced by the large Skeena River—can be quite choppy. It's a good idea to pre-plot your route across this open stretch in case of decreased visibility.

John & Réanne on bow watch

For sheltered anchorages along the way, Union Passage, Lowe Inlet, East Inlet, Baker Inlet, and Kumealon Inlet are all popular overnighters. The hike along the trail above Verney Falls in Nettle Basin (Lowe Inlet) is worth a stop in itself. Lawson Harbour, on the east side of Porcher Island, is a convenient anchorage just 18 miles south of Prince Rupert.

Grenville Channel
25.5 mi NW of Butedale
Entrance (S): 53°21.94'N, 129°19.33'W
Entrance (N): 53°55.25'N, 130°11.00'W

Grenville Channel has the appearance of a classic fiord and seldom gets serious seas. However, the ebb currents can be strong—we have seen as much as 6 knots off James Point at Lowe Inlet. Canadian Hydrographic Service has no current predictions for Grenville Channel. NOAA has secondary corrections based on Wrangell Narrows that has not been updated in a long time. All software predictions for current in Grenville Channel are based upon NOAA's information and may not be accurate. To take advantage of the currents, start your transit on the last of the flood. As you approach Klewnuggit Inlet, pick up the first of the ebb current and let it carry you the rest of the way through Grenville Channel. But don't let yourself or your crew be overcome by the natural beauty; drift logs and debris, as well as shoals near Morning Reef, present lurking hazards.

Sainty Point Cove (known as Camp Point) (position 53°22.43'N, 129°18.30'W), at the southeast entrance of Grenville Channel, has a good kayak haul-out beach on its northwest side—a good place to wait if current in Grenville Channel is contrary. This is a useful anchorage in northwest winds and the bottom is good.

Mosley Point, 9 miles northwest of Sainty Point (position: 53°28.40'N, 129°29.00'W), provides a good kayak campsite and haul-out beach.

Union Passage, Peters Narrows
(Squally Channel)
11.5 mi NW of MacDonald Bay
Position: 53°22.55'N, 129°27.49'W

Union Passage is a place few cruising boats visit. Both its southwest and northeast entrances are narrow and shallow, and larger boats may not be comfortable here. Although on spring tides this may be true, we've found that the window of access is quite wide during neap tides. Since you can see bottom all the way through the narrows, it is a good place to find sheltered waters or to have fun exploring. The fairway in Peters Narrows, although much like Hawkins Narrows, is deeper and its flow-rate less (7 knots maximum) and

Keep a sharp lookout for logs in Grenville Channel!

more laminar. Favor the east shore to avoid a shoal area along Pitt Island.

The Great Bear Rainforest Conservation Efforts

The Great Bear Rainforest (GBR) is a portion of the Pacific temperate rainforest eco-region. Extending along the British Columbia coast from northern Vancouver Island to the Alaskan border, it is about 250 miles long and 12,000 square miles in area—approximately the size of Vancouver Island. It is home to numerous unique species and sub-species of plants and animals, including sea wolves, spirit bears, and old growth forests.

In 2006, following decades of usage conflicts, a coalition of stakeholders reached preliminary agreement on GBR management. Participants included more than 20 First Nations tribes, industrial and commercial mining and timber interests, conservation organizations, and the government of British Columbia. On February 1, 2016, after years of complex negotiations, the Provincial government announced a final agreement that will protect much of the GBR from industrial logging and mining.

The agreement is a model for the effective mediation of a land use dispute among diverse interests. In addition to the sheer size of the area it protects, the agreement is unique in that the Provincial government negotiated with the First Nations governments as co-equals. This has allowed for the preservation of the cultural integrity of communities living in the disputed area—a primary goal of the negotiations. Studies show that the conservation lands already provide a significant boost to rural employment as well as providing economic benefits to the Province.

About 62% of the GBR has been placed under Ecosystem-Based Management (EBM), an ambitious but yet-to-be proven approach to forest management. Though EBM offers some stringent rules and guidelines, it still permits rotational forestry, road building, and other human activities that can be incompatible with the habitat needs of salmon, bears, wolves and many other old-growth dependent or associated species. Additionally, EBM allows

for expansive industrial logging of old-growth enclaves—which, at the time of the announcement was already taking place along the southern-most tip of the GBR. Although the historical and collaborative nature of the GBR agreement should be celebrated, headlines and government sound-bites oversimplify the complexity of the protection rules, leading the general public to believe—incorrectly—that the majority of the GBR is completely protected from clear-cutting and other industrial logging practices.

Assessing the effectiveness of the EBM framework will require accurate, ongoing, and current information. Pacific Wild, a non-profit located on Denny Island, in the heart of the GBR, is one organization that has taken on a monitoring role. Committed to defending wildlife and habitat on Canada's Pacific coast, Pacific Wild works to develop and implement solutions to conservation problems. In the GBR, their goal is to determine whether EBM actually sets a new standard for forest management, or is merely industrial logging rebranded. To learn more about their EBM monitoring work, please visit www.pacificwild.org

Additional environmental threats to the GBR—and the surrounding ocean—are likely to come from mining and oil and gas operations outside of the protected parts of the region. Kitimat and Prince Rupert are currently under intensive consideration as sites for the construction of new LNG (Liquefied Natural Gas) plants, oil refineries, and pipelines bringing crude oil and natural gas from Alberta. First Nations groups, the Union of British Columbia Municipalities, and environmental groups have all opposed construction of gas and oil transport pipelines in this area. Canadian Prime Minister Justin Trudeau's 2015 ban on oil tanker traffic along British Columbia's North Coast has ended the immediate threat of an oil pipeline.

—LW

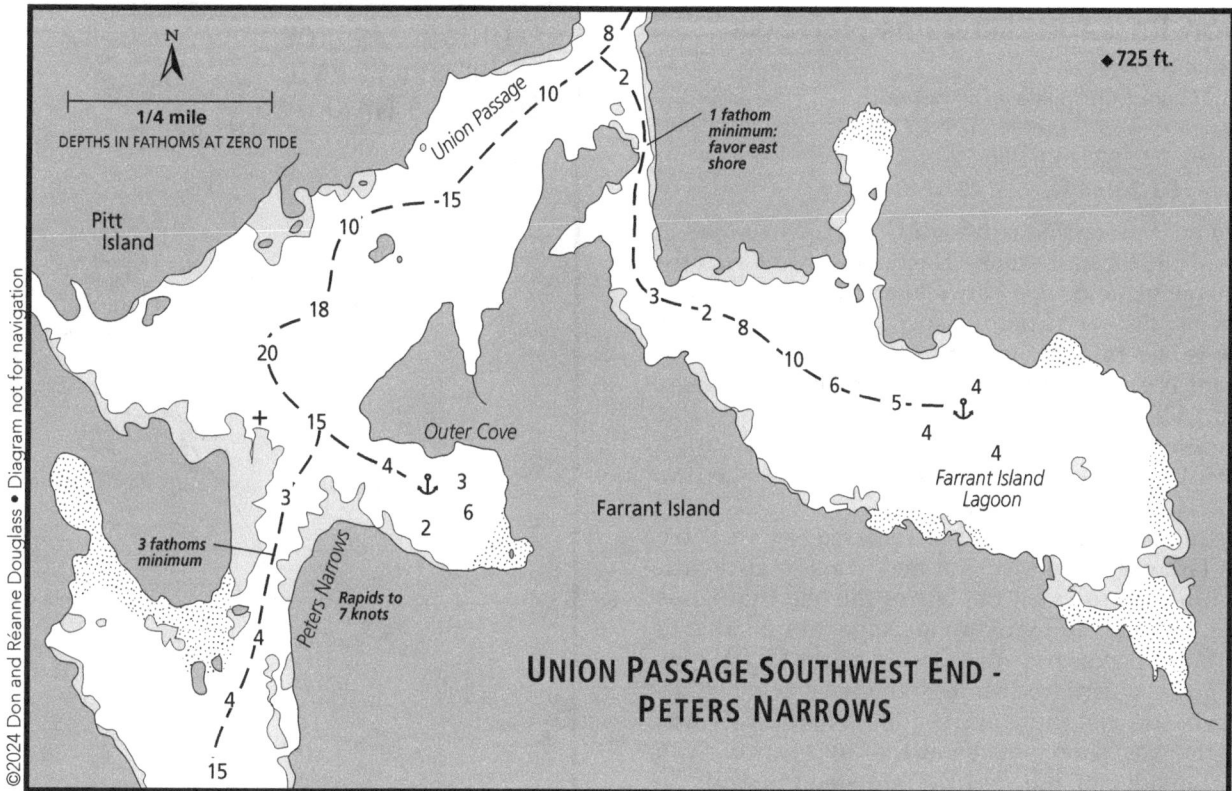

UNION PASSAGE SOUTHWEST END – PETERS NARROWS

Outer Cove (Union Passage)

2.4 mi SW of Hawkins Narrows
Entrance: 53°22.69'N, 129°27.34'W
Anchor: 53°22.62'N, 129°27.13'W

"Outer Cove," the anchor site immediately north of Peters Narrows, on the Farrant Island side, is easy to enter and offers splendid shelter. Upon entering the cove, avoid the grassy islet in the center. While the chart indicates that the islet dries at 19 feet, our observations indicated 15 feet. The outlet of 2-mile long Tsimtack Lake lies on the west shore, just north of Peters Narrows.

Anchor (center of cove) in 6 fathoms in the over sand, mud (and perhaps some logger's refuse); good holding.

Farrant Island Lagoon (Union Passage)

1.9 mi SW of Hawkins Passage
Entrance: 53°23.15'N, 129°26.81'W
Anchor: 53°22.72'N, 129°26.10'W

"Farrant Island Lagoon" is our name for the perfectly bombproof anchor site on the northwest side of Farrant Island. The south end of Union Passage, constricted due west of hill 725, has a depth of 6 to 8 fathoms. Just below this constriction, there is a small channel leading due south to Farrant Island lagoon.

The tidal currents from the north and south meet just north of this channel.

Entering the lagoon, favor the east shore which is steep-to. Minimum depth in the fairway is about one fathom at zero tide. The channel opens to the east in what must be one of the most remote and sheltered anchorages along the shores of the Inside Passage.

With the exception of a small 10-fathom hole, the entire lagoon has a flat 5-fathom bottom. There is plenty of swinging room, and the level tree branches along the high-tide line indicate that this cove sees hardly a ripple. Outer Cove "next door" is easier for boats to enter.

Anchor in 5 fathoms over mud with good holding.

Grenville Channel

Union Passage, Hawkins Narrows

(Grenville Channel)
4.3 mi NW of Grenville Channel entr.
Entrance (S): 53°21.93'N, 129°27.48'W
Entrance (N): 53°24.84'N, 129°24.79'W
Anchor: 53°23.64'N, 129°25.42'W

Entry to Hawkins Narrows off Grenville Channel is difficult to locate because Davenport Point is rather inconspicuous. Hawkins Narrows currents are known to flow at 8 knots on spring tides. High-water slack is the transit time of choice for larger boats. Farrant Island, on the south side of Union Passage, has a 1,130-foot peak that provides a landmark. Pitt Island, along the north side, is low and flat with a 200-foot-high peninsula; Hawkins Narrows is the slit between these two landmarks.

If this is your first visit to the area, on an entry from Grenville Channel you may want to approach Hawkins Narrows on the last of the ebb that flows north, in order to maintain steerage and be able to back out if necessary. We've found about 1.5 fathoms minimum at zero tide through the fairway.

Favor the east shore in the middle of the narrows, then the west shore as soon as the bay starts to open up. The sides of the narrows are steep-to and the shoal rocks indicated on the chart are not evident. There is a landing beach with a primitive campsite on the north point where kayakers could spend the night. The shores are covered with old-growth forest and appear to be undisturbed by man. Protection from southerlies can be found against the south shore, as indicated in the diagram.

Anchor in 6 fathoms over mud with fair holding.

Lowe Inlet Provincial Marine Park

(Grenville Channel)
14.3 mi NW of Hartley Bay
Entrance: 53°32.48'N, 129°35.94'W

Most of the uplands in Lowe Inlet are Provincial Park except for those along the east shore at Verney Falls which are Indian Reserve.

Nettle Basin/Verney Falls

(Lowe Inlet)
1.5 mi NE from inlet entrance
Anchor (Verney Falls): 53°33.60'N, 129°33.93'W
Anchor (Nettle Basin): 53°33.49'N, 129°34.17'W

For years, Nettle Basin in Lowe Inlet has been a popular overnight anchorage for cruising boats. Spectacular photo opportunities exist at low tide when Verney Falls doubles in height.

Land your dinghy on the north shore and from

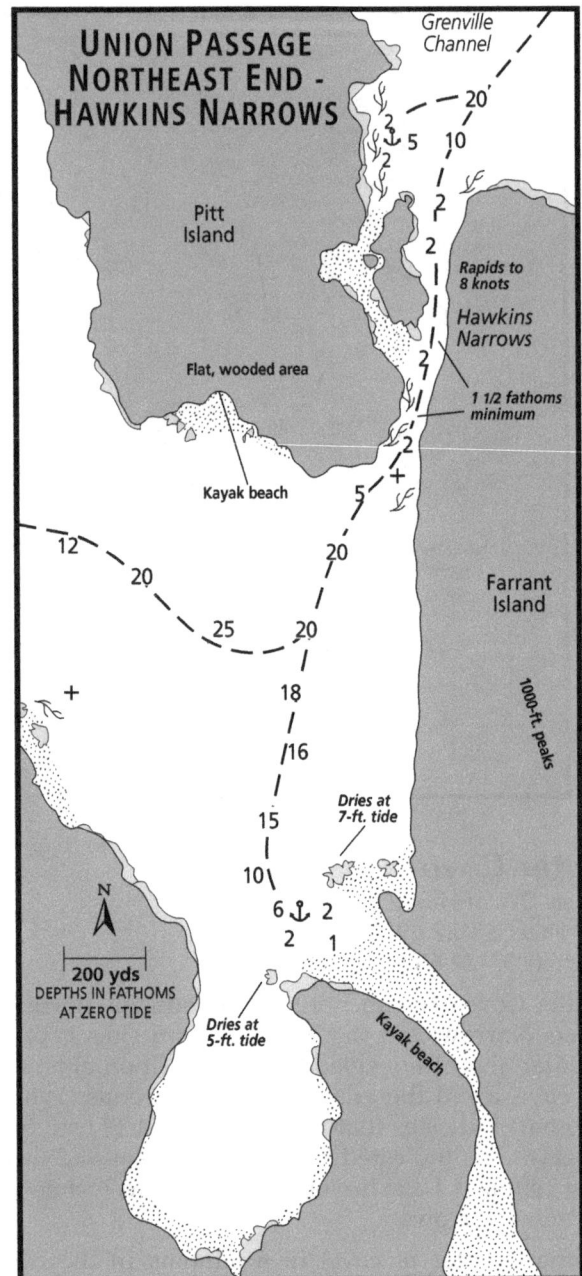

UNION PASSAGE
NORTHEAST END -
HAWKINS NARROWS

©2024 Don and Réanne Douglass • Diagram not for navigation

there, you can take a rough but passable trail that leads along the north side of short Kumowdah River, passing the first and second falls on its way to Lowe Lake. Bear like to poke around the drying flats along the beach at the head of Nettle Basin, so keep your whistle and binoculars handy. (The first time we went ashore here, we missed the trail and ran smack into a bear's den—empty, thank goodness!)

Although we like to anchor in the fast-moving stream below the falls for the full view, this site, with its gravel bottom and just fair holding is not to everyone's liking. (We had to set our anchor well, here!) Kayakers or canoeists should not approach the falls too closely. The reverse hydraulic flow here can carry a small boat directly into the falls where it can be swamped. (The reverse flow sucks down any floating object at the base of the falls—throw a stick and watch it!)

Most boats anchor in the quieter, less-exposed south end of Nettle Basin where the bottom provides better holding power and there's a good view of animals and birds combing the grassy shores.

Anchor (Verney Falls) in 5 fathoms over gravel with a strong westerly current; poor-to-fair holding.

Anchor (Nettle Basin) in 10 to 12 fathoms over mud with good holding.

Nabannah Bay

(Grenville Channel)
10 mi NW of Lowe Inlet
Entrance (N): 53°40.75'N, 129°46.19'W
Anchor (SE corner): 53°40.38'N, 129°45.30'W

Nabannah Bay, between Morning Point and Evening Point, is largely protected from the chop of Grenville Channel by Morning Reef and Barrier Rock. This site is a convenient lunch stop or a place to wait until the current in Grenville Channel starts to ebb. (The tides meet in this vicinity.)

The safest way to enter Nabannah Bay is from the north, passing just east of Morning Reef light. The fairway has a minimum of 5 fathoms, but keep a sharp lookout to avoid kelp patches marking the reef.

You can land a dinghy on the small gravel beach on the east side of the bay; avoid an uncharted rock

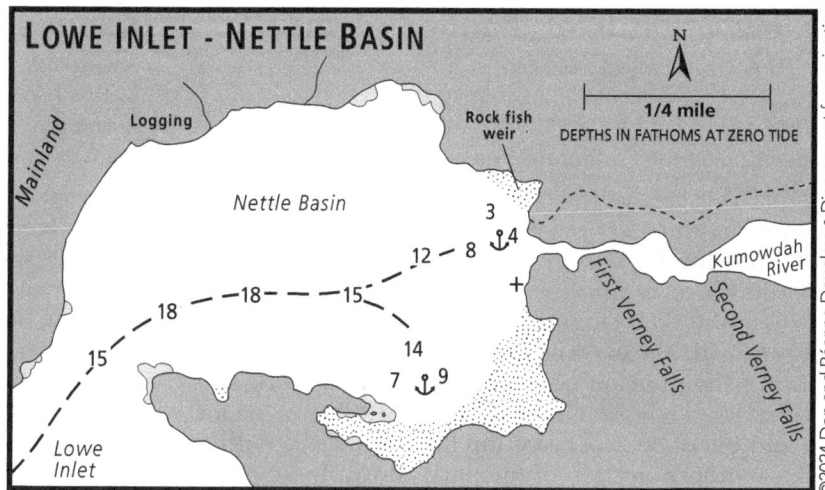

LOWE INLET - NETTLE BASIN

Mainland

Logging

Nettle Basin

Rock fish weir

Kumowdah River

First Verney Falls

Second Verney Falls

Lowe Inlet

1/4 mile
DEPTHS IN FATHOMS AT ZERO TIDE

©2024 Don and Réanne Douglass • Diagram not for navigation

about 100 feet from the shore, awash on an 8-foot tide.

A narrow dinghy pass, choked with kelp, about one-fathom deep at zero tide, exists between Evening Point and the southernmost tip of Barrier Rock. This pass can be used by small vessels near high water. Visibility in the water is about 6 feet.

Large boats can find anchorage in the southeast corner of the bay over a flat 10-fathom bottom, while small boats may want to use the nook on the north side between two kelp patches over a 4- to 6-fathom bottom.

Anchor (southeast corner) in 10 fathoms over sand, stones, and kelp, with poor-to-fair holding.

Anchor (north nook) in 6 fathoms off kayak haul-out and campsite.

Note for kayakers: Saunders Creek (position: 53°36.15'N, 129°42.39'W), 4 miles south of Nabannah Bay on the west shore of Grenville Channel, below a high waterfall, has a good haul-out beach and campsite. There are also two campsites on the opposite shore, between one and two miles to the south.

Thoughts of the North Coast by a *Baidarka* crewmember

Going through rapids; traversing rocky, twisting, narrow passages; crossing rough sounds or rounding difficult capes—these are the things that excite some people. As for me, I'm glad when that part of a cruise is over. After a day's run, I look forward to the adventure of finding the right cove for the night. I like the job of being the bow watch, and even though it might be freezing outside, this is one of the most thrilling adventures for me.

Of course I'm on the bow as an extra pair of eyes and my job is to inform the captain of any obstacles that might impede the smooth progress of the boat. I might see a pair of loons off to one side, a sea lion peering up with half-submerged face, large masses of undulating jellyfish, or walls of ferns and lichens. A stream, a bear, eagles, wildflowers and the forest walls hug the cove.

Sometimes I feel a change of temperature or a drop in the force of the wind. I love the shrill sound from all directions of a million small birds echoing through the branches. Wet earth and sea life have their own fragrance that means land and a quiet cove—a haven for the night.

—Gloria Burke, First mate, *Carousel*

Klewnuggit Inlet Marine Provincial Park (Grenville Channel)
10.5 mi NW of Lowe Inlet
Entrance: 53°41.27'N, 129°45.11'W
Klewnuggit Inlet is entered between Rogers Point and Silas Point.

Klewnuggit Inlet was established as a B.C. Provincial Marine Park in June of 1993. The north side of its entrance is marked by a dark, granite massif. Where the tidal currents of Grenville Channel meet just outside the entrance, a line of flotsam frequently marks the division point. East Inlet, the middle finger of Klewnuggit, is 2.7 miles long and has room for a number of boats. Brodie and Freda Lakes lie within the southern portion of the park. Morning Reef is a foul area that should be given wide berth.

The remains of a rock fish weir may be found, just north of the outlet of the falls in Nettle Basin.

Exposed Inlet (Klewnuggit Inlet)
2 mi SE of Morning Reef Inlet
Entrance: 53°40.00'N, 129°42.98'W
Anchor: 53°39.60'N, 129°42.37'W

Exposed Inlet, as its name implies, is exposed to prevailing northwesterlies; however, it is acceptable in fair weather or southerlies. Most cruising boaters, however, will prefer the more secure inner basin of East Inlet.

Along the east shore of Exposed Inlet, take a look at the unusual outlet of Freda and Brodie Lakes.

Anchor in 6 fathoms (south of the islet) over sand and mud; fair-to-good holding.

East Inlet, Inner Basin (Klewnuggit Inlet)
1.9 mi E of Morning Reef Lt.
Entrance: 53°40.34'N, 129°43.03'W
Anchor (inner basin): 53°42.84'N, 129°43.61'W

The inner basin of East Inlet, protected from channel winds and in calm waters, is a natural shelter for cruising boats, and there's enough swinging room for a whole yacht club. The view of the high peaks to the north and the east are splendid but at times williwaws may roar down these mountains, so be prepared to let out plenty of anchor rode if you hear their scream. To obtain shelter from southerly chop, tuck in behind the west point of the narrows.

Entry into the inner basin is easy, and the five miles to the anchor site at the head of the inlet is a lovely trip. Avoid the rock which dries a quarter-mile southeast of Inner Basin narrows.

Anchor (inner basin) in 7 fathoms over mud with good holding.

Kxngeal Inlet
(Grenville Channel)
3.9 mi NW of Morning Reef Lt.
Entrance: 53°44.05'N, 129°49.57'W
Anchor (beach): 53°45.17'N, 129°49.36'W

Kxngeal Inlet, which is easily accessible from Grenville Channel, offers shelter from north-and south-blowing winds and chop found in the channel. On entry, avoid a poorly marked rock, awash on a 16-foot tide. The fairway north of the rock carries a minimum of 11 fathoms.

The inlet can be a welcome relief from the chop of Grenville Channel. On a sunny day, with the high peaks visible above to the east, it can be quite pleasant. The head of the inlet shows little evidence that serious chop enters. Small boats can anchor over the drying flat with appropriate tide level, or on the sloping bottom just off the flat in about 6 fathoms. Larger boats can anchor anywhere in the center of the bay.

Anchor in 6 fathoms off the steep-to beach in sand, mud, and shells; fair-to-good holding.

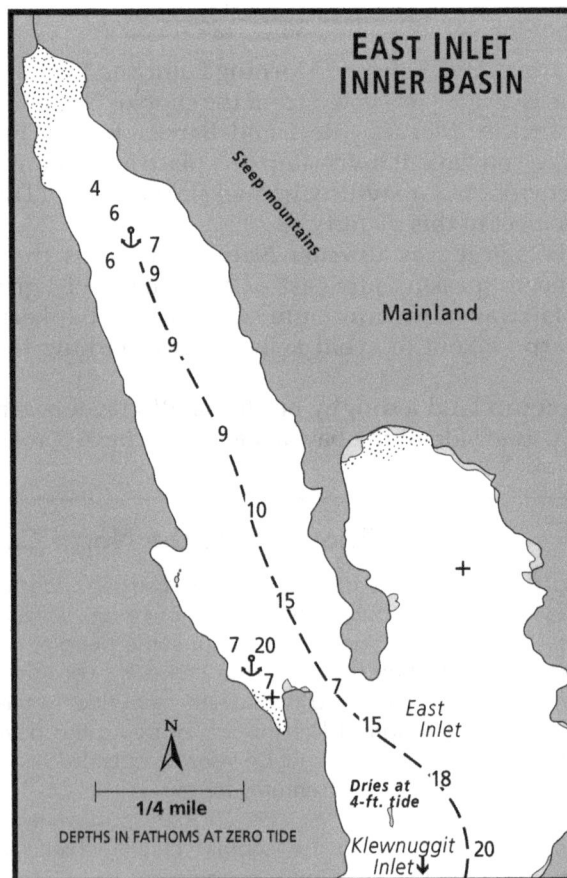

EAST INLET INNER BASIN

Steep mountains

Mainland

East Inlet

Dries at 4-ft. tide

Klewnuggit Inlet

N

1/4 mile

DEPTHS IN FATHOMS AT ZERO TIDE

©2024 Don and Réanne Douglass • Diagram not for navigation

Watts Narrows

(Grenville Channel)
10.4 mi NW of Morning Reef Lt.
Entrance (SW): 53°48.66'N, 129°57.31'W
Entrance (NE): 53°49.01'N, 129°56

Watts Narrows, the entrance to Baker Inlet, is a special place to seek beauty and solitude. We seldom pass it without a quick run inside to see our "old friend." Old-growth trees that line the shore create a rich overhead canopy, and the winding channel, with its turbulent but deep waters flooding in or out, is magical. The sides of the channel are fairly steep-to but the rocky shore causes the water to "boil" a bit. When the flood is running at 6 knots during spring tides, there's a two-foot drop along the length of Watts Narrows and you should wait for near slack water to transit. The window for passage during neap tides is quite wide.

Caution: Watts Narrows has limited visibility and sharply restricted maneuvering room in the fairway. It's a good idea to sound your horn upon entering and again halfway through. We also post alert lookouts on the bow and keep a finger on the button of our horn in case we see or hear an opposing boat. While the helmsman must respond quickly to stay in midchannel, no special techniques are required. The minimum depth in the fairway is 10 fathoms and, if the turbulence disturbs the readings of your echo sounder, don't be alarmed; you'll be fine as long as you maintain a near mid-channel route. If you experience anxiety during your approach to the entrance, wait until slack water when you feel more comfortable. Watts Narrows is a memorable experience, but it needn't give you white knuckles!

Baker Inlet

(Grenville Channel)
E of Wrangell Narrows
Anchor (south bight): 53°48.94'N, 129°56.74'W
Anchor (inlet head): 53°48.52'N, 129°51.13'W

Baker Inlet, entered via Watts Narrows, is the most protected and secure anchorage in Grenville Channel. You can find shelter from all weather inside this scenic basin where well-developed second-growth trees line the entire inlet. Perpetual snowfields tower high above Alvin Lake to 3,600 feet. At sea level, tree limbs extend over the water

in a perfectly horizontal line, giving testimony to the calmness of the basin. At the head of the inlet, behind a treed island, there is a lovely, serene basin where you can look up to glacier-scarred alpine slopes. The head of Baker Inlet is a special place. Wolves howl at night and bears roam the grassy margins of the drying mud flat and a pair of resident loons sometimes patrol the shore. The large creek dropping from Alvin Lake lulls you to sleep. The silence is broken only by the rushing creek water; there is no radio reception at the head of the inlet.

While depths in the inlet range from 30 to 50 fathoms, small boats can find many spots to anchor near shore along shoaling banks. This is a perfect place to linger before entering the busy ports ahead. It's a quiet place where you can spot bear, wolves, and deer. Avoid the numerous small crab-pot floats.

If you want to be close to Grenville Channel, you can anchor in the small bight to the south just past the narrows, off an old float. Otherwise you can continue to the head of the inlet, behind the treed islet, and anchor off the drying flat. Kayakers will find a good anchor spot across the channel at the outlet of Pa-aat River. *Caution:* We once snagged our anchor on a nylon line in the south bight.

Anchor (south bight) in 7 fathoms over mud with fair holding.

Anchor (head of the inlet) in 9 fathoms over mud with good holding.

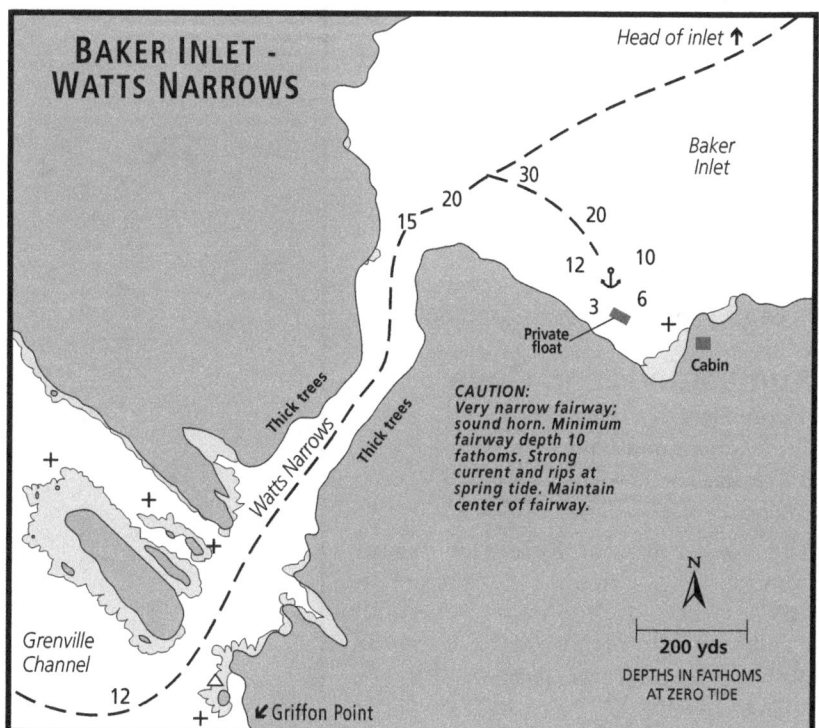

BAKER INLET - WATTS NARROWS

CAUTION: Very narrow fairway; sound horn. Minimum fairway depth 10 fathoms. Strong current and rips at spring tide. Maintain center of fairway.

200 yds
DEPTHS IN FATHOMS AT ZERO TIDE

©2024 Don and Réanne Douglass • Diagram not for navigation

Kumealon Inlet inner basin

Entrance to Watts Narrows

Kumealon Inlet (Grenville Channel)

3.2 mi NW of Baker Inlet
Entrance: 53°51.17'N, 130°00.67'W
Anchor (E shore): 53°52.04'N, 129°58.49'W

Kumealon Inlet, on the northeast corner of Grenville Channel, is a scenic inlet dotted with small tree-covered islands and islets, with an intricate channel into Kumealon Lagoon at its head. The eastern shore of the inner basin provides good protection in most weather. Upon entering the basin at the head of the inlet, favor the north shore until you have passed the treed islet in the center; avoid the group of rocks from the center to the south shore.

At one time, this site held a logging camp, so you may still find remnants on shore, but second-growth trees now line the shore. Deep within the inlet you can quickly find snug anchorage.

There is a small 5- to 6-fathom shelf on the eastern shore of the basin where one or two boats can find good shelter; larger vessels can anchor in the center of the basin in 12 to 15 fathoms.

Anchor (east shore) in 5 to 6 fathoms over grey mud with very good holding.

Kumealon Island Cove

(Grenville Channel)
N of Kumealon Island
Entrance: 53°51.49'N, 130°01.79'W
Anchor: 53°51.72'N, 130°01.63'W

The cove north of Kumealon Island provides excellent shelter from northerly winds and chop and gives good, quiet protection from southerly winds and chop. (One sleepless night, anchored in Kelp Passage Cove, we experienced 50-knot southeast gusts and were hanging on maximum scope. Twenty miles to the southeast, friends anchored in Kumealon Island Cove reported 10- to 20-knot winds and no discomfort.) Since the head of the cove dries rapidly, allow for a variation of more than 3 fathoms in tide level when you set your anchor.

Anchor in 6 fathoms over sand and mud with good holding.

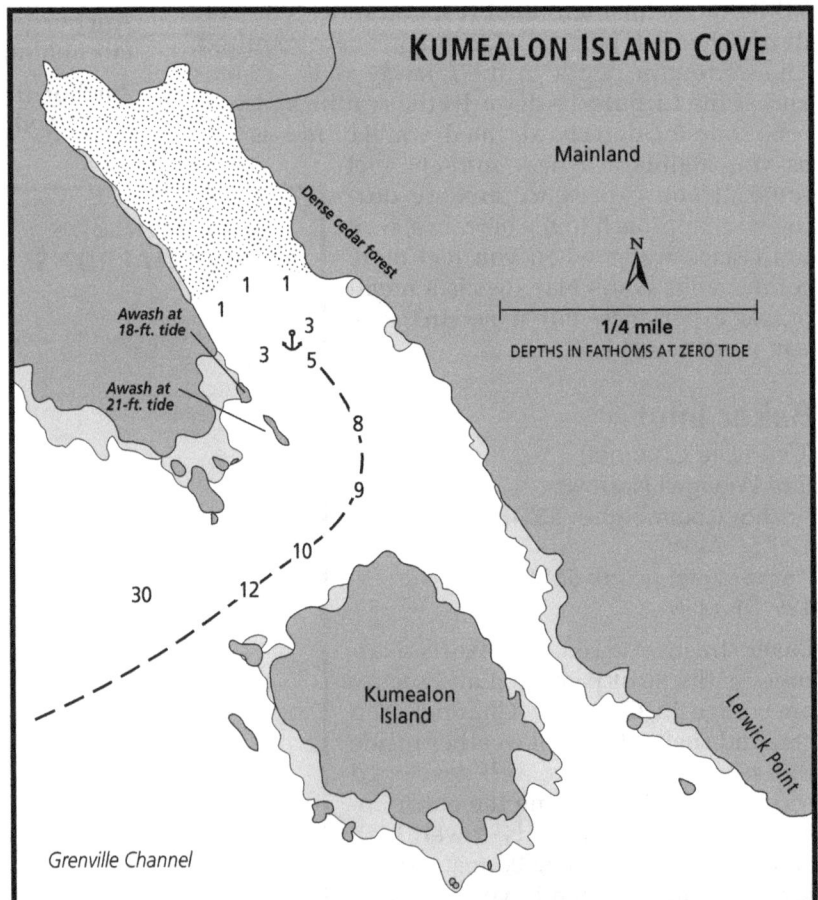

KUMEALON ISLAND COVE

Mainland

Dense cedar forest

Awash at 18-ft. tide

Awash at 21-ft. tide

N

1/4 mile
DEPTHS IN FATHOMS AT ZERO TIDE

Kumealon Island

Lerwick Point

Grenville Channel

©2024 Don and Réanne Douglass • Diagram not for navigation

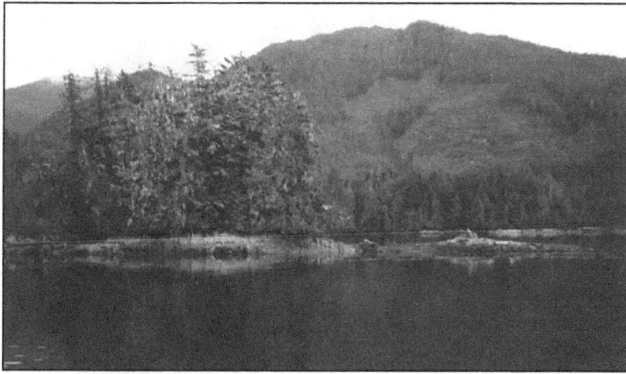

Stuart Anchorage

Stuart Anchorage (Grenville Channel)

1.8 mi W of Kumealon Island
Entrance: 53°51.52'N, 130°04.38'W
Anchor (westernmost cove): 53°51.08'N, 130°04.54'W

Stuart Anchorage provides shelter for large vessels west of Stag Rock next to Pitt Island; small vessels can find anchorage in the second cove west of Bon-wick Point as described below.

The first cove immediately west of Bonwick Point, which is fouled by a large center rock and patches of kelp, can be used only by small boats under 30 feet; even then, they must stern tie to shore on the south side of the center group of rocks.

We prefer the second small cove, west of Bonwick Point against Pitt Island. This cove offers good shelter from southeast winds or chop that blow up Grenville Channel, but it is partially exposed to northwest chop. (Gunboat Harbour is better in heavy northwesterlies.) Several isolated rocks, most marked by kelp in the summer, must be avoided. As you approach from the north, Stag Rock, which dries on an 18-foot tide, makes a good leading mark to identify the anchorage. Two or three small craft can find secure anchorage in this westernmost cove where the bottom remains flat at 6 to 8 fathoms for about 400 yards. The head of the cove is grassy, with easy dinghy access and primitive campsites for kayakers.

Anchor (westernmost cove) in 6 to 8 fathoms over grey mud; very good holding.

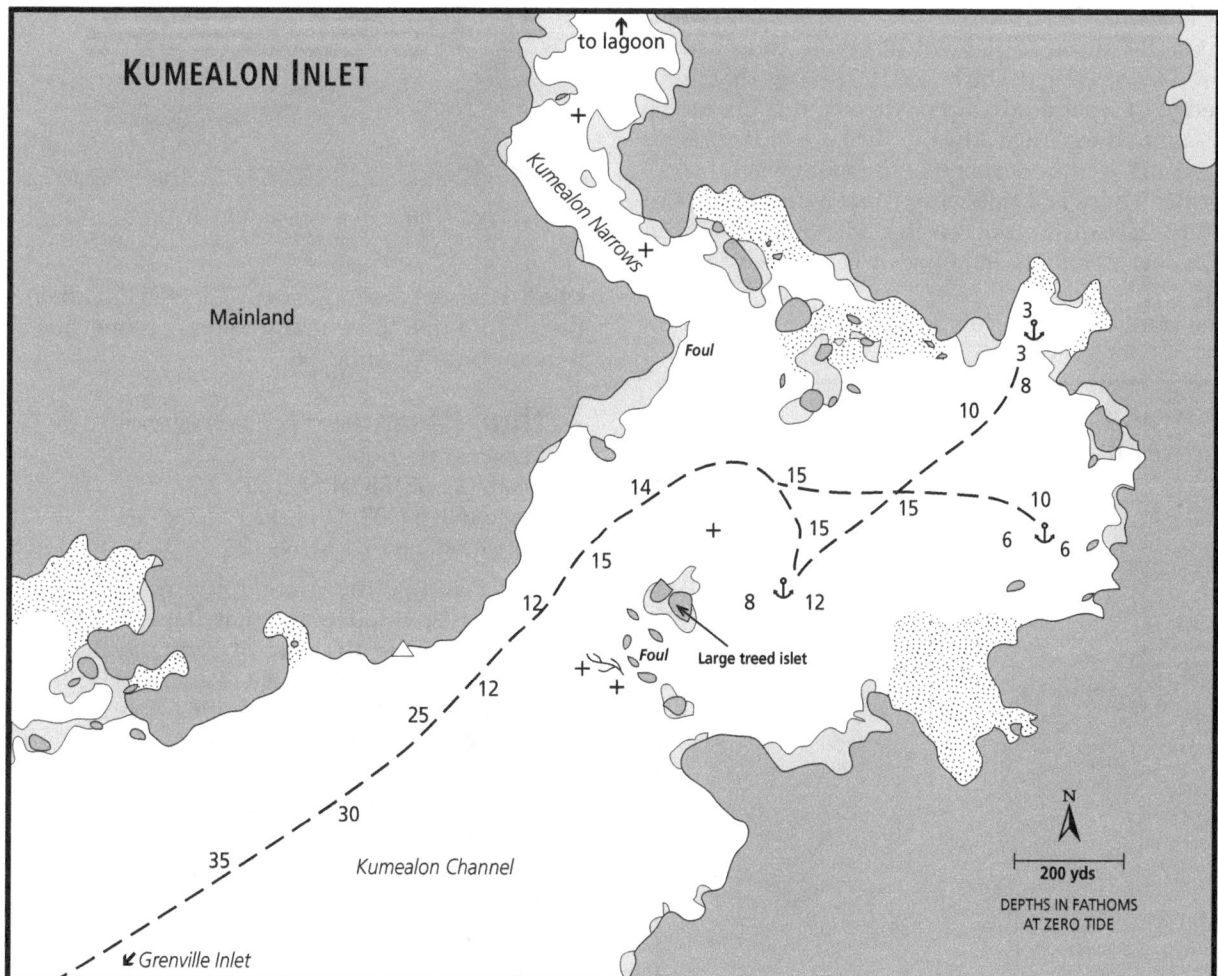

Gunboat Harbour (Gibson Island)
4.6 mi NW of Stuart Anchorage
Entrance: 53°55.16'N, 130°08.60'W
Anchor: 53°55.35'N, 130°08.67'W

Gunboat Harbour is a good, short rest stop where small boats can wait out the chop that occurs 2 miles to the north or find protection from prevailing north-westerlies or northeast outflow winds. Since it's completely open to the south, it does not provide shelter in a southerly storm.

Due to the outflow of the Skeena River from the east, the color of the water in the vicinity of Gibson Island changes to opaque beige. South of Kennedy Island, a moderate southwest wind against the strong, 3-knot ebb current from the Skeena River can cause nasty chop on your beam.

Anchor in 3 fathoms over sand and gravel with fair holding.

Oona River (Ogden Channel)
5 mi S of Lawson Harbour
Buoy position: 53°56.44'N, 130°14.20'W

The small fishing settlement of Oona River can be entered by passing to starboard the pilings that mark the edge of a shoal; the lip of the shoal is about 150 yards from the pilings. Line up the two white private range marks on the east end of the breakwater before entering. There is a tide gauge approximately 300m (1000 ft) east of the breakwater. At high water you can expect about 2½ fathoms in the fairway of the river.

The public dock is crowded with commercial and

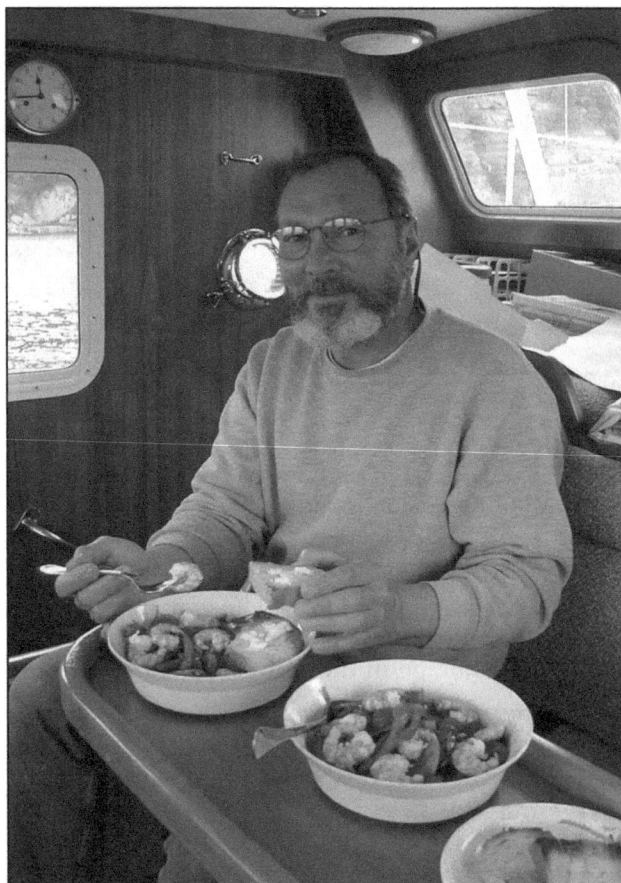

Master chef, John Leone, enjoys a fresh catch

small boats of various sizes. Water is available but there is no fuel. Like many villages along this coast, they monitor Channel 06.

Arthur Passage (Kennedy Island)
E of Lawson Harbour
Entrance (S): 53°58.81'N, 130°12.30'W
Entrance (N): 54°03.87'N, 130°16.09'W
Herbert Reefs: 54°01.45'N, 130°14.31'W

Arthur Passage, the main route north, avoids the Skeena River flood plain that flows through Telegraph Passage to the east of Kennedy Island. It is shallow and laden with silt. Lawson Harbour, just north of Herbert Reefs, provides good anchorage. Herbert Reefs can be carefully passed on either side.

Lawson Harbour (Lewis Island)
18 mi S of Prince Rupert
Entrance: 54°01.76'N, 130°15.25'W
Anchor: 54°01.37'N, 130°15.12'W

Lawson Harbour gives excellent protection from southeast winds and chop in Arthur Passage. How-

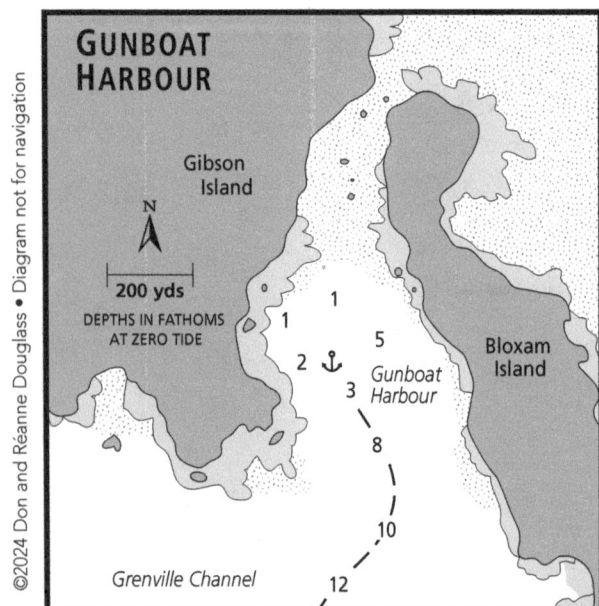

GUNBOAT HARBOUR

Gibson Island

N

200 yds

DEPTHS IN FATHOMS
AT ZERO TIDE

1

1

5

2 ⚓

Gunboat
Harbour

3

Bloxam
Island

8

10

Grenville Channel

12

©2024 Don and Réanne Douglass • Diagram not for navigation

ever, it is not good for westerlies and it is open to the north and the wake of passing ships.

Entry is easy, as long as you avoid both the underwater rock on the east side of the route, off the northwest corner of Break Island, and the charted reef in the western center of the harbor. Once past the Break Island rock, head straight for the narrow slit formed by a small peninsula of Lewis Island. Drop your hook just after you pass the charted mid-center reef, as indicated in the diagram.

Here it's easy to tell you're approaching Prince Rupert, since at night, you can see the glow of the city to the north.

Anchor in 4 fathoms over mud with good holding.

Bloxam Passage (Lewis Island)
N side of Lawson Harbour
Entrance (NE): 54°02.06'N, 130°15.22'W
Entrance (SW): 54°01.41'N, 130°16.08'W

Bloxam Passage separates Lewis Island, at its south and Elliott Island on its north.

Kelp Passage Cove
(Kelp Passage)
0.7 mi SW of Lawson Harbour
Anchor: 54°00.94'N, 130°15.86'W

"Kelp Passage Cove" is our name for the north end of Kelp Passage—a high-water route choked with kelp and reefs and not recommended except by dinghy. You can take anchorage tucked between the shallow reef and Lewis Island in the northwest corner of Kelp Passage as indicated on the diagram. We once took a full southeast gale here in windy and exciting but safe conditions.

Anchor in 3 fathoms over mud with very good holding.

Chalmers Anchorage (Arthur Passage)
1.5 mi N of Lawson Harbour
Entrance: 54°03.02'N, 130°16.53'W

Chalmers Anchorage provides good holding for large vessels in southeast winds; however, it is exposed to the northwest. Lawson Harbour, just south, is a better anchorage for smaller cruising boats.

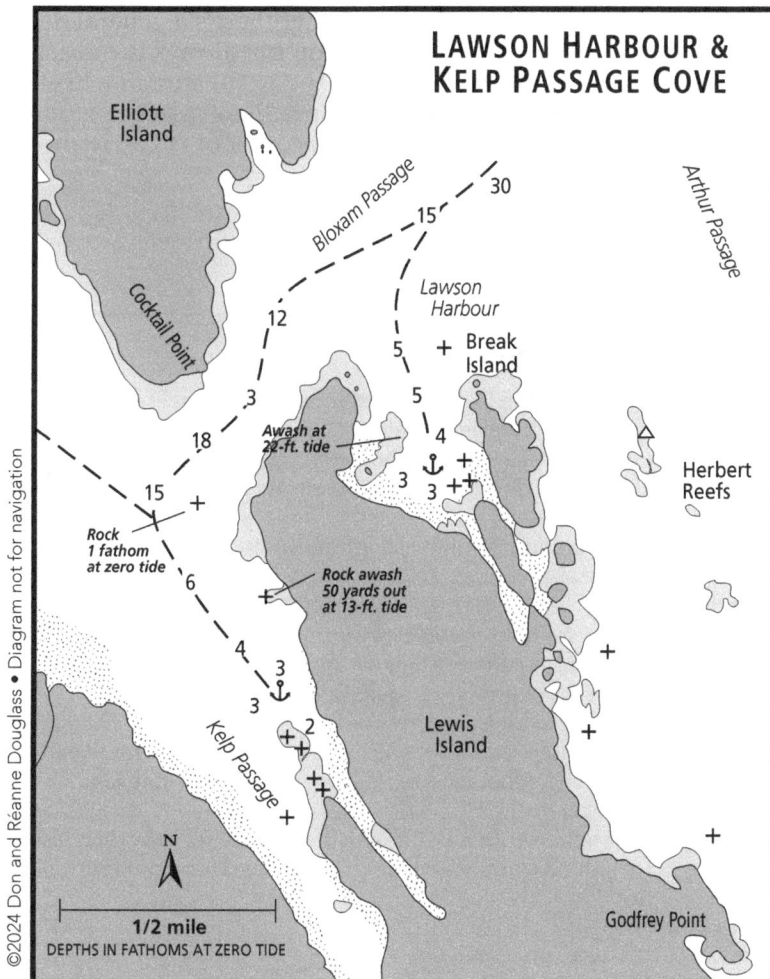

Réanne enjoys warm day at Lawson Harbour

Chatham Sound as winds pick up

Chismore Passage (Porcher Island)
1 mi W of Lawson Harbour
Entrance (SE): 54°02.12'N, 130°17.37'W
Entrance (NW): 54°04.47'N, 130°20.68'W

Chismore Passage, a well-sheltered smooth-water route, provides good anchorage almost anywhere in its south end.

Lawyer Islands (Chatham Sound)
5.3 mi N of Lawson Harbour
Position: 54°06.85'N, 130°20.62'W

Lawyer Islands consist of several islands, islets and drying reefs. The direct route to Prince Rupert passes between Lawyer and Genn islands.

Chatham Sound (Porcher Isl. to Dixon Entr.)
10 mi W of Prince Rupert
Entrance (S): 54°09.00'N, 130°25.00'W

Chatham Sound is the large body of water between Porcher Island, at its south end, and Dixon Entrance at its north. In our experience, it is either flat calm and featureless in haze, or active and lively, with winds on the nose and "square-wave" chop, uncomfortable for boats under 30 feet. More than once, at either end of the sound, we have had to reduce speed due to head seas. Currents are strong in the sound and, with any wind, it doesn't take long for nasty chop to build.

Entering Chatham Sound, you can head for Prince Rupert by passing to either side of the Lawyer Islands, staying east of Holland Island light, and favoring Kaien Island shore.

We suggest that you monitor conditions just south of Holland Island Light (shoal water and heavy Skeena River outflow), particularly in northwest or southeast winds. If unsure about proceeding, call the helpful Prince Rupert Coast Guard and ask if conditions are local or whether there's a general deterioration of the weather. You can always turn back or find temporary shelter. Pay careful attention to all entrance buoys and lights since there are dangerous foul patches off the southeast corner of Digby Island.

Telegraph Passage (Skeena River)
E of Kennedy Island
Entrance: 53°59.03'N, 130°07.32'W

The Skeena: River of Riches

Flowing unfettered from high in the coastal mountains of the Spatsizi Plateau to the ocean port of Prince Rupert, the Skeena River is the second largest river entirely within British Columbia. More than thirty tributaries join the river on its 350-mile journey as it travels generally southeast, turning west near Hazelton. The Skeena River traverses a number of Provincially-designated ecological reserves. These are selected areas that preserve natural ecosystems, rare and endangered flora and fauna, outstanding geographical phenomena, and other natural resources. Sitka and Pacific willows, black cottonwood, and red alder grow abundantly in the forests that bank the river. Townsend's and orange-crowned warblers, thrushes, and Steller's jays call the reserve home. Moose choose the area to calve and beavers dam the river's channels as it bends through the reserves. The rare wolverine occasionally makes an appearance.

The native Gitxsan people live in the valleys along the Skeena and gave the river its name. The Gitxsan word "Ksan" means "river of mist." A reconstructed Gitxsan village and museum are near the village of Gitanmaax, at the junction of the Skeena and the Bulkley Rivers. The museum acts as a cultural interpretative center for tourists and locals. In an effort to improve the economy of First Nations living in the area, local artists and craft persons display and sell their traditional arts and crafts.

Sport and commercial fishing contribute significantly to the local economy. Anglers come from all over the world during September and October to fish the river's idyllic waters for wild steelhead and salmon. The Skeena River holds the record not only for the largest hooked steelhead (36 lbs.), but also the largest Coho salmon (25 lbs.), and the largest "caught and released" Chinook salmon (99.5 lbs., 2001). More than five million salmon spawn in the Skeena each year, generating more than $100 million in revenue for the local economy.

The "river of mist" is a lush wonderland, providing visitors with exceptional wildlife viewing and fishing opportunities.

—KK

North Pacific Cannery on Inverness Passage

North Pacific Cannery museum is well worth a visit

Telegraph Passage is actually the continuation of the Skeena River that flows east of Kennedy Island. The drying banks in the approaches to the Skeena are constantly shifting, and skippers should be vigilant when navigating these waters. When southbound, leaving Eleanor Passage, head across the Skeena River toward Hegan Point. The ebb will carry you downstream, requiring you to crab to port to gain the east shore and carrying you past Robertson Banks with a 3-knot current. Beware of 4-knot ebb current on the east side of DeHorsey Island.

Marcus Passage (Skeena River)
N of Kennedy Island
Entrance (N): 54°07.16'N, 130°15.51'W

Vessels proceeding northbound in Telegraph Passage can avoid the strong ebb currents of the Skeena River by taking Marcus Passage west to Chatham Sound. See charts to avoid sizeable sandbars that can be dangerous on strong currents or falling tides. Shoals extend for roughly a mile east of Marked Tree Bluff.

Inverness Passage (Smith Island)
10 mi SE of Prince Rupert
Entrance (W): 54°09.59'N, 130°17.63'W
River entrance (Clara Point): 54°08.23'N, 130°07.70'W

Inverness Passage, which flows between the north shore of Smith Island and the Tsimpsean Peninsula, is part of a smooth-water route that crosses the outlet of the Skeena River, avoiding the south end of Chatham Sound. The grassy shore along the passage, once lined with canneries, holds the remains of two canneries: Cassiar and North Pacific. Cassiar has some heritage houses to rent and North Pacific is now a museum.

De Horsey Passage (known locally as Osland Passage), between Smith and De Horsey Islands, leads to the ruins of the Danish village, Osland. The passage dries 7 feet or more and is subject to very strong ebb currents. Entering this passage is not recommended unless you first reconnoiter a route. The color of the water in Inverness Passage is opaque pea green with little visibility due to outwash from the Skeena River.

As you pass Osborn Point and De Horsey Passage, you enter Eleanor Passage which connects with the Skeena River, 1.25 miles southeast. Avoid Clara Shoal at the east end of Eleanor Passage by favoring the DeHorsey Island shore.

We found minimum depths of 3 fathoms in Inverness Passage; in Eleanor Passage, depths were approximately 2 fathoms. However, just east of Clara Point, we found a narrow bar with just over one fathom of water at zero tide.

North Pacific Cannery Museum
(Inverness Passage)
5 mi E of Holland Island
Float position: 54°11.66'N, 130°13.58'W

The North Pacific Cannery, the oldest standing cannery on the west coast, was in operation from 1889 to 1968. Imagine what life was like when boatloads of salmon were brought in to be packed for shipment around the world! The cannery is a National Historic Site that has been preserved as a museum where the public can visit the company store, office and the workers' living quarters. The mess house has been converted into a cafe; there is also a gift store. The museum is open yearly from May through September. During the summer the museum offers demonstrations and tours. You can

North Pacific Cannery in the old days.

City of Vancouver Archives, CVA 783-175.

reach the museum by highway from Prince Rupert, where local bus service is available. A beach landing is required if you plan to arrive by dinghy. http://www.northpacificcannery.ca

Boat tours up the Skeena River can be arranged through Skeena Wilderness Safaries (tel: 800 485-7696, or 250-635-4686 (http://www.skeenaecotours.com)

Tsum Tsadai Inlet (Smith Island)

3 mi E of Holland Island
Entrance: 54°10.46'N, 130°16.75'W
Anchor: 54°10.49'N, 130°14.89'W

Tsum Tsadai Inlet, on the northwest shore of Smith Island, offers good protection from all weather and is worth braving the somewhat difficult entrance to profit from the quiet. The key to entering this inlet is to avoid the charted rocks and time your entrance to the narrow channel at or near high-water slack. Minimum depth in the fairway is about one foot at zero tide; this shallow spot lies slightly east of the 18-foot islet with a tall tree. Pass the islet on your starboard.

At the east end of the narrows—about 200 yards from the islet—there is a dangerous shoal, awash at 16 feet, which extends from the south shore to past mid-channel. Avoid this shoal by favoring the north shore and remaining about 25 feet from shore.

Anchor in 2 to 5 fathoms over brown sticky mud; very good holding.

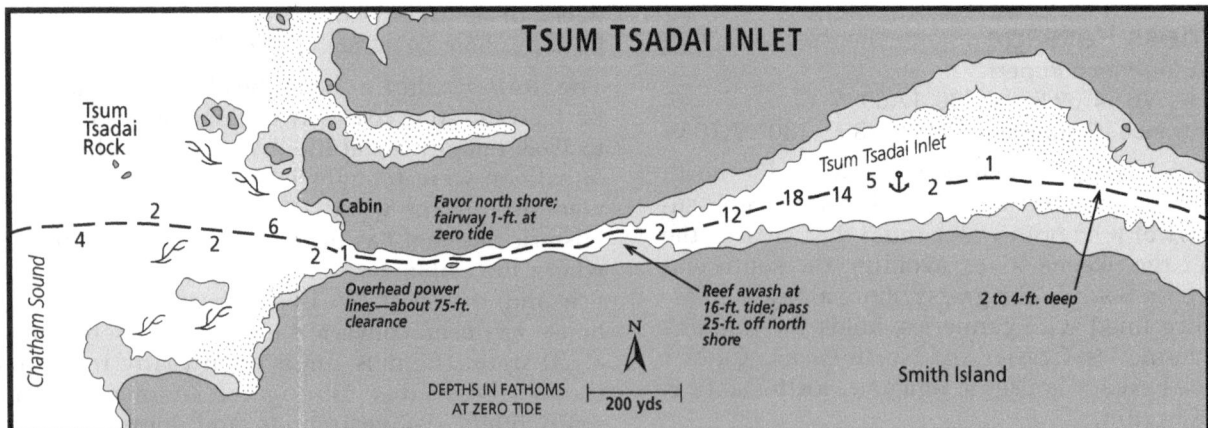

TSUM TSADAI INLET

Tsum Tsadai Rock

Chatham Sound

Cabin

Favor north shore; fairway 1-ft. at zero tide

Overhead power lines—about 75-ft. clearance

Reef awash at 16-ft. tide; pass 25-ft. off north shore

Tsum Tsadai Inlet

2 to 4-ft. deep

Smith Island

DEPTHS IN FATHOMS AT ZERO TIDE

200 yds

N

©2024 Don and Réanne Douglass • Diagram not for navigation

Porpoise Channel

1.8 mi SW of Port Edward
Range entrance: 54°11.52'N, 130°20.55'W
Deep water entrance: 54°12.25'N, 130°19.87'W

Prince Rupert Harbour (Kaien Island)

Spire Island entrance: 54°14.81'N, 130°20.94'W

Prince Rupert, located on Kaien Island, is a culturally diverse city that boasts the deepest natural harbor in North America. Coal, grain, lumber, minerals, pulp, and fish are exported all over the globe from here. The city is served by air, highway system, and rail. Full services are available for pleasure craft and commercial vessels. As you enter the harbor, monitor Vessel Traffic Services on VHF Channel for information about the approach of large ships.

Note that there is a strictly controlled 5-knot speed limit within 600 yards of the eastern shore from Fairview Small Craft marina to Rushbrook Floats in Prince Rupert Harbour.

For vessels headed southbound from Alaska, this is the first port of entry. To clear Customs call 888-226-7277 (in Hamilton, Ontario) from the dock at Cow Bay Marina, Rushbrook Floats or from Prince Rupert Yacht Club. Canadian Customs is available by phone 24 hours a day, seven days a week. Wait aboard until a Customs Officer clears you. Boaters with NEXUS phone 866-996-3987 at least 30 minutes before arrival.

Small craft can find moorage at several facilities: Cow Bay Marina, the Prince Rupert Rowing and Yacht Club (PRRYC) in Cow Bay, or the public floats at Rushbrook, a mile north of the yacht club. Rushbrook Floats and Fairview floats (south of the ferry docks) are mainly for fishing vessels and have limited guest moorage.

You can buy fuel at Northwest Fuels in Cow Bay, open daily - contact on VHF 71 or call 250-624-4106.

Safeway, three blocks from Cow Bay, has everything a skipper or first mate could possibly want. If you buy more than you can carry, taxi service is convenient and reasonable. There is a shopping mall in town with a Walmart. For marine supplies, charts and nautical books head to SeaSport Marine at 295–1st Avenue East (tel: 250-624-5337). (PRRYC provides a list of addresses and telephone numbers of businesses that cater to boats, including repairs and parts.)

Other services: propane tanks can be filled at Northwest Fuels one block from the yacht club. King Koin Laundromat at 745 W. 2nd Ave W. offers both self-service and wash-and-fold.

Cow Bay area in Prince Rupert Harbour

To learn about the cultural history of the area, visit the Museum of Northern British Columbia (tel. 250-624-3207), housed in the beautiful longhouse along the waterfront to the west of Mariners Memorial Park. In the park, of interest to boaters are the names of regional mariners who have been lost at sea—a sadly impressive number! In addition, on display is the *Kaza Maru*, a small, open Japanese wooden fishing boat that floated across the Pacific and washed ashore on the British Columbia coast; its owner was lost at sea off Japan.

Free brochures and a city map are available at the Tourist Centre. If you're tired of galley cooking, the city map contains a list of the numerous restaurants in town. Smile's Seafood cafe, a "landmark" famous for its fish and chips, and the Breakers Pub are in Cow Bay. If you feel like celebrating in fine style, the dining room of the Crest Motor Hotel (222-1st Avenue West) has consistently good quality food and excellent service.

Prince Rupert Visitor Information Centre, is a good source for information on the services and activities around town and in the region; see visitprincerupert.com There is daily air transportation to and from Rupert. Via Rail provides service to Jasper, Alberta—the western terminus of the trans-Canada railway line. (Ferry information and reservations: The Alaska Ferry (1-800-642-0066 U.S.); 1-250-627-1744 B.C. local); B.C. Ferries (1-877-223-8778) in Canada & U.S.; local: 250-624-9627.

Canadian Coast Guard recommends that you file a sail plan if you are heading out to Haida Gwaii. Contact the Marine Communications and Traffic Services Centre (MCTS) by telephone (250-627-3081) or by VHF. Be ready with the names of persons aboard, date and point of departure and return, route information, emergency equipment carried, description of your vessel, its make and license or documentation. A copy of Transport Canada Publication is available on their website. Be sure to cancel your float plan on the scheduled date.

Photo courtesy CHS, Pacific Region

Butze Rapids from Fern Passage "

Photo by Lorena Landon

Prince Rupert Rowing & Yacht Club in Cow Bay

Casey Cove (Prince Rupert Harbour)
1.1 mi SE of ferry docks
Entrance: 54°16.92'N, 130°22.22'W

Temporary anchorage can be found in Casey Cove out of the tidal stream and chop.

Anchor in 5 fathoms over an unrecorded bottom.

Dodge Cove (Prince Rupert Harbour)
1 mi E of ferry docks
Range entrance: 54°17.51'N, 130°22.26'W
Public float position: 54°17.35'N, 130°22.98'W

Good shelter can be found in Dodge Cove, on the southwest side of Prince Rupert Harbour. The public floats are generally crowded but rafting is encouraged. The cove is shallow, 1 to 2 feet at zero tide, but there is swinging room for several boats.

Russell Arm (Prince Rupert Harbour)
Entrance: 54°19.29'N, 130°21.66'W
Anchor: 54°19.59'N, 130°21.72'W

Russell Arm, on the north side of Prince Rupert Harbour, offers shelter from all but strong southerlies, 0.2 mile north of Burrowes Island.

Anchor in 3 fathoms over mud with good holding.

Prince Rupert Rowing & Yacht Club
(Prince Rupert Harbour)
1.8 mi NE of ferry docks
Entrance: 54°19.23'N, 130°19.13'W

The Yacht Club, a five-minute walk from town, has Wi-Fi, water, showers, ice, and garbage disposal. Electricity (30 amp) is available for an added fee.

Changes at the Port of Prince Rupert

Prince Rupert has a population of about 12,300 people (2021), making it one of the largest population centers between Vancouver and Juneau. The town is accessible by sea, air, road, and rail, but has little metropolitan congestion, making it an attractive location for a North American freight terminal. The Port of Prince Rupert is the deepest natural harbor in North America, with a main channel depth of 115 feet, compared with depths of 53 feet and 36 feet at the Ports of Los Angeles and Seattle respectively. The marine climate keeps the port ice free year-round, although the area can be subject to North Pacific gales in the winter time. Due to its position along the Great Circle shipping route, Prince Rupert is also significantly closer to Asian ports than other west coast ports, and comparison of shipping a container from Shanghai to Chicago via either Prince Rupert of Los Angeles favors the Canadian route by three to four days of travel time. The Port of Prince Rupert presently handles bulk cargo including grain and forest products as well as containerized freight, and the Port is seeing steady annual increases in volume.

In addition to containerized and bulk freight, Prince Rupert's proximity to the gas and oil fields of northern Alberta and British Columbia have created demand for construction of oil and gas facilities. At least twelve projects are in various stages of scoping and permitting, including crude oil refineries. Proposed pipelines and terminal facilities for handling crude oil, natural gas, and LNG pipeline have been under consideration in both Prince Rupert and Kitimat, fifty miles to the south.

The Prince Rupert Visitor Information Centre is also the Port's Interpretive Centre. The centre is open year-round, and knowledgeable guides can answer your questions about port operations as well as provide information about boating in the surrounding waters.

—LW

The dock managers of the club are friendly and helpful, and will gladly answer questions if you're unfamiliar with Prince Rupert. Call them on VHF Channel 73 to arrange for a slip as you arrive. Land telephone: 250-624-4317; email: info@prryc.com. The moorage is available to everyone, but reservations are recommended. When storms are expected, it's recommended you don't use the outermost float of the yacht club.

Cow Bay Marina breakwater in the foreground with slips beyond

Cow Bay Marina
(Prince Rupert Harbour)
1.7 mi NE of ferry docks
Entrance: 54°19.20'N, 130°19.25'W

Cow Bay Marina—a pleasure craft marina with slips for vessels up to 80 feet and breakwater side tie for vessels up to 140 feet. Located below Atlin Terminal and west of the yacht club. Water, 30, 50, & 100 amp power, washrooms; showers; Wi-Fi; garbage drop are available. Tel: 250-622-2628; www: cowbaymarina.ca; reservations recommended; monitors VHF 66A. Fuel is available at Northwest Fuels Ltd. Weather can be monitored on VHF Channel 08.

Rushbrook Floats (Prince Rupert Harbour)
0.5 mi E of Cow Bay
Entrance: 54°19.58'N, 130°18.36'W

Rushbrook Floats, about a mile north of town, has space for about 280 vessels. From June through August when the trawlers and gillnetters are active, commercial vessels have priority. Water and power are available; there are public washrooms and showers. The marina has a free public launch ramp. An old railway line, converted to a walking and cycling trail, connects Rushbrook Floats with Seal Cove, providing a beautiful evening walk along the waterfront. Land telephone: 250-624-9400; website: peharbourauthority.ca

Seal Cove (Prince Rupert Harbour)
1 mi E of Rushbrook Floats
Entrance: 54°19.99'N, 130°16.75'W

Fern Passage (Kaien Island)
1.1 mi E of Rushbrook Floats
Entrance (N): 54°20.02'N, 130°16.60'W

Butze Rapids (Fern Passage)
2 mi SE of Seal Cove
Position: 54°18.24'N, 130°14.89'W

Morse Basin (Fern Passage)
3 mi S of Seal Cove
North entrance: 54°17.93'N, 130°14.73'W

Morse Basin can be entered carefully by cruising boats only through Butze Rapids and then only at slack water. Many small sportfishing boats and some local cruising boats use Morse Basin as a protected and quiet retreat. Some of the attractions are:

Denise Inlet (Morse Basin)
Entrance: 54°15.85'N, 130°12.21'W

Kloiya Bay (Morse Basin)
Position: 54°15.74'N, 130°12.44'W

Miller Bay (Morse Basin)
Entrance: 54°16.03'N, 130°15.65'W

Tuck Inlet (Prince Rupert Harbour)
5.2 mi NE of Cow Bay
Entrance: 54°23.92'N, 130°15.35'W

Tuck Inlet is located at the northeast end of Prince Rupert Harbour. Landlocked by Tuck Narrows, the inlet is relatively sheltered but deep and steep-to and seldom visited.

Rushbrooke floats, aerial view

Gurd I.

Gunboat Hbr

Kumealon (West) Inlet

Kitkatla Channel

Gasboat Passage

Ogden Channel

Stuart Anchorage

Kumealon I. Cove

Grenville Channel

Baker Inlet

Watts Narrows

50'

Captain Cove

KITKATLA

Kxngeal Inlet

Ship Anchorage

Browning Entrance

Dolphin I.

Spicer I.

Connis Cove

Beaver Passage

Annie's Inlet

Petrel

East Inlet

Spicer Complex

Murder Cove

Newcombe Hbr

Klewnuggit Inlet

Channel

Exposed Inlet

40'

McCauley I.

Keswar Inlet

Hevenor Inlet

Larsen Hbr

Logan Bay

Port Canaveral

Squall Bay

Allcroft Point Cove

Markle Inlet

Wilson Inlet

Pitt

Nettle Basin

Lowe Lake

Griffith Hbr

Dixon I.

Dory Passage

Island

Verney Falls

Squall I.

Wright I.

Math Is.

Lowe Inlet

Kingkown Inlet

Colby Bay

Principe Channel

Anger I.

Ire Inlet

Nass Passage

Curtis Inlet

Miller Inlet

30'

Banks

Hodgson Cove

Moolock Cove

Bonilla I.

Island

Patterson Inlet

Hawkins Narrows

Farrant I. Lagoon

Limestone Bay

Mink Trap Bay

Lundy Cove

Buchan Inlet

Union Passage

Peters Narrows

Farrant I.

Port Stephens

Tuwartz Inlet

Mitchell Cove

Kooryet Bay

Foul Bay

Monckton Inlet

Fin I.

20'

Waller Bay

Nepean Sound

Dillon Cove

Grief Point

Otter Channel

Squally Channel

Gung Ho Bay

Harwood Bay

Terror Point

Calamity Bay

Otter Passage

Trutch I.

Estevan

Weinberg Inlet

10'

Geodetic Cove

Devlin Bay

Betteridge Inlet

Langley Passage

Sound

Ethedal Bay

Pryor I.

Trouble Pass

Campania I.

Barnard I.

McMicking Inlet

Oswald Bay

Lotbiniere I.

Murray Anch.

Dewdney

Gillen Hbr.

Pemberton Bay

53°N

N

0 2 4 6 8 10
NAUTICAL MILES

10

Estevan Sound,
Banks Island, Principe
and Petrel Channels

©2024 Don and Réanne Douglass • Diagram not for navigation

10

Estevan Sound, Banks Island, Principe and Petrel Channels

The area stretching from the south end of Esteven Sound to the northern tip of Banks Island is a continuation of the "wild" Outer Passage. Infrequently visited and still natural, these waters—which offer unlimited opportunities for summer cruising and kayaking—are a viable alternative to the "beaten track" of Grenville Channel. A major bird flyway lies along this route and fishing is excellent—so good that you may be surprised from time to time to encounter a hardy local who has come all the way from Kitimat in a small boat to catch his quota.

Ranking among the more interesting choices for exploring are the Estevan Group—a series of five islands and numerous islets at the head of Caamaño Sound—and the western shores of Campania and Pitt islands. McMiking Inlet on Campania Island has white sandy shores where sandhill cranes and loons can often be sighted. Among the many anchor sites along the Pitt Island shore, Monckton Inlet, Buchan Inlet, Lundy Cove, and Moolock Cove offer good protection. The waters around Anger Island, Ala Passage and the "Math Islands" are outstanding for their remoteness and possibilities for exploring by kayak and small boat.

Banks Island, whose Principe Channel shore includes relatively few indentations, has perhaps the most rugged western coastline of all the islands in this region—its history is written in names such as Calamity Bay, Terror Point, Grief Point and Foul Bay. Griffith Harbour, with its maze of islets is a prime example of this west coast ruggedness, and it is also considered a "jumping off" point for the Haida Gwaii. Both Pitt Island and Banks Island have innumerable lakes, ponds, and muskeg bogs. Although the inlets and islands along Principe Channel are sheltered, the channel does kick up nasty chop of three to four feet when winds oppose an ebbing tide, and currents are 2 knots or more. To minimize discomfort in such conditions, it's a good idea to get underway early in the morning in prevailing winds and seek shelter during storms.

Although you may see a cruise ships every so often in Principe Channel during summer season, this is wilderness cruising at its best—a place that opens new possibilities for human experience and understanding. But, along with the thrill of exploration, come marginal radio reception, a lack of navigational aids, and the possibility of strong winds or currents. When you venture along this Outer Passage have fun, but be prepared and be vigilant! (Please see sidebar under Principe Channel to determine how you can help keep this wonderful area natural and wild.)

Estevan Sound (Campania Island)
24 mi SW of Hartley Bay
Entrance (S): 52°56.77'N, 129°23.38'W
Entrance (N): 53°08.47'N, 129°37.51'W

Estevan Sound is one of the smaller and more remote of the B.C. sounds. Three miles wide and twelve miles long, it allows most boats to pass through it in just an hour or two. Somewhat isolated by Campania Sound, on the south, and Nepean Sound to the north, Estevan Sound is a small jewel worth at least a lunch stop, if not a full-scale exploration. The west coast of Campania Island has beautiful white sand beaches, small intricate channels—almost like lagoons—where you can easily get lost as you wander around in human-powered boats. Here there exists a strange, flat forest whose shores rise abruptly to a tree line where only stunted, twisted trees survive.

Langley Passage in the center of the Estevan Group of islands is a prelude to true wilderness. To sense this wildness firsthand, consider anchoring in Geodesic Cove and circumnavigating Trutch Island (18 miles) by paddle power in a kayak or dinghy; we're certain you won't be disappointed.

In Estevan Sound, between Hickey Islands, Dupont Island and west to Borthwick Rock, we have found a south-flowing current of 3 to 3.5 knots on spring ebbs. Under these conditions, the sound is lumpy with southwest swells and breaking whitecaps. On the flood we find 2 to 2.5 knots.

Baidarka exploring the outer passage

Estevan Group (Estevan Sound)
18 mi NW of Aristazabal Island

The Estevan Group is divided by Langley Passage on the north side. Most of the area to the south is charted only at a small scale and remains truly wild.

Pemberton Bay (Dewdney Island)
16 mi NW of Borrowman Bay
Entrance: 52°56.39'N, 129°35.89'W

Pemberton Bay, on the southwest side of the Estevan Group, can provide cruising boats with good protection tucked into the far corner of Gillen Harbour. The bay should be avoided in southerly weather or when a strong ebb is running with wind or southwest swell.

On crossing Hecate Strait from Moresby Island in Haida Gwaii, Gillen Harbour can offer quick shelter from northwest winds and chop. The navigation light

on Jacinto Island at the southwest end of Pemberton Bay makes a good leading mark when approaching the coast. Note that the exposed south side of Jacinto Island is devoid of vegetation for 60 to 70 feet above the water due to the pounding it receives during severe storms.

Gillen Harbour (Pemberton Bay)
1.7 mi N of Pemberton Bay
Entrance (S channel): 52°58.38'N, 129°36.19'W
Anchor (NE of Adams I.): 52°58.96'N, 129°35.58'W

Gillen Harbour has collected major driftwood over the decades, indicating that storm-force winds blow up its entrance. However, its far eastern end offers a calm setting regardless of outside conditions. We consider this a very good spot to ride out a gale. The flat 2-fathom bottom between Adams Island and the islet to the east is as bombproof as it gets on the west coast. Avoid the small rock pile which dries at 7 feet on the northeast side of Adams Island about 100 feet out that extends farther from shore than charts suggest. The inside waters are dark brown with poor visibility.

Anchor in 2 fathoms east of Adams Island over sticky mud with very good holding.

Gillen Harbour

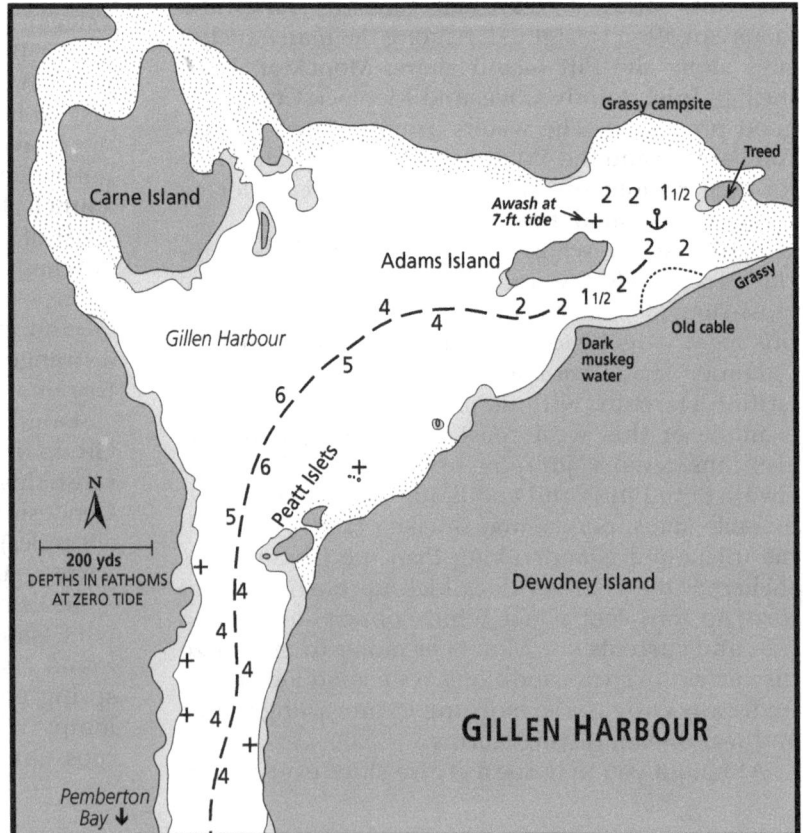

©2024 Don and Réanne Douglass • Diagram not for navigation

Devlin Bay (Gillespie Channel)

2.7 mi SE of Geodetic Cove
Entrance: 53°04.05'N, 129°35.25'W
Anchor: 53°03.63'N, 129°36.52'W

Devlin Bay, on the south side of Trutch Island, offers fair-to-good protection in most weather. Enter north of the wooded islet and avoid the reefs and fast current in the vicinity. A tender or kayak can use the interesting, convoluted passage that leads west to Hecate Strait via Langley Passage.

Anchor in 6 to 8 fathoms, over a mixed bottom with rocks, fair-to-good holding.

Gillespie Channel, Langley Passage

(Estevan Group)
0.2 mi SE of Devlin Bay
Northeast entrance: 53°03.99'N, 129°35.61'W
Southwest entrance: 53°02.93'N, 129°37.32'W

Gillespie Channel, the narrow east end of Langley Passage, offers a challenge to boaters due to its fast-moving water over an irregular bottom with rocks and kelp. The chart is inadequate for making navigation easy; transiting the channel should not be attempted in poor visibility or foul weather. On your first try, you may want to transit at or near slack

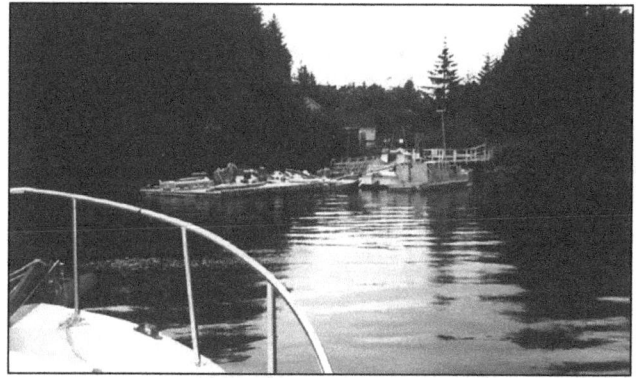

Ethelda Bay, Trutch Island

water. Read the river, stay in the fast-moving main channel, avoiding the kelp, breaking water, and turbulence on either side.

Langley Passage (Estevan Sound)

6 mi W of McMicking Inlet
Anchor (E): 53°02.82'N, 129°37.79'W
Anchor (W): 53°03.12'N, 129°39.72'W

Langley Passage is a lovely, intricate passage that connects Estevan Sound with Hecate Strait. Cruising boats should use only the east entrance. Seas are reported to break across the narrow western entrance in moderate weather. The passage is a quiet place with a charm of its own where wolves and deer roam the islands, and shrimp and crab abound.

The large antenna on the mountaintop at the south side of Trutch Island, which can be seen from Estevan Sound in clear weather, played an important role in the Cold War as part of the intercontinental ballistic early warning system to protect North America from potential incoming Russian missiles.

Anchor (east 0.3 mile southwest of buoy "ET4") in 10 fathoms, soft bottom; fair-to-good holding.

Anchor (west 0.7 mi SW of "ET3") in 8 fathoms over mud; good holding.

Ethelda Bay (Langley Passage)

2.4 mi W of Devlin Bay
Anchor (Ethelda Bay): 53°03.33'N, 129°40.61'W

Note: Ethelda Bay-Tennant Island Conservancy was designated as a conservancy in 2007. It was once the site of a radio beacon station (operated by the DOT, Ottawa) where a maintenance crew was housed. Dan and Danielle Pollock purchased the houses, dock, generator station, and helicopter pad from the federal government in 1996 to develop a tourist and fishing lodge and an abalone hatchery. All of that activity has ended, and the former dock has vanished.

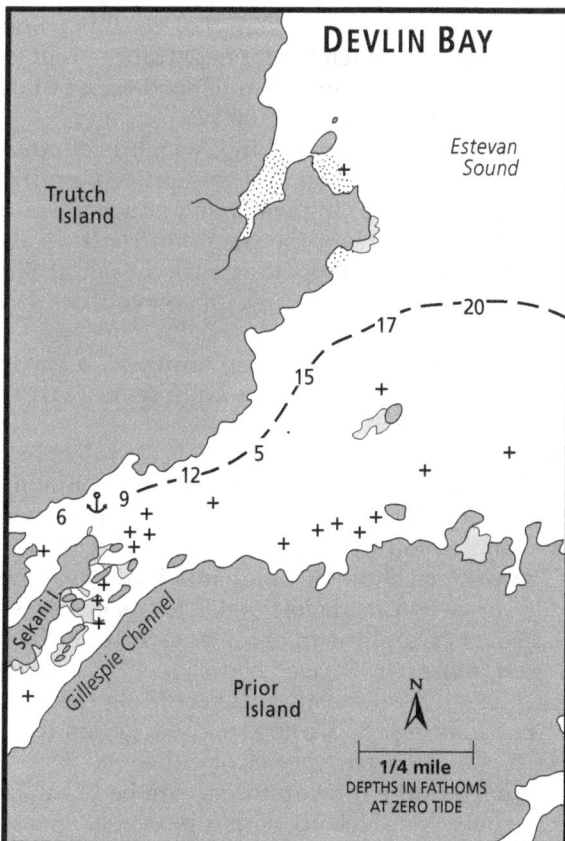

DEVLIN BAY

Estevan Sound

Trutch Island

20

17

15

12   5

6   9

Sekani

Gillespie Channel

Prior Island

N

1/4 mile
DEPTHS IN FATHOMS
AT ZERO TIDE

©2024 Don and Réanne Douglass • Diagram not for navigation

There are several good anchoring opportunities in Langley Passage. We list two of the better ones west and east that offer protection from both strong northwest and southeast winds as well as Ethelda Bay.

Anchor in Ethelda Bay in 12 to 14 fathoms over mud; good holding.

Geodetic Cove (Trutch Island)

2.5 mi N of Devlin Anchorage
Entrance: 53°06.07'N, 129°37.54'W
Anchor: 53°05.56'N, 129°37.79'W (See Caution)
Geodetic Cove is 2.3 miles NNW of Devlin Bay.

Geodetic Cove is seldom visited because it is narrow and only charted at small scale. We feel that the cove offers very good protection for small cruising boats, especially in southeast storms, deep near the head of the cove; swinging room within the entire cove is limited. Trees overhang the shore on either side of the 100-foot-wide cove, touching the water at high tide, and there are no drift logs. The flat sandy bottom shows no indication of rocks and holding is good.

Upon entering the cove, favor the west shore to avoid a rocky shoal that extends about 50 yards—or a third of the way—from the east shore. Watch your depth sounder in the narrows on low water. Vessels longer than 35-ft may prefer to anchor northeast of the narrows with a possible stern tie to shore to restrict swinging room. We comfortably rode out a two-day southerly anchored north of the narrows and felt just light wake caused by an occasional cruise ship. However, during periods of heavy outflow winds from Douglas Channel, this outer basin may be subject to chop. Vessels of less than 35 feet can find anchorage in the inner basin in 1½ to 2 fathoms where it appears to be free of any chop; swinging room is limited here, also. Larger boats that need more swinging room should consider Devlin Anchorage or one of the inlets on Campania Island.

Anchor (outer basin) in about 5 fathoms over sand and mud with some kelp; fair-to-good holding.

Anchor (inner basin) in about 1½ fathoms over a flat bottom of sand and soft brown mud and shells with some kelp and grass; good-to-very-good holding.

McMicking Inlet

(Campania Island)
15.5 mi NW of Surf Inlet
Entrance: 53°02.15'N, 129°27.56'W
Anchor: 53°04.83'N, 129°28.17'W

McMicking Inlet, a special place for boaters up to a navigational challenge, provides good landlocked

McMicking Inlet

protection north of the second narrows. The islands, islets, rocks and reefs that fill its southern entrance effectively diminish any swell. Avoid the rocks and shoals east of Logan Rock when approaching the entrance point.

The waters in the inlet are darkened by muskeg, causing poor underwater visibility. Entering the inlet requires careful piloting. The inner entrance point we use is located 0.7 mile due east of Logan Rock. Northbound boats can reach the inner entrance point from a southern outer entrance point 0.5 southeast of Cartwright Rocks (53°01.10'N, 129°26.50'W). Southbound boats can reach the inner entrance point from an outer entrance point 0.3 mile northwest of Logan Rock at (53° 02.80'N, 129°28.50'W).

The entrance to McMicking, which is circuitous, requires a sharp lookout and responsive helmsmanship. Avoid all breaking water and attached kelp. At the first narrows, favor the west shore (within about 75 feet); there is a dangerous rock awash at 3 or 4 feet on the end of the drying spit, on your starboard hand.

Don't explore this area in anything but a kayak or dinghy without the help of a large scale chart with good detail.

McMicking Inlet (as well as the two inlets immediately north) provides a wonderful environment for exploration. The maze of islands and islets can cause confusion if you don't pay attention, but it's worth it. The western shore of Campania Island, southeast of Jewsbury Peninsula, is notable for its lovely white sand beaches, and the inlet is a wonderful bird habitat. One morning we watched two elusive sandhill cranes feeding on the mud flats, ruffling their feathers and making their unusual calls. Loons like the area, too, as do many species of gulls.

A quarter-mile hike up the stream bed to the east takes you to a tableland with a peat-bog, "post-for-

GEODETIC COVE

Estevan Sound

20

10

Geodetic Cove

Favor
west
shore

5

Boats greater
than 35-ft.

5

3

1

Narrows to 100-ft.

Fallen
tree

Trutch
Island

1 1/2

Favor
east
shore

1 1/2

Antenna
on peak

1 1/2

Boats less than 35-ft.

N

100 yds

DEPTHS IN FATHOMS AT ZERO TIDE

©2024 Don and Réanne Douglass • Diagram not for navigation

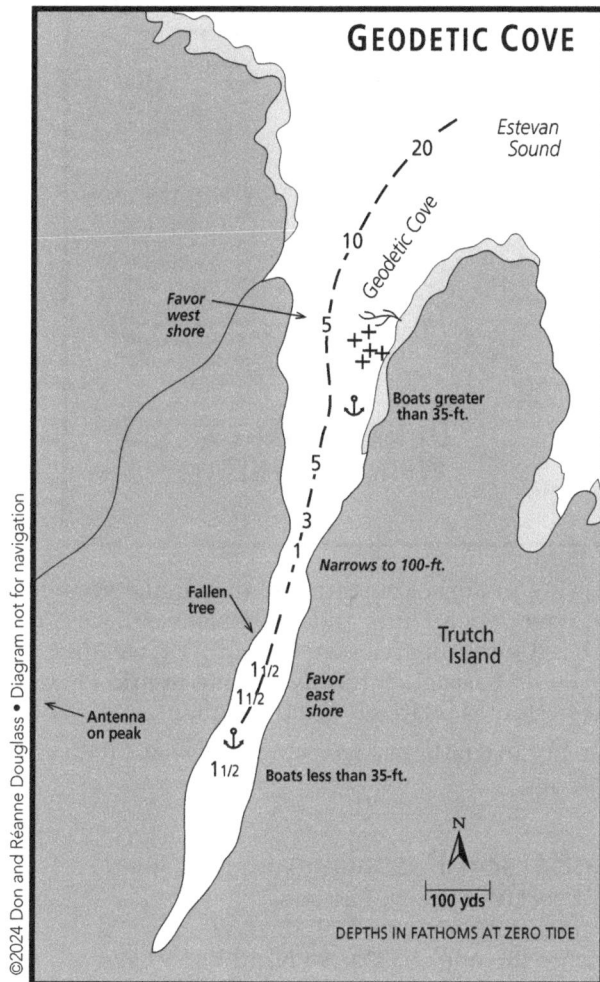

McMicking Narrows

est" environment, including bonsai-shaped trees, created after the original forest died off. An interesting—if speculative—theory postulates that because the lighter-colored mosses reflect sunlight, rather than absorbing it as trees do, the atmosphere will grow colder, contributing to a possible new ice age.

There are a number of possible anchor sites within the vicinity, especially using a stern tie. We prefer the protected anchor site in the small cove on the east side of the main basin, west of an island that dries on all but its west side. The water in the cove is reported to remain smooth even in 60-knot southeast storms. In a southeast storm, since McMicking Inlet faces south, the rocks would be a dangerous lee shore. Weinberg Inlet via Dunn Passage or Anderson Passage would be a safer entrance under such conditions.

Anchor (east cove) in 4 fathoms over sand and mud; very good holding.

Betteridge Inlet

(Campania Island)
2.5 mi NW of McMicking Inlet
Entrance (Hale Rock): 53°04.93'N, 129°29.99'W
Anchor: 53°06.17'N, 129°30.25'W

Betteridge Inlet can be a calm-water playground for dinghies or kayaks and a provider of secure anchorages. It can also be confusing, even a nightmare. Between Jewsbury and Finlayson peninsulas, there are dozens of unnamed islands and islets. Do not attempt to enter Betteridge Inlet without a large scale chart. Favor Hale Islet, a major islet with trees. The narrow entrance should not be attempted during strong southerlies or in limited visibility. An alert bow watch is recommended to help avoid the many charted rocks, reefs, and patches of kelp.

Hundreds of silver drift logs lie along the rocky shores and islets that have a southern exposure. The northwest shore, in particular, is littered with all sizes of drift logs. The northwest basin can provide shelter or solitude from prevailing northwesterlies during fair weather. For the adventurous, there is a route that circles east, then south to within 200 yards of the upper end of McMicking Inlet. This basin may be more protected from swells and chop than most of the anchorages on the west coast.

The anchor site listed above is a temporary one for reconnoitering the island maze to the east and south. The depth at this site is 9 fathoms over a soft bottom with poor to fair holding depending on how well you set anchor. Watch spring currents and maintain an anchor watch.

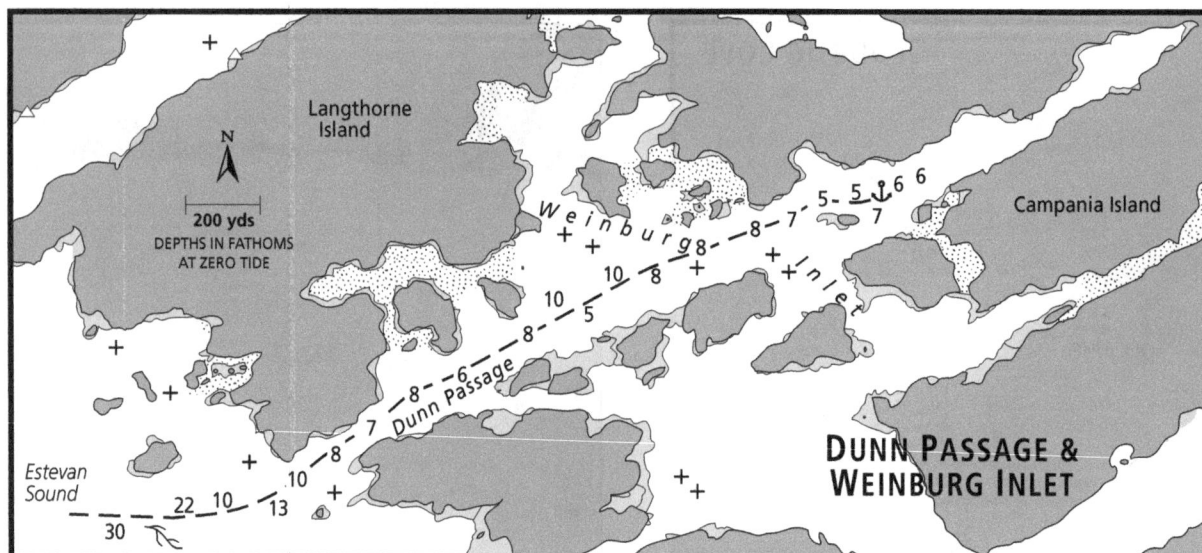

Dunn Passage & Weinburg Inlet

©2024 Don and Réanne Douglass • Diagram not for navigation

Dunn Passage/Weinburg Inlet

(Campania Island)

2.6 mi NW of Betteridge Inlet

Entrance: 53°06.85'N, 129°32.76'W

Anchor (Weinburg Inlet): 53°07.51'W, 129°30.96'W

Dunn Passage leads into a maze of islets and lagoons. Weinburg and Betteridge inlets to the south—with miniature archipelagos of over a hundred islets—are fun to explore by dinghy or kayak. Covered with stubby cedars, the islets give the feeling of being on a small pond in the midst of the Black Forest.)

The head of Dunn Passage in Weinberg Inlet (see diagram) is a bombproof anchorage for small boats or larger boats with a shore tie. No driftwood or chop enters here. The water is clear and schools of fish passing underneath your keel may make your echo sounder dance. Dunn and Anderson passages can be entered with relative ease in southerly weather. Enter Dunn Passage, carefully staying in mid-channel; the bottom is relatively flat throughout.

Anchor in 6 fathoms over sand and gravel with good holding.

Anderson Passage (Weinberg Inlet)

0.75 mi NW of Dunn Passage

Entrance: 53°07.53'N, 129°33.28'W

Anchor (SE nook): 53°07.94'N, 129°31.97'W

Anderson Passage leads to a large basin where there is a good anchorage, with swinging room, for several boats. This passage is the easiest way to enter

---

Banks Island

Off the British Columbia coast south of Prince Rupert, in Hecate Straight, there is a wing-shaped strip of land called Banks Island. Seventy-two kilometers (forty-five miles) long, it ranges from ten to eighteen kilometers (six to eleven miles) in width.

In 1787, British fur traders Charles Duncan and James Colnett pulled into Calamity Bay at the south end of Banks Island to make repairs on their vessels *Prince of Wales* and *Princess Royal*. Soon they became involved in skirmishes with the Kitkatla Band of the Tsimshian First Nations. The trouble escalated when one of the British long boats disappeared. Captains Duncan and Colnett ordered the use of muskets and cannons, resulting in several Kitkatla deaths. But despite the conflicts, the British remained on the island for eleven weeks, exploring and mapping the waterways of Principe Channel, Douglas Channel, and Laredo Sound. In 1788, the island was officially named after Sir Joseph Banks, who had encouraged British fur trading voyages to the Pacific Northwest.

Skirmishes on the island today are avian in nature. Banks Island is home to a significant number of seabird species. The most abundant species is the Rhinoceros Auklet, which nests in burrows or deep crevices. In 1988, observers tallied 91,640 nesting pairs, seven percent of the global population of this species. Other species nesting there include the Cassins auklet, pigeon guillemot, glaucous-winged gull, fork-tailed storm petrel, and Leach's storm petrel. Often sighted in this area are peregrine falcons, tufted and horned puffins, white-winged scoters, and marbled murrelets. While boating along the shore of Banks Islands in the summer, visitors can often spot these birds diving for fish.   —KK

Weinberg Inlet in limited visibility—especially for larger boats that can anchor in the center of the basin north of Langthorne Island in about 13 fathoms. Small boats can anchor in the more scenic and intimate southeast nook.

Anchor (southeast nook) in 5 fathoms over soft mud with fair-to-good holding.

Harwood Bay
(Campania Island)
1.2 mi NW of Anderson Passage
Entrance: 53°08.67'N, 129°34.04'W
Anchor (N basin): 53°09.13'N, 129°33.36'W
Anchor (E basin): 53° 08.82'N, 129° 33.20'W

We have found that Harwood Bay offers very good shelter for small boats in prevailing northwest summer winds. Its scenery is typical of Outer Passage wilderness. There is little driftwood in its north basin and none in its eastern basin, indicating safe protection. We would anchor here in all conditions except in a strong southwesterly or during a major storm front. If a major storm is expected, Dunn Passage is preferable.

Harwood Bay is one of the easiest anchorages to enter in Estevan Sound, and the only one to use under a radar approach. We tuck up in either the small far northern or the eastern basin, as indicated in the diagram. The basin is surrounded by old-growth forest, and the water is clear with visibility better than 12 feet. Larger vessels may find the east basin a bit tight and shallow. Anchor outside if necessary. Lindsay, 0.6 mi north, is rather exposed.

Anchor (north basin) in 5 fathoms, over brown sand and mud with good holding.

Anchor (east basin) in 5 fathoms, over sand and mud with good holding.

Otter Passage
(Estevan Group)
6.5 mi NW of Delvin Anchorage
Entrance (NE): 53°09.30'N, 129°42.62'W

Intricate Otter Passage requires sharp visual identification of all hazards; however, the kelp beds help identify submerged reefs in late summer and keep swell down. Watch for 6-knot current and transit on a slack during spring tides. Don't enter or exit on an ebb with southwest swells or chop running.

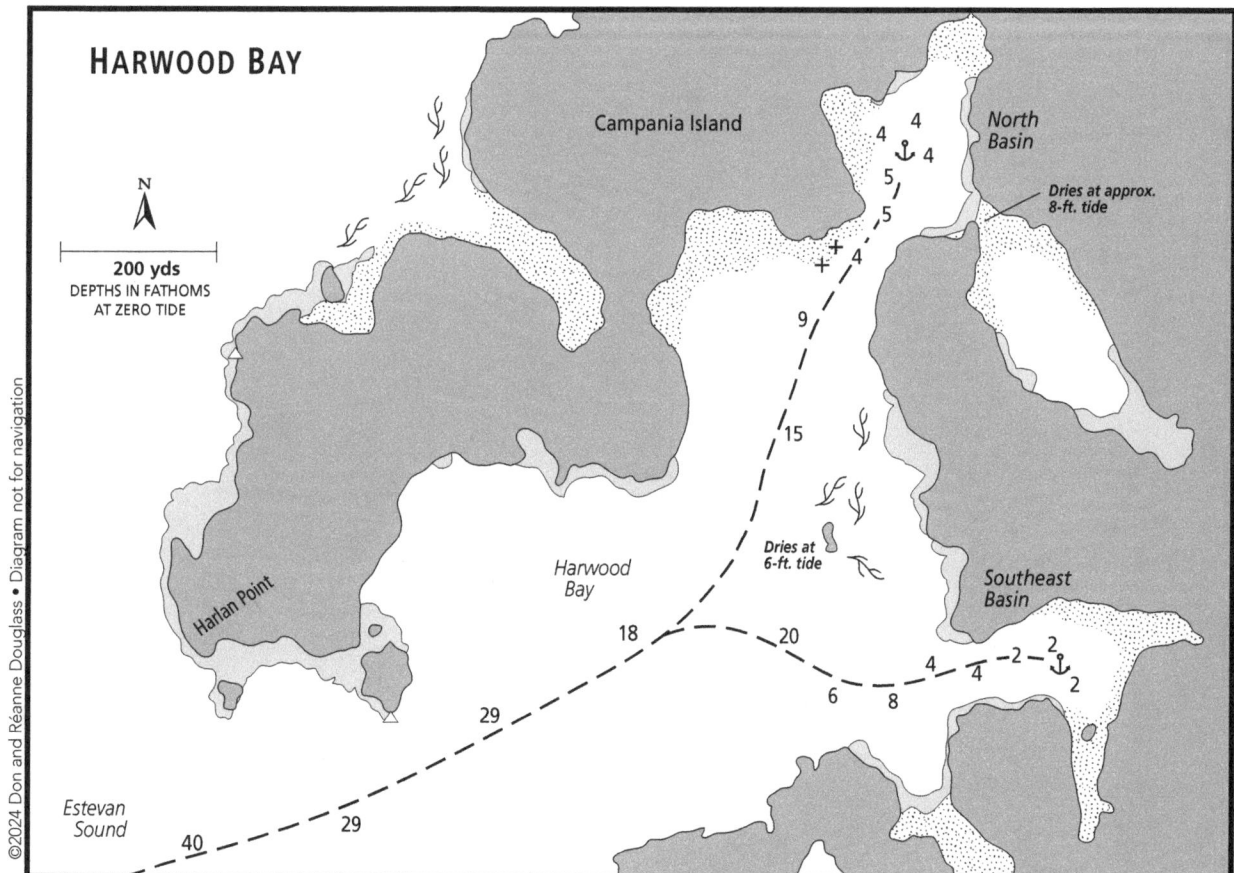

Gung Ho Bay (Banks Island)
6.7 mi NW of Geodetic Cove
Entrance: 53°10.75'N, 129°45.72'W
Anchor: 53°10.68'N, 129°46.63'W

Gung Ho Bay, frequently used as an anchorage by sea urchin divers, is the local name for a well-sheltered anchorage deep inside a labyrinth of rocks and islets northwest of Sisters Islands at the southeast tip of Banks Island. To safely enter the bay a sharp lookout and vigilant navigation are required. A high-water dinghy route south of the bay leads directly into Otter Passage. As many as four to five seiners may use this bay during fishing openings.

Anchor in 6 fathoms over sand, gravel and mud with fair-to-good holding.

Nepean Sound (Banks Island)
5 mi N of Otter Passage
Position: 53°12.46'N, 129°40.10'W

Nepean Sound, at the southern end of Banks Island, has little swell action due to the myriad islets and rocks protecting its western opening. During ebb tides and southeast gales, Nepean Sound can be ugly due to strong tidal currents. From this point, it is easy to regain Grenville or Princess Royal channels for a smooth-water route north or south. Turn east at Nepean Sound, transiting Otter Channel and Lewis Passage to Wright Sound. Peters Narrows at the south end of Union Passage is a well-protected anchorage.

Principe Channel (Banks Island)
52 mi NW of Meyers Passage
Entrance (S): 53°15.00'N, 129°42.00'W
Entrance (N): 53°39.32'N, 130°25.85'W

The flood tide in the south end of Principe Channel flows north while the ebb flows south. The opposite is true north of Anger Island where the currents mix. The south end of the channel can become rough when the tide sets against the wind.

Monckton Inlet (Principe Channel)
8.2 mi NE of Gungho BayEntrance: 53°18.55'N, 129°41.48'W
Anchor (laqoon): 53°18.99'N, 129°39.92'W
Anchor (0.5 mile north of Roy Island): 53°19.65'N, 129°36.89'W
Anchor (head of inlet): 53°19.00'N, i29°35.00'W

Monckton Inlet, near the southern tip of Pitt Island,

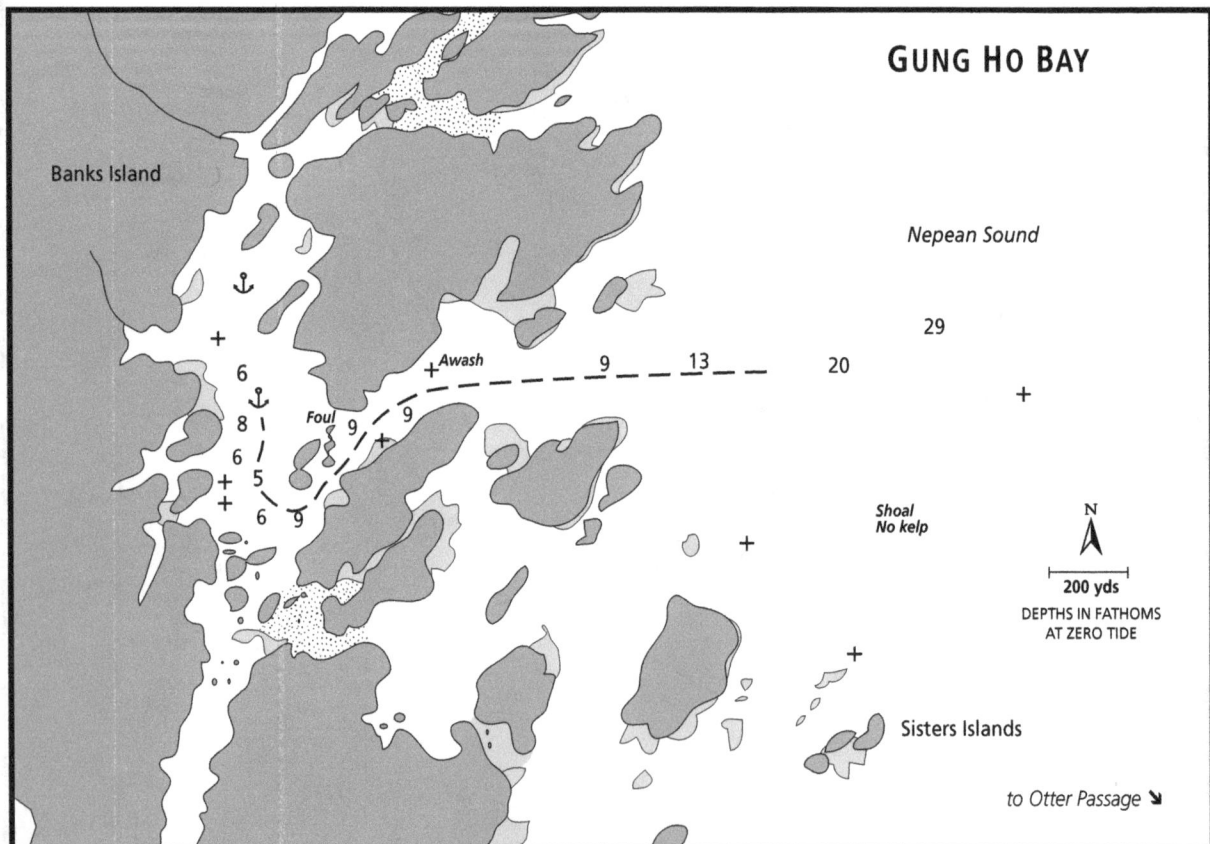

GUNG HO BAY

carves deep into the island. Trees laden with moss line the shore, and the area looks undisturbed—this is true Outer Passage wilderness. Within the inlet there are three good anchorages. The first lies at the far eastern end of the inlet; the second is in the bay north of Roy Island; the third is in the small lagoon northwest of Monckton Point. The far end of the inlet, which has the most swinging room, is recommended for larger boats.

Just a mile inside the entrance to the inlet, a small cove on the north side that doubles back to the west around Monckton Point offers excellent protection from all weather. Although the first part of this cove is roomy enough for two or three boats, we found the bottom to be somewhat irregular and rocky and the holding poor at best. However, the lagoon west of this cove can hold one or two small boats and is perfectly bombproof. Enter the lagoon through a narrows that carries a minimum of one fathom at zero tide. Inside the narrows a small 2- to 4-fathom hole provides complete protection from all weather. The steep, rocky shores of the lagoon are covered with lovely old-growth cedar. Anchor just east of the islet with several trees and silver snags, favoring the east shore.

Anchor (lagoon) in 2 fathoms over soft mud; good holding.

Anchor (north of Roy Island) in 6 to 8 fathoms over mud; good holding.

Anchor (head of inlet) in 10 fathoms over mud; good holding.

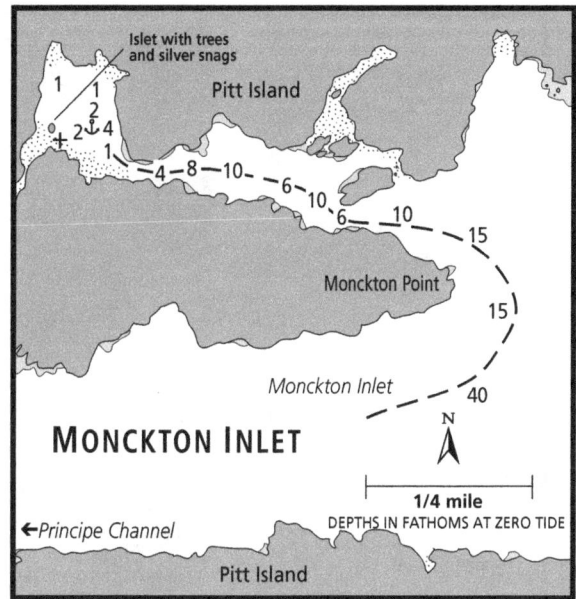

MONCKTON INLET

©2024 Don and Réanne Douglass • Diagram not for navigation

Port Stephens (Pitt Island)
1 mi N of Monckton Inlet
Entrance: 53°19.28'N, 129°42.61'W

Port Stephens, one mile north of Monckton Inlet, has a large area of sheltered water; however, the water is deep and the inner basin and lagoon have restricted passages. We have not anchored here; however, the small cove entered 0.35 mile northeast of Centre Point may offer cruising boats temporary anchorage. Leavitt Lagoon looks particularly interesting but requires reconnoitering and development of local knowledge.

Cancelling the Early Morning Take-off

Rain hits *Baidarka*'s deck; she tugs at anchor and rocks gently. Below, snuggled in our berth, we listen to the clatter, and in the light of early dawn, we watch raindrops create Rohrsacht patterns on the hatch glass. We are unwilling to hop up, raise anchor and head away from Geodetic Cove. It's autumn, already, and we're southbound on our homeward route, after another great summer.

Gusts of wind knock the boat and we hear a strange moaning sound on the anchor snubber—a sound that alternates between low and a high frequency. "It sounds like there's a sea lion under our bow. I'll go check." Don says.

He climbs out of bed and goes out on the bow and stands in the pouring rain, listening.

"You'll freeze," I shout from below. He comes back, dries himself and crawls into bed again. "I can't figure out that sound. . . . Do you want to get going?"

It's now 0700. "Could we be in Meyers Passage by high tide?" I ask.

"Hmm, probably not. But we might be able to anchor outside the narrows."

Neither of us makes a move.

"Let's listen to the weather forecast," I suggest.

Don gets up and climbs back to the pilothouse to retrieve one of the hand-held VHF radios. The weather channel has a lot of static, but we manage to decipher what we've already noticed visually—a southeasterly is blowing straight up Estevan Sound. White caps curl and race north like surf at the edge of a sandy beach.

"Well, maybe we should head south and get a little taste of misery. . . it's been so nice, we've almost forgotten how bad it can be," I say. A dark purple cloud passes over the hatch. Rain pelts the glass again.

"I'm losing my ambition," I tell Don.

"Do you mean you have no goal for today?"

"Yeah, exactly. Once I get up—if I have to—I'll have plenty of drive but I'm so comfortable here, I really don't want to get up."

"Then let's not. Let's just stay in Geodetic Cove as long as we feel like it."   —RHD

BUCHAN INLET

Pitt Island

Pitt Island

Elsfield Point

Tweedsmuir Point

Principe
Channel

2

5   4

8

16   10   6

5 ⚓ 7   6

**Rock dries at
9-ft. tide**

10   8   12

2

**Rock dries at
14-ft. tide**

2

**1 fathom at
zero tide:
favor west
shore**

3

4

+   10

16

+   14

10

12

20

25

22

25

50

+

+
+
*Dries at
10-ft. tide*

N

200 yds
DEPTHS IN FATHOMS AT ZERO TIDE

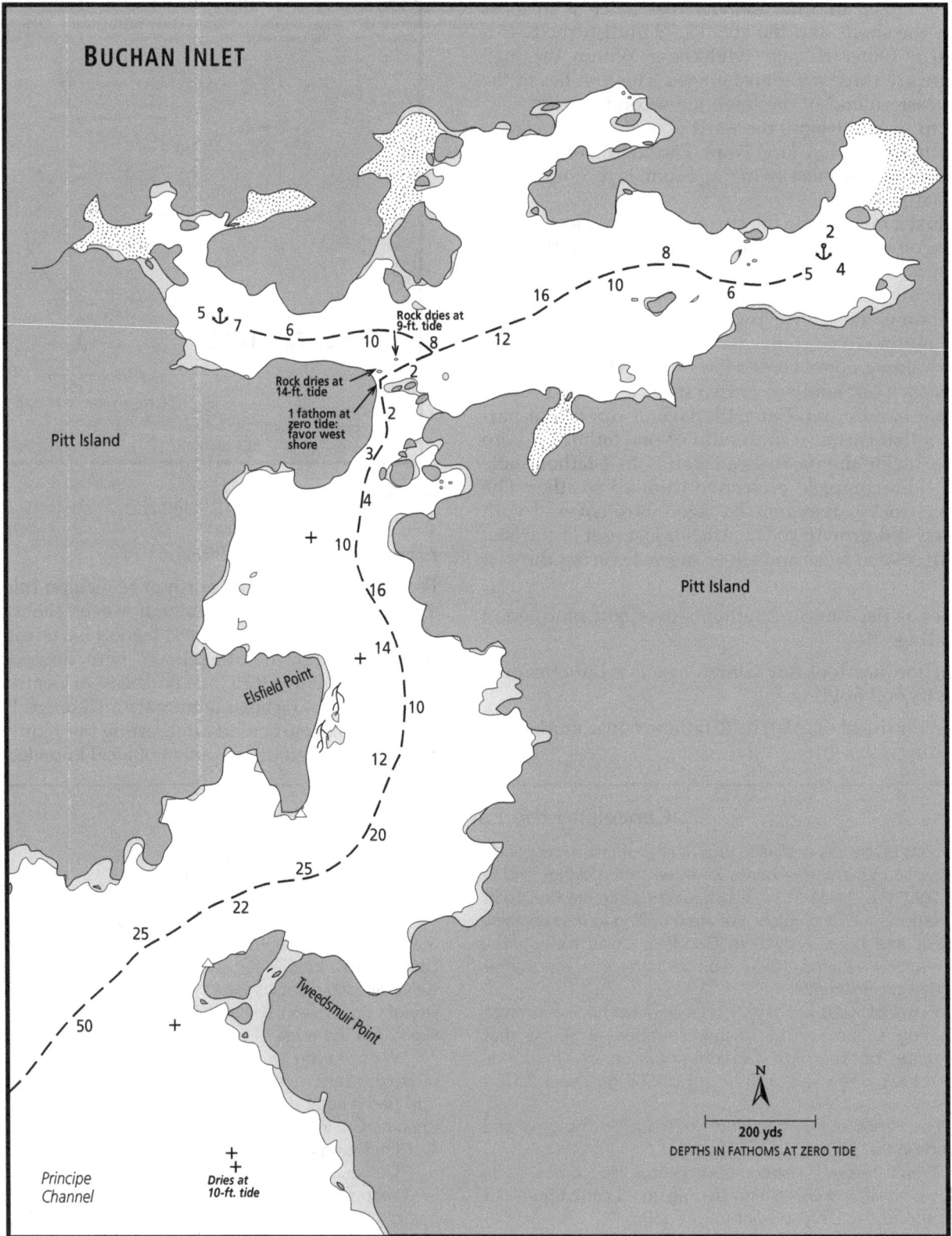

©2024 Don and Reanne Douglass • Diagram not for navigation

Kooryet Bay

(Banks Island)
10.1 mi N of Gungho Bay
Entrance: 53°20.17'N. 129°51.65'W
Anchor (S): 53°20.07*N, 129°51.88'W

Kooryet Bay—which lies east of Joseph Hill, a high peak with rocky tundra that makes a good landmark in clear weather—provides moderate protection. The center of the bay is filled with rocks and shoals, but shelter for small craft can be found in threes areas: off the creek outlet; off the south shore below Joseph Hill peak and on the northwest side of Kooryet Island. The south side of the south point receives a heavy concentration of drift logs; however, few find their way inside the bay. The outpourings of Keecha Creek create a lot of foam. Weather reception in this area is poor to non-existent. Although we explored the bay we did not test for holding power. Swinging room is quite limited and we would use Kooryet only as a temporary stop.

Anchor (south) in about 10 fathoms over a mixed bottom; unrecorded holding.

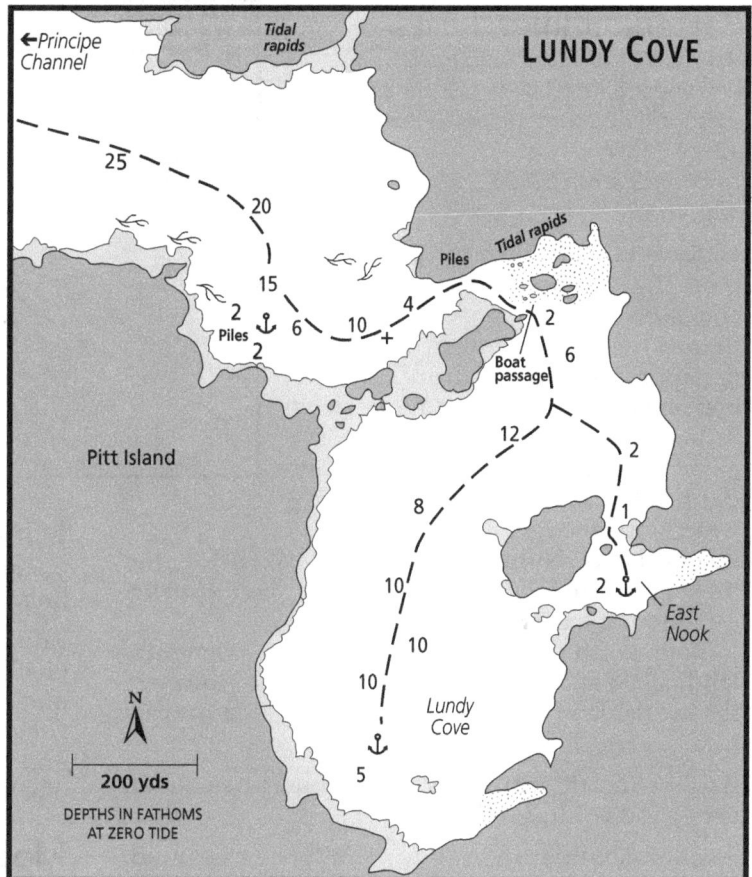

LUNDY COVE

←Principe Channel

Tidal rapids

Piles   Tidal rapids

Pitt Island

Boat passage

East Nook

Lundy Cove

N

200 yds

DEPTHS IN FATHOMS AT ZERO TIDE

©2024 Don and Réanne Douglass • Diagram not for navigation

Buchan Inlet

(Pitt Island)
4.8 mi NW of Monckton Inlet
Entrance: 53°22.06'N, 129°47.07'W
Anchor (W cove): 53°22.73'N, 129°46.79'W
Anchor (E cove): 53°22.79'N, 129°45.80'W

Buchan Inlet, which is moderate in size, has very complex topography with two dozen small islands and islets. For small boats it is a landlocked, intricate paradise in a natural West Coast environment and well worth exploring.

Our reported information is shown on the diagram. We advise caution as the bottom appears to be irregular and may contain uncharted hazards. The entrance is passable at high-water slack, but it is very narrow and shallow and should be reconnoitered before entering. There appear to be several very secure landlocked coves along the north shore suitable for small craft and kayaks.

Anchor (west cove) in 5 to 7 fathoms over an unrecorded bottom.

Anchor (east cove) in 3 to 4 fathoms over an unrecorded bottom.

Lundy Cove (Pitt Island)

8.5 mi NW of Monckton: 53°24.90'N, 129°50.96'W
Anchor (outerbay): 53°24.72'N, 129°50.32'W
Anchor (E nook): 53°24.52'N, 129°49.85'W

The outer bay of Lundy Cove, adjacent to the pilings, offers quick access to shelter from southerly weather. Additional protection can be found inside the cove south of the tidal rapids. Inner Lundy Cove offers very good shelter for small boats either in the east nook behind the islet on the east shore or at the south end of the cove for larger boats. The tidal rapids into the inner cove should be transited near slack water. The east nook can be entered from the north by favoring the island side of the passage and avoiding the mid-channel reef. We found the east nook to be very comfortable, however, swinging room is limited. Test your anchor set as the mud is like Jello.

Anchor (outer bay) in 2 to 6 fathoms over sand and mud with fair holding.
Anchor (east nook) in 1.5 fathoms (just east of 3-Fathom Hole) over soft mud, broken shells, gravel and kelp; poor-to-good holding depending on how well you set your anchor.

Patterson Inlet (Pitt Island)

9.3 mi NW of Monckton Inlet
Entrance: 53°26.08'N, 129°50.83'W
Anchor (N arm head): 53°27.43'N, 129°47.15'W
Anchor (S arm): 53°26.96'N, 129°46.99'W

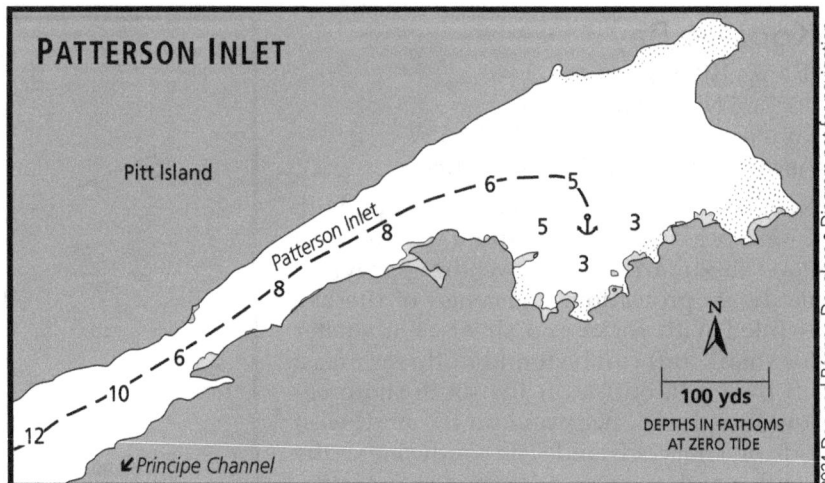

Patterson Inlet, which has perhaps the most straightforward entry of any anchor site in this region, can be entered in foul weather or at night under a radar approach. The disadvantage is that both arms of the inlet are 3 miles from Principe Channel. The north arm is a particularly beautiful place to stay and the head has a large area of shallow water with enough swinging room for several boats. Numerous hanging lakes below the high peaks and ridges furnish freshwater streams for mud-flat habitat.

Both north arm and south arm are essentially landlocked and provide very good shelter. However, the south arm has an old log booming area near its head and its depth requires a lot of scope.

Anchor (north arm head) in 5 fathoms over mud; very good holding.

Anchor (south arm) in 10 to 15 fathoms over mud; good holding.

Mink Trap Bay/Burns Bay (Pitt Island)

0.6 mi N of Patterson Inlet
Entrance: 53°26.51'N, 129°51.48'W

Mink Trap Bay has Burns Bay at its head and Moolock Cove to its east. Mink Trap, itself, is wide-open and exposed to the south. Burns Bay is too deep for convenient anchoring and it is exposed to the south and not safe to use in unstable weather. We find Moolock Cove to be quite sheltered.

Moolock Cove (Mink Trap Bay)

1 mi NE of Mink Trap Bay
Entrance: 53°27.21'N, 129°50.30'W
Anchor: 53°27.10'N, 129°49.27'W

Although Moolock Cove provides good shelter, depths tend to be too great for convenient anchorage unless you tuck far into its southeast corner. Entering Moolock, look for a mountain with an exposed white spot on its south flank that makes a prominent landmark. Favor the east shore as you cross the bar at the east end of the cove.

Small craft can anchor in the bight at the southeast corner of the cove, facing the landmark mountain. This bight, northeast of the neck that separates Moolock from Patterson Inlet, is somewhat out of the path of southeast winds and appears to offer good shelter in all weather. Summer water temperatures in this cove hover in the mid-sixties, providing fertile grounds for hundreds of sea nettles.

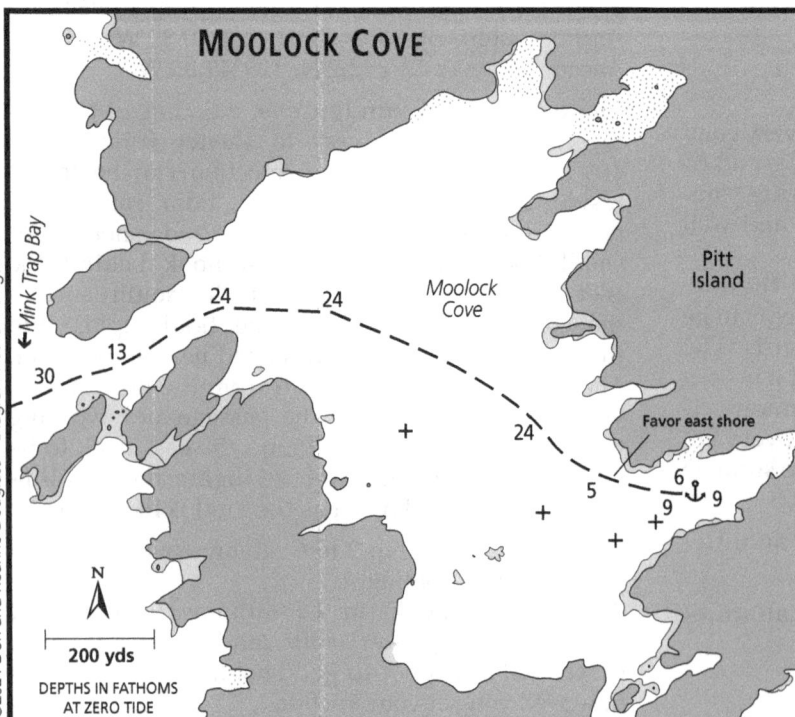

Anchor in 9 fathoms over a soft bottom; good holding with a well-set anchor.

Hodgson Cove (Pitt Island)

1.7 mi NW of Patterson Inlet
Entrance (outer): 53°27.03'N,
129°52.97'W
Anchor: 53°27.48'N, 129°52.03'W

Hodgson Cove has rocky, tree-lined steep-to shores and is totally land-locked. Its entrance is narrow and shallow, requiring a careful mid-channel approach between two underwater rocks that extend from rocky spits on either shore. The cove should not be entered in poor visibility.

Although the cove has excellent protection in all weather, we were unable—on three separate attempts—to set our Danforth test-anchor satisfactorily in depths of 8 to 9 fathoms. The pattern on our echo sounder indicated soft Jello-like matter along a fairly flat bottom, but over a hard rock base. Vessels with a different type of anchor and more chain may not experience the same problem. We've talked to boaters who cannot recall having a problem and who felt quite comfortable here.

If heavy weather is expected, Patterson Inlet or Monckton Inlet may be better alternatives.

Anchor in 9 fathoms over a very soft bottom; holding may be poor, depending on your type of anchor and amount of chain.

Rusty beachcombing on the west coast

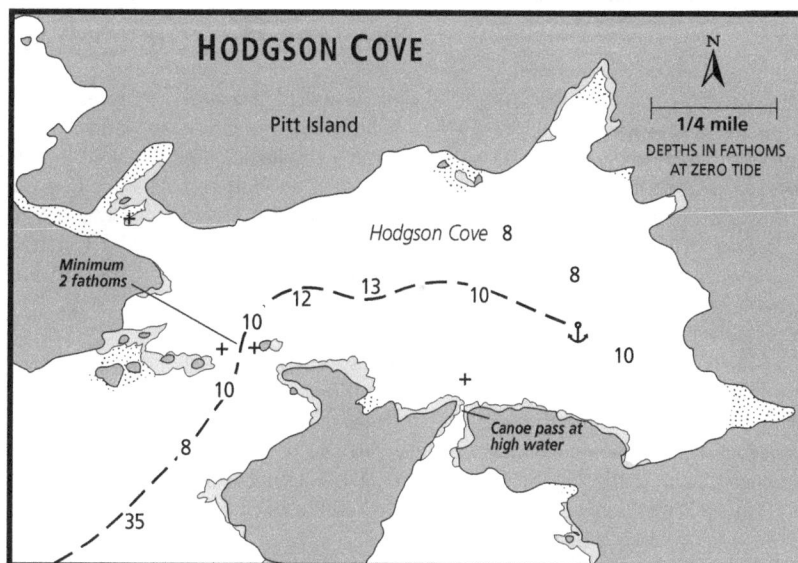

©2024 Don and Réanne Douglass • Diagram not for navigation

Ala Passage South (Principe Channel)

E of Trade Islets
Entrance (S): 53°27.14'N, 129°55.45'W

The south entrance to Ala Passage shown on charts leads to some remote waters that provide both challenges and rewards for intrepid explorers. (See Sidebar Beware of Horizontal Trees!) Hazardous Peck Shoal can be avoided easily by favoring Anger Island until you are directly north of Trade Islets. Caution: Avoid the dangerous mid-channel rock 0.3 mile south of the entrance to Ire Inlet, awash at mid-tide. Ala Passage requires an alert bow watch throughout.

Miller Inlet (Ala Passage)

1.2 mi NE of Ala Passage entr.
Entrance: 53°28.14'N, 129°54.38'W
Anchor (S basin): 53°28.19'N, 129°52.52'W

Miller Inlet, off the main Principe Channel, has an inner basin reported to be bombproof. Although there is anchorage at the head of the inlet, the inner basin on the south shore is more sheltered for smaller boats but swinging room is limited. The entrance is narrow and shallow with several charted rocks.

Anchor (inner basin south) in 4 to 5 fathoms; an unrecorded bottom.

Ire Inlet (Anger Island)

2.7 mi N of Ala Passage entr.
Entrance: 53°30.07'N, 129°54.59'W
Anchor: 53°29.98'N, 129°56.43'W

Ire Inlet is an example of a near-perfect and secure anchorage in the middle of wilderness. Although its

BEWARE OF HORIZONTAL TREES!

We were intrigued by the Douglass' description of the wild area around Anger Island in the first edition of this book and decided to explore it on our way north to Alaska. As we were entering Ire Inlet, we found more than half the entrance blocked by a horizontal, but still attached and growing tree. We managed to squeeze by in our 52' sloop *Mithrandir*, dodging the tree to port and a rock to starboard. We anchored safely and spent a rainy, windy night in the shelter of the inlet.

The next morning we got an early start to make it through Ala Narrows at slack tide. Since there was a new moon, the tides were running a little heftier than normal and exiting Ire Inlet wasn't quite as easy. We had to navigate our way around the horizontal tree with a 1-2 knot current running against us. It was still raining and 20 knots of wind seemed to swirl around us in all directions.

In order to avoid the poorly charted rock to port and the tree to starboard, Rick had to crank up the engine for more precise steerage. I was on the bow as lookout and kept warning him not to get too close to the rock on the left—at that point the tree seemed the lesser of the two problems. I was more worried that as we rounded the tree the stern would swing and the rudder would hit the rock.

When we seemed to be clear of the rock and came round the tree, Rick straightened the boat into the channel. The tip of the tree caught the handlebars of one of the bicycles we keep tied to the starboard stern rail. That was enough to deflect it inboard; it slid between the backstay and the radar pole mounted on the portside of the stern.

The force of the branches catching the backstay stopped the boat, swung her to starboard until the tree hit the shrouds and flattened the right side of the dodger and stopped laying against the steering wheel, holding the boat in this position in the channel. The bow was four feet from the rock face and the tree roots. The tree held *Mithrandir* firmly in place without moving and giving us a moment to assess our situation.

The dodger was completely crushed under the tree on the starboard side.

I dug out our little Sandvik handsaw and a machete and we started to saw and chop for dear life. I had kidded Rick for buying the machete a few days earlier—to me it carried memories of sugar cane fields in Barbados.

To protect the radar pole and its expensive equipment, we hurriedly cut the top of the tree which extended 7 feet past the stern of the boat. Next we attempted to cut the much thicker part of the tree that lay forward of the shrouds, attacking it as hard as our arms could manage. (The little Sandvik saw was shorter than the width of the trunk.) We took turns—one of us sawed, while the other tried to clear the branches. It was crucial to free the wheel so we could steer once we broke free and avoid further damage.

Finally we managed to saw and chop our way through the heavy trunk, but the tree didn't move enough to release the wheel. By going into forward and reverse, time and again, we managed to point the bow forward. But we couldn't steer the boat.

The current was taking us back into Ire Inlet, right up onto the rock we had worked so hard to avoid. *Mithrandir* hit the rock and shuddered. Somehow the impact moved the log enough to free the wheel so Rick could now steer. We let the current carry us back into the inlet which seemed calm compared to the rain and wind that had pelted us in the channel.

We dropped anchor, shocked, aching and wet, but otherwise unharmed. We sawed the tree into four sections and, using the spinnaker halyard, we lowered each one into the water. It took all day to clean up the worst of the mess.

The survey of damage at that point was:
- bent backstay rod
- bent dodger stainless frame
- dodger Sunbrella top destroyed
- four stanchions needed repair
- stern railing needed repair
- the crabtrap was flattened
- the BBQ lost its lid
- the downrigger was bent
- 2 twisted beyond repair mountain bikes

The good news was that, other than a few cuts and bruises, we weren't injured.

— Elke Cunningham — *S/V Mithrandir.*

Courtesy Elke Cunningham∞

S/V **Mithrandir** *in distress, Ire Inlet*

entrance is quite narrow, it is landlocked and secure from any weather. The entrance may look daunting (and it can be for larger boats), but the fairway is quite deep with about 2 knots at spring tides with a flat bottom. With the exception of rock and kelp on the north side, the 2-fathom bar at the west end of the narrows, and the remains of the "Mithrandir tree" at the entrance. We anchor behind the islet at the west end of Ire Inlet and feel that we are in one of the most remote places in the Northwest. Mithrandir's experience illustrates the need for caution and self-sufficiency when cruising in the wilds. (See Sidebar Beware of Horizontal Trees!)

Anchor in 4 fathoms over mud with good holding.

Curtis Inlet (Ala Passage)
0.6 mi E of Ire Inlet
Entrance: 53°30.04'N, 129°53.64'W

Curtis Inlet, which is fed by a series of large lakes, looks like a good place for kayak or dinghy exploring while your vessel is safely anchored in Ire Inlet. When we explored Curtis Inlet, the narrows carried 1 fathom through the fairway but our route was suddenly blocked at low tide: the 8-fathom hole inside the first narrows appears to offer very good shelter and intrigued us, but as we approached this hole near low water, our bow lookout observed an uncharted, submerged rock in the center of the passage. Lacking turning room, we were forced to back out. Remember, that throughout this wilderness of the Outer Passage, the waters are poorly charted, requiring caution and vigilance.

Wright Inlet (Ala Passage)
1.5 mi NE of Ire Inlet
Entrance (Wright Narrows): 53°31.14'N, 129°53.15'W

Wright Inlet, which lies behind a fortress of islets and reefs, could justly be called a lagoon. It is an "end-of-the-world place" that should be explored first by inflatable or kayak. Study the small-scale chart and you will see what a challenge entering the inlet can be. The two small coves and lagoon in the east end of Wright Inlet appear interesting. The narrows has a 7-foot tidal falls at low water.

Ala Narrows (Anger Island)
1.4 mi N of Ire Inlet
Position: 53°31.34'N, 129°53.64'W

Ala Narrows is best transited near slack water when you can make a slow approach with an alert bow lookout. Most of the rocks and reefs are marked by kelp. Study large scale charts and avoid the rock that dries at 7 feet near Anger Island, as well as the kelp and turbulent water. The fairway carries a minimum depth of about 3 fathoms. Currents are generally moderate but on spring tides they may be stronger. North of Ala Narrows, the bottom is irregular requiring careful navigation to avoid the many hazards.

Ala Passage North (Anger Island)
E of Cosine Island
Entrance (N): 53°32.91'N, 129°56.76'W

Northbound Ala Passage is clear of dangers once you are abeam of Anger Point. Southbound, the bottom is irregular, requiring vigilance. We do not recommend the passage in poor visibility. The small cove east of Anger Point has a U-shaped valley, a good leading point on a southbound route through Ala Passage from Logarithm Point.

Math Islands
(Ala Passage)
N of Anger Island
Position: 53°33.88'N, 129°57.15'W

We call this interesting area the "Math Islands" in honor of Sine, Cosine and Tangent islands. In 1949, the first surveyors to chart this maze of islands north of Anger Island faced the challenge of keeping track of their baseline. Visual distances are short and the channels and islands confusing. The survey must have required a lot of triangulation involving trigonometric functions, hence the island names. Nowadays we're fortunate to have GPS to help identify our turning points.

From Principe Channel, the Math Island complex can be entered via Evinrude or Markle passages. While exploring Math Islands, Wilson and Markle inlets, and Ala Passage, you can find good anchorage on the east side of Clear Passage. This area is an important spawning ground for herring in the spring.

Clear Passage
(Math Islands)
Between Sine & Cosine islets
Entrance (E): 53°33.14'N, 129°57.79'W
Anchor (E entrance): 53°33.16'N, 129° 58.46'W.

Clear Passage has very good anchorage just east of the 3-foot shoal; this site makes a good base camp from which to explore the vicinity by dinghy or inflatable.

Anchor (east entrance) in about 5 to 10 fathoms over sand and mud with good holding; limited swinging room.

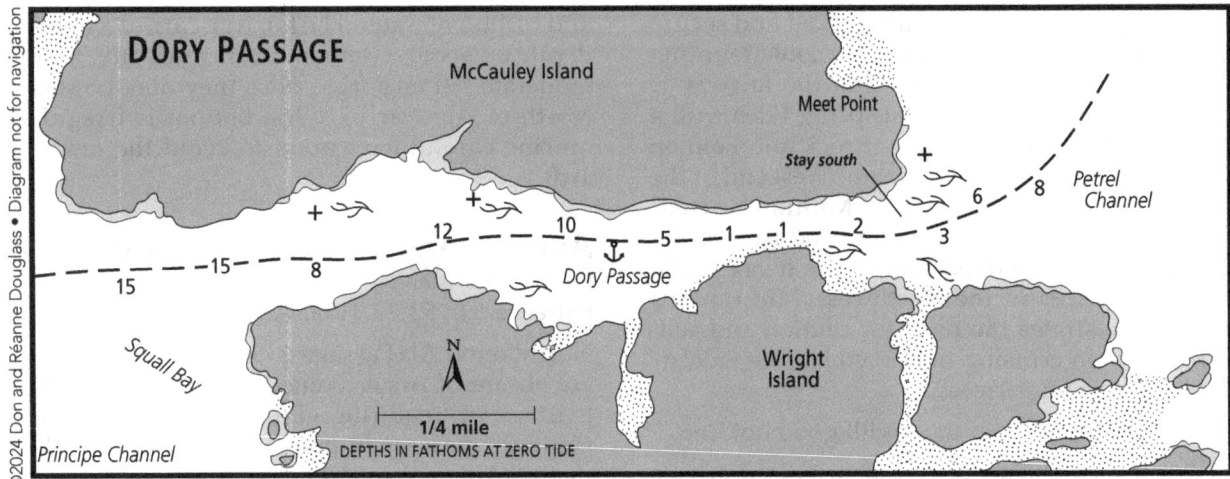

DORY PASSAGE

McCauley Island

Meet Point

Stay south

Petrel Channel

6　8

Dory Passage

12　10　—5—1—1—2　3

—15—　8

15

Squall Bay

Wright Island

Principe Channel

N

1/4 mile

DEPTHS IN FATHOMS AT ZERO TIDE

©2024 Don and Réanne Douglass • Diagram not for navigation

Anger Inlet (Anger Island)

S of Cosine Island
Entrance: 53°31.41'N, 129°58.47'W

Anger Inlet, an explorer's dream and a navigator's nightmare, is intricate, highly convoluted, shallow, with all kinds of menacing narrows—in short, a perfect place to explore by kayak or dinghy. Its southeastern end lies less than 100 yards from the head of Ire Inlet; its southwestern corner is only 100 yards from the backwater of Principe Channel. The overall appearance here is one of a swamp, and the bottom is irregular and rocky.

Wilson Inlet (Math Islands)

0.5 mi E of Sine Island
Entrance: 53°33.44'N, 129°56.82'W

Wilson Inlet—most easily entered south of Tangent Island—is landlocked and offers very good shelter at its head in 12 to 15 fathoms. Be careful to avoid the rocks shown on the chart; others may be lurking, too!

Markle Passage, Island (325) Bight

(Principe Channel)
N of Sine Island
Entrance (W): 53°33.66'N, 129°59.78'W
Entrance (E): 53°33.85'N, 129°57.41'W
Anchor (Island (325) bight): 53°34.36'N, 129°57.91'W

Markle Passage connects Petrel Channel to Ala Passage. Good shelter from southeast gales is reportedly found in the bight on the west side of island (325), 0.5 mile northeast of Markle Island.

Anchor (island [325] bight) in 14 fathoms with moderate holding.

Markle Inlet (Math Island)

0.6 mi N of Sine Point
Entrance: 53°34.23'N, 129°57.26'W

Markle Inlet, like the areas surrounding Ala Passage, is a labyrinth. The inlet has several possible anchor sites for small boats that are savvy enough to enter it safely. We have not unlocked its secrets yet, but it is on the list. The eastern cove just inside the entrance looks like a bombproof lagoon and the basin at the head of the inlet looks very good for small boats. Reconnoiter the inlet before you enter.

Colby Bay (Banks Island)

14.5 mi SE of Larson Hbr.
Entrance: 53°32.11'N, 130°10.15'W
Anchor: 53°31.81'N, 130°10.67'W

Colby Bay, 2 miles south of Dixon Island on the east side of Banks Island, provides very good protection. The entrance lies between a bare rock that extends about 100 feet from the north shore and a small bare rock topped with some grass on the south shore. Minimum depth in the fairway is about 4 fathoms. The

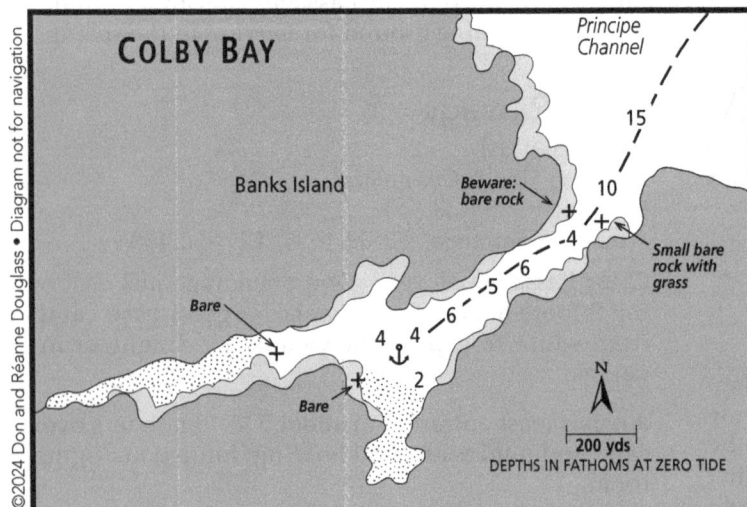

COLBY BAY

Principe Channel

Banks Island

Beware: bare rock

15

10

—4

Small bare rock with grass

Bare

—5—6

—6—5

4　4

2

Bare

N

200 yds

DEPTHS IN FATHOMS AT ZERO TIDE

©2024 Don and Réanne Douglass • Diagram not for navigation

shores in Colby Bay are edged with old-growth cedar. Inside there is swinging room for several small boats. The charted pilings are no longer evident.

Anchor in 4 fathoms over mud with good holding.

Dory Passage (McCauley Island)
N of Wright Island
Entrance (E): 53°33.81′N, 130°04.27′W
Entrance (W): 53°33.64′N, 130°06.20′W

Dory Passage connects Petrel Channel to Squall Bay at the southern tip of McCauley Island. Approaching from the north, Dory Passage is hard to see. To find the east entrance, head for the grassy flat south of Meet Point until the passage opens up. Kelp marks both the north and south sides of the entrance. Least depth through the narrows is one fathom, with sandy patches, grassy spots, and occasional bull kelp attached to the flat bottom. Locals sometimes use the area just west of the Dory Passage shoal for anchorage in 6 to 8 fathoms; with moderate protection from southerlies.

Squall Bay (McCauley Island)
0.7 mi NW of Dory Passage
Entrance (S): 53°33.09′N, 130°06.32′W
Anchor (N): 53°34.02′N, 130°07.36′W

Squall Bay, east of Squall Island, holds a picturesque group of islets and rocks. The small basin at its north side offers temporary anchorage for small boats although its bottom is irregular, hard and rocky, and swinging room is limited. To enter the bay, approach from the south or from Dory Passage. Post a bow lookout to avoid rocks and kelp patches. The intricate pattern of islets and rocks makes it difficult to enter in a major storm, but the bay is calm during a westerly. The 10-fathom hole in the northern part of the bay offers fair protection from southerlies. In foul weather Colby Bay, on the west side of Principe Channel, is the recommended anchorage since it provides better shelter and more swinging room than Squall Bay.

Anchor (north) in the 10-fathom hole over a hard rocky bottom; fair holding with a well-set anchor.

Jack and Linda Schreiber's Sanctuary

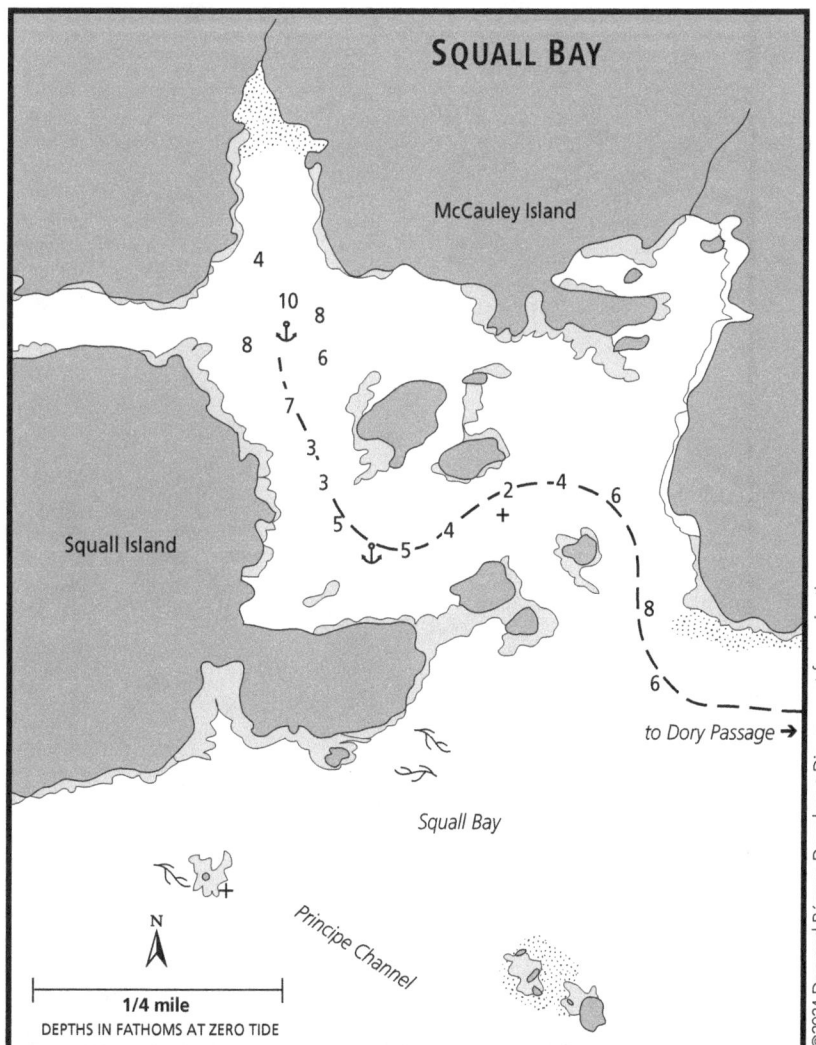

SQUALL BAY

McCauley Island

Squall Island

Squall Bay

Principe Channel

to Dory Passage →

N

1/4 mile
DEPTHS IN FATHOMS AT ZERO TIDE

©2024 Don and Réanne Douglass • Diagram not for navigation

Port Canaveral (McCauley Island)

2 mi NE of Colby Bay
Entrance (Port Canaveral): 53°33.82'N, 130°09.46'W
Anchor (W nook, Port Canaveral): 53°34.10'N, 130°08.68'W

In Port Canaveral shelter can be found at the southern end of McCauley Island, east of Red Point and Round Islet. Better shelter can be found at the north end of Dixon Island.

Anchor (west nook, Port Canaveral) in about 6 fathoms east of Round Island

Dixon Island Nook (McCauley Island)

2 mi NE of Colby Bay
Entrance (Dixon I. Nook): 53°34.29'N, 130°09.71'W
Anchor (Dixon I. Nook): 53°35.08'N, 130°10.31'W

"Dixon Island Nook" is what we call the fair weather

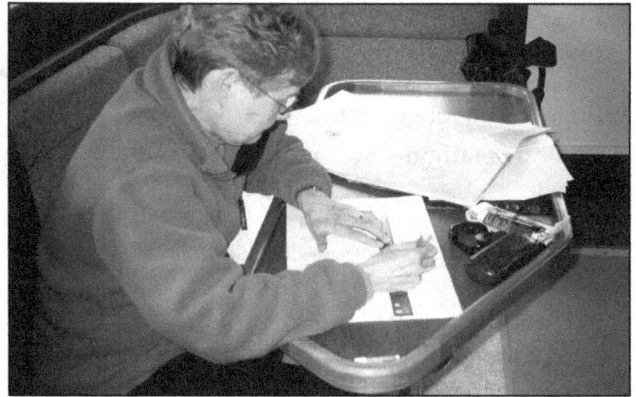

Réanne collecting data

hideaway at the north end of Dixon Island. Enter from the southeast avoiding the mid-channel rocks. **Anchor** in about 5 fathoms over sand and gravel; fair holding; limited swinging room.

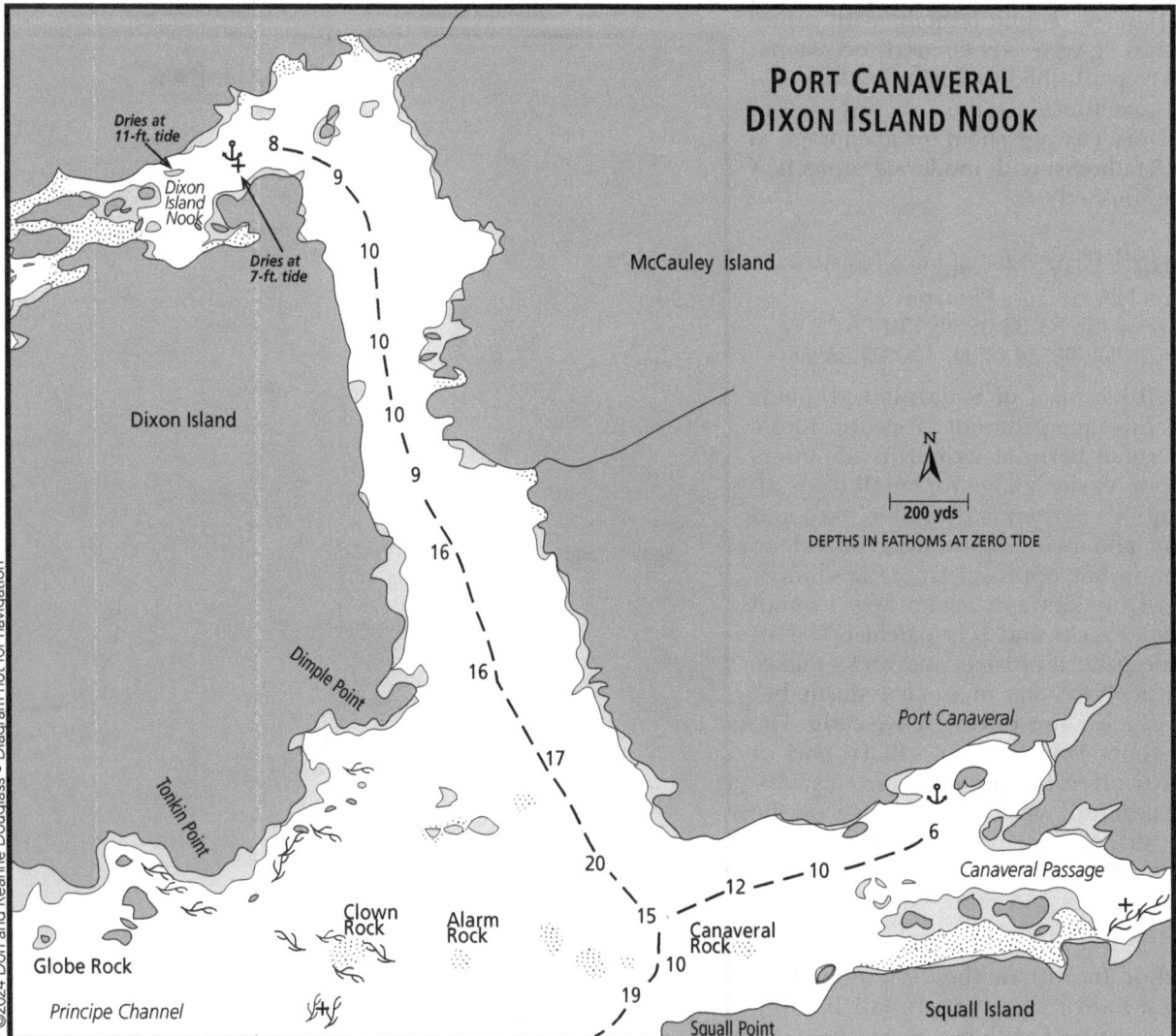

Authors kayaking during a rain storm on the west coast

Close look at Banks Island shore

Keswar Inlet (McCauley Island)

6.5 mi E of Larson Hbr.
Entrance: 53°38.46'N, 130°21.64'W
Anchor (inner basin): 53°38.41'N, 130°20.56'W

Keswar Inlet, on the McCauley Island shore at the north entrance to Principe Channel, provides very good shelter for small boats in its inner basin. In all weather except northwesterly gales, we feel comfortable here. The inner basin, which resembles a lagoon, has a nearly flat bottom between 2 and 4 fathoms. The absence of driftlogs and signs of stress indicates that little chop enters the basin.

The entrance to Keswar Inlet is very narrow with an irregular bottom; avoid rocks by favoring the north shore of island (240). Within the narrows, you can avoid what we call dangerous "Pin Rock" by hugging island (240) within 75 feet; Pin Rock, marked by kelp, lies mid-channel and is awash at mid-tide. Moderate current runs through the narrows. Visibility through the muskeg water is limited to about 2 feet.

Anchor (inner basin) in 2 to 3 fathoms over mud and grass with good holding.

Principe Channel, North Entrance

(Banks/McCauley Islands)
E of Banks Island
Entrance (N): 53°39.32'N, 130°25.85'W
(See Chapter 11 for Browning Entrance and Larsen Harbour.)

Principe Channel forms part of what we call the Outer Passage (one of our favorite routes). It is a wild and natural area with many sheltered anchorages. This channel is a major flyway for seabirds.

Petrel Channel South (McCauley/Pitt Isl.)

15 mi E of Larson Hbr.
Entrance (S): 53°33.71'N, 130°02.31'W

Petrel Channel is a shortcut to Principe Channel on either a north- or southbound trip to or from Prince Rupert.

Allcroft Point Cove (Petrel Channel)

0.3 mi SE of Allcroft Pt.
Entrance: 53°35.64'N, 130°03.42'W
Anchor: 53°35.74'N, 130°03.09'W

Allcroft Point Cove, 0.3 mile southeast of Allcroft Point, offers fair-to-good protection in southeasterlies and northerlies, and makes a temporary lunch stop for small boats. Swinging room is limited.

Anchor in the middle of the cove in 8 to 10 fathoms over a mixed bottom.

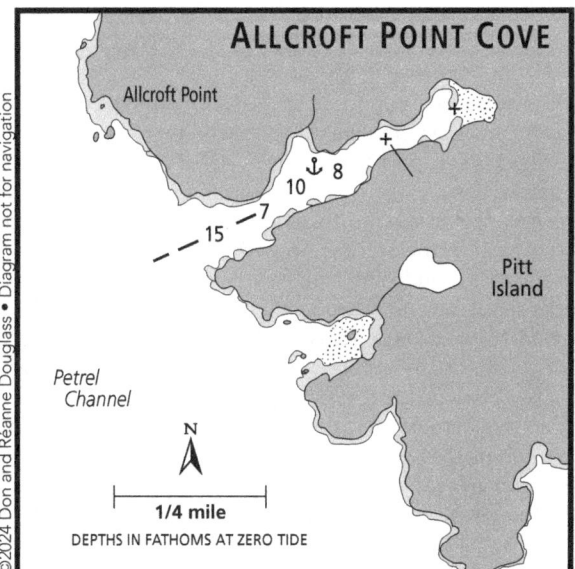

ALLCROFT POINT COVE
Allcroft Point
10 8
7
15
Pitt Island
Petrel Channel
N
1/4 mile
DEPTHS IN FATHOMS AT ZERO TIDE
©2024 Don and Réanne Douglass • Diagram not for navigation

NEWCOMBE HARBOUR
Use Chart 3895

Dries

Pitt Island

5

8 7 ⚓ 4

8

8 Northest Basin

Newcombe

9

Harbour

10

10

+
+   8 ⚓
9   8
10   East Nook

12

13   Islet with small trees

McCutcheon Point

13

10

Petrel
Channel   20

N

1/2 mile
DEPTHS IN FATHOMS AT ZERO TIDE

©2024 Don and Réanne Douglass • Diagram not for navigation

Newcombe Harbour (Petrel Channel)
4.4 mi N of Hevenor Inlet
Entrance: 53°41.83'N, 130°06.16'W
Anchor (E nook): 53°42.25'N. 130°05.58'W
Anchor (NE basin): 53°42.85'N, 130°05.17'W

Newcombe Harbour offers excellent protection from all weather for small craft transiting Petrel Channel. Enter south of McCutcheon Point, avoiding a shoal on the north side. The shores of the harbor are steep-to and forested, and absence of driftwood indicates good protection. Several creeks enter the head of the harbor at the north end, creating a large mud flat.

The nook on the east side provides good anchorage for one boat. Anchorage can also be found in the northeast basin of Newcombe Harbour off the mud flats.

Anchor (E nook) in 6 fathoms over soft gray mud with excellent holding.

Anchor (NE basin) in 7 fathoms over mud with excellent holding.

Petrel Channel Narrows
0.5 mi W of Newcombe Hbr.
Position: 53°42.7rN, 130°09.51'W

Petrel Channel narrows and turns northwest at McCutcheon Point then

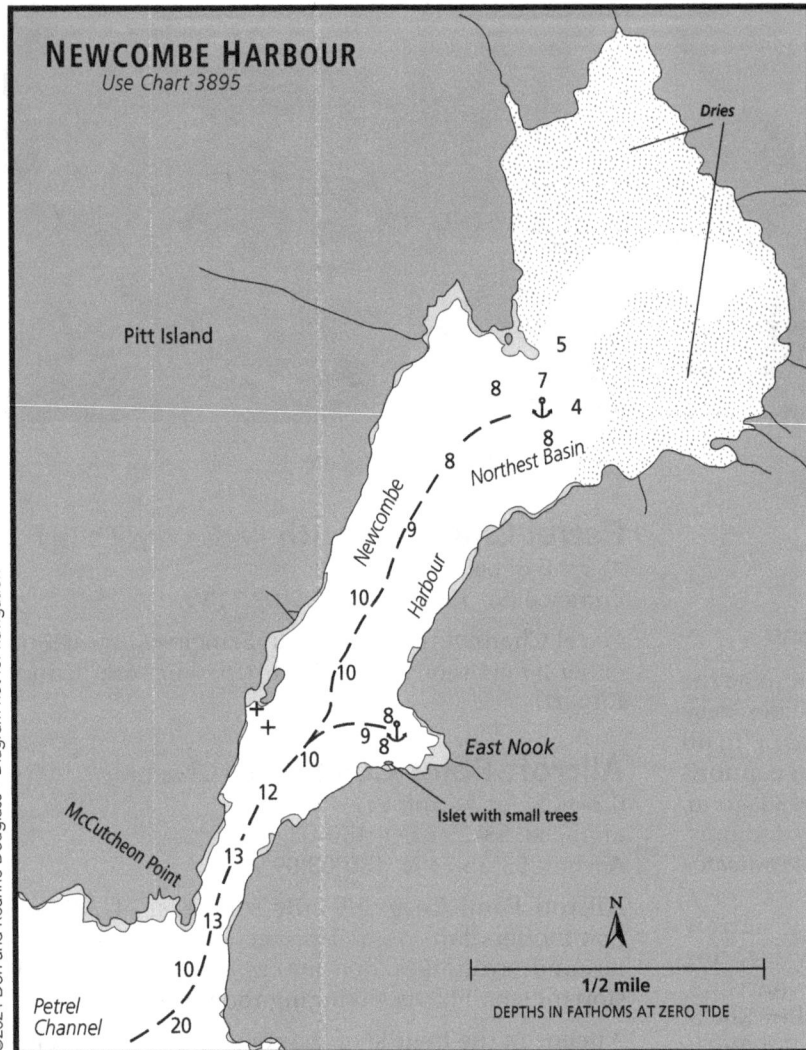

Photographing the Bald Eagle

Bald eagles are abundant in British Columbia and along the outer coast, making them easy to photograph. My husband Steve and I are cruising the North Coast waters aboard *Charisma*, our 26-foot Nordic tug. Looking around, you can see the white head and neck feathers of a bald eagle high in the trees. Known for its keenness of vision, the eagle is able to see a mile away. Steve fishes for salmon and halibut, saving a few small fish he would normally use as bait to feed the eagles. Making a small cut at the top of the fish, Steve is careful not to collapse its air bladder which would cause the fish to sink. Standing on the bow, I grab my camera and pre-focus on the water a few feet from where Steve is in the skiff. He attracts the eagle's attention by waving the fish above his head then tosses it into the air. Within seconds, the eagle swoops down and, with great strength and power, grabs the fish in his talons.

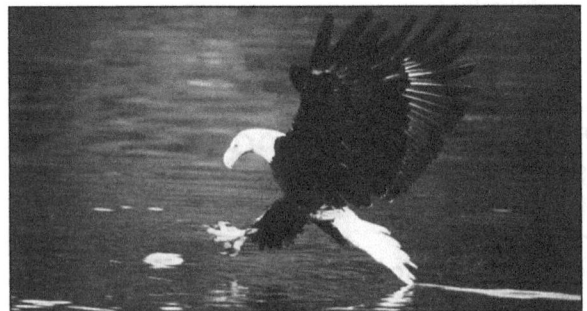

I click off several shots as water pours from his feathered legs. Capturing the beauty and grace of such a wonderful bird of prey makes a rare "Kodak moment."
—Robin Hill-Ward

turns north again just beyond Elbow Point. To the east of Elbow Point, stands Noble Mountain whose glistening slabs of granite covered with tundra rise to 2,885 feet. Due west of Noble Mountain, along the east side of Petrel Channel, several unmarked shoals extend about 100 yards into the channel.

The ebb flows south through the channel; the flood flows north. Near Elbow Point, the current may run up to 4 knots. Due to its proximity to the ocean, summer water temperatures in Petrel Channel tend to be in the low fifties. The narrows have moderate turbulence, and drift logs sometimes congregate near the Elbow.

Photo courtesy Kevin Monahan

Campania Island beach, south of McMicking Inlet

Coastal Bird Occurrences

Coastal cruising affords marvelous opportunities to expand one's appreciation of birds. You encounter species that land-bound birders never see, and often in numbers that are mind-boggling. An added advantage is that many inshore species are desensitized by the routine presence of boats. They thus allow you to approach quite close before taking evasive action.

As with terrestrial species, the most exciting times of the year for oceanic and inshore species are during spring and fall migrations. Thus, May will give you a chance to see Arctic-bound shorebirds and waterfowl, all decked out in their breeding colors to make identification easier. In August and September you can catch them returning, but many are in their drab fall colors and look frustratingly alike.

In autumn you also have a chance to see pelagic (oceanic) species like shearwaters and storm-petrels that come to inshore waters to feed before heading back out into the open Pacific.

Winter can be more interesting than high summer in coastal waters because species that nest far northward or inland come here to spend their winters. Four species of loons, many species of ducks (including the colorful Harlequin), and the alcids (murres, puffins, guillemots, murrelets and auklets) are winter familiars. Most of the alcids are also year-round residents. Bald eagles, Peregrine falcons and other raptors are also present year-round.

Birds go where their food is most abundant. Tidal flats and river estuaries are rich in shore birds, waterfowl of all kinds, gulls, and the birds like falcons and jaegers (in migration) that prey on them. Locations of heavy tidal upwellings, and places where migrant-feed species like herring and salmon are funneled into restricted passages, are where you'll find the fish-eaters. The excitement of getting close

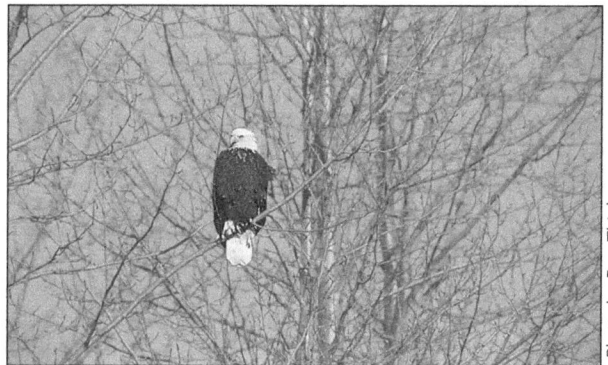

Photo by Ron Thiele

The magnificent bald eagle surveys the water

to a "herring ball" and a feeding frenzy of gulls, murres and shearwaters may be accentuated by the presence of a pod of dolphins that add their slapping and thrashing to the din of the excited birds.

A boat is an unsteady platform, but the recent development of binoculars with built-in stabilizers has helped correct this fault. With the push of a button they maintain a steady image. Not only has this helped smooth out wobbles from shaky hands and rocking decks, it has enabled the manufacturers to go well beyond the former 10-power upper limit of hand-held glasses. Some stabilizer binoculars now offer power that matches the lower magnifications of spotting scopes.

All in all, the north coast of British Columbia is a spectacular birding area of unending pleasure.

—Bob Waldon

Bob Waldon is a B.C. newspaper columnist and author of *Feeding Winter Birds in the Pacific Northwest.*

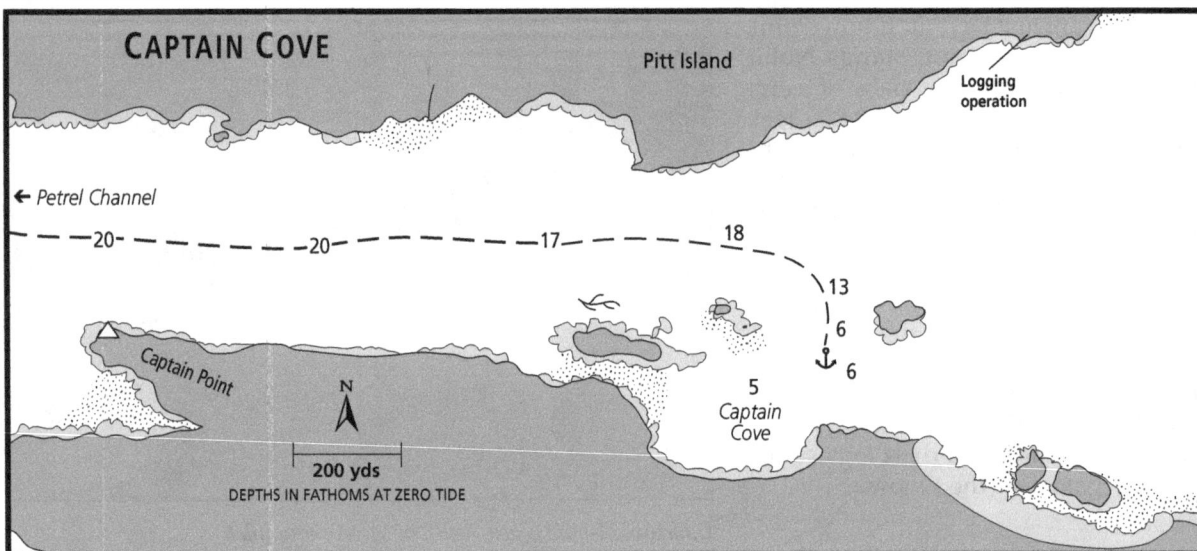

CAPTAIN COVE

Pitt Island

Logging operation

← Petrel Channel

20 — 20 — 17 — 18

13

6

5
Captain Cove

6

Captain Point

N

200 yds
DEPTHS IN FATHOMS AT ZERO TIDE

©2024 Don and Réanne Douglass • Diagram not for navigation

Captain Cove (Petrel Channel)
3.5 mi E of Ogden Channel
Entrance: 53°48.71′N, 130°13.23′W
Anchor: 53°48.59′N, 130°11.87′W

About 2.5 miles long, Captain Cove offers very good protection. Pretty location with opportunities to see wildlife on shore.

Small boats can anchor southwest of the last mid-channel islet. If a westerly chop picks up, you can tuck up against the western islets in 2 fathoms. In either case, several boats will have adequate swinging room. Large boats can have the entire end of the bay over a flat bottom of 12 fathoms.

Anchor in 7 fathoms, mud bottom, with good holding.

BEARS AND BOATS
by Roderick Frazier Nash and Honeydew Murray

Viewing bears is one of the highlights of a visit to northern British Columbia, and a cruising boat offers the best opportunity for an encounter, with minimal stress to either party. Indeed, your chances of seeing a bear other than from a boat are close to zero. Just as is the case with rhinos and big cats in Africa, bears fear humans on foot. Remember these guys are wild, not the campground Yogi-bears adept at raiding ice chests next to your tent. So your boat is your Land Rover safari vehicle. Bears don't associate it with danger nor do they think of the sea as the direction from which a threat might come.

Here are some tips that have helped us spot bear as we cruise B.C.'s north coast in *Forevergreen*.

1. *Maintain a constant shoreline watch.* Every time you round a point make it a habit to scan the shore carefully with binoculars. You'll see a hundred stumps and rocks that you will swear are bears. But suddenly one of those dark lumps will move and what you're seeing is a bear.

Although they come in a wide range of colors, including pure white, most British Columbia bears are startlingly blue-black. They have a distinctive long-legged profile that becomes easy to recognize. But movement is your litmus test, and bears on shore patrol are always on the move.

With the binoculars you can tell within a few seconds if you have the real thing.

2. *Let them come to you.* Since bears move most of the time, your chances of a sighting are good if you stay in one place—that is, at anchor. Keep looking around a full 360 degrees, and take advantage of the fact that north of Cape Caution in the summer, there is twilight most of the night. This means that you could sight a bear around the clock. When we wake up to use the head or check the anchor, we routinely take a look around; tell your crew to do the same. On one occasion a friend woke us at 5 a.m. to watch a female black bear and her two cubs working the shoreline rocks for crabs. They were only 50 feet away and totally oblivious to our presence. With amazing dexterity, the mother flipped rocks over and lapped up the goodies. Eventually they worked down the beach and into the timber. It was a peaceful moment in sharp contrast to the usual panicky human-bear encounters that occur on shore. We felt privileged to have witnessed this normal activity.

If bears are a priority of your cruising experience, select an anchorage at the head of an inlet (they love the grassy flats) or off the mouth of a river or stream.

3. *Approach quietly and stealthily.* If you spot a bear while

Petrel Channel North (Petrel Channel)
3 mi E of Captain Cove
Entrance: 53°48.88'N, 130°17.26'W

The north end of Petrel Channel, leads into Ogden Channel then north to Prince Rupert, or west into Kitkatla Inlet, or south into Beaver Passage, as described in Chapter 11. The west side of Petrel Channel, along McCauley Island, has low, rocky, wooded shores. The east side, along Pitt Island, is mountainous and forested. Moderate turbulence can be felt over a large area west of Comrie Head.

New deadhead

Walking the logs, west coast

underway, slow your engine and ease in toward shore. A bear is not threatened from the sea, and chances are good that he will not even look up until you are less than 100 yards away. He may stare at you for a moment and go right back to the food patrol. One trick we've used with great success is to position the boat in the direction the bear is moving, kill the engine and drift in to close range.

Once, with the engine off, we watched in awe as a big male grizzly walked directly past our position no more than 50 yards away—we were so close we could hear his 3-inch claws tap-tapping on the stones. The beach ended in a steep cliff and there was a sharp 30-foot cutbank right before it. We wondered if the big guy would wade around and turn back the way he had come. Instead, he scrambled right up the bank in a shower of dirt and gravel. The sight of his big haunch muscles bunching as he powered uphill is one we will always remember. It was especially nice to know that he was not fleeing from us but just "doing his thing." It hardly needs saying that such undetected, close-up sightings of grizzly are rare. Once again—the magic of a cruising boat!

4. *Shore encounters.* Your boat is your castle, but on land it's a different ball game. Now you are perceived as a threat—or as food! The basic axiom in dealing with bears on land is no surprises. Let large animals know you are coming and give them a chance to express their

natural fear of you by fleeing. We normally carry an air horn—found in many pilothouses for marine signaling—and make several blasts before walking into the forest. A whistle or a can with some pebbles, or merely talking and singing loudly, will also do the trick.

If a confrontation should occur, remember that when a bear rears on its hind legs, it is simply trying to gain a better vantage point to figure out what you are. Let him know. Stand still, speak in a normal voice, do not look directly at him. If there are several people in your group, stand together to increase your apparent size and hold packs or raingear over your heads. If the bear does not run off (which he almost always will), back away slowly. Never run.

Pepper spray specially designed for bears would be a last-ditch deterrent in the event of a charge. You can wear a can in a holster on your belt, but check Canadian regulations before importing it.

Finally, if you are near the mainland between Kynoch and Khutze inlets, think twice about landing. The bears in this region are so-called "problem" animals that have been trapped and relocated from the communities of Terrace and Kitimat. They are not afraid of people and they have a taste for garbage. Since they are decidedly smarter than the average bear, give them a wide berth!

Close encounters of the bear kind are a special treat in northern British Columbia. Good luck!

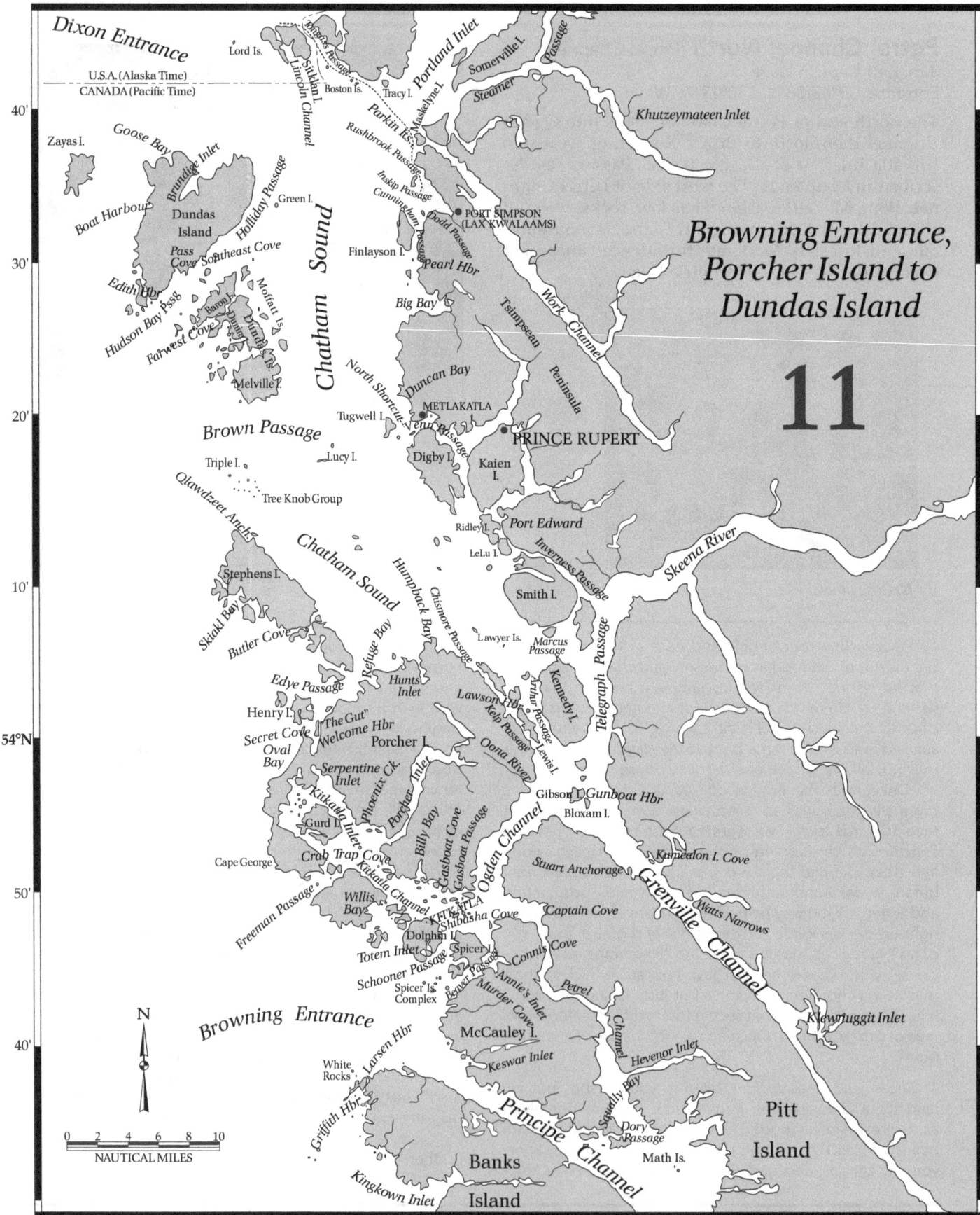

Dixon Entrance

U.S.A. (Alaska Time)
CANADA (Pacific Time)

40'

Zayas I.

Goose Bay

Lord Is.

Ghosts Passage

Silkan I.
Lincoln Channel

Boston Is.

Tracy I.

Parkin Is.

Portland Inlet

Maskelyne I.

Somerville I.

Steamer

Passage

Khutzeymateen Inlet

Brundige Inlet

Boat Harbour

Dundas
Island

Green I.

Rushbrook Passage

Inskip Passage

Cunningham Passage

Dodd Passage

PORT SIMPSON
(LAX KW'ALAAMS)

Pass
Cove

Holiday Passage

Southeast Cove

Chatham Sound

Finlayson I.

Pearl Hbr

Work Channel

30'

Edith Hbr

Hudson Bay Pssg

Farwest Cove

Moffatt Is.

Baron I.

Dundas Is.

Big Bay

North Shorecut

Duncan Bay

Tsimpsean

Peninsula

Melville I.

Brown Passage

Triple I.

Lucy I.

Tree Knob Group

Tugwell I.

METLAKATLA

Venn Passage

Digby I.

PRINCE RUPERT

Kaien
I.

20'

Qlawdzeet Anch.

Chatham Sound

Stephens I.

Skiakl Bay

Butler Cove

Humpback Bay

Chismore Passage

Lawyer Is.

Ridley I.

LeLu I.

Port Edward

Inverness Passage

Smith I.

Marcus
Passage

Skeena River

10'

Refuge Bay

Edye Passage

Hunts
Inlet

Lawson Hbr

Kelp Passage

Arthur Passage

Kennedy I.

Lewis I.

Telegraph Passage

Henry I.

Secret Cove

Oval
Bay

"The Gut"

Welcome Hbr

Porcher I

Oona River

Gibson I. Gunboat Hbr

Bloxam I.

54°N

Serpentine
Inlet

Phoenix Ck.

Porcher Inlet

Billy Bay

Gasboat Cove

Gasboat Passage

Kitkatla Inlet

Gurd I.

Stuart Anchorage

Kumealon I. Cove

Cape George

Crab Trap Cove

Kitkatla Channel

Captain Cove

Watts Narrows

Grenville Channel

50'

Willis
Bay

Freeman Passage

KITKATLA

Shibasha Cove

Connis Cove

Petrel

Dolphin I.

Spicer I.

Totem Inlet

Schooner Passage

Spicer Is.
Complex

Beaver Passage

Annie's Inlet

Murder Cove

Klewnuggit Inlet

Browning Entrance

McCauley I.

Channel

Hevenor Inlet

Pitt

Island

40'

White
Rocks

Larsen Hbr

Keswar Inlet

Squally Bay

Griffith Hbr

Dory
Passage

Math Is.

Principe Channel

Banks

Kingkown Inlet

Island

N

0 2 4 6 8 10
NAUTICAL MILES

©2024 Don and Réanne Douglass • Diagram not for navigation

11

Browning Entrance, and Porcher Island to Dundas Island

The complex of islands, islets and passages from Porcher Island to the Dundas Islands, along the west side of Chatham Sound, offers some fine remote cruising grounds that are seldom visited by cruising boats. Wonderful opportunities for kayaking, fishing and exploring exist in this area, both on the outer coast and in the smooth waters protected by islands and islets.

For small craft heading south from Alaska across Dixon Entrance, the islands covered in this chapter offer the first available shelter; for vessels crossing Hecate Strait to or from Haida Gwaii, Larsen Harbor on the northwest corner of Banks Island and Spicer Island on the north side of Beaver Passage have convenient and well-sheltered anchor sites. As the islands, beaches and campsites of this pristine environment are "discovered," wilderness cruising and kayaking are drawing increasing interest.

Beautiful Kitkatla Inlet and Welcome Harbour make good bases from which to explore Porcher Island and its surroundings. North of Melville Island and southeast of Edith Harbour, those with smaller boats and kayakers alike will discover beautiful places in this wonderful island complex.

Browning Entrance (Hecate Strait)
5 mi NW of Banks Island
Entrance: 53°41.39'N, 130°34.09'W

Browning Entrance is the jumping-off point for boats headed for or returning to Haida Gwaii.

Baidarka in Larsen Harbour

Larsen Harbour
(Browning Entrance)
N end of Banks Island
Entrance (outer): 53°38.32'N, 130°32.21'W
Entrance (inner): 53°37.79'N, 130°32.48'W
Anchor: 53°37.42'N, 130°33.09'

Larsen Harbour, strategically located on the northwest corner of Banks Island, is a gathering spot for cruising boats awaiting proper conditions to cross Hecate Strait to Haida Gwaii. Large swells from the northwest and kelp beds can sometimes make the entrance to Larsen Harbour intimidating. However, the kelp quickly knocks down the swell and chop and you can glide through in neutral for short periods without much difficulty. Boaters have reported in recent years that kelp no longer clogs Larsen Habour.

The fairway is somewhat difficult to discern so use your chart plotter to determine the point where you turn south toward the Larsen Harbour light. We have heard of boaters who had difficulty finding the fairway route and considered Spicer Anchorage a better place to hide from the weather.

However, Larsen is one of our favorites. We like its wild aspect—twisted, stunted trees, loons that moan, eagles that scream and, despite the windswept coastline, no swell or chop enters the harbor. We also like the "window" between the unnamed islets along the west side of the harbor that allow us to assess conditions in Hecate Strait.

Larsen Harbour is worth a visit on its own, no matter whether you're crossing Hecate Strait or not. It's a particularly good base from which to explore the wild and beautiful Griffith Harbour. After you manage the entrance to Larsen, once you're inside you'll find safe moorage. Anchorage for small craft can be found at the head of the bay off the drying mud flat with limited swinging room. Mooring buoys were removed years ago and anchoring is your only option.

Anchor (mud flat) in 1 to 2 fathoms over sand and mud with good holding.

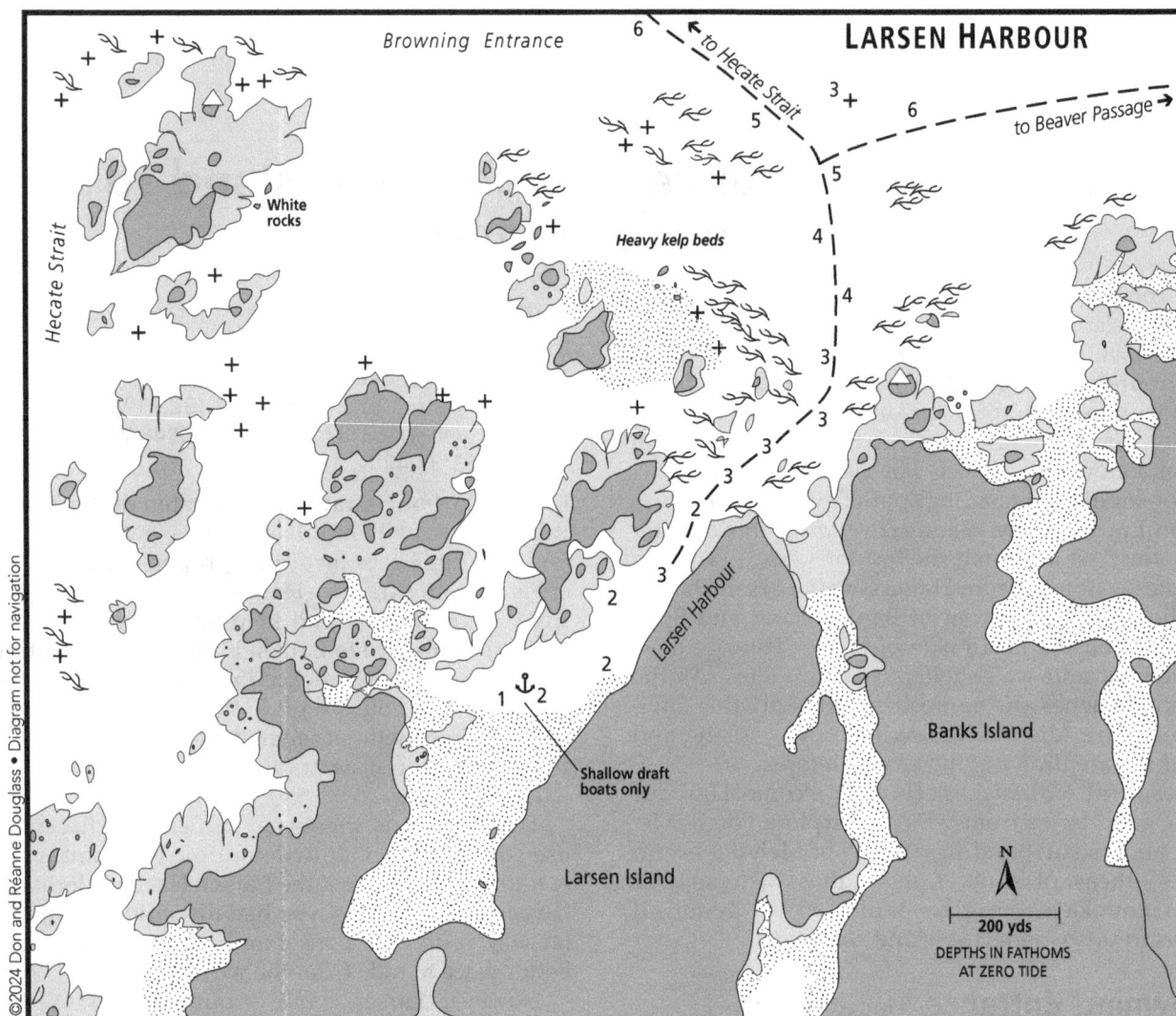

Browning Entrance

LARSEN HARBOUR

to Hecate Strait

to Beaver Passage

Hecate Strait

White rocks

Heavy kelp beds

©2024 Don and Reanne Douglass • Diagram not for navigation

Larsen Harbour

Shallow draft boats only

Banks Island

Larsen Island

N

200 yds

DEPTHS IN FATHOMS AT ZERO TIDE

Bonilla Island

(Hecate Strait)

9 mi SW of Larsen Harbour

Position (Bonilla Island light): 53°29.55'N, 130°38.22'W

Bonilla Island is strategically located close off the northwest corner of Banks Island. The lightstation gives critical reports for weather and sea conditions in Hecate Strait, and the lightkeepers collect and provide weather information for the MAREP program. The passageway between Bonilla and Banks Islands is notorious for nasty chop and swells whenever the currents and wind oppose each other. The west coast of Banks Island is generally considered off-the-chart cruising ground because of its reputation for rough seas, dangerous unmarked hazards to navigation, and the lack of published local knowledge.

Griffith Harbour (Banks Island)

3 mi S of Larsen Harbour

Entrance: 53°35.21'N, 130°33.43'W

Anchor: 53°35.96'N, 130°32.64'W

Griffith Harbour and Kingkown Inlet, 7 miles to the south, are major spawning grounds for aquatic life and are seldom visited by cruising boats. The entrance to Griffith Harbour is exposed to the south and has numerous rocks and reefs, making the approach dangerous during southeast gales. The vegetation is highly stressed by southeast winds that blow through the passage. More recently we reconnoitered Griffith Harbour by dinghy and found it much more interesting than we previously reported. We entered from the north through a narrow, drying passage east of Larsen Harbour, which is passable only on the upper reaches of high water. Griffith Harbour is a beautiful archipelago of small islands and islets covered with stunted, wind-

High water passage: Larsen Harbour to Griffith Harbour

blown trees. We found several 2- to 3-fathom holes far from the outer swell and chop that appear to offer good shelter. However, until the inner basins of the harbor are better charted, you are on your own to find the right channels to explore this region. During strong northwest winds the Boardman Group provide a significant shelter for the entrance zone. Chop was largely confined to the area west of Parlane Islet.

Anchor in 6 fathoms over mud at the anchor site shown on the chart.

Kingkown Inlet (Banks Island)
9.5 mi S of Larsen Harbour

We do not recommend Kingkown Inlet. Sailing Directions warns of numerous drying and below-water rocks and drying banks in the entrances to Kingkown Inlet.

Beaver Passage (Browning Entrance)
6.2 mi NE of Larsen Harbour
Entrance (W): 53°42.58'N, 130°25.06'W
Entrance (N): 53°47.87'N, 130°20.10'W

Beaver Passage is the shortest route for those crossing Hecate Strait to the protected waters of the Inside Passage. The shorter ocean ferryboat route from Daajing Giids (Queen Charlotte City) to Prince Rupert uses Edye Passage on the north side of Porcher Island. Ocean swell decreases rapidly east of Hankin Rock and disappears by Annie's Inlet.

Spicer Island Complex (Spicer Anchorage)
(Beaver Passage)
0.9 mi NW of Murder Cove
South Entrance: 53°44.57'N, 130°21.30'W
Anchor: 53°45.12'N, 130°21.60'W

"Spicer Anchorage," the local name for the popular anchor site between Spicer Island and South Spicer Island, is a well-sheltered and landlocked passage that offers very good anchorage out of all swells and chop. There are no drift logs and grass grows along the rocky shore. Bald eagles, mergansers and other waterfowl frequent this Spicer Island Complex. Small boats may want to anchor in the nook 0.25 mile south for a little more shelter; the bottom at this site is soft like Jello, however, with less swinging room.

Anchor (elbow) in 4 fathoms over grey mud with shells and kelp; good holding.

Anchor (unnamed island nook) in 1 to 2 fathoms over soft grey mud, shells and kelp; very good holding with a well-set anchor.

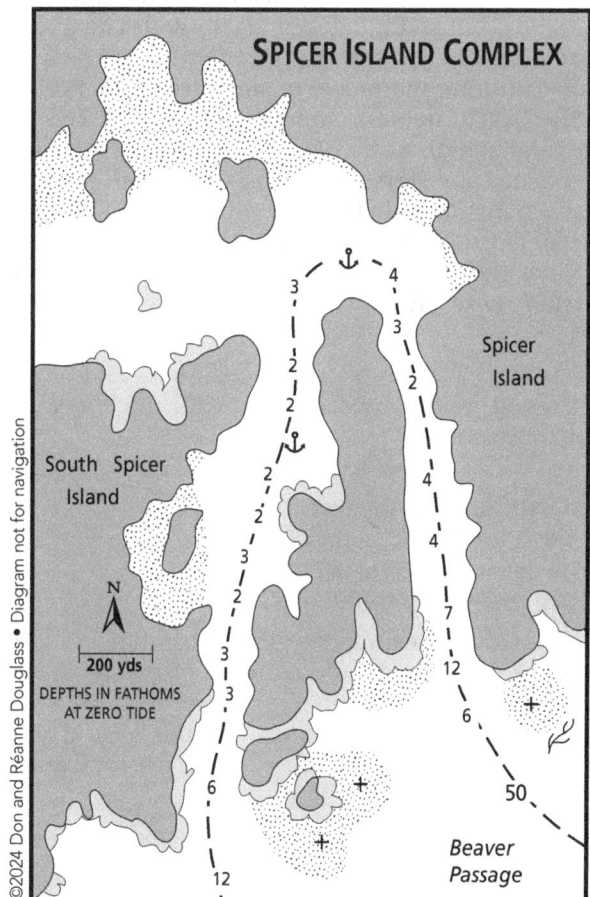

SPICER ISLAND COMPLEX

Spicer Island

South Spicer Island

N

200 yds

DEPTHS IN FATHOMS AT ZERO TIDE

Beaver Passage

©2024 Don and Réanne Douglass • Diagram not for navigation

Murder Cove (Beaver Passage)
1 mi SE of Spicer Is Complex
Entrance: 53°44.31'N, 130°19.92'W
Anchor: 53°44.24'N, 130°19.73'W

Murder Cove is a small indentation on the south shore of Beaver Passage. It can be used as a convenient lunch stop; however, it has limited swinging room for anything but one or two small boats. The cove is full of floating rockweed and there are no logs on shore, indicating good protection from southerly weather. Favor the north shore on entering to avoid a shoal area.

Anchor off the small waterfall in 2 to 3 fathoms over sand and gravel; fair holding.

Annie's Inlet (Beaver Passage)
0.8 mi S of Connis Light
Entrance: 53°44.76'N, 130°18.38'W
Anchor: 53°44.50'N, 130°18.34'W

We call this small, unnamed inlet "Annie's Inlet" where *Baidarka*'s First Mate, Réanne, found relief from the last of the swells in Hecate Strait and Browning Entrance. This is a well-protected anchor site for a small boat but swinging room is limited. The inlet is surrounded by old-growth cedar and silver snags—there's nothing manmade in sight; there are no logs on the beach, no surf, and cedar branches kiss the saltwater at high water. Here you can enjoy watching huge green sun stars in the clear water; Dall porpoises swim just outside the inlet and harbor seals play inside. This is an intimate and scenic place.

Favor the west side upon entering; there are uncharted rocks on the east side that dry at 8 and 10 feet.

Anchor in 3 fathoms over mud, grass and shells; very good holding. (Make sure your anchor is not fouled by grass.)

Connis Cove (Beaver Passage)
0.7 mi SE of Connis Light
Entrance: 53°45.36'N, 130°18.01'W
Anchor: 53°45.20'N, 130°17.83'W

Connis Cove is exposed to the north, but fair protection from most weather can be found tucked in behind the wooded islets on the south shore. River otters are busy on these islets and the large drying flat off the creek is a favorite resting place for Canada geese.

Anchor in 5 fathoms over mud and sand with some kelp; fair holding.

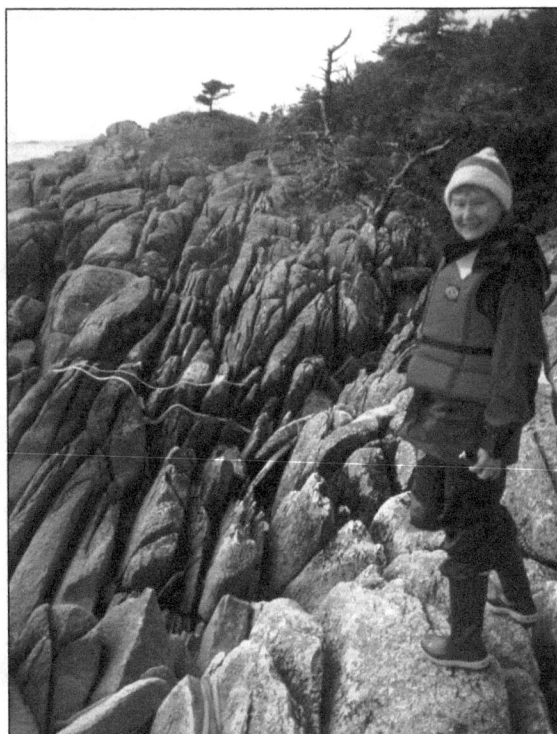

Rock formations on Parlane Islet near Griffith Harbour

Ogden Channel (SE of Porcher Island)
21 mi S of Prince Rupert
Entrance (S): 53°49.63'N, 130°18.77'W
Entrance (N): 53°55.49'N, 130°13.52'W

Ogden Channel separates Pitt Island from Porcher Island and leads north from Beaver Passage and Petrel Channel to Grenville Channel and Arthur Passage. It is deep and free of dangers in the fairway.

Ogden Channel carries part of the outflow of the opaque Skeena River to the sea. On spring tides, turbulence can be felt at its south entrance.

Skene Cove (Ogden Channel)
6.6 mi SW of Oona River
Entrance: 53°50.88'N, 130°20.43'W

The small nook in the south shore of Skene Cove can be useful as a lunch stop or emergency shelter; it is deep and steep-to. As an anchor site, we prefer either Captain Cove or Billy Bay.

Alpha Bay (Ogden Channel)
5 mi SW of Oona River
Position: 53°51.70'N, 130°17.26'W

Alpha Bay is a deep open bight and steep-to; it is also exposed to chop. Fishing boats sometimes anchor off the drying shoal in about 10 fathoms.

Schooner Passage (Browning Entrance)

3.5 mi S of Kitkatla
Entrance (SW): 53°44.44'N, 130°25.63'W
Entrance (N): 53°47.23'N, 130°23.37'W

Schooner Passage is used as a shortcut from Browning Entrance to Kitkatla Inlet. Totem Inlet and Shaman Cove offer anchorage.

Shaman Cove (Dolphin Island)

0.5 mi SW of Totem Inlet
Entrance: 53°45.14'N, 130°25.82'W

Anchorage can be found at the head of Shaman Cove. Favor the west shore to avoid rocks that extend from the east shore to mid-channel. Totem Inlet, immediately north, provides superior shelter for cruising boats.

Anchor in about 2 fathoms over unrecorded bottom.

Totem Inlet (Dolphin Island)

2.5 mi S of Kitkatla
Entrance: 53°45.35'N, 130°24.94'W
Anchor: 53°45.75'N, 130°25.52'W

Totem Inlet, on the southeast corner of Dolphin Island, is a scenic, landlocked inlet that provides good shelter for cruising boats. Several boats can find adequate room to anchor here. The entrance to the inlet is about 40 feet wide with about $2\frac{1}{2}$ fathoms in the fairway. The first basin is perfectly calm with grassy margins along the shore and rockweed floating in still waters. The inner lagoon can best be explored by dinghy as there is a mid-channel rock in the shallow narrows. Entering Totem Inlet during times of heavy southwest swells can be difficult, so under such conditions it's easier to head 1.5 miles north to Shibasha Cove.

Anchor in 3 fathoms over soft mud with good holding.

Shibasha Cove (Dolphin Island)

1.6 mi N of Totem Inlet
Entrance: 53°46.80'N, 130°23.93'W
Anchor: 53°46.99'N, 130°24.46'W

Shibasha Island, on the northeast corner of Dolphin Island, provides good protection in all weather. A large, dangerous reef in the middle of the entrance is awash on an 18-foot tide. Avoid this reef by favoring the south shore where the fairway carries about 2 fathoms. The reef is well marked with a large patch of kelp. A recent embankment and road now cross the grassy spit, giving even better protection to the cove. Watch for drift logs and kelp brought in on flood tides. The cove has swinging room for up to six boats. Anchorage can be taken anywhere off the drying flat.

Anchor in about 3 fathoms over soft grey mud with kelp and wood debris; good holding.

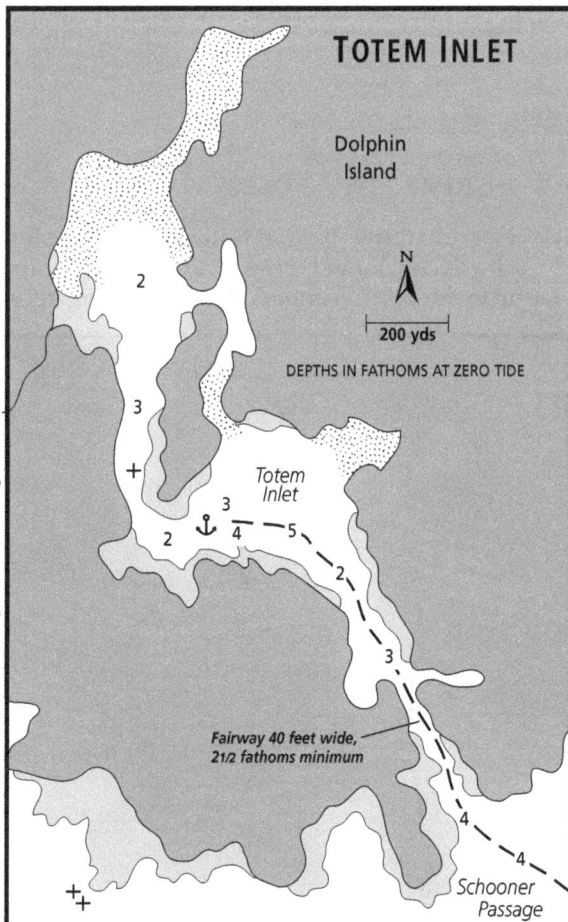

TOTEM INLET

Dolphin Island

N

200 yds

DEPTHS IN FATHOMS AT ZERO TIDE

Totem Inlet

Fairway 40 feet wide,
2½ fathoms minimum

Schooner Passage

©2024 Don and Réanne Douglass • Diagram not for navigation

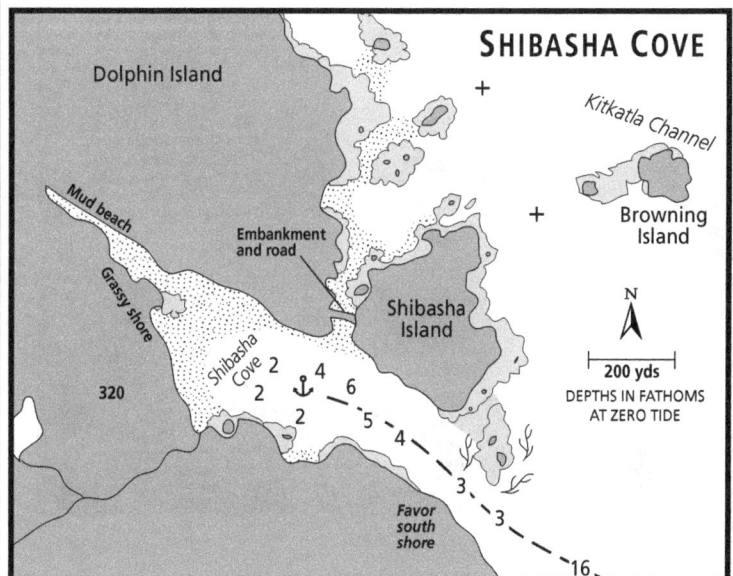

SHIBASHA COVE

Dolphin Island

Kitkatla Channel

Browning Island

Mud beach

Embankment and road

Shibasha Island

Grassy shore

Shibasha Cove

320

N

200 yds

DEPTHS IN FATHOMS AT ZERO TIDE

Favor south shore

©2024 Don and Réanne Douglass • Diagram not for navigation

Willis Bay (Goschen Island)
3 mi W of Kitkatla
Entrance: 53°48.06'N, 130°31.26'W

Willis Bay is frequently used by fishermen as shelter from prevailing westerlies. The tiny cove behind a reef complex at the western extremity of the bay has provided good shelter for small boats in all weather. Kitkatla Pass is used by locals to connect Willis Bay to Kitkatla Channel. The north end is very tricky and must be done on a proper tide, with local knowledge and with a good bow lookout. Schooner Passage on the south side of Dolphin Island is much safer.

Sailing Directions warns against navigating any of the narrow intricate channels around Shakes Islands due to the numerous drying reefs, rocks awash, and foul ground.

Dolphin Lagoon
(Dolphin Island)
1.5 mi SW of Kitkatla
Entrance: 53°46.68'N, 130°28.36'W

Dolphin Lagoon is filled with a sizable island and several islets. Although its topography looks interesting, its cruising potential is unknown.

Freeman Passage (Kitkatla Inlet)
6 mi NW of Kitkatla
Entrance (SW): 53°49.47'N, 130°39.59'W
Entrance (NE): 53°51.04'N, 130°34.46'W

Freeman Passage is the western entrance to Kitkatla Inlet. Mooring buoys have reportedly been removed and no longer available on Freeman Passage.

Freeman Passage Cove
7.6 mi NW of Kitkatla
Entrance: 53°50.53'N, 130°38.27'W

"Freeman Passage Cove" is what we call the small cove on the northwest shore of Freeman Passage, 1.3 miles northeast of the south entrance buoy "E98." The cove is well sheltered from all weather.

Absalom Cove (Freeman Passage)
1 mi E of Freeman Passage Cove
Entrance: 53°50.68'N, 130°36.54'W

"Absalom Cove" is what we call the small anchor site west of Absalom Island. It is a useful anchor site for small boats, or as a base camp for exploring the surrounding islets and reefs.

Kitkatla Channel (Porcher Island)
W of Beaver Passage
Entrance (SE): 53°47.13'N, 130°20.81'W
Entrance (NW): 53°51.29'N, 130°32.90'W

Kitkatla Channel connects Kitkatla and Porcher inlets to Beaver Passage. The village of Kitkatla is located on the south shore on the north side of Dolphin Island.

Kitkatla (Kitkatla Channel)
3.6 mi W of Beaver Passage
Public floats: 53°47.73'N, 130°26.27'W

Kitkatla is a thriving Native village. Its mission church spire is no longer clearly visible upon approach due to new construction. When entering keep

Calm anchorage, Porcher Island

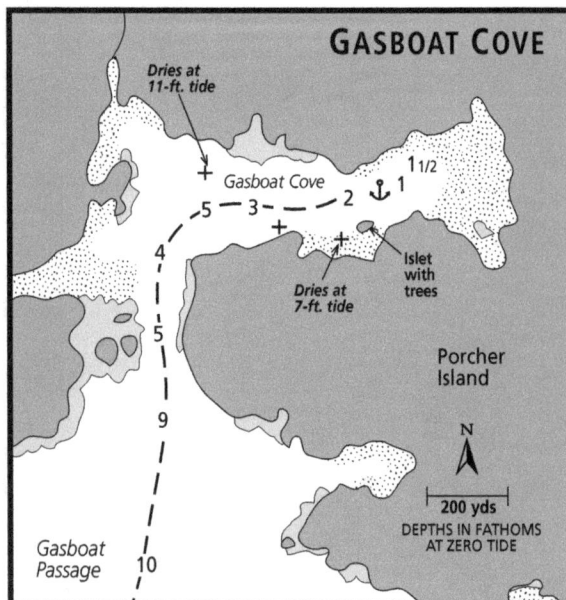

Buoy "E95" to port—the floats are on the west side of the village and most are taken up by local boats.

Gasboat Passage (Porcher Island)
3.5 mi NE of Kitkatla
Entrance (E): 53°49.59'N, 130°20.42'W
Entrance (W): 53°49.46'N, 130°25.07'W

Cruising boats should experience no problem using Gasboat Passage as a shortcut in or out of Kitkatla Inlet; however, there are a number of submerged rocks on the south side of the passage at its west entrance.

Gasboat Cove (Gasboat Channel)
2.4 mi N of Kitkatla
Entrance: 53°49.95'N, 130°25.35'W
Anchor: 53°50.19'N, 130°24.97'W

"Gasboat Cove" is what we call the small L-shaped cove on the northwest end of Gasboat Passage. The cove offers very good protection for small boats deep in the eastern part over a shallow, flat bottom; swinging room is limited, however.

On entering the cove, avoid the rocks on the west shore and the rock at the elbow that extends 150 feet from the north shore, awash at 11 feet. Also avoid the two rocks awash on 7 feet off the south shore of the inner cove. Anchor north of the uncharted wooded islet. Larger boats can find more swinging room in Billy Bay.

Anchor in 1 to 2 fathoms over soft grey mud with fair-to-good holding.

Billy Bay (Gasboat Channel)
2.1 mi N of Kitkatla
Entrance: 53°49.64'N, 130°25.80'W
Anchor: 53°50.42'N, 130°26.02'W

Billy Bay offers good shelter in the eastern section of the cove. Avoid the rock awash at 3 feet near the elbow at mid-channel. We prefer Gasboat Cove, a half-mile to the east, because it is more intimate.

Anchor in 4 fathoms over soft mud with fair-to-good holding.

Crab Trap Cove (Kitkatla Channel)
5 mi NW of Kitkatla
Entrance (S): 53°50.94'N, 130°31.00'W
Entrance (NW): 53°51.66'N, 130°30.84'W
Anchor: 53°51.14'N, 130°30.20'W

The Cessford Islands, at the north end of Kitkatla Channel, provide a well-sheltered basin to the east which we call Crab Trap Cove. The flat mud and grassy

bottom of Crab Trap Cove is a favorite location of crab fishermen. The northern entrance to the cove is more accessible; however, avoid shoals outside the entrance and sand spits that extend inside from both shores. The south entrance is usable, but very narrow with several reefs, some marked by kelp. In both cases a very slow entrance speed with bow lookout is prudent. There is a large, flat area with plenty of swinging room in the middle of the cove to accommodate several boats. The westernmost Cessford Island has a white sandy beach that makes an excellent kayak haul-out and campsite.

Anchor in 3 to 4 fathoms over soft mud with grass; very good holding.

Porcher Inlet (Porcher Island)
5.6 mi NW of Kitkatla
Entrance: 53°52.64'N, 130°30.90'W

Porcher Inlet, which nearly cuts Porcher Island in two, extends 8.2 miles from the entrance through a U-shaped, high-sided fiord to a 4-mile long salt lagoon. Its entrance is encumbered with a shallow bar with many isolated rocks. Porcher Narrows, 2 miles northeast of the entrance, has tidal streams that reach 7 knots on spring flood and ebb. The entrance to the salt lagoon at the head of the inlet has a convoluted channel that dries. The narrows has an irregular bottom with several drying rocks on both sides. Depths are too great for convenient anchorage.

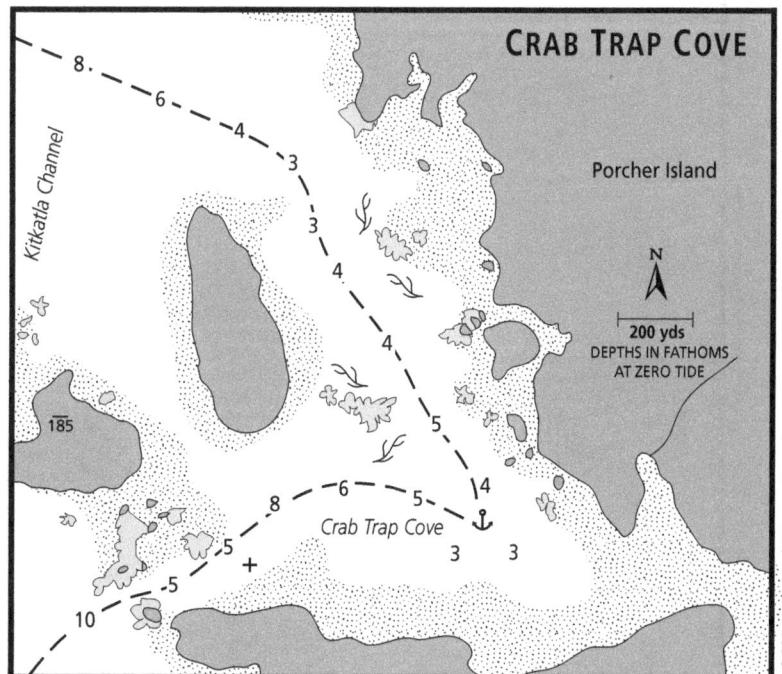
CRAB TRAP COVE

Kitkatla Inlet (Porcher Island)

8 mi NW of Kitkatla
Entrance: 53°51.94'N, 130°35.35'W

Kitkatla Inlet is a horseshoe-shaped basin on the west side of Porcher Island with Gurd Island in its center. Gurd Inlet is on the south side of Gurd Island; Serpentine Inlet is in the northwest corner of the basin and Dries Inlet is in the north corner of the basin. The inlet is exposed to southeast winds and chop.

Only one place in Kitkatla Inlet should be considered during a southeast blow: along the northwest side of Gurd Island. Anchor near 53°54.70'N, 130°39.10'W over a mud bottom with moderate holding close under the lee of Gurd Island; the closer to the island the better. Kevin Monahan anchored there in a 60-knot southeast wind and found it tolerable, but he had to maintain close anchor watch. In a normal southeast gale, he found the anchorage fine. But when southeasters blow 60 knots in Hecate Strait, it also blows 60 knots in Kitkatla Inlet. "In three years of working on the *Bahine Post*," Kevin reported, "this was the only time I ever dragged anchor. Anywhere else in Kitkatla Inlet proper is totally untenable in southeast gales."

Phoenix Creek Cove (Porcher Island)

6.5 mi NW of Kitkatla
Entrance (W): 53°53.62'N, 130°31.52'W
Anchor 53°53.52'N, 130°30.85'W

Another lagoon to explore!

We call the narrow passageway between Phoenix Islands and the outlet of Phoenix Creek, "Phoenix Creek Cove." This scenic, well-sheltered spot is a favorite of loons and eagles and there are grassy campsites on shore. Anchorage for a single, small boat can be found in the passage off the drying flat of Phoenix Creek. This is a scenic, quiet place to find solitude and it makes a good base camp from which to explore Porcher Inlet.

Anchor in 2 to 3 fathoms over sand and mud with good holding.

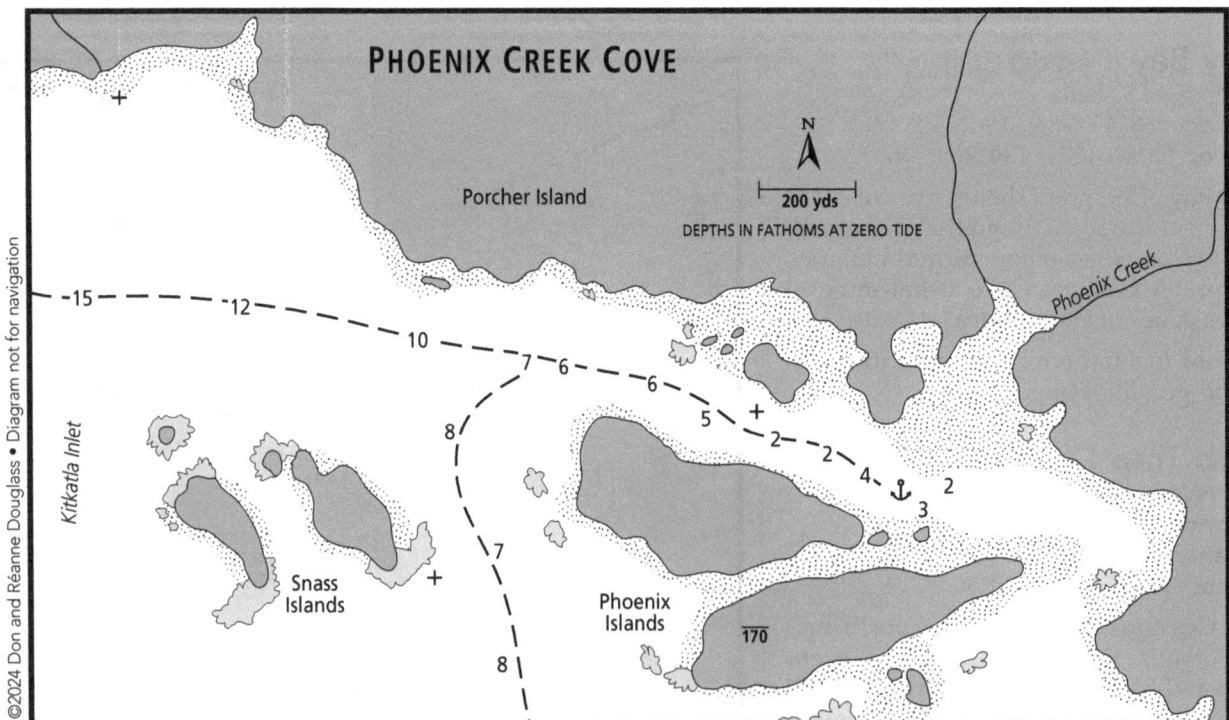

PHOENIX CREEK COVE

Porcher Island

N

200 yds

DEPTHS IN FATHOMS AT ZERO TIDE

Phoenix Creek

Kitkatla Inlet

-15 — -12 — -10 — -7 -6 — 6 —

8 5 2 — 2

7 4 2

3

Snass Islands

Phoenix Islands

170

8

©2024 Don and Reanne Douglass • Diagram not for navigation

Gurd Inlet (Kitkatla Inlet)
9.7 mi NW of Kitkatla
Entrance: 53°53.26'N, 130°39.26'W

Gurd Inlet is well sheltered and reported to have 5 to 7 fathoms at its east end. The entrance to the inlet is encumbered with a number of rocks and reefs and can be entered only at high-water slack with alert bow lookouts. We haven't been inside but this could be bombproof if it's accessible.

Wilcox Group Cove (Kitkatla Inlet)
10.8 mi NW of Kitkatla
Entrance: 53°55.03'N, 130°39.53'W
Anchor: 53°55.15'N, 130°39.90'W

The Wilcox Group consists of several islands on the northwest side of Gurd Island. Approaching from the east, you can anchor in the center of the Wilcox Group. We use this cove in prevailing northwest winds and like the window across the reef to the west; however, it is useful in stable weather only. At high water, some chop can be felt in the cove; however, at low water the reefs form a natural breakwater. The same conditions as those mentioned above by Kevin Monahan, pertain to this cove.

Anchor in 3 fathoms over soft mud with shells and weeds; fair-to-good holding.

Serpentine Inlet (Kitkatla Inlet)
11.5 mi NW of Kitkatla
Entrance: 53°55.87'N, 130°39.95'W
Anchor: 53°56.59'N, 130°40.86'W

Serpentine Inlet is well sheltered in westerlies but it is exposed to southeast winds and should be used

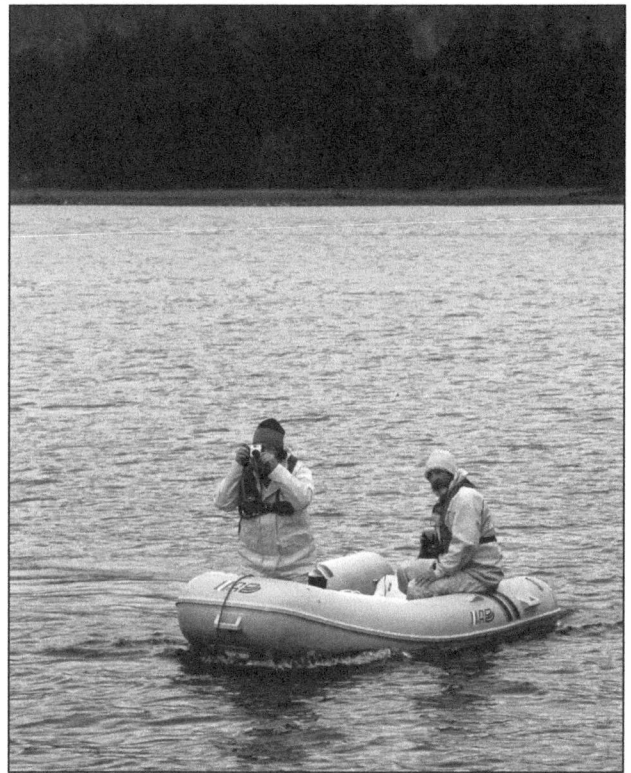

Baidarka *scouts at work*

as a fair weather anchorage only. The entrance is very narrow with drying flats on either side. *Caution:* a slow entrance with alert lookout is required. Anchorage can be found at the head of the inlet off a small grey-pebble beach. There are several abandoned cabins at the north end of the inlet. The sandy beach at Oval Bay is less than a half-mile away. We understand there may be a trail across to the beach but we have not been able to find it.

Anchor in 1 to 2 fathoms over a soft bottom with fair-to-good holding; good swinging room over a large flat area.

Dries Inlet
(Kitkatla Inlet)
1.7 mi NE of Serepentine Inlet
Entrance: 53°56.23'N, 130°37.22'W
Dries Inlet is a large, shallow area exposed to winds, especially from the south. Temporary anchorage can be taken anywhere short of the drying flats in 2 to 3 fathoms over a soft bottom. There is lots of swinging room for larger boats and it is easy to enter or leave at any time or tide.

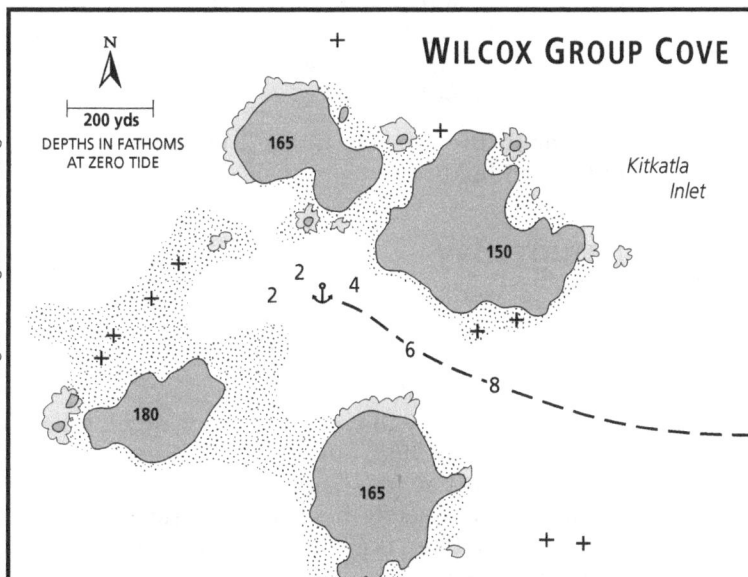

©2024 Don and Réanne Douglass • Diagram not for navigation

WILCOX GROUP COVE

N

200 yds
DEPTHS IN FATHOMS
AT ZERO TIDE

165

150

Kitkatla
Inlet

2
2   4
6
8

180

165

Chatham Sound
(Porcher Island to Dixon Entrance)

The western side of Chatham Sound, extending from the north end of Porcher Island to Dundas Island, offers fine, remote cruising and exploration by kayak with scenic and isolated anchorages. The three main passages between Chatham Sound and Hecate Strait and Dixon Entrance to the west are Edye Passage, north of Porcher Island, Brown Passage in the center, and Hudson Bay Passage on the south side of Dundas Island.

Currents can be strong in all of these passages especially on an ebb with Skeena River outflow. Nasty chop that requires boats to seek shelter can be encountered in Chatham Sound, as well as in the three passages when strong wind opposes the current.

Humpback Bay
(Porcher Island)
2.2 mi SW of Lawyer Islands
Entrance: 54°05.50'N, 130°23.20'W
Anchor: 54°05.26'N, 130°23.99'W

Humpback Bay, on the northeast corner of Porcher Island, once held an active fishing cannery known as "Porcher Island." Only the pilings, old cannery buildings, and the ruins of houses remain. The large flat south of the cannery dries at low water. The bay offers good temporary shelter from most weather—especially southeasterlies—in the narrow channel between the old pilings and the two islands on the north side. Swinging room is quite limited.

Anchor in 4 fathoms over mud and gravel with fair holding.

Hunt Inlet
(Porcher Island)
7.7 mi NW of Lawson Harbour
Entrance: 54°05.16'N, 130°27.25'W
Public float: 54°04.12'N, 130°26.68'W
Anchor: 54°03.29'N, 130°26.33'W

Two-mile-long Hunt Inlet, which indents the north end of Porcher Island, lies between the Creek Islands to the west and a group of unnamed islands, rocks and islets off the north end of Porcher Island. Use a large scale chart to identify the hazards. The inlet offers welcome protection from the weather of Chatham Sound.

Sheltered anchorage can be found in the middle of the inlet. Favor the west shore 0.4 mile north of the public dock. You may, however, experience nasty chop near the entrance when a strong northwest blows against an ebb tide. There's a small public

A mink combs the shore looking for dinner

dock at Hunts Inlet [sic]. It's largely filled with local boats, and there are a number of nice-looking homes with large wooden sheds.

The inner basin has a very narrow entrance channel with a least depth of one fathom and a mid-channel rock that dries on a 1-fathom tide. Favor the east side of the channel to avoid rocks and the treed islet. The narrows is chock full of kelp. At the bitter end, there are several private floats. The landlocked inner basin offers total shelter over a wide area. Larger boats will want to anchor southeast of the public dock in 6 to 8 fathoms.

Anchor in the inner basin in 2 fathoms over mud with good holding.

Refuge Bay
(Edye Passage)
3.4 mi W of Hunt Inlet
Entrance: 54°03.71'N, 130°32.57'W
Anchor: 54°03.25'N, 130°31.97'W

Refuge Bay is easy to enter and offers quick relief in nasty southeast chop, but for small boats it is rather open. Useless Bay (the next bay west) is well-named because it completely dries on low tides. South of Useless Point there is a long, sandy beach that can be used by kayakers.

Edye Passage (Porcher Island)

0.5 mi W of Refuge Bay
Entrance (W): 54°03.30'N, 130°39.75'W
Entrance (E): 54°04.20'N, 130°33.20'W

Approaching from the east, Edye Passage appears to be a landlocked dead-end until you are well south of Arthur Island. Occasional turbulence may be encountered on the south side of Arthur Island. Prescott Passage is the narrow, shallow channel (1 fathom minimum) on the north side of Arthur Island.

Seiner at work in the fog

Photo courtesy Kevin Monahan

The Sea Wolves of British Columbia

Ian McAllister/PacificWild.com

The term "marine mammal" brings to mind slick-skinned animals that spend most of their time in the ocean: whales, porpoises, dolphins, sea lions, seals, sea otters, and polar bears. Except for the latter, these mammals use fins, flippers, flukes, and tails to maneuver through water. There are at least 129 species of aquatic or semi-aquatic mammals that depend upon the oceans for their existence, feeding on fish, crustaceans, squid, and other sea mammals. But a unique mammal has been recently added to the list; it's a four-legged creature known for hunting caribou on the Alaskan tundra, or stalking deer in the forests of British Columbia. It belongs to the genus *Canis*, which includes wolves and dogs.

This sea wolf is a wily subspecies of the gray wolf. Because of their isolation on remote islands west of British Columbia and Southeast Alaska, they have adapted to subsisting on salmon, crustaceans, herring roe glued onto kelp fronds, and dead whales washed up on beaches, and they have been observed to swim several miles in order to surprise seals and sea lions hauled out on rocks.

Wildlife photographer Ian McAllister has watched sea wolves for years as they combed beaches and waded tide pools, searching for shellfish and salmon. In the early 2000s, he returned several times with Canadian wolf biologist Paul Paquet and documented the sea wolves feeding on fresh salmon.

With the support of First Nations and the Rainforest Conservation Foundation, graduate student Chris Darimont began a ten-year study of these elusive canines. At first Darimont assumed the wolves found on these isolated islands were gray wolves that traveled between the islands and the mainland where they supplemented their diet with deer. He soon discovered that the sea wolves live their entire lives on these rugged islands, with ninety percent of their diet coming from the ocean. They possess exceptional swimming prowess, and in 1996, a pair of wolves were observed on Dundas Island, eight miles from the nearest mainland shore. A small population has been discovered in Southeast Alaska, and at one time their range may have extended south along Washington State's coast.

Though sea wolves rarely come in contact with people, their future remains in jeopardy due to habitat loss from resource exploitation and industrial development along BC's remote north coast.

—KK

Information taken from the October 2015 issue of *National Geographic*: "In Search of the Elusive Sea Wolf Along Canada's Rugged Coast," by Susan McGrath, and the October 15 issue of the online magazine *Mother Nature Network*: "Tracking British Columbia's Secretive Sea Wolf," by Jaymi Heimbuch.

Welcome Harbour

(Porcher Island)
8 mi SW of Hunt Inlet
Entrance (N): 54°02.00'N, 130°37.38'W
Anchor: 54°00.14'N, 130°39.60'W

Welcome Harbour, in the northwest corner of Porcher Island, is well named—after a safe arrival you don't want to leave. The harbor is composed of a labyrinth of islands, islets, and reefs—at least 100 islets and reefs in an area less than five miles square—and without navigational aids or identifying features.

Entering the harbor can be a nightmare to a newcomer, or in poor visibility. The bottom is irregular and an echo sounder records a ragged pattern. It's best to consider entering on a low tide, rising, when rocks and kelp can be seen more easily. Plotting your course on a large scale chart is necessary; careful dead reckoning or judicious use of chart plotter to help identify turning points is vital.

Because of its intricate layout, Pacific swell does not enter Welcome Harbour; chop is present only in the strong tidal current off the northwest corner of Dancey Island or when strong winds are blowing. There is an almost unlimited number of nooks and crannies where anchorage can be taken, especially using a stern-tie. The area 0.8 mile west of the center of Dancey Island is designated by the B.C. Forest Service as Welcome Harbour. During the day you can hear crows, ravens, and bald eagles, and at night you may hear wolves howling.

Welcome Harbour has been almost entirely the playground of Prince Rupert residents. When cruising boaters learn about its fascinating geography, solitude, pristine hemlock and cedar forest, and nearby sandy beaches, the harbor may become a major boating destination. The bay south of Welcome Harbour, known locally as Campbells Place, is entered by way of "the gut" along the southwest corner of Dancey Island. The very narrow channel is chock full of bull kelp with rocks and reefs at either end. Secret Cove, the small outer bight with an extraordinary view of the exposed outer coast, is entered as noted below.

Anchor in 6 fathoms over sand, stone and seaweed; holding can be poor-to-good depending on the set of your anchor.

Secret Cove (Porcher Island)
0.3 mi W of Welcome Cove
Entrance (W): (Henry Island): 54°00.65'N,
130°41.44'W
Anchor: 54°00.10'N, 130°40.10'W

Secret Cove is secret—it takes imagination to see it and courage to enter. The cove, which lies on the exposed west side of Porcher Island, is surprisingly well sheltered by a complex of reefs and rocks that act as a breakwater at low tides, making the cove essentially landlocked. However, this is no place to be caught during storms—witness the large stumps and old drift logs that line the gravel beach. The shore has been eroded by storms, and the beach is steep-to. This is a small boat, fair weather route only.

Although this can be an interesting anchorage, or a good lunch stop, at high spring tides the rocks and reefs off Welcome Point (the "breakwater") largely disappear underwater, and the anchorage becomes quite rolly. Our crew wanted to return to Welcome Harbour after rolling below.

When entering Secret Cove from Welcome Harbour, avoid the rocks off the north end of the peninsula by favoring the Henry Island shore. Proceeding south, favor the east shore close to Porcher Island while passing east of the off-lying reefs. The narrow 40-foot-wide, or less, fairway has a minimum depth of about 1.5 fathoms. Kelp and rocks are on either side. Avoid patches of attached bull kelp since they indicate shoals or uncharted rocks. Moderately strong currents run in the fairway and the flood tide tends to cross the reef, setting you on the island. There is no passing or turning room on this route—it is for small boats only.

During a moderate southerly gale when we were once anchored here, breakers smashed on the rocks and reefs to the west, but only an occasional strong puff entered the cove. We don't recommend either entering or anchoring in Secret Cove in anything but fair weather. Enter on a low tide rising so that rocks and reefs can be more easily identified. An entry from Hecate Strait along the Henry Island shore or from Oval Bay to the south is not advised unless you reconnoiter first, and then only under ideal conditions. Approaching this coast from seaward would be hazardous under most conditions—we have seen one 40-foot fishing boat use the Oval Bay route at mid-tide.

Oval Bay, one mile south of Secret Cove, has a long, beautiful sandy beach that is best visited by hiking across from the protected anchorage on the east side of the peninsula, or by fast inflatable from Welcome Harbour.

Time to turn on the radar

Stephens Passage
5.5 mi NW of Refuge Bay
Position (drying passage): 54°07.06'N, 130°08.86'W

Stephens Passage is normally used only by skiffs near high water. We strongly recommend reconnoitering before use. On the chart, it looks very challenging.

Qlawdzeet (Squatterie) (Stephens Island)
12 mi SW of Digby Island
Entrance: 54°12.58'N, 130°46.11'W
Anchor: 54°12.47'N, 130°45.90'W

Qlawdzeet Anchorage, a fisherman's favorite, is located on the extreme northeast end of Stephens Island. Called locally "Squatterie" (emphasis on the last two letters), the site is reported to offer very good protection for small boats deep in the inner basin south of Dunn Island, tied to one or more of the old pilings or dolphins. Swinging room is limited. Larger boats anchor southwest of Dunn Island in about 8 to 10 fathoms.

Tree Nob Group (Rushton Island)
3 mi NW of Squatterie
Position: 54°15.70'N, 130°48.90'W

Temporary anchorage is reported in the Tree Nob Group on the east side of Rushton Island, 3 miles northwest of Squatterie. A large, flat area southwest of bell buoy "D72" can be used as an anchorage in fair weather. This is a useful anchorage as a lunch stop or for exploring the interesting rocks and islets of the Tree Nob Group, but inadequate in heavy weather. Tree Knob Group forms the south side of Brown Passage with Triple Island Light on its west side.

Anchor in 5 to 7 fathoms over an unrecorded bottom.

Brown Passage

(Chatham Sound)
12 mi W of Digby Island
Entrance (W): 54°15.19'N, 130°55.40'W

Triple island is a key lightstation on the south side of Brown Passage, 3 miles northwest of Rushton Island. The weather reports from Triple Island are an important indicator of conditions in Dixon Entrance.

Dundas Islands

(Chatham Sound)
9 to 24 mi NW of Digby Island
Entrance (W): (Hudson Bay Passage): 54°25.50'N, 130°58.50'W
Entrance (E): 54°33.00'N, 130°45.00'W

The Dundas Islands consist of hundreds of small islands in an intriguing pattern. Relief can be found inside these islands when northeast chop occurs in Chatham Sound during outflow gales in Portland Inlet. It is a great place to explore by kayak or small boat.

Farwest Cove (Dunira Island)

5.1 mi SE of Edith Cove
Position (Farwest Point): 54°25.55'N, 130°50.10'W
Entrance (cove): 54°25.94'N, 130°48.70'W

"Farwest Cove" is what we call the basin 1.5 miles northeast of Farwest Point, on the west side of Dunira Island. This cove, on the west side of Coast Mound—a 700-foot cone-shaped peak—appears to be well-sheltered in most weather. Its entrance is encumbered by a number of reefs and rocks but the inner basin has a fairly flat bottom with good swinging room for several boats.

Anchor in 8 fathoms over an unrecorded bottom.

Clam Inlet (Baron Island)

2.3 mi SW of Hudson Bay Passage Cove
Entrance: 54°29.95'N, 130°47.26'W
Anchor: 54°29.48'N, 130°47.19'W

Clam Inlet provides good shelter in fair weather. It is scenic and makes a good base camp to explore the many anchorages in the Dundas and Moffatt islands.

Cruising Crewless

My wife, Shirley and I have been cruising for the past 14 years and have visited many places, including Alaska, the Queen Charlotte Islands and the east and west coasts of Vancouver Island. When Shirley informed me that she wanted to take a year off, I thought this was bordering on insanity—boating is what we do in the summer. After much discussion and, to my chagrin, she convinced me that I should go cruising on my own. She helped me provision *Sea Cabana* and, as we were saying our goodbyes on the dock, she asked me when I was coming home. I replied, "I don't know."

I headed north from Vancouver across the Strait of Georgia, up Johnstone Strait and across Queen Charlotte Sound, stopping to visit favorites cove and harbors along the way. I decided before I left to rendezvous with my friends David and Noreen on *Pacific Voyager*. We agreed to travel together but to allow each other lots of space and I tried to anchor in a different cove several times a week.

With only one pair of hands, I found that I kept very busy. While under way, I hardly had time to leave the helm to hit the head. "Barney," my autopilot, helped me out here. Fishing, prawning, dropping or pulling anchor, deciding what to have for dinner, washing dishes, cleaning "house," making up the berth and doing all the other chores kept me going. It seems like there were always dishes in the sink!

In port I ran around buying fresh fruit and vegetables, propane, outboard motor fuel and doing laundry with the women. In an effort to be self-sustainable I made my own muffins (although the first batch turned out like hockey pucks), bread and I even baked a cake. Meal preparation turned into a challenge. I could never decide what to make and when I did, I had enough left-overs to feed a crew. Eating alone offered interesting feelings. I'd put on a Neil Diamond tape and my imaginary waiter would say, "Table for one, Sir? There's one by the window with an ocean view. Will it be red or white wine with your Kraft Dinner?"

Over the years I had become used to saying *we* and *our* in conversation with other boaters. I found it difficult to say *I* and *my*, and when I notice I was talking to myself, I realized how much I missed my mate. I certainly had not expected to spend a crewless summer, but as I reflected on the summer's special moments—a visit with the Pollocks in Ethelda Bay; a cruise up Kynoch Inlet in Fiordland; a dinghy cruise through Culpepper Lagoon; white-sided dolphins that played alongside the boat in Principe Channel and the odor of the west coast forest —one day at a time stretched into three enjoyable months at sea where the closeness with nature was almost spiritual!

—Lou Beke

Lou and Shirley Beke live near Vancouver, B.C. and spend their summers cruising the North Coast of B.C. and Alaska (usually together!) on their M/V *Sea Cabana*.

The passage west of Moffatt Islands is a smooth-water route when northeast winds blow in Chatham.

Anchor in 2 to 4 fathoms at the head of the inlet.

Hudson Bay Passage Cove
(Dundas Island)
4.7 mi NE of Edith Harbour
Entrance: 54°30.92'N, 130°50.52'W
Anchor: 54°30.90'N, 130°50.93'W

"Hudson Bay Passage Cove" is what we call the nook on the south side of Dundas Island opposite the Nares Islets. When current and northeast wind and chop combine to make life miserable in Chatham Sound, we head for Hudson Bay Passage Cove and wait for morning to make a smooth passage into Alaskan waters. This small cove has room for two or three boats.

Anchor in 6 to 8 fathoms over mud with good holding.

Edith Harbour
(Dundas Island)
10.5 mi SW of Green Island lt.
Entrance: 54°27.60'N, 130°56.75'W

Edith Harbour, a narrow, tiny landlocked passage on the extreme southeast corner of Dundas Island, is protected from the "slop" in Dixon Entrance or Hecate Strait. Anchorage can be found here, but swinging room is limited. This is a picturesque place and we feel right at home in its outer coast environment. It's also a marvelous place to explore by kayak.

Kayaking the outer coast

Crab for dinner anyone?

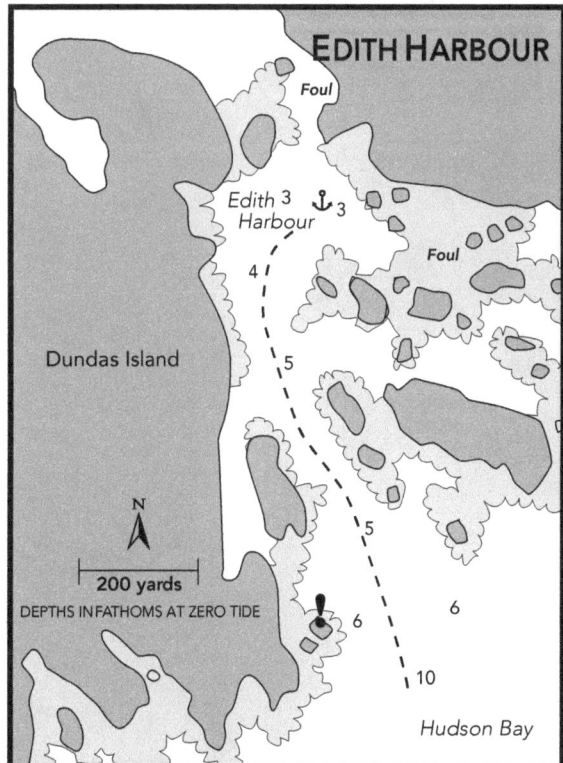

Brundige Inlet (Dixon Entrance)

5.3 mi NW of Green Island lt.
Entrance: 54°36.86'N, 130°50.63'W
Anchor (bitter end): 54°35.25'N, 130°53.54'W

Brundige Inlet, a narrow, 3-mile-long channel on the north side of Dundas Island, affords excellent shelter from all outside swells and chop. When you're anchored deep in the inlet, everything is so still, it's difficult to tell whether a tempest is blowing outside or not. The inlet has long been a favorite refuge for both north- and southbound cruising boats.

The only negative we've heard is the presence of pesky black flies when winds are slight or non-existent. However, we've been so thankful for this shelter after a rough crossing of Dixon Entrance that either we didn't notice the flies or they had left for the sea-son. It is said that there are no deer on Dundas Island because the black flies drain them of all their blood.

Although entering Brundige is not difficult, if you're arriving from the north it's easy to overshoot the entrance; the entrance is quite narrow. It helps to take a fix on Prospector Point. Stay mid-channel for the entire 3 miles but then favor the west shore at the beginning of the last narrows; there is a rock mid-channel with about 6 feet over it at zero tide.

We have anchored at the bitter end of the inlet and been perfectly comfortable during a major blow. There is shallower water and good swinging room on the south side of the lagoon south of Fitch Island or in the small basin 0.8 mile southwest of Fitch Island.

Anchor (bitter end) in 4 to 6 fathoms over mud with very good holding.

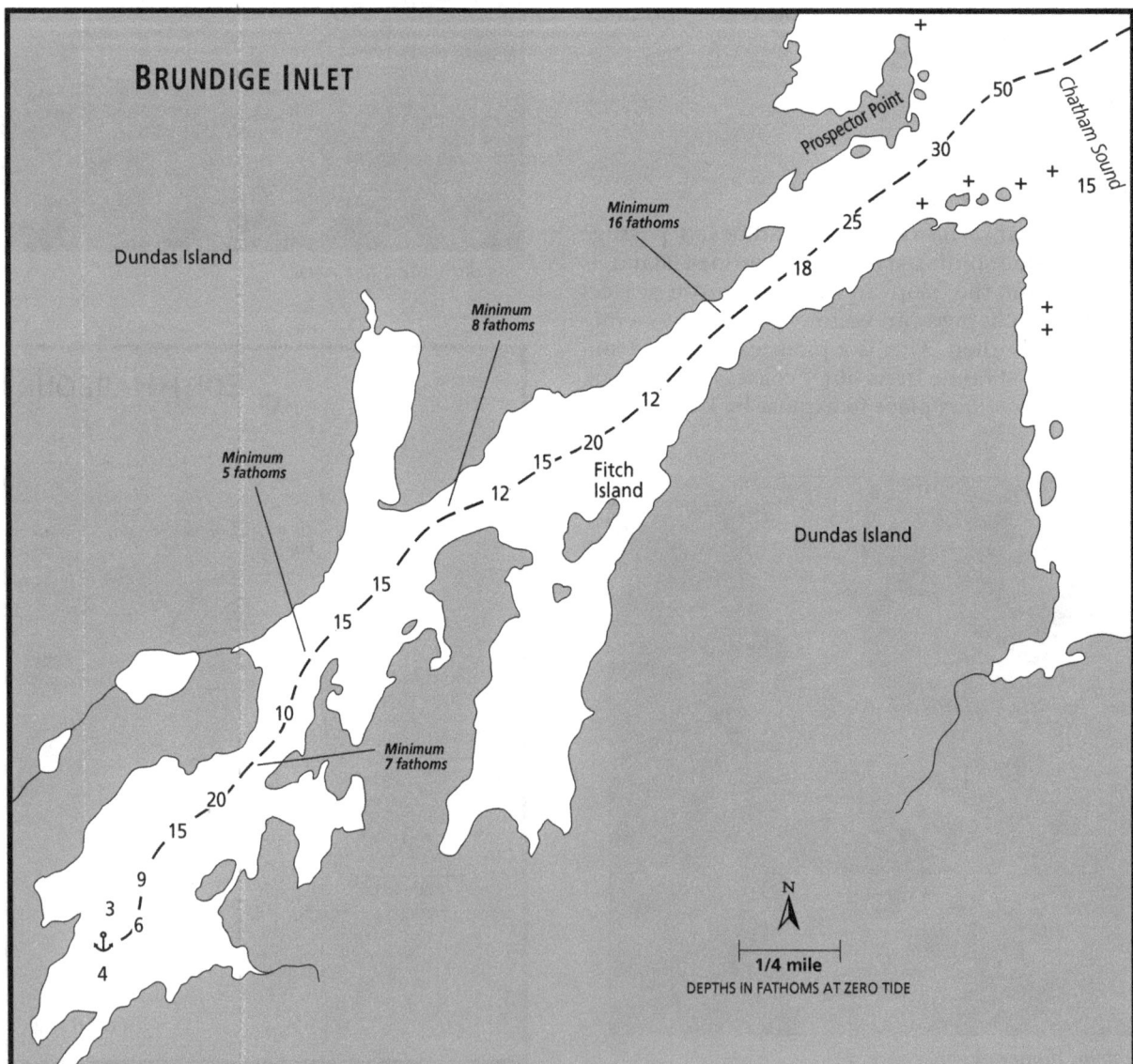

BRUNDIGE INLET

Dundas Island

Prospector Point

Chatham Sound

Minimum 16 fathoms

Minimum 8 fathoms

Minimum 5 fathoms

Fitch Island

Dundas Island

Minimum 7 fathoms

N

1/4 mile
DEPTHS IN FATHOMS AT ZERO TIDE

©2024 Don and Réanne Douglass • Diagram not for navigation

Drift on Dundas Island beach

Wreck on Baron Island

Green Island (Chatham Sound)
20.5 mi NW of Prince Rupert
Position (light): 54°34.12'N, 130°42.53'W

Green Island is an important weather observation station for boats crossing Dixon Entrance. Most small boats pass west of Green Island in Holiday Passage, using the lee of Dundas Island to avoid the westerly swells found in Dixon Entrance. The lighthouse is staffed, and the grounds of the lighthouse station are open, but the tower is closed.

The Green Island Lighthouse is the northernmost B.C. lighthouse. Construction began after the 1902 wreck of the coal steamer Bristol, which killed seven of the twenty-eight men aboard. The site is subject to extremely harsh conditions, and the keepers have endured many harrowing experiences in addition to the isolation and privation of this remote site during the 110 years of the light's operation. The Green Island lighthouse gained heritage status from Parks Canada in 2015. This ensures that the lighthouse will be maintained and protected to recognize its contribution to the culture and history of Northern British Columbia.

Goose Bay (Dundas Island)
1.2 mi W of Brundidge Inlet
Entrance: 54°37.83'N, 130°52.56'W
Anchor: 54°36.78'N, 130°52.60'W

Goose Bay is a fishing port that offers good protection deep in the south end. Reefs and submerged rocks extend over halfway across from the west shore. Favor the east shore until approaching island (36), then favor the west shore and anchor east of the tanks. Swinging room is limited here.

See what the west coast offers?

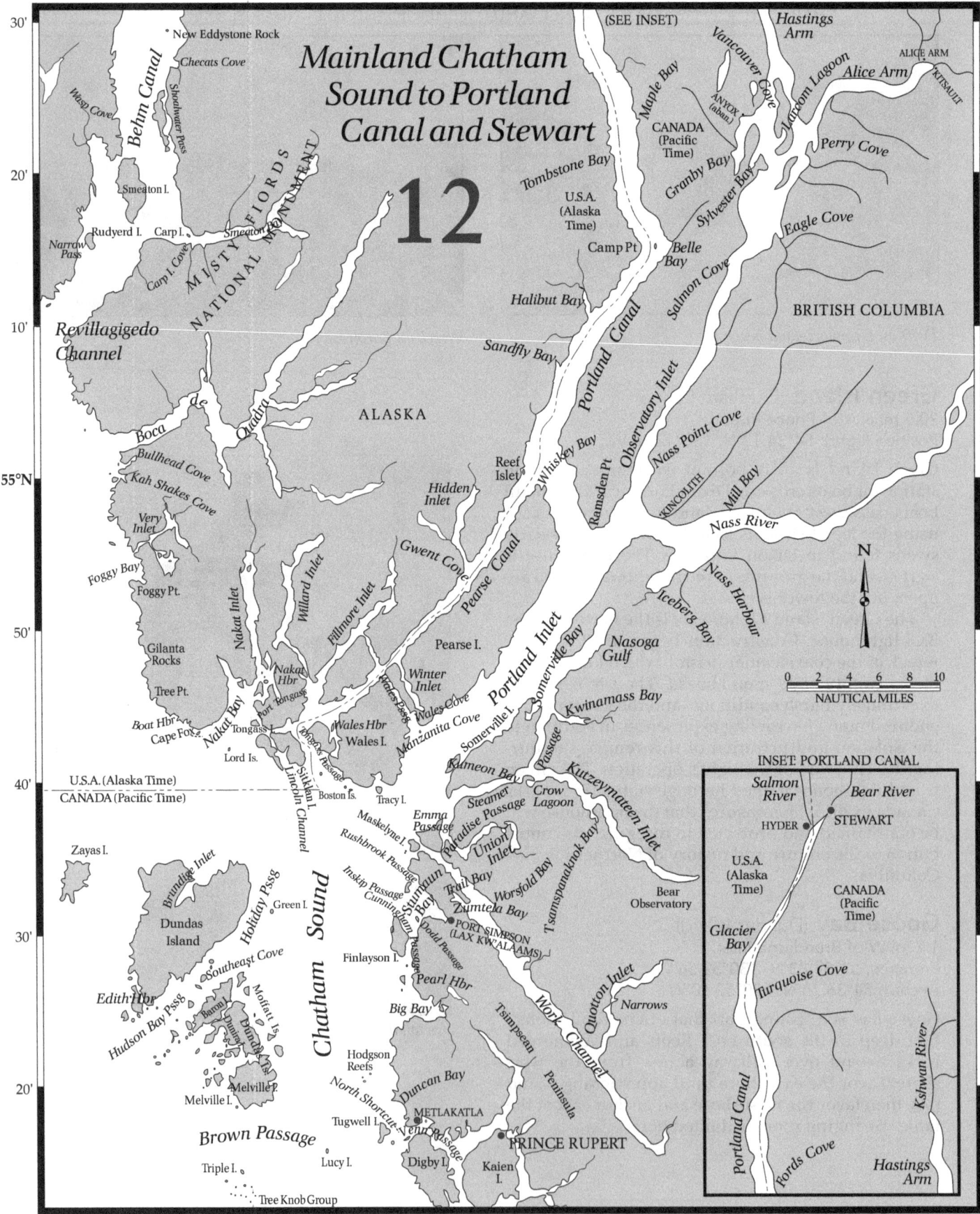

Mainland Chatham Sound to Portland Canal and Stewart

12

(SEE INSET)

ALASKA

BRITISH COLUMBIA

CANADA (Pacific Time)

U.S.A. (Alaska Time)

New Eddystone Rock

Checats Cove

Shoalwater Pass

Wasp Cove

Behm Canal

Smeaton I.

Rudyerd I. Carp I.

Carp I. Cove

Narrow Pass

MISTY FIORDS NATIONAL MONUMENT

Smeaton Bay

Revillagigedo Channel

Boca de Quadra

Bullhead Cove

Kah Shakes Cove

Very Inlet

Foggy Bay

Foggy Pt.

Gilanta Rocks

Tree Pt.

Boat Hbr

Cape Fox

Nakat Inlet

Willard Inlet

Fillmore Inlet

Nakat Bay

Nakat Hbr

Port Tongass

Tongass I.

Lord Is.

Hidden Inlet

Gwent Cove

Pearse Canal

Pearse I.

Winter Inlet

Wales Pass

Wales Cove

Wales Hbr

Wales I.

Manzanita Cove

Tombstone Bay

Camp Pt

Halibut Bay

Sandfly Bay

Reef Islet

Whiskey Bay

Portland Canal

Ramsden Pt

Maple Bay

Vancouver Cove

ANYOX (aban.)

Granby Bay

Sylvester Bay

Belle Bay

Salmon Cove

Observatory Inlet

Nass Point Cove

KINCOLITH

Mill Bay

Nass River

Hastings Arm

ALICE ARM

Larcom Lagoon

Alice Arm

KITSAULT

Perry Cove

Eagle Cove

Nass Harbour

Iceberg Bay

Nasoga Gulf

Somerville I.

Somerville Bay

Kwinamass Bay

Portland Inlet

Kameon Bay

Steamer Passage

Paradise Passage

Crow Lagoon

Union Inlet

Emma Passage

Maskelyne I.

Rushbrook Passage

Inskip Passage

Cunningham Passage

Stumaun Bay

Trail Bay

Zumtela Bay

Worsfold Bay

Tsamspanaknok Bay

Kutzeymateen Inlet

Bear Observatory

Work Channel

Quotoon Inlet

Narrows

Tsimpsean Peninsula

Zayas I.

Brundige Inlet

Green I.

Holiday Pssg

Dundas Island

Southeast Cove

Edith Hbr

Hudson Bay Pssg

Baron I.

Dundas Is.

Moffatt Is.

Melville P.

Melville I.

Finlayson I.

Dodd Passage

PORT SIMPSON (LAX KW'ALAAMS)

Pearl Hbr

Big Bay

Hodgson Reefs

North Shortcut

Duncan Bay

Tugwell I.

METLAKATLA

Venn Passage

Digby I.

Kaien I.

PRINCE RUPERT

Chatham Sound

Brown Passage

Triple I.

Lucy I.

Tree Knob Group

U.S.A. (Alaska Time)
CANADA (Pacific Time)

Boston Is.

Tracy I.

Lincoln Channel

Stikian L.

N

0 2 4 6 8 10
NAUTICAL MILES

INSET PORTLAND CANAL

Salmon River

Bear River

HYDER

STEWART

U.S.A. (Alaska Time)

CANADA (Pacific Time)

Glacier Bay

Turquoise Cove

Portland Canal

Fords Cove

Kshwan River

Hastings Arm

©2024 Don and Réanne Douglass • Diagram not for navigation

12

Mainland Chatham Sound to Portland Canal and Stewart

Portland Canal, a long, narrow inlet, is perhaps the longest fiord on the entire North American continent. Measured from Dixon Entrance to Stewart, B.C., it stretches more than 100 miles. The international boundary between Canada and Alaska runs mid-channel through Pearse and Portland Canals, north to Stewart. Largely pristine, and seldom visited, the shores along Portland Canal have stunning scenery. Floating trees or flotsam, common north of Fords Cove, require caution. Where the canal turns northeast at Belle Bay, the water becomes progressively more opaque, with very limited underwater visibility.

Narrower and more intimate than Alaskan fiords, Portland Canal generally requires less challenging navigation, although anchorages tend to be somewhat marginal and far apart. There is little to no radio reception throughout the canal. Locals report that upslope winds predominate in the summer and downslope winds in the winter. The winds tend to die off as you near Stewart, a phenomenon that becomes apparent near Hattie Island (Belle Bay) or a little farther north. Generally, summer nights are quiet and calm. Other than a few Stewart sportfishing boats, you are unlikely to see many pleasure craft.

Stewart, at the head of Portland Canal, is a small town of about 500 [in 2021] that caters to sportfish-

ing, snowmobiling and camping enthusiasts. Hyder, Alaska, just south of Stewart is a settlement with one or two pubs where "getting Hyderized" is one of the main attractions for visitors. One of the largest glaciers in the area lies 20 miles up the valley from Hyder. A visit to the Fish Creek Wildlife Observation Center about three miles north of Hyder, Alaska provides an unequaled opportunity to watch bears in the wild from boardwalks and platforms near a salmon spawning stream.

George Vancouver, who was the first recorded European to explore and write about the canal, named it after William Bentinck, Duke of Portland.

Venn Passage and Metlakatla Bay
(Prince Rupert Harbour)
2.5 mi W of Cow Bay
Entrance (E): 54°18.65'N, 130°23.22'W
Entrance (W) (Metlakatla Bay): 54°18.40'N, 130°30.37'W

Although narrow and intricate with strong currents, Venn Passage substantially shortens the route northbound to Chatham Strait. The passage is marked by three tri-sector, lighted ranges and several buoys. Be aware, however, that the buoys in Venn Passage are often dragged out of position after being hit by tows.

Be sure of your route before attempting the passage; use large scale charts to identify turning points, and line up with the range marks. As you leave Prince Rupert Harbour, the ranges are all behind you so have a spotter ready to help you. Both sides of the fairway carry shoal water close aboard, and currents run several knots. Slow to a no-wake speed when you pass the airport ferry dock at Du Vernay Point, and again off the Metlakatla Float. In summer, after a favorable weather forecast, there is frequently an early-morning exodus (0400 to 0500 hours) of boats heading north from Prince Rupert.

If you leave Rupert near or ahead of high water, you have favorable current all the way to Green Island. Ebb currents turn about one hour before high-water slack in Prince Rupert.

Slow for airport ferry in Venn Passage

METLAKATLA BAY & VENN PASSAGE

Duncan Bay

D80 red

Hecate Rock

Observation Point

Metlakatla

Chapman Point

CAUTION!

D81 grn

Doolan Point

Kelp Reef

D65 grn

DJ

D63 grn

Tugwell Island (IR)

D83 grn

D85 grn

Devastation Island

Pike Island (IR)

Metlakatla Bay

Knight Island

Armour Rock

N

Tugwell Reef

1/4 mile

DEPTHS IN FATHOMS AT ZERO TIDE

Scattered Reefs

to Chhatham Sound

to Venn Passage

©2024 Don and Réanne Douglass • Diagram not for navigation

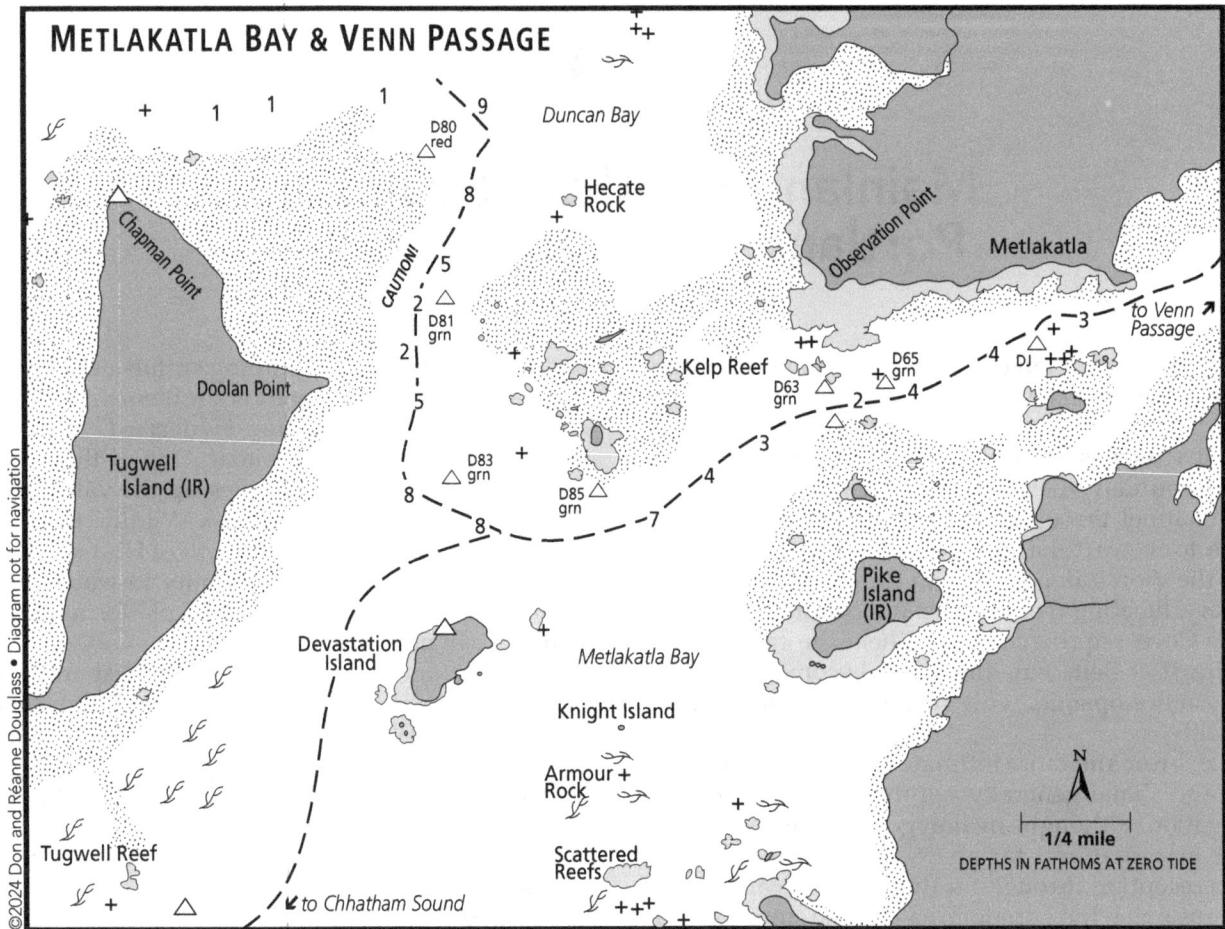

Fallen Human Bay, (Pillsbury Cove)

2.9 mi W of Cow Bay
Entrance: 54°19.00'N, 130°22.75'W
Anchor: 54°19.57'N, 130°23.93'W

"Fallen Human Bay"—also known as Pillsbury Cove—is the well-sheltered bay north of Anian Island. A fascinating petroglyph of "The Man Who Fell from Heaven" is located near Robertson Point near the high-tide line. The museum in Prince Rupert has an attractive replica and story of this petroglyph. (See if you think the figure looks like a man or a woman.)

Anchor in 5 fathoms over mud with good holding.

Carolina Island Anchorage (Venn Pass.)

0.5 mi S of Metlakatla Float
Entrance: 54°20.21'N, 130°25.63'W
Anchor: 54°20.41'N, 130°25.82'W

The bay northeast of Carolina Islands is busy with local boats. The site is well sheltered and out of the current and busy traffic of Venn Passage.

Anchor in 4 fathoms over mud with good holding.

Duncan Bay Shortcut (Venn Passage)

1.6 mi W of Metlakatla float
Entrance (S): 54°19.70'N, 130°29.40'W
Entrance (N): 54°20.57'N, 130°29.15'W

By leaving the west end of Venn Passage and entering Duncan Bay you can gain a half-hour when northbound using a shortcut across the sand bar. We call

Fallen Human, Venn Passage

this route "Duncan Bay Shortcut." Larger yachts may find this route too shallow and/or narrow; however, smaller yachts can safely cross the bar during the upper half of most tides, staying close to the buoys and monitoring the echo sounder carefully.

Leaving Prince Rupert via Duncan Bay, from a point 0.25 mile west of buoy "D82," 0.7 mile southwest of Ryan Point, head north (about 344°M) for Slippery Rock light via the channel inside Hodgson Reefs.

To enter the North Shortcut, turn north at buoy "D83" on the east side of Tugwell Island, due north of Devastation Island, and pass close on the west side of buoy "D81" that marks the shallow spot. Continue north and pass just east of buoy "D80" as you enter Duncan Bay. Minimum depth on the bar is about 1½ fathoms at zero tide. However, the channel is narrow and subject to shoaling or shifting. On a northbound route, do not cut west until 0.25 mile north of buoy "D80"—the Tugwell Island shoal extends well over a half-mile from shore. On a southbound route, red buoy "D80" is hard to see until you are fairly close; its position is about 54°20.48′N, 130°29.30′W.

On the Duncan Bay side, a large drying shoal extends well out from Tugwell Island, so avoid turning west too soon. Avoid the shoals 1.2 miles off Ryan Point, as well as Hodgson Reefs north of Duncan Bay.

Hodgson Reefs

(Chatham Sound)
1.5 mi NW of Ryan Point
Position: 54°22.35′N, 130°31.73′W

Caution: If you head directly for buoy "D84" from Duncan Bay, you will cross the south part of Hodgson Reefs; pay close attention to pass south of Hodgson Reefs or turn north before the reefs if you are taking the smooth-water route hugging the mainland shore.

Salmon Bight, Big Bay

(Chatham Sound)
7.4 mi N of Duncan Bay
Entrance (S): 54°27.45′N, 130°30.00′W
Anchor (Salmon Bight): 54°27.50′N, 130°25.00′W

Enter Salmon Bight at the extreme east end of Big Bay, between Curlew Rock and Swallow Island. Avoid the reef that extends northeast from Curlew Rock about 350 yards. You can find anchorage anywhere off the drying flat east of Curlew Rock, due south of One-Foot Rock. One-Foot Rock is a good guide when entering near high water.

Anchor (Salmon Bight) in 5 fathoms over sand and mud; fair-to-good holding.

Whales Watching Us!

In over two decades of cruising the North Coast, we've seen wonderful whales who have watched us just as much as we've watched them.

Our first adrenaline rush is recorded in the 1982 ship's log of our 22-foot Bayliner, *Sundancer.* While we were sightseeing one afternoon in golden sun, a huge humpback whale surfaced along our port beam, eyeball to eyeball—we're still not sure who was the more startled! On a steady course, our friendly whale kept an eye on us by resurfacing three times before continuing to other waters. We became hooked on all forms of British Columbia sea life, especially friendly whales, and we've never been disappointed.

In 1985, aboard our 35′ Uniflite, *Sea Señor II,* a once-in-a-lifetime show erupted from the depths. Traveling at cruising speed, ahead off the bow, we saw what appeared to be dynamite charges exploding repeatedly. Slowing, we discovered what we'd seen only in movies: two huge, frolicking whales leaping remarkably high, again and again. We watched, completely in awe and never tiring. Finally, in order to anchor for the night, we were forced to part company. If we had never seen another whale in our lives, we'd have been happy.

However, as whales watching us goes, we never have long to wait. Another day, while trolling slowly, a spectacular orca suddenly surfaced across the course of our bow—we were on a collision course. We stopped, and the bobbing eyes of this mammoth creature registered as much surprise as we felt. Needless to say, our friendly orca took a dive. Whales can literally take your breath away!

Recently, friends chatting with us aboard our 45′ *Sanctuary,* told us of their expedition in a much larger Hatteras. While trolling, their whale "show" turned into a giant whale-lifting and their damaged stern told the tale.

This whale watching and vice versa continues to fascinate us. And so we wait, cameras in hand, and ask ourselves: when will the next whale watch us?

—Linda Schrieber

Linda and Jack Schreiber, M/V *Sanctuary,* have spent over 20 years cruising B.C.'s North Coast waters.

Pearl Harbour (Chatham Sound)
2.5 mi N of Big Bay
Entrance (Boat Passage): 54°30.16'N, 130°28.16'W
Anchor: 54°30.27'N, 130°26.87'W

Very good protection from northeast winds can be obtained in the east side of Pearl Harbour. After clearing Sparrowhawk Rock, enter Pearl Harbour via the deepwater route on the west side of Flat Top Island. Small boats can use narrow Boat Passage, but the reef south of Mist Island must be identified and avoided. If passing north of Mist Island, be careful to avoid the drying spit to the north; many boats have gone aground here, expecting the reef to terminate farther south.

Anchor at the far eastern side of Pearl Harbour, due north of Pearl Point. The "pearl" in Pearl Point is a large glacial boulder 200 yards northwest of the point.

Anchor in 4 fathoms over sand and mud; fair-to-good holding.

Cunningham Passage (Finlayson Island)
0.7 mi N of Pearl Harbour
South entrance: 54°34.90'N, 130°28.50'W
North entrance: 54°34.40'N, 130°28.40'W

Cunningham Passage is an easy, smooth-water passage for cruising boats on the east side of Finlayson Island. The white triangle near Redcliff Point provides the leading point for the fairway between Pender and Centre rocks, both underwater. Avoid the reefs at the north end of Cunningham Passage.

Dodd Passage (Port Simpson)
0.7 mi NW of Port Simpson
Entrance (W): 54°33.72'N, 130°27.25'W

Dodd Passage is the shallow, narrow smooth-water route into Port Simpson. Pass north of buoy "D88" and south of buoy "D89" on a generally northeast heading. When you are north of One Tree Islet, round slowly for the Port Simpson breakwater. *Note:* Beware—we once found that buoy "D88" had drifted 200 or 300 yards southeast of its charted position!

Port Simpson (Lax Kw'alaams)
(Cunningham Passage)
13.2 mi N of Duncan Bay
Entrance (breakwater): 54°33.72'N, 130°25.79'W

Public floats, Port Simpson (Lax Kw'alaams)

The public floats in Port Simpson are located in the busy native community of Lax Kw'alaams. Three finger-floats for small boats on the south side of the Port Simpson breakwater are frequently crowded, in season, with sportfishing and commercial boats. Rafting may be necesssary. Avoid the shallow water east and south of the floats. Good water can be obtained from a hose at the foot of the gangway; fuel may be available during the fishing season; electricity is available for a reasonable fee. The village has a grocery store.

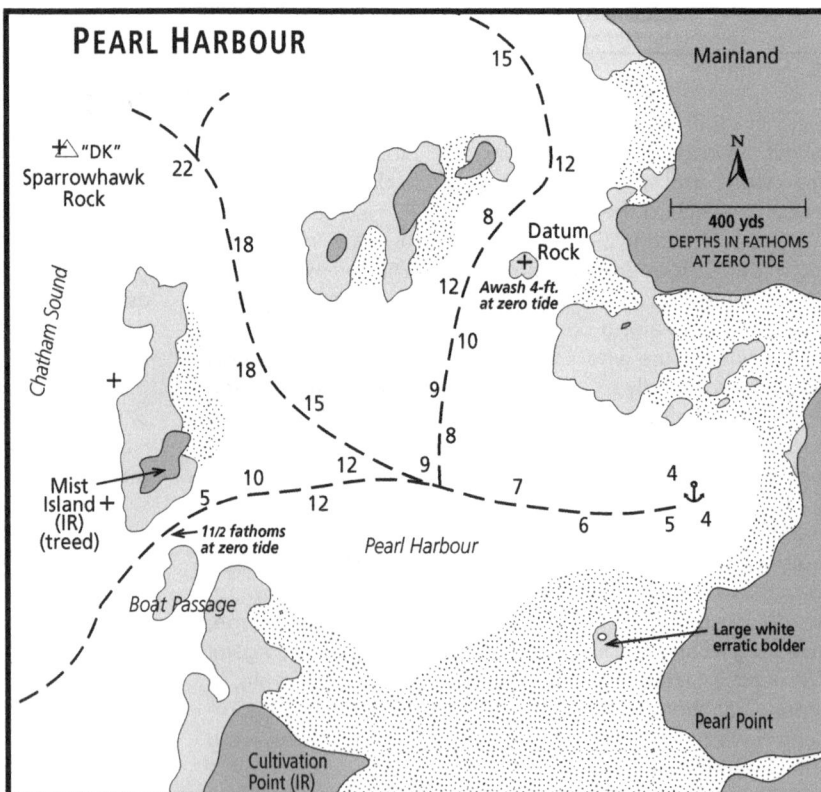

PEARL HARBOUR

Mainland
15
12
⌖ "DK"
Sparrowhawk Rock
22
18
8
Datum Rock
N
400 yds
DEPTHS IN FATHOMS
AT ZERO TIDE
12 Awash 4-ft. at zero tide
10
Chatham Sound
18
9
8
15
9
4 ⚓
12
9
Mist Island + (IR) (treed)
5
10
12
7
6
5 4
1½ fathoms at zero tide
Pearl Harbour
Boat Passage
Large white erratic boulder
Cultivation Point (IR)
Pearl Point

©2024 Don and Réanne Douglass • Diagram not for navigation

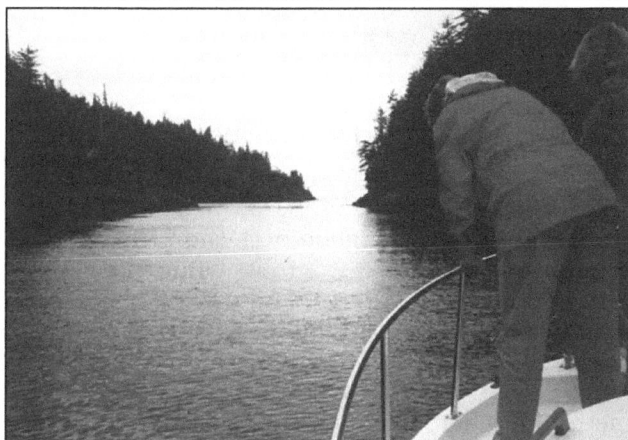

Paradise Passage, looking toward Work Channel

Stumaun Bay (Port Simpson)
1.3 mi E of La Kw'alaams
Position: 54°33.70'N, 130°23.44'W

Stumaun Bay, the far eastern end of Port Simpson, provides good protection from southeast blows off the drying flat in 12 fathoms. Avoid the private buoys and the offshore rock on the south side.

Rushbrook Passage (Birnie Island)
2.4 mi N of Port Simpson
Entrance (S): 54°36.08'N, 130°26.62'W
Entrance (N): 54°36.30'N, 130°26.95'W

Rushbrook Passage continues the mainland shore smooth-water route. The narrow fairway through Rushbrook Passage lies midway between two sets of reefs northeast of Birnie Island. Use caution as these reefs are steep-to. This route helps avoid chop in Chatham Sound.

Dudevoir Passage
(Work Channel)
4.2 mi N of Port Simpson
Entrance (S): 54°37.86'N, 130°26.71'W
Entrance (N): 54°38.29'N, 130°26.97'W

Dudevoir Passage is useful for avoiding the turbulent waters off the entrance to Work Channel. However, the passage, which is not well surveyed, has considerably less water than indicated on the chart—perhaps 6 feet less than charted depths—and it is useful only near high-water slack. The bar is stony and the bottom is clearly visible. There are two old cabins on the Work Channel side at the north entrance to Dudevoir. Temporary anchorage for reconnoitering the shoal area can be found inside either entrance. The bottom is flat with isolated patches of bull kelp, indicating a bottom of stone and gravel. We tied our Nordhavn to a piling to wait until the tide level increased enough for us to proceed and we crossed, more or less, in mid-channel.

Work Channel
(Portland Inlet)
4.8 mi SE of Tongass Passage
Entrance: 54°39.00'N, 130°26.70'W

We have seen breaking waves extend a half-mile from the entrance to Work Channel during strong outflow winds and spring ebb tides. Trail Bay and Zumtela Bay, 7 miles inside Work Channel, provide good summer anchorages. Most of the 28-mile long Work Channel is deep and steep to with only a few favorable anchoring locations. From here it is 4.8 miles to sheltered Tongass Passage—the smooth-water route to and from Ketchikan.

Lax Kw'alaams

Lax Kw'alaams (pronounced Lach-goo-alams, and meaning "place of wild roses") is a First Nations community located in Port Simpson. With a population of approximately 700, it is the largest of seven Tsimshian villages in British Columbia; the Tsimshian, in turn, are the most numerous First Nations people in the province.

An ancient camping place of the Gispaxlo'ot tribe, Lax Kw'alaams became the site of a Hudson's Bay Company trading post, Fort Simpson, in 1834. Seeking a share of the American-dominated maritime fur trade on the Pacific Coast, Company factor, Dr John Frederick Kennedy, married the daughter of a Gispaxlo'ot to facilitate establishment of the fort. Kennedy served there until 1856. The following year, Anglican missionary William Duncan brought Christianity to Lax Kw'alaams. He made converts of at least 800 of the natives—approximately one-third of the

population at that time—and persuaded them to leave the fort and its temptations and relocate to Metlakata, a few miles to the south. A further 500 villagers died of smallpox after Duncan's departure. The Metlakata group later moved to a reservation on Annette Island, in what is now Southeast Alaska.

In 1874, a new missionary, Rev. Thomas Crosby, a Methodist, arrived in Lax Kw'alaams. His wife, Emma, established a girls' home there; this later became a residential school. The community remains predominantly Methodist (United Church of Canada) to this day.

In 1931, Port Simpson (as it was known by that time) became home to B.C.'s first Native-run rights organization, the Native Brotherhood of British Columbia, with Gispaxlo'ot Chief William Jeffrey and Tsimshian ethnologist William Beynon among its founders.   —AC

Paradise Passage (Work Channel)
1.3 mi E of Dudevoir Passage
Entrance (S): 54°37.85'N, 130°23.60'W
Entrance (N): 54°38.90'N, 130°23.38'W

Paradise Passage, connecting Work Channel to Emma and Steamer passages, continues the smooth-water route north up Portland Inlet. To avoid rough water off Work Channel and beam seas when crossing Portland Inlet bound for Ketchikan, we like to follow the smooth-water through Paradise Passage to Sumner Island before crossing to the lee under Wales Point. Emma Passage can be transited during most phases of the tide, avoiding kelp patches in the vicinity of the islet. The fairway of the narrows east of the islet carries about one fathom; favor the east shore, avoiding the kelp. The islet, covered with rockweed, dries on about a 17-foot tide and is about 45 feet across. Ebb current flows northward in Paradise Passage.

Trail Bay
(Work Channel)
6 mi SE of channel entrance
Entrance: 54°34.28'N, 130°20.22'W
Anchor: 54°35.19'N, 130°21.97'W

Trail Bay, surrounded by old-growth cedar and silver snags, offers very good protection from prevailing west and northwest winds. Other than storm-force winds, the bay is out of the brunt of southerly winds. Large boats can find good anchorage over a wide, flat area of 7 to 9 fathoms, south of a predominant point on the north shore. Small craft wanting more "intimate" shelter can tuck in behind the point farther north in 4 fathoms with a stern-tie or in Zumtela Bay to the southwest.

Anchor in 8 fathoms over sand, gravel, and soft grey mud patches; fair holding.

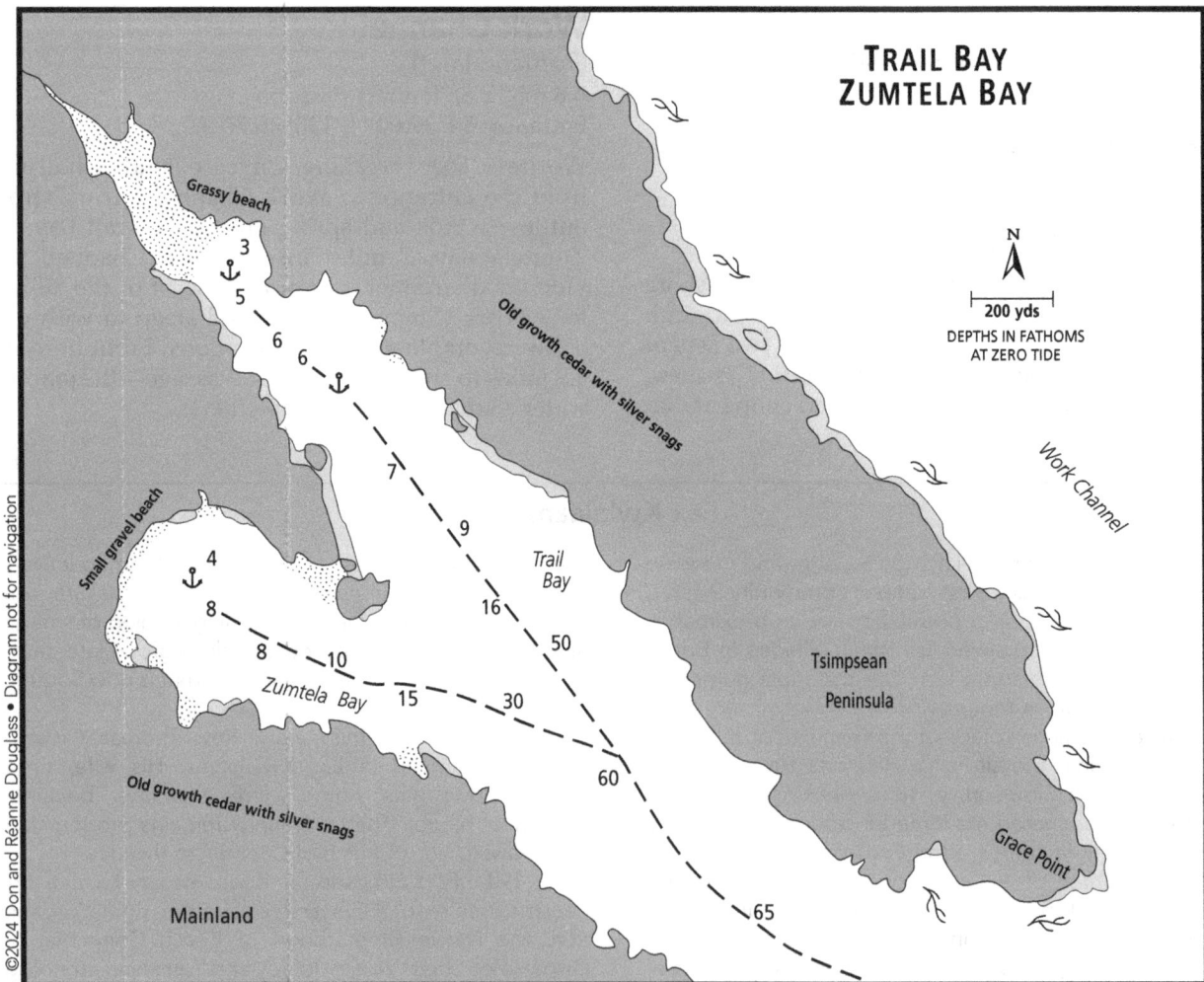

TRAIL BAY
ZUMTELA BAY

200 yds
DEPTHS IN FATHOMS
AT ZERO TIDE

Grassy beach

Old growth cedar with silver snags

Work Channel

Small gravel beach

Trail Bay

Zumtela Bay

Tsimpsean Peninsula

Old growth cedar with silver snags

Grace Point

Mainland

©2024 Don and Réanne Douglass • Diagram not for navigation

Zumtela Bay (Trail Bay)

0.3 mi W of Trail Bay
Entrance: 54°34.85'N, 130°21.75'W
Anchor: 54°34.95'N, 130°22.37'W

Zumtela Bay offers slightly more protection than Trail Bay with its wide, flat bottom of 7 to 9 fathoms. Anchor off the small gravel beach at the head of the bay.

Anchor in 8 fathoms over sand and gravel; fair holding.

Portland Inlet (East Dixon Entrance)

7.5 mi N of Port Simpson
Entrance: 54°42.06'N, 130°25.91'W

If Portland Inlet is choppy, cruising boats can follow a smooth-water route from Wales Passage to Pearse Canal to Portland Canal; or, for more protection, follow Steamer Passage as far north as Trefusis Point. Somerville Bay and Winter Inlet are two of the more protected anchor sites in the center of Portland Inlet.

Wales Passage (Wales Island)

6.7 mi N of Work Channel
Entrance (S): 54°45.53'N, 130°25.41'W
Entrance (N): 54°49.65'N, 130°29.55'W

When there's a blow in Portland Inlet or Pearse Canal, the water is generally smooth in Wales Passage. This passage frequently contains a number of crab pots marked by small floats. Temporary protection from downslope winds can be found in Wales Cove, 1.3 miles northeast of Manzanita Cove.

Manzanita Cove (Wales Passage)

0.6 mi W of Wales Passage Entrance
Entrance: 54°45.61'N, 130°26.24'W
Anchor: 54°45.45'N, 130°26.31'W

Manzanita Cove has a steep-to bottom with depths

inconvenient for anchoring and without flat areas. The small nook on the south side of the cove, immediately west of Swaine Point, which is protected in most weather, is useful for one or two small boats, using a stern-tie to shore.

At the head of the nook, stands one of four original stone masonry cabins built for the initial surveys of the Alaska border in 1896, under the direction of Captain Gaillard, U.S. Army Corps of Engineers. A stone plaque on the north corner of the ruined building says " . . . property, Do not Injure." The B.C./Alaska border was later established north of Wales and Pearse islands and, since then, someone chiseled out the "US" on the stone marker.

Anchor in 6 fathoms over rocks; poor holding; stern-tie to shore recommended.

Wales Cove (Wales Passage)

1.3 mi N of Manzanita Cove
Entrance: 54°46.71'N, 130°25.82'W
Anchor: 54°46.95'N, 130°25.72'W

"Wales Cove" is our name for the small bay in Wales Passage on the south side of Pearse Island, 1.3 miles northeast of Manzanita Cove. Temporary shelter can be found here when downslope winds are blowing in Portland Inlet. Depths in the cove are irregular, indicating a rocky bottom. Winter Inlet, just north, provides superior all-weather protection.

Anchor in about 6 fathoms over a rocky bottom; poor-to-fair holding.

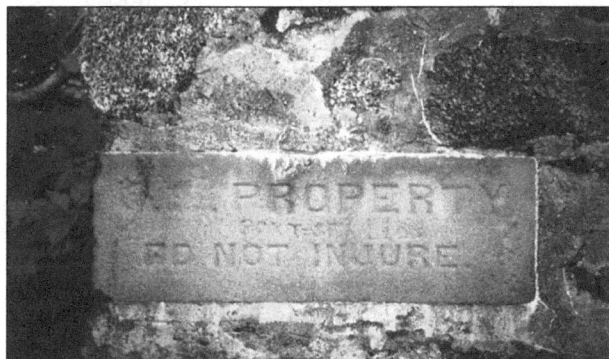

Sign on Customs House, U.S. has been obliterated

Exploring the former U.S. Customs House, now on Canadian soil (Manzanita Cove)

Steamer Passage (Portland Inlet)
3.5 mi NE of Work Channel
Entrance (SW): 54°41.16'N, 130°22.51'W
Entrance (NE): 54°47.13'N, 130°11.53'W

Steamer Passage, a smooth-water route from Chatham Sound to Portland Canal, has steep shores lined with granite cliffs, mostly forested. Several striking examples of climax avalanches are evident along both the south and north shores. The upper reaches of Steamer Passage, previously clearcut, show re-growth of small alders and bushes.

Kumeon Bay (Steamer Passage)
1.1 mi SW of Khutzeymateen Inlet
Entrance: 54°42.72'N, 130°14.79'W
Anchor: 54°42.56'N, 130°14.71'W

An attractive creek flows out of a lake just west of Kumeon Bay; the shoal lies directly off that creek. On the west side of the creek there is a log dump and a road that leads to the interior of the mainland. There are no drift logs on shore in the bay, indicating good protection in most weather.

Marine life

The west side of Kumeon Bay has a steep-to mud flat that rises rapidly to just 100 feet offshore. Rusting cables secured to a tree along the south shore indicate earlier use.

The best anchorage appears to be just west of the avalanche bluff. You can easily land your dinghy on the gravel beach and explore.

Anchor in the center of the bay in 5 fathoms over sand and gravel; good holding.

Somerville Bay (Portland Inlet)
5 mi N of Kumeon Bay
Entrance: 54°47.65'N, 130°12.50'W
Anchor (W): 54°46.80'N, 130°13.68'W
Anchor (E): 54°46.75'N, 130°13.46'W

Excellent protection can be found on the west side of the far head of Somerville Bay, tucked in behind Start Point. A stern tie makes this anchorage bombproof. Long used by fishermen, the central part of the bay is reported to have old rope and nets along the bottom that could foul an anchor. Small vessels can anchor near the head of the bay while larger vessels can anchor in deeper water. In either case, be sure to check that your anchor is not fouled.

Anchor (west) in 2 to 3 fathoms over mud with grass and kelp; fair-to-good holding.

Anchor (east) in 11 fathoms, over sand and shell with good holding.

Crow Lagoon (Khutzeymateen In.)
4.8 mi S of Somerville Bay
Entrance: 54°42.83'N, 130°12.89'W

Crow Lagoon is an unusual and amazing geological feature—a saltwater-filled volcano. The lagoon can be entered only on

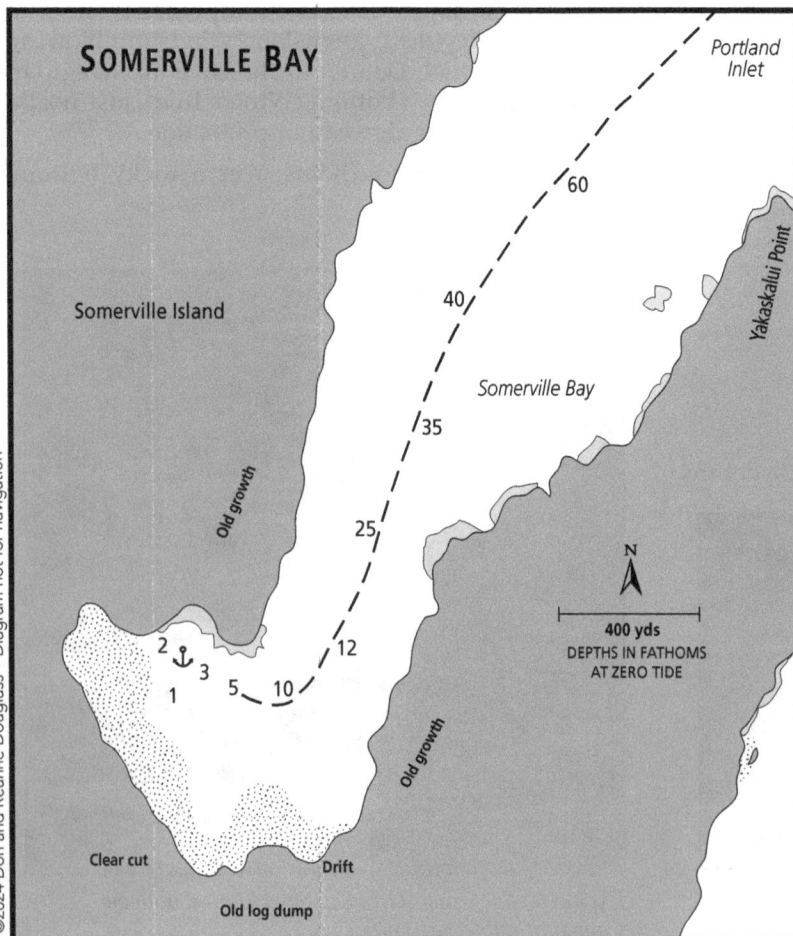

SOMERVILLE BAY

Somerville Island

Somerville Bay

Portland Inlet

Yakaskalui Point

Old growth

Old growth

Old growth

Clear cut

Drift

Old log dump

N

400 yds
DEPTHS IN FATHOMS
AT ZERO TIDE

60

40

35

25

12

2

3

5

10

1

©2024 Don and Réanne Douglass • Diagram not for navigation

Poplar III *anchored in Somerville Bay*

Heading for Alaska, Chatham Sound

high-water rising due to the shallow mud flat across its entrance. The rocky cliffs surrounding the steep-sided volcanic crater produce good echoes. We can only guess what the reverberations are inside when outside channel winds blow by its tiny entrance and set the lagoon howling.

Entirely landlocked, the lagoon is reached by crossing the shallow drying mud flat; unfortunately, depths inside the lagoon are too great for convenient anchoring. However, you may find that a stern tie works. No weather of any kind reaches inside the lagoon except a few circular gusts. You can tie temporarily to the boomsticks if it is still there. We passed the center rock that dries mid-tide on the north side of the narrows; however, but recommend that you reconnoiter the channel before entering, since conditions do change. Small boats can enter on the upper half of tide; the current is moderate.

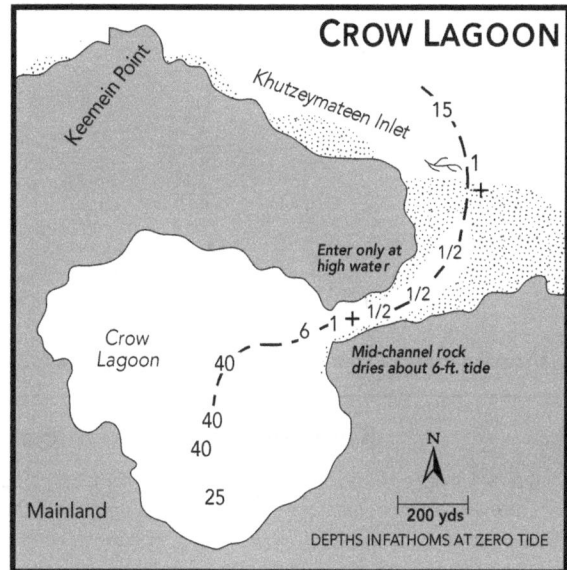

Fouled Prop—A High-Latitude Emergency

Crab pots littered the site where we had just anchored and they were catching more than just crabs—the engine gave a strangled cough and died making a dive necessary —a chilling prospect.

Making do with what I had, I donned a thin wet suit (1/8 of an inch is not enough), a light jacket, quilted hood, boots, and sailing gloves. My accessories included mask, snorkel and a fanny-pack of zinc weights.

We rigged a guide-line under the boat, rafted the dinghy as a work float, taped a hose to the snorkel, and went in. The water was the temperature of a martini with visibility like milk. Scary stuff. The snorkel kinked. No air. Straighten the snorkel and try again. No air. Shorten the hose. Still can't get air below 2 feet. Bag the snorkel.

The guide-line curves into the darkness. No prop here. We move the line three times before a shadowy prop materializes. Dive, search the murk for the rope end, unwrap a loop. One dive per wrap. After each dive the crew dumps very hot water (feels lukewarm) inside my wetsuit. Finally there's enough line free to bring the end to the surface. Heavy duty, expensive stuff; just like on our boat. Funny they would use it for crabbing. Hello??!! This isn't a crab pot float line. We have run over our own jib sheet. I take back what I said about crab fishermen. More hot water. Back down and under. I fantasize about hot showers. Only crab are comfortable here. My average dive lasts 10 seconds. Up on the dinghy, hot water down the wetsuit, drag myself down the guide-line. My lungs tell me to stop. Back to the dinghy for more blessed water. Only six more wraps to go. Last wrap. Warm up the champagne. Let's celebrate!

—Lachlan McGuigan

Lachlan and Becky McGuigan are long-time cruisers in their sailboat, *Xephyr*.

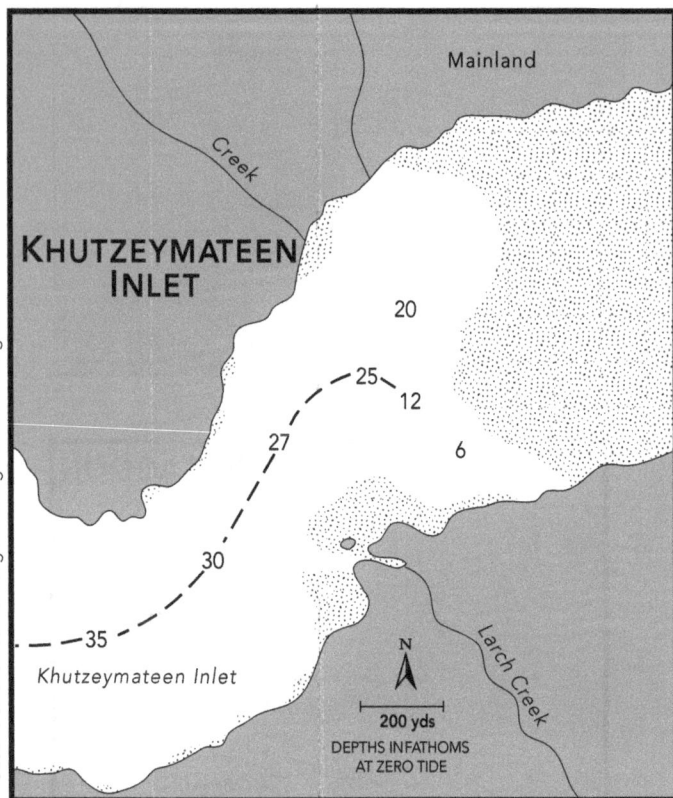

Map labels:
- Mainland
- Creek
- KHUTZEYMATEEN INLET
- 20
- 25
- 12
- 27
- 6
- 30
- 35
- Khutzeymateen Inlet
- Larch Creek
- N
- 200 yds
- DEPTHS IN FATHOMS AT ZERO TIDE
- ©2024 Don and Réanne Douglass • Diagram not for navigation

Khutzeymateen Inlet (Portland Inlet)
9 mi NE of Work Channel
Entrance: 54°43.21'N, 130°13.30'W
Floating Ranger Station: 54°36.52'N, 129°58.09'W

Khutzeymateen Inlet (Khutzeymateen Grizzly Bear Sanctuary, or Khutzeymateen Provincial Park, also called "Valley of the Grizzly") is scenic and deep with few options for anchoring. The inlet, which holds one of the largest concentrations of grizzlies along the British Columbia coast, is a designated sanctuary and an area of extreme sensitivity. The topography is diverse, with rugged peaks towering to 2100 metres above a valley of wetlands, old growth temperate rainforests and a large estuary. Visiting boaters wishing to view the bears must register at the floating ranger station near the head of the inlet (see the lat/long location noted above) for an orientation regarding responsible bear viewing. An interpretive center is located at the Ranger Station along with information about permitted tour guides. Land access without a guide is not permitted. It is critical to review the regulations on the Provincial Park Website: http://www.env.gov.bc.ca/bcparks/explore/park-pgs/khutzeymateen/

Khutzeymateen Provincial Park and Grizzly Bear Sanctuary

Forty-five kilometers northeast of Prince Rupert, BC, Khutzeymateen Provincial Park encompasses about 45,000 hectares (about 170 square miles) of the northern Kitimat Ranges and Khutzeymateen Inlet shoreline. The park's name is a Tsimshian First Nations word that means "sheltered place of fish and bears." Wetlands, river estuaries, and old-growth forests provide ideal habitat for a grizzly bear sanctuary. These inlet shorelines can be explored by boat, free of charge and without a commercial guide, but visitors must first register at the floating ranger station. Upon entering the park, visitors receive an orientation on responsible bear-viewing techniques. Viewing areas are set up so that visitors can observe grizzly bears in their natural environment. To access the river estuary for viewing, the public must sign up for a guided tour operated by approved commercial guides. Unguided tours in these areas are not permitted. A visit to the park's website offers a list of approved guides and a map showing the sanctuary boundaries and ranger station. https://bcparks.ca/khutzeymateen-park-aka-khutzeymateen-ktzim-a-deen-grizzly-sanctuary//

The Provincial government established the Khutzeymateen Provincial Park in 1994 to protect grizzlies and their habitat because of their declining numbers. The Inlet Conservancy was further enlarged and enhanced in 2008 to ensure protection of sufficient territory and biological diversity necessary for these animals. Scientists believe

Grizzly on Kutzeymateen shore

Photo courtesy Pacific Voyager/Sea Cabana

that approximately 25,000 grizzly bears roamed British Columbia before European settlement. By 2008, the population had dwindled to an estimated 16,000 bears in BC.

Grizzly bears are an umbrella species, meaning that when they and their habitat are protected, other species receive protection as well. Seeds, berries, insects, roots, and fungi are distributed as nutrients through the bears' scat, which helps other species in their habitat thrive. By feeding on elk and deer, grizzlies also keep those ungulates from overpopulating. Allowing grizzlies to live undisturbed in their natural habitat benefits the entire ecosystem.

—KK

Khutzey estuary

Three-year-old grizzly in Khutzeymateen Inlet

Kwinamass Bay (Portland Inlet)
1.3 mi E of Somerville Bay
Position: 54°47.10'N, 130°10.69'W

The south shore of Kwinamass Bay behind Gadu Point is steep-to; on the north shore the bottom shoals rapidly. The head of the bay at the outlet of Kwinamass River is filled with deadheads. The inlet, which does not appear as charted, should be entered only after reconnoitering with a dinghy. The water is opaque, with visibility limited to a foot or two. About a half-dozen cables along the north shore were formerly used for shore ties. On the north shore of Kwinamass Bay, next to the fishing triangles, notice that a climax avalanche started from the top of the ridge, scouring everything to bare rock and dumping rocks and trees at the bottom along shore.

Temporary shelter can be obtained off the north shore along the steep granite cliffs, northwest of the old log dump, in 2 to 3 fathoms; sand bottom with poor holding.

Nasoga Gulf (Portland Inlet)
2.4 mi NE of Somerville Bay
Entrance: 54°49.53'N, 130°10.35'W
Anchor: 54°53.70'N, 130°04.01'W

Nasoga Gulf, a five-mile-long inlet on the east shore of Portland Inlet, offers good protection from downslope winds. The head of the gulf is a deep U-shaped valley. Chambers Creek, which drains the land basin, flows northeast into Iceberg Bay on the Nass River. As you enter the gulf, high snowy peaks are visible above the north side of Nass River.

If you're headed up Portland Inlet, be aware that depths are about 7 fathoms in the fairway between the tip of Mylor Peninsula and the drying rock north of Ranger Islet. Remain about 50 yards off Trefusis Point on the tip of the peninsula.

Anchor in 10 fathoms over gravel with fair holding.

Nass River (Portland Inlet)
13.6 mi N of Somerville Bay
Entrance: 54°59.30'N, 130°00.50'W

Nass River, entered between Low Point on the south and Nass Point on the north, drains a watershed of over 21,000 square kilometers. A number of old pilings lie off Low Point, with stumps and logs along shore. Due to its current, constantly changing channels, and opaque waters, the river requires vigilant navigation.

Head up the river on a rising tide since the water, already opaque and light green, becomes increasingly milky and pale. If you're attempting to head up Nass River from Double Islet Point, the 2-knot current on springs could set you onto Ripple Tongue which dries at a minimum of 6 feet on zero tide and is marked by overfalls. Take the depths listed on charts with skepticism; we found many discrepancies in the area between Governors Bar and Ripple Tongue. A high-speed inflatable with echo sounder is the best way to explore the river.

The lower regions of the Nass are the traditional homeland of the Nisga'a. The name Nass comes from a Tlingit word meaning "food depot," since the river was the source of their food. Although Vancouver was the first to document the name, his men did not explore more than four miles beyond the entrance, considering it to be an "insignificant river." Landslip Mountain, south of Stevens Point, is an impressive half-dome of grey granite whose west-leading face appears to have been shaped by a huge cleaver. Iceberg Bay lies along the south shore of the Nass.

A classic U-shaped valley, with snow-covered peaks to the south, makes a lovely background to Nass Harbour. The river, itself—whose length is about 109 miles (175 kilometers)—is a favorite of river-rafters and kayakers who ride the many rapids and camp along its shore.

Kincolith (Nass River/Observatory Inlet))
1.2 mi SE of Nass Point
Entrance (boat harbour): 54°59.83'N, 129°58.66'W

Kincolith (Gingolx), a Nisga'a village of about 300, has a small-boat harbor crammed with local fishing boats. The harbor lacks room for anchoring. The village was established in 1867 by an Anglican minister. Its name comes from the fact that an Indian chief who, on returning from a raid to a neighboring tribe, nailed the scalps of his victims on the village trees. Kincolith means "Place of Scalps."

Iceberg Bay (Nass River)
2.5 mi SE of Kincolith
Entrance: 54°57.50'N, 129°56.50'W

If you wish to enter Iceberg Bay, remain on the south side of the Nass River entrance, along Mylor Peninsula which does not require crossing the shifting bar.

Echo Cove (Nass River)
0.7 mi SW of Nass Bay
Anchor: 54°55.67'N, 129°57.00'W

Lovely Echo Cove, the site of an abandoned cannery, provides good shelter. Remains of the wharf dolphins lie at the head of the cove. When strong upslope winds blow in Portland Inlet, winds from Nasoga Gulf whip across Chambers Creek. However, when there is a large logboom on the south side of

Salmon Cove, Observatory Inlet

the cove against the steep cliff, little chop enters the cove. The cove has grassy margins with granite cliffs on either side of its head and a low pass leading to Nass Harbour. A deep, U-shaped valley to the southwest leads to Nasoga Gulf. This area is a perfect place for those seeking solitude.

Anchor in 4 to 5 fathoms, between the island and the south shore, over sticky grey mud; very good holding.

Observatory Inlet (Portland Inlet)
31 mi NE of Port Simpson
Entrance: 55°00.62'N, 130°01.46'W

Observatory Inlet gets its name from George Vancouver who used a site at Salmon Cove, six miles to the north, for his astronomical observations. The inlet starts just north of Nass Bay and leads north to Alice and Hastings arms and the abandoned settlements of Anyox and Kitsault.

Nass Point Cove (Observatory Inlet)
2.5 mi N of Nass Point
Entrance: 55°02.79'N, 129°59.44'W
Anchor: 55°03.11'N, 129°59.12'W

"Nass Point Cove" is our name for the bight on the east shore that provides welcome relief from strong downslope winds. The cove is exposed to upslope winds, however, as evidenced by the many large stumps and old logs at the upper edge of the beach. An attractive sizable creek which enters the cove from a U-shaped valley, is fed by a small lake on the north side of Mt. Tomlinson. *Caution:* Avoid what we call Two-Foot Rock at the end of the western spit which has about 2 feet of water at zero tide, in addition to the fast-shoaling flat off the creek. Good protection from downslope winds can be found near the west end of the beach. We have anchored here overnight in fair weather on just our lunch hook with little concern.

Anchor in 2 to 3 fathoms over sand with fair-to-good holding.

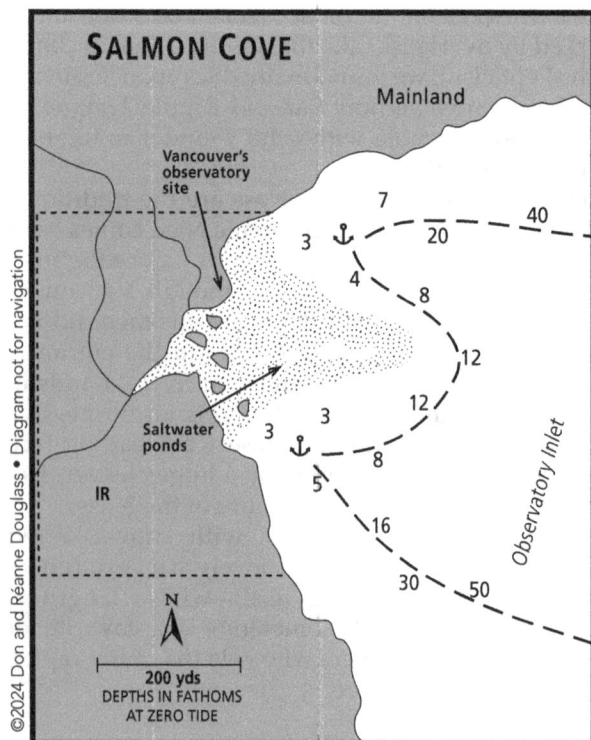

SALMON COVE

Mainland

Vancouver's observatory site

7

3 ⚓ 20   40

4   8

12

Saltwater ponds   3   3 ⚓

12

8

IR   5

16

Observatory Inlet

30   50

N

200 yds
DEPTHS IN FATHOMS
AT ZERO TIDE

©2024 Don and Réanne Douglass • Diagram not for navigation

Tidal ponds, Salmon Cove

Salmon Cove (Observatory Inlet)
6.5 mi NE of Observatory Inlet lt.
Entrance: 55°16.04'N, 129°50.46'W
Anchor: 55°16.20'N, 129°50.87'W

Salmon Cove, named by George Vancouver, is the site *Discovery* used as an anchorage while his men were exploring Observatory and Hastings inlets and Alice Arm. Vancouver established a base camp on the beach behind the drying flat where he made astronomical observations in order to check his latest Kendall chronometer. At low water there are a number of saltwater ponds on the drying flat and, with imagination, you can locate what may have been Vancouver's astronomical campsite along the north side of the creek.

The shoreline reveals a variety of marine creatures: colonies of leather stars, barnacles, mussels, and small clams. On the west side, landward of the shore, are two small ponds whose lower edges are lined with rocks; these appear to be old fish weirs. Hardly more than a wide bight, the mud flat is poorly charted.

The cove provides moderate protection from downslope winds on its north side, and upslope winds on its south side, tucked behind the large drying mud flats. As you proceed north of Salmon Cove, low islands at the head of the inlet come into view, along with high, snowy peaks that rise on either side of Hastings Arm.

Large vessels can anchor off the mouth of the creek in 20 fathoms, much as Captain Vancouver did in *Discovery*; small craft can anchor on a shallow spot next to the rock walls on either extreme of the extensive drying flats. A major creek divides the drying flat. The north side of the cove is rocky and steep-to, but you can conveniently use a shore tie to hold your boat in position.

Anchor (north side) in 3 fathoms over stones, sand, gravel and mud; good holding if you set your anchor well. A shore tie makes the anchorage more secure.

Eagle Cove, Stagoo Creek (Observatory Inlet)
3.8 mi NE of Salmon Cove
Entrance: 55°17.90'N, 129°45.00'W
Anchor: 55°17.65'N, 129°45.07'W

The cove off Stagoo Creek, 2.5 miles northeast of Dawkins Point, is a haven for eagles and seals. The raptors perch on the many snags and stumps on shore, while a dozen or more seals make their home in the harbor. This cove, which we call "Eagle Cove," provides good protection from upslope winds. The substantial creek drains a wide area that you can explore on foot.

Large boats can anchor in 16 fathoms; small craft can anchor, using a stern-tie, along the rocky shore at the southwest side of the cove.

Anchor in 4 to 16 fathoms over mud and shells with good holding.

Alice Arm (Observatory Inlet)
27 mi N of Nass Bay
Entrance: 55°24.41'N, 129°41.11'W

Alice Arm, a steep-sided fiord that trends 10.5 miles northeast to its head, is nearly landlocked by Liddle Island in its entrance. Along the north shore of Alice Arm, the 5,000-foot peaks of Chaloner Ridge are just a mile and a half above saltwater. Alice Peak, with its permanent ice field, is the source of a number of impressive waterfalls that tumble over forested granite slabs to the inlet below.

You can enter on either side of Liddle Island with Liddle Channel on its east side the recommended route. Perry Bay, just east of the arm entrance, provides very good shelter.

The head of the arm, a large U-shaped valley, is fed by four major streams: Kitsault River, Wilwauks Creek, Illiance River and Lime Creek. A gravel logging road from Kitsault, now abandoned, leads 130 kilometers to Terrace.

Alice Arm Settlement is located on the west shore at the outlet of Kitsault River. A substantial public dock and float are located on the north shore near the head of the bay; the village is about a mile away via a good gravel road

The Dolly Varden silver mine, whose ore was reported to be 85% pure, opened in the early years of the 20th Century. Located 18 miles up the Kitsault River, the mine was served by a narrow-gauge railroad that started in Alice Arm Settlement. You can hike a short portion of this old road to Falls Creek (known locally as Bug Creek), where you can watch salmon spawning in late summer and spot black bear in search of easy prey. A primitive trail paralleling the west side of the creek leads to beautiful falls whose source is the ice fields of Alice Peak; the creek is full of glacial "flour."

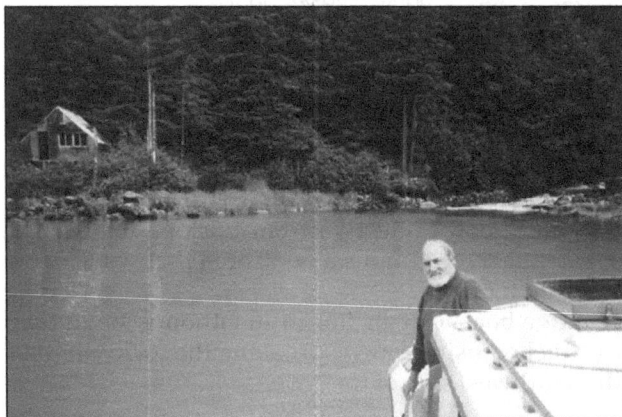

Hastings Arm: cabin, north end

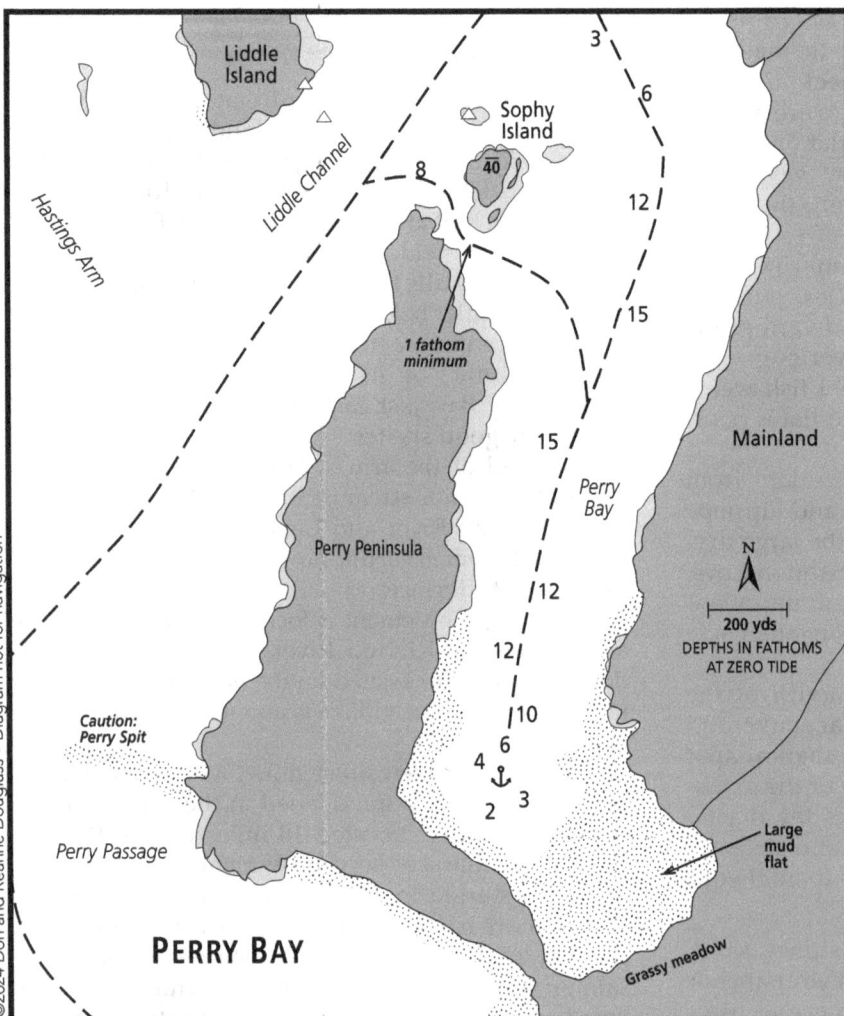

PERRY BAY

Perry Bay (Observatory Inlet)
0.5 mi E of Liddle Island
Entrance (N): 55°23.90'N, 129°40.90'W
Anchor (shelf): 55°22.77'N, 129°41.10'W

Perry Bay, one of the best anchorages at the head of Observatory Inlet, offers good protection from southeast storm winds or upslope winds. The head of the bay has a large, drying grassy flat. With no drift logs, the bay appears to offer calm shelter in most weather.

You can enter between Perry Peninsula and Sophy Island, carefully staying mid-channel between the two bodies of land; the fairway carries a minimum of one fathom.

Large boats can anchor anywhere in Perry Bay in 16 fathoms; small boats can anchor over a 3- to 4-fathom shelf at the south end of the bay just north of a large tree stump on shore. Good landing beaches and campsites can be found at the southeast corner of the bay.

Anchor (shelf) in 4 fathoms over a mixed bottom of sand, mud, gravel and stones, with poor-to-fair holding; good if your anchor is well set.

Kitsault (Alice Arm)
7.7 mi NE of Perry Bay
Position: 55°27.57'N, 129°28.88'W

The former mining town of Kitsault, on the north shore of Lime Creek, is entirely private property and closed to the public. Mining operations at Kitsault ceased in the early 1980s when the price of molybdenum made further operation unprofitable. The town has an interesting history—including its purchase in 2004 by a Virginia businessman. To read about its history, check both *Wikipedia* and *Business Vancouver*, July 17, 2015.

Hastings Arm (Observatory In.)
24 mi N of Nass Bay
Entrance (Vadso Rocks): 55°22.87'N, 129°45.90'W
Entrance (E fairway at Brooke Shoal): 55°23.00'N, 129°43.50'W

As you proceed northward into Hastings Arm, the water turns to the milky green of glacial runoff, and water runs down every crevice and canyon of the western side. The weather turns increasingly misty and rainy, and fog wafts up and down the mountainsides. This inlet is a spectacular treat!

There are a number of good anchor sites at the south end of Hastings Arm. At the north end of Hastings Arm, there are two old cabins on the east shore. Be careful as you approach the outlet of Kshwan River; the bottom shoals rapidly, and visibility is limited to about 3 inches in the glacial-melt water!

Strombeck Bay (Hastings Arm)
6.7 mi N of Salmon Cove
Entrance: 55°22.90'N, 129°46.90'W
Anchor: 55°22.46'N, 129°46.95'W

Strombeck Bay, although open to the north, provides good protection for small boats in fair weather from strong southerlies. Anchor deep in the bay avoiding the mid-bay rocks. You can easily land a dinghy on its gravel beaches and comb the grassy shores, but be alert for bears. South of the cluster of mid-bay rocks, there is a flat bottom of 6 fathoms with swinging room for several boats. Avoid these rocks by staying within 200 feet of the west shore. There is an uncharted rock 100 feet off the southwest beach that dries only at low water. Anchor on a line between the 2.7-meter rock on the west shore and the 3.7-meter rock on the east shore. If you want more protection or swinging room try Sylvester Bay.

Moving a pick-up truck from Kitsault to Alice Arm

Anchor in 5 fathoms over sand with good holding.

Sylvester Bay (Hastings Arm)
0.5 mi W of Strombeck Bay
Entrance: 55°23.20'N, 129°47.20'W
Anchor: 55°21.76'N, 129°48.30'W

Sylvester Bay, with its grassy, tree-covered shores, is well protected from southeasterlies and up-channel winds, and it makes a wonderful anchorage for pleasure craft. There are no drift logs along shore. You can often spot bears combing the shores, and get a rare glimpse of a marten or two. To the west, you have a magnificent view of a hanging glacier whose valley is drained by Cascade Creek.

After you pass south of Cane Rock and Fortier Point, favor the west shore to avoid the rocks shown on the chart two-thirds of the way down the bay. There is plenty of swinging room for a number of boats near the head of the bay. The bottom is flat over an extensive area.

Anchor in 4 fathoms, over sand, mud, and shells with good-to-very-good-holding.

Larcom Lagoon (Hastings Arm)
1.2 mi NE of Strombeck Bay
Entrance: 55°23.26'N, 129°45.14'W
Anchor (W center): 55°23.87'N, 129°44.42'W

Larcom Lagoon gives the best all-weather protection in upper Observatory Inlet. Inside its formidable entrance the lagoon is totally landlocked and comfortable. When a blustery southerly is blowing outside, no chop penetrates the lagoon, and because fetch is minimal, southerly winds and gusts raise little threat. The lagoon can be entered only at adequate tide levels and by careful piloting, using large scale charts.

The entrance to the lagoon is through a very nar-

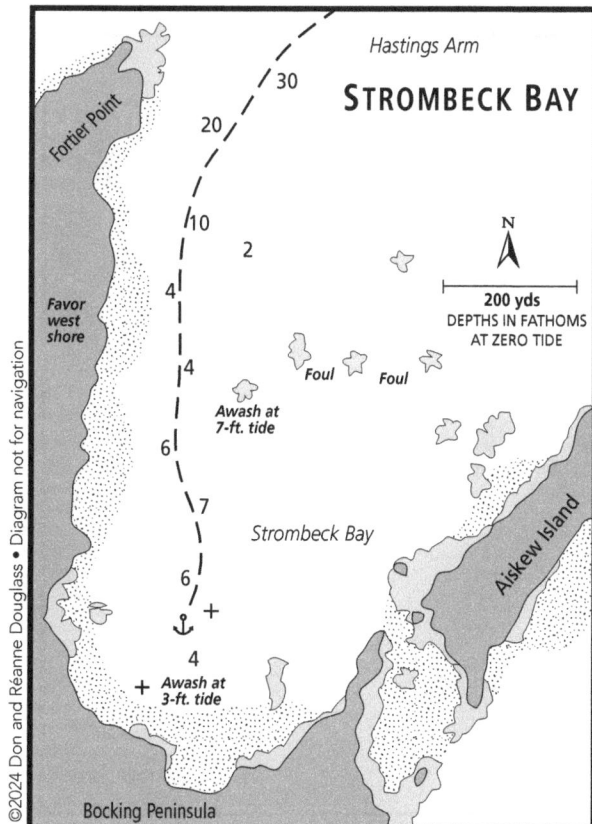

row channel where current runs at considerable strength. On a blustery south wind and ebb current, small standing waves occur just outside the entrance. We waited 2-3 hours to enter. West of the entrance, there are two isolated rocks awash at about 2 feet; stay close to the south shore to avoid these rocks.

Entering the narrows, favor the south shore; the fairway is fairly steep-to and composed of gravel and stone. On a 3.5-foot tide, there are no visible isolated rocks. The narrows carries about a foot of water in the center of the fairway at zero tide, so you should enter only at mid-tide or higher. (Slack water is within a few minutes of Prince Rupert.) The rock connected to the entrance island extends to mid-channel at high water so use caution at this point. At low water the fairway passes about 20 to 30 feet east of this rock. Larger boats may not be comfortable entering at any time but high-water slack.

Inside the lagoon, there is ample swinging room

for a number of boats. Avoid the charted rocks in mid-lagoon by favoring the west shore. Larger boats and those wanting plenty of swinging room will find convenient anchorage over an extended flat area of 3 to 4 fathoms in the center of the bay. Small boats can find good shelter in the small nook between the north end of the entrance island and Larcom Island's west shore, protected by a wide grassy spit.

Anchor (west center of lagoon) in 2 to 3 fathoms over mud; very good holding.

Anyox
(Hastings Arm)
9 mi N of Salmon Cove
Position: 55°25.10'N, 129°48.73'W

Two lovely old brick chimneys on Graves Point mark the site of a former copper smelter. Unfortunately, the chimneys are the only attractive part of the once-vast operation. The old buildings between Graves Point and the slag pile resemble a bombed-out village. Two additional stacks and ruined buildings lie along Anyox Creek.

Keep a sharp lookout as you pass Anyox. The large, drying flat off Anyox Creek extends into the bay, and you could easily be distracted while studying the ruins.

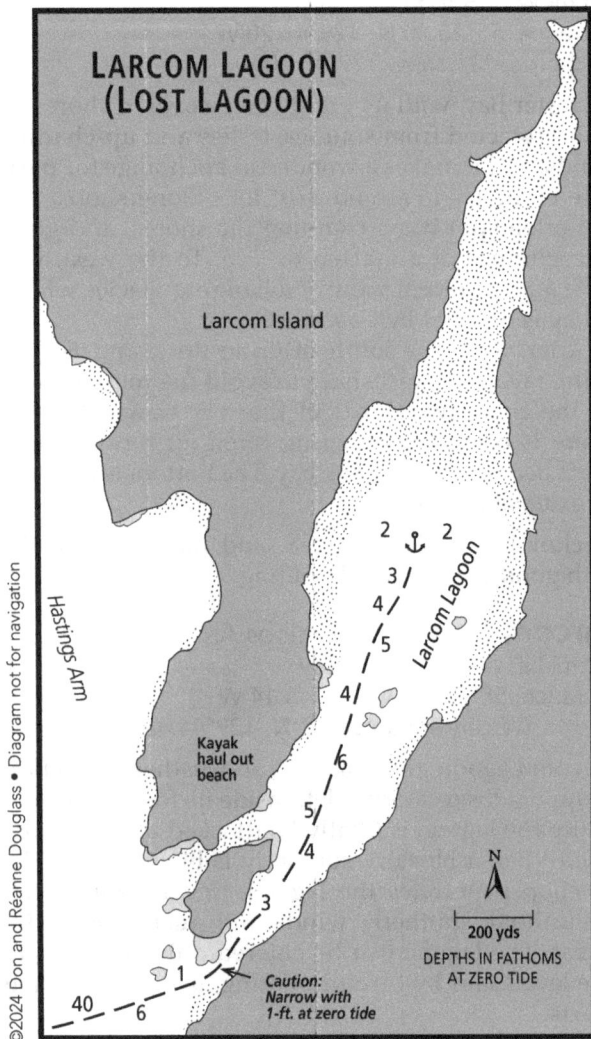

LARCOM LAGOON
(LOST LAGOON)

Larcom Island

Hastings Arm

Larcom Lagoon

Kayak haul out beach

2 ⚓ 2
3
4
5
4
6
5
4
3
1
40 6

Caution:
Narrow with
1-ft. at zero tide

N

200 yds

DEPTHS IN FATHOMS
AT ZERO TIDE

©2024 Don and Réanne Douglass • Diagram not for navigation

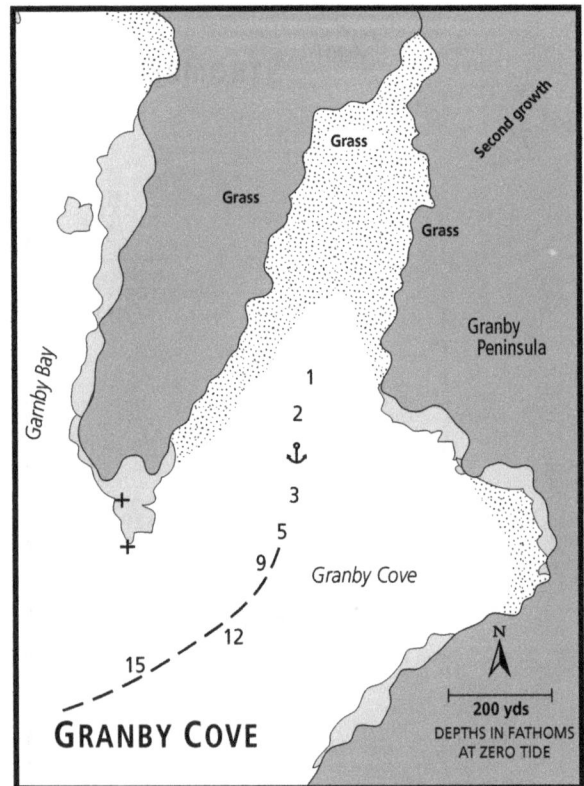

Gamby Bay

Grass
Grass
Grass
Grass

Second growth

Granby
Peninsula

1
2
⚓
3
5
9
12
15

Granby Cove

GRANBY COVE

N

200 yds

DEPTHS IN FATHOMS
AT ZERO TIDE

©2024 Don and Réanne Douglass • Diagram not for navigation

Anyox: remains of old smelter

Granby Cove (Hastings Arm)

6.6 mi N of Salmon Cove
Entrance: 55°22.85'N, 129°49.05'W
Anchor: 55°22.95'N, 129°48.80'W

Granby Cove (from Granby Consolidated Mining Company) is situated halfway down Granby Peninsula at its narrowest point, 2.2 miles south of Anyox. This cove—the only convenient anchorage for small craft in Granby Bay—is calm in all weather, as shown by the grassy shores without drift logs. Snowy peaks to the north and west provide a beautiful backdrop for the anchor site.

Anchor in 5 fathoms over mud with good holding.

Vancouver Cove (Hastings Arm)

2.3 mi NE of Anyox
Anchor (N side): 55°26.93'N, 129°46.37'W

Although George Vancouver's name is honored

Anyox (pronounced annie-ox)

Anyox, whose short history follows the pattern of so many other mining communities in British Columbia, was a thriving town of 1500 in the early part of the Twentieth Century. In 1913, the town boasted a hospital, electricity, a telegraph station and complete telephone system, as well as docks that could accommodate three or four freighters—remarkable facilities when you consider how remote the town was. Destroyed by fire in 1923, the town was completely rebuilt and, within a few years, was producing 35 million pounds of copper annually, in addition to gold and silver. During the Depression years, copper prices declined, and operations became unprofitable. The mine and the town were closed for good in 1934. When you study the destruction of vegetation along the western shore of Granby Bay, you can't help but wonder what effect years of breathing noxious smelter gas had on the lungs of the residents.

—RHD

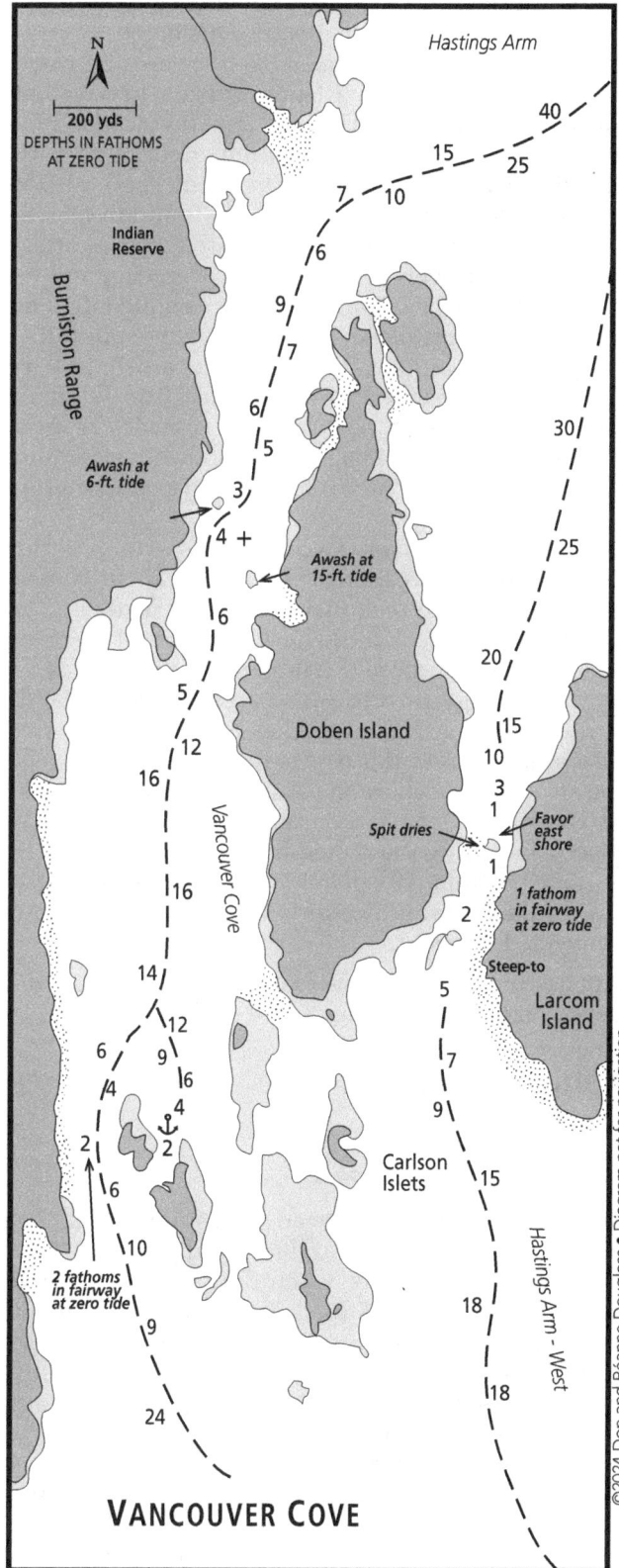

VANCOUVER COVE

©2024 Don and Réanne Douglass • Diagram not for navigation

in the major B.C city, to our knowledge there is no cove in Northern B.C. that carries his name. We understand that he and his men liked the area between Salmon Cove and these islands, thus we have called the small area west of Doben Island and Carlson Islets, "Vancouver Cove." This calm, quiet place with beautiful surroundings is totally landlocked; in fact it is the calmest anchorage we have found in Observatory Inlet, and its grassy, stress-free shores attest to the fact that very little wake or even chop enters these waters. This is bird heaven; we sighted dozens of tufted puffins, oldsquaw, loons, and small gulls. We also saw a large wolf combing the beach on Larcom Island. Fresh water is available from a small stream at the north narrows that cascades from a high ridge. We can imagine that Vancouver would have liked to linger here if he had had a good motor, charts and tide tables.

To enter Vancouver Cove from the north, find the narrow fairway west of Doben Island, about 50 feet to the west of the rock that dries at 5.5 meters. The south entrance to Vancouver Cove, east of Carlson Islets, has a minimum of 2 fathoms in the fairway.

The passage on the east side of Doben Island, known as "The Narrows," has a fairway of about one fathom at zero tide east of the drying rock. Favor the steep-to east shore to pass through the narrows. In Vancouver Cove, large craft can anchor in several places, including the center, in 12 to 15 fathoms over a gravel bottom. We prefer to anchor on the north side of the two southwesterly Carlson Islets that are connected by a spit.

Anchor (north side of the two islets) in about 2 fathoms over mud and stones; fair-to-good holding.

Kshwan River

(Hastings Arm)
10.1 mi N of Vancouver Cove
Position: 55°37.39'N, 129°47.64'W

Kshwan River enters the head of Hastings Arm. This area can be a very misty and mystical place. If you're lucky enough to arrive when the sky clears, you'll be treated to a view of a snow-covered peak that lies directly north of the river delta. The peaks here rise to 4,000 and 6,000 feet. We have heard that there are petroglyphs near the river's outlet but we have not been able to locate them.

There is a large steep-to mud flat, the extent of which is difficult to gauge due to the opacity of the water. Use caution when proceeding beyond the two cabins located on the east shore. There is no convenient anchorage here.

Portland Canal

78 mi N of Work Channel
Entrance (S): 55°03.39'N, 130°11.29'W

Portland Canal and Inlet, combined, is a long, narrow fiord, perhaps the longest on the entire North American continent. When measured from Dixon Entrance to Stewart, it is more than 100 miles long. The international boundary between Canada and Alaska runs mid-channel through Portland Canal. Its shoreline is sheer and steep and its waters are deep. Anchorage, which is marginal at best, depends entirely on the weather. The long fetch of the canal can create choppy seas from upslope and downslope winds. There is little or no VHF reception in the canal.

Whiskey Bay (Portland Inlet)

7 mi NW of Nass Bay
Anchor: 55°01.91'N, 130°11.17'W

Whiskey Bay is a good lunch stop, or an overnighter, if no downslope winds are expected. At the head of the bay there is a grassy meadow with a huge stump; the shoreline has a constant slope which can be used as a kayak haul-out. Upon entering, avoid the rocks awash on the east side of the bay and anchor in convenient depths short of the long, drying mud flat.

Anchor in 4 to 6 fathoms over sand and mud with good holding.

Reef Island (Portland Canal)

2.9 mi N of Whiskey Bay
Anchor (S cove): 55°04.72'N, 130°12.69'W
Anchor (W): 55°04.93'N, 130°12.38'W

Reef Island, on the west side of Portland Canal, has two small coves that provide some relief from downslope winds, but both are exposed to the south. The south cove is steep-to and temporary anchorage can be taken in 6 to 8 fathoms off the drying beach near a drift tree with limbs still attached.

Small craft can also find some protection directly west of Reef Island, off the stony beach, where there is a 100-foot-long tree lying onshore. The fairway on the west side of Reef Island has a minimum depth of about one fathom. There is a 1- to 2-fathom area in the passage between Reef Island and the shore. The level of the tree limbs indicates that the area is mostly free of chop. If you anchor in this passageway, a stern-tie to shore may be effective.

Anchor (south cove) in 6 to 8 fathoms over sand, stones and iridescent seaweed; fair holding.

Anchor (west Reef Island) in about 3 fathoms, mixed bottom, predominantly sand; fair-to-good holding.

Portland Canal: heading south from "Glacier Bay"

Portland Canal, looking north at head

Photo courtesy CHS, Pacific Region

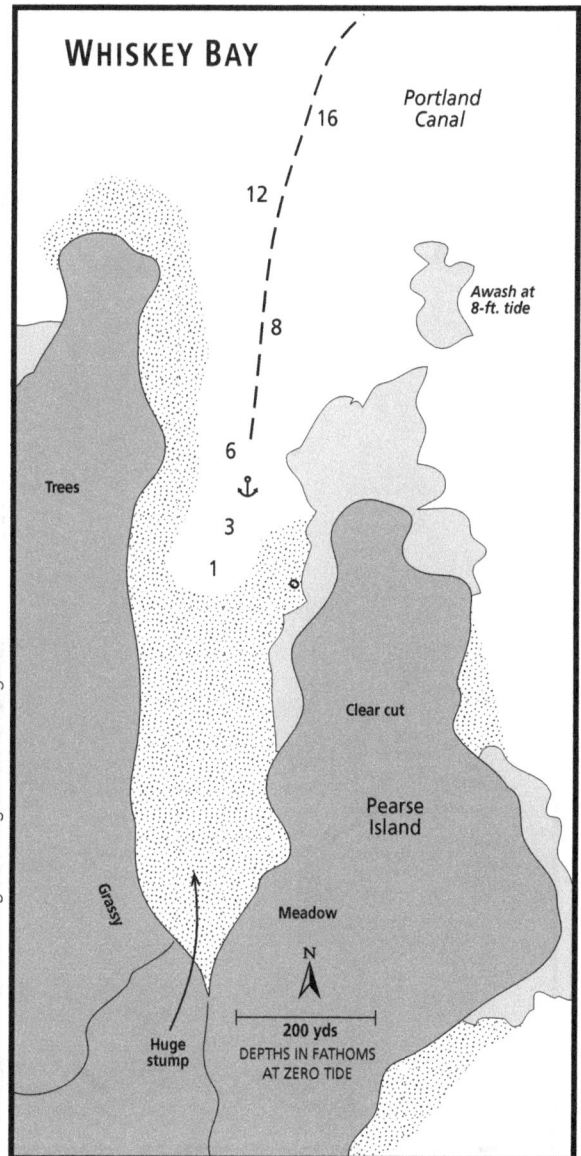

WHISKEY BAY

Portland Canal

16

12

Awash at 8-ft. tide

8

Trees

6

⚓

3

1

Clear cut

Pearse Island

Grassy

Meadow

N

Huge stump

200 yds
DEPTHS IN FATHOMS
AT ZERO TIDE

©2024 Don and Réanne Douglass • Diagram not for navigation

Sandfly Bay

(Portland Canal)
7.8 mi N of Whiskey Bay
Entrance: 55°09.49'N, 130°09.17'W
Anchor: 55°09.75'N, 130°09.22'W

Some temporary protection from downslope winds can be found in scenic Sandfly Bay. It is a good place for small craft to anchor only in fair weather. Sandfly Bay is steep-to off the creek outlet; the foreshore slope is less steep on the west side of the bay. Its grassy margins have little driftwood to indicate severe weather or chop. Avoid the charted rocks near the east shore.

Anchorage can be found about 100 yards from the white granite rocks on the west shore, 50 yards south of the drying gravel flat. This spot can provide reasonable anchoring for one or two boats in fair weather. There is easy landing access.

Anchor in 3 to 5 fathoms over sand with fair-to-good holding.

Halibut Bay (Portland Canal)

11.7 mi N of Whiskey Bay
Entrance: 55°13.03'N, 130°05.49'W
Anchor (E): 55°13.71'N, 130°05.83'W

Halibut Bay affords the best protection between Whiskey Bay and Maple Bay or Fords Cove but it is poorly charted. Convenient anchorage can be found in the entrance on the east shore, just off a tiny creek and stony beach, or on the west shore between a small creek and the rocky point. While the bay is open to the southeast, most of the summer up- and downslope winds blow by the entrance.

In the inner bay, there is a 3-fathom hole north of the large creek. The passage to this hole is very shallow. We found as little as 2 feet in the fairway at zero tide, with rapidly shoaling flats on either side. We once found it necessary to travel within a few yards of the east wall until we were abeam the low point north of the west creek. We would not recommend inner Halibut Bay until it is more fully charted.

Anchor (east shore) in 8 fathoms over sand, gravel and stone with good holding.

Anchor (west shore) in 6 fathoms off a tiny creek over sand, gravel and stone with good holding.

Car Point Notch (Portland Canal)

19.4 mi N of Whiskey Bay
Entrance: 55°20.24'N, 130°00.17'W

The head of the notch at Car Point holds a wonderful surprise—a stunning waterfall that tumbles vertically over somber, angular, grey and rust-colored granite. Although we encountered many lovely cascades along the eastern shore of Portland Inlet, this one got raves from all the crew. As we approached the notch, the water grew calm and we were able to approach within 10 feet of the waterfall. Ferns and delicate white flowers grow out of every small crevice, while hemlock and spruce sprout from unlikely vertical faces.

At the south end of Portland Canal, the water is tea-colored but becomes progressively greener as you proceed northward.

Tombstone Bay (Portland Canal)

22.8 mi N of Whiskey Bay
Entrance: 55°24.33'N, 130°33.00'W

On the north side of Tombstone Bay are overhanging cliffs from which hemlock and cedar grow. The bottom is steep-to with a rocky beach. This bight could offer shelter from north winds with an anchor placed close to the drying flat at its head.

The south end of Tombstone Bay is the watershed for an unnamed creek flowing from a perfect, U-shaped valley. Protection from southerly weather can be obtained; however, avoid the charted rocks and the drying flat off the creek.

Anchor off the drying flat in about 10 fathoms; unrecorded bottom.

Fords Cove (Portland Canal)

36 mi N of Whiskey Bay
Entrance: 55°37.78'N, 130°06.00'W
Anchor (small boats): 55°37.67'N, 130°05.85'W

Fords Cove, directly west of the hanging glacier affords good protection in southerly weather. Small

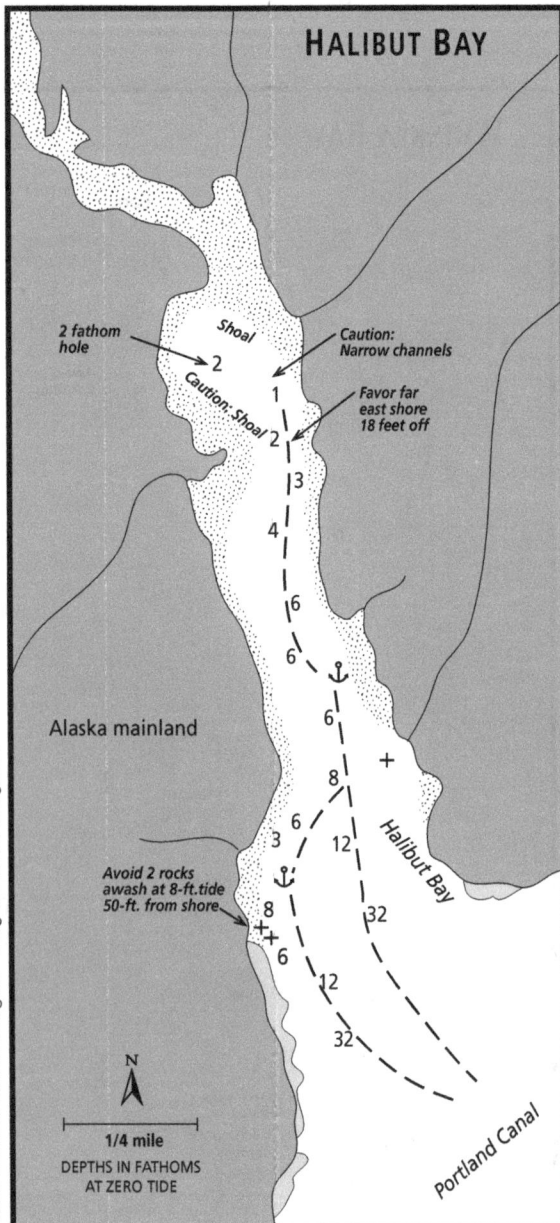

HALIBUT BAY

2 fathom hole

Shoal

Caution: Narrow channels

Caution: Shoal

Favor far east shore 18 feet off

Alaska mainland

Halibut Bay

Avoid 2 rocks awash at 8-ft.tide 50-ft. from shore.

Portland Canal

N

1/4 mile

DEPTHS IN FATHOMS AT ZERO TIDE

©2024 Don and Réanne Douglass • Diagram not for navigation

boats can anchor near the sandy beach in 3 fathoms; larger boats can anchor just outside in 5 to 7 fathoms.

Anchor (small boats) in 3 fathoms over sand with very good holding.

Turquoise Cove (Portland Canal)
10.8 mi S of Stewart
Entrance: 55°45.39'N, 130°08.15'W

"Turquoise Cove," on the east side of Portland Canal 0.5 mile south of Round Point, is our name for the tiny cove that has exquisitely brilliant turquoise-colored water. The cove can provide anchorage for one small boat only, out of southerly chop and with good protection in most summer weather. The V-shaped cove is deep with constant shoaling to the small beach at its head; a stern tie to shore is recommended. Visibility through the water is about a foot. From this cove you have a first-class view of high snowfields on the mountains to the west.

Anchor in the head of the cove in about 5 fathoms, soft silt bottom; fair holding.

Glacier Cove, Glacier Bay (Portland Canal)
7.2 mi Sw of Stewart
Entrance: 55°48.95'N, 130°07.60'W
Anchor (E cove): 55°49.38'N, 130°07.08'W
Anchor (west bay): 55°49.45'N, 130°07.62'W

The large bay south of Glacier Point, known locally as Glacier Bay, has two possibilities for anchorage in stable weather or in downslope winds. The easterly cove, just behind Glacier Point, is steep-to close to a rocky shore, with room for one or two boats in about 7 fathoms. Here a stern-tie to shore can be used effectively.

The western part of the bay is steep-to and more open, with swinging room for a number of boats.

Visibility through the water is limited to about a foot. Both anchor sites are completely open to the south.

An unnamed river enters the south end of Glacier Bay through a 40-foot cleft in a 100-foot-high cliff. It's an impressive sight to view from a dinghy. *Caution:* shoal water exists a quarter-mile off the shore of the river, contrary to what is indicated on charts. The waters of Glacier Bay take a close second in beauty to "Turquoise Cove."

Anchor (west bay) in 7 fathoms over sand or glacial silt, with fair holding.

Anchor (east cove) in 9 fathoms over sand or glacial silt, with fair holding.

Marmot Bay (Portland Canal)
2.1 mi S of Stewart
Entrance: 55°53.14'N, 130°00.58'W

Marmot Bay, on the British Columbia side of Portland Canal, offers some protection from downslope winds; however, the bay is filled largely with log booms, float houses, and steel dols. Consider temporary moorage tied to the boomsticks only if fog develops and you have no radar, or if you don't want to approach Hyder or Stewart in poor visibility.

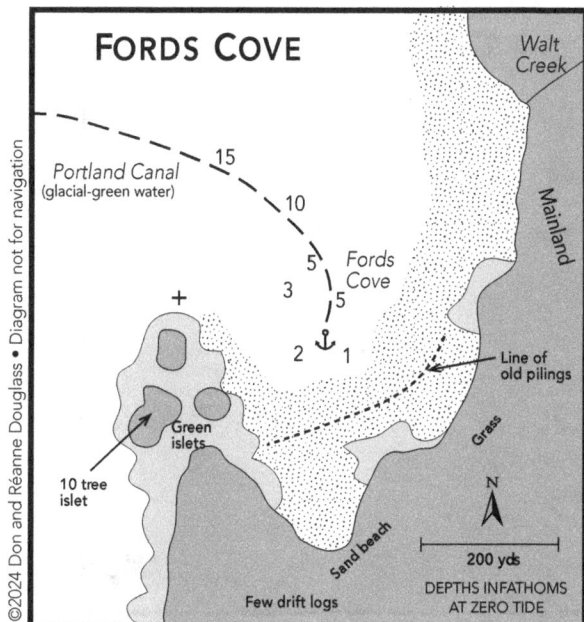

FORDS COVE

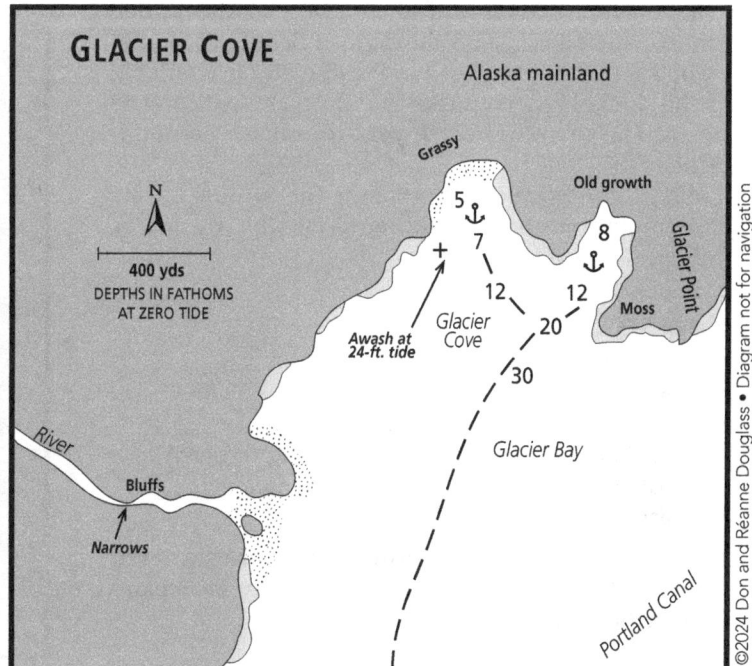

GLACIER COVE

Hyder, Alaska

(Portland Canal)
1 mi S of Stewart
Float position: 55°54.32'N, 130°00.62'W

Hyder (population 87 in 2010) still advertises itself as the friendliest ghost town in Alaska. The orthodox church with its golden ornaments is the only attractive building in town. Getting "Hyderized" is the main attraction in the village. The town, with its pot-holed road, largely exists as a duty-free zone for Stewart residents, and a waypoint for Salmon Glacier, some 30 miles up the Salmon River. Ketchikan, Alaska has the nearest Customs and Immigration facilities. There are none in Hyder; but there is a Canadian CBSA customs station - so bring your passport. Canadian Customs is closed at night.

The Hyder public dock is suitable for smaller vessels and is located on the U.S. side of the border.

Stewart

(Portland Canal)
54 mi N of Whiskey Bay
Breakwater entrance: 55°55.20'N, 130°00.47'W

The beautiful settings of Stewart (population about 500) and the upper canal make the 125-mile (200 km) cruise up Portland Canal worthwhile. The mountains are more precipitous, more glaciers are visible, and waterfalls increase. As you approach the head of the canal and pass Marmot Bay, Bear Glacier comes into view, looming high over the town and its harbor.

The Stewart Harbour Authority welcomes visiting boaters who will find moorage at the public wharf which lies just off the delta of Bear River on the Canadian side of the border. Fresh water is available at the dock. Hyder, Alaska is a 0.7-mile walk to the south. The town has three year-round accommodations.

The town is quite popular in the winter for its snowmobiling and heli-skiing, accessible by motor vehicle along Highway 37A.

Pearse Canal

(Portland Canal)
Marks Canada/Alaska border
Entrance (NE): 55°02.75'N, 130°12.24'W
Pearse Canal leads about 23 miles along the NW sides of Wales and Pearse Islands and connects Tongass

Pearse Canal, which is narrower and more sheltered than Portland Inlet, has interesting places to explore and anchor at its southern entrance.

Hidden Inlet

(Pearse Canal)
7.7 mi N of Winter Harbour
Entrance: 54°56.72'N, 130°19.86'W
Anchor: 54°57.13'N, 130°20.30'W

Hidden Inlet is located on the west side of Pearse Canal, just north of Gwent Cove. The entrance is narrow, set back from the canal, and easy to miss. The tree-covered Yelnu Islets, 300 yards off the west shore, are a leading mark.

Enter the inlet on or near slack, staying mid-channel—spring currents reach a rapid 10 knots. Watch the current as this inlet with a rolly, poor-holding bottom may not be safe. A bight 1.1 miles northwest may be better or stay in Gwent Cove and explore by dinghy. The fairway is quite wide, but entering favor slightly west of center at the south, and east of center in the narrows. The fairway has a fairly even bottom, that bounces between 3 and 5 fathoms. One hour after a low water of 6 feet, the flood current was 2 knots. Thirty minutes later, it had increased to 3 plus knots, with moderate turbulence forming.

Just beyond the narrows, on the west side of the inlet, is a grassy shore, off which lies a 2- to 3-fathom shoal where temporary anchorage can be found. The bottom is rocky and there are kelp patches on either side of the beach area. The shores are steep, with rocky slabs; high peaks can be seen nearby.

Anchor in 3 fathoms over a rocky bottom with kelp; poor holding.

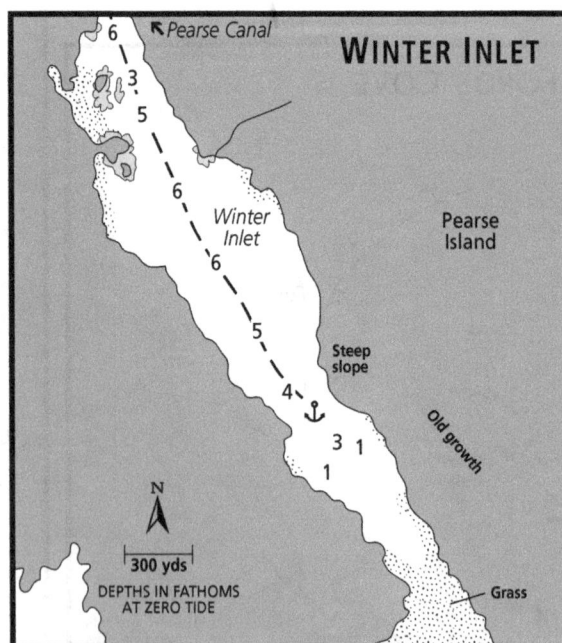

Gwent Cove (Pearse Canal)
0.2 mi S of Hidden Inlet
Entrance: 54°56.55'N, 130°19.70'W CHECK
Anchor: 54°56.56'N, 130°20.16'W

Gwent Cove, off the south entrance to Hidden Inlet, provides fair-weather anchorage directly in front of the old white cannery building with two smoke stacks. There is a 5-fathom flat area off the old wharf and small private float. The float is sometimes used as a sportfishing outstation.

The head of the cove shoals rapidly west of the wharf and, as the water is dark brown muskeg, you can't see more than a foot or two.

Anchor in 5 fathoms over sand and mud with shells; good holding.

Winter Inlet (Pearse Canal)
8.2 mi NE of Tongass Passage
Entrance: 54°50.41'N, 130°27.67'W
Anchor: 54°48.31'N, 130°25.95'W

Winter Inlet is one of the best sheltered anchorages east of Dixon Entrance. This is where we head when a storm is approaching. It is a long, scenic inlet and total protection can be found anywhere in reasonable depths past the small west shore islets with trees. There is a lot of swinging room and larger vessels can anchor in the center of the basin in 6 to 8 fathoms. Porpoises and seals like to play in the strong currents off the entrance. The creek outlet on the east shore has grassy margins, and at the head of

Stewart: public floats north of yacht club floats

the inlet there is a large grassy meadow.

Anchor in 3 to 5 fathoms over black sticky mud, small broken shells and wood debris; very good holding.

Wales Harbour, (West Cove) (Pearse Cn.)
1.7 mi NE of Tongass Passage
Entrance (main): 54°46.59'N, 130°36.78'W
Entrance (W cove): 54°45.61'N, 130°35.68'W
Anchor: 54°45.27'N, 130°35.80'W

The West Cove of Wales Harbour, which is shaped like a keyhole, offers very good protection from all weather. Intimate West Cove has room for one or two small boats over a flat bottom with steep, rocky shores and limited swinging room. Larger boats may feel more comfortable anchoring in the eastern arm where there is more swinging room to ride out a southeaster.

Anchor in 4 fathoms, soft bottom, with good holding.

Tongass Passage (Dixon Entrance)
4.5 mi NW of Work Channel
Entrance (SE): 54°42.10'N, 130°32.72'W
Entrance (S): 54°43.40'N, 130°37.72'W
Entrance (N): 54°45.83'N, 130°39.60'W

The channel between Protector and Boston islands is clear and well protected. Both sets of islands have beautiful sandy beaches for good kayak haul-outs and campsites. The head of the bay, on the south end of Wales Island, offers protection from downslope winds from Portland Inlet.

Boats taking the smooth-water route to Ketchikan will use Sitklan Passage and Port Tongass. Those going to Stewart/Hyder will want to use Pearse Canal.

See *Exploring Southeast Alaska* published by FineEdge. com for additional local knowledge.

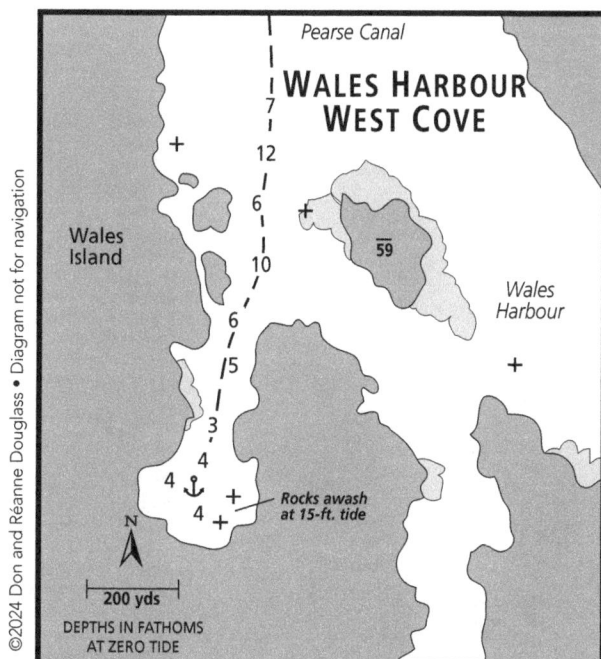

WALES HARBOUR
WEST COVE

Pearse Canal

Wales Island

Wales Harbour

Rocks awash at 15-ft. tide

N

200 yds

DEPTHS IN FATHOMS AT ZERO TIDE

©2024 Don and Reanne Douglass • Diagram not for navigation

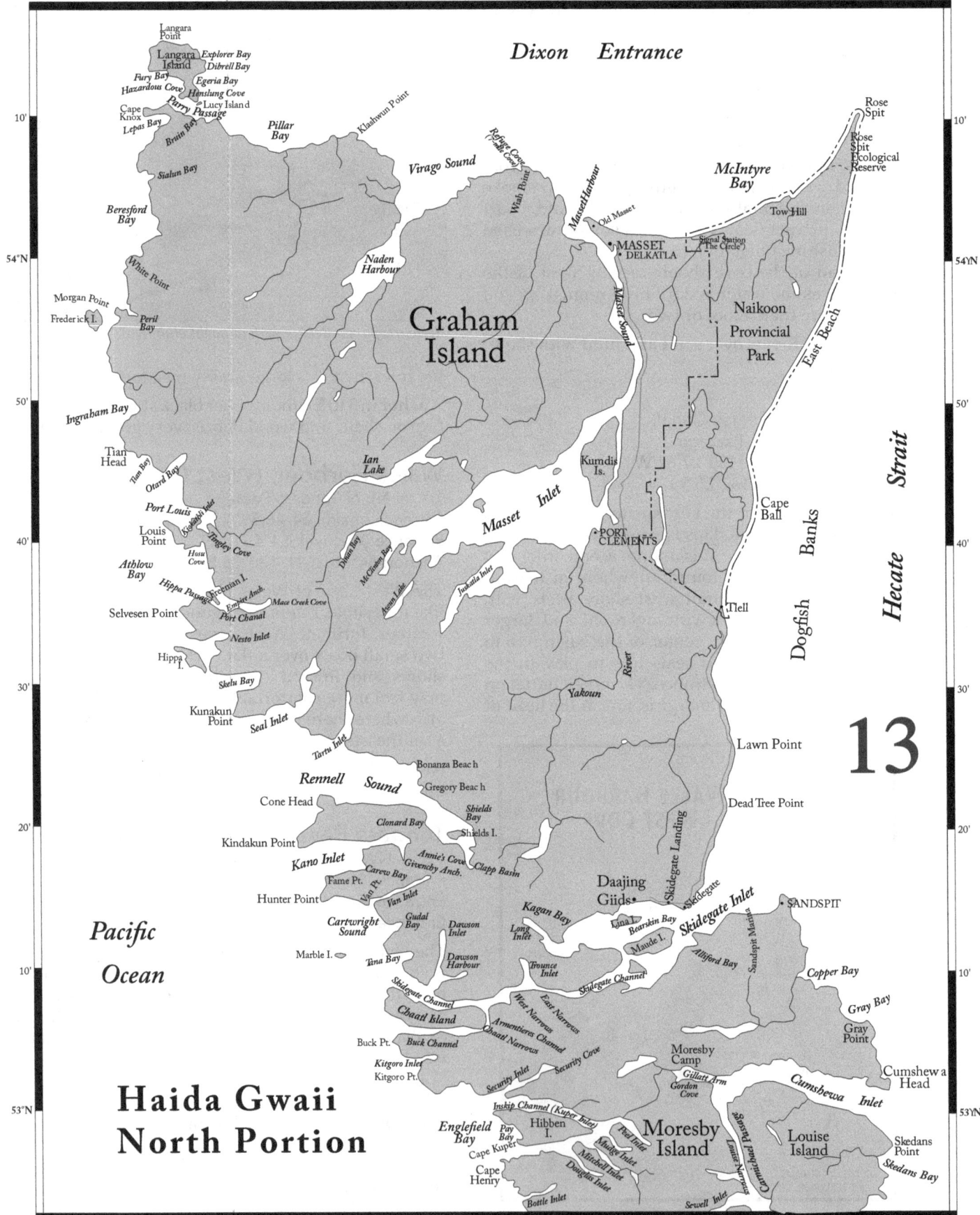

Dixon Entrance

Langara Point
Langara Island
Explorer Bay
Dibrell Bay
Egeria Bay
Henslung Cove
Parry Bay
Lucy Island
Fury Bay
Hazardous Cove
Cape Knox
Lepas Bay
Bruin Bay
Parry Passage
Pillar Bay
Klashwun Point
Virago Sound
Wiah Point
Refuge Cove
(Yan Cove)
Masset Harbour
Old Masset
Rose Spit
Rose Spit Ecological Reserve
McIntyre Bay
Tow Hill
Sialun Bay

Beresford Bay

54°N

White Point

Morgan Point
Frederick I.
Peril Bay

Naden Harbour

Graham Island

MASSET
DELKATLA
Signal Station
(The Circle)

Naikoon Provincial Park

East Beach

54°N

Ingraham Bay

50'

Tian Head
Tiun Bay
Otard Bay

Port Louis
Kano Inlet
Louis Point
Tingley Cove
Hosu Cove
Athlow Bay
Hippa Passage
Freeman I.
Empire Anch.
Mace Creek Cove
Selvesen Point
Port Chanal
Nesto Inlet
Hippa I.
Skelu Bay

Ian Lake
Dinan Bay
McClinton Bay
Awun Lake
Inskula Inlet

Masset Inlet

Kumdis Is.

PORT CLEMENTS

Cape Ball

Dogfish Banks

Hecate Strait

50'

40'

Yakoun River

Tlell

40'

Athlow Bay

30'

Kunakun Point
Seal Inlet
Tartu Inlet

Rennell Sound
Cone Head
Clonard Bay
Kindakun Point
Kano Inlet
Fame Pt.
Carew Bay
Van Pt.
Hunter Point
Van Inlet
Cartwright Sound
Gudal Bay
Marble I.
Tina Bay
Dawson Inlet
Dawson Harbour
Skidegate Channel
Chaatl Island
Buck Pt.
Buck Channel
Kitgoro Inlet
Kitgoro Pt.

Bonanza Beach
Gregory Beach
Shields Bay
Shields I.
Annie's Cove
Givenchy Anch.
Clapp Basin

Kagan Bay
Long Inlet

Lyna I.
Bearskin Bay
Maude I.

Daajing Giids

Skidegate Landing
Skidegate

Security Cove

West Narrows
East Narrows
Armentieres Channel
Chaatl Narrows

Trounce Inlet

Lawn Point

Dead Tree Point

13

30'

SANDSPIT

Skidegate Inlet

Sandspit Machine

Alliford Bay

Copper Bay

Gray Bay

Gray Point

Cumshewa Head

20'

Pacific Ocean

Englefield Bay
Pay Bay
Hibben I.
Cape Kuper
Cape Henry
Bottle Inlet
Sludge Inlet
Mitchell Inlet
Douglas Inlet

Moresby Camp
Gillatt Arm
Gordon Cove

Sewell Inlet

Moresby Island

Cumshewa Inlet

Louise Island

Skedans Point
Skedans Bay

10'

53°N

Haida Gwaii
North Portion

Inskip Channel (Kuper Inlet)

Security Inlet

Tasu Narrows
Carmichael Passage

53°N

©2024 Don and Réanne Douglass • Diagram not for navigation

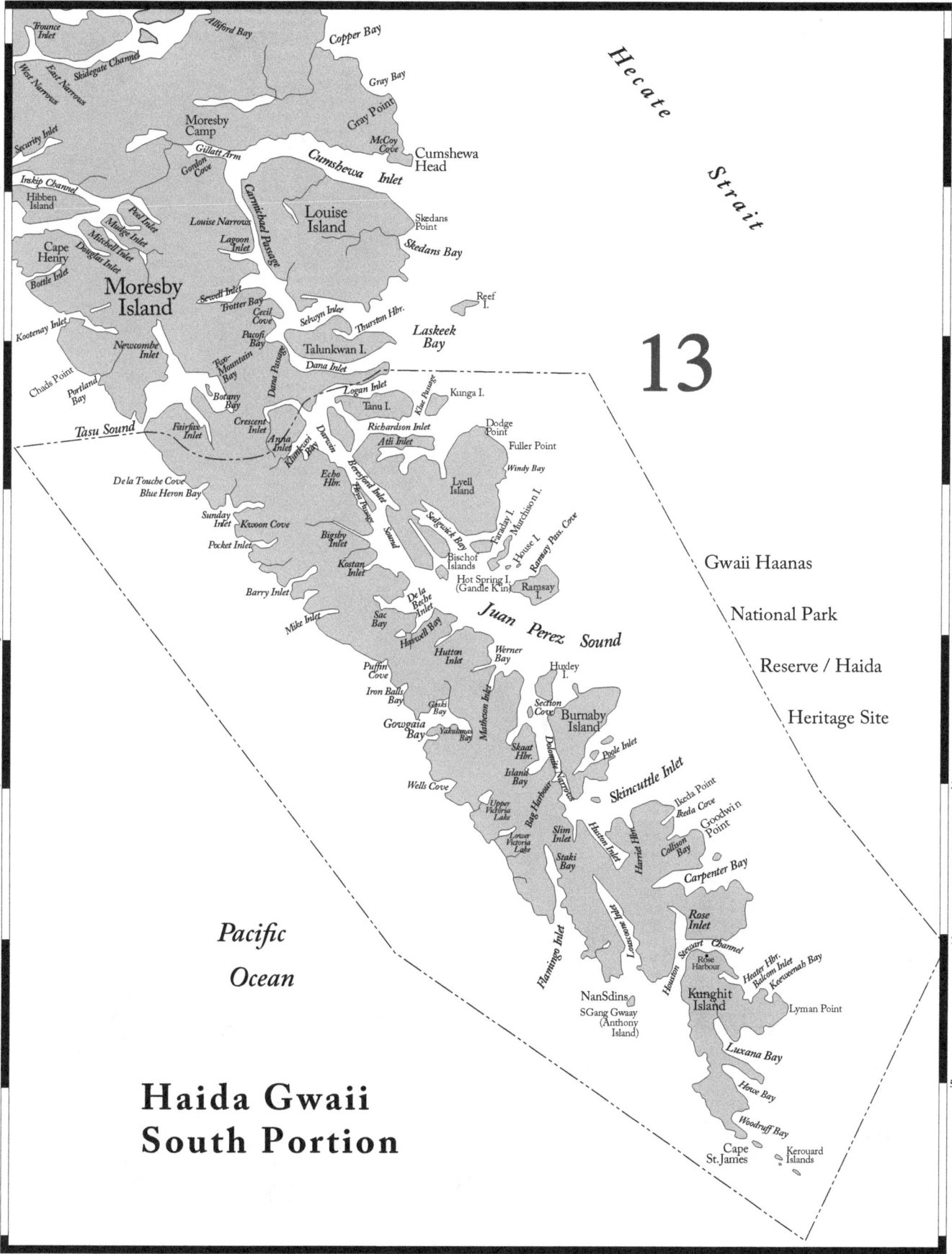

Haida Gwaii
South Portion

13

Hecate Strait

Pacific Ocean

Gwaii Haanas

National Park

Reserve / Haida

Heritage Site

Moresby Island

Trounce Inlet
West Narrows
East Narrows
Skidegate Channel
Alliford Bay
Copper Bay
Gray Bay
Security Inlet
Moresby Camp
Gillatt Arm
Gray Point
McCoy Cove
Cumshewa Head
Gordon Cove
Cumshewa Inlet
Inskip Channel
Hibben Island
Peel Inlet
Louise Narrows
Louise Island
Skedans Point
Cape Henry
Maude Inlet
Mitchell Inlet
Lagoon Inlet
Carmichael Passage
Skedans Bay
Douglas Inlet
Bottle Inlet
Sewell Inlet
Trotter Bay
Cecil Cove
Selwyn Inlet
Thurston Hbr.
Reef I.
Kootenay Inlet
Pacofi Bay
Talunkwan I.
Laskeek Bay
Newcombe Inlet
Two-Mountain Bay
Dana Passage
Dana Inlet
Chads Point
Botany Bay
Crescent Inlet
Logan Inlet
Kunga I.
Portland Bay
Fairfax Inlet
Anna Inlet
Tanu I.
Alse Passage
Tasu Sound
Klunkwoi Bay
Richardson Inlet
Dodge Point
Darwin Sound
Atli Inlet
Fuller Point
De la Touche Cove
Echo Hbr.
Beresford Inlet
Windy Bay
Blue Heron Bay
Peel Passage
Lyell Island
Sunday Inlet
Kwoon Cove
Sedgwick Bay
Faraday I.
Murchison I.
Pocket Inlet
Bigsby Inlet
Crescent Sound
House I.
Ramsay Pass. Cove
Kostan Inlet
Bischof Islands
Barry Inlet
De la Beche Inlet
Hot Spring I. (Gandle K'in)
Ramsay I.
Mike Inlet
Sac Bay
Hoskwell Bay
Juan Perez Sound
Puffin Cove
Hutton Inlet
Werner Bay
Huxley I.
Iron Balls Bay
Gidki Bay
Section Cove
Gowgaia Bay
Yakulanas Bay
Mathieson Inlet
Burnaby Island
Poole Inlet
Skincuttle Inlet
Skaat Hbr.
Dolomite Narrows
Ikeda Point
Wells Cove
Island Bay
Big Harbour
Ikeda Cove
Goodwin Point
Upper Victoria Lake
Slim Inlet
Collison Bay
Lower Victoria Lake
Huston Inlet
Harriet Hbr.
Carpenter Bay
Staki Bay
Flamingo Inlet
Louscoone Inlet
Rose Inlet
Stewart Channel
Heater Hbr.
Balcom Inlet
Keewenah Bay
Houston Stewart Channel
Rose Harbour
NanSdins
SGang Gwaay (Anthony Island)
Kunghit Island
Lyman Point
Luxana Bay
Howe Bay
Woodruff Bay
Cape St. James
Kerouard Islands

53°N 53'N
50' 50'
40' 40'
30' 30'
20' 20'
10' 10'
52°N 52'N

©2024 Don and Réanne Douglass • Diagram not for navigation

S/V **Duen** *crossing Hecate Strait under full canvas*

© Chris Cheadle

13

Haida Gwaii: Graham and Moresby Islands, Gwaii Haanas National Park Reserve, and Haida Heritage Site

Haida Gwaii, an archipelago of 150 islands, lies across Hecate Strait, 60 miles (98 kilometers) from the nearest point of the mainland coast. Sometimes referred to as the "Galapagos of Canada" for its diverse ecosystem, the archipelago has one of the finest remaining old-growth rain forests, as well as some of the highest densities of sea lions, sea birds, eagles and falcons found on the Pacific Coast. Scientists believe that portions of the islands escaped glaciation during the last ice age, providing refuge for flora and fauna that might otherwise have been eliminated. Haida Gwaii, the Haida name for these unique islands, means Islands of Beauty, and indeed, as you cruise through the pristine waters of the southern portion of Moresby Island, you become aware of this unrivaled beauty. Misty inlets, snow-capped mountains, and historic Haida village sites offer unforgettable experiences for cruising boaters.

The eastern side of Graham Island, north of Skidegate Inlet, is nearly flat, with many sandy beaches and no sheltered anchorages with the exception of Masset Sound, entered from the north end of Graham Island. By contrast, the southern half of Moresby Island—about 25% of Haida Gwaii's landmass—lies within the Gwaii Haanas National Park Reserve, National Marine Conservation Area, and Haida Heritage Site, and has mountainous terrain. Along the eastern shoreline of Moresby many small islands and passages provide opportunities to find sheltered anchorages, as well as a chance to visit Haida Watchmen sites.

Anyone wishing to visit Gwaii Haanas must attend an orientation of approximately 90 minutes held at the Haida Heritage Centre in Skidegate. Phone 250-559-7885 to make an appointment for your orientation, which is required annually to get a permit to visit Gwaii Haanas. Fees for daily or seasonal visits to Gwaii Haanas between May 1st and September 30th vary and depend on age and group size.

The island on the southwestern shore of Moresby Island now known as SGang Gwaa (known as Anthony Island in English and on many charts) is the home of the Haida village site of Nan Sdins (known as Ninstints in English). SGang Gwaay was named a UNESCO World Heritage Site.

Boaters not entering the Park itself still have many choices for exploration. The north portion of Moresby Island from Cumshewa Inlet to Dana Passage via Skedans Bay makes a good east coast loop trip.

Skidegate Inlet to Skidegate Channel and the wild west coast of Moresby, with Buck Channel and Englefield Bay to Kootenay Inlet (see Chapter 14) are particularly beautiful. Cruising boats leaving Masset and crossing the north end of Graham Island may enjoy Naden Harbour, Pillar Rock, Langara Island and the old Haida villages of Yaku and Kiusta. You and your crew may enjoy a hike from these villages through the moss-decorated forest to Lepas Bay, before you turn your boat southward to enjoy the beauty of the island's rugged and remote west coast. Protected anchor sites can be found from Port Louis south. The rusting remains of the bow portion of the *Usats Clarksdale Victory* can be seen on the rocks of the southwest side of Hippa Island. This Army Transport ship was wrecked at Thanksgiving time 1947 while en route from Whittier, Alaska to San Francisco with the loss of 49 of the 53 men aboard.

From mid-May to mid-September you may find a floating sports fishing lodge and its helicopter landing float moored in any of the sheltered bays or inlets along this coast from Langara Island to Tasu Sound.

With Marble Island in sight you are about ready to enter Skidegate Channel. Watch for avid salmon and halibut anglers trying for the large spring or tyee salmon. A circumnavigation of either Graham or Moresby Island offers some of the best wilderness cruising in North America.

The exposed nature of a Hecate Strait crossing,

the remoteness of the islands, and the wildness of the rugged, infrequently visited shores of Haida Gwaii demand careful planning and vigilant seamanship. If you're accustomed to sailing in protected, well-charted waters, approach Haida Gwaii with care and preparation; this is an area where fuel, water, and phones are rare; where weather can change rapidly; where radio reception is spotty, and where charts do not show all the hazards.

You can reach Haida Gwaii from either Hecate Strait or Dixon Entrance. The shortest route leads across Hecate Strait to Skidegate Inlet from Larsen Harbour *(see comments in Chapter 12)* at the north end of Banks Island. If you plan to visit Gwaii Haanas National Park Reserve, you can head straight for Skidegate and the Haida Heritage Centre for your orientation.

With a trailerable boat, you can catch the large BC Ferry vessel from Prince Rupert for the eight-hour trip to Skidegate (staterooms and meals are available). Check the BC Ferries website for schedules: <bcferries.com>.

Then cross to Alliford Bay (a 20-minute ferry ride), and drive on logging roads to Moresby Camp, at the

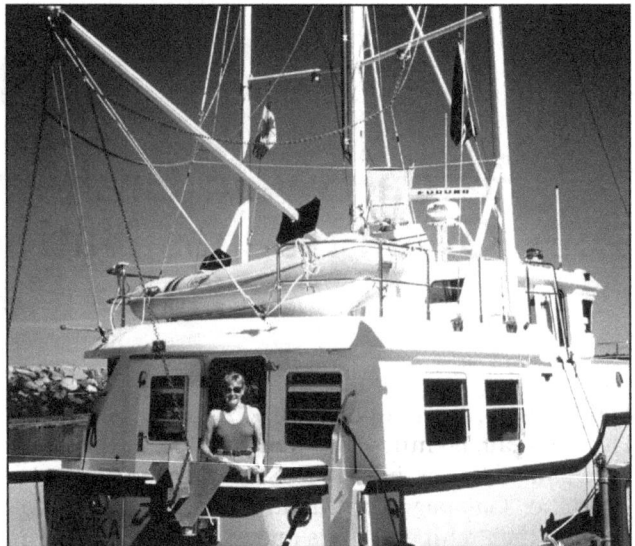

Sunny day in Sandspit

head of Cumshewa Inlet where you can launch and begin your adventurous trip. You can also put in at Masset and be able to reach the excellent fishing waters around Langara Island within a few hours. To

Haida Gwaii Reading List

The desire to visit the remote Haida Gwaii archipelago is frequently kindled by a magazine article displaying seductive photos of deserted anchorages and cultural relics returning to the forest. Once the daydreams end and actual preparations begin, the intrepid boater is faced with masses of data from numerous sources—a fleet of guidebooks that seem to be under constant revision, internet blog posts from other travelers, and invitations to cruising seminars and flotilla briefings. Safely visiting Haida Gwaii under your own command requires absorbing large amounts of data about weather, currents, and navigational hazards.

In order to develop a more profound understanding of the islands—beyond mere charts and logistics—the traveler should consider reading background material. Start with learning about the culture of the Haida people as reflected in their stories and lore, and appreciate its manifestation in their art. Deepen your understanding by reading some of the writings of early European explorers and settlers of Haida Gwaii, while remembering that time has changed the perceptions of the modern reader. It is both enjoyable and instructive to look at these islands through the eyes of earlier inhabitants and visitors. Below is suggested reading list.

Raven Steals the Light, Bill Reid and Robert Binghurst, 1996, University of Washington Press. Bill Reid was a renowned Haida artist. His drawings illuminate 10 stories of Haida mythology retold by Canadian poet Robert Binghurst.

The Golden Spruce, John Vaillant, W.W. Norton, 2006. Described in more detail in a sidebar below, this is the story of an ex-logger turned environmentalist who cut down an iconic tree in order to draw attention to the destruction of B.C.'s old-growth forests. This is a compelling book written in a vigorous style.

During My Time: Florence Edenshaw Davidson, a Haida Woman, Margaret Blackman and Florence Davidson, University of Washington Press, 1992. Born in Massett in 1896, Florence Davidson was the daughter of noted Haida chief Charles Edenshaw. This book is a narrative compiled from taped interviews in which she describes the culture of a bygone era, including female experiences not often captured in standard ethnography.

Ninstints, Haida World Heritage Site, George F. MacDonald, 1983, University of British Columbia Press. This is a guidebook to the village of the Kunghit Haida, which is now a UNESCO World Heritage Site. The book is an illustrated 60 page monograph with images of archeological reconstructions, photos of the remaining monumental poles, descriptions of village life, and a summary of European contact and its results.

Haida Eagle Treasures: Pansy Collison, Brush Education, 2017. Traditional Stories and Memories from a Teacher of the Tsath Lanas Eagle Clan. Pansy Collison, a Haida woman born and raised in Old Massett on Haida Gwaii, tells sto-

reach the west coast of Haida Gwaii via Skidegate Channel, you can launch near Skidegate, at Sandspit Harbour or Alliford Bay. Although it's possible to launch at Rennell Sound, a 4-wheel drive vehicle is recommended—the road is steep and rough!

The most favorable months for cruising Haida Gwaii are generally June, July and August, although other months can be good as well. Limited supplies, transportation, fuel, water and telephone service can be found in Masset, Port Clements, Daajing Giids, and Sandspit. Rental cars are available in Masset, Daajing Giids and Sandspit. The Sandspit Marina has fuel, water, pump out, showers and pay telephone. Parks maintains two water hoses in Gwaii Haanas; one opposite the west side of Shuttle Island and the other at Louscoone Inlet. *This water should be purified by boiling before use.*

Throughout most of the North Coast and Haida Gwaii, locals use Channel 06 as a "party line," where telephones are few and far between. In an emergency you *may* be able to summon local help more readily using Channel 06 than Channel 16, especially in areas of poor reception. Cell service is in and around the populated areas of Skidegate Inlet and Masset. With the imminent addition of cell service via low earth orbit systems there may soon be service throughout Haida Gwaii.

Before you head out to the Haida Gwaii by boat, you should submit a detailed cruising plan to Prince Rupert Coast Guard Radio; but be sure to close your plan on time—Coast Guard takes this seriously—we know!

Authors' notes: Please note that the preliminary soundings we recorded on our research vessel, *Baidarka*, as mentioned in our text and/or shown on our diagrams, have not been confirmed by CHS. The user must accept responsibility for their own verification. This is particularly important for the west coast of both Graham and Moresby islands, as well as for Dolomite Narrows, Louise Narrows and Skidegate Channel where groundings over the years have been all too common.

Réanne and I wish to acknowlege the contributions of Neil Carey of Sandspit, Moresby Island, for providing a great deal of accurate and updated local knowledge on many of the hazards and anchorages we describe in Chapters 13 and 14.

---

ries of her clan and community as well as personal narratives about her history and family. Haida Eagle Treasures embodies a strong Haida woman's voice offering a rare glimpse inside Haida culture.

Looking at Indian Art of the Northwest Coast, Hilary Stewart, 1979, University of Seattle Press. This book introduces the elements of indigenous art, describes their forms and cultural background, and includes some of the myths and legends shaping the motifs. This is an outstanding resource to enhance an appreciation of Northwest Coastal Art.

To the Charlottes, George Dawson's 1878 Survey of the Queen Charlotte Islands, edited by Douglas Cole and Bradley Lockner, University of British Columbia Press, 1993. The Canadian government sent the young but respected geologist George Dawson to the Queen Charlotte Islands in 1878 to inventory their resource potential. Dawson carried out a thorough survey of the islands, collecting geological samples and plant, animal, and fossil specimens. He also collected Haida artifacts and took some of the first photographs of Haida villages. Dawson was a trained observer, and an excellent writer. His journals capture his sympathetic impressions of a rapidly vanishing culture.

Exploration of the Queen Charlotte Islands, Newton H. Chittenden, 1984, Fireweed Enterprises. Originally published as: Official report of the exploration of the Queen Charlotte Islands for the government of British Columbia. Victoria, B.C., first published in Victoria, B.C. in 1884.

Chittenden was a veteran of the U.S. Civil War who became a professional explorer. In 1884, the government of B.C. commissioned him to spend several months assessing the Queen Charlotte Islands. He carried out his mission thoroughly, and wrote a report that is still enjoyable to read today. The report retells some Haida legends which Chittenden heard directly from the people he met, and objectively describes the cultural practices he observed.

The Ghostland People, Charles Lillard, Sono Nis Press, 1989. B.C. poet and historian Charles Lillard collected firsthand accounts of exploration and discovery in the Queen Charlotte Islands from the time of early fur traders to the period of settlement by farmers, fishermen, loggers, and miners.

Just East of Sundown, Charles Lillard, Horsdal and Schubart, 1995. A history of Haida Gwaii compiled from primary sources, this book tells the stories of key people in the islands' history.

The Queen Charlotte Islands, Volume 1: 1774-1996, Volume 2: Places and Names, by Kathleen Dalzell, Bill Ellis, 1988. The daughter of pioneering settlers, Kathleen Dalzell grew up on the Charlottes. Her narrative brings the history of the islands alive with tales and photographs. The second volume details more than 2,000 place names, retelling fascinating and little known stories with warmth and personal anecdotes.

—LW

Hecate Strait

Between Queen Charlotte Sound & Dixon Entrance
Position (Bonilla Island Lt.): 53°29.56'N, 130°38.24'W
Position (White Rocks Lt.): 53°38.07'N, 130°38.90'W
Lawn Point Light: 53°25.43'N, 131°54.99'W

Boats heading southbound from Alaska must clear Canadian Customs in Prince Rupert.

The shortest and most direct crossing of Hecate Strait, 55 miles, begins at Browning Entrance. East of Banks Island, the Spicer Islands complex, near Beaver Passage, is a well-protected anchorage used frequently as a convenient jumping-off place, with a number of coves where you can wait for favorable weather to make the crossing. Larson Harbour is our favorite anchor site before crossing Hecate Strait although kelp may lay across the entrance from time to time.

Some boats prefer to cross Queen Charlotte Sound directly to the south end of Moresby Island—a distance of 110 miles from Cape Scott to Cape St. James—or to cross from Ivory Island to the south end of Moresby—also 110 miles. Since these southern routes are exposed to swell and changing sea conditions, they are more appropriate for offshore sailboats.

Before you cross Hecate Strait, carefully monitor the weather forecasts, wait until the combined swell and sea height is expected to be one meter or less, then leave very early in the morning. That way you can anticipate a much smoother ride. If conditions deteriorate, you can turn around before the halfway point. Bonilla Island, a MAREP station, is happy to give you updates when they are monitoring Channel 69.

Before heading out, be sure your vessel is in proper condition and that you are self-sufficient for your stay. Fuel is not available at Skidegate Landing, but is available at Daajing Giids. At Daajing Giids, the fuel dock is adjacent to Queen Charlotte Harbour Authority docks. Shopping is limited to Daajing Giids, Skidegate, Sandspit, Port Clements, and Masset.

Neuron II approaching Lawn Point

Rose Point

(Graham Island)
28 mi NE of Masset

Rose Spit, which extends 8 miles northeast of Rose Point, has shallow water on its eastern side and currents tend to be quite strong in this area. Impressive "boiling" waters heap up when prevailing northwest winds blow counter to spring tides; stay away from the shoal areas during such conditions, or during strong southerlies. It helps to pick a waypoint, such as a mile northwest of whistle buoy C25 (a total of 9 miles or more off Rose Point), to ensure an adequate margin of safety. Although some kayakers and sport-fishing boaters report having made safe passage inside buoy C25, the overfalls create heavy turbulence, and it is risky to do so even in fair weather. Heading from Prince Rupert to Masset, you might consider staying overnight in Edith Harbour on Dundas Island which is only 51 miles from Masset (31 miles from Rose Point).

Lawn Point

(Graham Island)
51 mi W of Larsen Harbour
Entrance (NE): 53°18.94'N, 131°54.79'W
Position (Lawn Pt. Buoy "C14"): 53°25.58'N, 131°53.23'W

Lawn Point is the leading mark when heading for Skidegate Inlet, then Daajing Giids or Sandspit Harbour from the north end of Hecate Strait. Close off Lawn Point, marked by a series of buoys, is the entrance channel leading south behind the shallow 10-mile spit, which protrudes north from Sandspit.

Caution: The Prince Rupert Ferry and other high-speed traffic going both to and from Daajing Giids, Skidegate, or Sandspit Harbour, all converge at Lawn Point.

We find the direction of the currents in Hecate Strait somewhat confusing. During prevailing northwest summer winds, a smooth lee extends east of Graham Island for several miles.

Skidegate Inlet

(Hecate Strait)
Between Sandspit and Daajing Giids

When entering Skidegate Inlet from Hecate Strait, the safe course heads west for Lawn Point, then turns south at buoy C18. The safest, deepest water course would be to turn south at buoy C16. To enter this deep-water channel behind Dog Fish Banks the route passes north of Bar Rocks.

Shingle Bay (Skidegate Inlet)
Position (public wharf): 53°15.24'N, 131°49.39'W

Shingle Bay, known locally as Welcome Point, lies on the south side of the entrance to Skidegate Inlet, between Spit Point and Onward Point. A public wharf at the head of the bay is closed and in disrepair.

Homes and modest commercial buildings rim the shoreline of Shingle Bay, at the western edge of Sandspit village and Sandspit Airport—Haida Gwaii's main airport.

Vessel operators anchoring here should be aware of the great tidal range. During southeast gales, fishing vessels frequently find shelter by anchoring in Shingle Bay. When southeast weather occurs, recreational boaters may prefer moorage in Sandspit's small boat harbor, Sandspit Marina. The harbor monitors VHF channel 73.

Sandspit Marina (Moresby Island)
1.5 mi W of Sandspit
Entrance: 53°14.31'N, 131°51.47'W

Sandspit Marina lies 2 miles southwest of Spit Point on the east side of Haans Creek. A Canadian Coast Guard vessel and crew are based here. The harbor has well maintained moorage docks for 80 vessels. The moorage area is dredged to 9.8 feet and 16 feet at the outer dock. A crane—maximum lift 10,000 pounds—is located at the unloading dock. Berths have 15, 30, 50, and 100 amp electrical service and fresh, potable water. Diesel fuel and gasoline are available at a float, as is a holding tank pump station. Tel: 250-637-5700;

Showers, restrooms, long-term parking for vehicles and trailers, and launching ramp facilities are available. Fuel for trailered boats is available at the Cardlock facility 1/8 mile west of the harbor. Boaters have access by foot or taxi to the Sandspit Airport,

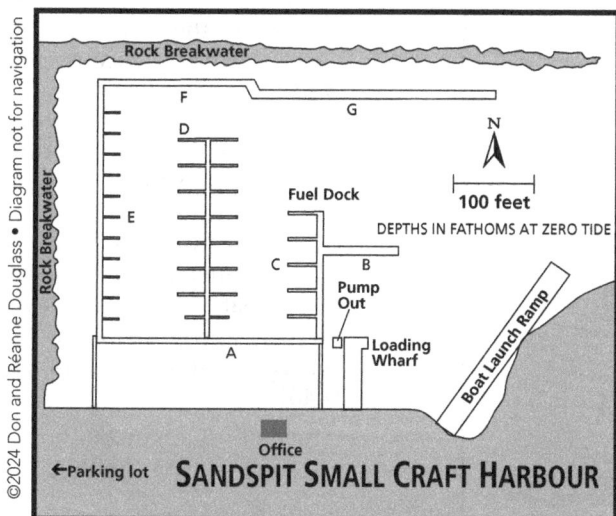

Baidarka *at Sandspit Marina*

stores, hotel, restaurants, facilities for recreation and small boat marine repairs, as well as to the Visitors Center and Gift Shop.

Alliford Bay (Moresby Island)
5.2 mi SW of Sandspit Marina
Entrance: 53°13.19'N, 132°00.58'W
Anchor: 53°12.61'N, 131°59.31'W

The ferry landing ramp lies a quarter of a mile south of the public float. The car ferry *Kwuna* runs from Alliford Bay to Skidegate (called Skidegate Landing by many old timers) on Graham Island, daily from 0720 to 1810. Anchor south of the ferry dock, avoiding private mooring buoys and the float-plane dock.

Anchor in 6 fathoms, clear of the float-plane area and mooring buoys; unrecorded bottom.

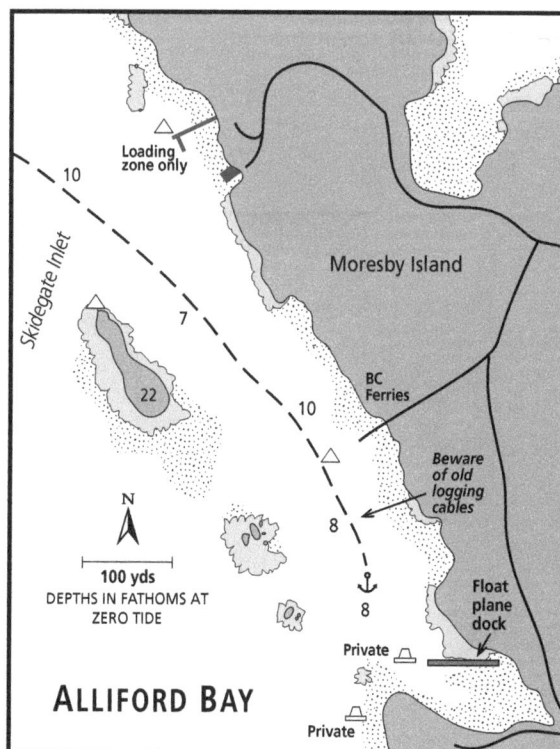

Public floats, Queen Charlotte Harbour Authority at Dajing Giids

Skidegate Landing (Graham Island)
E of Daajing Giids
Entrance: 53°14.63'N, 132°00.60'W
Ferry dock: 53°14.71'N, 132°00.65'W

It's about a kilometer's walk northeast from Skidegate Landing to the attractive Haida Museum and Heritage Centre. If you prefer not to enter Daajing Giids, Skidegate (the Haida village) has a co-op where you can find ample provisions. The most accessible fuel is available at the Fast Fuel LP dock located in Daajing Giids near the Queen Charlotte Harbor docks.

Daajing Giids (Bearskin Bay)
7.8 mi W of Sandspit Marina
Entrance (breakwater): 53°15.14'N, 132°04.45'W
Fast Fuel LP Float: 53°15.18'N, 132°04.53'W
Anchor (Bearskin Bay): 53°15.07'N, 132°04.73'W

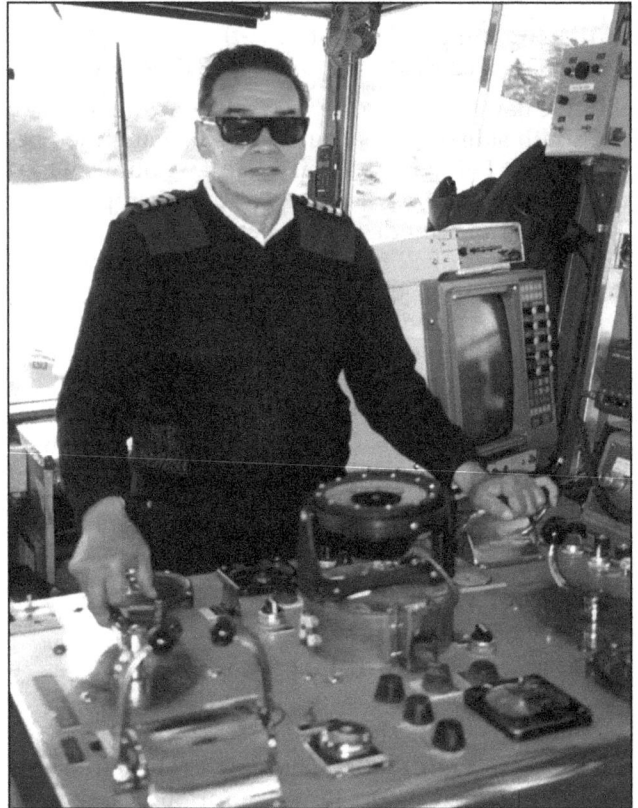

BC Ferries crossing to Skidegate Landing

Daajing Giids is the administrative hub for Haida Gwaii. The public floats offer visiting yachts a chance to re-supply and visit the attractive Visitors' Information Centre on Wharf Street. The main shopping center, credit union, ATM, post office, RCMP, and churches are west of the floats. Cell service is available. Car rentals are available here, and a number of guide services offer tours to out-of-the-way attractions.

Facilities for pleasure craft are limited here; the floats are often full and rafting is encouraged. Bearskin Bay has adequate space for anchoring over a wide, flat bottom, 0.2 mile southwest of the end of the breakwater, avoiding the shoal area west of the breakwater.

Fast Fuel LP float is located just west of the Queen Charlotte Harbour public floats. Gas and diesel. Attended daily mid-June to late August; open year-round for call-outs. (250) 559-4611

Anchor (Bearskin Bay) in 2 fathoms, mud and shell bottom with good holding.

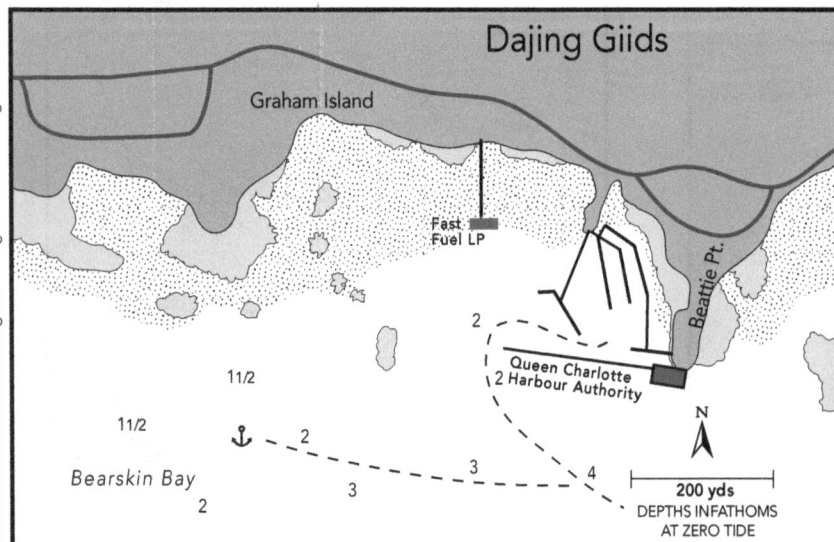

©2024 Don and Réanne Douglass • Diagram not for navigation

Dajing Giids
Graham Island
Fast Fuel LP
Beattie Pt.
2
Queen Charlotte Harbour Authority
1
2
11/2
11/2
⚓ 2
Bearskin Bay
2
3
3
4
N
200 yds
DEPTHS IN FATHOMS AT ZERO TIDE

Haida canoe at Haida Heritage Centre near Skidegate

Withered Point Coves (Lina Island)

3 mi SW of Daajing Giids
Anchor (E of spit): 53°13.22′N, 132°08.32′W
Anchor (W of spit): 53°13.33′N, 132°08.88′W

Lina Island, on the southwest side of Bearskin Bay, separates Bearskin Bay from Kagan Bay, both of which have a number of anchor sites. Lina Island has private homes on its east end, one of which is marked by a modern totem on the beach. Kagan Bay, to the west of Lina Island, has a number of anchor sites. Two petroglyphs are on tidal rocks on the west side of Lina Island.

You can find good protection during prevailing northwesterlies in the small, shallow cove just north of Withered Point, at the southwest tip of Lina Island. There's a 200-foot wooded hill on the south side of this cove, connected to Lina Island by a low, narrow spit with a landing beach of gray pebbles, sand and mud. In its shallow portion, east side of the spit, the flat bottom of 1 to 2 fathoms is covered with eelgrass. There is room for two to three moderate-sized boats; avoid the shallow drying portions of both coves. If there is southeast chop, anchorage can be found on the opposite (west) side of the spit.

Anchor (east of spit) in 1.5 fathoms, over sand with grass; very good holding.

Anchor (west of spit) in 1 to 2 fathoms over mud; very good holding.

Kagan Bay (Graham Island)

3.8 mi SW of Daajing Giids
Entrance: 53°12.85′N, 132°08.60′W

Kagan Bay connects Bearskin Bay to the east, and Skidegate Channel to the south, with Long Inlet to the west. This is an area of smooth water, full of intimate anchorages and abundant wildlife. The area to the north on Graham Island is slowly recovering from extensive clear-cutting done years ago. The northeast quadrant of the bay is still used as a log booming area. The mountain to the west is where the Haida quarried argillite for their carvings. A low grade of hard coal was once mined near Anthracite Point.

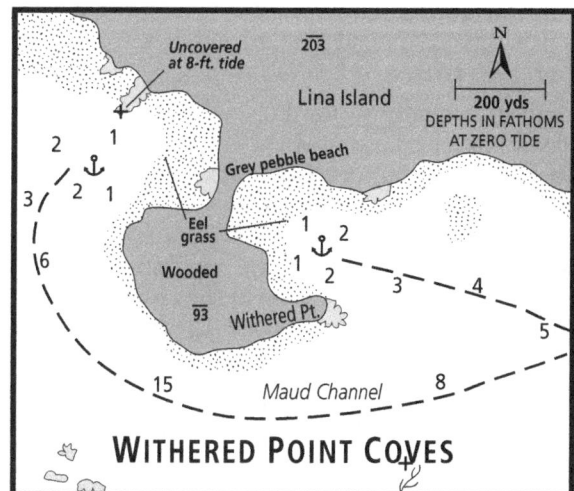

WITHERED POINT COVES

Christie Bay (Graham Island)

5.8 mi SW of Daajing Giids
Entrance: 53°12.60'N, 132°13.18'W
Anchor: 53°12.32'N, 132°12.85'W

Christie Bay, which offers the best protection for small craft in Kagan Bay, is one of our favorites. Well protected from all weather, it has nice views of the high peaks to the northwest. A fine, clear salmon stream meanders through this broad valley. There is swinging room for several boats. The easily-accessible landing beach of sand and cobblestones is backed by second-growth trees. Christie Bay and the mud flats to the south are favorite hangouts for ducks and shore birds.

The entrance to Christie Bay lies south of Canoe Point. The small passage to the west can be used by moderate-sized vessels; minimum depth is approximately 2 fathoms. Entering from the east there is a small-boat passage immediately west of Legace Island. Stay within 75 yards of its west end with 3 fathoms minimum.

Anchor in 2 fathoms, black sand and mud bottom, very good holding.

Anchor Cove (Graham Island)

6.7 mi SW of Daajing Giids
Entrance: 53°12.40'N, 132°14.49'W
Anchor: 53°12.38'N, 132°14.67'W

Anchor Cove, a small bight between Pier Point and Random Point on the far west side of Kagan Bay, provides good protection from strong westerlies. The small landing beach is steep-to.

Anchor in 2 fathoms over soft gray mud with shells; good holding.

Hallet Island Cove (Graham Island)

1 mi NW of Christie Bay
Entrance: 53°12.95'N, 132°14.30'W
Anchor: 53°13.10'N, 132°14.40'W

We call the shallow, flat-bottomed cove between Hallet Island and the drying flat south of the outlet to Saltchuck Creek, "Hallet Island Cove." Anchor on the west side of the wooded island. This is a good place from which to explore the surrounding islets and flats at the outlet of the creek. The cove is somewhat exposed to south winds.

Anchor in 2 to 3 fathoms over mud, shells, and patches of cobble and grass; fair-to-good holding.

Long Inlet (Graham Island)

6.5 mi SW of Daajing Giids
Entrance: 53°12.10'N, 132°14.00'W

The entrance to Long Inlet is encumbered with a number of small islands, reefs, and rocks, with drying flats along the shore. The head of the inlet is deep and steep-to with excellent views of the jagged peaks to the northwest. This inlet is a good place to explore by kayak or dinghy. Temporary fair-weather anchorage can be found along either side of the entrance.

Saltspring Bay (Graham Island)

0.5 mi SW of Christie Bay
Anchor: 53°11.88'N, 132°13.04'W

Saltspring Bay is mostly a long shallow bight that offers little in the way of protection; however, in fair weather, you can anchor temporarily just off the drying flats at its north end. The flats here and to the north and south are excellent places for viewing the local bear population. At low tide you can often find a mother bear with her cubs, combing the beach and turning rocks over, teaching the cubs to look for "goodies."

Anchor in one fathom or less over a combination of sand, gravel and mud; fair-to-good holding.

East Narrows (Skidegate Channel)

8.4 mi SW of Daajing Giids
Entrance (E): 53°08.72'N, 132°13.60'W
Entrance (W): 53°09.26'N, 132°18.02'W

East Narrows, Skidegate Channel, should not be at-

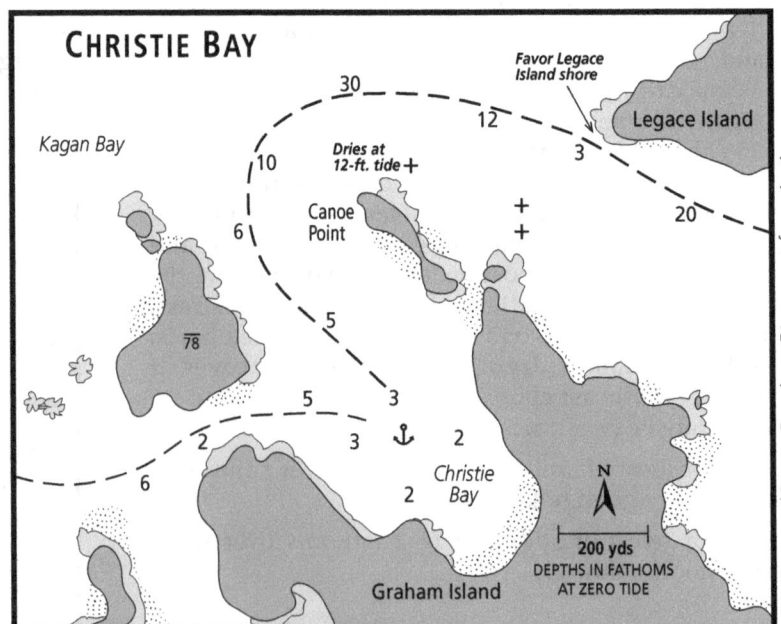

CHRISTIE BAY

Kagan Bay

Favor Legace
Island shore

Legace Island

Dries at
12-ft. tide

Canoe
Point

Christie
Bay

Graham Island

200 yds
DEPTHS IN FATHOMS
AT ZERO TIDE

©2024 Don and Réanne Douglass • Diagram not for navigation

tempted without large scale charts. You must feel comfortable in risky situations that require high performance and be willing to make your own judgments.

Note: For details on transiting Skidegate Channel, please see Chapter 14.

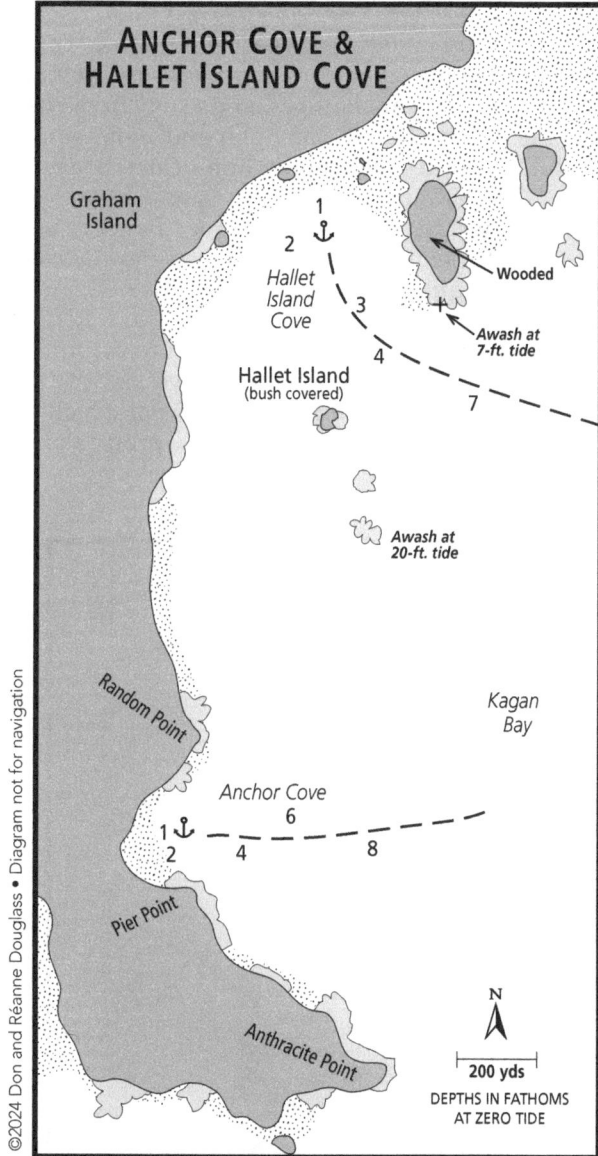

ANCHOR COVE & HALLET ISLAND COVE

Graham Island

Hallet Island Cove

Wooded

Awash at 7-ft. tide

Hallet Island (bush covered)

Awash at 20-ft. tide

Random Point

Kagan Bay

Anchor Cove

Pier Point

Anthracite Point

N

200 yds

DEPTHS IN FATHOMS AT ZERO TIDE

©2024 Don and Réanne Douglass • Diagram not for navigation

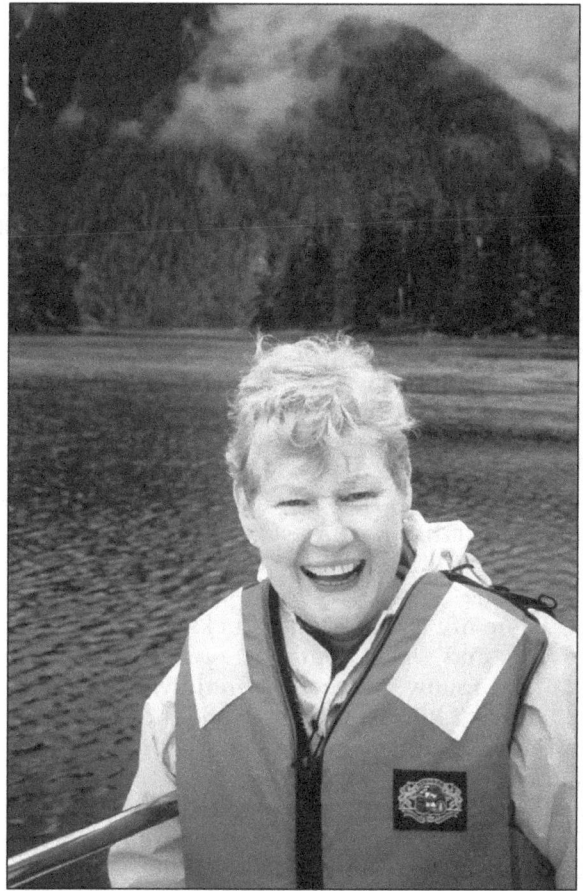

Smooth water agrees with Réanne

Unloading a day's catch

Hope is alive in Daajing Giids

MORESBY ISLAND'S EAST COAST

When you head south from Skidegate Inlet toward Gwaii Haanas National Park Reserve, you must first negotiate the classic, shallow bar that extends north from Sandspit all the way to Lawn Point and Rose Point. If you have a large vessel or one with deep draft, you may want to exit Skidegate Inlet by heading north to Lawn Point, then due east with 3 fathoms minimum depth. Others with a shallow draft vessel may cross two miles south of Bar Rocks. With local knowledge, boats of shallow draft may cross immediately north of the tidal sand/gravel north of the Sandspit airport.

If you head east from buoy C19, 5 miles northwest of Spit Point, you will cross the shoal in a little over 2 fathoms at zero tide. We have also crossed from a point 3.5 miles northwest of Spit Point (position: 53°18.50'N, 131°52.20'W) with just over one fathom at zero tide. The bar is steep-to and is essentially flat. There are a few isolated rocks, so check charts carefully and watch your drift or cross track error. Plan and follow your route carefully, since there is as much as 2 knots running on the shoal and no visual signs to guide you. The route south follows the 6-fathom curve as far as Gray Point, then stays offshore a mile or so, in 8 to 15 fathoms, until reaching Cumshewa Island and turning into Cumshewa Inlet. Avoid the rocks north of Gray Point.

Although both Sheldens and Gray bays appear to offer good temporary relief from southerly weather, their entrances are encumbered by submerged rocks and reefs and lots of kelp. Safe shelter is an illusion—neither locals nor *Sailing Directions* recommend using these bays.

Copper Bay; Sheldens Bay; Gray Bay
(Moresby Island)
Position (Copper Bay): 53°10.10'N, 131°46.54'W
Position (Sheldens Bay): 53°09.44'N, 131°43.76'W
Position (Gray Bay): 53°07.19'N, 131°40.75'W

Copper Bay is home to a small fishing lodge (Copper Bay Lodge, tel: 1-877-846-9153). Otherwise, as Neil Carey said in one of our earlier editions, "I don't know of anyone using Copper, Sheldens, or Gray bays for overnight anchorages, and rarely in the daytime. These bays are all too open and dangerous if the wind is from any combination of north, east or south. Sport salmon fishermen in small boats often troll these waters, especially Copper Bay. I've seen a salmon seiner wrecked in Copper Bay—a creek robber. An acquaintance of ours lost his homemade craft in Gray Bay."

The concrete boat launch ramp on the northeast side of Copper Bay is not always useable due to southeast rollers. The hard sand flats, which are shallow on about a quarter-tide, can be pretty sloppy.

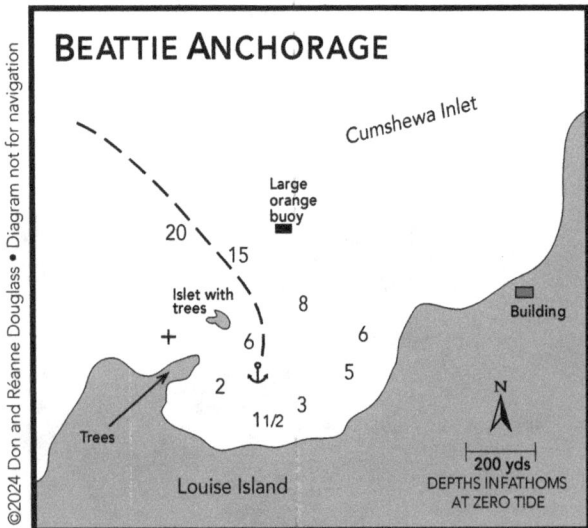

BEATTIE ANCHORAGE

©2024 Don and Réanne Douglass • Diagram not for navigation

Cumshewa Inlet

Large orange buoy

20

15

Islet with trees

8

Building

6

6

5

2

3

1 1/2

Trees

Louise Island

200 yds
DEPTHS IN FATHOMS
AT ZERO TIDE

N

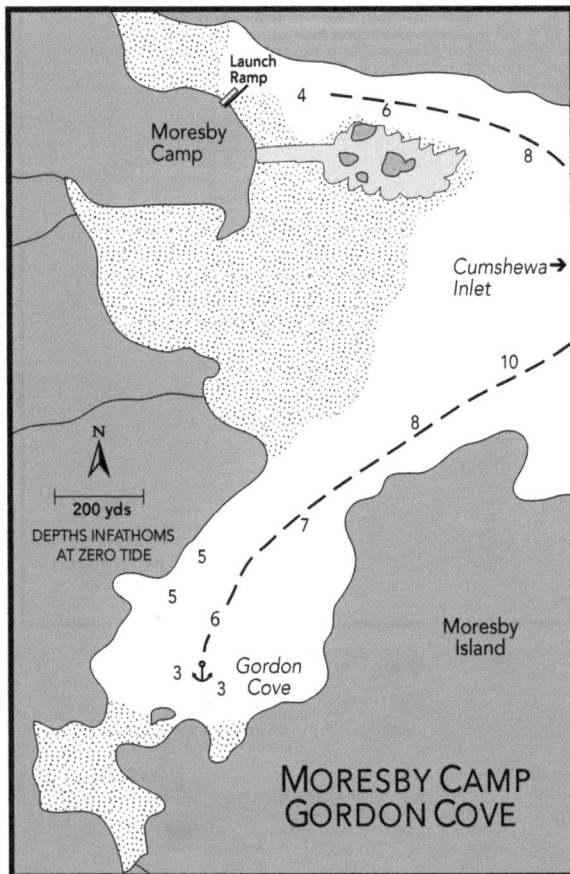

©2024 Don and Réanne Douglass • Diagram not for navigation

Launch Ramp

Moresby Camp

4

6

8

Cumshewa Inlet

10

8

N

200 yds
DEPTHS IN FATHOMS
AT ZERO TIDE

5

5

7

6

3

3

Gordon Cove

6

Moresby Island

MORESBY CAMP
GORDON COVE

Author with bones, Copper Bay

Cumshewa Inlet
(Moresby Island)
16.2 mi SW of Sandspit
Entrance: 53°01.40'N, 131°35.42'W

Cumshewa Inlet is entered between Cumshewa Island and Cumshewa Rocks to the southeast. Favor the north shore to clear Fairbairn, McLean, and Davies shoals on your port. When off McCoy Cove, follow the range lights, passing the green buoy on McLean Shoal to port. The large kelp beds on Fairbairn Shoals do a good job of knocking down southerly chop, and making Cumshewa Inlet a welcome haven in southerly weather.

Cumshewa (Cumshewa Inlet)
1 mi W of McCoy Cove
Position: 53°02.40'N, 131°40.96'W

Behind Haans Islet a few weathered and leaning totems amidst second growth forest mark this old village site. This was once home of the Cumshewa—reported to be one of the fiercest of the Haida peoples. An attractive traditional style longhouse was constructed here in the summer of 2000. Ask for permission before entering the site, remain on trails, and avoid damage to fallen artifacts.

Beattie Anchorage (Louise Island)
Entrance: 53°01.59'N, 131°54.21'W
Anchor: 53°01.33'N, 131°54.25'W

Beattie Anchorage, at the northwest corner of Louise Island, has the first safe anchorage in Cumshewa Inlet in the bight about 1 mile southwest of Renner Point. Small craft will find very good protection from southerly weather; anchor nearby in the islets to the west. This has been the site of logging and log dumping in the past. The surroundings were clearcut in the past and second growth is now filling in the bare spots. The landing beach is gravel.

Anchor in 2 fathoms over a mixed bottom of unknown holding.

Gillatt Arm (Cumshewa Inlet)
3 mi NW of Carmichael Passage

Gordon Cove at its west end is the most protected anchorage in the area.

Moresby Camp (Gillatt Arm)
0.65 mi N of Gordon Cove
Entrance: 53°02.80'N, 132°01.07'W
Public floats: 53°03.17'N, 132°01.29'W

Moresby Camp has a large parking lot, boat launch ramp and float used as a jumping off spot for small boats that are headed to South Moresby Island. A gravel logging road with numerous potholes connects to Sandspit via Alliford Bay. The nearby waters offer excellent salmon fishing due to the natural returns and enhancement in Pallant and Braverman creeks.

A shelter, picnic tables, and pit toilets are at Moresby Camp. Seven campsites are available and parking for vehicles.

Gordon Cove (Gillatt Arm)
15 mi W of Cumshewa Head
Entrance: 53°02.83'N, 132°01.03'W

Gordon Cove is a bombproof anchorage; the preferred anchor site is at the head of the cove. The cove is calm and quiet, with tree limbs extending over the water and no drift logs along the shore. Moresby Camp is out of sight to the northwest. Avoid the large shallow mud flat to the north when entering. Gordon Cove, whose shores are lined with second growth forest has great views of some of the tall peaks of Moresby Island. A service road that approaches the beach at the southwest corner of the cove is a good place to stretch your legs.

Anchor in about 4 fathoms over sand and mud with good holding.

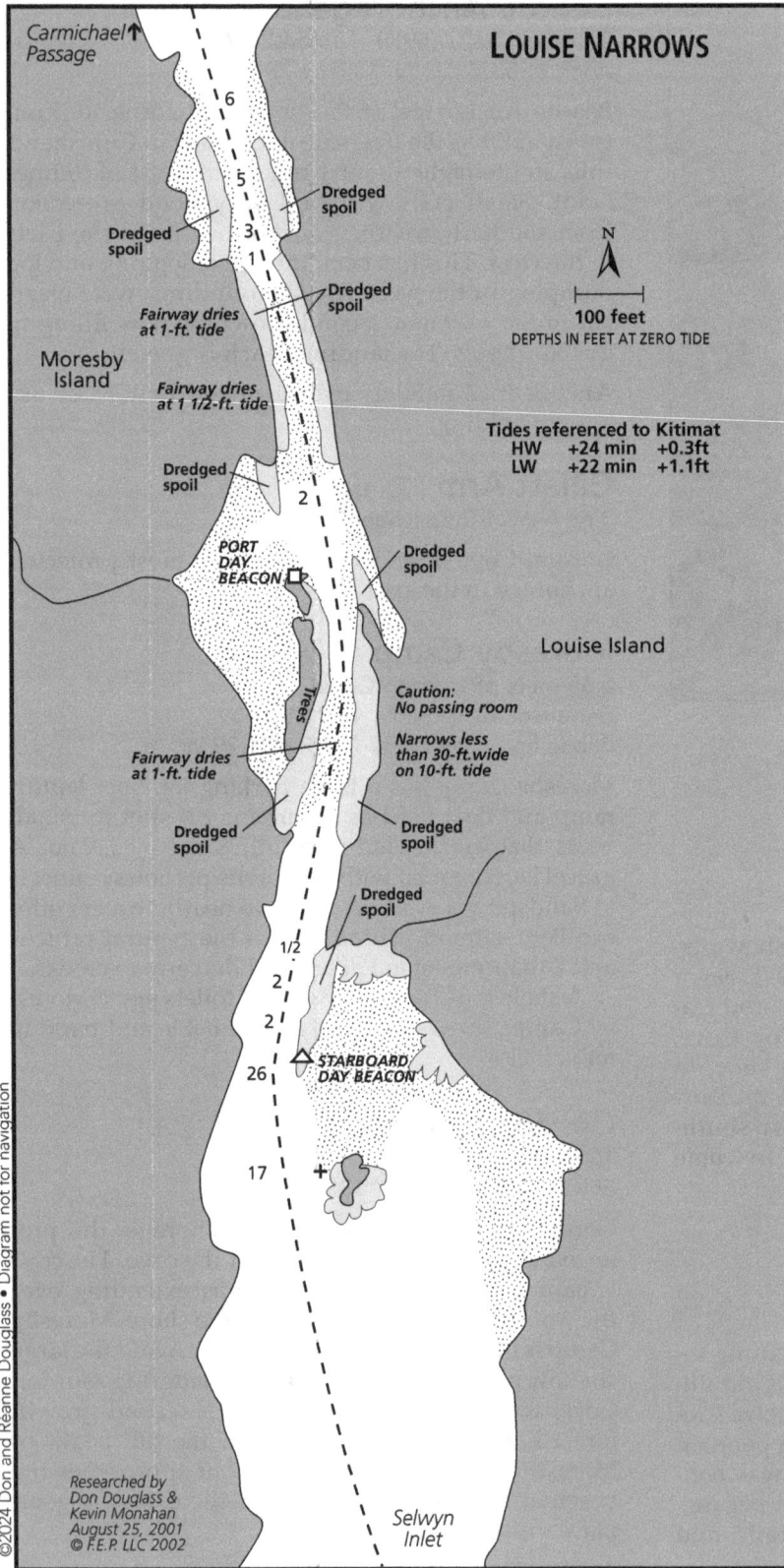

LOUISE NARROWS

Carmichael Passage

6
5
3
1

Dredged spoil

Dredged spoil

Dredged spoil

Fairway dries at 1-ft. tide

Fairway dries at 1 1/2-ft. tide

Moresby Island

Dredged spoil

2

PORT DAY BEACON

Dredged spoil

Louise Island

Trees

Caution: No passing room

Narrows less than 30-ft. wide on 10-ft. tide

Fairway dries at 1-ft. tide

Dredged spoil

Dredged spoil

Dredged spoil

1/2
2
2
26
17

STARBOARD DAY BEACON

N

100 feet
DEPTHS IN FEET AT ZERO TIDE

Tides referenced to Kitimat
HW +24 min +0.3ft
LW +22 min +1.1ft

Selwyn Inlet

Researched by
Don Douglass &
Kevin Monahan
August 25, 2001
© F.E.P. LLC 2002

©2024 Don and Réanne Douglass • Diagram not for navigation

Carmichael Passage (Moresby Island)

3.5 mi SE of Moresby Camp
Entrance (N): 53°01.19'N, 131°56.39'W
Entrance (S): 53°56.07'N, 131°54.13'W

Carmichael Passage is the first of several small-craft passages that provide a smooth-water route along the east side of Moresby Island. We have found Carmichael Passage to be nearly calm when southeast winds are blowing on the outside of Louise Island.

Water can be obtained from a nearby stream. The view from here is wonderful—high, thickly forested ridges with barren crowns.

Louise Narrows (Carmichael Passage)

7 mi SE of Moresby Camp
Entrance (N): 52°57.57'N, 131°54.30'W
Entrance (S): 52°56.57'N, 131°54.15'W

Louise Narrows, the small-boat passage between the west side of Louise Island and Moresby Island, is an interesting, narrow traverse in which the bottom can be followed visually all the way. The dredged channel seems to have filled in over the years. We measured as much as 1.5 feet above zero tide, as noted in the accompanying diagram, and the width of the channel is about 30 feet wide, with perhaps a bit more on the north end.

Once you are in the Louise Narrows channel, there is limited visibility and it's impossible to pass another boat (other than a dinghy) or to turn around. For this reason we recommend that each boat make a security radio call on Channel 16 before starting a transit to assure that there is no opposing traffic; be ready, also, to blow a loud horn if necessary.

The recommended time for traversing Louise Narrows is on a rising tide when the top of the dredged spoil banks are still visible; this way there is a clearly-defined dredged channel—more like a ditch—that you can easily follow. We have found the last of the flood flowing south at about 3 knots at the north end, then slowing to about half that near the treed islet. A painted arrow on the islet

Louise Narrows, heading north

Louise Narrows, north end looking south

Photo courtesy CHS, Pacific Region

reminds you to pass to the east side. A starboard-hand daybeacon is at the south entrance and a port-hand daybeacon on the north tip of the islet.

Gliding through this beautiful narrow channel, your bow watch will notice brightly-colored starfish on the bottom and large fish milling around.

Lagoon Inlet
(Moresby Island)
1 mi S of Louise Narrows
Entrance: 52°55.75'N, 131°54.46'W
Anchor (near pier): 52°55.76'N, 131°56.88'W

Lagoon Inlet, immediately south of Louise Narrows, is a place to wait for proper conditions in the narrows; it offers fairly good protection along the south shore when southeasterlies are blowing in Selwyn Inlet. This beautiful natural environment was last logged in 1963, but new growth has claimed the shores.

The salmon cannery is gone except for a few remnants and part of an old pier. There is an abandoned 30-foot wooden boat on the shore near the pier. Temporary anchorage can be found off the flat in front of the pier in about 8 fathoms.

For small boats that can safely enter it, the lagoon, west of the bottleneck and tidal rapids, appears almost bombproof; its sheltered waters have little fetch, even if the williwaws should come sweeping down the surrounding three thousand- to four thousand-foot peaks. The tidal rapids are shallow, rocky and crammed with bull kelp, so entrance should be attempted only at high-water slack. The irregular bottom at the entrance to the lagoon should be sounded by dinghy prior to entering. Bear often frequent the grassy flats at the head of the lagoon.

Anchor (near pier) in 7 fathoms over sand, gravel and mud bottom; fair holding. Caution: The bottom may still contain old bricks from the cannery and wire from the logging operation.

Anchor (lagoon) in 4 to 7 fathoms near the head; unrecorded bottom.

Kevin Monahan in Louise Narrows

S/V Takuli *waits at south entrance, Louise Narrows*

Photo courtesy of Neil Carey

Aerial of Lagoon Inlet looking east

Sewell Inlet (Moresby Island)
2.5 mi S of Louise Narrows
Entrance: 52°54.08'N, 131°53.80'W

Sewell Inlet, like Lagoon Inlet, cuts westward, deep into Moresby Island's spine. Its head is less than 3.5 air miles from Newcombe Inlet. One may hike the old logging road to Newcombe Inlet in Tasu Sound.

Trotter Bay (Moresby Island)
3.5 mi W of Louise Narrows
Entrance: 52°53.10'N, 131°52.84'W
Anchor: 52°55.87'N, 131°53.17'W

Trotter Bay is a tiny, cozy bay on Moresby Island that is slowly reverting to its natural condition since the log dump was abandoned. The bottoms may contain slash and a few underwater logs or cables from days past. When a southeaster blows outside, low clouds scud along the north shore and the trees sway, but there is little effect on the more protected south shore. An old "donkey" sits near the entrance on the south shore and the small beach is backed with alder trees.

Small craft can find good protection from westerlies, as well as protection from all but strong southeast winds, deep in the cove close along the south shore. You can avoid most chop by anchoring just off the drying flat on the south side of the cove. Avoid the shoal on the west and north sides, and any patches of kelp.

Anchor in 1 to 2 fathoms over soft mud, grass and small rocks; good holding with a well-set anchor.

Selwyn Inlet (connects Louise Narrows with Dana Passage)
S of Louise Island
West entrance: 52°51.09'N, 131°40.00'W

Selwyn Inlet, the east-west passage on the south side of Louise Island, connects Hecate Strait and Laskeek Bay to Carmichael Passage and Dana Inlet. Cecil Cove and Pacofi Bay, southwest of Point Selwyn, offer anchorage as do Rockfish Harbour on the north side of Selwyn Inlet (Louise Island) and Thurston Harbour on the south (Talunkwan Island).

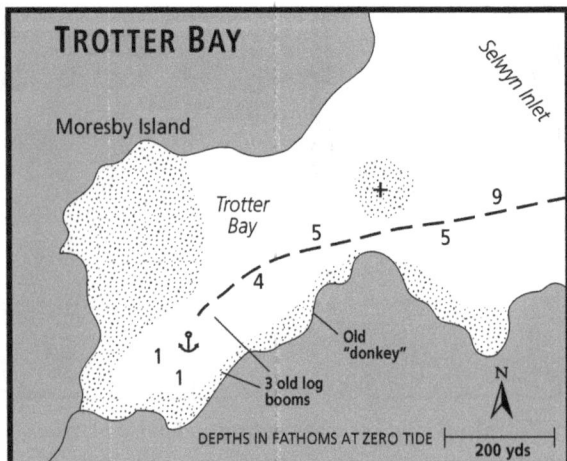

©2024 Don and Réanne Douglass • Diagram not for navigation

TROTTER BAY

Moresby Island

Selwyn Inlet

Trotter Bay

9

5

5

4

+

1

1

Old "donkey"

3 old log booms

N

DEPTHS IN FATHOMS AT ZERO TIDE   200 yds

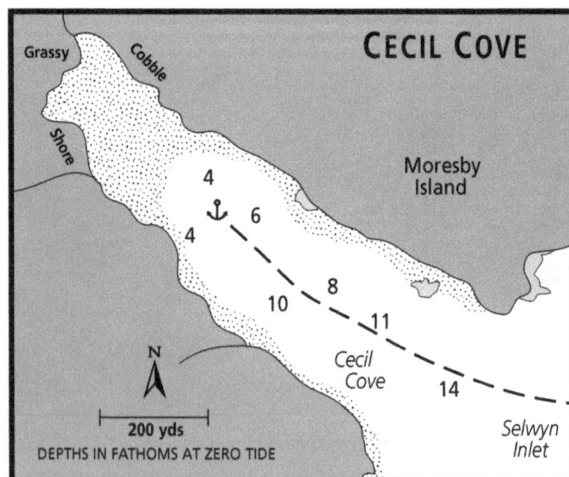

©2024 Don and Réanne Douglass • Diagram not for navigation

CECIL COVE

Grassy   Cobble

Shore

Moresby Island

4

4   6

10   8

11

N

Cecil Cove

14

200 yds

DEPTHS IN FATHOMS AT ZERO TIDE

Selwyn Inlet

Cecil Cove
(Moresby Island)
5.5 mi S of Louise Narrows
Entrance: 52°51.32'N, 131°51.60'W
Anchor: 52°51.64'N, 131°52.27'W

Cecil Cove is a convenient anchor site in prevailing westerlies. In strong southerlies, however, 2- to 3-foot chop funnels into the cove along with gusts. In easterly winds, favor the north shore to minimize chop. You can anchor anywhere off the drying mud flats, or farther out in 8 to 10 fathoms. The drying mud flats have a cobble shore and grassy beach. Watch for occasional deadheads in the cove.

Anchor in 4 to 6 fathoms over mud with good holding.

Pacofi Bay (Moresby Island)
1 mi W of Dana Passage
Entrance: 52°50.43'N, 131°51.71'W
Anchor: 52°50.14'N, 131°52.84'W

Pacofi Bay is a large, wide bay open to easterlies with a number of rocks and shoals. To avoid these hazards consult large scale charts of the area.

The Moresby Explorers float camp in Crescent Inlet is the last possible emergency communication and transportation connection for southbound boats until Rose Harbour. We have seen fishing boats take shelter from southeast storms at the northwest corner of Dana Passage on the south side of Beatrice Shoal in about 6 fathoms, as well as in a small indentation on the east side of Dana Passage.

Anchor (north of Locke Shoal) in 5 to 10 fathoms over mud; unrecorded holding.

Rockfish Harbour (Louise Island)
3.5 mi NW of Thurston Hbr.
Entrance: 52°52.92'N, 131°46.76'W
Anchor: 52°52.95'N, 131°49.12'W

Rockfish Harbour, on the southwest corner of Louise Island, is a good anchorage with excellent fishing nearby and in the harbor. However, in southeast gales, a strong easterly tends to blow through the harbor and across the low spit at its head. If white caps in the western section of Selwyn Inlet are any indication, easterly chop in the harbor could be substantial under these circumstances.

Anchor in 6 to 8 fathoms over mud with good holding.

Thurston Harbour (Talunkwan Island)
4.5 mi W of Dana Passage
Entrance: 52°50.61'N, 131°42.80'W
Anchor: 52°50.48'N, 131°44.80'W

Our first run into Thurston Harbour was at 1300 hours after the barometer had fallen about 4 millibars in the morning. We sat out what became an unpredicted front with easterly storm-force winds of 50-plus knots. The 2- to 3-foot easterly chop and strong wind gusts blew foam that nearly covered the buoys (placed there at that time). But this was nothing compared to the 10- to 12-foot chop we had encountered off Protector Rocks as we beat our way into the harbor. While Thurston Harbour was noisy and bouncy, we didn't feel particularly uncomfortable. The next morning the harbor was flat calm, proving that rapid and unpredictable changes in weather can occur during any month! Since then we have heard from readers who thought Thurston was

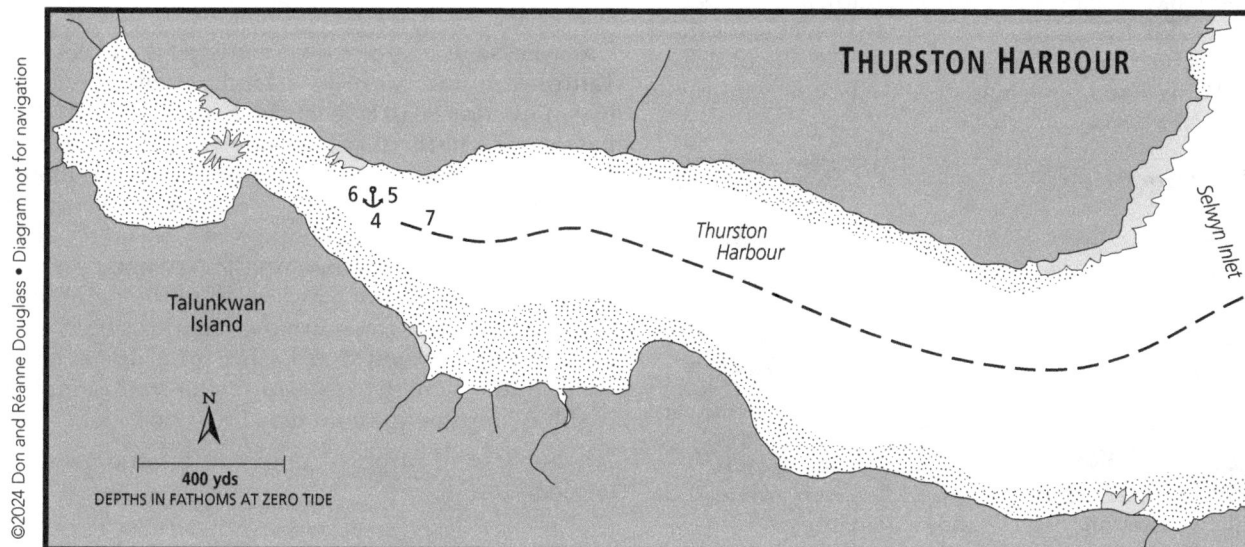

Thurston Harbour looking west

a terrible anchorage, so beware and make your own decision. We have heard that it can be difficult to get a solid anchor set in the western part of the bay, and that it's better closer to Thompson point.

The mountainsides of Thurston Harbour are recovering from prior logging activities and the overgrown logging roads are a good place to stretch your legs.

Anchor in 6 fathoms over sand and mud with good holding.

Skedans Bay (Louise Island)

5.4 mi S of Cumshewa Head
Entrance: 52°56.62'N, 131°36.86'W

Skedans Bay can be used as a temporary anchorage while you visit the Haida Historic Watchmen Site, located just west of Skedans Point, one mile north of the bay. Hail the watchmen on VHF 06 before going ashore. The bottom of the bay is irregular with isolated rocks and a lot of kelp patches. During calm weather, the tiny bay southwest of Skedans Point is also used as a daytime anchorage for small boats. Skedans Bay is exposed to strong southeast winds.

Listen for the "Drums of Skedans" when northeast seas beat into a sea cave on the east side of Skedans Point. Skedans Islands are a favorite haul-out spot for sea lions.

Pacific Voyager *and* Sea Cabana *rafted at Skedans*

Skedans totem pole

Dana Passage (Talunkwan Island)

6.5 mi S of Louise Narrows
Entrance (N): 52°50.26'N, 131°51.11'W
Entrance (S): 52°49.03'N, 131°49.90'W
Anchor (center of passage): 52°49.77'N, 131°50.46'W

Dana Passage is a narrow, scenic passage between Talunkwan and Moresby islands, easily navigated by small craft at all tide levels. Average depth of the passage is 10 fathoms. The narrows, which are about 100 yards wide, have a minimum depth of about 5 fathoms. High winds or chop seldom penetrate the passage. Temporary anchorage can be taken along the shore almost anywhere in the passage.

Along the east shore, just north of the point, midway along the narrows, are the remains of a burned barge. It is reported that local fishing boats sometimes find overnight or storm shelter in this shallow bight. A stern tie to shore may be a good idea.

Anchor (center of passage) in 3 to 5 fathoms; unrecorded bottom.

GWAII HAANAS NATIONAL PARK RESERVE/HAIDA HERITAGE SITE

The Gwaii Haanas National Park Reserve (NPR) is comprised of 138 islands having some 1,600 kilometers (nearly 1,000 miles) of shoreline, much of it exposed to the open North Pacific or turbulent Hecate Strait. Along the eastern side of Moresby Island, several small channels provide a smooth-water route to its south end.

Gwaii Haanas is a protected area. A permit and orientation are required in order to enter the park boundary. Contact the Haida Heritage Centre in Skidegate 250-559-7885; haidaheritagecentre.com; contact watchmen on VHF Ch 06 before going ashore at the five Haida Heritage sites of Skedans, Tanu, Windy Bay, Hotspring, and Anthony Island. Skedans Haida Heritage Watchmen Site is located outside of Gwaii Haanas Park boundary but requires a permit to visit the site.

The northern boundary of the Park lies along the center of Tangil Peninsula. Passing Porter Head, the swells from Laskeek Bay and Hecate Strait die off as soon as you enter Logan Inlet. Entering the Park directly from Hecate Strait, do not confuse Helmet Island in Dana Inlet for the similar-sized Flowerpot Island in Logan Inlet.

In Logan Inlet, you can use the shallow bight on the north side of Tanu Island for temporary protection from southerlies by tucking in close to shore. During periods of prevailing northwest winds, Stalkungi Cove can provide a central anchorage. However, a number of protected anchorages can be found along the Moresby Island shore, south of here, for the next several miles.

Logan Inlet (Moresby Island/Tangil Peninsula)
7 mi E of Dana Passage
Logan Inlet entrance (E): 52°47.73'N, 131°38.90'W

Logan Inlet, between Tangil Peninsula and Tanu Island, is entered from the east by passing to the north of Flower Pot Island and its nearby reef.

Stalkungi Cove (Tanu Island)
3.6 mi W of Flower Pot I.
Entrance: 52°45.75'N, 131°44.70'W
Anchor: 52°45.98'N, 131°44.90'W

If approaching Stalkungi Cove from the north, avoid the large reef off the point on the west side of the cove which dries on about a 17-foot tide; the reef is a major seal haul-out spot. The small landing beach is steep-to. Ashore, behind the beach in dense trees, notice a prominent burned-out stump, 9 feet wide—an example of the size of the old-growth trees. At this anchor site, you can use a stern tie to a log on shore. These logs give warning to avoid the cove in a strong southeast wind!

Anchor in about 5 fathoms over gravel and sand with fair-to-good holding.

Tanu (Tanu Island)
1.8 mi SE of Flower Pot I.
Position: 52°45.91'N, 131°36.74'W

This Watchmen site is located on the east shore of Tanu Island in Laskeek Bay. This early native village site of the mid-1800s had a population of 550 people, with 25 longhouses and 15 mortuary houses.

Anchor in fair weather off the beach in 35-50 feet. Holding is marginal and currents run strong. Swells roll in from Hecate Strait in northerly winds.

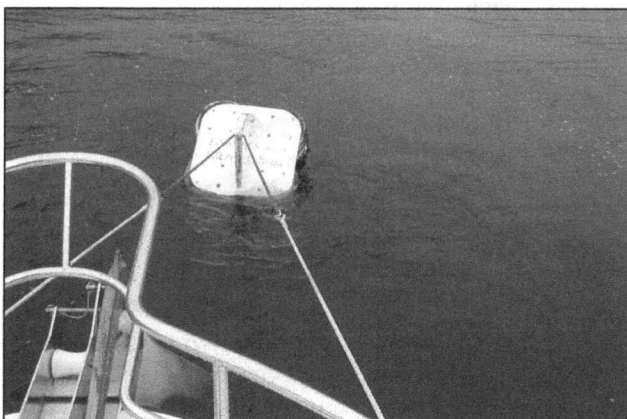

Testing buoy at Gordon Cove

Downed totem

Photo courtesy Pacific Voyager/Sea Cabana

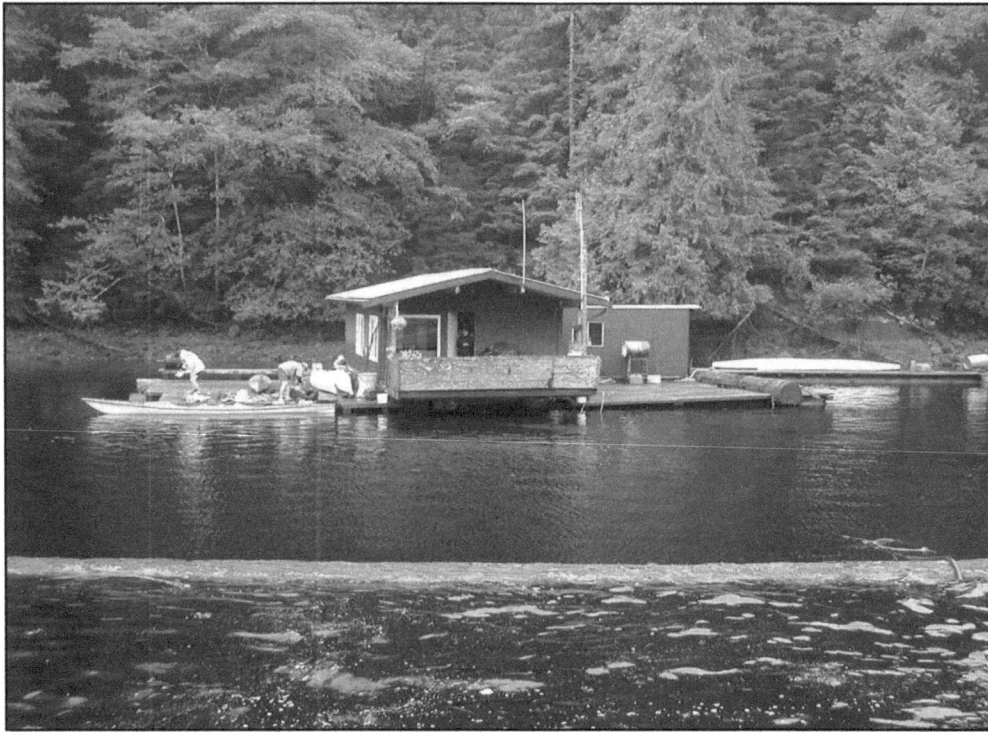

Moresby Explorers' float camp, Crescent Inlet

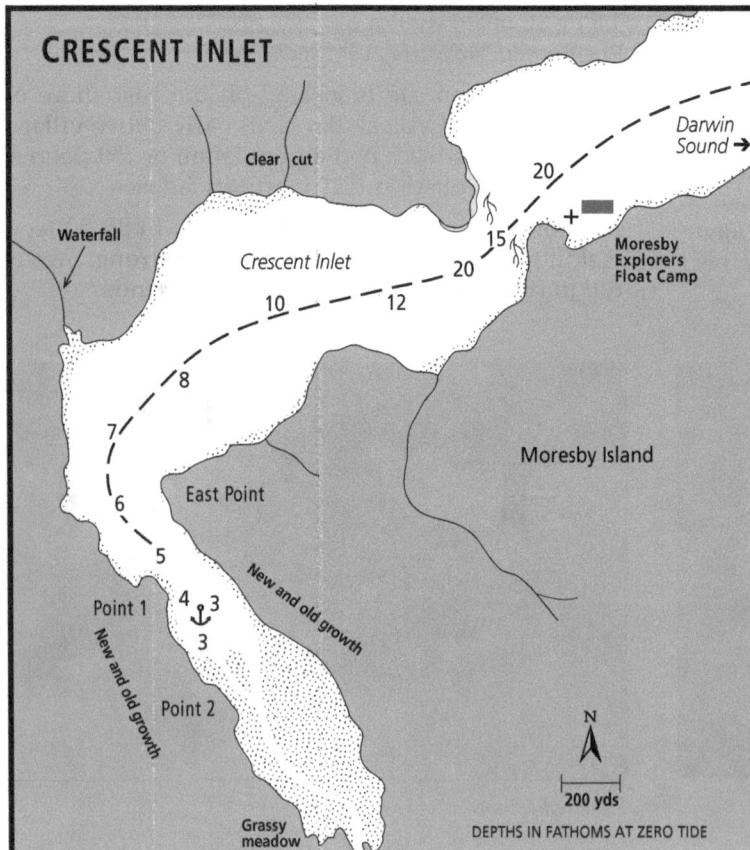

Crescent Inlet
(Moresby Island)
4 mi S of Dana Passage
Entrance: 52°45.03'N, 131°48.20'W
Anchor: 52°44.85'N, 131°52.95'W

Crescent Inlet is an attractive, winding inlet that offers isolation and a scenic environment deep in Moresby Island. We consider it the best bombproof anchorage south of Gordon Cove. The inner part of Crescent Inlet lies outside the Gwaii Haanas NPR borders. Moresby Explorers keeps an outstation here during the summer season, as indicated on the diagram, and you will generally find that the caretakers can provide excellent local knowledge; they can also make emergency radio calls.

The far head of the inlet offers solitude, a great view of old growth on all sides, a half-mile drying flat with a flowing stream, a grassy meadow, and high peaks in all directions—an excellent place for wildlife viewing. There are some beautiful old trees along the shore, but also indications of clearcutting. A dirt road crosses to Wilson Bay in Tasu Sound, then follows the shore to Newcombe Inlet where it crosses back over to Sewell Inlet.

At high water, it's easy to confuse the recommended anchor site. Two small points extend from the west shore. Point 1—about 0.5 mile south of the prominent waterfall, has two trees growing nearly horizontal to the water. Look for the anchor site south of this point—the drying flat before Point 2 is steep-to and dries at low water. Williwaws may blow off the peaks to the south, but chop should be minimal with the exception of high tide when fetch increases considerably. However, the shores show no signs of chop damage or driftwood.

Anchor in 3 fathoms over a flat mud bottom, with very good holding.

Klunkwoi Bay
(Moresby Island)
2 mi S of Crescent Inlet
Position: 52°43.39'N, 131°48.82'W

Anna Inlet
(Klunkwoi Bay)
2.5 mi S of Crescent inlet
Entrance: 52°42.92'N, 131°49.70'W
Anchor: 52°42.27'N, 131°50.53'W

Anna Inlet is a beautiful, small inlet perfect for cruising boats: good views of the high peaks in all directions; tall alders grow among second-growth evergreens, and a drying flat becomes a grassy meadow at low tide.

In mid-bay, the Klunkwoi Rocks are marked with a private cement pillar not indicated on the chart. The narrow entrance can be navigated without difficulty, and there is swinging room for a number of boats. The bottom is a little deep—10 fathoms—until the steep-to shore. Fifty feet from shore you may find your boat in 20 feet of water, so a stern tie is a good idea. We found excellent anchorage in 8 fathoms with more swinging room, 100 yards from shore. Although the cove on the west shore is well protected, it proved to have a rocky bottom with poor holding.

The old shake trail to Anna Lake near the stream on the northwest shore is not recommended. Just northeast of the entrance to Anna Inlet is the site of the abandoned settlement of Lockeport. Miners prospected, staked claims, drilled and blasted in this area, off and on from 1907 to 1988, without locating a worthwhile body of ore.

Anchor in 6 to 8 fathoms over brown mud with shells; very good holding.

McEchran Cove
(Moresby Island)
0.7 mi E of Anna Inlet
Entrance: 52°42.81'N, 131°48.85'W

McEchran Cove, immediately east of Anna Inlet, is full of rocks, reefs and kelp. Despite its kelp, we had a good lunch stop here, anchored just south of Raven Island. It's an interesting place to explore by dinghy or kayak.

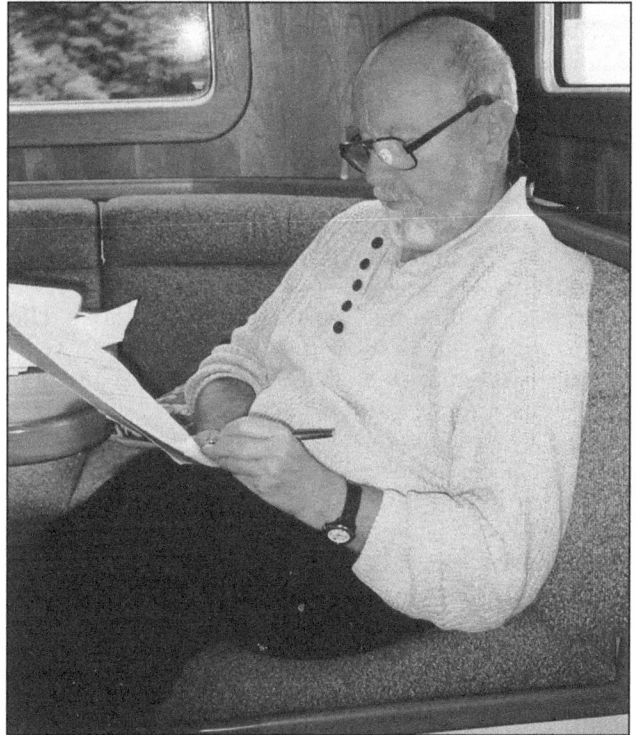

Don recording the day's observations

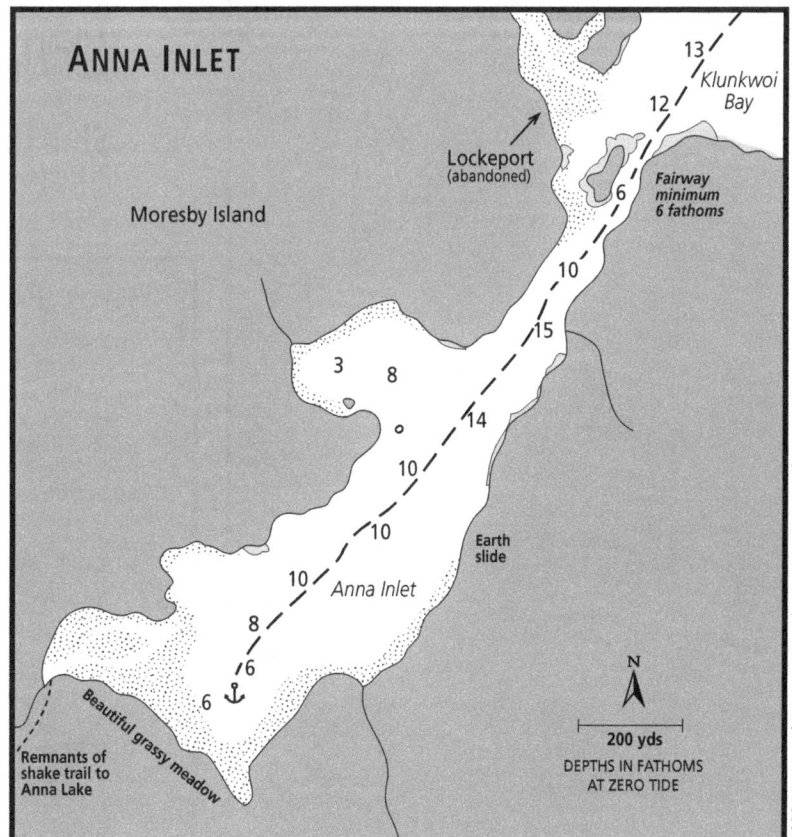

ANNA INLET

Klunkwoi Bay

Lockeport (abandoned)

Fairway minimum 6 fathoms

Moresby Island

Earth slide

Anna Inlet

Remnants of shake trail to Anna Lake

Beautiful grassy meadow

N

200 yds

DEPTHS IN FATHOMS AT ZERO TIDE

©2024 Don and Réanne Douglass • Diagram not for navigation

Echo Harbour (Moresby Island)

3.5 mi SE of Crescent Inlet
Entrance: 52°41.99'N, 131°45.88'W
Anchor: 52°41.57'N, 131°45.86'W

Well-protected Echo Harbour, along the smooth-water route south, makes a good stop and access is easy. The high peaks are picturesque and the landlocked inner cove is charming. When entering the harbor, favor the east shore in the narrows where depths run from 8 to 10 fathoms; the west shore is shoal. The mud flats at the head of the bay are steep-to with small grassy margins. While some small boats anchor in the inner cove at the head of Echo Harbour—paying due regard to tide levels—most stay outside and row in for a look.

On shore you can find evidence of an old homestead and several apple trees. You can enjoy a walk in the open forest behind the apple trees. But *beware*—bear are active in the mud flats and evidence of their presence can be found everywhere; they fish in the small waterfall at the head of the cove.

Anchor (harbor) in 6 fathoms over a mud bottom with good holding.

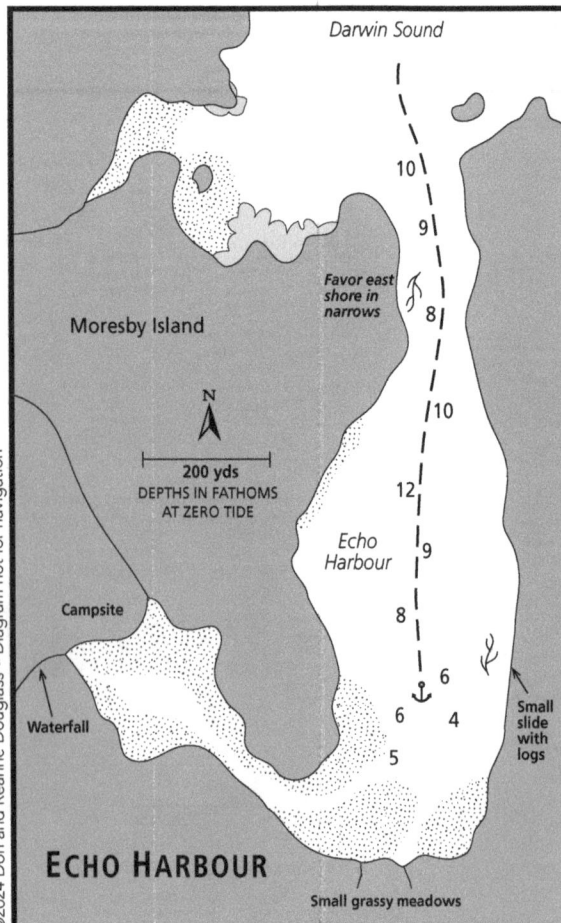

Shuttle & Hoya Passages

(Moresby/Lyell Islands)
E & W of Shuttle Island

Hoya Passage on the west side of Shuttle Island has a water hose, and a public float.

Hoya Passage, Freshwater Cove

(Moresby Island)
2.5 mi SE of Echo Harbour
Entrance: 52°40.05'N, 131°43.44'W
Anchor: 52°39.95'N, 131°43.71'W

"Freshwater Cove" is our name for Hoya Passage Cove, where welcome water flows continuously out of a large hose on the sizeable detached cement float on the west side. This is the only convenient place to get water south of Skidegate Inlet. Although the water tastes good, we recommend treating it. Freshwater Cove is a must stop; it may be the only time you tie to a float in the Park. If you plan to stay overnight, clear the float and anchor just to the south. Fishing, charter and cruising boats are likely to stop for water at any time. Swinging room is limited in the cove, and current during heavy runoffs is substantial. Approaching Freshwater Cove from the north, avoid a drying rock, 0.3 mile north of the cove near the Moresby shore.

Anchor in about 6 fathoms over sand and gravel with kelp; fair holding.

Shuttle Island (Shuttle Passage)

2.1 mi SE of Echo Harbour

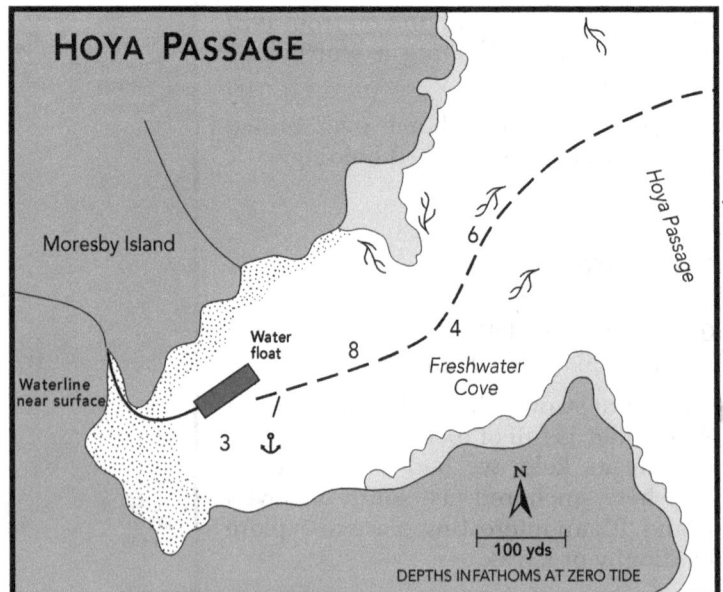

Lyell Bay (Lyell Island)
5 mi SE of Echo Harbour
Entrance: 52°39.31'N, 131°39.53'W
Anchor 52°38.94'N, 131°38.76'W

Lyell Bay is an indentation on Lyell Island on the east side of Shuttle Passage. Anchor near the head of the bay, avoiding the rocks and kelp. We have found the bay comfortable in moderate to strong southeast winds.

Anchor in about 8 fathoms over an irregular bottom with kelp; fair holding.

Bigsby Inlet (Moresby Island)
3.1 mi S of Echo Harbour
Entrance: 52°36.87'N, 131°41.53'W

Darwin Sound connects Hoya and Lyell passages to Juan Perez Sound and Hecate Strait. Bigsby Inlet, to the west, is steep-sided and deep throughout.

Reportedly, the stream that empties into Darwin Sound one mile northwest of Bigsby Point is a back-up source of water. This lake-fed stream, which is approachable at high water, can be found in the southwest corner of the unnamed cove.

Kostan Inlet (Moresby Island)
5 mi S of Freshwater Cove

Entrance: 52°35.31'N, 131°40.56'W
Anchor: 52°34.82'N, 131°42.24'W

Kostan Inlet is the first of a number of unusually beautiful, intimate, and intricate inlets and coves between Darwin Sound and Dolomite Narrows. The shoal narrows of Kostan Inlet are alive with a variety of colorful starfish, sea urchins, sea cucumbers, intertidal mollusks, and other beguiling marine life.

South of Darwin Point a residual swell from Juan Perez Sound can be felt. With winds from the southeast, this can be uncomfortable until you reach the lee of Burnaby Strait. Kostan Inlet is well protected and appears to be bombproof, with no sign of chop or serious winds. Gusts may swoop down from the surrounding high peaks but, in general, you never know what's happening outside.

The outer inlet has an irregular bottom with isolated patches of kelp. The inner inlet is totally landlocked and feels like an inner sanctum. The narrows is navigable for most cruising boats at upper half of neap tides, and near high-water slack at spring tides. We found a narrows-flooding current of 1.5 knots, 2 hours after a neap tide low water.

Approaching the narrows, stay mid-channel, avoiding the kelp off the two large bare rocks on the west shore. Head for what we call "Bread Rock" (it looks like an uncut loaf of bread). Pass within 20 feet of Bread Rock on a heading to pass mid-channel

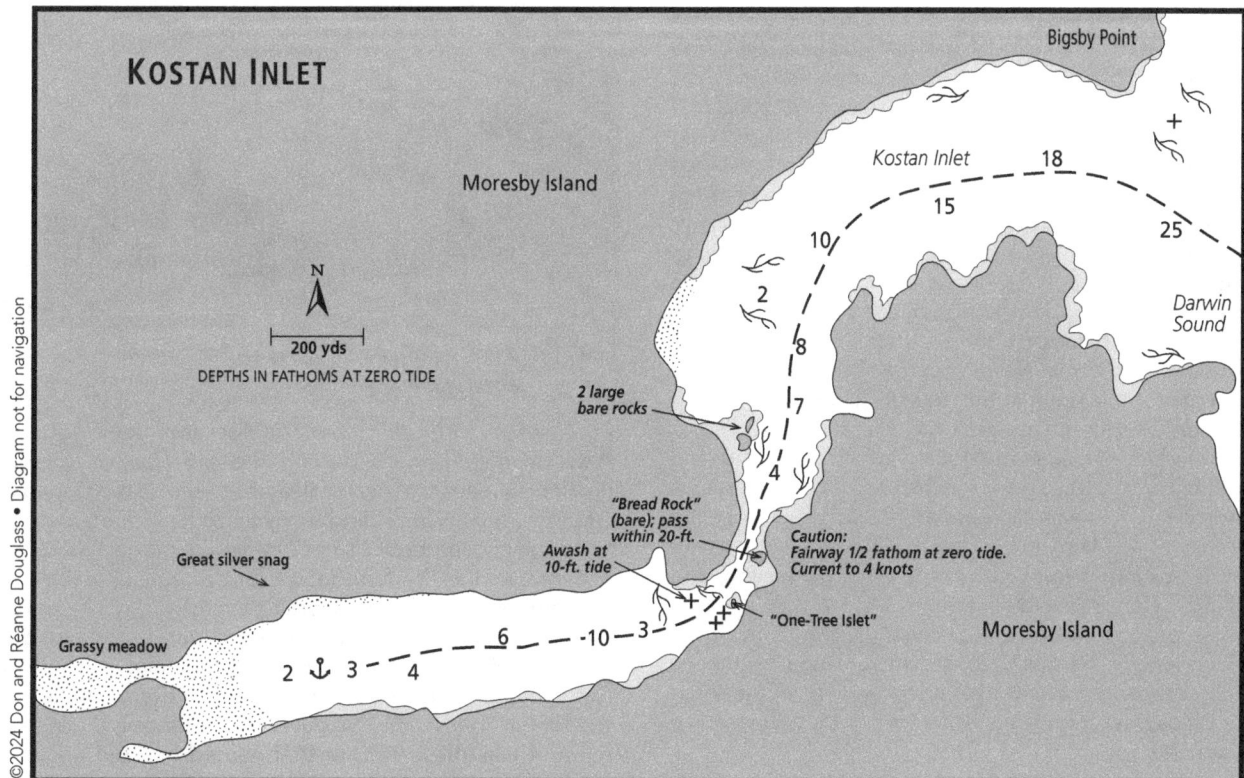

between "One Tree Islet" and a rock to starboard, awash on a 10-foot tide. We found a minimum fairway depth of about one-half fathom just north of Bread Rock. There is a gradual deepening to 3 fathoms as the inlet opens up. The depths are reasonable for anchoring anywhere in the inlet, and we prefer to anchor mid-channel near the head, abeam a giant silver snag with a split top which is on the north wall.

Inside Kostan Inlet, you will find a dramatic wilderness of striking proportions. Tall peaks with bare, slate-gray slopes and wind-carved bushes testify to strong westerlies on the San Christoval Range and Barry Inlet, less than 3 miles away on the west coast. If it is perfectly calm, the shoreline rocks are mirrored in the water, creating fascinating patterns and designs. In the stillness, you can hear many distant streams hidden in the rain forest, as they tumble down the steep mountainsides. In the evening, you may see Sitka deer grazing on the bank of the grassy meadow.

Anchor in 2 to 3 fathoms over brown mud bottom with big clamshells; very good holding.

Kostan Point Cove
(Darwin Sound)
5.4 mi S of Echo Hbr.
Entrance: 52°35.05'N, 131°40.42'W
Anchor (small boats): 52°34.92'N, 131°40.21'W

"Kostan Point Cove" is what we call the small cove immediately west of Kostan Point. This cove is open to the north, but somewhat protected by a line of kelp stretching from the island to the east shore. The east nook is for small boats; the west nook for large boats. The cove, generally out of the southeast swell of Juan Perez Sound, is useful only as a temporary stop in fair weather. This is a very good place to wait for optimal tide conditions before entering Kostan Inlet.

An alternative, Stevenson Cove, one mile to the southeast, which is deep and steep-to, with no flat bottom or shelf as shown on the chart, might be useful in a southeast storm, if you had a strong shore tie to a big tree.

Anchor in a 2- to 4-fathom hole just off the drying flat over a bottom of sand, kelp and eelgrass with poor-to-fair holding.

George Dawson and A Few Moresby Island Place Names

Eminent scientists and politicians have been commemorated in the names of landforms around the world, and even in features on other planets. Repeated memorials to Darwin and Huxley, among others, give a glimpse into the world view of the 19th century explorers and mappers who wished to acknowledge scientific inspiration as well as political and financial sponsorship. Nonetheless, it is a little surprising to sail into one of the world's most remote archipelagos to find inlets and islands named after a series of great scientists—Darwin Sound, Huxley Island, and Logan Inlet, among many others. These particular features were named by the Canadian geologist, surveyor, and anthropologist George Dawson, who has himself been commemorated in a series of place names.

Dawson was born in Nova Scotia in 1849. He contracted tuberculosis of the spine at the age of 11, which left him a hunchback. Despite his physical handicaps, he excelled in private studies. He entered McGill College, studying and publishing the results of geologic field research while still an undergraduate. He was then awarded a scholarship to the Royal School of Mines in London, U.K., where he received intensive training in many aspects of geology, mining, and metallurgy. He also studied natural history with Thomas Huxley, a proponent of Darwin's theories. Dawson's career was founded on his ability to accumulate and synthesize scientific observations and his understanding of the interrelationships between natural history, geology, and resource development.

Skidegate Native Village of the Haida tribe in the Queen Charlotte Islands, 1878.

Photo by George Dawson. By permission: Library and Archives Canada/Natural Resources Canada fonds/PA-037756.

Dawson worked as a naturalist and geologist with the Canadian party surveying the U.S.-Canada international boundary. He then took a position with the Canadian Geologic Survey, mapping many areas in western Canada. His original contributions to Canadian geology and natural history became the foundation for the agricultural development of the Canadian prairies, and his work formed the foundation for modern understanding of the complex geology of the Canadian Rocky Mountains and British Columbia. Dawson also reported on Native peoples with the intent of advising the government on policy development. It was these studies that earned him the unofficial

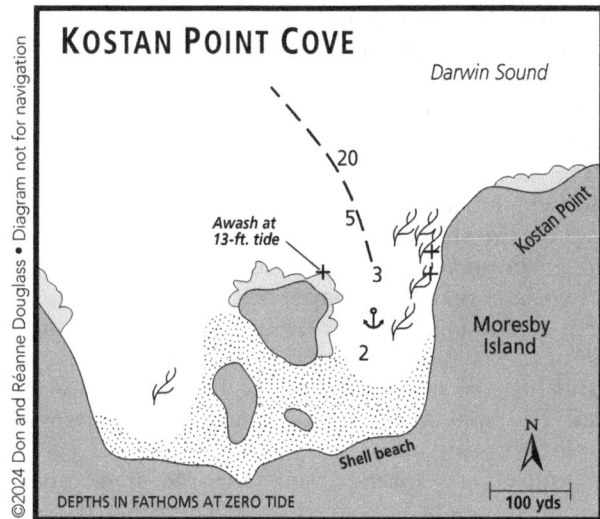

KOSTAN POINT COVE

Darwin Sound

Awash at 13-ft. tide

Kostan Point

Moresby Island

Shell beach

N

DEPTHS IN FATHOMS AT ZERO TIDE   100 yds

©2024 Don and Réanne Douglass • Diagram not for navigation

S/V Island Roamer, *Freshwater Cove*

Stevenson Cove (Moresby Island)

6.2 mi S of Echo Harbour
Entrance: 52°34.54'N, 131°38.87'W
Anchor: 52°34.29'N, 131°38.78'W

Stevenson Cove is a quick "in-and-out" anchorage with an unimpeded view northward into Hoya and Shuttle passages of Darwin Sound. Its small size should ensure privacy.

Anchor in the inner basin in 5 fathoms over sand; fair holding.

---

title of "Father of Canadian Anthropology."

In 1878, Dawson visited the so-called Queen Charlotte Islands (now Haida Gwaii) as part of a voyage surveying and charting the archipelago. He added ethnographic appendices, including a Haida vocabulary, as well as sketches and photographs, to his geologic report. This work reflected his great appreciation for the highly developed Native culture as seen in the art and design of the Haida villages.

After an expedition to survey the Yukon territory in 1887, Dawson's understanding of ore distribution and glacial deposition led him to predict the potential for commercial quantities of gold in the Yukon basin, inspiring an influx of mineral exploration. Although he never reached the Klondike, Dawson City, the heart of the 1898 gold rush, was named in his honor.

Dawson spent the remainder of his career dedicated to the cause of preserving Canadian artifacts in Canada, rather than allowing them to be dispersed to foreign museums. His legacy also includes the names of the many inlets and islands which Dawson charted and named for geologists and scientists who inspired him. Some of Dawson's place names on Moresby Island's east coast and their namesakes:

Dana Inlet: James Dwight Dana was a Yale professor of mineralogy and geology who mapped parts of the western U.S., including the Haro archipelago, now known as the San Juan Islands, on an expedition from 1838 to 1842. Dana developed much of the early understanding of Hawaiian volcanism. He was the author of standard textbooks on mineralogy still in use today. He was also a cousin of Richard Henry Dana, the author of the classic *Two Years*

Before the Mast.

Darwin Sound: Named for Charles Darwin, known for his contributions to evolutionary theory.

Hutton Inlet: James Hutton was a Scottish geologist who lived from 1726 until 1797. Known as the "Father of Geology," his observations and theories led to the theory of Uniformitarianism: the doctrine that the geologic processes active today have operated throughout geologic time and that these processes created the earth's features both ancient and modern.

Huxley Island: Thomas Huxley was a largely self-taught biologist and paleontologist who became a great advocate for Darwin's theory of evolution. He was the first to conclude that birds evolved from small carnivorous reptiles.

Logan Inlet: William Logan established the Canadian Geological Survey in 1842. He made many significant discoveries, and Mt. Logan, the tallest mountain in Canada at 19,551 feet, is named for him.

Lyell Island: Charles Lyell was one of foremost geologists of the 19th century. His book *Principles of Geology*, was published between 1830 and 1833. It supported and refined James Hutton's arguments for Uniformitarianism with the statement that "the present is the key to the past." He determined that the earth was older than the previously computed 6,000 years. Both Hutton and Lyell had a great influence on the young Charles Darwin, as he read their books while on the voyage of the *Beagle* from 1831 to 1836.

—LW

Juan Perez Sound (Hecate Strait)
18 mi SE of Dana Passage
Entrance (N): 52°34.24'N, 131°35.72'W

For many cruising boats, Juan Perez Sound is the heart of Moresby Island's east coast. There are many opportunities for interesting cruising and exploring among the several inlets. The refreshing hot springs of Hotspring Island lie on the east side of the sound. Afternoon or gale southeast winds can kick up a chop or southeast swell, but you are never more than a few miles from sheltered waters.

One Foot Rock Cove (Bischof Islands)
4 mi E of Kostan Inlet
Entrance (W): 52°34.37'N, 131°34.11'W
Anchor: 52°34.46'N, 131°33.54'W

"One Foot Rock Cove" is our name for the small bight in the center of the Bischof Islands. The islands, which are grouped in a small cluster, are fun to explore by dinghy, kayak and/or skin diving. The rocks, reefs and kelp beds are full of marine life. The anchor site should be used only in fair weather, and as a place to wait for optimal tide conditions before entering Beresford Inlet. Keep a careful lookout; the bottom is irregular and swinging room is limited. Some boats prefer the north nook, entered from the east, as shown in the diagram, where a shore tie may be useful.

Anchor southeast of "One-Foot Rock" in about 3 fathoms over a rocky kelp-and-sand bottom; poor-to-fair holding.

Beresford Inlet (Lyell Island)
0.5 mi N of Bischof Islands
Entrance: 52°35.39'N, 131°34.11'W
Anchor: 52°38.05'N, 131°37.20'W

Beresford Inlet is one of those places that appeals only to intrepid explorers looking for an experience we call "anchor at the ready" or "heads-up bow watch." The transit is not technically difficult, but information is minimal and the surroundings austere and foreboding. It may not be easy to retreat if you change your mind. The Careys, in typical understatement, call it simply "a unique experience." It is solitude *par excellence*.

The long, narrow inlet has a straight, mile-long drying section, which is relatively easy to navigate with sufficient tide. Its flat bottom of mud and large clam shells is clearly visible most of the time. However, remain alert and use caution at the north end of the flat where a wooded islet and a number of rocks choke the fairway. On a 15-foot tide, we found the minimum depth of the fairway to be 11 to 12 feet.

The course we followed was to approach the wooded islet, avoiding the two rocks off the eastern point on the starboard shore, pass about 75 feet east of the wooded islet, then resume a generally northeast course, reaching deeper water about 100 yards north of the islet. The rocks and reefs on the west side of the islet appear intricate and dangerous. We found little or no current in the inlet at high-water slack. The inlet could handle a number of boats with ample swinging room.

Small cedars interspersed with old silver snags line the shores of Beresford Inlet. The inner basin is pure wilderness with plenty of places to anchor. We anchored on the western side at the head of the inlet across from the two rocks on the east side. There may be a strong draw of southeast winds across the low pass to Lyell Bay to the northwest, but we found little evidence of strong winds or any chop in the inner basin.

Anchor in 4 fathoms over a brown mud bottom with shells and twigs with good holding.

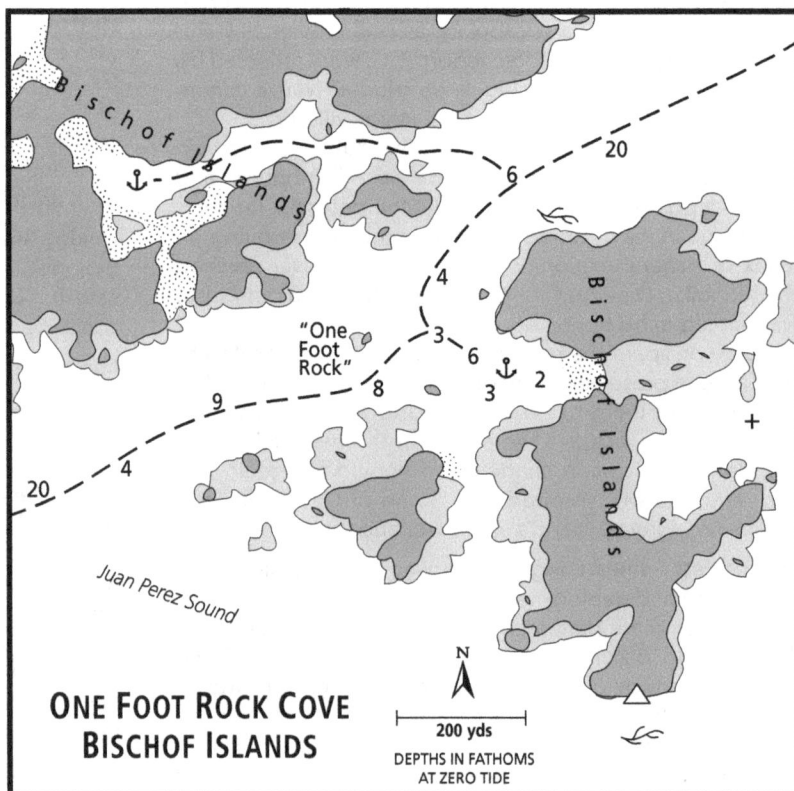

ONE FOOT ROCK COVE
BISCHOF ISLANDS

200 yds

DEPTHS IN FATHOMS
AT ZERO TIDE

©2024 Don and Réanne Douglass • Diagram not for navigation

Windy Bay (Lyell Island)
7 mi N of Hotspring Island
Position: 52°41.96'N, 131°26.41'W

Windy Bay, an exposed bight north of Gogit Point on the east side of Lyell Island, is the site of an old Haida village. In recent years, the Haida have built a modern longhouse, known as the Blinking Eye House, where Haida Watchmen welcome visitors in the summer. The shores surrounding the bay are known for their beautiful, old-growth spruce trees. Windy Bay is a fair-weather anchorage only. A beautifully carved and painted legacy pole was erected near the Windy Bay longhouse in *August 2013,* to commemorate the 20th year of cooperative management between the Government of Canada and the Council of the Haida Nation. This is the first monumental pole erected in Gwaii Haanas in 130 years.

Murchison Island (Juan Perez Sound)
3.5 mi E of Bischof Is.
Entrance: 52°35.88'N, 131°27.69'W
Buoys: 52°35.65'N, 131°28.00'W

Murchison Island, 3 miles east of the Bischof Islands, one mile northwest of Hotspring Island, has a well-protected and scenic cove on its north shore. The cove is surrounded by rocks and reefs and should be carefully entered from the northeast, avoiding the two shallow rocks nearly blocking the entrance. Anchorage can be found just northeast of the center of the cove. Current can be strong during parts of the tide cycle. On high tides, small boats can find a way out through the northwest "window." This area is popular as a haul-out for kayaks and other boaters waiting to visit the Hotspring Island. Two public mooring buoys are located in the south end of the island's cove.

Blinking eye house in Windy Bay

Hotspring Island (Ramsay Passage)
4.2 mi E of Bischof Is.
Position (springs): 52°34.45'N, 131°26.42'W
Anchor (E side): 52°34.60'N, 131°26.01'W

Hotspring Island has several of the most wonderful hot springs on the Pacific Coast of North America. Several rock-lined, natural hot pools are nicely maintained by Haida Watchmen, in residence during the summer season. Pools located uphill from the beach have unusually fine views and isolated surroundings. Boardwalks and trails connect the pools and a building with showers and changing rooms near the Watchmen house. Your friendly Haida guide will answer any questions you may have.

Visiting boats can anchor temporarily off the south shore in an exposed, rocky area. This marginal anchorage—which is the only site that gives you a chance to keep an eye on your boat—may become rough on a change of tide. We don't recommend leaving the mother ship unattended in this anchorage location. A more protected spot is located in the shallow area between Hotspring and House islands on the east side of the island. Visiting float planes land in this shallow passage, so be on the lookout.

Exploring the outdoor pool, Hotspring Island ˇ

Cabins at Hotspring Island

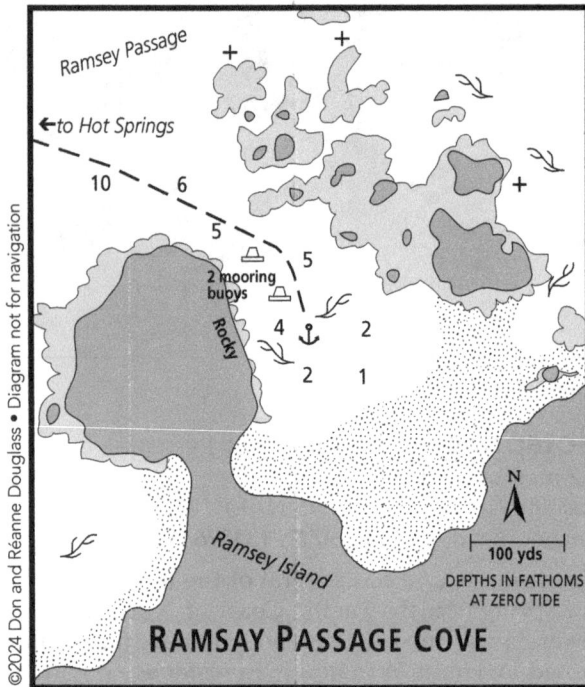

Mooring covered with kelp, Murchison Island

Ramsay Passage Cove (see below), the most protected place to leave your boat, involves a mile and a quarter crossing by outboard to Hotspring Island.

A trail that leads from the eastern shore through the center of the island directly to the springs is worth just the walk itself. The trail starts near the center of the eastern beach, and is marked here and there with white clamshells. The number of visitors on shore at any one time on Hotspring Island is limited to 12. Due to the increase in charter boat visitors, private cruising vessels should call the Watchman on Channel 06 to make arrangements to go ashore. The Watchman will notify you when it's your turn. A clothesline system for securing dinghies is located in front of the Watchmen house.

Anchor (east side) in 4 fathoms over stone and gravel; poor-to-fair holding.

Ramsay Passage Cove (Ramsay Island)
1.5 mi E of Hotsprings Island
Entrance: 52°34.47'N, 131°24.08'W
Buoys position: 52°334.40'N, 131°23.87'W

The reefs, rocks and kelp beds on the north side of Ramsay Passage Cove create good anchoring protection when you want to visit Hotspring Island. Small craft can work their way closer to shore through some kelp patches and find a clear 1.5-fathom hole. Two public mooring buoys are located in the cove on the northwest shore of Ramsay Island.

Anchor in 1.5 fathoms over a sand, mud and grass bottom with fair-to-good holding.

De la Beche Inlet (Moresby Island)
Entrance: 52°32.13'N, 131°36.89'W

De la Beche Inlet contains lots of surprises. Skittagetan Lagoon and the head of the inlet are especially interesting to explore by kayak and dinghy. Sac Bay has its own special environment.

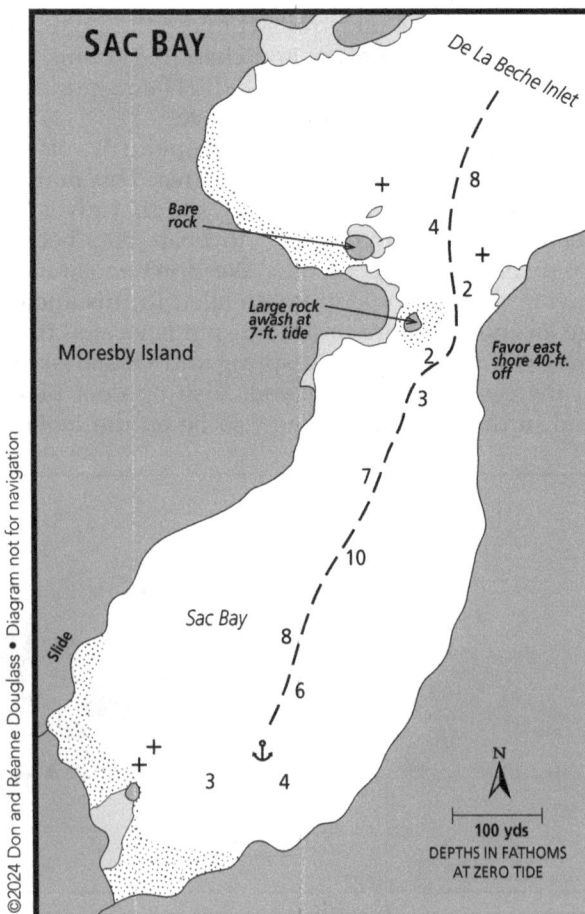

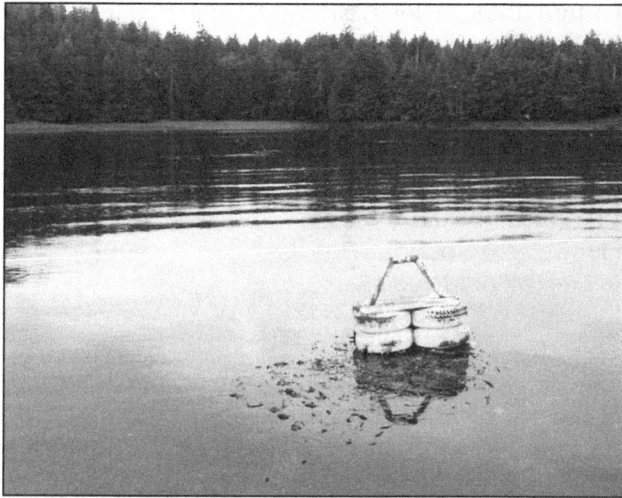

Buoy at Ramsay Passage Cove

Rain forest interior, Echo Harbour

De la Beche Cove (De la Beche Inlet)
15 mi SE of Crescent Inlet
Entrance: 52°32.11'N, 131°38.01'W
Anchor: 52°32.16'N, 131°38.49'W

"De la Beche Cove" is what we call the unnamed cove formed by a bight in the south shore of De la Beche Inlet; it is landlocked by a moderate-sized unnamed island on its north side. The west entrance isn't much more than a kayak passage; however, the eastern passage appears safe enough for small boats with 2 fathoms or more in the narrow fairway on the south side. The north side of the east passage has a shoal that dries at about 11-foot tide; pass south of the shoal by favoring the south shore (about 15 feet off). This is the former home of the Moresby Explorer, now located in Moresby Camp at Crescent Inlet. Although the bottom of the cove is somewhat irregular, indicating a rocky bottom, we found the northwest corner to be flat at about 4 fathoms with adequate and comfortable holding.

Anchor in 4 fathoms over sand and mud bottom; fair-to-good holding.

Sac Bay (De la Beche Inlet)
8.6 mi W of Hot Springs I.
Entrance: 52°32.33'N, 131°40.26'W
Anchor: 52°31.99'N, 131°40.48'W

Sac Bay, deep in the east side of Moresby Island, has much in common with the rugged Patagonian coast: high, black granite walls with stunted trees that struggle to survive in vertical and horizontal crevices. The trees hang on for dear life up to 1,800 feet, then give way to knobs of somber gray granite. This is a brooding place where the perpetually dark mus-

keg-colored water is made darker by the long shadows of the San Christoval Range. The mountains form a dinosaur ridge where Moresby Island narrows at its southern tip. Look up and try to imagine conditions on the trail to the southwest, where hikers climb, crossing to Puffin Cove on the west coast!

In *A Guide to the Queen Charlotte Islands*, Neil Carey describes Sac Bay so well: *After a rain, Sac Bay's dark waters – on the southwest side of rocky and baroque De la Beche Inlet – are brightened by mounds of foam riding seaward like miniature icebergs from two chattering waterfalls. The shore is rimmed with black lichen-covered rocks, decorated with golden rockweed. On windless days the still water mirrors the steep hillside, surrounding your boat with trees that appear to be standing on their delicate tops.*

Sac Bay is similar to Kostan Inlet. The narrows are tight and shallow. The western side of the narrows is largely a dangerous reef that dries on about a 7-foot tide. As you approach the narrows, after passing a bare rock mid-channel on the west side, move smartly to the east side and stay about three-quarters of the way to the east shore where you will find a narrow channel. This channel, at its narrowest part, is only 40 feet off the east shore, and over 2 fathoms deep at zero tide.

Because the entire Sac Bay is of moderate depth, you can anchor anywhere. We like the small bight just east of a small spit that extends from the head of the bay. (It lies east of the two waterfalls that tumble down the granite slopes at the south end of the bay.) Winds occasionally sweep down from the surrounding high peaks, so don't be lulled into complacency when checking your anchor set.

Anchor in 5 fathoms over mud with good holding.

Haswell Bay (Juan Perez Sound)

6.8 mi SW of Hot Springs Island
Entrance: 52°32.22'N, 131°34.93'W
Anchor: 52°30.53'N, 131°37.03'W

Haswell Bay is easily accessed from Juan Perez Sound and well sheltered from all weather. You can anchor in 7 fathoms or continue deeper into the bay, crossing a bar and its kelp patch into a flat-bottom mud hole. There you will barely move, no matter how badly it's blowing outside.

The bar, which carries depths of 8 to 13 feet at zero tide, extends from the west shore to the unnamed wooded island and the drying flat to its south. The mud hole has 3 fathoms of water with room where a couple of boats can anchor. Less intimidating than Sac Bay, Haswell Bay has good views of the tall peaks to the south with shores surrounded by old-growth cedar in every direction. You can frequently see a mother bear and her cubs browsing along the landing beach. This is another of our favorites. Larger boats will find more swinging room and easier entrance in Hutton Inlet.

Anchor in 3 fathoms over a soft, brown mud bottom with clam shells; very good holding.

Hutton Inlet (Juan Perez Sound)

2.5 mi E of Haswell Bay
Entrance: 52°31.51'N, 131°32.03'W
Anchor: 52°30.05'N, 131°33.98'W

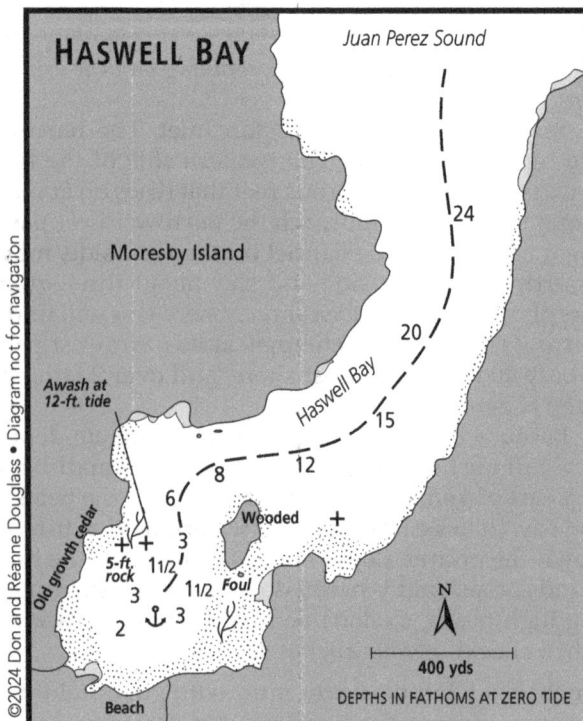

HASWELL BAY
Juan Perez Sound
Moresby Island
©2024 Don and Reanne Douglass • Diagram not for navigation
Awash at 12-ft. tide
Old growth cedar
5-ft rock
Wooded
Foul
24
20
15
12
8
6
3
1 1/2
3
1 1/2
2
3
N
400 yds
DEPTHS IN FATHOMS AT ZERO TIDE
Beach

Hutton Inlet, a long, straight inlet that gradually shallows to a long drying flat, is well sheltered. Off the drying flat, you can select your depth with plenty of swinging room.

Anchor in 5 fathoms over mud with good holding.

Hutton Island Cove

(Juan Perez Sound)
0.5 mi SW of Marco I.
Entrance: 52°31.08'N, 131°31.53'W
Anchor: 52°30.88'N, 131°31.50'W

"Hutton Island Cove" is our name for the small cove at the south side of the entrance to Hutton Inlet, 0.3 mile southeast of Hutton Island. The cove, which is frequently used as a campsite by kayakers, is close to good fishing grounds around Marco Island and the passage along the Moresby Island shore. Although it is open to the north, the cove provides shelter from all other directions. It has easy access to Juan Perez Sound and is a good base from which to explore the vicinity by kayak or dinghy. Avoid one bare and two wooded islets on the west side of the cove, and anchor off the steeply-sloping landing beach.

Anchor in about 4 fathoms over sand, shells and kelp; fair-to-good holding.

Marshall Inlet

(Juan Perez Sound)
2.6 mi SW of Marco Island
Entrance: 52°28.66'N, 131°28.19'W
Anchor: 52°28.04'N, 131°30.25'W

Marshall Inlet is an east-west channel off Werner Bay, west of the interesting tree-covered "All Alone Stone" in Juan Perez Sound. The inlet appears to offer fair protection in all but easterly winds. The head of the inlet has a large 5-fathom flat that makes a good anchor site; however, the gravel beach is steep-to with depths that rise from 5 fathoms to 1 fathom in two boat lengths.

Avoid the mid-channel shoal in the entrance by passing on either side. Note that the high rocky bluffs at the entrance are washed clean by waves from southeast storms. The swells and chop appear to diminish as you proceed west in the inlet. There is evidence that strong northwest winds funnel through the low valley to the northwest. Note that the south shore has predominately old-growth cedar with silver snags, while the south-facing north shore is a vibrant mixture of all kinds of trees and plants.

Anchor in the center of the 5-fathom flat, over mud and shells; good holding.

Matheson Inlet

(Juan Perez Sound)
3.2 mi SW of Marco Island
Entrance: 52°28.36'N, 131°27.59'W
Anchor: 52°27.06'N, 131°28.56'W

Matheson Inlet, immediately south of Marshall Inlet, offers better shelter than its northern cousin, but it is more difficult to enter. A bar extends from the west shore, marked during summer by large kelp patches. The fairway across the bar favors the east side, passing the kelp patches to starboard. Stay in mid-channel to avoid the drying banks in the narrows.

Secure anchorage can be found just beyond the small wooded island on the west shore, near the head of the inlet. Avoid the inshore rocks and the large reef across on the east shore. A kayak campsite is on the east shore south of the bar. Wildlife can be found in the grassy margins. This area offers excellent fishing for Coho (silver) and Chinook (king) salmon.

Anchor in 4 fathoms over soft, brown mud with eelgrass; fair-to-good holding.

Skaat Harbour

(Burnaby Strait)
4 mi NW of Dolomite Narrows
Entrance: 52°26.38'N, 131°24.75'W
Anchor: 52°23.07'N, 131°26.42'W

Skaat Harbour is a good place to wait for favorable tidal conditions in Dolomite Narrows or to use as a base camp for the general area. It has easy access and good protection from southerlies. On the west shore, just north of the 110-foot island, is a grassy rock; next to that is a low bare rock, a favorite haul-out rock for dozens of harbor seals.

We found harbor depths somewhat different than charted. Most of the southern part of the harbor is 7 to 8 fathoms and steep-to right to the shore. We found a 2.5-fathom ledge just south of the wooded islet and the bare rock, north of the drying flat and landing beach, which provided a scenic and convenient anchor site.

Anchor in 2.5 fathoms over sand and mud with fair-to-good holding.

Section Cove

(Burnaby Island)
3.8 mi N of Dolomite Narrows
Entrance: 52°25.52'N, 131°21.58'W
Buoy Position: 52°25.109'N, 131°21.762'W
Huxley Ranger Cabin: 52°26.05'N, 131°22.40'W

Section Cove is a convenient anchorage at the north end of Burnaby Strait. The preferred anchorage lies

Bottom of mud and clam shells, good holding!

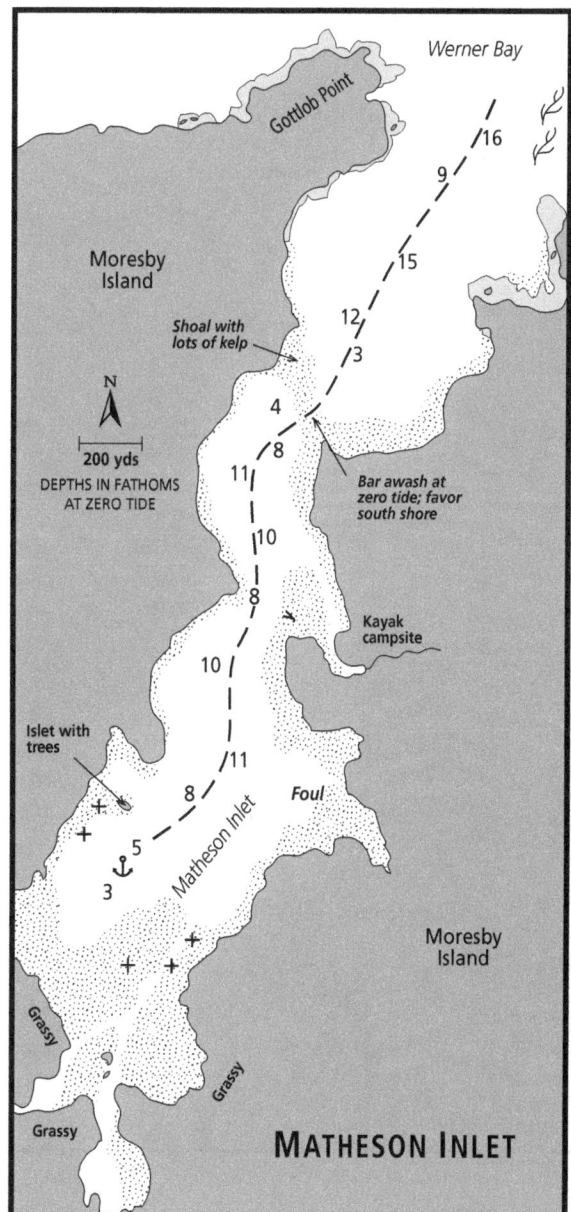

©2024 Don and Reanne Douglass • Diagram not for navigation

DOLOMITE NARROWS (BURNABY NARROWS)

CAUTION:
This diagram differs from Chart 3809

25

Log Cabin

20

Private range markers (white)

Dolomite Narrows

Moresby Island

Dries at 6-ft. tide

8

6

Private range markers (white)

6

Dries at 6-ft. tide

Dries at 16-ft. tide

6

Shake cabin

Dries at 2-ft. tide

Dries at 7-ft. tide

Dries at 12-ft. tide

Burnaby Island

1

Dries at 7-ft. tide

3

Exposed above HW

+ Foul

6

+

Grassy

Private range markers (white)

4

+ Grassy knob 3-ft. above HW

3

1

Private range markers (white)

+

Dries at 12-ft. tide

4

+

8

5

9

+

Dries at 12-ft. tide

9

+

Tide rip on south flow

5

N

2

0.1 mile

ALL DRYING HEIGHTS AND DEPTHS IN FEET AT ZERO TIDE (APPROXIMATE) SUBJECT TO USER VERIFICATION

12

18

Researched by Don Douglass & Kevin Monahan August 23, 2001
© F.E.P. LLC 2002

©2024 Don and Réanne Douglass • Diagram not for navigation

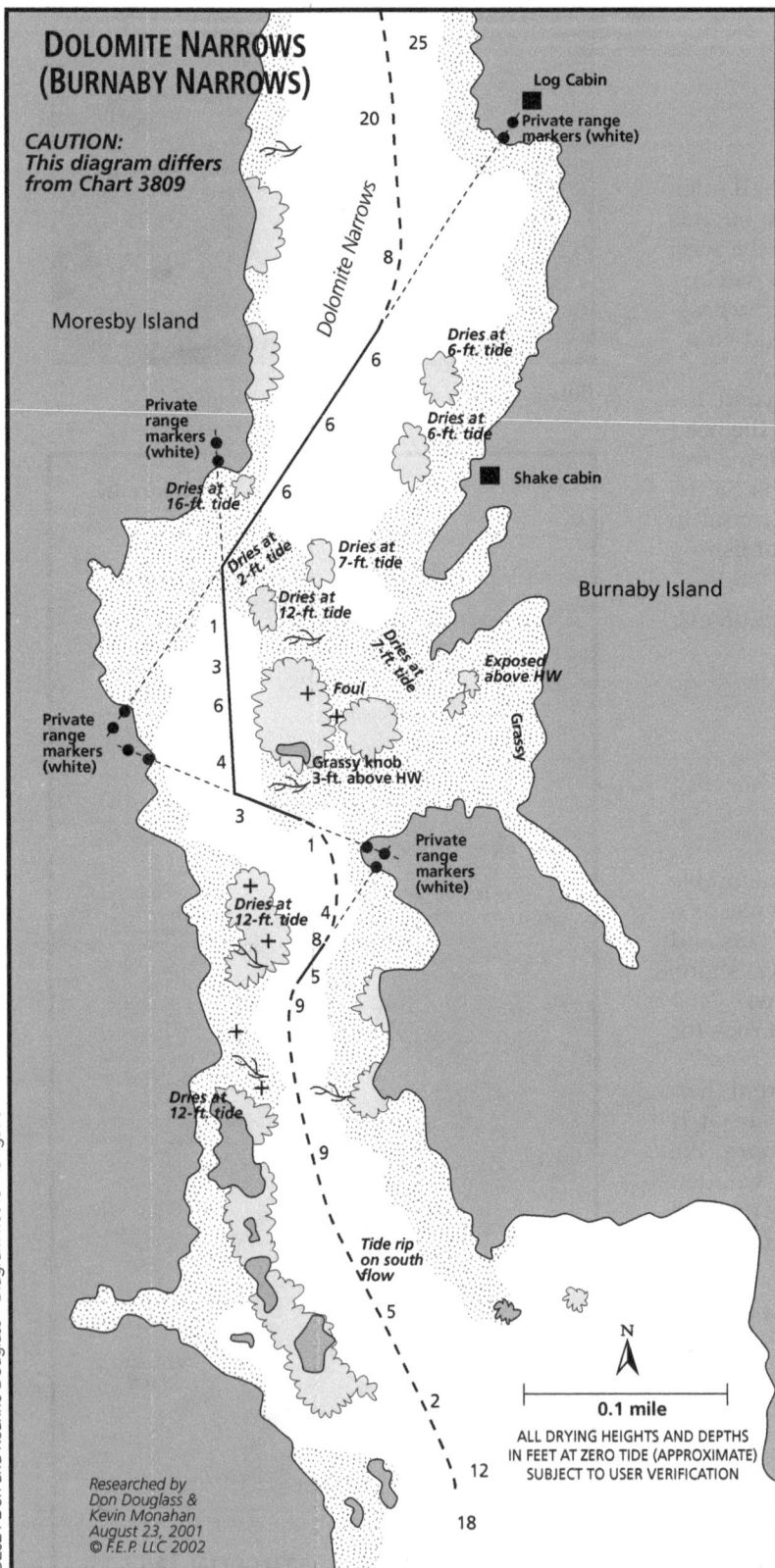

on the east side of Section Island in 9 fathoms over a flat bottom with good holding. Haida engaged in the herring roe on kelp fishery sometimes have rectangular pens moored to the buoy; fine mesh nets suspended within the log pens contain live herring and kelp fronds.

Burnaby Strait

W side of Burnaby Island
Entrance (N): 52°25.96'N, 131°23.54'W
Entrance (S): 52°19.22'N, 131°19.76'W

Burnaby Strait continues the smooth-water route south along the Moresby Island coast, sheltered by Burnaby Island. Because of the drying flats at Dolomite Narrows, which require careful timing, boats heading directly to SGang Gwaay may find it faster to follow Juan Perez Sound around the north side of Burnaby Island.

Island Bay

(Burnaby Strait)
1.4 mi NW of Dolomite Narrows
Entrance: 52°22.79'N, 131°22.31'W
Anchor (0.3 mi S of Dolomite Pt.): 52°22.31'N, 131°22.22'W
Anchor (large boats): 52°21.52'N, 131°24.10'W

Island Bay is a good area for photos with its tree-covered islets, bare rocks, and shoals. The bay is surrounded by green hills that climb westward to the bare, blunt stubs of Yatza Mountain. Kayakers and small boaters should savor many hours of smooth travel from the short point at the south end of Kat Island, around Island Bay to the entrance to Dolomite Narrows. We have enjoyed quiet nights anchored in seven fathoms southwest of Dolomite Point.

Small boats can anchor close to Dolomite Point, while larger boats or those wanting more swinging room can anchor near the head of the bay.

Anchor (small boats) in 7 fathoms over sand; fair holding.

Anchor (larger boats) in 6 fathoms over sand, gravel and shells; fair holding.

Dolomite Narrows, Burnaby Narrows

(Burnaby Strait)
SGang Gwaay
Entrance (N): 52°21.84'N, 131°21.12'W
Entrance (S): 52°21.03'N, 131°20.90'W

Dolomite Narrows, called locally Burnaby Narrows, is very poorly charted and a significant challenge for navigators. Any boat attempting a transit from either the north or south should reconnoiter the Narrows prior to entering. There has been no channel cut through this drying flat.)

This is our second diagram of Dolomite Narrows and still the only one we know of that has been published. *Note that it may contain errors or omissions and you should not use it without independent verification.* The current in the Narrows may be moderate but, if the current is with you, you will find your boat moving past the rocks and reefs faster than you would like. We found that the flood enters from both ends of the Narrows. At some point during the middle part of the flood, the current seems to change rapidly to a south-flowing stream the entire length of the Narrows and may reach 3 knots or more. If you are headed south on the last of the flood, it's important to move quickly east as you pass just south of the mid-channel grassy-covered islet.

We believe that this dogleg to the east—which is in the narrowest part of the channel—is the trickiest part of the channel due to a strong cross-current that occurs where you head east to deeper water off the range mark point. When the tide covers most of the dangerous reef, the south-flowing current tends to set you on the reef before you notice it. The water is shallow at both ends of Burnaby Narrows, and we recommend that you get in position early, anchor mid-channel, observe the flooding current and proceed when the water has risen sufficiently for

Dolomite Narrows, looking north

your boat and the situation. (If you're uncomfortable about transiting the Narrows, you can always take a route around the east side of Burnaby Island.)

The Narrows should be taken as a potentially serious navigation hazard!

On the brighter side, Dolomite Narrows is a marvelous place to observe marine life. Parks' surveys have found 293 species of tidal and intertidal life here. They calculate that more protein per square meter exists here than any place in the world. During high water in years past, our friends in *Clavella* spent many hours diving around these rocks, observing the unusual and beautiful creatures that live underwater here.

Every time we have transited Dolomite, we've seen deer browsing in the grassy flats just south of the cabin, and they don't seem to fear slow-moving humans. The Careys report: "On one occasion in the Narrows we had the thrill of watching a large black bear swim across to Moresby Island where it hauled out on the rocks, shook itself three or four times like a great black dog before swaggering into the bush."

Private range marks at Dolomite Narrows

S/V Tasman *transits the dogleg in Dolomite Narrows*

Bag Harbour

(Burnaby Strait)
15.3 mi NW of Rose Hbr.
Entrance: 52°20.88'N, 131°21.10'W
Anchor: 52°20.84'N, 131°21.82'W

Bag Harbour is an excellent small-boat harbor that offers good protection and welcome relief for boats completing the southbound transit of Dolomite Narrows. And it's a convenient place to wait for correct conditions on a northbound trip.

Grassy margins surrounding the harbor indicate that little chop penetrates here. With the flat bottom, it can be used by many boats, anchoring anywhere in the basin, but avoiding submerged rocks near the grassy margins. The forest is all old growth with several small creeks entering the west end. Except for a rusty boiler hidden in the brush on the north shore—the remnant of a clam cannery established here over 100 years ago—this is a quiet, peaceful place with nothing manmade in sight.

In late summer leaping, splashing, and finning (swimming with the dorsal fin above the surface) pink salmon waiting to go upstream to spawn will tantalize any fisherman anchored here. The larger and more sporting coho salmon are also fished here. Listening to the pleasing symphony of frolicking salmon is guaranteed to lull anyone into sleep after a sumptuous fresh fish dinner at the end of a satisfying day of exploring this enticing region.

Anchor in 2 fathoms over soft mud with good holding.

Bob Rockwell and Flying Colors *anchored in Bag Harbour*

Slim Inlet (Skincuttle Inlet)

3.5 mi S of Dolomite Narrows
Entrance: 52°18.19'N, 131°19.48'W
Anchor: 52°17.09'N. 131°19.39'W

In our estimation, Slim Inlet is underrated. We find it peaceful, scenic and intimate and a good anchor site. Many deer graze on the grassy margins and we like the feel of the place.

At the entrance, avoid the submerged rocks to the northwest, as well as all the poorly-defined isolated rocks and shoals en route to and from Dolomite Narrows. The entire shoreline of Slim Inlet is composed of gray sand and gravel or cobble beaches. Although we have seen no indication of strong southerly winds here, the low pass to the south leads to Louscoone Inlet on the west coast, which means gusts could blow through Slim Inlet during southerly storms. Since there are only low hills near the inlet, the chance of

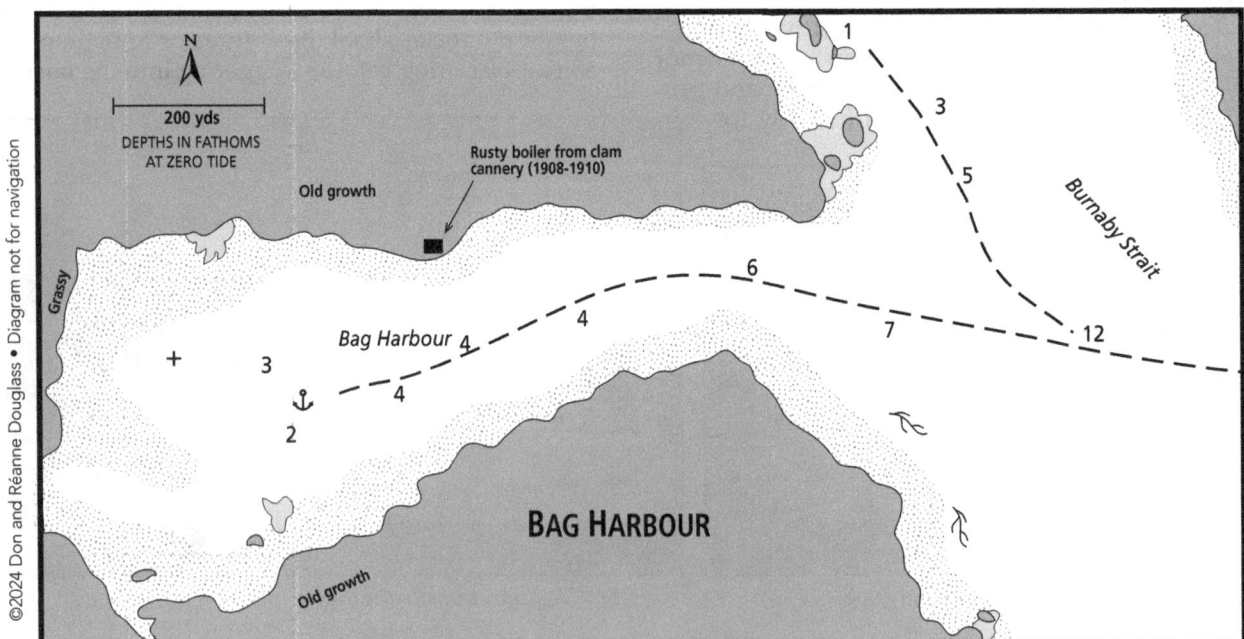

Kevin Monahan and Bob Rockwell at old log cabin, Dolomite Narrows

williwaws is greatly reduced. It is easy to land any-where along the shore.

There is no marked trail but it is possible to hike along the streams and through the lowland connecting Slim and Louscoone inlets. Carry a good compass and know how to use it while hiking in the bush.

Anchor in 3 fathoms over gray mud and shells; very good holding.

Jedway Bay (Skincuttle Inlet)
2.3 mi E of Slim Inlet
Entrance: 52°18.00'N, 131°15.84'W
Anchor: 52°17.30'N, 131°15.57'W

Jedway Bay is preferable over Huston Inlet which is much too large and open for our comfort, but we prefer either Slim Inlet or Ikeda Inlet. (See *Sailing Directions'* Caution about the entrance to Ikeda Inlet.)

Jedway Bay was the site of a saltery and cannery operated by Japanese before World War I, then later by Canadians. All such work ceased in the early 1930s and few signs of this activity remain.

Anchor in 5 fathoms over a mixed bottom of unrecorded holding.

Harriet Harbour (Skincuttle Inlet)
3.5 mi E of Slim Inlet
Entrance: 52°18.30'N, 131°14.00'W
Anchor: 52°17.85'N, 131°13.39'W

Harriet Harbour is the site of the abandoned Jedway mining ruins on Funter Point. This moderate-sized bay has fair-to-good protection in all but strong northerlies with plenty of swinging room for larger boats. However, winds in the harbor are unpredictable and heavy squalls can occur. The roads along the east shore can be used for hiking, but be on the lookout for open or hidden tunnels or pits.

Anchor in 4 fathoms over sand, mud and gravel.

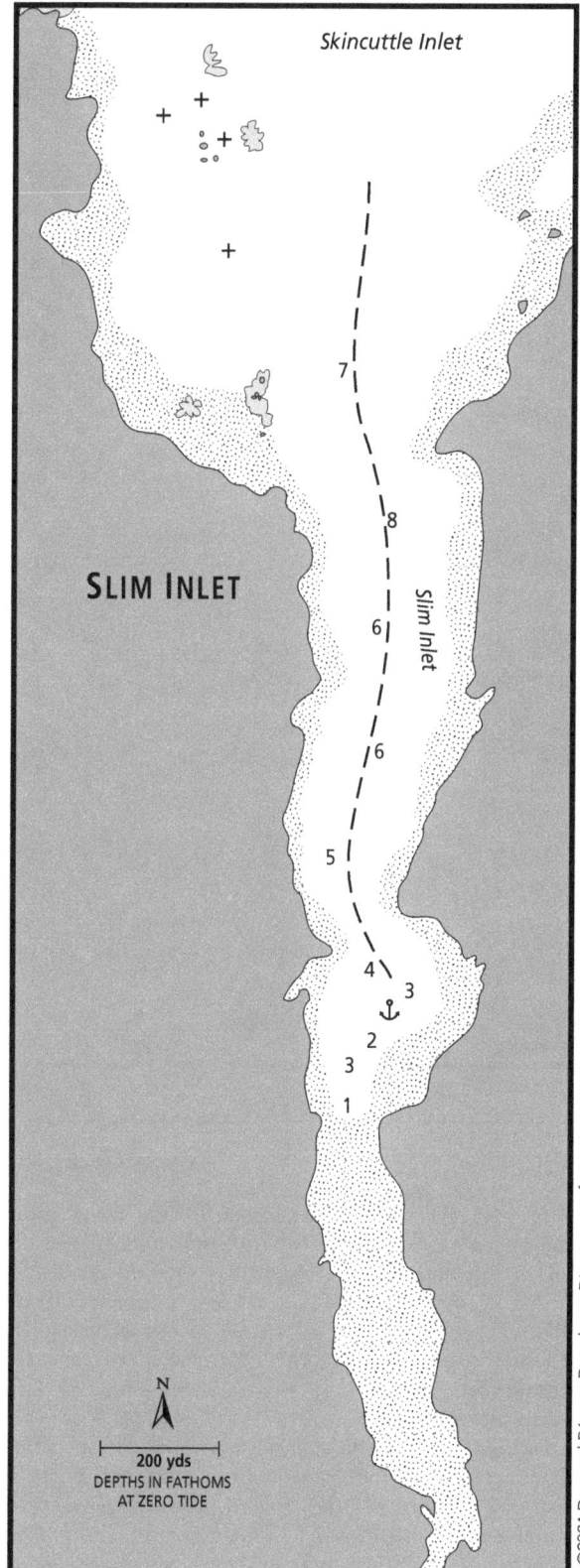

Skincuttle Inlet

SLIM INLET

Slim Inlet

N

200 yds
DEPTHS IN FATHOMS
AT ZERO TIDE

©2024 Don and Réanne Douglass • Diagram not for navigation

IKEDA COVE

Ikeda Point

Hecate Strait

Moresby Island

High ridge

Blow down

Awaya Point

12
8
6
7
8
7
10
11
10
8
7
6
5
4
4
3

Dries at 16-ft. tide

Dries at 8-ft. tide

Dries at 16-ft. tide

Ancient fish weir

Dries at 9-ft. tide

Dries at 10-ft. tide

Dries at 7-ft. tide

High peak

N

200 yds

DEPTHS IN FATHOMS AT ZERO TIDE

©2024 Don and Réanne Douglass • Diagram not for navigation

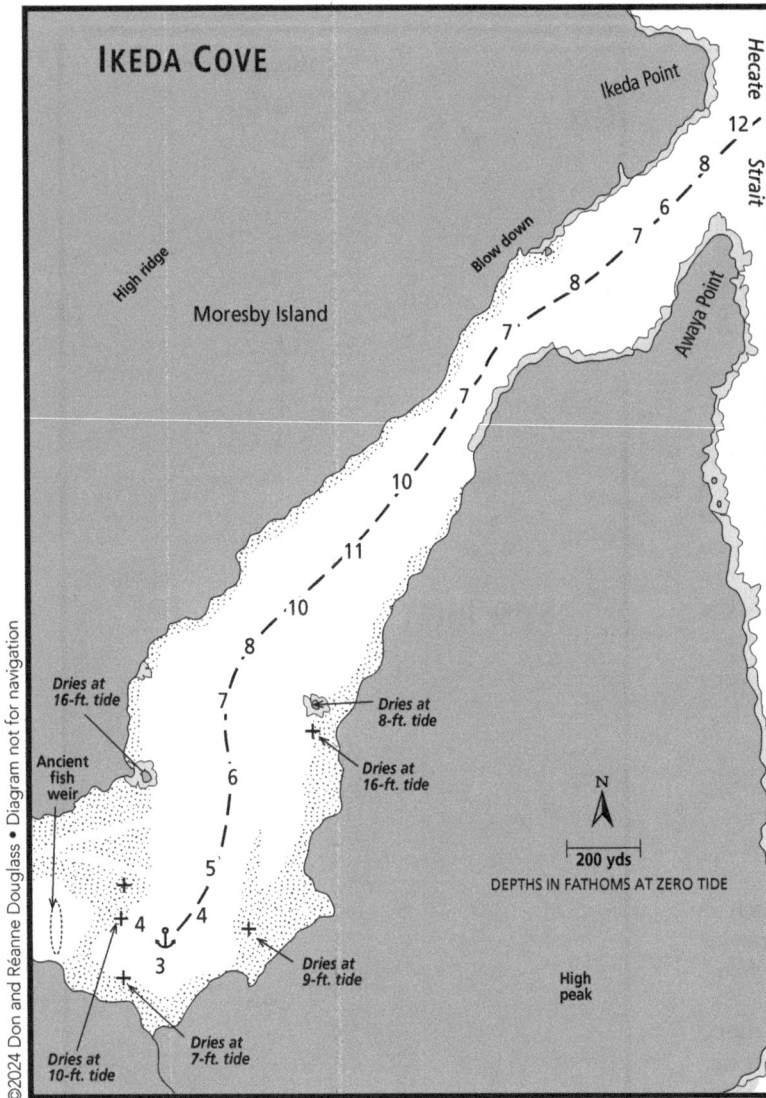

Ikeda Cove (Hecate Strait)
8.2 mi E of Dolomite Narrows
Entrance: 52°18.78'N, 131°08.17'W
Anchor: 52°17.76'N, 131°09.42'W

Ikeda Cove is a well-protected anchorage, subject to the entrance cautions found in the *Sailing Directions*. We found it quite comfortable and secure, with good holding. Due to strong currents along this coast, the entrance to Ikeda Cove may be treacherous during times of gales, confirmed by the rock wall on Ikeda Point that is washed bare and the wind-felled trees to the immediate west. The south side of the bitter end of the cove appears to be secure and, except for the williwaws off the high ridges, should get little chop.

The shore is fairly steep-to, but it might be possible to anchor close enough for a shore tie if southerly gales are expected. We find Ikeda Cove a convenient summer stopping place on the way to SGang Gwaay via Houston Stewart Channel.

What appears to be an ancient fishing weir lies at the head of the basin. In the mornings, deer often graze on the large grassy meadow; in the evening they graze along the outlet of the creek. Tailings on the ridge and service roads are scars left from the mining operations in Jedway. Summer water temperatures range in the low sixties—rather warm for Haida Gwaii! Here you may observe thousands of moon jellyfish so densely packed they give the appearance of a reef.

Rusty bolts secured in the bare sloping rock at Ikeda Point remain from a wireless station that operated from 1909 to 1920.

Texada Grounds in Dolomite Narrows

On 4 August 2000, the 92-foot vessel, *Texada*, ran aground on the eastern portion of the large reef while attempting to transit the narrows from south to north on an ebbing tide. Within three days diesel oil was pumped off into barrels with a minimum of damage to the ecology. The craft was moved ashore to the east where patching was accomplished. Nearly three weeks of working the tides passed before Dave Unsworth, owner of D&E Towing (of Port Clements), using his crane-barge and, assisted by a second tug and sailboat, were able to repair the battered 70-year-old, 99-ton, wooden hulled *Texada* to the point where she could be towed to Prince Rupert. From there she was towed to the drydocks in Vancouver where she was declared a total loss.

photo courtesy of Dave Unsworth

Texada aground in Dolomite Narrows

Farther north, in the forest, are blue-green stone and concrete walls, all that remains of the small quarters for the radio crew.

More than a century ago the old sternwheeler, *Dawson,* was set on a grid and converted into a bunkhouse for the miners. Its burned timbers and the grid may be seen a few yards north of the fish weir.

In the forest along the south side of the cove four miners are buried under marble gravestones that are engraved with old-style Japanese characters.

Anchor in 4 fathoms over sticky brown mud with large clam shells; good-to-excellent holding.

Collison Bay (Hecate Strait)
1.5 mi S of Ikeda Cove
Entrance: 52°17.30'N, 131°07.80'W
Anchor (small boats): 52°16.61'N, 131°09.10'W

Collison Bay offers good protection in most weather and is a pleasant anchorage. There are no drift logs on the beach and the tree limbs hang over the saltwater, indicating lack of shore stress. This is also a good place to watch bears ashore. Swells may enter the inlet, so consider using a stern anchor.

Anchor in 4 to 6 fathoms over soft brown mud with stones; fair-to-good holding.

Rankine Islands Ecological Reserve
(Hecate Strait)
3.1 mi SE of Collison Bay
Position: 52°15.48'N, 131°03.64'W

It's possible to pass inside Rankine Islands by avoiding all kelp patches.

Canoeists enjoy flat water in Gwaii Haanas NPR

Carpenter Bay (Hecate Strait)
3.3 mi S of Collison Bay
Entrance: 52°14.23'N, 131°03.92'W

Carpenter Bay is full of rocks, shoals and islets. Although anchorage can be found along the south shore in the south cove or in Koya Bay, the bottom in these sites is irregular. Collison Bay and Ikeda Cove offer much better shelter.

Houston Stewart Channel
(Hecate Strait)
16.5 mi SE of Dolomite Narrows
Entrance (E): 52°09.12'N, 131°01.00'W

Houston Stewart Channel, the protected route between Moresby and Kunghit islands, allows passage to the west coast of Moresby Island without the need to round Cape St. James. The channel has well-protected Rose Harbour on its south side, which is a good place to anchor when visiting.

Photo courtesy of Neil Carey
One of four grave markers of Japanese miners who died at Ikeda Cove copper mine 100 years ago

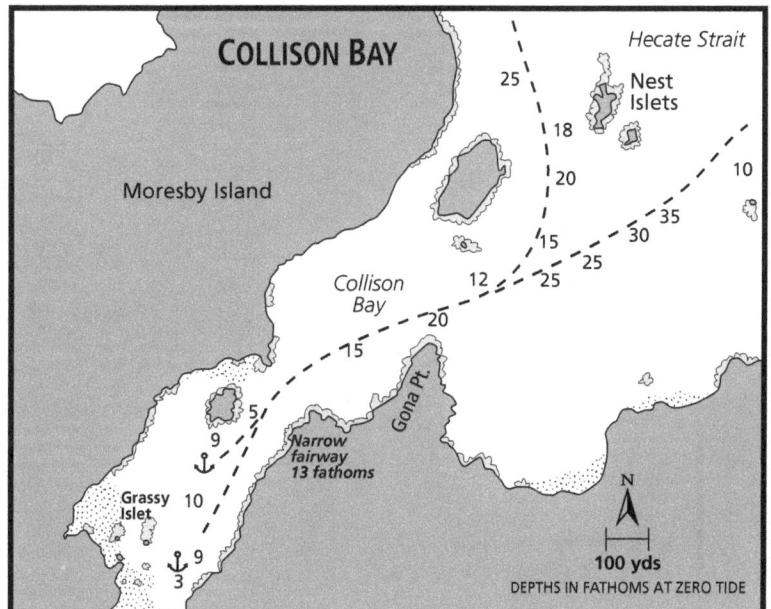
©2024 Don and Réanne Douglass • Diagram not for navigation

COLLISON BAY
Hecate Strait
Nest Islets
Moresby Island
Collison Bay
Gona Pt.
Narrow fairway 13 fathoms
Grassy Islet
N
100 yds
DEPTHS IN FATHOMS AT ZERO TIDE

Rose Harbour (Kunghit Island)

15.4 mi SW of Dolomite Narrows
Entrance: 52°09.39'N, 131°05.17'W
Mooring Buoy: 52°09.02'N, 131°05.19'W

Rose Harbour—an active whaling station in the first half of the 20th Century—is the only privately owned property within the Park boundaries, and the buildings on shore are occupied year-round. The harbor and the area near the public mooring buoy are out of the strong currents found in Houston Stewart Channel. The mooring buoy is often busy, and rafting is encouraged. Like all buoys, test them before you rely on them.

It may be possible for small boats to anchor in 2 fathoms south of the buoy; however, because swinging room is severely limited due to nearby shoals, kelp, and private buoys, a second stern anchor may be required. Larger boats may want to anchor north of the buoy or in a quieter location, such as Rose or Louscoone inlets. Float planes may land several times during the day near the buoy then taxi to shore

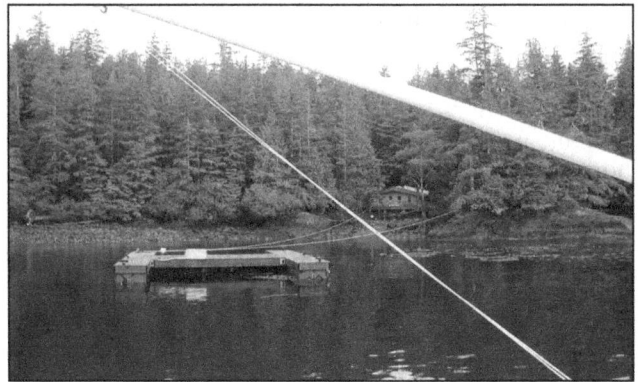

Warden's cabin and float, Rose Harbour

adding to the bustle and noise of Rose Harbour.

The building and metal float in the notch on the east side of Ellen Island are for a Park Ranger and Park boat use only. They are occupied during the tourist season. The narrow passage on the south side of Ellen Island can be carefully navigated by small craft and used as an anchor site, out of the main current.

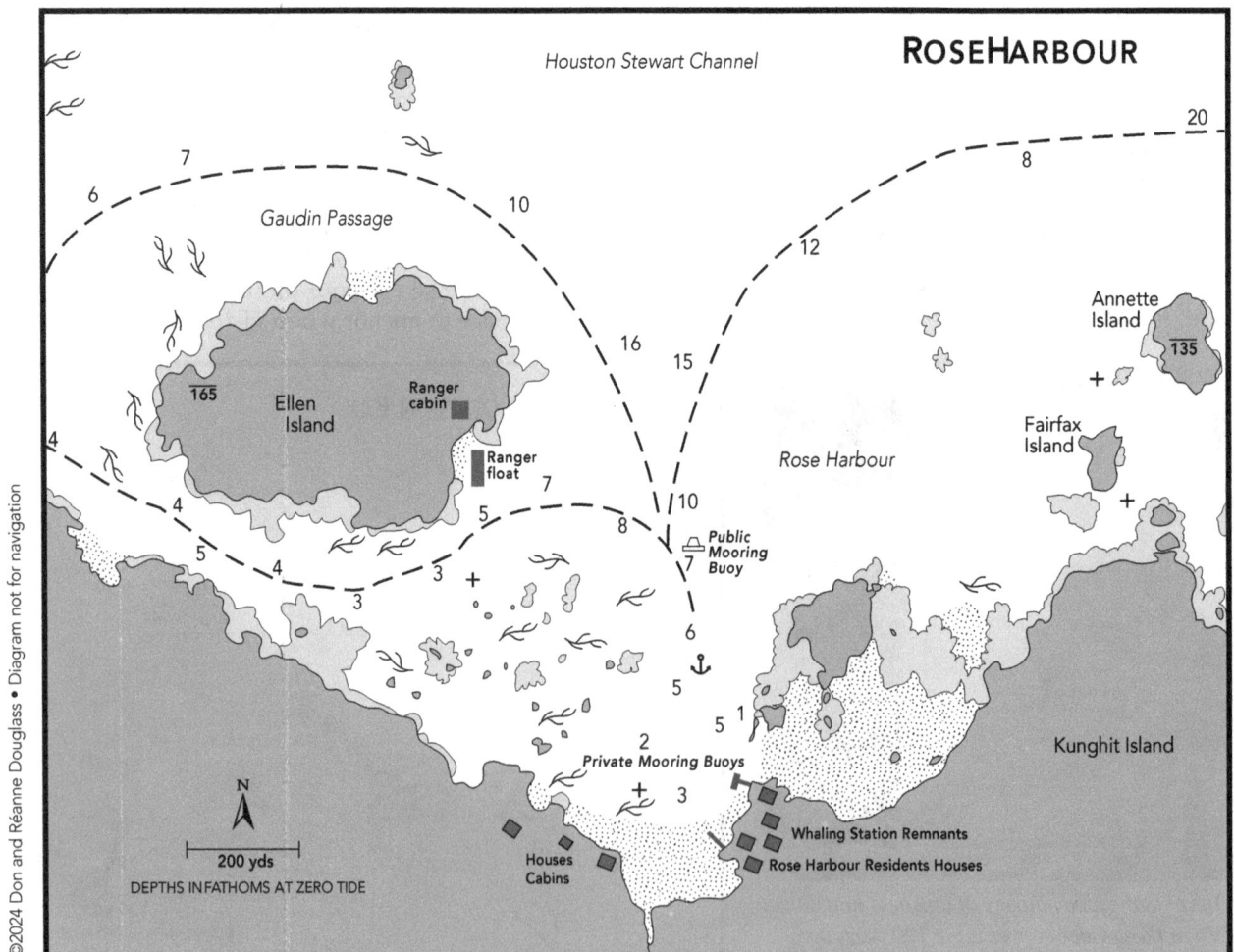

The houses and buildings at the historic whaling station house residents that seasonally provide accommodations and meals for various tour operators. On a space available basis, boaters may be able to join one of the group meals; hail "Rose Harbour Kitchen" on VHF 06 to inquire about available space. Payment is by cash only.

Raspberry Cove
(Houston Stewart Channel)
1 mi N of Rose Harbour
Entrance: 52°09.98'N, 131°04.92'W

Raspberry Cove, the small indentation on the north side of Houston Stewart Channel, nearly opposite Rose Harbour, has a gravel beach that makes it a favorite camping spot for the many kayakers who visit SGang Gwaay. Campers should be alert to the possibility of bears attracted by the smell of cooking food.

Rose Inlet (Houston Stewart Channel)
1.7 mi W of Rose Harbour
Entrance: 52°09.50'N, 131°05.14'W
Anchor: 52°11.33'N, 131°07.51'W

Larger vessels can find anchorage in Rose Inlet, 1.3 miles north of Denny Rocks with ample swinging room. Small boats may want to anchor east of Denny Rocks.

Anchor in 4 to 5 fathoms over sand and mud; good holding.

Flatrock Island (Houston Stewart Channel)
0.75 miles NW of Gordon Islands
Flatrock Island light: 52°06.46'N, 131°10.14'W

Flatrock Island, northeast of SGang Gwaay, is known

Pacific Voyager *at Rose Harbour buoys - Archive Photo*

for its large concentration and variety of nesting birds. There is a light on its 60-foot plateau. Flatrock Island marks the southwest entrance to Houston Stewart Channel and can be passed on either side.

Gordon Islands (Houston Stewart Channel)
2.5 miles E of SGang Gwaay
Position: 52°05.91'N, 131°08.53'W

The Gordon Islands are an interesting small-island complex. The flat, wind-swept terrain creates a fertile nesting area for birds. Temporary anchorage can be found on the east side of Gordon Islands just outside the kelp line; however, the current from Houston Stewart Channel blowing against a southerly wind makes this an uncomfortable anchorage. However, the Gordon Islands are a great place to explore from your dinghy or kayak in calm weather.

Louscoone Inlet (Moresby Island)
6 miles W of Rose Harbour
Entrance: 52°07.57'N, 131°13.05'W
Anchor (head of inlet): 52°13.84'N, 131°16.73'W
Buoy (Etches Pt. Cove): 52°10.03'N, 131°12.88'W
Water buoy: 52°11.64'N, 131°15.37'W

Small Cove, just east of Crooked Point, offers indifferent anchorage due to its rocky bottom and kelp. The most secure anchorage in the inlet—which we call "Etches Point Cove"—is 1.5 miles north of Small Cove between two unnamed islands that provide very good shelter from both up and down inlet winds.

You may also obtain reasonable shelter in an unnamed small cove one mile northwest of Etches Point Cove, 0.4 mile north of Cadman Point. There is room for one small vessel, but swinging room is limited.

A buoy with an attached water hose for year-around service is anchored near the western shore of Louscoone Inlet, due west of the north end of Skindaskun Island.

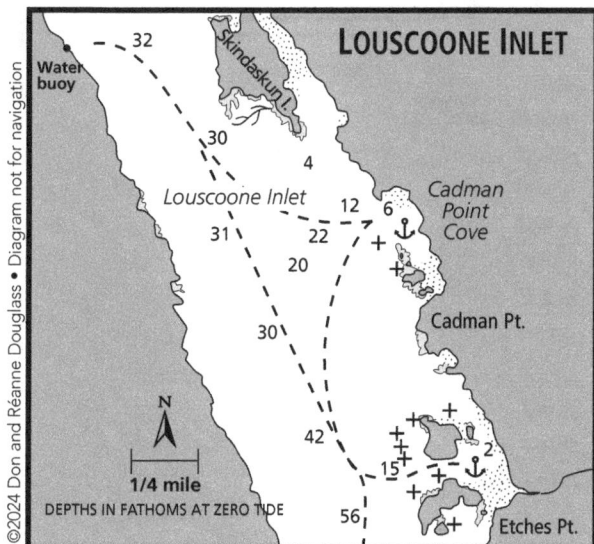

SGang Gwaay World Heritage Site

5.5 mi from Rose Harbour
Entrance (village site): 52°05.94'N, 131°12.85'W

For most tourists, a visit to historic SGang Gwaay llnagaay (Wailing Island Town) National Historic Site (formerly called Ninstints) on SGang Gwaay, is the highlight of their experience in Haida Gwaii. The greatest collection of Haida memorial, frontal, and mortuary poles in the entire Gwaii Haanas NPR stand in the forest only steps from the gravel and rock-covered landing beach. Standing and fallen poles, house pits, and the posts and beams of longhouses make up this outstanding example of a traditional Haida village. Original poles still standing in this old village site are maintained in a state of slowed decay by Watchmen who care-fully remove moss in an effort to minimize decay of the wood. Even with the present excellent care, each year sees the havoc of natural deterioration and ruthless storms, and in respect for traditional practice, the poles will no longer be raised when they fall. As you walk along the path viewing these giants, you can't help being moved by their originality and authenticity. Visitors are asked to remain on existing paths and not to touch or handle any standing or fallen wood.

The watchmen request that there be no anchoring of vessels (including kayaks) in front of the totem park. Anchorage is available in a cove to the northwest of the island and in Grays Cove, 0.25 mile to the southeast. Contact the watchmen on VHF Ch 06 for permission to come ashore. The number of visitors may be limited so be patient.

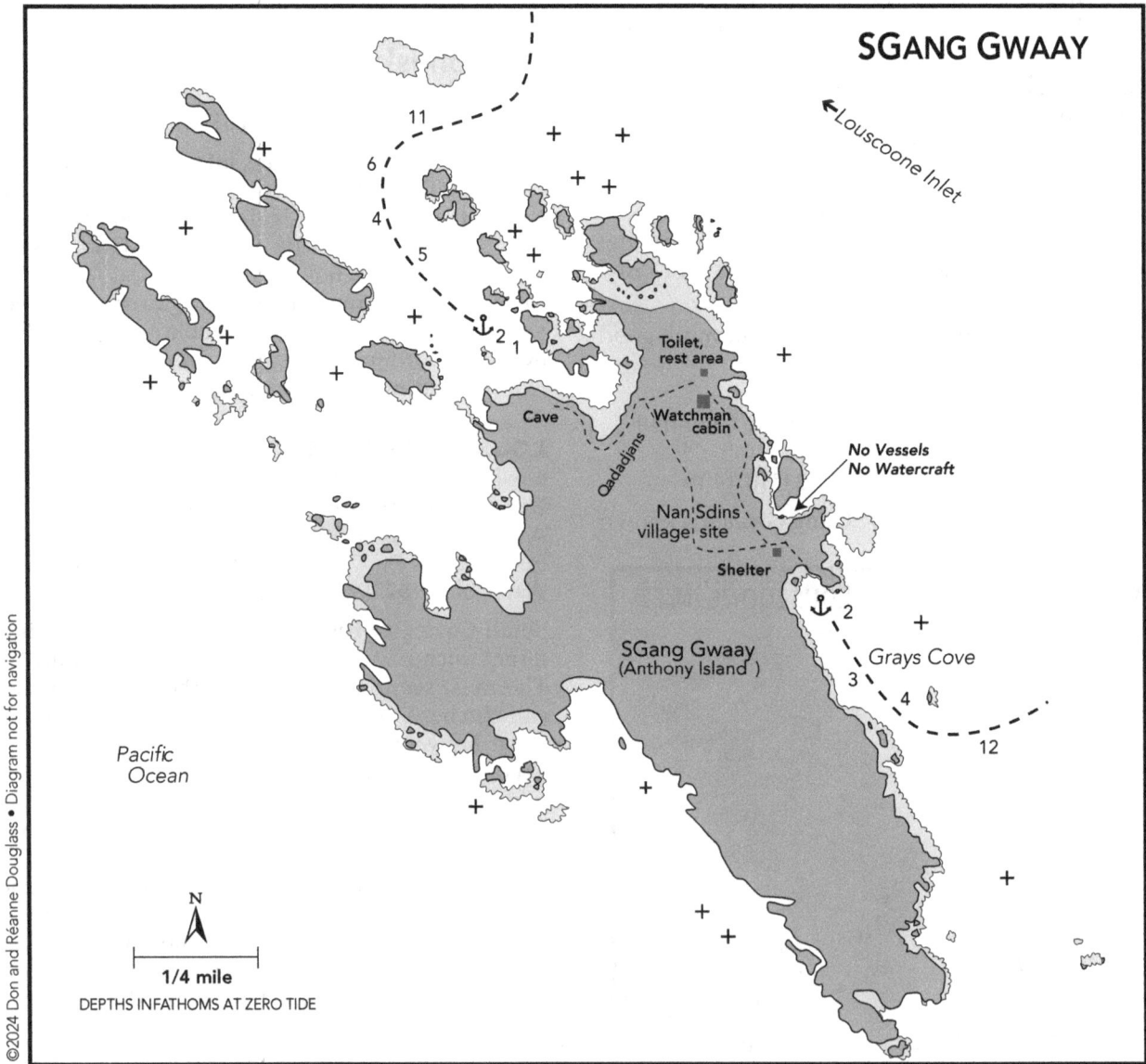

SGANG GWAAY

Louscoone Inlet

Toilet, rest area
Watchman cabin
Cave
Qadadjans
Nan Sdins village site
No Vessels No Watercraft
Shelter
Grays Cove
SGang Gwaay (Anthony Island)
Pacific Ocean

N
1/4 mile
DEPTHS IN FATHOMS AT ZERO TIDE

©2024 Don and Réanne Douglass • Diagram not for navigation

East beach, SGang Gwaay

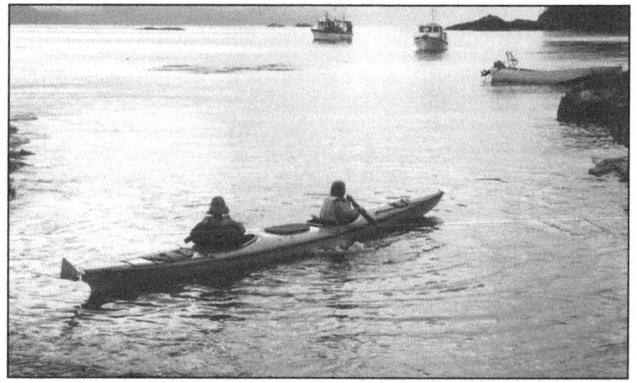

Landing beach and temporary anchorage, Grays Cove at SGang Gwaay

Grays Cove (SGang Gwaay)
5.5 mi SW of Rose Harbour
Entrance: 52°05.79′N, 131°12.56′W
Anchor: 52°05.75′N, 131°12.83′W

Three or four small craft can anchor in the small bight called Grays Cove on the east shoreline a quarter-mile southeast of Nan Sdins. This site is a fair-weather anchorage only and is completely open to south winds. Entry into the basin should be made from the south to avoid the rocks and kelp off the small gray rock point forming the east side of the cove. The west shore is composed of rocky bluffs where oyster catchers wade and otters play in the adjacent waters. A small but effective landing beach is in the northeast corner of the bight; the short trail to the historic site is located there.

In an emergency, the nearest protected anchorage is Etches Point, 4.5 miles north of SGang Gwaay, on the east side of Louscoone Inlet 0.6 mile north of Etches Point. Although Park personnel like to recommend anchoring in the tiny rocky cove on the north side of SGang Gwaay, this site is not favored by cruising boats for several reasons: its rocky bottom with marginal holding, its poor landing beach, and the fact that it is not visible from shore.

Anchor in 2 to 4 fathoms over a rocky bottom with some sand and kelp; poor-to-fair holding.

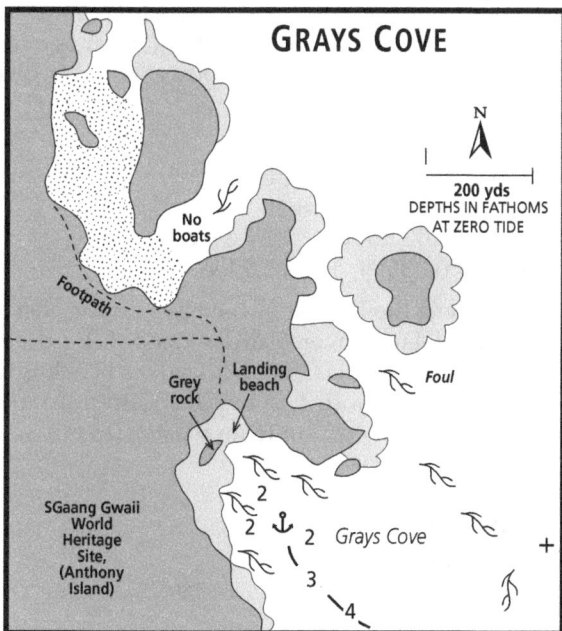

GRAYS COVE

N

200 yds
DEPTHS IN FATHOMS
AT ZERO TIDE

No boats

Footpath

Foul

Grey rock

Landing beach

SGaang Gwaii World Heritage Site, (Anthony Island)

Grays Cove

©2024 Don and Réanne Douglass • Diagram not for navigation

SGang Gwaay World Heritage Site

Looking northeast from beach at Nan Sdins village

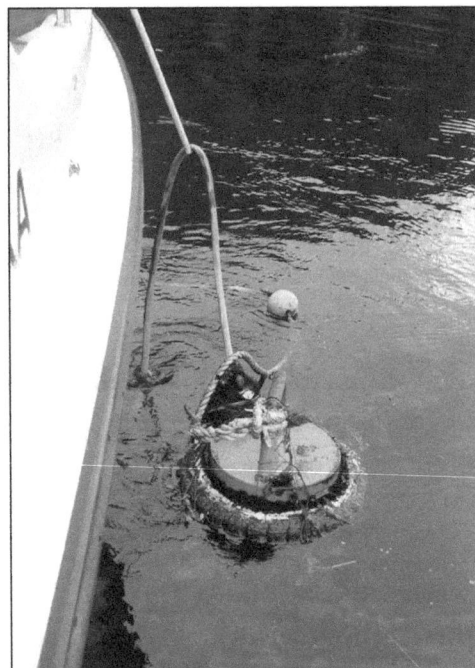

Baidarka picks up water hose, Louscoone Inlet

Heater Harbour (Kunghit Island)
2.5 mi SE of Rose Harbour
Entrance: 52°07.20'N, 130°01.22'W

Heater Harbour, on the east side of Kunghit Island, provides good protection from westerlies and southerlies, and moderate protection from easterlies. Small boats will find the anchorage in Rose Harbour superior to Heater Harbour. Heater Harbour has the best reputation for shelter on the east side of Kunghit Island. It is well protected in almost all weather, however, Rose Harbour would be preferable in gale-force southeast weather. Anchorage for small craft can be found anywhere.

Neil Carey does not recommend anchoring overnight in any of the open anchorages along the east and south coast of Kunghit Island from Montserrat Bay south to, and including, Woodruff Bay. All the sites are seldom free of swell.

Montserrat Bay (Kunghit Island)
4.5 mi SE of Rose Harbor
Entrance: 52°06.97'N, 130°58.58'W
Anchor: 52°06.32'N, 130°59.83'W

Anchorage can be found in Montserrat Bay near the head of the bay in 10 fathoms. Rainy Islands, at the entrance to the bay, provide moderate protection from northerlies but not from northeast winds.

Keeweenah Bay (Kunghit Island)
5.5 mi SE of Rose Harbour/10 mi S of Cape St. James
Entrance: 52° 06.59'N, 130° 57.73'W
Anchor: 52° 05.97'N, 130° 57.92'W

Keeweenah Bay is the first protection from southeast weather north of Cape St. James. It is open to the north, however, and provides little protection from northeast gales.

Treat Bay (Kunghit Island)
E side of Luxana Bay
Entrance: 52°03.28'N, 131° 00.65'W
Anchor: 52°03.84'N, 131°01.04'W

Treat Bay is open to the southeast which makes for a rolly anchorage. There is a nice sandy beach at the head of the bay with a creek and there are several submerged rocks along the shore. Treat Bay and the four anchorages to the south are considered rolly and uncomfortable for overnight anchorages even in calm weather; they are fully exposed and dangerous in southeast winds.

Luxana Bay (Kunghit Island)
8 mi N of Cape St. James lt.
Entrance: 52°02.38'N, 130°57.39 W
Anchor: 52°04.35'N, 131°03.94'W

Luxana Bay is the largest of the bays on the east side of Kunghit Island, over 5 miles deep. Like the two bays to the south, it has beautiful sandy beaches with interesting driftwood. The upper reaches of Luxana Bay offer good protection from westerlies but are exposed to the southeast.

Howe Bay (Kunghit Island)
3 mi N of Woodruff Bay
Entrance: 51°59.73'N, 130°59.88'W

Howe Bay provides reasonably good shelter from westerly winds except strong westerlies which blow down the valley. It is open and not protected from any southeast weather.

Woodruff Bay (Kunghit Island)
2 mi N of Cape St. James lt.
Entrance: 51°57.71′N, 131°00.47′W

While some protection may be afforded in westerly winds, it is exposed to the southeast and generally has swells breaking on its long, sandy beach.

Dave Unsworth (mentioned in the sidebar on the *Texada* grounding) tried anchoring here while towing away the demolished material from the lighthouse. He reported that the west and southwest winds charged through the low valley and made anchoring uncomfortable.

At the north end of the sandy beach, just south of the creek, there was once a bathtub used by the former lightkeepers. The bathtub was used by the construction crew working on the lighthouse building in 1963 but no one has seen it in years.

Cape St. James
13.5 mi S of Houston Stewart Channel
Light: 51°56.15′N, 131°00.96′W
N Channel (center position): 51°56.53′N, 131°01.22′W
S channel (center position): 51°55.98 N, 131°00.54′W

Cape St. James is located on the south end of St. James Island, the first island south of Kunghit Island and the northernmost of the Kerouard Islands. The lighthouse formerly located atop the 100-foot bluff on the south side of St. James Island, has been replaced by a small, automatic light and a helicopter pad. South St. James Channel carries 6-10 fathoms in the fairway and is passable by small craft under calm conditions. Strong winds blowing against the tidal stream can cause heavy dangerous seas in this passage. During times of spring tides, tide rips make this passage risky. The North Channel between St. James Island and Kunghit Island has only 5 fathoms in the fairway and is passable by small boats only in calm conditions.

Neil Carey writes: "I prefer the passage between Kunghit and St. James rather than the one south, unless I want to see the sea lions hauled out on one of the low rocks of the Kerouard Islands. Both passages are bouncy. Betty and I anchored overnight three times in the tiny, kelp encumbered notch on the east side of St. James Island."

Crescent beach of golden sand, Gilbert Bay

Photo courtesy of Neil Carey

Gilbert Bay (Kunghit Island)
6.5 mi NW of Cape St. James
Entrance (Kunghit Island): 52°01.45′N, 131°06.16′W
Anchor (N cove): 52°02.18′N, 131°05.12′W

Gilbert Bay is an open bight on the west side of Kunghit Island with a small, interesting cove on its northeast shore. There is a beautiful, sandy beach at the head of the cove and green grass along the large creek that flows from the north. Temporary anchorage for small boats can be found in about 3 fathoms over mud, sand with good holding. This is a good place for a lunch stop and to explore this attractive, remote area. Open to southerly weather, it should not be used as an overnight anchorage.

"In good weather," Neil Carey says, "a row or two of lazy breakers tumble onto the golden sand beach making this enticing spot a difficult place to land. We have found that the northwest corner near where sand and rocks meet is best for landing and launching. This southwest facing beach is a catchall of treasures from the sea. The addition of palm trees would make this a great setting for a South Seas movie."

Photo courtesy of Neil Carey

Kerouard Islands seen from St. James Island

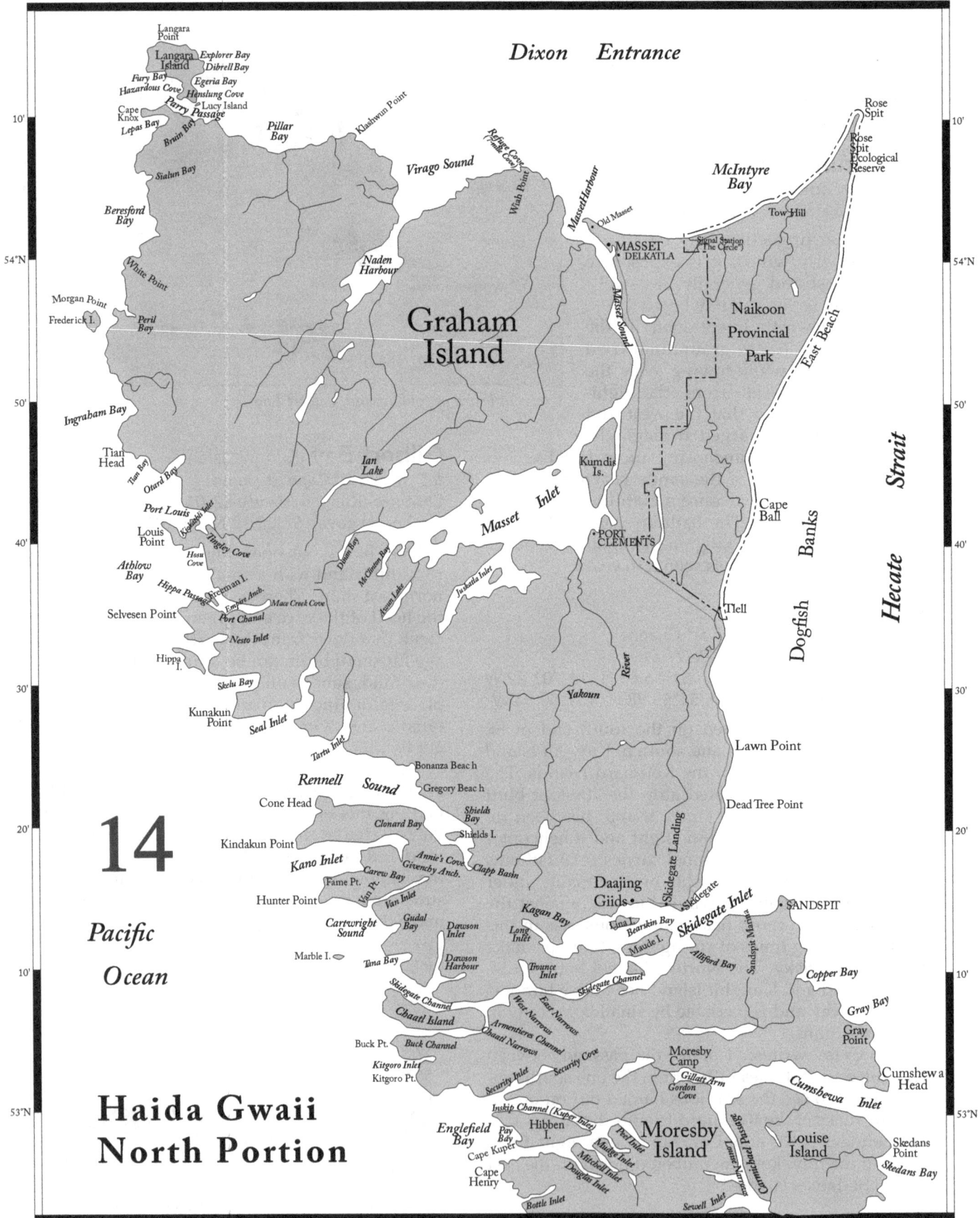

Langara Point
Langara Island
Explorer Bay
Dibrell Bay
Fury Bay
Hazardous Cove
Egeria Bay
Henslung Cove
Lucy Island
Cape Knox
Parry Passage
Lepas Bay
Bruin Bay
Sialun Bay
Klashwun Point
Pillar Bay
Virago Sound
Wiah Point
Refuge Cove (Yaku Cove)
Masset Harbour
Old Masset
Rose Spit
Rose Spit Ecological Reserve
McIntyre Bay
Tow Hill
Beresford Bay
White Point
MASSET DELKATLA
Signal Station (The Circle)
Morgan Point
Frederick I.
Peril Bay
Naden Harbour
Graham Island
Masset Sound
Naikoon Provincial Park
East Beach
Ingraham Bay
Tian Head
Tian Bay
Otard Bay
Ian Lake
Kumdis Is.
Port Louis
Seal Inlet
Louis Point
Beresford Inlet
Tingley Cove
Hosu Cove
Athlow Bay
Hippa Passage
Freeman I.
Empire Anch.
Masset Inlet
Dinan Bay
McClinton Bay
Awun Lake
Juskatla Inlet
PORT CLEMENTS
Cape Ball
Dogfish Banks
Hecate Strait
Selvesen Point
Port Chanal
Mace Creek Cove
Nesto Inlet
Tlell
Hippa I.
Skelu Bay
Yakoun
River
Kunakun Point
Seal Inlet
Tartu Inlet
Yakoun
Lawn Point
Dead Tree Point
14
Pacific Ocean
Rennell Sound
Bonanza Beach
Gregory Beach
Cone Head
Shields Bay
Shields I.
Kindakun Point
Clonard Bay
Kano Inlet
Annie's Cove
Givenchy Anch.
Clapp Basin
Skidegate Landing
Carew Bay
Fame Pt.
Van Pt.
Van Inlet
Daajing Giids
Skidegate
SANDSPIT
Hunter Point
Cartwright Sound
Gudal Bay
Dawson Inlet
Long Inlet
Kagan Bay
Lina I.
Bearskin Bay
Maude I.
Skidegate Inlet
Sandspit Marina
Copper Bay
Marble I.
Tina Bay
Dawson Harbour
Trounce Inlet
Skidegate Channel
Alliford Bay
Gray Bay
Gray Point
Skidegate Channel
Chaatl Island
East Narrows
West Narrows
Armentieres Channel
Chaatl Narrows
Security Cove
Moresby Camp
Cumshewa Inlet
Cumshewa Head
Buck Pt.
Buck Channel
Security Inlet
Gillatt Arm
Gordon Cove
Kitgoro Inlet
Kitgoro Pt.
Inskip Channel (Kuper Inlet)
Hibben I.
Peel Inlet
Moresby Island
Louise Island
Englefield Bay
Pay Bay
Cape Kuper
Mudge Inlet
Mitchell Inlet
Sewell Inlet
Skedans Point
Skedans Bay
Cape Henry
Douglas Inlet
Bottle Inlet

Haida Gwaii
North Portion

©2024 Don and Réanne Douglass • Diagram not for navigation

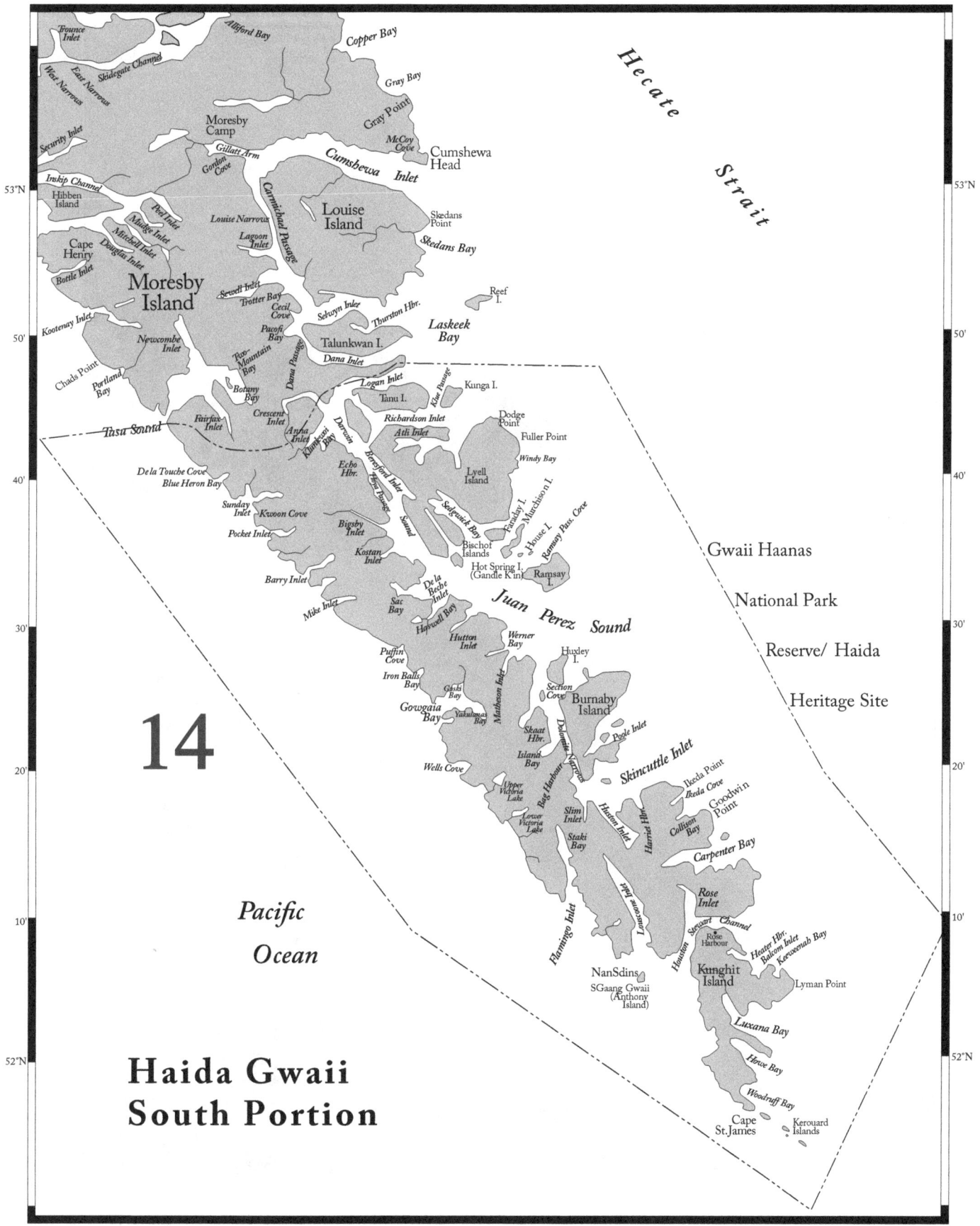

Haida Gwaii
South Portion

14

Pacific Ocean

Hecate Strait

Gwaii Haanas

National Park

Reserve/ Haida

Heritage Site

Moresby Island

Founce Inlet
Alliford Bay
Copper Bay
West Narrows
East Narrows
Skidegate Channel
Gray Bay
Security Inlet
Moresby Camp
Gray Point
McCoy Cove
Cumshewa Head
Cumshewa Inlet
Inskip Channel
Gillatt Arm
Gordon Cove
Hibben Island
Peel Inlet
Carmichael Passage
Louise Island
Skedans Point
Louise Narrows
Skedans Bay
Madge Inlet
Mitchell Inlet
Cape Henry
Douglas Inlet
Lagoon Inlet
Bottle Inlet
Sewell Inlet
Reef I.
Trotter Bay
Cecil Cove
Selwyn Inlet
Thurston Hbr.
Kootenay Inlet
Pacofi Bay
Laskeek Bay
Newcombe Inlet
Talunkwan I.
Two Mountain Bay
Dana Passage
Dana Inlet
Chads Point
Botany Bay
Logan Inlet
Portland Bay
Crescent Inlet
Kunga I.
Tasu Sound
Fairfax Inlet
Anna Inlet
Tanu I.
Kwe Passage
Klunkwoi Bay
Darwin Sound
Richardson Inlet
Dodge Point
De la Touche Cove
Echo Hbr.
Atli Inlet
Fuller Point
Blue Heron Bay
Beresford Inlet
Windy Bay
Sunday Inlet
Kwoon Cove
Klue Passage
Lyell Island
Pocket Inlet
Bigsby Inlet
Sedgwick Bay
Faraday I.
Murchison I.
Kostan Inlet
Bischof Islands
House I.
Ramsay Pass. Cove
Barry Inlet
Hot Spring I. (Gandle K'in)
Ramsay I.
De la Beche Inlet
Mike Inlet
Sac Bay
Hopwell Bay
Juan Perez Sound
Hutton Inlet
Werner Bay
Puffin Cove
Huxley I.
Iron Balls Bay
Gishi Bay
Section Cove
Gowgaia Bay
Yakulanas Bay
Matheson Inlet
Burnaby Island
Skaat Hbr.
Pogle Inlet
Wells Cove
Island Bay
Dolomite Narrows
Skincuttle Inlet
Upper Victoria Lake
Big Harbour
Ikeda Point
Lower Victoria Lake
Slim Inlet
Hutton Inlet
Ikeda Cove
Goodwin Point
Staki Bay
Harriet Hbr.
Collison Bay
Carpenter Bay
Flamingo Inlet
Rose Inlet
Luscombe Inlet
Stewart Channel
Houston Stewart Channel
Rose Harbour
Heater Hbr.
Balcom Inlet
Keerevenah Bay
NanSdins
Kunghit Island
Lyman Point
SGaang Gwaii (Anthony Island)
Luxana Bay
Howe Bay
Woodruff Bay
Cape St. James
Kerouard Islands

©2024 Don and Réanne Douglass • Diagram not for navigation

Exploring the beach in Buck Channel while Baidarka *circles*

14

Haida Gwaii: Dixon Entrance & the West Coast of Graham & Moresby Islands (including Skidegate Channel)

The west coast of Haida Gwaii has, in our opinion, the most stunningly beautiful coastline between the Mexican border and Southeast Alaska. Extruded shapes of volcanic rock, riddled with sea caves that, in many cases, are large enough for a boat to enter; sandy beaches; high granite walls that rise precipitously from the shores to snow-capped ridges; waterfalls that plunge directly into the Pacific. This is raw land that looks as if it had suddenly risen fully sculpted from the sea at the beginning of creation. In many ways the west coast of Haida Gwaii is the last cruising frontier of the Inside Passage since portions of the coastline are unsurveyed, uncharted or unsounded. To date, its remoteness and the lack of detailed information have drawn few pleasure vessels. But there are unparalleled rewards along Haida Gwaii's west coast for intrepid boaters who want to explore a world of outstanding natural beauty and solitude uncommon in the modern world and to participate in challenging navigation.

Haida Gwaii lies along an active earthquake fault. In August 1949, Canada's largest quake (magnitude 8.1) occurred along the Queen Charlotte Fault. The shaking was so severe that a geologist working on the north end of Graham Island reported he could not stand up and an oil storage tank collapsed in Cumshewa Inlet. People on the mainland in Terrace reported that standing on the street was "like being on the heaving deck of a ship at sea." Windows shattered and buildings swayed in Prince Rupert.

Canada's second most severe earthquake rolled and shook Haida Gwaii in the evening of October 28, 2012. This quake was centered a few miles northwest of Puffin Cove, Moresby Island and had a magnitude of 7.7. "I've retained my stability aboard ships during typhoons," says Neil Carey, "but this quake instantly dropped me to the deck. I was in my house. The quake rolled faster than any ship and I expected my place to be a pile of rubble." Surprisingly, only minor damage was done on Haida Gwaii, although it was felt on the mainland; mostly in Prince Rupert and Terrace.

It was soon discovered that warm and hot water had ceased to flow at Hotspring Island. This was cause for alarm and distress as the hot springs are a great attraction for visitors and local residents. Longtime residents recalled that this flow also ceased after the quake of 1949. Some correctly predicted the flow would start again. And, although the flow started out slow, it has returned with the joy and thankfulness of all.

Advice from a Local Expert

For sailors not fettered by a tight schedule—and adequate time is often synonymous with safety—the west coast of Haida Gwaii offers solitary magnificence and seafaring challenge. Weather and sea conditions may change abruptly. Shorelines, horizontal and vertical, change with random abandon from beaches of gleaming surf-smoothed sand to bare, blunt wave-scoured rocks, over 100 feet in height, crowned with silvered drift logs cast by deadly breakers. There are days when one can safely enjoy this North Pacific in a small rowboat; on other days, sailors pray for a snug harbor.

Weather forecasting is not a precise science, sources of information are not always available, and occasionally a local gale will develop without warning. Accept all the information available, then use your seaman's judgment. In winter months, west coast waters may be flat for days, due to islands sheltering the sea from the force of cold northeasterly winds. In summer, the coastal waters may be roughened for many successive days—even weeks—by northwesters blowing some 15 knots at night, building to as much as 45 knots from the mid-morning onward. Any sunny day will see the convection wind raise whitecaps before noon. Exquisite rainbows are a specialty of Haida Gwaii.

—Neil Carey

Neil and Betty Carey, long-time residents of Haida Gwaii, have extensively explored Graham and Moresby islands. Betty herself explored every inch of the west coast of Graham and Moresby islands in her dugout canoe.

Authors' notes: Since several west coast charts have unknown horizontal datums, all GPS waypoints should be taken with a healthy dose of skepticism until proven to your satisfaction. The authors have tried to use actual differential and WAAS GPS readings, rather than lat/longs taken off the chart, but in some cases, the chart values were all we had.

It is safe to say that large parts of the west coast of Haida Gwaii are poorly charted and documented. Little original hydrographic work has been done here in over 50 years. There are many errors and omissions in the government data, so *beware.* Approach this coast as an explorer out to see the unknown world, but always with an eagle eye for hazards.

Since many buoys and floats have been eliminated along the coast of Haida Gwaii, we suggest that, if you do find such, be sure to test for reliability.

Réanne and I are indebted to Francis Caldwell and Kevin Monahan who each spent three weeks aboard *Baidarka* with us as crew-members when we first explored the West Coast of Haida Gwaii, helping us conduct our research and keeping us off uncharted rocks.

Our short descriptions do not do justice to this bold and fascinating iron-bound coast, and we strongly recommend that boaters up to its mighty challenges take the earliest opportunity to see and explore what few others have.

The following italicized quotations come from *Canadian Sailing Directions, Vol. 2.* We had permission to quote this work in our 2nd Edition, Copyright 2002, and we feel that the following information is critical to know before you set out to the Haida Gwaii.

Anchorages—Caution—*Although a number of well enclosed anchorages are available in various inlets on the west coast of Haida Gwaii these are subject during strong SE gales to violent squalls from the valleys leading into them and, although no heavy seas are raised, the force of the squalls induces violent yawing. A sharp lookout should therefore be kept to guard against dragging.*

Surveys—Caution—*On the west coast of Haida Gwaii some of the smaller inlets have not been surveyed or have been only partially surveyed, and large stretches of the outer coast have not been surveyed inside a distance of 1 or 2 miles. Unsurveyed areas are inadvisable to enter without local knowledge.*

Winds—*From about October 1 to the latter part of December the prevailing winds are from the SE and east, and are frequently of gale force, accompanied by heavy rainfall . . . During May there are generally westerly winds, while during June, July, August and September, the more usual winds are from the south, SW and west . . .*

Baidarka *at Refuge Cove*

Refuge Cove (locally Seven Mile Cove)
(Graham Island)
8.7 mi NW of Masset Harbour
Entrance: 54 07.14'N, 132°18.32.'W
Float: 54°06.70'N, 132°18.60'W

Refuge Cove, the perfect cove in which to spend a night before crossing, used to be known locally as Seven Mile Cove. It is strategically located in a tiny

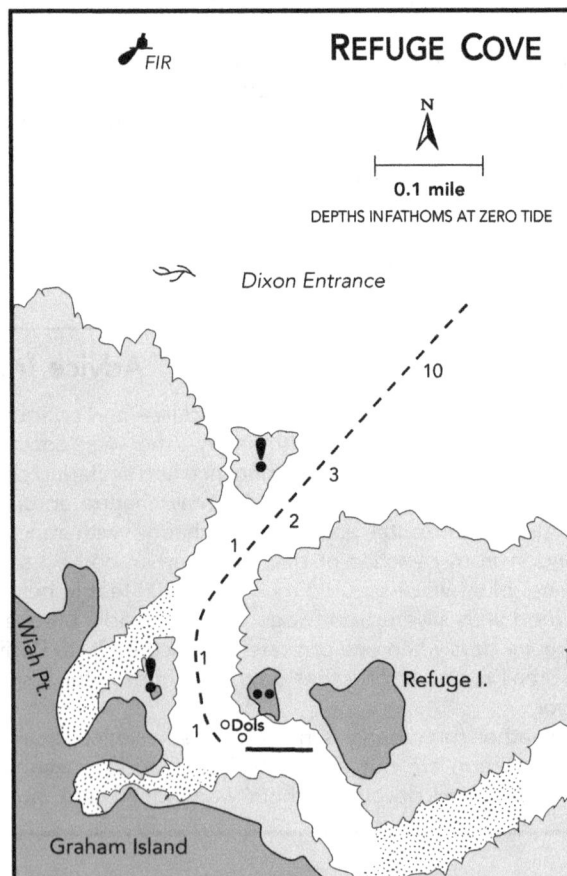

©2024 Don and Réanne Douglass • Diagram not for navigation

bay on the east side of Wiah Point south of Refuge Island, 23 miles from Rose Point to the east and Langara Island to the west. It provides an excellent rest stop where you can wait for the appropriate tide or wind conditions either entering or exiting Masset Harbour.

After safely anchoring in Refuge Cove it can be exciting to sit out a southeast gale and watch storm-force winds breaking along the north shore of Refuge Island. The narrow, shallow entrance channel should not be attempted at night or in foul weather when breakers are threatening or when steerage might be difficult. The fairway, which has a sector entrance light, is about 100 feet wide and has a minimum of 6 feet of water at zero tide. Outside swell diminishes quickly as you pass into the entrance channel. Keep the wooden light structure close to starboard on entering and maintain an alert lookout. Approach slowly, avoiding any big swells or kelp patches.

McIntyre Bay (Graham Island)
Between Rose and Wiah Points
Position: 54°07.22'N, 132°00.05'W
Anchor (Tow Hill): 54°06.49'N, 131°47.88'W

McIntyre Bay is the very wide bight of shallow water along the north side of Graham Island east of Rose Point. We have viewed the bay from Tow Hill during moderate southeast winds and observed a very good lee during these conditions; however, it is a dangerous breaking lee shore during heavy northwest winds and swell. Conspicuous Tow Hill, which rises 500 feet above an otherwise flat sandy beach, is reported to provide an open roadstead anchorage in fair or southeast winds 1 to 2 miles offshore.

McIntyre Bay leads to Masset Harbour via a set of range marks starting at buoy C29 from the northwest; you can also enter from the northeast by carefully crossing the Outer and Inner Bars and avoiding the dangerous Troup Bank east of buoy C31.

Anchor in southeast conditions, in 5 to 7 fathoms over hard sand; unrecorded holding.

Masset Harbour (Graham Island)
Entrance (Range at Outer Bar): 54°06.26'N, 132°13.81'W

The radio towers at Skonun Point appear as a large, tall, interconnected circular fence on the low, tree-covered land (locally known as The Elephant Cage). Rollers are likely to be breaking along the shallow, sandy shores of McIntyre Bay, encouraging seamen to stay well offshore. The safest route is to follow the charted range starting west of buoy C29 on a

Breaker hits entrance marker to Refuge Cove

Photo courtesy Pacific Voyager/Sea Cabana

course of 165° T. Approaching the entrance to Masset Harbour from the east, note that dangerous Troup Bank extends 1.5 miles north-northeast of Entry Point and must be given a wide berth. Locals use VHF Channel 06 as a party line for all kinds of communication.

Masset and Delkatla Inlet (Masset Sound)
4.2 miles SE of buoy C31
Delkatla Inlet Entrance: 54°00.19'N, 132°08.78'W
Public Floats: (Delkatla Inlet) 54°00.46'N, 132°08.49'W

As you head south into Masset Harbour, to your port hand is the rapidly growing Haida village of Old Massett with its mixture of new and older homes sprinkled with a few colorfully painted totems of recent origin. After passing about a mile of forest the cannery wharf is abeam, then the public wharf with a berthing face of 217 feet and a 90 foot float. A fuel float is inboard. The Delkatla Inlet boat basin, four blocks from the center of town, has two public floats, each 500 feet in length. The floats are often crowded and you will likely have to raft alongside another vessel. Potable water is available on the float and some electricity is available; make inquiry. A private marina on the east shore has slips for smaller vessels. Float-planes, commercial and private, use the airplane float on the east shore. Heads up! Airplane and helicopter traffic is heavy at all hours!

When turning around here or going alongside another vessel, take into consideration the velocity of water flooding into, or the strong flow ebbing out of Delkatla Inlet through the causeway at the head of the inlet.

The village of Masset has a population of about 885, while Old Massett is home to 600 Haida. Both villages are connected by road to Port Clements, Juskatla,

Tlell, Skidegate, and Daajing Giids, and to Sandspit by ferry and road. Masset has marine fuels at the public wharf, a post office, hospital, RCMP detachment, a motel, bed and breakfasts, grocery, hardware, liquor, and dry goods stores, credit union, churches, cafe/restaurants, and a public library. The Delkatla Wildlife Sanctuary is on the northeast side of the causeway crossing Delkatla Inlet. Dixon Entrance Maritime Museum, with exhibits on the early settlement and maritime history of Masset, is in the renovated 90-year old former hospital, several blocks north of the Delkatla Inlet boat basin. There is now a hospital midway between Masset and Old Massett.

Masset Sound
Connects Masset Harbour to Masset Inlet
Entrance: 53°59.84'N, 132°08.99'W

Masset Sound provides access for small boats to Graham Island's great inland waterway, Masset Inlet, as well as the village of Port Clements, and the logging camp at Juskatla. The tidal stream attains a maximum of 5.5 knots during the ebb and 5 knots during the flood on spring tides and we found that, although the water is fast, the flow is mostly laminar with minimum turbulence. The duration of slack water is brief, so local vessels use the channel during most parts of the tide.

Masset Inlet (Graham Island)
15 S of Delkatla Inlet Boat Basin
Entrance (N): 53°44.50'N, 132°15.50'W

Masset Inlet is an inland sea with a flat coastline on its eastern side and mountains on its west. Nearly 20 miles long with several fingers, channels and islets, the inlet is open to exploration by cruising vessels and kayaks and, other than major logging activity, it is sparsely visited or populated. Those who want to

Longhouse in Old Massett

explore the outer reaches of Masset Inlet may want to stop in the village of Port Clements to obtain local knowledge and conditions. Here you will find a Post Office, grocery store and a few other amenities. Sheltered anchor sites can be found around the perimeter of Masset Inlet, as well as Juskatla Inlet.

Port Clements
(Graham Island)
19 mi W of Delkatla Inlet Boat Basin
Entrance (breakwater): 53°41.42'N, 132°10.94'W

Juskatla Inlet and Narrows
(Graham Island)
6.1 mi W of Port Clements

Caution: At low water on an 11-foot tide, Juskatla Narrows has a 6-foot waterfall.

Virago Sound
(Graham Island)
14.5 mi W of Masset
Position: 54°06.00'N, 132°30.50'W

Virago Sound is a large open bight somewhat sheltered from westerly swell by Cape Naden and Marzarredo Islands. Naden Harbour provides anchorage over a wide flat bottom of moderate depth. Most vessels coming from Masset will use Smyth Passage to enter Naden Harbour and sportfishing boats use Hodgson Passage when headed to or from Langara Island. Use care in approaching Naden Harbour consulting charts, since the off lying sand bar is very shallow, and be sure to avoid the dangerous mid-channel Hastings and Haswell Reefs.

Once clear of The Bar and Hastings Reefs, favor the far east shore between Deepwater and George Point to avoid mid-channel Haswell Reef 0.6 mi NE of George Point.

Floats at Masset Harbour

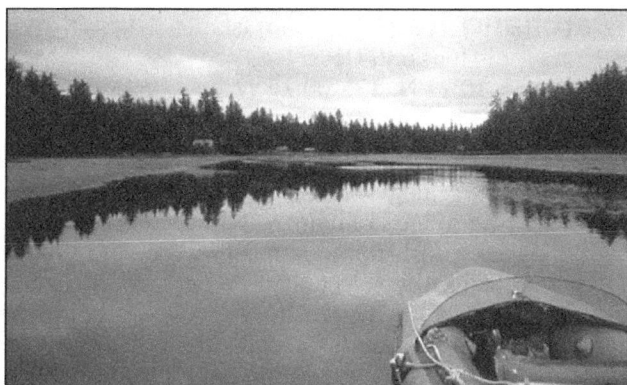

Photo courtesy *Pacific Voyager/Sea Cabana*

Port Clements

Naden Harbour (Graham Island)

9.6 mi SW of Refuge Cove
Anchor (SE Richard III Bnk): 54°01.25'N, 132°34.52'W
Anchor (Craft Bay): 54°00.04'N, 132°34.19'W

Naden Harbour is a large, landlocked body of water five miles long with a generally flat bottom that allows ample swinging room for a number of vessels. The only disappointment we had in anchoring here is that the bottom is very soft mud with a consistency of Jello. Although the harbor is protected in all weather, you may find that your anchor slowly drags when the wind blows with any strength. One commercial operator we know told us he sometimes drags from one side to the other, but that does not concern him since there's so much swinging room. We found that westerlies blowing in Dixon Entrance translate into southwesterlies in Naden Harbour.

There are several sportfishing resorts in the harbour. They run small sportfishing boats that leave the harbor early in the morning. The lodges are serviced by water taxis, helicopters, and float planes during the day.

Good anchorage can be found at two sites: on the east side of Richard III Bank, south of the two DFO mooring buoys; in Craft Bay between the log dump, on the south, and the log storage area, on the north. Anchorage can also be found anywhere at the south end of the bay in 3 to 4 fathoms.

Logging operations are conducted inland and the logs loaded and barged out of the harbor. Since some logs may escape the boom or fall off the barge, be alert for deadheads and driftwood. The old Haida village of Kung is located at Mary Point, where a few weathered totems remain. Naden Harbour was once the site of a whaling station. Closed during World War II, its only relic is a tall concrete tower in front of the fishing lodge at Germania Creek.

Anchor in 5 fathoms (southeast of Richard III Bank) over sand, gravel sea grass and kelp; fair holding.

Anchor (Craft Bay) in 4 fathoms over very soft grey mud; fair holding.

The Golden Spruce of Haida Gwaii

A 300-year old Sitka spruce with a rare genetic mutation that gave it a striking golden color grew near Port Clements, on northern Graham island in the Haida Gwaii archipelago. Known as *Kiidk'yaas*, the Golden Spruce, the mutation caused the tree's chloroplasts to break down when exposed to ultraviolet light. This would normally cause a plant's death, but the almost perpetual cloud cover over the stormy islands enabled the tree to survive. Lack of chlorophyll in the parts of the tree exposed to sunlight gave the needles a glowing golden color. Shaded parts of the tree retained enough chlorophyll for the tree to grow to 165 feet tall, with a symmetric conical form unusual in the Sitka spruce.

The love and respect the Haida people have for their island home are deeply embedded in their culture. The Haida who lived near the golden spruce claimed the ability to interpret the tree's feelings and it became a symbol of the tribe's existence. There are many variations of Haida stories about the unusual tree that has now become a metaphor for disruption and loss.

The Sitka spruce of old growth forests had escaped logging during the early years of industrial exploitation. After World War I, when it was discovered that the species' lightweight yet strong properties were a valuable commodity in building aircraft, the logging industry in British Columbia began unlimited clear-cutting of old-growth forests. Amid wider destruction, the golden spruce of Haida Gwaii was spared as a curiosity and cultural icon. In the 1990's, logger-turned-activist Grant Hadwin began advocating for cutting limits. Frustrated that policymakers were ignoring the protection of old growth forests while using the mutant tree as tourist bait, Hadwin came up with a delusional plan to publicize the devastation. One night in the winter of 1997, Hadwin took his chainsaw and nearly cut through its trunk, leaving the tree teetering. The next day, high winds brought the 165-foot tree crashing down, destroying every tree in its path. Hadwin was arrested. Local feeling ran extremely high against him, since his crime was viewed as a symbolic murder of the Haida people. On the day he was to appear in court, he paddled his sea kayak to the proceedings, but he never arrived, nor was he ever heard from again. Many believe he drowned in the rough seas while others suspect he was dealt with by the people he'd angered; some wondered if he simply fled into the wilderness.

Read John Vaillant's account in his book, *The Golden Spruce: A True Story of Myth, Madness, and Greed.*

—KK

Pillar Bay (Graham Island)
21.1 mi W of Refuge Cove
Entrance: 54°09.66'N, 132°54.33'W
Anchor: 54°09.06'N, 132°54.10'W

The distinctive 95-foot Pillar Rock in Pillar Bay is the outstanding attraction of Graham Island's north coast. The seaward side of Pillar Rock has a nearly vertical drying ledge where, if the tide is at the proper stage, you can pull alongside and step ashore to inspect and photograph it. Neil and Betty Carey sighted a nest of peregrine falcons atop Pillar Rock when they last visited the bay.

A sandy landing beach lies to the east of Pillar Rock. Anchorage can be found off this landing beach, in the lee of Seath Point in moderate southerly weather. Avoid the kelp beds off Seath Point and the kelp close to shore. Very little westerly swell penetrates Pillar Bay.

Anchor in 4 fathoms over sand and gravel; good-to-very good holding.

Parry Passage (Dixon Entrance)
S side of Langara Island
Entrance (E): 54°10.67'N, 132°57.41'W
Entrance (W): 54°11.60'N, 133°01.56'W

Bruin Bay (Parry Passage)
1.5 mi SE Henslung Cove
Entrance: 54°10.24'N, 132°58.72'W
Anchor: 54°10.10'N, 132°58.89'W

Lovely Bruin Bay can be used as a temporary anchor site for small boats in settled weather. Tucked up near the kelp beds, little current can be felt here during neap tides. Contrary to the chart, there were no remaining mooring buoys in the bay in 2001. A gray sand and gravel beach lies above the shoreline where a Haida Watchman's cabin, with a radio antenna and a sign, is partially hidden in the trees.

Anchor in 6 fathoms, over grey sand, gravel and kelp; fair holding if you set your anchor well.

Floundering buoy, Marchand Reef

Marchand Reef (Graham Island)
0.75 mi S of Henslung Cove
Anchor: 54°10.74'N, 133°00.77'W

Marchand Reef was once considered the place to anchor or moor while you were visiting the long-abandoned Haida villages of Kiusta and Yaku where a few decaying totems remain, or while hiking the low, well-marked forest trail to Lepas Bay. The old village sites were carefully selected to be near good fishing waters and beaches where heavy dugouts could be landed. Kiusta is known for its triple mortuary pole, now badly decayed, but visible from close offshore. There is a Haida cabin above the beach at this site at the start of the trail that leads across to Lepas Bay, where the Haida conduct a Rediscovery Program in the summer. Visitors who wish to go ashore at this location are asked to make prior arrangements in Old Massett.

Although you can anchor in the lee of the reef, out of most of the current, we would consider this a marginal site at best. Beal Cove would be a better choice in bad weather. Do not confuse Marchand Reef, which is submerged on a 10-foot tide, with Chanal Reef, a half-mile west and exposed at high water.

Anchor in 3 fathoms over grey sand and shells, gravel, eelgrass and kelp; fair holding.

Langara Island (also known as North Island)
31 mi NW of Masset Hbr.

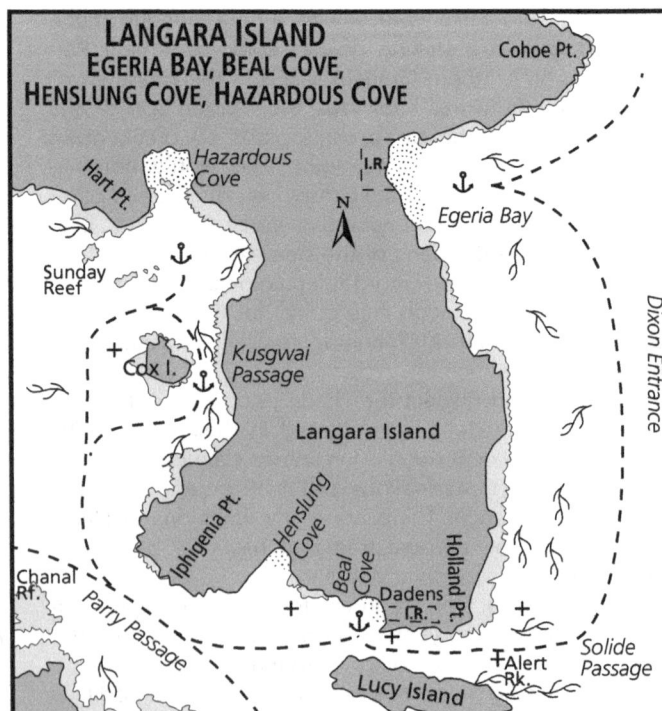

©2024 Don and Réanne Douglass • Diagram not for navigation

Pacific Voyager *at Pillar Rock*

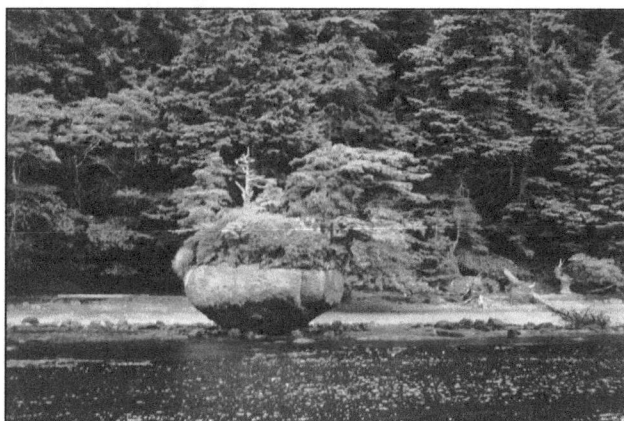

Testlatlints Rock, Parry Passage

Beal Cove
(Langara Island)
0.4 mi E of Henslung Cove
Anchor: 54°11.24'N, 132°59.45'W

Beal Cove, west of Village Point, offers perhaps the best protection from southeast winds on Langara Island, however, the small cove is largely filled with large floats for floating sport fishing lodges and lodges on shore. Anchorage can be found south of the floats; however there may be old buoy or lodge cables along the bottom. Helicopters and float planes come and go to lodges and resorts in Henslung Cove, just to the west, and Beal Cove, making Beal Cove a noisy place in summer. However, its proximity to Cape Knox makes it a convenient anchorage for one boat.

Anchor in 4 fathoms over a mixed bottom of sand, gravel, kelp and eelgrass; fair-to-good holding; limited swinging room. (If more swinging room is needed in a southeast blow, consider Kusgwai Passage.)

Testlatlints Rock
Position: 54°11.35'N, 132°59.71'W

This rock, which lies between Beal Cove and Henslung Cove, is a whimsical rock formation that resembles a gigantic flower bowl with small trees and bushes sprouting from its top.

Henslung Cove
(Langara Island)
17. mi NW of Naden Hbr.
Entrance: 54°11.33'N, 133°00.17'W

Henslung Cove is a busy, noisy place full of sportfishing boats that race around at all hours and float planes or helicopters that land and take off frequent-

ly. Shore-based and floating sportsfishing lodges operate here from about the second week in May until the second week of September. Guests are brought in and taken out by floatplanes or helicopters. In an emergency, it is sometimes possible to board a flight to Masset or Sandspit. (Inquire at the attractive lodge on the hillside.)

Kusgwai Passage
(Cox Island)
0.9 mi N of Henslung Cove
Kusgwai Passage Entrance S: 54°12.19'N, 133°00.88'W
Anchor: 54°12.22'N, 133°00.53'W

Kusgwai Passage, the charmingly scenic passage between Langara and Cox islands, can be used as a nice lunch stop or as an anchor site in fair weather. This site appears to be sheltered from southeast gales. One boat of less than 45 feet can anchor. Small Cox Island has several attractive pinnacle rocks over 100 feet high from whose summits sprout trees and shrubs. A sandy beach lies along its east shore and vertical cliffs line its western shore; a large hole lets light through the rocky pillar at its south side. The Langara shoreline has two fine gravel beaches where a dinghy or kayak can be beached.

In fair weather no northwest swell enters the passage and, while swinging room is restricted, we would not hesitate to anchor off the south side of Cox Island. Shallow-draft boats can traverse Kusgwai Passage when there is adequate tide as the fairway almost dries on zero tide; due to the clarity of the water you can see the sandy bottom throughout the passage.

Anchor (southeast of Cox Island) in 2 to 3 fathoms over sand and shells fair holding; hazardous limited swinging room.

Cloak Bay (Langara Island)
1.2 mi NW of Henslung Cove

Cloak Bay is exposed to southwest swell. Moderate protection can be found in Hazardous Cove, north of Sunday Reef, with good swinging room.

Hazardous Cove (Langara Island)
0.5 mi N of Kusgwai Passage
Entrance: 54°12.53'N, 133°00.96'W
Anchor: 54°12.81'N, 133°00.70'W

Hazardous Cove deserves its name. Although protected from the prevailing northwest swell by Sunday Reef, its foreshore and shoreline are quite rocky, and it is exposed to the southwest. It is useful only as a temporary anchor site in stable weather. There is a sand and gravel beach northeast of Hart Point. East winds may flow through the low saddle from Egeria Bay on Langara's east side.

Anchor in 9 fathoms over sand and gravel with fair holding.

Fury Bay (Langara Island)
1.4 mi W of Hazardous Cove
Position: 54°13.22'N, 133°02.88'W

Fury Cove lies behind a long reef and kelp beds that extend west of Rhodes Point. The sea breaks violently on this reef, even in stable weather, and the rocky shoreline is littered with logs and driftwood. The only landing beach is at the north side behind a small islet. We feel that this cove is of no interest for cruising vessels.

Neil Carey says: "Some of the candid old seamen had enchanting ways with words and names. We have been in these waters some four times, but never considered it prudent to anchor. Once, Betty and a friend were able to land and launch through light surf, while I remained aboard and underway. Peregrine falcons and their prey—ancient and marbled murrelets—nest in this wild and scenic area."

Langara Light Station

Kusgwai Passage anchor site

Langara Light Station (Langara Island)
4.5 mi NW of Henslung Cove
Position: 54°15.34'N, 133°02.53'W

Langara Light Station, considered to have the wildest winter weather on the B.C. coast, is one of the two dozen or more manned light stations remaining in B.C. A small cove northeast of the compound is used for loading and unloading supplies by boat or helicopter. If the weather is calm and your boat can maneuver the tight entrance, you may be able to visit the light station. A large sea lion colony lives on the Langara Rocks 1.5 miles east of Langara Light.

Explorer Bay and Dibrell Bay (Langara Island)
N of Egeria Bay (Explorer) 1.5 mi; (Dibrell) 0.9 mi
Anchor (Explorer): 54°14.45'N, 132°58.67'W
Anchor (Dibrell): 54°14.02'N, 132° 58.06'W

Explorer Bay, which is protected from the westerly swell, has room where two to three small vessels can anchor in 6 to 7 fathoms outside the line of kelp. Entering Explorer Bay from the northwest, clear the unnamed point south of Andrews Point before rounding into the bay. The shoreline is rocky with a small stony beach. Avoid the large rock awash at high water in the south side of the bay. We sighted numerous pigeon guillemots and Cassin's aucklets inside the bay.

Dibrell Bay is surrounded by a rocky foreshore and a thick forest. Temporary anchorage in fair weather can be found off the rocky foreshore or in front of the gravel beach. Drift logs on shore indicate lack of protection in stormy weather. During our anchor-test we fouled the anchor on seaweed and kelp and were unable to get a hold. Egeria Bay is the preferred anchorage during prevailing westerly weather.

Sportfishing boat, Egeria Bay

Oak Bay

Anchor (Explorer) in 6 to 7 fathoms over hard sand; fair holding.

Anchor (Dibrell) in 6 to 8 fathoms over hard sand and gravel with kelp; poor holding.

Egeria Bay
(Langara Island)
2 mi NE of Henslung Cove
Entrance: 54°13.02′N, 132°58.07′W
Anchor: 54°13.10′N, 132° 58.71′W

Egeria Bay, 1.5 miles north of Holland Point, affords the best anchorage in the vicinity; it is sheltered from all except east winds. In summer and autumn months kelp is visible growing in depths up to 8 fathoms. Anchorage may be obtained in Egeria Bay in about 15 fathoms, mud bottom.

Egeria Bay, a popular anchor site with trollers, provides excellent shelter from prevailing northwesterlies. Tucked in a quarter mile from shore in the northwest corner of the bay, boats will feel only a gentle swell. A gray sandy beach full of logs makes a good haul-out and campsite for kayakers, and a dinghy can be safely landed on the beach at the northwest corner.

When entering from the north, clear Cohoe Point by 200 yards then round into the bay. Kelp lines both the north and south shores; anchor east of the north kelp bed when it bears about 105°M.

A low spit on shore, just east of Cloak Bay allows the strong west wind to spill across the bay during the night, keeping swell to a minimum. In the early morning and at evening, deer like to graze in the rockweed along shore. The waters in this area are especially rich with salmon and halibut. Commercial salmon season has been greatly reduced but, when there are openings, numerous trollers work from dawn to dark around Langara Island, especially along the east side and well into Dixon Entrance. At night the waters from Naden Harbour, west to Graham Island's west coast are aglow with bioluminescence.

Neil Carey writes: "We have anchored in Egeria Bay, close to shore, while numerous salmon trollers, their poles rigged out, ready for the morrow, lay in deeper water. The tinkling of small bells attached to outrigged poles was lulling music. At dawn, engines were started, anchors hauled aboard and the day's work started. Okay, if you don't object to early reveille."

Anchor in 5 to 7 fathoms over sand and gravel; good holding. Pleasure craft over 50 feet and commercial fishing vessels anchor in deeper water.

Northern Dawn Lost on Langara Island

A few weeks after *Baidarka* left Haida Gwaii, we received a copy of the newspaper, *Observer* (18 October 2001 issue), reporting the loss of the 78-foot fishing boat, *Northern Dawn*. The wooden vessel had fished for halibut for decades in the Bering Sea, riding out incredible storms, only to meet her demise in one of the major storms that began hitting the North Coast in late August. *Northern Dawn* had taken refuge on an unspecified DFO buoy in Parry Passage. The buoy gave way in the middle of the night and the boat and buoy were thrown against the rocky shore where the vessel disintegrated underneath the crew. The crew managed to send a MAYDAY, and a USCG helicopter from Ketchikan was able to pluck them off the wreckage just in time, flying them to Prince Rupert. The next morning, viewers said there were very few pieces of *Northern Dawn* that wouldn't fit into a garbage bag.

We were unable to determine the specific buoy involved. But this disaster demonstrates the need to be self-sufficient with oversized anchor gear, and to be skeptical about using the few remaining DFO buoys without testing them first!
—DD

Sandy Beach at Lepas Bay

Photo courtesy Pacific Voyager/Sea Cabana

Solide Passage
N side of Lucy Island
Entrance (E): 54°11.20'N, 132°58.26'W
Entrance (W): 54°11.18'N, 132°59.46'W

For sportfishing boats, Solide Passage is the preferred route to the fishing grounds that lie along the east and north coasts of Langara. We used Solide Passage to regain Parry Passage from the north and found about 3 fathoms minimum in the fairway. Avoid Alert Rocks and all kelp patches.

Lepas Bay
(Graham Island)
0.83 mi S of Cape Knox
Position: 54°09.94'N, 133°04.11 W
Anchor (temporary): 54°10.38'N, 133°04.21
Kayak landing: 54°10.34'N, 133°04.14'W

Rounding Cape Knox to Lepas Bay you leave the sheltered waters of Parry Passage and pick up the swells of the open Pacific. Avoid the prolific reefs and kelp beds close to shore. The cape has numerous trees that have been blown down on its south side—evidence of fierce southerly storms. A flood tide from the south causes chaotic dancing waters off the cape and about 2 knots of current.

The foremost feature of Lepas Bay is a lovely sand beach—almost a mile wide—along its eastern side. The rocky north shore is covered with tall silver snags; "haystacks" with tree-topped summits lie along the foreshore. Massive, sharp headlands form the southwest side of the bay. Swells that break along the sandy beach make landing a dinghy problematic. However, kayakers and dinghies can land, in most weather, in the extreme northwestern cove of the bay, behind two islets 0.7 mile southeast of Cape Knox. *Baidarka* has found temporary anchorage here with minimal swell in prevailing northwest winds.

Even during fine weather, a swell is always felt in the main part of Lepas Bay. When entering the bay from the northwest, avoid three rocks, awash at low water.

Anchor (one boat) in the northwest corner, east of the two islets, in 4 to 5 fathoms over sand and gravel; good holding.

Neil Carey comments: "When approaching Parry Passage from the south during periods of low visibility it is possible to mistake open Lepas Bay for the entrance to Parry Passage—a bad mistake. The gently sloping sands of crescent-shaped Lepas Bay with its rows of breaking waves are easily and safely visited from the shoreside."

Caution: Heading south from Lepas Bay, it is best to pass west of Gatenby Rock. We found an uncharted seamount that breaks every two to three minutes at 54°07.886'N, 133°07.694'W, 0.229 nm west of a charted 6-foot rock and northwest of Lauder Point. We also found five distinct tooth-shaped rocks all showing above water on a 10-foot tide.

Sialun Bay (Graham Island)
5 mi S of Cape Knox
Position: 54°05.93'N, 133°05.30'W

Neil Carey writes: "Sialun Bay is another of the enticing sandy bays along this coast that are lovely to gaze at from a distance but often hazardous to become acquainted with. Wide open, this shallow bay gives little shelter and the hard packed sand bottom is poor for holding. When the sea is calm it is possible to land and leave through the low surf. When the tide is half out, a dinghy can land on the reef inside the south point. Sialun Creek flows into the middle of the bay from behind a high, storm-created sand bank. I once picked a Japanese glass ball, at shoulder height, from the perpendicular sand wall."

Beresford Bay (Graham Island)
8 mi S of Cape Knox
Position: 54°03.30'N, 133° 07.19'W

We found many large knots of floating kelp, 1 to 2 miles north of La Pérouse Reef. This coast is poorly charted and it's best to stay offshore. "I have never seen open Beresford Bay," writes Carey, "when at least one row of white capped waves was not breaking onto the wide and gently sloping sand shore. It is a tempting place but the sea is rarely willing to let you land. Large, fascinating rock formations decorate the upper portion of the north side. Beresford Creek drains the extensive tree covered lowland to the east."

La Pérouse Reef

(Graham Island)
10.6 mi S of Cape Knox
Position: 54°00.85'N, 133°11.02'W

One to 2 miles north of La Pérouse Reef there may be floating knots of unattached kelp that create ribbons of slick water, causing anxiety as you look through your binoculars. The reef has two rocks that show at high water and surf heaps up on a 4-fathom shoal to the north. On Hope Point, storms have sheered off the branches of trees (with a few exceptions)—to a height of 100 feet. *Because these shores are poorly charted, it is best to stay offshore.*

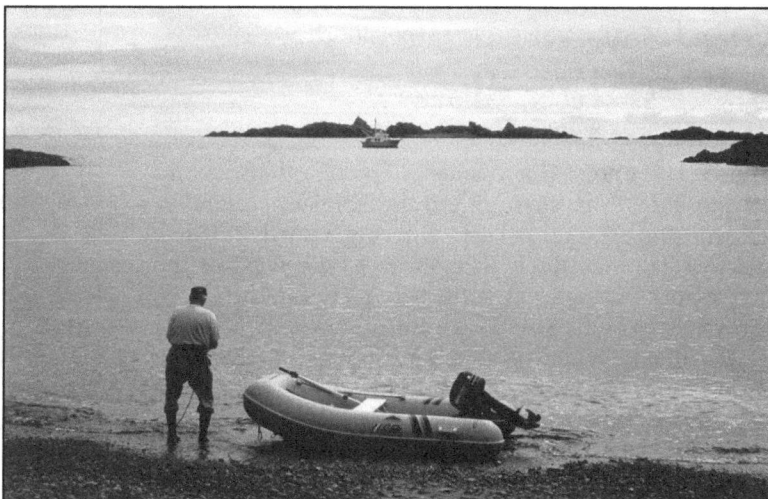

Frank Caldwell beachcombing with Baidarka *and Tian Islets in background*

Beehive Hill

(Graham Island)
0.6 mi SE of Morgan Pt.
Anchor: 53°55.96'N, 133°07.70'W

We found the nook on the east side of Beehive Hill to be a good rest stop in fair weather, since it's protected from northwest swells. There is a good landing beach with a tiny creek and lots of silvery drift logs. The bottom is flat all the way to 1 fathom. Anchor according to tide level and the draft of your boat about 100 yards offshore. We spotted several deer on shore among the shiny logs. Along the south side of the beach the trees have no lower limbs, a possible indication of fierce wind activity. Notice the large patch of downed trees on the southwest side of Frederick Island and along the coast farther south.

Anchor in 1 fathom over firm sand with some patches of kelp; good holding.

Tian Bay

(Graham Island)
11 mi S of Frederick Island
Entrance: 53°44.99'N, 133°04.10'W
Anchor (W): 53°46.13'N, 133°04.76'W
Anchor (E): 53°46.05'N, 133°04.02'W

Tian Bay is the first moderately sheltered anchorage in prevailing northwesterly weather, south of Cape Knox. The Tian Islets form a natural "breakwater" from northwest swells. The islets—a series of grassy knobs—are fun to explore by kayak or dinghy. Northwest swell is negligible in the lee of the islets. However, Tian Bay is exposed to southwest through southeast weather and swells and not recommended for overnight anchorage, except in calm weather. Otard Bay offers more shelter. The western part of Tian Bay has a small landing beach with a small stream, but it is filled with piles of driftlogs, showing the effect of southeast storms; the eastern part of the bay has a gravel beach with grassy shores where Blue Creek enters.

The Tian Islets are home to numerous species of sea birds. The Careys were once caught here by high winds and heavy rain and for two days found shelter for their dory inside the mouth of Blue Creek. The storm gave them time to hike around shore where they found deteriorating artifacts of two cultures: a few weathered and leaning Haida totems; rusted wire rope, drill rods, a steam engine, and a burbling six-inch pipe—remains of an oil drilling effort conducted just prior to WW I.

Anchor (west) in 4 fathoms over firm sand; very good holding.

Anchor (east) in 3 fathoms over sand and gravel with isolated kelp; good holding with a well-set anchor.

Entrance to Blue Creek, Tian Bay

Otard Bay (Graham Island)
3.6 mi E of Tian Head
Entrance: 53°44.60'N, 133°01.69'W
Anchor: 53°45.85'N, 132°59.88'W

Otard Bay, one of the loveliest of our Graham Island "discoveries," is surrounded by forested hillsides. The preferred channel for entering Otard Bay lies west of Thomas Rock. The shore to the west of the creek outlet is covered with driftwood that has been blown 20 to 30 feet above high water. The beach east of the creek, which is more sheltered and has just moderate drift, makes a good landing and camping site, but depths are shallow. We found good overnight shelter in the next bight south where we weathered a 20-knot southeast wind inside a line between the rocks off the north and south points of the east shore. The bottom at this site appears fairly flat to within about the 2-fathom curve. We don't know what this site would be like in a southeast gale, but it is the best available anchorage on a southbound voyage before reaching Port Louis.

A dark river flows in from behind a high sandbar at its head and, at high tide, you can take a dinghy upstream for about a half-mile, following mossy shores where there are no signs of human existence. We have heard reports that a trail follows the creek then leads to Naden Harbour; if so, we didn't notice it. The beach south of the creek has evidence of both old and new camping activity. We found a "culturally modified tree" (CMT) that was strip-barked by indigenous people. This is an excellent area for kayak haul-out and camping.

Anchor in about 2 to 3 fathoms over sand, broken shells and black mud; very good holding.

Cobble Beach, Otard Bay

Port Louis (Graham Island)
28.5 mi S of Cape Knox
Entrance: 53°42.75'N, 133°00.76'W

Port Louis is a region that could divert the hiker, birdwatcher, fisherman, or photographer for days. Steep hills surround most of this tree-shrouded region. In Port Louis shoals reduce the fairway to north and south of Queen Island. Commercial fishermen sometimes anchor near the island's east side in about 11 fathoms with a mud bottom. Deer are often seen browsing on the grassy flats at the head of Port Louis, near Coates River. A fish ladder has been constructed along the north side of the Coates River falls and Coho salmon are released here. This is creating a new fishery, and other species of salmon are expected to spawn in the stream and lakes draining into Coates River. Within Port Louis, very good anchorage can be found in Tingley Cove.

Tingley Cove (Port Louis)
1 mi SW of Port Louis
Entrance: 53°41.59'N, 132°57.23'W
Anchor: 53°41.17'N, 132°57.92'W

Tingley Cove, deep in Port Louis behind Alured Point, is the most secure anchorage between Cape Knox and Rennell Sound. The cove appears bombproof with no signs of shore stress. The water temperatures deep in Port Louis are typically several degrees warmer than the outer coast, inviting dozens of Lions Mane jellyfish.

In the far west corner of Tingley Cove, there is a dump for old fuel drums; oil drilling was conducted in this area years ago. Neil Carey says that the sight of the dawn sun striking on 1,865-foot Mt. Louis due east is well worth early reveille.

Anchor in 6 fathoms over soft brown mud with large clam and oyster shells and copper-colored shale rocks; very good holding.

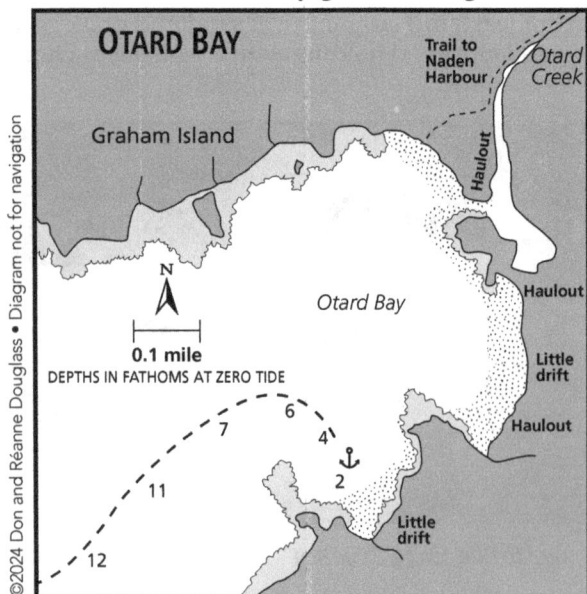

OTARD BAY

Trail to Naden Harbour · Otard Creek

Graham Island

Haulout

N

Otard Bay

Haulout

0.1 mile
DEPTHS IN FATHOMS AT ZERO TIDE

Little drift

6

7

4

Haulout

2

11

Little drift

12

©2024 Don and Réanne Douglass • Diagram not for navigation

Anchor site at Otard Bay

Coates Creek with salmon ladder, left, Port Louis

East Cove

(Port Louis)
1 mi NE of Tingley Cove
Anchor: 53°41.66'N, 132°56.52'W

The cove just west of Coates Creek outlet provides sheltered anchorage off the steep-to lagoon entrance. This is a good place to explore the eastern section of Port Louis and the Coates Creek. The lagoon to the south, as well as the margin along the Coates Creek peninsula, is a favorite of deer. We watched as four deer ate sea grass hanging from cedar limbs.

Anchor in about 10 fathoms over mud and shells; good holding.

Kiokathli Inlet

(Port Louis)
Entrance: 53°41.38'N, 133°00.10'W
Anchor: 53°40.76'N, 132°59.46'W

Short and narrow Kiokathli Inlet offers protected anchorage. Good anchorage can be found off the entrance to the saltchuck on the east shore. The saltchuck, which is larger than charted, is full of steamer clams.

Neil Carey writes: "A short hike across the neck of grassy low land on the inlet's south side takes you to the stony shore of Hosu Bay. If the sea is raging in from the west the bay may appear as a mass of flying scud. A vein of red jasper shows in a low cliff just a few minutes hike to the west."

Anchor in 6 fathoms over brown mud; good holding.

Athlow Bay

(Graham Island)
4 mi SW of Port Louis
Entrance: 53°87.10'N, 133°01.75'W

Athlow Bay is a rugged and fearsome coast with an irregular bottom. Our track showed a number of uncharted seamounts reaching to within 60 feet of the surface with surrounding waters of 40 to 60 fathoms.

Among the attractions of Athlow Bay are bold Celestial Bluff, caves, rocks and reefs with screaming or crashing breakers, beaches of sand, gravel, and rocks, salmon and halibut fishing. Perhaps you will see a fast-flying peregrine falcon or hear its long series of slurred notes.

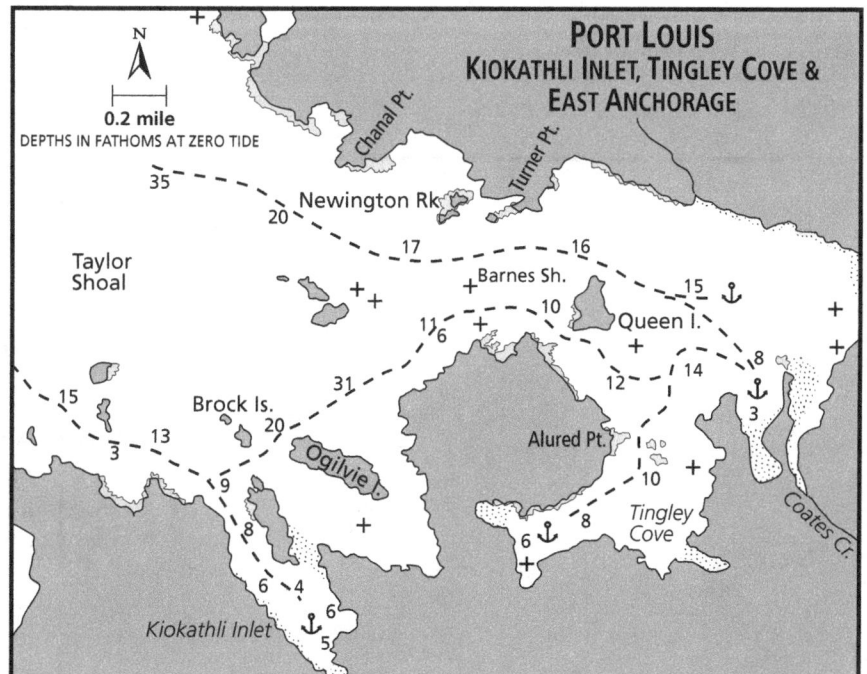

PORT LOUIS
KIOKATHLI INLET, TINGLEY COVE & EAST ANCHORAGE

N
0.2 mile
DEPTHS IN FATHOMS AT ZERO TIDE

©2024 Don and Réanne Douglass • Diagram not for navigation

Hosu Cove (Athlow Bay)
3 mi SW of Port Louis
Entrance: 53°39.25'N, 132°58.61'W

Hosu Cove is uncharted and appears to us to be filled with breakers across its north half. David and Noreen of *Pacific Voyager* visited Hosu Cove by hiking south from Kiokathli Inlet and said that it appears to be too rocky to enter by boat. Neil Carey writes that it is a fascinating water-land of flying spray and crashing breakers during westerly swells. "On calm days its seldom explored rocks, reefs, and jagged shoreline offer hours of entertainment, ashore or in a small boat; all with a background of steep, tree covered hillsides rising to bare or snow crowned mountains." When the sea is favorable, the small bay just east of Gillan Point is worthy of a stop and short hike across the low neck to the tiny, nearly identical bay to the north that opens on Hosu Cove.

Mace Creek anchorage, Port Chanal

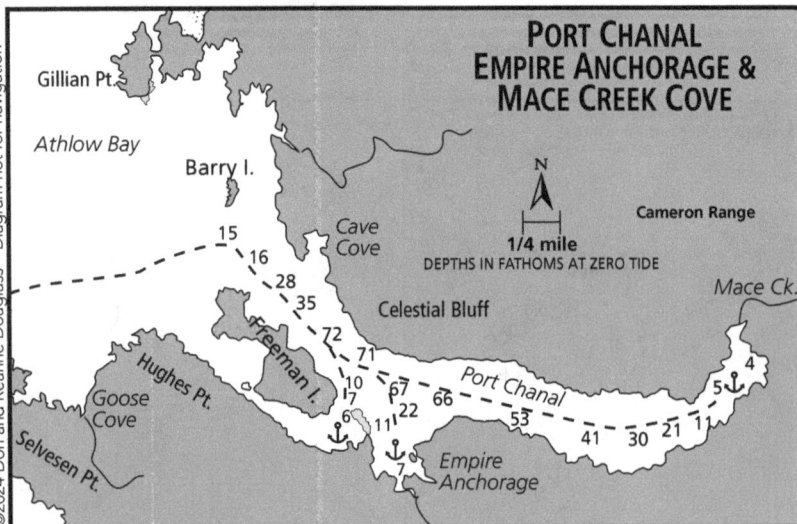

©2024 Don and Reanne Douglass • Diagram not for navigation

Port Chanal (Graham Island)
6 mi S of Port Louis
Entrance: 53°37.13'N, 132°57.02'W
Anchor: 53°36.06'N, 132°49.21'W

The region of Port Chanal is an Ecological Reserve with many places to explore. For a pleasant anchorage we prefer Mace Creek over Empire Anchorage. The word "Port" is just part of the name, not an indication of facilities usually associated with that word.

Cave Cove (Port Chanal)
0.5 mi E of S end of Barry Island

"Cave Cove"—our name for the small, uncharted cove with a big cave at its head east of Barry Island. This is another great place for the intrepid to explore. The bottom is irregular with numerous kelp patches, but temporary anchorage can be taken by small boats in about 2 fathoms half-way into the cove with limited swinging room. Although this site is protected from northwest winds, it is shallow and rocky and we recommend it only for its cave, not as an anchorage.

Anchor in 2 fathoms over sand patches, gravel and kelp and rocks with poor holding

Empire Anchorage (Port Chanal)
0.5 mi E of Goose Cove
Anchor: 53°35.24'N, 132°54.32'W

Empire Anchorage offers good protection from southeast winds but has poor holding. We found the bottom here was also irregular suggesting lots of rocks. We prefer the anchor site at Mace Creek.

Anchor in 8 to 10 fathoms over a hard rocky bottom; poor holding unless you can get a good set.

Mace Creek Cove (Port Chanal)
3 mi E of Empire Anchorage
Entrance: 53°35.55'N, 132°54.39'W
Anchor: 53°35.99'N, 132°49.41'W

"Mace Creek Cove" is our name for the attractive anchorage, nearly landlocked, off Mace Creek's drying mud flat at the head of Port Chanal. A large flat area that ranges between 3 and 5 fathoms provides ample swinging room for a number of boats. The cove appears to be relatively well sheltered and well worth the extra miles to find it. Keep a mid-channel route to avoid Chanal rocks on the south side and several smaller rocks off the north shore near the entrance. We found little stress along the shore to indicate strong winds but williwaws may descend from the high towering peaks on occasion.

Mace Creek Cove—one of the more attractive and remote anchorages on Graham Island's west coast—is surrounded by lovely, mist-covered peaks and forests of hemlock, spruce and cedar. We saw Canada geese grazing in grassy meadows along the creeks. We hope you like this site as much as we do!

Anchor in 5 fathoms over mud and shells with good holding.

Caution: We found several submerged uncharted sea mounts of 10 fathoms or less on our track between Selveson Island and Hippa Passage about 0.7 mile off the coast of Selveson Point.

Hippa Island (Pacific Ocean)
U.S.A.T.S. Clarksdale Victory bow: 53°31.41'N, 132°59.10'W

Hippa Island can be passed on either side. Its east side provides a lee for Nesto Inlet and Hippa Passage Cove. On the southwest corner behind an extensive reef lie the sea-battered and rusting remains of Army transport, *Clarksdale Victory* which, while heading south from Alaska without radar and in poor visibility, was blown 25 miles off course and onto the reef during the week of Thanksgiving in 1947. Forty-nine of the fifty-three crew members were lost. (See Neil Carey's *A Guide to the Queen Charlotte Islands*.) Use caution at the south entrance to Hippa Passage to avoid mid-channel reefs and kelp patches.

Tingley Cove

Nesto Inlet (Hippa Passage)
Entrance: 53°33.13'N, 132°56.75'W

Picturesque Nesto Inlet provides good shelter at the head of the inlet behind a number of rocks and reefs that must be avoided when entering. The curving fairway carries about 8 fathoms. Anchorage can be found in the center of the cove, but swinging room is limited. There are two kayak haulouts and campsites amidst large trees east of the islet. You may sight black bear in the inlet during late summer and early fall.

Anchor in 4 to 6 fathoms over soft brown sand and mud and newspaper kelp; holding is poor unless your anchor cuts the kelp.

HIPPA PASSAGE & NESTO INLET

Nesto Inlet

Hippa Passage

Hippa Pt.

N

1/4 mile

DEPTHS IN FATHOMS AT ZERO TIDE

©2024 Don and Réanne Douglass • Diagram not for navigation

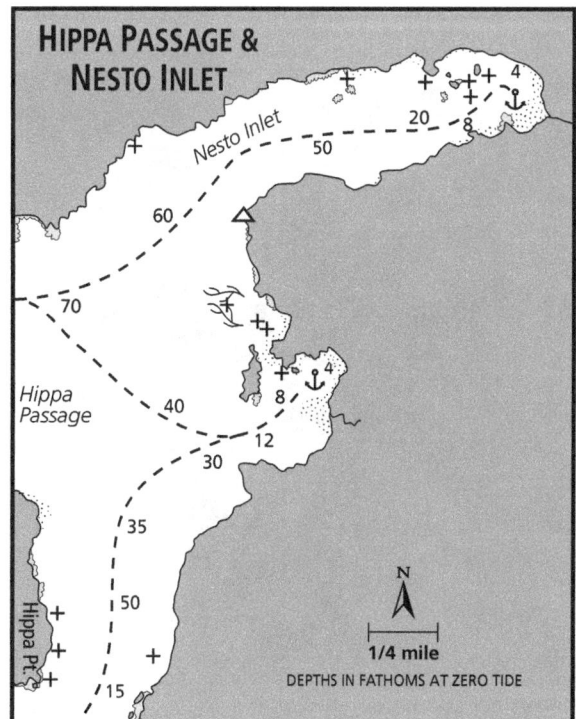

Sea cave, Port Chanal

Photo courtesy *Pacific Voyager/Sea Cabana*

Hippa Passage Cove (Hippa Island)

2.6 mi SE of Marchand Pt.
Entrance: 53°32.46'N, 132°55.97'W
Anchor: 53°32.66'N, 132°55.55'W

"Hippa Passage Cove," our name for the cove in the lee of Hippa Island, south of Nesto Inlet, is protected from prevailing northwest winds by an unnamed island. Good anchorage can be found in a 4-fathom hole; avoid a 1-fathom rock and shoal that extends from the eastern shore. Visibility through the muskeg water is limited. The sandy beach has a haul-out site with camping possibilities.

Anchor in the 4-fathom hole over sand and soft mud with kelp; fair-to-good holding.

Skelu Bay (Graham Island)

3.1 mi S of Nesto Inlet
Entrance: 53°30.24'N, 132°55.73'W

Skelu Bay is entered between Sadler Island and Skelu Point; it is wide open to all seas and winds from the west. The east end is charted only at small scale. On the north side precipitous, forested hills rise to more than 2,000 feet, while uncounted rocks guard the foreshore. The east and south hillsides are also steep and wooded. The bay is not recommended as an anchorage.

Note: From Skelu Point, southward along the entire coast to Cape St. James, the mountains rise in elevation, towering above the shores, and the volcanic formations, sea caves, and sea mounts increase in numbers and ruggedness.

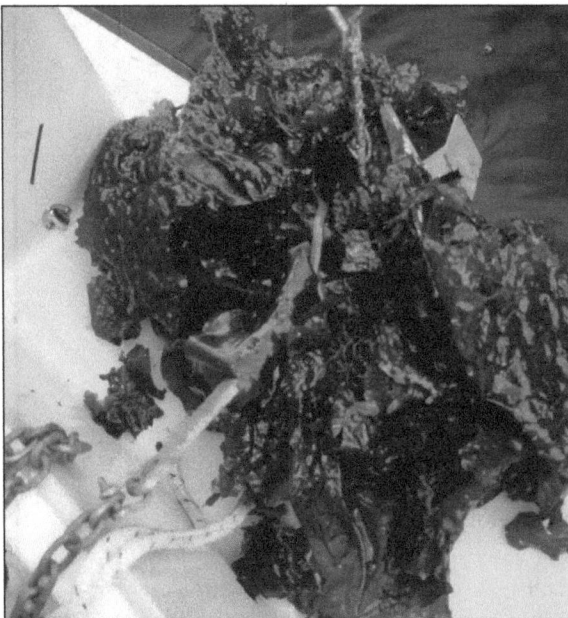

Newspaper kelp on test anchor, Hippa Passage Cove

Seal Inlet (Graham Island)

7 mi SE of Hippa Island
Entrance: 53°28.14'N, 132°48.50'W
Anchor (east): 53°31.33'N, 132°44.33'W
Anchor (head): 53°31.72'N, 132°44.38'W

Anchorage for small boats can be found at Lauder Island Cove inside the entrance to Seal Inlet, or at the head of the inlet on the eastern side of the bay, off the drying mud flat where swinging room is limited. Larger boats can anchor in deeper water, 0.4 mile farther north, in front of the outlet of the unnamed creek. In late summer and early fall salmon return to spawn in the numerous meandering streams draining the valley and surrounding hillsides, and spawning salmon attract black bear. Early one morning, we sighted four deer and three harbor seals here.

Anchor (east) in 8 fathoms over brown mud, small shale rocks and shells; fair-to-good holding; limited

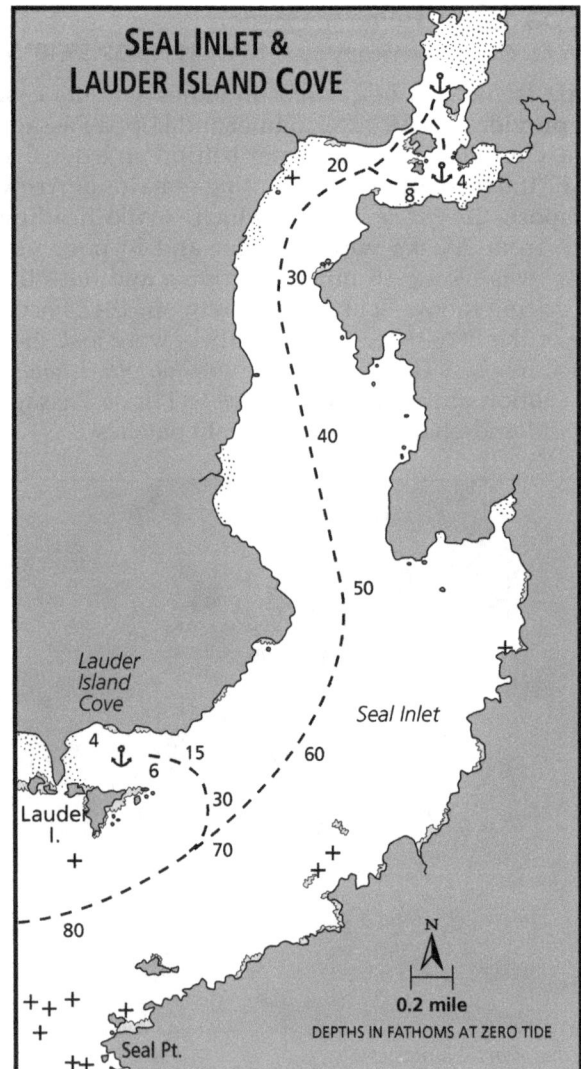

Réanne, creek exploration

swinging room.

Anchor (head) in 6 fathoms over mud and eelgrass with small rocks and shells; fair-to-good holding.

Lauder Island Cove (Seal Inlet)

4.4 mi E of Kunakun Pt.
Anchor: 53°29.01'N, 132°46.47'W

Lauder Island Cove offers good temporary anchorage in settled weather behind a low spit and kelp beds that connect to Lauder Island. There is a good landing beach at the head of the cove where kayakers might find a campsite. On the northeast side of the cove there is a small sea cave that fills on high water.

Anchor in 6 fathoms over gravel and kelp with fair holding.

Tartu Inlet

(Graham Island)
4.5 mi E of Seal Inlet
Entrance: 53°26.45'N, 132°41.57'W
Anchor: 53°29.49'N, 132°40.24'W

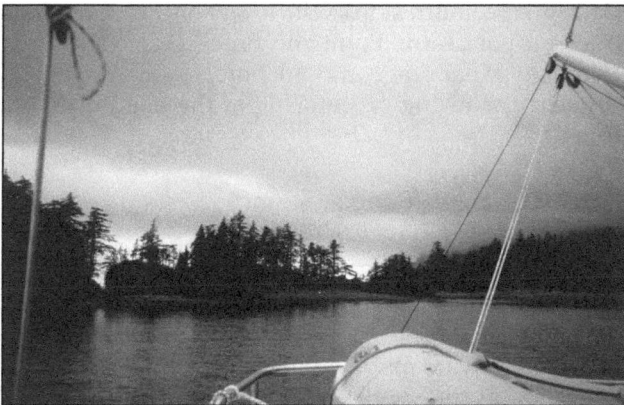

Lauder Island Cove, Seal Inlet

Slim, north-pointing Tartu Inlet on the north side of Rennell Sound is the site of recent logging which has been absent between Cape Knox and Seal Inlet. However, once you reach Tartu Inlet on Rennell Sound the clearcutting becomes obvious.

Near Tartu Point there are several caves whose volcanic rock is covered with bright shades of lichen. As you approach the inlet, 50 feet above the water, see if you can spot a rock formation that resembles a head. North of a log dump and booming area, on the east shore near the head of the inlet, are camp and fuel barges. A few decades ago a large landslide tore through the shore-based camp that was located here.

Anchorage for small boats can be found off the wide, grassy mud flat with stumps and new-growth alders; larger boats can anchor 0.6 mile south of the head of the bay. The hillsides behind the flats have been clearcut and there are numerous hikeable but dead-end roads.

Anchor (head of inlet) in 8-12 fathoms over very soft brown mud; fair-to-good holding.

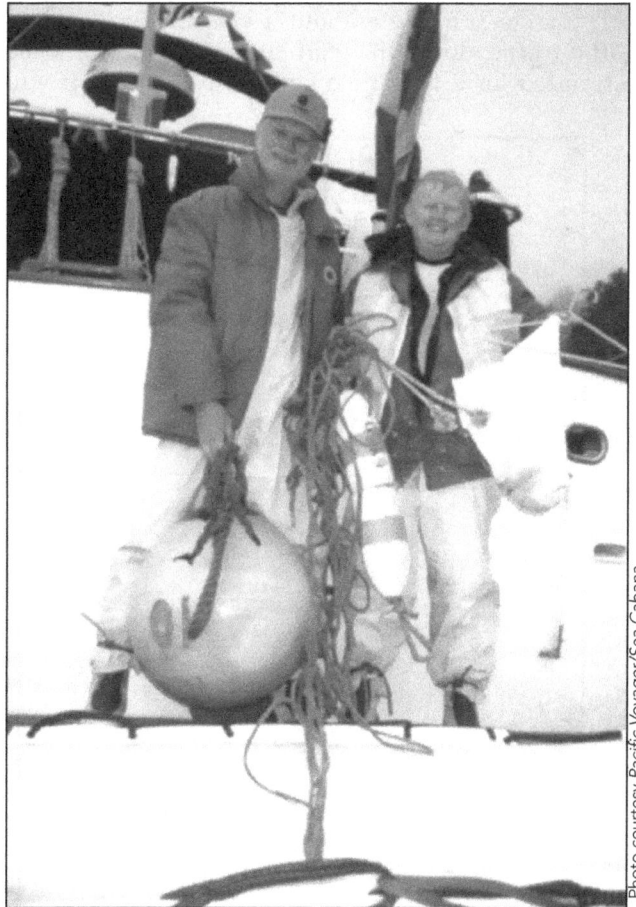

Photo courtesy Pacific Voyager/Sea Cabana

Beachcombing, Frederick Island

Rennell Sound (Graham Island)

14.8 mi N of Skidegate Channel
Entrance: 53°24.00'N, 132°40.50'W

Rennell Sound is the largest of the inlets along Graham Island's west coast; entering requires a 17-mile detour to reach Clapp Basin. Two reasons for making this detour are to seek shelter from storms or to find emergency assistance at the end of the cross-island road. Well-sheltered anchorages can be found from Ells Bay to Clapp Basin. Our favorite is what we call "Annie's Cove" (see below). Rennell Sound is a popular sportfishing and boating area due to its access to Queen Charlotte City via logging roads. Entering the sound is straightforward. Westerly winds follow you into Shields Bay but ocean swells decrease as you head east past Gospel Island.

You will see fishermen and hunters in pick-up trucks with their boat trailers camped along the beach between Shields Creek and Clapp Basin. The rocky, dirt road into Rennell Sound has grades as steep as 24% and locals recommend carrying two spare tires. We once got a flat tire as we approached Clapp Basin. We changed the tire, but had to return up the steep grade without a spare. There is very little traffic along this road, and a vehicle could be stranded for a long time here, so *be prepared* if you

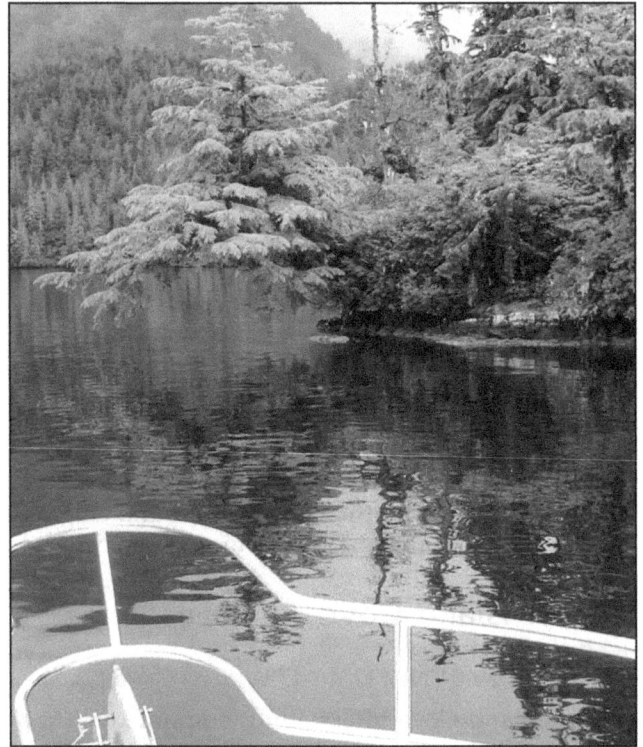

Tree growing over water, Clapp Basin anchorage

plan to put in at Clapp Basin. Occasionally a landslide blocks this or adjacent roads.

Neil Carey writes: "All of the waters from Shields Bay westward offer choice salmon trolling. Toss over a bright flasher and spoon while enjoying the varied scenery of the nearby northern rain forest. Jigging for halibut, ling cod, and red snapper is also a pleasant way of providing the main course for the next meal—or for several meals if you land a large halibut."

Neil continues with advice for boaters who want to avoid entering Rennell Sound. "If northbound, before reaching Rennell Sound, I'd anchor near the smooth sand beach of Carew Bay, east of Cadman Island, on the south side of the broad entrance to Kano Inlet. Or pass Kano Point and proceed into sheltered Givenchy Anchorage and anchor. If southbound, I'd suggest anchoring or mooring at the head of Nesto Inlet."

Shields Bay (Rennell Sound)

12 mi N of Skidegate Channel
Entrance: 53°22.40'N, 132°31.88'W

Shields Bay has a small boat-launch and car-camping area on the beach east of Shields Island and a float and private mooring bouy for a halibut charter operation at the south end of MacKenzie Passage as you enter Clapp Basin.

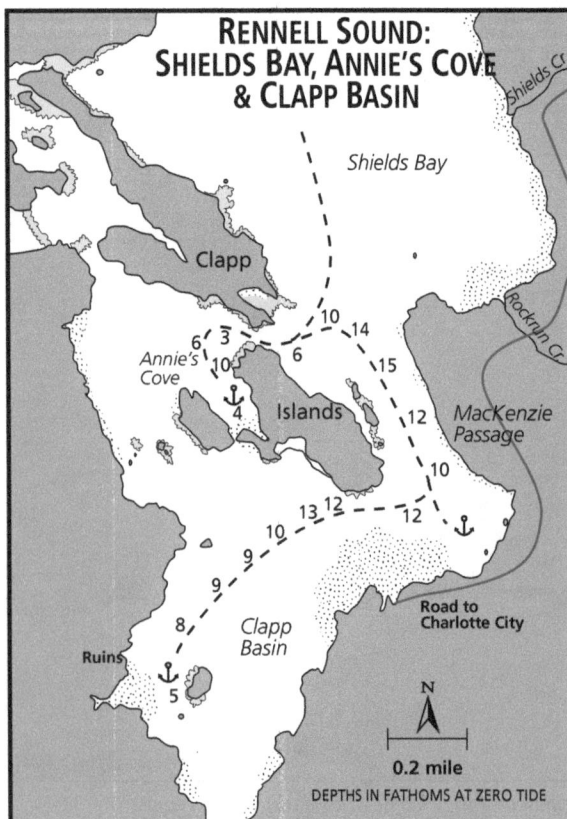

RENNELL SOUND:
SHIELDS BAY, ANNIE'S COVE
& CLAPP BASIN

©2024 Don and Réanne Douglass • Diagram not for navigation

Shields Cr.

Shields Bay

Clapp

Annie's Cove

Islands

Rocknun Cr.

MacKenzie Passage

Road to Charlotte City

Ruins

Clapp Basin

N

0.2 mile

DEPTHS IN FATHOMS AT ZERO TIDE

Réanne photographing tree fungus

Annie's Cove

Clonard Bay (Shields Bay, Rennell Sound)
1.5 mi NW of Shields Island
Anchor: 53°20.68'N, 132°30.61'W

Clonard Bay, an open bight on the west side of Shields Bay, is somewhat exposed to westerly chop and eastern winds. Larger boats that require swinging room may find good shelter at the south end of Ells Bay. The gravel beach, covered with stumps and logs, is backed by clearcuts. Annie's Cove and Clapp Basin are much more scenic and better protected.

Anchor in 8 fathoms; unrecorded bottom.

Clapp Basin (Shields Bay, Rennell Sound)
1 mi S of Shields Island
Entrance: 53°19.19'N, 132°25.42'W
Anchor: 53°18.39'N, 132°26.20'W

Landlocked Clapp Basin, at the bitter end of Rennell Sound, offers well-sheltered anchorage throughout. High snowy mountains tower above the anchorage with a classic steep sided U shaped valley heading inland. Favor the north shore on entering to avoid the large sand and gravel flat covered with stumps and grass extending north from the south shore (parking area) at the south end of MacKenzie Passage.

Our preferred anchorage lies just north of the small island at the west side of Clapp Basin. This site is off some ruins and a low valley with logging road to the southwest which crosses 2.5 miles to Van Inlet. This island will provide some shelter if williwaws blow down from the high peaks to the southeast. Annie's Cove will provide even more shelter from southeast williwaws.

Anchor in about 8 fathoms over soft brown mud with broken shells with fair to good holding.

Annie's Cove (Shields Bay, Rennell Sound)
0.5 mi NW of MacKenzie Passage
Anchor (nook): 53°18.97'N, 132°25.94'W
Anchor (basin center): 53 19.05'N, 132 26.14'W

Baidarka's first mate liked the small, intimate cove on the west side of the Clapp Islands that we now call "Annie's Cove." Although its entrance is narrow, inside, there is complete shelter without the views of the clearcutting that has occurred in Rennell Sound.

Entrance into Annie's Cove is from the east via a narrow channel between the two main Clapp Islands. Favor the north shore—there is a rock that dries on a 12-foot tide and a shoal that extends from the south island. The narrow fairway carries 3 to 4 fathoms minimum. The small nook on the south side is very calm and quiet with enough room for just a couple of boats in an intimate natural setting of unusual beauty and solitude. This is a place where river otters and harbor seals play and time passes slowly.

Small boats can anchor in this nook, north of a small window between two islands in 3 to 5 fathoms. Larger boats can anchor in the central basin in about 10 fathoms with more swinging room. The intricate waterway north of Annie's Cove is basically a saltwater lagoon and best explored by kayak or dinghy.

Anchor (nook) in 4 fathoms over soft brown mud and clam shells; good-to-very good holding.

Anchor (center of basin) in 10 fathoms over soft brown mud with good holding.

Kano Inlet (Graham Island)

9.8 mi NW of Skidegate Channel
Entrance: 53°17.41'N, 132°44.79'W

Kano Inlet is entered via the wide, deep-water channel between Fame Point and Kindakun Point. An automated weather station located on Kindakun Point gives important updates on the weather channels. You can carefully pass Kindakun Point inside the off-lying Kindakun Rocks, if visibility and conditions allow, in a fairway of about 12 fathoms.

Anchorage in fair weather can be found in Carew Bay or, for more complete shelter, in Givenchy Anchorage.

Givenchy Anchorage (Kano Inlet)

7.6 mi E of Kindakun Pt.
Entrance: 53°19.00'N, 132°33.47'W
Anchor: 53°18.31'N, 132°33.44'W

Landlocked Givenchy Anchorage, at the head of Kano Inlet, is fully sheltered.

From mid-May until mid-September you may find one of the floating sports fishing lodges moored or anchored here, or in some other well protected inlet or bay along the north or west coast of Haida Gwaii. If you do find one of these lodges, it is likely that you can tie alongside for a short time and fill up with fresh water. These lodges, whether ashore or afloat, provide a number of self-propelled boats for nearly three-dozen guests whom you will encounter long before sighting the lodge.

You may notice the unusual anthropomorphic formation of peaks and hills found at the south end of the inlet, sometimes called Kano Lady.

The bottom of the anchorage is mostly flat with depths of 11 to 14 fathoms. Use plenty of scope if southeast winds are forecast because of potential williwaws flowing down from Kano Lady.

Anchor in about 12 fathoms over soft brown mud with twigs; fair-to-good holding.

Carew Bay (Graham Island)

4.5 mi E of Kindakun Pt.
Entrance: 53°18.14'N, 132°38.96'W
Anchor: 53°17.57'N, 132°38.12'W

Carew Bay, on the south shore of Kano Inlet, provides moderate shelter in fair weather. Cad-

Basalt columns near Tana Bay

man Island forms the west side of this lovely sandy bay with a tombolo that connects to Graham Island awash on a mid tide. We have found some surge here when SW swells are running. A small stream flows across the sand beach. The prior DFO buoys are no longer here.

While Carew Bay is more convenient than Givenchy Anchorage, the bay is not calm. Its hard-packed sand and gravel beach behind some kelp patches has easy landing. The visibility through the water is good here as the water does not drain from muskeg. There are several small streams and a small amount of driftwood.

Anchor in 8 to 12 fathoms over a firm sand and gravel bottom with isolated kelp with fair holding unless well set.

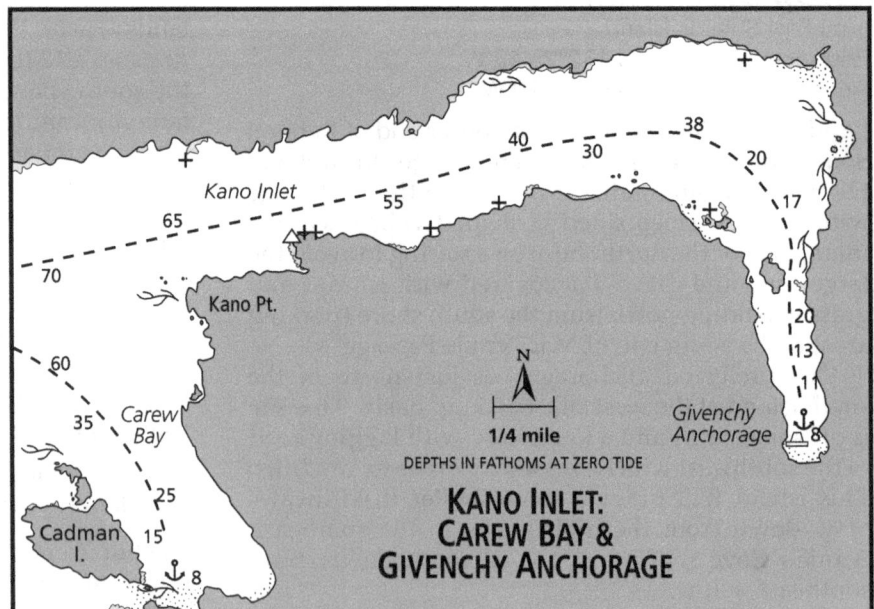

KANO INLET:
CAREW BAY &
GIVENCHY ANCHORAGE

©2024 Don and Réanne Douglass • Diagram not for navigation

S/V Faraway, *Givenchy Anchorage*

Marble Island, Gudal and Tana Bays
(Cartwright Sound)
5 mi NW of Skidegate Channel
Position: 53°13.00'N, 132°40.00'W

Marble Island is approximately midway on a direct line between Tcenakun and Hunter Points and a leading mark for boats headed to or from Skidegate Channel. The island is a bird sanctuary and a popular stop for whales around its prolific rocks and reefs. The bare summit of double-peaked La Pérouse Mountain (3,675 feet) looms large to the east. A radar station was erected atop 475-foot Marble Island during World War II and a few tumbled pieces of the buildings remain.

In summer and early fall sports and commercial fishermen from Sandspit and Queen Charlotte City will often be encountered in these fish-rich waters.

Gudal and Tana bays, on Cartwright Sound's eastern shore, do not offer safe anchorage. Tana Bay has some striking basalt columns on the north side of Ells Point; its steep gravel beach may attract beachcombers. Look for a blowhole where water spouts to 20 feet or more and notice the orange, light yellow, black and grey shades of the volcanic rock. The golden sands of Gudal Bay, with its stream, are tempting for the hiker.

Van Inlet (Cartwright Sound)
3 mi NE of Marble Island
Entrance: 53°14.62'N, 132° 37.73'W

Van Inlet is long, steep-sided and deep throughout. Although it appears to be well-protected, it is too deep for convenient anchorage. When entering the inlet, avoid the mid-channel rocks at the entrance.

A visit by Fisheries officers off Marble Island

Portions of the inlet's steep hillsides have been logged. A large sea-level cave is in the bold headland of Stiu Point. Indifferent anchorage in 10 fathoms at the head is not worth the time to make the nearly 5-mile trip.

Dawson Inlet (Graham Island)
4.8 mi W of West Narrows

Steep-sided Dawson Inlet is similar to Fiordland with the 3,675-foot La Pérouse Mountain towering above the west shore at the head of the inlet. Depths within the inlet are too great for convenient anchorage.

Dawson Harbour (Dawson Inlet)
4.2 mi W of West Narrows
Anchor: 53°09.71'N, 132°27.60'W

Our preferred place to anchor is on the south side of the small whale-shaped islet half-way up Dawson Harbour on its south shore. There is no evidence of shore stress; there are no driftlogs, and it is quiet and calm during southeast winds.

Anchor in 6½ fathoms over soft mud with broken shells and kelp; fair-to-good holding.

Armentières Channel (Moresby Island)

1.5 mi NE of Armentières Ch.
Entrance (N): 53°07.70'N, 132°23.90'W
Anchor (buoy): 53°06.65'N, 132°23.50'W

Armentières Channel offers the closest and most bombproof anchorage on the west side of Skidegate Channel. It's particularly convenient when you want to fish or explore the west coast of Haida Gwaii.

Southerly squalls sometimes rush out of the valley at the head but, if you're well anchored, you should have no problem. Anchor in depths comfortable for your boat at the head of Armentières Channel, north of the drying mud flats near the entrance to Chaatl Narrows where the bottom gradually shoals. The drying flat at the narrows seems to cover on a 7-foot tide and is 3 feet deep when high water kisses the lower tree limbs. The deepest water in the narrows into Buck Channel is about 40 feet off the tree limbs on the inside of the curve.

A few sportfishing boats headed south along Moresby Island coast use the uncharted Chaatl Narrows and Buck Channel near high water only. No vessel should attempt Chaatl Narrows, known locally as Canoe Pass, without local knowledge.

Anchor north of the drying flat, mid-channel in 4 to 6 fathoms, over mud and shells; good holding.

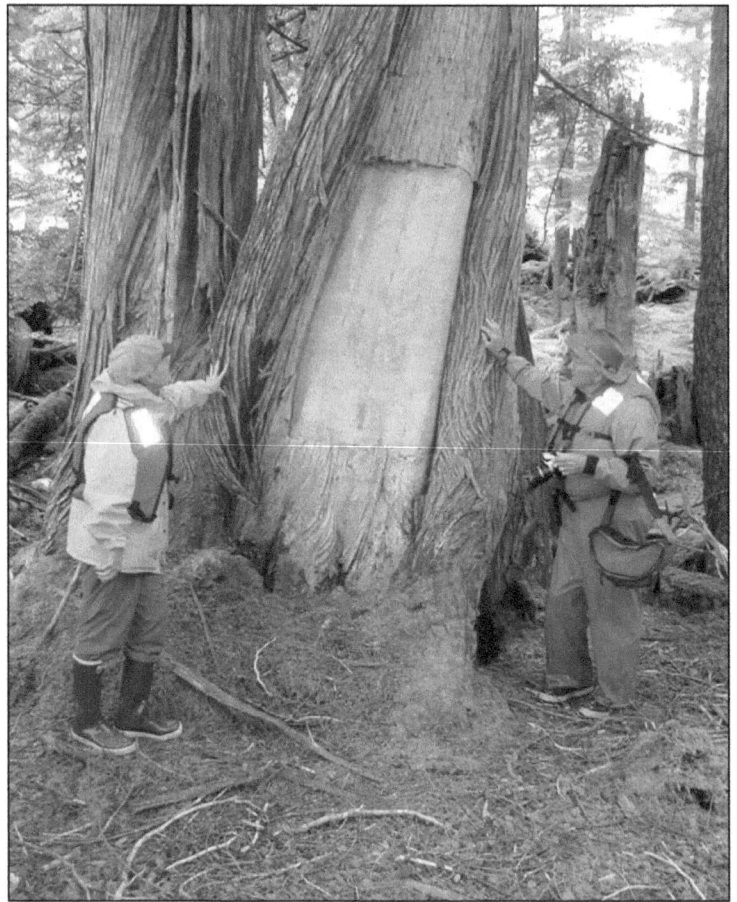

Examining a strip-barked cedar [CMT—culturally modified tree]

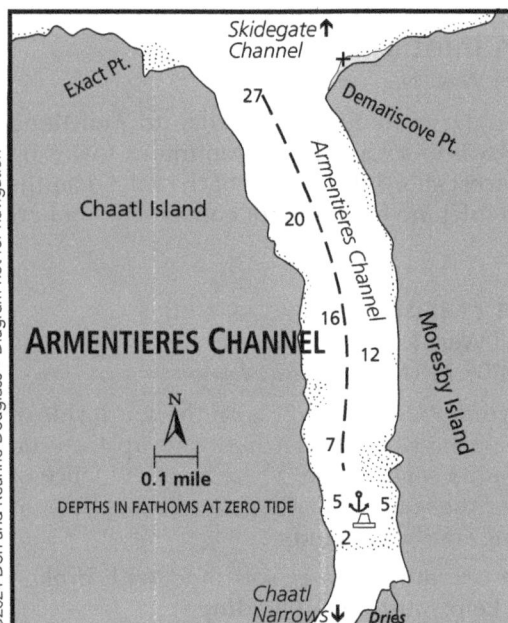

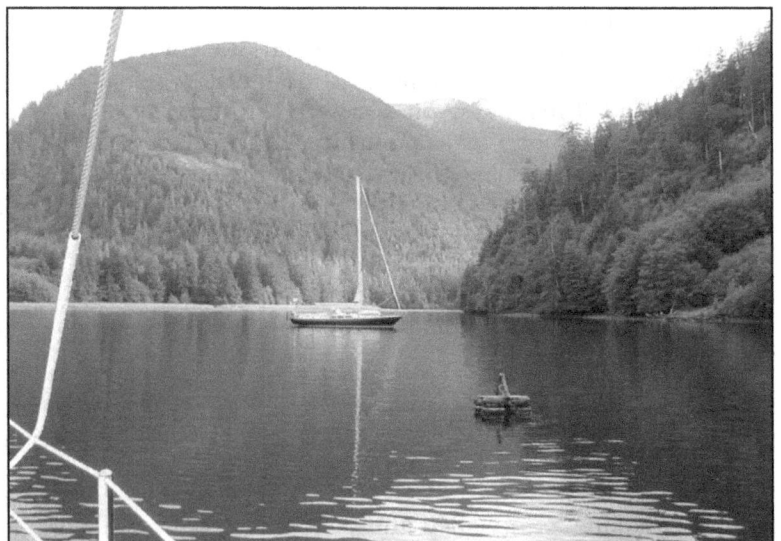

©2024 Don and Réanne Douglass • Diagram not for navigation

Skidegate Channel
Exact Pt.
27
Demariscove Pt.
Chaatl Island
Armentières Channel
20
ARMENTIERES CHANNEL
16
12
Moresby Island
N
7
0.1 mile
DEPTHS IN FATHOMS AT ZERO TIDE
5 ⚓ 5
2
Chaatl Narrows ↓ Dries

Mithrandir anchored at Armentières Channel

Skidegate Channel, East and West Narrows

7.4 mi W of West Narrows
Entrance (W): 53°08.92'N, 132°20.30'W
Entrance (E): 53°08.72'N, 132°13.60'W

Note: We quoted the following brief excerpt from *Canadian Sailing Directions* in our second edition ©2002, and we repeat it here because we feel the information is particularly significant. Note: not all references to Queen Charlotte city in the following dated quote have not been changed to the city's present day name of Daajing Giids.

Skidegate has shores which, for the most part, rise fairly steeply to mountain tops a short distance inland on each side. East Narrows, the central portion of Skidegate Channel, is narrow and winding with strong tidal streams. Although this very shallow narrows is navigated regularly at HW by fishing vessels with ample power, drawing up to 3 m (10 ft), it is recommended only for mariners with local knowledge. West Narrows, although shallow, is deeper, less winding and has weaker tidal streams than East Narrows.

Tides – There is a great difference in tide range between the east and west portions of Skidegate Channel. At Queen Charlotte, to the east of East Narrows, the range on a large tide is 7.8 m (26 ft). Therefore, the levels to which the tide rises above datum at various positions in East and West Narrows are much less than at Queen Charlotte (see table on chart). The times of HW at the positions in the table are up to 1 hour later than at Queen Charlotte.

Navigation of East Narrows – Because of the narrow and winding fairway though East Narrows and the strong currents, particularly near McLellan Point, vessels with low power are advised to navigate the narrows so as to pass McLellan Point at or near slack water. However, because slack water near McLellan Point occurs 3 to 3 1/2 hours after HW or LW at Queen Charlotte (see slack water note on chart), the depth of the water through East Narrows will decrease considerably between HW and the following slack water, thus limiting the draught at which a vessel can pass through safely. Accordingly, Masters of low powered vessels are strongly advised to navigate East Narrows only at or near the slack water preceding a HW at Queen Charlotte.

East Narrows has extensive drying banks, with drying rocks in places, extending from its shores. The fairway is narrow and winding but well marked with beacon ranges. The least depth in the fairway lies about 0.2 mile west of Mid Beacon. Two below-water rocks lie in the fairway close west and a shoal area lies in mid-channel 0.4 mile west of McLellan Point. Two small islets are close off the south shore SE of the shoal area. Note: The upstream direction for aids to navigation in East and West Narrows is when proceeding west.

A first transit of Skidegate Channel is a major undertaking that should be carefully researched. No authority seems to have a good handle on the behavior of the actual tide and current as it seems to be slightly different each time you transit. The good news is that day marks on steel poles have been installed and they greatly help to identify key turning points. We have made the transit several times in both directions with and without the marks and they are a great improvement. Study the aerial photo of East Narrows taken at low water to gain an idea of what is involved. We advise talking with local fishermen and following their boats when possible.

There is a sizeable fleet that leaves Sandspit Marina or Daajing Giids every morning to day-fish off Marble Island. Both East and West Narrows have a fairway that carries 2 to 3 feet at zero tide with a meandering course difficult to discern, with steep-to mud flats on either side. Many boats have gotten into trouble here because of the strong and unpredictable currents and the poorly defined channel.

The flood tide flowing from Hecate Strait to the east has a tidal range roughly twice as high as that from the Pacific to the west. This creates some interesting tidal dynamics, and we recommend taking any predictions of slack water time with a grain of salt. Don't be surprised—we find that the currents flow in directions and strengths that differ substantially from charts, the *Sailing Directions*, and local advice. Furthermore, since the ranges in East Narrows are designed for use in returning eastbound from the Pacific, on a westbound passage it is easy to overshoot your turning points.

The currents in West Narrows are approximately half those found in East Narrows; the challenge there is extensive kelp. Stay mid-channel between the 14-meter islet on the north and two small rocks off the northeast corner of Downie Island. Favoring the Graham Island side, avoid shoals and a dangerous reef off Downie Island.

While awaiting proper conditions, temporary anchorage can be taken on the east side of West Narrows along the north shore, west of the 28-meter island, or on the southeast side of Downie Island. The latter, however, can be exposed to chop from strong westerly winds.

East Narrows, Skidegate Channel, should not be attempted without large scale charts, and before having studied the tidal information, as well as *Sailing Directions*. You must feel comfortable in risky situations requiring high performance and be willing to make your own judgments.

Skidegate Channel, East Narrows, at low water

Photo courtesy Neil Carey

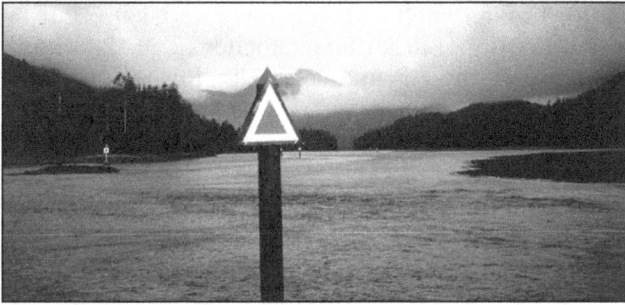

Day mark in Skidegate Channel

Trounce Inlet (Skidegate Channel)
0.6 mi W of East Narrows
Entrance: 53°09.34'N, 132°18.92'W
Anchor: 53°11.09'N, 132°20.14'W

Trounce Inlet is a good place to anchor when waiting for the appropriate tide to enter East Narrows. It is protected in most weather, as noted by the little shoredrift. The north shore has recent clearcuts halfway up its side, and logging roads that lead to and from old "stump farms." The head of the inlet terminates in a grassy mud flat with a rocky, steep-to foreshore. Several boats can find room to anchor here.

Anchor off the mud flat in 6 fathoms, brown sticky mud with clam shells; very good holding.

Root system of Sitka spruce forest, Chaatl Island

Chaatl Island (West Skidegate Channel)
South side of west Skidegate Channel

The south shore of Chaatl Island is the home of the fascinating Mosquito totem and a beautiful old growth Sitka spruce forest across the channel at Nesi.

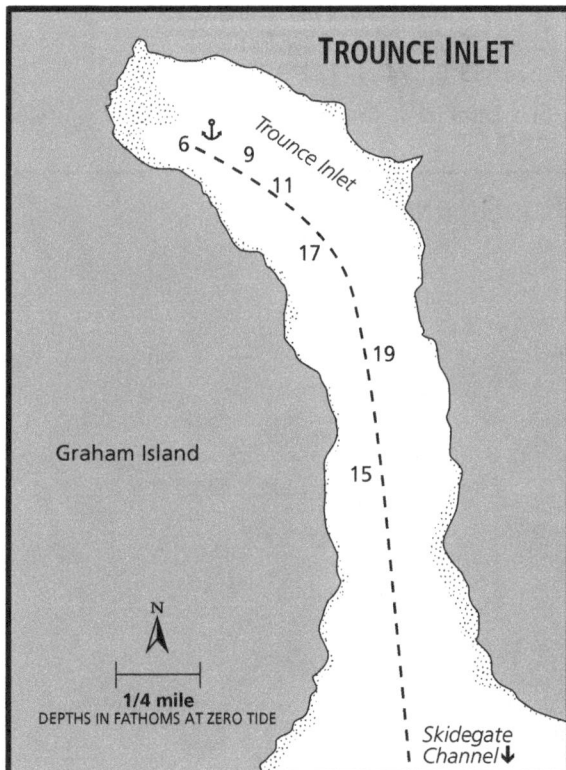

TROUNCE INLET

6 — 9
— 11

17

19

15

Graham Island

Trounce Inlet

N

1/4 mile
DEPTHS IN FATHOMS AT ZERO TIDE

Skidegate
Channel↓

©2024 Don and Réanne Douglass • Diagram not for navigation

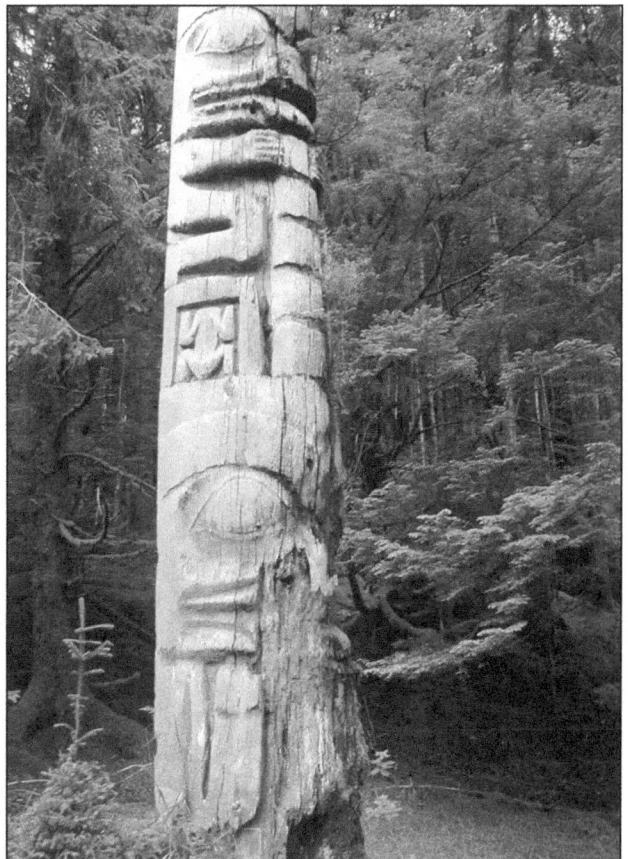

Trail leads through rain forest on Chaatl Island

Buck Channel (Chaatl Inlet)

2 mi S of Skidegate Ch W entr.
Entrance (NW): 53 07.49'N, 132 36.11'W
Anchor (old log dump): 53°05.80'N, 132°30.35'W
Anchor (head): 53°06.14'N, 132°24.70'W

Buck Channel is unsounded and has large offsets; the narrows are not used by any but a few local dinghies. An old log dump now used as a kayak campsite 2.0 miles east of Buck Point can serve as a temporary anchor site while you visit the Mosquito totem on Chaatl Island. However, a better place and the best anchor site lies 0.5 miles further east on the south side of the channel at the old village site of Nesi where there is also a kayak haulout spot and possible campsite. An underwater rock hazardous to navigation is located at 55°06'.8"n, 132°34'36.8"W; at a depth of 7.8 feet (observation courtesy of Steve Hulsizer, *S/V Osprey*.

The head of Buck Channel slowly shoals to a drying mud flat at its east end, west of Chaatl Narrows. Visibility through the water is good to 10 feet or more. Weather reception can be obtained only on Channel 1 at this site. Because this site is open to the west, it receives winds and fetch that can kick up an afternoon chop, causing anxiety for the crew. A cabin at the head of the channel is usually inhabited in the summer months.

The trail to the unique Mosquito Totem Pole starts from a small rocky beach near 53°07.49'N, 132°36.11'W. First visit the small cabin site to the west and two totems, then double back east following the trail which contours across a small grotto and creek and continue east for about half a mile to the pole which is situated in a small clearing about 100 feet above the rocky beach line. It is a privilege to visit this ancient native site so do your part by not disturbing anything and taking only photos and leaving nothing but footprints on the small trail.

Anchor (old log dump) in about 10 fathoms over a steep-to rocky bottom with poor to fair holding.

Anchor (east end of channel) in 5 to 7 fathoms off the drying mud flat over brown mud, broken shells, some gravel and kelp; fair-to-good holding. Larger boats anchor in 10-12 fathoms farther off the drying flats with lots of swinging room.

Nesi (Buck Channel)

2.5 mi E of Buck Point
Anchor (Nesi): 53°05.82'N, 132°30.33'W

Nesi, a small cove on the south side of Buck Channel, is a lovely temporary anchor site for one boat in stable weather. This is the only relatively safe place to anchor and leave your boat to view the Mosquito Totem. Its stony beach has no driftwood and shows no signs of stress. Two streams drain into the head of the cove, the larger of which (west) appears to run all year. Partially protected from easterly and westerly swells that spill down the inlet, it would be fairly well protected in southeast weather. The cove, which is surrounded by 200-foot tall spruce and mossy banks without underbrush, is an excellent example of mature Sitka Spruce forest and well worth a dinghy trip ashore. There is an uncharted island on the east side of the entrance to Nesi which can be passed on its east side with 4 fathoms in the fairway.

Anchor west of the islet in about 8 fathoms over black mud with shells; good holding but limited swinging room (a stern tie to shore is recommended).

Kitgoro Inlet (Moresby Island)

2.1 mi S of Skidegate Ch W Entr.
Entrance: 53°03.94'N, 132°32.02'W

Kitgoro Inlet is a temporary or emergency anchor-

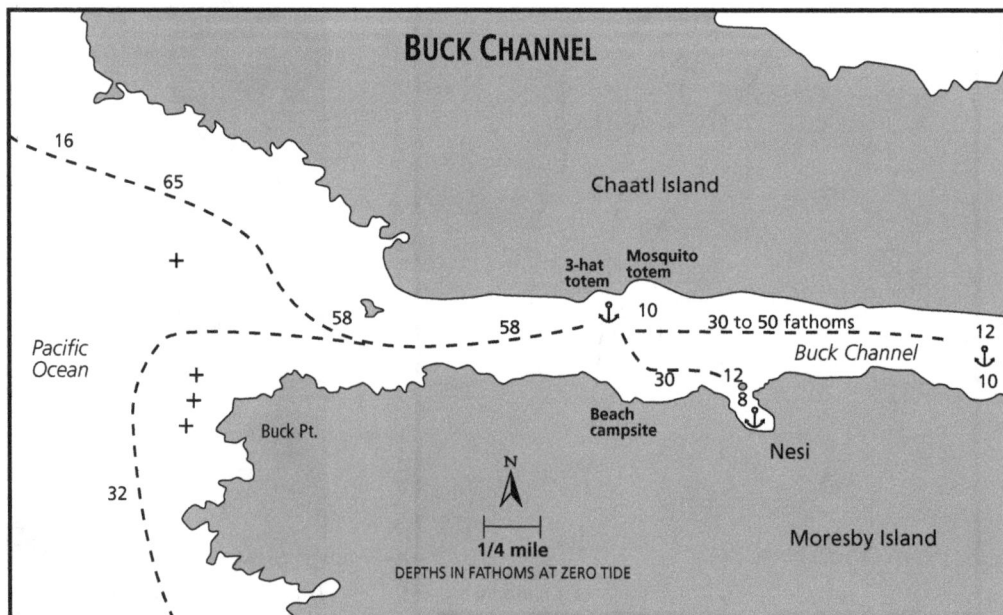

BUCK CHANNEL

Chaatl Island

Pacific Ocean

Buck Pt.

3-hat totem

Mosquito totem

30 to 50 fathoms

Buck Channel

Beach campsite

Nesi

Moresby Island

1/4 mile
DEPTHS IN FATHOMS AT ZERO TIDE

©2024 Don and Réanne Douglass • Diagram not for navigation

age only for shallow draft vessels. The narrowest part of the entrance is shallow and encumbered with kelp and upon entering, favor the south shore past the first kelp bed, then favor the north side to avoid a smaller kelp bed off the first treed islet. The swells quickly die off once inside this first kelp line. The bay shoals slowly to 1 to 2 fathoms with 2-foot boulders and has kelp beds everywhere. This is not a pleasant place other than giving temporary relief from outside swells. You can anchor over the hard sand, gravel and kelp bottom as the tide level allows with your draft. Two streams empty the head of the inlet through the drying flat.

Englefield Bay, 3.5 miles southeast, has much better anchor sites.

Englefield Bay

14 mi S of Skidegate Channel
Entrance: 52°58.73'N, 132°26.52'W

Englefield Bay has a variety of beautiful remote inlets worth exploring. The area is outside the Gwaii Haanas Park, therefore it gets a fair amount of local use that used to favor the east coast of Moresby Island before permits and fees were established.

On the south side of Englefield Bay, when the weather permitted, the Careys navigated their small dory between Cape Henry and the offlying rocks to save time and to miss much of the Denham Shoals. The area around the shoals, which is seldom calm, becomes nasty when tide and wind are in opposition. This lively water may continue until southeast of Freshfield Point. Moore Channel provides a welcome, relaxing waterway between the wooded hillsides of Hibben and Moresby islands. Although unsurveyed, our track line of mid-channel soundings indicates deep water. The south side of heavily forested Hibben Island is steep up to the shoreline and nearly straight without landing beaches.

Kaisun Harbour (Englefield Bay)

8.6 mi SE of Buck Channel
Entrance: 53°01.25'N, 132°29.15'W
Anchor (Site 1): 53°01.88'N, 132°28.27'W
Anchor (Site 2): 53°02.06'N, 132°22.60'W

Kaisun Harbour, the first possible anchor site inside Englefield Bay on a southbound route, offers good shelter, but it is rolling and becomes marginal in southerly gales. Kaisun Harbour, as well as many of the other bays and inlets in Englefield have not been surveyed or sounded by Canadian Hydrographic Service, and we have found numerous charting discrepancies, including shoals and rocks not indicated on charts. Use extreme caution when cruising Englefield Bay; maintain an alert bow watch and proceed slowly when exploring. Preliminary positions and soundings taken by *Baidarka* in 2001 have not been confirmed by CHS or any other authority and, as the user of our data, you must accept responsibility for your own verification.

The entrance to Englefield Bay lies between two small, unnamed islands (entrance islands) west of Saunders Island which forms the south side of the harbor. Approach Kaisun from a point approximately a half-mile south of these two islands before turning north to avoid large kelp patches off the westernmost islets. Maintain a minimum depth of 20 fathoms, avoiding all kelp patches that surround both unnamed islands until well into the fairway between them. We found 7 fathoms in the fairway between the two entrance islands, as indicated on the diagram.

Anchor Site 1, just west of two large kelp beds, is a marginal anchorage in a storm, but useful for larg-

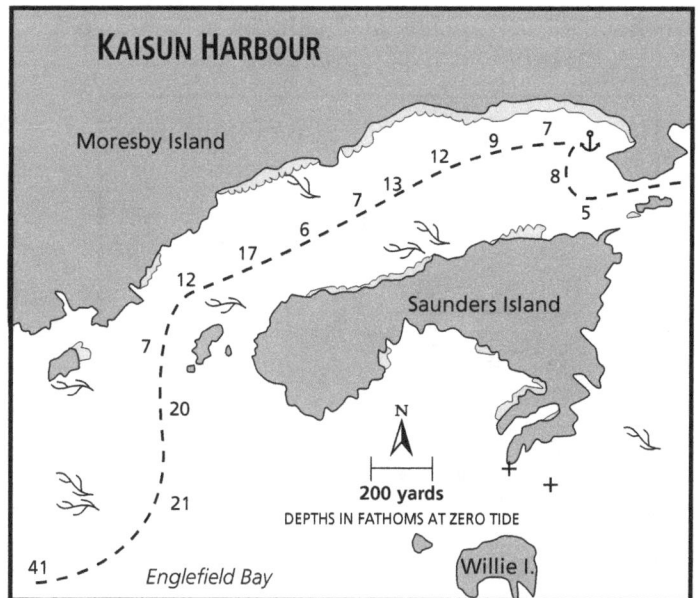

KITGORO INLET

N

200 yards
DEPTHS IN FATHOMS AT ZERO TIDE

Moresby Island

Cliff   Kitgoro Inlet

10 4 2
17

17

65   20

50

11

Pacific Ocean

Kitgoro Point

©2024 Don and Réanne Douglass • Not for navigation

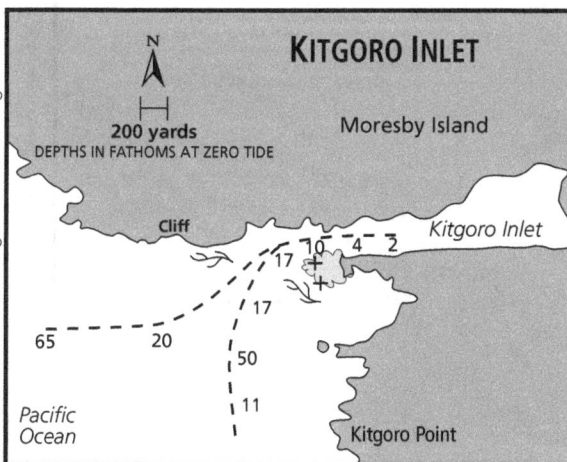

KAISUN HARBOUR

Moresby Island

7
12 9
7 13
7
8
6
5
17
12

7
20

7
21

41

N

200 yards
DEPTHS IN FATHOMS AT ZERO TIDE

Saunders Island

Englefield Bay   Willie I.

©2024 Don and Réanne Douglass • Diagram not for navigation

Anchor site, Dawson Harbour

er vessels that need a lot of swinging room and are willing to tolerate some rolling. Commercial fishermen usually anchor at this site for its swinging room and to avoid the kelp patches farther east.

Small vessels may want to anchor off the southernmost of two beaches that lie at the head of Kaisun, past the intermittent kelp patches (Anchor Site #2). This anchorage is the site of an old Haida village that was partially buried in a landslide during the 1980s. Site 2 is scenic and well-protected by islets and reefs to the southeast. These islets and rocks provide only marginal protection in southeast gales, especially at high water, and inadequate protection in southeast storms. When storm-force winds are forecast, Security Cove offers the only good protection; its flat bottom over an extensive area has almost unlimited swinging room.

We found the tiny pass east of Kaisun Harbour to carry a minimum of about 2 fathoms, as indicated on our diagram.

Anchor (Site 1): Anchor in 6 fathoms over hard sand; poor holding; rolly on tide changes or in foul weather.

Anchor (Site 2): Anchor in 7 fathoms over brown mud with shells and kelp; fair-to-good holding.

Kaisun Creek/Helgesen Island
(Englefield Bay)
0.75 mi E of Kaisun Harbour
Position: 53°02.19'N, 132°26.49'W

Kaisun Creek is largely protected on its south side by Helgesen Island. Two large reefs, awash on high water, lie off the extensive drying mud flats. The Careys found anchorage between these two reefs and the drying flats, but we would consider this site—as well as Boomchain Bay to the east—as temporary only. If Kaisun Harbour anchor site #2 does not provide enough protection in heavy weather, we recommend heading for Security Cove where there is substantially more swinging room and less exposure.

Boomchain Bay (Englefield Bay)
1.25 mi E of Kaisun Harbour
Anchor: 53°02.38'N, 132°25.72'W

Boomchain Bay is a temporary fair-weather anchorage only. The beach at its head takes a beating, as indicated by driftlogs above the high tide line. The bay is poorly protected from southwest winds and is not recommended for overnight anchorage. A gravel beach lies at the head but no streams drain into the bay.

Anchor (temporary only) in 6 fathoms over sand; poor-to-fair holding.

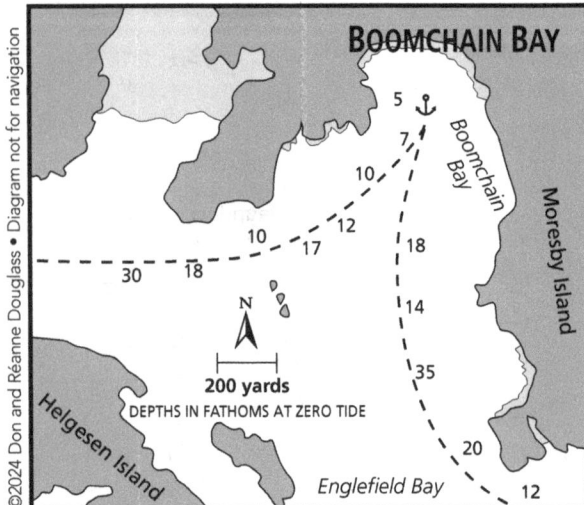

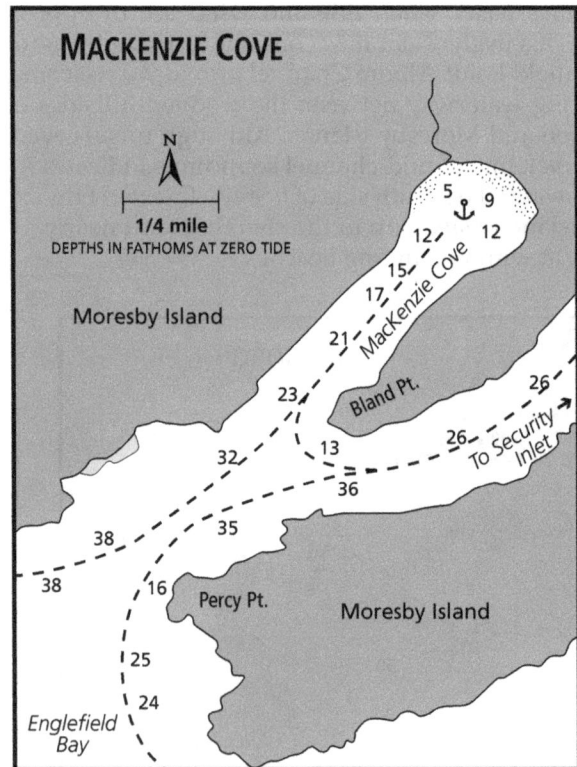

Mackenzie Cove (Englefield Bay)

4.5 mi E of Kaisun Harbour
Entrance: 53°02.08'N, 132°21.09'W
Anchor: 53°02.61'N, 132°20.42'W

Mackenzie Cove, the first cove inside Security Inlet on its north shore, offers protection from the northeast only—we found that prevailing westerlies curl around into the cove. Shelter is indifferent in fair weather, even when anchored well inside, near the northwest edge.

For decades the limestone formations in this area have attracted hopeful prospectors. Their abandoned shacks of logs or plastic used to be seen along the edge of the forest. A slide scar marks the northeast head, and a salmon stream quietly wends its way over the limestone rocks into the head of the cove.

Although Neil and Betty Carey spent many nights here one September while on Fisheries Patrol, anchoring in 3 fathoms close to the northwest shore, we would recommend anchoring in deeper water, as shown on our diagram. We spent several hours sounding the cove while the track on our electronic chart indicated we were crossing over land—a rather disturbing experience!

Anchor in 12 fathoms over soft brown-black sand and mud with broken shells and some kelp. The bottom matter has a consistency like Naden Harbour "Jello," and holding varies from fair-to-good.

Security Inlet

(Englefield Bay)
5 mi E of Kaisun Harbour
Entrance: 53°01.70'N, 132°21.90'W

The first well-protected anchorage south of Skidegate Channel on Moresby Island's west coast is Security Cove, a beautiful spot at the head of Security Inlet. Neil Carey told us that, in a storm, he preferred to anchor in Security Inlet, rather than Security Cove.

Security Cove (Englefield Bay)

7 mi E of Kaisun Harbour
Anchor: 53°03.44'N, 132°16.54'W

Security Cove, which forms the east-west-lying head of Security Inlet, provides protection in all weather. Past Security Point, southwest swells felt in Mackenzie Cove and the northeast-trending Security Inlet die off and the waters calm. Tall spruce trees line the shore, with no sign of logging. The cove shoals to a small, flat, grassy mar-

gin that shows little stress from weather. The most northerly of the creeks that drain into the cove can be explored at high water.

The drying flat, at the head of the cove extends a long way into the water, so it's a good idea to anchor in the middle of the cove in not less than 5 to 7 fathoms. The bottom in Security Cove is composed of soft brown mud with broken shells and twigs, not unlike what we call Naden Harbour "Jello," which means you must set your anchor slowly and with a fine touch. Our initial attempts to anchor were unsuccessful because we applied too much pressure too soon. When we set the anchor slowly with adequate scope, we found good holding. Neil Carey reported that during a storm his anchor dragged from near the north creek to near the east creek and that he preferred to anchor close to a small notch on the south shore of Security Inlet rather than in Security Cove. A large fishing boat also anchored nearby during one storm. His experience emphasizes the need to set an anchor carefully with adequate chain and scope for this condition of very soft mud.

We found large horseflies to be a nuisance here—the worst along Moresby's west coast. However, we would not let this deter us from anchoring here in foul weather.

Anchor in 5 to 6 fathoms over soft brown mud, broken shells and twigs; poor-to-fair holding unless you set your anchor well with lots of scope; good-to-very-good if well set.

Larger vessels can anchor in Security Inlet, mid-channel in 17 fathoms, between Kennedy Point and Security Point. The past skipper of CCG Vessel *Sooke Post* (length over 60 feet) found this to be a better anchor site than at the head of Security Cove where his anchor also dragged.

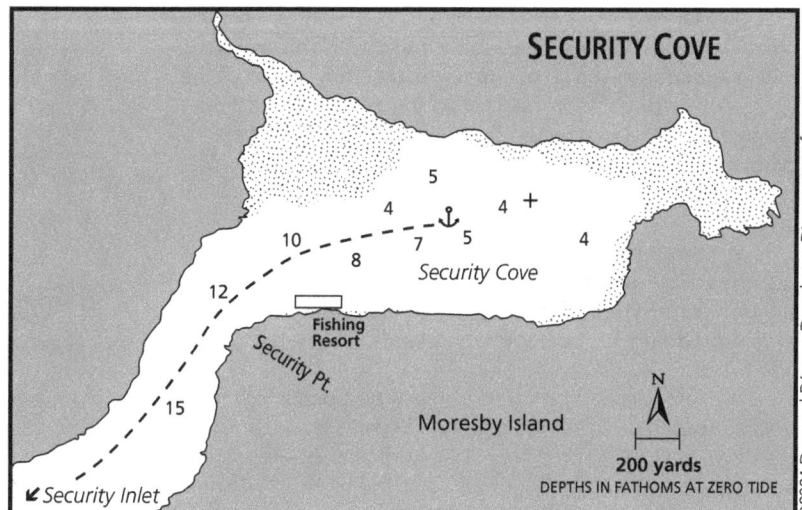

SECURITY COVE

Security Cove

Fishing Resort

Security Pt.

Moresby Island

Security Inlet

N

200 yards
DEPTHS IN FATHOMS AT ZERO TIDE

©2024 Don and Réanne Douglass • Diagram not for navigation

Test anchor pulls up newspaper kelp

Baylee Bay (Englefield Bay)
5 mi E of Kaisun Harbour
Entrance (W): 53°01.37'N, 132°19.63'W

We find Baylee Bay in Inskip Channel north of Hibben Island is too open for adequate shelter. Heavy concentrations of drift logs and surf-swept gravel above the high-water line are the proof. It is a scenic spot that can be used for a temporary anchorage only to go ashore on the sandy landing beach. We found depths of between 7 and 18 fathoms in Baylee Bay and a 2 to 3 fathoms shoal that extends well out from the east end of Instructor Island.

Hastings Point (Englefield Bay)
8 mi SE of Kaisun Harbour

Passing on either side of the small islet north of Hastings Point and entering the winding cove about 1/4 mile, small boats can find room to anchor. Neil and Betty Carey—in their dory—were blown out of here one moonless night by an unexpected southeaster. We found the swinging room inadequate for anything more than a lunch stop, unless you have a boat of 25 feet or less and use shore ties.

Glacially Induced Sea Level Changes Along the British Columbia Coast

British Columbia's spectacular fjords and inlets are the result of glacial erosion from the most recent Ice Age combined with the effects of relative sea level changes. Two primary mechanisms control sea level variations. The first is eustatic sea level change, which is the global rise or fall of sea level due to changes in the volume of water in the ocean. For example, during a period of maximum global glacial extent, much of the earth's water is incorporated in continental ice sheets, which has the effect of lowering sea level around the world. The second mechanism is isostatic elevation change. The weight of a massive ice sheet will actually depress the earth's crust into the mantle, and the crust will rebound when the load is removed. This results in local variations in sea level due to relative movement of the shore up or down with respect to the ocean. In addition, relative elevation changes can also occur due to vertical crustal movements associated with tectonic activity like faulting. During the most recent Ice Age, the Haida Gwaii archipelago and the BC mainland experienced different glacial histories that resulted in different relative sea level changes. In addition, the two regions are composed of different rock types which vary in their resistance to glacial erosion, adding to the variation in landforms between the two areas.

The last glacial period, or Ice Age, occurred from approximately 110,000 years to 12,000 years ago, although there were significant differences in glacial development among the various continents around the world. The most

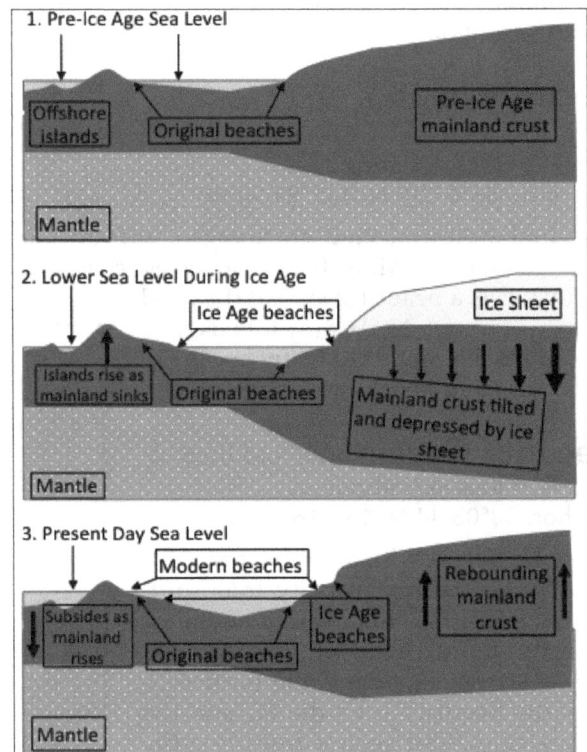

recent period of maximum glacial extent in North America

Réanne on bow entering Leopold Island Narrows

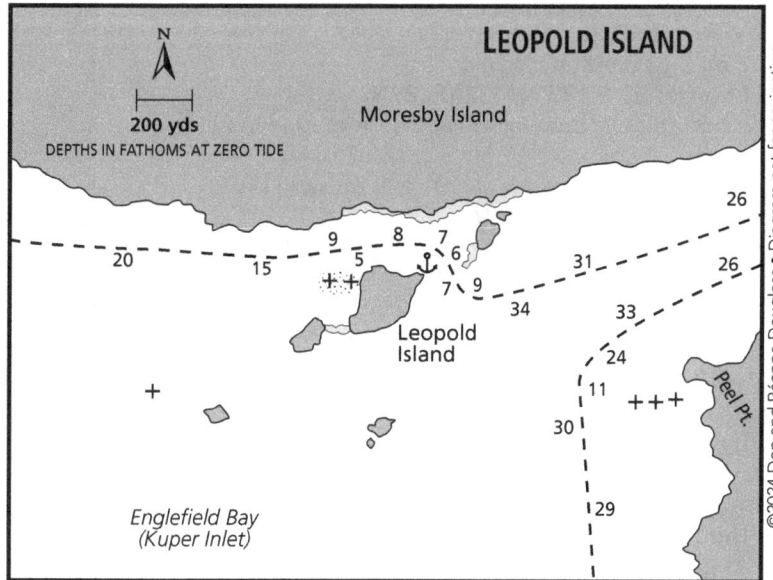

Leopold Island (Englefield Bay)
Intersection of Moore and Inskip Ch
Anchor: 52°59.55'N, 132°10.07'W

The small area to the east of Leopold Island and the gravelly Moresby Island shore can be used as a fair-weather anchorage for one boat. Most of the light westerly breeze blows by in Inskip Channel. *Note:* Chart positioning for this area is not accurate, so do not depend on your GPS.

Anchor in 6 fathoms over gravel and newspaper kelp; holding is poor unless your anchor penetrates the kelp.

---

was part of the Wisconsin Glacial Episode, which began between 30,000 and 25,000 years ago. During this episode, the so-called Cordilleran ice sheet covered much of British Columbia and parts of the Yukon Territory, Alaska, Washington, and Idaho. Mountain glaciers coalesced and thickened into a continental ice sheet that reached its maximum regional extent approximately 15,000 to 14,000 years ago. Some of the glacial lobes penetrated as far south as Puget Sound and the Strait of Juan de Fuca, and tidewater glaciers carved fjords along the Pacific coast.

The Wisconsin glacial maximum led to significantly lower global sea level. Land bridges formed when shallow sea floors became exposed in many parts of the world, including the Bering Strait and Bering Sea. However, even though the global oceans contained significantly less water during this period, the weight of the Cordilleran ice sheet on the BC mainland depressed the continental crust so far into the mantle that sea level along the BC coast actually rose to more than a hundred meters higher than it is today. This progressive isostatic loading of the coast by the Cordilleran ice sheet and the resulting crustal subsidence more than outpaced the eustatic fall in sea level due to the global ice age. Evidence for ancient shorelines has been mapped by geomorphologists who analyze the erosional and depositional features of the near-shore and beach environments that are now found hundreds of feet above today's sea level.

Meanwhile the continental shelf west of the Cordilleran ice sheet experienced eustatic sea level fall due to sequestration of the world's ocean in the global ice sheets. In addition, the region experienced a simultaneous isostatic uplift, lowering sea level even further. This uplift occurred when glacial loading of the BC mainland created a forebulge to the west where the crust was not loaded. Some features along the coast of the Pacific Northwest that are underwater today were exposed to air during this period of lower sea-level, including the Bowie Seamount west of Haida Gwaii. Shallow portions of the continental shelf surrounding Haida Gwaii became dry land. The relatively thin glaciers of the Haida Gwaii archipelago receded about 2,000 years earlier than the thick continental ice sheet on the BC mainland, creating a unique and isolated ecological zone.

Rapid deglaciation of the BC mainland at the end of the Wisconsin glacial period inverted the earlier sea level changes. Vertical uplift of the mainland, the result of isostatic rebound following glacial unloading, has outpaced eustatic sea level rise due to melting ice. This accounts for the beach deposits now found hundreds of feet above the present-day shoreline. Meanwhile, global eustatic sea level rise has loaded the western continental shelf, causing isostatic depression and crustal subsidence. Lands that were above sea level during the glacial maximum have been inundated during this sea level rise, effectively further isolating the unique plant and animal life of the archipelago from the mainland. The story of both local and global responses to the most recent Ice Age is written in relict coastal features along the BC coast and islands.

—LW

Peel Inlet (Englefield Bay)

12 mi E of Kaiksun Harbour
Entrance: 52°59.73'N, 132°08.29'W
Anchor (Site 1, base of valley where road leads to
Moresby Camp): 52°59.50'N, 132°07.07'W
Anchor (Site 2, S of islet [120] & N of islet [110])
52°59.09'N, 132°06.54'W
Anchor (Site 3, 0.28 mi SE of Laing Pt): 52°58.51'N,
132°05.87'W
Anchor (Site 4, head of inlet): 52°58.01'N,
132°04.87'W

Peel Inlet, which is unsounded, is almost landlocked and provides very good protection from all chop. High peaks on either side of the inlet and calm waters bring to mind a Swiss lake. Except for the power line poles that cross the inlet from ridge to ridge, this offers a lovely wilderness experience. Tree limbs that hang low over the water show no evidence of storm stress although, in some conditions, williwaws may refract off the high ridges above. The inner basin has a flat bottom starting at 30 fathoms off Laing Point that slowly rises to about 10 fathoms off its drying head. The head is steep-to, with depths to 13 fathoms just off the drying flat. The northeast side of the head of Peel Inlet is almost completely closed off by a drying mud and sand flat that extends from the creek. A narrow, shallow channel leads south only 40 feet from island [120] with a fairway of about 3 fathoms.

Northwest of Laing Point, there are two sites where one small vessel can find anchorage. The first (Site 1) is the "pothole" near the base of the road that leads to Moresby Camp; swinging room is limited here, so a stern tie to the trees is recommended. This site is exposed to westerlies that may make their way into Peel Inlet.

A small boat can find protection at Site 2 from strong northwesterlies between islets [120] and [110]. This site is well protected from chop but care must be taken to avoid the mud flat to the north and the wide reef on the southwest side that dries at 14 feet.

Both Sites 1 and 2 have stoney bottoms, so take care in anchoring. Larger vessels find better holding and more swinging room in deeper water, 0.28 mile southeast of Laing Point, in 19 to 20 fathoms (Site 3) or off the head of the inlet in about 13 fathoms (Site 4). Site 4 is steep-to and shoals rapidly after 10-fathoms.

Entering Peel Inlet

The old logging road leading to Moresby Camp can be used by hikers who are ready to ford fast flowing streams during the rainy season—or anytime. It is possible for a determined ATV operator to transit this abandoned road during the dry season.

Anchor (Site 1) in 10 fathoms over a stony bottom with poor holding.

Anchor (Site 2) in 7 to 9 fathoms over a stony bottom with poor holding.

Anchor (Site 3) in 21 fathoms over soft brown mud with twigs; fair-to-good holding.

Anchor (Site 4) in 13 fathoms over soft brown mud with twigs; fair-to-good holding.

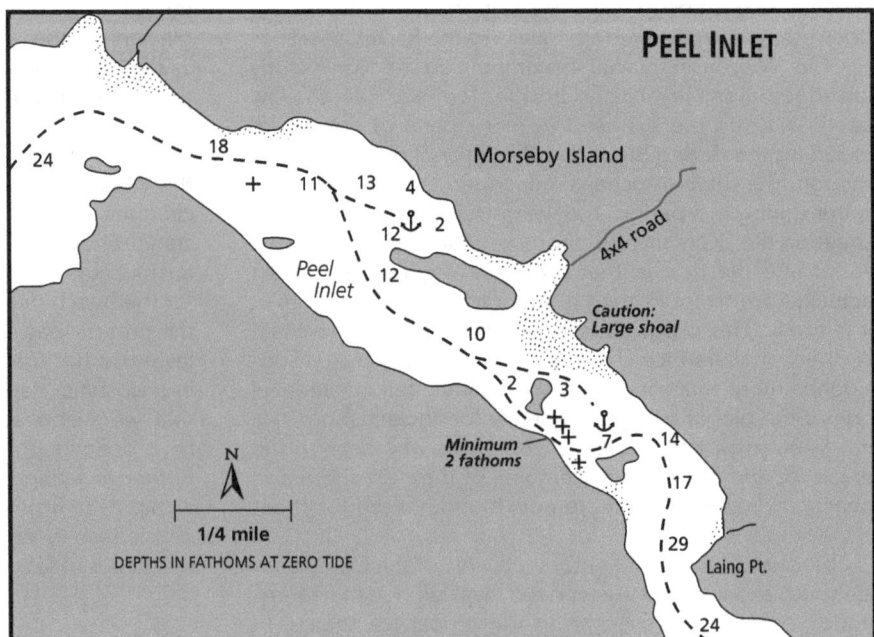

©2024 Don and Réanne Douglass • Diagram not for navigation

Kevin Monahan collecting data

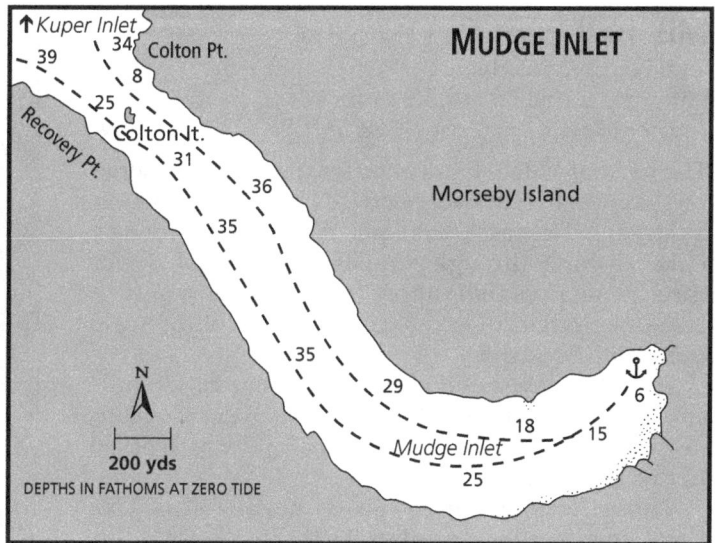

Mudge Inlet (Englefield Bay)
8.5 mi NE of Cape Henry
Entrance: 52°58.66'N, 132°09.62'W
Anchor (Site 1): 52°57.71'N, 132°06.92'W
Anchor (Site 2): 52°57.73'N, 132°06.89'W

Mudge Inlet is surrounded by high, forested ridges that were logged or burned years ago before clearcutting began. The inlet shows few signs of stress at its head. Many small avalanche scars along its precipitous sides indicate heavy winter damage. A remarkable giant spruce snag on the southwest shore drew our attention; we call it the "totem tree" and we imagined that the ancient people might have drawn their ideas from snags such as this one.

Weather reception on Weather Channel 8 is poor-to-nil in Mudge, and the inlet may be subject to willi-waws in stormy weather. We had trouble getting our test anchor to set at both sites. (At Site 1, our set was inconclusive.) Site 2 was overlaid with newspaper-sized kelp, making holding difficult.

Anchor (Site 1) in 8 to 9 fathoms with inconclusive holding.

Anchor (Site 2) in 7 fathoms over a bottom of stones and black mud overlaid with kelp; poor to fair holding unless your anchor is well set.

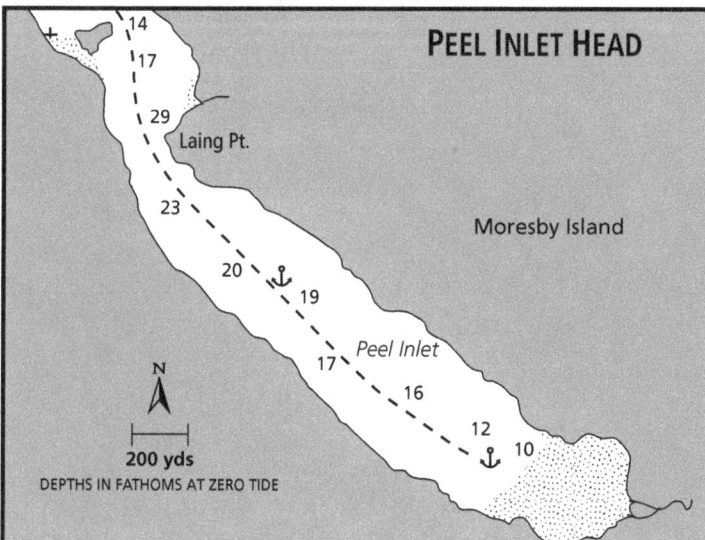

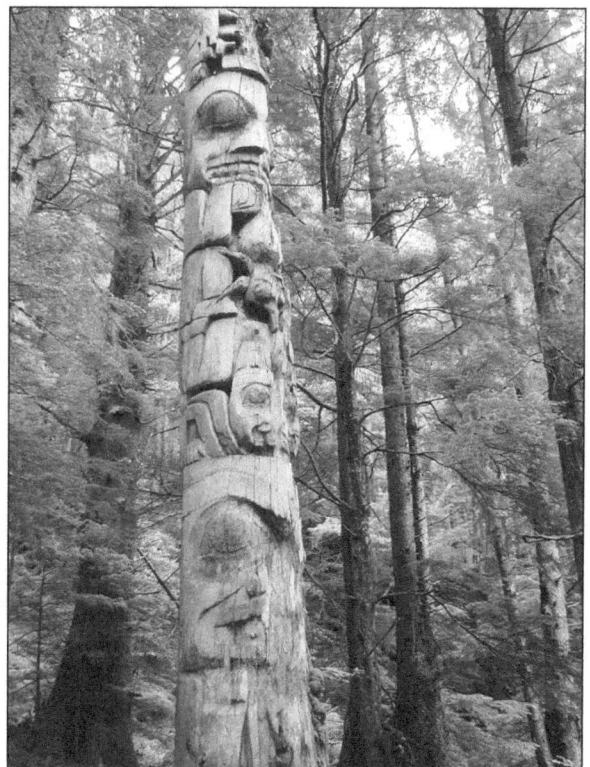

Mysterious Mosquito Totem, Chaatl Island

Mitchell Inlet (Englefield Bay)

7 mi NE of Cape Henry
Entrance: 52°58.00'N, 132°11.85'W
Anchor (Thetis Anchorage): 52°56.12'N, 132°08.19'W

The head of Mitchell Inlet houses the power-generating plant that provides electricity for Daajing Giids, Skidegate, Tlell and Sandspit. Water from Moresby Lake rushing through an 1100-foot tunnel drives three generators that supply this electrical power. A resident electrician here has telephone communications with Sandspit.

A rusting crusher and decaying boards, 1/8 mile south of Una Point, are the remains of former visions of great fortunes—a small vein of gold was worked in this area in 1851.

Thorn Rock, about 200 yards northwest of Una Point, may not be seen—but it's there! We found its actual position to be about 200 yards to the northwest of the position noted on charts. Thorn Rock is actually a large, rock and sand shoal, 250 feet from north to south, with the shoalest part at its north end. It rises steeply from a depth of 18 fathoms or more from all sides and appears to be covered with rockweed; it is slightly submerged or awash at zero tide.

Thetis Anchorage, at the head of the inlet, gained its name from the British frigate, *Thetis,* which used this anchor site in the winter of 1852 during its survey of Gold Harbour. In 1981, Thetis Rock was reported to lie mid-channel in Thetis Anchorage, 0.3 mile southeast of Sansum Island. We made several passes crisscrossing over its reported position and could not find any depths shallower than 15 fathoms; there was no indication of anything other than a fairly flat bottom. Use caution in the vicinity until this mystery is resolved!

We found it possible to pass Sansum Island on either side; the fairway on the east side carries 6 fathoms minimum and, on the west 13 fathoms. The east shore of Mitchell Inlet near Sansum Island, as charted, appears to be about 200 feet west of its GPS position.

Anchor in 8 fathoms over soft brown mud with twigs; fair-to-good holding.

Neil Carey writes: "Large vessels may anchor southeast of Sansun Island. Small craft anchor near the head on the south side in 5 fathoms. Mud bottom. Kayakers may choose to enter the small rock-bound pocket a quarter-mile northeast of Sansun Island. We have carefully slipped between the rocks at high tide and spent a quiet night in this deep and sheltered pocket, landlocked until high tide the next day."

Power station in Mitchell Inlet

Douglas Inlet

(Englefield Bay)
9.2 mi SE of Kaisun Harbour
Entrance: 52°57.65'N, 132°14.48'W
Entrance (Leslie Pt. Cove): 52°56.85'N, 132°13.25'W
Anchor (Leslie Pt. Cove): 52°56.77'N, 132°13.23'W
Entrance (Leg Nook): 52°56.56'N, 132°12.67'W
Anchor (head of inlet): 52°55.84'N, 132°10.28'W
Water buoy: 52°56.01'N, 132°10.73'W

Steep-sided Douglas Inlet is a lovely wilderness whose head lies at the base of a large U-shaped valley lined with tall, old growth trees and silver snags. Fissures, faults and avalanche scars show the effect of geologic and storm activity; windswept, knobby, sub-alpine ridges where gnarled and bent shore pines take hold give evidence of storm-force winds and poor soil. Strong northwest winds often charge in through Moore Channel, then veer, creating white-

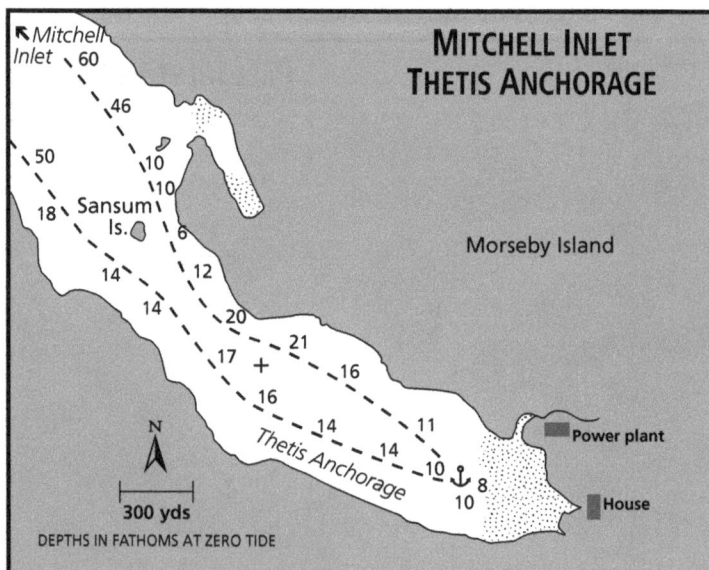

MITCHELL INLET
THETIS ANCHORAGE

Mitchell Inlet
60
46
50
10
10
18 Sansum Is.
6
14
12
14
20
17 + 16
16
Thetis Anchorage
14 11
14
10 8
10

Morseby Island

Power plant

House

N

300 yds

DEPTHS IN FATHOMS AT ZERO TIDE

Diagram not for navigation
©2024 Don and Réanne Douglass

Water hose, Douglas Inlet

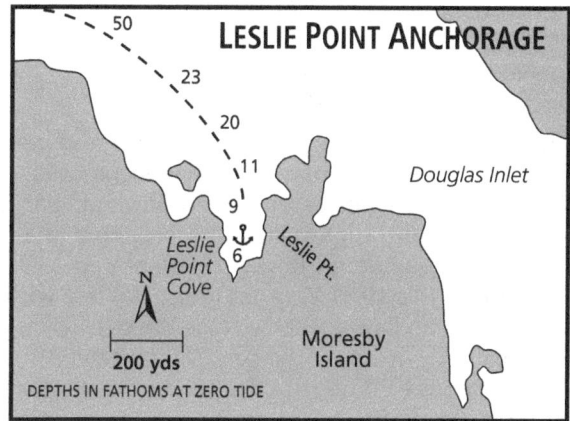

caps all the way to the head of Douglas Inlet.

Douglas Inlet is shaped like a human leg, the knee just below Leslie Point, and the shoal head the big toe. Anchorage can be found at three sites within the inlet. The first, which we call "Leslie Point Cove"— has room for one or two small boats; this site has a gravel beach and kayak haul-out with marginal

camping. A number of shore pines (*Pinus contorta*) surround the point and the cove, and there is little evidence of shore stress. Swinging room at this site is limited.

While the second notch south of Leslie Point, used by the Careys as an anchor site, is attractive, it appears too restricted for anything but a vessel shorter than 30 feet; the cove is only about 50 to 75 feet wide. This site does, however, offer protection from southerly weather. We found a dozen or more seals hauled out on the point. The site west of Leslie Point has a line across it about 50 feet from shore where one small boat could find protection from southerly weather; a gravel beach can be used as a kayak haul-out with marginal camping.

In 2015, a fishing lodge was moored near the head of Douglas Inlet. A white cross on shore marks a small 300-foot cascading stream. A cement catchment dam can be seen on the slope, from where a plastic hose with good water flow leads to the edge of shore. Several old stern tie lines hang from trees above.

The creek at the head of the inlet takes an abrupt turn to the south behind the grassy shoal. Due west of the head of the inlet, there is a good kayak haul-out spot along the rocky beach.

Anchor in Leslie Point Cove in 7 to 9 fathoms over gravel and stone; fair holding. Two shore ties are needed for a serious blow.

Anchor in 7 to 13 fathoms (head of the inlet) over soft brown mud with broken shells and newspaper kelp; fair-to-good holding depending on the set of your anchor; good swinging room.

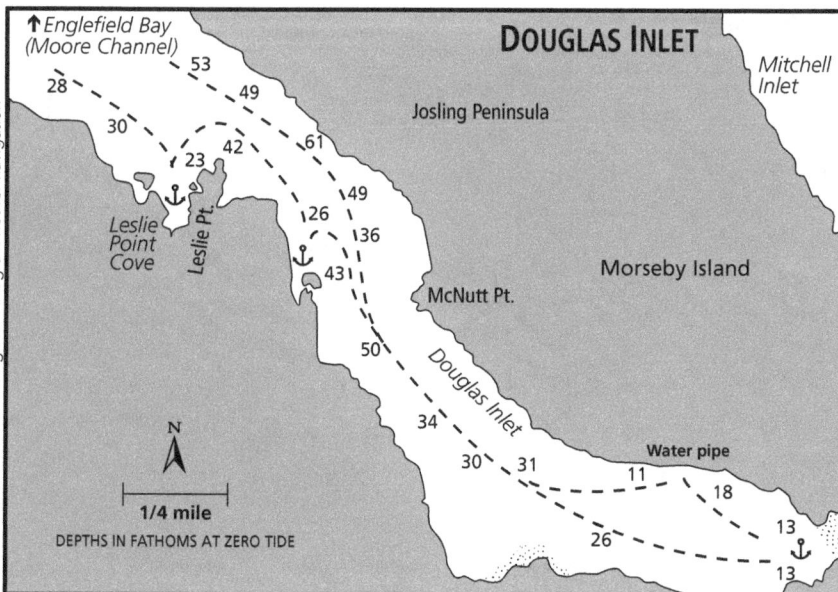

Hewlett Bay (Englefield Bay)
1.1 mi NE of Denham Point
Entrance: 52°57.30'N, 132°19.91'W

Hewlett Bay is largely choked with kelp and useful only as a temporary or emergency anchor site. A small gravel beach can be used as a haulout. Large driftlogs above the high-water line on shore make this site an untenable anchorage. We entered as far as 52°57.15'N, 132°19.81'W, 4 fathoms, but left without making an anchor check because the bay seemed too restricted for us under the conditions at that time. The anchor sites east of Cape Kuper, one mile north of Hewlett Bay, offer more protection and swinging room. *Caution:* The charted shoreline of Hewlett appears to have sizeable offsets from its GPS position.

Pay Bay (Englefield Bay)
3.4 mi NE of Cape Henry
Entrance: 52°58.86'N, 132°20.00'W
Anchor (Site 1, E side Cape Kuper): 52°58.17'N, 132°19.98'W
Anchor (Site 2): 52°58.40'N, 132°19.59'W
Anchor (Site 3): 52°58.61'N, 132°19.41'W

Pay Bay, which takes its name from Paymaster Luxmoore who sailed aboard the frigate, *Thetis*, during an 1852 survey of the area, has three anchor sites to choose from. The first site, immediately east of Cape Kuper, is our first choice for its scenic qualities and its good protection from southerly weather. The tidal split through Luxmoore Island should attract the photographer, as will the sea lions that often haul out on the nearby Moresby Islets. We felt no signs of northwest swells in this site.

Entrance to Site 1 can be made from the south via a narrow passage immediately west of Cape Kuper, southeast of Luxmoore Island, avoiding large kelp beds off each point. We found 12 fathoms minimum in the fairway. This site can also be entered east of Luxmoore Island by avoiding the submerged rock marked by kelp or through a tiny passage between Pay Bay, south of Rogers Island, favoring the south shore where the fairway carries 5 fathoms. *Caution:* several submerged rocks and kelp beds extend south of Rogers Island. Cape Kuper is separated from Hibben Island by a small rocky passage through which a kayak can pass on a tide level of 8 feet or more.

Site 2, southeast of Rogers Island, seems quite well protected, although we did not test the bottom. Like Site 1, it has no landing beach.

Site 3, Pay Bay, is more exposed to northwest winds than either Sites 1 or 2, as evidenced by driftlogs above the highwater line on shore. A skiff or kayak can be landed on the sandy beach in all but northwest gales; the south shore is rocky and full of kelp. Several caves are located north of the beach. Although this site feels the effect of outside swells more than the other two sites, holding is better.

The steep west end of Hibben Island is scarred with numerous natural landslides.

Anchor (Site 1, east side of Cape Kuper) in 7 to 10 fathoms near the head of the bay over a rocky bottom; poor-to-fair holding.

Anchor (Site 2) in the middle of the bay in 6 to 8 fathoms over an undetermined bottom—probably stony.

Anchor (Site 3, Pay Bay) in 4 to 6 fathoms over sand and gravel with fair-to-good holding.

Denham Point Bay
0.3 mi E of Denham Pt.
Entrance: 52°56.50'N, 132°21.28'W

The small, unnamed bay immediately to the east of Denham Point provides day shelter for kayakers or small boats from all but westerly and northwest

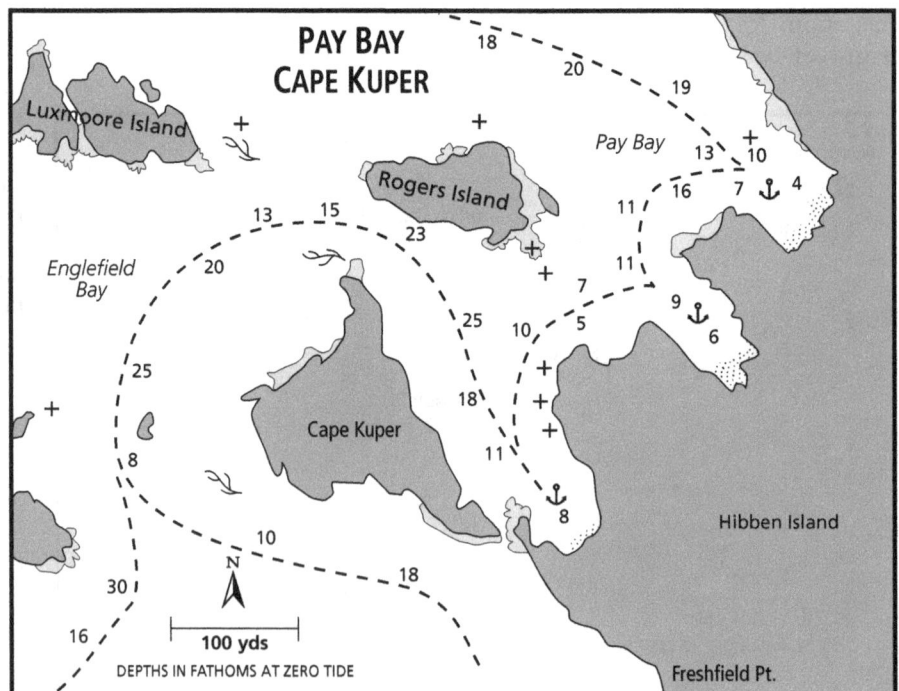

PAY BAY
CAPE KUPER

Luxmoore Island
Rogers Island
Pay Bay
Englefield Bay
Cape Kuper
Hibben Island
Freshfield Pt.

100 yds
DEPTHS IN FATHOMS AT ZERO TIDE

©2024 Don and Réanne Douglass • Diagram not for navigation

winds and seas; it is somewhat sheltered from southwest swells by the offshore kelp beds. Avoid the numerous rocks and reefs that extend from the north entrance point. Neil Carey suggests that, for northbound small boaters, this site could be the first rest stop after rounding Cape Henry or—when heading south along Moresby Island's coast—the last chance to prepare a meal before entering the open ocean.

Denham Shoals
(Englefield Bay)
Off the S entrance to Englefield Bay

Charts note that Denham Shoals have not been examined. The ten or more rocks that rise from more than 50 fathoms to a few feet of the surface should be treated with great caution and respect, especially in foul weather or under limited visibility. Although some dangers are marked by kelp patches, we would advise remaining off the coast a *minimum* of three miles in any but ideal weather.

Neil Carey claims there is a small-craft route close along shore between Cape Henry and Denham Point. However, we would suggest its use only for experienced kayakers who like to keep one foot on the beach. We found a deep-water route 0.6 mile off Cape Denham where we followed a course of 195°M until northwest of Cape Henry in 75 fathoms.

Depths along this route, which were irregular, lay between 30 and 60 fathoms. On all three sides of Denham Shoals depths are on the order of 100 fathoms and because the shoals rise so steeply and suddenly a depth sounder is of little help in avoiding these shoals.

The area west of Denham Point can be rough, especially on strong ebbs during westerly winds. The breaking surf on the shoals about 4 miles offshore reminds us of the shoals off Cabo Rugged at Canal Trinidad in Southern Chile, where the channel is the alternative to Magellan Strait. Denham Point is at about 50°N latitude, while Canal Trinidad is at roughly 50°S latitude, and neither is a good experience in foul weather!

Antiquary Bay
(Moresby Island)
0.85 mi SE of Cape Henry
Entrance: 52°55.18'N, 132°20.92'W

Antiquary Bay is open to all weather and not useful as an anchorage. Its entrance is identified by large rocks—one is a tall rock with flat "balconies" where old bull sea lions guard their harems. The bay's steep beach is rocky and its bottom gravel. Offshore kelp dampens the waves that slope ashore.

A Thirty-year Perspective from Puffin Cove

Kayakers, singly or in groups, men and women, have visited us in Puffin Cove while paddling around Moresby Island. None ever mentioned that their trip was anything less than an extremely satisfying and memorable experience. Betty rowed much of Haida Gwaii's coast in her trusty and durable 14-foot dugout. As a family of four, we crossed Hecate Strait and cruised around Haida Gwaii in a 19-foot codfish dory powered by an outboard. For thirty years Betty and I cruised Haida Gwaii during all months, especially the west coast, experiencing the joy of flat seas and the demands of savage storms, always thankful to return to the safety and calm of our cabin in Puffin Cove on Moresby Island's enticing west coast.

There are more than two dozen bays or inlets on Haida Gwaii's west coast where you can find shelter for mooring or anchoring. These vary greatly in safety, depending upon the wind's direction and velocity, and the size of your craft. We have used all of these and more. Though our converted 26-foot lifeboat would usually stay put with a 35-pound Danforth, 50 feet of 3/8-inch chain and fathoms of line, we sometimes found it necessary to add, on the same cable, a 35-pound CQR anchor. And when we started to drag, I'd slide a 25-pound lead down until it was stopped by the

cable/chain shackle. We have endured gales and storms tied bow and stern to trees near an indentation in the rocky shore, our skiff alongside as a fender while the anchor (or anchors) held us off. Most storms pass within a complete tidal cycle. A few last longer. It never ceases to amaze me how fast the sea can change from an angry killer to a pacified friend. *Heavy anchor gear is necessary on the west coast.* You should also have long, strong lines for tying to the shore if all else fails.

Ashore you encounter beaches littered or piled with logs lost from forest harvests; occasionally a redwood from California, a Douglas fir from Vancouver Island, or a Sitka spruce from Alaska. Most logs are local spruce, red cedar, and hemlock. Treasures to pick up are the Japanese glass fishing floats of assorted sizes and shapes, bamboo from the Philippines, some item lost from a shipping container wrenched from the decks of a storm-wrecked vessel, even a message in a bottle cast overboard months or years past.

—Neil and Betty Carey are considered modern pioneers of the Queen Charlotte Islands. Their adventures on the west coast of Moresby Island are shared in their classic book, Puffin Cove. *(Please see Bibliography.)*

Entrance to Bottle Inlet

Anchored, head of Bottle Inlet

Bottle Inlet

(Moresby Island)
2.5 mi S of Cape Henry
Entrance: 52°54.12'N, 132°20.12'W
Position of cave: 52°54.10'N, 132°18.91'W
Anchor: 52°54.96'N, 132°15.93'W

Caution: a dangerous uncharted rock, about 0.3 mile west of the northernmost outer entrance point to Bottle Inlet is located at 52°54.475'N, 132°20.377'W. We found, on mid-tide and moderate southwest swells, that the water covering this rock heaps up and breaks approximately once every five minutes. Depths of 70 to 80 fathoms lie on either side of this rock and the eruption of a sudden breaker could catch you by surprise. Note that charts may have inaccuracies on Bottle Bay and should *not* be relied upon.

Bottle Inlet is notable for its stunning basaltic rock columns that comprise the south shore of its entrance, east of Bottle Point. A prominent and large sea cave, 40 feet high and about 10 feet wide, has been carved out of these formations. We were able to approach the cave to within about 40 feet in 8 fathoms of water. The south side of the narrows, west of the cave, is composed of large, angular basaltic columns.

Ocean swells die off rapidly once you have passed inside the narrows giving a welcome contrast. Neil Carey writes: "This is the quickest transition from rough to smooth on Haida Gwaii's west coast that I can think of. Of course, the reverse may be true upon departing!"

Several waterfalls cascade off the south wall—one of which takes its source from a hanging lake high above—adding to the feeling of relief and calm. The inlet culminates in a grassy flat where a large creek is bordered by mature spruce trees. An uncharted rock lies near the north shore, 0.2 mile from the flat, at 52°54.90'N, 132°16.03'W. This rock, which bares 2 feet above high water, is about 60 feet long and extends 40 feet north. A fairway of about 6 fathoms lies on both the north and south side of the rock. A second uncharted rock lies about 50 yards off the north entrance shore at approximately 52°54.221'N, 132°19.056'W. We found good anchorage in 5 to 7 fathoms east of this rock. Reception on Weather Channel 1 is marginal; otherwise this is a near-perfect anchorage.

Bottle Inlet, like many inlets on Moresby's west coast, has its own micro-climate. We noticed that, on warm sunny afternoons, a locally brisk westerly wind is sucked up the inlet by thermals that rise above the high ridges. As Neil Carey noted at the beginning of this chapter, these are convection winds.

Anchor in 5 to 7 fathoms over soft brown mud with fair-to-good holding; very good holding if you set your anchor well.

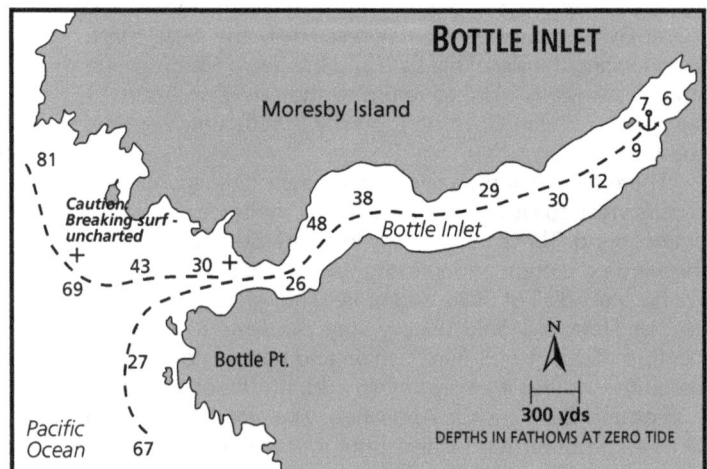

BOTTLE INLET

Moresby Island

81

Caution!
Breaking surf -
uncharted

43   30

69

38   29   30   12

48   Bottle Inlet

26

27

Bottle Pt.

Pacific
Ocean   67

7 6
9

N

300 yds
DEPTHS IN FATHOMS AT ZERO TIDE

©2024 Don and Reanne Douglass • Diagram not for navigation

Kootenay Inlet (Moresby Island)

9 mi N of Tasu Narrows (unsurveyed & uncharted)
Entrance: 52°51.50'N, 132°15.49'W
Anchor (Haystack Cove): 52°51.50'N, 132°15.49'W
Anchor (North Arm): 52°52.54'N, 132°12.52'W
Anchor (East Arm): 52°50.87'N, 132°12.30'W

Kootenay Inlet has two arms that penetrate deep into the 3000-foot mountain range. In our opinion, this is one of the best kept secrets on the west coast of Haida Gwaii and, like Englefield Bay, this inlet lies outside the Gwaii Haanas Park boundaries. Just inside the entrance on the south shore is a moderate-sized cove that has the most convenient anchor site with good shelter from southerly weather. The north arm offers particularly beautiful scenery with good anchorage at moderate depths throughout its length.

The 3-mile-long east arm is entered through a narrow, strikingly lovely channel about three-quarters of a mile in length and a hundred feet wide before opening into a large basin with several small islands. Floating down the entrance channel to the east arm, with the current pushing you gently forward, is a magical experience. The shores are lined with a thick forest of spruce, yellow and red cedar, hemlock, coast pines, alder, and maidenhair fern. Almost totally landlocked, the east arm offers protection from all winds and there is no fetch to speak of. The basin terminates in a large drying mud flat.

We found that, in using the electronic version of charts, our track occasionally crossed land on the south side of the inlet, well before reaching its charted eastern terminus. Therefore, alert bow lookouts are critical in unsounded and unsurveyed areas such as this! Well-protected anchorage can be found

Two outside rocks and entrance reef, to west, Kootenay Inlet

in East Basin, due south of the eastern end of the narrows. An old gold mine can be found on the north side of East Arm by hiking up a stream about a mile from the head.

From the outside, the entrance to Kootenay Inlet appears to have a lot of foam and it looks like seas break behind the two rocks just off the north entrance point. This white water turns out to be foam from the uncharted mid-channel reef awash in the center of the entrance. You must round the north side of this reef in about 7 to 9 fathoms.

The inlet is best entered from the north by heading for a point halfway between Kootenay Point and the almost-hidden entrance, 1.6 miles to the north-north-east. The entrance waypoint given above should be reached (30 fathoms) before turning due east in order to pass south of two rocks that extend from a small peninsula on the north shore. On the south shore you pass a "haystack" that stands guard close in. A yellow dike about 40 feet wide cuts diagonally across the rock at a 60° angle.

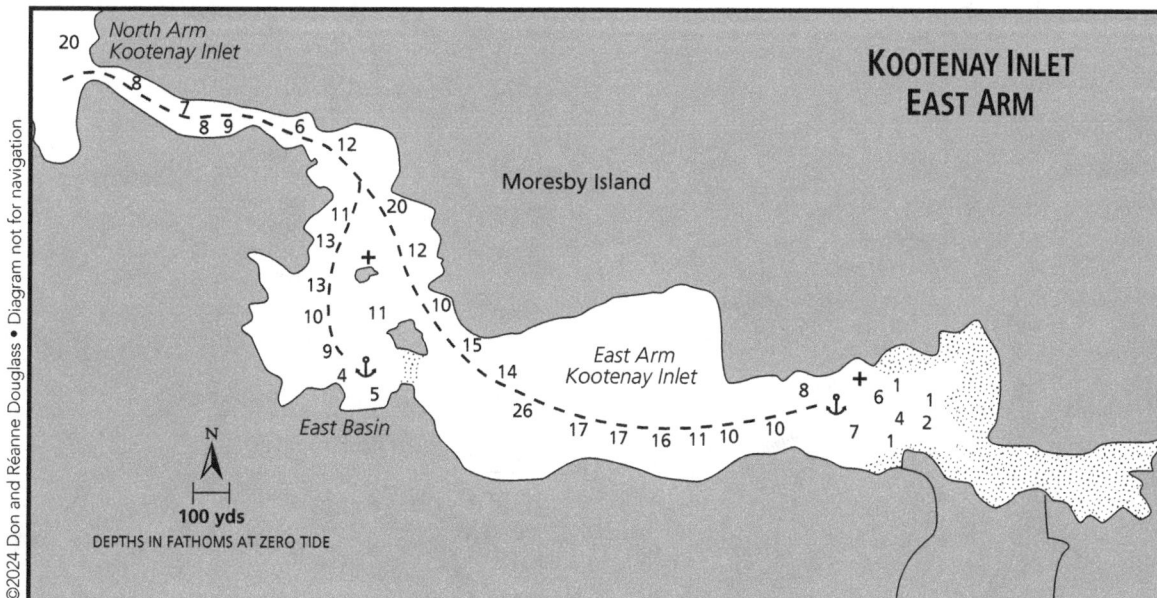

Once due south of the easternmost of the two entrance rocks, turn northeast for about 0.27 mile in order to take to starboard a large uncharted reef that lies mid-channel and is awash at mid-tide. Once safely past the entrance reef, turn east and enter a large basin with a tall island which we call "Haystack Island." Southeast of this island is the cove we call "Haystack Cove"—the most convenient anchorage within the inlet; this cove offers good protection in southerly weather in 1 to 2 fathoms. However, we prefer to anchor in the more sheltered North Arm or the basin in the East Arm.

The north arm of Kootenay Inlet has four small islands on the west side of its entrance, the northernmost of which we call "Silver Snag Island." The fairway lies to the east of these islands. Favor the east shore as you start through the narrows. When past the first three islands, as you approach Silver Snag Island favor the west shore of the channel—a dangerous shoal extends about 100 feet from the east shore to near mid-channel. The shoal is really a wide rock, awash on about a 2-foot tide, that rises sharply from a 10-fathom bottom. The shore along Silver Snag Island is steep-to, and the entire fairway carries between 8 to 15 fathoms. Once inside the north arm, turn northeast into the basin where the bottom gradually rises from 11 fathoms to about 4 fathoms 100 yards from a drying grassy flat. The flat, which is about 100 feet wide, has a salmon stream at its north arm.

Neil Carey notes that seas break heavily clear across the entrance to Kootenay Inlet during heavy westerlies.

Approaching north arm of Kootenay Inlet

Anchor (Haystack Cove) in 1 to 2 fathoms over brown mud, broken shells and cobble with newspaper kelp; poor-to-fair holding unless you set your anchor well. Avoid a 4-foot long rock at the head of the bay between the two streams, awash on a 3-foot tide. Shoal areas lie on either side of the cove north of both streams.

Anchor (North Arm) in the center of the basin in 4 to 11 fathoms over very soft brown mud with clam shells and twigs; fair holding unless you set your anchor well.

Anchor (East Arm) at the south end of the basin west of two islands, as indicated on the diagram in 6 to 8 fathoms over brown mud, broken shells and cobble; fair-to-good holding.

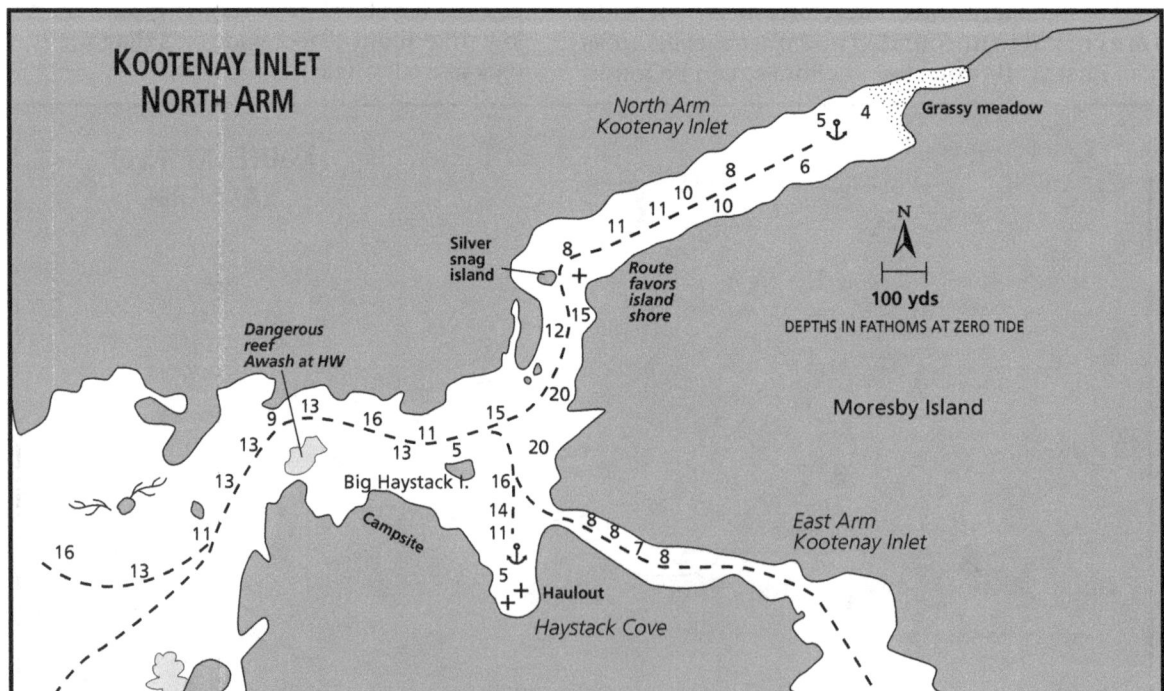

KOOTENAY INLET
NORTH ARM

North Arm
Kootenay Inlet

Grassy meadow

Silver snag island

Route favors island shore

N

100 yds
DEPTHS IN FATHOMS AT ZERO TIDE

Dangerous reef
Awash at HW

Moresby Island

Big Haystack I.

Campsite

East Arm
Kootenay Inlet

Haulout

Haystack Cove

©2024 Don and Réanne Douglass • Diagram not for navigation

Entrance to north arm, Kootenay Inlet

Portland Bay (Moresby Island)
4.5 mi N of Tasu Narrows
Entrance: 52°47.40'N, 132°11.67'W

Portland Bay is exposed to the seas and weather and offers no shelter. *Caution:* there can be strong tide rips off Chad's Point. Neil Carey writes: "The broad waterfall tumbling into Portland Bay is alluring and, if the sea is amenable, it is possible to make a quick landing and hike up to the rock-bound, water lily speckled lake where small shrubs and knee-high bonsai-like trees grow from crevasses in the granite rock. Landing is easiest before the tide changes to flood as the incoming flood often rolls ashore with enough force to make launching a small boat a rough and wet experience. Sea conditions can change so quickly that it is never prudent to anchor here overnight. I saw one sailboat anchored here overnight because the crew could not re-board after an evening picnic on the rocky beach. Luckily, the anchor caught between large rocks and the cable did not chafe through. They were rescued by helicopter the next forenoon—despite having told friends in Tasu that they were going to sail south and would be back by dark. So much for changing travel plans without notifying a responsible person."

Finger Inlet (Moresby Island)
0.5 mi W of Davidson Point
Entrance: 52°44.60'N, 132°07.54'W

"Finger Inlet" is what we call the narrow, steep-sided inlet just northwest of the entrance to Tasu Sound. This little inlet offers adequate temporary protection for one small boat wanting a few hours rest, a quiet meal, or time to make minor repairs. Kelp near the entrance dampens the sea within the inlet. A small stream pours in through logs trapped on the left side of an upswept gravel beach.

Anchor in 3 to 4 fathoms, gravel bottom; poor-to-fair holding.

Tasu Head entering Tasu Sound

Tasu Sound
(Moresby Island)
31 mi S of Skidegate Channel
Entrance: 52°44.29'N, 132°06.78'W

You can frequently find sea lions basking on their rocky haulouts along the iron-bound coast below Mt. De la Touche and Tasu Sound. One of the most sheltered anchorages between Skidegate Channel and Cape St. James can be found inside Tasu Sound at Two Mountain Bay, 5.5 miles northeast of Tasu Narrows.

With the closing of the extensive mining activities in Tasu Sound there are no longer any facilities or inhabitants. The only form of communication with civilization is by hiking the old logging road that extends from the north end of Newcombe Inlet over to the abandoned and cleared land that was once the Sewell Inlet logging camp on the eastern side of Moresby Inlet.

Tasu Head, across Moresby Island to Tangil Peninsula, marks the northern boundary of Gwaii Haanas National Park Reserve.

Neil Carey writes: "Tasu is a good place to fish for salmon and halibut as well as trout in its many streams. Two Mountain Bay is a fine all weather anchorage. We anchored north and east of the small island in 6-8 fathoms. This is another year-round, all-weather anchorage. Fossils can sometimes be found along the bay's rocky and treed west and south border. When not caring to take time to fully enter the sound, we have anchored in either of the two notches just inside the entrance in the southeast. Both are protected and offer a chance for a quick check outside to see if it is feasible to proceed."

Beach at Lomgon Bay

Baidarka exiting Two Mountain Bay

Two Mountain Bay (Tasu Sound)

5.5 mi NE of Tasu Narrows
Entrance: 52°47.46′N, 131°59.36′W
Anchor: 52°47.89′N, 132°00.16′W

Two Mountain Bay is a land-locked, half-mile-long cove that affords good shelter in nearly all conditions. The center of the bay has a large area of between 10-15 fathoms where anchorage can be found for several vessels. The bay is entered east of Flyaway Islet avoiding the rocks on the west side of the entrance and a 1.5-fathom shoal in the center of the fairway. Although the mountainside to the east has been clearcut, brush and small alders have begun to take hold.

Anchor in 12 fathoms over sand and gravel; fair-to-good holding.

Barrier Bay (Tasu Sound)

Immediately E of Two Mountain Bay
Entrance: 52°47.40′N, 131°58.84′W

If you are this close to the secure anchorage of Two Mountain Bay, don't bother to drop your anchor in open Barrier Bay.

Neil Carey: "In the early 1970s an agreement between Canada and the USSR allowed Russian vessels fishing in the North Pacific to enter Tasu Sound for the purpose of being resupplied by large freighters from Vladivostok or Black Sea ports; they then loaded processed fish products for transport home. The crews were not authorized to go ashore. For a few years we frequently saw a num-

ber of these ships anchored east of Reid Point and on the north edge of Wilson Bay. Women as well as men crewed the large, rusty, hard-working draggers and the fine, well-maintained freighters. Covered lifeboats that appeared suitable for surviving in any weather hung from davits mounted at bridge level on these fine ships."

Botany Inlet (Tasu Sound)

7 mi E of Tasu Narrows
Entrance: 52°45.37′N, 131°57.86′W
Anchor (Botany Island): 52°45.58′N, 131°58.70′W
Anchor (head): 52°43.03′N, 131°55.19′W

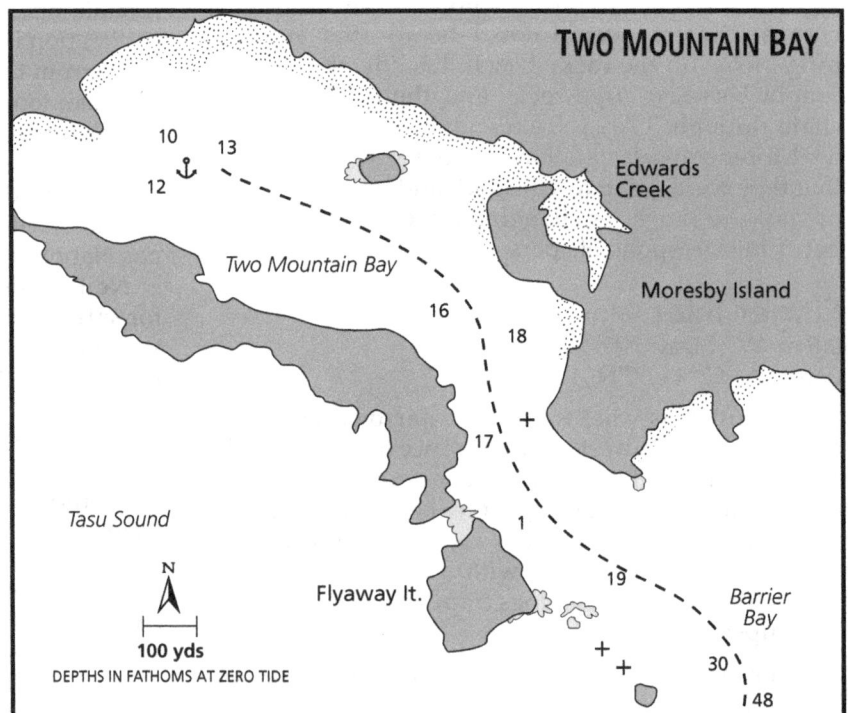

TWO MOUNTAIN BAY

Edwards Creek

Moresby Island

Two Mountain Bay

Tasu Sound

Flyaway It.

Barrier Bay

N

100 yds
DEPTHS IN FATHOMS AT ZERO TIDE

©2024 Don and Réanne Douglass • Diagram not for navigation

Islet in Botany Bay

Botany Inlet is a lovely largely unexplored finger of water set between high, steep, forested ridges. For cruising vessels, it offers wonderful possibilities as an anchorage to wait out stormy weather or to enjoy a quiet peaceful area. Landlocked by Botany Island and a peninsula across from the island at its entrance, it can offer excellent protection in almost any weather. The preferred entrance into Botany Inlet lies between the southeast corner of Botany Island and the mid-channel islet.

At the head of the inlet, a valley that opens to the south is bordered by abrupt, high mountains that rise to over 2,000 feet. Several small creeks drain this valley, creating a wide grassy flat that shoals 200 yards into the inlet. No indication of clearcutting exists and, although it appears to have been logged decades ago (probably A-frame logging), second growth prevails. The grassy valley floor is predominantly alder with some young spruce and cedar.

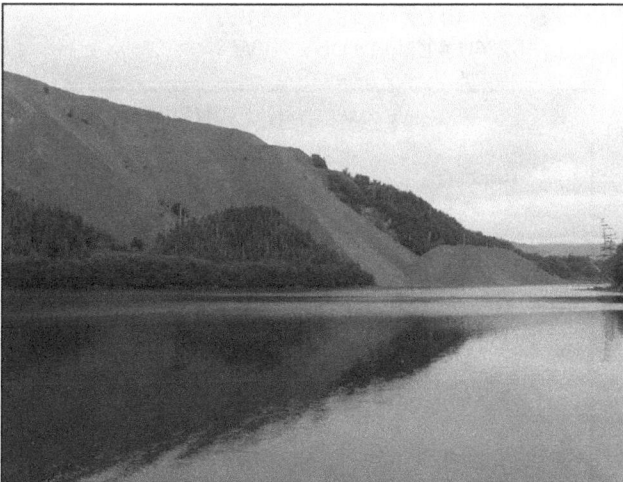

Old tailings visible in Hunger Harbour

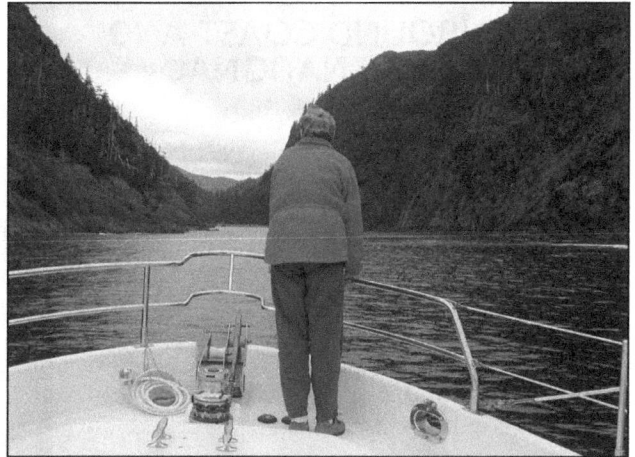

Entrance to Finger Inlet

Anchor (Botany Island) in 8 to 10 fathoms over a soft bottom; fair holding.

Anchor (head) in 6 fathoms over sticky brown mud; very good holding.

Fairfax Inlet
(Tasu Sound)
2 mi SW of Two Mountain Bay
Entrance: 52°46.13'N, 132°01.77'W

Fairfax Inlet is the first inlet on the south side of Tasu Sound. Hunger Harbour lies just inside its entrance, at the west side.

Hunger Harbour
(Fairfax Inlet)
3 mi NE of Tasu Narrows
Entrance: 52°45.52'N, 132°01.36'W
Anchor: 52°45.75'N, 132°02.31'W

Hunger Harbour is the former mining townsite where 400 people once lived and worked. Nearly all of the townsite has been demolished and the area seeded to grass and clover for deer. Landing on the causeway at the head of the harbor can offer a few miles of old roads for hiking. The dark mine tailings that rise steeply along the west side of the inlet are an ugly reminder of the devastation created years earlier. Access to the underground portion of the mine has been blocked with waste rock. Bushes are slowly reclaiming this hillside, but for nearly 20 years Tasu, which was reported to be the best looking settlement in Haida Gwaii, provided a great variety of amenities.

Anchorage can be found at the northwest corner of Hunger Harbour in 10 to 15 fathoms where it is protected by a causeway. Avoid submerged cables and other debris left from the mining operations.

THE IRONBOUND COAST AND GWAII HAANAS NATIONAL PARK RESERVE

The section of Moresby's west coast between Tasu Sound and Gowgaia Bay is so rugged and wild that we call it "The Creation Coast." The entire distance is unsurveyed, uncharted, and pristine. Vessels that venture into this uninhabited and remote area must be able to rely on their own observations and resources where risks to vessel and life can become extreme. Strong and sometimes violent southeast winds can occur in this area, and although you can find anchorage in a number of inlets, be prepared for such weather.

The boundary of Gwaii Haanas National Park Reserve/Haida Heritage Site lies south of Tasu Head.

Ironbound Coast

De la Touche Cove (Moresby Island)
4.3 mi SE of Tasu Head
Entrance: 52°40.77'N, 132°02.23'W
Anchor: 52°41.04'N, 132°01.82'W

"De la Touche Cove" is what we call the unnamed cove to the west of De la Touche Mountain—a mountain that rises nearly vertically from sea level to 3,685 feet, creating one of the most magnificent panoramas along the North Pacific coast. The last 1,000 feet of the dark granite mountain are so precipitous that snow cannot get a hold on its sides. Although the cove, which faces southwest, does not provide good storm anchorage, the surrounding views are so intoxicating that a crew could almost forget the need to haul up anchor and get underway.

The entrance to De la Touche Cove, which is uncharted, can be intimidating as it leads through large patches of kelp. Our diagram does not show

the full extent of the unidentified hazards. Although the cove makes a wonderful lunch stop in stable weather, its hard stony bottom with poor holding does not qualify it for an overnight anchor site until it is more thoroughly explored. The kelp seems to knock down the bulk of outside swell; however, in strong southwesterly gales, this protection may be inadequate. The cove's flat bottom and the two small beaches composed of white stones seem to indicate that the cove might offer serious cruising possibilities. This cove may possibly be the long-lost village of Saolangai referred to in Kathleen Dalzell's book on the Queen Charlottes.

Anchor in about 8 fathoms over a hard, stony bottom; poor holding.

Blue Heron Bay (Moresby Island)
2.5 mi NW of Sunday Inlet
Entrance: 52°40.09'N, 132°00.64'W
Anchor: 52°40.41'N, 131°59.98'W

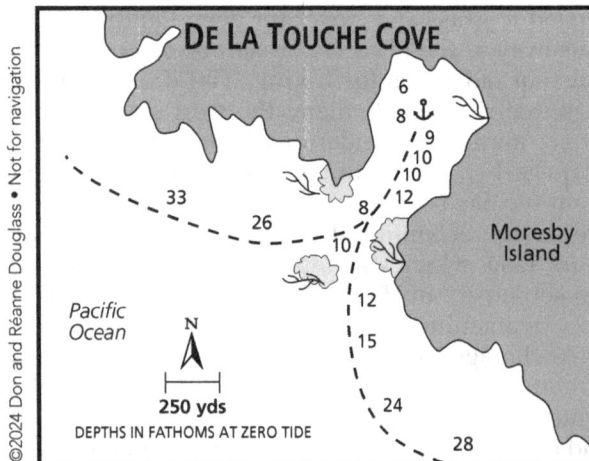
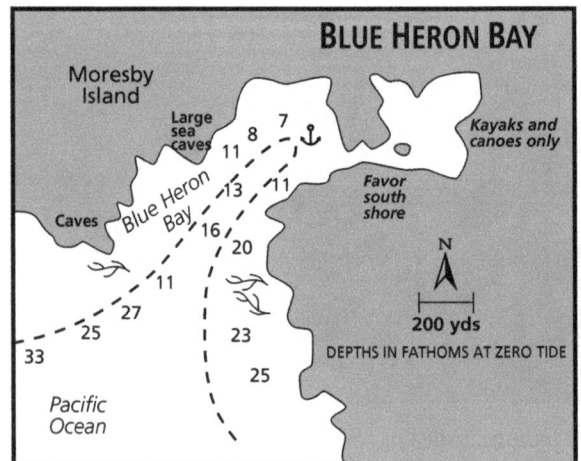

Entrance to Blue Heron Basin

Entering De La Touche Cove

We found the steep-to western shore of Blue Heron Bay excellent for inspecting the sea caves near its entrance. Farther in is a little boulder beach. Moderate depths are found in 8 to 15 fathoms from the small boulder beach across the bay to the entrance to Blue Heron Pond. This pond has the shape of a maple leaf and is fed by a sizeable lake that drops from a cirque high in the mountains. It can be entered by kayaks and small sportfishing boats; hug the south shore until well into the pond itself.

The pond is fully sheltered from outside chop. Temporary anchorage can be found west of the entrance to the pond, southwest of a cleavage line that goes from the water to the top of a nearby peak. Although the shore has just a moderate amount of driftwood, the trees appear to have been blasted by strong winds. Experienced hikers may want to hike up through brush on the north side of the creek to the cirque via a series of glaciated benches.

Neil Carey reports that they anchored during a storm near the steep north shore off the falls inside the pond in deep water, using a kedge anchor and a line to shore. This uncharted bay was named by Neil and Betty for the blue herons that reside here.

Exiting the bay, avoid two large kelp beds off the south entrance point where we found a minimum of 22 fathoms in the vicinity.

Anchor in 8 to 10 fathoms over an unrecorded bottom.

Sea cave at entrance to Blue Heron Bay

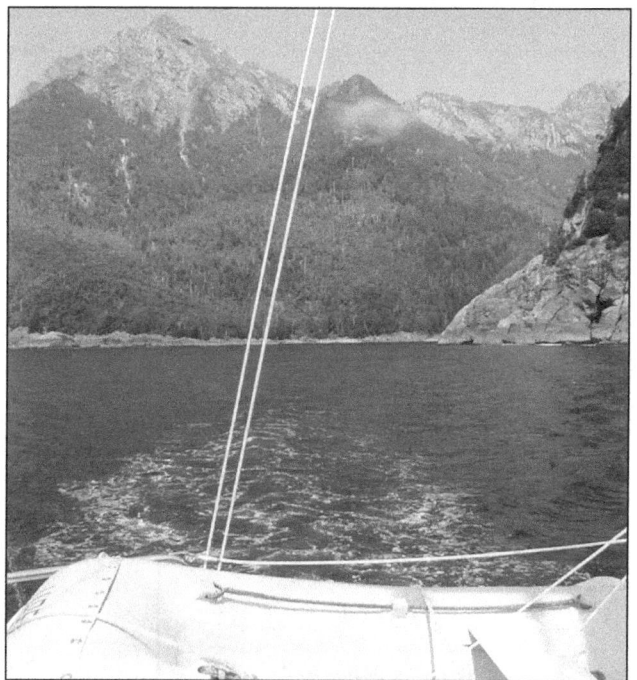

Leaving De La Touche Cove

From the ridge, Blue Heron Bay

Rocks near Sunday Inlet entrance

Sunday Inlet (Pacific Ocean)

8 mi SE of Tasu Sound
Entrance: 52°38.75'N, 131°56.58'W
Anchor: 52°38.86'N, 131°53.25'W

Sunday Inlet can be entered between a rock off the north entrance point that resembles a witch's hat and two submerged mid-channel rocks; the fairway carries 15 fathoms or more. These mid-channel rocks are not visible on a 7-foot tide, but they break on moderate swells. The north arm of the inlet has two small beaches at its north end but this site is too exposed and too deep (30 to 60 fathoms) for convenient anchoring. Entering the first narrows of Sunday Inlet there is an uncharted rock with 3 fathoms of water over it, marked by kelp, 0.1 mile south of the north shore (see diagram). Charts have large offsets—our

track crossed land on more that one occasion.

The bottom of the inlet has irregular depths all the way to its head where a small cove indents the south shore. Referring to this small cove, Neil Carey says, "Sunday Inlet is one of the few places on Moresby Island's west coast where I feel comfortable anchoring during any storm, year around."

We anchored in 10 fathoms halfway into this cove and set our anchor in a hard rocky bottom with kelp. (Be sure to test your anchor's set before relying on it!) Farther in, near the head of the cove, is a 6-fathom bench that may have better holding but swinging room is more limited at this site. (Neil Carey recalls a mud bottom closer to the creek.)

Anchor in 10 fathoms over a hard rocky bottom with kelp; poor holding.

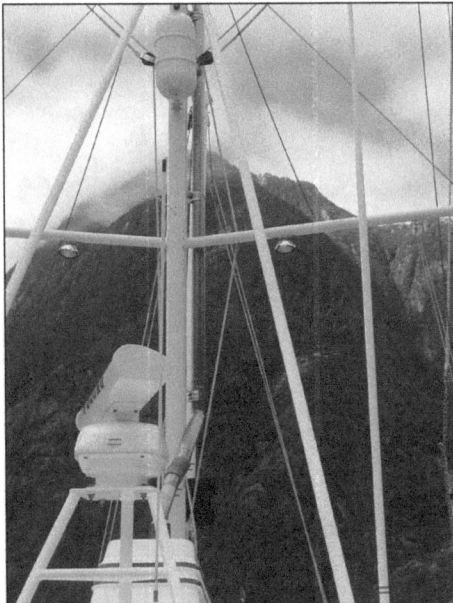

Anchored below the towering peaks of Sunday Inlet

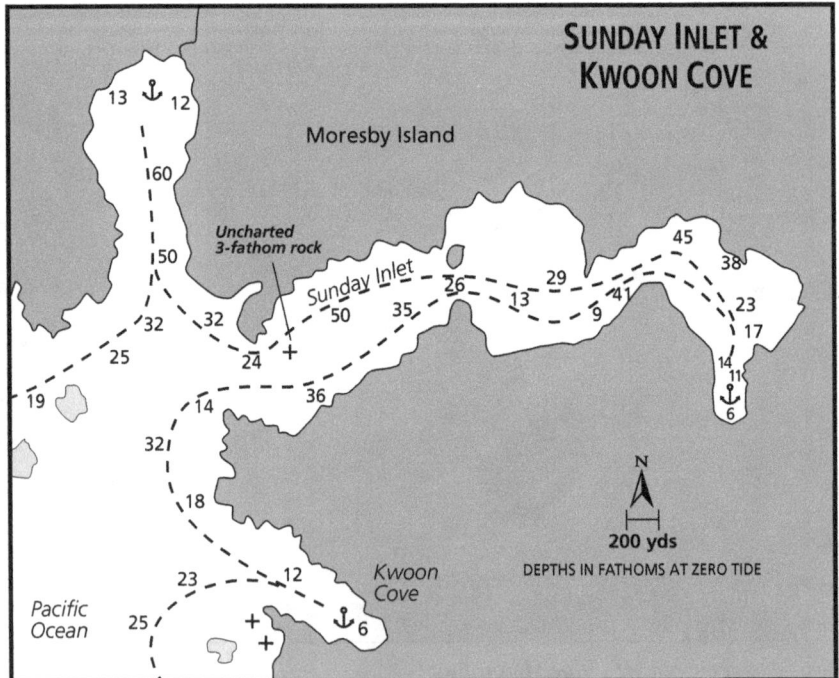

Sunday Inlet

Entrance cave, Pocket Inlet

Kwoon Cove (Moresby Island)
S side of Sunday Inlet
Entrance: 52°38.01'N, 131°56.47'W
Anchor: 52°37.88'N, 131°55.89'W

Kwoon Cove, immediately south of Sunday Inlet, is wide open to westerly swell and chop; its eastern shore is piled high with driftlogs—excellent for beachcombing but indicative of its exposure. Despite a beautiful white sand beach at its south end that could serve as a good campsite under tall trees, we do not recommend that you leave your boat unattended.

The southwest entrance to Kwoon Cove has many smooth-sided pinnacles that protrude about 100 feet above the ocean. Be alert for a rock awash on a 5- to 6-foot tide 0.7 mile southwest of Kwoon Cove and 0.3 mile offshore. This rock is located 0.5 mile northwest of what we call the "Four Fangs"—pinnacle-shaped rocks more than 100 feet high, west of the entrance to Pocket Inlet.

Anchor in 6 to 8 fathoms over hard cobble with kelp; poor-to-fair holding.

Pocket Inlet (Moresby Island)
1.5 mi N of Murray Cove
Entrance: 52°36.42'N, 131°55.28'W
Anchor: 52°36.84'N, 131°51.91.'W

Pocket Inlet, another jewel tucked into the rocky west coast, offers good protection at its head, out of sight of the entrance. The Four Fangs, west of the entrance to Pocket, are a major landmark visible all the way from Tasu Head, 10 miles to the northwest. Just 200 yards northwest of the entrance to the inlet there is a large sea cave filled with boulders. Inside the entrance, silvery driftlogs have been flung high onto shore above the high tide line. The southern shores of the inner basin have rocky slopes with hanging valleys from which plunges a particularly beautiful waterfall. The north shore has rocky slopes with stunted pine trees and low brush. Neil Carey found satisfactory anchorage here in winter, indicating its potential in heavier weather.

Anchor in 12 to 15 fathoms over sand and gravel with some kelp; fair-to-good holding.

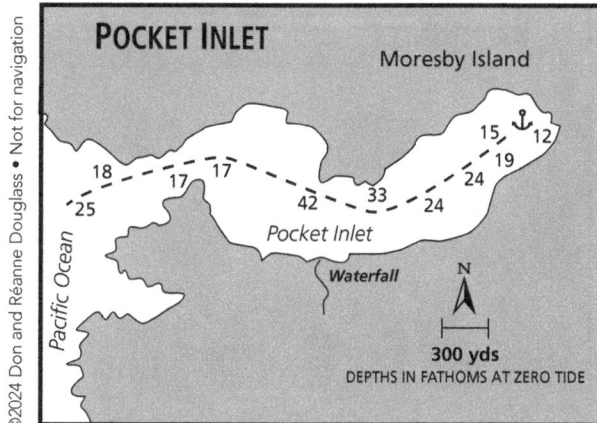

©2024 Don and Réanne Douglass • Not for navigation

Sand beach in Kwoon Cove

Entrance to Murray Cove

Cobble beach, Murray Cove

Murray Cove (Moresby Island)
2.5 mi N of Barry Inlet
Entrance: 52°35.03'N, 131°53.98'W

Murray Cove is easily identified by the tall pinnacle rock just off the south side of the entrance between headlands of bare rocks. The cove is wide open to the west and not suitable for overnight anchoring, nor does it offer much attraction. A small stream rolls over the large granite rocks at the head. Landing on the rocks with a boat or kayak can be a bumpy experience!

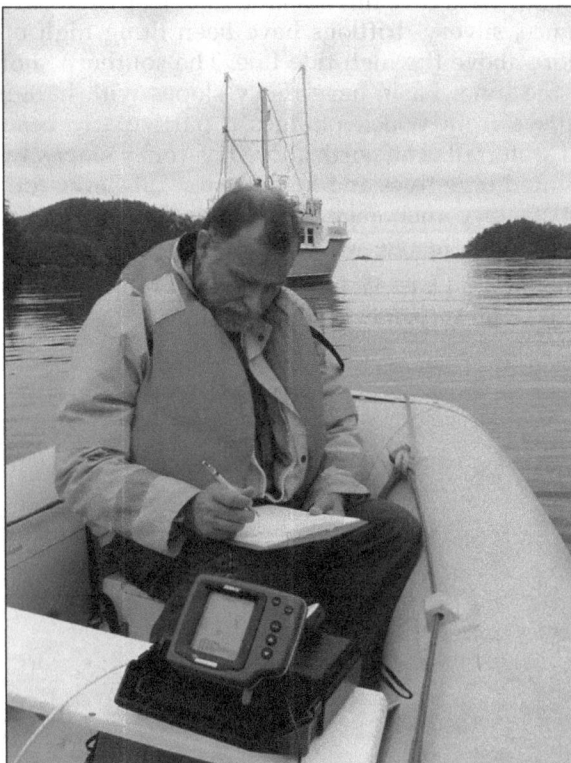

Kevin Monahan collecting depth data in Kootenay Inlet

Carey writes, "It was rewarding one mid-September when we found a lone man who had tried hiking along the coast to Tasu from a lake just south of Barry Inlet. As the raven flies, he'd done four miles in 15 days. I have no guess as to how many miles this experienced hiker had actually covered. He had to climb part of the San Christoval Range to get around Barry Inlet then finally to reach Murray Cove. He was in good physical condition, but early fall storms and the impossible coastal hike were too much. He had tied bright plastic beachcombings to a small tree by his campsite to attract attention but it was bursts from the flash unit of his camera that caught our eyes. He was rescued because he had left a schedule with his fiancée, who alerted the RCMP (we just found him first!). And the lady's prize—a loving and grateful future husband."

Barry Inlet
(Moresby Island)
3 mi N of Mike Inlet
Entrance: 52°33.58'N, 131°50.89'W
Anchor: 52°33.90'N, 131°50.72'W

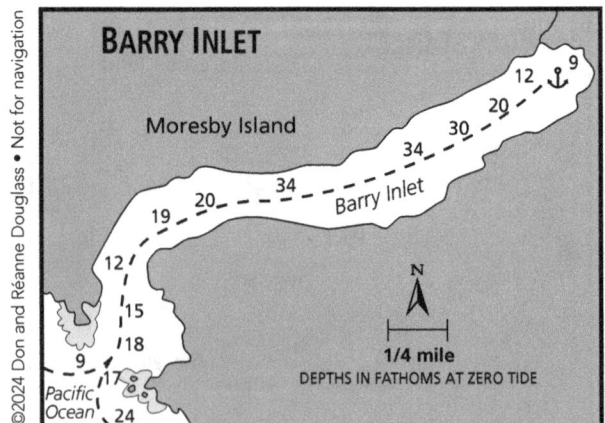

Mike Inlet

Entrance to Mike Inlet

Barry Inlet is a dramatically rugged inlet that extends three miles to the San Christoval Range. The walls of the inlet appear to have been carved out of solid granite and the headwall itself rises over 3,000 feet to the heights of the mountain range. The entrance fairway is rather narrow; rocks, reefs and kelp extend from either side of the entrance point. Upon entering, slightly favor the north shore to avoid a rock off the south entrance point that dries at 10 feet and has patches of kelp on either side; the rock and kelp extend about 100 feet from shore.

Most of the inlet is too deep for anchoring; the bottom rises rapidly to 20 fathoms then slowly decreases to 10 fathoms off the gravel and grassy beach at its head. The north shore seems to have little evidence of stress and the south shore has many standing silver snags. Neil Carey writes, "Deer and bear feed near the clear, meandering stream."

Anchor in 10 fathoms over sand and gravel with fair holding.

Mike Inlet (Moresby Island)

3.5 mi N of Puffin Cove
Entrance: 52°31.47′N, 131°48.07′W
Anchor: 52°31.93′N, 131°45.07′W

Mike Inlet is surrounded by steep, forested hills with a stream that descends at its northeast end over a series of rocky steps. Kelp extends for a distance of 0.20 mile west of the south entrance point. We found 26 fathoms on the north side of the islet and 7 on the south. The bottom has irregular depths. We tried anchoring on the south shore just east of the peninsula and found the bottom stony with poor holding. Anchorage can be found at 10 fathoms off the head of the inlet south of the islet; however we fouled and nearly lost our anchor at this site on what appeared to be large rocks. We cannot recommend it because of this. Neil Carey reports that he anchored here a dozen times or more and sometime fouled his anchor as well. The inlet may be subject to strong williwaws blowing down from the San Christoval Range.

Head of Barry Inlet

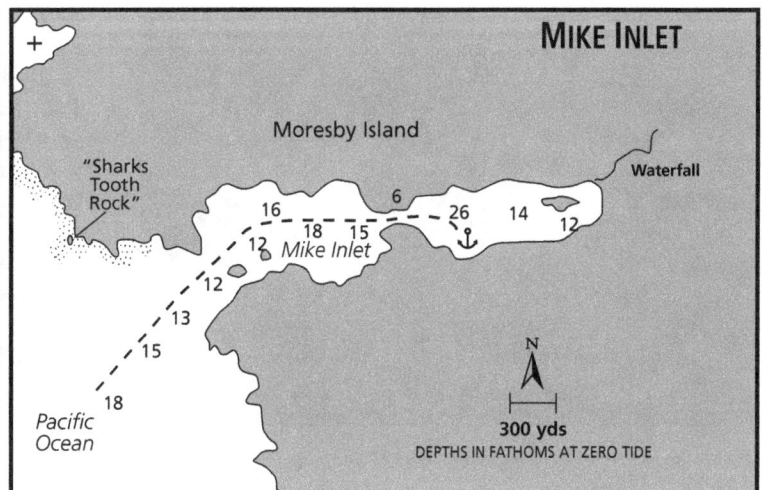

Puffin Cove (Moresby Island)

7.5 mi N of Gowgaia Bay
Entrance: 52°29.61'N, 131°43.96'W
Entrance (inner cove): 52°29.70'N, 131°43.75'W

Puffin Cove does not offer anchorage for cruising boats. In fair weather it is possible to stand off the rocky beach along the north shore, which is strewn with masses of drift logs, and to enter Puffin Cove's salt lagoon with a dinghy when tides are adequate. The entrance to the lagoon, which is hidden behind a tall, rocky peninsula with several detached rocks, carries about 3 feet at low water. In any westerly it's likely that you won't get near enough to the rocks to see the entrance—from 100 yards off our bridge we were unable to see it. Winter storms have scrubbed clean the outer rocks to a height of about 50 feet.

Neil and Betty Carey, who built a log cabin high above the shore of the lagoon, documented their unusual pioneering life on the west cove in their book, *Puffin Cove*. Their cabin, which now lies within Gwaii Haanas National Park Reserve, can no longer be permanently occupied.

Neil Carey writes: "Waves deflected from the rocky shore always kept us off the north rock wall. Unseen rocks create a hazard on the south half of the narrow, short entrance. Inside, the water quickly shoals over the sandy bottom."

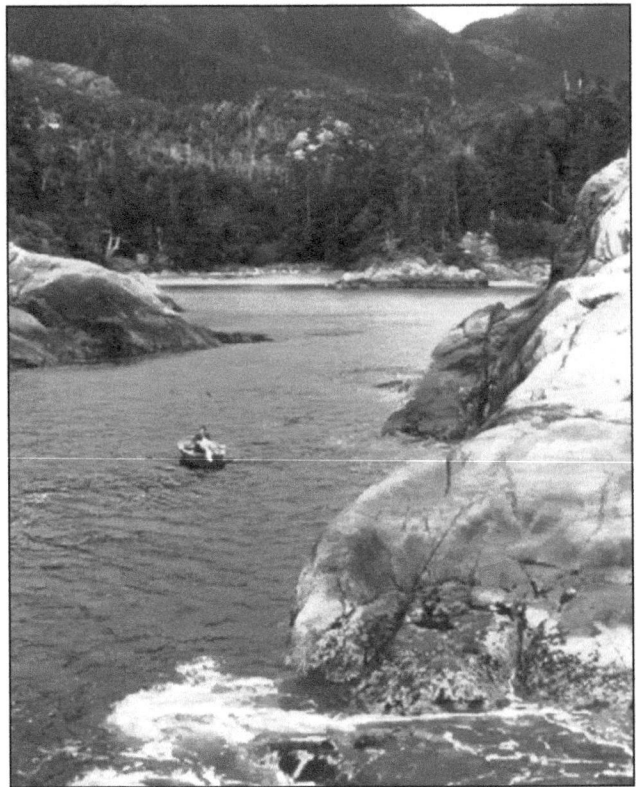

Photo courtesy Neil Carey

Aerial photograph of Puffin Cove with lagoon in foreground

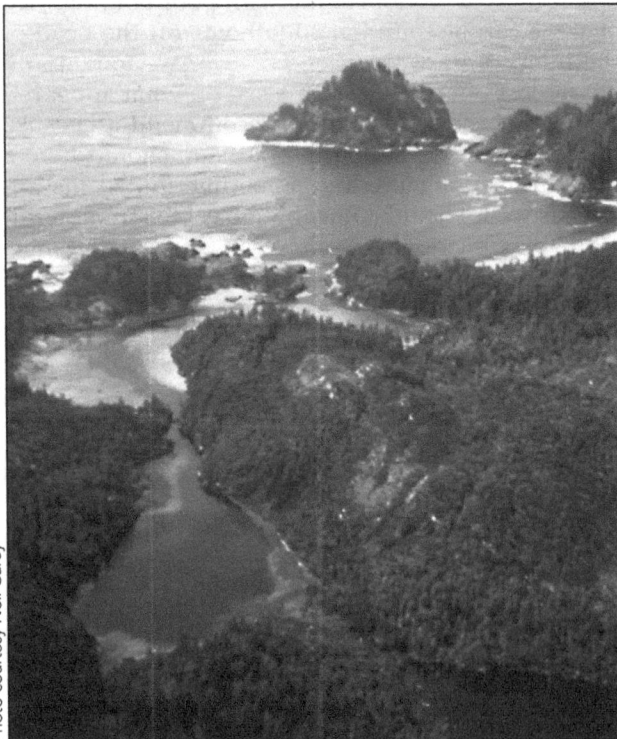

Photo courtesy Neil Carey

Entering Puffin Cove Lagoon

Two Buck Bay (Moresby Island)

4.5 mi N of Nangwai Islands
Entrance: 52°28.57'N, 131°40.04'W

Two Buck Bay, although lovely as a daytime stop, is not recommended for overnight anchoring. While living in Puffin Cove, Neil and Betty Carey bagged two bucks from this bay—thus the name "Two Buck Bay." It is also known as Husband Harbour in Neil Frazer's *Boat Camping in Haida Gwaii*. The upper reaches of the bay are too shallow for deep-draft boats, but good for small boats and kayaks. The sandy beach on the west side of the head can be used as a nice kayak haul-out and campsite.

Due to several offlying islets and kelp patches, Two Buck Bay is surprisingly calm considering its southern exposure. The easiest entrance is to pass west and north of the offlying islets where the fairway carries about 11 fathoms. There is also a route east of the major islet that has about 5 fathoms in its fairway.

Silver driftwood forms an obstacle course along the storm-wracked shore where the trees have been savagely windswept. You can choose between beaches of golden sand, small gravel, or grey rocks where falls and small streams drop into the bay. Sand comprises most of the bay's bottom.

Entrance to Iron Balls Bay

Pyramid Island, Two Buck Bay

Iron Balls Bay (Moresby Island)

2.3 mi NW of Nangwai Islands
Entrance (N): 52°26.83′N, 131°38.66′W
Entrance (S): 52°26.70′N, 131°38.12′W

Iron Balls Bay is wide open to southwesterlies and is rolly under almost all conditions. It can serve as an emergency or temporary anchorage but is not recommended for overnight use. The bay has a uniform depth of about 10 to 12 fathoms. There is a gravel and rock beach on the west shore where logs have been thrown high above the high-tide line; a boulder beach lies at the head of the bay.

The north entrance has a very narrow fairway of 60 feet width with depths of 6 fathoms. The south entrance is wider with 11 fathoms in its fairway, however there are rocks and kelp patches off the entrance islets as well as off the south entrance point.

Neil Carey found a number of metal floats used by draggers while beachcombing here. We, too, noticed a number of these floats on the beach.

Gowgaia Bay

(Moresby Island)
23 mi NW of SGaang Gwaii
Entrance: 52°24.06′N, 131°36.78′W

Gowgaia Bay, Tasu Sound, and Flamingo Inlet are the only three major inlets on the southernmost portion of Moresby Island's west coast. Within Gowgaia, we consider Yakulanas Bay to have the best all-around shelter and holding power. The seas break heavily on the rocks and shoals south of Nangwai Islands where a large seal population lives.

Neil and Betty Carey reported that their boat, *Skylark,* couldn't enter Gowgaia Bay due to huge breakers and they had to run south to Flamingo Inlet for shelter when the seas were some 50 feet between crest and trough. There is a large resident seal population among these islands.

Carey also reports he found good protection in a deep cove behind the larger of the Gowdas Islands located 0.5 mile southwest of Gowgaia Point. He noted that the beaches in this unnamed cove have no driftwood.

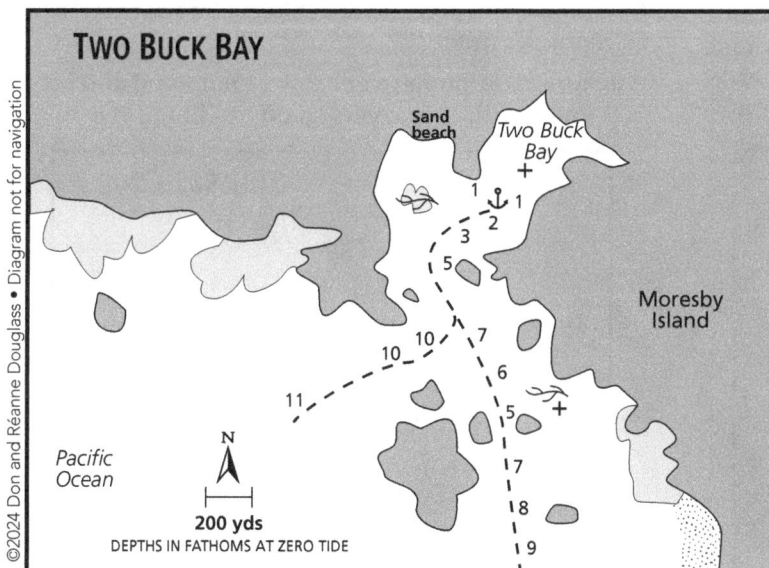

TWO BUCK BAY

Sand beach

Two Buck Bay

Moresby Island

Pacific Ocean

200 yds
DEPTHS IN FATHOMS AT ZERO TIDE

©2024 Don and Réanne Douglass • Diagram not for navigation

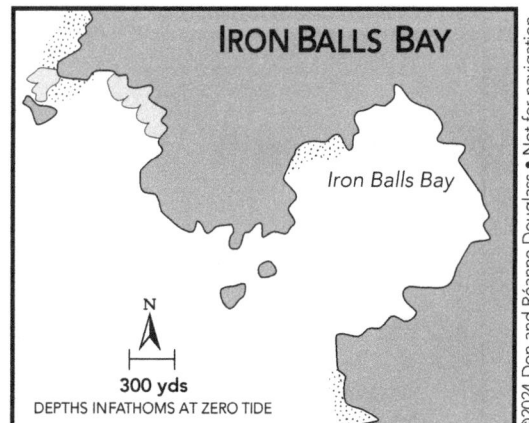

IRON BALLS BAY

Iron Balls Bay

300 yds
DEPTHS IN FATHOMS AT ZERO TIDE

©2024 Don and Réanne Douglass • Not for navigation

©2024 Don and Réanne Douglass • Not for navigation

GOSKI BAY

Moresby Island

4   4
6
7
8
5
Goski Bay
14
5
15   Goski Island

Gowgaia Bay

N

200 yds

DEPTHS IN FATHOMS AT ZERO TIDE

Head of Yakalunas Bay,

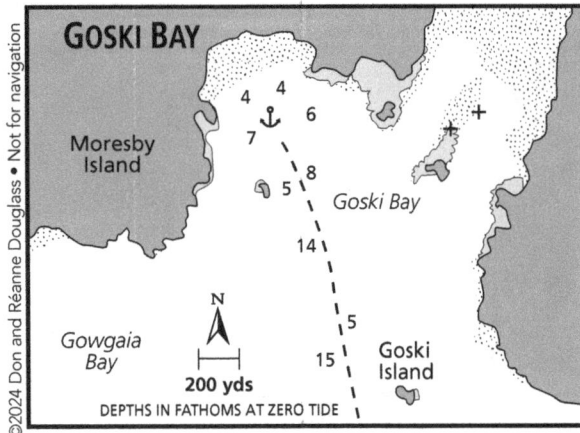

Goski Bay (Gowgaia Bay)
2 mi NE of Gowgaia Point lt.
Entrance: 52°25.75'N, 131°33.87'W
Anchor: 52°25.87'N, 131°34.09'W

The west arm of Goski Bay is known to be a good anchorage in westerly weather. There is a campsite off a small stream at its head. Open to the southeast with considerable fetch, the bay is not recommended in such weather. The large drying sand and mud flat in the northeast corner of the bay, which catches a lot of driftwood in southerlies, is home to a resident population of Canada geese, called homesteaders. Small boats can anchor in shallower water northwest of the west islet in 2 to 3 fathoms.

Anchor in 7 fathoms, fine sand and mud with fair-to-good holding with lots of scope.

Yakulanas Bay (Gowgaia Bay)
3 mi E of Gowgaia Point lt.
Entrance: 52°24.65'N, 131°32.28'W
Anchor: 52°23.78'N, 131°30.58'W

Yakulanas Bay, for our money, is the best anchorage in Gowgaia Bay. It has more protection from north-westerlies than Soulsby. It does not receive south-

west swells and is not exposed to the southeast, as is Goski. It has by far the best holding of any sites we tested in Gowgaia. The shores are lined with mixed old growth forest with large spruce trees at the head of the bay. The head has a possible haul-out spot and campsite. The flat gravel beach bares at low water and drops off to 6 fathoms. Avoid the rocky shoal area off the east shore.

Neil Carey writes that the surrounding hillsides are steep, forested, and marked by new and old landslides. The beaches are narrow whether they are composed of sand, gravel, stones, or rocks. At any time but high tide, deer wander the shore selecting choice pieces of kelp, and bear amble along sniffing and flipping rocks, searching for a meal of small crabs. Starting near the mouth of an east-tending stream at the head of Yakulanas Bay, it is possible to hike across the low land, locate and follow an east flowing stream and arrive at Skaat Harbour, north of Burnaby Narrows.

Anchor in 8 fathoms over brown mud, sand and broken shells with twigs; very good holding.

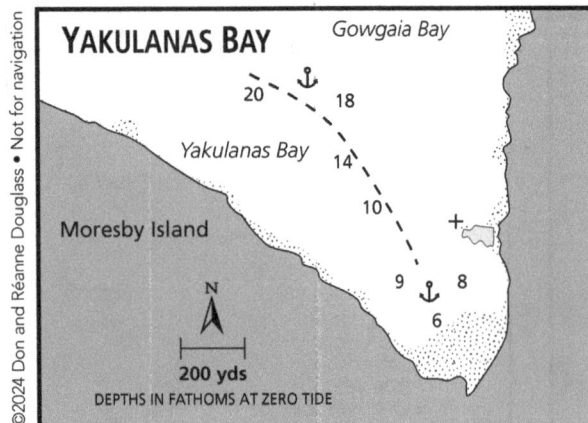

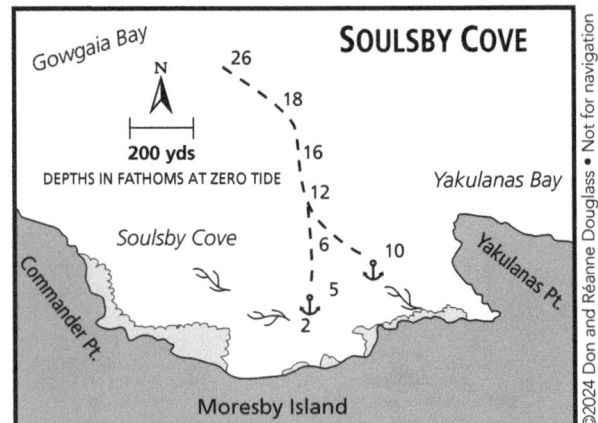

©2024 Don and Réanne Douglass • Not for navigation

YAKULANAS BAY   Gowgaia Bay

20   18
Yakulanas Bay
14
10
Moresby Island
9   8
6

N

200 yds

DEPTHS IN FATHOMS AT ZERO TIDE

©2024 Don and Réanne Douglass • Not for navigation

Gowgaia Bay   SOULSBY COVE

26
18
N
16
200 yds
12
DEPTHS IN FATHOMS AT ZERO TIDE
Yakulanas Bay
Soulsby Cove
6
6   10
5
Commander Pt.
2
Yakulanas Pt.

Moresby Island

Soulsby Cove (Gowagai Bay)

1.5 mi NE of Gowgaia Point lt.
Entrance: 52°24.63'N, 131°33.28'W
Anchor: 52°24.39'N, 131°33.16'W

Soulsby Cove offers some protection from southeast winds, but as Neil Carey reports, holding is marginal and strong southwest winds curl into the cove. Depths are greater than charted and the three anchor tests we made in *Baidarka* proved that the bottom is not stony, but very hard sand with some kelp and poor holding.

Anchor in 8 fathoms over a hard bottom; poor holding.

Tcuga Cove and Lagoon (Gowgaia Bay)

0.5 mi S of Gowgaia Pt.
Entrance: 52°23.90'N, 131°35.86
Anchor: 52°23.52'N, 131°35.64'W

The bay on the east side of the Gowdas Islands offers surprisingly good shelter and the shores have no drift or signs of stress deep in the southern arm. The east arm was the site of the Haida village of Tcuga at the outlet of a large lagoon that can be entered by small craft only at high water. The narrows becomes a rapids on spring tide. Anchorage can be found off its south arm in appropriate depths as the cove shoals before reaching the kelp patch and sandy beach.

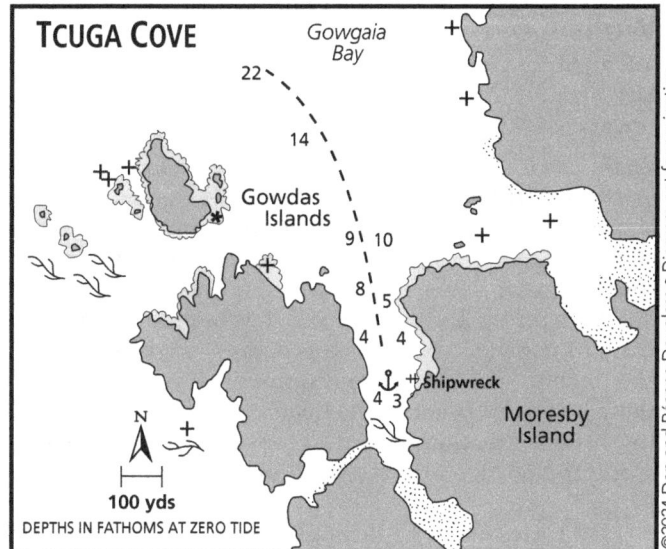

TCUGA COVE
Gowgaia Bay
Gowdas Islands
Shipwreck
Moresby Island
N
100 yds
DEPTHS IN FATHOMS AT ZERO TIDE
©2024 Don and Réanne Douglass • Diagram not for navigation

On our visit to shore with the Park's boat (see Sidebar below) we found spongey earth underneath a canopy of old-growth forest where shells of all kinds—red abalone, turban, clam, scallop, sea urchin—and in sizes from exquisitely small to eight inches wide—had taken permanent hold. The abalone shells, alone, had been polished to a pearly, thin surface.

Anchor in 3 to 4 fathoms over sand and gravel; fair-to-good holding.

West Coast Mystery Shipwreck and the Reuniting of a Captain and a Workhorse

As *Baidarka* was leaving Gowgaia Bay we received a call on the radio from *Gwaii Haanas II*, the NPR's bright red vessel that was making its initial shakedown to the west coast. Aboard were Richelle Leonard, the retiring Park Superintendent and other Park personnel, as well as Heather Toews, a UBC graduate student conducting research on ecology.

"Did you see the wreck inside Tcuga Cove?" the skipper asked. We hadn't, and he wanted our opinion on what it might be and asked if we'd like to raft alongside so they could show it to us. A shipwreck? Of course!

We headed back into the small cove we had visited earlier, somehow missing the shipwreck. Outside the small lagoon that leads to the old village site of Tcuga we rafted alongside 60-foot *Gwaii Haanas II.*

Ken Brillon, the new skipper, welcomed us aboard. Kevin Monahan remarked that the *Gwaii Haanas II* looked like the *Robson Reef*—a Fisheries Patrol boat on which he had served as Captain for several years. "It WAS the *Robson Reef*," Ken replied, proceeding to ply Kevin with lots of questions on the ship's systems. Kevin was delighted to visit his former vessel and go over the systems with Ken.

Shortly afterwards, the entire crew of both boats jumped in two Park inflatables to go ashore and inspect the strange hull somewhat hidden behind a rock outcropping above high water south of the lagoon's entrance.

This was the Park boat's first visit to the area and they had come across something unexpected. Kevin and Don pondered what this craft might have been. It was fairly old but unlike an ordinary or commercial fishing vessel. None of us could remember having seen anything like this.

The heavy partial wooden hull was constructed with thick planks that, in some places, had a double layer. Sawn knees were fastened by both wooden pegs and old iron bolts, and there was a large flat overhang on the exposed end.

By process of elimination, Kevin and Don surmised that this was an Asian vessel—perhaps a coastal trading boat or a river vessel for fishing in shallow waters. It had some similarities in shape to the small Japanese fishing boat now resting in Mariners Memorial Park in Prince Rupert that was blown ashore years ago off Dixon Entrance without its crew. Could this be an old Chinese boat that had traveled the distance across the Pacific Ocean to find its resting place? With more questions than answers the crews walked the head of the inlet enjoying the lovely west coast rain forest and looking for other clues.   —RHD

Wells Cove (Moresby Island)

4.3 mi SE of Gowgaia Bay
Entrance: 52°20.10′N, 131°34.88′W
Anchor: 52°20.66′N, 131°32.60

Wells Cove offers moderate protection in fair weather tucked in behind the inner islands on the north shore. When approaching the cove from the north, stay off the north point at least 0.45 mile to avoid several rocks, reefs and kelp beds. There are rocks and kelp off the south inner point. From the entrance waypoint given above it's almost a straight shot to the anchor site. There are a number of driftlogs on the white sand beach at the head of the cove, indicating little protection in southwest storms. The beach along the north shore is a good place to stretch your legs.

Neil Carey writes: "If caught by a sudden gale or storm and the tide is high, shelter may be obtained for shallow-draft vessels by entering the stream at the north side of the sand beach at the head of the cove and tying to the trees. Low tide will most likely leave your boat grounded on soft sand."

We found strong turbulence off the south entrance point of Wells Cove and a 2-knot north-flowing current two hours after local high water.

Anchor in 7 fathoms over sand and rock with some kelp; fair holding.

Flamingo Inlet (Anvil, Short Inlet, Sperm Bay & Staki Bay)

7 mi NW of Louscoone Inlet
Entrance: 52°10.43′N, 131°21.11′W

Flamingo Inlet offers the best shelter along this part of the coast and is reportedly easier to enter under difficult conditions than Gowgaia and other inlets north of here. Anvil Cove, 1.5 miles northeast of Nagas Point, and Short Inlet, 0.75 mile northwest of Anvil Cove, have not been surveyed; they are exposed

Kevin Monahan inspects Asian shipwreck

to southerly weather and are recommended for day use only, not as overnight anchorages.

Entering Flamingo, avoid the shoals and reefs located mostly on the eastern half of the inlet. When southbound in good visibility we have taken the shortcut north of Nagas Rocks, recommended by Neil Carey, where the fairway carries about 20 fathoms.

The bottom of the inlet is highly irregular with numerous rocks and patches of kelp. Kevin Monahan's research aboard *Baidarka* indicates that po-

WELLS COVE — Moresby Island

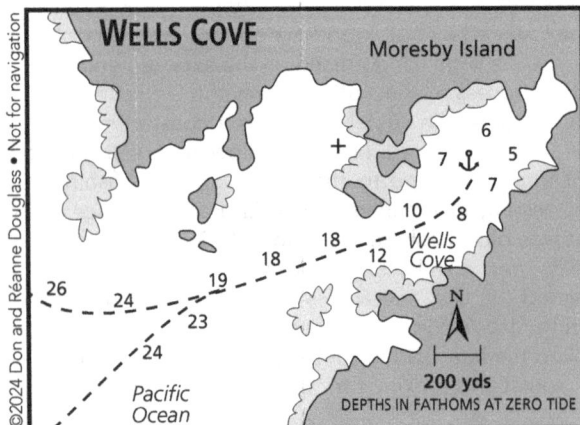

6
7 ⚓ 5
7
10 8
18 8
18 12 *Wells Cove*
19
26 24 23
24

©2024 Don and Réanne Douglass • Not for navigation

Pacific Ocean

200 yds
DEPTHS IN FATHOMS AT ZERO TIDE

Baidarka rafted to Gwaii Haanas II *in Tcuga*

sitions taken by DGPS must be moved 150-meters northwards and eastwards to agree with charts. As an example, while traversing the center of Flamingo Inlet north of Sperm Bay, our track crossed over land on the west shore. CHS has notified NDI, and this error may be corrected on future paper and electronic charts.

Sperm Bay offers good shelter in prevailing westerly winds and fair in southerlies; Staki Bay, east of Staki Point offers very good shelter in southeast gales.

Neil Carey writes: "Approaching Flamingo Inlet from either Nagas Point or Cape Freeman and sighting the scattered breakers slamming onto widely dispersed above and below surface rocks and shoals may discourage the skipper from investigating the wild beauty of this area. With caution, it is feasible to enjoy a quiet anchorage in Flamingo Inlet,

Group explores the mystery ship

perhaps basing your explorations in Sperm or Staki bays and enjoying the beachcombing or photographing at the low head of the inlet or enjoying Short Inlet, Anvil Cove, and the wild, low, rocky shores of Cape Freeman. Photo opportunities are always great and, due to Cape Freeman's location, challenging access and isolation, the beachcombing possibilities are vast. We have found many Japanese glass fishing floats, bones and teeth of a sperm whale, and liferings. The deer, bear, seals, eagles, and numerous waterfowl resident here have rarely seen a human."

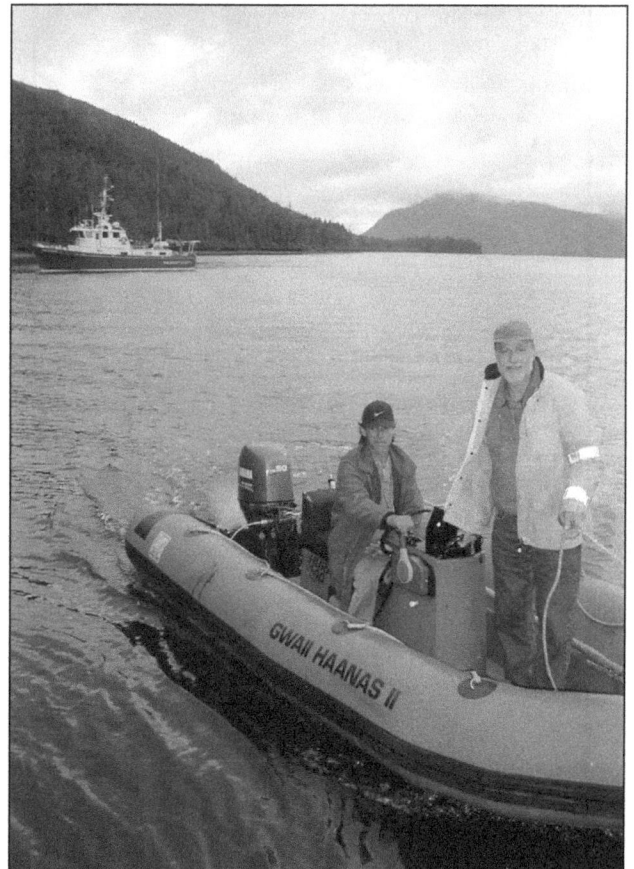

Gwaii Haanas II *prepares for* Baidarka *to raft alongside*

Kevin Monahan and Ken Brillon come alongside Baidarka

Sperm Bay (Flamingo Inlet)
2 mi N of Nagas Point
Entrance: 52°12.85'N, 131°21.05'W
Anchor: 52°13.35'N, 131°20.88'W

Sperm Bay offers good shelter in westerlies and fair shelter in southerlies. Small boats will anchor in shallow water just north of the northern island connected to Moresby Island by a tidal sand bar with limited swinging room; larger boats can anchor a little north of this sand bar, in the center of the bay where there is more swinging room. Sperm Bay is uncharted and should be entered carefully, favoring the north shore to avoid the small rocks and associated shoal and kelp patches off the south entrance point island of the south shore. Loop around the northern island following a near mid-channel course over an irregular bottom which bounces from 4 to 12 fathoms. The shore is rimmed with small trees and many over-

Entrance to Sperm Bay

hanging branches and a few small beaches. Because of the limited swinging room and mixed bottom, we would recommend moving to Staki Bay east of Staki Point if SE gales are forecasted.

Neil Carey reports being stormbound in Sperm Bay in his boat *Skylark* and having anchored on the north side of the island in the center of the bay where he found the shelter reasonable. "We anchored here often. Once during a northwest fall storm that lasted nearly three days, we dragged only a short distance."

Anchor (small boats) in 2-4 fathoms, larger boats in 6 fathoms over a sand, mud and gravel bottom with some kelp; fair-to-good holding.

Staki Bay (Flamingo Inlet)
3.5 mi N of Nagas Point
Entrance: 52°14.25'N, 131°21.75'W
Anchor Head: 52°15.95'N, 131°22.20'W
SE Corner: 52°14.35'N, 131°21.31'W

Staki Bay has a large area of moderate depths for anchoring off the large drying mud flat near its head in prevailing winds and stable weather. The bay is poorly charted so use caution when underway and thoroughly check your expected swinging circle. The bight in the southeast corner of Staki Bay, 0.25 mile northeast of Staki Point, is well protected in southeast gales. When entering Staki Bay, avoid the large shoal and kelp bed with isolated rocks that extend nearly 0.3 mile northwest of Staki Point, as well as some other isolated small shoals and kelp patches.

The waters of the southeast bight appear to have little interchange and there are no signs of stress along shore. The flat at the head of the bight dries 1 to 2 feet and good anchorage can be found a short distance north. In this way you will have almost unlimited swinging room to the northwest in case you need it in a SE blow.

Anchor in 6 fathoms over a soft brown mud with twigs and broken shells; fair-to-good holding.

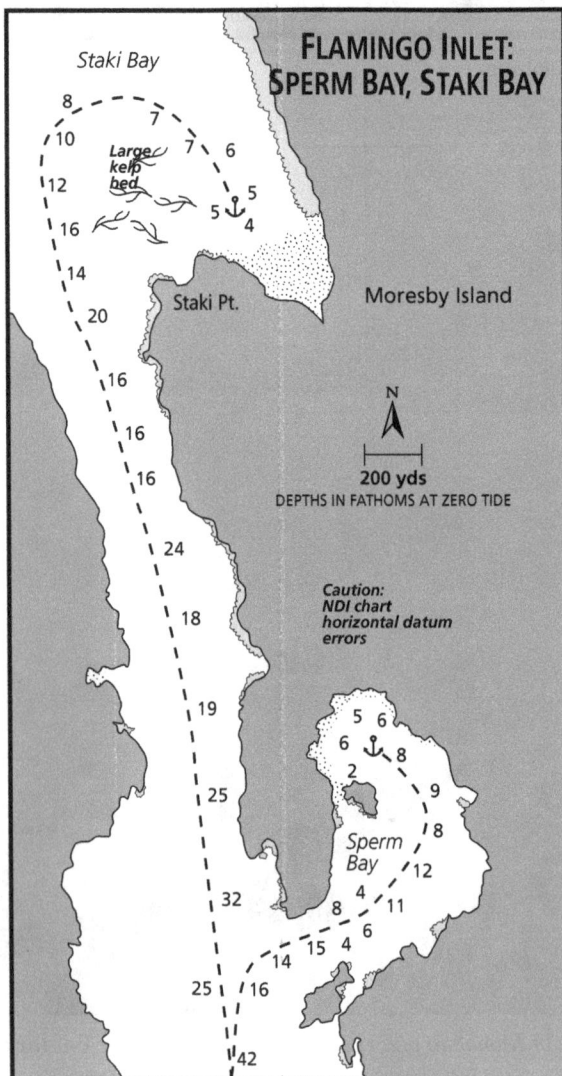

Map

FLAMINGO INLET: SPERM BAY, STAKI BAY

Staki Bay

Large kelp bed

Staki Pt.

Moresby Island

N

200 yds
DEPTHS IN FATHOMS AT ZERO TIDE

Caution:
NDI chart
horizontal datum
errors

Sperm Bay

Depths shown: 8, 7, 10, 7, 6, 12, 5, 5, 4, 16, 14, 20, 16, 16, 16, 24, 18, 19, 25, 32, 5, 6, 6, 8, 2, 9, 8, 12, 8, 4, 11, 15, 4, 6, 14, 25, 16, 42

©2024 Don and Réanne Douglass • Diagram not for navigation

Storm-washed vertical shoreline along Creation Coast

Entrance to Puffin Cove Lagoon

Finis

If you are making a circumnavigation of Moresby Island, Congratulations!—most of the hard work is behind you. You have also visited what we call the "Creation Coast" one of the world's premier cruising frontiers. We hope you enjoyed it as much as we did.

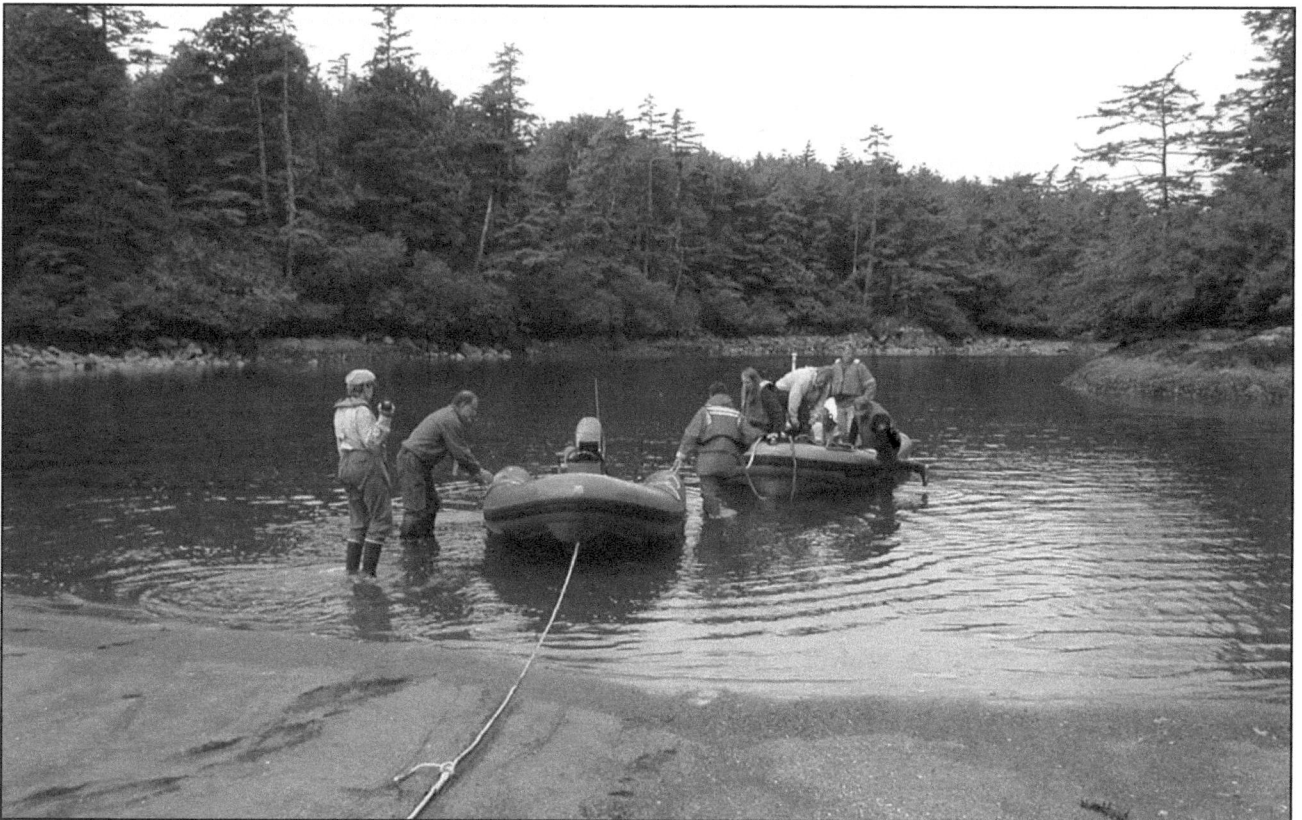

Landing party goes ashore

Foreword to the First Edition

by Kevin Monahan

Throughout my time at sea, it has been the tiny harbours that appealed to me the most. No matter how stimulated by the drama of the coast, one must eventually find refuge. Diminutive but secure, such places are scattered throughout this coastline in vast numbers, providing privacy and contentment for the spirit. Indeed, after beating my way through gale-force winds or worse, weaving my boat into a quiet anchorage brings on a kind of euphoria, a joy that cannot be understood without the experience.

Though the North Coast of British Columbia provides numerous protected passages and anchorages, let there be no doubt that these waters can be as hazardous as any. While it may seem that a benevolent creator has scattered numerous islands to protect the inner coast from the Aleutian low and its devastating weather systems, this comforting shield of forested rock also focuses the power of wind and sea into narrow confines. To anyone who has experienced the frigid outflow of gales in Douglas Channel or the treacherous tide rips of Nahwitti Bar, these conditions will come as no surprise. As is true of any waters, those of the British Columbia coast are at times placid and nurturing (a truly *Pacific* ocean), or deadly and menacing. Yet, for those of us who go down to the sea in boats, it is precisely these qualities that attract us. I have made my living in West Coast waters for more than twenty years; first as a fisherman and later as a professional mariner. At times I have been terrified. At other times I have been astonished by the sublime beauty and power of this place. And sometimes I have felt all those emotions at once. But never have I grown tired of the spectacle.

In the remoter parts of the North Coast, some areas have not been charted at all, while other areas are charted only at small scale, so that many sheltered bays and coves barely show, and it is only local knowledge that can bring us safely out of the weather. True, one can plan one's cruising so that well-charted harbours break up the journey, but then one misses the truly unique and refreshing places, many of which are used only by fishermen in season and a few locals who live in these remote areas. Some are sacred to native communities. All are populated by waterfowl and marine and terrestrial mammals. Yet others are punctuated by waterfalls and tidal rapids, or by salmon runs and white Kermodei bears.

In my first meeting with Don Douglass I recognized a fellow mariner. In Réanne Hemingway-Douglass I subsequently discovered another. While I was surveying a herring spawn in Smith Inlet, I steered my inflatable boat into a small bay. A trim little powerboat turned in from the opposite point. I approached the boat and came face-to-face with *Baidarka* and her crew who were gathering information for their books. One small boat, exquisitely neat and seemingly so roomy, could barely contain the force of Don's enthusiasm. Indeed, he fills his own personal space to overflowing and his presence is generous enough to enfold all those with whom he comes in contact. Since that time, I have seen *Baidarka* at work in many out-of-the-way places.

In this new edition of *Exploring the North Coast of British Columbia—Blunden Harbour to Dixon Entrance, Including the Queen Charlotte Islands*—as in their previous publications—Don and Réanne present an atlas of local knowledge for the amateur and professional alike. Together, with uncommon skill and integrity, they have systematically observed and recorded the exacting details of local knowledge for this very complex area.

This guidebook captures the North Coast like never before. Designed to be a constant wheelhouse companion, it easily fills our expectations. The local knowledge found inside helps us understand the North Coast waters, and more importantly, helps us safely to our destination. And may you all have safe and eventful voyages!

Kevin Monahan, a retired Canadian Coast Guard officer, lives in Qualicum Beach, B.C.

Foreword to the Second Edition

by George Eaton

Remote, silent and sparsely populated, a maze of islands and rock-strewn channels frequently clothed in low-lying clouds, British Columbia's northern coast offers both challenges and rewards for the capable and self-sufficient mariner. Travels in these locations can be enjoyed safely if the mariner's skills and the environment of strong currents, wind, and weather are critically assessed and fully respected.

Official CHS charts and related publications provide a strong framework of knowledge essential for navigation, but other sources of information are invaluable. *Exploring the North Coast of British Columbia* by Don Douglass and Réanne Hemingway-Douglass is one such trusted source.

Nothing can replace what is commonly referred to as local knowledge, and *Exploring the North Coast* provides excellent local knowledge from a seasoned research and writing team. The Douglasses, in their vessel *Baidarka,* have personally researched several thousand anchor sites over the entire coast. Documenting anchor sites and passages as never before with invaluable local knowledge, their guidebooks have become a standard for countless commercial and recreational skippers.

The Douglasses present vital local knowledge in a logical and effective manner using GPS waypoints, detailed anchoring diagrams, photos and personal observations. Their unique pilothouse style allows navigators to quickly assimilate the knowledge they need for determining approaches to unfamiliar territory, for making passages, and for finding refuge or anchor sites.

This newly expanded edition of *Exploring the North Coast of British Columbia* deals not only with the northern mainland coast and its archipelagos, but now reaches across Hecate Strait to provide information previously unavailable about the Queen Charlotte Islands and their remote west coast. The Douglasses, along with Kevin Monahan, have researched many unsurveyed coves and harbours on Moresby Island and, in sharing their new local knowledge with CHS, have helped increase safety for all sailors via the *Notice to Mariners.*

Exploring the North Coast of British Columbia published by FineEdge.com should be kept close at hand for all those attracted to these northern waters.

George Eaton
Director, Hydrography
Pacific Region

Fisheries and Oceans   Pêches et Océans
Canada   Canada

CANADIAN HYDROGRAPHIC SERVICE
Pacific Region
Institute of Ocean Sciences
9860 West Saanich Rd., PO Box 6000
Sidney, B.C. V8L 4B2
Canada

Nautical Charts Protect Lives, Property and the Marine Environment
Les cartes marines protègent la vie, la propriété et l'environnement marin

Foreword to the Third Edition

by Marianne Scott

Early in the summer of 2014, we provisioned our Hanse 411, s/v *Beyond the Stars,* and set off for Alaska's Panhandle. It was our first time travelling along the Inside Passage further northwest than Bella Bella, and besides detailed electronic and paper charts, we needed precise information on the various routes to take, anchorages to hook down in, and new sites to experience. The second edition of *Exploring the North Coast of British Columbia from Blunden Harbour to Dixon Entrance* was the perfect resource.

Plenty of cruising guides can direct boaters through such popular destinations as the Gulf Islands, the San Juans, Desolation Sound and even the Broughtons. But cruise further north than Port Hardy, and information is slim. That is why *Exploring the North Coast* became invaluable to us and will become even more so in this revamped, updated edition.

Don Douglass and Réanne Hemingway Douglass have first-hand experience describing the vast waterways and thousands of islands that mark the central and north coast of British Columbia. Like Captain Vancouver in the 1790s, they explored the bays, inlets and channels on their own boat, or aboard other vessels with crew interested in helping explore every nook and cranny of these wild shores. The team provides direct experience of the places they visited, many of them more than once. For a range of locations, they have been the first to describe bays and anchorages as not all of British Columbia has been charted at large scale, especially in parts of Haida Gwaii.

So how did we use the second edition? To begin with, we marked the places in the book we could reach during a daily passage. We would plot the distance integrating weather conditions and tides. A double check on our route and we'd locate hidey-holes or secondary anchorages in case we were delayed. We'd read the descriptions of these isolated places and plan accordingly. As just one example, when reaching Baker Inlet off Grenville Channel, we waited some time in the Channel before entering Watts Narrows that lead into the Inlet. *Exploring the North Coast* had warned us the Narrows could "boil a bit" at high tide or ebb. We could describe many other experiences where the book guided us to safety—or to the enjoyment of a particularly enchanting location.

Exploring the North Coast is complete and consistent. The descriptions are practical, informative and personal. The "personal" aspect is part of what makes the guide appealing. We travel with Don and Réanne and, along the way, make our own personal discoveries.

Some people call the Douglass-Hemingway cruising guides the "bible." We agree with that assessment, especially for the volume that describes the area north of Vancouver Island. If you plan to set your course into Queen Charlotte Sound and beyond, don't leave home without it.

Marianne Scott
Nautical author
Victoria, British Columbia

Acknowledgments

Over the years of cruising the waters of the beautiful North Coast, we have met many wonderful people whose help, encouragement, and contributions played an important part in the making of this guidebook.

We would like to thank, in particular, those who reviewed parts of the manuscript and provided invaluable comments, and to those who provided reports or sidebars: Neil and Betty Carey, pathfinders of the Queen Charlottes for their many contributions to our data; our fellow explorer Kevin Monahan, who has more year-round experience on this coast than anyone we know; Roderick Frazier Nash, for his Guest Essay and help in documenting Spiller Channel; Honeydew Murray for co-authoring Bears and Boats; David Hoar and Noreen Rudd, *Pacific Voyager*, for use of their recipes and photos, Lou Beke, *Sea Cabana*, for photos and sidebar; Elke and Rick Cunningham, *Mithrandir*; Lach McGuigan, *Landfall*; Linda and Jack Schreiber, *Sanctuary*; Sally Isaksen, Jo-Anne Kumpula and Don Suttis of Ocean Falls; Don and Merilyn Baldwin, former owners of SeaSport Marine, Prince Rupert; Andy Macdonald, Hakai Recreation Ranger; Ian Douglas, Quadra Island, for his article on *Hakai Ranger*; Bob Waldon for his sidebar on birds; David Scharf, Portland, and John P. McCormack, San Francisco for kayakers' viewpoints; Don Pearson, Moon Bay Marina, for his local knowledge of Douglas Canal; Ron Thiele for information on the Kermodei bear and his excellent photographs; Norm Wagner, Kitimat, for his sidebar on Jesse Falls; Robin Hill-Ward for contributions and photographs; Glen Craig, Kemano, for information on anchor sites in Gardner Canal; John De Boeke, skipper of *Clavella*, for sharing his notes on Moresby Island; Don Radford, Division of Forestry, Prince Rupert, and Tom Tabacco, Victoria, for information on the Griffin Passage Mayday; and to Kathleen Kaska and Lisa Wright for contributing several new sidebars to this third edition. Thanks to Iain McAllister of Pacific Wild for the pictures of the sea wolf and spirit bear, and to Mike Pignéguy and Elsie Hulsizer for their photos. We want to express our appreciation to Canadian Hydrographic Service Pacific Region: George Eaton, David Prince, David Fisher, and Brian Watt and Dick MacDougall, Ottawa, for their support and timely responses; and to Maggie Stronge, Gwaii Haanas National Park Reserve/Haida Heritage Site for her help and information.

We are grateful to the many boaters and residents along the waterways who volunteered information or checked our observations: Warren and Laurie Miller, *Sacalaurie*; Dr. Thomas Harding, *La Sonrisa II*, Bill Swain, *High Flight III*; Terry Jack, *Seasons in the Sun*; John and Randi Sanger, *Misty*; the skipper and crew of the *Narwhal*; Jim Robinson, Hartley Bay; Danielle and the late Dan Pollock, Langley Passage; Wendy and Mike Clark, Stewart; Tonnae Hennigan, Vancouver. And to the many boaters along the way who took time to write us or radio us, we thank you, too!

A special acknowledgement to our lightstation friends on Egg Island, Ivory Island, and to the crew of the MAREP stations at Cape Scott and Bonilla Islands. They all do a fantastic job for the benefit of every boater. Thanks as well as to the staff of the Prince Rupert Coast Guard and to the crew at the former Comox station. Their high standards and superior abilities match any we have encountered in 165,000 miles of world cruising.

To our *Baidarka* crew members who offered valuable insights of their own and endured long work days as we carried out our research: John Leone, the late Francis Caldwell, Herb and Wendy Nickles, and Tom and Gloria Burke. In addition, our gratitude goes out to the late Frank and Margy Fletcher, whose enthusiasm for the North Coast encouraged our initial explorations. And last, but never least, we owe our deepest thanks to our shore crew, without whose long "watches" we would never have been able to bring this project to a conclusion: Elayne Wallis, Rae Kozloff, Arlene Cook, Melanie Haage, and Lisa Wright.

Appendices and References

APPENDIX A
Marine Weather Information

Environment Canada Guide to Marine Weather Forecasts
http://www.ec.gc.ca/meteo-weather/default.asp?lang=En&n=2EC4EC51-1

Environment Canada Marine Weather for the Pacific - North Coast
http://www.weather.gc.ca/marine/region_e.html?mapID=01

Weather Radio Channels

CHANNEL	FREQUENCY (MHz)	LOCATIONS	SOURCE
WX 1	162.55	Klemtu, Van Inlet (Graham Island)	Prince Rupert CG radio
WX 2	162.40	Barry Inlet (Moresby Island), Calvert Island, Dundas Island, Mt. Gil	Prince Rupert CG radio
WX 3	162.475	Cumshewa, Naden Harbour (Graham Island), Estevan Point	Prince Rupert CG radio
WX 4	162.425	Masset	Weatheradio Canada
WX 5	162.450		
WX 6	162.500	Queen Charlotte Sound	Weatheradio Canada
WX 7	162.525	Prince Rupert	Weatheradio Canada
CH 21B	161.65	Mt. Dent, Mt. Hays	Prince Rupert CG radio

APPENDIX B
Emergency Contacts and Radio Information

Canadian Coast Guard	VHF Channel 16
Canadian Coast Guard (cellular — emergencies only)	star(*)16
Canadian Coast Guard District Office - Prince Rupert	250-624-0036
Rescue Co-ordination Center (emergencies only)	800-567-5111
Rescue Co-ordination Center (inquiries)	250-413-8933
Coast Guard Emergency/Pollution Response Hotline	800-663-3456

VHF Channels

5A   Vessel Traffic Service Seattle: Strait of Juan de Fuca west of Victoria

6   Intership Safety Communications - Working Channel in remote areas of Northern BC and Haida Gwaii

9   Intership and Vessel Traffic Systeml

11   Vessel Traffic Service Victoria: Strait of Juan de Fuca east of Victoria; Haro Strait; Boundary Passage; Gulf Islands; Southern Strait of Georgia

11   Vessel Traffic Service Prince Rupert: North of Cape Caution

12   Vessel Traffic Service Vancouver: Vancouver Harbour and Howe Sound

16   International Hailing Channel: Hailing, distress, urgent traffic, and safety calls only

67   Intership and ship-shore: working channel

68   Intership and ship-shore: working channel

69   Intership and ship-shore: working channel

70   Digital Selective Calling (no voice)

71   Vessel Traffic Service Victoria: Northern Strait of Georgia to Cape Caution

71   Vessel Traffic Service Prince Rupert: Prince Rupert, Dixon Entrance and Chatham Sound

72   Intership: working channel

73   Intership and ship-shore, working channel

74   Vessel Traffic Service Prince Rupert: West of Vancouver Island

83A Coast Guard Liaison: Primary Canadian Coast Guard Safety & Communications Channel

Vessel Traffic Services and Pleasure Craft Usage

Vessels less than 20 meters in length are not required to participate in the Vessel Traffic System. However, in areas where large commercial vessels are operating, it is recommended to monitor the appropriate radio channel.

Victoria   250-363-6333
Prince Rupert   250-627-8899

Traffic Area	Area Description	VHF Channel
Prince Rupert Sector 1	Prince Rupert Harbour & approaches, including the north end of Grenville Channel, Chatham Sound, and all of Dixon Entrance to Langara Island	71
Prince Rupert Sector 2	Hecate Strait, Cape Caution north to Alaska, and the west side of Haida Gwaii	11

APPENDIX C
Distance Tables

Port Hardy to Prince Rupert

Inside Passage via Milbanke Sound.
For routes via Jackson Pass add 14 miles.

Copyright © 1996 Shipwrite Productions
Used by permission (see Sources)

Key to points (diagonal / leg distance in miles):

No.	Location	Leg
1	PRINCE RUPERT (Fairview)	—
2	Glenn Island	13
3	Watson Rock	12
4	Kumealon (Entrance)	7
5	Morning Reef	14
6	Lowe Inlet	11
7	Sainty Point	14
8	Point Cumming	7
9	Kingcome Point	15
10	Butedale	11
11	Khutze Inlet	8
12	Sarah Head	13
13	Split Head	5
14	KLEMTU	10
15	Jorkins Point	15
16	Ivory Island	11
17	Idol Point	6
18	BELLA BELLA	9
19	Pointer Island	11
20	NAMU	13
21	Kelpie Point (East Hakai)	9
22	Safety Cove	13
23	Dugout Rocks	11
24	Egg Island	7
25	Cape Caution	5
26	Storm Islands	8
27	Pine Island	4
28	Scarlett Point	9
29	Duval Point	8
30	PORT HARDY	3
31	Pulteney Point	16
32	Cape Scott	54

Distance matrix (row = from-point No., columns 1–31 = to-point No.):

No.	1	2	3	4	5	6	7	8	9	10	11	12	13	14	15	16	17	18	19	20	21	22	23	24	25	26	27	28	29	30	31
2	13																														
3	25	12																													
4	32	19	7																												
5	46	33	21	14																											
6	57	44	32	25	11																										
7	71	58	46	39	25	14																									
8	78	65	53	46	32	21	7																								
9	86	73	61	54	40	29	15	8																							
10	97	84	72	65	51	40	26	19	11																						
11	105	92	80	73	59	48	34	27	19	8																					
12	116	103	91	84	70	59	45	38	30	19	11																				
13	129	116	104	97	83	72	58	51	43	32	24	13																			
14	134	121	109	102	88	77	63	56	48	37	29	18	5																		
15	144	131	119	112	98	87	73	66	58	47	39	28	15	10																	
16	155	142	130	123	109	98	84	77	69	58	50	39	26	21	11																
17	161	148	136	129	115	104	90	83	75	64	56	45	32	27	17	6															
18	170	157	145	138	124	113	99	92	84	73	65	54	41	36	26	15	9														
19	181	168	156	149	135	124	110	103	95	84	76	65	52	47	37	26	20	11													
20	194	181	169	162	148	137	123	116	108	97	89	78	65	60	50	39	33	24	13												
21	203	190	178	171	157	146	132	125	117	106	98	87	74	69	59	48	42	33	22	9											
22	216	203	191	184	170	159	145	138	130	119	111	100	87	82	72	61	55	46	35	22	13										
23	227	214	202	195	181	170	156	149	141	130	122	111	98	93	83	72	66	57	46	33	24	11									
24	234	221	209	202	188	177	163	156	148	137	129	118	105	100	90	79	73	64	53	40	31	18	7								
25	239	226	214	207	193	182	168	161	153	142	134	123	110	105	95	84	78	69	58	45	36	23	12	5							
26	247	234	222	215	201	190	176	169	161	150	142	131	118	113	103	92	86	77	66	53	44	31	20	13	8						
27	251	238	226	219	205	194	180	173	165	154	146	135	122	117	107	96	90	81	70	57	48	35	24	17	12	4					
28	260	247	235	228	214	203	189	182	174	163	155	144	131	126	116	105	99	90	79	66	57	44	33	26	21	13	9				
29	268	255	243	236	222	211	197	190	182	171	163	152	139	134	124	113	107	98	87	74	65	52	41	34	29	21	17	8			
30	271	258	246	239	225	214	200	193	185	174	166	155	142	137	127	116	110	101	90	77	68	55	44	37	32	24	20	11	3		
31	283	270	258	251	237	226	212	205	197	186	178	167	154	149	139	128	122	113	102	89	80	67	56	49	44	36	32	23	19	16	
32	271	258	246	239	225	214	200	193	185	174	166	155	142	137	127	116	110	101	90	77	68	55	44	37	32	29	28	44	36	42	54

APPENDIX C
Distance Tables

Bella Bella to Kitimat

Routes, including Bella Bella and McInnes Island, are via Milbanke Sound

Copyright © 1996 Shipwrite Productions
Used by permission (see Sources)

#	Place	1	2	3	4	5	6	7	8	9	10	11	12	13	14	15	16	17	18	19	20	21	22	23	24	25	26	27	28	29	30	31	32
1	KITIMAT																																
2	Nanakwa Shoal	11																															
3	Loretta Anchorage	18	6																														
4	Staniforth Bank	25	14	9																													
5	Europa Bay	38	27	22	13																												
6	KEMANO	55	45	40	31	18																											
7	Kitkiata (Old Town)	30	19	16	24	37	55																										
8	HARTLEY BAY	43	32	27	24	36	54	13																									
9	Sainty Point	49	38	33	26	39	57	19	6																								
10	Peters Narrows	56	45	40	33	46	64	26	13	8																							
11	Tuwartz Narrows	60	49	46	35	48	66	30	17	13	9																						
12	Man Islet, Otter Passage	71	60	57	50	63	81	41	28	24	22	18																					
13	Gillen Harbour	85	74	69	63	76	94	53	40	36	37	30	16																				
14	Barnard Harbour	66	55	50	45	58	76	36	23	21	24	29	24	23																			
15	Duckers Islands	78	67	62	57	70	88	45	32	28	28	25	16	12	12																		
16	Evinrude Inlet	87	76	71	66	79	97	54	41	37	34	38	22	16	22	9																	
17	Ramsbotham Islands	93	82	77	72	85	103	60	47	43	40	40	28	21	27	15	6																
18	Kettle Inlet	93	82	77	72	85	103	59	46	42	36	39	21	15	27	15	15	16															
19	Weeteeam Bay	117	106	101	96	109	127	84	71	67	67	66	41	39	51	39	28	21	21														
20	Point Cumming	50	39	33	24	37	55	21	8	19	28	17	32	24	40	32	26	35	40	20													
21	Bishop Bay	44	33	27	18	31	49	37	28	39	48	37	52	44	60	52	46	52	60	40	65												
22	Kingcome Point	62	51	45	23	47	67	33	16	27	37	35	40	38	48	39	35	39	56	32	39	12											
23	Butedale	73	62	56	34	60	78	44	27	28	18	19	32	30	57	52	43	37	52	38	31	8	11										
24	Khutze inlet	77	66	60	51	61	82	48	35	35	30	18	33	30	63	57	49	37	57	44	43	19	20	8									
25	Sarah head	89	78	72	63	75	94	60	47	46	38	28	46	36	63	57	49	43	63	55	52	31	33	20	12								
26	Split Head	102	91	85	76	80	107	65	60	57	30	39	52	61	74	63	55	43	73	52	57	43	37	25	18	13							
27	KLEMTU	107	96	90	81	85	112	76	65	61	38	40	46	66	72	74	61	45	79	39	61	44	49	30	34	18	5						
28	Wingate Point	104	98	106	97	74	128	61	55	40	12	28	39	40	52	48	40	35	75	32	57	54	64	46	37	24	21	3					
29	Wilby Point	105	99	107	98	75	129	62	56	47	13	19	35	41	79	15	43	32	75	57	67	57	67	49	37	24	24	3	3				
30	Quigley Creek	104	98	106	97	74	128	61	55	46	12	18	34	40	75	21	40	30	75	57	67	57	67	49	37	24	24	3	3	6			
31	Kipp Islet, West Higgins Pass	109	103	111	102	79	133	66	60	57	17	23	32	45	81	14	30	23	85	63	73	43	55	30	35	9	6	9	6	12	
32	McInnes Island	136	125	110	123	90	141	70	77	61	30	36	45	57	86	20	38	30	74	63	55	19	26	22	49	30	14	26	19		
33	BELLA BELLA	171	131	125	116	129	147	112	102	101	100	111	84	72	47	57	63	65	57	47	65	92	96	84	73	65	40	35	49	46	52	41	27

APPENDIX C
Distance Tables

Distances in Juan de Fuca Strait, Admiralty Inlet, Puget Sound and the S.E. Part of the Strait of Georgia

From *Sailing Directions*, Vol. 1, 15th Edition, 1990; used with permission of CHS.

Column abbreviations: NB = Noah Bay, Wash.; PR = Port Renfrew, B.C.; SH = Sooke Harbour, B.C. (Entrance); RR = Race Rocks Lt. Ho. brg. 000°, 1.5 miles; PA = Port Angeles, Wash.; Vic = Victoria, B.C. (Ogden Point); PW = Point Wilson Lt. Ho. brg. 225°, 1 mile; PT = Port Townsend, Wash.; PL = Port Ludlow, Wash.; PG = Port Gamble, Wash.; Eve = Everett, Wash. (See Note 3); EH = Eagle Harbour, Wash.; Sea = Seattle, Wash.; Bre = Bremerton, Wash.; Tac = Tacoma, Wash.; Oly = Olympia, Wash.; Ana = Anacortes, Wash.; Bel = Bellingham, Wash.; Bla = Blaine, Wash.; NW = New Westminster, B.C.; Nan = Nanaimo, B.C.; Van = Vancouver, B.C. (Brockton Point).

From	NB	PR	SH	RR	PA	Vic	PW	PT	PL	PG	Eve	EH	Sea	Bre	Tac	Oly	Ana	Bel	Bla	NW	Nan	Van
Nanaimo																						34
New Westminster																					46	40
Blaine																			47	53	47	
Bellingham																		37	70	74	70	
Anacortes																	16	35]	69	74	68	
Olympia																110	124	139	172	178	173	
Tacoma															34	86	100	115	148	154	149	
Bremerton														29	50	75	89	104	137	143	138	
Seattle													14	25	50	66	80	95	128	134	129	
Eagle Harbour												8	13	25	50	66	80	95	128	134	129	
Everett											29	29	38	49	73	49	63	78	111	116	111	
Port Gamble										28	34	34	44	55	79	47	61	76	109	115	110	
Port Ludlow									10	25	32	32	41	52	76	42	56	71	104	110	105	
Port Townsend								16	21	34	40	40	49	60	84	29	43	58	91	97	92	
Point Wilson							3	16	21	34	40	40	49	60	84	26	40	55	88	94	89	
Victoria						31	34	47	52	65	71	71	80	91	115	35	49	53	79	85	80	
Port Angeles					19	29	32	45	50	63	69	69	78	89	113	42	55	65	91	100	92	
Race Rocks				12	10	33	36	49	54	67	73	73	82	93	117	41	55	60	87	92	87	
Sooke Harbour			10	21	20	43	46	59	64	77	83	83	92	103	128	51	65	70	97	102	97	
Port Renfrew		36	44	54	54	77	80	93	98	111	117	117	126	137	161	85	99	104	131	136	131	
Noah Bay	14	35	43	54	53	76	79	92	97	110	116	116	125	136	160	84	98	103	130	135	130	
Cape Flattery	10	16	43	51	61	61	84	87	100	105	118	124	124	133	144	168	92	106	111	138	143	138

Cape Flattery, Wash. (Tatoosh Id. Lt. Ho. brg. 140°, 3.5 miles)

APPENDIX C
Distance Tables

Principal Distances within the Inside Passage between Vancouver Island and the Mainland

From *Sailing Directions*, Vol. 1, 15th Edition, 1990; used with permission of CHS.

Distances (nautical miles) — Alert Bay area

	Blinkhorn Peninsula	Beaver Cove	Alert Bay	Port McNeill	Sointula
Beaver Cove	5				
Alert Bay	7½	4½			
Port McNeill	9	6	6		
Sointula	14	10	10	5	
Pulteney Point	15	12	12	7	3

Principal distances table

Column key (from left to right, 1–25):

1. Cape Caution Light (Cape Scott Lt. Ho.; brg. 078°, 2.2 miles)
2. Cape Scott Lt. Ho.; brg. 150°, 1.3 miles
3. Pine Island Lt. Ho.; brg. 030°, 1 mile
4. Bull Harbour (Entrance)
5. Port Hardy
6. Alison Harbour
7. Blunden Harbour
8. Pulteney Point
9. Blinkhorn Peninsula
10. Broken Islands (See Note 4)
11. Port Neville (Entrance)
12. Kelsey Bay
13. Stuart Island (Settlement) (See Note 3)
14. Seymour Narrows
15. Campbell River
16. Comox
17. Powell River
18. Blubber Bay
19. Pender Harbour (Entrance) (See Note 2)
20. Halfmoon Bay
21. Northwest Bay
22. Nanoose Bay (Richards Point)
23. Nanaimo
24. Vancouver Bay (Brockton Point)
25. New Westminster

From \ To	1	2	3	4	5	6	7	8	9	10	11	12	13	14	15	16	17	18	19	20	21	22	23	24	25
Cape Scott (150°)	32																								
Pine Island	12	30																							
Bull Harbour	22	20	11																						
Port Hardy	32	43	20	22																					
Alison Harbour	16	39	9	21	21																				
Blunden Harbour	27	49	20	29	14	16																			
Pulteney Point	42	55	31	34	17	30	18																		
Blinkhorn Peninsula	58	87	46	50	33	45	33	15																	
Broken Islands	76	89	65	69	51	64	52	34	19																
Port Neville	85	97	73	77	59	72	60	42	27	8															
Kelsey Bay	91	104	80	84	66	79	67	49	34	15	7														
Stuart Island	127	139	115	119	102	115	103	85	69	50	43	36													
Seymour Narrows	125	138	114	117	100	113	101	83	68	49	41	34	41												
Campbell River	133	146	122	126	108	121	109	91	76	57	50	43	33	8											
Comox	167	179	155	158	141	154	142	124	109	90	82	75	54	41	33										
Powell River	165	177	153	157	140	153	141	123	107	88	81	74	39	39	31	21									
Blubber Bay	162	175	151	154	137	150	138	120	105	86	78	72	42	37	29	18	5								
Pender Harbour	186	199	174	179	161	174	162	144	129	110	102	96	64	61	53	42	26	25							
Halfmoon Bay	196	208	184	188	171	184	172	154	138	120	112	105	74	70	62	52	35	35	11						
Northwest Bay	192	204	180	184	167	180	168	150	134	116	108	101	75	66	58	37	41	37	21	18					
Nanoose Bay	202	215	191	194	177	190	178	160	145	126	118	112	85	77	69	48	46	46	25	18	12				
Nanaimo	208	221	197	201	183	196	184	166	151	132	125	118	91	83	75	54	52	52	30	21	20	13			
Vancouver Bay (Brockton Point)																									
New Westminster	248	260	236	240	222	235	223	205	190	175	156	148	142	109	107	99	79	70	70	48	35	46	40	34	
Victoria (Ogden Point) (See Note 1)	277	289	265	269	251	264	252	234	219	200	193	186	156	151	143	122	118	117	95	85	88	81	76	73	72

APPENDIX C
Distance Tables

Inside Passage—Prince Rupert to Cape Caution
via Grenville, Princess Royal, and Seaforth Channels,
Lama Passage, Fitz Hugh Sound

From *Sailing Directions*, Vol. 2, 12th Edition, 1991;
used with permission of CHS.

Note. — The distances given in the tables on this and subsequent pages are approximate only. They are based on the most frequently used tracks which may not be suitable for all vessels.

Prince Rupert														
72	Sainty Point													
100	28	Butedale												
121	49	67	Kitimat											
158	58	65	57	Kemano										
135	63	35	102	104	Boat Bluff									
161	89	61	126	128	26	Susan Rock								
180	108	80	147	145	45	20	Bella Bella							
190	118	90	157	155	55	30	10	Pointer Island (E. end Lama Pass)						
210	138	110	167	176	63	50	30	20	Ocean Falls					
255	183	165	213	211	119	86	61	56	54	Bella Coola via Burke Chan.				
203	131	103	181	179	68	42	23	12	33	56	Namu			
222	150	122	189	191	87	61	42	32	51	66	20	Safety Cove		
232	160	132	199	201	98	71	52	42	61	86	30	10	Dugout Rocks	
245	173	145	212	214	110	84	65	55	74	99	43	23	13	Cape Caution 078° 2.2 miles

Figure at the intersection of columns opposite places in question is the approximate distance in nautical miles between the two.

APPENDIX C
Distance Tables

Inside Passage—Seattle, Washington to Cape Spencer, Alaska

From *United States Coast Pilot*, Vol. 8, 20th Edition, 1993

Place coordinates:
- Seattle, Wash. — 47-36.2'N, 122-20.3'W
- Victoria, Canada — 48-25.0'N, 123-28.5'W
- DIXON ENTRANCE, ALASKA — 54-26.0'N, 132-52.0'W
- Hyder, Alaska — 55-54.2'N, 130-00.6'W
- Cape Chacon, Alaska — 54-40.6'N, 131-59.7'W
- Metlakatla, Alaska — 55-07.8'N, 131-34.2'W
- Ketchikan, Alaska — 55-20.5'N, 131-38.7'W
- Craig, Alaska — 55-28.7'N, 133-09.2'W
- Wrangell, Alaska — 56-28.2'N, 132-23.2'W
- CAPE DECISION, ALASKA — 55-59.4'N, 134-08.1'W
- Port Alexander, Alaska — 56-14.8'N, 134-38.8'W
- Petersburg, Alaska — 56-48.9'N, 132-57.8'W
- Sitka, Alaska — 57-03.1'N, 135-20.5'W
- Pelican, Alaska — 57-57.6'N, 136-13.8'W
- Juneau, Alaska — 58-17.9'N, 134-24.7'W
- Haines, Alaska — 59-13.8'N, 135-26.1'W
- Skagway, Alaska — 59-26.8'N, 135-19.3'W
- Gustavus, Alaska — 58-23.3'N, 135-43.6'W
- CAPE SPENCER, ALASKA — 58-10.0'N, 136-38.3'W

From \ To	Victoria	Dixon Entrance	Hyder	Cape Chacon	Metlakatla	Ketchikan	Craig	Wrangell	Cape Decision	Port Alexander	Petersburg	Sitka	Pelican	Juneau	Haines	Skagway	Gustavus	Cape Spencer
Seattle	72	664	690	640	660	659	716	749	788	812	771	883	969	879	950	962	938	976
Victoria		612	638	568	608	608	664	697	737	761	719	832	937	827	898	910	886	924
Dixon Entrance			169	34	66	79	77	157	126	150	180	221	332	288	359	371	290	319
Hyder				136	148	144	212	234	273	297	256	368	464	364	435	447	423	451
Cape Chacon					32	45	76	123	125	149	146	220	331	254	325	337	289	318
Metlakatla						16	109	104	143	167	126	238	334	235	305	317	293	321
Ketchikan							121	89	129	153	112	224	320	220	291	303	278	307
Craig								111	49	73	113	144	255	206	253	264	213	242
Wrangell									75	99	40	170	248	148	219	231	208	235
Cape Decision										24	76	95	206	157	204	215	164	193
Port Alexander											100	82	166	140	186	198	147	173
Petersburg												159	207	108	179	191	166	195
Sitka													79	162	176	187	136	85
Pelican														123	136	148	45	18
Juneau															88	100	82	110
Haines																14	96	124
Skagway																	106	136
Gustavus																		32

Distances to Sitka are partly outside.

APPENDIX D
Procedures Used in Documenting Local Knowledge

1. Coves, bays or bights that seem to offer full or limited protection from different weather situations are identified and visited by the authors.
2. Routes are sketched and photographed.
3. Perusal of a possible anchor site was made with a dual-frequency recording echo sounder; major underwater obstacles identified; depth and flatness of the bottom over the expected swinging area checked; depths then recorded on the sketches.
4. A sample test of the bottom was made by using a small "lunch hook" attached to light line and six feet of chain for maximum responsiveness and feel of the bottom.
5. The response of the anchor to the bottom noted (i.e. soft or hard mud, sand, gravel, rocky, etc.; digging power, bounce, fouling with kelp, pull-out, etc.).
6. Additional line let out to fully set the anchor.
7. A pull-down, with the engine in reverse, was made against the anchor to test holding power of the bottom.
8. Upon retrieving the anchor, authors inspect the residue on its flukes to verify bottom material, as well as the type of grass, kelp, etc.
9. Discussions were held with local residents and fishermen about anchorages, names, etc., and their comments are noted on the sketches. In some cases rough drafts of the manuscript were sent to experts for review.
10. The information gathered from tests, or that submitted by local experts, is consolidated and edited and becomes the local knowledge presented in diagrams and text.

APPENDIX E
Sources for Fishing Regulations

British Columbia is home to some of the most productive fishing waters in the world, and opportunities for quality fishing are endless. For current fishing regulations, download the British Columbia Sport Fishing Guide from

http://www.pac.dfo-mpo.gc.ca/fm-gp/rec/index-eng.html

Read it online at
http://www.pac.dfo-mpo.gc.ca/fm-gp/rec/know-savoir-eng.html

In-season regulatory updates are not in the .pdf version of the Fishing Guide, but they can be found on the website or heard on continuous weather broadcasts. You may also phone the Fishing Information Line at 604-666-0384 for updates, or subscribe to the Fishery notification service to receive automatic regulatory updates via email.

APPENDIX F
Canadian Holidays

New Year's Day (January 1)
Family Day (third Monday in February)
Good Friday (Friday before Easter Sunday)
Easter Monday (Government employees & some banks only)
Victoria Day (the Monday before May 25)
Canada Day (July 1st, or July 2nd if July 1st is a Sunday
B.C. Day (first Monday in August)

Labour Day (first Monday in September)
Thanksgiving Day (second Monday in October)
Remembrance Day (November 11)
Christmas Day (December 25)
Boxing Day (December 26)

APPENDIX G
Sources of Nautical Supplies & Other Information
Fine Edge Nautical and Recreational Publishing

Publications of Fine Edge Nautical and Recreational Publishing (www.FineEdge.com) include the products of several subsidiaries, including the Waggoner Guide, the Dreamspeaker Guides, Ports and Passes, among others. These publications can be found at most ship's chandlers and nautical bookstores.

BOOKSTORES, CHART SALES, PUBLISHERS

Waggoner Media Group
910 B 25th Street
Anacortes, WA 98221
Tel: 360-299-8500
http://www.waggonerguidebooks.com
E-mail: orders@fineedge.com

Harbour Marine Chandler
52 Esplanade
Nanaimo, BC Y9R 4Y7
Tel: 250-753-2425
https://www.harbourchandler.ca

Seasport Marine
295 First Ave. East
Prince Rupert, BC V8J1A7
Tel: 250-624-5337
http://seasport.ca
E-mail: sales@seasport.ca

Tanners Books and Gifts
2436 Beacon Street
Sidney, BC V8L 4X3
Tel: 250-656-2345
http://www.tannersbooks.com
E-mail: service@tannersbooks.com

TOURIST OFFICES

Tourism British Columbia's excellent website has a pull-down list of 130 visitor's centres around BC. Use this site as an entry page to find activities, facility information, and contacts for many of the places listed in this guidebook.

Tourism British Columbia
P.O. Box 9830
Station Provincial Govt. 1803 Douglas Street, 3rd Floor
Victoria, BC V8W 9W5
www.hellobc.com

Prince Rupert Tourism
https://visitprincerupert.com
250-624-5637

BRITISH COLUMBIA MARINE PROVINCIAL PARKS

Although many of B.C.'s coastal parks are on the South and West Coasts, there are more than twenty marine parks, conservancies, and reserves on the Central and Northern Coasts. The BC Provincial Marine Parks website is the entry to the pages for these amazing destinations. Many of the recreational sites offer facilities for cruising boats free of charge, and some have mooring buoys.

For more information, visit the website: http://www.env.gov.bc.ca/bcparks/recreation/marine_parks/

Gwaii Haanas National Park Reserve and Haida Heritage Site

Gwaii Haanas National Park Reserve and Haida Heritage Site has a complicated regulatory history. By the 1980s, the Haida Nation were seeking to protect the southern third of the Haida Gwaii archipelago from logging. In 1985, the area was designated as the Haida Heritage Site, but logging continued in spite of legal and political battles. Continued negotiation and administrative measures eventually led to creation of The National Park Reserve and Heritage Site that now protects land and sea areas of 138 islands at the southern end of the archipelago. The Gwaii Haanas Park Reserve also includes the Ninstints UNESCO World Heritage Site on Anthony Island at the southern end of the archipelago.

#2 2 Beach Rd
Skidegate, BC V0T 1S1
Tel: 250-559-8818
E-mail: gwaii.haanas@pc.gc.ca
http://www.pc.gc.ca/eng/pn-np/bc/gwaiihaanas/natcul.aspx

ENVIRONMENTAL ORGANIZATIONS

Ecotrust Canada
Vancouver Headquarters
225 West 8th Avenue Ste 300
Vancouver, BC V5y 1N3
Tel: 604-682-4141

Ecotrust Canada
Prince Rupert Office
425-309 2nd Avenue West
Prince Rupert, BC V8J 3T1
Tel: 250.624.4191
www.ecotrust.ca

Pacific Wild
1529 Amelia Street
Victoria, BC V8W 2K1
Tel: 250-380-0547
Email: info@pacificwild.org
http://pacificwild.org

Raincoast Conservation Foundation
P.O. Box 2429
Sidney, BC V8L 3Y3
Tel: 250-655-1229
E-mail: greatbear@raincoast.org
http://www.raincoast.org

The Nature Conservancy Canada
366 Adelaide Street East, Suite 331
Toronto, ON M5A 3X9
Tel: 250-479-3191 Victoria
604-331-0722 Vancouver
E-mail: bcoffice@natureconservancy.ca
http://natureconservancy.ca

TOUR AND CHARTER SERVICES

Bluewater Adventures
#3-252 East First Street
North Vancouver, BC V7L 1B3
Tel: 888-877-1770
E-mail: explore@bluewateradventures.ca
http://bluewateradventures.ca

APPENDIX G (continued)

The Natural Coast Sailing Adventures
PO Box: 398
Brentwood Bay, BC V8M 1R3
Tel: 250-896 8227
E-mail: explore@thenaturalcoast.com
http://www.thenaturalcoast.com

Khutzeymateen Wilderness Lodge
PO Box 1096
Prince Rupert, BC V8J 4H6
Tel: 250-641-0957
E-mail: info@khutzlodge.com
http://grizzlytour.com

Moresby Explorers
365 Beach Rd.
Sandspit, B.C. VOT 1T0
Tel: 250-637-2215
E-mail: info@moresbyexplorers.com
http://www.moresbyexplorers.com

Ocean Light II Adventures
PO Box 64594
Coquitlam, B.C. V3S 7V7
Tel: 604-328-5339

Inland Air Charters
Box 592
Prince Rupert BC V8J 3R5
Tel: 250-624-2577
E-mail: info@inlandair.bc.ca
http://inlandaircharters.ca

Kingfisher Wilderness Adventures
PO Box 1318
Port McNeill, BC, Canada, V0N 2R0
Tel: 250-956-4617
E-mail: info@kingfisher.ca
https://kingfisher.ca/about-us/

APPENDIX H
Websites of Interest

Georgia Strait Alliance
http://georgiastrait.org/work/cleanmarinebc/

RCMP Canadian Firearms Information
http://www.rcmp-grc.gc.ca

Canadian Coast Guard
https://www.ccg-gcc.gc.ca/index-eng.html

Canada Border Services Agency
http://www.cbsa-asfc.gc.ca/menu-eng.html

Parks Canada
http://www.pc.gc.ca/eng/index.aspx

Fisheries and Oceans Canada
http://www.dfo-mpo.gc.ca/index-eng.html

BC Parks
http://www.bcparks.ca

Canadian Hydrographic Services
https://www.charts.gc.ca/index-eng.html

U.S. Department of Homeland Security
https://www.dhs.gov/how-do-i/cross-us-borders

APPENDIX I
Summer Wind Reports

The following wind reports show percentages of wind speeds for May through September
for typical Inside Passage areas:

Herbert Island *(North of Goletas Channel near Pine Island where Queen Charlotte Strait meets Queen Charlotte Sound)*

May, winds less than 20 knots 88%; 20 to 33 knots 8%;
   winds greater than 34 knots 3%
June, winds less than 20 knots 94%; 20 to 33 knots 6%
July, winds less than 20 knots 97%; 20 to 33 knots 3%
August, winds less than 20 knots 97%; 20 to 33 knots 3%
September, winds less than 20 knots 94%; 20 to 33 knots 5%;
   winds greater than 34 knots 1%

Egg Island *(Queen Charlotte Sound, east)*

May, winds less than 20 knots 92%; 20 to 30 knots 8%;
   winds greater than 34 knots 1%
June, winds less than 20 knots 94%; 20 to 30 knots 5%;
   winds greater than 34 knots 1%
July, winds less than 20 knots 96%; 20 to 30 knots 3%;
   winds greater than 34 knots nil
August, winds less than 20 knots 95%; 20 to 30 knots 4%; winds
   greater than 34 knots nil
September, winds less than 20 knots 92%; 20 to 30 knots 7%;
   winds greater than 34 knots 1%

Bonilla Island *(B.C. coast, central, west of Banks Island)*

May, winds less than 20 knots 75%; 20 to 30 knots 23%;
   winds greater than 34 knots 2%
June, winds less than 20 knots 82%; 20 to 30 knots 17%;
   winds greater than 34 knots 1%
July, winds less than 20 knots 88%; 20 to 30 knots 11%;
   winds greater than 34 knots nil
August, winds less than 20 knots 86%; 20 to 30 knots 13%;
   winds greater than 34 knots 1%
September, winds less than 20 knots 77%; 20 to 30 knots 22%;
   winds greater than 34 knots 1%

Triple Island *(Dixon Entrance, east of Dundas Island)*

May, winds less than 20 knots 84%; 20 to 30 knots 15%;
   winds greater than 34 knots 1%
June, winds less than 20 knots 87%; 20 to 30 knots 13%;
   winds greater than 34 knots nil
July, winds less than 20 knots 92%; 20 to 30 knots 8%;
   winds greater than 34 knots nil
August, winds less than 20 knots 91%; 20 to 30% 9%;
   winds greater than 34 knots nil
September, winds less than 20 knots 85%; 20 to 30 knots 14%;
   winds greater than 34 knots 1%

Cape St. James *(off South Moresby Island)*

May, winds less than 20 knots 71%; 20 to 33 knots 26%;
   winds greater than 36 knots 3%
June, winds less than 20 knots 74%; 20 to 33 knots 24%;
   winds greater than 36 knots 2%
July, winds less than 20 knots 75%; 20 to 33 knots 24%;
   winds greater than 36 knots 1%
August, winds less than 20 knots 79%; 1 20 to 33 knots 20%;
   winds greater than 36 knots 1%
September, winds less than 20 knots 74%; 20 to 33 knots 23%;
   winds greater than 36 knots 3%

APPENDIX J
Float Plan

1. EMERGENCY PHONE NUMBERS

Coast Guard: Prince Rupert	**250-624-0036**
Coast Guard: Campbell River	**800-465-7735**
Coast Guard: Alaska	**907-463-2000**

2. DESCRIPTION OF THE BOAT

Boat Name:

Skipper: Age:

Hailing Port:

Type & Make:

Length: Beam: Draft:

Color Hull: Cabin: Deck:

Trim: Dodger:

Distinguishing Features:

Documentation or Registration Number:

Sail Number:

Engine(s) Type:

Horsepower: Cruising Speed:

Fuel Capacity:

Fuel Aboard (quantity):   Estimated Cruising Range:

Electronics/Safety Equipment Aboard:

VHF Radio:	Call Sign:	Loran:
GPS:	Depth Sounder:	Radar:
EPRRIB:	Other:	
Raft:	Dinghy:	

3. TRIP DETAILS

Name of Person Filing Report:

Phone:

Additional Persons Aboard, Total:

Name: Age:
Phone:

Name: Age:
Phone:

Name: Age:
Phone:

Name: Age:
Phone:

Departure:

Date: Time:

Return No Later Than:

Depart From:

Marina: Phone:

Destination (or most northerly) Port:

ETA: No Later Than: Phone:

Anticipated Stopover Ports:

     ETA: No Later Than:
Phone:

     ETA: No Later Than:
Phone:

     ETA: No Later Than:
Phone:

Plan Filed With:

Name: Phone:

Special Instructions:

YOU MAY COPY THIS FINE EDGE FLOAT PLAN AS NEEDED AND LEAVE WITH A RESPONSIBLE PARTY

Bibliography & References

Anderson, Hugo. *North to Alaska*. Anacortes, Washington: Anderson Publishing Company, 1993.

Secrets of Cruising The New Frontier, British Columbia Coast and Undiscovered Inlets. Anacortes, Washington: Anderson Publishing Company, 1995.

Blackman, Margaret and Davidson, Florence. *During My Time: Florence Edenshaw Davidson, a Haida Woman*. Seattle, WA: University of Washington Press, 1992.

Waggoner Cruising Guide. Anacortes, WA: Fine Edge Publishing, published annually.

Canadian Tide and Current Tables, Pacific Coast, Vols. 5 and 6 [issued annually]. Ottawa: Department of Fisheries and Oceans.

Carey, Neil G. *A Guide to the Queen Charlotte Islands*. Vancouver: Raincoast Books, 12th Ed., 1998.

Carey, Neil G. *Puffin Cove, Escape to the Wilderness of the Queen Charlotte Islands*. Surrey, B.C.: Columbia: Hancock House Publishers Ltd., 1989.

Chappell, John. *Cruising Beyond Desolation Sound*. Surrey, B.C.: Naikoon Marine, 1979, revised edition 1987.

To the Charlottes. George Dawson's 1878 Survey of the Queen Charlotte Islands. Edited by Douglas Cole and Bradley Lockner. Vancouver, UBC Press, 1993.

Chittenden, Newton H. *Exploration of the Queen Charlotte Islands*. Burnaby, B.C.: Fireweed Enterprises Inc., 1984, first published in Victoria, B.C, 1884.

Christensen, Bev. *Too Good to Be True*, Alcan's Kemano Completion Project. Vancouver: Talonbooks, 1995.

Dalzell, Kathleen E. *The Queen Charlotte Islands 1774–1966 (Volume 1)*. Queen Charlotte City, B.C.: Bill Ellis, Publisher, 1988.

Dalzell, Kathleen E. *The Queen Charlotte Islands, Places and Names (Volume 2)*. Madeira Park, B.C.: Harbour Publishing, 1973; (3rd printing 1993)

Dawson, Will. *Coastal Cruising*. Vancouver: Mitchell Press, 1959.

Douglass, Don, and Hemingway-Douglass, Réanne, *Exploring Vancouver Island's West Coast, A Cruising Guide, 2nd Edition*. Anacortes, Washington: Fine Edge Productions, LLC, 1999.

Douglass, Don & Reanne. *Exploring Southeast Alaska — Dixon Entrance to Skagway 4th Edition*. Anacortes, Washington: Fine Edge Productions, LLC, 2022.

Douglass, Don & Reanne. *Exploring the South Coast of British Columbia, Gulf Islands and Desolation Sound to Port Hardy & Blunden Harbour, 4th Edition*, Anacortes, Washington: Fine Edge Productions, LLC, 2022.

Encyclopedia of British Columbia. Edited by Daniel Francis, Maderia Park, B.C.: Harbour Publishing Ltd., 2000.

Fox, William T. *At the Sea's Edge*. New York: Prentice Hall Press, 1983.

Frazer, Neil. *Boat Camping Haida Gwaii: A Small-Vessel Guide to the Queen Charlotte Islands*, Maderia Park, B.C.: Harbour Publishing, 2001.

Graham, Donald. *Lights of the Inside Passage*. Madeira Park, B.C.: Harbour Publishing Co. Ltd., 1986.

Harbo, Rick M. *Guide to the Western Seashore*. Surrey, B.C.: Hancock House Publishers Ltd., 1988.

Hill, Beth and Ray. *Indian Petroglyphs of the Pacific Northwest*. Saanichton, B.C.: Hancock House Publishers Ltd., 1974.

Hoar, David, and Rudd, Noreen. *Cooks Afloat!*. Madeira Park, B.C.: Harbour Publishing, 2001.

Hordwood, Dennis and Parkin, Tom. *Haida Gwaii — The Queen Charlotte Islands*. Surrey, B.C.: Heritage House Publishing Co., Ltd.

Horn, Elizabeth L. *Coastal Wildflowers of the Pacific Northwest*. Missoula: Mountain Press Publishing Company, 1994.

Hulsizer, Elsie. *Glaciers, Bears and Totems: Sailing in Search of the Real Southeast Alaska*. British Columbia: Harbour Publishing, 2010.

The Journals and Letters of Sir Alexander Mackenzie. Edited by W. Kaye Lamb. Cambridge: The Hakluyt Society, 1970.

Kopas, Cliff. *Bella Coola*. Vancouver: Tenastiktik Publishing, 1974 (3rd printing, 1990).

Kozloff, Eugene N. *Plants and Animals of the Pacific Northwest*. Seattle: University of Washington Press, 1976.

Large, R. Geddes. *The Skeena, River of Destiny*. Surrey, B.C.: Heritage House Publishing Company Ltd., 1996.

Lawrence, Iain. *Far-Away Places, 50 Anchorages on the Northwest Coast*. Victoria: Orca Book Publishers, 1995.

Sea Stories of the Inside Passage. Bishop, CA: Fine Edge Productions: 1997

Lillard, Charles. *The Ghostland People*. Winlaw, B.C.: Sono Nis Press, 1989

Lillard, Charles. *Just East of Sundown, the Queen Charlotte Islands*. Victoria: Horsdal & Schubart, 1995.

Loudon, Pete. *Anyox, The Town That Got Lost*. Sidney, B.C.: Gray's Publishing Ltd., 1973.

MacDonald, George F. *Ninstints: Haida World Heritage Site*. Vancouver: University of British Columbia Press, 1983.

Marine Weather Hazards Manual, a guide to local forecasts and conditions, 2nd Edition. Vancouver: Environment Canada, 1990.

McAllister, Ian and Karen with Cameron Young. *The Great Bear Rainforest, Canada's Forgotten Coast*. San Francisco: Sierra Club Books, 1997.

Monahan, Kevin & Douglass, Don. *GPS Instant Navigation*, 2nd Ed., Anacortes, Washington: Fine Edge Productions, 2000.

Monahan, Kevin. *Local Knowledge, a Skipper's Reference*. Anacortes, WA: Fine Edge, 2005.

Nehls, Harry B. *Familiar Birds of the Northwest*. Portland: Portland Audubon Society, 1981.

Pacific Coast, List of Lights, Buoys and Fog Signals. Canadian Coast Guard, Marine Navigation Services.

Petersen, Dale R. *Day by Day to Alaska – Queen Charlotte Islands and Around Vancouver Island*. Victoria: Trafford Publishing, 2000.

Ramsey, Bruce. *Rain People, the Story of Ocean Falls*, 2nd Edition. Kamloops, B.C.: Wells Gray Tours Ltd., 1997.

Reid, Bill and Binghurst, Robert. *Raven Steals the Light*. Seattle, WA: University of Washington Press, 1996.

Renner, Jeff. *Northwest Marine Weather, from the Columbia River to Cape Scott*. Seattle: The Mountaineers, 1993.

Rogers, Fred. *Shipwrecks of British Columbia*. West Vancouver: J.J. Douglas Ltd., 1973.

Sailing Directions – PAC 200 General Information Pacific Coast. Ottawa: Canadian Hydrographic Service, Department of Fisheries and Oceans, 2022

Sailing Directions – PAC 205 Inner Passage - Queen Charlotte Sound to Chatham Sound. Ottawa: Canadian Hydrographic Service, Department of Fisheries and Oceans, 2023

Sailing Directions – PAC 206 Hecate Strait, Dixon Entrance, Portland Inlet, and Adjacent Waters and Haida Gwaii. Ottawa: Canadian Hydrographic Service, Department of Fisheries and Oceans, 2023

Small Fishing Vessel Safety Manual. Ottawa: Minister of Supply and Services, 1993.

Snively, Gloria. *Exploring the Seashore*. West Vancouver: Gordon Soules Book Publishers Ltd., 1978, sixth printing, 1985.

Stewart, Hilary. *Looking at Indian Art of the Northwest Coast*. Seattle, WA: University of Seattle Press, 1979.

Terdal, Leif G. *Small Boat Cruising to Alaska*. Seattle: Hara Publishing, 2000.

Thomson, Richard E. *Oceanography of the British Columbia Coast*. Ottawa: Department of Fisheries and Oceans, Fisheries and Aquatic Sciences 56, 1981.

Upton, Joe. *Journeys through the Inside Passage*. Bothell, Washington: Alaska Northwest Books, 1992.

Valliant, John. *The Golden Spruce: A True Story of Myth, Madness, and Greed*. New York, NY: W.W. Norton & Co., 2006.

The Voyage of George Vancouver 1791–1795. Volumes I–IV. Edited by W. Kaye Lamb. London: The Hakluyt Society, 1984.

Walbran, Captain John T. *British Columbia Coast Names*. Vancouver: Douglas & McIntyre, 1971.

Walbran, John, T. *British Columbia Place Names, 1592-1906*. First published by the Government Printing Bureau, Ottawa, in 1909, republished in the U.S. by University of Washington Press, 1977.

Enjoy these other publications from Fine Edge

Waggoner Cruising Guide - Published Annually

The most comprehensive and up-to-date information for marinas, anchorages, and waterways from Olympia, Washington to Skagway, Alaska, this guidebook is consistently attested as a "must-have" resource for Northwest boaters. The Compendium section includes topics to help boaters plan, stay safe, and get the most out of cruising the Inside Passage. The Waggoner Cruising Guide is updated annually and includes a wealth of information about cruising the Pacific Northwest. Editors of the Waggoner continue to maintain its high standard for being the Most Trusted Source for Northwest Boating Information; our readers have told us it's their bible for Northwest cruising.

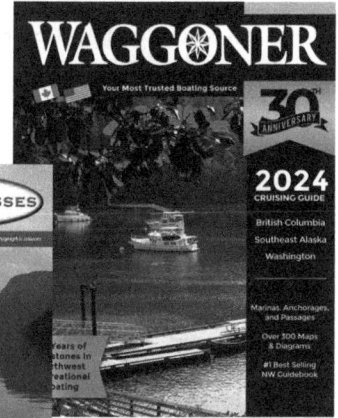

Ports & Passes - Published Annually

Ports and Passes has reliable and convenient tide and current information. Ports and Passes uses official government data updated every year. It is corrected for Daylight Savings Time and presented in an easy to read format. Ports and Passes is the most complete reference guide for tide and current information.

Exploring Southeast Alaska
Dixon Entrance to Glacier Bay and Icy Point
Don Douglass and Réanne Hemingway-Douglass
Almost completely protected, these waters give access to a pristine wilderness of breathtaking beauty—thousands of islands, deeply-cut fiords, tidewater glaciers and icebergs.

Exploring the Pacific Coast—San Diego to Seattle
Don Douglass and Réanne Hemingway-Douglass
All the places to tie up or anchor your boat from the Mexican border to Victoria/ Seattle. Over 500 of the best marinas and anchor sites, starting from San Diego to Santa Barbara—every anchor site in the beautiful Channel Islands, the greater SF Bay Area, the lower Columbia River, and the greater Puget Sound.

Exploring Vancouver Island's West Coast
Don Douglass and Réanne Hemingway-Douglass
With five great sounds, sixteen major inlets, and an abundance of spectacular wildlife, the largest island on the west coast of North America is a cruising paradise.

Exploring the South Coast of British Columbia
Gulf Islands & Desolation Sound to Port Hardy & Blunden Harbour
Don Douglass and Réanne Hemingway-Douglass
Descriptions of marinas, marine parks, and anchorages covering these popular cruising areas. Includes Government *Sailing Directions* quotes and other helpful information.

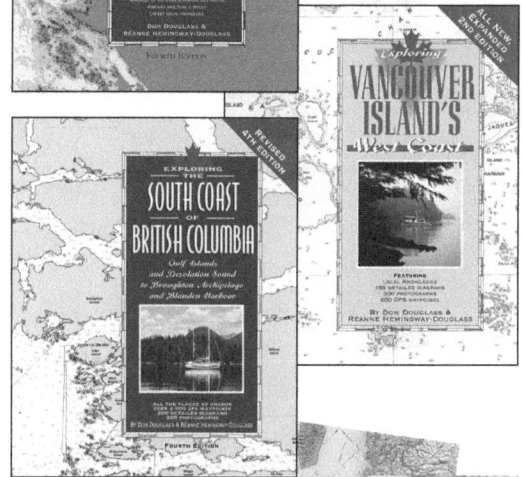

Inside Passage Route Planning Maps North and South portions
Our maps include an index to all harbors and coves in this superb wilderness allowing you to customize your own routes.
Fine Edge Publishing

Inside Passage North Portion and South Portion
Over 4,000 place names alphabetically indexed on these laminated maps in full color with geographical locations, chart numbers, and GPS waypoints.

San Juan and Gulf Islands Nautical and Recreational Planning Map

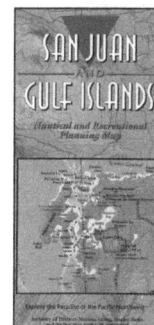

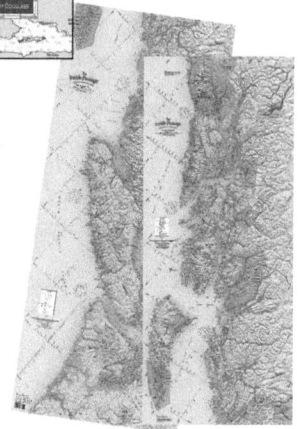

The Nautical Knowledge Series from Fine Edge

Local Knowledge: A Skipper's Reference
Tacoma to Ketchikan
Kevin Monahan
A must-have reference for the skipper of any boat traveling the Inside Passage! Includes over 50 pages of handy distance tables and strategies for managing tides and currents in Johnstone Strait and Cordero Channel, time, distance and speed tables, weather data and much, much more!

The Radar Book
Kevin Monahan
The complete picture on how to maximize the use of your marine radar system. By using practical examples, illustrated with screen displays and the corresponding charts, the newcomer to radar as well as the experienced mariner will learn how to tune a radar system, interpret the display in a variety of conditions, take advantage of all of the built-in features and use radar effectively as a real-time navigational tool.

Cape Horn
One Man's Dream, One Woman's Nightmare – 2nd Ed.
Réanne Hemingway-Douglass
"This is the sea story to read if you read only one." – McGraw Hill, International Marine Catalog "Easily the hairy-chested adventure yarn of the decade, if not the half-century." – Peter H. Spectre, *Wooden Boat*

Trekka Round the World
John Guzzwell
Long out-of-print, this international classic is the story of Guzzwell's circumnavigation on his 20-foot yawl, Trekka. Includes previously unpublished photos and a foreword by America's renowned bluewater sailor-author Hal Roth.

Destination Cortez Island A sailor's life along the BC Coast
June Cameron
A nostalgic memoir of the lives of coastal pioneers – the old timers and their boats, that were essential in the days when the ocean was the only highway.

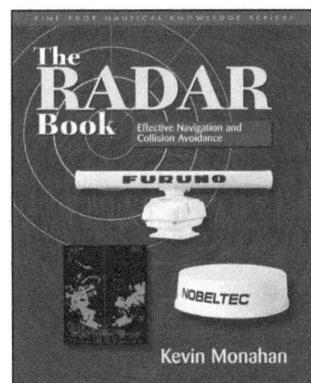

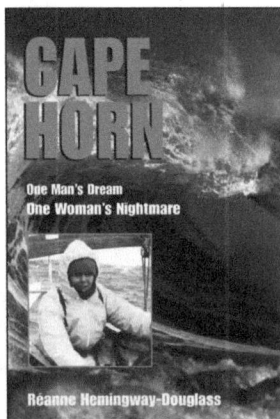

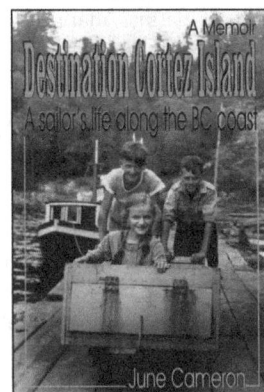

The late **Don Douglass and the late Réanne Hemingway-Douglass** logged more than 170,000 cruising miles over 35 years—from 60°N to 63°S latitude. They spent their summers cruising on their trawler, *Baidarka*, gathering data for new titles and updating their acclaimed *Exploring* series of nautical guidebooks. Together they documented 6,000 anchor sites between San Diego and the Alaska Peninsula.

Don began exploring Alaskan waters as a youth living in Ketchikan. He sailed the West Coast and the Inside Passage on everything from a 21-foot sailboat to a commercial fish boat and a Coast Guard icebreaker. He held a BSEE degree from California State University and a Masters in Business Economics from Claremont Graduate University. Don was an honorary member of the International Association of Cape Horners. He authored several mountain biking guidebooks. As a father of the sport, he was elected to the Mountain Biking Hall of Fame.

Réanne, who held a BA degree in French from Pomona College, attended Claremont Graduate University and the University of Grenoble, France. Sailor, writer, cyclist and language teacher, Réanne's articles appeared in numerous outdoor magazines. Her classic, *Cape Horn: One Man's Dream, One Woman's Nightmare* has been published in French and Italian. Réanne led the first women's bicycling team to cross Tierra del Fuego at the tip of South America. In 2008, she signed the register atop Cape Horn Island during Don's second visit.

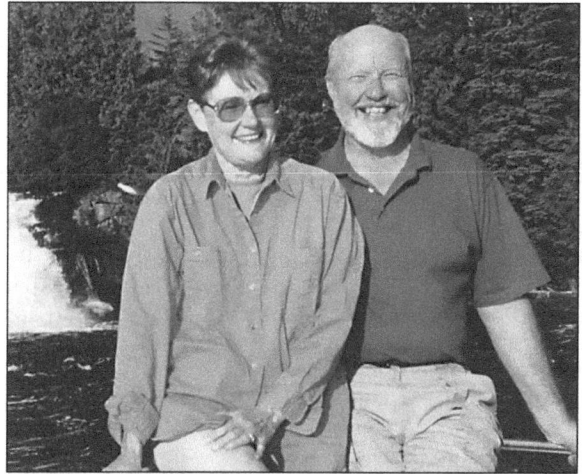

Réanne Hemingway-Douglass and Don Douglass

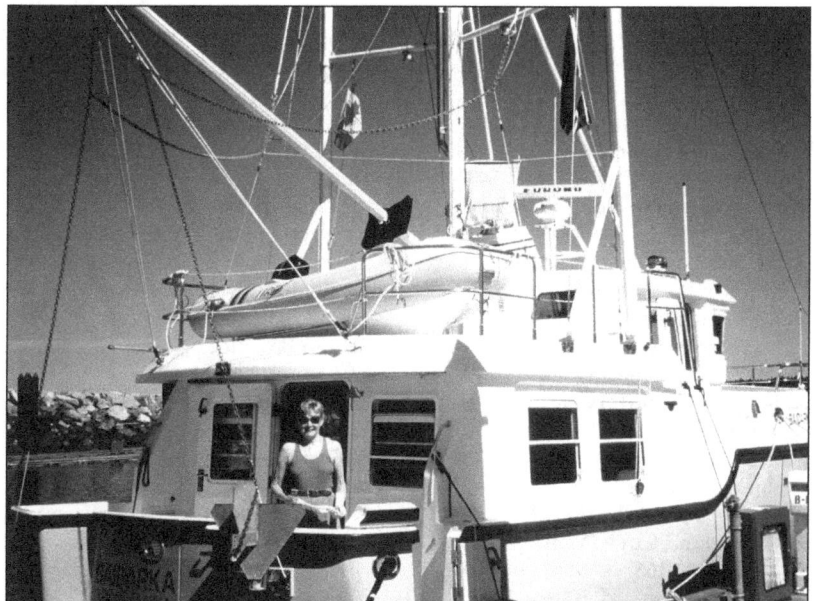

Réanne enjoying a sunny day in Sandspit

Index

Please Note: Names in italics refer to sidebars

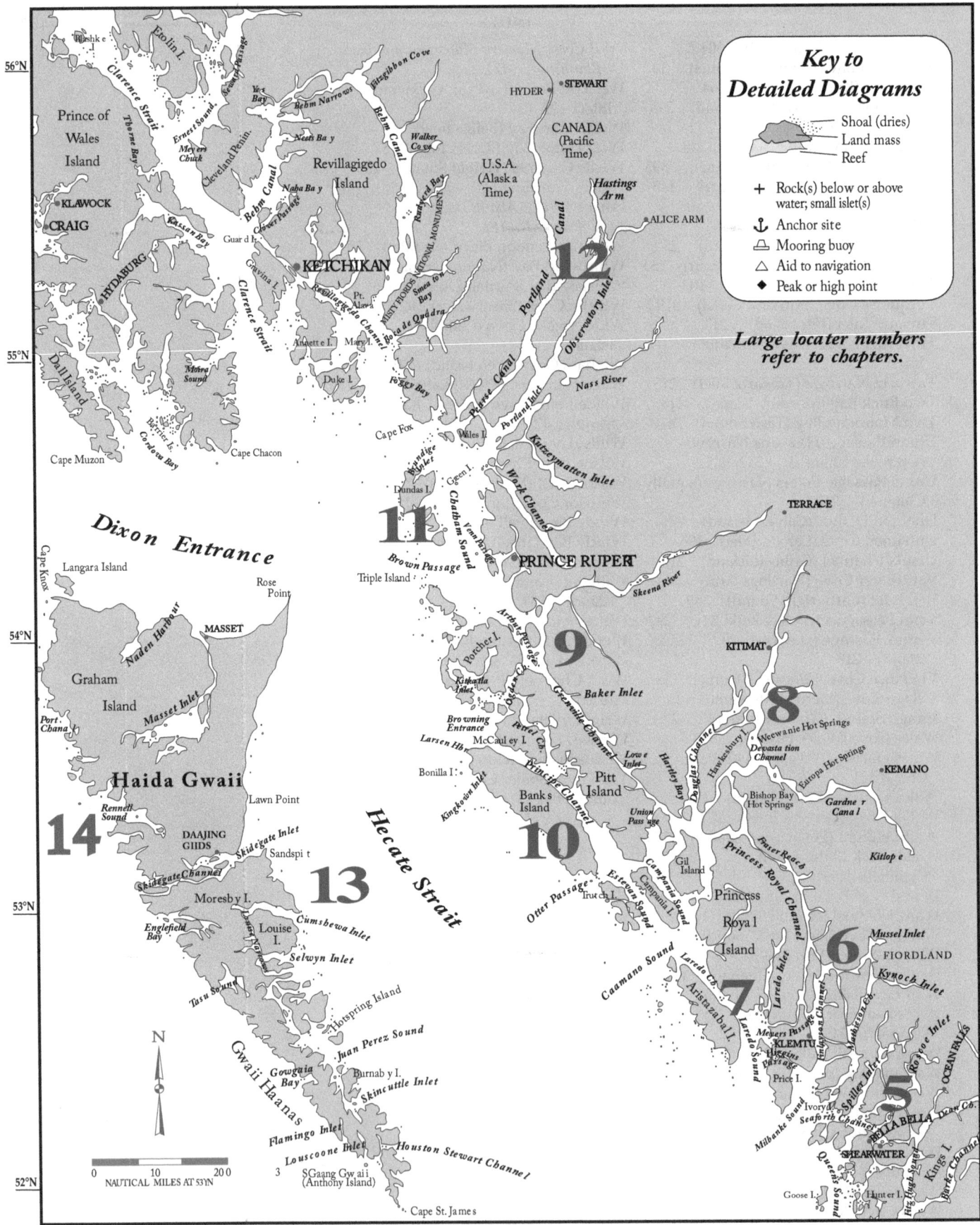

Key to Detailed Diagrams

Key to Detailed Diagrams

- Shoal (dries)
- Land mass
- Reef

+ Rock(s) below or above water; small islet(s)
⚓ Anchor site
⛴ Mooring buoy
△ Aid to navigation
◆ Peak or high point

Large locater numbers refer to chapters.

56°N
55°N
54°N
53°N
52°N

Washke e
Etolin I.
Clarence Strait
Sumner Passage
Thorne Bay
Ernest Sound
Meyers Chuck
Cleveland Penin.
Prince of Wales Island
Behm Narrows
Yes Bay
Neets Bay
Naha Bay
Behm Canal
Fitzgibbon Cove
Walker Cove
Revillagigedo Island

HYDER
STEWART
CANADA (Pacific Time)
Hastings Arm
ALICE ARM
U.S.A. (Alaska Time)

Portland Canal
Observatory Inlet

KLAWOCK
CRAIG
Kassan Bay
Guard I.
Gravina I.
Revillagigedo Channel
Carrow Passage
MISTY FJORDS NATIONAL MONUMENT
Rudyerd Bay
Smeaton Bay
KETCHIKAN
Pt. Alava
Boca de Quadra

HYDABURG
Clarence Strait
Annette I.
Mary I.
Duke I.
Foggy Bay
Pearse Canal
Portland Inlet
Nass River
Katzeymatten Inlet

Dall Island
Barrier Is.
Cordova Bay
Cape Muzon
Mehta Sound
Cape Chacon
Cape Fox
Wales I.
Windige I.
Green I.
Dundas I.
Work Channel

TERRACE
Skeena River

Dixon Entrance
Cape Knox
Langara Island
Naden Harbour
Rose Point
MASSET
Masset Inlet
Graham Island
Port Chana

Haida Gwaii
Rennell Sound
DAAJING GIIDS
Lawn Point
Sandspit
Skidegate Inlet
Skidegate Channel

14
13

Chatham Sound
Brown Passage
Triple Island
Venn Passage
PRINCE RUPERT

11

9
Porcher I.
Arthur Passage
Baker Inlet
KITIMAT
Kitkatla Inlet
Oskar Ch.
Browning Entrance
McCauley I.
Larsen Hb.
Bonilla I.
Kingkown Inlet
Banks Island
Principe Channel
Petrel Ch.
Greenville Channel
Low e Inlet
Hartley Bay
Douglas Channel
Hawkesbury
Weewanie Hot Springs
Devastation Channel
Europa Hot Springs
KEMANO
Bishop Bay Hot Springs
Gardner Canal

8

Pitt Island
Union Passage
Gil Island
Fraser Reach
Kitlope
Princess Royal Channel
Princess Royal Island

6
Mussel Inlet
FIORDLAND
Kynoch Inlet

10
Otter Passage
Iruch I.
Estevan Sound
Campania I.
Campania Sound
Caamano Sound
Laredo Ch.
Laredo Inlet
Aristazabal I.
Laredo Sound
Meyers Passage

7

Hecate Strait

Moresby I.
Cumshewa Inlet
Louise I.
Selwyn Inlet
Englefield Bay
Dana Narrows
Tasu Sound
Hotspring Island
Juan Perez Sound
Gwaii Haanas
Gowgaia Bay
Burnaby I.
Skincuttle Inlet
Flamingo Inlet
Louscoone Inlet
Houston Stewart Channel
SGaang Gwaii (Anthony Island)
Cape St. James

KLEMTU
Higgins Passage
Price I.
Jackson Channel
Mathieson Channel
Roscoe Inlet
Spiller Inlet
OCEAN FALLS

5
Ivory I.
Seaforth Channel
BELLA BELLA
SHEARWATER
Kings I.
Dean Ch.
Burke Channel
Milbanke Sound
Fitz Hugh Sound
Queens Sound
Goose I.
Hunter I.

N

0   10   20 0
NAUTICAL MILES AT 53°N
3

12

DARK HORIZON TRILOGY

THE CHILDREN OF THE GODS SERIES BOOKS 80-82

I. T. LUCAS

Dark Horizon Trilogy is a work of fiction! Names, characters, places, and incidents are products of the author's imagination or are used fictitiously and are not to be construed as real. Any similarity to actual persons, organizations, and/or events is purely coincidental.

Copyright © 2024 by I. T. Lucas

All rights reserved.

No part of this book may be reproduced in any form or by any electronic or mechanical means, including information storage and retrieval systems, without written permission from the author, except for the use of brief quotations in a book review.

Published by Evening Star Press

EveningStarPress.com

ISBN: 978-1-962067-52-2